陕西统计年鉴 2015

SHAANXI STATISTICAL YEARBOOK

陕 西 省 统 计 局
国家统计局陕西调查总队 编

中国统计出版社
China Statistics Press

图书在版编目（CIP）数据

陕西统计年鉴. 2015 = Shanxi Statistical Yearbook 2015 : 汉英对照 / 陕西省统计局，国家统计局陕西调查总队编. -- 北京 : 中国统计出版社，2015.8
ISBN 978-7-5037-7529-1

Ⅰ. ①陕… Ⅱ. ①陕… ②国… Ⅲ. ①统计资料－陕西省－2015－年鉴－汉、英 Ⅳ. ①C832.41-54

中国版本图书馆 CIP 数据核字（2015）第 187946 号

陕西统计年鉴—2015

作　　者 / 陕西省统计局　国家统计局陕西调查总队
责任编辑 / 郭　栋
封面设计 / 翟　竞
出版发行 / 中国统计出版社
通信地址 / 北京市丰台区西三环南路甲 6 号　邮政编码 /100073
电　　话 / 邮购（010）63376909　书店（010）68783171
网　　址 /http://www.zgtjcbs.com/
印　　刷 / 河北天普润印刷厂
经　　销 / 新华书店
开　　本 /880mm×1230mm　1/16
字　　数 /1190 千字
印　　张 /36.5　彩页 1.25 印张
版　　别 /2015 年 8 月第 1 版
版　　次 /2015 年 8 月第 1 次印刷
定　　价 /398.00 元

本书附同版本 CD-ROM 一张，光盘内容以书面文字为准。
如有印装差错，由本社发行部调换。

陕西一日

86179
财政收入（万元）

187
离 婚（对）

1046
结 婚（对）

647
死 亡（人）

1047
出 生（人）

3.28
粮食产量（万吨）

367914
个人储蓄额（万元）

1707
油料产量（吨）

7296
入境旅游人数（人次）

42575
水果产量（吨）

3693
进口总额（万美元）

47252
蔬菜产量（吨）

3816
出口总额（万美元）

3199
肉类产量（吨）

206
客运量（万人）

生产总值（亿元）	第一产业	第二产业	第三产业
48.47	4.29	26.24	17.94

10
原油产量（万吨）

430
货运量（万吨）

11236
天然气（万立方米）

43860
发电量（万千瓦小时）

1027
汽车产量（辆）

30.75
能源消费量（万吨标准煤）

162156
社会消费品零售额（万元）

生产总值（亿元）

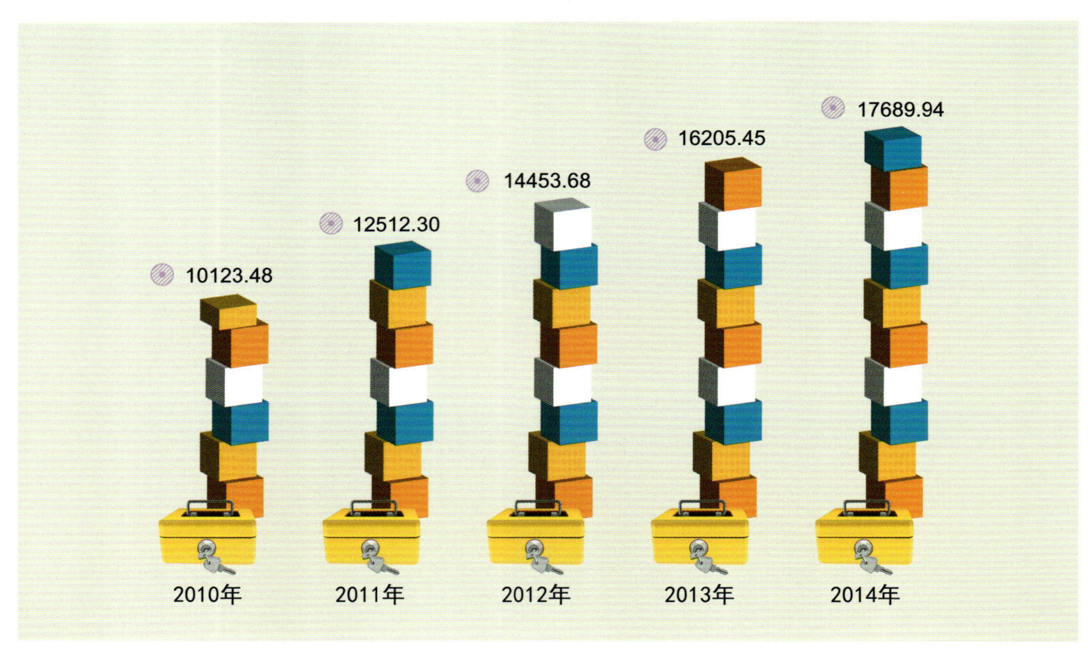

人均生产总值（元）

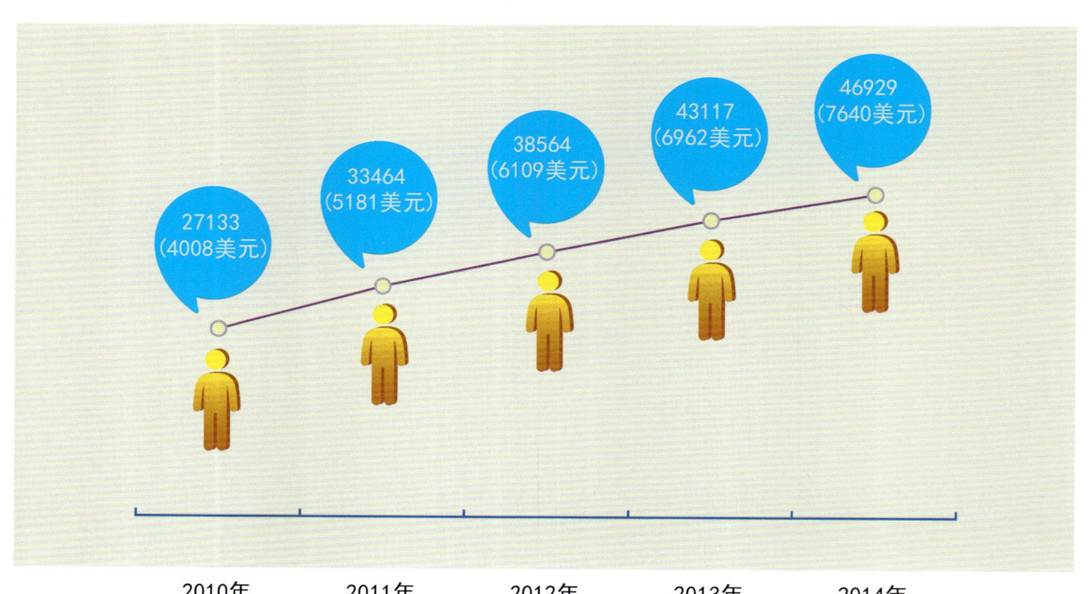

年底常住人口（万人）

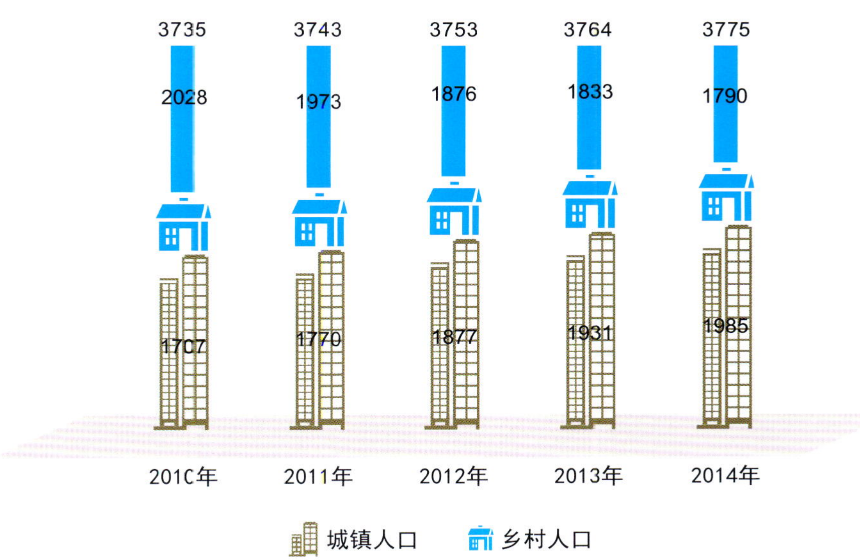

城镇人口比重（%）

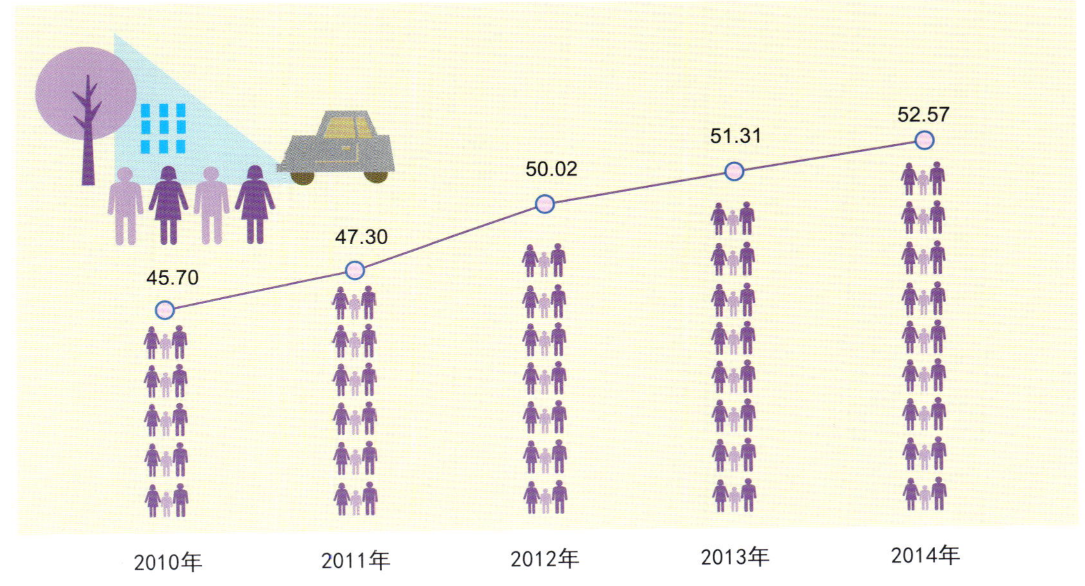

全社会固定资产投资

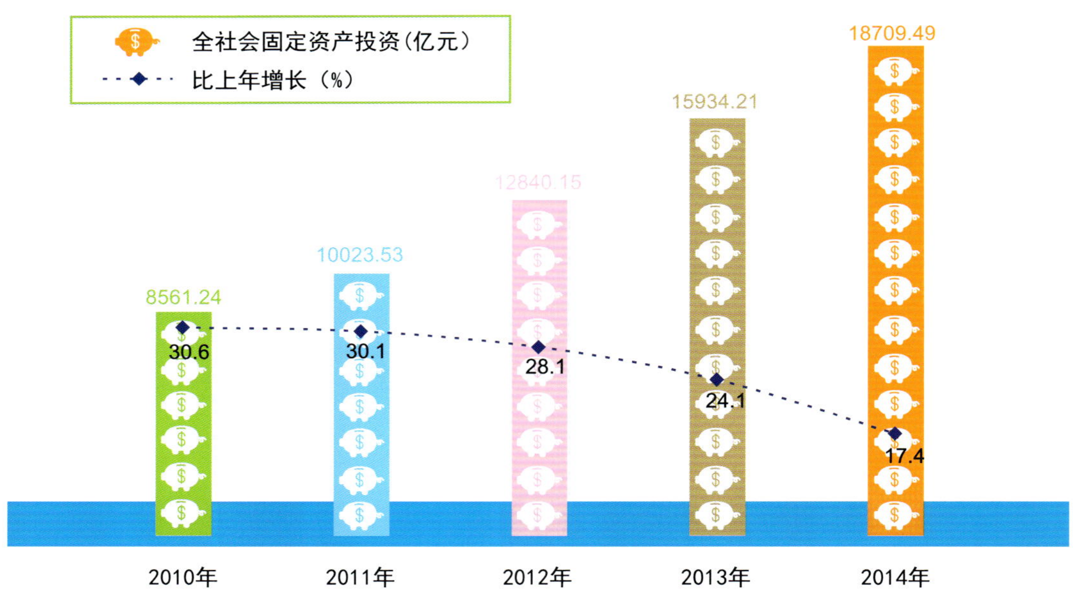

财政收支(亿元)

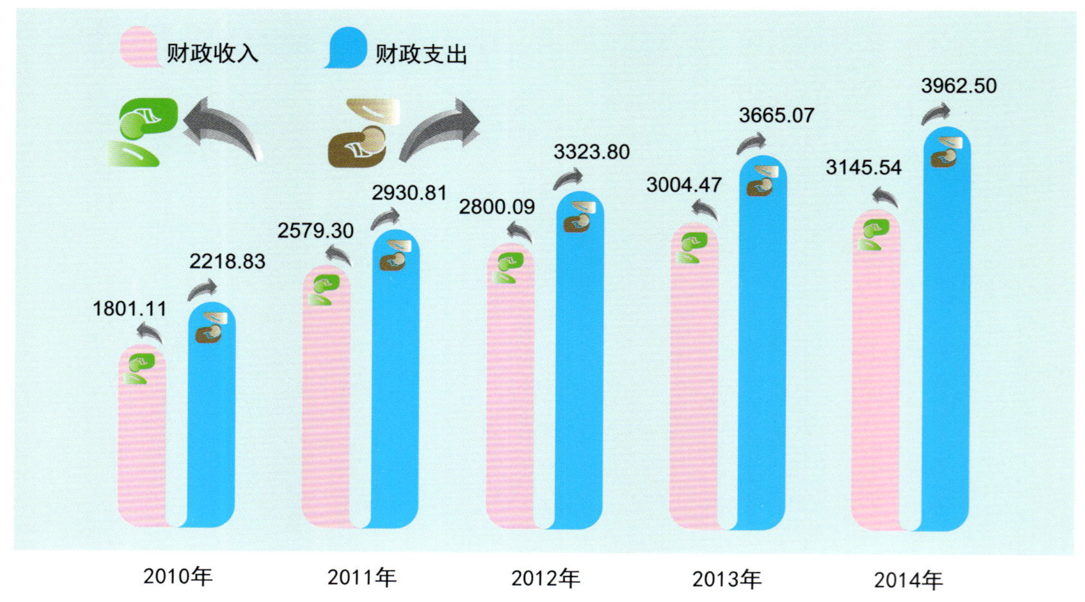

能源生产总量（万吨标准煤）

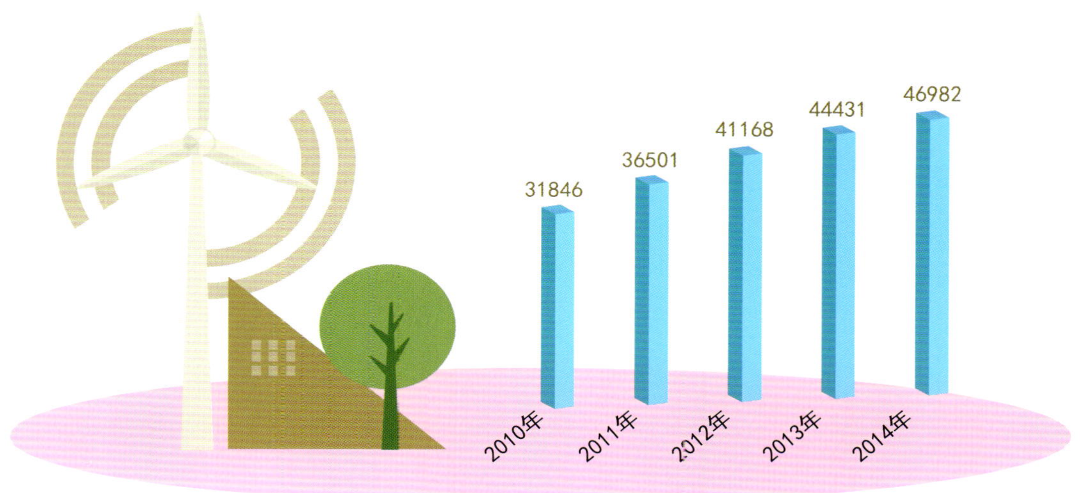

能源消费总量（万吨标准煤）

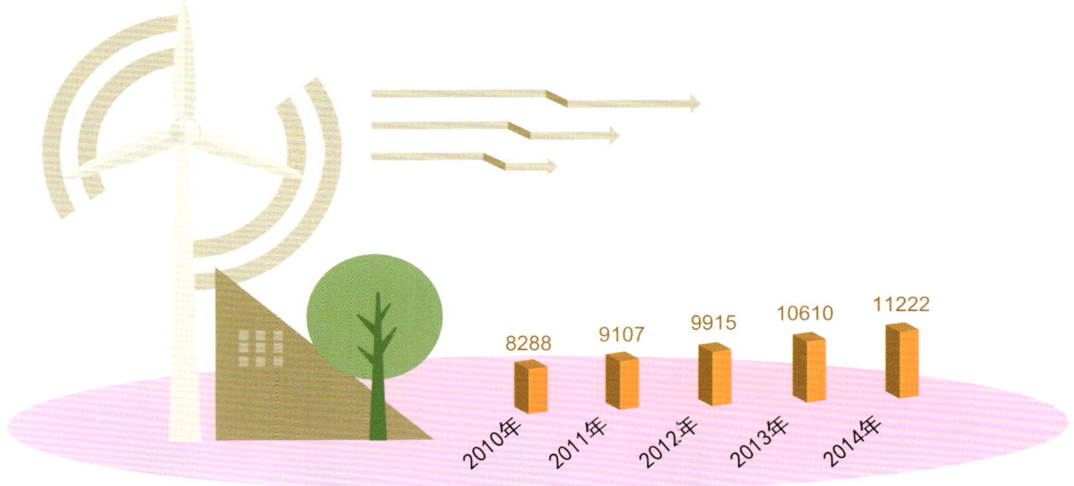

农村居民人均收入（元）

城镇居民人均可支配收入（元）

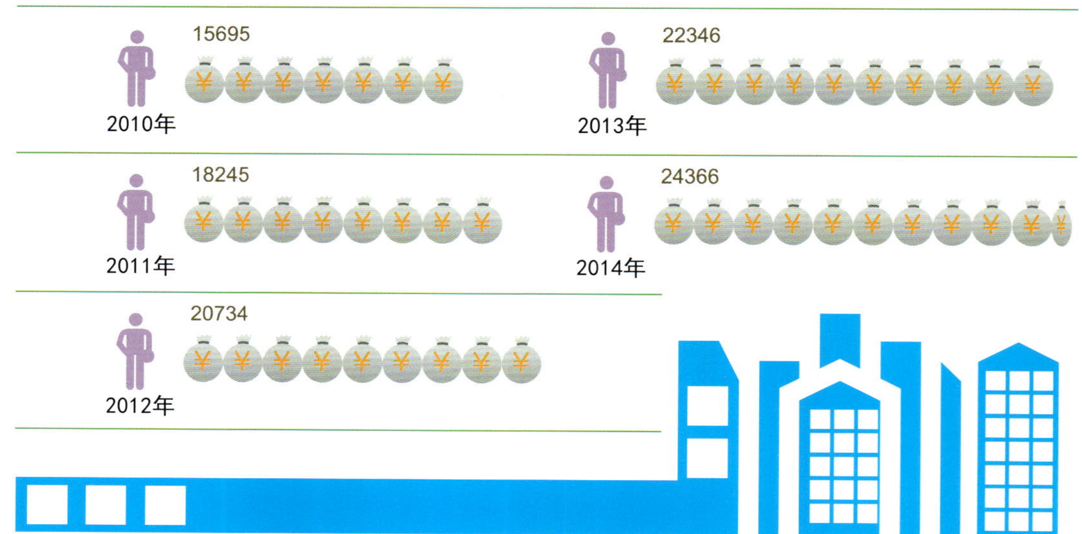

居民家庭人均生活消费支出构成

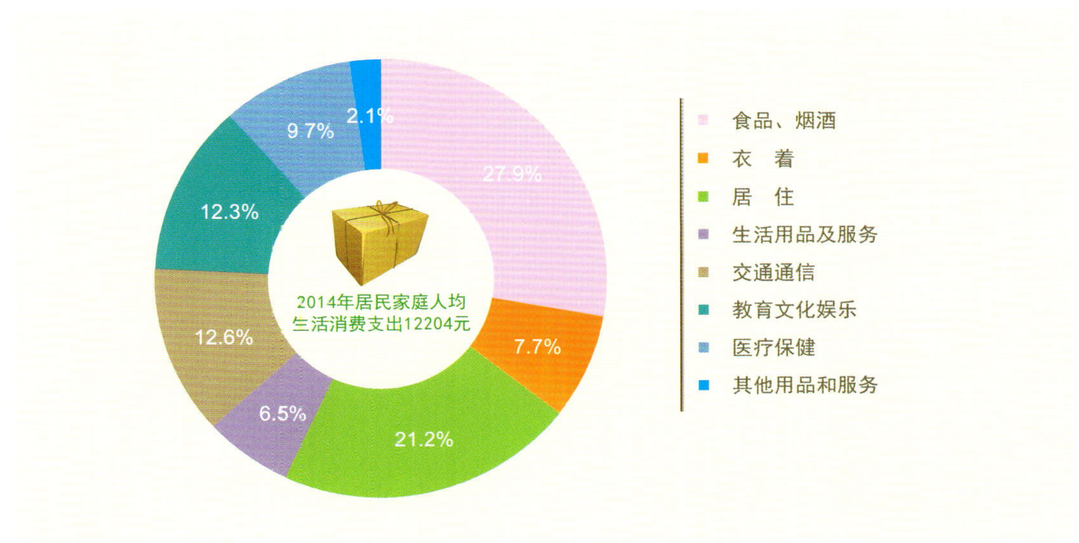

个人储蓄存款余额

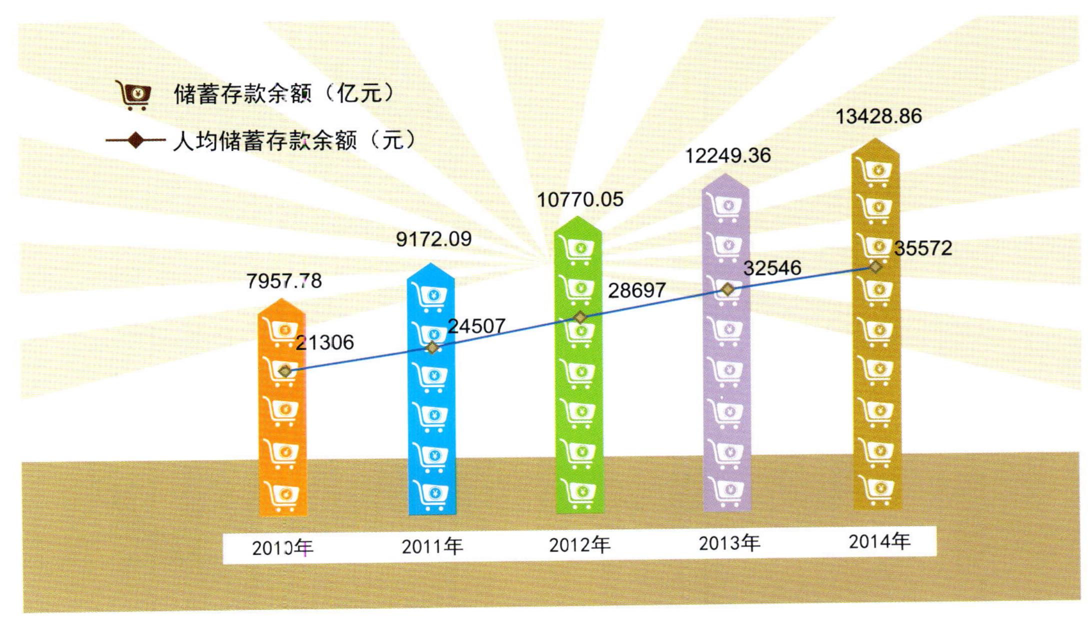

高速公路里程（公里）

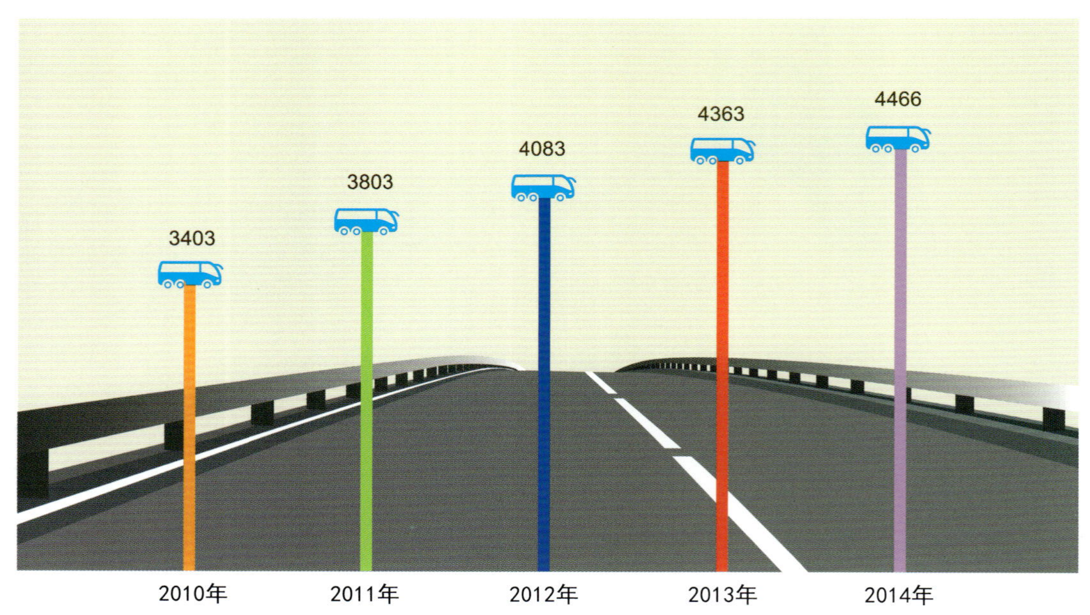

私人汽车拥有量（万辆）

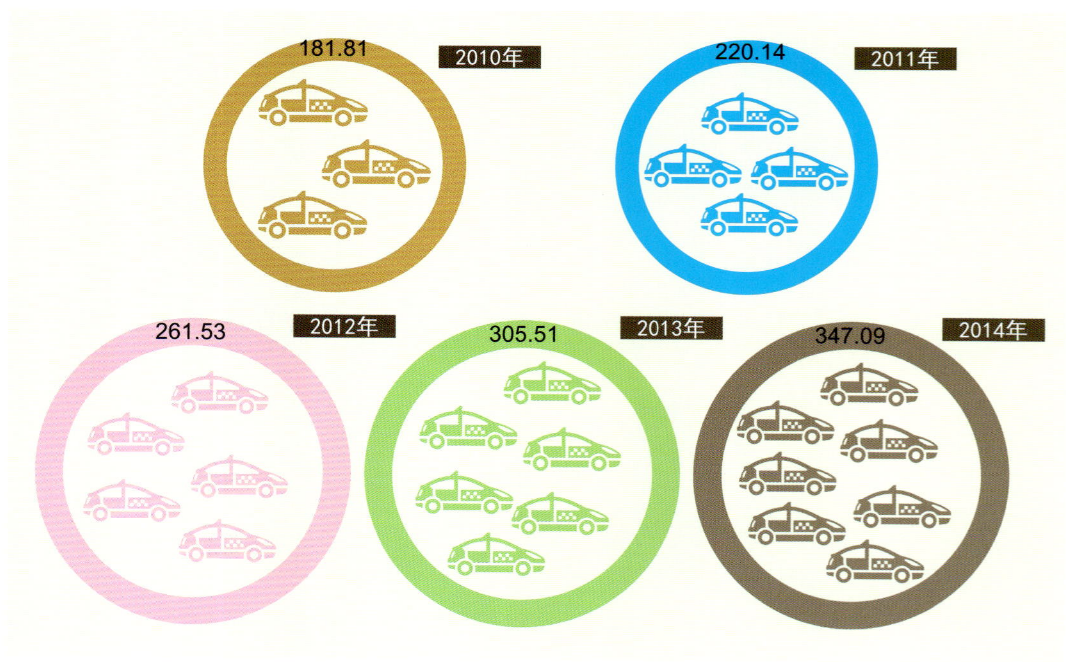

粮食产量（万吨）

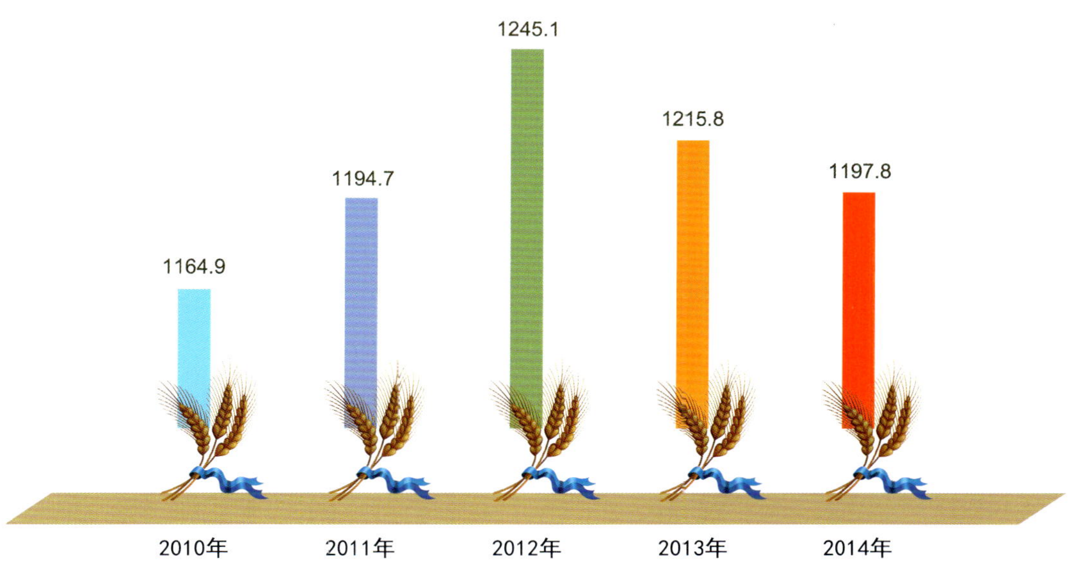

苹果产量（万吨）

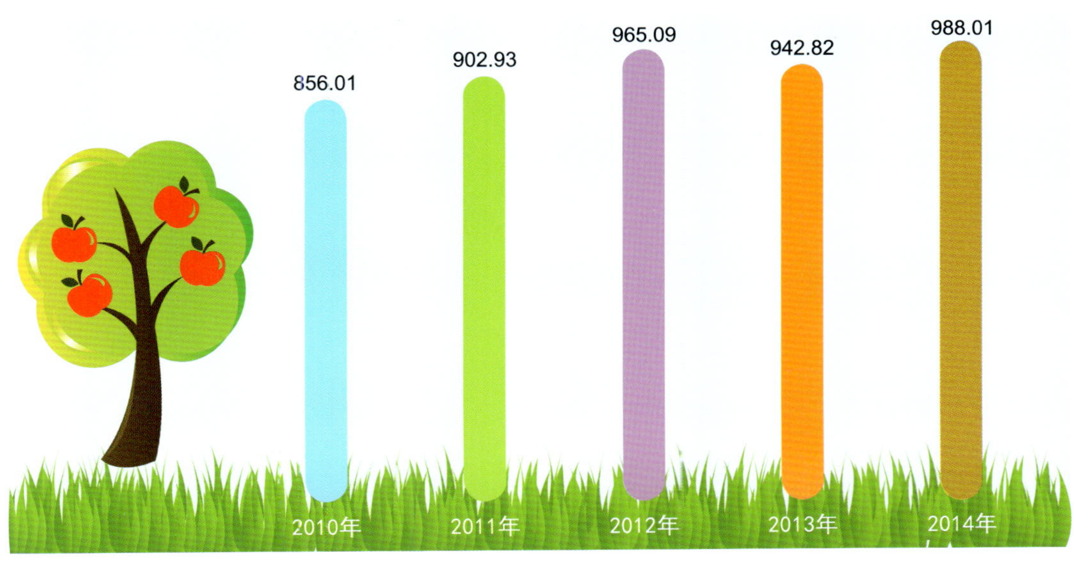

发电量（亿千瓦小时）

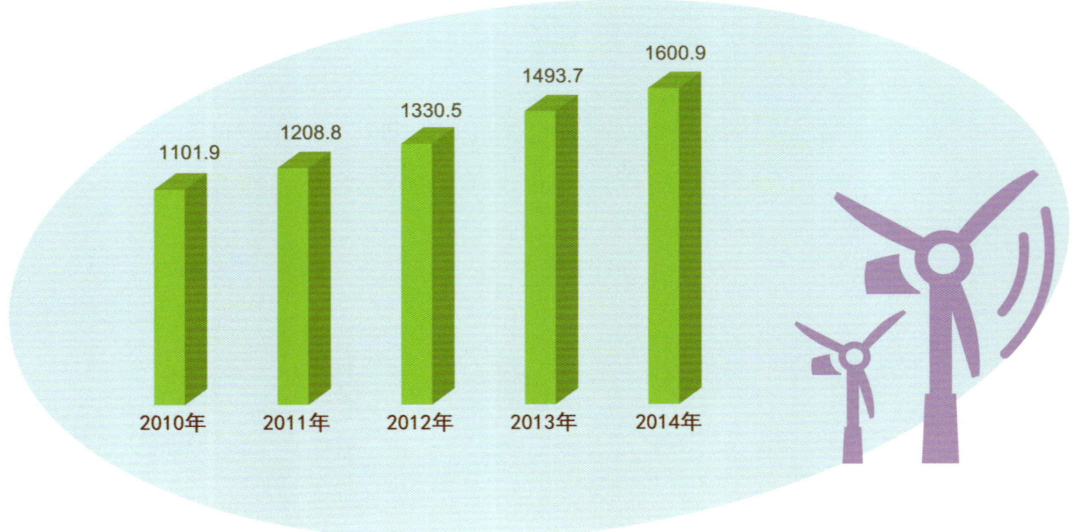

原油产量（万吨）

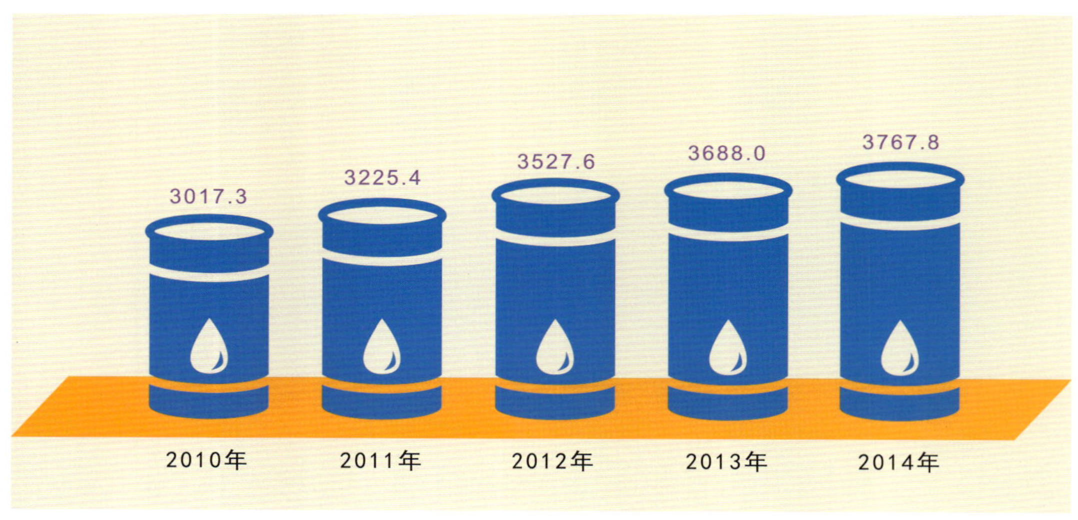

天然气产量（亿立方米）

汽车产量（万辆）

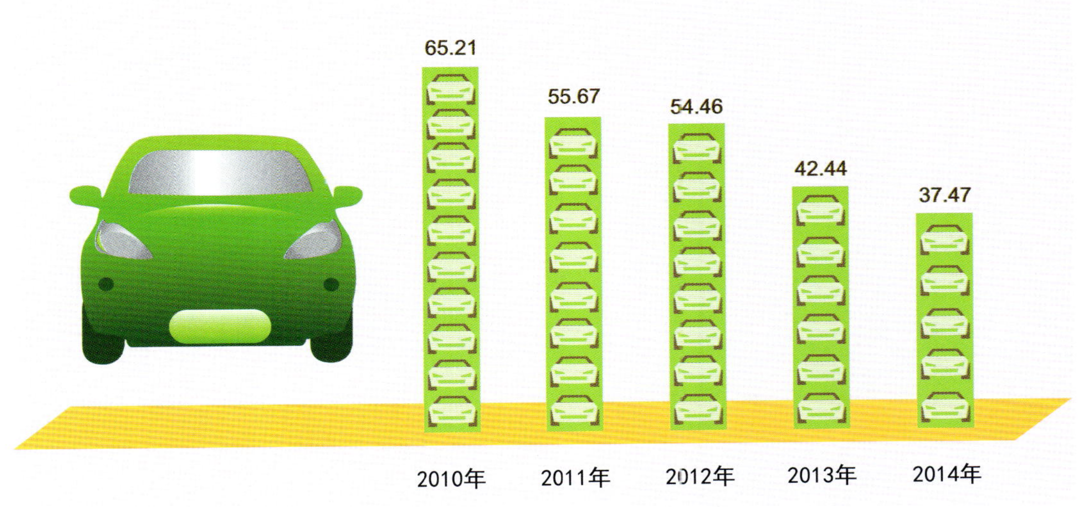

移动电话年末用户（万户）

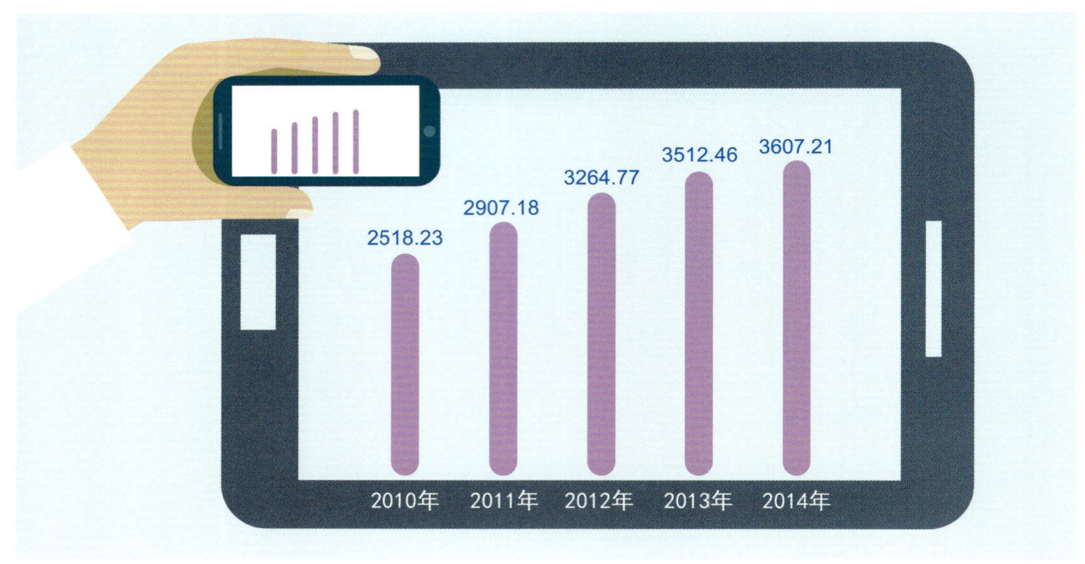

社会消费品零售总额

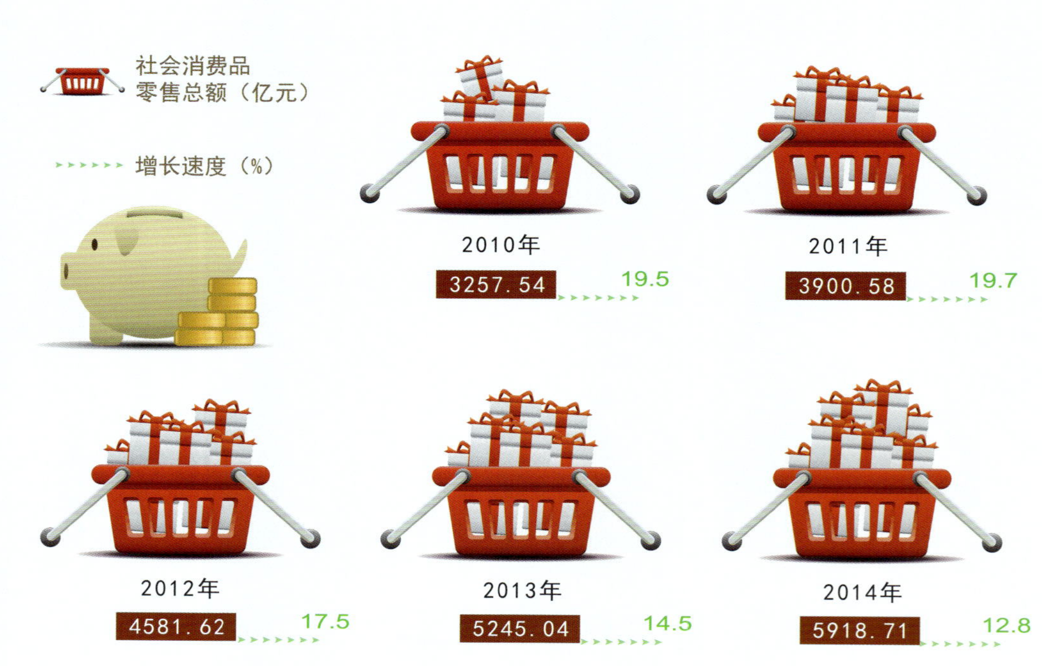

进出口总额（亿美元）

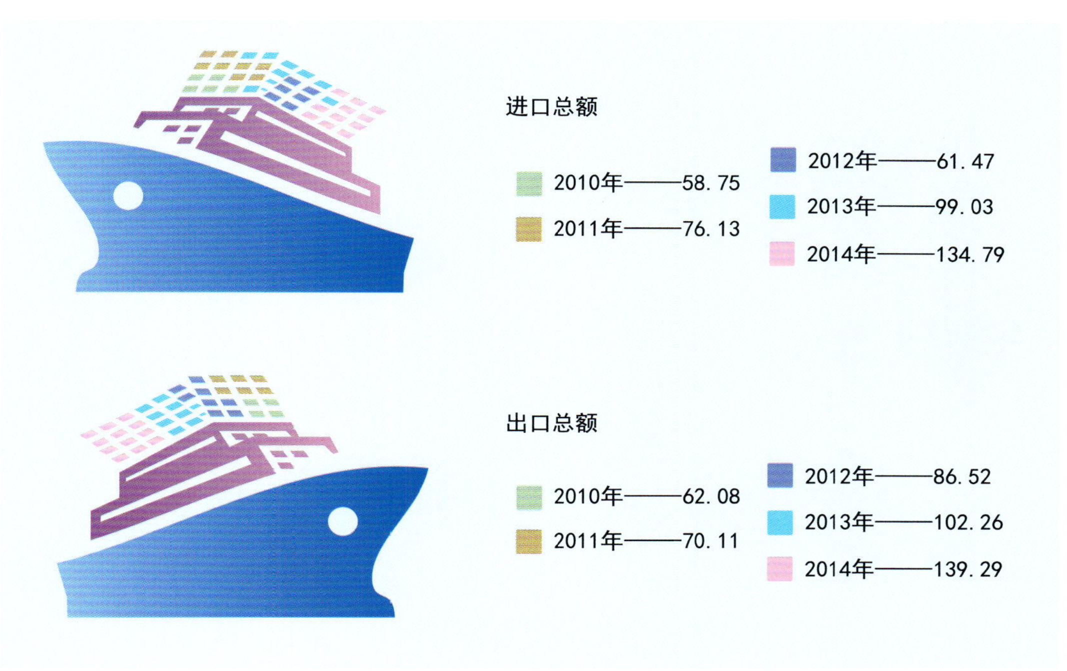

实际利用外资额

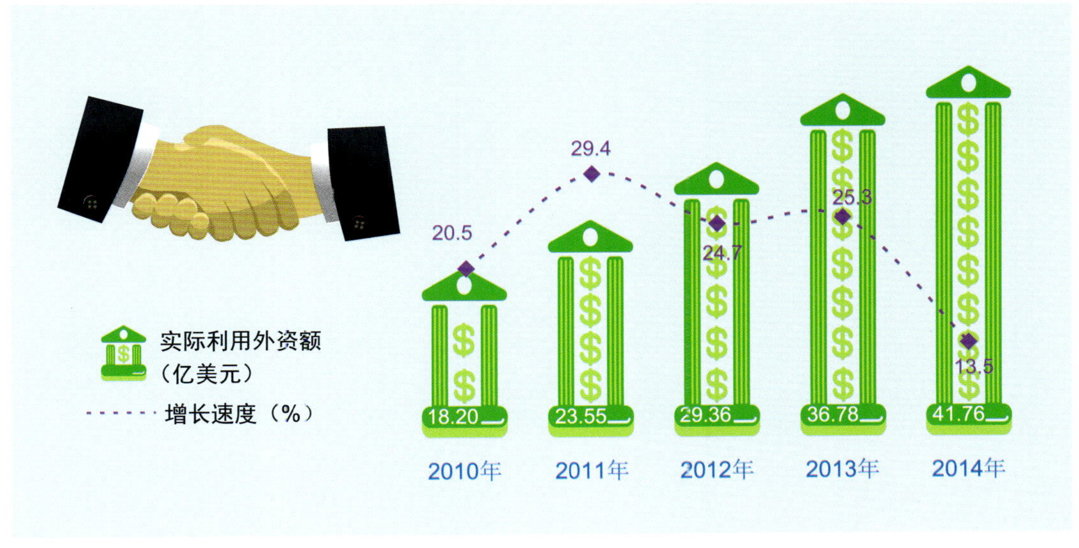

研究与试验发展经费(R&D)内部支出 (亿元)

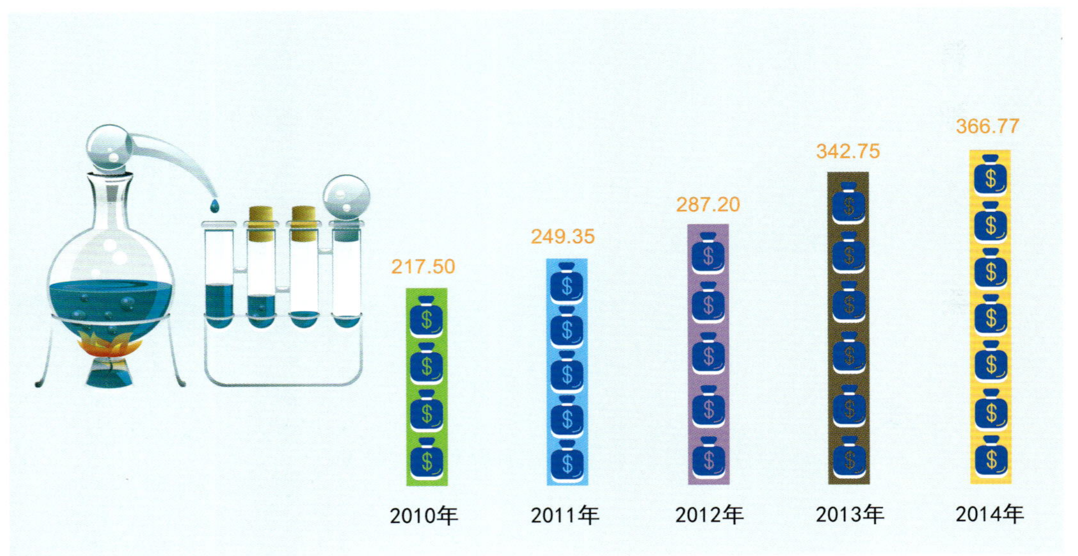

高等学校毕业生数 (万人)

《陕西统计年鉴－2015》

编委会和编辑工作人员名单

Shaanxi Statistical Yearbook - 2015

EDITORIAL BOARD AND EDITORIAL STAFF

I. Editorial Board

II. Editorial Staff

编 者 说 明

一、《陕西统计年鉴－2015》是一部全面系统反映陕西省经济、社会、科技发展状况的资料性年刊。书中资料根据全省各专业统计年报加工而成，并收录了各市、县及省级有关部门的统计数据。

二、全书内容分为22部分：1．行政区划和自然资源；2．综合；3．国民经济核算；4．人口；5．就业人员和职工工资；6．固定资产投资；7．能源；8．财政；9．价格指数；10．人民生活；11．环境和城市；12．农业；13．工业；14．建筑业；15．运输和邮电；16．国内贸易；17．对外经济贸易和旅游；18．金融和保险；19．教育、科技和文化；20．体育、卫生和其他；21．水利；22．全国各省、市、自治区主要指标。附录为2014年陕西省统计局大事记、2014年陕西调查总队大事记、陕西省统计局机构一览表、陕西调查总队机构一览表。为方便读者使用，各篇章前设有简要说明，列示主要统计指标提要和统计图，后面附主要统计指标解释。

三、本年鉴数据以2014年为主，主要指标列示改革开放以来重点年份的资料。

四、本年鉴依据第三次经济普查结果对国民经济核算、能源和国内贸易等部分近年数据进行了调整，凡与本年鉴有出入的，均以本年鉴为准。

五、2012年韩城市试点设立省内计划单列市，本年鉴在各市（区）主要指标中增加了韩城市的数据。

六、本年鉴全国及各省、市、自治区主要指标资料来源于《中国统计摘要－2015》，部分数据为初步统计数，正式数据以《中国统计年鉴－2015》为准。

七、本年鉴表中的符号使用说明："..."表示数据不足本表最小单位；"空格"表示该项统计指标数据不详或无该项数据；"#"表示其中项。

EDITOR'S NOTES

Ⅰ. *Shaanxi Statistical Yearbook-2015* is an annual statistical publication, which reflects various aspects of province's economic, social science and technology development.

The major data sources of the publication are statistical annual report of different sectors. Also some other statistical data of city, county, and relevant departments are filled.

Ⅱ. The yearbook contains the following twenty-two chapters:

1. Divisions of Administrative Areas and Natural Resources;
2. General Survey;
3. National Accounts;
4. Population;
5. Employment and Wages;
6. Investment in Fixed Assets;
7. Energy;
8. Government Finance;
9. Price Indices;
10. People's Livelihood;
11. Environment and Cities;
12. Agriculture;
13. Industry;
14. Construction;
15. Transport, Post and Telecommunication Services;
16. Domestic Trade;
17. Foreign Trade and Tourism;
18. Banking and Insurance;
19. Education, Science, Technology and Culture;
20. Sports, Public Health and Others;
21. Irrigation;
22. Main Indicators of National Economy by Countrywide, Province, Municipality and Autonomous Region.

The addenda include chronicle of events of Shaanxi Provincial Bureau of Statistics in 2014, chronicle of events of NBS Survey Office in Shaanxi in 2014 list of institutions of Shaanxi Provincial Bureau of Statistics and list of institutions of NBS Survey Office in Shaanxi.

As a matter of convenience for readers, we make Brief Introduction, abstract of major indicators and statistical charts at the beginning of each chapter and explanatory notes on main statistical indicators at the end of each chapter.

Ⅲ. The yearbook is based on data of 2014. Each part includes statistical materials for historically important years, especially from 1978.Since then we have been implementing the reform and opening policy.

Ⅳ. The yearbook is based on data of the third economic census results, National Accounts , Energy ,Industry, Domestic Trade and some other of historical data has been adjusted previously published some relevant data. If there are some differences between this yearbook with others, refer to this yearbook please.

Ⅴ.The Hancheng city has established the city specifically designated in the province plan in 2012. So, the main index by city(district) has added the data of Hancheng city in the yearbook-2015.

Ⅵ.The rough data of the nation and other provinces are taken from *China Statistical Abstract-2015* The official data should refer to *China Statistical Yearbook-2015* later.

Ⅶ.Explanatory symbol for notations used in this yearbook:

"..." indicates that the figure is not large enough to be measured with the smallest unit in the table;

"   " (blank) indicates that the data not available;

"#" indicates that the major items of the total.

目 录

CONTENTS

一、行政区划和自然资源

Divisions of Administrative Areas and Natural Resources

简要说明……2
Brief Introduction

1-1 陕西省行政区划(2014 年)……4
Divisions of Administrative Areas in Shaanxi (2014)

1-2 陕西省行政区划一览(2014 年)……5
Divisions List of Administrative Areas in Shaanxi (2014)

1-3 自然状况及资源……8
Natural Conditions and Resources

1-4 主要山脉……9
Main Mountain Ranges

1-5 主要河流……9
Major Rivers

1-6 主要矿产保有储量(2014 年)……9
Ensured Reserves of Major Mineral (2014)

1-7 陕西重要矿产保有储量在全国和西部的位次(2014 年)……10
Precedence of Shaanxi Major Mineral Ensured Reserves in China and Western China(2014)

1-8 陕西矿产保有储量居全国前十位的矿种(2014 年)……10
Mineral Kinds of Shaanxi Mineral Ensured Reserves Within the Top Ten Places in China (2014)

1-9 主要城市气候基本情况(2014 年)……11
Basic Statistics on Climate of Major Cities (2014)

1-10 主要城市平均气温(2014 年)……11
Monthly Average Temperature of Major Cities(2014)

1-11 主要城市降水量(2014 年)……12
Monthly Precipitation of Major Cities(2014)

1-12 主要城市日照时数(2014 年)……12
Monthly Sunshine Hours of Major Cities(2014)

1-13 历届陕西省人民代表大会代表人数……13
Number of Deputies to All the Previous Shaanxi Province People's Congresses

1-14 历届陕西省政治协商会议委员人数……13
Number of Deputies to All the Previous Shaanxi Province People's Political Consultative Conferences

主要统计指标解释……14
Explanatory Notes on Main Statistical Indicators

二、综合
General Survey

	简要说明 Brief Introduction	18
2-1	陕西一日 Selected Indicators on Average Daily Social and Economic Activities	20
2-2	陕西省主要国民经济指标占全国比重(2014 年) Percentage of Shaanxi Main Indicators on National Economic to National Total(2014)	21
2-3	国民经济和社会发展总量与速度指标 Principal Aggregate Indicators on National Economic and Social Development and Growth Rates	22
2-4	国民经济主要结构指标 Main Composition Indicators on National Economy	30
2-5	国民经济和社会发展比例与效益指标 Indicators on Proportions and Efficiency in National Economic and Social Development	33
2-6	社会经济主要指标平均每人水平 Per Capita Main Indicators on Society and Economy	36
2-7	人均工农业主要产品产量 Per Capita Output of Major Industrial and Agricultural Products	37
2-8	各市(区)国民经济主要指标(2014 年) Main Indicators on National Economic by City(District)(2014)	38
	主要统计指标解释 Explanatory Notes on Main Statistical Indicators	40

三、国民经济核算
National Accounts

	简要说明 Brief Introduction	46
3-1	生产总值 Gross Domestic Product	48
3-2	生产总值指数 Indices of Gross Domestic Product	49
3-3	生产总值指数 Indices of Gross Domestic Product	50
3-4	分行业增加值 Value-added of the Tertiary Industry	51
3-5	分行业增加值指数 Indices of Value-added of the Tertiary Industry	52
3-6	分行业增加值指数 Indices of Value-added of the Tertiary Industry	53
3-7	三次产业贡献率 Share of the Contributions of the Three Strata of Industry to the Increase of the GDP	54
3-8	三次产业拉动率 Contribution of the Three Strata of Industry to GDP Growth	54
3-9	分行业增加值构成 Value-added by Sector	55
3-10	非公有制经济增加值 Value-added of Non-public Economy	55
3-11	各市(区)生产总值 Gross Domestic Product by City(District)	56
3-12	各市(区)生产总值指数 Indices of Gross Domestic Product by City(District)	60

3-13 各市(区)非公有制经济增加值……64
Value-added of Non-public Economy by City(District)
3-14 各县(市、区)生产总值(2014 年)……65
Gross Domestic Product by County (City and District)(2014)
主要统计指标解释……67
Explanatory Notes on Main Statistical Indicators

四、人口
Population

简要说明……72
Brief Introduction
4-1 人口数和构成……74
Population and Its Composition
4-2 人口自然变动情况……75
Population Natural Changes
4-3 各市(区)常住人口和自然增长率……75
Usual Residents and Natural Growth Rate by City(District)
4-4 人口年龄构成和抚养比……76
Age Composition and Dependency Ration of Population
4-5 各市、县(市、区)常住人口……77
Usual Residents by City and County (City and District)
4-6 各市、县(市、区)总户数和户籍人口数(2014 年)……79
Total Households and Population by City and County (City and District)(2014)
主要统计指标解释……82
Explanatory Notes on Main Statistical Indicators

五、就业人员和职工工资
Employment and Wages

简要说明……86
Brief Introduction
5-1 就业人员人数……88
Number of Employed Persons
5-2 分行业就业人员人数(2014 年)……89
Number of Employed Persons by Sector (2014)
5-3 城镇非私营单位企业、事业、机关人数和工资(2014 年)……90
Persons and Wages of Urban Non-private Enterprises, Institutions and State Organs (2014)
5-4 城镇非私营单位分行业就业人员年末人数(2014 年)……91
Number of Fully Employed Staff and Workers in Urban Non-private Units at Year-end by Sector (2014)
5-5 各市(区)城镇非私营单位就业人员年末人数(2014 年)……92
Number of Fully Employed Staff and Workers in Urban Non-private Units at Year-end by City(District)(2014)
5-6 城镇非私营单位就业人员年末人数和工资……92
Total Persons and Wages of Employed Staff and Workers in Urban Non-private Units
5-7 职工平均工资和指数……93
Average Wage of Staff and Workers and Related Indices
5-8 城镇非私营单位就业人员分行业工资总额(2014 年)……94
Earnings of Employed Persons by Sector in Urban Non-private Units (2014)
5-9 城镇非私营单位就业人员分行业平均工资(2014 年)……95
Average Earnings of Employed Persons by Sector in Urban Non-private Units (2014)
5-10 城镇非私营单位在岗职工分行业平均工资(2014 年)……96
Average Wage of Employed Staff and Workers in Urban Non-private Units by Sector (2014)
5-11 城镇私营单位分行业就业人员平均工资……97

Average Wage of Employed Persons in Urban Private Units by Sector
5-12 各市(区)城镇非私营单位就业人员工资总额(2014 年)……98
Earnings of Employed Persons and Total Wages Bill of Fully Employed Staff in Urban Non-private Units by City(District)(2014)
5-13 各市(区)城镇非私营单位就业人员平均工资(2014 年)……98
Average Earnings of Employed Persons and Average Wage of Fully Employed Staff and Workers in Urban Non-private Units by City(District)(2014)
5-14 城镇登记失业人数及失业率……99
Registered Urban Unemployment Persons and Unemployment Rate
5-15 社会保障基本情况……99
Basic Statistics on Social Security
5-16 参加基本养老保险的职工及离退休人员(2014 年)……100
Staff and Workers, Retired and VCSR Joined Basic Pension Insurance(2014)
5-17 失业保险基本情况……100
Basic Statistics on Unemployment Insurance
主要统计指标解释……101
Explanatory Notes on Main Statistical Indicators

六、固定资产投资
Investment in Fixed Assets

简要说明……106
Brief Introduction
6-1 全社会固定资产投资……108
Total Investment in Fixed Assets of the Whole Province
6-2 按经济类型分的全社会固定资产投资……109
Total Investment in Fixed Assets of the Whole Province by Economic Type
6-3 全社会新增固定资产……110
Total Newly Increased Fixed Assets of the Whole Province
6-4 全社会竣工住宅建筑面积……111
Total Floor Space of Residential Buildings Completed of the Whole Province
6-5 全社会固定资产投资主要指标及构成(2014 年)……112
Main Indicators and Composition of Total Investment in Fixed Asset of the Whole Province (2014)
6-6 各市(区)全社会固定资产投资……114
Total Investment in Fixed Assets of the Whole Province by City(District)
6-7 各行业按构成分的固定资产投资(2014 年)……115
Investment by Sector and Use of Funds in the Whole Province (2014)
6-8 分行业固定资产投资施工、投产项目个数及新增固定资产(2014 年)……118
Number of Investment Projects under Construction and Put into Use and Newly Increased Fixed Assets by Sector in the Whole Province(2014)
6-9 固定资产投资新增生产能力或效益(2014 年)……121
Newly Increased Production Capacity or Project Efficiency through Investment(2014)
6-10 分行业工业投资(2014 年)……122
Investment of Industrial by Sector(2014)
6-11 民间投资(2014 年)……123
Private Investment(2014)
6-12 基础设施投资(2014 年)……123
Investment for Basic Infrastructure(2014)
6-13 七大战略性新兴产业投资(2014 年)……124
Investment of Seven Strategic Emerging Industries(2014)
6-14 文化产业投资(2014 年)……124
Culture Industry Investment(2014)
6-15 全社会固定资产投资财务拨款资金来源(2014 年)……125

Source of Funds of Investment in Fixed Assets for Finance Allocation in the Whole Province(2014)
6-16 固定资产投资资金来源(2014 年)……125
Source of Funds of Investment (2014)
6-17 各市(区)固定资产投资资金来源(2014 年)……126
Source of Funds of Investment by City(District)(2014)
6-18 各市(区)国有经济单位投资资金来源(2014 年)……127
Source of Funds of Investment in State-Owned Units by City(District)(2014)
6-19 各市(区)按国民经济行业分的固定资产投资(2014 年)……128
Investment by Sector and City(District)(2014)
6-20 各市(区)工业投资(2014 年)……129
Investment of Industry by City(District) (2014)
6-21 各市(区)按登记注册类型分的固定资产投资(2014 年)……129
Investment by Registration Status and City (District)(2014)
6-22 各市(区)按隶属关系分的固定资产投资(2014 年)……130
Investment in Urban Area by Jurisdiction of Management and City (District)(2014)
6-23 各市(区)能源工业投资(2014 年)……130
Investment in Energy Industry by City(District)(2014)
6-24 各市(区)按构成分的固定资产投资 (2014 年)……131
Investment by Use of Funds and City(District)(2014)
6-25 各市(区)按建设性质分的固定资产投资(2014 年)……131
Investment by Type of Construction and City(District)(2014)
6-26 各市(区)固定资产投资施工、投产项目个数及新增固定资产(2014 年)……132
Number of Investment Projects under Construction and Put into Use and Newly Increased Fixed Assets by City(District)(2014)
6-27 各市(区)固定资产投资房屋建筑面积及造价(2014 年)……132
Floor Space and Cost of Buildings in Investment by City(District)(2014)
6-28 房地产开发投资主要指标及构成(2014 年)……133
Main Indicators and Composition of Investment for Real Estate Development(2014)
6-29 房地产开发投资资金来源(2014 年)……135
Sources of Funds of Investment for Real Estate Development (2014)
6-30 各市(区)房地产开发投资和新增固定资产(2014 年)……135
Investment for Real Estate Development and Newly Increased Fixed Assets by City(District)(2014)
6-31 各市(区)按构成和工程用途分的房地产开发投资(2014 年)……136
Investment for Real Estate Development by Use of Funds and Projects by City(District)(2014)
6-32 房地产开发面积及造价(2014 年)……136
Floor Space and Cost of Buildings in Real Estate Development(2014)
6-33 商品房屋销售情况(2014 年)……137
Seal of Commercialized Buildings(2014)
6-34 房地产开发经营情况(2014 年)……138
Operating Statistics on Enterprises for Real Estate Development(2014)
6-35 房地产开发企业基本情况(2014 年)……138
Basic Statistics on Real Estate Development Enterprises (2014)
主要统计指标解释……139
Explanatory Notes on Main Statistical Indicators

七、能源
Energy

简要说明……148
Brief Introduction
7-1 能源生产、消费总量及构成……150
Total Production and Consumption of Energy and Its Composition
7-2 主要能源平衡情况(2014 年)……152

Main Energy Balance Sheet(2014)
7-3 能源生产弹性系数······154
Elasticity Ratio of Energy Production
7-4 平均每万人能源生产量······154
Energy Production Per 10 000 Population
7-5 能源加工转换效率······154
Efficiency of Energy Conversion
7-6 单位 GDP 能耗······155
Energy Consumption Per Unit of GDP by City (District)
7-7 单位工业增加值能耗······156
Energy Consumption Per Unit of Value Added of Industry
7-8 能源消费弹性系数······157
Elasticity Ratio of Energy Consumption
7-9 平均每天各种能源消费量······157
Average Daily Energy Consumption by Variety
7-10 全省用电总量······158
Total Electricity Consumption in the Whole Province
7-11 主要能源按行业分组消费量(2014 年)······159
Consumption of Main Energy by Sector (2014)
7-12 平均每万元工业总产值能源消费量(2014 年)······161
Energy Consumption Per 10 000 Yuan of Gross Industrial Output Value(2014)
7-13 各市(区)规模以上工业企业能源消费量(2014 年)······162
Industrial Enterprises above Designated Size Consumption of Energy by City(District) (2014)
7-14 规模以上工业企业主要能源按行业分组消费量(2014 年)······164
Industrial Enterprises above Designated Size Consumption of Main Energy by Sector (2014)
主要统计指标解释······166
Explanatory Notes on Main Statistical Indicators

八、财政
Government Finance

简要说明······170
Brief Introduction
8-1 财政收支总额······172
Government Revenue and Expenditure
8-2 财政分项目收支······173
Government Revenue and Expenditure by Item
8-3 各市、县(市、区)财政收支(2014 年)······174
Government Revenue and Expenditure by City and County (City and District) (2014)
主要统计指标解释······177
Explanatory Notes on Main Statistical Indicators

九、价格指数
Price Indices

简要说明······182
Brief Introduction
9-1 商品零售价格和居民消费价格指数······184
Retail Price Indices and Consumer Price Indices
9-2 商品零售价格分类指数(2014 年)······185
Retail Price Indices by Category (2014)
9-3 居民消费价格分类指数(2014 年)······187
Consumer Price Indices by Category (2014)

9-4　十九个市、县商品零售价格分类指数(2014 年)……189
Retail Price Indices by Category of 19 Cities and Counties(2014)
9-5　十九个市、县居民消费价格分类指数(2014 年)……190
Consumer Price Indices by Category and Region of 19 Cities and Counties(2014)
9-6　农业生产资料价格指数……191
Price Indices for Means of Agricultural Production
9-7　工业生产者出厂价格指数……192
Producer Price Index for Industrial Products
9-8　工业生产者购进价格指数……193
Purchasing Price Index for Industrial Products
9-9　固定资产投资价格指数……193
Price Index of Investment in Fixed Assets
9-10　农产品生产价格指数……194
Producers' Price Indices for Farm Products
9-11　西安市住宅销售价格指数……194
Sales Price Index of Residential Buildings and Second-hand House in Xi'an
主要统计指标解释……195
Explanatory Notes on Main Statistical Indicators

十、人民生活
People's Livelihood

简要说明……198
Brief Introduction
10-1　城乡居民家庭人均收入及指数……200
Per Capita Annual Income of Urban and Rural Households
10-2　各市(区)城乡居民人均收入……201
Per Capita Income in Urban and Rural Households by City(District)
10-3　城乡居民人民币储蓄存款(年底余额)……201
Savings Deposit of Urban and Rural Households at Year-end
10-4　全省居民家庭基本情况……202
Basic Conditions of All Households
10-5　全省居民家庭人均可支配收入……203
Per Capita Annual Disposable Income of All Households
10-6　全省居民家庭人均生活消费支出……204
Per Capita Living Expenditure of All Households
10-7　全省居民家庭人均购买主要商品数量……205
Per Capita Annual Purchases of Major Commodities of All Households
10-8　全省居民家庭每百户耐用消费品拥有情况……206
Ownership of Major Durable Consumer Goods Per 100 All Households
10-9　全省居民家庭年末居住情况……207
Housing Conditions of All Households
10-10　城镇常住居民家庭基本情况……208
Basic Conditions of Urban Households
10-11　城镇常住居民不同收入层次家庭基本情况(2014 年)……209
Basic Conditions of Urban Households by Income Percentile(2014)
10-12　城镇常住居民不同收入层次家庭人均可支配收入 (2014 年)……210
Per capita Annual Disposable Income of Urban Households by Income percentile(2014)
10-13　城镇常住居民不同收入层次家庭人均生活消费支出(2014 年)……212
Per Capita Living Expenditure of Urban Households by Income Percentile(2014)
10-14　城镇常住居民不同收入层次家庭人均购买主要商品数量（2014 年）……213
Per Capita Annual Purchases of Major Commodities of Urban Households by Income Percentile(2014)
10-15　城镇常住居民不同收入层次家庭每百户耐用消费品拥有情况 (2014 年)……214

Ownership of Major Durable Consumer Goods Per 100 Urban Households by Income Percentile(2014)
10-16 城镇常住居民家庭年末居住情况 ······215
Housing Conditions of Urban Households
10-17 农村常住居民家庭基本情况······216
Basic Conditions of Urban Households
10-18 农村常住居民不同收入层次家庭基本情况(2014 年) ······217
Basic Conditions of Rural Households by Income Percentile(2014)
10-19 农村常住居民不同收入层次家庭人均可支配收入(2014 年)······218
Per capita Annual Disposable Income of Rural Households by Income percentile(2014)
10-20 农村常住居民不同收入层次家庭人均生活消费支出(2014 年)······220
Per Capita Living Expenditure of Rural Households by Income Percentile(2014)
10-21 农村常住居民不同收入层次家庭人均购买主要商品数量(2014 年)······221
Per Capita Annual Purchases of Major Commodities of Rural Households by Income Percentile(2014)
10-22 农村常住居民不同收入层次家庭每百户耐用消费品拥有情况 (2014 年)······222
Ownership of Major Durable Consumer Goods Per 100 Rural Households by Income Percentile(2014)
10-23 农村常住居民家庭年末居住情况 ······223
Housing Conditions of Rural Households
10-24 各县(市、区)城乡居民人均收入(2014 年)······224
Per Capita Income in Urban and Rural Households by County (City and District)(2014)
主要统计指标解释······226
Explanatory Notes on Main Statistical Indicators

十一、环境和城市
Environment and Cities

简要说明 ······230
Brief Introduction
11-1 环境保护基本情况······232
Basic Statistics on Environmental Protection
11-2 各市(区)工业固体废物排放及处理情况(2014 年) ······235
Production and Treatment of Industrial Solid Wastes by City(District)(2014)
11-3 各市(区)工业废水排放及处理量(2014 年)······235
Discharge and Treatment of Industrial Waste Water by City(District)(2014)
11-4 各市(区)工业废气排放及处理情况(2014 年)······236
Emission and Treatment of Industrial Waste Gas by City(District)(2014)
11-5 城市设施水平(2014 年)······236
Level of Public Facilities in Cities(2014)
11-6 城市市政设施(2014 年)······237
Municipal Infrastructure in Cities(2014)
11-7 城市供水情况(2014 年)······237
Basic Statistics on Tap Water Supply in Cities (2014)
11-8 城市园林绿化情况(2014 年) ······238
Basic Statistics on Parks, Gardens and Green Areas in Cities(2014)
11-9 城市环境卫生情况(2014 年) ······238
Basic Statistics on Urban Sanitation in Cities(2014)
11-10 城市燃气情况(2014 年)······239
Basic Statistics on Supply of Gas in Cities(2014)
11-11 国家级风景名胜区(2014 年) ······239
State Scenic Spots at National Level (2014)
主要统计指标解释······240
Explanatory Notes on Main Statistical Indicators

十二、农业
Agriculture

简要说明 ……246
Brief Introduction

12-1 常用耕地面积 ……248
Area of Cultivated Land

12-2 各市(区)常用耕地面积(2014 年) ……248
Area of Cultivated Land by City(District)(2014)

12-3 农林牧渔业总产值 ……249
Gross Output Value of Agriculture, Forestry, Animal Husbandry and Fishery

12-4 各市(区)农林牧渔业总产值(2014 年) ……249
Gross Output Value of Agriculture, Forestry, Animal Husbandry and Fishery by City(District)(2014)

12-5 农林牧渔业总产值指数(1978 年=100) ……250
Indices of Gross Output Value of Agriculture, Forestry, Animal Husbandry and Fishery (year of 1978=100)

12-6 农林牧渔业总产值指数(上年=100) ……250
Indices of Gross Output Value of Agriculture, Forestry, Animal Husbandry and Fishery (preceding year=100)

12-7 农林牧渔业分项产值 ……251
Gross Output Value of Agriculture, Forestry, Animal Husbandry and Fishery by Item

12-8 农林牧渔业增加值 ……252
Value Added of Agriculture, Forestry, Animal Husbandry and Fishery

12-9 各市(区)农林牧渔业增加值(2014 年) ……252
Value Added of Farming, Forestry, Animal Husbandry Fishery by City(District)(2014)

12-10 主要农作物播种面积 ……253
Total Sown Areas of Major Farm Crops

12-11 各市(区)主要农作物播种面积(2014 年) ……254
Total Sown Areas of Major Farm Crops by City(District)(2014)

12-12 主要农作物产品产量 ……255
Output of Major Farm Products

12-13 各市(区)主要农产品产量(2014 年) ……256
Output of Major Farm Products by City(District)(2014)

12-14 主要农产品单位面积产量 ……257
Output of Major Farm Products Per Hectare

12-15 各市(区)主要农作物单位面积产量(2014 年) ……258
Output of Major Farm Products Per Hectare by City(District)(2014)

12-16 茶、桑、果面积及产量 ……259
Areas and Output of Tea Plantation, Cocoon, Orchards

12-17 水果生产情况 ……259
Production of Fruit

12-18 各市(区)茶、桑、果面积及产量(2014 年) ……260
Areas and Output of Tea Plantation, Cocoon, Orchards by City(District)(2014)

12-19 主要林产品产量 ……261
Output of Major Forest Products

12-20 各市(区)主要林产品产量(2014 年) ……261
Output of Major Forest Products by City(District)(2014)

12-21 各市(区)造林情况(2014 年) ……262
Area of Afforestation by City(District)(2014)

12-22 畜牧业和渔业生产情况 ……263
Production of Animal Husbandry and Fishery

12-23 各市(区)牲畜存栏情况 (2014 年) ……264
Livestock by City(District)(2014)

12-24 各市(区)主要畜产品和水产品产量(2014 年) ……265
Output of Livestock and Aquatic Products by City(District)(2014)

12-25 粮食生产大县情况 266
Large County of Food Production
12-26 商品棉基地县情况 267
Base County of Marketable Cotton
12-27 烤烟主产县情况 267
Base County of Flue-cured Tobacco
12-28 苹果基地县情况 268
Base County of Apple
12-29 梨基地县情况 269
Base County of Pear
12-30 猕猴桃基地县情况 269
Base County of Kiwi
12-31 各市(区)灾情(2014 年) 270
Conditions in Natural Disaster by City(District)(2014)
12-32 农业现代化情况 270
Agriculture Modernization
12-33 各市(区)农业现代化情况 (2014) 271
Agriculture Modernization by City(District) (2014)
12-34 各市、县(市、区)农村经济主要指标(2014 年) 272
Main Indicators of Rural Economy by City and County (City and District) (2014)
主要统计指标解释 281
Explanatory Notes on Main Statistical Indicators

十三、工业
Industry

简要说明 286
Brief Introduction
13-1 全部工业总产值 288
Gross Industrial Output Value
13-2 规模以上工业企业主要经济指标(1998-2014 年) 289
Main Indicators of Industrial Enterprises above Designated Size (1998-2014)
13-3 规模以上工业企业主要经济效益指标(1998-2014 年) 289
Main Indicators on Economic Benefit of Industrial Enterprises above Designated Size(1998-2014)
13-4 规模以上工业企业主要经济指标(2014 年) 290
Main Indicators of Industrial Enterprises above Designated Size(2014)
13-5 规模以上工业企业分行业主要经济指标(2014 年) 298
Main Indicators of Industrial Enterprises above Designated Size by Industrial Sector (2014)
13-6 国有及国有控股工业企业主要经济指标(2014 年) 302
Main Indicators of State-owned and State-holding Industrial Enterprises (2014)
13-7 外商及港澳台商投资工业企业主要经济指标(2014 年) 306
Main Indicators of Industrial Enterprises with Hong Kong, Macao, Taiwan and Foreign Funds (2014)
13-8 大中型工业企业主要经济指标(2014 年) 310
Main Indicators of Large and Medium-sized Industrial Enterprises(2014)
13-9 八大工业支柱产业主要经济指标(2014 年) 314
Main Indicators of Industrial Enterprises(2014)
13-10 规模以上工业企业主要经济效益指标(2014 年) 316
Main Indicators on Economic Benefit of Industrial Enterprises above Designated Size (2014)
13-11 规模以上工业企业分行业主要经济效益指标(2014 年) 318
Main Indicators on Economic Benefit of Industrial Enterprises above Designated Size by Industrial Sector (2014)
13-12 国有及国有控股工业企业主要经济效益指标(2014 年) 319
Main Indicators on Economic Benefit of State-owned and State-holding Industrial Enterprises(2014)
13-13 外商及港澳台商投资工业企业主要经济效益指标(2014 年) 320

Main Indicators on Economic Benefit of Industrial Enterprises with Hong Kong, Macao, Taiwan and Foreign Funds (2014)
13-14 大中型工业企业主要经济效益指标(2014 年) ······ 321
Main Indicators on Economic Benefit of Large and Medium-sized Industrial Enterprises(2014)
13-15 主要工业产品产量 ······ 322
Output of Major Industrial Products
13-16 各市(区)规模以上工业企业工业总产值(1995-2014 年) ······ 324
Gross Industrial Output Value above Designated Size by City(District)(1995-2014)
13-17 各市(区)规模以上工业企业主要经济指标(2014 年) ······ 325
Main Indicators of Industrial Enterprises above Designated Size by City(District)(2014)
主要统计指标解释 ······ 326
Explanatory Notes on Main Statistical Indicators

十四、建筑业
Construction

简要说明 ······ 332
Brief Introduction
14-1 建筑业总产值 ······ 335
Gross Output Value of Construction
14-2 具有资质等级的建筑业企业主要指标(2014 年) ······ 336
Main Production Indicators of Construction Enterprises Which Possess Qualification Grades(2014)
14-3 施工总承包和专业承包建筑业企业主要指标(2014 年) ······ 340
Main Indicators of General Contracting and Professional Contracting in Construction Enterprises (2014)
14-4 劳务分包建筑业企业主要指标(2014 年) ······ 348
Main Production Indicators of Labor Subcontracting in Construction Enterprises (2014)
14-5 各市(区)建筑业企业个数(2014 年) ······ 350
Number of Construction Enterprises by City(District) (2014)
14-6 各市(区)建筑业企业直接从事生产经营活动平均人数(2014 年) ······ 350
Number of Employed Persons at Year-end of Construction Enterprises by City(District)(2014)
14-7 各市(区)建筑业企业年末从业人数(2014 年) ······ 351
Annual Average Persons of Construction Enterprises by City(District)(2014)
14-8 各市(区)建筑业企业总产值(2014 年) ······ 351
Gross Output Value of Construction Enterprises by City(District)(2014)
14-9 各市(区)建筑业企业劳动生产率(2014 年) ······ 352
Labor Productivity of Construction Enterprises by City(District)(2014)
14-10 各市(区)建筑业企业竣工产值(2014 年) ······ 352
Output Value of Buildings Completed in Construction Enterprises by City(District)(2014)
14-11 各市(区)建筑业企业房屋建筑施工面积(2014 年) ······ 353
Floor Space of Building under Construction in Construction Enterprises by City(District)(2014)
14-12 各市(区)建筑业企业房屋建筑竣工面积(2014 年) ······ 353
Floor Space of Building Completed in Construction Enterprises by City(District)(2014)
14-13 各市(区)建筑业企业竣工房屋价值(2014 年) ······ 354
Valuation of Building Completed in Construction Enterprises by City(District)(2014)
14-14 各市(区)建筑业企业资产合计(2014 年) ······ 354
Total Assets of Construction Enterprises by City(District)(2014)
14-15 各市(区)建筑业企业负债合计(2014 年) ······ 355
Total Liability of Construction Enterprises by City(District)(2014)
14-16 各市(区)建筑业企业固定资产(2014 年) ······ 355
Fixed Assets of Construction Enterprises by City(District)(2014)
14-17 各市(区)建筑业企业流动资产(2014 年) ······ 356
Circulating Assets of Construction Enterprises by City(District)(2014)
14-18 各市(区)建筑业企业实收资本(2014 年) ······ 356

Contributed Capital of Construction Enterprises by City(District)(2014)
14-19 各市(区)建筑业主营业务收入(2014 年)……357
Revenue from Principal Business of Construction Enterprises by City(District)(2014)
14-20 各市(区)建筑业企业利润总额(2014 年)……357
Total Profits of Construction Enterprises by City(District)(2014)
14-21 各市(区)建筑业企业税金总额(2014 年)……358
Total Tax of Construction Enterprises by City(District)(2014)
14-22 各市(区)建筑业企业年末应收工程款(2014 年)……358
Account Receivable of Projects at Year-end of Construction Enterprises by City(District)(2014)
14-23 各市(区)建筑业企业主要经济效益指标(2014 年)……359
Main Indicators on Economic Efficiency of Construction Enterprises by City(District)(2014)
主要统计指标解释……360
Explanatory Notes on Main Statistical Indicators

十五、运输和邮电
Transport, Post and Telecommunication Services

简要说明……364
Brief Introduction
15-1 运输线路里程、质量和运输网密度……366
Length, Quality and Density of Transportation Routes
15-2 铁路、公路线路长度及民航航线……367
Length of Railways, Highways and Civil Aviation
15-3 运输工具……368
Transportation
15-4 各市(区)公路里程(2014 年末)……368
Length of Highways by City(District)(2014)
15-5 客运量、旅客周转量及构成……369
Passenger Traffic, Passenger-Kilometers and Composition
15-6 货运量、货物周转量及构成……370
Freight Traffic, Freight Ton-Kilometers and Composition
15-7 民用汽车拥有量(2014 年末)……371
Possession of Civil Vehicles(2014)
15-8 私人车辆拥有量(2014 年末)……371
Possession of Private Vehicles(2014)
15-9 公路部门营运载客车拥有量(2014 年末)……372
Possession of Vehicles in Operation for Highway Transportation(2014)
15-10 公路部门营运载货车拥有量(2014 年末)……373
Possession of Vehicles in Operation for Highway Transportation(2014)
15-11 城市公共汽车情况(2014 年)……374
Basic Statistics on Bus in Cities (2014)
15-12 城市出租汽车情况(2014 年)……374
Basic Statistics on Taxi in Cities (2014)
15-13 铁路客货运输量……375
Passenger and Freight Traffic of Railways
15-14 全省公路客货运输量(2014 年)……375
Passenger and Freight Traffic of Highway Departments(2014)
15-15 铁路运输主要经济技术指标……376
Principal Economic and Technical Indicators of Railway Transport
15-16 铁路分品类货物发送量及装车数……376
Volume of Freight Dispatched and Loaded Cars of Railways by Category of Cargo
15-17 邮电业务总量……377
Total Business Volume of Post and Telecommunication Services

15-18 邮电通信水平……377
Level of Post and Telecommunication Services
15-19 各市(区)邮政业务量(2014 年)……378
Total Business Volume of Post Services by City(District)(2014)
15-20 各市(区)电信业务量(2014 年)……378
Total Business Volume of Telecommunication Services by City(District)(2014)
15-21 各市(区)邮电局所及邮递线路(2014 年)……379
Postal and Telecommunication Offices and Postal Routes by City(District)(2014)
15-22 邮电通信企业主要财务指标……379
Principal Financial Indicators of Postal and Telecommunication Services Enterprises
主要统计指标解释……380
Explanatory Notes on Main Statistical Indicators

十六、国内贸易
Domestic Trade

简要说明……384
Brief Introduction
16-1 限额以上批发和零售业、住宿和餐饮业法人企业数和从业人员数(2014 年)……386
Number of Corporation Enterprises above Designated Size in Wholesale and Retail Trades, Hotels and Catering Services and Employed Persons(2014)
16-2 社会消费品零售总额……387
Total Retail Sales of Consumer Goods in the Whole Province
16-3 各市(区)社会消费品零售总额……388
Total Retail Sales of Consumer Goods by City(District)
16-4 各市(区)按销售单位所在地和消费形态分的社会消费品零售总额(2014 年)……389
Total Retail Sales of Consumer Goods by Location of Establishments and Consumption Patterns by City(District)(2014)
16-5 各市、县(市、区)社会消费品零售总额……390
Total Retail Sales of Consumer Goods by City and County(City and District)
16-6 限额以上批发和零售企业(单位)商品零售类值……393
Total Sales of Enterprises above Designated Size in Retail Trades by Category of Commodities
16-7 限额以上批发业商品购进、销售、库存总额(2014 年)……394
Total Purchases, Sales and Inventory of Enterprises above Designated Size in Wholesale Trades(2014)
16-8 限额以上零售业商品购进、销售、库存总额(2014 年)……398
Total Purchases, Sales and Inventory of Enterprises above Designated Size in Retail Trades (2014)
16-9 各市(区)限额以上批发业商品购进总额(2014 年)……404
Total Purchases of Enterprises above Designated Size in Wholesale Trades by City(District)(2014)
16-10 各市(区)限额以上零售业商品购进总额(2014 年)……405
Total Purchases of Enterprises above Designated Size in Retail Trades by City(District)(2014)
16-11 各市(区)限额以上批发业商品销售总额(2014 年)……406
Total Sales of Enterprises above Designated Size in Wholesale Trades by City(District)(2014)
16-12 各市(区)限额以上零售业商品销售总额(2014 年)……407
Total Sales of Enterprises above Designated Size in Retail Trades by City(District)(2014)
16-13 各市(区)限额以上批发业商品库存总额(2014 年)……408
Total Inventory of Enterprises above Designated Size in Wholesale Trades by City(District)(2014)
16-14 各市(区)限额以上零售业商品库存总额(2014 年)……409
Total Inventory of Enterprises above Designated Size in Retail Trades by City(District)(2014)
16-15 限额以上住宿业经营情况(2014 年)……410
Management of Enterprises above Designated Size of Hotels(2014)
16-16 限额以上餐饮业经营情况(2014 年)……412
Management of Enterprises above Designated Size of Catering Services(2014)
16-17 各市(区)限额以上住宿业和餐饮业经营情况(2014 年)……414
Management of Enterprises above Designated Size in Hotels and Catering Services by City(District)(2014)

16-18 限额以上批发业主要财务指标(2014 年) ……416
Main Financial Indicators of Enterprises above Designated Size in Wholesale Trades(2014)
16-19 限额以上零售业主要财务指标(2014 年) ……420
Main Financial Indicators of Enterprises above Designated Size in Retail Trades(2014)
16-20 限额以上住宿业主要财务指标(2014 年) ……424
Main Financial Indicators in Hotels above Designated Size(2014)
16-21 限额以上餐饮业主要财务指标(2014 年) ……426
Main Financial Indicators of Enterprises above Designated Size in Catering Services(2014)
16-22 批发和零售业、住宿和餐饮业连锁经营情况(2014 年) ……428
Chain Management of Enterprises of Wholesale, Retail Trades, Hotels and and Catering Services(2014)
16-23 限额以上产业活动单位和个体户批发业商品购、销、存总额(2014 年) ……429
Total Purchases, Sales and Inventory of Industrial Activity Units and Individuals above Designated Size in Wholesale Trades(2014)
16-24 限额以上产业活动单位和个体户零售业商品购、销、存总额(2014 年) ……430
Total Purchases, Sales and Inventory of Industrial Activity Units and Individuals above Designated Size in Retail Trades(2014)
16-25 限额以上产业活动单位和个体户住宿业经营情况(2014 年) ……432
Management of Industrial Activity Units and Individuals above Designated Size of Hotels(2014)
16-26 限额以上产业活动单位和个体户餐饮业经营情况(2014 年) ……433
Management of Industrial Activity Units and Individuals above Designated Size of Catering Services(2014)
16-27 重点交易市场情况(2014 年) ……434
Focus on Transaction Markets(2014)
16-28 重点交易市场商品销售类值(2014 年) ……435
Total Sales at Main Trade Markets by Category of Commodities(2014)
16-29 重点交易市场成交情况(2014 年) ……436
Turnover of Main Commodity Transaction Markets(2014)
16-30 成品油批发企业能源购进、销售与库存(2014 年) ……437
Total Purchases, Sales and Inventory of Energy of Petroleum Products Enterprises in Wholesale Trades in the Whole Province(2014)
16-31 各市(区)成品油批发企业能源购进量(2014 年) ……437
Total Purchases of Energy of Petroleum Products Enterprises in Wholesale Trades by City(District)(2014)
16-32 各市(区)成品油批发企业能源销售量(2014 年) ……438
Total Sales of Energy of Petroleum Products Enterprises in Wholesale Trades by City(District)(2014)
16-33 各市(区)成品油批发企业能源年末库存量(2014 年) ……438
Inventory of Energy of Petroleum Products Enterprises in Wholesale Trades by City(District) at Year-end(2014)
主要统计指标解释 ……439
Explanatory Notes on Main Statistical Indicators

十七、对外经济贸易和旅游
Foreign Trade and Tourism

简要说明 ……444
Brief Introduction
17-1 外贸进出口总值 ……446
Total Value of Imports and Exports in Foreign Trade
17-2 按贸易方式分外贸进口总值 ……447
Total Value of Imports in Foreign Trade by Type of Trade
17-3 按贸易方式分外贸出口总值 ……447
Total Value of Exports in Foreign Trade by Type of Trade
17-4 按国别(地区)分外贸进出口总值(2014 年) ……448
Total Value of Imports and Exports in Foreign Trade by Country (Region)(2014)
17-5 进出口商品分类金额(2014 年) ……452
Value of Imports and Exports by HS Section and Division(2014)

17-6 主要出口商品数量、金额(2014 年)……457
Main Export Commodities in Volume and Value(2014)
17-7 主要进口商品数量、金额(2014 年)……462
Main Import Commodities in Volume and Value(2014)
17-8 利用外资情况……466
Utilization of Foreign Capital
17-9 外商投资情况……467
Foreign Investment
17-10 旅游总收入和总人数……469
Total Income and Number of Visitors
17-11 旅游业发展情况……469
Development of Tourism
17-12 分国别入境旅游人数……470
Number of Oversea Visitor Arrivals by Country/Region
17-13 各市(区)对外经济和国际旅游情况(2014 年)……470
Foreign Economy Trade and International Tourism by City(District)(2014)
17-14 主要星级饭店基本情况(2014 年)……471
Basic Conditions of Main Star-Degree-Hotels(2014)
主要统计指标解释……473
Explanatory Notes on Main Statistical Indicators

十八、金融和保险
Banking and Insurance

简要说明……476
Brief Introduction
18-1 金融机构(含外资)人民币信贷收支(年底余额)……478
Summary of Sources & Uses of Funds of Financial Institutions in RMB (Uncluding Foreign Currency at Year-end)
18-2 证券业主要情况……479
General Statistics on Securities Markets
18-3 保险业保费收入(2014 年)……479
Premium of Insurance Transactions (2014)
主要统计指标解释……480
Explanatory Notes on Main Statistical Indicators

十九、教育、科技和文化
Education, Science, Technology and Culture

简要说明……482
Brief Introduction
19-1 各级各类教育基本情况(2014 年)……484
Basic Statistics on Schools by Level and Type of School(2014)
19-2 普通高等学校基本情况……485
Basic Statistics on Regular Institutions of Higher Education
19-3 中等职业学校基本情况……485
Basic Statistics on Vocational Secondary Schools
19-4 普通中学基本情况……486
Basic Statistics on Regular Secondary Schools
19-5 普通小学基本情况……486
Basic Statistics on Regular Primary Schools
19-6 技工学校基本情况(2014 年)……487
Basic Statistics on Technical Schools(2014)

19-7 全省科技活动情况……487
Scientific and Technological Activities in the Whole Province
19-8 全省地方登记的科技成果……488
Achievements in Science and Technology in the Whole Province
19-9 地方公有经济企业专业技术人才分行业情况(2014 年)……489
Situation of Professional and Technical Personnel in Local Public Economy Enterprises(2014)
19-10 规模以上工业企业研究与试验发展(R&D)人员和经费支出情况(2014 年)……490
R&D Personnel and Expenditure of Industrial Enterprises above Designated (2014)
19-11 规模以上工业企业研究与试验发展(R&D)项目情况(2014 年)……492
The Situation of Industrial Enterprises above Designated Projects (2014)
19-12 规模以上工业企业新产品开发、生产及销售情况(2014 年)……494
Developing, Producing and Sales of Industrial Enterprises above Designated (2014)
19-13 规模以上工业企业自主知识产权保护情况(2014 年)……496
Proprietary Intellectual Property Rights of Industrial Enterprises above Designated (2014)
19-14 专利项目……500
Patent Items
19-15 各类技术合同签定情况……500
Statistics on Technical Contracts Signed by Type
19-16 文化事业……501
Development of Culture Industry
19-17 文化事业机构和人员……501
Number of Institution and Personnel in Cultural Industry
19-18 群众艺术馆、文化馆(站)活动情况……502
Activities Statistics on Mass Art Centers and Cultural Centers(Stations)
19-19 文物事业……502
Development of Cultural Relics
19-20 广播电视基本情况……503
Basic Statistics on Radio and Television
19-21 图书出版……504
Number of Books Published
19-22 杂志、报纸出版……505
Number of Magazines and Newspapers Published
19-23 各市(区)文化事业情况(2014 年)……505
Basic Statistics on Cultural Industry by City(District)(2014)
主要统计指标解释……506
Explanatory Notes on Main Statistical Indicators

二十、体育、卫生和其他
Sports, Public Health and Others

简要说明……510
Brief Introduction
20-1 体育事业……512
Statistics on Sports Industry
20-2 等级运动员发展人数(2014 年)……512
Number of Athletes in Grades by Type of Sports (2014)
20-3 卫生机构、床位及人员数……513
Number of Health Units, Beds and Staff
20-4 各类卫生机构、床位及人员数(2014 年)……514
Number of Various Health Units, Beds and Staff (2014)
20-5 传染病发病率和死亡率(2014 年)……515
The Incidence and Death of Infectious Diseases(2014)
20-6 出院病人前十位疾病构成（2014 年）……516

Discharged Patients Diseases of the Top Ten (2014)
20-7 各市(区)卫生机构、床位及人员数(2014 年)……517
Number of Health Institutions, Beds and Persons Engaged by City(District) (2014)
20-8 农村村级卫生组织情况(2014 年)……517
Situations of Health Institutions in Rural Village (2014)
20-9 社区卫生服务中心(站)情况(2014 年)……518
Statistics on Community Health Service Centers (Stations) (2014)
20-10 新型农村合作医疗情况……518
Statistics on New Cooperative Medical System
20-11 社会福利事业、企业单位机构和人员……519
Social Welfare, Business Unit Organizations and Personnel
20-12 社会福利事业单位基本情况(2014 年)……519
Basic Statistics on Social Welfare Institutions (2014)
20-13 社会福利企业基本情况(2014 年)……520
Basic Statistics on Social Welfare Enterprises (2014)
20-14 城镇社区服务设施(2014 年)……520
Urban Welfare Facilities (2014)
20-15 律师、公证及人民调解工作(2014 年)……521
Lawyers, Notarization and Mediation of Civil Disputes (2014)
20-16 国内公证文书分类(2014 年)……521
Domestic Notarized Documents by Type (2014)
20-17 婚姻登记情况……522
Registered Marriages
20-18 各市(区)婚姻登记情况(2014 年)……522
Registered Marriages by City(District) (2014)
20-19 交通事故情况……523
Basic Statistics on Traffic Accidents
20-20 火灾事故情况……523
Basic Statistics on Fires
20-21 各类伤亡事故情况(2014 年)……524
Statistics on Various Fatal Accident (2014)
20-22 社会捐赠和收养登记情况(2014 年)……524
Statistics on Social Donation and Adopting Registration (2014)
主要统计指标解释……525
Explanatory Notes on Main Statistical Indicators

二十一、水利
Irrigation

简要说明……528
Brief Introduction
21-1 水利建设投资情况(2014 年)……530
Construction Investment Situation of Hydroproject(2014)
21-2 灌溉面积(2014 年)……531
Irrigated Areas(2014)
21-3 易涝耕地面积治理情况(2014 年)……532
Management Situation of Areas of Floating Plowland (2014)
21-4 用水总量(2014 年)……532
Water Use (2014)
21-5 水利工程供水总量(2014 年)……533
Water Supply by Water Projects(2014)
21-6 堤防情况(2014 年)……534
Dikes Situation(2014)

21-7 水库情况(2014 年) 535
Situation of Reservoir (2014)
21-8 万亩以上灌区基本情况(2014 年) 535
Basic Irrigated Area above 10 000 Acres (2014)
21-9 农村饮水安全达标情况(2014 年) 536
Basic Statistics on Rural Drinking Water Safety Standards(2014)
21-10 水土保持情况(2014 年) 536
Basic Statistics on Soil and Water Conservation(2014)
21-11 农村水电装机情况(2014 年) 537
Basic Statistics on Rural Hydropower Installed Capacity(2014)
主要统计指标解释 538
Explanatory Notes on Main Statistical Indicators

二十二、全国各省、市、自治区主要指标
Main Indicators of National Economy by Countrywide, Province, Municipality and Autonomous Region

简要说明 544
Brief Introduction
22-1 生产总值(2014 年) 545
Gross Domestic Product(2014)
22-2 年末常住人口 546
Resident Population and Per Capita GDP
22-3 固定资产投资 547
Investment in Fixed Assets
22-4 房地产开发企业投资和商品房销售额 548
Total Investment in Real Estate Development and Total Sale of Commercialized Buildings
22-5 居民消费价格分类指数(2014 年) 549
Consumer Price Index by Category(2014)
22-6 城乡居民人均收入 550
Per Capita Income of Urban and Rural Residents
22-7 农林牧渔业总产值(2014 年) 551
Gross Output Value of Farming, Forestry, Animal Husbandry and Fishery (2014)
22-8 主要农产品产量(2014 年) 552
Output of Major Farm Crops (2014)
22-9 主要工业产品产量(2014 年) 553
Output of Major Industrial Products(2014)
22-10 社会消费品零售总额和进出口总额 554
Total Retail Sales of Consumer Goods and Total Import and Export

附录 2014 年陕西省统计局大事记 555
2014 年陕西调查总队大事记 558
陕西省统计局机构一览表 563
陕西调查总队机构一览表 564
统计职业道德规范 565
陕西统计人精神 566

一、行政区划和自然资源

Divisions of Administrative Areas and Natural Resources

资料整理：李　娟　潘英杰

简 要 说 明

一、本篇资料反映陕西行政区划、自然资源的开发和利用等情况。自然资源包括土地、气候、森林、水利、矿产资源情况。

二、本篇资料来源：行政区划、矿产资源、森林资源、水利、气象资料分别由省民政厅、省国土资源厅、省林业厅、省水利厅、省气象局提供，土地资源资料取自省国土资源厅《陕西省国土资源公报（2012年度）》。

Brief Introduction

Ⅰ.This chapter reflects the data on administrative division's areas and the exploitation and utilization of the natural resources of Shaanxi Province. Natural resources cover land, climate, forest, water conservancy and mineral resources.

Ⅱ.Data resources: the data on administrative divisions, mineral resources, forest resources, water conservancy and meteorology are provided by Shaanxi Province Department of Civil Affairs, Shaanxi Province Department of Land and Resources, Shaanxi Province Forestry Department, Shaanxi Province Water Department of Resources and Shaanxi Province Meteorological Bureau. The data on land resources are obtained from "Shaanxi Territorial Resources communiqué (2012)".

1.行政区划和自然资源

陕西位于东经105° 29′ －111° 15′ 和北纬31° 42′ －39° 35′ 之间，东隔黄河与山西相望，西连甘肃、宁夏，北临内蒙古，南连四川、重庆，东南与河南、湖北接壤。2014年全省设西安、铜川、宝鸡、咸阳、渭南、延安、汉中、榆林、安康、商洛10个省辖市和杨凌农业高新技术产业示范区，有 3 个县级市，80个县和24个市辖区，1142个镇，74个乡，204个街道办事处。

全省面积为20.56万平方公里。地势南北高、中间低，西部高、东部低，地形复杂多样，北部为陕北黄土高原，中部为号称“八百里秦川”的关中平原，南部为陕南秦巴山地。

全省以秦岭为界南北河流分属长江水系和黄河水系。主要有渭河、泾河、洛河、无定河和汉江、丹江、嘉陵江等。陕西属大陆性季风气候，年平均气温13.5摄氏度，年降水量685.6毫米，南北差异明显。

全省自然资源丰富，矿产多，储量大，探明矿产储量居全国前十位的矿种有60多种。

主要城市降水量（毫米）

（2014年）

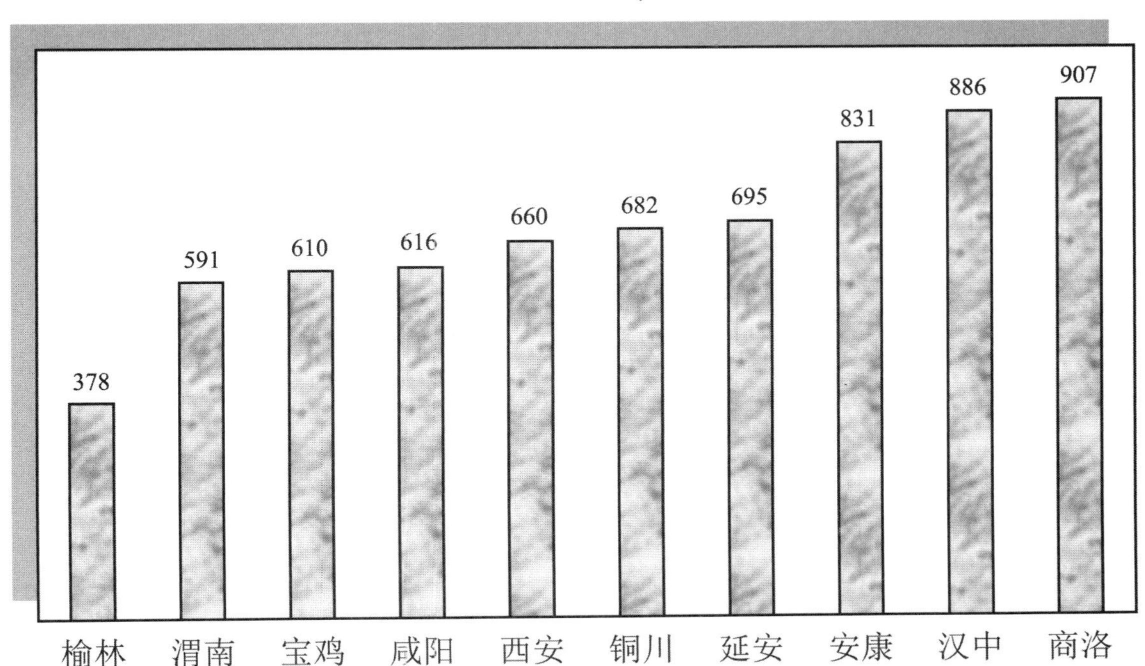

1-1 陕西省行政区划(2014年)
Divisions of Administrative Areas in Shaanxi (2014)

单位：个 (unit)

地　　区	Region	地级市 Cities at Prefecture Level	县级市 Cities at County Level	县 Counties	市辖区 Districts under the Jurisdiction of Cities	镇 Towns	乡 Townships	街道办事处 Street Communities
全　　省	**Shaanxi**	**11**	**3**	**80**	**24**	**1142**	**74**	**204**
西安市	Xi'an	1		4	9	67		111
铜川市	Tongchuan	1		1	3	23	5	13
宝鸡市	Baoji	1		9	3	105		15
咸阳市	Xianyang	1	1	10	2	126		25
渭南市	Weinan	1	2	8	1	130		12
延安市	Yan'an	1		12	1	91	31	3
汉中市	Hanzhong	1		10	1	180		8
榆林市	Yulin	1		11	1	138	38	7
安康市	Ankang	1		9	1	157		4
商洛市	Shangluo	1		6	1	122		4
杨凌示范区	Yangling	1			1	3		2

1-2 陕西省行政区划一览(2014年)
Divisions List of Administrative Areas in Shaanxi (2014)

单位：个 (unit)

地　　区	Region	镇 Towns	乡 Townships	街道办事处 Street Communities	村民委员会 Village Committees	居民委员会 Neighbourhood Committees
全　　省	**Shaanxi**	**1142**	**74**	**204**	**26519**	**2218**
西 安 市	**Xi'an**	**67**		**111**	**2957**	**812**
新城区	Xincheng			9		101
碑林区	Beilin			8		100
莲湖区	Lianhu			9	5	129
灞桥区	Baqiao			9	218	42
未央区	Weiyang			12	140	129
雁塔区	Yanta			8	83	129
阎良区	Yanliang	2		5	80	23
临潼区	Lintong			23	284	42
长安区	Chang'an			25	646	65
蓝田县	Lantian	22			519	9
周至县	Zhouzhi	22			376	14
户　县	Huxian	16			518	21
高陵县	Gaoling	5		3	88	8
铜 川 市	**Tongchuan**	**23**	**5**	**13**	**543**	**69**
王益区	Wangyi	1	1	5	39	20
印台区	Yintai	7		3	107	24
耀州区	Yaozhou	9	1	5	219	23
宜君县	Yijun	6	3		178	2
宝 鸡 市	**Baoji**	**105**		**15**	**1729**	**165**
渭滨区	Weibin	5		5	104	55
金台区	Jintai	4		7	102	51
陈仓区	Chencang	15		3	332	15
凤翔县	Fengxiang	12			233	4
岐山县	Qishan	10			144	14
扶风县	Fufeng	8			169	6
眉　县	Meixian	8			123	7
陇　县	Longxian	12			158	3
千阳县	Qianyang	8			98	2
麟游县	Linyou	7			100	2
凤　县	Fengxian	9			100	4
太白县	Taibai	7			66	2
咸 阳 市	**Xianyang**	**126**		**25**	**2766**	**219**
秦都区	Qindu	1		11	146	100
渭城区	Weicheng	1		9	130	46
三原县	Sanyuan	11			208	9
泾阳县	Jingyang	13			231	8
乾　县	Qianxian	16			256	8

1-2 续表 1 continued

单位：个 (unit)

地区	Region	镇 Towns	乡 Townships	街道办事处 Street Communities	村民委员会 Village Committees	居民委员会 Neighbourhood Committees
礼 泉 县	Liquan	12			317	13
永 寿 县	Yongshou	11			249	5
彬 县	Binxian	13			247	4
长 武 县	Changwu	9			160	1
旬 邑 县	Xunyi	11			187	2
淳 化 县	Chunhua	12			204	2
武 功 县	Wugong	8			212	6
兴 平 市	Xingping	8		5	219	15
渭 南 市	**Weinan**	**130**		**12**	**3185**	**210**
临 渭 区	Linwei	16		8	508	54
华 县	Huaxian	10			228	27
潼 关 县	Tongguan	6			78	15
大 荔 县	Dali	18			400	26
合 阳 县	Heyang	12			353	5
澄 城 县	Chengcheng	10			266	14
蒲 城 县	Pucheng	17			360	7
白 水 县	Baishui	10			194	11
富 平 县	Fuping	17			337	9
韩 城 市	Hancheng	10		2	275	26
华 阴 市	Huayin	4		2	186	16
延 安 市	**Yan'an**	**91**	**31**	**3**	**3386**	**92**
宝 塔 区	Baota	11	5	3	611	31
延 长 县	Yanchang	7	2		288	6
延 川 县	Yanchuan	8	2		346	7
子 长 县	Zichang	9	1		358	8
安 塞 县	Ansai	8	1		211	6
志 丹 县	Zhidan	7	1		200	5
吴 起 县	Wuqi	6	3		164	3
甘 泉 县	Ganquan	3	3		117	4
富 县	Fuxian	9	1		240	5
洛 川 县	Luochuan	7	5		371	2
宜 川 县	Yichuan	6	3		202	4
黄 龙 县	Huanglong	4	3		87	3
黄 陵 县	Huangling	6	1		191	8
汉 中 市	**Hanzhong**	**180**		**8**	**2630**	**188**
汉 台 区	Hantai	7		8	189	65
南 郑 县	Nanzheng	22			397	17
城 固 县	Chenggu	18			392	9
洋 县	Yangxian	20			357	13
西 乡 县	Xixiang	18			261	18
勉 县	Mianxian	19			233	10
宁 强 县	Ningqiang	21			269	11
略 阳 县	Lueyang	18			183	20
镇 巴 县	Zhenba	21			192	23
留 坝 县	Liuba	8			98	1
佛 坪 县	Foping	8			59	1

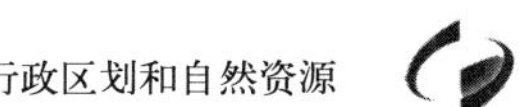

1-2 续表 2 continued

单位：个 (unit)

地　区	Region	镇 Towns	乡 Townships	街道办事处 Street Communities	村民委员会 Village Committees	居民委员会 Neighbourhood Committees
榆 林 市	**Yulin**	**138**	**38**	**7**	**5380**	**128**
榆 阳 区	Yuyang	14	7	7	488	49
神 木 县	Shenmu	15			631	8
府 谷 县	Fugu	15			232	10
横 山 县	Hengshan	12	2		361	6
靖 边 县	Jingbian	11	6		213	10
定 边 县	Dingbian	15	5		335	6
绥 德 县	Suide	12	4		661	8
米 脂 县	Mizhi	8	2		396	4
佳 县	Jiaxian	11	5		653	7
吴 堡 县	Wubu	6			221	5
清 涧 县	Qingjian	8	4		639	4
子 洲 县	Zizhou	11	3		550	11
安 康 市	**Ankang**	**157**		**4**	**2270**	**179**
汉 滨 区	Hanbin	30		4	744	52
汉 阴 县	Hanyin	14			179	8
石 泉 县	Shiquan	11			193	18
宁 陕 县	Ningshan	12			98	9
紫 阳 县	Ziyang	21			210	20
岚 皋 县	Langao	15			188	6
平 利 县	Pingli	11			190	6
镇 坪 县	Zhenping	9			78	4
旬 阳 县	Xunyang	22			266	52
白 河 县	Baihe	12			124	4
商 洛 市	**Shangluo**	**122**		**4**	**1605**	**138**
商 州 区	Shangzhou	19		4	390	28
洛 南 县	Luonan	19			351	30
丹 凤 县	Danfeng	16			183	25
商 南 县	Shangnan	13			164	3
山 阳 县	Shanyang	23			198	41
镇 安 县	Zhen'an	19			202	6
柞 水 县	Zhashui	13			117	5
杨凌示范区	**Yangling**	**3**		**2**	**68**	**18**
杨 陵 区	Yangling	3		2	68	18

1-3 自然状况及资源
Natural Conditions and Resources

指　　标	Item	2014
一、自然状况	**Natural Conditions**	
1.土　地	Land	
土地总面积　(万平方公里)	Land Area　(10 000 sq.km)	20.56
2.气　候	Climate	
全省年平均降水量　(毫米)	Annual Average Precipitation in the Whole Province　(mm)	685.6
全省年平均气温　(摄氏度)	Annual Average Temperature in the Whole Province　(℃)	13.5
全省年平均日照时数　(小时)	Annual Average Sunshine Hours in the Whole Province　(hour)	2001.4
全省年平均风速　(米/秒)	Annual Average Wind Speed in the Whole Province　(m/s)	1.8
全省年平均无霜期　(天)	Annual Average Frost-free Period in the Whole Province　(day)	237.5
二、自然资源	**Natural Resources**	
1.土地资源	Land Resources	
耕地面积　(万公顷)	Area of Cultivated Land　(10 000 hectares)	398.5
园地面积　(万公顷)	Area of Plantation Land　(10 000 hectares)	83.3
林地面积　(万公顷)	Area of Forestland　(10 000 hectares)	1121.[illegible]
草地面积　(万公顷)	Area of Grassland　(10 000 hectares)	287.8
居民点及工矿用地　(万公顷)	Residential Purpose, Manufacturing and Mining Land(10 000 hectares)	76.6
交通用地　(万公顷)	Transportation Land　(10 000 hectares)	24.4
水利设施用地　(万公顷)	Water-conservancy Projects Land　(10 000 hectares)	31.0
其他土地面积　(万公顷)	Area of Unused Land　(10 000 hectares)	33.5
2.林木资源	Forest Resources	
森林面积　(万公顷)	Forest Area　(10 000 hectares)	887.00
森林覆盖率　(%)	Forest-coverage Rate　(%)	43.06
林木蓄积量　(亿立方米)	Stock Volume of the Forest　(100 million cu.m)	4.79
3.水利资源	Water Resources	
全年自产河川年径流总量　(亿立方米)	Natural Annual Flow　(100 million cu.m)	575.51
黄河流域	Yellow River (Huanghe River) Drainage Area	114.42
长江流域	Yangtze River (Changjiang River)Drainage Area	461.09
平原区浅层地下水资源总量(亿立方米)	Total Ground Water Volume of Plain　(100 million cu.m)	63.65
水力资源理论蕴藏量　(万千瓦)	Theoretical Hydropower Resources　(10 000 kw)	1438.46
黄河流域	Yellow River (Huanghe River)Drainage Area	580.37
长江流域	Yangtze River(Changjiang River)Drainage Area	858.09
水力资源的可开发量　(万千瓦)	Developable Hydropower Resources　(10 000 kw)	666.66
黄河流域	Yellow River (Huanghe River) Drainage Area	234.06
长江流域	Yangtze River (Changjiang River)Drainage Area	432.60

注：本表土地资源数据为2012年数。

a) The data of land resources in this table are 2012.

1-4 主要山脉
Main Mountain Ranges

名 称	Mountain Range	海拔高度(米) Altitude above Sea Level (m)
太白山	Taibai Mountains	3767
化龙山	Hualong Mountains	2917
首阳山	Shouyang Mountains	2719
终南山	Zhongnan Mountains	2604
华 山	Huashan Mountains	2160
白于山	Baiyu Mountains	1823
巴 山	Bashan Mountains	1500～2000
子午岭	Ziwuling Mountains	1400～1600

1-5 主要河流
Major Rivers

名 称	River	流域面积(平方公里) Drainage Area (sq.km)	河 长(公里) Length (km)
无定河	Wudinghe River	30261	491.2
延 河	Yanhe River	7687	284.3
泾 河	Jinghe River	45421	455.1
渭 河	Weihe River	62440	818.0
北洛河	Beiluohe River	26905	680.3
嘉陵江	Jialingjiang River	9930	244.0
汉 江	Hanjiang River	61959	652.0
丹 江	Danjiang River	7551	244.0

1-6 主要矿产保有储量(2014年)
Ensured Reserves of Major Mineral (2014)

矿 种	Item	保有储量 Ensured Reserves
钠 盐 (亿吨)	Sodium Salt NaCl (100 million tons)	8855.33
煤 (亿吨)	Coal (100 million tons)	1642.70
石油(剩余可采储量) (万吨)	Petroleum(Surplus Developable Resources) (10 000 tons)	36300.80
天然气(剩余可采储量) (亿立方米)	Natural Gas(Surplus Developable Resources) (100 million cu.m)	8047.88
岩 金 (金属吨)	Rock Gold (Metal,ton)	338.44
砂 金 (金属吨)	Placer Gold (Metal,ton)	14.81
伴生金 (金属吨)	Associated Gold (Metal,ton)	4.59
钼 (金属万吨)	Molybdenum (Metal, 10 000 tons)	130.54
铅 (金属万吨)	Lead (Metal, 10 000 tons)	227.68
锌 (金属万吨)	Zinc (Metal, 10 000 tons)	301.10
汞 (金属吨)	Mercury (Metal, 10 000 tons)	1792.15
锑 (金属吨)	Antimony (Metal, 10 000 tons)	35800.00
水泥用石灰岩 (矿石亿吨)	Cement Limestone (Ore, 100 million tons)	77.49
玻璃用石英岩 (矿石亿吨)	Glass Quartzite (Ore, 100 million tons)	1.89
铁 (矿石亿吨)	Iron (Ore, 100 million tons)	7.76

1-7 陕西重要矿产保有储量在全国和西部的位次(2014年)
Precedence of Shaanxi Major Mineral Ensured Reserves in China and Western China(2014)

矿种 Item		位次 Precedence 全国 National Total	西部 West	矿种 Item		位次 Precedence 全国 National Total	西部 West
煤	Coal	4	3	钼矿	Molybdenum	7	3
石油	Petroleum	3	2	金矿	Gold	10	6
天然气	Natural Gas	4	4	银矿	Silver	24	9
铁矿	Iron	19	7	硫铁矿	Pyrite Ore	17	8
铜矿	Copper	18	8	磷矿	Phosphorus Ore	7	4
铅矿	Lead	12	8	盐矿	Sodium Salt NaCl	1	1
锌矿	Zinc	15	10	水泥用灰岩	Cement Limestone	4	2
铝土矿	Bauxite	12	6				

1-8 陕西矿产保有储量居全国前十位的矿种(2014年)
Mineral Kinds of Shaanxi Mineral Ensured Reserves Within the Top Ten Places in China (2014)

位次 Precedence	矿种 Item	矿种数 Types
1	盐矿、水泥配料用黄土、透辉石、片麻岩 Salt, Cement batching with loess, Diopside, Gneiss	4
2	煤层气、铼矿、毒重石、制碱用灰岩、饰面用板岩、透闪石 CBM, Rhenium ore, Witherite, Soda limestone, Finishes with slate,Tremolite	6
3	钛矿(金红石)、锶矿、镁盐($MgCl_2$)、镁盐($MgSO_4$)、高岭土、蛭石、石榴子石(矿物)、蓝石棉 Titanium ores(rutile TiO_2), Strontium, Magnesium($MgCl_2$), Magnesium($MgSO_4$), Kaolin Ore, Vermiculite, Garnet(mineral), Blue asbestos	8
4	煤矿、石油、天然气、碲矿、矽线石、伴生硫、长石、玻璃用石英岩、水泥用灰岩、海泡石粘土、陶粒页岩、陶粒用粘土 Coal, Petroleum, Natural Gas, Tellurium ore, Sillmanite, Associated with sulfur,Feldspar, Glass with quartz, Cement with limestone,Sepiolite clay,Haydite shale,Ceramsite clay	12
5	汞矿、重晶石、电石用灰岩、化肥用蛇纹岩、石墨(隐晶质) Mercury,Barite, Calcium carbide with limestone,Fertilizer with serpentinite, Graphite(aphanitic),	5
6	岩金、钒矿、锗矿、石榴子石(矿石)、饰面用大理岩、石棉、富铬矿(Cr_2O_3>32%) Rock gold, Vanadium,Germanium,Garnet (mineral), Marble,Asbestin, Chromium ore (Cr_2O_3> 32%)	7
7	石煤、油页岩、钛矿(原生钛[磁]铁矿)、钼矿、铌矿、磷矿、石墨(晶质) Stone coal,Oil shale, Titanium (Ti-native [magnetic] iron ore), Molybdenum ore, Niobium, Phosphate,Graphite (crystalline)	7
8	镍矿、铍矿(绿柱石矿)、冶金用石英岩、云母(片云母) Nickel, Berylliume(Beryl mineral), Metallurgical quartzite, Mica (mica)	4
9	砂金、钛矿(钛铁砂矿矿物)、冶金用白云岩、冶金用脉石英、自然硫、玻璃用白云岩 Gold dust, Titanium (ilmenite placer minerals),Metallurgical dolomite, Metallurgical vein quartz, Natural sulfur, Glass with dolomite	6
10	滑石、红柱石 Talc, Andalusite	2

1-9 主要城市气候基本情况(2014年)
Basic Statistics on Climate of Major Cities (2014)

城 市 City	平均气温(摄氏度) Average Temperature (℃)	日照时数(小时) Sunshine Hours (hour)	平均风速(米/秒) Average Wind Speed (m/s)	相对湿度(%) Relative Humidity (%)	无霜期(天) Frost-free Period (day)	气 压(百帕) Pressure (hPa)	降水量(毫米) Precipitation (mm)
西安市 Xi'an	15.2	1941.8	2.3	61	226	969	660
铜川市 Tongchuan	11.1	2293.9	2.1	68	237	906	682
宝鸡市 Baoji	14.3	1568.4	1.2	61	233	946	610
咸阳市 Xianyang	13.9	2091.9	2.1	66	226	961	616
渭南市 Weinan	15.4	1617.6	1	63	255	975	591
延安市 Yan'an	9.8	2598.1	2	60	205	884	695
汉中市 Hanzhong	15.6	1288.3	1.1	75	287	957	886
榆林市 Yulin	10.0	2830.8	2.9	47	217	886	378
安康市 Ankang	16.3	1584.5	1.2	72	264	982	831
商洛市 Shangluo	13.3	2199.1	2.2	66	225	932	907

1-10 主要城市平均气温(2014年)
Monthly Average Temperature of Major Cities(2014)

单位：摄氏度 (℃)

月 份 Month	西安市 Xi'an	铜川市 Tongchuan	宝鸡市 Baoji	咸阳市 Xianyang	渭南市 Weinan	延安市 Yan'an	汉中市 Hanzhong	榆林市 Yulin	安康市 Ankang	商洛市 Shangluo
一 月 Jan.	2.9	-0.6	2.4	0.6	3.0	-2.5	4.4	-3.8	5.0	2.4
二 月 Feb.	2.3	-1.1	2.2	1.6	2.4	-2.5	5.1	-3.2	5.7	2.0
三 月 Mar.	12.0	7.9	10.8	10.6	12.2	6.8	11.7	6.6	13.4	10.4
四 月 Apr.	16.1	12.3	14.8	15.0	16.2	11.9	16.8	12.9	17.5	14.4
五 月 May	21.1	16.4	19.6	19.5	21.5	16.3	19.6	17.4	20.0	17.3
六 月 June	26.0	21.6	24.7	25.1	26.4	20.1	24.3	22.0	24.6	22.8
七 月 July	29.1	24.0	28.5	28.6	28.9	21.9	27.6	22.8	28.0	25.9
八 月 Aug.	25.1	20.9	24.3	24.2	25.1	18.9	25.4	20.6	25.5	22.8
九 月 Sept.	20.3	16.8	19.2	19.5	20.5	16.0	20.9	16.7	22.1	18.5
十 月 Oct.	16.4	12.3	14.8	15.1	16.3	11.7	16.7	11.9	17.5	14.0
十一月 Nov.	8.9	4.8	7.8	7.3	9.2	3.4	10.3	2.2	11.4	7.7
十二月 Dec.	2.2	-2.1	1.9		2.5	-5.0	3.8	-6.7	4.9	1.8
极端最高 Highest	40.6	35.5	40.3	41.0	40.4	34.2	38.2	33.7	39.2	39.1
极端最低 Lowest	-6.0	-11.5	-7.0	-10.6	-7.6	-18.7	-3.5	-21.1	-3.7	-8.8
年平均 Annual Average	15.2	11.1	14.3	13.9	15.4	9.8	15.6	10.0	16.3	13.3

1-11 主要城市降水量(2014年)
Monthly Precipitation of Major Cities(2014)

单位：毫米 (millimeters)

月份 Month	西安市 Xi'an	铜川市 Tongchuan	宝鸡市 Baoji	咸阳市 Xianyang	渭南市 Weinan	延安市 Yan'an	汉中市 Hanzhong	榆林市 Yulin	安康市 Ankang	商洛市 Shangluo
一 月 Jan.	0.3	0.2	0.0	0.0	0.1	0.3	2.0	0.0	0.4	0.5
二 月 Feb.	16.2	22.3	23.3	13.4	19.7	27.2	9.9	10.3	8.7	25.2
三 月 Mar.	13.9	22.6	25.2	15.4	19.1	19.8	37.3	5.2	29.1	16.2
四 月 Apr.	65.6	79.2	78.6	67.5	68.4	64.0	117.1	50.4	68.7	113.5
五 月 May	53.4	50.7	43.8	47.2	56.5	56.8	68.3	28.3	90.9	73.3
六 月 June	62.7	71.1	38.2	47.6	25.9	46.7	84.7	58.8	131.5	51.9
七 月 July	80.3	92.4	16.0	71.1	64.1	147.0	71.5	58.4	110.6	118.3
八 月 Aug.	96.8	120.4	112.1	106.8	97.6	139.9	108.3	29.0	91.6	149.5
九 月 Sept.	230.3	196.2	226.2	206.1	201.2	172.4	269.0	99.7	201.9	267.2
十 月 Oct.	20.7	11.2	24.4	20.9	19.2	8.3	80.5	35.0	59.6	41.0
十一月 Nov.	19.5	13.3	21.2	19.2	18.1	11.1	36.7	3.2	38.2	49.7
十二月 Dec.	0.5	2.4	0.7	0.6	0.7	1.4	0.7	0.0	0.2	0.4
全 年 Annual Total	660.2	682.0	609.7	615.8	590.6	694.9	886.0	378.3	831.4	906.7

1-12 主要城市日照时数(2014年)
Monthly Sunshine Hours of Major Cities(2014)

单位：小时 (hours)

月份 Month	西安市 Xi'an	铜川市 Tongchuan	宝鸡市 Baoji	咸阳市 Xianyang	渭南市 Weinan	延安市 Yan'an	汉中市 Hanzhong	榆林市 Yulin	安康市 Ankang	商洛市 Shangluo
一 月 Jan.	181.5	213.7	162.5	185.8	152.1	240.4	95.1	241.5	143.2	198.1
二 月 Feb.	55.4	64.9	51.3	49.7	20.1	127.8	24.9	146.4	73.7	80.0
三 月 Mar.	162.5	204.1	158.5	192.7	167.8	255.8	92.1	277.0	149.4	191.0
四 月 Apr.	126.0	149.3	90.0	135.0	84.8	178.3	101.9	220.4	120.6	169.6
五 月 May	209.3	258.5	164.2	222.7	201.3	286.0	141.1	317.0	146.8	221.8
六 月 June	193.9	244.5	149.5	212.8	174.2	253.1	122.6	297.7	126.7	221.9
七 月 July	288.0	298.9	220.9	303.9	280.9	287.8	239.2	274.8	267.5	282.8
八 月 Aug.	191.4	218.3	153.1	214.9	182.4	238.8	172.3	245.3	156.4	211.5
九 月 Sept.	112.0	122.2	64.4	103.6	72.7	125.8	80.4	170.5	97.0	109.1
十 月 Oct.	105.0	159.0	102.5	149.4	54.0	206.3	73.1	214.4	94.6	172.6
十一月 Nov.	141.0	154.7	102.1	132.3	93.2	167.7	49.9	184.0	66.9	138.6
十二月 Dec.	175.8	205.8	149.4	189.1	134.1	230.3	95.7	241.8	141.7	202.1
全 年 Annual Total	1941.8	2293.9	1568.4	2091.9	1617.6	2598.1	1288.3	2830.8	1584.5	2199.1

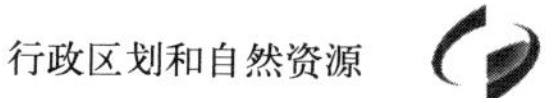

1-13 历届陕西省人民代表大会代表人数
Number of Deputies to All the Previous Shaanxi Province People's Congresses

单位：人 (person)

届 次	Congress	年 份 Year	代表人数 Number of Deputies	# 女代表 Female Deputies		# 少数民族代表 Ethnic Minority Deputies	
				人 数 Number	占代表总数% As Percentage to Total Deputies (%)	人 数 Number	占代表总数% As Percentage to Total Deputies (%)
第一届	First Congress	1954	386	51	13.2	9	2.3
第二届	Second Congress	1959	400	67	16.8	12	3.0
第三届	Third Congress	1964	520	84	16.0	15	2.9
第四届	Fourth Congress	1975					
第五届	Fifth Congress	1978	1186	234	19.7	26	2.2
第六届	Sixth Congress	1983	727	168	23.1	29	4.0
第七届	Seventh Congress	1988	600	117	19.3	19	3.2
第八届	Eighth Congress	1993	602	118	19.6	22	3.7
第九届	Ninth Congress	1998	566	129	22.8	19	3.4
第十届	Tenth Congress	2003	565	117	20.7	18	3.2
第十一届	Eleventh Congress	2008	574	142	24.9	19	3.3
第十二届	Twelfth Congress	2013	578	132	22.8	18	3.1

1-14 历届陕西省政治协商会议委员人数
Number of Deputies to All the Previous Shaanxi Province People's Political Consultative Conferences

单位：人 (person)

届 次	Congress	年 份 Year	委员人数 Number of Deputies	中国共产党党员代表 Deputies from the Communist Party of China		民主党派和无党派爱国人士代表 Deputies from Democratic Parties and Non-partisan Patriot	
				人 数 Number	占代表总数% As Percentage to Total Deputies (%)	人 数 Number	占代表总数% As Percentage to Total Deputies (%)
第一届	First Congress	1955	165	42	25.5	123	74.5
第二届	Second Congress	1958	262	85	32.4	177	67.6
第三届	Third Congress	1963	275	91	33.1	184	66.9
第四届	Fourth Congress	1977	420	205	48.8	215	51.2
第五届	Fifth Congress	1983	428	162	37.9	266	62.1
第六届	Sixth Congress	1988	502	191	38.0	311	62.0
第七届	Seventh Congress	1993	506	244	48.2	262	51.8
第八届	Eighth Congress	1998	539	216	40.1	323	59.9
第九届	Ninth Congress	2003	590	235	39.8	355	60.2
第十届	Tenth Congress	2008	627	248	39.6	379	60.4
第十一届	Eleventh Congress	2013	648	258	39.8	390	60.2

主要统计指标解释

行政区划 指国家对行政区域的划分。根据有关法规规定，我国的行政区域划分如下: (1)全国分为省、自治区、直辖市; (2)省、自治区分为自治州、县、自治县、市; (3)自治州分为县、自治县、市; (4)县、自治县分为乡、民族乡、镇; (5)直辖市和较大的市分为区、县; (6)国家在必要时设立的特别行政区。

气候 指地球与大气之间长期能量交换与质量交换所形成的一种自然环境状态，它是多种因素综合作用的结果。气候既是人类生活和生产的环境要素之一，又是供给人类生活和生产的重要资源。气温、降水、湿度等气象要素的多年平均值是用来描述一个地区气候状况的主要参数，而各种气象要素某年、某月的平均值(或总量)则可以反映出该时期天气气候状况的重要特征。

自然资源 指人类可以直接从自然界获得，并用于生产和生活的物质资源。自然资源一般可以分成可再生资源和非再生资源两大类。可再生资源指在较短时间内可以再生、可以循环利用的资源，包括土地资源、水资源、气候资源、生物资源和海洋资源等。非再生资源指在使用后不能再生的资源，包括矿产资源和地热能源。

土地资源 土地指陆地的表层部分，它主要由岩石、岩石的风化物和土壤构成。土地资源按利用类型可以分为农用地、建筑用地和未利用地。农用地包括耕地、园地、林地、牧草地和水面。建筑用地包括居民点及工矿用地、交通用地和水利设施用地。未利用地指农用地和建筑用地以外的土地，包括滩涂、荒漠、戈壁、冰川和石山等。

森林面积 指由乔木树种构成，郁闭度 0.2 以上(含 0.2)的林地或冠幅宽度 10 米以上的林带的面积，即有林地面积。森林面积包括天然起源和人工起源的针叶林面积、阔叶林面积、针阔混交林面积和竹林面积，不包括灌木林地面积和疏林地面积。

森林蓄积量 指一定森林面积上存在着的林木树干部分的总材积。它是反映一个国家或地区森林资源总规模和水平的基本指标之一，也是反映森林资源的丰富程度、衡量森林生态环境优劣的重要依据。

森林覆盖率 指一个国家或地区森林面积占土地总面积的百分比。森林覆盖率是反映森林资源的丰富程度和生态平衡状况的重要指标。在计算森林覆盖率时，森林面积包括郁闭度 0.2 以上的乔木林地面积和竹林地面积，国家特别规定的灌木林地面积、农田林网以及四旁(村旁、路旁、水旁、宅旁)林木的覆盖面积。计算公式为:

$$森林覆盖率(\%)=\frac{森林面积}{土地总面积}\times 100\%$$

径流 指陆地上接受降水后扣除损耗外，从地表和地下向流域出口断面汇集的水流。径流可分为地表径流、地下径流和壤中流。地表径流指沿地表向河流、湖泊、沼泽、海洋等汇集的水流; 地下径流指沿潜水层或隔水层间的含水层，向河流、湖泊、沼泽、海洋等汇集的地下水水流。

径流量 指在一定时段内通过河流某一过水断面的水量，用以反映一个国家或地区水资源的丰歉程度。计算公式为:

径流量=降水量-蒸发量

矿产资源 矿产资源指由地质作用形成的，具有利用价值的，呈固态、液态、气态的自然资源，是社会生产发展的重要物质基础。目前我国已发现矿种有 170 多种，按其特点和用途，可分为能源矿产(如煤炭、石油、天然气、地热)、金属矿产(如铁矿、锰矿、铜矿、铅矿、铝土矿)、非金属矿产(如金刚石、石灰岩、粘土)和水气矿产(如地下水、矿泉水、二氧化碳气)四大类。其中: 金属矿产按其物质成份和性质又可分为: 黑色金属矿产、有色金属矿产、贵金属矿产、稀有金属矿产、稀土金属矿产、分散元素金属矿产六类。

气温 指空气的温度，我国一般以摄氏度(℃)为单位表示。气象观测的温度表是放在离地面约 1.5 米处通风良好的百叶箱里测量的，因此，通常说的气温指的是离地面 1.5 米处百叶箱中的温度。其统计计算方法为:

月平均气温是将全月各日的平均气温相加，除以该月的天数而得。

年平均气温是将 12 个月的月平均气温累加后除以 12 而得。

降水量 指从天空降落到地面的液态或固态(经融化后)水，未经蒸发、渗透、流失而在地面上积聚的深度。其统计计算方法为:

月降水量是将全月各日的降水量累加而得。

年降水量是将 12 个月的月降水量累加而得。

日照时数 指太阳实际照射地面的时间。其统计方法与降水量相同。

Explanatory Notes on Main Statistical Indicators

Divisions of Administrative Areas refers to the division of administrative areas by the State. The relative laws stipulate that 1) the whole country is divided into provinces, autonomous regions and municipalities directly under the Central Government; 2) provinces and autonomous regions are further divided into autonomous prefectures, counties, autonomous counties and cities; 3) autonomous prefectures are further divided into counties, autonomous counties and cities; 4) counties and autonomous counties are further divided into townships, ethnic townships and towns; 5) municipalities directly under the Central Government and large cities are divided into districts and counties, 6) the State shall, when necessary, establish special administrative regions.

Climate refers to the natural environmental status formed by the long-term exchange of energy and mass between the earth and the atmosphere, and is the result of interaction of many factors. Climate is both one of the environment factors and also the important resources for living and production activities of the human being. The average values across several years of meteorological factors such as temperature, rainfall and humidity are used as important parameters to describe the climate of a region, while the average values (or total values) of a given year or month of meteorological factors reflect the key characteristics of climate for that period of time.

Natural Resources refers to material resources that could be obtained from the nature by human being and used for production and living. Natural resources in general can be classified as renewable resources and non-renewable resources. Renewable resources refer to resources that could be renewed and recycled during a relatively short period of time, including land resource, water resource, climate resource, biology resource and marine resource. Non-renewable resources include resources that could not be renewed, such as minerals and geothermal resource.

Land Resource Land refers to the surface of the earth, consisting of mainly rocks and its weathering and earth. Land resource can be classified, by its utilization, as land for agriculture, land for construction and unused land. Land for agriculture includes cultivated land, plantation land, forestland, grassland and waters. Land for construction includes land for residential purpose, for manufacturing and mining, for transportation and for water-conservancy projects. Unused land refers to land other than land for agriculture and construction, including beaches, deserts, Gobi, glaciers and rock mountains

Forest Area refers to the area of forest where trees and bamboo grow with canopy density above 0.2, including land of natural woods and planted woods, but excluding bush land and thin forest land. It reflects the total areas of afforestation.

Stock Volume of Forest refers to total stock volume of wood growing in forest area, which shows the total size and level of forest resources of a country or a region. It is also an important indicator illustrating the richness of forest resource and the status of forest ecological environment.

Forest Coverage Rate refers to the ratio of area of afforested land to total land area. It is a very important indicator that reflects the status of abundance of forest resource and balance of the ecosystem. Forest area includes the area of trees and bamboo grow with canopy density above 0.2, the area of shrubby tree according to regulations of the government, the area of forest land inside farm land and the area of trees planted by the side of villages, farm houses and along roads and rivers. The formula for calculating forest coverage rate is as follows:

$$\text{Forestry coverage rate (\%)} = \frac{\text{Area of Afforested Land}}{\text{Area of Total Land}} \times 100\%$$

Runoff refers to the water gathered at the way out of the cross section of drainage area either from the surface or underground after deducting the wastage of the precipitation on the land. Runoff can be divided into surface runoff, underground runoff and within soil runoff. Surface runoff refers to water flowing to the rivers, lakes, swamps, and seas on the surface of the earth. Underground runoff refers to water flow to rivers, lakes, swamps, and seas through the water-bearing stratum of confined layer or unconfined layer.

Volume of Runoff refers to the total volume of water running through a certain cross section of a river during a certain period of time, reflecting the water resource condition in a country or a region. The formula for calculating volume of runoff is as follows:

Runoff=Precipitation-Evaporation

Mineral Resources refers to useful minerals, with solid state, liquid state, gaseity, due to the geological process. Minerals are important natural resources, and important material base for social development. At present, there are more than 170 types of minerals discovered in China. They can be categorized into four groups: energy producing minerals (including coal, petroleum, natural gas and terrestrial heat), metallic minerals (including iron, manganese, copper, lead and bauxite), non metallic minerals (including diamond, limestone and clay), and water/gas related minerals (including ground water, mineral water and carbon dioxide). Metallic minerals can be further classified as ferrous, non-ferrous, noble metal, rare metal, rare earth metal and dispersed metals.

Temperature refers to the air temperature. China uses centigrade as the unit. The thermometry used for weather observation is put in a breezy shutter, which is 1.5 meters high from the ground. Therefore, the commonly used temperature refers to the temperature in the breezy shutter 1.5 meters away from the ground. The calculation method is as follows:

Monthly average temperature is the summation of average daily temperature of one month divided by the actual days of that particular month.

Annual average temperature is the summation of monthly average of a year divided by 12 months.

Volume of Precipitation refers to the deepness of liquid state or solid state (thawed) water falling from the sky to the ground that has not been evaporated, infiltrated or run off. The calculation method is as follows:

Monthly precipitation is the summation of daily precipitation of a month.

Annual precipitation is the summation of 12 months precipitation of a year.

Sunshine Hours refers to the actual hours of sun irradiating the earth. The calculation method is the same as that of the precipitation.

二、综　合

资料整理：马　靖

简 要 说 明

一、本篇资料反映陕西经济、科技、社会等方面的规模、水平、速度、结构、比例、效益情况，并收录了基本单位统计情况。

二、国民经济综合资料是抽取全书的精华，通过对各篇章主要统计指标及其速度、结构、比例和效益等的加工计算，来反映国民经济和社会发展的总体情况。

三、本篇资料根据各专业统计年报资料以及国家统计局、省级有关部门提供的统计资料加工整理而成。

Brief Introduction

Ⅰ.This chapter reflects the scale, level, speed, structure, proportion and efficiency of the national economy, science and technology and the social development of Shaanxi Province.

Ⅱ. The summary data on the national economy reflect the overall situation of the economic and social development by presenting further processed statistics including growth, structure, ratio, and efficiency data derived from other chapters.

Ⅲ.The summary data are processed and prepared on the basis of the annual reports of various specialized fields provided by Statistics Bureau of Shaanxi Province and the statistics provided by the National Bureau of Statistics and some related departments of Shaanxi Province.

2.综　合

2014年全省

生产总值	17689.94	亿元	比1978年增长	41.7倍
全社会固定资产投资	18709.49	亿元	比1978年增长	918.2倍
财政收入	3145.54	亿元	比1978年增长	158.2倍
社会消费品零售总额	5918.71	亿元	比1978年增长	176.4倍
出口总额	139.29	亿美元	比1978年增长	1169.5倍
城镇居民人均可支配收入	24366	元		
农村居民人均可支配收入	7932	元		

生产总值增长速度

（比上年增长%）

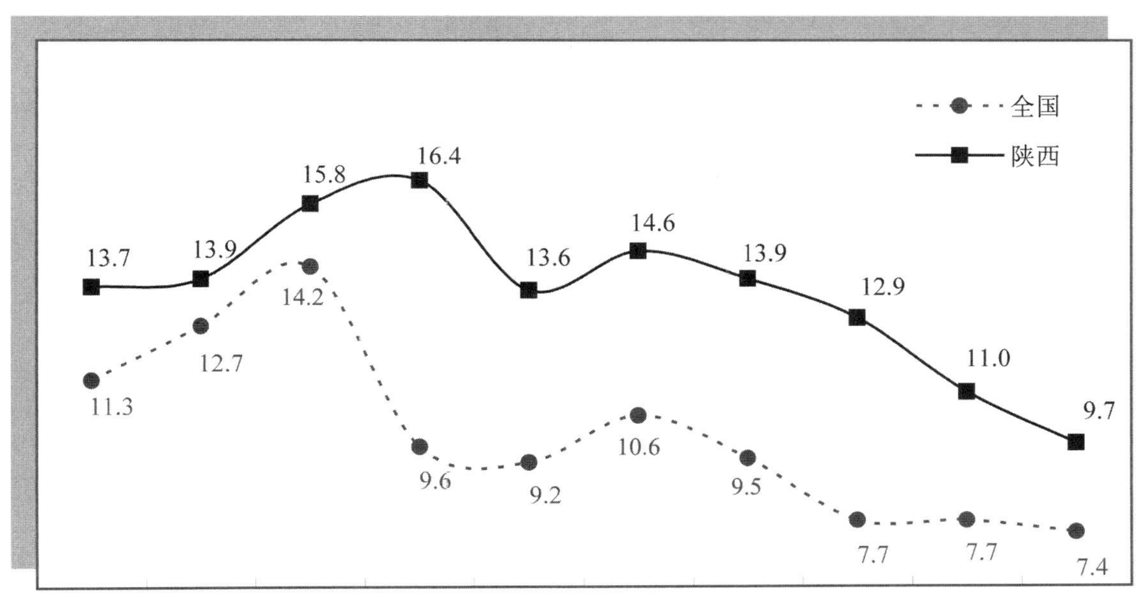

2-1 陕 西 一 日

Selected Indicators on Average Daily Social and Economic Activities

指 标		Item		2000	2005	2010	2013	2014
每天创造的财富		**Daily Production**						
生产总值	(万元)	Gross Domestic Product	(10 000 yuan)	49425	107773	277356	443985	484656
第一产业		Primary Industry		7075	11939	27081	40027	42875
第二产业		Secondary Industry		21441	53462	149208	244174	262390
第三产业		Tertiary Industry		20910	42372	101067	159785	179391
财政收入	(万元)	Government Revenue	(10 000 yuan)	5123	14494	49345	82314	86179
粮 食	(万吨)	Grain	(10 000 tons)	2.98	3.12	3.19	3.33	3.28
棉 花	(吨)	Cotton	(ton)	75	213	190	159	116
油 料	(吨)	Oil-bearing Crops	(ton)	1062	1242	1536	1631	1707
肉 类	(吨)	Meat	(ton)	2524	3674	2812	3083	3199
布	(万米)	Cloth	(10 000 m)	196.71	217.26	206.16	157.26	167.04
发 电 量	(万千瓦小时)	Electricity	(10 000 kwh)	7460	13834	30189	40922	43860
原 油	(吨)	Crude Oil	(ton)	20450	48717	82665	101042	103228
粗 钢	(吨)	Crude Steel	(ton)	1470	8419	16570	26852	28445
每天消费量		**Daily National Consumption**						
能源消费量	(万吨标准煤)	Energy Consumption	(10 000 tons of SCE)		15.26	22.71	29.07	30.75
社会消费品零售额	(万元)	Total Retail Sales of Consumer Goods	(10 000 yuan)	19880	36475	89248	143700	162156
每天其他经济活动		**Other Daily Economic Activities**						
货 运 量	(万吨)	Freight Traffic	(10 000 tons)	82.12	125.27	286.09	418.39	430.34
客 运 量	(万人)	Passenger Traffic	(10 000 persons)	78.61	107.16	257.41	324.14	206.05
邮电业务总量	(万元)	Business Volume of Postal and Telecommunication Services	(10 000 yuan)	2330	9072	24736	11438	15525
进出口总额	(万美元)	Total Value of Imports and Exports	(USD 10 000)	586.33	1253.93	3310.36	5514.74	7509.17
# 出口总额		Total Exports		358.91	842.69	1700.75	2801.69	3816.23
入境旅游人数	(人次)	Number of Overseas Visitor Arrivals	(person-times)	1953	2544	5813	9646	7296
个人储蓄额	(万元)	Outstanding Amount of Savings Deposit	(10 000 yuan)	41713	96821	218021	335599	367914
每天人口变动和婚姻		**Daily Population Changes and Marriages**						
出 生	(人)	Births	(person)	1244	1013	994	1031	1047
死 亡	(人)	Deaths	(person)		608	613	633	647
结 婚	(对)	Marriages	(couples)	557	571	950	1085	1046
离 婚	(对)	Divorces	(couples)	71	64	122	173	187

注：1.本表价值量指标中，除邮电业务总量按不变价格计算，其余均按当年价格计算。
2.工业产品产量为规模以上企业数据。
3.能源消费量按等价值计算。

a) Figures in value terms in this table are at current prices, except that on the business volume of postal and telecommunication services which is at constant prices.
b) Output of industrial products are obtained from above designated size enterprises.
c) Energy consumption are calculated at equivalent value.

2-2　陕西省主要国民经济指标占全国比重(2014年)

Percentage of Shaanxi Main Indicators on National Economic to National Total(2014)

指　　标		Item		陕　西 Shaanxi	全　国 National Total	陕西占全国% Shaanxi as Percentage of National Total (%)
年底总人口	(万人)	Population at Year-end	(10 000 persons)	3775	136782	2.8
就业人员	(万人)	Number of Employed Persons	(10 000 persons)	2067	77253	2.7
生产总值	(亿元)	Gross Domestic Product	(100 million yuan)	17689.94	636463	2.8
第一产业		Primary Industry		1564.94	58332	2.7
第二产业		Secondary Industry		9577.24	271392	3.5
第三产业		Tertiary Industry		6547.76	306739	2.1
全社会固定资产投资总额	(亿元)	Total Investment in Fixed Assets	(100 million yuan)	18709.49	512761	3.6
地方一般预算收入	(亿元)	Local General Bugetary Revenue	(100 million yuan)	1890.40	75860	2.5
主要产品产量		Output of Major Products				
粮　　食	(万吨)	Grain	(10 000 tons)	1197.78	60702.6	2.0
棉　　花	(万吨)	Cotton	(10 000 tons)	4.22	617.8	0.7
油　　料	(万吨)	Oil-bearing Crops	(10 000 tons)	62.30	3507.4	1.8
肉　　类	(万吨)	Meat	(10 000 tons)	116.76	8706.7	1.3
水　　果	(万吨)	Fruits	(10 000 tons)	1553.98	26142.2	5.9
原　　油	(万吨)	Crude Oil	(10 000 tons)	3767.81	21142.9	17.8
天 然 气	(亿立方米)	Natural Gas	(100 million cu.m)	410.11	1301.6	31.5
发 电 量	(亿千瓦小时)	Electricity	(100 million kwh)	1600.88	56495.8	2.8
粗　　钢	(万吨)	Crude Steel	(10 000 tons)	1038.26	82269.8	1.3
水　　泥	(万吨)	Cement	(10 000 tons)	9083.49	247613.5	3.7
化　　肥	(万吨)	Fertilizers	(10 000 tons)	179.33	6887.2	2.6
纱	(万吨)	Yarn	(10 000 tons)	40.05	3379	1.2
布	(亿米)	Cloth	(100 million m)	6.10	893.7	0.7
汽　　车	(万辆)	Motor Vehicles	(10 000 units)	37.47	2372.5	1.6
货物周转量	(亿吨公里)	Total Freight Ton-kilometers	(100 million ton-km)	3522.54	185397.8	1.9
邮电业务总量	(亿元)	Business Volume of Postal and Telecommunication Services	(100 million yuan)	566.66	21845.6	2.6
社会消费品零售总额	(亿元)	Total Retail Sales of Consumer Goods	(100 million yuan)	5918.71	271896.1	2.2
进出口总额	(亿美元)	Total Value of Imports and Exports	(USD 100 million)	274.08	43030.4	0.6
# 出口额		Exports		139.29	23427.5	0.6
入境旅游人数	(万人次)	Number of Overseas Visitor Arrivals	(10 000 person-times)	266.30	5562.2	4.8
国际旅游外汇收入	(亿美元)	Foreign Exchange Earnings from International Tourism	(USD 100 million)	14.16	569.1	2.5
大学生在校学生数	(万人)	Students Enrollment of College and University	(10 000 persons)	109.96	2547.7	4.3
图书出版量	(亿册)	Number of Books Published	(100 million copies)	1.89	84	2.3
杂志出版量	(亿册)	Number of Magazines Published	(100 million copies)	0.53	32	1.7
报纸出版量	(亿份)	Number of Newspapers Published	(100 million copies)	6.82	465	1.5

2-3 国民经济和社会发展总量与速度指标

指　　标		Item		1978	2000
人口与就业		**Population and Employment**			
人　口		Population			
年底总人口	(万人)	Population at Year-end	(10 000 persons)	2779	3644
城镇人口		Urban		454	1176
乡村人口		Rural		2325	2468
男性人口		Male		1444	1896
女性人口		Female		1335	1748
就　业		Employment			
就业人员	(万人)	Number of Employed Persons	(10 000 persons)	1078	1813
# 职工人数		Number of Staff and Workers		257	328
城镇登记失业人数	(万人)	Registered Unemployment in Urban Areas	(10 000 persons)		11.39
宏观经济		**Macro Economy**			
国民经济核算		National Accounting			
生产总值	(亿元)	Gross Domestic Product	(100 million yuan)	81.07	1804.00
第一产业		Primary Industry		24.70	258.22
第二产业		Secondary Industry		42.13	782.58
第三产业		Tertiary Industry		14.24	763.20
固定资产投资		Investment in Fixed Assets			
全社会固定资产投资总额	(亿元)	Total Investment in Fixed Assets	(100 million yuan)	20.35	745.85
# 固定资产投资		Investment in Fixed Assets			
# 房地产开发投资		Investment in Real Estate Development			78.89
财　政		Government Finance			
财政收入	(亿元)	Government Revenue	(100 million yuan)	19.76	187.00
# 地方一般预算收入		Local General Bugetary Revenue			114.97
财政支出	(亿元)	Government Expenditures	(100 million yuan)	18.30	271.76
物价指数	(上年=100)	Price Indices	(preceding year=100)		
商品零售价格指数		Retail Price Index		100.5	98.3
居民消费价格指数		Consumer Price Index		100.6	99.5
利用外资		Utilization of Foreign Capital			
签订利用客商直接投资协议额	(万美元)	Contracted Value of Direct Investments	(USD 10 000)		49931
实际利用客商直接投资额	(万美元)	Actually Utilized Value of Direct Investments	(USD 10 000)		28842
能源生产与消费(等价值)		Production and Consumption of Energy	(Equivalent Value)		
能源生产总量	(万吨标准煤)	Total Energy Production	(10 000 tons of SCE)		
能源消费总量	(万吨标准煤)	Total Energy Consumption	(10 000 tons of SCE)		

注：1.本表价值量指标中，除邮电业务总量按不变价格计算，其余指标均按当年价格计算。

2.2000年及以后工业产品产量、财务指标为规模以上企业数据。
3.1998年及以后职工人数、职工工资总额、职工平均工资为在岗职工数据。
4.本表速度指标中，生产总值及三次产业增加值、物价指数、农林牧渔业增加值、工业增加值、城乡居民收入和职工平均工资指标均按不变价格计算。固定资产投资平均增长速度按累计法计算。
5.2014年财政收入、入境旅游人数和旅游外汇收入增长速度为同口径增长速度。

Principal Aggregate Indicators on National Economic and Social Development and Growth Rates

2005	2010	2013	2014	2014年为下列年份% 2014as Percentage of the Following Years(%)					1979-2014 平均增长% Average Annual Growth Rate(%)
				1978	2000	2005	2010	2013	
3690	3735	3764	3775	135.8	103.6	102.3	101.1	100.3	0.9
1374	1707	1931	1985	437.2	168.8	144.5	116.3	102.8	4.2
2316	2028	1833	1790	77.0	72.5	77.3	88.3	97.7	-0.7
1899	1930	1944	1949	135.0	102.8	102.6	101.0	100.3	0.8
1791	1805	1820	1826	136.8	104.5	102.0	101.2	100.3	0.9
1976	2074	2058	2067	191.7	114.0	104.6	99.7	100.4	1.8
323	343	471	479	186.4	146.0	148.3	139.7	101.7	1.7
21.54	21.42	21.06	22.35		196.3	103.7	104.3	106.1	
3933.72	10123.48	16205.45	17689.94	4266.3	547.9	312.9	156.6	109.7	11.0
435.77	988.45	1460.97	1564.94	626.8	213.4	166.2	123.4	105.1	5.2
1951.36	5446.10	8912.34	9577.24	6423.2	707.3	357.5	166.9	110.9	12.3
1546.59	3688.93	5832.14	6547.76	7777.1	504.5	301.6	150.5	108.9	12.9
1982.04	8561.24	15934.21	18709.49	91916.8	2508.5	944.0	218.5	117.4	20.4
		15583.58	18357.84					117.8	
298.95	1159.47	2240.17	2426.49		3075.8	811.7	209.3	108.3	
529.02	1801.11	3004.47	3145.54					108.3	15.1
275.32	958.21	1748.33	1890.40					113.7	
638.96	2218.83	3665.07	3962.50	21650.0	1458.1	620.1	178.6	108.1	16.1
100.1	103.6	101.8	100.7	516.4	131.0	130.0	109.9	100.7	4.7
101.2	104.0	103.0	101.6	638.7	143.0	134.9	113.7	101.6	5.3
158237	221030	372078	585453		1172.5	370.0	264.9	157.4	
62839	182006	367800	417557		1447.7	664.5	229.4	113.5	
14576	31846	44431	46982			322.3	147.5	105.7	
5571	8288	10610	11222			201.4	135.4	105.8	

a) Figures in value terms in this table are at current prices, except that on the business volume of postal and telecommunication services which is at constant prices.

b) Since 2000, Output of industrial products and financial indicators are obtained from above designated size enterprises.

c) Figures on number of staff and workers ,total wage bill and average wage refer to fully employed staff and workers since 1998 .

d) The indices and growth rates of the follow indicators are calculated at constant prices: gross domestic product, value-added of the three strata of industry,price indices,value-added of agriculture, forestry, animal husbandry and fishery ,value-added of industry, per capita income of urban and rural residents, average wage of staff and workers. The average annual growth rate of total investment in fixed assets is calculated at the accumulate method.

e) The increase rates of government revenue、 number of overseas visitor arrivals and foreign exchange earnings from tourism are the same requirements data in the 2014.

2-3 续表 1

指 标	Item	1978	2000
产 业	**Industry**		
农 业	Agriculture		
常用耕地面积 (千公顷)	Cultivated Land (1 000 hectares)	3854	3114
农林牧渔业增加值 (亿元)	Value-added of Agriculture, Forestry, Animal Husbandry and Fishery (100 million yuan)	24.70	258.22
主要农产品产量	Output of Major Farm Products		
粮 食 (万吨)	Grain (10 000 tons)	800	1089
棉 花 (万吨)	Cotton (10 000 tons)	10.54	2.74
油 料 (万吨)	Oil-bearing Crops (10 000 tons)	5.65	38.76
烤 烟 (万吨)	Flue-Cured Tobacco (10 000 tons)	1.38	7.36
茶 叶 (吨)	Tea (ton)	1408	6126
水 果 (万吨)	Fruits (10 000 tons)	33.41	493.79
蔬 菜 (万吨)	Vegetables (10 000 tons)		556.53
肉 类 (万吨)	Meat (10 000 tons)	14.20	92.12
工 业	Industry		
工业增加值 (亿元)	Value-added of Industry (100 million yuan)	36.52	629.88
主要工业产品产量	Output of Major Industrial Products		
纱 (万吨)	Yarn (10 000 tons)	13.85	15.68
布 (亿米)	Cloth (100 million m)	5.81	7.18
原 油 (万吨)	Crude Oil (10 000 tons)	6.03	746.44
天然气 (亿立方米)	Natural Gas (100 million cu.m)		21.10
发电量 (亿千瓦小时)	Electricity (100 million kwh)	66.10	272.28
粗 钢 (万吨)	Crude Steel (10 000 tons)	24.29	53.65
钢 材 (万吨)	Rolled Steel (10 000 tons)	17.38	57.70
水 泥 (万吨)	Cement (10 000 tons)	210.66	989.44
化 肥 (万吨)	Fertilizers (10 000 tons)	13.69	93.90
汽 车 (万辆)	Motor Vehicles (10 000 units)		1.93
规模以上工业企业	Industrial Enterprises above Designated Size		
资产总计 (亿元)	Original Value of Fixed Assets (100 million yuan)		2683.07
主营业务收入 (亿元)	Revenue from Principal Business (100 million yuan)		1133.82
利润和税金总额 (亿元)	Total Profits and Tax (100 million yuan)		155.51
交通运输	Transportation		
货物运输量 (万吨)	Freight Traffic (10 000 tons)	7160	29973
# 铁 路	Railways	2400	4697
公 路	Highways	4733	25200
货物周转量 (亿吨公里)	Freight Ton-kilometers (100 million ton-km)	176.11	593.24
# 铁 路	Railways	165.58	448.15
公 路	Highways	10.39	143.64
旅客运输量 (万人)	Passenger Traffic (10 000 persons)	5628	28693
# 铁 路	Railways	2009	2661
公 路	Highways	3605	25600
旅客周转量 (亿人公里)	Passenger-Kilometers (100 million passenger-km)	60.73	376.99
# 铁 路	Railways	47.56	178.89
公 路	Highways	12.95	151.04

continued

2005	2010	2013	2014	2014年为下列年份% 2014 as Percentage of the Following Years(%)					1979-2014 平均增长% Average Annual Growth Rate(%)
				1978	2000	2005	2010	2013	
2788	2861	2871	2866	74.4	92.0	102.8	100.2	99.8	-0.8
435.77	988.45	1526.05	1635.85	628.0	213.8	166.5	123.6	105.2	5.2
1140	1165	1216	1198	149.7	110.0	105.1	102.8	98.5	1.1
7.78	6.92	5.79	4.22	40.0	153.9	54.2	60.9	72.8	-2.5
45.35	56.08	59.52	62.30	1102.6	160.7	137.4	111.1	104.7	6.9
5.88	6.73	8.54	7.20	521.7	97.8	122.4	107.0	84.3	4.7
11382	25052	40656	49128	3489.2	802.0	431.6	196.1	120.8	10.4
765.74	1238.50	1487.38	1553.98	4651.2	314.7	202.9	125.5	104.5	11.3
869.93	1384.02	1629.36	1724.68		309.9	198.3	124.6	105.9	
134.11	102.64	112.52	116.76	822.3	126.7	87.1	113.8	103.8	6.0
1650.63	4558.97	7507.34	7993.39	7162.9	743.8	359.7	169.2	110.8	12.6
19.43	27.12	35.55	40.05	289.2	255.4	206.1	147.7	112.7	3.0
7.93	7.52	5.74	6.10	104.9	84.9	76.9	81.0	106.2	0.1
1778.16	3017.28	3688.04	3767.81	62484.4	504.8	211.9	124.9	102.2	19.6
80.59	223.47	371.65	410.11		1943.6	508.9	183.5	110.3	
504.94	1101.91	1493.66	1600.88	2421.9	588.0	317.0	145.3	107.2	9.3
307.28	604.82	980.08	1038.26	4274.4	1935.2	337.9	171.7	105.9	11.0
337.10	994.89	1565.22	1683.92	9688.8	2918.4	499.5	169.3	107.6	13.5
1972.13	5463.79	8545.52	9083.49	4311.9	918.0	460.6	166.2	106.3	11.0
122.86	82.74	103.04	179.33	1309.9	191.0	146.0	216.7	174.0	7.4
4.26	65.21	42.44	37.47		1940.5	879.2	57.5	88.3	
5085.90	14688.70	22443.11	24371.44		908.3	479.2	165.9	108.6	
3302.50	10888.80	17763.00	18622.14		1642.4	563.9	171.0	104.8	
676.50	2401.96	3352.07	3506.18		2254.7	518.3	146.0	104.6	
45724	104423	152712	157074	2193.8	524.1	343.5	150.4	102.9	9.0
12123	27121	35804	37483	1561.8	798.0	309.2	138.2	104.7	7.9
33483	77123	116711	119343	2521.5	473.6	356.4	154.7	102.3	9.4
1115.31	2465.99	3472.92	3522.54	2000.2	593.8	315.8	142.8	101.4	8.7
905.76	1267.90	1514.69	1603.38	968.3	357.8	177.0	126.5	105.9	6.5
207.85	1195.91	1956.54	1917.45	18454.8	1334.9	922.5	160.3	98.0	15.6
39137	93954	118312	75208	1336.3	262.1	192.2	80.0	63.6	7.5
3600	5411	6123	7077	352.3	265.9	196.6	130.8	115.6	3.6
34780	87457	110963	66720	1850.8	260.6	191.8	76.3	60.1	8.4
571.60	851.45	1051.14	964.66	1588.4	255.9	168.8	113.3	91.8	8.0
279.08	362.60	421.38	464.74	977.2	259.8	166.5	128.2	110.3	6.5
206.54	383.99	514.90	339.02	2617.9	224.5	164.1	88.3	65.8	9.5

2-3 续表 2

指　　标		Item		1978	2000
邮电通信业		Postal and Telecommunication Services			
邮电业务总量	(亿元)	Business Volume of Postal and Telecommunication Services	(100 million yuan)	0.50	85.04
函　件	(万件)	Number of Letters Delivered	(10 000 pieces)	9188	17444
报刊期发数	(万份)	Number of Newspapers and Magazines Distributed	(10 000 copies)	319	454
固定电话	(万户)	Number of Fixed Telephone Subscribers	(10 000 subscribers)	4.65	345.24
城　市		Urban Telephone Subscribers		3.24	252.86
农　村		Rural Telephone Subscribers		1.41	92.39
移动电话	(万户)	Number of Mobile Telephone Subscribers	(10 000 subscribers)		151.67
互联网宽带用户	(万户)	Number of Internet Subscribers	(10 000 subscribers)		19.87
国内商业		Domestic Trade			
社会消费品零售总额	(亿元)	Total Retail Sales of Consumer Goods	(100 million yuan)	33.37	725.64
对外贸易和旅游		Foreign Trade and Tourism			
进出口总额	(万美元)	Total Value of Imports and Exports	(USD 10 000)		214009
进口额		Imports			83006
出口额		Exports		1190	131003
国际旅游		International Tourism			
入境旅游人数	(万人次)	Number of Overseas Visitor Arrivals	(10 000 person-times)	1.37	71.28
旅游外汇收入	(万美元)	Foreign Exchange Earnings from Tourism	(USD 10 000)	177	28025
金　融		Financial Intermediation			
金融机构(含外资)人民币存款	(亿元)	Deposits of National Banking System in RMB (Including Foreign Currency)	(100 million yuan)		
金融机构(含外资)人民币贷款	(亿元)	Loans of National Banking System in RMB (Including Foreign Currency)	(100 million yuan)		
教育·科技·文化		**Education, Science and Technology and Culture**			
教　育		Education			
专任教师数	(万人)	Full-time Teachers	(10 000 persons)		
普通高等学校		Regular Institutions of Higher Education		1.07	2.07
中等职业学校		Vocational Secondary Schools		0.33	2.17
普通中学		Secondary Schools		9.17	12.23
小　学		Primary Schools		17.30	18.23
在校学生数	(万人)	Students Enrollment	(10 000 persons)		
普通高等学校		Regular Institutions of Higher Education		3.44	24.17
中等职业学校		Vocational Secondary Schools		2.93	36.37
普通中学		Secondary Schools		193.47	230.52
小　学		Primary Schools		450.51	480.93
科　技		Science and Technology			
全省从事科技活动人员数	(万人)	Personnel Engaged in S&T Activities in the Whole Province	(10 000 persons)		15.51
R&D经费内部支出	(亿元)	Internal Expenditure on Research and Development	(100 million yuan)		
文　化		Culture			
出版数量		Number of Publication			
图　书	(万册)	Books	(10 000 copies)	7661	15958
杂　志	(万册)	Magazines	(10 000 copies)	1423	4944
报　纸	(万份)	Newspapers	(10 000 copies)		70389
制作电视节目	(小时)	Time for TV Programs Production	(hour)		16174

continued

2005	2010	2013	2014	2014年为下列年份% 2014 as Percentage of the Following Years(%)					1979-2014 平均增长% Average Annual Growth Rate(%)
				1978	2000	2005	2010	2013	
331.13	902.85	417.50	566.66	112768.2	666.4	171.1	62.8	135.7	21.6
15119	9734	4914	3310	36.0	19.0	21.9	34.0	67.4	-2.8
286	517	346	375	117.6	82.6	131.1	72.5	108.4	0.5
859.32	781.89	769.29	750.79	16161.2	217.5	87.4	96.0	97.6	15.2
561.84	519.55	555.02	556.61	17202.8	220.1	99.1	107.1	100.3	15.4
297.47	262.34	214.27	194.17	13771.2	210.2	65.3	74.0	90.6	14.7
938.10	2518.23	3512.46	3607.21		2378.3	384.5	143.2	102.7	
236.90	368.83	506.24	552.44		2779.7	233.2	149.8	109.1	
1331.35	3257.54	5245.04	5918.71	17736.6	815.7	444.6	181.7	112.8	15.5
457684	1208283	2012881	2740847		1280.7	598.9	226.8	136.2	
150103	587510	990265	1347921		1623.9	898.0	229.4	136.1	
307580.8	620773	1022617	1392926	117052.6	1063.3	452.9	224.4	136.2	21.7
92.84	212.17	352.07	266.30					105.1	
44625	101596	167620	141630					105.5	
		25577.19	28111.34					109.9	
		16219.84	18837.20					116.1	
4.29	5.83	6.42	6.50	607.3	313.5	151.6	111.5	101.2	5.1
2.85	3.46	3.30	2.75	833.6	126.7	96.3	79.4	83.2	6.1
15.91	17.05	16.75	16.44	179.2	134.4	103.3	96.4	98.2	1.6
18.66	17.52	16.28	14.75	85.3	80.9	79.0	84.2	90.6	-0.4
66.69	92.78	107.76	109.96	3196.5	454.9	164.9	118.5	102.0	10.1
55.84	89.93	60.56	50.26	1715.4	138.2	90.0	55.9	83.0	8.2
304.56	259.91	210.13	196.83	101.7	85.4	64.6	75.7	93.7	…
340.09	261.04	227.33	226.41	50.3	47.1	66.6	86.7	99.6	-1.9
13.49	20.69	22.94	24.91		160.6	184.6	120.4	108.6	
92.15	217.50	342.75	366.77			398.0	168.6	107.0	
17628	19830	19328	18925	247.0	118.6	107.4	95.4	97.9	2.5
6450	7522	5498	5305	372.8	107.3	82.3	70.5	96.5	3.7
68219	62239	68281	68245		97.0	100.0	109.6	99.9	
71983	83275	118154	110336		682.2	153.3	132.5	93.4	

2-3 续表 3

指 标	Item	1978	2000
家庭·生活·环境	**Family, People's Living Conditions and Environment**		
家 庭	Family		
家庭总户数 (万户)	Total Number of Households (10 000 households)	560.82	948.06
居民家庭平均每户居住人口 (人)	Average Household Size of All Households (person)		
城镇居民平均每户居住人口 (人)	Average Household Size in Urban Areas (person)		
农村居民平均每户居住人口 (人)	Average Household Size in Rural Areas (person)		
婚 姻	Marriages and Divorces		
结婚数 (对)	Number of Marriages (couples)	136230	203598
离婚数 (对)	Number of Divorces (couples)		26031
居 住	Housing		
居民家庭人均住房建筑面积(平方米)	Per Capita Floor Space of All Households (sq.m)		
城镇居民人均住房建筑面积(平方米)	Per Capita Floor Space of Urban Residents (sq.m)		
农村居民人均住房建筑面积(平方米)	Per Capita Floor Space of Rural Residents (sq.m)		
生 活	People's Living Conditions		
居民人均可支配收入 (元)	Per Capita Annual Disposable Income of All Households (yuan)		
城镇居民人均可支配收入 (元)	Per Capita Annual Disposable Income of Urban Households (yuan)		
农村居民人均可支配收入 (元)	Per Capita Annual Disposable Income of Rural Households (yuan)		
居民人均生活消费支出 (元)	Per Capita Living Expenditure of All Households (yuan)		
城镇居民人均生活消费支出 (元)	Per Capita Living Expenditure of Urban Households (yuan)		
农村居民人均生活消费支出 (元)	Per Capita Living Expenditure of Rural Households (yuan)		
个人储蓄存款余额 (亿元)	Personal Saving Deposits (100 million yuan)	7.79	1522.53
工 资	Wages		
职工工资总额 (亿元)	Total Wages of Staff and Workers (100 million yuan)	16.44	257.28
职工平均工资 (元)	Average Wage of Staff and Workers (yuan)	654	7804
卫 生	Health Care		
医院数 (个)	Number of Hospitals (unit)	3064	2779
医生数 (万人)	Number of Doctors (10 000 persons)	3.43	6.43
医院床位数 (万张)	Number of Hospital Beds (10 000 units)	4.99	9.26
市政建设	Municipal Works		
自来水供应量 (万立方米)	Volume of Tap Water Supply (10 000 cu.m)	21119	67062
排水管道长度 (公里)	Length of Sewer Pipelines (km)	431	1856
城市天然气供应量 (万立方米)	Volume of Natural Gas Supply in Urban Areas (10 000 cu.m)		17770
道路长度 (公里)	Length of Paved Roads (km)	639	2537
园林绿地面积 (公顷)	Area of Green Land (hectare)	488	9079
环境、灾害	Environment and Disaster		
环境污染治理投资总额 (万元)	Total Investment in the Treatment of Environmental Pollution (10 000 yuan)		
突发环境事件次数 (次)	Environmental Disasters (time)		
火灾发生数 (起)	Number of Fire Disasters (unit)		3818
火灾损失 (万元)	Loss of Fire Disasters (10 000 yuan)		2613
交通事故发生数 (件)	Number of Traffic Accidents (unit)	3979	11846
交通事故损失 (万元)	Loss of Traffic Accidents (10 000 yuan)	165	3978

continued

2005	2010	2013	2014	2014年为下列年份% 2014 as Percentage of the Following Years(%)					1979-2014 平均增长% Average Annual Growth Rate(%)
				1978	2000	2005	2010	2013	
1055.74	1198.37	1263.50	1265.65	225.7	133.5	119.9	105.6	100.2	2.3
		3.28	3.21					98.1	
		3.00	2.96					98.8	
		3.46	3.38					97.6	
208421	346645	396187	381682	280.2	187.5	183.1	110.1	96.3	2.9
23447	44402	63292	68328		262.5	291.4	153.9	108.0	
		35.02	35.99					102.8	
		29.95	30.58					102.1	
		39.65	41.01					103.4	
		14372	15837					108.5	
		22346	24366					107.3	
		7092	7932					109.9	
		11217	12204					108.8	
		16399	17546					107.0	
		6488	7252					111.8	
3533.97	7957.78	12249.36	13428.86	172286.4	882.0	380.0	168.8	109.6	23.0
477.97	1176.33	2311.59	2542.73	15466.7	988.3	532.0	216.2	110.0	15.0
14796	34299	48853	52119	1191.2	483.6	262.7	134.2	105.0	7.1
2674	2639	2634	2587	84.4	93.1	96.7	98.0	98.2	-0.5
6.03	6.28	7.44	7.65	223.0	119.0	126.9	121.9	102.8	2.3
10.34	13.72	17.93	18.57	372.1	200.5	179.6	135.3	103.6	3.7
71170	81335	88990	87921	416.3	131.1	123.5	108.1	98.8	4.0
3250	5666	6766	6925	1606.7	373.1	213.1	122.2	102.3	8.0
76285	164654	238667	279088		1570.6	365.8	169.5	116.9	
3191	4810	5802	5794	906.7	228.4	181.6	120.5	99.9	6.3
15003	26063	33853	34496	7068.9	380.0	229.9	132.4	101.9	12.6
		2216819	2763183					124.6	
		118	82					69.5	
7490	4620	12127	13137		344.1	175.4	284.4	108.3	
4683	8354	16220	13875		531.0	296.3	166.1	85.5	
12011	6004	5952	5055	127.0	42.7	42.1	84.2	84.9	0.7
6242	3311	3696	3652	2213.3	91.8	58.5	110.3	98.8	9.0

2-4 国民经济主要结构指标
Main Composition Indicators on National Economy

单位：% (%)

指 标	Item	2000	2005	2010	2013	2014
人口与就业	**Population and Employment**					
人 口	Population					
城乡结构	Urban and Rural Composition					
城 镇	Urban	32.3	37.2	45.7	51.3	52.6
乡 村	Rural	67.7	62.8	54.3	48.7	47.4
性别结构	Sexual Composition					
男	Male	52.0	51.5	51.7	51.6	51.6
女	Female	48.0	48.5	48.3	48.4	48.4
宏观经济	**Macro Economy**					
国民经济核算	National Accounting					
生产总值产业结构	Industrial Composition					
第一产业	Primary Industry	14.3	11.1	9.8	9.0	8.8
第二产业	Secondary Industry	43.4	49.6	53.8	55.0	54.1
第三产业	Tertiary Industry	42.3	39.3	36.4	36.0	37.0
生产总值地区结构	By Region					
关 中	Guanzhong	72.5	66.2	62.8	62.1	62.7
陕 南	Southern Shaanxi	14.2	12.2	11.1	12.4	12.9
陕 北	Northern Shaanxi	13.3	21.6	26.1	25.5	24.4
投 资	Investment					
固定资产投资结构	Composition of Investment in Fixed Assets					
第一产业	Primary Industry	2.7	2.7	5.7	5.5	5.5
第二产业	Secondary Industry	36.2	34.1	35.1	35.2	31.2
第三产业	Tertiary Industry	61.1	63.2	59.2	59.3	63.4
固定资产投资经济类型结构	Compositione of Investment in Fixed Assets by Registration Status					
国有经济	State-Owned Units	63.5	51.3	49.3	41.4	42.2
集体经济	Collective-Owned Units	5.6	3.9	4.8	3.2	3.3
其他经济	Others	18.4	38.1	42.8	52.6	52.2
个 体	Individuals	12.5	6.7	3.0	2.8	2.2

2-4 续表 1 continued

单位：%　　(%)

指　标	Item	2000	2005	2010	2013	2014
能　源	Energy					
能源生产总量结构	Composition of Total Energy Production					
原　煤	Coal		74.7	76.5	76.5	76.1
原　油	Crude Oil		17.4	13.5	11.9	11.5
天然气	Natural Gas		6.7	9.1	10.8	11.6
水电、风电及其他能发电	Hydro-power, Wind Power and Others		1.1	0.9	0.9	0.9
能源消费总量结构	Composition of Total Energy Consumption					
煤　品	Coal		75.6	70.5	72.3	72.4
油　品	Petroleum		17.4	17.1	15.6	15.1
天然气	Natural Gas		4.1	9.0	8.5	8.9
水电、风电及其他能发电	Hydro-power, Wind Power and Others		3.0	3.4	3.6	3.6
产　业	**Industry**					
农　业	Agriculture					
农林牧渔业产值结构	Composition of Gross Output Value of Agriculture, Forestry,Animal Husbandry and Fishery					
农　业	Farming	70.5	64.7	66.5	66.9	68.2
林　业	Forestry	5.9	3.4	2.1	2.6	2.7
牧　业	Animal Husbandry	22.9	27.2	26.1	25.1	23.6
渔　业	Fishery	0.8	0.8	0.5	0.7	0.7
农林牧渔服务业	Services in Support of Agriculture,Forestry,Animal Husbandry and Fishery		3.9	4.8	4.6	4.7
工　业	Industry					
轻重工业产值结构	Composition of Gross Output Value of Light and Heavy Industry					
轻 工 业	Light Industry	35.1	24.0	18.9	19.9	21.3
重 工 业	Heavy Industry	64.9	76.0	81.1	80.1	78.7
交通运输业	Transportation					
客运量结构	Composition of Passenger Traffic					
铁　路	Railways	9.3	9.2	5.8	5.2	9.4
公　路	Highways	89.2	88.9	93.1	93.8	88.7
水　运	Waterways	0.8	0.9	0.3	0.3	0.5
民用航空	Civil Aviation	0.8	1.1	0.8	0.7	1.4
货运量结构	Composition of Freight Traffic					
铁　路	Railways	15.7	26.5	26.0	23.4	23.9
公　路	Highways	84.1	73.2	73.9	76.4	76.0
水　运	Waterways	0.2	0.3	0.2	0.1	0.1
民用航空	Civil Aviation	…	…	…	…	…

2-4 续表 2 continued

单位：% (%)

指　　标	Item	2000	2005	2010	2013	2014
国内贸易	Domestic Trade					
社会消费品零售总额构成	Composition of Total Retail Sales of Consumer Goods					
城　镇	Urban			87.0	88.1	88.4
乡　村	Rural			13.0	11.9	11.6
国际旅游	International Tourism					
入境旅游人数结构	Composition of Overseas Visitor Arrivals					
外国人	Foreigners	82.0	80.3	73.2	71.3	69.8
港澳台同胞	Hong Kong, Macao and Taiwan Compatriots	18.0	19.7	26.8	28.7	30.2
生活 · 环境	**People's Living Conditions and Environment**					
生　活	People's Living Conditions					
居民可支配收入结构	Annual Per Capita Disposable Income					
工资性收入	Wages Income				56.9	55.9
经营净收入	Net Income from Business				15.4	15.2
财产净收入	Property Income				6.1	6.5
转移净收入	Transfer Income				21.5	22.4
居民消费支出结构	Annual Per Capita Consumption Expenditure					
食品、烟酒	Food,Tobacco and Alcohol				27.3	27.9
衣　着	Clothing				8.1	7.7
居　住	Residence				21.3	21.2
生活用品及服务	Living Articles and Services				6.5	6.5
交通通信	Transportation and Communications				12.3	12.6
教育文化娱乐	Recreation, Education and Culture Services				12.8	12.3
医疗保健	Medicine and Medical Services				9.6	9.7
其他用品和服务	Others				2.1	2.1
环　境	Environment					
工业污染防治投资结构	Consumption of Investment in the Treatment of Industrial Pollution					
治理废水	Waste Water Treatment				14.5	19.7
治理废气	Waste Gas Treatment				76.9	70.3
治理固体废物	Solid Wastes Treatment				2.4	0.6
治理噪音	Noise Abatement				0.2	0.4
其　他	Others				6.0	9.0

2-5　国民经济和社会发展比例与效益指标
Indicators on Proportions and Efficiency in National Economic and Social Development

指　　标	Item	2000	2005	2010	2013	2014
人　口	Population					
出生率 (‰)	Birth Rate (‰)		10.02	9.73	10.01	10.13
死亡率 (‰)	Death Rate (‰)		6.01	6.01	6.15	6.26
自然增长率 (‰)	Natural Growth Rate (‰)		4.01	3.72	3.86	3.87
就　业	Employment					
城镇登记失业率 (%)	Registered Unemployment Rate in Urban Areas(%)	2.7	4.2	3.9	3.3	3.4
国民经济核算	National Accounting					
一、二、三产业增加值比例 (%) (第一产业＝100)	Ratio of Value-added by Type of Industry(%) (Value added in Primary Industry=100)					
第一产业	Primary Industry	100.0	100.0	100.0	100.0	100.0
第二产业	Secondary Industry	303.1	447.8	551.0	610.0	612.0
第三产业	Tertiary Industry	295.6	354.9	373.2	399.2	418.4
人均生产总值 (元)	Per Capita GDP (yuan)	4968	10674	27133	43117	46929
固定资产投资	Investment in Fixed Assets					
全社会固定资产投资相当于生产总值比例 (%)	Proportion of Investment in Fixed Assets to GDP (%)	41.3	50.4	84.6	98.3	105.8
全社会房屋建筑面积竣工率 (%)	Rate of Total Floor Space of Buildings Completed (%)	75.5	49.2	22.9	22.0	21.0
财　政	Government Finance					
财政收入相当于生产总值比例 (%)	Proportion of Government Revenue to GDP (%)	10.4	13.4	17.8	18.5	17.8
财政支出相当于生产总值比例 (%)	Proportion of Government Expenditures to GDP (%)	15.1	16.2	21.9	22.6	22.4
利用外资	Utilization of Foreign Capital					
实际利用外资额相当于签订利用外资额比例 (%)	Proportion of Actually Utilization of Foreign Capital to Signed Utilization of Foreign Capital (%)	57.8	39.7	82.3	98.9	71.3
能　源	Energy					
能源生产弹性系数	Elasticity Ratio of Energy Production (%)		1.14	1.15	0.73	0.59
能源消费弹性系数	Elasticity Ratio of Energy Consumption(%)		0.99	0.72	0.64	0.59
每万元生产总值消耗的能源(吨标准煤)	Energy Consumption Per 10 000 yuan of GDP (ton of SCE)		1.416	0.818	0.734	0.708

注：本表能源生产用等价值折算,2005年每万元生产总值消耗的能源GDP按2005年价格计算，2010年及以后GDP按2010年价格计算。

a) Energy production in this table are converted on the basis of equal value.Energy Consumption Per 10 000 yuan of GDP in 2005 is calculated at 2005 constant prices. The Figure are calculated at 2010 constant prices since 2010.

2-5 续表 1 continued

指　　标	Item	2000	2005	2010	2013	2014
农　业	Agriculture					
人均耕地面积 (公顷)	Per Capita Cultivated Land (hectare)	0.09	0.08	0.08	0.08	0.08
每公顷耕地农业机械总动力 (千瓦)	Total Power of Agricultural Machinery per Hectare of Cultivated Land (kw)	3.36	5.04	6.60	8.10	8.90
每公顷耕地化肥施用量 (公斤)	Chemical Fertilizer Consumption per Hectare of Cultivated Land (kg)	421	527	688	842	803
每公顷耕地生产的农业产值 (元)	Agricultural Output Value per Hectare of Cultivated Land (yuan)	14929	26205	58243	89255	95667
每公顷播种面积农产品产量(公斤)	Output of Farm Crops per Hectare of Sown Area (kg)					
粮　食	Grain	2850	3300	3687	3915	3893
棉　花	Cotton	911	1107	1361	1577	1358
油　料	Oil-bearing Crops	1277	1638	1861	1992	2071
工　业	Industry					
总资产贡献率 (%)	Ratio of Total Assets to Industrial Output Value (%)	7.8	15.4	17.1	16.0	15.7
资产负债率 (%)	Assets-Liability Ratio (%)	68.2	62.2	56.8	56.1	56.8
流动资产周转次数 (次/年)	Number of Times of Annual of Turnover Circulating Funds (times/year)	1.1	1.7	1.7	2.0	2.2
成本费用利润率 (%)	Ratio of Profits to Industrial Cost (%)	6.1	14.5	16.1	12.9	11.5
产品销售率 (%)	Proportion of Products Sold (%)	96.7	97.7	96.9	95.2	95.5
建筑业	Construction					
产值利润率 (%)	Ratio of Per-tax Profits to Gross Output Value (%)	0.6	1.5	1.9	3.9	2.8
全员劳动生产率 (元/人)	Overall Labor Productivity (yuan/person)	59672	135356	269553	331957	327323
运输邮电通信业	Transportation, Postal and Telecommunication Services					
铁路网密度 (公里/平方公里)	Railway Density (km/sq.km)	0.011	0.016	0.019	0.022	0.022
公路网密度 (公里/平方公里)	Highway Density (km/sq.km)	0.214	0.265	0.717	0.804	0.813
铁路客运密度 (万人公里/公里)	Density of Passenger Traffic (10 000 person-km/km)	658.0	850.8	1004.4	1072.3	1137.9
铁路货运密度 (万吨公里/公里)	Railway Freight Traffic Density (10 000 ton/km)	1634.6	2686.1	2863.5	3386.2	3405.7
固定电话普及率 (部/百人)	Access to Fixed Telephones (set/100 persons)	9.47	23.28	20.93	20.44	19.89
城市电话普及率 (部/百人)	Access to Urban Telephones(set/100 persons)	21.50	40.89	30.44	28.74	28.05
移动电话普及率 (部/百人)	Access to Mobile Telephones (set/100 persons)	4.16	25.42	67.42	93.32	95.55

2-5 续表 2 continued

指 标	Item	2000	2005	2010	2013	2014
国内商业	Domestic Trade					
人均消费品零售额 (元)	Per Capita Retail Sales of Consumer Goods (yuan)	1998	3612	8731	13956	15702
对外贸易	Foreign Trade					
进出口额相当于生产总值比例 (%)	Proportion of Total Value of Imports and Exports to GDP (%)	9.8	9.5	8.1	7.7	9.5
金 融	Financial Intermediation					
金融机构存款相当于生产总值比例 (%)	Deposits of Financial Institutions as Percentage of GDP (%)				157.8	158.9
金融机构贷款相当于生产总值比例 (%)	Loans of Financial Institutions as Percentage of GDP (%)				100.1	106.5
教育、科技	Education, Science and Technology					
每万人大学生数 (人)	Number of College and University Students per 10 000 Population (person)	66	181	248	286	291
R&D经费内部支出相当于生产总值比例 (%)	Internal Expenditure on Research and Development as Percentage of GDP (%)		2.35	2.15	2.12	2.07
文 化	Culture					
每万人有艺术表演团体 (个)	Number of Troupesper 10 000 Population (unit)	0.03	0.03	0.03	0.02	0.02
每万人有公共图书馆 (个)	Number of Public Libraries per 10 000 Population (unit)	0.03	0.03	0.03	0.03	0.03
每万人有博物馆 (个)	Number of Museums per 10 000 Population (unit)	0.02	0.02	0.03	0.06	0.06
广播电视	Radio and Television					
广播人口覆盖率 (%)	Radio Coverage of Population (%)	90.3	93.2	96.7	97.4	97.8
电视人口覆盖率 (%)	TV Coverage of Population (%)	91.4	94.4	97.7	98.3	98.5
卫 生	Health Care					
每万人医院数 (个)	Number of Hospitals per 10 000 Population (unit)	0.8	0.7	0.7	0.7	0.7
每万人医生数 (人)	Number of Doctors per 10 000 Population (person)	18	16	17	20	20
每万人医院病床数 (张)	Number of Hospital Beds per 10 000 Population (unit)	25	28	37	48	49
市政建设	Municipal Works					
城市用水普及率 (%)	Coverage Rate of Urban Population with Access to Tap Water (%)	96.50	93.20	99.39	96.52	96.25
城市燃气普及率 (%)	Coverage Rate of Urban Population with Access to Gas (%)	74.53	79.80	90.39	93.75	95.77
人均公园绿地面积 (平方米)	Per Capita Public Green Area(hectare)			10.67	11.77	12.58
灾 害	Disasters					
平均每起火灾损失 (元)	Average Loss of per Fire Disaster (yuan)	7028	6253	18082	13375	10562
平均每起交通事故损失 (元)	Average Loss of per Traffic Accident (yuan)	3358	5197	5515	6210	7225

2-6 社会经济主要指标平均每人水平
Per Capita Main Indicators on Society and Economy

单位：元 (yuan)

年 份 Year	生产总值 Gross Domestic Product	工农业总产值 Gross Industrial and Agricultural Output Value	工业总产值 Gross Industrial Output Value	农林牧渔业总产值 Gross Output Value of Agriculture, Forestry, Animal Husbandry and Fishery	社会消费品零售总额 Total Retail Sales of Consumer Goods
1978	291	480	349	131	121
1980	334	539	390	149	154
1985	604	910	644	267	268
1990	1241	1881	1359	522	490
1995	2965	4147	3056	1091	1141
1996	3446	4583	3312	1271	1346
1997	3834	4892	3611	1281	1553
1998	4070	5019	3681	1338	1680
1999	4415	5416	4162	1254	1824
2000	4968	6001	4721	1280	1998
2001	5511	6649	5336	1312	2218
2002	6161	7423	6031	1392	2482
2003	7057	8781	7387	1394	2757
2004	8638	10992	9220	1771	3163
2005	10674	13133	11150	1983	3612
2006	12840	16430	14206	2224	4175
2007	15546	20495	17787	2708	4961
2008	19700	25954	22512	3442	6241
2009	21947	29257	25665	3592	7322
2010	27133	37759	33293	4465	8731
2011	33464	47796	42290	5506	10433
2012	38564	55752	49607	6145	12225
2013	43117	62214	55396	6818	13956
2014	46929	65491	58218	7274	15702

2-6 续表 continued

年 份 Year	职工平均工资(元) Average Wage of Staff and Workers (yuan)	人均储蓄存款余额(元) Per Capita Balance of Saving Deposits (yuan)	每万人有 Per 10 000 Population		
			大学生(人) College and University Students (person)	医院床位(张) Hospital Beds (unit)	医生数(人) Doctors (unit)
1978	654	28	12	18	12
1980	785	48	19	19	13
1985	1122	149	27	22	17
1990	2042	617	29	24	18
1995	4396	2089	37	26	18
1996	4882	2659	38	26	18
1997	5184	3054	39	25	17
1998	6029	3453	42	25	17
1999	6931	3792	50	25	18
2000	7804	4178	66	25	18
2001	9120	4841	87	26	18
2002	10351	5756	112	26	16
2003	11461	6863	136	27	16
2004	13024	8010	159	27	16
2005	14796	9577	181	28	16
2006	16918	10997	196	29	16
2007	21296	11538	209	31	16
2008	25942	14778	226	33	16
2009	30185	18094	240	35	16
2010	34299	21306	248	37	17
2011	39043	24507	258	39	18
2012	44330	28697	273	43	19
2013	48853	32546	286	48	20
2014	52119	35572	291	49	20

2-7　人均工农业主要产品产量
Per Capita Output of Major Industrial and Agricultural Products

年份 Year	粮食 (公斤) Grain (kg)	棉花 (公斤) Cotton (kg)	油料 (公斤) Oil-bearing Crops (kg)	蔬菜 (公斤) Vegetables (kg)	水果 (公斤) Fruits (kg)	肉类 (公斤) Meat (kg)	禽蛋 (公斤) Poultry Eggs (kg)	水产品 (公斤) Aquatic Products (kg)
1978	289.3	3.8	2.0		12.1	5.1	0.9	0.1
1980	268.5	2.9	3.9		9.9	8.2	1.1	0.1
1985	319.0	1.4	10.0	99.6	11.2	10.1	3.8	0.2
1990	328.7	2.4	10.3	112.8	19.0	14.4	5.7	0.6
1995	261.2	1.1	10.9	103.8	81.2	22.7	11.5	1.1
1996	345.0	0.9	10.6	122.1	102.7	19.3	10.2	1.2
1997	293.7	0.6	10.3	110.0	91.8	20.8	11.2	1.3
1998	363.7	0.6	9.9	128.3	120.2	23.8	11.1	1.4
1999	299.9	0.5	8.8	138.6	136.8	23.8	11.1	1.6
2000	299.9	0.8	10.7	153.3	136.0	25.4	11.7	1.7
2001	267.7	1.4	10.3	144.0	146.4	26.4	11.6	1.7
2002	274.9	1.2	11.2	180.6	157.9	28.9	12.7	1.8
2003	264.1	1.4	11.3	193.3	169.4	31.1	13.4	1.8
2004	315.6	2.2	12.5	213.6	200.1	33.3	13.2	1.9
2005	309.2	2.1	12.3	236.0	207.8	36.4	13.2	2.0
2006	282.0	2.4	11.2	229.7	238.7	27.5	11.1	1.3
2007	288.4	2.4	10.6	250.6	253.9	25.9	11.7	1.4
2008	310.0	2.7	13.3	287.4	287.5	30.0	12.9	1.4
2009	303.9	2.3	14.6	337.8	309.1	26.5	12.9	1.5
2010	312.2	1.9	15.0	371.0	331.9	27.5	12.6	1.6
2011	319.5	1.8	15.8	383.1	356.4	26.6	13.5	2.2
2012	332.2	1.8	16.1	407.1	383.6	28.6	13.8	2.8
2013	323.5	1.5	15.8	433.5	395.7	29.9	14.7	3.3
2014	317.8	1.1	16.5	457.5	412.3	31.0	14.5	3.7

2-7　续表　continued

年份 Year	纱 (公斤) Yarn (kg)	布 (米) Cloth (m)	机制纸及纸板 (公斤) Machine-made Paper and Paperboard (kg)	原油 (公斤) Crude Oil (kg)	发电量 (千瓦小时) Electricity (kwh)	粗钢 (公斤) Crude Steel (kg)	钢材 (公斤) Rolled Steel (kg)	水泥 (公斤) Cement (kg)
1978	5.0	21.0	2.4	2.2	239.1	8.8	6.3	76.2
1980	5.3	23.4	3.2	3.0	280.7	8.7	6.6	81.4
1985	5.3	21.5	6.3	7.4	364.5	11.6	8.1	128.6
1990	4.6	22.4	12.9	21.5	459.7	15.0	9.5	162.7
1995	4.0	22.6	24.6	47.8	677.1	15.4	16.9	243.6
1996	3.6	20.8	24.2	62.6	761.6	15.3	13.6	259.6
1997	3.9	22.2	25.5	80.4	758.6	13.5	11.9	327.8
1998	3.9	17.9	6.3	89.6	686.5	14.7	13.7	239.7
1999	4.0	19.1	6.5	178.3	707.1	14.0	17.1	274.4
2000	4.3	19.8	6.6	205.6	749.9	14.8	15.9	272.5
2001	4.3	18.9	7.8	251.0	831.8	19.0	17.6	304.3
2002	4.8	19.9	6.6	290.8	939.2	24.0	22.4	363.2
2003	4.9	20.2	8.7	345.6	1121.4	47.4	36.0	418.4
2004	5.1	20.3	14.2	415.6	1308.2	60.0	54.7	489.7
2005	5.3	21.5	10.9	482.5	1370.1	83.4	91.5	535.1
2006	5.1	21.1	13.8	538.3	1562.6	105.2	135.3	643.0
2007	5.8	22.2	19.2	611.8	1886.8	107.0	151.1	817.1
2008	5.9	19.9	19.8	663.5	2264.3	82.1	134.9	965.0
2009	6.6	20.0	20.0	724.2	2415.6	140.4	238.4	1199.4
2010	7.3	20.2	23.2	808.7	2953.4	162.1	266.7	1464.4
2011	7.3	16.4	24.8	862.7	3233.2	201.0	274.2	1720.0
2012	7.7	17.3	21.4	941.2	3550.0	221.1	342.5	2015.2
2013	9.5	15.3	21.4	981.3	3974.2	260.8	416.5	2273.7
2014	10.6	16.2	21.3	999.6	4247.0	275.4	446.7	2409.8

2-8 各市(区)国民经济主要指标(2014年)

指 标	Item	关中 Guanzhong	西安市 Xi'an
年底常住人口 (万人)	Number of Usual Residents in the Households Surveyed at Year-end (10 000 persons)	2372.86	862.75
城镇非私营单位就业人员年末人数 (万人)	Number of Fully Employed Staff and Workers in Urban Non-private Units at Year-end (10 000 persons)	351.86	193.82
生产总值 (亿元)	Gross Domestic Product (100 million yuan)	11066.91	5492.64
全社会固定资产投资总额 (亿元)	Total Investment in Fixed Assets (100 million yuan)	12710.56	5903.98
# 固定资产投资	Investment in Fixed Assets	12211.17	5697.26
# 房地产开发投资	Investment in Real Estate Development	2171.98	1761.88
地方一般预算收入 (亿元)	Local General Bugetary Revenue (100 million yuan)	844.77	583.79
财政支出 (亿元)	Government Expenditures (100 million yuan)	1725.52	819.54
城镇非私营单位就业人员工资总额 (亿元)	Total Wages Bill of Fully Employed Staff and Workers in Urban Non-private Units (100 million yuan)	1784.78	1106.57
城镇非私营单位就业人员平均工资 (元)	Average Wage of Fully Employed Staff and Workers in Urban Non-private Units (yuan)		53974
城镇居民人均可支配收入 (元)	Per Capita Annual Disposable Income of Urban Households (yuan)		36100
农村居民人均纯收入 (元)	Per Capita Net Income of Rural Residents (yuan)		14462
农林牧渔业总产值 (亿元)	Gross Output Value of Agriculture, Forestry, Animal Husbandry and Fishery (100 million yuan)	1646.31	367.21
粮食产量 (万吨)	Grain (10 000 tons)	735.40	175.61
棉花产量 (吨)	Cotton (ton)	40737	328
油料产量 (万吨)	Oil-bearing Crops (10 000 tons)	15.85	0.98
规模以上工业总产值 (亿元)	Gross Industrial Output Value above Designated Size (100 million yuan)	12333.18	4420.06
邮电业务总量 (亿元)	Business Volume of Postal and Telecommunication Services (100 million yuan)	396.63	247.13
固定电话 (万户)	Number of Fixed Telephone Subscribers (10 000 subscribers)	545.38	322.91
移动电话 (万户)	Number of Mobile Telephone Subscribers (10 000 subscribers)	2526.34	1462.32
社会消费品零售总额 (亿元)	Total Retail Sales of Consumer Goods (100 million yuan)	4713.97	3093.89
进出口总额 (亿元)	Total Value of Imports and Exports (100 million yuan)	1639.75	1532.15
# 出 口	Exports	820.86	734.68
实际利用外商直接投资额 (万美元)	Actually Utilized Value of Direct Investments (USD 10 000)	392609	370318
卫生机构数 (个)	Health Care Institutions (unit)	18682	5742
卫生机构床位数 (张)	Number of Beds (unit)	126762	51065
卫生技术人员 (人)	Medical Technical Personnel (person)	171344	76375

注：本表价值量指标中，除邮电业务总量按不变价格计算，其余均按当年价格计算。

Main Indicators on National Economic by City(District)(2014)

铜川市 Tongchuan	宝鸡市 Baoji	咸阳市 Xianyang	渭南市 Weinan	# 韩城市 Hancheng	杨凌示范区 Yangling	陕南 Southern Shaanxi	汉中市 Hanzhong	安康市 Ankang	商洛市 Shangluo	陕北 Northern Shaanxi	延安市 Yan'an	榆林市 Yulin
84.51	375.32	495.68	534.30	39.71	20.30	842.43	343.15	264.20	235.08	559.82	221.43	338.39
12.13	40.23	54.53	46.75		4.40	67.66	30.87	17.63	19.17	76.93	34.83	42.10
325.36	1642.90	2085.15	1423.75	303.01	97.11	2267.26	1002.83	689.44	574.99	4306.67	1386.09	2920.58
327.63	2105.59	2492.43	1765.63	252.39	115.31	2075.76	845.04	605.56	625.16	3188.11	1541.07	1647.04
298.57	2058.98	2398.57	1646.34	248.79	111.46	1844.90	705.33	541.78	597.78	2694.10	1297.53	1396.56
31.66	93.14	195.95	81.35	9.23	7.99	153.93	82.10	53.48	18.35	100.59	26.66	73.93
22.06	78.06	85.46	67.46	17.00	7.93	98.02	40.89	28.09	29.04	435.96	168.10	267.85
83.01	235.60	272.44	293.41	30.79	21.52	601.88	234.00	204.74	163.14	733.73	310.41	423.32
53.67	174.60	228.66	198.62		22.65	282.35	136.81	74.49	71.06	429.63	187.95	241.68
45665	43603	42434	42508		50915		44417	42714	37870		53651	56321
27237	31560	31530	26725	30071	36008		24605	25011	24727		30588	29665
9169	9421	9612	8534	11400	14046		7933	7468	7035		9779	9730
41.88	280.90	559.99	384.46	27.69	11.86	655.17	325.51	163.75	165.92	453.24	203.20	250.03
23.39	144.32	184.14	206.01	7.28	1.93	239.99	101.75	86.04	52.20	236.78	78.68	158.10
	60	130	40219	120		38	1	35	2	1051	931	120
0.80	1.92	4.77	7.36	0.12	0.01	35.86	18.91	14.79	2.16	10.59	2.27	8.32
565.91	2274.97	3002.05	1959.32		110.86	2295.63	873.55	787.97	634.11	5157.76	1708.57	3449.20
9.95	40.27	49.33	49.95			77.34	34.91	26.16	16.28	92.69	34.52	58.18
13.43	64.91	61.67	82.46			116.96	53.31	36.69	26.96	88.45	34.70	53.75
66.71	266.46	367.88	362.98			529.07	234.63	174.22	120.22	551.80	213.75	338.04
96.64	539.67	528.84	441.98	36.99	12.95	611.76	281.65	193.18	136.92	592.98	218.24	374.74
1.37	52.43	35.39	14.17		4.25	31.01	6.37	2.17	22.47	10.07	7.14	2.93
1.36	41.21	28.28	11.91		3.42	25.03	4.54	2.17	18.32	9.69	7.14	2.55
2100	8008	10356	1216		611	7478	4005	3000	473	8329	1063	7266
947	2916	4683	4203		191	10055	3858	3190	3007	8510	3571	4939
5179	21478	27148	20832		1060	43391	19805	12595	10991	29219	11971	17248
7048	22784	37596	25780		1761	46187	20065	14351	11771	35080	13835	21245

a) Figures in value terms in this table are at current prices, except that on the business volume of postal and telecommunication services which is at constant prices.

主要统计指标解释

平均增长速度 平均增长速度表明社会经济现象在一个较长的时期内逐期平均增长变化的程度，它不能根据各个环比增长速度直接求得，但与平均发展速度之间存在着一定的数量关系：平均增长速度＝平均发展速度－1。

平均发展速度是一种根据环比发展速度计算的序时平均数,由于各时期对比的基础不同，所以计算平均发展速度不能采用一般的序时平均数的计算方法，计算方法分为水平法和累计法。水平法，又称几何平均法，即将环比发展速度按连乘法用几何平均数公式计算。累计法，也称方程法，根据一段时期内各年发展水平总和与基期水平的关系，列出方程式计算平均发展速度。水平法着重考虑最后一年所达到的发展水平；累计法着重考虑整个时期累计发展水平的总量。

本《年鉴》内所列的平均增长速度，除固定资产投资用“累计法”计算外，其余均用“水平法”计算。从某年到某年平均增长速度的年份，均不包括基期年在内。如建国六十年以来的平均增长速度是以 1949 年为基期计算的，则写为 1950-2009 年平均增长速度，其余类推。

企业(单位)登记注册类型 是以在工商行政管理机关登记注册的各类企业为划分对象，以工商行政管理部门对企业登记注册的类型为依据，将企业登记注册类型分为内资企业、港澳台商投资企业和外商投资企业三大类。内资企业包括国有企业、集体企业、股份合作企业、联营企业、有限责任公司、股份有限公司、私营公司和其他企业；港澳台商投资企业和外商投资企业分别包括合资经营企业、合作经营企业、独资经营企业和股份有限公司。对不在工商行政管理部门进行登记注册的行政机关、事业单位和社会团体，主要按其经费来源和管理方式进行划分。

国有企业 指企业全部资产归国家所有，并按《中华人民共和国企业法人登记管理条例》规定登记注册的非公司制的经济组织。不包括有限责任公司中的国有独资公司。

集体企业 指企业资产归集体所有，并按《中华人民共和国企业法人登记管理条例》规定登记注册的经济组织。

股份合作企业 指以合作制为基础，由企业职工共同出资入股，吸收一定比例的社会资产投资组建，实行自主经营，自负盈亏，共同劳动，民主管理，按劳分配与按股分红相结合的一种集体经济组织。

联营企业 指两个及两个以上相同或不同所有制性质的企业法人或事业单位法人，按自愿、平等、互利的原则，共同投资组成的经济组织。联营企业包括国有联营企业、集体联营企业、国有与集体联营企业和其他联营企业。

有限责任公司 指根据《中华人民共和国公司登记管理条例》规定登记注册，由两个以上、五十个以下的股东共同出资，每个股东以其所认缴的出资额对公司承担有限责任，公司以其全部资产对其债务承担责任的经济组织。有限责任公司包括国有独资公司以及其他有限责任公司。

股份有限公司 指根据《中华人民共和国公司登记管理条例》规定登记注册，其全部注册资本由等额股份构成并通过发行股票筹集资本，股东以其认购的股份对公司承担有限责任，公司以其全部资产对其债务承担责任的经济组织。

私营企业 指由自然人投资设立或由自然人控股，以雇佣劳动为基础的营利性经济组织。包括按照《公司法》、《合伙企业法》、《私营企业暂行条例》规定登记注册的私营有限责任公司、私营股份有限公司、私营合伙企业和私营独资企业。

其他企业 指上述企业之外的其他内资经济组织。

与港澳台商合资经营企业 指港澳台地区投资者与内地企业依照《中华人民共和国中外合资经营企业法》及有关法律的规定，按合同规定的比例投资设立、分享利润和分担风险的企业。

与港澳台商合作经营企业 指港澳台地区投资者与内地企业依照《中华人民共和国中外合作经营企业法》及有关法律的规定，依照合作合同的约定进行投资或提供条件设立、分配利润和分担风险的企业。

港澳台商独资经营企业 指依照《中华人民共和国外资企业法》及有关法律的规定，在内地由港澳台地区投资者全额投资设立的企业。

港澳台商投资股份有限公司 指根据国家有关规定，经原外经贸部依法批准设立，其中港、澳、台商的股本占公司注册资本的比例达 25% 以上的股份有限公司。凡其中港、澳、台商的股本占公司注册资本的比例小于 25%的，属于内资企业中的股份有限公司。

中外合资经营企业 指外国企业或外国人与中国内地企业依照《中华人民共和国中外合资经营企业法》及有关法律的规定，按合同规定的比例投资设立、分享利润和分担风险的企业。

中外合作经营企业 指外国企业或外国人与中国内地企业依照《中华人民共和国中外合作经营企业法》及有关法律的规定，依照合作合同的约定进行投资或提供条件设立、分配利润和分担风险的企业。

外资企业 指依照《中华人民共和国外资企业法》及有关法律的规定，在中国内地由外国投资者全额投资设立的企业。

外商投资股份有限公司 指根据国家有关规定，经原外经贸部依法批准设立，其中外资的股本占公司注册资本的比例达 25% 以上的股份有限公司。凡其中外资股本占公司注册资本的比例小于 25%的，属于内资企业中的股份有限公司。

行政机关、事业单位和社会团体 参照企业登记注册类型，主要按其经费来源和管理方式划分。具体规定如下：

⑴行政机关：包括国家机关和政党机关，原则上均列为

“国有”。但有特殊规定的，如供销社等，则列为“集体”。

⑵事业单位：包括经国家机构编制部门和有关业务主管部门批准成立的各类事业单位，不包括实行企业化管理的事业单位。事业单位的划分办法如下：

①由国家财政预算拨款或列入财政预算外资金管理以及经费主要来源于国有主管部门或国有上级单位的事业单位，列为“国有”。

②经费主要来源于集体单位的事业单位，列为“集体”。

③公民个人(或个人合伙)开办的事业单位，列为“私营”。

④上述以外的其他事业单位，如果其经费来源不明确，按管理方式进行归类。

⑶社会团体：包括经民政部门批准成立以及未纳入社会团体管理条例范围的工会、妇联等各类社会团体。社会团体的划分办法如下：

①未纳入民政部社会团体管理条例范围的工会、妇联、共青团、青联、工商联、科协、侨联等社会团体，国家拨款设立的基金会或基金管理组织以及经费主要来源于国有业务主管部门或国有上级单位的社会团体，列为“国有”。

②经费主要来源于集体单位的社会团体，列为“集体”。

③公民个人(或个人合伙)开办的社会团体，划为“私营”。

④上述以外的其他社会团体，如果其经费来源不明确，改按管理方式进行归类。

Explanatory Notes on Main Statistical Indicators

Average Annual Growth Rate shows the average growth rate of social and economic development during a longer period. It can not be directly calculated by chain based growth rate. The relation is:

Average Annual Growth Rate = Average Speed of Development – 1

Average speed of development is the time series average of speed which calculated by chain based. Because the reference bases during the different periods are not same, average speed of development can not be calculated by the general method. Level approach and accumulative approach for calculating average speed of development rate are applied. The "level approach", or the method of calculating the geometric average, is derived by the formula of geometric average of the chain-based speeds of development, or comparing the level of the last year of the interval with that of the beginning year; the other is called the "accumulative approach" or the "algebraic average", "equation" method, which is derived by the summation of the actual figure of each year in the interval divided by the figure in the base year. The level approach focuses on the level of the last year, while the accumulative approach emphasizes the aggregate development in the duration.

The average annual growth rates listed in the Yearbook are calculated by the level approach except for the growth rate of investment in fixed assets. The base year is not listed in the duration for which average annual growth rates are computed. For instance, the average annual growth rate of the 60 years since 1949 is shown as the average annual growth rate of 1950-2009 without showing the base year 1949.

Registration Status of Enterprises Enterprises are classified into 3 categories, namely domestic-funded enterprises, enterprises with investment from Hong Kong, Macau and Taiwan, and enterprises with foreign investment, according to the registration status of an enterprise in industrial and commercial administration agencies. Domestic-funded enterprises include State-owned enterprises, collective-owned enterprises, cooperative enterprises, joint ownership enterprises, limited liability corporations, share-holding corporations Ltd., private enterprises and other enterprises. Included in the enterprises with investment from Hong Kong, Macau and Taiwan and enterprises with foreign investment are joint-venture enterprises, cooperative enterprises, sole investment enterprises and share-holding corporations Ltd. For government agencies, institutions and social organizations which are not registered in industrial and commercial administration agencies, they are classified mainly by their sources of funding and manner of management.

State-owned Enterprises refer to non-corporation economic units where the entire assets are owned by the State and which have been registered in accordance with the *Regulation of the People's Republic of China on the Management of Registration of Corporate Enterprises.* Not included from this category are solely State-funded corporations in the limited liability corporations.

Collective-owned Enterprises refer to economic units where the assets are owned collectively and which have been registered in accordance with the *Regulation of the People's Republic of China on the Management of Registration of Corporate Enterprises.*

Cooperative Enterprises refer to a form of collective economic units (enterprises) where capitals come mainly from employees as their shares, with certain proportion of capital from the outside, where production is organized on the basis of independent operation, independent accounting for profits and losses, joint work, democratic management, and a distribution system that integrates remuneration according to work with dividend according to capital share.

Joint Ownership Enterprises refer to economic units established by two or more corporate enterprises or corporate institutions of the same or different ownership, through joint investment on the basis of voluntary participation, equality, and mutual benefits. They include State joint ownership enterprises; collective joint ownership enterprises; joint State-collective enterprises; and other joint ownership enterprises.

Limited Liability Corporations refer to economic units established with investment from 2-50 investors and registered in accordance with the *Regulation of the People's Republic of China on the Management of Registration of Corporations*, each investor bearing limited liability to the corporation depending on its share of investment, and the corporation bearing liability to its debt to the maximum of its total assets. Limited liability corporations include solely State-funded limited liability corporations and other limited liability corporations.

Share-holding Corporations Ltd. refer to economic units registered in accordance with the *Regulation of the People's Republic of China on the Management of Registration of Corporations*, with total registered capital divided into equal shares and raised through issuing stocks. Each investor bears limited liability to the corporation depending on the holding of shares, and the corporation bears liability to its debt to the maximum of its total assets.

Private Enterprises refer to profit-making economic units invested and established by natural persons, or controlled by natural persons using employed labour. Included in this category are private limited liability corporations, private share-holding corporations Ltd., private partnership enterprises and private-funded enterprises registered in accordance with the *Company Law, the Law on Partnership Business* and *Interim Regulations on Private Enterprises* .

Other Domestic-funded Enterprises refer to

domestic-funded economic units other than those mentioned above.

Joint Venture Enterprises with Funds from Hong Kong, Macau and Taiwan are enterprises established by investors from Hong Kong, Macau and Taiwan with enterprises in the mainland of China in accordance with the *Law of the People's Republic of China on Sino-foreign Equity Joint Ventures* and other relevant laws, where the establishment of the investment and the sharing of profits and risks are stipulated under joint venture contracts.

Cooperative Enterprises with Funds from Hong Kong, Macau and Taiwan established by investors from Hong Kong, Macau and Taiwan with enterprises in the mainland of China in accordance with the *Law of the People's Republic of China on Sino-foreign Contractual Joint Venture* and other relevant laws, where the investment or provision of facilities and the sharing of profits and risks are stipulated under cooperative contracts.

Enterprises with Sole (exclusive) Investment from Hong Kong, Macau and Taiwan refer to enterprises established in the mainland of China with exclusive investment from investors from Hong Kong, Macau and Taiwan in accordance with the *Law of the People's Republic of China on Wholly Foreign-owned Enterprises* and other relevant laws.

Share-holding Corporations Ltd. with Investment from Hong Kong, Macau and Taiwan refer to share-holding corporations Ltd. established with the approval from the former Ministry of Foreign Trade and Economic Relations in line with relevant State regulations, where the share of investment from Hong Kong, Macau or Taiwan businessmen exceeds 25% of the total registered capital of the corporation. In case the share of investment from Hong Kong, Macau or Taiwan is less than 25% of the total registered capital, the enterprise is to be classified as domestic-funded share-holding corporation Ltd.

Joint Venture Enterprises with Foreign Investment refer to enterprises jointly established by foreign enterprises or foreigners with enterprises in the mainland of China in accordance with the *Law of the People's Republic of China on Sino-foreign Equity Joint Ventures* and other relevant laws, where the sharing of investment, profits and risks is stipulated under contract.

Cooperative Enterprises with Foreign Investment refer to enterprises jointly established by foreign enterprises or foreigners with enterprises in the mainland of China in accordance with the *Law of the People's Republic of China on Sino-foreign Contractual Joint Venture* and other relevant laws, where the investment or provision of facilities and the sharing of profits and risks are stipulated under cooperative contracts.

Enterprises with Sole (exclusive) Foreign Investment refer to enterprises established in the mainland of China with exclusive investment from foreign investors in accordance with the *Law of the People's Republic of China on Wholly Foreign-owned Enterprises* and other relevant laws.

Share-holding Corporations Ltd. with Foreign Investment refer to share-holding corporations Ltd. established with the approval from the former Ministry of Foreign Trade and Economic Relations in line with relevant State regulations, where the share of investment from foreign investors exceeds 25% of the total registered capital of the corporation. In case the share of foreign investment is less than 25% of the total registered capital, the enterprise is to be classified as domestic-funded share-holding corporation Ltd.

Government Agencies, Institutions and Social Organizations are classified into the following categories by source of funds and manner of management taking reference of the registration status of enterprises:

(1) Government agencies: include State and party agencies, classified in principle as State-owned. There are exceptions, such as supply and marketing cooperatives which are classified as collective-owned.

(2) Institutions: include institutions of various types established with the approval by organization and staffing departments of the government, but exclude institutions where enterprise management system is introduced. Institutions are further classified as follows:

(a) Institutions for which their main budgets are from government budget appropriations or extra-budget funds, or allocated from the budget of their competent government agencies. Such institutions are classified as state-owned.

(b) Institutions for which their budget mainly come from collective units. Such institutions are classified as collective-owned.

(c) Social institutions established by individual or a group of citizens, which are classified as private.

(d) Institutions other than those mentioned above for which their sources of budget are not clear. Such institutions are classified by the manner of management.

(3) Social organizations: include social organizations established with the approval from the Ministry of Civil Affairs, and organizations that are not covered by social organization management regulations such as trade unions, women's federations etc.. Social organizations are further classified as follows:

(a) Social organizations that are not covered by social organization management regulations of the Ministry of Civil Affairs such as trade unions, women federations, communist youth leagues, youth associations, industrial and commerce associations, scientist associations, overseas Chinese associations, etc., foundations and fund management organizations established with funds from the state, and social organizations whose funds mainly come from the budget of their competent government agencies. Such institutions are classified as State-owned.

(b) Social organizations for which their budget mainly come from collective units. Such institutions are classified as collective-owned.

(c) Social organizations established by individual or a group of citizens, which are classified as private.

(d) Social organizations other than those mentioned above for which their sources of budget are not clear. Such organizations are classified by the manner of management.

三、国民经济核算

National Accounts

资料整理：萨　慧　何晓红　孙小芳　王阿耕
李　阳　乔　波　杨　磊　张　巧

简 要 说 明

一、本篇资料反映陕西国民经济核算情况。

二、国民经济核算资料主要包括生产总值及其有关资料。生产总值是根据不同产业部门、不同支出构成的特点和资料来源情况而采用不同方法计算的。

三、本年鉴公布的国民经济核算资料，如果遇到普查，在能够获得更详细的基础资料情况下，历史数据也会调整。根据2008年全国第二次经济普查结果，对2005-2008年生产总值进行了调整，根据2013年全国第三次经济普查结果，对2013年生产总值进行了最终核实和修订。

四、2012年，根据国家质检总局和国家标准委颁布的《国民经济行业分类》（GB/T 4754—2011），国家统计局对《三次产业划分规定》进行了修订，将“农、林、牧、渔业”中的“农、林、牧、渔服务业”，“采矿业”中的“开采辅助活动”，“制造业”中的“金属制品、机械和设备修理业”等三个大类一并调入第三产业。本年鉴2013-2014年三次产业增加值为修订后的三次产业数据。

五、国民经济核算数据绝对数按当年价格计算，速度按可比价格计算。

Brief Introduction

Ⅰ. This chapter reflects the national accounts of Shaanxi Province.

Ⅱ. The data on national accounts mainly include gross domestic product (GDP) and related data. Data on GDP are calculated with various approaches in accordance with the features of various industrial sectors, various expenditure structures and the data resources.

III. The data of past years may also be revised on the basis of more detailed basic data obtained during a census year. GDP data from 2005 to 2008 were adjusted in accordance with the result of the second national economic census in 2008. GDP data of 2013 was adjusted in accordance with the result of the third national economic census in 2013. Data published in this yearbook are adjusted data.

IV. “Classification Rules of Three Strata of Industry” was adjusted by National Bureau of Statistics of China in accordance with “Industrial Classification for National Economic Activities” (GB/T 4754—2011) in 2012, which was promulgated by AQSIQ and SAC. Services in support of agriculture, forestry, animal husbandry and fishery, support activities for mining, repair service of metal products, machinery and equipment are categorized into tertiary industry. Data in 2013 and 2014 published in this yearbook are adjusted data.

Ⅴ. The data on national accounts are calculated at current prices, and the growth rates are calculated at constant prices.

3.国民经济核算

2014年全省				
生产总值	17689.94	亿元	比上年增长	9.7%
第一产业	1564.94	亿元	比上年增长	5.1%
第二产业	9577.24	亿元	比上年增长	10.9%
第三产业	6547.76	亿元	比上年增长	8.9%
人均生产总值	46929	元	比上年增长	9.4%

生产总值构成

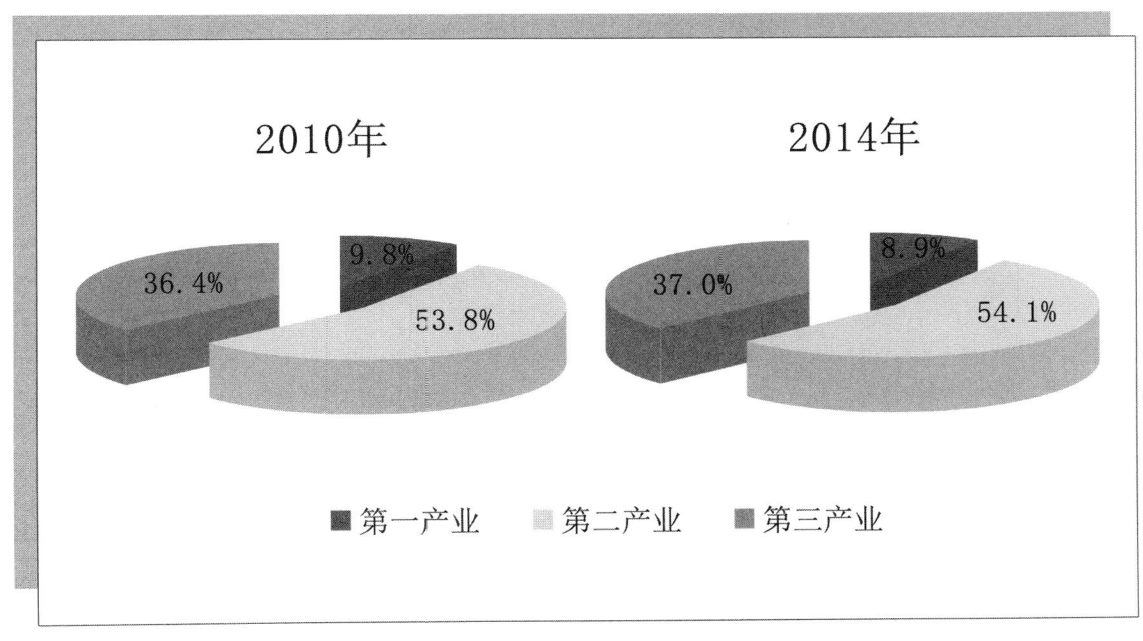

3-1 生产总值
Gross Domestic Product

年份 Year	生产总值 (亿元) Gross Domestic Product (100 million yuan)	第一产业 Primary Industry	第二产业 Secondary Industry	第三产业 Tertiary Industry	人均生产总值 (元) Per Capita GDP (yuan)
1978	81.07	24.70	42.13	14.24	291
1979	94.52	32.52	44.67	17.33	336
1980	94.91	28.47	47.74	18.70	334
1981	102.09	35.40	46.25	20.44	356
1982	111.95	37.02	50.36	24.57	385
1983	123.39	40.00	55.15	28.24	420
1984	149.35	51.05	63.12	35.18	504
1985	180.87	53.39	81.96	45.52	604
1986	208.31	58.00	93.48	56.83	688
1987	244.96	67.84	108.20	68.92	794
1988	314.48	82.69	138.58	93.21	1004
1989	358.37	91.28	158.50	108.59	1124
1990	404.30	105.56	166.95	131.79	1241
1991	468.37	116.88	197.54	153.95	1402
1992	531.63	116.71	232.07	182.85	1571
1993	678.20	148.24	297.49	232.47	1981
1994	839.03	171.81	364.40	302.82	2424
1995	1036.85	217.27	441.67	377.91	2965
1996	1215.84	250.58	514.27	450.99	3446
1997	1363.60	255.42	567.25	540.93	3834
1998	1458.40	266.92	607.82	583.66	4070
1999	1592.64	254.57	681.43	656.64	4415
2000	1804.00	258.22	782.58	763.20	4968
2001	2010.62	263.63	878.82	868.17	5511
2002	2253.39	282.21	1007.56	963.62	6161
2003	2587.72	302.66	1221.17	1063.89	7057
2004	3175.58	372.28	1553.10	1250.20	8638
2005	3933.72	435.77	1951.36	1546.59	10674
2006	4743.61	484.81	2452.44	1806.36	12840
2007	5757.29	592.63	2986.46	2178.20	15546
2008	7314.58	753.72	3861.12	2699.74	19700
2009	8169.80	789.64	4236.42	3143.74	21947
2010	10123.48	988.45	5446.10	3688.93	27133
2011	12512.30	1220.90	6935.59	4355.81	33464
2012	14453.68	1370.16	8073.87	5009.65	38564
2013	16205.45	1460.97	8912.34	5832.14	43117
2014	17689.94	1564.94	9577.24	6547.76	46929

注：1.本表按当年价格计算。
　　2.人均生产总值1991年及以后按常住人口计算,2001-2009年按2010年人口普查修正的常住人口计算。

a) Data in this table are calculated at current prices.

b) Per Capita GDP are calculated at usual residents since 1991.Per Capita GDP were calculated at usual residents which adjusted according to the national population census in 2010 from 2001-2009.

3-2 生产总值指数
Indices of Gross Domestic Product

(上年=100) (preceding year=100)

年 份 Year	生产总值 Gross Domestic Product	第一产业 Primary Industry	第二产业 Secondary Industry	第三产业 Tertiary Industry	人均生产总值 Per Capita GDP
1978	111.0	98.4	114.7	122.2	115.5
1979	107.5	109.1	102.7	123.7	110.0
1980	107.3	109.0	106.4	107.9	98.0
1981	104.5	113.7	96.3	108.1	103.5
1982	109.1	106.5	108.5	115.3	107.6
1983	107.3	101.5	109.5	112.7	106.3
1984	117.8	112.5	120.0	121.9	116.9
1985	116.5	99.3	121.9	131.0	115.1
1986	108.7	104.6	105.9	118.2	107.7
1987	110.0	101.8	110.8	116.6	107.8
1988	121.0	105.3	125.0	127.9	119.2
1989	103.3	106.5	102.8	101.6	101.4
1990	103.4	105.3	101.8	104.5	101.3
1991	107.2	106.8	105.2	110.2	105.7
1992	108.3	103.0	110.4	109.9	106.9
1993	112.1	108.1	115.0	111.5	110.8
1994	108.6	97.0	116.4	106.9	107.4
1995	110.4	104.0	115.2	108.0	109.3
1996	110.9	109.6	112.8	108.9	109.9
1997	110.7	99.7	112.6	114.8	109.8
1998	111.6	107.3	113.8	110.7	110.8
1999	110.3	97.7	112.4	113.7	109.6
2000	110.4	104.0	111.1	112.1	109.6
2001	109.8	101.9	111.2	111.2	109.3
2002	111.1	103.5	113.4	111.0	110.9
2003	111.8	104.1	115.8	109.8	111.5
2004	112.9	108.6	116.7	109.7	112.6
2005	113.7	107.7	116.1	112.5	113.5
2006	113.9	107.4	114.6	114.9	113.7
2007	115.8	105.0	117.5	116.5	115.6
2008	116.4	107.6	118.5	115.8	116.1
2009	113.6	104.9	113.8	115.3	113.3
2010	114.6	105.8	118.0	112.1	114.4
2011	113.9	105.9	116.4	112.5	113.7
2012	112.9	106.0	114.8	111.6	112.6
2013	111.0	104.6	112.6	110.1	110.7
2014	109.7	105.1	110.9	108.9	109.4

注：本表按不变价格计算。
a) Data in this table are calculated at constant prices.

3-3 生产总值指数

Indices of Gross Domestic Product

(1978年=100) (year of 1978=100)

年份 Year	生产总值 Gross Domestic Product	第一产业 Primary Industry	第二产业 Secondary Industry	第三产业 Tertiary Industry	人均生产总值 Per Capita GDP
1979	107.5	109.1	102.7	123.7	110.0
1980	115.3	118.9	109.3	133.5	107.8
1981	120.5	135.2	105.3	144.3	111.6
1982	131.5	144.0	114.3	166.4	120.1
1983	141.1	146.2	125.2	187.5	127.7
1984	166.2	164.5	150.2	228.6	149.3
1985	193.6	163.3	183.1	299.5	171.8
1986	210.4	170.8	193.9	354.0	185.0
1987	231.4	173.9	214.8	412.8	199.4
1988	280.0	183.1	268.5	528.0	237.7
1989	289.2	195.0	276.0	536.4	241.0
1990	299.0	205.3	281.0	560.5	244.1
1991	320.5	219.3	295.6	617.7	258.0
1992	347.1	225.9	326.3	678.9	275.8
1993	389.1	244.2	375.2	757.0	305.6
1994	422.6	236.9	436.7	809.2	328.2
1995	466.6	246.4	503.1	873.9	358.7
1996	517.5	270.1	567.5	951.7	394.2
1997	572.9	269.3	639.0	1092.6	432.8
1998	639.4	289.0	727.2	1209.5	479.5
1999	705.3	282.4	817.4	1375.2	525.5
2000	778.7	293.7	908.1	1541.6	575.9
2001	855.0	299.3	1009.8	1714.3	629.5
2002	949.9	309.8	1145.1	1902.9	698.1
2003	1062.0	322.5	1326.0	2089.4	778.4
2004	1199.0	350.2	1547.4	2292.1	876.5
2005	1363.3	377.2	1796.5	2578.6	994.8
2006	1552.8	405.1	2058.8	2962.8	1131.1
2007	1798.1	425.4	2419.1	3451.7	1307.6
2008	2093.0	457.7	2866.6	3997.1	1518.1
2009	2377.6	480.1	3262.2	4608.7	1720.0
2010	2724.7	507.9	3849.4	5166.4	1967.7
2011	3103.4	537.9	4480.7	5812.2	2237.3
2012	3503.7	570.2	5143.8	6486.4	2519.2
2013	3889.1	596.4	5791.9	7141.5	2788.8
2014	4266.3	626.8	6423.2	7777.1	3050.9

注：本表按不变价格计算。

a) Data in this table are calculated at constant prices.

3-4 分行业增加值
Value-added of the Tertiary Industry

单位：亿元 (100 million yuan)

年 份 Year	生产总值 Gross Domestic Product	农、林、牧、渔业 Agriculture, Forestry, Animal Husbandry and Fishery	工 业 Industry	建筑业 Construc-tion	交通运输仓储和邮政业 Transport, Storage and Post	批发和零售业 Wholesale and Retail Trades	住宿和餐饮业 Hotels and Catering Services	金融业 Financial Intermedi-ation	房地产业 Real Estate	其 他 Others
1978	81.07	24.70	36.52	5.61	3.15	5.46		1.72	0.99	2.92
1979	94.52	32.52	39.38	5.29	3.83	6.00		2.01	1.21	4.28
1980	94.91	28.47	42.22	5.52	3.91	6.52		2.31	1.22	4.74
1981	102.09	35.40	40.08	6.17	3.65	7.02		2.67	1.37	5.73
1982	111.95	37.02	43.31	7.05	4.69	7.91		4.13	1.47	6.37
1983	123.39	40.00	47.48	7.67	5.48	8.53		4.45	1.62	8.16
1984	149.35	51.05	53.82	9.30	7.79	9.33		4.87	1.72	11.47
1985	180.87	53.39	68.81	13.15	9.95	10.58		5.63	2.28	17.08
1986	208.31	58.00	78.81	14.67	11.57	13.26		6.52	3.15	22.33
1987	244.96	67.84	90.47	17.73	15.60	15.03		7.54	4.11	26.64
1988	314.48	82.69	117.77	20.81	21.17	17.46		8.73	5.99	39.86
1989	358.37	91.28	136.40	22.10	25.45	21.83		10.10	5.86	45.35
1990	404.30	105.56	143.28	23.67	33.79	25.50		11.69	6.78	54.03
1991	468.37	116.88	168.28	29.26	35.36	35.70		13.52	6.81	62.56
1992	531.63	116.71	198.93	33.14	42.32	41.79		15.65	8.22	74.87
1993	678.20	148.24	250.07	47.42	59.59	48.30		18.10	11.30	95.18
1994	839.03	171.81	307.46	56.94	77.31	59.90		20.95	16.87	127.79
1995	1036.85	217.27	377.91	63.76	90.60	86.71		24.24	19.06	157.30
1996	1215.84	250.58	439.66	74.61	99.56	111.91		28.04	22.56	188.92
1997	1363.60	255.42	477.35	89.90	111.71	130.64		32.45	33.62	232.51
1998	1458.40	266.92	500.26	107.56	115.32	138.05		37.55	41.36	251.38
1999	1592.64	254.57	549.01	132.42	127.03	152.28		43.44	47.18	286.71
2000	1804.00	258.22	629.88	152.70	151.75	175.62		50.27	59.42	326.14
2001	2010.62	263.63	706.62	172.20	182.96	202.17		58.16	68.11	356.77
2002	2253.39	282.21	819.51	188.05	203.15	228.35		67.30	77.68	387.14
2003	2587.72	302.66	1006.92	214.25	217.50	256.16		77.87	83.90	428.46
2004	3175.58	372.28	1306.50	246.60	267.10	311.00		90.10	95.90	486.10
2005	3933.72	435.77	1650.63	300.73	246.48	322.13	88.23	127.58	108.62	653.55
2006	4743.61	484.81	2094.02	358.42	291.76	391.68	107.03	152.25	125.20	738.44
2007	5757.29	592.63	2544.42	442.04	326.99	449.39	132.66	231.03	153.98	884.15
2008	7314.58	753.72	3274.57	586.55	378.63	568.68	165.35	287.16	193.27	1106.65
2009	8169.80	789.64	3501.25	735.17	423.24	707.39	175.01	336.21	239.92	1261.97
2010	10123.48	988.45	4558.97	887.13	474.60	856.65	218.16	384.75	315.95	1438.82
2011	12512.30	1220.90	5857.92	1077.67	552.54	1036.35	266.92	432.11	398.03	1669.86
2012	14453.68	1370.16	6847.41	1226.46	617.39	1166.90	312.27	551.20	450.12	1911.77
2013	16205.45	1526.05	7507.34	1452.79	611.11	1289.60	338.51	738.52	518.60	2222.93
2014	17689.94	1635.85	7993.39	1645.65	675.66	1413.16	365.85	948.93	579.44	2432.01

注：本表按当年价格计算。
a) Data in this table are calculated at current prices.

3-5 分行业增加值指数
Indices of Value-added of the Tertiary Industry

(上年＝100) (preceding year=100)

年 份 Year	生产总值 Gross Domestic Product	农、林、牧、渔业 Agriculture, Forestry, Animal Husbandry and Fishery	工 业 Industry	建筑业 Construction	交通运输仓储和邮政业 Transport, Storage and Post	批发和零售业 Wholesale and Retail Trades	住宿和餐饮业 Hotels and Catering Services	金融业 Financial Intermediation	房地产业 Real Estate	其 他 Others
1978	111.0	98.4	114.7	114.7	122.2	122.2				
1979	107.5	109.1	102.7	102.7	121.6	121.7		121.3	122.2	119.7
1980	107.3	109.0	106.4	106.4	102.1	77.9		156.1	100.8	122.9
1981	104.5	113.7	96.2	96.3	92.3	113.0		114.3	111.5	107.2
1982	109.1	106.5	108.5	108.4	123.3	92.9		152.3	102.2	109.6
1983	107.3	101.5	109.5	109.6	114.6	100.2		106.4	108.6	110.5
1984	117.8	112.5	120.0	119.9	139.0	125.1		106.2	104.0	106.8
1985	116.5	99.3	121.9	122.0	101.0	140.1		108.1	122.3	111.6
1986	108.7	104.6	105.9	105.0	138.1	119.3		109.2	131.3	108.9
1987	110.0	101.8	110.8	110.2	128.8	103.6		106.5	118.3	112.1
1988	121.0	105.3	125.0	121.0	132.3	138.1		97.1	132.6	114.1
1989	103.3	106.5	104.0	95.4	102.9	68.2		97.8	93.2	109.3
1990	103.4	105.3	102.2	96.1	112.2	116.9		114.3	105.2	101.8
1991	107.2	106.8	105.3	104.6	102.5	119.8		109.1	112.4	110.4
1992	108.3	103.0	111.2	105.7	105.9	116.1		105.6	116.3	109.1
1993	112.1	108.1	116.1	107.8	117.2	115.9		103.4	115.6	107.1
1994	108.6	97.0	118.1	104.9	115.2	99.5		97.1	113.4	107.1
1995	110.4	104.0	116.4	106.2	110.4	107.0		105.2	110.3	107.1
1996	110.9	109.6	113.8	104.5	109.5	107.6		106.3	111.2	109.2
1997	110.7	99.7	112.7	111.5	112.5	117.1		110.2	112.6	116.3
1998	111.6	107.3	113.6	115.4	111.2	110.1		115.8	118.1	108.7
1999	110.3	97.7	111.6	119.7	111.6	110.8		116.4	113.9	116.1
2000	110.4	104.0	111.3	109.3	112.5	113.4		114.1	116.6	110.2
2001	109.8	101.9	111.8	108.6	114.9	113.6		113.8	114.2	107.2
2002	111.1	103.5	115.2	106.0	113.9	111.4		115.6	114.0	107.9
2003	111.8	104.1	116.8	111.2	110.6	112.0		113.8	107.1	108.0
2004	112.9	108.6	118.6	107.7	110.4	112.1		110.2	102.0	109.4
2005	113.7	107.7	115.9	117.6	110.5	111.4	116.8	109.9	108.1	114.5
2006	113.9	107.4	114.5	115.2	110.7	116.7	119.7	117.6	112.5	139.9
2007	115.8	105.0	118.1	114.0	111.2	114.4	117.3	119.6	116.9	118.8
2008	116.4	107.6	118.7	117.1	109.3	115.8	111.7	112.5	110.4	120.2
2009	113.6	104.9	111.6	126.5	109.3	122.0	109.0	117.3	120.3	113.8
2010	114.6	105.8	118.7	114.6	108.5	113.5	115.8	110.3	121.3	111.0
2011	113.9	105.9	117.1	112.6	110.2	115.4	113.9	106.1	118.9	111.6
2012	112.9	106.0	115.7	110.1	107.8	109.9	111.2	122.9	109.9	111.3
2013	111.0	104.7	112.7	113.0	101.0	108.6	103.6	128.9	111.8	108.8
2014	109.7	105.2	110.8	111.8	107.4	108.8	104.1	117.0	107.8	107.7

注：本表按不变价计算。

a) Data in this table are calculated at constant prices.

3-6　分行业增加值指数
Indices of Value-added of the Tertiary Industry

(1978年=100)　　(year of 1978=100)

年 份 Year	生产总值 Gross Domestic Product	农、林、牧、渔业 Agriculture, Forestry, Animal Husbandry and Fishery	工 业 Industry	建筑业 Construction	交通运输仓储和邮政业 Transport, Storage and Post	批发和零售业 Wholesale and Retail Trades	住宿和餐饮业 Hotels and Catering Services	金融业 Financial Intermediation	房地产业 Real Estate	其 他 Others
1978	100.0	100.0	100.0	100.0	100.0	100.0		100.0	100.0	100.0
1979	107.5	109.1	102.7	102.7	121.6	121.7		121.3	122.2	119.7
1980	115.3	118.9	109.3	109.3	124.2	94.8		189.3	123.2	147.1
1981	120.5	135.2	105.1	105.3	114.6	107.1		216.4	137.3	157.7
1982	131.5	144.0	114.0	114.1	141.3	99.5		329.6	140.4	172.8
1983	141.1	146.2	124.8	125.1	161.9	99.7		350.7	152.4	191.0
1984	166.2	164.5	149.8	150.0	225.1	124.8		372.5	158.5	204.0
1985	193.6	163.3	182.6	183.0	227.3	174.8		402.6	193.9	227.6
1986	210.4	170.8	193.4	192.2	313.9	208.5		439.7	254.6	247.9
1987	231.4	173.9	214.3	211.8	404.3	216.0		468.2	301.2	277.9
1988	280.0	183.1	267.9	256.3	535.0	298.3		454.7	399.3	317.1
1989	289.2	195.0	278.6	244.5	550.5	203.5		444.7	372.2	346.6
1990	299.0	205.3	284.7	235.0	617.6	237.8		508.3	391.5	352.8
1991	320.5	219.3	299.8	245.8	633.1	284.9		554.5	440.1	389.5
1992	347.1	225.9	333.4	259.8	670.4	330.8		585.6	511.8	424.9
1993	389.1	244.2	387.1	280.1	785.7	383.4		605.5	591.7	455.1
1994	422.6	236.9	457.2	293.8	905.2	381.5		587.9	670.9	487.4
1995	466.6	246.4	532.2	312.0	999.3	408.2		618.5	740.1	522.0
1996	517.5	270.1	605.6	326.0	1094.2	439.2		657.4	822.9	570.1
1997	572.9	269.3	682.5	363.5	1231.0	514.3		724.5	926.6	663.0
1998	639.4	289.0	775.3	419.5	1368.9	566.3		839.0	1094.4	720.7
1999	705.3	282.4	865.2	502.1	1527.7	627.4		976.6	1246.5	836.7
2000	778.7	293.7	963.0	548.8	1718.6	711.5		1114.3	1453.4	922.0
2001	855.0	299.3	1076.6	596.0	1974.7	808.2		1268.0	1659.8	988.4
2002	949.9	309.8	1240.2	631.8	2249.2	900.4		1465.8	1892.1	1066.5
2003	1062.0	322.5	1448.6	702.6	2487.6	1008.4		1668.1	2026.5	1151.8
2004	1199.0	350.2	1718.0	756.7	2746.3	1130.5		1838.3	2067.0	1260.1
2005	1363.3	377.2	1991.2	889.9	3034.7	1259.3		2020.3	2234.4	1442.8
2006	1552.8	405.1	2279.9	1025.2	3359.4	1469.6		2375.8	2513.7	2018.5
2007	1798.1	425.4	2692.6	1168.7	3735.6	1681.3		2841.5	2938.5	2398.0
2008	2093.0	457.7	3196.1	1368.5	4083.0	1946.9		3196.7	3244.2	2882.3
2009	2377.6	480.1	3566.8	1731.2	4462.8	2375.2		3749.7	3902.7	3280.1
2010	2724.7	507.9	4233.8	1984.0	4842.1	2665.9		4135.9	4734.0	3640.9
2011	3103.4	537.9	4957.8	2234.0	5336.0	3111.1		4388.2	5628.7	4063.2
2012	3503.7	570.2	5736.2	2459.6	5752.2	3419.1		5393.1	6185.9	4522.3
2013	3889.1	597.0	6464.7	2779.3	5809.7	3713.1		6951.7	6915.8	4920.3
2014	4266.3	628.0	7162.9	3107.3	6239.6	4039.9		8133.5	7455.3	5299.2

注：本表按不变价计算。

a) Data in this table are calculated at constant prices.

3-7 三次产业贡献率

Share of the Contributions of the Three Strata of Industry to the Increase of the GDP

单位：% (%)

年 份 Year	生产总值 Gross Domestic Product	第一产业 Primary Industry	第二产业 Secondary Industry	第三产业 Tertiary Industry
2000	100.0	5.9	54.5	39.6
2001	100.0	2.8	49.1	48.1
2002	100.0	4.2	53.4	42.4
2003	100.0	4.3	60.1	35.6
2004	100.0	7.7	60.4	31.9
2005	100.0	6.5	56.7	36.8
2006	100.0	9.1	51.8	39.1
2007	100.0	3.3	55.2	41.5
2008	100.0	4.4	57.0	38.6
2009	100.0	3.1	52.1	44.8
2010	100.0	3.2	63.4	33.4
2011	100.0	4.1	63.2	32.7
2012	100.0	4.2	63.4	32.4
2013	100.0	3.4	63.6	33.0
2014	100.0	4.0	63.3	32.7

注：三次产业贡献率指各产业增加值增量与GDP增量之比。

a) Share of the contributions of the three strata of industry to the increase of the GDP refers to the proportion of the increment of the value-added of each industry to the increment of GDP.

3-8 三次产业拉动率

Contribution of the Three Strata of Industry to GDP Growth

单位：% (%)

年 份 Year	生产总值 Gross Domestic Product	第一产业 Primary Industry	第二产业 Secondary Industry	第三产业 Tertiary Industry
2000	10.4	0.6	5.7	4.1
2001	9.8	0.3	4.8	4.7
2002	11.1	0.5	5.9	4.7
2003	11.8	0.5	7.1	4.2
2004	12.9	1.0	7.8	4.1
2005	13.7	0.9	7.8	5.0
2006	13.9	1.3	7.2	5.4
2007	15.8	0.5	8.7	6.6
2008	16.4	0.7	9.4	6.3
2009	13.6	0.4	7.1	6.1
2010	14.6	0.5	9.2	4.9
2011	13.9	0.6	8.8	4.5
2012	12.9	0.5	8.2	4.2
2013	11.0	0.4	7.0	3.6
2014	9.7	0.4	6.1	3.2

注：三次产业拉动率指GDP增长速度与各产业贡献率之乘积。

a) Contribution of the three strata of industry to GDP growth refers to the growth rate of GDP multiplied by the contribution share of every industry.

3-9 分行业增加值构成
Value-added by Sector

行业	Sector	增加值(亿元) Value Added (100 million yuan) 2013	2014	构成(%) Composition (%) 2013	2014	2014年比2013年增长% Growth Rate in 2014 over 2013(%)
总计	**Total**	**16205.45**	**17689.94**	**100.0**	**100.0**	**9.7**
农、林、牧、渔业	Agriculture, Forestry, Animal Husbandry and Fishery	1526.05	1635.85	9.4	9.2	5.2
工业	Industry	7507.34	7993.39	46.3	45.2	10.8
建筑业	Construction	1452.79	1645.65	9.0	9.3	11.8
交通运输、仓储和邮政业	Traffic, Transport, Storage and Post	611.11	675.66	3.8	3.8	7.4
批发和零售业	Wholesale and Retail Trades	1289.60	1413.16	8.0	8.0	8.8
住宿和餐饮业	Hotels and Catering Services	338.51	365.85	2.1	2.1	4.1
金融业	Financial Intermediation	738.52	948.93	4.6	5.4	17.0
房地产业	Real Estate	518.60	579.44	3.2	3.3	7.8
其他服务业	Others	2222.93	2432.01	13.7	13.7	7.7
营利性服务业	Profit Services	652.02	725.20	4.0	4.1	10.7
非营利性服务业	Non-profit Services	1570.91	1706.81	9.7	9.6	6.4
第一产业	Primary Industry	1460.97	1564.94	9.0	8.9	5.1
第二产业	Secondary Industry	8912.34	9577.24	55.0	54.1	10.9
第三产业	Tertiary Industry	5832.14	6547.76	36.0	37.0	8.9

注：本表增加值及构成按当年价格计算,增长速度按不变价格计算。

a) Value added and Compositionin in this table are calculated at current prices.The growth rates are calculated at constant prices.

3-10 非公有制经济增加值
Value-added of Non-public Economy

年份 Year	非公有制经济增加值(亿元) Value-added of Non-public Economy (100 million yuan)	第一产业 Primary Industry	第二产业 Secondary Industry	第三产业 Tertiary Industry	非公有制经济增加值占生产总值比重(%) Value-added of Non-public Economy as Percentage of GDP(%)	第一产业 Primary Industry	第二产业 Secondary Industry	第三产业 Tertiary Industry
2005	1651.14	129.53	728.34	793.27	43.3	29.7	37.6	54.4
2006	2059.16	144.64	991.70	922.82	44.4	29.8	40.9	53.1
2007	2599.06	177.49	1313.63	1107.94	45.6	30.0	44.3	51.6
2008	3462.21	245.79	1817.01	1399.41	47.3	32.6	47.1	51.8
2009	3971.78	248.74	1998.65	1724.39	48.6	31.5	47.2	54.9
2010	5011.39	294.56	2583.52	2133.31	49.5	29.8	47.4	57.8
2011	6318.20	359.80	3355.98	2602.43	50.5	29.5	48.4	59.8
2012	7398.04	488.74	3955.51	2953.79	51.2	35.7	49.0	59.0
2013	8459.01	463.91	4551.32	3443.78	52.2	32.6	51.1	59.0
2014	9323.58	455.75	4999.02	3868.80	52.7	30.1	52.2	59.1

注：本表按当年价格计算。

a) Data in this table are calculated at current prices.

3-11 各市(区)生产总值
Gross Domestic Product by City(District)

地 区 年 份 Region Year	生产总值 (亿元) Gross Domestic Product (100 million yuan)	第一产业 Primary Industry	第二产业 Secondary Industry	第三产业 Tertiary Industry	人 均 生产总值 (元) Per Capita GDP (yuan)
西安市 Xi'an					
2000	646.13	44.65	277.13	324.35	9484
2001	734.86	45.87	312.90	376.09	10628
2002	826.68	47.77	353.58	425.33	11831
2003	946.66	50.72	407.38	488.56	13341
2004	1102.39	60.21	476.92	565.26	15294
2005	1313.93	66.01	540.50	707.42	16406
2006	1538.94	70.44	645.65	822.85	18890
2007	1856.63	82.51	781.94	992.18	22463
2008	2318.14	103.45	981.58	1233.11	27794
2009	2724.08	110.38	1144.75	1468.95	32411
2010	3241.69	140.06	1406.72	1694.91	38343
2011	3862.58	173.14	1674.31	2015.13	45475
2012	4366.10	195.59	1881.75	2288.76	51166
2013	4924.97	200.45	1998.82	2725.70	57464
2014	5492.64	214.55	2194.78	3083.31	63794
铜川市 Tongchuan					
2000	34.55	4.02	15.53	15.00	4171
2001	37.08	3.85	16.42	16.81	4448
2002	40.90	4.12	18.50	18.28	4889
2003	48.69	4.10	23.26	21.33	5804
2004	59.49	5.02	30.56	23.91	7069
2005	71.84	5.87	38.67	27.30	8582
2006	86.41	6.33	49.08	31.00	10993
2007	102.81	7.84	58.81	36.16	12331
2008	129.87	9.68	77.94	42.25	15508
2009	154.40	10.81	93.73	49.86	18375
2010	187.73	14.18	116.50	57.05	22509
2011	232.63	17.41	147.41	67.81	27806
2012	273.31	19.47	176.82	77.02	32556
2013	323.27	20.96	210.85	91.46	38402
2014	325.36	22.61	204.88	97.87	38550

注：1.本表按当年价格计算。
2.人均生产总值2004年以前按户籍人口计算，2005年及以后按常住人口计算。

a) Data in this table are calculated at current prices.

b) Per Capita GDP are calculated at usual residents since 2005，while were were taken from the statistics of household registration before 2004.

3-11 续表 1 continued

地 区 年 份 Region Year	生产总值 (亿元) Gross Domestic Product (100 million yuan)	第一产业 Primary Industry	第二产业 Secondary Industry	第三产业 Tertiary Industry	人 均 生产总值 (元) Per Capita GDP (yuan)
宝鸡市 Baoji					
2000	195.34	25.18	98.32	71.84	5425
2001	221.88	25.59	114.88	81.41	6097
2002	250.37	27.07	132.18	91.12	6863
2003	287.35	30.66	154.30	102.39	7847
2004	353.24	40.06	196.67	116.51	9594
2005	414.52	44.30	240.13	130.09	11103
2006	490.31	49.70	293.45	147.16	13082
2007	578.78	60.86	345.91	172.01	15402
2008	714.07	78.30	434.70	201.07	19071
2009	806.54	85.18	491.08	230.28	21525
2010	976.09	104.20	614.42	257.47	26274
2011	1175.75	128.56	749.25	297.94	31579
2012	1374.33	143.26	895.92	335.15	36826
2013	1545.91	157.65	1007.72	380.54	41327
2014	1642.90	161.33	1051.65	429.92	43824
咸阳市 Xianyang					
2000	234.46	52.45	102.33	79.68	4980
2001	257.08	53.62	109.26	94.20	5402
2002	281.89	55.36	122.17	104.36	5879
2003	316.77	60.43	140.82	115.52	6564
2004	374.77	74.82	169.77	130.18	7698
2005	432.49	89.10	191.99	151.40	8683
2006	483.87	98.34	220.41	165.12	9721
2007	588.48	120.39	271.39	196.70	11804
2008	764.55	148.97	382.65	232.93	15285
2009	873.20	157.41	434.02	281.77	17434
2010	1098.68	203.29	573.27	322.12	22469
2011	1361.32	252.46	740.40	368.46	27751
2012	1573.68	283.10	876.78	413.80	31982
2013	1860.39	299.56	1073.73	487.10	37695
2014	2085.15	321.72	1227.70	535.73	42128
渭南市 Weinan					
2000	165.47	37.43	60.42	67.62	3149
2001	181.44	39.45	64.56	77.43	3424
2002	201.53	41.55	73.93	86.05	3790
2003	230.39	44.34	91.08	94.97	4320
2004	280.71	52.96	119.81	107.94	5267
2005	330.17	58.66	148.71	122.80	6052
2006	377.40	63.13	171.83	142.44	6907
2007	456.95	80.19	206.06	170.70	8402
2008	563.09	96.26	256.22	210.61	10378
2009	636.96	100.55	294.44	241.97	11728
2010	801.42	128.94	394.55	277.93	15149
2011	1028.97	160.47	545.19	323.31	19424
2012	1157.32	171.54	610.67	375.11	21783
2013	1321.81	193.09	710.74	417.98	24816
2014	1423.75	207.16	751.34	465.25	26675

3-11 续表 2 continued

地 区 年 份 Region Year	生产总值 (亿元) Gross Domestic Product (100 million yuan)	第一产业 Primary Industry	第二产业 Secondary Industry	第三产业 Tertiary Industry	人 均 生产总值 (元) Per Capita GDP (yuan)
延安市 Yan'an					
2000	130.63	19.13	78.69	32.81	6690
2001	158.33	22.68	98.38	37.27	8021
2002	179.71	24.94	113.35	41.42	9010
2003	218.33	23.03	151.00	44.30	10746
2004	275.36	25.86	188.99	60.51	13289
2005	394.65	29.47	286.90	78.28	18815
2006	541.86	34.52	415.77	91.57	25567
2007	647.46	41.32	498.40	107.74	30432
2008	760.84	52.15	578.20	130.49	35555
2009	728.26	55.07	515.89	157.30	33898
2010	885.42	71.19	635.49	178.74	40621
2011	1113.35	86.69	815.45	211.21	50807
2012	1271.02	97.06	934.85	239.11	57876
2013	1354.14	105.00	974.39	274.75	61493
2014	1386.09	113.70	968.89	303.50	62714
汉中市 Hanzhong					
2000	119.23	31.41	38.41	49.41	3250
2001	129.32	31.55	42.28	55.49	3503
2002	141.31	32.91	47.45	60.95	3819
2003	163.44	36.79	56.57	70.08	4402
2004	192.94	43.01	75.49	74.44	5172
2005	217.72	48.07	85.38	84.27	6255
2006	249.83	55.64	99.01	95.18	7158
2007	299.71	66.77	115.39	117.55	8562
2008	366.19	87.64	135.03	143.52	10435
2009	415.64	91.71	152.48	171.45	11819
2010	509.70	110.39	199.50	199.81	14907
2011	647.48	142.29	267.58	237.61	18952
2012	754.57	159.47	320.42	274.68	22084
2013	890.31	171.52	391.01	327.78	26020
2014	1002.83	183.98	453.60	365.25	29252
榆林市 Yulin					
2000	105.05	13.98	46.60	44.47	3264
2001	129.31	13.03	62.10	54.18	3942
2002	162.83	17.68	83.37	61.78	4953
2003	204.76	19.31	113.30	72.15	6176
2004	278.53	26.24	171.05	81.24	8310
2005	447.63	28.34	260.06	159.23	13602
2006	592.34	35.33	358.05	198.96	17943
2007	795.98	47.47	503.92	244.59	24007
2008	1172.76	66.11	796.10	310.55	35177
2009	1302.31	70.09	860.78	371.44	38950
2010	1756.67	92.16	1205.77	458.74	52436
2011	2292.25	111.91	1629.66	550.68	68358
2012	2669.88	125.88	1928.53	615.47	79587
2013	2779.46	134.88	1915.09	729.49	82633
2014	2920.58	145.04	1966.78	808.76	86482

3-11 续表 3 continued

地 区 年 份 Region Year	生产总值 (亿元) Gross Domestic Product (100 million yuan)	第一产业 Primary Industry	第二产业 Secondary Industry	第三产业 Tertiary Industry	人 均 生产总值 (元) Per Capita GDP (yuan)
安康市 Ankang					
2000	74.80	22.76	20.29	31.75	2561
2001	80.74	23.50	21.33	35.91	2758
2002	91.08	24.59	24.42	42.07	3107
2003	105.03	26.61	28.72	49.70	3577
2004	121.97	31.50	35.18	55.29	4141
2005	143.76	36.71	42.83	64.22	5413
2006	163.57	42.44	49.05	72.08	6175
2007	191.37	48.69	60.71	81.97	7218
2008	241.24	63.79	79.42	98.03	9087
2009	274.95	65.59	96.83	112.53	10341
2010	327.06	67.07	130.95	129.04	12428
2011	407.17	72.01	183.13	152.03	15477
2012	496.91	80.95	243.47	172.49	18878
2013	604.55	88.73	315.99	199.83	22938
2014	689.44	93.01	371.03	225.4	26117
商洛市 Shangluo					
2000	56.35	16.66	20.08	19.61	2382
2001	59.52	17.29	17.88	24.35	2529
2002	67.10	17.29	21.74	28.07	2842
2003	92.43	18.71	32.43	41.29	3902
2004	105.03	22.92	35.47	46.64	4393
2005	114.43	25.43	37.25	51.75	4800
2006	137.77	28.31	46.64	62.82	5787
2007	160.40	33.87	55.19	71.34	6737
2008	197.45	44.57	71.18	81.70	8272
2009	224.47	46.65	83.75	94.07	9383
2010	285.90	58.05	117.82	110.03	12194
2011	362.95	70.61	163.03	129.31	15513
2012	423.31	79.43	195.14	148.74	18097
2013	510.88	85.20	258.97	166.71	21795
2014	574.99	90.82	298.39	185.78	24484
杨凌示范区 Yangling					
2000	6.20	0.83	2.06	3.31	4941
2001	7.71	0.89	2.63	4.19	5887
2002	9.29	0.94	3.47	4.88	6796
2003	12.33	1.06	5.23	6.04	8805
2004	15.39	1.31	7.19	6.89	10125
2005	17.36	1.42	8.05	7.89	11193
2006	20.75	1.83	9.46	9.46	13233
2007	26.66	2.21	12.73	11.72	16642
2008	30.32	2.78	13.16	14.38	18873
2009	35.59	3.01	15.45	17.13	19670
2010	47.63	3.75	23.50	20.37	23689
2011	61.20	5.31	31.54	24.35	30373
2012	68.17	5.76	34.36	28.05	33771
2013	85.51	6.44	46.91	32.16	42290
2014	97.11	6.92	53.95	36.24	47910

3-12 各市(区)生产总值指数
Indices of Gross Domestic Product by City(District)

(上年=100) (preceding year=100)

地 区 年 份 Region Year	生产总值 Gross Domestic Product	第一产业 Primary Industry	第二产业 Secondary Industry	第三产业 Tertiary Industry	人 均 生产总值 Per Capita GDP
西安市 Xi'an					
2000	113.0	103.5	115.1	111.5	111.4
2001	113.1	102.5	115.3	112.6	111.4
2002	113.3	103.1	115.0	113.0	112.1
2003	113.5	101.8	117.5	111.2	111.7
2004	113.5	106.7	115.9	112.0	111.7
2005	114.0	107.5	112.3	116.3	112.2
2006	114.0	107.1	113.7	114.9	112.9
2007	115.6	104.5	115.7	116.4	113.9
2008	116.3	107.6	116.4	116.9	115.3
2009	114.5	106.3	114.0	115.5	113.7
2010	114.5	106.9	118.0	112.5	113.8
2011	113.8	106.7	114.9	113.4	113.2
2012	111.8	106.0	111.8	112.2	111.3
2013	111.1	104.7	113.6	109.7	110.6
2014	109.9	105.1	109.3	110.7	109.4
铜川市 Tongchuan					
2000	108.3	108.1	108.5	108.1	107.7
2001	107.2	98.5	105.8	110.9	106.5
2002	110.0	104.8	111.8	109.5	109.6
2003	111.5	105.8	113.2	111.3	111.2
2004	112.4	116.1	113.9	110.3	112.0
2005	112.7	106.9	113.2	113.2	113.3
2006	115.0	108.0	119.5	110.2	115.8
2007	115.3	104.9	118.5	112.7	115.0
2008	117.1	107.8	119.9	114.3	116.6
2009	115.2	106.3	114.0	118.9	114.9
2010	115.6	107.7	118.1	112.8	115.3
2011	116.0	107.3	118.0	114.2	115.7
2012	115.8	106.3	119.4	110.5	115.4
2013	113.8	104.9	117.2	107.8	113.4
2014	110.5	104.8	111.0	110.6	110.2

注：本表按不变价格计算。
a) Data in this table are calculated at constant prices.

3-12 续表 1 continued

(上年=100) (preceding year=100)

地 区 年 份 Region Year	生产总值 Gross Domestic Product	第一产业 Primary Industry	第二产业 Secondary Industry	第三产业 Tertiary Industry	人 均 生产总值 Per Capita GDP
宝鸡市 Baoji					
2000	110.5	100.6	112.4	111.1	109.1
2001	109.7	101.9	110.2	111.3	107.0
2002	110.5	103.8	113.0	109.0	110.2
2003	112.9	107.2	116.3	109.7	112.5
2004	115.1	112.0	119.2	109.7	114.4
2005	113.0	110.2	116.1	108.9	113.1
2006	113.1	108.0	116.4	108.8	112.7
2007	114.8	104.4	117.9	112.2	114.5
2008	115.5	107.4	118.3	112.3	115.9
2009	115.0	106.2	116.7	113.9	115.4
2010	114.4	106.9	117.5	109.4	114.0
2011	114.5	106.1	117.5	111.0	114.3
2012	115.1	105.7	118.5	109.9	114.8
2013	113.0	104.5	115.3	109.5	112.7
2014	110.8	104.9	111.9	109.4	110.6
咸阳市 Xianyang					
2000	111.7	106.5	111.3	115.4	107.8
2001	109.0	104.3	105.7	116.2	107.8
2002	112.0	102.5	117.9	110.6	111.3
2003	113.2	107.6	117.5	110.8	112.0
2004	114.9	110.6	119.3	111.2	113.5
2005	112.6	108.1	114.1	113.2	110.1
2006	111.5	107.1	114.7	110.1	111.6
2007	112.3	104.5	115.5	112.4	112.1
2008	116.0	107.5	119.3	116.1	115.6
2009	114.2	106.3	115.1	117.0	114.1
2010	114.5	107.8	118.7	111.7	114.3
2011	114.2	107.2	119.6	109.1	113.9
2012	114.5	106.1	119.8	109.3	114.1
2013	113.1	104.3	116.5	110.7	112.6
2014	110.9	105.0	113.5	108.2	110.5
渭南市 Weinan					
2000	108.2	104.3	107.5	112.0	107.2
2001	108.3	104.4	107.2	111.4	107.4
2002	110.4	104.1	113.9	110.7	110.0
2003	109.5	101.5	116.4	107.3	109.2
2004	112.6	106.3	119.1	109.2	112.2
2005	112.4	105.5	117.7	110.6	111.2
2006	112.9	107.3	114.8	113.3	112.7
2007	114.2	104.9	115.5	116.8	114.7
2008	116.3	107.6	117.3	118.7	116.6
2009	114.3	106.5	116.3	114.7	114.2
2010	115.0	107.3	120.7	110.6	115.1
2011	115.0	107.0	120.6	110.9	114.9
2012	114.5	106.1	119.6	110.3	114.1
2013	112.0	104.6	115.3	109.5	111.7
2014	110.5	104.9	112.1	109.7	110.2

3-12 续表 2 continued

(上年=100) (preceding year=100)

地区 年份 Region Year	生产总值 Gross Domestic Product	第一产业 Primary Industry	第二产业 Secondary Industry	第三产业 Tertiary Industry	人均生产总值 Per Capita GDP
延安市 Yan'an					
2000	109.8	103.1	114.9	109.5	108.7
2001	112.4	101.0	116.4	109.5	111.2
2002	112.3	104.0	114.9	109.9	111.2
2003	115.5	102.0	121.5	106.6	113.3
2004	119.8	105.7	126.0	107.7	117.5
2005	116.2	110.2	118.8	110.0	114.8
2006	116.5	110.6	118.3	112.2	115.3
2007	115.1	104.5	115.4	117.6	114.6
2008	116.3	107.1	117.0	116.6	115.6
2009	112.2	106.3	110.5	120.2	111.7
2010	113.6	107.0	114.8	111.0	112.7
2011	111.0	107.4	110.9	112.8	110.4
2012	110.5	106.1	110.3	112.7	110.3
2013	106.5	104.3	105.6	110.1	106.2
2014	106.2	105.5	105.3	109.3	105.8
汉中市 Hanzhong					
2000	108.2	103.8	109.3	110.2	107.5
2001	106.6	102.5	108.0	109.0	105.9
2002	107.2	101.7	108.7	109.2	107.0
2003	109.1	105.9	111.8	108.4	108.7
2004	110.9	109.1	115.9	107.8	110.4
2005	111.9	109.2	112.0	113.0	111.2
2006	112.1	108.1	115.6	110.8	111.8
2007	113.9	106.0	114.9	117.3	113.6
2008	113.8	107.9	113.8	116.8	113.5
2009	114.5	106.4	113.6	119.3	114.3
2010	115.1	106.6	119.6	114.3	115.2
2011	115.5	106.6	122.2	113.7	115.6
2012	115.2	105.8	121.8	112.9	115.1
2013	112.7	105.3	118.6	109.3	112.5
2014	111.6	105.4	115.5	109.5	111.4
榆林市 Yulin					
2000	114.3	128.0	113.3	109.1	112.5
2001	114.2	92.4	116.3	118.9	112.4
2002	112.7	115.9	116.2	108.3	112.1
2003	117.5	120.3	121.9	112.0	116.6
2004	117.9	104.2	125.3	112.9	116.6
2005	120.0	103.1	124.7	115.8	119.4
2006	119.3	108.7	122.6	115.9	119.0
2007	121.4	106.4	124.3	118.9	120.9
2008	125.3	108.3	125.7	127.1	124.6
2009	113.3	106.6	111.6	117.2	113.0
2010	118.3	107.8	119.1	118.2	118.3
2011	115.0	106.0	116.3	113.5	114.9
2012	112.0	105.9	113.6	108.8	111.9
2013	108.8	104.5	109.6	107.4	108.5
2014	109.0	105.4	109.9	107.2	108.6

3-12 续表 3 continued

(上年=100) (preceding year=100)

地 区 年 份 Region Year	生产总值 Gross Domestic Product	第一产业 Primary Industry	第二产业 Secondary Industry	第三产业 Tertiary Industry	人 均 生产总值 Per Capita GDP
安康市 Ankang					
2000	105.8	106.0	102.8	108.9	105.6
2001	106.4	104.6	102.9	109.9	106.1
2002	108.6	101.3	110.9	112.1	108.5
2003	108.6	98.8	113.1	112.1	108.4
2004	109.2	109.2	113.2	106.7	108.9
2005	109.8	110.4	109.1	109.9	109.6
2006	110.4	108.0	112.5	110.4	110.7
2007	112.8	106.3	116.5	113.9	112.7
2008	115.4	107.7	121.6	115.2	115.3
2009	115.0	106.2	120.2	115.5	114.8
2010	115.0	106.4	121.5	113.9	115.0
2011	115.5	106.5	122.9	112.6	115.5
2012	115.2	105.7	123.6	110.5	115.1
2013	113.4	105.1	119.8	109.5	113.3
2014	111.7	105.5	115.7	109.1	111.5
商洛市 Shangluo					
2000	111.2	104.5	118.5	110.8	110.9
2001	110.5	102.3	114.6	113.3	110.4
2002	111.0	104.0	113.6	113.6	110.6
2003	109.8	105.4	114.0	108.5	109.4
2004	109.4	107.7	108.0	111.4	109.2
2005	109.9	107.7	110.4	110.6	109.6
2006	110.8	106.5	111.2	112.6	110.5
2007	112.8	106.3	114.6	114.5	112.5
2008	115.8	107.2	119.9	116.6	115.5
2009	114.1	106.4	115.8	115.8	113.8
2010	114.9	106.5	119.5	114.7	115.3
2011	115.1	106.5	121.2	113.1	115.3
2012	114.8	105.9	120.7	112.5	114.9
2013	112.6	105.0	118.0	109.3	112.3
2014	111.0	104.6	115.2	108.1	110.7
杨凌示范区 Yangling					
2000	117.7	105.3	110.9	125.0	113.4
2001	123.8	105.9	127.3	126.2	118.5
2002	117.5	104.2	127.8	113.8	112.6
2003	121.0	106.7	131.8	116.1	118.1
2004	116.7	115.5	127.0	108.6	115.9
2005	115.1	114.2	117.6	112.9	112.8
2006	113.4	114.8	108.2	118.4	112.1
2007	119.4	106.7	117.9	122.9	116.8
2008	113.2	107.1	105.3	120.3	112.5
2009	112.9	106.7	113.3	113.4	111.4
2010	115.5	108.0	119.1	113.9	115.3
2011	116.5	108.1	120.4	113.6	116.3
2012	114.7	106.9	119.9	109.8	114.5
2013	114.0	105.2	117.2	111.1	113.8
2014	112.5	104.9	114.5	110.8	112.2

3-13 各市(区)非公有制经济增加值
Value-added of Non-public Economy by City(District)

地 区	Region	非公有制经济增加值(亿元) Value-added of Non-public Economy (100 million yuan)					
		2005	2010	2011	2012	2013	2014
全 省	**Shaanxi**	**1651.14**	**5011.39**	**6318.20**	**7398.04**	**8459.01**	**9323.58**
西 安 市	Xi'an	568.45	1611.28	1952.78	2244.25	2569.20	2892.90
铜 川 市	Tongchuan	30.27	82.13	107.48	129.00	154.62	158.20
宝 鸡 市	Baoji	183.72	471.30	578.48	681.17	773.29	822.60
咸 阳 市	Xianyang	191.52	532.92	668.87	786.81	944.95	1072.42
渭 南 市	Weinan	127.68	350.19	459.62	526.82	610.86	676.86
延 安 市	Yan'an	55.91	151.47	201.55	235.25	266.65	292.62
汉 中 市	Hanzhong	91.83	252.35	327.03	387.88	467.60	516.86
榆 林 市	Yulin	134.13	632.37	828.49	1004.65	1081.25	1179.98
安 康 市	Ankang	60.58	156.53	198.52	247.20	307.86	364.78
商 洛 市	Shangluo	44.28	138.93	180.09	211.78	260.15	296.60
杨凌示范区	Yangling	7.61	23.05	29.68	32.43	43.08	49.17

3-13 续表 continued

地 区	Region	非公有制经济增加值占生产总值比重(%) Value-added of Non-public Economy as Percentage of GDP (%)					
		2005	2010	2011	2012	2013	2014
全 省	**Shaanxi**	**43.3**	**49.5**	**50.5**	**51.2**	**52.2**	**52.7**
西 安 市	Xi'an	43.3	49.7	50.6	51.4	52.2	52.7
铜 川 市	Tongchuan	42.1	43.8	46.2	47.2	48.1	48.6
宝 鸡 市	Baoji	44.3	48.3	49.2	49.6	50.0	50.1
咸 阳 市	Xianyang	44.6	48.5	49.1	50.0	50.8	51.4
渭 南 市	Weinan	38.7	43.7	44.7	45.7	46.2	47.5
延 安 市	Yan'an	14.2	17.1	18.1	18.5	19.7	21.1
汉 中 市	Hanzhong	42.2	49.5	50.5	51.4	52.5	51.5
榆 林 市	Yulin	30.0	36.0	36.1	37.6	38.9	40.4
安 康 市	Ankang	42.1	47.9	48.8	49.8	50.9	52.9
商 洛 市	Shangluo	44.2	48.6	49.6	50.0	50.9	51.6
杨凌示范区	Yangling	43.6	48.7	48.8	48.1	50.5	50.6

3-14 各县(市、区)生产总值(2014年)

Gross Domestic Product by County (City and District)(2014)

地 区	Region	生产总值(亿元) Gross Domestic Product (100 million yuan)	生产总值比上年增长(%) Growth Rate of GDP over Preceding Year(%)
西安市	**Xi'an**		
新城区	Xincheng	506.05	9.0
碑林区	Beilin	591.72	10.8
莲湖区	Lianhu	552.53	9.0
灞桥区	Baqiao	293.30	11.1
未央区	Weiyang	675.20	10.1
雁塔区	Yanta	1066.15	10.7
阎良区	Yanliang	194.72	9.9
临潼区	Lintong	231.45	5.0
长安区	Chang'an	420.70	11.3
蓝田县	Lantian	128.45	8.8
周至县	Zhouzhi	97.20	8.8
户 县	Huxian	161.96	7.8
高陵县	Gaoling	300.09	12.0
铜川市	**Tongchuan**		
王益区	Wangyi	82.16	13.8
印台区	Yintai	77.94	9.0
耀州区	Yaozhou	150.78	13.6
宜君县	Yijun	29.54	14.0
宝鸡市	**Baoji**		
渭滨区	Weibin	445.70	8.5
金台区	Jintai	295.45	12.0
陈仓区	Chencang	173.64	8.8
凤翔县	Fengxiang	131.81	10.5
岐山县	Qishan	149.10	12.1
扶风县	Fufeng	100.57	12.0
眉 县	Meixian	104.63	16.1
陇 县	Longxian	57.16	13.0
千阳县	Qianyang	35.06	16.9
麟游县	Linyou	55.75	18.9
凤 县	Fengxian	145.61	15.7
太白县	Taibai	17.11	12.1
咸阳市	**Xianyang**		
秦都区	Qindu	425.01	12.7
渭城区	Weicheng	316.43	10.8
三原县	Sanyuan	160.13	12.3
泾阳县	Jingyang	152.03	11.0
乾 县	Qianxian	145.04	11.6
礼泉县	Liquan	145.00	10.8
永寿县	Yongshou	44.83	10.3
彬 县	Binxian	186.10	12.6
长武县	Changwu	60.61	12.4
旬邑县	Xunyi	116.02	10.2
淳化县	Chunhua	53.54	10.0
武功县	Wugong	110.03	10.5
兴平市	Xingping	182.77	11.1
渭南市	**Weinan**		
临渭区	Linwei	303.79	11.5
华 县	Huaxian	115.75	9.2
潼关县	Tongguan	41.10	10.4
大荔县	Dali	112.37	9.6
合阳县	Heyang	71.39	8.9
澄城县	Chengcheng	85.29	10.0
蒲城县	Pucheng	151.62	9.7
白水县	Baishui	66.30	8.6
富平县	Fuping	135.51	11.2
韩城市	Hancheng	303.01	11.2
华阴市	Huayin	78.35	11.8

3-14 续表 continued

地 区	Region	生产总值(亿元) Gross Domestic Product (100 million yuan)	生产总值比上年增长(%) Growth Rate of GDP over Preceding Year(%)	地 区	Region	生产总值(亿元) Gross Domestic Product (100 million yuan)	生产总值比上年增长(%) Growth Rate of GDP over Preceding Year(%)
延安市	**Yan'an**			横山县	Hengshan	136.09	9.4
宝塔区	Baota	243.39	10.2	靖边县	Jingbian	365.19	9.3
延长县	Yanchang	41.09	7.9	定边县	Dingbian	338.39	8.1
延川县	Yanchuan	100.17	10.6	绥德县	Suide	54.09	8.1
子长县	Zichang	81.12	6.2	米脂县	Mizhi	48.66	7.1
安塞县	Ansai	106.44	6.2	佳 县	Jiaxian	41.47	6.8
志丹县	Zhidan	166.62	5.6	吴堡县	Wubu	17.80	7.1
吴起县	Wuqi	211.51	4.1	清涧县	Qingjian	39.40	5.0
甘泉县	Ganquan	22.44	4.4	子洲县	Zizhou	52.26	4.9
富 县	Fuxian	38.95	12.0	**安康市**	**Ankang**		
洛川县	Luochuan	229.44	-2.1	汉滨区	Hanbin	210.39	11.0
宜川县	Yichuan	22.72	7.4	汉阴县	Hanyin	68.44	13.4
黄龙县	Huanglong	11.11	8.2	石泉县	Shiquan	54.76	13.3
黄陵县	Huangling	111.36	10.8	宁陕县	Ningshan	22.22	9.1
汉中市	**Hanzhong**			紫阳县	Ziyang	64.79	11.5
汉台区	Hantai	203.89	12.9	岚皋县	Langao	35.11	11.5
南郑县	Nanzheng	154.04	11.9	平利县	Pingli	60.59	13.3
城固县	Chenggu	168.84	13.2	镇坪县	Zhenping	12.06	8.3
洋 县	Yangxian	94.40	12.5	旬阳县	Xunyang	112.37	11.9
西乡县	Xixiang	75.38	12.9	白河县	Baihe	48.27	13.9
勉 县	Mianxian	111.41	12.8	**商洛市**	**Shangluo**		
宁强县	Ningqiang	61.94	12.7	商州区	Shangzhou	117.65	10.0
略阳县	Lueyang	63.20	2.0	洛南县	Luonan	92.06	12.3
镇巴县	Zhenba	56.42	13.0	丹凤县	Danfeng	73.20	12.1
留坝县	Liuba	11.42	12.1	商南县	Shangnan	63.39	11.5
佛坪县	Foping	6.65	13.1	山阳县	Shanyang	95.51	12.5
榆林市	**Yulin**			镇安县	Zhen'an	77.50	11.5
榆阳区	Yuyang	508.57	11.6	柞水县	Zhashui	64.18	10.9
神木县	Shenmu	968.24	11.3	**杨凌示范区**	**Yangling**		
府谷县	Fugu	436.53	8.7	杨陵区	Yangling	93.20	12.5

注：本表数据为快报数。
a) Data in this table are from annual statistical reporting forms.

主要统计指标解释

三次产业 指根据社会生产活动历史发展的顺序对产业结构的划分。目前我国的三次产业划分是:

第一产业是指农、林、牧、渔业（不含农、林、牧、渔服务业）。

第二产业是指采矿业（不含开采辅助活动），制造业（不含金属制品、机械和设备修理业），电力、热力、燃气及水生产和供应业，建筑业。

第三产业即服务业，是指除第一产业、第二产业以外的其他行业。

国内生产总值(GDP) 指按市场价格计算的一个国家(或地区)所有常住单位在一定时期内生产活动的最终成果。国内生产总值有三种表现形态，即价值形态、收入形态和产品形态。从价值形态看，它是所有常住单位在一定时期内生产的全部货物和服务价值超过同期投入的全部非固定资产货物和服务价值的差额，即所有常住单位的增加值之和；从收入形态看，它是所有常住单位在一定时期内创造并分配给常住单位和非常住单位的初次收入之和；从产品形态看，它是所有常住单位在一定时期内最终使用的货物和服务价值与货物和服务净出口价值之和。在实际核算中，国内生产总值有三种计算方法，即生产法、收入法和支出法。三种方法分别从不同的方面反映国内生产总值及其构成。

对于一个地区来说，称为地区生产总值或地区 GDP。

劳动者报酬 指劳动者因从事生产活动所获得的全部报酬。包括劳动者获得的各种形式的工资、奖金和津贴，既包括货币形式的，也包括实物形式的，还包括劳动者所享受的公费医疗和医药卫生费、上下班交通补贴、单位支付的社会保险费、住房公积金等。

生产税净额 指生产税减生产补贴后的余额。生产税指政府对生产单位从事生产、销售和经营活动以及因从事生产活动使用某些生产要素(如固定资产、土地、劳动力)所征收的各种税、附加费和规费。生产补贴与生产税相反，指政府对生产单位的单方面转移支出，因此视为负生产税，包括政策亏损补贴、价格补贴等。

固定资产折旧 指一定时期内为弥补固定资产损耗按照规定的固定资产折旧率提取的固定资产折旧，或按国民经济核算统一规定的折旧率虚拟计算的固定资产折旧。它反映了固定资产在当期生产中的转移价值。各类企业和企业化管理的事业单位的固定资产折旧是指实际计提的折旧费；不计提折旧的政府机关、非企业化管理的事业单位和居民住房的固定资产折旧是按照统一规定的折旧率和固定资产原值计算的虚拟折旧。原则上，固定资产折旧应按固定资产当期的重置价值计算，但是目前我国尚不具备对全社会固定资产进行重估价的基础，所以暂时只能采用上述办法。

营业盈余 指常住单位创造的增加值扣除劳动者报酬、生产税净额和固定资产折旧后的余额。它相当于企业的营业利润加上生产补贴，但要扣除从利润中开支的工资和福利等。

支出法国内生产总值 是从最终使用的角度反映一个国家(或地区)一定时期内生产活动最终成果的一种方法，包括最终消费支出、资本形成总额及货物和服务净出口三部分。计算公式为:

支出法国内生产总值=最终消费支出+资本形成总额+货物和服务净出口

最终消费支出 指常住单位为满足物质、文化和精神生活的需要，从本国经济领土和国外购买的货物和服务的支出。它不包括非常住单位在本国经济领土内的消费支出。最终消费支出分为居民消费支出和政府消费支出。

居民消费支出 指常住住户在一定时期内对于货物和服务的全部最终消费支出。居民消费支出除了直接以货币形式购买的货物和服务的消费支出外，还包括以其他方式获得的货物和服务的消费支出，即所谓的虚拟消费支出。居民虚拟消费支出包括如下几种类型：单位以实物报酬及实物转移的形式提供给劳动者的货物和服务；住户生产并由本住户消费了的货物和服务，其中的服务仅指住户的自有住房服务和付酬的家庭雇员提供的家庭和个人服务；金融机构提供的金融媒介服务。

政府消费支出 指政府部门为全社会提供的公共服务的消费支出和免费或以较低的价格向居民住户提供的货物和服务的净支出，前者等于政府服务的产出价值减去政府单位所获得的经营收入的价值，后者等于政府部门免费或以较低价格向居民住户提供的货物和服务的市场价值减去向住户收取的价值。

资本形成总额 指常住单位在一定时期内获得减去处置的固定资产和存货的净额，包括固定资本形成总额和存货增加两部分。

固定资本形成总额 指常住单位在一定时期内获得的固定资产减处置的固定资产的价值总额。固定资产是通过生产活动生产出来的，且其使用年限在一年以上、单位价值在规定标准以上的资产，不包括自然资产。可分为有形固定资本形成总额和无形固定资本形成总额。有形固定资本形成总额包括一定时期内完成的建筑工程、安装工程和设备工器具购置(减处置)价值，以及土地改良、新增役、种、奶、毛、娱乐用牲畜和新增经济林木价值。无形固定资本形成总额包括矿藏的勘探、计算机软件等获得减处置。

存货增加 指常住单位在一定时期内存货实物量变动的市场价值，即期末价值减期初价值的差额，再扣除当期由于价格变动而产生的持有收益。存货增加可以是正值，也可以是负值，正值表示存货上升，负值表示存货下降。存货包括生产单位购进的原材料、燃料和储备物资等存货，以及生产单位生产的产成品、在制品和半成品等存货。

货物和服务净出口 指货物和服务出口减货物和服务进口的差额。出口包括常住单位向非常住单位出售或无偿转让的各种货物和服务的价值；进口包括常住单位从非常住单位购买或无偿得到的各种货物和服务的价值。由于服务活动的提供与使用同时发生，一般把常住单位从非常住单位得到的服务作为进口，非常住单位从常住单位得到的服务作为出口。货物的出口和进口都按离岸价格计算。

Explanatory Notes on Main Statistical Indicators

Three Strata of Industry Classification of economic activities into three strata of industry is a common practice in the world, although the grouping varies to some extent from country to country. In China economic activities are categorized into the following three strata of industry:

Primary industry refers to agriculture, forestry, animal husbandry and fishery(do not include services in support of these industries).

Secondary industry refers to mining and quarrying (do not include support activities for mining), manufacturing (do not include repair service of metal products, machinery and equipment), production and supply of electricity, water and gas, and construction.

Tertiary industry refers to all other economic activities not included in the primary or secondary industries.

Gross Domestic Product (GDP) refers to the final products at market prices produced by all resident units in a country (or a region) during a certain period of time. Gross domestic product is expressed in three different perspectives, namely value, income, and products respectively. GDP in its value perspective refers to the total value of all goods and services produced by all resident units during a certain period of time, minus the total value of input of goods and services of the nature of non-fixed assets; in other words, it is the sum of the value-added of all resident units. GDP from the perspective of income includes the primary income created by all resident units and distributed to resident and non-resident units. GDP from the perspective of products refers to the value of all goods and services for final demand by all resident units plus the net exports of goods and services during a given period of time. In the practice of national accounting, gross domestic product is calculated from three approaches, namely production approach, income approach and expenditure approach, which reflect gross domestic product and its composition from different angles.

For a region, it is called as Gross Regional Product(GRP) or regional GDP.

GDP by Expenditure Approach refers to the method of measuring the final results of production activities of a country (region) during a given period from the perspective of final uses. It includes final consumption expenditure, gross capital formation and net export of goods and services. The formula for computation is.:

GDP by expenditure approach = final consumption expenditure + gross capital formation + net export of goods and services

Final Consumption Expenditure refers to the total expenditure of resident units for purchases of goods and services from both the domestic economic territory and abroad to meet the needs of material, cultural and spiritual life. It does not include the expenditure of non-resident units on consumption in the economic territory of the country. The final consumption expenditure is broken down into household consumption expenditure and government consumption expenditure.

Household Consumption Expenditure refers to the total expenditure of resident households on the final consumption of goods and services. In addition to the consumption of goods and services bought by the households directly with money, the household consumption expenditure also includes expenditure on goods and services obtained by the households in other ways, i.e. the so-called imputed consumption expenditure, which includes the following: (a) the goods and services provided to households by employers in the form of payment in kind and transfer in kind; (b) goods and services produced and consumed by the households themselves, in which the services refer to the owner-occupied housing and services offered by payed family employees; (c) financial intermediate services provided by financial institution.

Government Consumption Expenditure refers to the consumption expenditure spent for the provision of public services provided by the government to the whole country and the net expenditure on the goods and services provided by the government to households free of charge or at reduced prices. The former equals to the output value of the government services minus the value of operating income obtained by the government departments. The latter equals to the market value of the goods and services provided by the government free of charge or at reduced prices to the households minus the value received by the government from the households.

Gross Capital Formation refers to the fixed assets acquired less disposals and the net value of inventory, thus including gross fixed capital formation and changes in inventories.

Gross Fixed Capital Formation refers to the value of acquisitions less those disposals of fixed assets during a given period. Fixed assets are the assets produced through production activities with unit value above a specified amount and which could be used for over one year. Natural assets are not included. Gross fixed capital formation can be categorized into total tangible fixed capital formation and total intangible fixed capital formation. Total tangible fixed capital formation includes the value of the construction projects and installation projects completed and the equipment, apparatus and instruments purchased (less those disposed) as well as the value of land improved, the value of draught animals, breeding stock and animals for milk, for wool and for recreational purposes and the newly increased forest with economic value. Total intangible fixed capital formation includes the prospecting of minerals and the acquisition of computer software minus the disposal of them.

Changes in Inventories refers to the market value of the change in the physical volume of inventory of resident units during a given period, i.e. the difference between the values at the beginning and at the end of the period minus the gains due to the change in prices. The changes in inventories can have a positive or a negative value. A positive value indicates an increase in inventory while a negative value indicates a decrease in inventory. The inventory includes raw materials, fuels and reserve materials purchased by the production units as well as the inventory of finished products, semi-finished products and work-in-progress.

Net Export of Goods and Services refers to the exports of goods and services subtracting the imports of goods and services. Exports include the value of various goods and services sold or gratuitously transferred by resident units to non-resident units. Imports include the value of various goods and services purchased or gratuitously acquired resident units from non-resident units. Because the provision of services and the use of them happen simultaneously, the acquisition of services by resident units from abroad is usually treated as import while the acquisition of services by non-resident units in this country is usually treated as export. The exports and imports of goods are calculated at FOB.

四、人　口

Population

资料整理：马　瑜

简 要 说 明

一、本篇资料反映陕西人口发展变化基本情况，主要内容和数据来源:

1. 年末常住人口、性别比例、年龄比例、城镇人口比例以及人口出生率、人口死亡率和人口自然增长率等，数据根据人口普查、1%人口抽样调查或年度人口变动情况抽样调查推算所得，2001-2009年年末常住人口根据2010年第六次全国人口普查数据进行了调整。

2. 户籍人口资料数据来源于省公安厅人口统计年报。

二、人口统计调查方法

目前人口统计调查有: 在逢“0”的年份进行全国人口普查; 在逢“5”的年份进行全国1%人口抽样调查; 其余年份进行人口变动情况抽样调查。

Brief Introduction

Ⅰ. This chapter reflects the basic conditions of development and changes of population in Shaanxi, including mainly:

1. Permanent population at the year-end, proportion of population by sex, proportion of population by age, proportion of urban population, birth rate, death rate and natural growth rate of population. The data are estimated by Shaanxi Provincial Bureau of Statistics on the basis of population censuses, the one percent sample survey on population, or annual sample surveys on population changes. Permanent Population at the Year-end from 2001 to 2009 have been adjusted in accordance with the flash sums of the 6th National Population Census in 2010.

2. The total population with residence registration are obtained from the annual reports of population of Shaanxi Provincial Department of Public Security.

Ⅱ. Sampling Methodology

The statistical surveys on population are as follows:

The national population census is conducted in the year ending with 0; the national 1 percent population sample survey is conducted in the year ending with 5; sample surveys on population changes are conducted in the rest of the years.

4.人 口

2014 年全省			
年底总人口	3775	万人	比上年增长 0.3%
# 城镇人口	1985	万人	占总人口比重为 52.57%
人口自然增长率	3.87	‰	比上年上升 0.01个千分点
男女性别比（以女性为100）	106.71		
人口密度	184	人/平方公里	

人口年龄构成

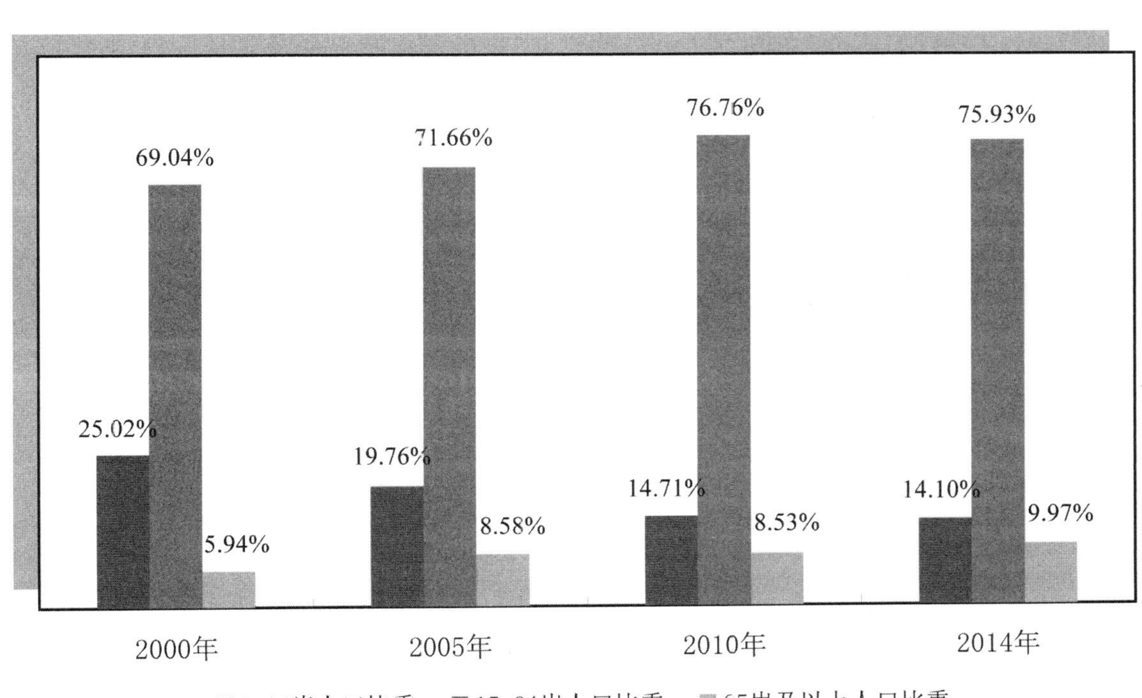

4-1 人口数和构成
Population and Its Composition

单位：万人 (10 000 persons)

年 份 Year	年底总人口 Total Population at Year-end	按性别分 By Sex 男 Male	 女 Female	按城乡分 By Residence 城 镇 Urban	 乡 村 Rural	按农业、非农业分 By Agriculture and Non-agriculture 农 业 Agriculture	 非农业 Non-agriculture
1978	2779	1444	1335	454	2325	2371	408
1979	2807	1456	1351	469	2339	2381	426
1980	2831	1468	1363	522	2309	2390	441
1981	2865	1486	1379	535	2329	2405	459
1982	2904	1507	1397	548	2356	2433	471
1983	2931	1525	1406	577	2354	2446	484
1984	2966	1546	1420	1111	1865	2457	509
1985	3002	1566	1436	1167	1834	2462	540
1986	3042	1588	1454	1203	1839	2501	541
1987	3088	1613	1476	1244	1844	2530	558
1988	3140	1640	1500	1405	1735	2565	574
1989	3198	1671	1527	1438	1759	2604	594
1990	3316	1727	1589	1501	1815	2699	617
1991	3363	1754	1609	1539	1824	2730	633
1992	3405	1777	1628	1576	1829	2748	657
1993	3443	1799	1644	1654	1789	2769	674
1994	3481	1819	1662	1668	1813	2784	697
1995	3513	1836	1677	1738	1775	2791	722
1996	3543	1842	1701	1939	1604	2799	744
1997	3570	1866	1704	2279	1291	2803	767
1998	3596	1879	1717	2547	1049	2812	784
1999	3618	1892	1726	2593	1025	2816	802
2000	3644	1896	1748	1176	2468	2812	832
2001	3653	1879	1774	1228	2425	2802	851
2002	3662	1882	1780	1268	2394	2787	875
2003	3672	1883	1789	1305	2367	2772	900
2004	3681	1893	1788	1338	2343	2765	916
2005	3690	1899	1791	1374	2316	2755	935
2006	3699	1902	1797	1447	2252	2699	1000
2007	3708	1906	1802	1506	2202	2686	1022
2008	3718	1911	1807	1565	2153	2677	1041
2009	3727	1916	1811	1621	2106	2603	1124
2010	3735	1930	1805	1707	2028	2460	1275
2011	3743	1931	1812	1770	1973	2411	1332
2012	3753	1938	1815	1877	1876	2361	1392
2013	3764	1944	1820	1931	1833	2333	1431
2014	3775	1949	1826	1985	1790	2319	1456

注：1.1990年以前为公安年报数，1990年及以后为人口普查及人口变动情况抽样调查推算的常住人口数。
2.2001-2009年人口数根据2010年人口普查进行了修正。
3.城乡人口2000年以前按行政区划统计，2000年及以后为人口普查和人口变动抽样调查推算数。
4.农业、非农业人口1990年及以后为按照公安年报推算的常住人口。

a) Data before 1990 were taken from the statistics of household registration.Since 1990, data have been estimated on the basis of the national population census or usual residents of the annual national sample surveys on population changes.
b) Data of population from 2001 to 2009 were adjusted according to the national population census in 2010.
c) Data by residence before 2000 were from the divisions of administrative areas. Since 2000, data have been estimated on the national population census and the basis of the annual national sample surveys on population changes.
d) Since 1990, data by agriculture and non-agriculture have been estimated on the basis of the statistics of household registration.

4-2 人口自然变动情况
Population Natural Changes

年 份 Year	出生人口 (万人) Births (10 000 persons)	死亡人口 (万人) Deaths (10 000 persons)	出生率 (‰) Birth Rate (‰)	死亡率 (‰) Death Rate (‰)	自然增长率 (‰) Natural Growth Rate (‰)
1953	53.4	18.0	34.00		
1964	83.1	33.3	40.00	16.00	24.00
1982	54.9	19.3	19.02	6.70	12.30
1990	77.2	21.4	23.48	6.52	16.96
1991	66.2	21.7	19.82	6.51	13.31
1992	63.8	22.2	18.85	6.57	12.28
1993	60.4	22.4	17.63	6.55	11.08
1994	60.9	22.9	17.59	6.60	10.99
1995	55.7	23.0	15.93	6.57	9.36
1996	52.9	23.0	14.99	6.51	8.48
1997	49.5	22.4	13.91	6.29	7.62
1998	48.6	23.0	13.56	6.43	7.13
1999	45.1	23.0	12.51	6.38	6.13
2000	45.4				
2001	38.4	23.2	10.50	6.34	4.16
2002	38.4	23.3	10.48	6.36	4.12
2003	39.2	23.4	10.67	6.38	4.29
2004	39.0	23.3	10.59	6.33	4.26
2005	37.0	22.2	10.02	6.01	4.01
2006	37.7	22.8	10.19	6.15	4.04
2007	37.9	22.8	10.21	6.16	4.05
2008	38.3	23.1	10.29	6.21	4.08
2009	38.2	23.3	10.24	6.24	4.00
2010	36.3	22.4	9.73	6.01	3.72
2011	36.5	22.7	9.75	6.06	3.69
2012	38.0	23.4	10.12	6.24	3.88
2013	37.6	23.1	10.01	6.15	3.86
2014	38.2	23.6	10.13	6.26	3.87

注：1.本表为人口普查、人口变动情况抽样调查数。
2.2001—2009年数据根据2010年人口普查进行了修正。

a) Data in this table are obtained from the national population census and the annual national sample surveys on population changes.
b) Data of population from 2001 to 2009 were adjusted according to the national population census in 2010.

4-3 各市(区)常住人口和自然增长率
Usual Residents and Natural Growth Rate by City(District)

地 区	Region	2013				2014			
		常住人口 (万人) Usual Residents (10 000 persons)	出生率 (‰) Birth Rate (‰)	死亡率 (‰) Death Rate (‰)	自然增长率 (‰) Natural Growth (‰)	常住人口 (万人) Usual Residents (10 000 persons)	出生率 (‰) Birth Rate (‰)	死亡率 (‰) Death Rate (‰)	自然增长率 (‰) Natural Growth (‰)
全 省	**Shaanxi**	**3763.70**	**10.01**	**6.15**	**3.86**	**3775.12**	**10.13**	**6.26**	**3.87**
西安市	Xi'an	858.81	9.57	5.37	4.20	862.75	10.11	5.47	4.64
铜川市	Tongchuan	84.28	9.72	6.03	3.69	84.51	9.83	6.04	3.79
宝鸡市	Baoji	374.46	9.62	6.01	3.61	375.32	9.66	6.11	3.55
咸阳市	Xianyang	494.22	10.08	6.06	4.02	495.68	10.14	6.16	3.98
渭南市	Weinan	533.17	9.82	6.21	3.61	534.30	9.74	6.28	3.46
延安市	Yan'an	220.61	10.49	6.03	4.46	221.43	10.54	6.20	4.34
汉中市	Hanzhong	342.50	9.82	7.19	2.63	343.15	9.77	7.35	2.42
榆林市	Yulin	337.03	11.48	6.07	5.41	338.39	11.49	6.34	5.15
安康市	Ankang	263.76	10.01	7.16	2.85	264.20	9.96	7.24	2.72
商洛市	Shangluo	234.61	10.49	7.07	3.43	235.08	10.39	7.11	3.28
杨凌示范区	Yangling	20.24	8.33	4.03	4.30	20.30	8.88	3.95	4.93

注：本表数据根据人口变动抽样调查结果评估推算。

a) Data in the table are estimated from the annual national sample surveys on population changes.

4-4 人口年龄构成和抚养比
Age Composition and Dependency Ration of Population

单位：% (%)

年 份 Year	各年龄段人口比重 Percentage to Tatal Population By Age			总抚养比 Gross Dependency Ratio	少年儿童 Children Dependency Ratio	老年人口 Old Dependency Ratio
	0-14岁 Aged 0-14	15-64岁 Aged 15-64	65岁及以上 Aged 65 and Over			
1953	36.71	59.25	4.04	68.78	61.96	6.82
1964	41.26	55.23	3.51	81.06	74.71	6.35
1982	33.06	62.40	4.57	60.30	52.98	7.32
1990	28.88	65.98	5.15	51.57	43.77	7.80
1991	30.21	64.07	5.72	56.08	47.15	8.93
1992	30.15	64.19	5.66	55.78	46.96	8.82
1993	29.30	65.09	5.61	53.64	45.02	8.62
1994	28.31	66.43	5.26	50.53	42.62	7.91
1995	28.88	65.40	5.72	52.90	44.16	8.74
1996	28.90	65.11	6.00	53.59	44.38	9.21
1997	27.63	66.52	5.85	50.33	41.54	8.79
1998	27.15	66.15	6.70	51.16	41.04	10.12
1999	26.28	66.58	7.14	50.21	39.48	10.73
2000	25.02	69.04	5.94	44.84	36.24	8.60
2001	24.49	68.78	6.73	45.39	35.61	9.78
2002	22.35	69.64	8.01	43.60	32.09	11.51
2003	20.90	71.35	7.75	40.15	29.29	10.86
2004	19.81	72.54	7.65	37.86	27.31	10.55
2005	19.76	71.66	8.58	39.55	27.57	11.97
2006	18.70	72.70	8.60	37.55	25.72	11.83
2007	18.13	72.91	8.96	37.16	24.87	12.29
2008	17.75	73.28	8.97	36.46	24.22	12.24
2009	17.05	73.84	9.11	35.43	23.09	12.34
2010	14.71	76.76	8.53	30.27	19.16	11.11
2011	14.55	76.74	8.71	30.31	18.96	11.35
2012	14.42	76.61	8.97	30.53	18.82	11.71
2013	14.30	76.27	9.43	31.11	18.75	12.36
2014	14.10	75.93	9.97	31.70	18.57	13.13

注：本表为人口普查、人口变动情况抽样调查数。抚养比指0-14岁、65岁及以上人口占15-64岁人口的比重。

a) Data in this table are obtained from the national population census and the annual national sample surveys on population changes. Dependency ratio refers to the population aged 0-14,65 and over as percentage of the population aged 15-64.

4-5　各市、县(市、区)常住人口
Usual Residents by City and County (City and District)

单位：万人　　(10 000 persons)

地　区	Region	2013	2014	地　区	Region	2013	2014
全　省	**Shaanxi**	**3763.70**	**3775.12**	千阳县	Qianyang	12.49	12.52
西安市	**Xi'an**	**858.81**	**862.75**	麟游县	Linyou	9.14	9.16
新城区	Xincheng	59.64	59.86	凤　县	Fengxian	10.63	10.65
碑林区	Beilin	62.23	62.40	太白县	Taibai	5.13	5.14
莲湖区	Lianhu	70.43	70.68	**咸阳市**	**Xianyang**	**494.22**	**495.68**
灞桥区	Baqiao	60.50	60.82	秦都区	Qindu	51.17	51.31
未央区	Weiyang	81.84	82.28	渭城区	Weicheng	44.14	44.23
雁塔区	Yanta	119.29	119.74	三原县	Sanyuan	40.76	40.89
阎良区	Yanliang	28.40	28.53	泾阳县	Jingyang	49.33	49.50
临潼区	Lintong	66.81	67.16	乾　县	Qianxian	53.08	53.20
长安区	Chang'an	110.03	110.59	礼泉县	Liquan	45.21	45.34
蓝田县	Lantian	52.07	52.30	永寿县	Yongshou	18.62	18.69
周至县	Zhouzhi	57.24	57.57	彬　县	Binxian	32.66	32.79
户　县	Huxian	56.32	56.60	长武县	Changwu	16.95	17.01
高陵县	Gaoling	34.01	34.22	旬邑县	Xunyi	26.45	26.54
铜川市	**Tongchuan**	**84.28**	**84.51**	淳化县	Chunhua	19.50	19.57
王益区	Wangyi	20.21	20.26	武功县	Wugong	41.61	41.74
印台区	Yintai	21.88	21.94	兴平市	Xingping	54.72	54.87
耀州区	Yaozhou	23.93	24.00	**渭南市**	**Weinan**	**533.17**	**534.30**
新　区	Xinqu	9.01	9.03	临渭区	Linwei	88.88	89.07
宜君县	Yijun	9.25	9.28	华　县	Huaxian	32.53	32.60
宝鸡市	**Baoji**	**374.46**	**375.32**	潼关县	Tongguan	15.76	15.79
渭滨区	Weibin	45.15	45.26	大荔县	Dali	69.75	69.90
金台区	Jintai	39.75	39.84	合阳县	Heyang	43.93	44.02
陈仓区	Chencang	59.95	60.09	澄城县	Chengcheng	38.95	39.03
凤翔县	Fengxiang	48.71	48.82	蒲城县	Pucheng	74.59	74.75
岐山县	Qishan	46.25	46.36	白水县	Baishui	28.27	28.33
扶风县	Fufeng	41.95	42.05	富平县	Fuping	74.78	74.94
眉　县	Meixian	30.22	30.29	韩城市	Hancheng	39.63	39.71
陇　县	Longxian	25.08	25.14	华阴市	Huayin	26.13	26.19

4-5 续表 continued

单位：万人 (10 000 persons)

地 区	Region	2013	2014	地 区	Region	2013	2014
延安市	**Yan'an**	**220.61**	**221.43**	横山县	Hengshan	29.26	29.55
宝塔区	Baota	47.85	48.15	靖边县	Jingbian	35.94	36.32
延长县	Yanchang	12.61	12.64	定边县	Dingbian	32.11	32.20
延川县	Yanchuan	16.97	17.01	绥德县	Suide	29.52	29.64
子长县	Zichang	21.72	21.76	米脂县	Mizhi	15.54	15.54
安塞县	Ansai	17.38	17.43	佳 县	Jiaxian	20.49	20.50
志丹县	Zhidan	14.24	14.31	吴堡县	Wubu	7.47	7.48
吴起县	Wuqi	14.70	14.76	清涧县	Qingjian	12.45	12.40
甘泉县	Ganquan	7.82	7.84	子洲县	Zizhou	17.61	17.65
富 县	Fuxian	15.15	15.21	**安康市**	**Ankang**	**263.76**	**264.20**
洛川县	Luochuan	22.32	22.38	汉滨区	Hanbin	87.26	87.41
宜川县	Yichuan	11.86	11.92	汉阴县	Hanyin	24.68	24.72
黄龙县	Huanglong	4.96	4.97	石泉县	Shiquan	17.17	17.20
黄陵县	Huangling	13.03	13.05	宁陕县	Ningshan	7.06	7.08
汉中市	**Hanzhong**	**342.50**	**343.15**	紫阳县	Ziyang	28.47	28.52
汉台区	Hantai	53.76	53.91	岚皋县	Langao	15.46	15.49
南郑县	Nanzheng	47.31	47.43	平利县	Pingli	19.36	19.39
城固县	Chenggu	46.62	46.74	镇坪县	Zhenping	5.11	5.12
洋 县	Yangxian	38.47	38.54	旬阳县	Xunyang	42.79	42.87
西乡县	Xixiang	34.28	34.36	白河县	Baihe	16.39	16.42
勉 县	Mianxian	38.87	38.95	**商洛市**	**Shangluo**	**234.61**	**235.08**
宁强县	Ningqiang	30.86	30.88	商州区	Shangzhou	53.29	53.37
略阳县	Lueyang	20.19	20.18	洛南县	Luonan	44.24	44.32
镇巴县	Zhenba	24.78	24.80	丹凤县	Danfeng	29.58	29.64
留坝县	Liuba	4.34	4.34	商南县	Shangnan	22.21	22.28
佛坪县	Foping	3.01	3.02	山阳县	Shanyang	42.28	42.35
榆林市	**Yulin**	**337.03**	**338.39**	镇安县	Zhen'an	27.64	27.70
榆阳区	Yuyang	64.42	64.89	柞水县	Zhashui	15.37	15.43
神木县	Shenmu	45.86	45.92	**杨凌示范区**	**Yangling**	**20.24**	**20.30**
府谷县	Fugu	26.36	26.30				

注：本表数据根据人口变动抽样调查结果评估推算。
a) Data in the table are estimated from the annual national sample surveys on population changes.

4-6 各市、县(市、区)总户数和户籍人口数(2014年)
Total Households and Population by City and County (City and District)(2014)

地 区	Region	总户数(户) Total Households (household)	户籍总人口(人) Total Population(person) 合计 Total	男 Male	女 Female	# 非农业人口 Non-agriculture
全 省	**Shaanxi**	**12656542**	**39405902**	**20362167**	**19043735**	**15195105**
西安市	**Xi'an**	**2502603**	**8152948**	**4124642**	**4028306**	**4181557**
新城区	Xincheng	172413	508001	257686	250315	508001
碑林区	Beilin	213811	710201	361763	348438	710201
莲湖区	Lianhu	227813	657547	330961	326586	657547
灞桥区	Baqiao	178443	535999	263864	272135	255980
未央区	Weiyang	189300	587030	292064	294966	445922
雁塔区	Yanta	266297	832517	415964	416553	735312
阎良区	Yanliang	79282	262620	131919	130701	89954
临潼区	Lintong	206780	718452	363306	355146	120043
长安区	Chang'an	313506	1059260	527481	531779	218027
蓝田县	Lantian	190642	654541	339387	315154	57649
周至县	Zhouzhi	178589	687859	362350	325509	64176
户 县	Huxian	184023	609844	314173	295671	135502
高陵县	Gaoling	101704	329077	163724	165353	183243
铜川市	**Tongchuan**	**278983**	**840529**	**437735**	**402794**	**445665**
王益区	Wangyi	71078	199983	101854	98129	165014
印台区	Yintai	70964	217631	116583	101048	136968
耀州区	Yaozhou	105304	330050	170167	159883	98283
宜君县	Yijun	31637	92865	49131	43734	45400
宝鸡市	**Baoji**	**1150185**	**3838387**	**1974939**	**1863448**	**2025530**
渭滨区	Weibin	146258	434760	219055	215705	367370
金台区	Jintai	131183	382634	180801	201833	324557
陈仓区	Chencang	168743	604567	313341	291226	176288
凤翔县	Fengxiang	155446	522550	269566	252984	246713
岐山县	Qishan	139236	476951	245726	231225	231682
扶风县	Fufeng	119430	451823	238766	213057	211702
眉 县	Meixian	92229	326441	168581	157860	215936
陇 县	Longxian	78988	271415	142654	128761	123891
千阳县	Qianyang	41618	133891	70209	63682	16906
麟游县	Linyou	26526	87359	49367	37992	27795
凤 县	Fengxian	33330	96402	50285	46117	73318
太白县	Taibai	17198	49594	26588	23006	9372
咸阳市	**Xianyang**	**1565985**	**5266828**	**2720934**	**2545894**	**1840707**
秦都区	Qindu	157116	504545	254238	250307	317183
渭城区	Weicheng	124689	415705	208431	207274	240500
三原县	Sanyuan	137414	415782	209757	206025	141762
泾阳县	Jingyang	155089	537994	272460	265534	87295
乾 县	Qianxian	173306	600131	313401	286730	58043
礼泉县	Liquan	149468	482660	251100	231560	55610

4-6 续表 1 continued

地 区	Region	总户数(户) Total Households (household)	户籍总人口（人） Total Population(person) 合 计 Total	男 Male	女 Female	# 非农业人口 Non-agriculture
永寿县	Yongshou	59548	206678	108608	98070	29500
彬 县	Binxian	97629	366607	193205	173402	170239
长武县	Changwu	56510	186944	97613	89331	18918
旬邑县	Xunyi	90227	291220	155923	135297	122424
淳化县	Chunhua	65273	192708	99872	92836	23301
武功县	Wugong	132194	445616	232738	212878	196595
兴平市	Xingping	167522	620238	323588	296650	379337
渭南市	**Weinan**	**1765615**	**5614285**	**2852592**	**2761693**	**2466363**
临渭区	Linwei	308541	962859	486086	476773	408435
华 县	Huaxian	109766	350424	179227	171197	126911
潼关县	Tongguan	53819	161290	81936	79354	81575
大荔县	Dali	208490	734058	371046	363012	202821
合阳县	Heyang	142518	456257	231056	225201	200913
澄城县	Chengcheng	132595	403421	205070	198351	146819
蒲城县	Pucheng	224996	788256	399998	388258	401158
白水县	Baishui	109791	294794	152031	142763	147923
富平县	Fuping	266203	803481	407830	395651	351956
韩城市	Hancheng	126592	402606	207420	195186	259644
华阴市	Huayin	82304	256839	130892	125947	138208
延安市	**Yan'an**	**858052**	**2343357**	**1214817**	**1128540**	**812019**
宝塔区	Baota	178173	464885	234642	230243	237108
延长县	Yanchang	60190	154888	81095	73793	36551
延川县	Yanchuan	73495	198269	103142	95127	50417
子长县	Zichang	91814	267971	139207	128764	59178
安塞县	Ansai	67594	193666	100811	92855	30769
志丹县	Zhidan	63489	158324	82414	75910	77906
吴起县	Wuqi	42748	141891	73685	68206	37534
甘泉县	Ganquan	34968	88867	46202	42665	24369
富 县	Fuxian	53842	154823	81455	73368	44045
洛川县	Luochuan	76800	220772	115791	104981	79522
宜川县	Yichuan	46370	123040	64694	58346	43555
黄龙县	Huanglong	19774	50220	26417	23803	20432
黄陵县	Huangling	48795	125741	65262	60479	70633
汉中市	**Hanzhong**	**1307447**	**3841313**	**2003054**	**1838259**	**923571**
汉台区	Hantai	211119	571971	291903	280068	305451
南郑县	Nanzheng	189207	565867	292246	273621	154656
城固县	Chenggu	186209	535497	275848	259649	94919
洋 县	Yangxian	139138	445502	234329	211173	75266
西乡县	Xixiang	147753	418517	222317	196200	62957
勉 县	Mianxian	143333	428052	220371	207681	73335
宁强县	Ningqiang	111619	327685	172947	154738	32474

4-6 续表 2 continued

地 区	Region	总户数 (户) Total Households (household)	户籍总人口（人） Total Population(person) 合 计 Total	男 Male	女 Female	# 非农业人口 Non-agriculture
略阳县	Lueyang	64895	187384	100104	87280	51422
镇巴县	Zhenba	87858	284985	152335	132650	59267
留坝县	Liuba	14765	42695	22713	19982	7349
佛坪县	Foping	11551	33158	17941	15217	6475
榆林市	**Yulin**	**1310783**	**3738414**	**1959585**	**1778829**	**762050**
榆阳区	Yuyang	219020	555437	283388	272049	197422
神木县	Shenmu	166305	430877	226461	204416	183019
府谷县	Fugu	94517	245671	129162	116509	47119
横山县	Hengshan	105332	372016	194586	177430	34735
靖边县	Jingbian	103653	343965	179614	164351	48616
定边县	Dingbian	95405	344983	179219	165764	54242
绥德县	Suide	134876	356921	186733	170188	58816
米脂县	Mizhi	80185	220183	115537	104646	38531
佳 县	Jiaxian	100048	266528	141345	125183	32859
吴堡县	Wubu	34752	84299	47325	36974	13977
清涧县	Qingjian	64437	215024	115305	99719	28546
子洲县	Zizhou	112253	302510	160910	141600	24168
安康市	**Ankang**	**1053958**	**3062070**	**1647319**	**1414751**	**494992**
汉滨区	Hanbin	342410	1025759	548956	476803	227085
汉阴县	Hanyin	106085	312862	168873	143989	34193
石泉县	Shiquan	68628	181292	97454	83838	29668
宁陕县	Ningshan	26894	74035	39738	34297	14652
紫阳县	Ziyang	109865	342141	184909	157232	40532
岚皋县	Langao	66334	167951	91287	76664	23618
平利县	Pingli	97551	230968	124969	105999	33404
镇坪县	Zhenping	21493	59247	31440	27807	8877
旬阳县	Xunyang	149454	455522	243123	212399	57638
白河县	Baihe	65244	212293	116570	95723	25325
商洛市	**Shangluo**	**810960**	**2517449**	**1329403**	**1188046**	**1127188**
商州区	Shangzhou	165091	563878	297043	266835	215129
洛南县	Luonan	149392	460659	241433	219226	225052
丹凤县	Danfeng	100031	310153	163532	146621	119142
商南县	Shangnan	94437	246095	129184	116911	109822
山阳县	Shanyang	145284	474003	250286	223717	237949
镇安县	Zhen'an	102129	300480	161455	139025	144826
柞水县	Zhashui	54596	162181	86470	75711	75268
杨凌示范区	**Yangling**	**51971**	**190322**	**97147**	**93175**	**115463**

注：本表为公安部门统计数。
a) Data in this table are obtained from the annual reports of the bureau of public secruity.

主要统计指标解释

人口数 指一定时点、一定地区范围内有生命的个人总和。

年度统计的年末人口数指每年12月31日24时的人口数。年度统计的全国人口总数内未包括香港、澳门特别行政区和台湾省以及海外华侨人数。

城镇人口和乡村人口 城镇人口是指居住在城镇范围内的全部常住人口；乡村人口是除上述人口以外的全部人口。

出生率(又称粗出生率) 指在一定时期内(通常为一年)一定地区的出生人数与同期内平均人数(或期中人数)之比，用千分率表示。本资料中的出生率指年出生率，其计算公式为:

$$出生率=\frac{年出生人数}{年平均人数}\times 1000‰$$

式中：出生人数指活产婴儿，即胎儿脱离母体时(不管怀孕月数)，有过呼吸或其他生命现象。年平均人数指年初、年底人口数的平均数，也可用年中人口数代替。

死亡率(又称粗死亡率) 指在一定时期内(通常为一年)一定地区的死亡人数与同期内平均人数(或期中人数)之比，用千分率表示。本资料中的死亡率指年死亡率，其计算公式为:

$$死亡率=\frac{年死亡人数}{年平均人数}\times 1000‰$$

人口自然增长率 指在一定时期内(通常为一年)人口自然增加数(出生人数减死亡人数)与该时期内平均人数(或期中人数)之比，用千分率表示。计算公式为:

$$人口自然增长率=\frac{本年出生人数-本年死亡人数}{年平均人数}\times 1000‰$$

$$=人口出生率-人口死亡率$$

总抚养比 也称总负担系数。指人口总体中非劳动年龄人口数与劳动年龄人口数之比。通常用百分比表示。说明每100名劳动年龄人口大致要负担多少名非劳动年龄人口。用于从人口角度反映人口与经济发展的基本关系。计算公式为:

$$GDR=\frac{P_{0\sim14}+P_{65^+}}{P_{15\sim64}}\times 100\%$$

其中：GDR 为总抚养比；

$P_{0\sim14}$ 为0～14岁少年儿童人口数；

P_{65}^{+} 为65岁及65岁以上的老年人口数；

$P_{15\sim64}$ 为15～64岁劳动年龄人口数。

老年人口抚养比 也称老年人口抚养系数。指某一人口中老年人口数与劳动年龄人口数之比。通常用百分比表示。用以表明每100名劳动年龄人口要负担多少名老年人。老年人口抚养比是从经济角度反映人口老化社会后果的指标之一。计算公式为:

$$ODR=\frac{P_{65^+}}{P_{15\sim64}}\times 100\%$$

其中：ODR 为老年人口抚养比；

P_{65}^{+} 为65岁及65岁以上的老年人口数；

$P_{15\sim64}$ 为15～64岁的劳动年龄人口数。

少年儿童抚养比 也称少年儿童抚养系数。指某一人口中少年儿童人口数与劳动年龄人口数之比。通常用百分比表示。以反映每100名劳动年龄人口要负担多少名少年儿童。计算公式为:

$$CDR=\frac{P_{0\sim14}}{P_{15\sim64}}\times 100\%$$

其中：CDR 为少年儿童抚养比；

$P_{0\sim14}$ 为0～14岁少年儿童人口数；

$P_{15\sim64}$ 为15～64岁劳动年龄人口数。

Explanatory Notes on Main Statistical Indicators

Total Population refers to the total number of people alive at a certain point of time within a given area.

The annual statistics on total population is taken at midnight, the 31st of December, not including residents in Taiwan province, Hong Kong SAR and Macao SAR and Chinese national residing abroad.

Urban Population and Rural Population Urban population refers to all people residing in cities and towns, while rural population refers to population other than urban population.

Birth Rate (or Crude Birth Rate) refers to the ratio of the number of births to the average population (or mid-period population) during a certain period of time (usually a year), expressed in ‰. Birth rate in the chapter refers to annual birth rate. The following formula is used:

$$\text{Birth Rate} = \frac{\text{Number of Births}}{\text{Annual Average Population}} \times 1000‰$$

Number of births in the formula refers to live births, i.e. when a baby has breathed or showed any vital phenomena regardless of the length of pregnancy.

Annual average population is the average of the number of population at the beginning of the year and that at the end of the year. Sometimes it is substituted by the mid-year population.

Death Rate (or Crude Death Rate) refers to the ratio of the number of deaths to the average population (or mid-period population) during a certain period of time (usually a year), expressed in ‰. Death rate in the chapter refers to annual death rate. The following formula is used:

$$\text{Death Rate} = \frac{\text{Number of Deaths}}{\text{Annual Average Population}} \times 1000‰$$

Natural Growth Rate of Population refers to the ratio of natural increase in population (number of births minus number of deaths) in a certain period of time (usually a year) to the average population (or mid-period population) of the same period, expressed in ‰. The following formula is applied:

$$\text{Natural Growth Rate of Population} = \frac{\text{Number of Births - Number of Deaths}}{\text{Annual Average Population}} \times 1000‰$$

Natural Growth Rate of Population = Birth Rate-Death Rate

Gross Dependency Ratio also called gross dependency coefficient, refers to the ratio of non-working-age population to the working-age population, express in %. Describing in general the number of non-working-age population that every 100 people at working ages will take care of, this indicator reflects the basic relation between population and economic development from the demographic perspective. The gross dependency ratio is calculated with the following formula:

$$GDR = \frac{P_{0\sim14} + P_{65^+}}{P_{15\sim64}} \times 100\%$$

Where: GDR is the gross dependency ratio,

P_{0-14} is the population of children aged 0-14,

P_{65+} is the elderly population aged 65 and over, and

P_{15-64} is the working-age population aged 15-64.

Old Dependency Ratio also called old dependency coefficient, refers to the ratio of the elderly population to the working-age population, express in %. It describes the number of the elderly population that every 100 people at working ages will take care of. Old dependency ratio is one of the indicators reflecting the social implication of population aging from the economic perspective. The old dependency ratio is calculated with the following formula:

$$ODR = \frac{P_{65^+}}{P_{15\sim64}} \times 100\%$$

Where: ODR is the old dependency ratio,

P_{65+} is the elderly population aged 65 and over, and

P_{15-64} is the working-age population aged 15-64.

Children Dependency Ratio also called children dependency coefficient, refers to the ratio of the children population to the working-age population, express in %. It describes the number of children population that every 100 people at working ages will take care of. The children dependency ratio is calculated with the following formula:

$$CDR = \frac{P_{0\sim14}}{P_{15\sim64}} \times 100\%$$

Where: CDR is the children dependency ratio,

P_{0-14} is the children population aged 0-14, and

P_{15-64} is the working-age population aged 15-64.

五、就业人员和职工工资

Employment and Wages

资料整理：张　峰

简 要 说 明

一、本篇资料反映陕西劳动就业与工资的基本情况。主要内容包括全社会就业人员数、城镇非私营单位就业人员数、城镇私营企业和个体工商业就业人数、城镇非私营单位就业人员工资、城镇私营单位就业人员工资、城镇登记失业率、社会保障情况等。

二、本篇资料中，城镇登记失业人数及失业率、社会保障情况、城镇私营及个体就业人员资料由省人力资源和社会保障厅、省民政厅、省工商行政管理局等部门提供并加工整理。

三、统计范围和调查方法

1. 城镇非私营单位：指城镇地区全部非私营法人单位，具体包括国有单位、城镇集体单位、联营经济、股份制经济、外商投资经济、港澳台投资经济等单位。工资统计是统计单位的就业人员，个体就业人员、自由职业者等非单位就业人员不在工资统计范围内。对城镇非私营单位工资统计采用全面调查的方法。

2. 城镇私营单位：主要是指在内资法人单位中由自然人投资设立或由自然人控股，以雇佣劳动为基础的营利性经济组织，包括按照《公司法》、《合伙企业法》、《私营企业暂行条例》规定登记注册的私营有限责任公司、私营股份有限公司、私营合伙企业和私营独资企业。对城镇私营单位工资统计采用全面调查和抽样调查相结合的方法。

Brief Introduction

Ⅰ. This chapter reflects the basic conditions of labour employment and wages of Shaanxi Province, mainly including the number of all employed persons, number of urban non-private units, number of urban private enterprise and private industry and commerce, wages of urban non-private units employed persons, wages of urban private enterprise employed persons, registered urban unemployment rate, the social security situation and etc.

Ⅱ. The data on registered urban unemployment and unemployment rate, social security, number of the persons employed in urban private enterprises and self-employed persons in industry and commerce are processed and prepared from figures provided by Shaanxi Provincial Department of Labour and Social Security, Shaanxi Provincial Department of Civil Affairs, Shaanxi Provincial Administration for Industry and Commerce and etc.

Ⅲ. The Statistical Coverage and Investigation Methods

a) The urban non-private units: are all non-private legal units in urban area, including state-owned units, urban collective-owned units, joint ownership units, cooperative units, foreign funded units and units with funds from Hong Kong, Macao & Taiwan etc. Wage of employed persons in urban non-private units are the persons employed in those units, except self-employed and freelancers. The investigation method of Wage of employed persons in urban non-private units is comprehensive survey.

b) The Urban private units: are established by natural person or controlled by natural person in legal units invested by domestic, are for-profit units based on wage-labor, including private limited liability corporations, private share holding corporations Ltd., partnership corporations and private sole proprietorship corporations registered in accordance with the "company law", "partnership enterprise law" and "Provisional Regulations". The investigation method of Wage of employed persons in urban private units is combined with comprehensive survey and sampling survey.

5.就业人员和职工工资

2014 年全省

年底就业人员	2067	万人	比上年增长 0.4%
# 城镇非私营单位在岗职工	479	万人	比上年增长 1.7%
城镇非私营单位就业人员平均工资	50535	元	比上年增长 6.5%
城镇私营单位就业人员平均工资	30483	元	比上年增长 15.2%
城镇登记失业率	3.41	%	

在岗职工年末人数（万人）

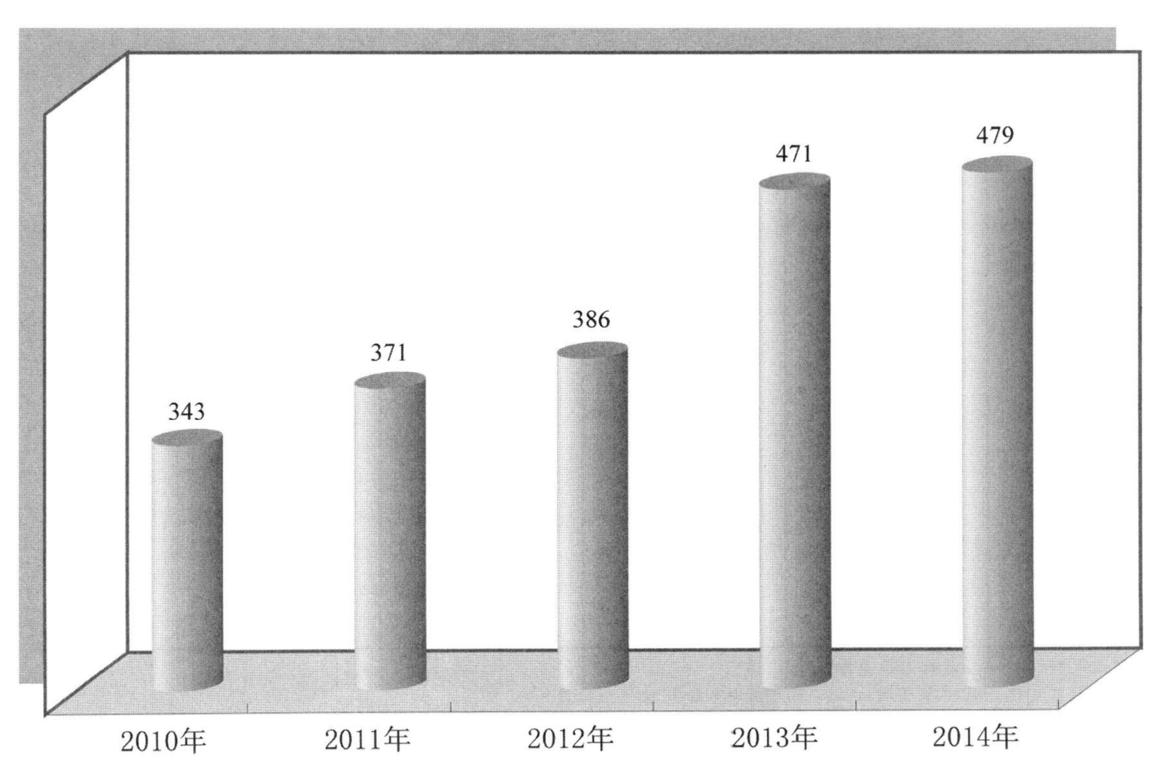

5-1 就业人员人数
Number of Employed Persons

单位：万人 (10 000 persons)

年份 Year	就业人员 人数 Number of Employed Persons	第一产业 Primary Industry	第二产业 Secondary Industry	第三产业 Tertiary Industry	年末职工 人数 Number of Staff & Workers at Year-end	#国有单位 State-owned Units	#城镇集体单位 Urban Collective-owned Units	城镇私营及个体就业人员 Employed Persons in Private Enterprises, Self-employed Individuals in Urban Areas	乡村就业人员 Rural Employed Persons	其他就业人员 Others
1978	1078	766	193	119	257	222	35	…	821	
1979	1105	794	191	120	264	225	40		840	
1980	1158	831	199	128	282	239	43	1	875	
1981	1202	874	188	140	297	250	47	2	903	
1982	1250	904	198	148	309	258	50	3	939	
1983	1285	925	199	161	312	261	51	4	969	
1984	1337	936	217	184	324	260	63	7	1007	
1985	1375	888	287	200	337	271	65	9	1029	
1986	1409	874	303	232	350	282	67	10	1049	
1987	1449	905	311	233	358	289	68	14	1077	
1988	1494	950	299	245	366	298	68	15	1112	
1989	1529	973	298	258	374	304	68	17	1138	
1990	1576	1010	302	264	379	311	67	17	1180	
1991	1640	1054	314	272	390	321	68	18	1232	
1992	1672	1069	321	283	395	326	67	19	1258	
1993	1708	1061	335	312	398	326	66	24	1272	14
1994	1720	1055	333	332	392	327	60	32	1283	13
1995	1748	1056	341	351	395	333	56	42	1298	13
1996	1776	1053	341	382	398	336	54	59	1308	11
1997	1792	1053	339	400	396	335	52	63	1322	11
1998	1788	1055	300	433	335	270	36	99	1342	12
1999	1808	1052	304	452	335	271	32	109	1353	11
2000	1813	1010	299	504	328	265	29	133	1343	9
2001	1785	994	297	494	324	258	27	118	1333	9
2002	1874	1003	308	563	322	253	25	179	1363	10
2003	1912	997	364	551	319	246	23	185	1397	11
2004	1941	965	361	615	319	243	22	184	1425	13
2005	1976	957	368	651	323	242	21	205	1437	11
2006	1986	956	375	655	324	247	21	227	1425	11
2007	2013	933	401	679	331	240	19	257	1414	11
2008	2039	909	420	710	332	240	19	275	1420	12
2009	2060	876	493	691	335	233	16	282	1425	17
2010	2074	856	561	657	343	239	14	333	1376	22
2011	2059	824	585	650	371	251	14	359	1307	22
2012	2061	797	298	458	386	272	15	351	1298	25
2013	2058	779	322	475	471	223	18	297	1256	35
2014	2067	782	335	528	479	229	17	355	1196	37

注：1.本表职工人数1998年及以后为在岗职工数。
2.由于统计制度变化，2012年及以后二、三产业中未含乡村就业人员。

a) Data in this table refer to number of staff and workers since 1998.

b) Number of employed persons in secondary industry and tertiary industry does not include rural employed persons because of the statistical system since 2012.

5-2 分行业就业人员人数(2014年)
Number of Employed Persons by Sector (2014)

单位：万人 (10 000 persons)

行业	Sector	合计 Total	国有单位 State-owned Units	城镇集体单位 Urban Collective-owned Units	其他单位 Units of Other Types of Ownership	私营企业 Private Enterprises	城镇个体 Urban Self-employed Individuals	乡村就业人员 Rural Employed Persons
总　　计	**Total**	**2067.4**	**244.4**	**18.6**	**253.5**	**170.2**	**184.7**	**1196.0**
第一产业	Primary Industry	782.6	2.2	0.05	0.1	3.4	2.9	774.0
农、林、牧、渔业	Agriculture, Forestry, Animal Husbandry and Fishery	782.6	2.2	0.05	0.1	3.4	2.9	774.0
第二产业	Secondary Industry	335.0	47.2	12.2	166.5	97.5	11.6	
采矿业	Mining	45.2	6.8	0.3	29.0	8.7	0.4	
制造业	Manufacturing	165.5	22.9	2.7	80.5	49.2	10.2	
电力、燃气及水生产和供应业	Production and Distribution of Electricity,Gas and Water	13.8	5.9	0.1	6.7	1.1	0.04	
建筑业	Construction	110.5	11.6	9.1	50.3	38.6	0.9	
第三产业	Tertiary Industry	527.7	195.1	6.3	86.9	69.3	170.2	
批发和零售业	Wholesale and Retail Trades	148.7	3.7	1.1	21.6	22.0	100.3	
交通运输、仓储和邮政业	Traffic, Transport, Storage and Post	35.4	19.5	0.5	8.7	4.9	1.7	
住宿和餐饮业	Hotels and Catering Services	55.6	1.2	0.2	10.4	10.5	33.4	
信息传输、软件和信息技术服务业	Information Transmission, Software and Information Services	15.8	0.5	0.01	9.9	3.2	2.2	
金融业	Financial Intermediation	16.5	3.6	1.8	10.7	0.4	…	
房地产业	Real Estate	19.5	2.1	0.1	8.5	8.2	0.6	
租赁和商务服务业	Leasing and Business Services	16.4	2.3	1.1	5.1	5.7	2.2	
科学研究和技术服务业	Scientific Research, Technology Services	21.2	13.1	0.2	4.4	2.8	0.6	
水利、环境和公共设施管理业	Management of Water Conservancy, Environment and Public Facilities	10.6	8.1	0.1	1.7	0.8	0.02	
居民服务、修理和其他服务业	Residents Service, Repair and other Services	29.5	0.7	0.1	0.9	2.5	25.3	
教　育	Education	63.4	56.8	0.2	2.6	3.7	0.05	
卫生和社会工作	Health, Social Work	28.5	23.3	0.9	1.4	2.6	0.5	
文化、体育和娱乐业	Culture, Sports and Entertainment	8.9	3.4	0.1	1.1	1.9	2.5	
公共管理、社会保障和社会组织	Public Management, Social Security and Social Organization	57.7	56.9	0.02	0.02		0.8	

注：本表第二、三产业就业人员中未含乡村就业人员422万。

a) Data in this table Number of employed persons in secondary industry and tertiary Industry does not include rural employed persons(4.22 million).

5-3 城镇非私营单位企业、事业、机关人数和工资(2014年)

Persons and Wages of Urban Non-private Enterprises, Institutions and State Organs (2014)

指标	Item	合计 Total	企业 Enter-prises	事业 Institu-tions	机关 Agencies & Organi-zations	民间非盈利组织 Civil Non-profit Organization	其他 Others
一、就业人员年末人数 (人)	Employed Persons in Urban Units at Year-end (person)	5165162	3526525	1129801	481284	9158	18394
# 女 性	Female	1777039	1075824	544195	143418	5102	8500
# 在岗职工人数	Number of Staff and Workers	4793985	3254784	1065440	446811	8691	18259
1.国有单位	State-owned Units	2291251	792085	1049056	446579	761	2770
2.集体单位	Urban Collective-owned Units	174812	163429	10762	14	239	368
3.其他单位	Units of Other Types of Ownership	2327922	2299270	5622	218	7691	15121
二、就业人员工资总额 (万元)	Earning of Employed Persons in Urban Units (10 000 yuan)	26624087	18607844	5721237.3	2176316	31426	87264
# 在岗职工工资总额	Number of Staff and Workers	25427259	17610667	5583563	2115809	30457	86764
三、就业人员平均工资 (元)	Average Earning of Employed Persons in Urban Units (yuan)	50535	51634	49511	45159	35086	47871
四、在岗职工平均工资 (元)	Average Wage of Staff and Workers (yuan)	52119	53135	51227	47247	35857	48024
1.国有单位	State-owned Units	51919	55190	51284	47254	51875	38666
2.集体单位	Urban Collective-owned Units	43562	43659	42451	41143	42556	34022
3.其他单位	Units of Other Types of Ownership	52965	53037	57163	32229	34016	50067

注：本表在岗职工人数及工资含劳务派遣人员。

a)Data in this table refer to number and wages of staff and workers including labor dispatch personnel.

5-4 城镇非私营单位分行业就业人员年末人数(2014年)
Number of Fully Employed Staff and Workers in Urban Non-private Units at Year-end by Sector (2014)

单位：人 (person)

行业	Sector	年末人数 Number at Year-end	国有单位 State-owned Units	城镇集体单位 Urban Collective-owned Units	其他单位 Units of Other Types of Ownership
总计	**Total**	**5165162**	**2444150**	**186035**	**2534977**
农、林、牧、渔业	Agriculture, Forestry, Animal Husbandry and Fishery	23587	21939	460	1188
采矿业	Mining	360986	67622	3273	290091
制造业	Manufacturing	1061298	228758	27215	805325
电力、燃气及水生产和供应业	Production and Distribution of Electricity, Gas and Water	126775	59194	504	67077
建筑业	Construction	709790	116116	91169	502505
批发和零售业	Wholesale and Retail Trades	263715	36555	11177	215983
交通运输、仓储和邮政业	Traffic, Transport, Storage and Post	287338	195275	4989	87074
住宿和餐饮业	Hotels and Catering Services	117718	12278	1768	103672
信息传输、软件和信息技术服务业	Information Transmission, Software and Information Services	103733	4919	56	98758
金融业	Financial Intermediation	160669	35632	18302	106735
房地产业	Real Estate	106751	21017	1195	84539
租赁和商务服务业	Leasing and Business Services	84993	22945	10562	51486
科学研究和技术服务业	Scientific Research, Technology Services	177691	131305	2460	43926
水利、环境和公共设施管理业	Management of Water Conservancy, Environment and Public Facilities	97752	80658	512	16582
居民服务、修理和其他服务业	Residents Service, Repair and other Services	17161	6564	1188	9409
教育	Education	596054	568072	2003	25979
卫生和社会工作	Health, Social Work	254779	232577	8521	13681
文化、体育和娱乐业	Culture, Sports and Entertainment	45262	33967	517	10778
公共管理、社会保障和社会组织	Public Management, Social Security and Social Organization	569110	568757	164	189

5-5 各市(区)城镇非私营单位就业人员年末人数(2014年)
Number of Fully Employed Staff and Workers in Urban Non-private Units at Year-end by City(District)(2014)

单位：人 (person)

地　区	Region	总　计 Total	国有单位 State-owned Units	城镇集体单位 Urban Collective-owned Units	其他单位 Others	# 港澳台投资 Funds from Hong Kong, Macao & Taiwan	# 外商投资 Foreign Funded
全　省	**Shaanxi**	**5165162**	**2444150**	**186035**	**2534977**	**51749**	**146378**
西安市	Xi'an	1938154	792372	66715	1079067	33172	116844
铜川市	Tongchuan	121292	54695	2971	63626		1304
宝鸡市	Baoji	402339	162898	16688	222753	3026	5246
咸阳市	Xianyang	545290	255333	35174	254783	10677	11552
渭南市	Weinan	467477	249315	11723	206439	562	5335
延安市	Yan'an	348333	185069	9709	153555	391	198
汉中市	Hanzhong	308716	155189	19143	134384	1332	1706
榆林市	Yulin	420979	224065	8911	188003	259	1641
安康市	Ankang	176259	102502	5801	67956	1130	447
商洛市	Shangluo	191671	115956	9195	66520	1102	863
杨凌示范区	Yangling	44028	15512	5	28511	98	1242

注：全省数据含省级直报单位。
a) The data of Shaanxi is include the direct reporting organization.

5-6 城镇非私营单位就业人员年末人数和工资
Total Persons and Wages of Employed Staff and Workers in Urban Non-private Units

指　标	Item	年末人数(人) Number of Staff and Workers (person)		工资总额(万元) Total Wages Bill (10 000 yuan)		平均工资(元) Average Wage (yuan)	
		2013	2014	2013	2014	2013	2014
总　计	**Total**	**5053327**	**5165162**	**24094226**	**26624087**	**47446**	**50535**
国有单位	State-owned Units	2370488	2444150	11641044	12766130	48381	50355
集体单位	Urban Collective-owned Units	188936	186035	712800	796191	38455	42932
其他单位	Units of Other Types of Ownership	2493903	2534977	11740382	13061766	47212	51267
(一)内　资	Domestic Funds	2305839	2336850	10829241	12040479	47069	51219
1.股份合作制	Cooperative	18324	19692	89274	106904	46089	53273
2.联　营	Joint Ownership	8849	9265	45845	45749	51756	50585
3.有限责任公司	Limited Liability Corporations	1763867	1797146	7853618	8816511	44557	48941
4.股份有限公司	Share-holding Corporations Ltd.	475253	467182	2724058	2925612	57861	61214
5.其　它	Others	39546	43565	116446	145703	29804	34470
(二)港、澳、台投资	Funds from Hong Kong, Macao & Taiwan	51133	51749	216047	247932	42354	48223
(三)外商投资	Foreign Funded	136931	146378	695094	773354	51482	53116

5-7 职工平均工资和指数
Average Wage of Staff and Workers and Related Indices

年份 Year	平均工资(元) Average Wage (yuan)	# 国有单位 State-owned Units	# 城镇集体单位 Urban Collective-owned Units	指数(1978年=100) Indices (1978 year=100)					
				平均货币工资 Average Wage	# 国有单位 State-owned Units	# 城镇集体单位 Urban Collective-owned Units	平均实际工资 Average Real Wage	# 国有单位 State-owned Units	# 城镇集体单位 Urban Collective-owned Units
1978	654	669	558	100.0	100.0	100.0	100.0	100.0	100.0
1979	705	728	570	107.8	108.8	102.2	106.3	107.3	100.7
1980	785	811	636	120.0	121.2	114.0	112.3	113.4	106.6
1981	780	812	609	119.3	121.4	109.1	107.7	109.6	98.6
1982	797	831	619	121.9	124.2	110.9	109.1	111.2	99.3
1983	824	857	652	126.0	128.1	116.8	111.0	112.9	102.9
1984	973	1024	757	148.8	153.1	135.7	126.7	130.4	115.6
1985	1122	1182	869	171.6	176.7	155.7	135.8	139.9	123.3
1986	1291	1363	987	197.4	203.7	176.9	146.7	151.4	131.4
1987	1409	1493	1054	215.4	223.2	188.9	146.6	151.8	128.5
1988	1680	1788	1206	256.9	267.3	216.2	145.5	151.4	122.5
1989	1856	1975	1319	283.8	295.2	236.4	136.7	142.2	113.9
1990	2042	2174	1425	312.2	325.0	255.4	146.6	152.6	119.9
1991	2198	2332	1554	336.1	348.6	278.5	147.1	152.6	121.9
1992	2434	2594	1634	372.2	387.7	292.8	146.5	152.6	115.2
1993	2890	3077	1918	441.9	459.9	343.7	152.5	158.8	118.6
1994	3803	4050	2299	581.5	605.4	412.0	156.6	163.0	110.9
1995	4396	4639	2795	672.2	693.4	500.9	153.4	158.2	114.3
1996	4882	5142	3082	746.5	768.6	552.3	154.4	159.0	114.3
1997	5184	5452	3177	792.7	814.9	569.4	155.9	160.2	111.9
1998	6029	6257	3823	921.9	935.3	685.1	185.5	188.2	137.9
1999	6931	7162	4318	1059.8	1070.6	773.8	219.4	221.6	160.2
2000	7804	8043	4920	1193.3	1202.2	881.7	246.3	248.2	182.0
2001	9120	9440	5293	1394.5	1411.1	948.6	287.6	291.0	195.6
2002	10351	10700	6080	1582.7	1599.4	1089.6	332.4	335.9	228.8
2003	11461	11833	6858	1752.4	1768.8	1229.0	365.1	368.5	256.0
2004	13024	13333	7373	1991.4	1992.9	1321.3	402.8	403.1	267.2
2005	14796	15223	7926	2262.3	2275.5	1420.4	453.5	456.1	284.7
2006	16918	17139	9086	2586.8	2561.9	1628.3	507.9	502.5	319.4
2007	21296	21653	11289	3256.3	3236.6	2023.1	607.7	603.5	377.2
2008	25942	26516	13523	3966.7	3963.5	2423.5	697.1	695.9	425.5
2009	30185	31537	16415	4615.4	4710.1	2941.8	810.3	827.6	516.5
2010	34299	35495	20650	5244.5	5305.7	3700.7	887.9	898.2	626.5
2011	39043	41291	27336	5969.9	6172.0	4898.9	956.2	988.6	784.7
2012	44330	46810	33142	6778.3	6997.0	5939.4	1058.2	1092.3	927.2
2013	48853	49815	39141	7469.9	7446.1	7014.6	1134.4	1130.8	1065.2
2014	52119	51919	43562	7969.3	7760.7	7806.8	1191.2	1160.0	1166.8

注：本表不含城镇私营单位和个体，1998年及以后数据为在岗职工平均工资，指数据此推算。

a) Data in this table do not include urban private enterprises and self-employed individuals. The data refer to average wage of fully employed staff and workers since 1998 and the indices was calculated on it.

5-8 城镇非私营单位就业人员分行业工资总额(2014年)
Earnings of Employed Persons by Sector in Urban Non-private Units (2014)

单位：万元 (10 000 yuan)

行业	Sector	工资总额 Total Wages Bill	国有单位 State-owned Units	城镇集体单位 Urban Collective-owned Units	其他单位 Others
总计	**Total**	**26624087**	**12766130**	**796191**	**13061766**
农、林、牧、渔业	Agriculture, Forestry, Animal Husbandry and Fishery	90479	84602	1742	4135
采矿业	Mining	2498464	444281	19169	2035014
制造业	Manufacturing	5196629	1301003	121312	3774314
电力、燃气及水生产和供应业	Production and Distribution of Electricity, Gas and Water	788650	349253	2905	436493
建筑业	Construction	3126538	507199	350610	2268730
批发和零售业	Wholesale and Retail Trades	982270	190900	27265	764105
交通运输、仓储和邮政业	Traffic, Transport, Storage and Post	1674928	1250800	20350	403778
住宿和餐饮业	Hotels and Catering Services	343132	36918	3860	302355
信息传输、软件和信息技术服务业	Information Transmission, Software and Information Services	945264	26784	271	918210
金融业	Financial Intermediation	1259949	260574	146595	852780
房地产业	Real Estate	458143	83569	4785	369790
租赁和商务服务业	Leasing and Business Services	370044	84754	30632	254658
科学研究和技术服务业	Scientific Research, Technology Services	1225506	849564	14349	361592
水利、环境和公共设施管理业	Management of Water Conservancy, Environment and Public Facilities	360991	287241	1666	72084
居民服务、修理和其他服务业	Residents Service, Repair and other Services	54518	22305	4241	27972
教育	Education	3149185	3036406	9792	102988
卫生和社会工作	Health, Social Work	1328596	1237800	34386	56410
文化、体育和娱乐业	Culture, Sports and Entertainment	212710	155650	1611	55450
公共管理、社会保障和社会组织	Public Management, Social Security and Social Organization	2558090	2556528	654	909

5-9　城镇非私营单位就业人员分行业平均工资(2014年)

Average Earnings of Employed Persons by Sector in Urban Non-private Units (2014)

单位：元　　(yuan)

行　　业	Sector	平均工资 Average Wage	国有单位 State-owned Units	城镇集体单位 Urban Collective-owned Units	其他单位 Others
总　　计	**Total**	**50535**	**50355**	**38455**	**51267**
农、林、牧、渔业	Agriculture, Forestry, Animal Husbandry and Fishery	38418	37272	35953	34690
采矿业	Mining	69920	65116	45092	70705
制造业	Manufacturing	46636	37509	36209	46279
电力、燃气及水生产和供应业	Production and Distribution of Electricity, Gas and Water	62907	53172	50221	67854
建筑业	Construction	43454	43603	34748	44162
批发和零售业	Wholesale and Retail Trades	37709	47434	22422	35876
交通运输、仓储和邮政业	Traffic, Transport, Storage and Post	57904	51973	38224	47245
住宿和餐饮业	Hotels and Catering Services	28929	27772	23137	28970
信息传输、软件和信息技术服务业	Information Transmission, Software and Information Services	91423	55789	32667	93312
金融业	Financial Intermediation	74340	74113	70312	74587
房地产业	Real Estate	43865	36523	26255	45138
租赁和商务服务业	Leasing and Business Services	43471	40598	30835	49455
科学研究和技术服务业	Scientific Research, Technology Services	63478	64265	50646	84342
水利、环境和公共设施管理业	Management of Water Conservancy, Environment and Public Facilities	36846	34940	32231	44700
居民服务、修理和其他服务业	Residents Service, Repair and other Services	32890	39037	24655	30994
教　育	Education	51856	51411	48516	41185
卫生和社会工作	Health, Social Work	49447	50876	40755	42774
文化、体育和娱乐业	Culture, Sports and Entertainment	47853	45371	33211	56697
公共管理、社会保障和社会组织	Public Management, Social Security and Social Organization	44915	44873	41906	48330

5-10 城镇非私营单位在岗职工分行业平均工资(2014年)
Average Wage of Employed Staff and Workers in Urban Non-private Units by Sector (2014)

单位：元 (yuan)

行业	Sector	平均工资 Average Wage	国有单位 State-owned Units	城镇集体单位 Urban Collective-owned Units	其他单位 Others
总计	**Total**	**52119**	**51919**	**43562**	**52965**
农、林、牧、渔业	Agriculture, Forestry, Animal Husbandry and Fishery	38749	38976	37863	34920
采矿业	Mining	70487	67059	62743	71349
制造业	Manufacturing	47116	48326	44230	46813
电力、燃气及水生产和供应业	Production and Distribution of Electricity, Gas and Water	63934	58590	58624	68977
建筑业	Construction	44694	45681	38874	45741
批发和零售业	Wholesale and Retail Trades	38103	54017	24268	36072
交通运输、仓储和邮政业	Traffic, Transport, Storage and Post	59231	64415	38260	48210
住宿和餐饮业	Hotels and Catering Services	30594	30122	21647	30810
信息传输、软件和信息技术服务业	Information Transmission, Software and Information Services	91892	54609	48393	93772
金融业	Financial Intermediation	87777	72026	82305	95780
房地产业	Real Estate	44551	40111	39581	45762
租赁和商务服务业	Leasing and Business Services	44059	36760	30188	50170
科学研究和技术服务业	Scientific Research, Technology Services	65376	59468	59015	85776
水利、环境和公共设施管理业	Management of Water Conservancy, Environment and Public Facilities	39658	38134	32931	47402
居民服务、修理和其他服务业	Residents Service, Repair and other Services	32886	34803	41265	30588
教育	Education	52954	53449	49058	41477
卫生和社会工作	Health, Social Work	50899	51680	41305	42829
文化、体育和娱乐业	Culture, Sports and Entertainment	49461	47360	32565	57266
公共管理、社会保障和社会组织	Public Management, Social Security and Social Organization	46980	46982	39854	48330

5-11　城镇私营单位分行业就业人员平均工资
Average Wage of Employed Persons in Urban Private Units by Sector

单位：元　　　　(yuan)

行　业	Sector	2011	2012	2013	2014
总　计	**Total**	**18844**	**22753**	**26454**	**30483**
农、林、牧、渔业	Agriculture, Forestry, Animal Husbandry and Fishery	14606	19514	22478	23228
采矿业	Mining	23581	30298	32114	36760
制造业	Manufacturing	17360	22450	25582	31542
电力、燃气及水生产和供应业	Production and Distribution of Electricity, Gas and Water	18729	21277	25194	29532
建筑业	Construction	19578	23290	26140	29540
批发和零售业	Wholesale and Retail Trades	19010	22306	24392	28568
交通运输、仓储和邮政业	Traffic, Transport, Storage and Post	21377	23220	25359	28968
住宿和餐饮业	Hotels and Catering Services	17958	20264	23418	24460
信息传输、软件和信息技术服务业	Information Transmission, Software and Information Services	22211	26518	33455	36580
金融业	Financial Intermediation	20486	25584	30309	33370
房地产业	Real Estate	24642	27613	34150	37493
租赁和商务服务业	Leasing and Business Services	21519	24531	26870	29915
科学研究和技术服务业	Scientific Research, Technology Services	27924	34187	35280	37802
水利、环境和公共设施管理业	Management of Water Conservancy, Environment and Public Facilities	15474	20493	26815	30534
居民服务、修理和其他服务业	Residents Service, Repair and Other Services	18306	20881	24315	25713
教　育	Education	23002	25160	28344	29707
卫生和社会工作	Health, Social Work	21240	21051	27224	29447
文化、体育和娱乐业	Culture, Sports and Entertainment	19358	23631	24069	25549

5-12 各市(区)城镇非私营单位就业人员工资总额(2014年)

Earnings of Employed Persons and Total Wages Bill of Fully Employed Staff in Urban Non-private Units by City(District)(2014)

单位：万元 (10 000 yuan)

地区	Region	就业人员工资总额 Total Wages Bill of Employed Persons	国有单位 State-owned Units	城镇集体单位 Urban Collective-owned Units	其他单位 Others	# 港澳台投资 Funds from Hong Kong, Macao & Taiwan	# 外商投资 Foreign Funded
全省	**Shaanxi**	**26624087**	**12766130**	**796191**	**13061766**	**247932**	**773354**
西安市	Xi'an	11065718	4695908	269388	6100421	162243	640575
铜川市	Tongchuan	536733	229359	7546	299828		5453
宝鸡市	Baoji	1745965	772136	59603	914226	15616	23487
咸阳市	Xianyang	2286628	1106791	123679	1056158	44795	49287
渭南市	Weinan	1986232	1096942	38160	851130	1616	18290
延安市	Yan'an	1879507	885317	50431	943758	2857	882
汉中市	Hanzhong	1368063	731077	105586	531400	6629	7631
榆林市	Yulin	2416775	1181696	69877	1165202	1226	12265
安康市	Ankang	744891	475227	32236	237427	7337	2525
商洛市	Shangluo	710572	455387	39667	215517	5247	7279
杨凌示范区	Yangling	226541	105055	16	121470	367	5675

注：全省数据含省级直报单位。下表同。

a) The data of Shaanxi is include the direct reporting organization. The same applies to the table following.

5-13 各市(区)城镇非私营单位就业人员平均工资(2014年)

Average Earnings of Employed Persons and Average Wage of Fully Employed Staff and Workers in Urban Non-private Units by City(District)(2014)

单位：元 (yuan)

地区	Region	就业人员平均工资 Average Wage of Employed Persons	国有单位 State-owned Units	城镇集体单位 Urban Collective-owned Units	其他单位 Others	# 港澳台投资 Funds from Hong Kong, Macao & Taiwan	# 外商投资 Foreign Funded
全省	**Shaanxi**	**50535**	**50355**	**42932**	**51267**	**48223**	**53116**
西安市	Xi'an	53974	52729	41006	55766	49623	55079
铜川市	Tongchuan	45665	42802	27960	48951		43005
宝鸡市	Baoji	43603	47447	36504	41301	50966	44575
咸阳市	Xianyang	42434	43567	35481	42252	41892	42775
渭南市	Weinan	42508	43641	32402	41695	29699	36463
延安市	Yan'an	53651	48140	52088	60213	73079	40815
汉中市	Hanzhong	44417	47253	53448	39795	48848	43604
榆林市	Yulin	56321	53198	71231	59097	47689	75345
安康市	Ankang	42714	46624	56834	35547	59843	56115
商洛市	Shangluo	37870	40073	43230	33249	48268	79295
杨凌示范区	Yangling	50915	68226	31200	41755	36740	45114

5-14 城镇登记失业人数及失业率
Registered Urban Unemployment Persons and Unemployment Rate

年 份 Year	年末城镇登记实有失业人数(人) Registered Unemployed Persons in Urban Areas (person)	城镇登记失业率(%) Registered Unemployment Rate in Urban Areas (%)	年 份 Year	年末城镇登记实有失业人数(人) Registered Unemployed Persons in Urban Areas (person)	城镇登记失业率(%) Registered Unemployment Rate in Urban Areas (%)
1980	216209	7.1	2002	135094	3.3
1985	67044	1.9	2003	139490	3.7
1990	112345	3.0	2004	184617	3.77
1991	100790	3.0	2005	215414	4.18
1992	90844	3.0	2006	215432	4.03
1993	108306	3.0	2007	209546	4.02
1994	99800	3.3	2008	208337	3.91
1995	85700	3.2	2009	214757	3.94
1996	125700	3.3	2010	214206	3.85
1997	151600	3.4	2011	209061	3.59
1998	122100	3.1	2012	194807	3.22
1999	107000	2.6	2013	210600	3.32
2000	113861	2.7	2014	223486	3.41
2001	140082	3.2			

5-15 社会保障基本情况
Basic Statistics on Social Security

指 标	Item	2011	2012	2013	2014
城镇居民最低生活保障户数 (万户)	Number of Families Receiving Minimum Living Allowance in Urban Areas (10 000 households)	38.03	35.10	32.10	28.20
城镇居民最低生活保障人数 (万人)	Number of Persons Receiving Minimum Living Allowance in Urban Areas (10 000 persons)	84.60	74.80	67.10	57.70
参加失业保险职工人数 (万人)	Unemployment Insurance Contributors (10 000 persons)	338.67	339.14	339.67	344.27
参加养老保险职工人数 (万人)	Pension Insurance Contributors (10 000 persons)	530.68	582.81	684.51	716.36
参加医疗保险职工人数 (万人)	Medical Care Insurancce Contributors (10 000 persons)	540.26	547.49	571.74	574.23
城镇居民基本医疗保险参保人数 (万人)	Basic Medical Care Insurancce Contributors in Urban Areas (10 000 persons)	550.18	571.32	672.53	671.93
参加工伤保险职工人数 (万人)	Work Injury Insurance Contributors (10 000 persons)	326.84	350.40	378.06	403.98
参加生育保险职工人数 (万人)	Maternity Insurance Contributors (10 000 persons)	211.55	223.66	240.25	250.79

5-16 参加基本养老保险的职工及离退休人员(2014年)
Staff and Workers, Retired and VCSR Joined Basic Pension Insurance(2014)

单位：人 (person)

指　　标	Item	职工人数 Number of Employees	离退休职工 Number of Retirees
总　计	**Total**	**4715250**	**1825482**
一、企　业	Enterprises	3782298	1567830
(一)内资企业	Domestic Units	3638663	1563908
1.国有企业	State-owned Units	1673371	1079700
2.集体企业	Collective-owned Units	118680	206718
3.其　他	Others	1846612	277490
(二)港澳台及外资企业	Funds from Hong Kong,Macao,Taiwan and Foreign	143635	3922
二、其　他	Others	932952	257652

5-17 失业保险基本情况
Basic Statistics on Unemployment Insurance

单位：人 (person)

指　　标	Item	2011	2012	2013	2014
参加失业保险人数	Unemployment Insurance Contributors	3386654	3391398	3396683	3442679
一、企　业	Enterprises	2587450	2598333	2589069	2628934
(一)内资企业	Domestic Units	2529174	2538295	2521002	2554277
1.国有企业	State-owned Units	1798876	1745195	1443128	1442201
2.集体企业	Collective-owned Units	248106	219047	227066	228901
3.其　他	Others	482192	574053	850808	883175
(二)港澳台及外资企业	Funds from Hong Kong,Macao,Taiwan and Foreign	58276	60038	68067	74657
二、事业单位	Institutions	783183	775584	791636	794414
三、其他单位	Others	16021	17481	15978	19331
领取失业保险金人数	Beneficiaries of Unemployment Insurance Fund	89018	63500	56759	29064

主要统计指标解释

就业人员 指在一定年龄以上，有劳动能力，为取得劳动报酬或经营收入而从事一定社会劳动的人员。具体指年满16周岁，为取得报酬或经营利润，在调查周内从事了1小时（含1小时）以上的劳动或由于学习、休假等原因在调查周内暂时处于未工作状态，但有工作单位或场所的人口。

单位就业人员 指报告期末最后一日24时在本单位中工作，并取得工资或其他形式劳动报酬的人员数。该指标为时点指标，不包括最后一日当天及以前已经与单位解除劳动合同关系的人员，是在岗职工、劳务派遣人员及其他就业人员之和。就业人员不包括：

(1)离开本单位仍保留劳动关系，并定期领取生活费的人员；

(2)利用课余时间打工的学生及在本单位实习的各类在校学生；

(3)本单位因劳务外包而使用的人员。

城镇私营和个体就业人员 城镇私营就业人员指在工商管理部门注册登记，其经营地址设在县城关镇(含县城关镇)以上的私营企业就业人员，包括私营企业投资者和雇工。城镇个体就业人员指在工商管理部门注册登记，并持有城镇户口或在城镇长期居住，经批准从事个体工商经营的就业人员，包括个体经营者和在个体工商户劳动的家庭帮工和雇工。

国有单位 指资产归国家所有的经济组织。包括按《中华人民共和国企业法人登记管理条例》规定登记注册的非公司制的经济组织，以及中央、地方各级国家机关、事业单位和社会团体。

集体单位 指生产资料归集体所有，并按《中华人民共和国企业法人登记管理条例》规定登记注册的经济组织。

其他单位 包括股份合作单位、联营单位、有限责任公司、股份有限公司、港澳台商投资单位以及外商投资单位等其他登记注册类型单位。

在岗职工 指在本单位工作且与本单位签订劳动合同，并由单位支付各项工资和社会保险、住房公积金的人员，以及上述人员中由于学习、病伤、产假等原因暂未工作仍由单位支付工资的人员。在岗职工还包括：

(1)应订立劳动合同而未订立劳动合同人员(如使用的农村户籍人员)；

(2)处于试用期人员；

(3)编制外招用的人员；

(4)派往外单位工作，但工资仍由本单位发放的人员(如挂职锻炼、外派工作等情况)。

工资总额 指根据《关于工资总额组成的规定》(1990年1月1日国家统计局发布的一号令)进行修订，在报告期内(季度或年度)直接支付给本单位全部就业人员的劳动报酬总额。包括计时工资、计件工资、奖金、津贴和补贴、加班加点工资、特殊情况下支付的工资，是在岗职工工资总额、劳务派遣人员工资总额和其他就业人员工资总额之和。

工资总额是税前工资，包括单位从个人工资中直接为其代扣或代缴的房费、水费、电费、住房公积金和社会保险基金个人缴纳部分等。

工资总额不论是计入成本的还是不计入成本的，不论是以货币形式支付的还是以实物形式支付的，均应列入工资总额的计算范围。

平均工资 指单位就业人员在一定时期内平均每人所得的工资额。它表明一定时期工资收入的高低程度，是反映就业人员工资水平的主要指标。计算公式为：

$$\text{平均工资}=\frac{\text{报告期就业人员工资总额}}{\text{报告期就业人员平均人数}}$$

平均工资指数 指报告期就业人员平均工资与基期就业人员平均工资的比率，是反映不同时期就业人员货币工资水平变动情况的相对数。计算公式为：

$$\text{平均工资指数}=\frac{\text{报告期就业人员平均工资}}{\text{基期就业人员平均工资}}\times 100\%$$

平均实际工资指数 就业人员平均实际工资指扣除物价变动因素后的就业人员平均工资。就业人员平均实际工资指数是反映实际工资变动情况的相对数，表明就业人员实际工资水平提高或降低的程度。计算公式为：

$$\text{平均实际工资指数}=\frac{\text{报告期就业人员平均工资指数}}{\text{报告期城镇居民消费价格指数}}\times 100\%$$

城镇登记失业人员 指有非农业户口，在一定的劳动年龄内(16周岁至退休年龄)，有劳动能力，无业而要求就业，并在当地就业服务机构进行求职登记的人员。

城镇登记失业率 城镇登记失业人员与城镇单位就业人员(扣除使用的农村劳动力、聘用的离退休人员、港澳台及外方人员)、城镇单位中的不在岗职工、城镇私营业主、个体户主、城镇私营企业和个体就业人员、城镇登记失业人员之和的比。

Explanatory Notes on Main Statistical Indicators

Employed Persons refers to persons above a specified age who had labour capacity and performed some social work for compensation or business gains. Specifically, it refers to all persons, aged 16 and over, who performed some work for compensation or business gains for one hour or more during the reference period; or who had work units or sites but were temporarily not at work during the reference period,

Persons Employed in Various Units refer to the total number of employees who work at his unit and obtain wages or other forms of payment at the end of the reporting period. This indicator is a kind of time point index and it equals to the sum of the number of employed staff and workers, labor dispatch personnel and other employed persons. Employed persons do not include:

1)persons who have left their working units while keeping their labour contract (employment relation) unchanged and receiving regular alimony;

2)students who do part-time jobs in spare time and all kinds of enrolled students who do internship in various units;

3)persons employed due to labor outsourcing;

4)persons who dissolve labor contracts with their units on the last day of reporting period or before.

Persons Employed in Private Enterprises and Self-Employed Individuals in Urban Areas Persons employed in private enterprises refer to the persons employed in the private enterprises which have been registered at the departments of industrial and commercial administration for which the business operation are situated at a county town (i.e. a town where the county government is located), or at urban areas with administrative hierarchy higher than a county town. The self-employed individuals in urban areas refer to persons who hold the certificates of residence in urban areas or have resided in the urban areas for a long time and have been registered at the departments of industrial and commercial administration and approved to be engaged in individual industrial or commercial business, including self-employed persons as well as helpers and hired laborers who work in individual households.

State-owned Units refer to economic units whose assets are owned by the state, including non-corporation units registered according to *Regulation of the People's Republic of China on the Registration of Enterprises and Corporations*, state organs, institutions and social organizations at the central-level and local levels.

Collective-owned Units refer to economic units registered according to *Regulation of the People's Republic of China on the Registration of Enterprises and Corporations* where the means of production are collectively owned.

Units of Other Types of Ownership refer to units registered with other types of ownership, including cooperative units, joint ownership units, limited liability corporations, share holding corporations, units funded by entrepreneurs from Hong Kong, Macao, and Taiwan, and foreign- funded units.

Employed Staff and Workers refer to persons who signed labor contracts with working units and working units would pay wages, social insurance and housing funds for them. Persons who have their work posts but are temporarily absent from work for reasons of study or on sick, injury or maternal leave and still receive wages from their working units are also included. Employed staff and workers also include:

1)Persons who should have signed the labor contracts but not (like people with rural household registration);

2)Employees on probation;

3)Employees beyond the staffing quota;

4)Employees who are sent to other working units but still obtain wages from their original units (situations like on-the-job placement, expatriated assignment, etc.)

Total Wage Bill It is revised according to the "Provision of Composition of Total Wages" (Order No.1 by National Bureau of Statistics on January, 1st, ,1990), total wage bill refers to the total remuneration payment to all employed persons in various units during the reporting period (by quarter or by year), including hourly-paid wages, piece-rate wages, bonuses, allowance and subsidies, overtime wages and wages paid under special circumstances. It equals to the sum of total wages of employed staff and workers, dispatch labors and other employed persons.

Total wage bill is pre-tax wages, including the room charges, utility bills, housing funds and social insurance paid or withheld by employee's units.

Total wage bill, whether or not included in cost, whether or not paid in money or in kind, shall be included in the calculation of total wage.

Average Wage refers to the average per capita wage during a certain period of time for employed persons. It shows the general level of wage income during a certain period of time, one major indicator to reflect the wage level. It is calculated as follows:

$$\text{Average Wage}=\frac{\text{Total Wage Bill of Employed Persons at Reference Time}}{\text{Average Number of Persons Employed at Reference Time}}$$

Average Wage Indices refers to the ratio of average wage of employed persons the reporting period to that at the base period, which reflects the change of wage of employed persons at the different period. It is calculated as follows:

$$\text{Average Wage Indices} = \frac{\text{Average Wage of Employed Persons at Reference Time}}{\text{Average Wage of Persons Employeds at Base Period}} \times 100\%$$

Average Real Wage Indices average real wage of employed persons refers to the average wage of employed persons after removing the effects of the price changes and average real wage indices of employed persons refers to the change of real wage, which reflects the relative increasing or decreasing level of real wage of employed persons ,which is calculated as follows:

$$\text{Average Real Wage Indices} = \frac{\text{Average Wage Indices of Employed Persons at the Reference Time}}{\text{Urban Consumer Price Indices at Reference Time}} \times 100\%$$

Registered Unemployed Persons in Urban Areas refer to the persons with non-agricultural household registration at certain working ages (16 years old to retirement age), who are capable of working, unemployed and willing to work, and have been registered at the local employment service agencies to apply for a job.

Registered Unemployment Rate in Urban Areas refers to the ratio of the number of the registered unemployed persons to the sum of the number of persons employed in various units (minus the employed rural labour force, re-employed retirees, and Hong Kong, Macao, Taiwan or foreign employees), laid-off staff and workers in urban units, owners of private enterprises in urban areas, owners of self-employed individuals in urban areas, employees of private enterprises in urban areas, employee of self-employed individuals in urban areas, and the registered unemployed persons in urban areas.

六、固定资产投资

资料整理：袁军会　郑　娟　穆　丹　刘海燕　刘卫斌

简 要 说 明

一、本篇资料反映陕西固定资产投资的基本情况，主要包括：全社会固定资产投资，房地产开发投资，商品房及保障房情况。

二、固定资产投资统计的范围包括：城乡建设项目投资，房地产开发投资，国防、人防建设项目投资及农户投资。

三、固定资产投资统计的资料来源主要为统计局的全面统计报表。除农户固定资产投资统计采用抽样调查方法外，其他均为全面统计报表。

四、统计口径的变化

自1997年起，除房地产开发投资、非农户投资、农户投资及城镇和工矿区私人建房投资外，固定资产投资的统计起点由5万元提高到50万元。

自2006年起，非农户固定资产投资统计改为按项目统计，调查方法由抽样调查改为全面统计报表，起点提高到50万元。城镇和工矿区私人建房投资改为按项目统计，起点为50万元。

自2011年起，提高固定资产投资统计起点标准，从计划总投资额50万元提高到500万元。投资统计的范围从城镇扩大到农村企事业组织，并将这一统计范围定义为“固定资产投资（不含农户）”。

Brief Introduction

Ⅰ.This chapter reflects the basic conditions of investment in fixed assets of Shaanxi Province, mainly including total investment in fixed assets in the whole province, real estate development, commercial residential building and security housing.

Ⅱ.Statistics on the investment in fixed assets cover investments in capital construction projects in urban and rural areas, investments in real estate development, as well as investments in national defence projects and civil defence projects, and rural household investment.

Ⅲ.The data sources for the statistics of investment in fixed assets mainly come from complete statistical report forms. Investment in fixed assets by farm households are calculated with sample survey, and the others come from complete statistical report forms.

Ⅳ. Changes in Statistical Scope

Since 1997, the cut-off point of projects covered by statistics of investment in fixed assets are raised from an investment of 50,000 yuan to 500,000 yuan, except investment in real estate development, farm household investment, non-farm household investment and private investment in housing construction in urban areas and industrial and mining areas.

Since 2006, statistics on investments in fixed assets of rural non-farm households are changed to project-based. Survey method is changed from sample survey to the system of reporting form with complete enumeration. The cut-off point has been raised to 500,000 yuan. Statistics on private investment in housing construction in urban areas and industrial and mining areas have become project-based. The cut-off point has been raised to 500,000 yuan.

Since 2011, the cut-off point of statistics on investments in fixed assets are raised, amount of intended investment are raised from 500,000 yuan to 5,000,000 yuan. The scope of investment statistics expends from urban to rural enterprises, and this scope of statistics is defined “investments in fixed assets(non-farm)”.

6.固定资产投资

2014年全省

全社会固定资产投资	18709.49	亿元	比上年增长	17.4%
# 房地产开发投资	2426.49	亿元	比上年增长	8.3%
全社会新增固定资产	10851.44	亿元	比上年增长	20.0%
全社会竣工住宅建筑面积	5647.91	万平方米	比上年增长	-2.7%

房地产开发投资（亿元）

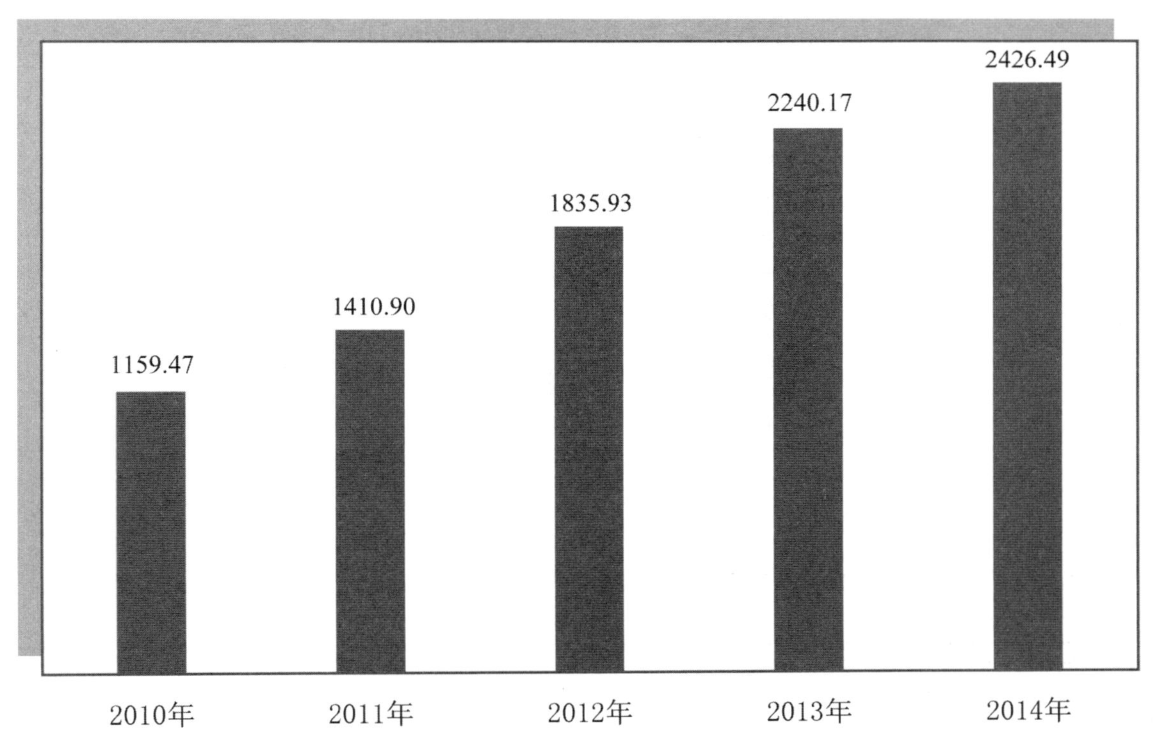

6-1 全社会固定资产投资
Total Investment in Fixed Assets of the Whole Province

单位：亿元 (100 million yuan)

年 份 Year	全社会固定资产投资 Total Investment	固定资产投资 Investment in Fixed Assets	# 房地产开发 Real Estate Development	农户固定资产投资 Rural Investment in Fixed Assets
1978	20.35	19.11		1.24
1979	21.16	19.48		1.68
1980	27.80	25.51		2.29
1981	22.92	19.81		3.11
1982	29.48	26.12		3.36
1983	30.83	26.08		4.74
1984	40.39	31.31		9.08
1985	57.99	44.08		13.91
1986	63.53	51.49		12.04
1987	80.89	65.52		15.37
1988	94.72	75.26		19.46
1989	95.18	73.21		21.97
1990	103.72	80.82		22.90
1991	124.93	94.75		30.18
1992	142.47	116.27		26.20
1993	228.21	197.46		30.74
1994	283.29	235.47	18.19	47.82
1995	324.33	268.78	28.28	55.54
1996	372.00	305.16	30.13	66.84
1997	424.10	353.35	29.53	70.74
1998	544.89	473.78	51.35	71.11
1999	619.27	536.72	68.33	82.55
2000	745.85	675.53	78.89	70.32
2001	850.66	774.12	99.79	76.54
2002	974.63	888.20	123.57	86.43
2003	1278.72	1179.99	188.56	98.73
2004	1544.19	1442.28	231.17	101.91
2005	1982.04	1872.06	298.95	109.98
2006	2610.22	2490.74	394.86	119.48
2007	3642.13	3507.12	535.32	135.01
2008	4851.41	4668.12	762.23	183.29
2009	6553.39	6353.51	943.73	199.88
2010	8561.24	8340.99	1159.47	220.25
2011	10023.53	9701.43	1410.90	322.10
2012	12840.15	12501.43	1835.93	338.72
2013	15934.21	15583.58	2240.17	350.63
2014	18709.49	18357.84	2426.49	351.65

注：2011年起，城镇固定资产投资数据发布口径改为固定资产投资(不含农户)。固定资产投资(不含农户)等于原口径的城镇固定资产投资加上非农户投资(以下相关表同)。

a) Urban Investment in Fixed Assets has changed to Investment in fixed assets (excluding rural households) since 2011. Investment in fixed assets (excluding rural households) is the Urban Investment in Fixed Assets and Non-farm Households(The related tables is the same).

6-2 按经济类型分的全社会固定资产投资
Total Investment in Fixed Assets of the Whole Province by Economic Type

单位：亿元 (100 million yuan)

年 份 Year	合 计 Total	国有经济 单 位 State-owned Units	固定资产投 资 Urban Investment in Fixed Assets	房地产开 发 Real Estate Development	集体经济 单 位 Collective-owned Units	# 农 村 Rural	其他经济 单 位 Others	城乡个人 Urban and Rural Individuals	# 农 村 Rural
1978	20.35	17.20	17.20		1.91	1.75		1.24	1.23
1979	21.16	17.47	17.47		2.02	1.82		1.68	1.66
1980	27.80	23.25	23.25		2.27	1.89		2.29	2.25
1981	22.92	17.47	17.47		2.34	1.97		3.11	3.05
1982	29.48	23.32	23.32		2.80	2.09		3.36	3.22
1983	30.83	24.99	24.99		1.10	0.59		4.74	4.53
1984	40.39	28.07	28.07		3.24	2.68		9.08	8.76
1985	57.99	39.81	39.81		4.27	2.96		13.91	13.35
1986	63.53	47.25	47.25		4.24	2.75		12.04	11.19
1987	80.89	58.11	58.11		7.41	5.63		15.37	14.34
1988	94.72	67.08	67.08		8.18	6.26		19.46	18.15
1989	95.18	67.13	67.13		6.08	4.55		21.97	20.41
1990	103.72	73.85	73.85		6.96	5.38		22.90	21.51
1991	124.93	85.36	85.36		9.39	7.27		30.18	28.89
1992	142.47	108.71	108.71		7.56	5.06		26.20	24.09
1993	228.21	171.86	162.05	9.81	14.01	9.72	11.60	30.74	26.93
1994	283.29	202.92	190.31	12.61	17.89	13.50	14.66	47.82	43.20
1995	324.33	226.61	211.95	14.67	21.53	12.63	20.64	55.54	51.32
1996	372.00	256.48	239.52	16.96	22.00	15.62	26.68	66.84	61.89
1997	424.10	287.64	271.06	16.57	24.74	17.69	40.98	70.74	67.40
1998	544.89	382.89	350.63	32.26	27.07	21.01	63.83	71.11	55.70
1999	619.27	407.76	367.89	39.87	38.96	30.22	89.99	82.55	63.74
2000	745.85	473.53	426.88	46.65	41.66	31.14	137.11	93.54	70.32
2001	850.66	523.92	484.95	38.97	46.41	34.05	169.14	111.19	76.54
2002	974.63	555.41	506.60	48.80	54.52	33.48	212.91	151.79	86.43
2003	1278.72	713.37	664.71	48.66	62.78	30.91	373.28	129.29	98.73
2004	1544.19	814.51	784.47	30.04	71.15	28.52	515.34	143.20	101.91
2005	1982.04	1017.13	985.00	32.13	77.63	31.34	754.18	133.11	109.98
2006	2610.22	1295.31	1258.48	36.84	132.32	75.50	1059.67	122.92	119.48
2007	3642.13	1779.70	1715.68	50.21	227.13	47.51	1494.01	141.29	135.01
2008	4851.41	2208.95	2155.79	53.16	398.62	144.71	2041.99	201.85	183.29
2009	6553.39	3015.64	2941.63	74.00	392.96	158.65	2912.48	232.32	199.88
2010	8561.24	4223.83	4101.13	122.70	412.17	173.51	3664.17	261.07	220.25
2011	10023.53	4462.54	4380.27	82.27	407.69	140.33	4760.71	392.59	322.10
2012	12840.15	5540.89	5378.84	162.05	439.49	71.82	6423.68	436.09	338.72
2013	15934.21	6604.23	6404.38	199.85	503.65	62.02	8374.46	451.87	350.63
2014	18709.49	7900.07	7700.73	199.34	622.26	103.90	9769.70	417.46	351.65

6-3 全社会新增固定资产
Total Newly Increased Fixed Assets of the Whole Province

单位：亿元 (100 million yuan)

年份 Year	合计 Total	国有经济单位 State-owned Units	固定资产投资 Urban Investment in Fixed Assets	房地产开发 Real Estate Development	集体经济单位 Collective-owned Units	#农村 Rural	其他经济单位 Others	城乡个人 Urban and Rural Individuals	#农村 Rural
1978	30.66	27.97	27.97		1.45	1.33		1.24	1.23
1979	16.66	13.45	13.45		1.53	1.38		1.68	1.66
1980	18.39	14.37	14.37		1.73	1.44		2.29	2.25
1981	18.69	13.77	13.77		1.80	1.50		3.11	3.05
1982	27.82	22.31	22.31		2.15	1.57		3.36	3.22
1983	26.51	20.72	20.72		1.04	0.59		4.74	4.53
1984	34.05	21.77	21.77		3.20	2.68		9.08	8.76
1985	41.35	23.67	23.67		3.78	2.96		13.91	13.35
1986	48.32	32.50	32.50		3.78	2.75		12.04	11.19
1987	62.71	40.25	40.25		7.09	5.63		15.37	14.34
1988	72.09	44.89	44.89		7.74	6.26		19.46	18.15
1989	70.96	43.21	43.21		5.78	4.55		21.97	20.41
1990	97.20	67.42	67.42		6.88	5.38		22.90	21.51
1991	102.48	63.82	63.82		8.49	7.25		30.18	28.89
1992	129.09	96.58	96.58		6.31	4.61		26.20	24.09
1993	144.64	98.85	95.21	3.64	11.80	8.96	3.24	30.74	26.93
1994	201.82	134.43	125.05	9.39	11.30	7.75	8.27	47.82	43.20
1995	247.96	161.77	152.39	9.38	16.79	11.24	13.86	55.54	51.32
1996	278.20	189.25	179.65	9.61	17.29	12.79	7.47	64.19	59.24
1997	288.92	189.49	174.92	14.57	21.42	16.06	7.27	70.74	67.40
1998	374.98	255.96	240.03	15.93	23.16	17.70	30.46	65.40	49.99
1999	520.87	349.21	309.81	39.40	37.41	30.35	58.39	75.86	57.05
2000	607.27	403.96	365.37	38.59	37.96	28.48	79.22	86.13	62.91
2001	683.46	430.00	393.43	36.56	40.01	28.16	116.19	97.26	68.35
2002	717.17	341.10	311.12	29.98	45.06	31.15	189.83	141.19	85.35
2003	851.54	447.63	412.17	35.46	46.26	28.39	230.31	127.33	97.20
2004	883.55	448.02	424.67	23.35	50.68	26.34	243.34	141.51	101.05
2005	1258.49	612.05	594.89	17.15	50.75	23.39	453.40	142.29	118.94
2006	1579.34	844.35	831.14	13.21	88.82	59.25	511.79	134.38	131.71
2007	2144.45	1176.79	1141.89	23.01	138.38	40.19	673.19	156.09	151.83
2008	2545.29	1155.80	1138.63	17.17	292.87	75.11	899.77	196.85	183.29
2009	3202.24	1462.70	1433.33	29.37	334.55	133.95	1175.23	229.77	199.88
2010	3655.85	1649.70	1622.98	26.72	175.73	108.02	1589.13	241.29	220.25
2011	4860.55	2219.49	2199.68	19.81	264.17	186.55	2002.80	374.09	322.10
2012	6733.66	3132.10	3080.39	51.71	283.33	61.44	2901.45	416.78	338.72
2013	9039.75	4406.64	4354.21	52.43	392.77	51.58	3805.74	434.60	350.63
2014	10851.44	4589.25	4548.68	40.57	507.69	105.56	5340.73	413.77	351.65

 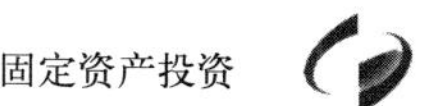

6-4 全社会竣工住宅建筑面积
Total Floor Space of Residential Buildings Completed of the Whole Province

单位：万平方米 (10 000 sq.m)

年 份 Year	合 计 Total	国有经济 单 位 State-owned Units	固定资产投 资 Urban Investment in Fixed Assets	房地产开 发 Real Estate Development	集体经济 单 位 Collective-owned Units	# 农 村 Rural	其他经济 单 位 Others	城乡个人 Urban and Rural Individuals	# 农 村 Rural
1978	706.09	135.61	135.61		32.61	30.33		537.87	535.55
1979	951.05	187.73	187.73		35.90	31.47		727.42	722.78
1980	1277.11	249.08	249.08		39.08	32.84		988.95	979.67
1981	1627.18	250.48	250.48		39.13	34.10		1337.57	1322.56
1982	1598.73	289.49	289.49		32.65	21.77		1276.59	1242.54
1983	2400.03	304.84	304.84		17.81	9.31		2077.38	2032.45
1984	1930.28	290.78	290.78		70.40	63.07		1569.10	1521.75
1985	2622.98	339.80	339.80		84.86	77.06		2198.32	2136.94
1986	2336.38	350.84	350.84		110.02	97.91		1875.52	1801.08
1987	2295.25	305.51	305.51		110.66	103.67		1879.08	1796.30
1988	2943.49	263.75	263.75		65.49	56.85		2614.25	2534.19
1989	1630.46	224.30	224.30		48.26	37.48		1357.90	1290.77
1990	2257.86	250.12	250.12		94.12	85.82		1913.62	1850.44
1991	2583.58	267.14	267.14		60.15	54.00		2256.29	2202.00
1992	1943.91	309.04	309.04		5.32			1629.55	1566.80
1993	2072.95	372.39	308.06	64.33	25.93	10.90	2.97	1671.66	1561.00
1994	2613.12	434.00	334.67	99.33	29.61	11.35	14.09	2135.42	2009.83
1995	3111.15	485.16	375.18	109.98	45.28	10.56	29.86	2550.85	2470.00
1996	2814.39	462.62	349.19	113.43	51.86	15.44	29.97	2269.94	2198.42
1997	2581.69	529.29	393.80	135.49	39.67	9.29	40.19	1972.54	1899.26
1998	2645.52	549.82	402.82	147.00	52.54	20.90	71.73	1971.43	1641.62
1999	3133.31	961.31	549.36	411.95	79.30	42.00	120.57	1972.13	1531.00
2000	4947.36	942.36	566.19	376.17	88.87	44.85	157.30	3758.83	3246.86
2001	4990.18	813.17	543.47	269.70	75.31	18.45	233.44	3868.26	3311.05
2002	4317.24	712.33	470.77	241.56	87.16	10.99	241.10	3276.65	2649.75
2003	4269.44	805.99	581.35	224.64	104.63	17.88	466.63	2892.19	2379.92
2004	3301.31	507.95	384.34	123.61	76.78	28.35	406.56	2310.02	1625.09
2005	3292.40	544.63	440.67	103.96	78.65	6.29	662.86	2006.26	1451.64
2006	2764.55	553.46	455.91	97.55	136.29	54.30	697.17	1377.63	1366.27
2007	3469.95	646.99	546.89	96.99	213.97	25.78	927.84	1681.15	1668.69
2008	4190.59	668.92	575.41	93.51	243.83	92.48	1020.74	2257.10	2242.44
2009	3696.33	694.14	597.95	96.19	177.70	36.85	871.84	1952.65	1880.73
2010	3451.16	401.50	299.83	101.67	74.98	19.79	804.17	2170.51	2155.24
2011	4986.63	478.86	370.75	108.11	210.43	125.83	1434.52	3073.25	3029.77
2012	5883.83	989.96	825.23	164.73	300.06	9.04	1589.79	3004.01	2972.08
2013	5804.35	866.06	735.92	130.14	358.98	14.51	1489.71	3089.59	3074.95
2014	5647.91	756.78	620.91	135.87	257.68	30.17	2330.33	2303.12	2228.74

6-5 全社会固定资产投资主要指标及构成(2014年)
Main Indicators and Composition of Total Investment in Fixed Asset of the Whole Province (2014)

单位：万元 (10 000 yuan)

指 标	Item	合计 Total	内资 Domestic	国有 State-owned	集体 Collective-owned
一、投资总额	Total Investment	187094903	177176604	79000700	6222583
1.按隶属关系分	By Jurisdiction of Management				
中 央	Central Investment	14306168	14306168	7323639	10188
地 方	Local Investment	172788735	162870436	71677061	6212395
2.按构成分	By Use of Funds				
建筑工程	Construction	132706714	126737870	58189791	4737981
安装工程	Installation	14555010	14216352	5860375	606959
设备工器具购置	Purchase of Equipment and Instruments	25158032	22036111	8307980	473635
其他费用	Others	14675147	14186271	6642554	404008
# 土地购置费	Purchase of Land	5950819	5780716	1935393	142305
3.按建设性质分	By Type of Construction				
# 新 建	New Construction	122861316	118508806	60962091	5031946
扩 建	Expansion	15593037	15536214	5549747	243297
改建和技改	Reconstruction and Technical Transformation	10876391	10663898	5525992	494729
4.按产业构成分	By Type of Industry				
第一产业	Primary Industry	10240218	6498913	2188680	457579
第二产业	Secondary Industry	58312024	54791536	18761447	523073
第三产业	Tertiary Industry	118542661	115886155	58050573	5241931
二、本年新增固定资产	Newly Increased Fixed Assets This Year	108514390	103030373	45892518	5076871
三、房屋建筑面积及竣工价值	Floor Space and Value of Buildings				
本年施工房屋面积(万平方米)	Floor Space of Buildings under Construction This Year (10 000 sq.m)	35076.71	31061.54	7142.41	1208.92
# 住 宅	Residential Buildings	22765.40	19236.00	3669.28	859.21
本年竣工房屋面积(万平方米)	Floor Space of Buildings Completed This Year (10 000 sq.m)	7376.40	4884.44	1268.94	362.58
# 住 宅	Residential Buildings	5647.91	3273.20	756.78	257.68
本年竣工房屋价值	Value of Buildings Completed This Year	15618975	12755476	3391146	785993
# 住 宅	Residential Buildings	10617197	8160025	1761939	514191

6-5 续表 continued

单位：万元 (10 000 yuan)

指标	Item	其他 Others	港澳台商投资 Funds from Hong Kong, Macao & Taiwan	外商投资 Foreign Funded	个体经营 Self-employed Individual
一、投资总额	Total Investment	91953321	1461468	4282214	4174617
1.按隶属关系分	By Jurisdiction of Management				
中　央	Central Investment	6972341			
地　方	Local Investment	84980980	1461468	4282214	4174617
2.按构成分	By Use of Funds				
建筑工程	Construction	63810098	842047	1675915	3450882
安装工程	Installation	7749018	137903	154325	46430
设备工器具购置	Purchase of Equipment and Instruments	13254496	412283	2201862	507776
其他费用	Others	7139709	69235	250112	169529
# 土地购置费	Purchase of Land	3703018	56134	101922	12047
3.按建设性质分	By Type of Construction				
# 新　建	New Construction	52514769	410558	3344904	597048
扩　建	Expansion	9743170	6490	34389	15944
改建和技改	Reconstruction and Technical Transformation	4643177	85110	93334	34049
4.按产业构成分	By Type of Industry				
第一产业	Primary Industry	3852654	18152	47100	3676053
第二产业	Secondary Industry	35507016	547943	2915531	57014
第三产业	Tertiary Industry	52593651	895373	1319583	441550
二、本年新增固定资产	Newly Increased Fixed Assets This Year	52060984	386054	960256	4137707
三、房屋建筑面积及竣工价值	Floor Space and Value of Buildings				
本年施工房屋面积(万平方米)	Floor Space of Buildings under Construction This Year (10 000 sq.m)	22710.21	493.11	538.97	2983.09
# 住　宅	Residential Buildings	14707.51	363.97	337.36	2828.08
本年竣工房屋面积(万平方米)	Floor Space of Buildings Completed This Year (10 000 sq.m)	3252.93	61.07	17.46	2413.42
# 住　宅	Residential Buildings	2258.74	59.43	12.16	2303.12
本年竣工房屋价值	Value of Buildings Completed This Year	8578337	169843	152818	2540838
# 住　宅	Residential Buildings	5883895	166557	78945	2211670

6-6 各市(区)全社会固定资产投资
Total Investment in Fixed Assets of the Whole Province by City(District)

地 区	Region	投资额(亿元) Total Investment(100 million yuan)				比上年增长(%) Growth Rate(%)			
		2011	2012	2013	2014	2011	2012	2013	2014
西安市	Xi'an	3352.12	4243.43	5134.56	5903.98	30.2	26.6	21.0	15.0
铜川市	Tongchuan	145.96	201.81	260.02	327.63	32.6	38.3	28.0	26.0
宝鸡市	Baoji	1008.03	1311.69	1669.78	2105.59	31.9	30.1	27.3	26.1
咸阳市	Xianyang	1263.10	1616.47	2054.53	2492.43	31.3	28.0	27.1	21.3
渭南市	Weinan	912.94	1172.21	1467.61	1765.63	30.2	28.4	25.2	20.3
# 韩城市	Hancheng	120.40	156.56	200.79	252.39	27.4	30.0	28.3	25.7
延安市	Yan'an	815.21	1032.06	1321.04	1541.07	29.2	26.6	28.0	16.7
汉中市	Hanzhong	411.33	534.86	679.27	845.04	30.2	30.0	27.0	24.4
榆林市	Yulin	1378.73	1771.23	1827.91	1647.04	32.1	28.5	3.2	-9.9
安康市	Ankang	304.49	380.27	482.56	605.56	29.2	24.9	26.9	25.5
商洛市	Shangluo	308.36	391.60	496.16	625.16	30.9	27.0	26.7	26.0
杨凌示范区	Yangling	55.01	76.08	91.37	115.31	45.5	38.3	20.1	26.2

6-7 各行业按构成分的固定资产投资(2014年)
Investment by Sector and Use of Funds in the Whole Province (2014)

单位：万元 (10 000 yuan)

行业	Sector	投资额 Investment	建筑工程 Construction	安装工程 Installation	设备工器具购置 Purchase of Equipment and Instruments	其他费用 Other Expenses
全省总计	**Total**	**183578393**	**129750810**	**14555010**	**24708243**	**14564330**
农、林、牧、渔业	Agriculture, Forestry, Animal Husbandry and Fishery	8281937	5835058	528864	708650	1209365
农业	Farming	3573278	2535567	216715	287060	533936
林业	Forestry	1069266	660535	102664	30981	275086
畜牧业	Animal Husbandry	1907832	1431772	105644	205266	165150
渔业	Fishery	173332	127373	13760	13985	18214
农、林、牧、渔服务业	Service in Support of Agriculture	1558229	1079811	90081	171358	216979
采矿业	Mining	16752714	12131235	1529261	2013725	1078493
煤炭开采和洗选业	Mining and Washing of Coal	7615352	4959266	621368	1204162	830556
石油和天然气开采业	Extraction of Petroleum and Natural Gas	6814559	5513682	763622	362453	174802
黑色金属矿采选业	Mining and Processing of Ferrous Metal Ores	248550	155996	22103	60687	9764
有色金属矿采选业	Mining and Processing of Non-Ferrous Metal Ores	703607	518988	17599	147859	19161
非金属矿采选业	Mining and Processing of Non-metal Ores	469813	253091	41025	151359	24338
开采辅助活动	Support Activities for Mining	885493	714872	63544	87205	19872
其他采矿业	Mining of Other Ores	15340	15340			
制造业	Manufacturing	33942730	16869657	3218353	11724378	2130342
农副食品加工业	Processing of Food from Agricultural Products	1779553	1065047	154320	430618	129568
食品制造业	Manufacture of Foods	1046568	383172	86589	545786	31021
酒、饮料和精制茶制造业	Manufacture of Liquor, Beverages and Refined Tea	1131235	713321	62659	297818	57437
烟草制品业	Manufacture of Tobacco	98931	49557	10079	30311	8984
纺织业	Manufacture of Textile	431392	208946	65616	137872	18958
纺织服装、服饰业	Manufacture of Textile, Wearing Apparel and Accessories	214696	110017	8747	86553	9379
皮革、毛皮、羽毛及其制品和制鞋业	Manufacture of Leather, Fur, Feather and Related Products and Footwear	44182	17470	2636	23096	980
木材加工和木、竹、藤、棕、草制品业	Processing of Timber, Manufacture of Wood, Bamboo, Rattan,Palm and Straw Products	139663	78029	6321	51321	3992
家具制造业	Manufacture of Furniture	339398	266512	33038	32432	7416
造纸和纸制品业	Manufacture of Paper and Paper Products	616029	347838	76571	165278	26342
印刷和记录媒介复制业	Printing and Reproduction of Recording Media	258115	162706	14278	73560	7571
文教、工美、体育和娱乐用品制造业	Manufacture of Articles for Culture, Education, Arts and Crafts, Sport and Entertainment Activities	119616	78018	4120	29375	8103
石油加工、炼焦和核燃料加工业	Processing of Petroleum, Coking and Processing of Nuclear Fuel	1996494	919547	264543	664175	148229
化学原料和化学制品制造业	Manufacture of Raw Chemical Materials and Chemical Products	3578419	1250798	593343	1184405	549873
医药制造业	Manufacture of Medicines	1077351	671974	85071	251694	68612
化学纤维制造业	Manufacture of Chemical Fibres	56350	9058	17594	29698	
橡胶和塑料制品业	Manufacture of Rubber and Plastics Products	673118	422121	47648	177129	26220
非金属矿物制品业	Manufacture of Non-metallic Mineral Products	2837334	1486941	332249	913926	104218
黑色金属冶炼和压延加工业	Smelting and Pressing of Ferrous Metals	732067	340193	48852	300951	42071
有色金属冶炼和压延加工业	Smelting and Pressing of Non-ferrous Metals	1439493	627136	146189	588085	78083
金属制品业	Manufacture of Metal Products	1119301	756980	99836	222843	39642
通用设备制造业	Manufacture of General Purpose Machinery	1908336	815051	146792	869036	77457

6-7 续表 1 continued

单位：万元 (10 000 yuan)

行业	Sector	投资额 Investment	建筑工程 Construction	安装工程 Installation	设备工器具购置 Purchase of Equipment and Instruments	其他费用 Other Expenses
专用设备制造业	Manufacture of Special Purpose Machinery	3450210	1888407	507666	812074	242063
汽车制造业	Manufacture of Automobiles	1240236	702322	65864	397931	74119
铁路、船舶、航空航天和其他运输设备制造业	Manufacture of Railway, Ship, Aerospace and Other Transport Equipments	1489894	432648	70147	916505	70594
电气机械和器材制造业	Manufacture of Electrical Machinery and Apparatus	2155257	1240720	130522	585193	198822
计算机、通信和其他电子设备制造业	Manufacture of Computers, Communication and Other Electronic Equipment	2874471	1073285	47442	1681943	71801
仪器仪表制造业	Manufacture of Measuring Instruments and Machinery	676673	481279	64123	123269	8002
其他制造业	Other Manufacture	141486	91470	5379	36265	8372
废弃资源综合利用业	Utilization of Waste Resources	164097	107289	13623	36472	6713
金属制品、机械和设备修理业	Repair Service of Metal Products, Machinery and Equipment	112765	71805	6496	28764	5700
电力、热力、燃气及水生产和供应业	Production and Supply of Electricity, Heat, Gas and Water	7357762	3481528	1058775	2431470	385989
电力、热力生产和供应业	Production and Supply of Electric Power and Heat Power	4879197	1744935	774213	2118882	241167
燃气生产和供应业	Production and Supply of Gas	1472211	955012	221766	235581	59852
水的生产和供应业	Production and Supply of Water	1006354	781581	62796	77007	84970
建筑业	Construction	1257076	521991	28580	683267	23238
房屋建筑业	Construction of Buildings	381105	104165	6310	269912	718
土木工程建筑业	Civil Engineering	742368	376843	21670	321635	22220
建筑安装业	Building Installation	69311	20739	600	47672	300
建筑装饰和其他建筑业	Building Decoration and Other Constructions	64292	20244		44048	
批发和零售业	Wholesale and Retail Trades	6517948	4824767	563637	585386	544158
批发业	Wholesale Trade	2477504	1874885	148970	219030	234619
零售业	Retail Trade	4040444	2949882	414667	366356	309539
交通运输、仓储和邮政业	Transport, Storage and Post	16945865	13666944	635037	647475	1996409
铁路运输业	Railway Transport	3142170	1732112	45084	100342	1264632
道路运输业	Road Transport	10828247	9805544	209191	230213	583299
水上运输业	Water Transport					
航空运输业	Air Transport	127785	100112	9896	3851	13926
管道运输业	Transport Via Pipelines	354565	201454	64584	66450	22077
装卸搬运和运输代理业	Loading, Unloading and Forwarding Agency	476739	372694	31158	46799	26088
仓储业	Storage	1969059	1411968	274444	198580	84067
邮政业	Post	47300	43060	680	1240	2320
住宿和餐饮业	Hotels and Catering Services	2975524	2346727	228953	228355	171489
住宿业	Hotels	2226970	1834310	141649	119559	131452
餐饮业	Catering Services	748554	512417	87304	108796	40037
信息传输、软件和信息技术服务业	Information Transmission, Software and Information Technology	1642850	647438	246193	663808	85411
电信、广播电视和卫星传输服务	Telecommunication, Radio and Television and Satellite Transmission Service	1053658	369805	163867	493754	26232
互联网和相关服务	Internet and Related Service	95203	15585	5223	70984	3411
软件和信息技术服务业	Software and Information Technology	493989	262048	77103	99070	55768

6-7 续表 2 continued

单位：万元 (10 000 yuan)

行业	Sector	投资额 Investment	建筑工程 Construction	安装工程 Installation	设备工器具购置 Purchase of Equipment and Instruments	其他费用 Other Expenses
金融业	Financial Intermediation	318672	271702	15139	21471	10360
货币金融服务	Monetary and Financial Service	229473	189896	11589	19228	8760
资本市场服务	Capital Market Service	1558			1558	
保险业	Insurance	16042	16042			
其他金融业	Other Financial Activities	71599	65764	3550	685	1600
房地产业	Real Estate	48994075	39997121	4016129	716477	4264348
房地产业	Real Estate	48994075	39997121	4016129	716477	4264348
租赁和商务服务业	Leasing and Business Services	2456356	1822161	240334	242014	151847
租赁业	Leasing	37130	22510	150	13050	1420
商务服务业	Business Services	2419226	1799651	240184	228964	150427
科学研究和技术服务业	Scientific Research and Technical Services	3383038	1416932	161116	1579892	225098
研究和试验发展	Research and Experimental Development	906973	529954	40247	274721	62051
专业技术服务业	Professional Technical Services	1486084	522973	27163	894503	41445
科技推广和应用服务业	Science and Technology Popularization and Application Services	989981	364005	93706	410668	121602
水利、环境和公共设施管理业	Management of Water Conservancy, Environment and Public Facilities	22239377	18446547	1338418	871906	1582506
水利管理业	Management of Water Conservancy	4503841	4177077	128400	92059	106305
生态保护和环境治理业	Ecological Protection and Environmental Treatment	876805	577148	75369	164998	59290
公共设施管理业	Management of Public Facilities	16858731	13692322	1134649	614849	1416911
居民服务、修理和其他服务业	Service to Households, Repair and Other Services	767248	513333	100818	126336	26761
居民服务业	Service to Households	544770	401164	73439	49904	20263
机动车、电子产品和日用产品修理业	Repair of Motor Vehicle, Electronics and Household Products	161784	71028	19699	67659	3398
其他服务业	Other Services	60694	41141	7680	8773	3100
教　育	Education	2216471	1788822	107287	199705	120657
教　育	Education	2216471	1788822	107287	199705	120657
卫生和社会工作	Health and Social Service	2277073	1181464	172668	855665	67276
卫　生	Health	1958789	911019	149310	845823	52637
社会工作	Social Service	318284	270445	23358	9842	14639
文化、体育和娱乐业	Culture, Sports and Entertainment	2033840	1339603	130444	308001	255792
新闻和出版业	Journalism and Publishing Activities	35454	31254	4200		
广播、电视、电影和影视录音制作业	Radio, Television, Motion Picture and Videotape Programme Production Services	109263	50126	4955	36562	17620
文化艺术业	Cultural and Art Activities	1147393	794781	60232	104073	188307
体　育	Sports Activities	264996	205718	41061	8900	9317
娱乐业	Entertainment	476734	257724	19996	158466	40548
公共管理、社会保障和社会组织	Public Management, Social Security and Social Organization	3217837	2647780	235004	100262	234791
中国共产党机关	Organs of Communist Party of China	11776	10736	1040		
国家机构	Government Agencies	2225651	1866770	162156	51678	145047
人民政协、民主党派	People's Political Consultative Conference and Democratic Parties	19800	18410	1390		
社会保障	Social Security	121401	88821	19881	6430	6269
群众团体、社会团体和其他成员组织	Non-Governmental Organizations, Social Organizations and Membership Organizations	377027	272582	21178	15290	67977
基层群众自治组织	Grass Roots Self-Governing Organizations	462182	390461	29359	26864	15498

6-8 分行业固定资产投资施工、投产项目个数及新增固定资产(2014年)
Number of Investment Projects under Construction and Put into Use and Newly Increased Fixed Assets by Sector in the Whole Province(2014)

行业	Sector	施工项目（个）Number of Projects under Construction (unit)	全部建成投产项目（个）Number of Projects Completed and Put into Use (unit)	施工项目计划总投资（万元）Total Planned Investment of Projects under Construction (10 000 yuan)	本年完成投资额（万元）Investment Completed This Year (10 000 yuan)	本年新增固定资产（万元）Newly Increased Fixed Assets This Year (10 000 yuan)
全省总计	**Total**	**20680**	**12985**	**503382740**	**183578393**	**104997880**
农、林、牧、渔业	Agriculture, Forestry, Animal Husbandry and Fishery	2292	1773	12907744	8281937	7095800
农业	Farming	885	681	5631496	3573278	3180217
林业	Forestry	276	204	1926516	1069266	784350
畜牧业	Animal Husbandry	563	439	2884080	1907832	1583172
渔业	Fishery	60	48	270154	173332	163318
农、林、牧、渔服务业	Service in Support of Agriculture	508	401	2195498	1558229	1384743
采矿业	Mining	744	485	37007237	16752714	7693835
煤炭开采和洗选业	Mining and Washing of Coal	297	191	26279606	7615352	2588027
石油和天然气开采业	Extraction of Petroleum and Natural Gas	135	63	6512358	6814559	3216135
黑色金属矿采选业	Mining and Processing of Ferrous Metal Ores	36	23	729873	248550	149038
有色金属矿采选业	Mining and Processing of Non-Ferrous Metal Ores	94	73	1474401	703607	682856
非金属矿采选业	Mining and Processing of Non-metal Ores	110	77	949307	469813	284823
开采辅助活动	Support Activities for Mining	68	56	1002616	885493	769356
其他采矿业	Mining of Other Ores	4	2	59076	15340	3600
制造业	Manufacturing	3351	2263	90513200	33942730	20914394
农副食品加工业	Processing of Food from Agricultural Products	364	248	3056023	1779553	1404461
食品制造业	Manufacture of Foods	128	93	1488715	1046568	930508
酒、饮料和精制茶制造业	Manufacture of Liquor, Beverages and Refined Tea	185	121	1993216	1131235	1048767
烟草制品业	Manufacture of Tobacco	10	4	443519	98931	78819
纺织业	Manufacture of Textile	76	62	940828	431392	551907
纺织服装、服饰业	Manufacture of Textile, Wearing Apparel and Accessories	24	19	519156	214696	92391
皮革、毛皮、羽毛及其制品和制鞋业	Manufacture of Leather, Fur, Feather and Related Products and Footwear	10	7	64860	44182	30230
木材加工和木、竹、藤、棕、草制品业	Processing of Timber, Manufacture of Wood, Bamboo, Rattan,Palm and Straw Products	33	26	201943	139663	99543
家具制造业	Manufacture of Furniture	30	25	1364550	339398	198796
造纸和纸制品业	Manufacture of Paper and Paper Products	68	55	1033874	616029	437241
印刷和记录媒介复制业	Printing and Reproduction of Recording Media	31	21	463545	258115	195918
文教、工美、体育和娱乐用品制造业	Manufacture of Articles for Culture, Education, Arts and Crafts, Sport and Entertainment Activities	16	9	151563	119616	96380
石油加工、炼焦和核燃料加工业	Processing of Petroleum, Coking and Processing of Nuclear Fuel	69	42	10161045	1996494	1260415
化学原料和化学制品制造业	Manufacture of Raw Chemical Materials and Chemical Products	222	138	17227954	3578419	1826421
医药制造业	Manufacture of Medicines	147	90	2828194	1077351	646581
化学纤维制造业	Manufacture of Chemical Fibres	4	4	66185	56350	66185
橡胶和塑料制品业	Manufacture of Rubber and Plastics Products	97	67	1121925	673118	623051
非金属矿物制品业	Manufacture of Non-metallic Mineral Products	457	332	4550364	2837334	2495871
黑色金属冶炼和压延加工业	Smelting and Pressing of Ferrous Metals	68	55	2274610	732067	531003
有色金属冶炼和压延加工业	Smelting and Pressing of Non-ferrous Metals	152	106	6057756	1439493	878072
金属制品业	Manufacture of Metal Products	157	108	2001301	1119301	744317
通用设备制造业	Manufacture of General Purpose Machinery	235	174	3471703	1908336	1269438

6-8 续表 1 continued

行 业	Sector	施工项目 (个) Number of Projects under Construc-tion (unit)	全部建成投产项目 (个) Number of Projects Completed and Put into Use (unit)	施工项目计划总投资 (万元) Total Planned Investment of Projects under Con-struction (10 000 yuan)	本年完成投资额 (万元) Investment Completed This Year (10 000 yuan)	本年新增固定资产 (万元) Newly Increased Fixed Assets This Year (10 000 yuan)
专用设备制造业	Manufacture of Special Purpose Machinery	224	151	5539894	3450210	2504782
汽车制造业	Manufacture of Automobiles	102	67	3348743	1240236	558228
铁路、船舶、航空航天和其他运输设备制造业	Manufacture of Railway, Ship, Aerospace and Other TransportEquipments	94	46	2767852	1489894	620967
电气机械和器材制造业	Manufacture of Electrical Machinery and Apparatus	168	93	8154347	2155257	776393
计算机、通信和其他电子设备制造业	Manufacture of Computers, Communication and Other Electronic Equipment	76	37	7153444	2874471	456597
仪器仪表制造业	Manufacture of Measuring Instruments and Machinery	33	21	1029702	676673	243061
其他制造业	Other Manufacture	18	7	356488	141486	37681
废弃资源综合利用业	Utilization of Waste Resources	35	21	225535	164097	106073
金属制品、机械和设备修理业	Repair Service of Metal Products, Machinery and Equipment	18	14	454366	112765	104297
电力、热力、燃气及水生产和供应业	Production and Supply of Electricity, Heat, Gas and Water	795	512	16635444	7357762	3670872
电力、热力生产和供应业	Production and Supply of Electric Power and Heat Power	390	248	11828007	4879197	1986849
燃气生产和供应业	Production and Supply of Gas	182	114	2704841	1472211	1006337
水的生产和供应业	Production and Supply of Water	223	150	2102596	1006354	677686
建筑业	Construction	168	122	1767579	1257076	1013413
房屋建筑业	Construction of Buildings	46	33	551336	381105	332986
土木工程建筑业	Civil Engineering	109	79	990638	742368	625692
建筑安装业	Building Installation	7	5	161383	69311	28231
建筑装饰和其他建筑业	Building Decoration and Other Constructions	6	5	64222	64292	26504
批发和零售业	Wholesale and Retail Trades	818	585	14043093	6517948	4590033
批发业	Wholesale Trade	255	181	6585738	2477504	1408398
零售业	Retail Trade	563	404	7457355	4040444	3181635
交通运输、仓储和邮政业	Transport, Storage and Post	1233	805	47464456	16945865	6532820
铁路运输业	Railway Transport	31	8	13241687	3142170	726285
道路运输业	Road Transport	838	558	27977932	10828247	3771619
水上运输业	Water Transport					
航空运输业	Air Transport	9	4	283835	127785	67847
管道运输业	Transport Via Pipelines	25	9	585119	354565	191390
装卸搬运和运输代理业	Loading, Unloading and Forwarding Agency	45	31	1037359	476739	365408
仓储业	Storage	278	191	4263936	1969059	1370381
邮政业	Post	7	4	74588	47300	39890
住宿和餐饮业	Hotels and Catering Services	365	272	6891724	2975524	2731212
住宿业	Hotels	211	148	5679858	2226970	2093046
餐饮业	Catering Services	154	124	1211866	748554	638166
信息传输、软件和信息技术服务业	Information Transmission, Software and Information Technology	169	112	3568950	1642850	989755
电信、广播电视和卫星传输服务	Telecommunication, Radio and Television and Satellite Transmission Service	115	80	2054537	1053658	761481
互联网和相关服务	Internet and Related Service	15	13	95641	95203	55535
软件和信息技术服务业	Software and Information Technology	39	19	1418772	493989	172739

6-8 续表 2 continued

行业	Sector	施工项目(个) Number of Projects under Construction (unit)	全部建成投产项目(个) Number of Projects Completed and Put into Use (unit)	施工项目计划总投资(万元) Total Planned Investment of Projects under Construction (10 000 yuan)	本年完成投资额(万元) Investment Completed This Year (10 000 yuan)	本年新增固定资产(万元) Newly Increased Fixed Assets This Year (10 000 yuan)
金融业	Financial Intermediation	30	17	785350	318672	66296
货币金融服务	Monetary and Financial Service	22	14	442881	229473	50036
资本市场服务	Capital Market Service			1558	1558	
保险业	Insurance	2		84465	16042	
其他金融业	Other Financial Activities	6	3	256446	71599	16260
房地产业	Real Estate	4484	1764	188872828	48994075	24725553
房地产业	Real Estate	4484	1764	188872828	48994075	24725553
租赁和商务服务业	Leasing and Business Services	202	123	7486482	2456356	1282953
租赁业	Leasing	5	3	70549	37130	21776
商务服务业	Business Services	197	120	7415933	2419226	1261177
科学研究和技术服务业	Scientific Research and Technical Services	271	188	7658099	3383038	1903361
研究和试验发展	Research and Experimental Development	59	31	3480936	906973	417587
专业技术服务业	Professional Technical Services	132	101	2251888	1486084	914951
科技推广和应用服务业	Science and Technology Popularization and Application Services	80	56	1925275	989981	570823
水利、环境和公共设施管理业	Management of Water Conservancy, Environment and Public Facilities	3573	2476	47267928	22239377	14448137
水利管理业	Management of Water Conservancy	695	524	7382902	4503841	2106515
生态保护和环境治理业	Ecological Protection and Environmental Treatment	185	142	1449033	876805	743784
公共设施管理业	Management of Public Facilities	2693	1810	38435993	16858731	11597838
居民服务、修理和其他服务业	Service to Households, Repair and Other Services	178	133	1292751	767248	435816
居民服务业	Service to Households	115	82	931415	544770	300167
机动车、电子产品和日用产品修理业	Repair of Motor Vehicle, Electronics and Household Products	32	28	225101	161784	99339
其他服务业	Other Services	31	23	136235	60694	36310
教　育	Education	555	384	4049029	2216471	1783418
教　育	Education	555	384	4049029	2216471	1783418
卫生和社会工作	Health and Social Service	348	240	4393810	2277073	1498638
卫　生	Health	256	175	3825187	1958789	1316929
社会工作	Social Service	92	65	568623	318284	181709
文化、体育和娱乐业	Culture, Sports and Entertainment	323	211	4779801	2033840	1264029
新闻和出版业	Journalism and Publishing Activities	10	7	177680	35454	7090
广播、电视、电影和影视录音制作业	Radio, Television, Motion Picture and Videotape Programme Production Services	21	15	223637	109263	82136
文化艺术业	Cultural and Art Activities	158	97	3030203	1147393	586345
体　育	Sports Activities	72	47	529633	264996	140560
娱乐业	Entertainment	62	45	818648	476734	447898
公共管理、社会保障和社会组织	Public Management, Social Security and Social Organization	781	520	5997235	3217837	2357545
中国共产党机关	Organs of Communist Party of China	2	1	20090	11776	7616
国家机构	Government Agencies	562	382	4445667	2225651	1514866
人民政协、民主党派	People's Political Consultative Conference and Democratic Parties	1	1	19800	19800	19800
社会保障	Social Security	54	23	148929	121401	58580
群众团体、社会团体和其他成员组织	Non-Governmental Organizations,Social Organizations and Membership Organizations	40	16	642997	377027	443131
基层群众自治组织	Grass Roots Self-Governing Organizations	122	97	719752	462182	313552

6-9 固定资产投资新增生产能力或效益(2014年)
Newly Increased Production Capacity or Project Efficiency through Investment(2014)

名称	Item	能力或效益 Capacity or Efficiency
原煤开采 (万吨／年)	Coal Mining (10 000 tons/year)	3420.86
洗煤 (万吨／年)	Coal Washing (10 000 tons/year)	2063
焦炭 (万吨／年)	Coke (10 000 tons/year)	500
天然原油开采 (万吨／年)	Petroleum Extraction (10 000 tons/year)	810.32
天然气开采 (亿立方米／年)	Natural Gas Extraction (100 million cu.m/year)	28.63
石油加工：蒸馏设备能力 (处理万吨/年)	Petroleum Processing: Distillation Equipment Capacity (Processing 10 000 tons/year)	244
铁矿开采(原矿) (万吨／年)	Iron-Ore Mining (10 000 tons/year)	135
铁矿选矿处理原矿量 (万吨／年)	Iron Ore Processing Ore Quantity (10 000 tons/year)	120
粗钢 (万吨／年)	Crude Steel (10 000 tons/year)	160.52
铁合金 (万吨／年)	Ferroalloy (standard ton/year)	71
钢材 (万吨／年)	Rolled Steel (10 000 tons/year)	2361.2
铜选矿：处理原矿 (万吨／年)	Copper Processing:Processing Ore (10 000 tons/year)	46
铜冶炼 (吨／年)	Copper Smelting (ton/year)	90
铅锌采矿(原矿) (万吨／年)	Lead and Zinc Mining (10 000 tons/year)	40.1
铅锌选矿：处理原矿 (万吨／年)	Lead-zinc Ore:Processing Ore (10 000 tons/year)	35.8
铅含量 (吨／年)	Lead Content (ton/year)	580
镍冶炼 (吨／年)	Nickel Smelting (ton/year)	119
铝加工 (吨／年)	Aluminium Fabrication (ton/year)	89564
铜加工材 (吨／年)	Copper Processing Material (ton/year)	4518
黄金 (公斤／年)	Gold (kilogram /year)	4113.73
水力发电 (万千瓦)	Hydraulic Power (10 000 kw)	30.72
火力发电 (万千瓦)	Thermal Power (10 001 kw)	60
风力发电 (万千瓦)	Wind Power (10 000 kw)	176.69
太阳能发电 (万千瓦)	Solar Energy (10 000 kw)	13.22
其他发电 (万千瓦)	Others (10 000 kw)	1.28
输电线路长度(11万伏及以上) (公里)	Length of Transmission Lines (above 110 000 VA) (km)	2198.6
水泥 (万吨／年)	Cement (10 000 tons/year)	557.9
平板玻璃 (万重量箱／年)	Plate Glass (10 000 Weight-boxs/year)	540
氮肥 (吨／年)	Nitrogen Fertilizers (ton/year)	313078
磷肥 (吨／年)	Phosphate Fertilizer (ton/year)	74800
钾肥 (吨／年)	Potash Fertilizer (ton/year)	5000
化学农药原药 (吨／年)	Chemical Pesticide (ton/year)	1150
塑料树脂及共聚物 (吨／年)	Plastic Resin and Copolymer (ton/year)	66986
合成橡胶 (吨／年)	Synthetic Rubber (ton/year)	4103
轿车制造 (辆／年)	Car Manufacturing (unit/year)	60000
化学纤维 (吨／年)	Chemical Fiber (ton/year)	6893
棉纺锭 (锭)	Cotton Spirit (unit)	99000
毛纺锭 (锭)	Wool Spinning (unit)	3000
啤酒 (万吨／年)	Beer (10 000 tons/year)	20
白酒 (万吨／年)	White Spirit (10 000 tons/year)	1.8
其他酒 (万吨／年)	Other Alcohols (10 000 tons/year)	0.56
新建铁路里程 (公里)	Newly Railway (km)	170.2
复线里程	Double-Tracking Length	231.3
高速铁路里程	Length of High-speed Railway	137.8
新建公路 (公里)	Newly Highways (km)	2608.29
# 高速公路	Expressway	94
一级公路	First Class	36.22
二级公路	Second Class	181.35
改建公路 (公里)	Reconstructed Highways (km)	3464.04
# 高速公路	Expressway	16
一级公路	First Class	165.04
二级公路	Second Class	820.83
新建独立公路桥梁 (延长米)	New-built Separate Highway Bridge (linear-meter)	6293.71
新建独立公路桥梁 (座)	New-built Separate Highway Bridge (unit)	36.8
新建独立公路隧道 (延长米)	New-built Separate Highway Tunnel (linear-meter)	290
新建独立公路隧道 (处)	New-built Separate Highway Tunnel (unit)	1
新(扩)建客、货运站 (个)	New (expanded) Passenger and Freight Stations (unit)	13
新(扩)建客、货运站 (平方米)	New (expanded) Passenger and Freight Stations (sq.m)	45302
城市自来水供水能力 (万吨／日)	Tap Water Supply Capacity in City (10 000 tons/day)	66.1
城市污水处理能力 (万吨／日)	Waste Water Treated Capacity in City (10 000 tons/day)	69.2

6-10 分行业工业投资(2014年)
Investment of Industrial by Sector(2014)

单位：万元 (10 000 yuan)

行 业	Sector	投资额 Investment	# 改建和技术改造 Reconstruction and Technical Transformation
工业投资合计	**Total of Industrial Investment**	**58053206**	**3890012**
采矿业	Mining	16752714	1013131
煤炭开采和洗选业	Mining and Washing of Coal	7615352	683712
石油和天然气开采业	Extraction of Petroleum and Natural Gas	6814559	31989
黑色金属矿采选业	Mining and Processing of Ferrous Metal Ores	248550	50789
有色金属矿采选业	Mining and Processing of Non-Ferrous Metal Ores	703607	85646
非金属矿采选业	Mining and Processing of Non-metal Ores	469813	40986
开采辅助活动	Support Activities for Mining	885493	120009
其他开采业	Mining of Other Ores	15340	
制造业	Manufacturing	33942730	2243540
农副食品加工业	Processing of Food from Agricultural Products	1779553	117425
食品制造业	Manufacture of Foods	1046568	51534
酒、饮料和精制茶制造业	Manufacture of Liquor, Beverages and Refined Tea	1131235	57043
烟草制品业	Manufacture of Tobacco	98931	12829
纺织业	Manufacture of Textile	431392	38909
纺织服装和服饰业	Manufacture of Textile, Wearing Apparel and Accessories	214696	10530
皮革、毛皮、羽毛(绒)及其制品业	Manufacture of Leather, Fur, Feather and Related Products and Footwear	44182	
木材加工及木、竹、藤、棕、草制品业	Processing of Timber, Manufacture of Wood, Bamboo, Rattan, Palm and Straw Products	139663	40022
家具制造业	Manufacture of Furniture	339398	12444
造纸及纸制品业	Manufacture of Paper and Paper Products	616029	48263
印刷业和记录媒介的复制	Printing and Reproduction of Recording Media	258115	16810
文教体育用品制造业	Manufacture of Articles for Culture, Education, Arts and Crafts, Sport and Entertainment Activities	119616	12300
石油加工、炼焦及核燃料加工业	Processing of Petroleum, Coking and Processing of Nuclear Fuel	1996494	31704
化学原料及化学制品制造业	Manufacture of Raw Chemical Materials and Chemical Products	3578419	105307
医药制造业	Manufacture of Medicines	1077351	134481
化学纤维制造业	Manufacture of Chemical Fibres	56350	1210
橡胶和塑料制品业	Manufacture of Rubber and Plastics Products	673118	97936
非金属矿制品业	Manufacture of Non-metallic Mineral Products	2837334	351933
黑色金属冶炼和压延加工业	Smelting and Pressing of Ferrous Metals	732067	99065
有色金属冶炼和压延加工业	Smelting and Pressing of Non-ferrous Metals	1439493	214025
金属制品业	Manufacture of Metal Products	1119301	74685
通用设备制造业	Manufacture of General Purpose Machinery	1908336	240299
专用设备制造业	Manufacture of Special Purpose Machinery	3450210	146268
汽车制造业	Manufacture of Automobiles	1240236	21994
铁路、船舶、航空航天等制造业	Manufacture of Railway, Ship, Aerospace and Other Transport Equipments	1489894	113520
电气机械及器材制造业	Manufacture of Electrical Machinery and Apparatus	2155257	99512
计算机、通信和其他电子设备制造业	Manufacture of Computers, Communication and Other Electronic Equipment	2874471	36647
仪器仪表制造业	Manufacture of Measuring Instruments and Machinery	676673	34025
其他制造业	Other Manufacture	141486	8126
废弃资源综合利用业	Utilization of Waste Resources	164097	8794
金属制品、机械和设备修理业	Repair Service of Metal Products, Machinery and Equipment	112765	5900
电力、热力、燃气及水的生产和供应业	Production and Supply of Electricity, Heat, Gas and Water	7357762	633341
电力、热力的生产和供应业	Production and Supply of Electric Power and Heat Power	4879197	563321
燃气生产和供应业	Production and Supply of Gas	1472211	45371
水的生产和供应业	Production and Supply of Water	1006354	24649

6-11 民间投资(2014年)
Private Investment(2014)

行业	Sector	投资额(万元) Investment (10 000 yuan)	占民间投资比重(%) Rate (%)
民间投资合计	**Total of Private Investment**	**84316639**	**100.0**
农、林、牧、渔业	Agriculture, Forestry, Animal Husbandry and Fishery	5186217	6.2
采矿业	Mining	4529041	5.4
制造业	Manufacturing	21748935	25.8
电力、燃气及水的生产和供应业	Production and Supply of Electricity, Heat, Gas and Water	1565232	1.9
建筑业	Construction	389545	0.5
批发和零售业	Wholesale and Retail Trades	5446830	6.5
交通运输、仓储和邮政业	Transport, Storage and Post	2485004	2.9
住宿和餐饮业	Hotels and Catering Services	2221170	2.6
信息传输、软件和信息技术服务业	Information Transmission, Software and Information Technology	391836	0.5
金融业	Financial Intermediation	57298	0.1
房地产业	Real Estate	29436109	34.9
租赁和商务服务业	Leasing and Business Services	1138174	1.3
科学研究和技术服务业	Scientific Research and Technical Services	1861404	2.2
水利、环境和公共设施管理业	Management of Water Conservancy, Environment and Public Facilities	5061336	6.0
居民服务、修理和其他服务业	Service to Households, Repair and Other Services	403046	0.5
教育	Education	503935	0.6
卫生和社会工作	Health and Social Service	605365	0.7
文化、体育和娱乐业	Culture, Sports and Entertainment	862105	1.0
公共管理、社会保障和社会组织	Public Management, Social Security and Social Organization	424057	0.5

6-12 基础设施投资(2014年)
Investment for Basic Infrastructure(2014)

行业	Sector	投资额(万元) Investment (10 000 yuan)	占基础设施投资比重(%) Rate (%)
基础设施投资合计	**Total Investment of Infrastructure**	**42700002**	**100.0**
一、交通运输、仓储和邮政业	Transport, Storage and Post	16945865	39.7
铁路运输业	Railway Transport	3142170	7.4
道路运输业	Road Transport	10828247	25.4
水上运输业	Water Transport		
航空运输业	Air Transport	127785	0.3
管道运输业	Transport Via Pipelines	354565	0.8
装卸搬运和运输代理业	Loading, Unloading and Forwarding Agency	476739	1.1
仓储业	Storage	1969059	4.6
邮政业	Post	47300	0.1
二、信息传输、软件和信息技术服务业	Information Transmission, Software and Information Technology	1642850	3.8
三、电网建设	Grid Construction	1871910	4.4
四、水利、环境和公共设施管理业	Management of Water Conservancy, Environment and Public Facilities	22239377	52.1
水利管理业	Management of Water Conservancy	4503841	10.5
生态保护和环境治理业	Ecological Protection and Environmental Treatment	876805	2.1
公共设施管理业	Management of Public Facilities	16858731	39.5

6-13 七大战略性新兴产业投资(2014年)
Investment of Seven Strategic Emerging Industries(2014)

行 业	Sector	投资额 (万元) Investment (10 000 yuan)	占战略性新兴产业投资比重(%) Rate (%)
七大战略性新兴产业投资合计	**Total Investment of Seven Strategic Emerging Industries**	**20843414**	**100.0**
节能环保产业	Energy Conservation and Environment Protection	7190603	34.5
新一代信息技术产业	New Generation of Enformation Technology	2901919	13.9
生物产业	Living Things	2091475	10.0
高端装备制造业	Manufacture of High-end Equipment	2784709	13.4
新能源产业	New Energy	2522146	12.1
新材料产业	New Material	3089931	14.8
新能源汽车产业	New Energy Automobile	262631	1.3

6-14 文化产业投资(2014年)
Culture Industry Investment(2014)

行 业	Sector	投资额 (万元) Investment (10 000 yuan)	占文化产业投资比重(%) Rate (%)
文化产业投资合计	**Total Investment of Culture Industry**	**7720526**	**100.0**
新闻出版发行服务	News Publishing Service	38054	0.5
广播电视电影服务	Broadcasting Television and Film Service	109263	1.4
文化艺术服务	Arts and Cultural Service	1421925	18.4
文化信息传输服务	Cultural Information Transmission Service	200619	2.6
文化创意和设计服务	Cultural Creative and Design Service	281370	3.6
文化休闲娱乐服务	Cultural and Recreational Service	4278400	55.4
工艺美术品的生产	Arts and Crafts Production	255629	3.3
文化产品生产的辅助生产	Subsidiary Production of Cultural Product	494114	6.4
文化用品的生产	Stationery Production	476924	6.2
文化专用设备的生产	Cultural Special Equipment Production	164228	2.1

6-15 全社会固定资产投资财务拨款资金来源(2014年)

Source of Funds of Investment in Fixed Assets for Finance Allocation in the Whole Province(2014)

单位：万元 (10 000 yuan)

指 标	Item	合 计 Total	固定资产投资 Investment in Fixed Assets	房地产开发 Real Estate Development	农户投资 Farm Households
一、本年资金来源合计	Total of Sources of Funds This Year	189604573	152384570	33703493	3516510
1.上年末结余资金	Funds of Last Year-end	12577220	5721527	6855693	
2.本年资金来源小计	Subtotal of Sources of Funds This Year	177027353	146663043	26847800	3516510
国家预算内资金	State Budget	11743195	11743195		
国内贷款	Domestic Loans	15883095	11628490	3912758	341847
债 券	Bond	496250	496250		
利用外资	Foreign Investment	1102600	1102600		
# 外商直接投资	Foreign Direct Investment	958253	958253		
自筹资金	Self-raising Fund	130489023	114621464	12745677	3121882
# 企事业单位自有资金	Enterprises and Institutions-owned Funds	23522743	18652297	4870446	
其他资金来源	Others	17313190	7071044	10189365	52781
二、本年各项应付款合计	Total Payment of this year	26648512	20460359	6188153	
# 工程款	Project Payment	7554211	4201298	3352913	

6-16 固定资产投资资金来源(2014年)

Source of Funds of Investment (2014)

单位：万元 (10 000 yuan)

指 标	Item	总 计	按经济类型分 By Owership		按隶属关系分 By Jurisdiction of Management	
		Total	国有经济单位 State-owned	其他经济单位 Others	中央单位 Central	地方单位 Local
一、本年实际到位资金合计	Total of Actual Funds This Year	152384570	72011850	80372720	7948590	144435980
1.上年末结余资金	Funds of Last Year-end	5721527	1911116	3810411	208058	5513469
2.本年实际到位资金小计	Subtotal of Actual Funds This Year	146663043	70100734	76562309	7740532	138922511
国家预算资金	State Budget	11743195	10117008	1626187	1020920	10722275
国内贷款	Domestic Loans	11628490	6438734	5189756	1317217	10311273
债 券	Bond	496250	495000	1250	482000	14250
利用外资	Foreign Investment	1102600	79607	1022993	2110	1100490
# 外商直接投资	Foreign Direct Investment	958253	20520	937733		958253
自筹资金	Self-raising Fund	114621464	49251672	65369792	4902018	109719446
# 企事业单位自有资金	Enterprises and Institutions-owned Funds	18652297	6318653	12333644	1381306	17270991
其他资金来源	Others	7071044	3718713	3352331	16267	7054777
二、本年各项应付款合计	Total Payment of this Year	20460359	11317474	9142885	6043696	14416663
# 工程款	Project Payment	4201298	2238647	1962651	149621	4051677

注：本表不含房地产开发投资。
a) Data in this table do not include those of real estate development.

6-17 各市(区)固定资产投资资金来源(2014年)
Source of Funds of Investment by City(District)(2014)

单位：万元 (10 000 yuan)

地区	Region	本年实际到位资金合计 Total of Actual Funds This Year	上年末结余资金 Funds of Last Year-end	本年实际到位资金小计 Subtotal of Actual Funds This Year	国家预算资金 State Budget	国内贷款 Domestic Loans	债券 Bond
全省	**Shaanxi**	**152384570**	**5721527**	**146663043**	**11743195**	**11628490**	**496250**
西安市	Xi'an	42304354	3858429	38445925	1659455	1714223	
铜川市	Tongchuan	2877083	6030	2871053	399042	148307	
宝鸡市	Baoji	18828356	178176	18650180	1322951	1298201	3000
咸阳市	Xianyang	24338692	657037	23681655	522729	2757846	
渭南市	Weinan	14436872	557217	13879655	1056037	477418	
# 韩城市	Hancheng	2357069	23219	2333850	190545	176661	
延安市	Yan'an	11659506	7140	11652366	2226678	86139	
汉中市	Hanzhong	5580465	173744	5406721	450679	215750	10000
榆林市	Yulin	14444328	122697	14321631	1179711	882245	
安康市	Ankang	4885399	68019	4817380	666768	86822	
商洛市	Shangluo	5684513	35759	5648754	992686	287677	1250
杨凌示范区	Yangling	1117857	17767	1100090	129178	102136	
不分地区	Not Classified by Region	6227145	39512	6187633	1137281	3571726	482000

6-17 续表 continued

单位：万元 (10 000 yuan)

地区	Region	利用外资 Foreign Investment	#外商直接投资 Foreign Direct Investment	自筹资金 Self-raising Fund	#企事业单位自有资金 Enterprises and Institutions-owned Funds	其他资金来源 Others	本年各项应付款合计 Total Payment of This Year	#工程款 Project Payment
全省	**Shaanxi**	**1102600**	**958253**	**114621464**	**18652297**	**7071044**	**20460359**	**4201298**
西安市	Xi'an	808018	738665	32962838	7796236	1301391	803973	352117
铜川市	Tongchuan			2080258	41689	243446	63808	47420
宝鸡市	Baoji	77862	76202	14764323	673399	1183843	1578337	560464
咸阳市	Xianyang	81450	53800	18900794	5044098	1418836	336887	219274
渭南市	Weinan	62274	55782	11272841	1434124	1011085	1673094	1264871
# 韩城市	Hancheng			1733654	124362	232990	156313	29644
延安市	Yan'an	13440	520	8978686	759091	347423	2679029	186487
汉中市	Hanzhong	27481	14900	4343451	749928	359360	1500892	662432
榆林市	Yulin	15084	15084	11854585	174326	390006	726110	97900
安康市	Ankang	11790	3300	3855247	284494	196753	673783	590769
商洛市	Shangluo	2200		3932945	741738	431996	469084	219564
杨凌示范区	Yangling	3001		847789	246262	17986		
不分地区	Not Classified by Region			827707	706912	168919	9955362	

注：本表不含房地产开发投资。
a) Data in this table do not include those of real estate development.

6-18 各市(区)国有经济单位投资资金来源(2014年)
Source of Funds of Investment in State-Owned Units by City(District)(2014)

单位：万元 (10 000 yuan)

地 区	Region	本年实际到位资金合计 Total of Actual Funds This Year	上年末结余资金 Funds of Last Year-end	本年实际到位资金小计 Subtotal of Actual Funds This Year	国家预算资金 State Budget	国内贷款 Domestic Loans	债券 Bond
全 省	**Shaanxi**	**72011850**	**1911116**	**70100734**	**10117008**	**6438734**	**495000**
西安市	Xi'an	17913460	1375918	16537542	1167417	1269382	
铜川市	Tongchuan	1389143	2301	1385842	377891	115834	
宝鸡市	Baoji	7543747	53485	7490262	1065411	173798	3000
咸阳市	Xianyang	7458735	70216	7383519	401905	1116558	
渭南市	Weinan	6148348	214011	5934337	981982	151662	
#韩城市	Hancheng	955341	8864	945477	170669	120815	
延安市	Yan'an	10252962	7140	10245822	1929082	62971	
汉中市	Hanzhong	2459113	70255	2383858	401586	84717	10000
榆林市	Yulin	8548831	68675	8480156	1113594	288745	
安康市	Ankang	1953000	19371	1933629	633721	34557	
商洛市	Shangluo	2733100	3391	2729709	779960	30946	
杨凌示范区	Yangling	657574	11958	645616	127178	83736	
不分地区	Not Classified by Region	4953837	14395	4939442	1137281	3025828	482000

6-18 续表 continued

单位：万元 (10 000 yuan)

地 区	Region	利用外资 Foreign Investment	#外商直接投资 Foreign Direct Investment	自筹资金 Self-raising Fund	#企事业单位自有资金 Enterprises and Institutions-owned Funds	其他资金来源 Others	本年各项应付款合计 Total Payment of This Year	#工程款 Project Payment
全 省	**Shaanxi**	**79607**	**20520**	**49251672**	**6318653**	**3718713**	**11317474**	**2238647**
西安市	Xi'an	40535	3000	13707719	2583716	352489	306503	165234
铜川市	Tongchuan			735484	22069	157633	63758	47420
宝鸡市	Baoji	800		5504594	213867	742659	559402	199830
咸阳市	Xianyang	17000	17000	5246241	901661	606815	186497	143870
渭南市	Weinan	6492		4307715	1143993	486486	690040	456126
#韩城市	Hancheng			532665	100468	122328	136205	27742
延安市	Yan'an	12840	520	7911963	718074	328966	2491623	183015
汉中市	Hanzhong			1711568	244037	180987	798311	554443
榆林市	Yulin			6717907	148788	359910	524474	56075
安康市	Ankang	440		1132155	29806	132756	343643	329025
商洛市	Shangluo	1500		1734196	225630	183107	182161	103609
杨凌示范区	Yangling			416716	81598	17986		
不分地区	Not Classified by Region			125414	5414	168919	5171062	

注：本表不含房地产开发投资。
a) Data in this table do not include those of real estate development.

6-19 各市(区)按国民经济行业分的固定资产投资(2014年)
Investment by Sector and City(District)(2014)

单位：万元 (10 000 yuan)

地 区	Region	总 计 Total	农、林、牧、渔业 Agriculture, Forestry, Animal Husbandry and Fishery	采矿业 Mining	制造业 Manufacturing	电力、热力燃气及水生产和供应业 Production and Supply of Electricity, Heat,Gas and Water	建筑业 Construction	批发和零售业 Wholesale and Retail Trades	交通传输仓储和邮政业 Transport, Storage and Post	住宿和餐饮业 Hotels and Catering Services	信息传输、软件和信息技术服务业 Information Transmission, Software and Information Technology
全 省	**Shaanxi**	**183578393**	**8281937**	**16752714**	**33942730**	**7357762**	**1257076**	**6517948**	**16945865**	**2975524**	**1642850**
西安市	Xi'an	56972552	860369	5500	9939453	1809658	574900	1923772	2761882	931034	694217
铜川市	Tongchuan	2985661	242737	316062	601032	107036		113942	105491	83136	
宝鸡市	Baoji	20589752	2012961	437340	5703192	791161	147609	968692	1119774	560022	222907
咸阳市	Xianyang	23985718	1040151	729753	6589437	548520	73807	1531063	1556195	319598	303413
渭南市	Weinan	16463384	1993019	1167642	2819013	484879	13948	1115295	678467	597637	4536
#韩城市	Hancheng	2487942	89186	558310	604102	48072		48103	126389	83251	
延安市	Yan'an	12975342	267010	3652469	2586571	885423	49335	116399	561456	79990	39826
汉中市	Hanzhong	7053333	372483	350091	1097051	282728	39647	174223	348951	79424	161875
榆林市	Yulin	13965619	415916	3447634	2292117	1706830	56906	441347	1302777	27983	126402
安康市	Ankang	5417825	612799	202359	945469	108345	7339	28238	224703	119531	13286
商洛市	Shangluo	5977835	443889	426976	1057789	238175	223369	88777	315990	137558	73808
杨凌示范区	Yangling	1114648	20603		300576	185756	32183	16200	107057	39611	2580
不分地区	Not Classified by Region	16076724		6016888	11030	209251	38033		7863122		

6-19 续表 continued

单位：万元 (10 000 yuan)

地 区	Region	金融业 Financial Intermediation	房地产业 Real Estate	租赁和商务服务业 Leasing and Business Services	科学研究和技术服务业 Scientific Research and Technical Services	水利、环境和公共设施管理业 Management of Water Conservancy, Environment and Public Facilities	居民服务、修理和其他服务业 Services to Households, Repair and Other Services	教 育 Education	卫生和社会工作 Health and Social Service	文化、体育和娱乐业 Culture, Sports and Entertainment	公共管理、社会保障和社会组织 Public Management Social Security and Social Organization
全 省	**Shaanxi**	**318672**	**48994075**	**2456356**	**3383038**	**22239377**	**767248**	**2216471**	**2277073**	**2033840**	**3217837**
西安市	Xi'an	261473	27387264	1290780	1833111	3935719	223700	746923	965177	363129	464491
铜川市	Tongchuan	3600	645134	18345	26318	539708	26286	43809	63152	12854	37019
宝鸡市	Baoji	22566	2917111	334425	396224	3257680	259780	301457	288474	214617	633760
咸阳市	Xianyang		5131176	333788	531464	3715552	15361	163955	303661	808850	289974
渭南市	Weinan	4099	3045614	152623	266980	3201850	52041	263790	175219	261564	165168
#韩城市	Hancheng		327793	7618		448279	22979	48448	23801	46601	5010
延安市	Yan'an	12385	1943596	138023	137228	1065822	49537	133836	41150	109928	1105358
汉中市	Hanzhong	700	2186148	19373	36608	1409175	30198	102471	110310	47382	204495
榆林市	Yulin	12649	2285972	117108	68581	1048179	50239	174838	177852	119876	92413
安康市	Ankang		1872114	29135	46781	918191	13135	100037	65423	61100	49840
商洛市	Shangluo	1200	1334186	21256	39008	1133111	11815	156004	74430	28920	171574
杨凌示范区	Yangling		245760	1500	735	75990	35156	29351	12225	5620	3745
不分地区	Not Classified by Region					1938400					

6-20 各市(区)工业投资(2014年)
Investment of Industry by City(District) (2014)

单位：万元 (10 000 yuan)

地区	Region	投资额 Investment	# 改建和技术改造 Reconstruction and Technical Transformation
全省	**Shaanxi**	**58053206**	**3890012**
西安市	Xi'an	11754611	335944
铜川市	Tongchuan	1024130	161834
宝鸡市	Baoji	6931693	1290055
咸阳市	Xianyang	7867710	377865
渭南市	Weinan	4471534	810099
# 韩城市	Hancheng	1210484	402068
延安市	Yan'an	7124463	95064
汉中市	Hanzhong	1729870	405534
榆林市	Yulin	7446581	149676
安康市	Ankang	1256173	68757
商洛市	Shangluo	1722940	109763
杨凌示范区	Yangling	486332	65939
不分地区	Not Classified by Region	6237169	19482

6-21 各市(区)按登记注册类型分的固定资产投资(2014年)
Investment by Registration Status and City (District)(2014)

单位：万元 (10 000 yuan)

地区	Region	合计 Total	内资 Domestic	国有 State-owned	集体 Collective-owned	其他 Other	港澳台商投资 Funds from Hong Kong, Macao and Taiwan	外商投资 Foreign Investment	个体经营 Self-Employed Individual
全省	**Shaanxi**	**159313479**	**154194623**	**77007276**	**6070299**	**71117048**	**745018**	**3715731**	**658107**
西安市	Xi'an	39353734	35790439	16540822	1815517	17434100	421369	3103619	38307
铜川市	Tongchuan	2669076	2666241	1306965	108008	1251268	745		2090
宝鸡市	Baoji	19658305	19236869	7768368	1271681	10196820	92705	254299	74432
咸阳市	Xianyang	22026213	21741762	6784461	323708	14633593	153562	114227	16662
渭南市	Weinan	15649847	15461700	6631046	808946	8021708	712	82905	104530
# 韩城市	Hancheng	2395619	2391619	1003830	56659	1331130		4000	
延安市	Yan'an	12708770	12699250	11546071	413898	739281	990		8530
汉中市	Hanzhong	6232338	6101753	3023084	575389	2503280	23120	75511	31954
榆林市	Yulin	13226336	13031899	8007926	392490	4631483	24565	65522	104350
安康市	Ankang	4883009	4592907	1943344	41597	2607966	8050	4800	277252
商洛市	Shangluo	5794372	5775172	2811434	318565	2645173	19200		
杨凌示范区	Yangling	1034755	1019907	610552	500	408855		14848	
不分地区	Not Classified by Region	16076724	16076724	10033203		6043521			

注：本表不含房地产开发投资。
a) Data in this table do not include those of real estate development.

6-22 各市(区)按隶属关系分的固定资产投资(2014年)
Investment in Urban Area by Jurisdiction of Management and City (District)(2014)

单位：万元 (10 000 yuan)

地区	Region	总计 Total	# 地方 Local	省 Province	市 City	县 County	其他 Others
全省	**Shaanxi**	**159313479**	**120185405**	**15133691**	**16653655**	**43188458**	**45209601**
西安市	Xi'an	39353734	32129627	2352758	8671960	7282354	13822555
铜川市	Tongchuan	2669076	1935416	331276	237697	839883	526560
宝鸡市	Baoji	19658305	14799616	379972	1068916	5597750	7752978
咸阳市	Xianyang	22026213	17490683	2709568	1609606	6616435	6555074
渭南市	Weinan	15649847	12299671	627619	963362	5007733	5700957
# 韩城市	Hancheng	2395619	1684394	251686	239068	897998	295642
延安市	Yan'an	12708770	11315977	2132647	1960019	6673119	550192
汉中市	Hanzhong	6232338	5123310	173092	448043	1973370	2528805
榆林市	Yulin	13226336	13146116	3064437	1261207	4797293	4023179
安康市	Ankang	4883009	3749820	60191	175672	1588842	1925115
商洛市	Shangluo	5794372	4481610	97322	217568	2771301	1395419
杨凌示范区	Yangling	1034755	604416	95666	39605	40378	428767
不分地区	Not Classified by Region	16076724	3109143	3109143			

注：本表不含房地产开发投资。下表同。
a) Data in this table do not include those of real estate development. The same applies to the table following.

6-23 各市(区)能源工业投资(2014年)
Investment in Energy Industry by City(District)(2014)

单位：万元 (10 000 yuan)

地区	Region	能源工业投资 Energy Industry	煤炭开采及洗选业 Mining and Washing of Coal	石油和天然气开采业 Extraction of Petroleum and Natural Gas	石油加工、炼焦及核燃料加工业 Processing of Petroleum,Coking, Processing of Nuclear Fuel	电力、热力生产和供应业 Production and Supply of Electric Power and Heat Power
全省	**Shaanxi**	**21305602**	**7615352**	**6814559**	**1996494**	**4879197**
西安市	Xi'an	1881828			304991	1576837
铜川市	Tongchuan	375907	222150	82930	6165	64662
宝鸡市	Baoji	619160	103568		11326	504266
咸阳市	Xianyang	957543	569161		142392	245990
渭南市	Weinan	1077360	702713	92886	77970	203791
# 韩城市	Hancheng	527621	361261	72831	59196	34333
延安市	Yan'an	4187492	525522	2625679	895735	140556
汉中市	Hanzhong	264439	39327		1583	223529
榆林市	Yulin	5379705	2551555	880476	556332	1391342
安康市	Ankang	90267	17056			73211
商洛市	Shangluo	124827				124827
杨凌示范区	Yangling	120935				120935
不分地区	Not Classified by Region	6226139	2884300	3132588		209251

6-24 各市(区)按构成分的固定资产投资（2014年）
Investment by Use of Funds and City(District)(2014)

单位：万元 (10 000 yuan)

地 区	Region	总 计 Total	建筑工程 Construction	安装工程 Installation	设备工具器具购置 Purchase of Equipment and Instruments	其他费用 Others	#土地购置费 Total Value of Land Purchased
全 省	**Shaanxi**	**159313479**	**111386338**	**11966426**	**24416185**	**11544530**	**4097716**
西 安 市	Xi'an	39353734	26558000	1973221	8692147	2130366	1103789
铜 川 市	Tongchuan	2669076	1746895	222277	497824	202080	40635
宝 鸡 市	Baoji	19658305	11662325	1738063	4949492	1308425	185425
咸 阳 市	Xianyang	22026213	15332754	2073957	3225231	1394271	846179
渭 南 市	Weinan	15649847	11142226	1072009	2021624	1413988	392702
# 韩城市	Hancheng	2395619	1353256	283943	493296	265124	69288
延 安 市	Yan'an	12708770	9728259	1522503	744951	713057	94175
汉 中 市	Hanzhong	6232338	4396422	392161	749704	694051	281321
榆 林 市	Yulin	13226336	6869914	2116847	2344146	1895429	836816
安 康 市	Ankang	4883009	3999431	270109	272045	341424	113356
商 洛 市	Shangluo	5794372	4853584	338467	438638	163683	65413
杨凌示范区	Yangling	1034755	656847	33853	293881	50174	29305
不分地区	Not Classified by Region	16076724	14439681	212959	186502	1237582	108600

注：本表不含房地产开发投资。下表同。
a) Data in this table do not include those of real estate development. The same applies to the table following.

6-25 各市(区)按建设性质分的固定资产投资(2014年)
Investment by Type of Construction and City(District)(2014)

单位：万元 (10 000 yuan)

地 区	Region	总 计 Total	新 建 New Construction	扩 建 Expansion	改建和技改 Reconstruction and Technological Transformation	单纯建造生活设施 Construction of Living Facilities	迁 建 Removal Construction	恢 复 Reestablishment	单纯购置 Purchase of Equipment
全 省	**Shaanxi**	**159313479**	**122861316**	**15593037**	**10876391**	**1348639**	**1051379**	**189785**	**7392932**
西 安 市	Xi'an	39353734	28312592	1080426	2732388	811357	544278	72830	5749863
铜 川 市	Tongchuan	2669076	2143127	99242	312888		2607		111212
宝 鸡 市	Baoji	19658305	14243265	1730527	2305075	40540	48115	30915	1259868
咸 阳 市	Xianyang	22026213	18975053	1916011	630622	388797	60833	670	84227
渭 南 市	Weinan	15649847	13019924	955007	1430861	43951	128495	31786	39823
# 韩城市	Hancheng	2395619	1625512	127459	543544	41951	28905	23434	4814
延 安 市	Yan'an	12708770	10012237	2060610	422935	39740	102338	26806	44104
汉 中 市	Hanzhong	6232338	4271618	444485	1343806	12404	108627	7616	43782
榆 林 市	Yulin	13226336	12442722	469512	284142	1400	22680	140	5740
安 康 市	Ankang	4883009	4622489	94356	148679		7549	8322	1614
商 洛 市	Shangluo	5794372	5141298	344892	270320	9600	17562	10700	
杨凌示范区	Yangling	1034755	882964	49814	68039	850	8295		24793
不分地区	Not Classified by Region	16076724	8794027	6348155	906636				27906

6-26 各市(区)固定资产投资施工、投产项目个数及新增固定资产(2014年)
Number of Investment Projects under Construction and Put into Use and Newly Increased Fixed Assets by City(District)(2014)

地区	Region	施工项目(个) Number of Project under Construction (unit)	全部建成投产项目(个) Number of Project Completed and Put into Use (unit)	施工项目计划总投资(万元) Total Investment Planned under Construction (10 000 yuan)	本年完成投资额(万元) Investment Completed This Year (10 000 yuan)	本年新增固定资产(万元) Newly Increased Fixed Assets of This Year (10 000 yuan)	固定资产交付使用率(%) Rate of Projects of Fixed Assets Completed and Put into Use (%)
全省	**Shaanxi**	**18696**	**12830**	**374760575**	**159313479**	**97729532**	**61.3**
西安市	Xi'an	2225	1391	98551889	39353734	19978793	50.8
铜川市	Tongchuan	657	409	7433571	2669076	1898191	71.1
宝鸡市	Baoji	4193	3591	27526762	19658305	16317271	83.0
咸阳市	Xianyang	2067	1251	55953532	22026213	16693164	75.8
渭南市	Weinan	2264	1769	27456407	15649847	14878759	95.1
#韩城市	Hancheng	375	260	4818039	2395619	2493645	104.1
延安市	Yan'an	1478	885	21796138	12708770	8190418	64.4
汉中市	Hanzhong	1598	1044	14213228	6232338	5333587	85.6
榆林市	Yulin	1340	758	61274105	13226336	5559174	42.0
安康市	Ankang	1574	1018	10523503	4883009	3584852	73.4
商洛市	Shangluo	984	581	15248317	5794372	3404914	58.8
杨凌示范区	Yangling	212	123	3206508	1034755	483294	46.7
不分地区	Not Classified by Region	104	10	31576615	16076724	1407115	8.8

注：本表不含房地产开发投资。下表同。
a) Data in this table do not include those of real estate development. The same applies to the table following.

6-27 各市(区)固定资产投资房屋建筑面积及造价(2014年)
Floor Space and Cost of Buildings in Investment by City(District)(2014)

地区	Region	本年施工房屋面积(万平方米) Floor Space of Buildings under Construction This Year (10 000 sq.m)	#住宅 Residential Buildings	本年竣工房屋面积(万平方米) Floor Space of Buildings Completed this Year (10 000 sq.m)	#住宅 Residential Buildings	本年竣工房屋价值(万元) Value of Buildings Completed This Year (10 000 yuan)	#住宅 Residential Buildings
全省	**Shaanxi**	**128363241**	**46069941**	**28919085**	**15561572**	**7309169**	**3626074**
西安市	Xi'an	39330595	8500909	4287911	1553994	1404312	582024
铜川市	Tongchuan	1681668	288135	109587	96100	15900	13395
宝鸡市	Baoji	13379947	4162345	5237533	1885618	1634275	512993
咸阳市	Xianyang	22241556	11303513	4716389	3432183	1363074	938881
渭南市	Weinan	13882527	3720818	5050840	2857592	951306	498792
#韩城市	Hancheng	2609111	477276	183169	88556	42945	12000
延安市	Yan'an	6341868	3662317	694938	591003	141253	101485
汉中市	Hanzhong	12711359	8361305	4025028	2845592	831631	531339
榆林市	Yulin	2920520	266991	311703	65971	80540	23900
安康市	Ankang	9349204	4235713	3445579	1856588	716796	380170
商洛市	Shangluo	5344197	1342740	1024828	362182	168730	41743
杨凌示范区	Yangling	1170064	225155	14749	14749	1352	1352
不分地区	Not Classified by Region	9736					

 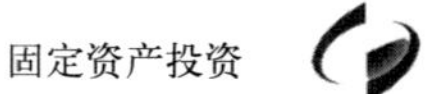

6-28 房地产开发投资主要指标及构成(2014年)
Main Indicators and Composition of Investment for Real Estate Development(2014)

指标	Item	房地产开发 Real Estate Development	# 地方 Local Governments	# 省属 Provincial Owned
一、企业(单位)个数 (个)	Number of Enterprises (unit)	1941	1859	58
二、本年完成投资 (万元)	Investment Completed This Year (10 000 yuan)	24264914	23448056	991736
# 配套工程投资	Investment of Related Project			
1.按隶属关系分	Group by Jurisdiction of Management			
中央	Central	816858		
地方	Local	23448056	23448056	991736
# 市县属	City and County Level	22456320	22456320	
2.按构成分	By Composition of Funds			
建筑工程	Construction	18364472	17759210	636036
安装工程	Installation	2588584	2569391	133067
设备工器具购置	Purchase of Equipment and Instruments	292058	279463	8960
其他费用	Others	3019800	2839992	213673
# 旧建筑物购置费	Purchase of Used Buildings	109048	109048	
土地购置费	Total Value of Land Purchased	1853103	1721420	106756
3.按工程用途分	By Use of Projects			
住宅	Residential Buildings	18696850	18039200	787866
# 别墅、高档公寓	Villas,High-grade Apartments	479339	479339	
办公楼	Office Buildings	1051474	1019438	40657
商业营业用房	Houses for Business Use	2857338	2830083	82874
其他	Others	1659252	1559335	80339
三、本年新增固定资产(万元)	Newly Increased Fixed Assets of This Year (10 000 yuan)	7268348	7128033	329461
四、房屋建筑面积及竣工价值	Floor Space of Buildings Completed and Value of Buildings Completed			
施工面积 (万平方米)	Floor Space of Buildings under Construction (10 000 sq.m)	19466.10	19100.48	874.06
# 住宅	Residential Buildings	15475.10	15189.15	740.30
竣工面积 (万平方米)	Floor Space of Buildings Completed (10 000 sq.m)	2188.91	2145.13	121.50
# 住宅	Residential Buildings	1863.01	1829.07	109.17
竣工价值 (亿元)	Value of Buildings Completed (100 million yuan)	595.88	581.85	31.82
# 住宅	Residential Buildings	491.40	480.82	25.76

6-28 续表 continued

指标	Item	按登记注册类型分 By Status of Registration					
		内资 Domestic Funded	国有 State-owned	集体 Collective-owned	其它 Others	港澳台投资 Funds from Hong Kong, Macao and Taiwan	外商投资 Foreign Funded
一、企业(单位)个数 (个)	Number of Enterprises (unit)	1903	120	14	1769	20	18
二、本年完成投资 (万元)	Investment Completed This Year (10 000 yuan)	22981981	1993424	152284	20836273	716450	566483
# 配套工程投资	Investment of Related Project						
1.按隶属关系分	Group by Jurisdiction of Management						
中央	Central	816858	361588	10188	445082		
地方	Local	22165123	1631836	142096	20391191	716450	566483
# 市县属	City and County Level	21176516	1520796	142096	19513624	716450	563354
2.按构成分	By Composition of Funds						
建筑工程	Construction	17312125	1589891	83748	15638486	606702	445645
安装工程	Installation	2468671	89635	13860	2365176	53618	66295
设备工器具购置	Purchase of Equipment and Instruments	286161	6115	300	279746	5368	529
其他费用	Others	2915024	307783	54376	2552865	50762	54014
# 旧建筑物购置费	Purchase of Used Buildings	109048	2045		107003		
土地购置费	Total Value of Land Purchased	1762731	184371	43200	1535160	47154	43218
3.按工程用途分	By Use of Projects						
住宅	Residential Buildings	17621647	1661020	108049	15852578	624643	450560
# 别墅、高档公寓	Villas,High-grade Apartments	411046	62461		348585	32764	35529
办公楼	Office Buildings	1037702	50009	730	986963	4972	8800
商业营业用房	Houses for Business Use	2744204	121105	5690	2617409	49891	63243
其他	Others	1578428	161290	37815	1379323	36944	43880
三、本年新增固定资产(万元)	Newly Increased Fixed Assets of This Year (10 000 yuan)	6966762	405729	8639	6552394	170093	131493
四、房屋建筑面积及竣工价值	Floor Space of Buildings Completed and Value of Buildings Completed						
施工面积 (万平方米)	Floor Space of Buildings under Construction (10 000 sq.m)	18554.01	1789.16	111.31	16653.54	466.30	445.79
# 住宅	Residential Buildings	14774.38	1502.37	102.90	13169.11	363.97	336.76
竣工面积 (万平方米)	Floor Space of Buildings Completed (10 000 sq.m)	2112.54	153.80	4.02	1954.71	61.07	15.30
# 住宅	Residential Buildings	1791.42	135.87	4.02	1651.53	59.43	12.16
竣工价值 (亿元)	Value of Buildings Completed (100 million yuan)	565.77	38.86	0.86	526.05	16.98	13.13
# 住宅	Residential Buildings	466.85	31.97	0.86	434.01	16.66	7.89

6-29 房地产开发投资资金来源(2014年)

Sources of Funds of Investment for Real Estate Development (2014)

单位：万元 (10 000 yuan)

指标	Item	总计 Total	内资 Domestic	国有 State-owned	集体 Collective-owned	其他 Others	港澳台投资 Funds from Hong Kong, Macao and Taiwan	外商投资 Foreign Investment
一、本年资金来源合计	Total of Sources of Funds This Year	33703493	30738219	2545486	210619	27982114	1661191	1304083
1.上年末结余资金	Funds of Last Year-end	6855693	5673965	618898	35066	5020001	565274	616454
2.本年资金来源小计	Subtotal of Sources of Funds This Year	26847800	25064254	1926588	175553	22962113	1095917	687629
国内贷款	Domestic Loans	3912758	3662488	196710	3450	3462328	172220	78050
# 银行贷款	Loans from Bank	2982493	2843673	175785	2950	2664938	60770	78050
非银行金融机构贷款	Loans from Non-bank	930265	818815	20925	500	797390	111450	
利用外资	Foreign Investment							
# 外商直接投资	Foreign Direct Investment							
自筹资金	Self-raising Funds	12745677	12481306	871493	105765	11504048	200431	63940
# 自有资金	Self-owned Funds	4870446	4723783	359967	85787	4278029	139727	6936
其他资金来源	Others	10189365	8920460	858385	66338	7995737	723266	545639
# 定金及预收款	Booked and Prepayed Money	6296876	5592856	603445	27612	4961799	380516	323504
个人按揭贷款	Individual Credit	2688855	2222988	174148	25969	2022871	260798	205069
二、本年各项应付款合计	Total Payment of this year	6188153	5819115	568609	4132	5246374	203728	165310
# 工程款	Project Payment	3352913	3094973	296998	4132	2793843	177713	80227

6-30 各市(区)房地产开发投资和新增固定资产(2014年)

Investment for Real Estate Development and Newly Increased Fixed Assets by City(District)(2014)

单位：万元 (10 000 yuan)

地区	Region	计划总投资 Total Investment Planed	自开始建设至本年底累计完成投资 Accumulative Investment Actually Completed Since Start of Construction up to the end of This Year	本年完成投资 Investment Completed This Year	本年新增固定资产 Newly Increased Fixed Assets of This Year
全省	**Shaanxi**	**128622165**	**76801148**	**24264914**	**7268348**
西安市	Xi'an	94642056	57096491	17618818	5314364
铜川市	Tongchuan	1707200	1040872	316585	65240
宝鸡市	Baoji	4646275	2820545	931447	166523
咸阳市	Xianyang	8734926	4561322	1959505	60522
渭南市	Weinan	4547244	2786589	813537	607042
# 韩城市	Hancheng	423227	315644	92323	102537
延安市	Yan'an	2083372	1090926	266572	45105
汉中市	Hanzhong	3819566	2719325	820995	435717
榆林市	Yulin	4446786	2316046	739283	329124
安康市	Ankang	2191906	1364157	534816	140489
商洛市	Shangluo	888369	431779	183463	71264
杨凌示范区	Yangling	914465	573095	79893	32958

6-31 各市(区)按构成和工程用途分的房地产开发投资(2014年)
Investment for Real Estate Development by Use of Funds and Projects by City(District)(2014)

单位：万元 (10 000 yuan)

地区	Region	按构成分 by Use of Founds 建筑安装工程 Construction and Installation Projects	设备工器具购置 Purchase of Equipment and Instruments	其他费用 Others	# 土地购置费 Total Value of Land Purchased	按工程用途分 by Use of Projects 住宅 Residential Buildings	# 别墅、高档公寓 Villas, High-grade Apartments	办公楼 Office Buildings	商业营业用房 Houses for Business Use	其他 Others
全　省	**Shaanxi**	**20953056**	**292058**	**3019800**	**1853103**	**18696850**	**479339**	**1051474**	**2857338**	**1659252**
西安市	Xi'an	14904160	150426	2564232	1547646	13344332	348915	840013	2101737	1332736
铜川市	Tongchuan	280885	220	35480	30344	206448		45474	49345	15318
宝鸡市	Baoji	802474	35197	93776	73555	662936	3978	24637	175027	68847
咸阳市	Xianyang	1871968	4338	83199	57922	1818377	112641	48538	59734	32856
渭南市	Weinan	716204	45556	51777	36941	627743		27587	127040	31167
# 韩城市	Hancheng	80157	1111	11055	8160	82071		1450	7895	907
延安市	Yan'an	242171	2475	21926	14634	219141		5613	28850	12968
汉中市	Hanzhong	717940	13664	89391	50588	604177	700	10500	119313	87005
榆林市	Yulin	686951	23327	29005	14899	503074	1500	47792	134490	53927
安康市	Ankang	507292	9392	18132	5613	470016	11540	260	43805	20735
商洛市	Shangluo	153403	6680	23380	20961	162410		960	17149	2944
杨凌示范区	Yangling	69608	783	9502		78196	65	100	848	749

6-32 房地产开发面积及造价(2014年)
Floor Space and Cost of Buildings in Real Estate Development(2014)

地区	Region	施工房屋面积(万平方米) Floor Space of Buildings Construction (10 000 sq.m)	# 住宅 Residential Buildings	竣工房屋面积(万平方米) Floor Space of Buildings Completed (10 000 sq.m)	# 住宅 Residential Buildings	竣工房屋价值(亿元) Value of Buildings Completed (100 million yuan)	# 住宅 Residential Buildings	竣工房屋造价(元/平方米) Cost of Buildings Completed (yuan/sq.m)	# 住宅 Residential Buildings
全　省	**Shaanxi**	**19466.10**	**15475.10**	**2188.91**	**1863.01**	**595.88**	**491.40**	**2722**	**2638**
西安市	Xi'an	12422.10	9727.60	1533.70	1307.64	442.74	368.25	2887	2816
铜川市	Tongchuan	444.69	349.76	23.72	23.42	6.47	6.37	2729	2718
宝鸡市	Baoji	828.63	637.62	26.79	24.01	7.31	6.35	2729	2644
咸阳市	Xianyang	1226.08	1128.91	30.35	30.23	6.05	6.04	1994	1999
渭南市	Weinan	1030.81	834.11	218.55	182.10	50.81	39.78	2325	2184
# 韩城市	Hancheng	121.87	98.09	19.71	16.71	4.91	4.24	2492	2538
延安市	Yan'an	523.59	462.22	14.85	14.09	2.22	2.10	1497	1492
汉中市	Hanzhong	901.19	745.25	130.66	110.28	31.48	25.08	2409	2274
榆林市	Yulin	1054.55	686.00	98.42	66.83	28.71	18.80	2917	2813
安康市	Ankang	578.91	490.51	67.91	61.08	11.64	10.35	1714	1694
商洛市	Shangluo	251.32	211.54	30.62	29.98	6.22	6.05	2030	2018
杨凌示范区	Yangling	204.21	201.60	13.33	13.33	2.23	2.23	1674	1674

6-33 商品房屋销售情况(2014年)
Seal of Commercialized Buildings(2014)

地区	Region	商品房销售面积(平方米) Floor Space of Commercialized Buildings Sold(sq.m)	住宅 Residential Buildings	#别墅、公寓 Villas, High-grade Apartments	办公楼 Office Buildings	商业营业用房 Houses for Business Use	其他 Others
全省	**Shaanxi**	**30936432**	**28366946**	**423870**	**474780**	**1374270**	**720436**
西安市	Xi'an	17077090	15259483	396271	458300	819227	540080
铜川市	Tongchuan	320586	314328			6258	
宝鸡市	Baoji	2631901	2571295		4301	50124	6181
咸阳市	Xianyang	2185832	2161631	12058	100	24101	
渭南市	Weinan	3252567	2828549		8500	305616	109902
#韩城市	Hancheng	389873	370308			19565	
延安市	Yan'an	584346	552756		3235	27824	531
汉中市	Hanzhong	1271553	1189220	3635		61453	20880
榆林市	Yulin	1067552	1018468		344	25634	23106
安康市	Ankang	1383916	1336073	11906		28087	19756
商洛市	Shangluo	756088	730142			25946	
杨凌示范区	Yangling	405001	405001				

6-33 续表 continued

地区	Region	商品房销售额(万元) Total Sale of Commercialized Buildings (10 000 yuan)	住宅 Residential Buildings	#别墅、公寓 Villas, High-grade Apartments	办公楼 Office Buildings	商业营业用房 Houses for Business Use	其他 Others
全省	**Shaanxi**	**15980360**	**13681219**	**422745**	**437401**	**1477739**	**384001**
西安市	Xi'an	11007099	9287428	406194	428372	1025376	265923
铜川市	Tongchuan	100077	96249			3828	
宝鸡市	Baoji	886903	849679		3129	31417	2678
咸阳市	Xianyang	924447	903903	10453	40	20504	
渭南市	Weinan	1203557	834899		3575	262265	102818
#韩城市	Hancheng	122461	116097			6364	
延安市	Yan'an	185406	162396		1890	20990	130
汉中市	Hanzhong	402996	352804	815		44925	5267
榆林市	Yulin	496918	463658		395	29931	2934
安康市	Ankang	454805	426548	5283		24006	4251
商洛市	Shangluo	205598	191101			14497	
杨凌示范区	Yangling	112554	112554				

6-34 房地产开发经营情况(2014年)
Operating Statistics on Enterprises for Real Estate Development(2014)

单位：万元 (10 000 yuan)

地区	Region	主营业务收入 Revenue from Principal Business	土地转让收入 Land Transferred	商品房屋销售收入 Commercialized Building Sold	房屋出租收入 House Leased	其它收入 Others	主营业务成本 Operating Costs of Main Business	主营业务税金及附加 Operating Tax and Extra Charge on Main Business
全省	**Shaanxi**	**13838977**	**16217**	**13326922**	**117291**	**378548**	**10093567**	**1171371**
西安市	Xi'an	10609512	9253	10169702	88848	341709	7460757	943001
铜川市	Tongchuan	61800		58755	244	2801	51605	5665
宝鸡市	Baoji	537919	10	526882	3496	7531	424298	39110
咸阳市	Xianyang	770968	20	759605	8293	3050	593467	60992
渭南市	Weinan	299814	30	298220	1191	374	232304	16781
# 韩城市	Hancheng	26693		26573		120	24514	709
延安市	Yan'an	156479	12	146955	7265	2246	123725	12189
汉中市	Hanzhong	383248	914	380772	1000	561	333321	31166
榆林市	Yulin	460278	4909	449824	2053	3492	426961	27548
安康市	Ankang	338254	1068	320364	4706	12117	273087	21410
商洛市	Shangluo	100168	2	97736	194	2236	80950	5519
杨凌示范区	Yangling	120538		118107		2431	93092	7991

6-35 房地产开发企业基本情况(2014年)
Basic Statistics on Real Estate Development Enterprises (2014)

地区	Region	开发公司个数(个) Number of Enterprises for Real Estate Development (unit)	实收资本金总计(万元) Total Capital Held (10 000 yuan)	资产总计(万元) Total Assets (10 000 yuan)	本年折旧(万元) Depreciation This Year (10 000 yuan)	负债合计(万元) Total Liabilities (10 000 yuan)	所有者权益合计(万元) Owners' Equity (10 000 yuan)	全部从业人员年平均人数(人) Average Number of Employed Persons (persons)	本年应付工资总额(万元) Total Wages This Year (10 000 yuan)
全省	**Shaanxi**	**1941**	**10095131**	**85493456**	**104184**	**70599378**	**14894079**	**81398**	**454821**
西安市	Xi'an	784	7216254	61563303	58587	51725577	9837726	45714	318449
铜川市	Tongchuan	66	133899	1102617	1568	900317	202300	1793	6637
宝鸡市	Baoji	187	497760	5377957	10755	3742494	1635463	4612	18514
咸阳市	Xianyang	151	375288	3635113	6700	3119540	515573	7369	33331
渭南市	Weinan	128	284407	2294277	3744	1900495	393782	5642	17760
# 韩城市	Hancheng	15	32506	329899	236	302698	27200	521	1444
延安市	Yan'an	82	339362	2174792	3691	1734213	440579	2751	8673
汉中市	Hanzhong	207	343273	2703829	4939	2249365	454464	4842	16156
榆林市	Yulin	151	379395	3031430	6502	2471830	559600	3510	13713
安康市	Ankang	116	338173	2369604	4988	1787982	581622	3359	11679
商洛市	Shangluo	48	102543	511480	1862	349626	161854	1174	5732
杨凌示范区	Yangling	21	84777	729055	849	617939	111116	626	4178

主要统计指标解释

全社会固定资产投资　是以货币形式表现的在一定时期内全社会建造和购置固定资产的工作量以及与此有关的费用的总称。该指标是反映固定资产投资规模、结构和发展速度的综合性指标,又是观察工程进度和考核投资效果的重要依据。全社会固定资产投资按登记注册类型可分为国有、集体、个体、联营、股份制、外商、港澳台商、其他等。

固定资产投资（不含农户）　指城镇和农村各种登记注册类型的企业、事业、行政单位及城镇个体户进行的计划总投资500万元及500万元以上的建设项目投资和房地产开发投资,包含原口径的城镇固定资产投资加上农村企事业组织项目投资，该口径自2011年起开始使用。

房地产开发投资　指各种登记注册类型的房地产开发法人单位统一开发的包括统代建、拆迁还建的住宅、厂房、仓库、饭店、宾馆、度假村、写字楼、办公楼等房屋建筑物和配套的服务设施，土地开发工程（如道路、给水、排水、供电、供热、通讯、平整场地等基础设施工程）的投资；不包括单纯的土地交易活动。

固定资产投资的资金来源　根据固定资产投资的资金来源不同，分为国家预算内资金、国内贷款、利用外资、自筹资金和其他资金。

(1)国家预算内资金：分为财政拨款和财政安排的贷款两部分。包括中央财政的基本建设基金(分经营性基金和非经营性基金两部分)、专项支出(如煤代油专项等)、收回再贷、贴息资金，财政安排的挖潜改造和新产品试制支出、城建支出、商业部门简易建筑支出、不发达地区发展基金等资金中用于固定资产投资的资金；地方财政中由国家统筹安排的资金等。

(2)国内贷款：指报告期固定资产投资单位向银行及非银行金融机构借入的用于固定资产投资的各种国内借款，包括银行利用自有资金及吸收的存款发放的贷款、上级主管部门拨入的国内贷款、国家专项贷款、地方财政专项资金安排的贷款、国内储备贷款、周转贷款等。

(3)利用外资：指报告期收到的用于固定资产建造和购置的国外资金(包括设备、材料、技术在内)。包括对外借款(外国政府、国际金融组织贷款、出口信贷、外国银行商业贷款、对外发行债券和股票)、外商直接投资及外商其他投资。不包括我国自有外汇资金(国家外汇、地方外汇、留成外汇、调剂外汇和中国银行自有资金发行的外汇贷款等)。计算利用外资时，需要折算成人民币，折算中所使用的外汇汇率按现汇计算，即按使用外汇时的汇率计算。

(4)自筹资金：指固定资产投资单位报告期收到的，由各地区、各部门及企、事业单位筹集用于固定资产投资的预算外资金，包括中央各部门、各级地方和企、事业单位的自筹资金。

(5)其他资金：指在报告期收到的除以上各种资金之外其他用于固定资产投资的资金，包括企业或金融机构通过发行各种债券筹集到的资金、群众集资、个人资金、无偿捐赠的资金及其他单位拨入的资金等。

固定资产投资按国民经济行业分　根据建设项目建成投产后的主要产品或主要用途及社会经济活动性质来确定国民经济行业。一般情况下，一个建设项目或一个企业、事业单位只能属于一种国民经济行业。

固定资产投资按隶属关系分　是按建设单位或企业、事业、行政单位的主管上级机关确定的。

（1）中央：是指中共中央、人大常委会和国务院各部、委、局、总公司以及直属机构直接领导的建设项目和企业、事业、行政单位。这些单位的固定资产投资计划由国务院各部门直接编制和下达，建设中所需物资、主要设备以及建设中的问题都由中央有关部门安排和解决。

（2）地方：是由省（自治区、直辖市）、地区（州、盟、省辖市）、县（旗、县级市）三级政府及业务主管部门直接领导和管理的建设项目、企业、事业、行政单位。地方项目还包括不隶属以上各级政府及主管部门的建设项目和企业、事业单位，如外商投资企业和无主管部门的企业等。

固定资产投资按建设性质分　根据整个建设项目情况来确定。建设项目的性质一般分为新建、扩建、改建和技术改造、迁建、恢复。房地产开发单位、农村投资、城镇工矿区私人建房投资不划分建设性质。

(1)新建：一般指从无到有开始建设的企业、事业和行政单位或建设项目。有的单位原有基础很小，经过建设后新增的固定资产价值超过该企、事业、行政单位原有固定资产价值(原值)三倍以上的也应作为新建。

(2)扩建：指在厂内或其他地点，为扩大原有产品的生产能力(或效益)或增加新的产品生产能力，而增建主要的生产车间(或主要工程)、分厂、独立的生产线。行政、事业单位在原单位增建业务用房(如学校增建教学用房、医院增建门诊部、病房等)也作为扩建。

现有企、事业单位为扩大原有主要产品生产能力或增加新的产品生产能力，增建一个或几个主要生产车间(或主要工程)、分厂，同时进行一些更新改造工程的，也应作为扩建。

(3)改建和技术改造：指现有企业、事业单位，对原有设施进行技术改造或更新(包括相应配套的辅助性生产、生活福利设施）的建设项目。现有企业、事业单位为适应市场变化的需要，而改变企业的主要产品种类(如军工企业转产民用品等）的建设项目，应作为改建。原有产品生产作业线由于各工序(车间)之间能力不平衡，为填平补齐充分发挥原有生产能力而增建不增加本企业主要产品设计能力的车间，也应作为改建。技术改造是指企业、事业单位在现有基础上，用先进的技术代替落后的技术，用先进的工艺和装备代替落后的工艺和装备，以改变企业落后的技术经济面貌，实现以内涵为主的扩大再生产，达到提高产品质量、促进产品更新换代、节约能源、降低消耗、扩大生产规模、全面提高社会经济效益的目的。技术改造具体包括以下内容：机器设备和工具的更新改造；生产工艺改革、节约能源和原材料的改造；厂房建筑和公共设施的改造；劳动条件和生产环境的改造等。

固定资产投资按构成分 固定资产投资活动按其工作内容和实现方式分为建筑安装工程，设备、工具、器具购置，其他费用三个部分。

(1)建筑安装工程(建筑安装工作量)：指各种房屋、建筑物的建造工程和各种设备、装置的安装工程。包括各种房屋建造工程；各种用途设备基础和各种工业窑炉的砌筑工程及金属结构工程；为施工而进行的各种准备工作和临时工程以及完工后的清理工作等；铁路、道路的铺设，矿井的开凿及石油管道的架设等；水利工程；防空地下建筑等特殊工程；列入房屋工程预算内的暖气、卫生、通风、照明、煤气等设备的价值及装设油饰工程；列入建筑工程预算内的各种管道(蒸汽、压缩空气、石油、给排水等管道)、电力、电讯电缆导线等的敷设工程；以及各种机械设备的安装工程；为测定安装工程质量，对设备进行的试运工作；房地产开发单位进行的商品房屋开发建设工程、土地开发工程。

在安装工程中，不包括被安装设备本身的价值。

(2)设备、工具、器具购置：指建设单位或企、事业单位购置或自制的，达到固定资产标准的设备、工具、器具的价值。新建单位及扩建单位的新建车间，按照设计或计划要求购置或自制的全部设备、工具、器具，不论是否达到固定资产标准均计入“设备、工具、器具购置”中。

(3)其他费用：指在固定资产建造和购置过程中发生的，除上述几项内容以外的各种应分摊计入固定资产的费用。

施工项目 指报告期内进行过建筑或安装施工活动的项目。凡是报告期内施过工的建设项目，不论施工时间长短，均作为施工项目统计。施工项目个数可以反映一定时期固定资产投资的实际规模，与同期全部建成投产项目个数相比，可以从建设速度的角度反映固定资产投资的效果。根据建设项目施工活动的不同性质，施工项目又分为：本年正式施工项目、本年收尾项目和以前年度全部停缓建项目。

全部建成投产项目 工业项目指设计文件规定形成生产能力的主体工程及其相应配套的辅助设施全部建成，经负荷试运转，证明具备生产设计规定合格产品的条件，并经过验收鉴定合格或达到竣工验收标准，与生产性工程配套的生活福利设施可以满足近期正常生产的需要，正式移交生产的建设项目。非工业项目指设计文件规定的主体工程和相应的配套工程全部建成，能够发挥设计规定的全部效益，经验收鉴定合格或达到竣工验收标准，正式移交使用的建设项目。

新增生产能力(或工程效益) 指通过固定资产投资活动而增加的设计能力(或工程效益)，该指标是以实物形态表现的反映固定资产投资成果的指标，也是考核投资经济效果的重要依据之一。

新增生产能力(或工程效益)一般有以下几种表现形式：

(1)用产品数量表示，以工程在单位时间内(一般是一年)所能生产的产品数量(即年产量)表示。如原煤开采用万吨／年表示，化学农药用吨／年表示，拖拉机制造用台／年表示等。某些化工产品由于含量差别较大，按其设计含量计算折合量表示，如硫酸、纯碱、烧碱等。

(2)用单位时间内所能处理的原料数量表示，以工程每天(或小时)所能处理原料的数量表示。如机制糖工程日处理原料吨，食用植物油日处理原料吨，城市污水处理能力用万吨／日表示等。

(3)用新增加的主要设备的数量或容量表示，如新增棉布织机、丝织机等台数，毛纺锭等锭数，发电厂新增发电机组容量用千瓦表示等。

(4)用建筑物容积、容量、面积、长度表示，是非工业项目或工程新增效益的一种表现形式。如铁路投产里程、新建公路、水库容量、粮食仓库、学校学生席位、医院病床、有效灌溉面积等。

根据工程的特点，有时需要用两种或两种以上的复合计量单位表示新增生产能力(或工程效益)，如新增内燃机生产能力同时用年产台数、千瓦数表示等。

为了规范新增生产能力(或工程效益)的名称和计算单位，国家统计局制订了《新增生产能力(或工程效益)目录及代码》。各固定资产投资单位在统计新增生产能力(或工程效益)时，必须按目录中规定的名称、计量单位和代码填报。

房屋建筑面积 指房屋建筑物勒脚以上外墙外围的水平截面面积，包括房屋建筑物的有效面积和结构面积。该指标是从实物形态上反映建设规模和建设成果的重要指标之一，也是检查工程形象进度、计算工程造价、分析投资效果、研究施工任务和建筑材料之间平衡情况的重要依据。

住宅建筑面积 指施工和竣工房屋建筑面积中供居住用的房屋建筑面积。

施工面积 指报告期内施工的全部房屋建筑面积。包括本期新开工的面积和上期开工跨入本期继续施工的房屋面积，以及上期已停建在本期恢复施工的房屋面积。本期竣工和本期施工后又停缓建的房屋，其建筑面积仍计入本期房屋施工面积中。

竣工面积 指在报告期内房屋建筑按照设计要求已经全部完工，达到住人和使用条件，经验收鉴定合格(或达到竣工验收标准)，正式移交使用单位的各栋房屋建筑面积的总和。

房屋建筑面积竣工率 指一定时期内房屋竣工面积占同期房屋施工面积的比率。

新增固定资产 指报告期内已经完成建造和购置过程，

并已交付生产或使用单位的固定资产价值。该指标是表示固定资产投资成果的价值指标，也是反映建设进度，计算固定资产投资效果的重要指标。

项目建成投产率 指一定时期内全部建成投产项目个数与同期施工项目个数的比率。该指标是从建设单位建设速度的角度反映投资效果的指标。

固定资产交付使用率 指一定时期新增固定资产与同期完成投资额的比率。该指标是反映固定资产动用速度，衡量建设过程中宏观投资效果的综合指标。由于新增固定资产是较长时期内形成的结果，而投资额则是当年完成的，因此，该指标一般适宜于反映较长时期内固定资产的动用情况。

商品房销售面积 指报告期内出售商品房屋的合同总面积(即双方签署的正式买卖合同中所确定的建筑面积)。由现房销售建筑面积和期房销售建筑面积两部分组成。

商品房销售额 指报告期内出售商品房屋的合同总价款(即双方签署的正式买卖合同中所确定的合同总价)。该指标与商品房销售面积同口径，由现房销售额和期房销售额两部分组成。

Explanatory Notes on Main Statistical Indicators

Total Investment in Fixed Assets in the Whole Country refers to the volume of activities in construction and purchases of fixed assets of the whole country and related fees, expressed in monetary terms during the reference period. It is a comprehensive indicator which shows the size, structure and growth of the investment in fixed assets, providing a basis for observing the progress of construction projects and evaluating results of investment. Total investment in fixed assets in the whole country includes, by type of ownership, the investment by State-owned units, collective-owned units, individuals, joint ownership units, share-holding units, as well as investments by entrepreneurs from foreign countries and from Hong Kong, Macao and Taiwan, and by other units.

Investment in Fixed Assets (Excluding Rural Households) refers to the investment in construction projects with a total planned investment of 5 million yuan and over by enterprises of various ownerships, institutions, administrative units and urban self-employed individuals, and the investment in real estate development in both urban and rural areas. Since 2011, it covers the urban investment in fixed assets under the previous statistical coverage plus project investments by rural enterprises and institutions.

Investment in Real Estate Development refers to investment by real estate development companies, commercialized buildings construction companies and other real estate development units of various types of ownership in the construction of buildings, such as residential buildings, factory buildings, warehouses, hotels, guesthouses, holiday villages, office buildings, the complementary service facilities and land development projects, such as roads, water supply, water drainage, power supply, heating supply, telecommunications, land leveling and other infrastructural projects. It does not include activities in pure land transactions.

Sources of Funds for Investment in Fixed Assets are categorized as funds from the State budget, domestic loans, foreign investment, self-raised funds, and others, depending on the sources of investment.

(1) Fund from the State budget consists of budgetary appropriation and loans from the State budget. More specifically, it includes, from the budget of the central government, capital construction fund (operation fund and non-operational fund), special expenses (e.g. expenses on substituting petroleum with coal), loans from repayment, discount fund, expenses on innovation and trial production of new products, expenses on urban construction, expenses on temporary construction from business departments, development fund for less developed areas, as well as local budgetary fund transferred from the central budget.

(2) Domestic loans refer to loans of various forms borrowed by investing units from banks and non-bank financial institutions during the reference period for the purpose of investment in fixed assets, including loans issued by banks from their self-owned funds and deposit, loans appropriated by higher authorities, special loans by government, loans arranged by local government from special funds, domestic reserve loan, and working loan.

(3) Foreign investment refers to foreign funds received during the reference period for the construction and purchase of investment in fixed assets (covering equipment, materials and technology), including foreign borrowings (loans from foreign governments and international financial institutions, export credit, commercial loans from foreign banks, issue of bonds and stocks overseas), foreign direct investment and other foreign investments. Excluded from this category is capital in foreign exchanges owned by China (foreign exchanges owned by the central and local governments, foreign exchanges retained by enterprises, foreign exchanges by enterprises through the regulating mechanism, loans in foreign exchanges issued by the Bank of China with its own fund, etc.). In calculating the utilization of foreign capital, foreign currencies are converted into Chinese Renminbi applying the current exchange rate when the foreign capitals are actually used.

(4) Self-raised funds refer to extra-budgetary funds for investment in fixed assets received during the reference period by investing units from central government ministries, local governments, enterprises and institutions, including their self-raised funds.

(5) Others refer to funds for investment in fixed assets received from sources other than those listed above, including capital raised through issuing bonds by enterprises or financial institutions, funds raised from individuals and through donations, and funds transferred from other units.

Investment in Fixed Assets by Sector The classification of construction projects by sector is determined by the major products or the purpose of the projects when they are put into production or use, and by the nature of their social economic activities. In general, one project or one enterprise or institution can only be classified into one sector.

Investment in Fixed Assets by Jurisdiction of Management refers to the classification of investment by the competent authorities under which investment is made by construction units, enterprises, institutions or administrative units.

(1) Central investment refers to the investment in projects or by enterprises, institutions or administrative units which are under the direct leadership and management of the State Council and of the national commissions, ministries, agencies and State-owned large corporations. Various ministries and departments of the State Council prepare and implement plans for investment in fixed assets by those departments, and

arrange and ensure the supply of materials and key equipment required for the projects.

(2) Local investment refers to the investment in projects or by enterprises, institutions or administrative units which are under the direct leadership and management of departments under the provincial, prefecture and county governments. Also included are projects by foreign-invested enterprises and enterprises without competent managing authorities.

Investment in Fixed Assets by Type of Construction Construction projects in general can be classified, by the type of construction, into new construction, expansion, reconstruction and technical transformation, moving and restoration. However, investment by type of construction is not applied to investment by real-estate development units, investment in rural areas and private investment in housing construction in urban areas and in industrial and mining areas.

(1) New construction in general refers to construction projects, which start from scratch, of enterprises, institutions, administrative agencies. In case the size of the existing unit is quite small, and the value of newly added fixed assets is more than three times of the original value, the expansion will be considered as new construction.

(2) Expansion refers to construction of new major production workshop, branch factory or independent production line within a factory or in other locations, for the purpose of increasing the production capacity (or improving efficiency) or adding new production capacity. Newly constructed accommodation for the operation of institutions and administrative organizations (such as newly constructed buildings for teaching in schools, buildings for clinics or wards in hospitals, etc.) are also classified as expansion.

Also included in expansion are investments by existing enterprises or institutions in building major production line(s) or branch factory(ies) along with some work on innovation, for the purpose of expanding the production capacity of original products or producing new products.

(3) Reconstruction and technical transformation refers to construction projects by existing enterprises or institutions in innovation or technical transformation of the old facilities (including auxiliary production equipment and welfare facilities). Also considered as reconstruction is the construction of new workshops by the existing enterprises or institutions to change the variety of products to meet the market demand (such as the production of civil products by defence industries), or to bring the designed production capacity into full play through a more balanced production process on production lines. Technical transformation refers to replacement of old technology or equipment by new technology or equipment, in order to expand the reproduction through improvement of technology contents in production, to improve product quality, to promote new products, to save energy, to reduce consumption, to expand the production scale and to improve overall social-economic efficiency. Contents of technical transformation include: updating of machinery, equipment and tools; reforming production process by using energy or materials saving technology; construction of factory workshops and transformation of public facilities; improvement of working conditions and environment, etc.

Investment in Fixed Assets by Structure By their contents and the mode of implementation, investment activities are classified into 3 categories, i.e. construction and installation, purchase of equipment and instrument, and other expenses.

(1) Construction and installation (work volume of construction and installation) refers to the construction of houses and buildings and the installation of various kinds of equipment and instruments. They include construction of houses; equipment foundations, industrial kilns and stoves, and metal structure work; preparation works and temporary works for project construction, and clearing up works post project construction; pavement of railways and roads, drilling of mines and putting up of oil pipes; construction of water conservancy; construction of underground air-raid shelters and construction of other special projects; value of equipment for heating, sanitation, ventilation, lighting, gas, painting, etc. that are covered by the budget of housing projects; laying out of various pipelines (for steam, compressed air, petroleum, tap water and sewage) and wiring and cabling for electric power and for communications; installation of various machinery and equipment; testing operation for pre-testing the quality of installation projects, and land and other development work conducted by real estate developers for commercialized housing. The value of equipment installed is itself not included in the value of installation projects.

(2) Purchase of equipment and instruments refers to the total value of equipment, tools, and instruments purchased or self-produced which come up to the cut-off point for fixed assets by the construction units or investing enterprises or institutions. Equipment, tools and instruments purchased or self-produced for new workshops by newly established or expanded units are categorized as "purchase of equipment and instruments" no matter whether they come up to the cut-off point for fixed assets.

(3) Other expenses refer to expenses arising during the construction or purchase of fixed assets other than those mentioned above.

Projects under Construction refer to projects with construction and installation activities undertaken in the reference period. All projects that have construction activities undertaken during the reference period are reported as projects under construction irrespective of the length of construction work. The number of projects under construction can reflect the actual size of investment in fixed assets during a given period, and when compared with the number of projects completed and put into use during the same period, it demonstrates the results of investment in fixed assets from the angle of the speed of the construction. Depending on the nature of construction activities, projects under construction can also be classified into projects beginning construction in current year, winding-up projects in current year and stopped or suspended projects in previous years (with resumption of work in current year).

Projects Completed and Put into Use Industrial projects refer to the major projects and anxilliary facilities having been completed in accordance with the design documents, resulting in forming production capacity and having checked and accepted after relevant tests, while the living and welfare facilities having been completed and being capable of ensuring normal production. Non-industrial projects refer to the major projects and anxilliary facilities which have been completed in accordance with the design documents; have been checked, accepted after relevant examination; and have been formally delivered for use.

Newly Increased Production Capacity (or Project Efficiency) refers to the increase in design capacity (or project efficiency) through investment in fixed assets, which reflects the accomplishment of investment in fixed assets in physical form and serves as an important basis for evaluating the economic efficiency of investment.

The newly increased production capacity (project efficiency) are usually expressed in one of the following forms:

(1) Volume of output of products, i.e. the volume of output that the project can produce during a given period (usually a year). For instance, the capacity in coal mining is expressed in 10,000 tons/year, the capacity in producing chemical pesticides expressed in ton/year, the capacity in producing tractors in tractor/year, etc. For some chemical products where the effective contents differ significantly, the production capacity is expressed as the designed effective content equivalent, such as in the case of sulphuric acid, soda ash, caustic soda, etc;

(2) Volume of raw materials processed per unit of time, i.e. the volume of raw materials that could be processed by the project per day (or per hour), such as tons of materials processed per day by a sugar refining project or edible vegetable oil project, or tons of urban sewage processed per day;

(3) Number or capacity of major equipment increased, such as number of cotton or silk looms increased, wool spindles increased, or capacity (in kilowatts) of power generators increased; and

(4) Physical measures (volume, capacity, area, and length) of construction, which is typical for non-industrial projects, for instance, the length of railways put into operation, the length of highways, the capacity of reservoirs, the capacity of warehouses, the floor space of housing projects, capacity for new students in schools or beds in hospitals, areas under new irrigation project, etc.

The special features of projects may sometimes call for the combined use of two or more measurements to reflect the increase in production capacity (or project efficiency); for instance, the new capacity for the production of internal combustion engines is expressed in sets per year and kilowatts per year simultaneously.

To standardize the nomenclature and unit of measurement for newly increased production capacity (or project efficiency), the National Bureau of Statistics has developed the *Nomenclature and Codes for New Production Capacity (Project Efficiency)*. All reporting units with investment activities are required to follow these two nomenclatures in reporting statistics on new production capacity (project efficiency).

Floor Space of Buildings under Construction refers to the total floor space of the horizontal section of outer walls above the plinth of the building, including the effective area and the area occupied by the structure. This indicator is one of the important indicators in physical terms to reflect the scale and accomplishment of the construction industry and also an important basis for monitoring the progress, calculating the cost, analyzing the efficiency and studying the supply of building materials in relation to the construction projects.

Floor Space of Residential Buildings refers to the floor space of the residential buildings among the total space of buildings under construction or completed.

Floor Space under Construction refers to total floor space of all buildings under construction during the reference period, including floor space of newly started buildings during the reference period, floor space of construction extended from the previous period to the current period, and floor space of construction suspended during the previous period and resumed in the current period. Floor space of construction completed in the current period, and floor space of construction started and then suspended in the current period are also included in the floor space under construction of the current year.

Floor Space Completed refers to the floor space of all buildings completed in the reference period, which have been appraised and accepted (or come up to the designed standards) and have been transferred to owner units.

Completion Rate of Floor Space of Buildings refers to the ratio of the floor space of buildings completed in a certain period of time to the floor space of buildings under construction in the same period.

Newly Increased Fixed Assets refer to the newly increased value of fixed assets, constructed or purchased, that have been transferred to the investors. This is an indicator that demonstrates the results of investment in fixed assets in monetary terms, and an important indicator to reflect the speed of construction and to calculate the efficiency of investment.

Rate of Construction Projects Completed and Put into Use refers to the ratio of the number of construction projects completed and put into use in a certain period of time to the number of projects under construction in the same period. This reflects the investment efficiency from the perspective of the speed of projects construction.

Rate of Projects of Fixed Assets Completed and Put into Operation refers to the ratio of the newly increased fixed assets to the total investment made in the same period. This is a comprehensive indicator reflecting the speed of the employment of fixed assets and the investment efficiency at the macro-level. As the newly increase fixed assets is the result of a long period while the investment is completed in the current year, this indicator is expected to be used to reflect the employment of fixed assets over a long period of time.

Area of Commercialized Housing Sold refers to total contracted area of commercialized housing (i.e. area of floor space as designated in the formal contracts signed by both sides) during the reference time. It constitutes floor space of completed housing and floor space of future housing.

Value of Commercialized Housing Sold refers to the total contracted value (i.e. value of sales/purchase for selling/purchase of commercialized housing as designated in the contract signed by both sides) during the reference time. This indicator has the same coverage as the area of commercialized housing sold, which constitutes floor space of completed housing and floor space of housing yet to be completed.

七、能　源

资料整理：蔡军辉

简 要 说 明

一、本篇资料反映陕西能源生产、消费和能耗水平等情况。主要内容有能源生产、消费及品种构成，能源生产和消费弹性系数，分行业、分主要能源品种的消费量，能源加工转换效率及生活用能源消费量、单位生产总值能耗等指标。

二、关于数据口径与计算的说明：

1. 能源生产与消费弹性系数分别以能源生产、消费增长速度与地区生产总值增长速度相比求得。

2. 能源平衡表中，进口量和出口量采用海关统计数据，电力折算标准煤系数按平均发电煤耗计算。

3. 能源加工转换效率表中的电力折算标准煤系数采用当量值计算，每千瓦小时折0.1229千克标准煤。

4. GDP和工业增加值按不变价格计算。

Brief Introduction

Ⅰ. This chapter reflects the energy production, consumption and efficiency of Shaanxi Province, mainly including energy production, consumption and composition, elasticity ratio of energy production and consumption, consumption of energy by sector and by types of energy, efficiency of energy processing and conversion and the consumption of energy for non-production uses, energy consumption of unit gross domestic product.

Ⅱ. Data coverage and calculation:

1. The elasticity ratio of energy production is calculated as the quotient of the growth rate of energy production divided by the growth rate of GDP; and the elasticity ratio of energy consumption is calculated as the quotient of the growth rate of energy consumption divided by the growth rate of GDP.

2. In the energy balance sheet, the data on the imports and exports are data from the customs statistics. The ratio for converting electric power into the standard coal equivalent is calculated according to the average consumption of coal for generating electricity.

3. In the table on the efficiency of energy conversion, the ratio for converting electric power into the standard coal equivalent is calculated on the basis of heat value equivalent. One kilowatt is equal to 0.1229 kg SCE.

4. Gross domestic product and industrial value-added are calculated at constant price.

7.能　源

2014 年全省			
能源生产总量	46981.85	万吨标准煤（等价值）	比上年增长 5.7%
能源消费总量	11222.46	万吨标准煤（等价值）	比上年增长 5.8%
平均每天消费能源	30.75	万吨标准煤	
# 原　煤	60.70	万　吨	
原　油	6.16	万　吨	
天然气	2006	万立方米	
电　力	33589	万千瓦小时	

能源消费总量构成

（2014年）

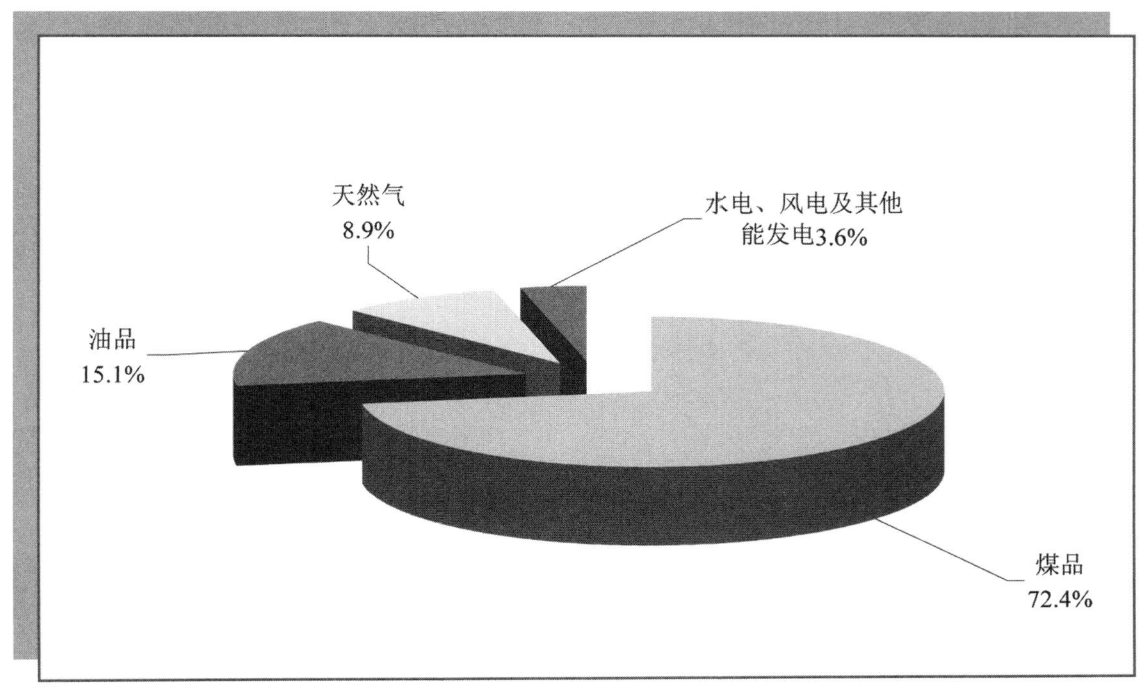

7-1 能源生产、消费总量及构成
Total Production and Consumption of Energy and Its Composition

指　标	Item	2010 当量值 Equivalent Weight	2010 等价值 Equivalent Value	2011 当量值 Equivalent Weight	2011 等价值 Equivalent Value	2012 当量值 Equivalent Weight	2012 等价值 Equivalent Value
能源生产总量 （万吨标准煤）	**Total Energy Production (10 000 tons of SCE)**	**31673.56**	**31845.63**	**36328.31**	**36500.59**	**40995.50**	**41168.40**
原　煤	Coal	24370.38	24370.38	27991.63	27991.63	31847.45	31847.45
原　油	Crude Oil	4310.49	4310.49	4607.83	4607.83	5039.48	5039.48
天然气	Natural Gas	2885.46	2885.46	3620.42	3620.42	3998.94	3998.94
水电、风电及其他能发电	Hydro-power,Wind Power and Others	107.23	279.30	108.43	280.71	109.63	282.53
能源生产构成 （%）	**Energy Production Composition (%)**	**100.00**	**100.00**	**100.00**	**100.00**	**100.00**	**100.00**
原　煤	Coal	76.94	76.53	77.46	77.10	77.69	77.36
原　油	Crude Oil	13.61	13.54	12.46	12.40	12.29	12.24
天然气	Natural Gas	9.11	9.06	9.79	9.74	9.75	9.71
水电、风电及其他能发电	Hydro-power,Wind Power and Others	0.34	0.88	0.29	0.76	0.27	0.69
能源消费总量 （万吨标准煤）	**Total Energy Consumption (10 000 tons of SCE)**	**8643.63**	**8287.63**	**9475.12**	**9107.48**	**10301.84**	**9914.53**
煤　品	Coal	6373.02	5844.95	7102.52	6562.60	7816.19	7255.99
油　品	Crude Oil	1421.13	1421.13	1444.03	1444.03	1571.34	1571.34
天然气	Natural Gas	742.26	742.26	820.15	820.15	804.67	804.67
水电、风电及其他能发电	Hydro-power,Wind Power and Others	107.23	279.30	108.43	280.71	109.63	282.53
能源消费构成 （%）	**Energy Consumption Composition (%)**	**100.00**	**100.00**	**100.00**	**100.00**	**100.00**	**100.00**
煤　品	Coal	73.73	70.53	74.96	72.06	75.87	73.19
油　品	Crude Oil	16.44	17.15	15.24	15.86	15.25	15.85
天然气	Natural Gas	8.59	8.96	8.66	9.01	7.81	8.12
水电、风电及其他能发电	Hydro-power,Wind Power and Others	1.24	3.37	1.14	3.08	1.06	2.85

注：1.当量值指电力按自身的热功当量换算成标准煤，等价值指电力按当年平均火力发电煤耗换算成标准煤。
2.2010-2013年数据根据第三次经济普查结果进行了调整。

a) The equivalent weight refers to the value that electric power converts to standard coal by its heat equivalent, equivalent value refers to the value of average standard coal consumption by thermal power in the current year.

b) Adjustment has been done for the data of 2010-2013, due to the 3rd Economic Census.

7-1　续表　continued

指　标	Item	2013 当量值 Equivalent Weight	2013 等价值 Equivalent Value	2014 当量值 Equivalent Weight	2014 等价值 Equivalent Value
能源生产总量（万吨标准煤）	**Total Energy Production (10 000 tons of SCE)**	**44200.01**	**44431.03**	**46733.83**	**46981.85**
原　煤	Coal	33997.02	33997.02	35736.98	35736.98
原　油	Crude Oil	5268.73	5268.73	5382.69	5382.69
天然气	Natural Gas	4786.41	4786.41	5454.46	5454.46
水电、风电及其他能发电	Hydro-power, Wind Power and Others	147.85	378.87	159.70	407.72
能源生产构成　(%)	**Energy Production Composition (%)**	**100.00**	**100.00**	**100.00**	**100.00**
原　煤	Coal	76.92	76.52	76.47	76.07
原　油	Crude Oil	11.92	11.86	11.52	11.46
天然气	Natural Gas	10.83	10.77	11.67	11.61
水电、风电及其他能发电	Hydro-power, Wind Power and Others	0.33	0.85	0.34	0.87
能源消费总量（万吨标准煤）	**Total Energy Consumption (10 000 tons of SCE)**	**11070.39**	**10610.48**	**11728.08**	**11222.46**
煤　品	Coal	8362.78	7671.85	8879.56	8125.91
油　品	Crude Oil	1652.66	1652.66	1690.24	1690.24
天然气	Natural Gas	907.10	907.10	998.58	998.58
水电、风电及其他能发电	Hydro-power, Wind Power and Others	147.85	378.87	159.70	407.72
能源消费构成　(%)	**Energy Consumption Composition (%)**	**100.00**	**100.00**	**100.00**	**100.00**
煤　品	Coal	75.54	72.30	75.71	72.41
油　品	Crude Oil	14.93	15.58	14.41	15.06
天然气	Natural Gas	8.19	8.55	8.51	8.90
水电、风电及其他能发电	Hydro-power, Wind Power and Others	1.34	3.57	1.36	3.63

7-2　主要能源平衡情况(2014年)
Main Energy Balance Sheet(2014)

指　标	Item	综合能源(万吨标准煤) Comprehensive Energy (10 000 tons of SCE)	原　煤(万吨) Coal (10 000 tons)	天然气(亿立方米) Natural Gas (100 million cu.m)	电　力(亿千瓦小时) Electricity (100 million kwh)	原　油(万吨) Crude Oil (10 000 tons)
一、可供本地区消费能源	**Volume of total Energy Available for Consumption**	**11229.03**	**22166.29**	**93.64**	**-264.89**	**2249.60**
年初库存	Stock at the Beginning of the Year	1058.58	881.15	0.25		82.25
一次能源生产量	Primary Energy Output	46981.85	52225.61	410.11	129.94	3767.81
外省(区、市)调入量	Inflow from Other Provinces (Regions, Cities)	1169.59	674.52			89.64
本省(区、市)调出量(-)	Outflow from this Provinces (Regions, Cities)	-36855.53	-30670.37	-316.47	-394.83	-1594.27
出口量(-)	Exports	-70.79	-104.04			
年末库存(-)	Stock at Year-end	-1054.68	-840.58	-0.25		-95.83
二、加工转换投入(-)产出(+)量	**Input (−) or Output (+) of Processing and Transformation**	**-890.99**	**-18392.22**	**-21.11**	**1490.90**	**-2095.79**
火力发电	Thermal Power	0.00	-4858.59	-0.59	1490.90	
供　热	Heating	-83.25	-456.68	-0.36		
煤炭洗选	Separation Coal	-312.54	-8347.58			
炼　焦	Coke Making	-469.87	-4728.06			
炼油及煤制油	Oil Refining and Coal to Make Oil	-155.56				-2095.79
天然气液化	Natural Gas Liquefaction	-24.13		-20.16		
煤制品加工	Processing of Coal Products	-0.07	-1.30			
回收能	Recovery of Energy	215.29				
三、损失量	**Loss Volume**					
四、终端消费	**Final Consumption**	**10331.46**	**3763.32**	**72.54**	**1226.01**	**153.81**
第一产业	Primary Industry	213.27	23.92		38.60	
农、林、牧、渔业	Agriculture, Forestry, Animal Husbandry and Fishery	213.27	23.92		38.60	
第二产业	Secondary Industry	7028.37	2960.63	46.76	823.99	153.81
工　业	Industry	6804.09	2941.56	46.76	794.81	153.81
建筑业	Construction	224.28	19.07		29.18	
第三产业	Tertiary Industry	1753.61	315.16	10.19	185.82	
交通运输、仓储和邮政业	Transportation, Storage and Post Services	928.17	28.58	2.61	53.14	
批发、零售业和住宿、餐饮业	Wholesale and Retail Trades, Hotels and Catering Services	393.07	92.23	7.16	50.55	
其　他	Others	432.37	194.35	0.42	82.14	
生活消费	Household Consumption	1336.21	463.61	15.58	177.60	
城　镇	Urban Areas	898.05	204.22	15.08	107.18	
乡　村	Rural Area	438.16	259.39	0.50	70.42	

注：综合能源消费电力按等价值折算。

a) Comprehensive energy consumption Electric power and heat are converted on the basis of equal value.

7-2 续表 continued

指 标	Item	汽 油 (万吨) Gasoline (10 000 tons)	煤 油 (万吨) Kerosene (10 000 tons)	柴 油 (万吨) Diesel Oil (10 000 tons)	燃料油 (万吨) Fuel Oil (10 000 tons)
一、可供本地区消费能源	**Volume of total Energy Available for Consumption**	**-536.25**	**0.98**	**-356.32**	**-1.15**
年初库存	Stock at the Beginning of the Year	40.26	3.25	62.01	0.71
一次能源生产量	Primary Energy Output				
外省(区、市)调入量	Inflow from Other Provinces (Regions, Cities)	94.65	42.73	247.27	1.36
本省(区、市)调出量(-)	Outflow from this Provinces (Regions, Cities)	-622.53	-43.13	-610.18	-2.23
出口量(-)	Exports				
年末库存(-)	Stock at Year-end	-48.63	-1.87	-55.42	-0.99
二、加工转换投入(-)产出(+)量	**Input (-) or Output (+) of Processing and Transformation**	**766.18**	**35.28**	**895.30**	**13.45**
火力发电	Thermal Power			-0.43	
供 热	Heating			-0.02	
煤炭洗选	Separation Coal				
炼 焦	Coke Making				
炼油及煤制油	Oil Refining and Coal to Make Oil	766.18	35.28	895.75	18.68
天然气液化	Natural Gas Liquefaction				
煤制品加工	Processing of Coal Products				
回收能	Recovery of Energy				
三、损失量	**Loss Volume**				
四、终端消费	**Final Consumption**	**229.92**	**36.26**	**538.98**	**12.30**
第一产业	Primary Industry	7.97		45.16	
农、林、牧、渔业	Agriculture, Forestry, Animal Husbandry and Fishery	7.97		45.16	
第二产业	Secondary Industry	36.12	3.03	122.20	1.19
工 业	Industry	25.83	3.03	72.11	0.16
建筑业	Construction	10.29		50.09	1.02
第三产业	Tertiary Industry	114.88	33.23	365.81	11.12
交通运输、仓储和邮政业	Transportation, Storage and Post Services	91.86	33.23	327.36	10.09
批发、零售业和住宿、餐饮业	Wholesale and Retail Trades, Hotels and Catering Services	16.36		26.12	1.03
其 他	Others	6.66		12.34	
生活消费	Household Consumption	70.95		5.80	
城 镇	Urban Areas	57.53		0.46	
乡 村	Rural Area	13.42		5.34	

注：综合能源消费电力按等价值折算。

a) Comprehensive energy consumption Electric power and heat are converted on the basis of equal value.

7-3 能源生产弹性系数
Elasticity Ratio of Energy Production

指　　标	Item	2010	2011	2012	2013	2014
能源生产增长速度(%)	Growth Rate of Energy Production over Preceding Year (%)	16.7	14.6	12.8	7.9	5.7
电力生产增长速度(%)	Growth Rate of Electricity Production over Preceding Year (%)	23.4	11.7	7.0	10.8	7.2
生产总值增长速度(%)	Rate of Gross Domestic Product (GDP) over Preceding Year (%)	14.6	13.9	12.9	11.0	9.7
能源生产弹性系数	Elasticity Ratio of Energy Production	1.15	1.05	0.99	0.73	0.59
电力生产弹性系数	Elasticity Ratio of Electricity Production	1.62	0.84	0.54	0.98	0.74

注：1.生产总值增长速度按不变价计算，能源生产用等价值折算。
2.2010-2013年数据根据第三次经济普查结果进行了调整。

a) The growth rates of GDP are calculated at constant prices. Energy production are converted on the basis of equal value.

b) Adjustment has been done for the data of 2010-2013, due to the 3rd Economic Census.

7-4 平均每万人能源生产量
Energy Production Per 10 000 Population

品　种	Item	2010	2011	2012	2013	2014
生产总量(吨标准煤)	**Total Production (ton of SCE)**	**85257.56**	**97527.36**	**109692.02**	**118051.47**	**124451.29**
原　煤(吨)	Coal(ton)	96819.15	109910.44	124610.17	133707.19	138341.59
原　油(吨)	Crude Oil(ton)	8077.92	8618.12	9399.09	9798.97	9980.64
天然气(万立方米)	Natural Gas(10 000 cu. m)	598.28	727.33	825.63	987.46	1086.35
电　力(万千瓦小时)	Electricity(10 000 kwh)	3017.17	3363.89	3589.91	4017.34	4293.48

注：能源生产总量用等价值折算，2010-2013年数据根据第三次经济普查结果进行了调整。

a) Total energy production are converted on the basis of equal value.
Adjustment has been done for the data of 2010-2013,due to the 3rd Economic Census.

7-5 能源加工转换效率
Efficiency of Energy Conversion

指　　标	Item	2010	2011	2012	2013	2014
总效率(%)	**Total Efficiency (%)**	**71.77**	**75.47**	**77.77**	**79.13**	**79.33**
火力发电	Thermal Power	38.41	38.63	38.80	38.78	39.17
供　　热	Heating	78.12	76.71	75.39	76.28	76.87
洗　　煤	Separation Coal	90.64	95.37	95.35	95.28	94.53
炼　　焦	Coke Making	82.98	86.69	89.16	89.12	90.07
炼　　油	Oil Refining	93.81	95.55	95.23	95.09	94.88

7-6 单位GDP能耗
Energy Consumption Per Unit of GDP by City (District)

单位：吨标准煤/万元 (ton of SCE/10 000 yuan)

地 区	Region	GDP按2005年价格计算 GDP are calculated at 2005 constant prices						GDP按2010年价格计算 GDP are calculated at 2010 constant prices				
		2005	2006	2007	2008	2009	2010	2010	2011	2012	2013	2014
全 省	**Shaanxi**	**1.416**	**1.368**	**1.306**	**1.228**	**1.172**	**1.129**	**0.818**	**0.789**	**0.761**	**0.734**	**0.708**
西安市	Xi'an	1.030	0.987	0.930	0.869	0.820	0.803	0.575	0.555	0.535	0.516	0.486
铜川市	Tongchuan	2.160	2.123	2.017	1.917	1.798	1.720	1.666	1.606	1.548	1.466	1.369
宝鸡市	Baoji	1.460	1.399	1.328	1.249	1.186	1.162	0.734	0.708	0.682	0.658	0.631
咸阳市	Xianyang	1.380	1.330	1.264	1.201	1.143	1.102	0.740	0.714	0.689	0.665	0.642
渭南市	Weinan	3.510	3.429	3.263	3.085	2.946	2.807	1.593	1.535	1.480	1.424	1.362
延安市	Yan'an	0.980	0.952	0.907	0.865	0.826	0.782	0.691	0.667	0.644	0.621	0.600
汉中市	Hanzhong	1.800	1.739	1.655	1.563	1.494	1.440	1.099	1.059	1.022	0.986	0.946
榆林市	Yulin	2.510	2.426	2.343	2.195	2.072	2.000	1.020	0.983	0.948	0.912	0.877
安康市	Ankang	1.380	1.340	1.276	1.198	1.148	1.103	0.701	0.677	0.652	0.631	0.602
商洛市	Shangluo	1.080	1.066	1.024	0.975	0.926	0.896	0.596	0.575	0.555	0.537	0.520
杨凌示范区	Yangling	0.710	0.695	0.670	0.628	0.597	0.582	0.406	0.393	0.383	0.373	0.359

7-6 续表 continued

地 区	Region	比上年增长(%) Growth Rates over Preceding Year(%)								
		2006	2007	2008	2009	2010	2011	2012	2013	2014
全 省	**Shaanxi**	**-3.41**	**-4.55**	**-5.94**	**-4.56**	**-3.64**	**-3.56**	**-3.54**	**-3.55**	**-3.58**
西安市	Xi'an	-4.15	-5.75	-6.65	-5.56	-2.02	-3.56	-3.51	-3.57	-5.89
铜川市	Tongchuan	-1.70	-5.01	-4.95	-6.21	-4.31	-3.62	-3.62	-5.31	-6.62
宝鸡市	Baoji	-4.20	-5.05	-5.96	-5.06	-2.01	-3.53	-3.64	-3.53	-4.10
咸阳市	Xianyang	-3.63	-4.97	-4.97	-4.81	-3.59	-3.61	-3.50	-3.50	-3.35
渭南市	Weinan	-2.30	-4.85	-5.44	-4.51	-4.72	-3.60	-3.61	-3.81	-4.33
延安市	Yan'an	-2.85	-4.78	-4.56	-4.54	-5.38	-3.50	-3.50	-3.50	-3.40
汉中市	Hanzhong	-3.40	-4.80	-5.60	-4.38	-3.63	-3.61	-3.56	-3.51	-4.05
榆林市	Yulin	-3.35	-3.42	-6.30	-5.60	-3.46	-3.60	-3.60	-3.80	-3.80
安康市	Ankang	-2.90	-4.75	-6.15	-4.20	-3.89	-3.50	-3.63	-3.33	-4.50
商洛市	Shangluo	-1.30	-3.96	-4.78	-5.01	-3.20	-3.51	-3.38	-3.32	-3.08
杨凌示范区	Yangling	-2.10	-3.65	-6.22	-5.00	-2.48	-3.20	-2.62	-2.60	-3.68

注：能源消耗按等价值计算，2010-2013年数据根据第三次经济普查结果进行了调整。

a) The energy consumption are converted on the basis of equal value.
Adjustment has been done for the data of 2010-2013, due to the 3rd Economic Census.

7-7 单位工业增加值能耗
Energy Consumption Per Unit of Value Added of Industry

单位：吨标准煤/万元 (ton of SCE/10 000 yuan)

地 区	Region	工业增加值按2005年价格计算 VAI are calculated at 2005 constant prices						工业增加值按2010年价格计算 VAI are calculated at 2010 constant prices				
		2005	2006	2007	2008	2009	2010	2010	2011	2012	2013	2014
全 省	**Shaanxi**	**2.620**	**2.460**	**2.270**	**2.009**	**1.892**	**1.770**	**1.323**	**1.249**	**1.178**	**1.110**	**1.052**
西安市	Xi'an	1.220	1.100	1.092	0.915	0.800	0.703	0.593	0.502	0.449	0.369	0.313
铜川市	Tongchuan	4.100	4.150	3.455	4.739	4.142	3.955	2.893	2.623	2.330	2.114	1.681
宝鸡市	Baoji	3.010	2.840	2.101	1.712	1.434	1.374	1.115	1.090	0.893	0.810	0.696
咸阳市	Xianyang	3.090	2.730	2.505	2.158	1.896	1.933	1.329	1.273	1.219	1.066	0.930
渭南市	Weinan	7.760	8.040	7.153	5.742	4.801	4.116	3.898	3.392	3.082	2.762	2.472
延安市	Yan'an	0.640	0.560	0.746	0.737	0.611	0.567	0.561	0.519	0.503	0.496	0.474
汉中市	Hanzhong	4.720	4.210	3.490	2.803	2.563	2.388	2.369	2.009	1.791	1.609	1.468
榆林市	Yulin	3.650	3.800	2.987	2.805	2.464	2.312	1.432	1.421	1.353	1.365	1.473
安康市	Ankang	2.080	1.840	1.583	1.259	1.079	0.952	0.895	0.825	0.642	0.546	0.462
商洛市	Shangluo	2.050	2.410	2.400	2.071	2.015	1.729	0.898	0.799	0.717	0.616	0.609
杨凌示范区	Yangling	1.590	1.620	1.204	0.352	0.277	0.304	0.159	0.130	0.128	0.111	0.108

7-7 续表 continued

地 区	Region	比上年增长(%) Growth Rates over Preceding Year(%)								
		2006	2007	2008	2009	2010	2011	2012	2013	2014
全 省	**Shaanxi**	**-7.09**	**-7.81**	**-11.48**	**-5.82**	**-6.83**	**-5.60**	**-5.65**	**-5.83**	**-5.18**
西安市	Xi'an	-3.04	-12.56	-13.43	-10.48	-12.18	-15.44	-10.56	-17.69	-15.21
铜川市	Tongchuan	-1.09	-8.02	0.70	-15.46	-4.51	-9.33	-11.18	-9.26	-20.47
宝鸡市	Baoji	-11.41	-13.27	-14.07	-22.44	-4.18	-2.30	-18.07	-9.27	-14.13
咸阳市	Xianyang	-11.37	-10.85	-14.06	-11.46	1.92	-4.24	-4.26	-12.51	-12.83
渭南市	Weinan	-2.09	-10.51	-18.84	-3.41	-14.26	-12.98	-9.12	-10.39	-10.50
延安市	Yan'an	-2.61	-8.60	-3.28	-2.71	-7.22	-7.51	-3.01	-1.32	-4.61
汉中市	Hanzhong	-7.34	-11.32	-19.55	-6.57	-6.82	-15.21	-10.86	-10.13	-8.76
榆林市	Yulin	-10.22	1.38	-5.95	0.60	-6.14	-0.72	-4.82	0.91	7.91
安康市	Ankang	-9.25	-4.81	-14.97	11.93	-11.72	-7.91	-22.11	-15.02	-15.33
商洛市	Shangluo	19.32	-0.72	-17.14	-10.13	-14.23	-11.08	-10.24	-14.00	-1.13
杨凌示范区	Yangling	1.23	-11.79	-0.06	-41.93	9.95	-18.60	-1.15	-13.69	-2.12

注：本表统计范围是年主营业务收入2000万元及以上的法人工业企业；能源消耗按当量值计算。

a) Statistical scope in this table is industrial enterprises with annual principal business sales over 20 million yuan. The energy consumption are converted on the basis of equal value.

7-8 能源消费弹性系数
Elasticity Ratio of Energy Consumption

指 标	Item	2010	2011	2012	2013	2014
能源消费增长速度(%)	Growth Rate of Energy Consumption over Preceding Year (%)	10.43	9.89	8.86	7.02	5.77
电力消费增长速度(%)	Growth Rate of Electricity Consumption over Preceding Year (%)	16.09	14.34	8.58	8.01	6.40
生产总值增长速度(%)	Growth Rate of Gross Domestic Product (GDP) over Preceding Year (%)	14.45	13.90	12.90	11.00	9.70
能源消费弹性系数	Elasticity Ratio of Energy Consumption	0.72	0.71	0.69	0.64	0.59
电力消费弹性系数	Elasticity Ratio of Electricity Consumption	1.11	1.03	0.67	0.73	0.66

注：生产总值增长速度按不变价计算，能源消费用等价值折算。

a) The growth rates of GDP are calculated at constant prices. Energy consumption are converted on the basis of equal value.

7-9 平均每天各种能源消费量
Average Daily Energy Consumption by Variety

品 种	Item	2010	2011	2012	2013	2014
消费总量(万吨标煤)	**Total Consumption (10 000 tons of SCE)**	**22.71**	**24.95**	**27.09**	**29.07**	**30.75**
原 煤 (万吨)	Coal (10 000 tons)	32.37	36.63	45.15	57.78	60.70
焦 炭 (吨)	Coke (ton)	20034	21745	24466	25622	26714
原 油 (吨)	Crude Oil (ton)	57661	57416	61966	61113	61633
汽 油 (吨)	Gasoline (ton)	5126	5422	5809	6054	6299
煤 油 (吨)	Kerosene (ton)	613	696	854	884	993
柴 油 (吨)	Diesel Oil (ton)	12558	13127	13846	14298	14779
天然气 (万立方米)	Natural Gas (10 000 cu.m)	1575	1689	1688	1906	2006
电 力(万千瓦小时)	Electricity (10 000 kwh)	23540	26917	29146	31568	33589

注：能源消费总量用等价值折算，2010-2013年数据根据第三次经济普查结果进行了调整。

a) Total energy consumption are converted on the basis of equal value.
Adjustment has been done for the data of 2010-2013, due to the 3rd Economic Census.

7-10 全省用电总量
Total Electricity Consumption in the Whole Province

单位：亿千瓦时 (100 million kwh)

指标	Item	2012	2013	2014
全省用电量总计	**Total Electricity Consumption in the Whole Province**	**1066.75**	**1152.22**	**1226.01**
农、林、牧、渔、水利用电	Electricity Consumption for Agriculture,Forestry, Animal Husbandry, Fishery and Water Conservancy	42.65	45.29	38.60
# 排灌用电	Electricity Consumption for drainage and irrigation	29.59	30.63	21.85
工业用电	Electricity Consumption for Industry	705.63	750.97	794.81
轻工业	Light Industry	62.21	61.20	59.08
重工业	Heavy Industry	643.42	689.77	735.73
# 自来水生产和供应业	Production and Supply of Water	5.59	6.43	6.94
# 电力、热力生产供应业	Production and Supply of Electric Power and Heat Power	172.22	178.93	197.90
# 厂用电量	Electricity Consumption for factory	92.24	91.42	102.05
# 线路损失电量	Loss of power lines	78.11	84.96	91.65
建筑业用电	Construction electricity	18.45	22.57	29.18
交通运输、仓储和邮政业用电	Electricity Consumption for Transport, Storage and Post	47.48	49.47	53.14
交通运输业	Transport	45.09	46.78	50.27
邮政业	Post	1.52	1.76	1.98
仓储业	Storage	0.87	0.93	0.90
信息传输、计算机服务和软件业用电	Electricity Consumption for Information Transmission, Computer Services and Software	6.85	7.54	8.65
商业、住宿和餐饮用电	Electricity Consumption for Commercial, Hotels and Catering Services	37.17	43.10	50.55
批发和零售业	Wholesale and Retail Trades	23.89	28.31	35.03
住宿和餐饮业	Hotels and Catering Services	13.28	14.79	15.52
金融、房地产、商务及其他服务业用电	Electricity Consumption for Financial Intermediation, Real Estate, Business and others Services	23.55	26.07	28.29
公共事业及其管理组织用电	Electricity Consumption for the Non-profit Organization and the Management Organization	36.80	42.51	45.20
城乡居民生活用电	Electricity Consumption for Cities and Rural Areas Residential	148.16	164.70	177.60
乡村用电	Electricity Consumption for Rural Areas	87.92	96.98	107.18
城市用电	Electricity Consumption for Cities	60.24	67.72	70.42

7-11　主要能源按行业分组消费量(2014年)
Consumption of Main Energy by Sector (2014)

行　业	Sector	原煤(万吨) Coal (10 000 tons)	焦炭(万吨) Coke (10 000 tons)	汽油(万吨) Gasoline (10 000 tons)	柴油(万吨) Diesel Oil (10 000 tons)	电力(亿千瓦时) Electricity (100 million kwh)
采矿业	**Mining**	**8214.72**		**9.32**	**42.08**	**131.12**
煤炭开采和洗选业	Mining and Washing of Coal	8178.17		1.29	14.32	61.27
石油和天然气开采业	Extraction of Petroleum and Natural Gas	9.99		7.05	21.04	43.36
黑色金属矿采选业	Mining and Processing of Ferrous Metal Ores	1.57		0.07	1.41	5.13
有色金属矿采选业	Mining and Processing of Non-Ferrous Metal Ores	10.73		0.29	0.92	13.75
非金属矿采选业	Mining and Processing of Non-metal Ores	5.14		0.02	1.15	2.68
开采辅助活动	Support Activities for Mining	9.11		0.60	3.24	
其他采矿业	Mining of Other Ores					4.94
制造业	**Manufacturing**	**8038.85**	**968.67**	**14.80**	**28.41**	**450.71**
农副食品加工业	Processing of Food from Agricultural Products	43.28		0.63	0.47	7.05
食品制造业	Manufacture of Foods	61.45		0.69	0.32	1.60
酒、饮料和精制茶制造业	Manufacture of Beverages	40.27		0.23	0.18	2.67
烟草制品业	Manufacture of Tobacco	4.20		0.05	0.08	2.38
纺织业	Manufacture of Textile	18.21		0.09	0.02	7.14
纺织服装、服饰业	Manufacture of Textile Wearing Apparel,	0.56		0.03	…	1.74
皮革、毛皮、羽毛及其制品和制鞋业	Manufacture of Leather, Fur, Feather and Related Products	0.76		0.29		0.44
木材加工及木、竹、藤、棕、草制品业	Processing of Timber, Manufacture of Wood, Bamboo, Rattan,Palm and Straw Products	1.42		0.05	…	3.20
家具制造业	Manufacture of Furniture	0.14		0.06	0.04	1.25
造纸及纸制品业	Manufacture of Paper and Paper Products	30.34		0.08	0.07	4.48
印刷业和记录媒介的复制	Printing, Reproduction of Recording Media	0.30		0.20	0.04	1.14
文教、工美、体育和娱乐用品制造业	Manufacture of Articles for Culture, Education, Arts and Crafts, Sport and Entertainment Activities		0.01	0.01	…	0.17
石油加工、炼焦及核燃料加工业	Processing of Petroleum, Coking and Processing of Nuclear Fuel		4.29	0.99	2.38	39.62
化学原料及化学制品制造业	Manufacture of Raw Chemical Materials and Chemical Products		198.48	2.66	2.19	107.66
医药制造业	Manufacture of Medicines	23.21		1.08	0.04	2.58
化学纤维制造业	Manufacture of Chemical Fibres	0.83		…	…	0.99
橡胶和塑料制品业	Manufacture of Rubber and Plastics	22.53	0.32	0.29	1.09	5.61
非金属矿物制品业	Manufacture of Non-metallic Mineral Products	1042.70	2.02	1.23	13.43	62.07
黑色金属冶炼及压延加工业	Smelting and Pressing of Ferrous Metals	135.92	743.82	0.12	0.71	71.40
有色金属冶炼及压延加工业	Smelting and Pressing of Non-ferrous Metals	809.95	19.00	0.48	2.83	50.25
金属制品业	Manufacture of Metal Products	4.91	0.13	0.31	0.11	17.47

7-11 续表 continued

行业	Sector	原煤(万吨) Coal (10 000 tons)	焦炭(万吨) Coke (10 000 tons)	汽油(万吨) Gasoline (10 000 tons)	柴油(万吨) Diesel Oil (10 000 tons)	电力(亿千瓦时) Electricity (100 million kwh)
通用设备制造业	Manufacture of General Purpose Machinery	3.94	0.09	0.63	0.27	8.09
专用设备制造业	Manufacture of Special Purpose Machinery	4.83	0.47	1.47	0.50	9.02
汽车制造业	Manufacture of Automobiles	5.88		1.15	2.04	16.72
铁路、船舶、航空航天和其他运输设备制造业	Manufacture of Railway, Ship, Aerospace and Other TransportEquipments	5.96	0.03	0.39	0.26	3.71
电气机械及器材制造业	Manufacture of Electrical Machinery and Apparatus	0.67	…	0.81	0.17	8.87
计算机、通信和其他电子设备制造业	Manufacture of Computers, Communication and Other Electronic Equipment	1.55		0.24	0.06	5.43
仪器仪表制造业	Manufacture of Measuring Instruments and	0.14		0.43	1.05	1.21
其他制造业	Manufacture of Other Manufacturing	1.64		0.07	0.05	5.74
废弃资源综合利用业	Recycling and Disposal of Waste	0.16				0.30
金属制品、机械和设备修理业	Repair Service of Metal Products, Machinery and Equipment	0.11		0.03	0.01	0.70
电力、燃气及水的生产和供应业	Electric Power, Gas and Water Production and Supply	5080.21	6.40	1.71	2.07	212.99
电力、热力生产和供应业	Production and Supply of Electric Power and Heat Power	5080.14	6.34	1.25	2.04	197.90
燃气生产和供应业	Production and Supply of Gas			0.29	0.02	8.15
水的生产和供应业	Production and Supply of Water	0.07	0.07	0.17	0.01	6.94
建筑业	Construction	19.07		10.29	50.09	29.18
房屋和土木工程建筑业	Housing and Civil Engineering Construction	19.07		7.35	28.45	29.18
建筑安装业	Building Installation			1.37	16.23	
建筑装饰业	Building Construction Decoration			0.46		
其他建筑业	Other Construction			1.12	5.41	
交通运输储运业和邮政业	Transport and Posts	28.58		91.86	327.36	53.14
铁路运输业	Railway Transport	25.58		5.38	9.89	37.75
道路运输业	Road Transport	0.95		83.29	309.11	0.81
水上运输业	Water Transport			0.11	0.68	
航空运输业	Air Transport			0.87		
管道运输业	Pipeline Transport			0.06	1.32	5.32
装卸搬运及其他运输服务业	Loading,Unloading and Other Transport Services	0.66		1.32	4.82	6.39
仓储业	Storage	0.68		0.37	0.21	1.98
邮政业	Posts	0.71		0.46	1.34	0.90

注：消费量包括中间消费和损失量。

a) Consumption includes middle expense and stock losses.

7-12　平均每万元工业总产值能源消费量(2014年)
Energy Consumption Per 10 000 Yuan of Gross Industrial Output Value(2014)

行　业	Sector	能源消费量(万吨标准煤) Total Energy Consumption (10 000 tons of SCE)	产值能耗(吨标准煤/万元) Output Energy Consumption (ton of SCE/10 000 yuan)
工　业	**Industry**	**8081.97**	**0.40**
采矿业	**Mining**	**1179.03**	**0.24**
煤炭开采和洗选业	Mining and Washing of Coal	387.70	0.17
石油和天然气开采业	Extraction of Petroleum and Natural Gas	740.72	0.38
黑色金属矿采选业	Mining and Processing of Ferrous Metal Ores	15.46	0.09
有色金属矿采选业	Mining and Processing of Non-Ferrous Metal Ores	10.72	0.04
非金属矿采选业	Mining and Processing of Non-metal Ores	13.62	0.14
开采辅助活动	Support Activities for Mining	10.81	0.35
制造业	**Manufacturing**	**3981.03**	**0.29**
农副食品加工业	Processing of Food from Agricultural Products	40.38	0.04
食品制造业	Manufacture of Foods	49.52	0.11
酒、饮料和精制茶制造业	Manufacture of Liquor, Beverages and Refined Tea	35.52	0.08
烟草制品业	Manufacture of Tobacco	3.42	0.02
纺织业	Manufacture of Textile	30.31	0.14
纺织服装、服饰业	Manufacture of Textile, Wearing Apparel and Accessories	0.99	0.02
皮革、毛皮、羽毛及其制品和制鞋业	Manufacture of Leather, Fur, Feather and Related Products and Footwear	0.86	0.07
木材加工及木、竹、藤、棕、草制品业	Processing of Timber, Manufacture of Wood, Bamboo, Rattan,Palm and Straw Products	3.72	0.06
家具制造业	Manufacture of Furniture	0.47	0.02
造纸及纸制品业	Manufacture of Paper and Paper Products	23.33	0.20
印刷业和记录媒介的复制	Printing and Reproduction of Recording Media	3.00	0.03
文教、工美、体育和娱乐用品制造业	Manufacture of Articles for Culture, Education, Arts and Crafts, Sport and Entertainment Activities	0.10	
石油加工、炼焦及核燃料加工业	Processing of Petroleum, Coking and Processing of Nuclear Fuel	798.58	0.42
化学原料及化学制品制造业	Manufacture of Raw Chemical Materials and Chemical Products	1292.83	1.53
医药制造业	Manufacture of Medicines	21.01	0.04
化学纤维制造业	Manufacture of Chemical Fibres	3.76	0.22
橡胶和塑料制品业	Manufacture of Rubber and Plastics Products	19.09	0.05
非金属矿物制品业	Manufacture of Non-metallic Mineral Products	704.19	0.63
黑色金属冶炼及压延加工业	Smelting and Pressing of Ferrous Metals	533.11	0.59
有色金属冶炼及压延加工业	Smelting and Pressing of Non-ferrous Metals	287.62	0.20
金属制品业	Manufacture of Metal Products	8.61	0.04
通用设备制造业	Manufacture of General Purpose Machinery	9.15	0.02
专用设备制造业	Manufacture of Special Purpose Machinery	17.32	0.03
汽车制造业	Manufacture of Automobiles	27.60	0.02
铁路、船舶、航空航天和其他运输设备制造业	Manufacture of Railway, Ship, Aerospace and Other TransportEquipments	5.87	0.02
电气机械及器材制造业	Manufacture of Electrical Machinery and Apparatus	23.84	0.03
计算机、通信和其他电子设备制造业	Manufacture of Computers, Communication and Other Electronic Equipment	27.16	0.09
仪器仪表制造业	Manufacture of Measuring Instruments and Machinery	1.86	0.02
其他制造业	Other Manufacture	4.88	0.19
废弃资源综合利用业	Utilization of Waste Resources	2.66	0.22
金属制品、机械和设备修理业	Repair Service of Metal Products, Machinery and Equipment	0.28	0.07
电力、热力、燃气及水生产和供应业	**Production and Supply of Electricity, Heat, Gas and Water**	**2921.91**	**2.01**
电力、热力的生产和供应业	Production and Supply of Electric Power and Heat Power	2893.33	2.25
燃气生产和供应业	Production and Supply of Gas	25.66	0.17
水的生产和供应业	Production and Supply of Water	2.93	0.16

注：本表能源消费量为当量值，工业总产值为现价；统计范围是年主营业务收入2000万元及以上的法人工业企业。

a) Energy consumption in this table is the equivalent weight, the gross industrial output value is at current prices.Statistical scope in this table is industrial enterprises with annual principal business sales over 20 million yuan.

7-13 各市(区)规模以上工业企业能源消费量(2014年)

单位：万吨标煤

行业	Sector	西安市 Xi'an	铜川市 Tongchuan	宝鸡市 Baoji
工业	**Industry**	**557.05**	**322.05**	**579.15**
采矿业	**Mining**	**0.99**	**21.47**	**6.68**
煤炭开采和洗选业	Mining and Washing of Coal		20.41	3.22
石油和天然气开采业	Extraction of Petroleum and Natural Gas		0.27	
黑色金属矿采选业	Mining and Processing of Ferrous Metal Ores	0.01		
有色金属矿采选业	Mining and Processing of Non-Ferrous Metal Ores			2.99
非金属矿采选业	Mining and Processing of Non-metal Ores		0.78	0.48
开采辅助活动	Support Activities for Mining	0.98		
制造业	**Manufacturing**	**195.55**	**180.40**	**315.25**
农副食品加工业	Processing of Food from Agricultural Products	14.81	0.44	2.31
食品制造业	Manufacture of Foods	10.29	0.50	24.98
酒、饮料和精制茶制造业	Manufacture of Liquor, Beverages and Refined Tea	12.82	0.33	5.37
烟草制品业	Manufacture of Tobacco	0.04		1.28
纺织业	Manufacture of Textile	3.05	1.30	6.03
纺织服装、服饰业	Manufacture of Textile, Wearing Apparel and Accessories	0.10	0.01	0.04
皮革、毛皮、羽毛及其制品和制鞋业	Manufacture of Leather, Fur, Feather and Related Products and Footwear	0.07		0.66
木材加工和木、竹、藤、棕、草制品业	Processing of Timber, Manufacture of Wood, Bamboo, Rattan,Palm and Straw Products	1.27	0.33	0.005
家具制造业	Manufacture of Furniture	0.17	0.02	0.01
造纸及纸制品业	Manufacture of Paper and Paper Products	1.54	0.08	10.44
印刷和记录媒介复制业	Printing and Reproduction of Recording Media	2.10		0.54
文教、工美、体育和娱乐用品制造业	Manufacture of Articles for Culture, Education, Arts and Crafts, Sport and Entertainment Activities	0.07		
石油加工、炼焦及核燃料加工业	Processing of Petroleum, Coking and Processing of Nuclear Fuel	23.37	0.43	
化学原料及化学制品制造业	Manufacture of Raw Chemical Materials and Chemical Products	8.43	0.17	53.47
医药制造业	Manufacture of Medicines	4.55	0.40	1.78
化学纤维制造业	Manufacture of Chemical Fibres	3.17		0.38
橡胶和塑料制品业	Manufacture of Rubber and Plastics Products	4.82	0.22	0.64
非金属矿物制品业	Manufacture of Non-metallic Mineral Products	30.44	168.83	134.34
黑色金属冶炼及压延加工业	Smelting and Pressing of Ferrous Metals	3.93	1.86	5.79
有色金属冶炼及压延加工业	Smelting and Pressing of Non-ferrous Metals	8.18	4.60	49.39
金属制品业	Manufacture of Metal Products	3.42	0.37	1.35
通用设备制造业	Manufacture of General Purpose Machinery	1.72	0.05	3.12
专用设备制造业	Manufacture of Special Purpose Machinery	4.75	0.12	4.02
汽车制造业	Manufacture of Automobiles	21.14	0.27	5.10
铁路、船舶、航空航天和其他运输设备制造业	Manufacture of Railway, Ship, Aerospace and Other TransportEquipments	3.44		2.11
电气机械及器材制造业	Manufacture of Electrical Machinery and Apparatus	12.42	0.02	0.14
计算机、通信和其他电子设备制造业	Manufacture of Computers, Communication and Other Electronic Equipment	13.51		1.93
仪器仪表制造业	Manufacture of Measuring Instruments and Machinery	1.77		0.01
其他制造业	Other Manufacture	0.12	0.04	
废弃资源综合利用业	Utilization of Waste Resources		0.004	
金属制品、机械和设备修理业	Repair Service of Metal Products, Machinery and Equipment	0.03		
电力、热力、燃气及水生产和供应业	**Production and Supply of Electricity, Heat, Gas and Water**	**360.50**	**120.18**	**257.22**
电力、热力的生产和供应业	Production and Supply of Electric Power and Heat Power	358.10	120.05	256.92
燃气生产和供应业	Production and Supply of Gas	1.11	0.02	0.22
水的生产和供应业	Production and Supply of Water	1.29	0.12	0.08

注：本表能源消费量为当量值，统计范围是年主营业务收入2000万元及以上的法人工业企业。

Industrial Enterprises above Designated Size Consumption of Energy by City(District) (2014)

(10 000 tons of SCE)

咸阳市 Xianyang	渭南市 Weinan	延安市 Yan'an	汉中市 Hanzhong	榆林市 Yulin	安康市 Ankang	商洛市 Shangluo	杨凌示范区 Yangling
852.76	**1491.81**	**422.96**	**415.68**	**2966.28**	**82.12**	**78.73**	**3.52**
12.99	**41.21**	**214.65**	**4.03**	**546.47**	**5.43**	**15.29**	
12.85	38.79	33.50	0.03	278.24	0.65	0.02	
		180.60		256.57			
	0.13		2.92		1.32	11.07	
	1.14		0.70	0.28	1.66	3.97	
0.15	1.15		0.38	8.64	1.80	0.24	
		0.54		2.74			
468.83	**804.72**	**145.28**	**359.66**	**1377.08**	**72.18**	**58.91**	**3.10**
8.44	3.47	0.23	2.92	0.37	3.04	3.36	0.99
9.85	1.13		0.78	1.41	0.34	0.09	0.14
8.75	3.06	0.92	1.44	1.01	1.43	0.23	0.15
0.49	0.06	0.55	0.81		0.18		
14.42	0.94		1.72	0.03	2.75	0.06	0.01
0.63			0.15	0.03	0.02	0.00	
0.11				0.00		0.02	
0.11	0.45		0.01	0.033	0.11	0.32	1.07
0.23	0.01				0.01		0.04
9.40	0.81			0.08	0.99		
0.31	0.00		0.04		0.01		0.01
	0.003			0.00		0.00	0.015
40.34	128.89	142.66		462.37	0.00		
180.13	293.85	0.01	40.34	706.56	7.31	2.37	0.09
4.23	0.33	0.04	3.48	0.30	3.38	2.24	0.27
0.13	0.07						
10.63	1.12	0.38	0.27	0.30	0.623	0.17	0.20
151.85	80.27	0.16	44.23	23.21	45.16	25.69	
5.99	255.34		229.91	26.99	0.36	2.95	
0.43	18.19		29.32	153.75	5.60	18.16	
1.86	0.50		0.65	0.01	0.39	0.02	0.03
3.23	0.29	0.00	0.64	0.01	0.05		0.04
3.56	4.25	0.28	0.04	0.22	0.05		0.03
0.80		0.03	0.02	0.09	0.08		0.01
0.08	0.05		0.12		0.08		
1.32	6.88	0.01	0.11		0.15	2.78	0.01
11.10	0.16		0.00		0.02	0.44	
			0.08				
0.12	4.59				0.00		0.01
0.023	0.01		2.57		0.06		
0.25							
370.93	**645.88**	**63.03**	**51.98**	**1042.74**	**4.51**	**4.52**	**0.42**
370.11	645.80	59.26	51.85	1022.17	4.21	4.45	0.41
0.48	0.07	3.63		19.89	0.23		0.01
0.35	0.01	0.15	0.13	0.67	0.07	0.07	

a) Energy consumption in this table is the equivalent weight, Statistical scope in this tableis industrial enterprises with annual principal business sales over 20 million yuan.

7-14 规模以上工业企业主要能源按行业分组消费量(2014年)

行业	Sector	煤炭(万吨) Coal (10 000 tons)	焦炭(万吨) Coke (10 000 tons)	天然气(气态)(亿立方米) Natural Gas (100 million cu.m)
工业	**Industry**	**23660.03**	**583.81**	**62.92**
采矿业	**Mining**	**8254.78**	**0.00**	**29.41**
煤炭开采和洗选业	Mining and Washing of Coal	8146.65		0.00
石油和天然气开采业	Extraction of Petroleum and Natural Gas	72.49		28.79
黑色金属矿采选业	Mining and Processing of Ferrous Metal Ores	8.05		
有色金属矿采选业	Mining and Processing of Non-Ferrous Metal Ores	4.81	0.00	
非金属矿采选业	Mining and Processing of Non-metal Ores	13.51		
开采辅助活动	Support Activities for Mining	9.27		0.62
制造业	**Manufacturing**	**8941.95**	**551.17**	**20.32**
农副食品加工业	Processing of Food from Agricultural Products	38.55		0.03
食品制造业	Manufacture of Foods	52.91		0.33
酒、饮料和精制茶制造业	Manufacture of Liquor, Beverages and Refined Tea	34.01		0.13
烟草制品业	Manufacture of Tobacco	3.54		0.010
纺织业	Manufacture of Textile	15.43		0.002
纺织服装、服饰业	Manufacture of Textile, Wearing Apparel and Accessories	0.47		0.002
皮革、毛皮、羽毛及其制品和制鞋业	Manufacture of Leather, Fur, Feather and Related Products and Footwear	0.64		
木材加工和木、竹、藤、棕、草制品业	Processing of Timber, Manufacture of Wood, Bamboo, Rattan,Palm and Straw Products	1.20		
家具制造业	Manufacture of Furniture	0.12		0.002
造纸及纸制品业	Manufacture of Paper and Paper Products	25.76		
印刷和记录媒介复制业	Printing and Reproduction of Recording Media	0.25		0.05
文教、工美、体育和娱乐用品制造业	Manufacture of Articles for Culture, Education, Arts and Crafts, Sport and Entertainment Activities	0.03		
石油加工、炼焦及核燃料加工业	Processing of Petroleum, Coking and Processing of Nuclear Fuel	5271.16	3.44	9.18
化学原料及化学制品制造业	Manufacture of Raw Chemical Materials and Chemical Products	1528.76	101.26	5.59
医药制造业	Manufacture of Medicines	19.65		0.10
化学纤维制造业	Manufacture of Chemical Fibres	0.71		0.00
橡胶和塑料制品业	Manufacture of Rubber and Plastics Products	21.01	0.18	0.019
非金属矿物制品业	Manufacture of Non-metallic Mineral Products	842.70	0.76	1.23
黑色金属冶炼及压延加工业	Smelting and Pressing of Ferrous Metals	161.93	435.22	0.48
有色金属冶炼及压延加工业	Smelting and Pressing of Non-ferrous Metals	898.10	10.04	0.63
金属制品业	Manufacture of Metal Products	4.21	0.03	0.13
通用设备制造业	Manufacture of General Purpose Machinery	3.32	0.02	0.03
专用设备制造业	Manufacture of Special Purpose Machinery	4.08	0.06	0.41
汽车制造业	Manufacture of Automobiles	4.96		0.53
铁路、船舶、航空航天和其他运输设备制造业	Manufacture of Railway, Ship, Aerospace and Other TransportEquipments	5.01	0.01	0.04
电气机械及器材制造业	Manufacture of Electrical Machinery and Apparatus	0.56		0.59
计算机、通信和其他电子设备制造业	Manufacture of Computers, Communication and Other Electronic Equipment	1.30		0.79
仪器仪表制造业	Manufacture of Measuring Instruments and Machinery	0.13		0.02
其他制造业	Other Manufacture	1.24		
废弃资源综合利用业	Utilization of Waste Resources	0.13	0.16	
金属制品、机械和设备修理业	Repair Service of Metal Products, Machinery and Equipment	0.06		
电力、热力、燃气及水生产和供应业	**Production and Supply of Electricity, Heat, Gas and Water**	**6463.31**	**32.63**	**13.18**
电力、热力的生产和供应业	Production and Supply of Electric Power and Heat Power	6463.18	32.62	0.319
燃气生产和供应业	Production and Supply of Gas			12.80
水的生产和供应业	Production and Supply of Water	0.13	0.01	0.06

注：消费量包括中间消费和损失量；统计范围是年主营业务收入2000万元及以上的法人工业企业；煤炭包括：原煤、洗精煤、其它洗煤、煤制品。

Industrial Enterprises above Designated Size Consumption of Main Energy by Sector (2014)

原 油 (万吨) Crude Oil (10 000 tons)	汽 油 (万吨) Gasoline (10 000 tons)	煤 油 (万吨) Eerosene (10 000 tons)	柴 油 (万吨) Diesel Oil (10 000 tons)	热 力 (万百万千焦) Heat (10 billion kilo-joule)	电 力 (亿千瓦时) Electricity (100 million kwh)
2249.60	**8.18**	**0.18**	**37.21**	**1834.71**	**876.85**
153.12	**2.94**	**0.08**	**21.72**	**54.18**	**134.94**
	0.41	0.03	7.39		51.56
153.12	2.21		10.86	9.84	62.25
	0.02		0.72		7.77
	0.09	0.05	0.48		7.59
	0.008		0.60		3.40
	0.19		1.67	44.34	2.36
2096.48	**4.71**	**0.10**	**14.63**	**1623.50**	**531.69**
	0.19	0.01	0.25	119.10	10.31
	0.21	0.00	0.17	39.30	5.23
	0.08		0.09	49.77	6.19
	0.02		0.04	0.72	0.77
	0.03	0.001	0.01	34.63	16.08
	0.01		0.000		0.52
	0.12			1.26	0.15
	0.01		0.003		2.35
	0.02		0.02		0.26
	0.03		0.04	2.94	3.58
	0.06		0.03	8.14	1.48
	0.00		0.001		0.06
2096.48	0.33		1.23	213.22	60.28
	0.84		1.10	97.46	113.23
	0.34		0.02	25.30	3.48
	0.002		0.001	77.14	0.46
	0.09	0.000	0.55	0.22	8.61
	0.39	0.002	6.93	13.48	85.84
	0.04	0.000	0.37	613.81	56.56
	0.15	0.07	1.46	62.13	99.89
	0.10	0.001	0.06	0.73	3.19
0.000	0.20	0.01	0.14	1.13	5.16
	0.46	0.004	0.26	18.56	7.24
	0.36	0.00	1.05	58.90	11.39
	0.12	0.00	0.13	10.76	2.16
	0.25	0.004	0.09	103.63	9.93
	0.08		0.03	70.50	12.50
	0.14		0.55	0.67	0.38
	0.02		0.03		3.71
			0.00		0.52
	0.01		0.00		0.18
	0.53	**0.000**	**0.86**	**157.02**	**210.22**
	0.39	0.000	0.84	157.02	201.37
	0.09		0.01		6.95
	0.05		0.004		1.91

a) Consumption covers intermediate consumption and loss. The scope of statistics include corporate industrial enterprises with revenue from principal business over 20 million yuan. The coals include raw coal, cleaned coal, other coal washing and coal products.

主要统计指标解释

能源生产总量　指一定时期内，一次能源生产量的总和。该指标是观察能源生产水平、规模、构成和发展速度的总量指标。一次能源生产量包括原煤、原油、天然气、水电、核能及其他动力能(如风能、地热能等)发电量，不包括低热值燃料生产量、生物质能、太阳能等的利用和由一次能源加工转换而成的二次能源产量。

能源消费总量　是指一定地域内，国民经济各行业和居民家庭在一定时间消费的各种能源的总和。包括：原煤、原油、天然气、水能、核能、风能、太阳能、地热能、生物质能等一次能源；一次能源通过加工转换产生的洗煤、焦炭、煤气、电力、热力、成品油等二次能源和同时产生的其他产品；其他化石能源、可再生能源和新能源。其中水能、风能、太阳能、地热能、生物质能等可再生能源，是指人们通过一定技术手段获得的，并作为商品能源使用的部分。在核算过程中，一次能源、二次能源消费不能重复计算。能源消费总量分为终端能源消费量、能源加工转换损失量和能源损失量三部分。

(1)终端能源消费量：指一定时期内，全国生产和生活消费的各种能源在扣除了用于加工转换二次能源消费量和损失量以后的数量。

(2)能源加工转换损失量：指一定时期内，全国投入加工转换的各种能源数量之和与产出各种能源产品之和的差额。该指标是观察能源在加工转换过程中损失量变化的指标。

(3)能源损失量：指一定时期内，能源在输送、分配、储存过程中发生的损失和由客观原因造成的各种损失量，不包括各种气体能源放空、放散量。

能源生产弹性系数　是研究能源生产增长速度与国民经济增长速度之间关系的指标。计算公式：

$$能源生产弹性系数=\frac{能源生产总量年平均增长速度}{国民经济年平均增长速度}$$

国民经济年平均增长速度，可根据不同的目的或需要，用国民生产总值、国内生产总值等指标来计算，本年鉴是采用国内生产总值指标计算的。

电力生产弹性系数　是研究电力生产增长速度与国民经济增长速度之间关系的指标。一般来说，电力的发展应当快于国民经济的发展，也就是说电力应超前发展。计算公式为：

$$电力生产弹性系数=\frac{电力生产量年平均增长速度}{国民经济年平均增长速度}$$

能源消费弹性系数　反映能源消费增长速度与国民经济增长速度之间比例关系的指标。计算公式为：

$$能源消费弹性系数=\frac{能源消费量年平均增长速度}{国民经济年平均增长速度}$$

电力消费弹性系数　反映电力消费增长速度与国民经济增长速度之间比例关系的指标。计算公式为：

$$电力消费弹性系数=\frac{电力消费量年平均增长速度}{国民经济年平均增长速度}$$

能源加工转换效率　指一定时期内，能源经过加工、转换后，产出的各种能源产品的数量与同期内投入加工转换的各种能源数量的比率。该指标是观察能源加工转换装置和生产工艺先进与落后、管理水平高低等的重要指标。计算公式为：

$$能源加工转换效率=\frac{能源加工转换产出量}{能源加工转换投入量}\times 100\%$$

单位生产总值能耗　指一定时期内，一个国家或地区每生产一个单位的生产总值所消耗的能源。计算公式为：

$$单位生产总值能耗=\frac{能源消费总量}{生产总值}$$

单位生产总值电耗　指一定时期内，一个国家或地区每生产一个单位的生产总值所消耗的电力。计算公式为：

$$单位生产总值电耗=\frac{全社会用电量}{生产总值}$$

单位工业增加值能耗　指一定时期内，一个国家或地区每生产一个单位的工业增加值所消耗的能源。计算公式为：

$$单位工业增加值能耗=\frac{工业能源消费量}{工业增加值}$$

Explanatory Notes on Main Statistical Indicators

Total Energy Production refers to the total production of primary energy by all energy producing enterprises in the country in a given period of time. It is a comprehensive indicator to show the level, scale, composition and pace of development of energy production of the country. The production of primary energy includes that of coal, crude oil, natural gas, hydro-power and electricity generated by nuclear energy and other means such as wind power and geothermal power. However, it does not include the production of fuels of low calorific value, bio-energy, solar energy and secondary energy converted from primary energy.

Total Energy Consumption refers to the total consumption of energy of various kinds by the production sectors of the economy and the households in a given period of time. It includes the primary kinds of energy such as coal, crude oil, natural gas, hydro-power, nuclear power, wind power, solar power, geothermal power and bio-energy; the secondary kinds of energy and their products which are transformed from the primary energy such as washed coal, coke, coal gas, electricity, heating, and petroleum products; and other kinds of fossil energy, renewable energy and new energy. The renewable energy, including hydro-power, wind power, solar power, geothermal power and bio-energy, refers to the part attained with some given technical means and used for commercial purposes. Total energy consumption can be divided into three parts: end-use energy consumption; loss during the process of energy conversion; and energy loss.

(1) End-use Energy Consumption: It refers to the total energy consumption by the production sectors and the households in the country (region) in a given period of time. It does not include the consumption during the conversion of primary energy into secondary energy and the loss in the process of energy conversion.

(2) Loss During the Process of Energy Conversion: It refers to the total input of various kinds of energy for conversion, minus the total output of various kinds of energy in the country in a given period of time. It is an indicator to show the loss that occurs during the process of energy conversion.

(3) Energy Loss: It refers to the total of the loss of energy during the course of energy transport, distribution and storage and the loss caused by any objective reason in a given period of time. The loss of various kinds of gas due to gas discharges and stocktaking is not included.

Elasticity Ratio of Energy Production is an indicator to show the relationship between the growth rate of energy production and the growth rate of the national economy. The formula is:

$$\text{Elasticity Ratio of Energy Production} = \frac{\text{Average Annual Growth Rate of Energy Production}}{\text{Average Annual Growth Rate of National Economy}}$$

The average annual growth rate of the national economy can be measured by indicators such as the Gross National Product and the Gross Domestic Product, depending on the purposes or needs. The Gross Domestic Product has been used in the calculation of the ratio in this Yearbook.

Elasticity Ratio of Electricity Production is an indicator to show the relationship between the growth rate of electricity production and the growth rate of the national economy. Generally speaking, the growth rate of electricity production should be higher than that of the national economy. Its formula is:

$$\text{Elasticity Ratio of Electricity Production} = \frac{\text{Average Annual Growth Rate of Electricity Production}}{\text{Average Annual Growth Rate of National Economy}}$$

Elasticity Ratio of Energy Consumption is an indicator to show the relationship between the growth rate of energy consumption and the growth rate of the national economy. The formula is:

$$\text{Elasticity Ratio of Energy Consumption} = \frac{\text{Average Annual Growth Rate of Energy Consumption}}{\text{Average Annual Growth Rate of National Economy}}$$

Elasticity Ratio of Electricity Consumption is an indicator to show the relationship between the growth rate of electricity consumption and the growth rate of the national economy. The formula is:

$$\text{Elasticity Ratio of Electricity Consumption} = \frac{\text{Average Annual Growth Rate of Electricity Consumption}}{\text{Average Annual Growth Rate of National Economy}}$$

Efficiency of Energy Processing and Conversion refers to the ratio of the total output of energy products of various kinds after processing and conversion to the total input of energy of various kinds for processing and conversion in the same reference period. It is an important indicator to show the current conditions of energy processing and conversion equipment, production technique and management. The formula is:

$$\text{Efficiency of Energy Processing \& Conversion} = \frac{\text{Output of Energy After Processing \& Conversion}}{\text{Input of Energy for Processing \& Conversion}} \times 100\%$$

Energy Consumption per Unit of GDP refers to the energy consumption per unit of Gross Domestic Product in a country or the Gross Regional Product in a region in the same reference period. The formula is:

$$\frac{\text{Energy Consumption}}{\text{per Unit of GDP}} = \frac{\text{Total Energy Consumption}}{\text{Gross Domestic Product}}$$

Electricity Consumption per Unit of GDP refers to the electricity consumption per unit of Gross Domestic Product in a country or the Gross Regional Product in a region in the same reference period. The formula is:

$$\frac{\text{Electricity Consumption}}{\text{per Unit of GDP}} = \frac{\text{Total Electricity Consumption}}{\text{Gross Domestic Product}}$$

Energy Consumption per Unit of Industrial Value-added refers to the energy consumption per unit of industrial value-added in a country or region in the same reference period. The formula is:

$$\frac{\text{Energy Consumption per}}{\text{Unit of Industrial Value-added}} = \frac{\text{Total Energy Consumption}}{\text{Industrial Value-added.}}$$

八、财　政

资料整理：张应剑

简 要 说 明

一、本篇资料反映陕西财政收支情况，内容包括财政总收入、一般预算收入及分项目收入，分项目支出。

二、本篇资料由省财政厅提供。

Brief Introduction

Ⅰ. This chapter reflects the basic situation of local government general budgetary revenue and expenditure of Shaanxi Province, mainly including total revenue, general budget revenue, item of income and item of expenditure.

Ⅱ. The data are provided by Finance Department of Shaanxi Provincial.

8. 财 政

2014年全省		
财政收入	3145.54 亿元	比上年增长 8.3%
# 地方一般预算收入	1890.40 亿元	比上年增长 13.7%
财政支出	3962.50 亿元	比上年增长 8.1%

财政收支（亿元）

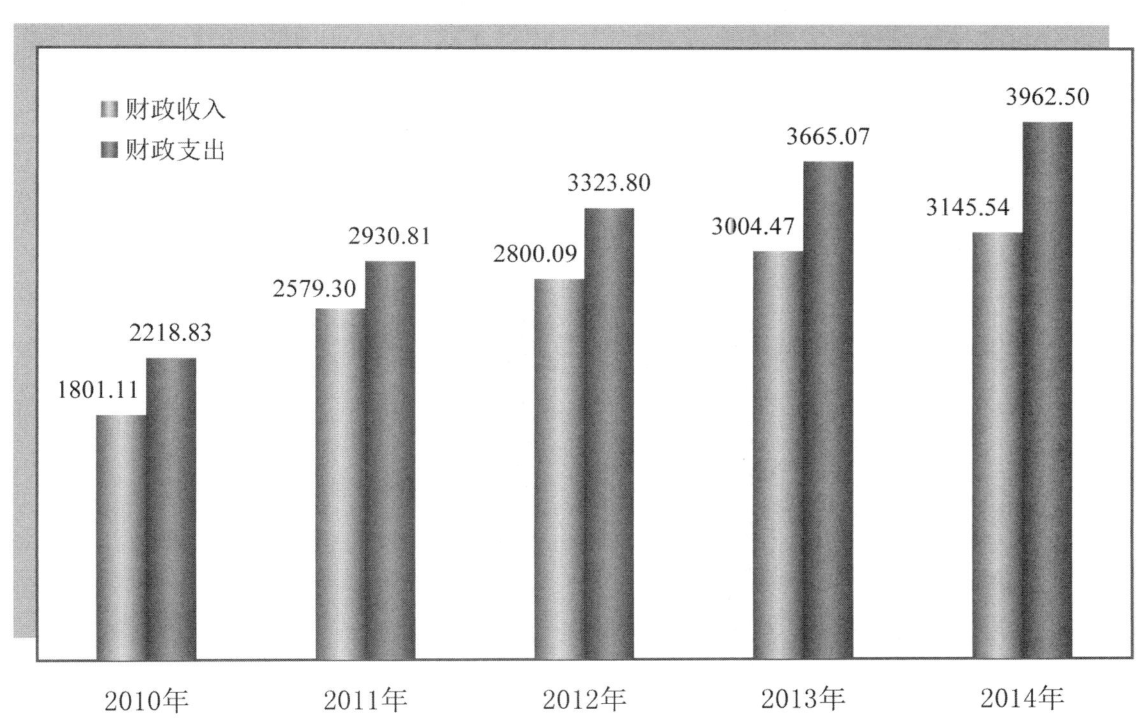

8-1 财政收支总额
Government Revenue and Expenditure

单位：万元 (10 000 yuan)

年 份 Year	财政收入 Government Revenue	# 地方一般预算收入 Local General Bugetary Revenue	财政支出 Government Expenditure	收支差额 Balance of Payment	比上年增长(%) Increase Rates(%) 财政收入 Government Revenue	地方一般预算收入 Local General Bugetary Revenue	财政支出 Government Expenditure
1978	197587		183026	14561	31.5		32.4
1979	168010		195617	-27607	-15.0		6.9
1980	158105		182837	-24732	-5.9		-6.5
1981	134538		163887	-29349	-14.9		-10.4
1982	135622		172993	-37371	0.8		5.6
1983	145407		188076	-42669	7.2		8.7
1984	153124		227471	-74347	5.3		20.9
1985	202967		275007	-72040	32.6		20.9
1986	240907		355931	-115024	18.7		29.4
1987	281805		378051	-96246	17.0		6.2
1988	338788		445835	-107047	20.2		17.9
1989	389603		507870	-118267	15.0		13.9
1990	411901		539062	-127161	5.7		6.1
1991	451391		582781	-131390	9.6		8.1
1992	509539		652654	-143115	12.9		12.0
1993	628982		753985	-125003	23.4		15.5
1994	833111	425886	855158	-22047	32.5	41.0	13.4
1995	951946	513011	1026917	-74971	14.3	20.5	20.1
1996	1172231	676022	1217909	-45678	23.1	31.8	18.6
1997	1400474	841178	1445338	-44864	19.5	24.4	18.7
1998	1569228	933309	1661955	-92727	12.0	11.0	15.0
1999	1729712	1064033	2065173	-335461	10.2	14.0	24.3
2000	1870019	1149711	2717597	-847578	8.1	8.1	31.6
2001	2259822	1358109	3500506	-1240684	20.8	18.1	28.8
2002	2522809	1502934	4049114	-1526305	11.6	10.7	15.7
2003	3269421	1773300	4182008	-912587	29.6	18.0	3.3
2004	4154957	2149586	5163052	-1008095	27.1	21.2	23.5
2005	5290241	2753183	6389627	-1099386	27.3	28.1	23.8
2006	6967712	3621295	8215522	-1247810	31.7	31.5	28.6
2007	8930217	4752398	10539665	-1609448	28.2	31.2	28.3
2008	11043550	5914750	14285208	-3241658	23.7	24.5	35.5
2009	13911343	7352704	18416388	-4505045	26.0	24.3	28.9
2010	18011071	9582065	22188283	-4177212	29.5	30.3	20.5
2011	25793001	15001838	29308100	-3515099	43.2	56.6	32.1
2012	28000912	16006862	33238020	-5237108	18.6	24.9	13.4
2013	30044699	17483305	36650665	-6605966	11.5	16.9	10.3
2014	31455438	18904044	39625042	-8169604	8.3	13.7	8.1

注：2012-2014年财政收入增长速度为同口径增长速度。
a)The increase rates of government revenue is the same requirements data in 2012-2014.

8-2 财政分项目收支
Government Revenue and Expenditure by Item

单位：万元 (10 000 yuan)

项 目	Item	2012	2013	2014
地方一般预算收入	**Local General Bugetary Revenue**	**16006862**	**17483305**	**18904044**
税收收入	Total Tax Revenue	11315534	12562435	13356844
增值税	Value Added Tax	1894574	1892494	1866029
改征增值税			123953	640316
营业税	Business Tax	3929029	4284411	3992796
企业所得税	Corporate Income Tax	1609186	1567633	1565329
企业所得税退税	Corporate Income Tax Drawback			
个人所得税	Individual Income Tax	420501	487616	468686
资源税	Resource Tax	615942	787736	848975
固定资产投资方向调节税	Fixed Assets Investment Orientation Regulation Tax			
城市维护建设税	City Maintenance and Construction Tax	824660	838326	869334
房产税	House Property Tax	269962	303449	376126
印花税	Stamp Tax	160605	179574	199506
城镇土地使用税	Urban Land Use Tax	226649	225476	280679
土地增值税	Land Appreciation Tax	370335	460131	500714
车船税	Tax on Vehicles and Boat Operation	103448	120503	137349
耕地占用税	Farm Land Occupation Tax	442450	635751	787190
契 税	Deed Tax	424310	627122	802702
烟叶税	Tobacco Leaf Tax	23783	28260	21113
其他税收收入	Other Tax Revenue			
非税收入	Total Non-tax Revenue	4691328	4920870	5547200
专项收入	Special Program Receipts	1747701	1477752	1234197
行政事业性收费收入	Charge of Administrative and Institutional Units	872300	1254668	1464778
罚没收入	Penalty Receipts	290680	392221	362077
国有资本经营收入	Operation Income of State-owned Assets	264141	300810	445565
国有资源(资产)有偿使用收入	Income from Use of State-owned Resources (Assets)	938036	836075	1268121
其他收入	Other Non-tax Receipts	578470	659344	772462
一般预算支出	**General Bugetary Expenditure**	**33238020**	**36650665**	**39625042**
一般公共服务	Expenditure for General Public Services	4071146	4142859	3663175
外 交	Expenditure for Foreign Affairs			
国 防	Expenditure for National Defense	38391	33484	38961
公共安全	Expenditure for Public Security	1490363	1568945	1614255
教 育	Expenditure for Education	7033359	7101107	6938334
科学技术	Expenditure for Science and Technology	349351	380165	448632
文化体育与传媒	Expenditure for Culture, Sport and Media	918055	1004420	932331
社会保障和就业	Expenditure for Social Safety Net and Employment Effort	4211552	4977519	5414037
医疗卫生	Expenditure for Medical and Health Care	2223015	2571363	3134521
环境保护	Expenditure for Environment Protection	941427	1097656	1125076
城乡社区事务	Expenditure for Urban and Rural Community Affairs	1820515	2594226	3305721
农林水事务	Expenditure for Agriculture, Forestry and Water Conservanc	3764492	4196218	4459710
交通运输	Expenditure for Transportation	2482441	2653469	3714896
工业商业金融等事务	Expenditure for Industry, Commerce and Banking			
其他支出	Other Expenditure	3893913	4329234	4835393

8-3 各市、县(市、区)财政收支(2014年)

Government Revenue and Expenditure by City and County (City and District) (2014)

单位：万元 (10 000 yuan)

地 区	Region	地方一般预算收入 Local General Bugetary Revenue	一般预算支出 General Bugetary Expenditure	收支差额 Balance of Payment
西安市	**Xi'an**	**5837888**	**8195366**	**-2357478**
市本级	City level	2631142	4492621	-1861479
新城区	Xincheng	355811	311201	44610
碑林区	Beilin	432276	282868	149408
莲湖区	Lianhu	471313	339115	132198
灞桥区	Baqiao	236711	220305	16406
未央区	Weiyang	355092	239836	115256
雁塔区	Yanta	470617	326731	143886
阎良区	Yanliang	120355	186987	-66632
临潼区	Lintong	121441	293966	-172525
长安区	Chang'an	354267	494189	-139922
蓝田县	Lantian	38387	251369	-212982
周至县	Zhouzhi	35218	284284	-249066
户县	Huxian	82748	269178	-186430
高陵县	Gaoling	132510	202716	-70206
铜川市	**Tongchuan**	**220647**	**830052**	**-609405**
市本级	City level	91028	300140	-209112
王益区	Wangyi	21568	96420	-74852
印台区	Yintai	15176	101861	-86685
耀州区	Yaozhou	71726	234651	-162925
宜君县	Yijun	21149	96980	-75831
宝鸡市	**Baoji**	**780571**	**2356018**	**-1575447**
市本级	City level	406781	725691	-318910
渭滨区	Weibin	51757	132242	-80485
金台区	Jintai	47402	126698	-79296
陈仓区	Chencang	36868	183899	-147031
凤翔县	Fengxiang	44915	190019	-145104
岐山县	Qishan	32262	172759	-140497
扶风县	Fufeng	27579	176399	-148820
眉县	Meixian	29963	164704	-134741
陇县	Longxian	26805	138954	-112149
千阳县	Qianyang	10353	97571	-87218
麟游县	Linyou	19188	90789	-71601
凤县	Fengxian	37655	82366	-44711
太白县	Taibai	9043	73927	-64884
咸阳市	**Xianyang**	**854644**	**2724395**	**-1869751**
市本级	City level	292571	488134	-195563
秦都区	Qindu	100079	178070	-77991
渭城区	Weicheng	85564	149388	-63824
三原县	Sanyuan	43389	188235	-144846
泾阳县	Jingyang	40056	218719	-178663
乾县	Qianxian	23960	223096	-199136
礼泉县	Liquan	21728	195649	-173921

8-3 续表 1 continued

单位：万元 (10 000 yuan)

地　区	Region	地方一般预算收入 Local General Bugetary Revenue	一般预算支出 General Bugetary Expenditure	收支差额 Balance of Payment
永寿县	Yongshou	14096	117655	-103559
彬　县	Binxian	108287	210943	-102656
长武县	Changwu	32013	110419	-78406
旬邑县	Xunyi	20261	145102	-124841
淳化县	Chunhua	6066	115757	-109691
武功县	Wugong	15274	172433	-157159
兴平市	Xingping	51300	210795	-159495
渭南市	**Weinan**	**674648**	**2934111**	**-2259463**
市本级	City level	129258	392622	-263364
临渭区	Linwei	64761	380995	-316234
华　县	Huaxian	34300	151161	-116861
潼关县	Tongguan	28010	118600	-90590
大荔县	Dali	19174	262388	-243214
合阳县	Heyang	24568	211500	-186932
澄城县	Chengcheng	40180	200369	-160189
蒲城县	Pucheng	61600	304836	-243236
白水县	Baishui	23700	167935	-144235
富平县	Fuping	40365	308006	-267641
韩城市	Hancheng	170031	307921	-137890
华阴市	Huayin	38701	127778	-89077
延安市	**Yan'an**	**1681035**	**3104128**	**-1423093**
市本级	City level	467819	805266	-337447
宝塔区	Baota	131976	281407	-149431
延长县	Yanchang	34562	136330	-101768
延川县	Yanchuan	34133	181568	-147435
子长县	Zichang	65998	157032	-91034
安塞县	Ansai	142521	209096	-66575
志丹县	Zhidan	254706	283425	-28719
吴起县	Wuqi	355688	371574	-15886
甘泉县	Ganquan	33017	91394	-58377
富　县	Fuxian	30844	114500	-83656
洛川县	Luochuan	26100	140935	-114835
宜川县	Yichuan	11152	105068	-93916
黄龙县	Huanglong	4226	99232	-95006
黄陵县	Huangling	88293	127301	-39008
汉中市	**Hanzhong**	**408910**	**2340003**	**-1931093**
市本级	City level	101940	439558	-337618
汉台区	Hantai	93427	216471	-123044
南郑县	Nanzheng	64961	264583	-199622
城固县	Chenggu	23730	227081	-203351
洋　县	Yangxian	19942	221117	-201175
西乡县	Xixiang	22069	199500	-177431
勉　县	Mianxian	31020	195829	-164809
宁强县	Ningqiang	16072	169701	-153629

8-3 续表 2 continued

单位：万元 (10 000 yuan)

地 区	Region	地方一般预算收入 Local General Bugetary Revenue	一般预算支出 General Bugetary Expenditure	收支差额 Balance of Payment
略阳县	Lueyang	17016	131970	-114954
镇巴县	Zhenba	11270	157028	-145758
留坝县	Liuba	4346	61465	-57119
佛坪县	Foping	3117	55700	-52583
榆林市	**Yulin**	**2678541**	**4233196**	**-1554655**
市本级	City level	1175867	970927	204940
榆阳区	Yuyang	239352	405025	-165673
神木县	Shenmu	540203	688726	-148523
府谷县	Fugu	231055	298998	-67943
横山县	Hengshan	37826	197425	-159599
靖边县	Jingbian	200008	327688	-127680
定边县	Dingbian	210812	327717	-116905
绥德县	Suide	8261	236000	-227739
米脂县	Mizhi	8041	160265	-152224
佳县	Jiaxian	9002	176687	-167685
吴堡县	Wubu	3256	105906	-102650
清涧县	Qingjian	6600	161229	-154629
子洲县	Zizhou	8258	176603	-168345
安康市	**Ankang**	**280886**	**2047357**	**-1766471**
市本级	City level	78843	299682	-220839
汉滨区	Hanbin	52206	409899	-357693
汉阴县	Hanyin	19900	171001	-151101
石泉县	Shiquan	12985	133666	-120681
宁陕县	Ningshan	7181	80040	-72859
紫阳县	Ziyang	21342	192310	-170968
岚皋县	Langao	10192	128389	-118197
平利县	Pingli	12807	161892	-149085
镇坪县	Zhenping	5944	69333	-63389
旬阳县	Xunyang	46460	258860	-212400
白河县	Baihe	13026	142285	-129259
商洛市	**Shangluo**	**290387**	**1631442**	**-1341055**
市本级	City level	39121	181074	-141953
商州区	Shangzhou	46010	242143	-196133
洛南县	Luonan	50240	243928	-193688
丹凤县	Danfeng	29822	195950	-166128
商南县	Shangnan	31983	180405	-148422
山阳县	Shanyang	38003	252670	-214667
镇安县	Zhen'an	27689	200995	-173306
柞水县	Zhashui	27519	134277	-106758
杨凌示范区	**Yangling**	**79339**	**215243**	**-135904**
市本级	City level	52750	135811	-83061
杨陵区	Yangling	26589	79432	-52843

主要统计指标解释

财政收入 指国家财政参与社会产品分配所取得的收入，是实现国家职能的财力保证。主要包括：

（1）各项税收：包括国内增值税、国内消费税、进口货物增值税和消费税、出口货物退增值税和消费税、营业税、企业所得税、个人所得税、资源税、城市维护建设税、房产税、印花税、城镇土地使用税、土地增值税、车船税、船舶吨税、车辆购置税、关税、耕地占用税、契税、烟叶税等。

（2）非税收入：包括专项收入、行政事业性收费、罚没收入和其他收入。

财政支出 指国家财政将筹集起来的资金进行分配使用，以满足经济建设和各项事业的需要。主要包括：

（1）一般公共服务：指政府提供基本公共管理与服务的支出，包括人大事务、政协事务、政府办公厅（室）及相关机构事务、发展与改革事务、统计信息事务、财政事务、税收事务、审计事务、海关事务、人力资源事务、纪检监察事务、人口与计划生育事务、商贸事务、知识产权事务、工商行政管理事务、国土资源事务、海洋管理事务、测绘事务、地震事务、气象事务、民族事务、宗教事务、港澳台侨事务、档案事务、共产党事务、民主党派事务及工商联事务、群众团体事务、彩票事务等。

（2）外交：指政府外交事务支出，包括外交行政管理、驻外机构、对外援助、国际组织、对外合作与交流、边界勘界联检等方面的支出。

（3）国防：指政府用于国防方面的支出，包括用于现役部队、预备役部队、民兵、国防科研事业、专项工程、国防动员等方面的支出。

（4）公共安全：指政府维护社会公共安全方面的支出，包括武装警察、公安、国家安全、检察、法院、司法行政、监狱、劳教、国家保密、缉私警察等。

（5）教育：指政府教育事务支出，包括教育行政管理、学前教育、小学教育、初中教育、普通高中教育、普通高等教育、初等职业教育、中专教育、技校教育、职业高中教育、高等职业教育、广播电视教育、留学生教育、特殊教育、干部继续教育、教育机关服务等。

（6）科学技术：指用于科学技术方面的支出，包括科学技术管理事务、基础研究、应用研究、技术研究与开发、科技条件与服务、社会科学、科学技术普及、科技交流与合作等。

（7）文化教育与传媒：指政府在文化、文物、体育、广播影视、新闻出版等方面的支出。

（8）社会保障和就业：指政府在社会保障与就业方面的支出，包括社会保障和就业管理事务、民政管理事务、财政对社会保险基金的补助、补充全国社会保障基金、行政事业单位离退休、企业改革补助、就业补助、抚恤、退役安置、社会福利、残疾人事业、城市居民最低生活保障、其他城镇社会救济、农村社会救济、自然灾害生活救助、红十字事务等。

（9）医疗卫生：指政府医疗卫生方面的支出，包括医疗卫生管理事务支出、医疗服务支出、医疗保障支出、疾病预防控制支出、卫生监督支出、妇幼保健支出、农村卫生支出等。

（10）环境保护：指政府环境保护支出，包括环境保护管理事务支出、环境监测与监察支出、污染治理支出、自然生态保护支出、天然林保护工程支出、退耕还林支出、风沙荒漠治理支出、退牧还草支出、已垦草原退耕还草、能源节约利用、污染减排、可再生能源和资源综合利用等支出。

（11）城乡社区事务：指政府城乡社区事务支出，包括城乡社区管理事务支出、城乡社区规划与管理支出、城乡社区公共设施支出、城乡社区住宅支出、城乡社区环境卫生支出、建设市场管理与监督支出等。

（12）农林水事务：指政府农林水事务支出，包括农业支出、林业支出、水利支出、扶贫支出、农业综合开发支出等。

（13）交通运输：指政府交通运输和邮政业方面的支出，包括公路运输支出、水路运输支出、铁路运输支出、民用航空运输支出、邮政业支出等。

（14）工业商业金融等事务：指政府对工业、商业及金融等方面的支出，包括采掘业支出、制造业支出、建筑业支出、工业和信息产业监管支出、国有资产监管支出、商业流通事务支出、金融业监管支出、旅游业管理与服务支出等。

中央财政收入和地方财政收入 指按现行分税制财政体制划分的中央本级收入和地方本级收入。属于中央财政的收入包括关税，进口货物增值税和消费税，出口货物退增值税和消费税，消费税，铁道部门、各银行总行、各保险公司总公司等集中交纳的营业税和城市维护建设税，增值税75%部分，纳入共享范围的企业所得税60%部分，未纳入共享范围的中央企业所得税、中央企业上交的利润，个人所得税60%部分，车辆购置税，船舶吨税，证券交易印花税97%部分，海洋石油资源税，中央非税收入等。属于地方财政的收入包括营业税（不含铁道部门、各银行总行、各保险公司总公司集中交纳的营业税），地方企业上交利润，城市维护建设税（不含铁道部门、各银行总行、各保险公司总公司集中交纳的部分），房产税，城镇土地使用税，土地增值税，车船税，耕地占用税，契税，烟叶税，印花税，增值税25%部分，纳入共享范围的企业所得税40%部分，个人所得税40%部分，证券交易印花税3%部分，海洋石油资源税以外的其他资源税，地方非税收入等。

Explanatory Notes on Main Statistical Indicators

Government Revenue refers to income for the government finance through participating in the distribution of social products. It is the financial guarantee to ensure government functioning. The contents of government revenue include the following main items:

(1) Various tax revenues, including domestic value added tax (VAT), domestic consumption tax, VAT and consumption tax from imports, VAT and consumption tax rebate for exports, business tax, corporate income tax, individual income tax, resource tax, city maintenance and construct tax, house property tax, stamp tax, urban land use tax, land appreciation tax, tax on vehicles and boat operation, ship tonnage tax, vehicle purchase tax, tariffs, farm land occupation tax, deed tax, and tobacco leaf tax, etc.

(2) Non-tax revenue, including special program receipts, charge of administrative and institutional units, penalty receipts and others non-tax receipts.

Government Expenditure refers to the distribution and use of the funds which the government finance has raised, so as to meet the needs of economic construction and various causes. It includes the following main items:

(1) Expenditure for general public services: It refers to the spending on the basic public management and services which provided by governments, including the expense on affairs of People's Congress, affairs of People's Political Consultative Conference, affairs of government general office and relative institutions, affairs of development and reform, affairs of statistics, affairs of finance, affairs of taxation, affairs of audit, affairs of customs, affairs of human resources and social security, affairs of discipline inspection and supervision, affairs of population and family planning, affairs of commerce and trade, affairs of intellectual property, affairs of administration for industry and commerce, affairs of land and resources, affairs of oceanic administration, affairs of surveying and mapping, affairs of earthquake, ethnic affairs, religious affairs, affairs of Hong Kong, Macao, Taiwan, and Overseas Chinese, affairs of archives administration, affairs of Chinese Communist Party, affairs of democratic parties and federation of industry and commerce, affairs of mass organization, and affairs of lottery, etc.

(2) Expenditure for foreign affairs: It refers to the spending of government on foreign affairs, including the expense on administration of foreign affairs, missions overseas, external assistance, international organizations, foreign cooperation and communication, surveying and joint inspection on borderline, etc.

(3) Expenditure for national defence: It refers to the spending of government on national defence, including the expense on active force, reserve force, militia, scientific research on national defence, special projects, mobilization of national defence, etc.

(4) Expenditure for public security: It refers to the spending of government on maintaining social and public security, including the expense on armed police force, public security, state security, prosecution, courts, justice, prison, labour education and rehabilitation, protection of state secrecy, anti-smuggling police, etc.

(5) Expenditure for education: It refers to the spending of government on education, including the expense on the administration of education, pre-primary education, primary education, secondary education, high school education, regular higher education, primary vocational education, secondary vocational education, technical school education, vocational high school education and higher vocational education, radio and television education, student abroad education, special education, on the job training of cadres, education authorities services, etc.

(6) Expenditure for science and technology: It refers to the spending of government on science and technology (S&T), including the expense on the administration of S&T, basic research, applied research, research and development, conditions and services of S&T, popularization of social science, science and technology, exchanges and cooperation of S&T, etc.

(7) Expenditure for culture, sport and media: It refers to the spending of government on culture, cultural heritage, sports, radio, film, television, press and publication, etc.

(8) Expenditure for social safety net and employment effort: It refers to the spending of government on social safety net and employment, including the expense on administration of social safety net and employment, civil affairs, budgetary subsidy on the social insurance funds, subsidy on National Social Security Fund, retirees of administrative units and institutions, subsidy on enterprise reform, subsidy on employment effort, pension, placement of ex-serviceman, social welfare, the handicapped undertakings, the system of cost of living allowances for urban residents, other urban social relief, rural social relief, living relief of natural disasters, affairs of Red Cross Society, etc.

(9) Expenditure for medical and health care: It refers to the spending of government on medical and health care, including the expense on administration of medical and health care, medical services, health care, disease prevention and control, health inspection and supervision, women and children's health, rural health care, etc.

(10) Expenditure for environment protection: It refers to the spending of government on environment protection, including the expense on administration of environment protection, environment monitoring and supervision, pollution control, natural ecology protection, project of virgin forests

protection, reforesting farmland, controlling the sources of dust storms, returning pastureland to grassland, returning pastureland to grassland, returning cultivated land to grassland, energy conservation, emissions reduction, comprehensive utilization of renewable energy and resources, etc.

(11) Expenditure for urban and rural community affairs: It refers to the spending of government on urban and rural community affairs, including the expense on administration of urban and rural community, planning and management of urban and rural community, public facilities of urban and rural community, housing of urban and rural community, sanitation of urban and rural community, management and supervision on the construction market, etc.

(12) Expenditure for agriculture, forestry and water conservancy: It refers to the spending of government on agriculture, forestry and water conservancy, including the expense on agriculture, forestry, water conservancy, poverty alleviation, comprehensive agricultural development, etc.

(13) Expenditure for transportation: It refers to the spending of government on transportation and postal services, including the expense on road transportation, waterway transportation, railway transportation, civil aviation transportation, and postal services.

(14) Expenditure for industry, commerce and banking: It refers to the spending of government on industry, commerce and banking, including the expense on mining, manufacturing, construction, industry and information technology supervision and administration, State-owned assets supervision and administration, commerce and circulation affairs, financial intermediation supervision and administration, tourism administration and service, etc.

Revenue of the Central Government and Revenue of the Local Governments refers to the revenue collected by the Central Government and that by the local governments as defined by the decentralized taxation system. In accordance with this system, the revenue of the Central Government includes tariff, VAT and consumption tax from imports, VAT and consumption tax rebate for exports, consumption tax, business tax and city maintenance and construct tax from the Ministry of Railways, head offices of banks, head offices of insurance company, which are handed over to the government in a centralized way, 75% of the value added tax, 60% the share part of the corporate income tax, unshared part of corporate income tax of the central enterprises, profit handed in by the central enterprises, 60% of individual income tax, vehicle purchase tax, ship tonnage tax, 97% of stamp tax on securities transactions, resource tax on the offshore petroleum resources. The revenue of the local governments includes business tax (excluding the part of the Ministry of Railways, head offices of banks, head offices of insurance company, which are handed over to the government in a centralized way), profit handed in by the local enterprises, city maintenance and construct tax (excluding the part of the Ministry of Railways, head offices of banks, head offices of insurance company, which are handed over to the government in a centralized way), house property tax, urban land use tax, land appreciation tax, tax on vehicles and boat operation, farm land occupation tax, deed tax, and tobacco leaf tax, stamp tax, 25% of the value added tax, 40% the share part of the corporate income tax, 40% of individual income tax, 3% of stamp tax on securities transactions, resource tax other than the tax on offshore petroleum resources, local non-tax revenue, etc.

九、价格指数

Price Indices

资料整理：王国强　沈小梅　姚小清　种都权　邹　悦

简 要 说 明

一、本篇资料反映生产、流通、消费与投资等环节的价格变动情况。主要包括居民消费价格指数、商品零售价格指数、农业生产资料价格指数、工业生产者价格指数、农产品生产价格指数、固定资产投资价格指数和房地产价格指数。

二、本篇资料由国家统计局陕西调查总队提供。

三、居民消费价格指数、商品零售价格指数采用抽样调查和重点调查相结合的方法编制，即选择不同经济区域的市、县以及有代表性的商品和服务项目作为样本，对其市场价格进行定期调查，以样本推断总体。

四、工业生产者价格指数采用重点调查与典型调查相结合的方法统计。重点调查对象为规模以上工业企业，典型调查对象为规模以下工业企业。

五、固定资产投资价格指数采用重点调查与典型调查相结合的方法统计。

六、农产品生产价格指数采用抽样调查和重点调查相结合的调查方法进行统计。

Brief Introduction

Ⅰ. This chapter reflects price changes in production, circulation, consumption and investment, mainly including consumer price indices, retail price indices, price indices of means of agricultural production, industrial producers' price indices, producers' price indices for farm products, price indices for investment in fixed assets and real estate price indices.

Ⅱ. The data are provided by NBS Survey Office in Shaanxi.

Ⅲ. The data for the calculation of consumer price indices and retail price indices in the province are collected through stratified random sampling. Cities and counties distributed in different economic regions of the province are selected as sample areas, and representative commodities and services are selected as sample commodities and services. Regular surveys are conducted to collect data on market prices. The data on the population are estimated on the basis of the sample.

Ⅳ. The industrial producers price indices are collected through key-point survey combined with typical survey. The key investigation objects are the industrial enterprises above designated size. The typical investigation objects are the industrial enterprises below designated size.

Ⅴ. The data for the calculation of price indices of investment in fixed assets are collected through key-point survey combined with typical survey.

VI. The data for the calculation of producers' price indices of farm products are collected through sampling survey combined with key-point survey.

9.价格指数

2014年全省	
商品零售价格指数(上年=100)	100.7
# 城 市	100.7
居民消费价格指数(上年=100)	101.6
# 城 市	101.6

居民消费价格指数

(上年=100)

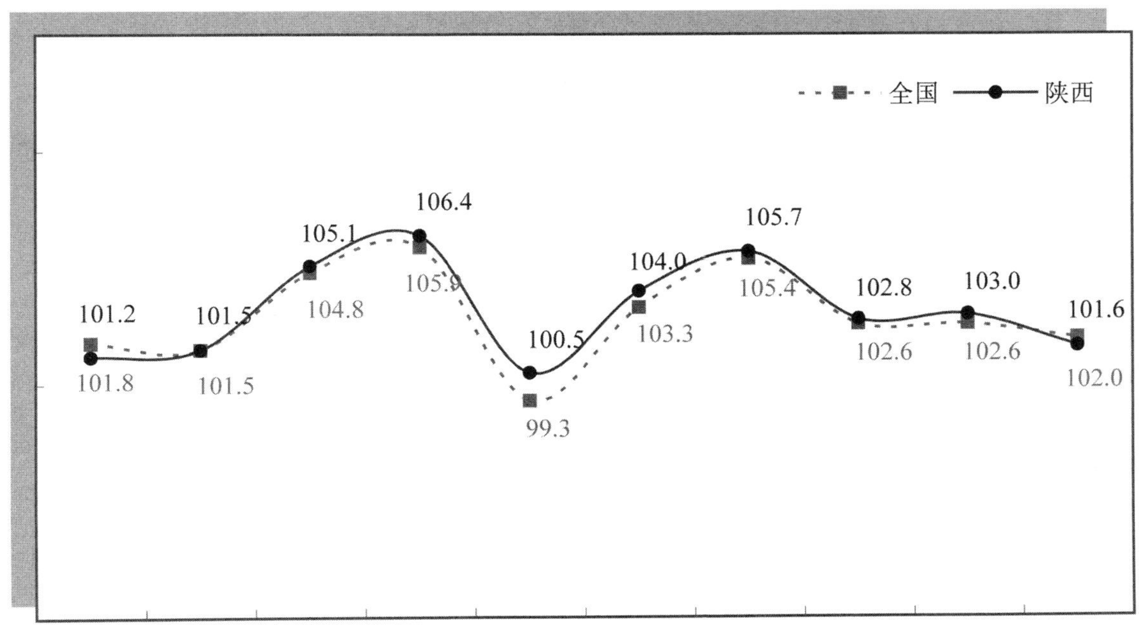

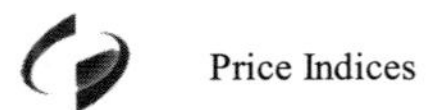

9-1 商品零售价格和居民消费价格指数
Retail Price Indices and Consumer Price Indices

年 份 Year	上年价格=100 preceding year=100			1978年价格=100 1978=100		
	商品零售价格指数 Retail Price Index	居民消费价格指数 Consumer Price Index	# 城市居民 Urban Household	商品零售价格指数 Retail Price Index	居民消费价格指数 Consumer Price Index	# 城市居民 Urban Household
1979	101.6	101.7	101.4	101.6	101.7	101.4
1980	104.7	105.3	105.4	106.4	107.1	106.9
1981	103.0	103.6	103.6	109.6	111.0	110.7
1982	101.0	101.4	100.4	110.7	112.6	111.7
1983	101.5	101.5	102.2	112.4	114.3	113.5
1984	103.9	103.0	103.4	116.8	117.7	117.4
1985	106.5	107.0	107.6	124.4	125.9	126.3
1986	105.2	106.0	106.6	130.9	133.5	134.6
1987	108.6	108.6	109.2	142.2	145.0	147.0
1988	119.0	119.1	120.1	169.2	172.7	176.5
1989	118.8	118.3	117.6	201.0	204.3	207.6
1990	101.6	101.3	102.6	204.2	207.0	213.0
1991	105.8	106.0	107.3	216.0	219.4	228.5
1992	109.5	109.7	111.2	236.5	240.7	254.1
1993	111.8	111.8	114.0	264.4	269.1	289.7
1994	125.9	126.7	128.2	332.9	340.9	371.4
1995	117.0	119.0	118.0	389.5	405.7	438.3
1996	108.1	109.7	110.3	421.0	445.1	483.4
1997	101.6	104.8	105.2	427.7	466.5	508.6
1998	96.2	98.4	97.7	411.4	459.0	496.9
1999	97.5	97.8	97.2	401.1	448.9	483.0
2000	98.3	99.5	100.3	394.3	446.7	484.4
2001	99.1	101.0	100.1	390.8	451.2	484.9
2002	98.6	98.9	98.2	385.3	446.2	476.2
2003	100.5	101.7	100.8	387.2	453.8	480.0
2004	102.5	103.1	103.0	396.9	467.9	494.4
2005	100.1	101.2	100.9	397.3	473.5	498.8
2006	101.8	101.5	102.1	404.5	480.6	509.3
2007	105.0	105.1	105.2	424.7	505.1	535.8
2008	106.9	106.4	106.2	454.0	537.4	569.0
2009	99.9	100.5	100.0	453.5	540.1	569.0
2010	103.6	104.0	103.7	469.8	561.7	590.1
2011	104.8	105.7	105.7	492.4	593.7	623.7
2012	102.3	102.8	102.6	503.7	610.3	639.9
2013	101.8	103.0	102.8	512.8	628.6	657.8
2014	100.7	101.6	101.6	516.4	638.7	668.3

9-2 商品零售价格分类指数(2014年)
Retail Price Indices by Category (2014)

(上年价格=100) (preceding year=100)

项目	Item	全省 Provincial Indices	城市 Urban Indices	农村 Rural Indices
商品零售价格总指数	**Retail Price Index**	**100.7**	**100.7**	**100.6**
一、食品	**Food**	**102.6**	**102.7**	**102.5**
1.粮食	Grain	103.2	103.2	102.9
2.淀粉及制品	Starches and Tubers	98.3	97.7	101.1
3.干豆类及豆制品	Beans and Bean Products	110.1	110.6	107.4
4.油脂	Oil or Fat	93.5	92.9	96.1
5.肉禽及其制品	Meat, Poultry and Processed Products	99.1	99.1	99.5
(1)食用畜肉及副产品	Starches	96.5	96.3	97.6
(2)禽	Bean and Its Products	109.9	110.5	105.7
(3)肉禽加工制品	Poultry Product	100.5	100.4	100.8
6.蛋	Eggs	109.5	109.7	107.9
7.水产品	Aquatic Products	103.2	103.2	103.6
(1)鱼	Fish	100.0	99.6	104.3
(2)其它水产品	Others	112.5	113.5	101.3
8.菜	Vegetables	95.6	95.1	98.9
9.调味品	Flavoring	102.8	102.9	102.0
10.糖	Sugar	101.6	101.7	100.8
11.干鲜瓜果	Dried and Fresh Melons and Fruits	114.5	114.8	112.2
12.糕点饼干面包	Cake, Biscuit and Bread	103.4	103.5	102.5
13.液体乳及乳制品	Milk and Its Products	113.5	114.0	107.7
14.在外用膳食品	Outward Dinner Food	103.2	103.1	103.6
15.其它食品	Other Foods	100.8	100.6	101.5
二、饮料、烟酒	**Beverages, Tobacco and Liquor**	**99.9**	**99.9**	**100.0**
1.茶及饮料	Tea and Beverages	102.9	102.9	102.3
(1)茶叶	Tea	103.4	103.4	103.2
(2)饮料	Beverages	102.5	102.6	101.7
2.烟草	Tobacco	99.9	99.9	100.0
3.酒	Liquor	96.8	96.6	98.0
三、服装、鞋帽	**Garments, Shoes and Hats**	**100.8**	**100.7**	**101.2**
1.服装	Garments	101.1	101.0	101.9
(1)男式服装	Man's Garments	100.6	100.5	100.7
(2)女式服装	Woman's Garments	100.9	100.8	101.6
(3)儿童服装	Children's Garments	104.0	103.8	104.4
2.鞋袜帽	Footgear and Hats	100.2	100.2	100.1
(1)鞋	Shoes	100.1	100.1	99.5
(2)袜子	Socks and Stockings	101.3	101.0	102.3
(3)帽子	Hats	102.8	102.6	103.3
3.其它	Others	99.0	98.7	100.7

9-2 续表 continued

(上年价格=100) (preceding year=100)

项 目	Item	全 省 Provincial Indices	城 市 Urban Indices	农 村 Rural Indices
四、纺织品	**Textiles**	**101.4**	**101.4**	**101.1**
1.衣着材料	Clothing	101.6	101.4	102.4
2.床上用品	Bedding	101.3	101.5	100.0
五、家用电器及音像器材	**Household Appliances, Music and Video Equipment**	**98.1**	**98.1**	**97.6**
1.家庭设备	Household Facilities	99.5	99.6	99.2
2.文娱用耐用消费品	Durable Consumer Goods for Recreation	94.9	94.8	95.2
3.音像器材	Audiovisual Articles	99.9	99.9	99.9
六、文化办公用品	**Cultural and Office Appliances**	**98.5**	**98.3**	**99.8**
七、日用品	**Articles for Daily Use**	**100.8**	**100.7**	**101.9**
1.日用百货	General Merchandise for Daily Use	100.1	99.8	101.4
2.日用杂品	Miscellaneous for Daily Use	101.6	101.5	102.5
3.洗涤用品	Washing Goods	101.5	101.5	101.4
4.其它日用品	Others	100.6	100.3	102.8
八、体育娱乐用品	**Sports and Recreation Articles**	**100.2**	**99.9**	**102.3**
1.体育用品	Sports Articles	100.3	100.2	102.0
2.娱乐用品	Recreational Articles	100.0	99.8	102.7
九、交通、通信用品	**Transportation and Communication Appliances**	**98.3**	**98.7**	**95.2**
1.交通运输机械	Means of Transportation	100.0	100.1	98.7
2.通讯器材	Means of Communication	91.7	91.2	92.5
十、家 具	**Furniture**	**99.1**	**98.9**	**100.2**
十一、化妆品	**Cosmetics**	**101.5**	**101.6**	**100.8**
十二、金银珠宝	**Gold, Silver and Jewelry**	**91.1**	**91.2**	**90.5**
十三、中西药品及医疗保健用品	**Traditional Chinese and Western Medicines and Health Care Articles Care Articles**	**104.7**	**104.9**	**102.9**
1.医疗器具及用品	Medical Apparatus and Article	103.7	104.1	100.1
2.中药材及中成药	Traditional Chinese Medicinal Materials and Medicines	109.2	109.7	105.0
3.西 药	Western Medicines	101.3	101.3	101.9
4.保健器具及用品	Health Care Equipment and Articles	101.7	102.0	100.3
十四、书报杂志及电子出版物	**Books, Newspapers, Magazines and Electronic Publications**	**103.1**	**103.3**	**101.4**
1.教材及参考书	Teaching Materials and Reference Books	102.5	102.6	102.4
2.书报杂志	Newspapers and Magazines	105.1	105.8	100.9
3.电子音像制品	Electronic Audiovisual Products	100.9	101.0	100.4
十五、燃 料	**Fuels**	**98.2**	**98.1**	**98.7**
1.煤炭及制品	Coal and Coal Products	95.0	94.5	97.7
2.石油及制品	Petroleum and its Products	99.2	99.2	99.1
十六、建筑材料及五金电料	**Building Materials and Hardware**	**96.5**	**95.9**	**100.2**
1.建筑装璜材料	Building Decoration Materials	95.3	94.5	100.0
2.五金电料	Hardware	99.8	99.7	100.4

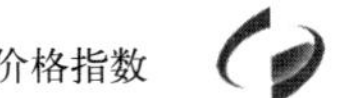

9-3 居民消费价格分类指数(2014年)
Consumer Price Indices by Category (2014)

(上年价格=100) (preceding year=100)

项　目	Item	全省 Provincial Indices	城市 Urban Indices	农村 Rural Indices
居民消费价格总指数	**Consumer Price Index**	**101.6**	**101.6**	**101.8**
非食品价格指数	Non-food Price Index	101.0	100.9	101.2
服务项目价格指数	Services Price Index	102.2	102.1	102.5
扣除鲜菜鲜果总指数	Index net of Fresh Vegetables and Fruit	101.5	101.5	101.6
消费品价格指数	Consumer Price Index	101.4	101.4	101.5
一、食　品	**Food**	**102.8**	**102.9**	**102.7**
1.粮　食	Grain	103.3	103.4	103.0
2.淀粉及制品	Starches and Tubers	99.6	98.1	101.7
3.干豆类及豆制品	Beans and Bean Products	109.7	110.9	107.2
4.油　脂	Oil or Fat	94.2	93.0	96.2
5.肉禽及其制品	Meat, Poultry and Processed Products	98.9	98.7	99.5
(1)食用畜肉及副产品	Poultry Meat and By-product	96.6	96.1	97.6
(2)禽	Poultry	108.9	110.6	106.1
(3)加工肉禽	Poultry Product	100.6	100.5	100.8
6.蛋	Eggs	109.2	110.0	107.6
7.水产品	Aquatic Products	104.0	104.1	103.5
(1)鱼	Fish	101.6	100.7	104.2
(2)其它水产品	Others	110.8	113.2	101.4
8.菜	Vegetables	96.7	95.2	99.8
9.调味品	Flavoring	102.4	102.8	102.0
10.糖	Carbohydrate	101.9	102.3	101.1
11.茶及饮料	Tea and Beverages	102.3	102.4	102.0
(1)茶　叶	Tea	102.9	102.9	102.9
(2)饮　料	Beverages	102.0	102.2	101.4
12.干鲜瓜果	Dried and Fresh Melons and Fruits	114.2	115.2	112.0
13.糕点饼干面包	Cake, Biscuit and Bread	103.3	103.7	102.2
14.液体乳及乳制品	Milk and Its Products	112.8	114.1	107.7
15.在外用膳食品	Dining Out	103.4	103.3	103.7
16.其它食品	Other Foods	99.8	99.1	101.1
二、烟　酒	**Tobacco and Liquor**	**98.8**	**98.7**	**99.1**
1.烟　草	Tobacco	99.9	99.8	100.0
2.酒	Liquor	97.2	97.0	97.9
三、衣　着	**Clothing**	**101.1**	**100.9**	**101.6**
1.服　装	Garments	101.3	101.0	101.9
(1)男式服装	Man's Garments	100.7	100.6	101.1
(2)女式服装	Woman's Garments	101.0	100.9	101.5
(3)儿童服装	Children's Garments	104.4	104.3	104.5
2.衣着材料	Clothing Material	102.1	101.0	103.0
3.鞋袜帽	Footgear and Hats	100.0	100.0	100.0
(1)鞋	Shoes	99.6	99.8	99.3
(2)袜　子	Socks and Stockings	101.7	101.0	102.7
(3)帽　子	Hats	103.7	102.7	104.7
4.衣着加工服务费	Clothing Manufacturing Services	107.5	107.9	106.8

9-3 续表 continued

(上年价格=100) (preceding year=100)

项 目	Item	全省 Provincial Indices	城市 Urban Indices	农村 Rural Indices
四、家庭设备用品及维修服务	**Household Facilities, Articles and Services**	**101.0**	**101.1**	**100.9**
1.耐用消费品	Durable Consumer Goods	99.4	99.2	100.0
(1)家 具	Furniture	99.5	99.1	100.7
(2)家庭设备	Household Facilities	99.3	99.3	99.5
2.室内装饰品	Interior Decorations	100.1	99.7	100.7
3.床上用品	Bed Articles	100.2	100.4	99.8
4.家庭日用杂品	Daily Use Household Articles	100.8	100.6	101.6
5.家庭服务及加工维修服务	Household Services and Maintenance and Renovation	111.0	113.5	104.5
五、医疗保健和个人用品	**Health Care and Personal Articles**	**102.7**	**103.1**	**101.7**
1.医疗保健	Health Care	103.5	104.1	102.2
(1)医疗器具及用品	Medical Instrument and Articles	102.0	103.5	100.0
(2)中药材及中成药	Traditional Chinese Medicine	108.3	109.8	104.6
(3)西 药	Western Medicine	101.4	101.3	101.8
(4)保健器具及用品	Health Care Appliances and Articles	101.5	102.0	100.2
(5)医疗保健服务	Health Care Services	100.9	101.1	100.5
2.个人用品及服务	Personal Articles and Services	100.6	100.6	100.7
(1)化妆美容用品	Cosmetics	101.6	101.6	101.6
(2)清洁化妆用品	Sanitation Articles	100.6	100.3	101.1
(3)个人饰品	Personal Ornaments	95.8	94.9	97.1
(4)个人服务	Personal Services	102.6	102.9	102.1
六、交通和通信	**Transportation and Communication**	**99.9**	**100.0**	**99.9**
1.交 通	Transportation	101.5	101.6	101.3
(1)交通工具	Transportation Facility	99.9	99.8	100.1
(2)车用燃料及零配件	Fuels and Parts	98.9	98.7	99.4
(3)车辆使用及维修费	Fees for Vehicles Use and Maintenance	105.6	106.3	104.4
(4)市区公共交通费	Incity Traffic Fare	100.5	100.1	101.7
(5)城市间交通费	Intercity Traffic Fare	103.2	103.6	102.0
2.通 信	Communication	98.3	98.3	98.3
(1)通信工具	Communication Facility	89.7	87.6	92.6
(2)通信服务	Communication Service	100.0	100.0	100.0
七、娱乐教育文化用品及服务	**Recreation, Education and Culture Articles**	**100.7**	**100.3**	**101.7**
1.文娱用耐用消费品及服务	Durable Consumer Goods for Cultural and Recreational Use and Services	95.7	95.3	96.5
2.教 育	Education	101.8	101.5	102.6
(1)教材及参考书	Teaching Materials and Reference Books	102.5	102.2	102.9
(2)教育服务	Education Services	101.7	101.3	102.5
3.文化娱乐	Cultural and Recreational Articles	102.8	103.2	101.8
(1)文化娱乐用品	Cultural Articles	100.8	100.3	101.8
(2)书报杂志	Newspapers and Magazines	104.1	105.6	101.1
(3)文娱费	Expenditure on Culture and Recreation	103.8	104.2	102.2
4.旅 游	Touring and Outing	99.1	97.3	105.4
八、居 住	**Residence**	**101.2**	**100.9**	**101.7**
1.建房及装修材料	Building and Building Decoration Materials	97.2	95.5	100.4
2.住房租金	Renting	103.4	103.2	103.8
3.自有住房	Private Housing	103.3	103.4	103.1
4.水、电、燃料	Water, Electricity and Fuels	99.8	99.7	100.1

9-4 十九个市、县商品零售价格分类指数(2014年)
Retail Price Indices by Category of 19 Cities and Counties(2014)

(上年价格=100) (preceding year=100)

地 区	Region	总指数 General Index	一、食品 Food	二、饮料烟酒 Beverages, Tobacco and Liquor	三、服装鞋帽 Garments, Shoes and Hats	四、纺织品 Textiles	五、家用电器及音像器材 Household Appliances, Music and Video Equipment	六、文化办公用品 Cultural and Office Appliances	七、日用品 Articles for Daily Use	八、体育娱乐用品 Sports and Recreation Articles
全 省	**Shaanxi**	**100.7**	**102.6**	**99.9**	**100.8**	**101.4**	**98.1**	**98.5**	**100.8**	**100.2**
国家调查点	**National Survey Points**									
西 安 市	Xi'an	100.7	103.0	100.4	100.9	101.1	98.7	97.9	100.4	98.8
宝 鸡 市	Baoji	100.3	103.2	97.7	99.4	100.5	94.4	99.9	99.9	100.7
汉 台 区	Hantai	102.2	103.8	100.1	104.6	109.1	96.9	101.5	103.5	105.3
咸 阳 市	Xianyan	101.3	104.8	100.6	100.2	100.9	95.4	95.9	100.7	100.4
榆 阳 区	Yuyang	100.4	101.1	102.4	100.2	102.3	98.5	100.3	103.8	101.5
汉 滨 区	Hanbin	100.1	102.6	97.8	100.6	98.7	96.4	100.3	101.2	99.8
三 原 县	Sanyuan	99.8	104.4	98.2	94.7	100.2	95.3	98.0	98.9	100.0
商 州 区	Shangzhou	102.4	103.7	101.8	102.2	110.5	99.7	101.8	107.6	110.9
省级调查点	**Provincial Survey Points**									
铜 川 市	Tongchuan	100.8	103.3	99.6	97.9	100.7	100.4	100.0	98.2	101.0
宝 塔 区	Baota	99.9	102.0	100.0	100.4	88.4	97.1	95.7	102.6	102.0
临 渭 区	Linwei	101.0	101.8	100.4	101.0	101.1	99.0	97.2	100.9	104.7
西 乡 县	Xixiang	100.7	102.9	100.5	102.8	99.4	98.6	99.7	101.1	100.9
陇 县	Longxian	102.1	103.6	100.8	96.9	102.9	97.8	100.5	103.4	108.3
洛 南 县	Luonan	100.6	102.9	99.4	106.0	100.8	99.9	97.4	100.6	100.1
蒲 城 县	Puchneng	100.3	102.0	99.1	101.2	100.0	95.8	101.1	101.4	100.0
户 县	Huxian	101.7	103.4	101.7	103.9	101.4	99.3	99.0	102.5	106.4
绥 德 县	Suide	99.1	100.2	98.2	98.4	98.0	95.0	100.5	100.1	100.6
华 阴 市	Huayin	100.4	103.1	101.6	103.6	99.6	98.8	99.2	101.0	100.0
略 阳 县	Lueyang	100.6	102.0	100.3	103.5	100.1	98.0	97.6	100.8	100.0

9-4 续表 continued

(上年价格=100) (preceding year=100)

地 区	Region	九、交通通信用品 Transportation and Communication Appliances	十、家具 Furniture	十一、化妆品 Cosmetics	十二、金银珠宝 Gold, Silver and Jewelry	十三、中西药品及医疗保健用品 Traditional Chinese and Western Medicines and Health	十四、书报杂志及电子出版物 Books, Newspapers, Magazines and Electronic Publications	十五、燃料 Fuels	十六、建筑材料及五金电料 Building Materials and Hardware
全 省	**Shaanxi**	**98.3**	**99.1**	**101.5**	**91.1**	**104.7**	**103.1**	**98.2**	**96.5**
国家调查点	**National Survey Points**								
西 安 市	Xi'an	98.8	98.2	101.5	91.2	104.5	104.1	98.5	94.2
宝 鸡 市	Baoji	98.9	100.8	101.9	91.1	102.7	101.2	96.2	98.1
汉 台 区	Hantai	94.3	102.6	100.5	92.6	105.9	100.4	100.4	102.8
咸 阳 市	Xianyan	98.3	100.3	103.9	95.4	102.5	98.8	99.7	100.4
榆 阳 区	Yuyang	90.8	100.3	101.3	98.2	102.4	101.3	97.8	102.2
汉 滨 区	Hanbin	94.5	100.0	99.7	89.4	101.1	102.4	99.7	100.2
三 原 县	Sanyuan	91.5	98.3	98.2	84.2	103.4	98.8	98.2	100.0
商 州 区	Shangzhou	99.0	104.4	107.3	85.9	100.2	105.6	100.2	98.8
省级调查点	**Provincial Survey Points**								
铜 川 市	Tongchuan	96.7	100.0	99.8	92.9	104.0	100.0	100.1	101.6
宝 塔 区	Baota	98.5	99.6	102.7	92.9	101.3	101.8	95.8	99.6
临 渭 区	Linwei	99.3	101.5	99.6	97.3	103.4	101.1	101.2	100.6
西 乡 县	Xixiang	91.8	104.5	99.9	81.9	102.8	101.0	99.4	101.0
陇 县	Longxian	103.4	108.0	100.9	92.2	103.8	103.7	101.4	100.7
洛 南 县	Luonan	84.9	99.8	100.5	90.0	102.6	100.0	98.4	98.8
蒲 城 县	Puchneng	98.6	100.1	100.0	89.9	104.1	100.3	97.0	99.7
户 县	Huxian	98.8	100.3	101.1	90.9	103.7	100.5	100.7	98.1
绥 德 县	Suide	92.9	93.4	100.0	93.2	105.5	101.2	97.4	104.0
华 阴 市	Huayin	92.9	99.8	101.4	93.4	102.4	103.0	95.4	97.7
略 阳 县	Lueyang	95.2	102.6	100.1	88.5	100.3	102.9	99.7	100.6

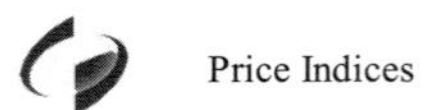

9-5 十九个市、县居民消费价格分类指数(2014年)
Consumer Price Indices by Category and Region of 19 Cities and Counties(2014)

(上年价格=100) (preceding year=100)

地区 Region	总指数 General Index	一、食品 Food	二、烟酒 Tobacco and Liquor	三、衣着 Clothing	四、家庭设备用品及维修服务 Household Facilities, Articles and Services	五、医疗保健和个人用品 Health Care and Personal Articles	六、交通和通信 Transportation and Communication	七、娱乐教育文化用品及服务 Recreation, Education and Culture Articles	八、居住 Residence
全省 Shaanxi	**101.6**	**102.8**	**98.8**	**101.1**	**101.0**	**102.7**	**99.9**	**100.7**	**101.2**
国家调查点 National Survey Points									
西安市 Xi'an	101.4	102.9	98.4	101.1	101.9	102.8	100.2	100.1	99.8
宝鸡市 Baoji	101.9	103.7	98.3	99.7	99.4	103.2	100.4	100.2	101.7
汉台区 Hantai	103.1	103.7	99.8	104.8	103.4	104.3	99.7	101.3	103.7
咸阳市 Xianyan	102.2	104.7	100.5	100.6	98.3	105.1	99.4	100.2	101.0
榆阳区 Yuyang	101.1	100.9	101.2	100.3	101.2	101.4	100.3	103.3	101.0
汉滨区 Hanbin	101.0	102.3	96.8	100.1	99.0	100.6	99.5	101.0	101.3
三原县 Sanyuan	101.5	104.5	97.0	95.1	99.0	102.0	100.7	99.2	102.1
商州区 Shangzhou	102.5	103.8	100.9	103.5	105.2	102.1	100.4	103.0	99.9
省级调查点 Provincial Survey Points									
铜川市 Tongchuan	101.8	103.2	99.6	99.6	100.8	101.4	100.1	101.5	102.4
宝塔区 Baota	101.4	102.0	99.7	100.4	99.0	101.7	99.9	101.3	102.2
临渭区 Linwei	101.6	102.0	100.3	101.1	101.4	101.8	100.1	101.0	102.2
西乡县 Xixiang	101.9	102.7	100.1	102.6	103.2	102.0	100.1	102.4	100.4
陇县 Longxian	102.8	103.8	100.4	98.8	104.3	103.0	101.1	102.5	103.8
洛南县 Luonan	103.1	103.4	98.4	105.8	100.8	100.7	99.1	101.4	106.6
蒲城县 Puchneng	101.1	102.1	98.1	101.6	99.2	101.8	100.2	102.1	99.4
户县 Huxian	102.0	103.4	100.4	104.1	100.5	101.9	99.7	100.0	101.0
绥德县 Suide	101.0	100.4	98.1	98.9	99.6	103.2	98.1	101.5	103.9
华阴市 Huayin	102.2	103.1	100.4	103.5	101.4	102.0	100.8	103.8	99.9
略阳县 Lueyang	101.7	101.8	100.3	103.9	102.4	100.3	99.8	102.4	102.1

9-6 农业生产资料价格指数
Price Indices for Means of Agricultural Production

(上年价格=100) (preceding year=100)

类 别	Item	2013	2014
总指数	**General Index**	**102.6**	**100.9**
一、农用手工工具	Farm Handtools	104.4	101.3
二、饲 料	Forage	105.7	103.4
混合饲料	Mixed Forage	105.8	103.4
其 他	Others	105.5	103.4
三、产品畜	Commodity Animals	102.7	97.9
幼禽家畜	Poultry and Livestock	102.7	97.9
四、半机械化农具	Semi-mechanized Farm Tools	103.0	100.7
五、机械化农具	Mechanized Farm Machinery	101.0	101.7
农用机械	Farm Machinery	101.0	101.7
六、化学肥料	Chemical Fertilizer	98.1	96.8
氮 肥	Nitrogenous Fertilizer	96.8	95.7
磷 肥	Phosphate Fertilizer	100.9	96.3
钾 肥	Potash Fertilizer	98.6	100.3
复合肥料	Compound Fertilizer	99.3	99.5
七、农药及农药械	Pesticide and Its Appliances	103.3	102.0
化学农药	Chemical Pesticide	103.8	102.2
杀虫剂	Insecticide	101.8	100.9
杀菌剂	Bactericide	107.3	102.8
除草剂	Herbicide	105.0	105.3
农药器械	Appliances for Pesticide	101.0	101.4
八、农用机油	Oil for Farm Machinery	99.6	99.1
九、其他农业生产资料	Other Means of Agricultural Production	105.9	104.9
农用种子	Seeds for Farming	108.0	105.8
其 他	Others	102.4	103.3
农用薄膜	Pellicle for Farming	101.7	103.7
其 他	Others	104.4	102.3
十、农业生产服务	Service for Agricultural Production	108.2	105.6
排灌费	Expenditure of Irrigation and Drainage	110.5	108.1
机械作业费	Expenditure of Mechanical Operations	107.9	104.4
农业用电	Agricultural Electricity	100.4	100.2
农业用工	Agricultural Labor	112.0	107.7

9-7 工业生产者出厂价格指数
Producer Price Index for Industrial Products

(上年价格=100) (preceding year=100)

类 别	Item	2013	2014
总指数	**General Index**	**97.3**	**97.1**
按轻重工业分	Grouped by Light & Heavy Industries		
轻工业	Light Industry	100.9	101.4
以农产品为原料	Agricultural Products as Raw Materials	101.0	101.0
以非农产品为原料	Non-agricultural Products as Raw Materials	100.2	103.0
重工业	Heavy Industry	96.8	96.5
采掘工业	Mining & Quarrying Industry	94.5	93.9
原料工业	Raw Materials Industry	96.2	96.3
加工工业	Processing Industry	99.0	98.4
按用途分	Grouped by Use		
生产资料	Means of Production	96.8	96.5
采掘工业	Mining & Quarrying Industry	94.5	93.9
原料工业	Raw Materials Industry	96.1	96.3
加工工业	Processing Industry	99.0	98.5
生活资料	Consumer Goods	100.6	100.9
食 品	Food	101.0	101.8
衣 着	Clothing	102.5	102.4
一般工业品	Articles for Daily Use	99.6	100.9
耐用消费品	Durable Consumer Goods	100.5	98.0
按工业部门分	By Department of Industry		
1.冶金工业	Metallurgical Industry	95.0	97.0
2.电力工业	Power Industry	101.0	99.0
3.煤炭及炼焦工业	Coal and Coking Industry	87.2	86.0
4.石油工业	Petroleum Industry	97.6	97.6
5.化学工业	Chemical Industry	97.5	98.1
6.机械工业	Machine Industry	100.4	99.8
7.建筑材料工业	Building Materials Industry	98.7	97.9
8.森林工业	Forestry Industry	102.2	101.1
9.食品工业	Food Industry	100.9	101.6
10.纺织工业	Textile Industry	103.4	97.9
11.缝纫工业	Tailoring Industry	102.8	102.6
12.皮革工业	Leather Industry	99.9	99.7
13.造纸工业	Paper Making Industry	98.6	98.0
14.文教艺术用品工业	Cultural, Education & Handicrafts Article	97.6	95.7
15.其它工业	Other Industry	103.4	102.9

9-8 工业生产者购进价格指数
Purchasing Price Index for Industrial Products

(上年价格=100)

类　别	Item	2013	2014
总指数	**General Index**	**99.3**	**98.5**
一、燃料、动力类	Fuels	98.4	97.1
二、黑色金属材料类	Ferrous Metal Materials	97.0	97.7
钢　材	Steel	96.8	97.0
其　它	Others	97.3	99.0
三、有色金属材料类和电线类	Non-ferrous Metals	96.5	98.9
四、化工原材料类	Chemical Raw Materials	95.2	96.6
五、木材及纸浆类	Timber and Paper Pulp	99.2	99.6
六、建筑材料类及非金属矿类	Building Materials and Non-metal Mineral	99.4	97.5
七、其它工业原材料及半成品	Other Industrial Raw Materials and Half-products	99.4	99.6
八、农副产品类	Farm Products	104.8	101.0
九、纺织原材料类	Textile Raw Materials	101.3	101.6

9-9 固定资产投资价格指数
Price Index of Investment in Fixed Assets

(上年价格=100)

类　别	Item	2013	2014
总指数	**General Index**	**102.0**	**101.1**
一、建筑安装工程	Construction and Installation	102.3	101.2
1.材料费	Material	98.8	97.9
钢　材	Steel	95.8	93.9
木　材	Timber	103.8	104.4
水　泥	Cement	99.1	99.8
地方材料	Local Construction Material	102.9	101.4
化工材料	Chemical Material	102.7	100.4
电　料	Electric Material	101.2	99.4
其它材料	Others	104.5	101.8
2.人工费	Labour	109.8	108.0
3.机械使用费	Machinery	103.1	102.3
二、设备工器具购置	Purchase of Equipment,Tools and Instruments	99.5	99.9
三、其它费用	Others	103.7	101.8

9-10 农产品生产价格指数
Producers' Price Indices for Farm Products

(上年价格=100) (preceding year=100)

类 别	Item	2013	2014
总指数	**General Index**	**107.4**	**102.1**
一、农业产品	Planting Products	110.3	104.8
# 小 麦	Wheat	111.0	104.4
玉 米	Corn	102.5	103.4
油 料	Oil-bearing Crops	107.9	95.9
水 果	Fruit	112.3	110.9
二、林业产品	Forestry Products	95.2	98.9
三、饲养动物及其产品	Animal Feeding and Products	102.0	96.6
# 活 猪	Live pigs	97.1	90.6
鸡 蛋	Eggs	105.8	107.0
四、渔业产品	Fishery Products	104.6	101.5

9-11 西安市住宅销售价格指数
Sales Price Index of Residential Buildings and Second-hand House in Xi'an

(上年价格=100) (preceding year=100)

类 别	Item	2013	2014
新建住宅销售价格指数	**Sales Price Index of New Residential Buildings**	**106.2**	**103.7**
新建商品住宅	New Commercialized Residential Buildings	107.3	104.1
1.90平方米以下	Less Than 90 Sq.m	107.9	104.2
2.90－144平方米	90-144 Sq.m	106.1	103.5
3.144平方米以上	144 Sq.m and more	106.9	105.1
二手住宅销售价格指数	**Sales Price Index of Second-hand House**	**102.7**	**99.8**
1.90平方米以下	Less Than 90 Sq.m	104.1	99.7
2.90－144平方米	90-144 Sq.m	101.4	99.8
3.144平方米以上	144 Sq.m and more	103.8	100.1

主要统计指标解释

居民消费价格指数 是反映一定时期内城乡居民所购买的生活消费品价格和服务项目价格变动趋势和程度的相对数，是对城市居民消费价格指数和农村居民消费价格指数进行综合汇总计算的结果。该指数可以观察和分析消费品的零售价格和服务项目价格变动对城乡居民实际生活费支出的影响程度。

城市居民消费价格指数 是反映一定时期内城市居民家庭所购买的生活消费品价格和服务项目价格变动趋势和程度的相对数。该指数可以观察和分析消费品的零售价格和服务项目价格变动对城镇职工货币工资的影响，作为研究职工生活和确定工资政策的依据。

农村居民消费价格指数 是反映一定时期内农村居民家庭所购买的生活消费品价格和服务项目价格变动趋势和程度的相对数。该指数可以观察农村消费品的零售价格和服务项目价格变动对农村居民生活消费支出的影响，直接反映农村居民生活水平的实际变化情况，为分析和研究农村居民生活问题提供依据。

商品零售价格指数 是反映一定时期内城乡商品零售价格变动趋势和程度的相对数。商品零售价格的变动直接影响到城乡居民的生活支出和国家的财政收入，影响居民购买力和市场供需的平衡，影响到消费与积累的比例关系。因此，该指数可以从一个侧面对上述经济活动进行观察和分析。

农业生产资料价格指数 指反映一定时期内农业生产资料价格变动趋势和程度的相对数。其编制目的是了解农业生产中物质资料投入价格的变动状况，服务于国民经济核算。1994 年以前，农业生产资料价格指数仅仅是商品零售价格指数的一个类别，此后，从商品零售价格指数中分离出来，单独编制。

农产品生产价格指数 是反映一定时期内，农产品生产者出售农产品价格水平变动趋势及幅度的相对数。该指数可以客观反映全国农产品生产价格水平和结构变动情况，满足农业与国民经济核算需要。其中某代表品生产价格指数是通过对全部有出售该产品行为的调查单位的个体指数进行几何平均求得的，类价格指数是通过对其所属的类（或代表品）的价格指数进行加权平均求得的。季度累计价格指数的计算方法与分季指数的计算方法相同。

工业生产者价格 包括工业企业产品第一次出售时的出厂价格和企业作为中间投入的原材料、燃料、动力购进价格（简称工业生产者购进价格）。

工业生产者出厂价格指数 是反映一定时期内全部工业产品出厂价格总水平的变动趋势和程度的相对数，包括工业企业销售给本企业以外所有单位的各种产品和直接售给居民用于生活消费的产品。该指数可以观察出厂价格变动对工业总产值及增加值的影响。

工业生产者购进价格指数 是反映工业企业作为生产投入，而从物资交易市场和能源、原材料生产企业购买原材料、燃料和动力产品时，所支付的价格水平变动趋势和程度的统计指标，是扣除工业企业物质消耗成本中的价格变动影响的重要依据。

固定资产投资价格指数 是反映一定时期内固定资产投资品及取费项目的价格变动趋势和程度的相对数。固定资产投资额是由建筑安装工程投资完成额、设备工器具购置投资完成额和其他费用投资完成额三部分组成的。编制固定资产投资价格指数应首先分别编制上述三部分投资的价格指数，然后采用加权算术平均法求出固定资产投资价格总指数。

该指数可以准确地反映固定资产投资中涉及的各类投资品和取费项目价格变动趋势和变动幅度，消除按现价计算的固定资产投资指标中的价格变动因素，真实地反映固定资产投资的规模、速度、结构和效益，为国家科学地制定、检查固定资产投资计划并提高宏观调控水平，为完善国民经济核算体系提供科学的、可靠的依据。

Explanatory Notes on Main Statistical Indicators

Consumer Price Indices reflect the trend and degree of changes in prices of consumer goods and services purchased by urban and rural households during a given period. They are obtained by combining Consumer Price Indices of Urban Household and Consumer Price Indices of Rural Household. The Indices enable the observation and analysis of the degree of impact of the changes in the prices of retailed goods and services on the actual living expenses of urban and rural residents.

Consumer Price Indices of Urban Household reflect the trend and degree of changes in prices of consumer goods and services purchased by urban households during a given period. It can be used to observe and analyze the impact of price changes in consumer goods and services on wages (in monetary terms) of urban staff and workers, and provide a basis for research on the livelihood of staff and workers and policy-making concerning wages.

Consumer Price Indices of Rural Household reflect the trend and degree of changes in prices of consumer goods and services purchased by rural households during a given period. It can be used to observe the impact of change in retail prices of consumer goods and service prices in rural areas on living expenditure of rural households, and to show the changes in the living standard of rural households. It provides a basis for analysis and research on the condition of life in rural areas.

Retail Price Indices reflect the trend and degree of change in retail prices of commodities during a given period. The change in retail prices of commodities directly affect the living expenses of urban and rural residents, government revenue, purchasing power of residents and the equilibrium of market supply and demand, and the ratio of consumption to accumulation. Therefore, the retail price indices are useful from an oblique perspective for observing and analyzing the changes of the above economic activities.

Price Indices for Means of Agricultural Production reflect the trend and degree of changes in the prices of the means of agricultural production during a given period. Compilation of these indices helps to understand the changes in prices of input into agricultural production and facilitate the compilation of national accounts statistics. Before 1994, price indices for means of agricultural production were a sub-category in the retail price indices for commodities, and it has been compiled separately since 1994.

Producer Prices Indices for Farm Products reflect the trend and degree of changes in producers' prices received by farmers when they sell farm products during a given period. These indices depict the change in the level and structure of producer prices for farm products of the country and meet the needs of agricultural statistics and national accounts statistics. The producer price index for a given product is calculated as the geometrical mean of individual indices for all surveyed units which sell such product, and the indices for a product category is obtained as the weighted mean of price indices for all products in the category. Method for calculating accumulative quarterly indices is the same as for calculating the individual quarterly indices.

Industrial Producer Price includes the ex-factory price when the products were first sold and the purchasing price of raw materials, fuel and power as intermediate input by enterprises (short for Industrial Producer Price).

Ex-factory Price Indices of Industrial Producer are to reflect ex-factory general price level of all industrial products in a given period the number of fluctuant trend and degree, including products sold to other units by industrial enterprises and products sold to residents for living. The index shows that ex-factory price changes influence on gross industrial output value and value-added.

Purchase price Indices of Industrial Producer are the statistical Indices to reflect the fluctuant trend and degree of the price as production inputs by industrial enterprises, which are paid for raw materials, fuel and power products, purchasing from material trading market and energy and raw materials production enterprises. It's the important basis of subtracting effects from price changes of industrial enterprises material cost.

十、人民生活

资料整理：于秋白　张应剑　李　宁　孙士梅

简 要 说 明

一、本篇资料反映陕西城乡居民生活状况，主要包括全省居民家庭常住人口、可支配收入、生活消费支出、主要商品购买数量、耐用消费品拥有情况、居住情况等。

二、本篇资料来源:

全省居民、城镇居民和农村居民生活状况数据来源于国家统计局陕西调查总队城镇住户抽样调查和农村住户抽样调查。

各市（区）城乡居民收入及县（市、区）城乡居民收入由省统计局地方经济调查中心调查统计。

三、2012年四季度起国家统计局实施全国统一的城乡一体化居民收支调查。由于2013年调查样本为全新抽取样本，且与往年城镇居民、农村居民抽选总体、方法不同，调查范围更广，统计口径发生变化，与老口径数据存在差异。本年鉴2013年、2014年全省数据为新口径数据，市及县（市、区）为老口径数据。

Brief Introduction

Ⅰ. This chapter reflects the people's living conditions in Shaanxi, consisting of the resident population , disposable income, living expenditure, the main commodity purchase quantity, consumer durables situation, the inhabit situation and etc.

Ⅱ. Sources of Data:

The data on the livelihood of province residents, urban residents and rural residents are obtained from sample surveys on urban and rural households conducted by the Division of Urban and Rural Household Survey under Shaanxi Survey Office of the National Bureau of Statistics.

The incomes of both urban and rural residents of cities (districts) and counties(cities, districts) are collected by the local economic survey center of the Statistic Bureau of Shaanxi Province.

Ⅲ. National Bureau of Statistic conducted the urban-rural integration revenue and expenditure investigation all over the nation since fourth-quarter in 2012. Because of investigation samples in 2013 are brand new samples, the selected population and methods are different from urban and rural residents chosen in previous years. The field of investigation are broader, statistics range have been changed, they are different from the old range data. The total of province in 2013 and 2014 yearbook are new range data. The data of counties (cities, districts) are old range data.

10.人民生活

2014 年全省			
居民人均可支配收入	15837	元	比上年增长 10.2% （实际增长 8.5%）
农村居民人均可支配收入	7932	元	比上年增长 11.8% （实际增长 9.9%）
城镇居民人均可支配收入	24366	元	比上年增长 9.0% （实际增长 7.3%）
居民个人年末人均储蓄存款	35572	元	比上年增长 9.3%

居民人均可支配收入（元）

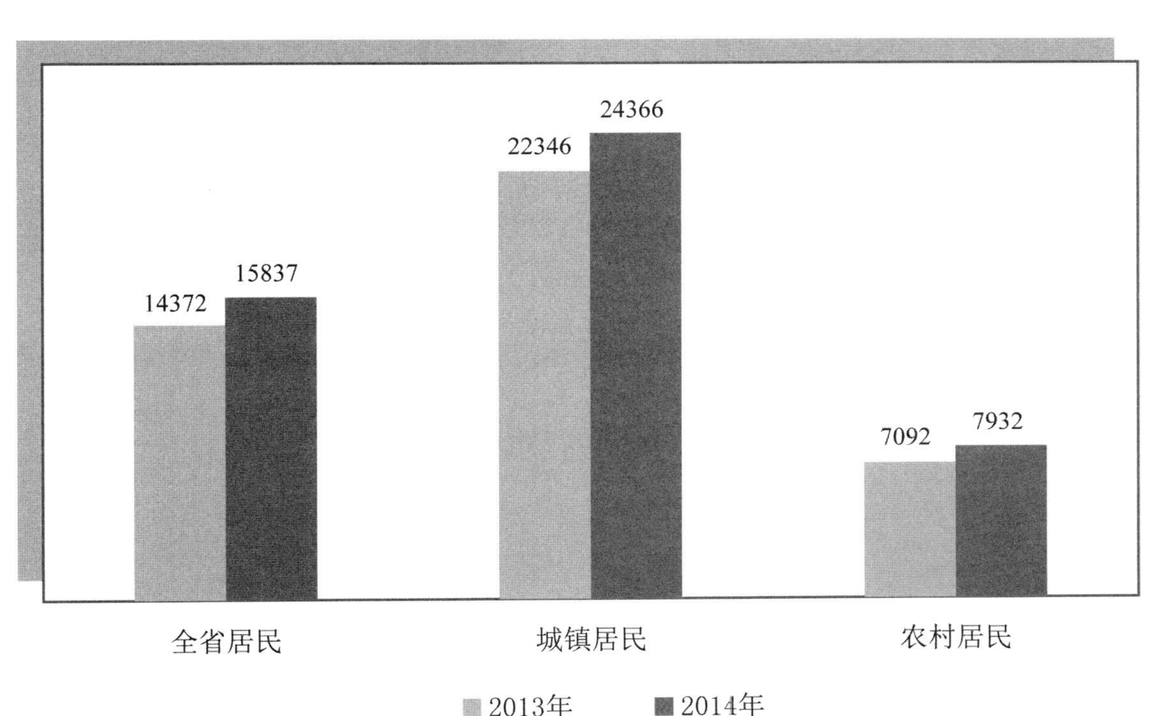

10-1 城乡居民家庭人均收入及指数
Per Capita Annual Income of Urban and Rural Households

年 份 Year	农村居民家庭人均纯收入 Per Capita Annual Net Income of Rural Households			城镇居民家庭人均可支配收入 Per Capita Annual Disposable Income of Urban Households		
	绝对数 (元) Value (yuan)	指 数 Index (上年=100) (preceding year=100)	指 数 Index (1978年=100) (year of 1978=100)	绝对数 (元) Value (yuan)	指 数 Index (上年=100) (preceding year=100)	指 数 Index (1978年=100) (year of 1978=100)
1978	134		100.0	310		100.0
1979	150	111.0	111.0			
1980	142	92.6	102.8	407		122.8
1981	177	122.8	126.1	427	101.3	124.4
1982	218	121.6	153.4	452	104.9	130.5
1983	236	107.4	164.8	488	106.3	138.7
1984	263	108.9	179.5	552	109.4	151.7
1985	295	106.7	191.4	650	109.5	166.0
1986	299	96.8	185.3	814	117.5	195.1
1987	329	103.8	192.5	905	101.8	198.6
1988	404	106.6	205.3	1040	95.7	190.1
1989	434	89.7	184.1	1239	101.3	192.5
1990	530	104.2	191.9	1369	107.7	207.3
1991	534	96.3	184.7	1498	102.0	211.5
1992	559	98.2	181.4	1705	102.4	216.5
1993	653	106.2	192.6	2102	108.1	234.1
1994	805	97.3	187.4	2684	99.6	233.1
1995	963	99.4	186.2	3310	104.5	243.6
1996	1165	110.0	204.8	3810	104.4	254.2
1997	1285	102.4	209.6	4001	99.8	253.8
1998	1406	113.1	237.1	4220	108.0	274.0
1999	1456	106.6	252.7	4654	113.5	310.8
2000	1470	103.3	261.0	5124	109.8	341.2
2001	1520	101.3	264.3	5484	106.9	364.8
2002	1596	104.6	276.5	6331	117.6	428.9
2003	1676	102.2	282.6	6806	106.6	457.4
2004	1867	106.3	300.4	7492	106.9	488.9
2005	2052	106.9	321.1	8272	109.4	534.9
2006	2260	107.9	346.5	9268	109.7	586.9
2007	2645	110.0	381.1	10763	110.5	648.5
2008	3136	110.6	421.5	12858	112.5	729.6
2009	3438	109.2	460.3	14129	109.9	801.8
2010	4105	112.0	515.5	15695	107.1	858.7
2011	5028	114.3	589.3	18245	110.0	944.6
2012	5763	111.2	655.3	20734	110.8	1046.6
2013	6503	109.4	716.8	22858	107.2	1122.0
2014	7932	109.9		24366	107.3	

注：1.本表绝对数按当年价格计算，指数按可比价格计算。

2.实施城乡住户调查一体化后，统计口径发生变化，新老口径数据存在差异。本表2014年为新口径城乡居民人均可支配收入。

a) Level data in this table are calculated at current prices while indices at constant prices.

b) After the rban-rural integration Investigation has been conducted, the statistical range has been changed, data of new and old ranges are different. Per capita annual disposable income of urban and rural households data of 2014 in this table is new range data.

10-2 各市(区)城乡居民人均收入
Per Capita Income in Urban and Rural Households by City(District)

单位：元 (yuan)

地区	Region	城镇居民人均可支配收入 Per Capita Annual Disposable Income of Urban Households 2013	2014	2014年比2013年增长% Increase of 2014 over 2013 (%)	农村居民人均纯收入 Per Capita Annual Net Income of Rural Households 2013	2014	2014年比2013年增长% Increase of 2014 over 2013 (%)
西安市	Xi'an	33100	36100	9.1	12930	14462	11.8
铜川市	Tongchuan	24495	27237	11.2	8140	9169	12.6
宝鸡市	Baoji	28509	31560	10.7	8376	9421	12.5
咸阳市	Xianyang	28488	31530	10.7	8538	9612	12.6
渭南市	Weinan	24164	26725	10.6	7565	8534	12.8
延安市	Yan'an	27643	30588	10.7	8681	9779	12.7
汉中市	Hanzhong	22167	24605	11.0	7053	7933	12.5
榆林市	Yulin	26820	29665	10.6	8687	9730	12.0
安康市	Ankang	22533	25011	11.0	6624	7468	12.7
商洛市	Shangluo	22257	24727	11.1	6223	7035	13.0
杨凌示范区	Yangling	33007	36008	9.1	12435	14046	13.0

10-3 城乡居民人民币储蓄存款(年底余额)
Savings Deposit of Urban and Rural Households at Year-end

年份 Year	城乡居民年末储蓄存款余额(亿元) Savings Deposit of Urban and Rural Households (100 million yuan)	城乡居民年末人均储蓄存款余额(元) Per Capita Balance of Saving Deposit (yuan)	年份 Year	城乡居民年末储蓄存款余额(亿元) Savings Deposit of Urban and Rural Households (100 million yuan)	城乡居民年末人均储蓄存款余额(元) Per Capita Balance of Saving Deposit (yuan)
1978	7.79	28	1997	1090.43	3054
1979	10.20	36	1998	1241.63	3453
1980	13.51	48	1999	1371.88	3792
1981	16.65	58	2000	1522.53	4178
1982	20.51	71	2001	1768.47	4841
1983	25.43	87	2002	2107.83	5756
1984	33.17	112	2003	2519.93	6863
1985	44.77	149	2004	2948.34	8010
1986	62.47	205	2005	3533.97	9577
1987	88.37	286	2006	4067.70	10997
1988	108.65	346	2007	4278.41	11538
1989	150.11	469	2008	5494.53	14778
1990	204.57	617	2009	6743.81	18094
1991	263.28	783	2010	7957.78	21306
1992	329.22	967	2011	9172.09	24507
1993	403.81	1173	2012	10770.05	28697
1994	547.20	1572	2013	12249.36	32546
1995	734.04	2089	2014	13428.86	35572
1996	942.21	2659			

注：2006年起含外资银行人民币储蓄存款。
a) Since 2006 Savings Deposit of Urban and Rural Households including Foreign.

10-4 全省居民家庭基本情况
Basic Conditions of All Households

指　　标	Item	2013	2014
调查户数　(户)	Number of Households Surveyed (household)	4351	4292
调查户人口　(人)	Number of Residents in the Household Surveyed(person)		
1.常住人口	Permanent Residents	14252	13789
2.平均每户常住人口	Average Household Size	3.3	3.2
3.平均每户劳动力人数	Labours Per Households	2.2	2.1
平均每户整劳动力人数	Ablebodied Labours Per Households	1.3	1.1
平均每户半劳动力人数	Semiablebodied Labours Per Households	0.9	1.0
4.平均每劳动力负担人口	Average Number of Persons Supported by a Laborer	1.5	1.5
平均每人可支配收入　(元)	Annual Per Capita Disposable Income (yuan)	14372	15837
工资性收入	Wages Income	8184	8849
经营净收入	Net Income from Business	2217	2404
财产净收入	Property Income	874	1033
转移净收入	Transfer Income	3097	3551
平均每人生活消费支出　(元)	Annual Per Capita Consumption Expenditure (yuan)	11217	12204
食品、烟酒	Food,Tobacco and Alcohol	3066	3406
衣　着	Clothing	912	945
居　住	Residence	2384	2586
生活用品及服务	Living Articles and Services	730	796
交通通信	Transportation and Communications	1374	1535
教育文化娱乐	Recreation, Education and Culture Services	1438	1500
医疗保健	Medicine and Medical Services	1081	1178
其他用品和服务	Others	232	258
平均每人年末现住房建筑面积（平方米）	Floor Area per Capita at Year-end (sq.m)	35.0	36.0

10-5 全省居民家庭人均可支配收入
Per Capita Annual Disposable Income of All Households

单位：元 (yuan)

指　　标	Item	2013	2014
可支配收入	**Disposable Income**	**14371.5**	**15836.7**
一、工资性收入	**Wages Income**	**8183.6**	**8848.5**
(一)工资	Wage	7382.9	8100.2
1.按月发放的工资	The wages by monthly	6243.9	6897.4
2.补发工资	Retroactive pay	116.1	75.0
3.不按月发放的奖金、津贴、过节费等	The Bonus, allowance, holiday fee etc.by no-monthly	1022.9	1127.8
(二)实物福利	Benefits in kind	52.2	47.0
1.从单位或雇主得到的实物产品折价	The Discount of Real Products from the Company or Employer	7.3	10.9
2.从单位或雇主得到的服务折价	The Discount of Services from the Company or Employer	31.7	36.1
3.单位或雇主实物福利报销所得	The Reimbursement Income in kind from the Company or Employer	13.2	
(三)其他	Others	748.5	701.3
1.住房公积金	Housing Funds	314.8	365.9
2.辞退金	Dismissal Payments	2.2	9.1
3.自由职业劳动所得(如稿费、翻译费)	Income by liberal work (Such as Remuneration, Translation Fee)	17.6	17.8
4.安家费	Settling-in Allowance	4.1	4.5
5.股票期权	Stock Options	0.5	0.1
6.其他劳动所得	Others	409.3	303.9
二、经营净收入	**Net Income from Business**	**2217.3**	**2404.4**
(一)第一产业经营净收入	Net Income from Primary Industry Business	1037.8	1111.0
1.农业	Agricultural	885.0	972.8
2.林业	Forestry	70.4	49.2
3.牧业	Animal Husbandry	81.7	88.3
4.渔业	Fishery	0.7	0.7
(二)第二产业经营净收入	Net Income from Secondary Industry Business	77.0	129.0
(三)第三产业经营净收入	Net Income from Tertiary Industry Business	1102.5	1164.4
1.批发和零售业	Wholesale and Retail Trades	568.7	594.9
2.交通运输、仓储和邮政业	Transport, Storage and Post	205.7	229.9
3.住宿和餐饮业	Hotels and Catering Services	95.5	105.5
4.房地产业	Real Estate	0.9	-3.1
5.租赁和商务服务业	Leasing and Business Services	7.7	9.7
6.居民服务、修理和其他服务业	Services to Households and Other Services	155.2	157.7
7.农林牧渔服务业	Services to Agriculture, Forestry, Animal Husbandry and Fishery	24.1	32.9
8.其他	Others	44.7	36.9
三、财产净收入	**Net Income from Properties**	**874.1**	**1033.4**
# 利息净收入	Net Interests	28.1	36.9
红利收入	Bonus	76.5	106.8
储蓄性保险净收益	Net Benefits of Savings Insurance	1.0	3.8
转让承包土地经营权租金净收入	The Rent Income by Transfer of Land Rights	17.6	23.4
出租房屋财产性收入	The Property Income by Renting House	315.1	406.7
出租机械、专利、版权等资产的收入	The Income by Renting Assets like Mechanical, Patents, Copyright ect.	10.5	8.3
四、转移净收入	**Net Income from Transfer**	**3096.5**	**3550.4**
(一)转移性收入	Income from Transfer	3649.7	4186.0
1.养老金或离退休金	Pension or Retired Pension	2578.4	2861.7
2.社会救济和补助	Social Relief and Aid	65.8	82.7
3.政策性生活补贴	Policy Allowance	32.1	38.3
4.报销医疗费	Reimbursement of Medical treatment	121.3	213.4
5.家庭外出从业人员寄回带回收入	Income from Family Outings Employees	476.8	477.0
6.赡养收入	Alimony Income	219.6	296.2
7.其他经常转移收入	Others Recurring Income from Transfer	66.6	124.0
8.从政府和组织得到的实物产品和服务折价	The Discount of Real Products and Services from the Governments and Organizations	12.2	12.6
9.现金政策性惠农补贴	The Cash Policy Subsidies for Agricultural	76.9	80.1
(二)转移性支出	Transfer Expenditure	553.2	635.6
1.个人所得税	Personal Income Tax	27.6	19.8
2.社会保障支出	Expenditure for Social Security	397.7	453.2
3.外来从业人员寄给家人的支出	Expenditure for Family from Migrant Workers	9.8	5.7
4.赡养支出	Expenditure for Alimony	75.2	99.4
5.其他	Others	42.9	57.5

10-6 全省居民家庭人均生活消费支出
Per Capita Living Expenditure of All Households

单位：元 (yuan)

指　标	Item	2013	2014
生活消费支出	**Total Living Expenditure**	**11217.3**	**12203.6**
一、食品、烟酒	**Food,Tobacco and Alcohol**	**3066.0**	**3406.1**
1.食　品	Food	2142.0	2281.1
# 谷　物	Grain	365.3	472.4
薯　类	Potato	56.3	61.6
豆　类	Beans	37.9	41.1
食用油	Edible Oil	137.2	148.0
蔬菜和食用菌	Vegetables and Edible Mushrooms	327.2	340.9
肉　类	Meat	358.4	390.1
禽　类	Poultry	43.3	45.5
水产品	Aquatic Products	43.0	46.4
蛋　类	Eggs	55.1	61.8
奶　类	Milk	166.2	184.7
干鲜瓜果类	Fresh and Dried Fruits	221.5	245.3
糖果糕点类	Candy and Pastry	84.6	87.9
2.烟　酒	Tobacco and Alcohol	306.0	341.3
# 烟　草	Tobacco	202.9	233.4
酒　类	Alcohol	100.0	108.0
3.饮　料	Beverages		68.0
4.饮食服务	Catering Services	618.0	715.7
二、衣　着	**Clothing**	**912.1**	**944.6**
# 衣　类	Garments	699.0	725.3
鞋　类	Footwear	203.5	219.3
三、居　住	**Residence**	**2383.8**	**2585.8**
# 租赁房房租	Rental Housing Rent	207.3	213.9
住房维修及管理	Housing Repair and Management	357.3	465.0
水电燃料及其他	Water,Electric Power Fuel and Others	595.2	652.6
四、生活用品及服务	**Living Articles and Services**	**729.8**	**796.2**
# 家具及室内装饰品	Furniture and External Decorations	123.3	153.3
家用器具	Household Appliances	215.9	205.8
家用纺织品	Household textile	66.0	71.5
家庭日用杂品	Household Articles of Daily Use	196.1	208.9
个人用品	Personal Items	87.3	104.9
家庭服务	Household Services	31.8	51.9
五、交通通信	**Transportation and Communications**	**1374.2**	**1535.4**
# 交　通	Transportation	857.4	993.0
通　信	Communications	514.5	542.4
六、教育文化娱乐	**Recreation, Education and Culture Services**	**1438.1**	**1500.4**
# 教　育	Education	974.5	994.4
文化娱乐	Recreation	463.0	506.0
七、医疗保健	**Medicine and Medical Services**	**1081.2**	**1178.2**
医疗器具及药品	Medical Instruments and Medicines	360.8	398.8
医疗服务	Medical Services	720.4	779.3
八、其他用品和服务	**Others**	**232.1**	**256.9**

10-7 全省居民家庭人均购买主要商品数量
Per Capita Annual Purchases of Major Commodities of All Households

品名		Item		2013	2014
小麦	（公斤）	Wheat	(kg)	2.0	1.6
面粉	（公斤）	Flour	(kg)	27.6	27.7
大米	（公斤）	Rice	(kg)	17.5	16.8
薯类	（公斤）	Potato	(kg)	9.2	9.5
豆类	（公斤）	Beans	(kg)	6.6	6.6
食用植物油	（公斤）	Edible Vegetable Oil	(kg)	9.5	9.9
鲜菜	（公斤）	Fresh Vegetables	(kg)	63.1	62.3
猪肉	（公斤）	Pork	(kg)	8.7	9.2
牛肉	（公斤）	Beef	(kg)	0.6	0.7
羊肉	（公斤）	Mutton	(kg)	0.7	0.7
鸡	（公斤）	Chicken	(kg)	1.4	1.5
鸭	（公斤）	Duck	(kg)	0.1	0.1
鱼类	（公斤）	Fish	(kg)	1.5	1.5
虾类	（公斤）	Shrimp	(kg)	0.2	0.1
鲜蛋	（公斤）	Fresh Eggs	(kg)	5.4	5.6
鲜奶	（公斤）	Fresh Milk	(kg)	7.2	7.5
酸奶	（公斤）	Yogurt	(kg)	2.1	2.0
奶粉	（公斤）	Milk Powder	(kg)	0.7	0.6
鲜瓜果	（公斤）	Fresh Fruits	(kg)	33.0	33.4
糕点	（公斤）	Cake	(kg)	2.8	2.6
茶叶	（公斤）	Tea	(kg)	0.2	0.2
卷烟	（盒）	Cigarette	(box)	27.1	27.1
啤酒	（公斤）	Beer	(kg)	3.2	2.8
白酒	（公斤）	Liquor	(kg)	1.1	1.0
果酒	（公斤）	Wine	(kg)	0.2	0.2
鞋	（双）	Footwear	(pair)	2.1	2.3
水	（吨）	Water	(ton)	17.3	15.6
电	（度）	Electricity	(kwh)	455.7	453.1
煤炭	（公斤）	Coal	(kg)	97.0	123.5
管道天燃气	（立方米）	Pipeline Natural Gas	(cu.m)	53.1	41.2
罐装液化石油气	（公斤）	Canned Liquified Petroleum Gas	(kg)	4.1	3.2

10-8 全省居民家庭每百户耐用消费品拥有情况
Ownership of Major Durable Consumer Goods Per 100 All Households

指　　标		Item		2013	2014
家用汽车	（辆）	Automobile	(unit)	11.4	13.6
摩托车	（辆）	Motorcycle	(unit)	35.6	42.3
助力车	（台）	Strength-aid Cycle	(unit)	25.2	28.8
洗衣机	（台）	Washing Machine	(unit)	89.4	91.4
电冰箱(柜)	（台）	Refrigerator	(unit)	71.9	76.0
微波炉	（台）	Microwave Oven	(unit)	23.5	23.3
彩色电视机	（台）	Color TV Set	(unit)	108.9	111.0
# 接入有线电视		Cable TV Set		62.8	61.5
空　调	（台）	Air Conditioner	(unit)	51.1	54.6
热水器	（台）	Water Heater	(unit)	53.0	55.4
# 太阳能热水器		Solar Water Heater		28.9	31.3
消毒碗柜	（台）	Sterilizing Cupboard	(unit)	2.6	2.8
洗碗机	（台）	Dish Washer	(unit)	0.2	0.4
排油烟机	（台）	Exhauster	(unit)	36.4	37.1
固定电话	（线）	Ordinary Telephone	(unit)	36.2	41.9
移动电话	（部）	Mobile Telephone	(unit)	223.2	233.2
# 接入互联网		Access to the Internet		50.3	59.0
计算机	（台）	Computer	(unit)	40.0	43.7
# 接入互联网		Access to the Internet		31.9	34.6
摄像机	（台）	Pickup Camera	(unit)	3.2	3.2
照相机	（台）	Camera	(unit)	19.0	19.1
中高档乐器	（架）	High-end Instruments	(unit)	1.5	1.8
健身器材	（台）	Setting-up Apparatus	(unit)	1.0	1.4
组合音响	（套）	Music Center	(set)	4.5	4.6

10-9 全省居民家庭年末居住情况
Housing Conditions of All Households

指 标	Item	2013	2014
调查户数 (户)	Number of Households Surveyed (household)	4351	4292
平均每户居住人口 (人)	Average Number of Resident Population (person)	3.3	3.2
平均每人建筑面积 (平方米)	The Average Floor Area Per Person (sq.m)	35.0	36.0
一、按住户居住空间样式分 (%)	By Style of Living Space (%)	100.0	100.0
单栋楼房	Dependent Building	16.6	16.9
单栋平房	Single-storey House	33.0	32.9
四居室及以上单元房	Four Bedrooms	0.8	0.8
三居室单元房	Three Bedrooms	13.8	14.1
二居室单元房	Two Bedrooms	20.9	20.8
一居室单元房	One Bedroom	1.7	1.6
筒子楼或连片平房	Tube-shaped Apartment or Lace Single-storey Houses	10.6	10.5
其他	Others	2.6	2.4
二、按主要建筑材料分 (%)	By Main Building Materials (%)	100.0	100.0
钢筋混凝土	Reinforced Concrete	13.4	13.4
砖混材料	Brick-and-concrete Buildings	65.8	66.3
砖瓦砖木	Brick and Brick-wood Structure	16.8	16.4
竹草土坯	Bamboo Grass and Sun-dried Mud Brick	2.5	2.4
其他	Others	1.5	1.5
三、按现住房房屋来源分 (%)	By Source of Housing (%)	100.0	100.0
租赁公房	Public-rent Housing	1.0	1.0
租赁私房	Private-rent Housing	8.6	8.6
自建住房	Self-establish Housing	55.4	54.9
购买商品房	Commercial Residential Housing	16.1	16.5
购买房改住房	Private Housing through Housing Reform	11.0	11.4
购买保障性住房	Indemnificatory Housing	1.8	1.9
拆迁安置房	Resettlement Housing	2.2	2.1
继承或获赠住房	Inheriting and Donation Housing	0.9	0.9
免费借用房	Free Housing	1.5	1.4
雇主提供免费住房	Free Housing from Employer	0.8	0.8
其他	Others	0.7	0.5
四、按住宅外道路路面情况分 (%)	By Pavement Condition Outside (%)	100.0	100.0
水泥或柏油路面	Cement or Asphalt Pavement	77.7	79.1
沙石或石板等硬质路面	Hard Sand or Stone Pavement	9.8	9.3
其他	Others	12.5	11.6
五、按住宅有管道供水情况分 (%)	By Piped Water Supply Condition (%)	100.0	100.0
管道供水入户	Pipe water into People's Homes	85.0	86.2
管道供水至公共取水点	Pipe water to Public Watering Points	1.6	1.2
没有管道设施	No Pipeline Facilities	13.4	12.6
六、按住户主要饮用水来源情况分 (%)	By Source of main Drinking Water (%)	100.0	100.0
经过净化处理的自来水	Purified Tap Water	68.4	68.7
受保护的井水和泉水	Protected Wells and Springs	17.7	17.8
不受保护的井水和泉水	Unprotected Wells and Springs	9.1	9.0
江河湖泊水	Rivers and Lakes Water	1.0	0.9
收集雨水	Collected Rainwater	1.6	1.7
桶装水	Barrels Water	0.2	0.1
其他	Others	2.0	1.8
七、按住户厕所类型分 (%)	By Household Lavatory Type (%)	100.0	100.0
水冲式卫生厕所	Sanitary Water Closet	48.1	48.2
水冲式非卫生厕所	Insanitary Water Closet	1.6	1.9
卫生旱厕	Sanitary Latrine	6.8	6.7
普通旱厕	Latrine	41.3	41.6
无厕所	No Lavatory	2.2	1.6
八、按住户主要取暖设备状况分 (%)	By Heating Facilities Condition (%)	100.0	100.0
由市政或小区集中供暖	Central Heating	20.1	21.1
自行供暖	Self Heating	52.2	52.2
无取暖设备	Without Heating Equipment	27.7	26.7
九、按主要炊用能源状况分 (%)	By Cocking Fuel Condition (%)	100.0	100.0
柴草	Firewood	26.0	26.1
煤炭	Coal	16.1	14.7
罐装液化石油气	Canned Liquified Petroleum Gas	11.0	9.5
管道液化石油气	Pipeline Liquified Petroleum Gas	0.3	0.3
管道煤气	Pipeline Gas	0.6	0.3
管道天然气	Pipeline Natural Gas	26.8	27.4
电	Electricity	17.6	20.4
沼气	Methane	0.8	0.8
其他	Others	0.8	0.5

10-10 城镇常住居民家庭基本情况
Basic Conditions of Urban Households

指　　标	Item	2013	2014
调查户数　(户)	Number of Households Surveyed　(household)	1760	1707
调查户人口　(人)	Number of Residents in the Household Surveyed(person)		
1.常住人口	Permanent Residents	5277	5055
2.平均每户常住人口	Average Household Size	3.0	3.0
3.平均每户劳动力人数	Labours Per Households	2.1	2.1
平均每户整劳动力人数	Ablebodied Labours Per Households	1.3	1.2
平均每户半劳动力人数	Semiablebodied Labours Per Households	0.8	0.9
4.平均每劳动力负担人口	Average Number of Persons Supported by a Laborer	1.5	1.4
平均每人可支配收入　(元)	Annual Per Capita Disposable Income　(yuan)	22346	24366
工资性收入	Wages Income	13987	14926
经营净收入	Net Income from Business	1876	2031
财产净收入	Property Income	1733	2019
转移净收入	Transfer Income	4750	5390
平均每人生活消费支出　(元)	Annual Per Capita Consumption Expenditure　(yuan)	16399	17546
食品、烟酒	Food,Tobacco and Alcohol	4484	4800
衣　着	Clothing	1453	1470
居　住	Residence	3426	3620
生活用品及服务	Living Articles and Services	1085	1176
交通通信	Transportation and Communications	2157	2447
教育文化娱乐	Recreation, Education and Culture Services	2068	2148
医疗保健	Medicine and Medical Services	1386	1496
其他用品和服务	Others	340	389
平均每人年末现住房建筑面积（平方米）	Floor Area per Capita at Year-end　(sq.m)	29.9	30.6

10-11 城镇常住居民不同收入层次家庭基本情况(2014年)

Basic Conditions of Urban Households by Income Percentile(2014)

指标	Item	总平均 Average	低收入户 Low Income Households	中低收入户 Lower Middle Income Households	中等收入户 Middle Income Households	中高收入户 Upper Middle Income Households	高收入户 High Income Households
调查户数 (户)	Number of Households Surveyed (household)	1707	342	341	341	341	342
调查户人口 (人)	Number of Residents in the Household Surveyed (person)						
1.常住人口	Permanent Residents	5055	1219	1127	1027	901	781
2.平均每户常住人口	Average Household Size	3.0	3.6	3.3	3.0	2.6	2.3
3.平均每户劳动力人数	Labours Per Households	2.1	2.2	2.2	2.2	1.9	1.9
平均每户整劳动力人数	Ablebodied Labours Per Households	1.2	1.5	1.4	1.2	1.0	0.8
平均每户半劳动力人数	Semiablebodied Labours Per Households	0.9	0.8	0.7	1.0	0.9	1.1
4.平均每劳动力负担人口	Average Number of Persons Supported by a Laborer	1.4	1.6	1.5	1.4	1.4	1.2
平均每人可支配收入 (元)	Per Capita Annual Disposable Income (Yuan)	24365.8	9957.6	17327.0	23837.4	31842.2	48048.5
平均每人生活消费支出 (元)	Per Capita Annual Consumption Expenditure (yuan)	17546.0	9334.2	12828.8	17928.6	21881.8	31091.0
平均每人年末现住房建筑面积	Housing Area per Capita at Year-end (sq.m)	30.6	24.9	27.2	30.8	33.5	40.3

10-12 城镇常住居民不同收入层次家庭人均可支配收入（2014年）
Per capita Annual Disposable Income of Urban Households by Income Percentile(2014)

单位：元 (yuan)

指 标	Item	总平均 Average	低收入户 Low Income Households	中低收入户 Lower Middle Income Households	中等收入户 Middle Income Households	中高收入户 Upper Middle Income Households	高收入户 High Income Households
可支配收入	**Disposable Income**	**24365.8**	**9957.6**	**17327.0**	**23837.4**	**31842.2**	**48048.5**
一、工资性收入	**Wages Income**	**14925.9**	**6702.3**	**11609.4**	**15257.2**	**18607.0**	**27324.5**
(一)工资	Wage	13802.6	6152.4	11077.6	14287.1	17409.4	24402.7
1.按月发放的工资	The wages by monthly	12698.9	5229.5	10276.0	13547.8	16039.9	22445.5
2.补发工资	Retroactive pay	114.5	36.4	83.8	103.2	276.1	106.4
3.不按月发放的奖金、津贴、过节费等	The Bonus,allowance,holiday fee etc.by no-monthly	989.2	886.4	717.8	636.1	1093.4	1850.8
(二)实物福利	Benefits in kind	89.6	17.3	64.2	129.6	95.8	176.4
1.从单位或雇主得到的实物产品折价	The Discount of Real Products from the Company or Employer	18.8	3.5	13.0	17.1	36.5	32.2
2.从单位或雇主得到的服务折价	The Discount of Services from the Company or Employer	70.8	13.8	51.2	112.4	59.3	144.2
(三)其他	Others	1033.7	532.6	467.6	840.5	1101.8	2745.4
1.住房公积金	Housing Funds	740.9	39.8	286.6	685.3	731.8	2508.9
2.辞退金	Dismissal Payments	18.5		5.3	40.6	51.2	
3.自由职业劳动所得(如稿费、翻译费)	Income by liberal work (Such as Remuneration, Translation Fee)	13.7	5.9	14.6	11.0	32.5	6.2
4.安家费	Settling-in Allowance	9.4	0.7			51.3	
5.股票期权	Stock Options	0.1		0.5			
6.其他劳动所得	Others	251.1	486.2	160.6	103.6	235.0	230.3
二、经营净收入	**Net Income from Business**	**2030.6**	**1174.1**	**1515.4**	**1272.2**	**2558.3**	**4394.6**
(一)第一产业经营净收入	Net Income from Primary Industry Business	55.4	69.0	94.0	37.6	60.6	-2.9
(二)第二产业经营净收入	Net Income from Secondary Industry Business	223.0	46.0	49.0	40.4	76.0	1128.4
(三)第三产业经营净收入	Net Income from Tertiary Industry Business	1752.2	1059.1	1372.4	1194.2	2421.7	3269.1
1.批发和零售业	Wholesale and Retail Trades	1004.6	428.2	702.5	737.3	1503.8	2064.2
2.交通运输、仓储和邮政业	Transport, Storage and Post	249.4	192.9	163.4	223.6	294.7	436.0
3.住宿和餐饮业	Hotels and Catering Services	183.5	166.0	37.7	97.4	288.6	404.4
4.房地产业	Real Estate	0.8	-0.7	3.0	0.4		1.2
5.租赁和商务服务业	Leasing and Business Services	20.3	6.3		18.1	84.3	
6.居民服务、修理和其他服务业	Services to Households and Other Services	229.1	254.8	399.1	95.9	60.6	309.7
7.农林牧渔服务业	Services to Agriculture, Forestry, Animal Husbandry and Fishery	0.3	0.5	-0.5	1.4	0.0	
8.其他	Others	64.2	11.1	67.2	20.1	189.7	53.6

10-12 续表 continued

单位：元 (yuan)

指 标	Item	总平均 Average	低收入户 Low Income Households	中低收入户 Lower Middle Income Households	中等收入户 Middle Income Households	中高收入户 Upper Middle Income Households	高收入户 High Income Households
三、财产净收入	**Net Income from Properties**	**2018.8**	**773.3**	**1283.3**	**2259.9**	**2466.7**	**4108.1**
# 利息净收入	Net Interests	59.3	0.1	-52.9	32.6	111.7	279.7
红利收入	Bonus	199.7	60.0	176.1	186.0	236.2	417.9
储蓄性保险净收益	Net Benefits of Savings Insurance	7.3		0.4	23.0		16.6
出租房屋财产性收入	The Property Income by Renting House	809.9	240.6	526.9	1086.8	833.2	1685.1
出租机械、专利、版权等资产的收入	The Income by Renting Assets like Mechanical,Patents,Copyright ect.	12.8		0.3	9.1	51.0	11.1
四、转移净收入	**Net Income from Transfer**	**5390.4**	**1307.9**	**2919.0**	**5048.1**	**8210.1**	**12221.3**
(一)转移性收入	Income from Transfer	5483.1	1936.9	3801.3	6240.7	9268.7	14217.0
1.养老金或离退休金	Pension or Retired Pension	5370.6	1285.5	3072.3	5440.7	8294.5	11325.9
# 离退休金	Retired Pension	5248.8	1110.3	2935.3	5283.3	8248.7	11264.5
城镇居民社会养老保险	Urban Employee Social Pension Insurance	55.8	112.5	42.4	64.8	22.1	16.3
2.社会救济和补助	Social Relief and Aid	86.6	259.5	39.4	30.9	42.6	13.9
3.政策性生活补贴	Policy Allowance	34.7	21.0	16.4	42.4	35.4	70.4
4.报销医疗费	Reimbursement of Medical treatment	310.7	89.5	166.9	300.4	294.9	874.8
5.家庭外出从业人员寄回带回收入	Income from Family Outings Employees	36.7	51.5	71.2	0.6	42.3	4.9
6.赡养收入	Alimony Income	427.3	124.9	209.6	316.3	316.4	1450.4
7.其他经常转移收入	Others Recurring Income from Transfer	197.9	89.3	204.1	96.9	216.0	458.5
8.从政府和组织得到的实物产品和服务折价	The Discount of Real Products and Services from the Governments and Organizations	14.4	9.7	12.4	10.2	25.9	16.6
9.其他	Others	4.2	6.0	9.0	2.3	0.7	1.6
(二)转移性支出	Transfer Expenditure	1092.7	629.0	882.3	1192.6	1058.6	1995.7
1.个人所得税	Personal Income Tax	39.4	4.5	3.4	20.3	35.3	171.1
2.社会保障支出	Expenditure for Social Security	750.7	394.0	650.9	755.3	826.9	1333.3
(1)个人缴纳的养老保险	Pension Insurance Personal Rendered	483.3	261.6	443.0	483.7	513.4	837.2
(2)个人缴纳的医疗保险	Medical Care Insurance Personal Rendered	212.9	124.7	167.5	203.3	255.9	372.4
(3)个人缴纳的失业保险	Unemployment Insurance Personal Rendered	40.5	7.7	28.1	45.6	52.9	86.7
(4)其他社会保障支出	Others	14.0	0.0	12.3	22.7	4.7	37.0
3.外来从业人员寄给家人的支出	Expenditure for Family from Migrant Workers	10.4		1.8	45.3	5.1	
4.赡养支出	Expenditure for Alimony	191.3	125.7	103.4	268.6	114.9	402.0
5.其他	Others	100.9	104.8	122.8	103.1	76.4	89.3

10-13 城镇常住居民不同收入层次家庭人均生活消费支出(2014年)
Per Capita Living Expenditure of Urban Households by Income Percentile(2014)

单位：元 (yuan)

指标	Item	总平均 Average	低收入户 Low Income Households	中低收入户 Lower Middle Income Households	中等收入户 Middle Income Households	中高收入户 Upper Middle Income Households	高收入户 High Income Households
生活消费支出	**Total Living Expenditure**	**17546.0**	**9334.2**	**12828.8**	**17928.6**	**21881.8**	**31091.0**
一、食品、烟酒	**Food,Tobacco and Alcohol**	**4800.2**	**2732.2**	**3732.9**	**5041.8**	**5920.2**	**7827.3**
1.食　品	Food	3065.6	2023.1	2550.6	3262.8	3683.8	4403.8
# 谷　物	Grain	551.5	438.3	457.8	558.8	628.3	757.0
薯　类	Potato	52.6	44.1	49.8	53.9	55.2	64.9
豆　类	Beans	56.9	43.7	51.3	59.8	62.6	74.8
食用油	Edible Oil	163.9	138.0	149.6	163.7	177.0	208.6
蔬菜和食用菌	Vegetables and Edible Mushrooms	463.8	323.6	433.2	498.3	508.0	623.6
肉　类	Meat	545.6	324.6	433.9	567.2	664.7	871.7
禽　类	Poultry	70.8	39.9	51.5	86.3	94.9	97.8
水产品	Aquatic Products	81.2	35.7	61.1	87.9	124.0	120.8
蛋　类	Eggs	79.4	55.1	67.6	84.4	93.1	110.8
奶　类	Milk	263.2	141.8	199.1	321.3	343.4	371.5
干鲜瓜果类	Fresh and Dried Fruits	389.5	195.9	299.3	435.2	498.0	626.1
糖果糕点类	Candy and Pastry	134.7	70.3	100.1	144.5	183.0	212.5
2.烟　酒	Tobacco and Alcohol	391.4	195.7	294.0	421.1	502.2	658.5
# 烟　草	Tobacco	254.8	134.6	198.3	297.3	307.7	401.0
酒　类	Alcohol	136.6	61.1	95.8	123.8	194.5	257.5
3.饮　料	Beverages	92.4	50.6	72.6	83.8	119.4	163.5
4.饮食服务	Catering Services	1250.8	462.8	815.7	1274.1	1614.8	2601.5
二、衣　着	**Clothing**	**1470.4**	**791.4**	**1096.9**	**1467.8**	**1849.2**	**2587.1**
# 衣　类	Garments	1121.8	589.0	826.4	1105.7	1410.5	2028.7
鞋　类	Footwear	348.6	202.4	270.5	362.1	438.7	558.4
三、居　住	**Residence**	**3620.4**	**2002.5**	**2767.2**	**3807.4**	**4382.5**	**6145.4**
# 租赁房房租	Rental Housing Rent	415.2	243.3	379.3	397.5	409.3	751.8
住房维修及管理	Housing Repair and Management	571.4	373.3	266.2	757.8	557.2	1078.6
水电燃料及其他	Water,Electric Power Fuel and Others	953.6	527.5	791.8	1007.5	1178.8	1497.0
四、生活用品及服务	**Living Articles and Services**	**1176.0**	**447.4**	**722.0**	**1151.2**	**1724.0**	**2317.2**
# 家具及室内装饰品	Furniture and External Decorations	209.9	32.4	69.6	107.1	429.7	553.8
家用器具	Household Appliances	278.5	89.1	201.1	308.6	401.1	494.7
家用纺织品	Household textile	99.1	56.4	73.6	104.7	129.1	158.3
家庭日用杂品	Household Articles of Daily Use	309.9	188.2	237.4	315.5	391.4	494.6
个人用品	Personal Items	187.7	67.8	119.9	216.6	261.7	342.5
家庭服务	Household Services	90.9	13.5	20.4	98.7	111.0	273.3
五、交通通信	**Transportation and Communications**	**2447.1**	**1203.3**	**1785.0**	**2165.5**	**2976.2**	**4996.2**
# 交　通	Transportation	1639.9	755.4	1128.3	1350.2	1948.3	3699.0
通　信	Communications	807.2	447.9	656.7	815.3	1027.9	1297.2
六、教育文化娱乐	**Recreation, Education and Culture Services**	**2147.5**	**1220.6**	**1685.7**	**2619.0**	**2638.4**	**3037.1**
# 教　育	Education	1254.5	956.7	1124.9	1660.3	1354.7	1258.9
文化娱乐	Recreation	893.0	263.9	560.8	958.7	1283.7	1778.2
七、医疗保健	**Medicine and Medical Services**	**1495.9**	**802.0**	**819.7**	**1332.4**	**1880.6**	**3256.1**
医疗器具及药品	Medical Instruments and Medicines	566.6	324.6	345.5	564.2	780.9	1000.6
医疗服务	Medical Services	929.3	477.4	474.2	768.2	1099.7	2255.5
八、其他用品和服务	**Others**	**388.5**	**134.8**	**219.4**	**343.5**	**510.7**	**924.6**

10-14 城镇常住居民不同收入层次家庭人均购买主要商品数量（2014年）
Per Capita Annual Purchases of Major Commodities of Urban Households by Income Percentile(2014)

品名		Item		总平均 Average	低收入户 Low Income Households	中低收入户 Lower Middle Income Households	中等收入户 Middle Income Households	中高收入户 Upper Middle Income Households	高收入户 High Income Households
小麦	(公斤)	Wheat	(kg)	0.1	0.0	0.0	0.0		0.7
面粉	(公斤)	Flour	(kg)	28.8	30.0	28.8	27.0	29.7	28.2
大米	(公斤)	Rice	(kg)	20.3	18.0	18.3	19.1	22.9	25.2
薯类	(公斤)	Potato	(kg)	14.4	12.7	14.6	14.8	13.2	17.4
豆类	(公斤)	Beans	(kg)	8.9	7.8	8.4	8.9	9.3	10.8
食用植物油	(公斤)	Edible Vegetable Oil	(kg)	10.8	10.1	10.1	10.5	10.9	12.9
鲜菜	(公斤)	Fresh Vegetables	(kg)	86.3	67.5	83.9	89.8	90.4	109.0
猪肉	(公斤)	Pork	(kg)	11.4	8.7	10.5	12.0	12.8	14.3
牛肉	(公斤)	Beef	(kg)	1.2	0.4	0.8	1.3	1.4	2.5
羊肉	(公斤)	Mutton	(kg)	1.1	0.6	0.8	1.1	1.4	1.9
鸡	(公斤)	Chicken	(kg)	2.2	1.3	1.7	2.8	3.0	2.9
鸭	(公斤)	Duck	(kg)	0.1	0.1	0.1	0.1	0.1	0.1
鱼类	(公斤)	Fish	(kg)	2.4	1.4	1.9	2.7	3.1	3.3
虾类	(公斤)	Shrimp	(kg)	0.3	0.1	0.2	0.3	0.5	0.4
鲜蛋	(公斤)	Fresh Eggs	(kg)	7.4	5.3	6.5	7.7	8.4	10.0
鲜奶	(公斤)	Fresh Dairy Products	(kg)	13.0	6.6	9.5	15.1	17.1	20.3
酸奶	(公斤)	Yogurt	(kg)	3.1	2.0	2.0	2.9	4.1	5.1
奶粉	(公斤)	Milk Powder	(kg)	0.5	0.4	0.5	0.7	0.6	0.5
鲜瓜果	(公斤)	Fresh Fruit	(kg)	47.7	29.7	40.0	53.2	57.1	68.0
糕点	(公斤)	Cake	(kg)	3.8	2.2	3.0	4.0	5.4	5.4
茶叶	(公斤)	Tea	(kg)	0.2	0.2	0.2	0.2	0.3	0.4
卷烟	(盒)	Cigarette	(box)	22.0	15.0	19.4	25.8	24.4	28.4
啤酒	(公斤)	Beer	(kg)	2.4	1.4	1.8	2.4	2.9	3.8
白酒	(公斤)	Liquor	(kg)	1.0	0.6	0.9	0.9	1.3	1.4
果酒	(公斤)	Wine	(kg)	0.2	0.1	0.1	0.2	0.2	0.3
鞋	(双)	Footwear	(pair)	2.7	2.2	2.3	2.8	3.0	3.6
水	(吨)	Water	ton)	25.0	14.2	21.7	26.5	30.5	37.5
电	(度)	Electricity	(kwh)	615.1	389.2	547.0	631.3	697.2	936.0
煤炭	(公斤)	Coal	(kg)	105.3	138.0	112.5	89.5	87.2	86.7
管道天燃气	(立方米)	Gas pipeline	(cu.m)	82.6	31.5	73.7	84.8	115.7	131.4
罐装液化石油气	(公斤)	Bottled LPG	(kg)	4.1	3.6	2.9	3.5	4.9	6.4

10-15 城镇常住居民不同收入层次家庭每百户耐用消费品拥有情况（2014年）
Ownership of Major Durable Consumer Goods Per 100 Urban Households by Income Percentile(2014)

指　标		Item		总平均 Average	低收入户 Low Income House-holds	中低收入户 Lower Middle Income House-holds	中等收入户 Middle Income House-holds	中高收入户 Upper Middle Income House-holds	高收入户 High Income House-holds
家用汽车	（辆）	Automobile	(unit)	18.9	7.3	15.3	19.5	22.8	29.5
摩托车	（辆）	Motorcycle	(unit)	19.9	26.2	28.0	17.9	13.2	14.5
助力车	（台）	Strength-aid Cycle	(unit)	24.7	25.0	22.9	29.2	22.1	24.3
洗衣机	（台）	Washing Machine	(unit)	95.0	93.2	93.6	95.7	96.5	95.8
电冰箱(柜)	（台）	Refrigerator	(unit)	88.5	73.2	87.8	91.4	92.3	97.9
微波炉	（台）	Microwave Oven	(unit)	38.6	17.7	28.0	41.5	48.3	57.5
彩色电视机	（台）	Color TV Set	(unit)	108.5	104.0	110.3	105.8	112.6	110.0
# 接入有线电视		Cable TV Set		86.3	71.2	85.6	88.0	93.6	93.2
空　调	（台）	Air Conditioner	(unit)	85.2	35.7	66.9	88.1	107.8	127.1
热水器	（台）	Water Heater	(unit)	71.2	47.0	67.9	73.5	83.1	84.5
# 太阳能热水器		Solar Water Heater		32.1	28.5	36.2	33.8	31.1	30.9
消毒碗柜	（台）	Sterilizing Cupboard	(unit)	4.9	3.1	1.4	1.9	7.3	11.0
洗碗机	（台）	Dish Washer	(unit)	0.6	0.4	0.1	1.0	0.5	0.8
排油烟机	（台）	Exhauster	(unit)	65.9	43.7	62.5	69.5	72.7	80.9
固定电话	（线）	Ordinary Telephone	(unit)	51.6	38.0	45.6	49.2	60.5	64.5
移动电话	（部）	Mobile Telephone	(unit)	225.0	221.8	241.6	224.2	223.2	214.1
# 接入互联网		Access to the Internet		72.3	53.9	67.7	74.6	78.7	86.6
计算机	（台）	Computer	(unit)	65.5	44.8	59.4	66.7	71.8	84.5
# 接入互联网		Access to the Internet		54.5	35.5	48.4	54.3	60.5	73.8
摄像机	（台）	Pickup Camera	(unit)	5.8	0.2	4.1	5.0	8.5	10.9
照相机	（台）	Camera	(unit)	32.7	8.1	24.7	37.0	39.8	53.6
中高档乐器	（架）	High-end Instruments	(unit)	3.0	0.2	2.1	4.4	4.6	3.7
健身器材	（台）	Setting-up Apparatus	(unit)	2.6	0.2	1.5	1.8	3.4	6.2
组合音响	（套）	Music Center	(set)	5.3	3.0	3.3	5.4	6.8	8.1

10-16 城镇常住居民家庭年末居住情况
Housing Conditions of Urban Households

指标	Item	2013	2014
调查户数 (户)	Number of Households Surveyed (household)	1760	1707
平均每户居住人口 (人)	Average Number of Resident Population (person)	3.0	3.0
平均每人建筑面积 (平方米)	The Average Floor Area Per Person (sq.m)	29.9	30.6
一、按住户居住空间样式分 (%)	By Style of Living Space (%)	100.0	100.0
单栋楼房	Dependent Building	8.6	8.7
单栋平房	Single-storey House	8.0	8.3
四居室及以上单元房	Four Bedrooms	1.3	1.3
三居室单元房	Three Bedrooms	26.4	26.6
二居室单元房	Two Beedrooms	40.2	39.7
一居室单元房	One Beedroom	3.2	3.1
筒子楼或连片平房	Tube-shaped Apartment or Lace Single-storey Houses	11.8	11.8
其他	Others	0.5	0.5
二、按主要建筑材料分 (%)	By Main Building Materials (%)	100.0	100.0
钢筋混凝土	Reinforced Concrete	23.0	22.4
砖混材料	Brick-and-concrete Buildings	70.8	71.6
砖瓦砖木	Brick and Brick-wood Structure	5.6	5.5
竹草土坯	Bamboo Grass and Sun-dried Mud Brick	0.2	0.2
其他	Others	0.4	0.3
三、按现住房房屋来源分 (%)	By Source of Housing (%)	100.0	100.0
租赁公房	Public-rent Housing	1.8	1.9
租赁私房	Private-rent Housing	15.8	14.7
自建住房	Self-establish Housing	17.5	18.1
购买商品房	Commercial Residential Housing	30.4	31.1
购买房改住房	Private Housing through Housing Reform	21.0	21.7
购买保障性住房	Indemnificatory Housing	3.5	3.6
拆迁安置房	Resettlement Housing	4.2	3.9
继承或获赠住房	Inheriting and Donation Housing	0.7	0.8
免费借用房	Free Housing	2.6	2.3
雇主提供免费住房	Free Housing from Employer	1.3	1.4
其他	Others	1.2	0.5
四、按住宅外道路路面情况分 (%)	By Pavement Condition Outside	100.0	100.0
水泥或柏油路面	ement or Asphalt Pavement	89.7	90.7
沙石或石板等硬质路面	Hard Sand or Stone Pavement	7.4	6.6
其他	Others	2.9	2.7
五、按住宅有管道供水情况分 (%)	By Piped Water Supply Condition (%)	100.0	100.0
管道供水入户	Pipe water into People's Homes	96.1	96.9
管道供水至公共取水点	Pipe water to Public Watering Points	1.7	1.1
没有管道设施	No Pipeline Facilities	2.2	2.0
六、按住户主要饮用水来源情况分 (%)	By Source of main Drinking Water (%)	100.0	100.0
经过净化处理的自来水	Purified Tap Water	93.1	93.0
受保护的井水和泉水	Protected Wells and Springs	5.2	5.4
不受保护的井水和泉水	Unprotected Wells and Springs	1.0	1.1
江河湖泊水	Rivers and Lakes Water	0.3	0.2
收集雨水	Collected Rainwater		
桶装水	Barrels Water	0.3	0.2
其他	Others	0.1	0.1
七、按住户厕所类型分 (%)	By Household Lavatory Type (%)	100.0	100.0
水冲式卫生厕所	Sanitary Water Closet	85.4	84.4
水冲式非卫生厕所	Insanitary Water Closet	1.4	1.6
卫生旱厕	Sanitary Latrine	2.4	2.6
普通旱厕	Latrine	9.1	9.8
无厕所	No Lavatory	1.7	1.6
八、按住户主要取暖设备状况分 (%)	By Heating Facilities Condition (%)	100.0	100.0
由市政或小区集中供暖	Central Heating	38.3	39.9
自行供暖	Self Heating	49.7	48.6
无取暖设备	Without Heating Equipment	12.0	11.5
九、按主要炊用能源状况分 (%)	By Cooking Fuel Condition (%)	100.0	100.0
柴草	Firewood	0.9	0.7
煤炭	Coal	10.3	10.1
罐装液化石油气	Canned Liquified Petroleum Gas	15.4	12.8
管道液化石油气	Pipeline Liquified Petroleum Gas	0.6	0.5
管道煤气	Pipeline Gas	1.2	0.5
管道天然气	Pipeline Natural Gas	51.3	51.5
电	Electricity	19.3	23.0
沼气	Methane		
其他	Others	1.0	0.9

10-17　农村常住居民家庭基本情况
Basic Conditions of Urban Households

指　　标		Item		2013	2014
调查户数	(户)	Number of Households Surveyed	(household)	2591	2585
调查户人口	(人)	Number of Residents in the Household Surveyed(person)			
1.常住人口		Permanent Residents		8975	8734
2.平均每户常住人口		Average Household Size		3.5	3.4
3.平均每户劳动力人数		Labours Per Households		2.3	2.2
平均每户整劳动力人数		Ablebodied Labours Per Households		1.2	1.1
平均每户半劳动力人数		Semiablebodied Labours Per Households		1.0	1.1
4.平均每劳动力负担人口		Average Number of Persons Supported by a Laborer		1.5	1.5
平均每人可支配收入	(元)	Annual Per Capita Disposable Income	(yuan)	7092	7932
工资性收入		Wages Income		2887	3217
经营净收入		Net Income from Business		2530	2751
财产净收入		Property Income		90	120
转移净收入		Transfer Income		1585	1844
平均每人生活消费支出	(元)	Annual Per Capita Consumption Expenditure	(yuan)	6488	7252
食品、烟酒		Food,Tobacco and Alcohol		1772	2112
衣　着		Clothing		418	457
居　住		Residence		1432	1627
生活用品及服务		Living Articles and Services		406	444
交通通信		Transportation and Communications		660	691
教育文化娱乐		Recreation, Education and Culture Services		863	900
医疗保健		Medicine and Medical Services		803	884
其他用品和服务		Others		134	137
平均每人年末现住房建筑面积	(平方米)	Floor Area per Capita at Year-end	(sq.m)	39.6	41.0

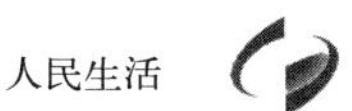

10-18 农村常住居民不同收入层次家庭基本情况(2014年)
Basic Conditions of Rural Households by Income Percentile(2014)

指　　标	Item	总平均 Average	低收入户 Low Income Households	中低收入户 Lower Middle Income Households	中等收入户 Middle Income Households	中高收入户 Upper Middle Income Households	高收入户 High Income Households
调查户数 (户)	Number of Households Surveyed (household)	2585	515	519	518	519	514
调查户人口 (人)	Number of Residents in the Household Surveyed (person)						
1.常住人口	Permanent Residents	8734	1989	1897	1795	1663	1390
2.平均每户常住人口	Average Household Size	3.4	3.9	3.7	3.5	3.2	2.7
3.平均每户劳动力人数	Labours Per Households	2.2	2.3	2.3	2.2	2.2	2.0
平均每户整劳动力人数	Ablebodied Labours Per Households	1.1	1.3	1.2	1.1	1.1	0.9
平均每户半劳动力人数	Semiablebodied Labours Per Households	1.1	1.0	1.0	1.1	1.1	1.1
4.平均每劳动力负担人口	Average Number of Persons Supported by a Laborer	1.5	1.7	1.6	1.6	1.5	1.3
平均每人可支配收入 (元)	Per Capita Annual Disposable Income (Yuan)	7932.2	2591.5	5227.8	7362.2	10137.3	17308.7
平均每人生活消费支出 (元)	Per Capita Annual Consumption Expenditure (yuan)	7252.4	5207.8	5697.6	7210.0	8126.4	11294.2
平均每人年末现住房建筑面积 (平方米)	Housing Area per Capita at Year-end (sq.m)	41.0	34.2	35.9	40.3	44.4	54.4

10-19 农村常住居民不同收入层次家庭人均可支配收入(2014年)

Per Capita Annual Disposable Income of Rural Households by Income Percentile(2014)

单位：元 (yuan)

指标	Item	总平均 Average	低收入户 Low Income Households	中低收入户 Lower Middle Income Households	中等收入户 Middle Income Households	中高收入户 Upper Middle Income Households	高收入户 High Income Households
可支配收入	**Disposable Income**	**7932.2**	**2591.5**	**5227.8**	**7362.2**	**10137.3**	**17308.7**
一、工资性收入	**Wages Income**	**3216.8**	**1069.8**	**2000.3**	**3141.8**	**4232.4**	**6812.4**
(一)工资	Wage	2815.2	867.8	1676.9	2765.1	3704.7	6139.1
1.按月发放的工资	The wages by monthly	1520.6	232.0	704.0	1408.1	2109.7	3909.0
2.补发工资	Retroactive pay	38.3	27.7	9.5	14.7	28.1	135.8
3.不按月发放的奖金、津贴、过节费等	The Bonus, allowance, holiday fee etc.by no-monthly	1256.3	608.1	963.4	1342.3	1566.9	2094.3
(二)实物福利	Benefits in kind	7.6	1.6	1.5	3.5	8.2	29.0
1.从单位或雇主得到的实物产品折价	The Discount of Real Products from the Company or Employer	3.5	1.6	0.5	2.1	2.3	13.6
2.从单位或雇主得到的服务折价	The Discount of Services from the Company or Employer	4.1		1.0	1.4	5.9	15.4
(三)其他	Others	394.0	200.4	321.9	373.2	519.5	644.3
1.住房公积金	Housing Funds	18.4		1.3	4.1	15.9	89.4
2.辞退金	Dismissal Payments	0.3			1.1		0.4
3.自由职业劳动所得(如稿费、翻译费)	Income by liberal work (Such as Remuneration,Translation Fee)	21.6	16.4	8.1	12.5	65.7	6.9
4.其他劳动所得	Others	353.7	184.0	312.5	355.5	437.9	547.6
二、经营净收入	**Net Income from Business**	**2750.7**	**857.2**	**1975.7**	**2380.5**	**3592.8**	**5968.0**
(一)第一产业经营净收入	Net Income from Primary Industry Business	2089.3	729.5	1572.9	1794.4	2585.1	4510.5
1.农业	Agricultural	1838.5	861.7	1419.9	1611.9	2312.7	3522.7
2.林业	Forestry	87.6	52.9	42.9	52.0	68.3	266.6
3.牧业	Animal Husbandry	161.8	-184.8	109.8	131.8	195.1	721.4
4.渔业	Fishery	1.4	-0.3	0.3	-1.3	9.0	-0.2
(二)第二产业经营净收入	Net Income from Secondary Industry Business	41.9	-10.8	45.6	47.6	11.1	140.0
(三)第三产业经营净收入	Net Income from Tertiary Industry Business	619.5	138.5	357.2	538.5	996.6	1317.5
1.批发和零售业	Wholesale and Retail Trades	215.3	94.9	102.6	162.6	470.4	306.2
2.交通运输、仓储和邮政业	Transport, Storage and Post	211.8	22.2	130.8	140.7	200.2	696.3
3.住宿和餐饮业	Hotels and Catering Services	33.1	10.4	11.4	19.9	90.7	43.8
4.房地产业	Real Estate	-6.6	-29.4				
5.租赁和商务服务业	Leasing and Business Services	0.0	-5.8	-0.2	2.9	3.1	1.0
6.居民服务、修理和其他服务业	Services to Households and Other Services	91.5	39.9	77.5	134.6	120.9	93.3
7.农林牧渔服务业	Services to Agriculture, Forestry, Animal Husbandry and Fishery	63.0	-2.0	25.8	72.8	92.9	157.9
8.其他	Others	11.4	8.3	9.3	5.0	18.4	19.0

10-19 续表 continued

单位：元 (yuan)

指　　标	Item	总平均 Average	低收入户 Low Income Households	中低收入户 Lower Middle Income Households	中等收入户 Middle Income Households	中高收入户 Upper Middle Income Households	高收入户 High Income Households
三、财产净收入	**Net Income from Properties**	**120.1**	**39.0**	**40.4**	**81.7**	**208.0**	**289.8**
# 利息净收入	Net Interests	16.2	-10.8	-5.5	17.6	49.2	43.0
红利收入	Bonus	20.6	8.7	2.2	9.7	30.6	65.2
储蓄性保险净收益	Net Benefits of Savings Insurance	0.6		1.3		0.9	1.0
转让承包土地经营权租金净收入	The Rent Income by Transfer of Land Rights	35.7	28.1	18.4	40.5	49.6	47.4
出租房屋财产性收入	The Property Income by Renting House	33.0	11.2	1.6	11.3	63.1	99.2
出租机械、专利、版权等资产的收入	The Income by Renting Assets like Mechanical, Patents,Copyright ect.	4.2	0.3	11.5	-0.3	0.6	9.4
四、转移净收入	**Net Income from Transfer**	**1844.5**	**625.5**	**1211.4**	**1758.1**	**2104.1**	**4238.5**
(一)转移性收入	Income from Transfer	2057.2	803.0	1381.8	1943.6	2329.0	4579.8
1.养老金或离退休金	Pension or Retired Pension	536.5	168.4	225.4	339.8	563.3	1705.9
# 离退休金	Retired Pension	366.0	7.4	65.7	156.3	383.2	1534.9
新型农村养老保险	Urban Employee Social Pension Insurance	150.8	153.6	144.9	166.9	148.0	137.6
2.社会救济和补助	Social Relief and Aid	79.1	65.4	84.0	67.3	72.6	114.4
3.政策性生活补贴	Policy Allowance	41.7	30.5	33.9	49.9	37.2	63.1
4.报销医疗费	Reimbursement of Medical treatment	123.3	47.8	77.5	164.8	94.1	274.0
5.家庭外出从业人员寄回带回收入	Income from Family Outings Employees	885.0	278.3	705.2	939.1	1075.7	1692.2
6.赡养收入	Alimony Income	174.7	50.3	100.4	166.3	220.9	408.8
7.其他经常转移收入	Others Recurring Income from Transfer	55.6	23.1	19.1	55.0	65.6	140.0
8.从政府和组织得到的实物产品和服务折价	The Discount of Real Products and Services from the Governments and Organizations	10.9	6.9	12.9	13.7	7.6	14.1
9.现金政策性惠农补贴	The Cash Policy Subsidies for Agricultural	150.4	132.3	123.4	147.7	192.0	167.3
(二)转移性支出	Transfer Expenditure	212.7	177.5	170.4	185.5	224.9	341.3
1.个人所得税	Personal Income Tax	1.6	0.4		0.2	0.1	9.2
2.社会保障支出	Expenditure for Social Security	177.4	151.7	143.3	163.7	197.8	254.2
(1)个人缴纳的养老保险	Pension Insurance Personal Rendered	81.5	72.1	54.6	69.8	96.5	128.7
(2)个人缴纳的医疗保险	Medical Care Insurance Personal Rendered	92.8	79.1	86.1	88.6	99.3	119.0
(3)个人缴纳的失业保险	Unemployment Insurance Personal Rendered	1.1	0.3		0.6	0.8	4.8
(4)其他社会保障支出	Others	2.0	0.2	2.6	4.7	1.2	1.7
3.外来从业人员寄给家人的支出	Expenditure for Family from Migrant Workers	1.3				1.7	6.1
4.赡养支出	Expenditure for Alimony	14.2	12.0	8.0	3.6	12.3	41.5
5.其他	Others	18.2	13.4	19.1	18.0	13.0	30.3

10-20 农村常住居民不同收入层次家庭人均生活消费支出(2014年)
Per Capita Living Expenditure of Rural Households by Income Percentile(2014)

单位：元 (yuan)

指标	Item	总平均 Average	低收入户 Low Income Households	中低收入户 Lower Middle Income Households	中等收入户 Middle Income Households	中高收入户 Upper Middle Income Households	高收入户 High Income Households
生活消费支出	**Total Living Expenditure**	**7252.4**	**5207.8**	**5697.6**	**7210.0**	**8126.4**	**11294.2**
一、食品、烟酒	**Food,Tobacco and Alcohol**	**2112.2**	**1579.6**	**1804.3**	**2012.5**	**2400.6**	**3073.9**
1.食品	Food	1554.0	1224.4	1384.9	1504.6	1732.2	2104.0
# 谷物	Grain	399.0	331.8	372.0	393.1	425.7	506.8
薯类	Potato	69.9	79.3	70.8	62.5	69.0	66.0
豆类	Beans	26.3	21.3	22.5	25.3	30.2	35.6
食用油	Edible Oil	133.2	108.5	124.9	131.2	147.1	165.9
蔬菜和食用菌	Vegetables and Edible Mushrooms	227.0	160.6	206.5	229.2	259.1	308.2
肉类	Meat	245.9	199.0	203.2	224.2	284.5	353.4
禽类	Poultry	22.1	16.7	20.1	17.1	28.5	31.2
水产品	Aquatic Products	14.1	8.1	11.0	12.0	16.6	26.5
蛋类	Eggs	45.5	39.5	40.2	43.3	49.5	59.2
奶类	Milk	112.0	80.2	102.8	121.0	117.2	151.8
干鲜瓜果类	Fresh and Dried Fruits	111.8	75.7	83.4	102.7	131.1	190.5
糖果糕点类	Candy and Pastry	44.5	26.0	35.6	43.1	52.0	75.5
2.烟酒	Tobacco and Alcohol	295.0	201.8	243.7	265.6	344.7	475.9
# 烟草	Tobacco	213.5	146.8	176.3	200.1	247.3	335.8
酒类	Alcohol	81.5	55.0	67.4	65.4	97.4	140.1
3.饮料	Beverages	45.4	32.8	39.6	37.1	50.9	75.3
4.饮食服务	Catering Services	217.8	120.5	136.1	205.2	272.9	418.7
二、衣着	**Clothing**	**457.3**	**321.3**	**360.2**	**436.6**	**540.9**	**710.7**
# 衣类	Garments	357.9	248.9	276.7	340.3	422.9	569.5
鞋类	Footwear	99.4	72.3	83.5	96.3	118.1	141.2
三、居住	**Residence**	**1627.0**	**1250.5**	**1271.1**	**1469.1**	**1794.0**	**2653.8**
# 租赁房房租	Rental Housing Rent	27.5	23.6	21.2	28.6	29.1	38.1
住房维修及管理	Housing Repair and Management	366.4	185.9	223.5	347.3	435.4	760.3
水电燃料及其他	Water,Electric Power Fuel and Others	373.5	295.8	320.6	337.8	414.8	553.1
四、生活用品及服务	**Living Articles and Services**	**444.2**	**250.5**	**336.2**	**394.6**	**517.5**	**843.4**
# 家具及室内装饰品	Furniture and External Decorations	100.9	36.9	75.0	64.9	118.1	252.8
家用器具	Household Appliances	138.3	68.6	99.2	140.6	173.2	246.0
家用纺织品	Household textile	45.8	31.2	32.3	37.8	46.0	95.4
家庭日用杂品	Household Articles of Daily Use	115.3	89.0	103.6	111.5	126.7	160.1
个人用品	Personal Items	28.2	18.0	20.2	26.0	32.7	51.0
家庭服务	Household Services	15.7	6.8	5.9	13.8	20.8	38.1
五、交通通信	**Transportation and Communications**	**690.5**	**412.9**	**448.2**	**750.9**	**821.5**	**1182.0**
# 交通	Transportation	393.5	190.6	211.2	461.5	499.8	717.0
通信	Communications	297.0	222.3	237.0	289.4	321.7	465.0
六、教育文化娱乐	**Recreation, Education and Culture Services**	**900.6**	**654.2**	**785.5**	**1004.5**	**993.5**	**1162.4**
# 教育	Education	753.3	566.1	691.7	875.6	813.0	873.5
文化娱乐	Recreation	147.3	88.1	93.8	128.9	180.5	288.9
七、医疗保健	**Medicine and Medical Services**	**883.7**	**666.2**	**603.9**	**1018.5**	**894.9**	**1388.0**
医疗器具及药品	Medical Instruments and Medicines	243.3	208.5	183.1	247.1	259.5	351.3
医疗服务	Medical Services	640.4	457.7	420.8	771.4	635.4	1036.7
八、其他用品和服务	**Others**	**136.9**	**72.6**	**88.2**	**123.3**	**163.5**	**280.0**

10-21 农村常住居民不同收入层次家庭人均购买主要商品数量(2014年)
Per Capita Annual Purchases of Major Commodities of Rural Households by Income Percentile(2014)

品名		Item		总平均 Average	低收入户 Low Income Households	中低收入户 Lower Middle Income Households	中等收入户 Middle Income Households	中高收入户 Upper Middle Income Households	高收入户 High Income Households
小麦	(公斤)	Wheat	(kg)	3.0	2.9	3.0	2.7	3.2	3.2
面粉	(公斤)	Flour	(kg)	26.8	27.2	25.2	25.2	25.5	31.9
大米	(公斤)	Rice	(kg)	13.5	12.3	13.9	12.1	14.2	15.6
薯类	(公斤)	Potato	(kg)	5.0	4.2	4.4	4.1	5.6	7.1
豆类	(公斤)	Beans	(kg)	4.5	3.6	3.7	4.4	5.2	6.3
食用植物油	(公斤)	Edible Vegetable Oil	(kg)	9.1	7.8	8.7	8.6	9.9	11.3
鲜菜	(公斤)	Fresh Vegetables	(kg)	40.1	27.9	34.8	41.1	45.5	57.0
猪肉	(公斤)	Pork	(kg)	7.1	5.7	5.8	6.7	7.8	10.5
牛肉	(公斤)	Beef	(kg)	0.2	0.1	0.1	0.2	0.2	0.3
羊肉	(公斤)	Mutton	(kg)	0.4	0.4	0.3	0.2	0.5	0.5
鸡	(公斤)	Chicken	(kg)	0.7	0.6	0.7	0.5	0.9	1.0
鸭	(公斤)	Duck	(kg)	0.0	0.0	0.0	0.1	0.0	0.0
鱼类	(公斤)	Fish	(kg)	0.7	0.4	0.5	0.6	0.8	1.1
虾类	(公斤)	Shrimp	(kg)	0.0	0.0	0.0	0.0	0.0	0.1
鲜蛋	(公斤)	Fresh Eggs	(kg)	3.9	3.5	3.4	3.7	4.3	5.2
鲜奶	(公斤)	Fresh Dairy Products	(kg)	2.4	2.3	1.7	2.4	2.5	3.5
酸奶	(公斤)	Yogurt	(kg)	1.0	0.7	1.0	1.1	1.3	1.3
奶粉	(公斤)	Milk Powder	(kg)	0.6	0.5	0.6	0.7	0.7	0.7
鲜瓜果	(公斤)	Fresh Fruit	(kg)	20.1	14.3	14.9	19.2	24.0	32.3
糕点	(公斤)	Cake	(kg)	1.5	1.0	1.2	1.5	1.7	2.4
茶叶	(公斤)	Tea	(kg)	0.2	0.1	0.2	0.2	0.2	0.3
卷烟	(盒)	Cigarette	(box)	31.8	23.9	27.2	31.4	35.6	45.2
啤酒	(公斤)	Beer	(kg)	3.2	2.0	2.8	2.7	4.6	4.7
白酒	(公斤)	Liquor	(kg)	1.1	0.8	1.1	0.9	1.5	1.4
果酒	(公斤)	Wine	(kg)	0.2	0.1	0.1	0.2	0.3	0.3
鞋	(双)	Footwear	(pair)	1.8	1.5	1.7	1.9	2.1	2.3
水	(吨)	Water	ton)	6.9	7.0	6.4	6.1	7.1	8.4
电	(度)	Electricity	(kwh)	302.8	225.3	261.4	287.2	338.9	446.9
煤炭	(公斤)	Coal	(kg)	140.4	141.0	125.4	124.5	147.7	172.2
管道天燃气	(立方米)	Gas pipeline	(cu.m)	2.8	0.5	0.8	1.7	3.5	9.1
罐装液化石油气	(公斤)	Bottled LPG	(kg)	2.3	1.4	2.1	2.5	2.9	3.1

10-22 农村常住居民不同收入层次家庭每百户耐用消费品拥有情况（2014年）

Ownership of Major Durable Consumer Goods Per 100 Rural Households by Income Percentile(2014)

品　名	Item		总平均 Average	低收入户 Low Income Households	中　低 收入户 Lower Middle Income Households	中　等 收入户 Middle Income Households	中　高 收入户 Upper Middle Income Households	高收入户 High Income Households
家用汽车	(辆) Automobile	(unit)	7.9	6.6	5.1	7.5	9.2	11.2
摩托车	(辆) Motorcycle	(unit)	66.3	61.8	66.3	70.5	67.8	64.9
助力车	(台) Strength-aid Cycle	(unit)	33.2	29.6	31.8	36.9	32.9	34.7
洗衣机	(台) Washing Machine	(unit)	87.5	81.0	85.1	89.1	88.8	93.4
电冰箱(柜)	(台) Refrigerator	(unit)	62.5	51.7	57.0	60.8	68.6	74.2
微波炉	(台) Microwave Oven	(unit)	6.8	5.7	3.9	6.0	6.2	12.0
彩色电视机	(台) Color TV Set	(unit)	113.6	111.1	112.1	115.8	112.8	116.2
# 接入有线电视	Cable TV Set		34.8	26.7	27.9	33.3	39.1	46.6
空　调	(台) Air Conditioner	(unit)	21.8	12.1	15.6	21.1	25.6	34.5
热水器	(台) Water Heater	(unit)	38.3	28.2	28.2	35.5	45.0	54.6
# 太阳能热水器	Solar Water Heater		30.4	22.9	20.9	29.3	35.8	43.0
消毒碗柜	(台) Sterilizing Cupboard	(unit)	0.6		0.5	0.8	0.3	1.4
洗碗机	(台) Dish Washer	(unit)	0.2		0.2	0.7	0.2	
排油烟机	(台) Exhauster	(unit)	6.1	3.1	3.6	4.2	6.6	12.9
固定电话	(线) Ordinary Telephone	(unit)	31.6	33.0	29.2	30.6	30.2	34.9
移动电话	(部) Mobile Telephone	(unit)	242.0	226.8	238.2	243.2	251.1	250.6
# 接入互联网	Access to the Internet		44.7	35.0	37.8	43.6	53.2	53.6
计算机	(台) Computer	(unit)	20.3	15.8	16.5	19.4	21.9	28.0
# 接入互联网	Access to the Internet		13.1	9.6	9.9	12.6	16.0	17.5
摄像机	(台) Pickup Camera	(unit)	0.4	0.2	0.4	0.4	0.2	0.8
照相机	(台) Camera	(unit)	4.4	3.1	1.8	3.2	4.7	9.1
中高档乐器	(架) High-end Instruments	(unit)	0.5	0.1	0.8	0.4	0.9	0.4
健身器材	(台) Setting-up Apparatus	(unit)	0.1			0.4	0.2	
组合音响	(套) Music Center	(set)	3.8	2.8	2.5	3.1	5.3	5.0

10-23 农村常住居民家庭年末居住情况
Housing Conditions of Rural Households

指　　标	Item	2013	2014
调查户数 (户)	Number of Households Surveyed (household)	2591	2585
平均每户居住人口 (人)	Average Number of Resident Population (person)	3.5	3.4
平均每人建筑面积 (平方米)	The Average Floor Area Per Person (sq.m)	39.6	41.0
一、按住户居住空间样式分 (%)	By Style of Living Space (%)	100.0	100.0
单栋楼房	Dependent Building	25.2	25.7
单栋平房	Single-storey House	60.1	59.4
四居室及以上单元房	Four Bedrooms	0.2	0.2
三居室单元房	Three Bedrooms	0.2	0.6
二居室单元房	Two Beedrooms	0.1	0.6
一居室单元房	One Beedroom		0.0
筒子楼或连片平房	Tube-shaped Apartment or Lace Single-storey Houses	9.4	9.2
其他	Others	4.8	4.3
二、按主要建筑材料分 (%)	By Main Building Materials (%)	100.0	100.0
钢筋混凝土	Reinforced Concrete	3.0	3.6
砖混材料	Brick-and-concrete Buildings	60.3	60.6
砖瓦砖木	Brick and Brick-wood Structure	28.9	28.1
竹草土坯	Bamboo Grass and Sun-dried Mud Brick	5.1	4.7
其他	Others	2.7	3.0
三、按现住房房屋来源分 (%)	By Source of Housing (%)	100.0	100.0
租赁公房	Public-rent Housing	0.1	0.1
租赁私房	Private-rent Housing	0.7	2.1
自建住房	Self-establish Housing	96.5	94.5
购买商品房	Commercial Residential Housing	0.6	0.9
购买房改住房	Private Housing through Housing Reform	0.1	0.3
购买保障性住房	Indemnificatory Housing	0.1	0.2
拆迁安置房	Resettlement Housing		0.2
继承或获赠住房	Inheriting and Donation Housing	1.1	1.1
免费借用房	Free Housing	0.4	0.4
雇主提供免费住房	Free Housing from Employer	0.2	0.1
其他	Others	0.2	0.1
四、按住宅外道路路面情况分 (%)	By Pavement Condition Outside (%)	100.0	100.0
水泥或柏油路面	Cement or Asphalt Pavement	64.7	66.7
沙石或石板等硬质路面	Hard Sand or Stone Pavement	12.4	12.2
其他	Others	22.9	21.1
五、按住宅有管道供水情况分 (%)	By Piped Water Supply Condition (%)	100.0	100.0
管道供水入户	Pipe water into People's Homes	73.1	74.7
管道供水至公共取水点	Pipe water to Public Watering Points	1.5	1.4
没有管道设施	No Pipeline Facilities	25.4	23.9
六、按住户主要饮用水来源情况分 (%)	By Source of main Drinking Water (%)	100.0	100.0
经过净化处理的自来水	Purified Tap Water	41.7	42.5
受保护的井水和泉水	Protected Wells and Springs	31.1	31.2
不受保护的井水和泉水	Unprotected Wells and Springs	18.0	17.5
江河湖泊水	Rivers and Lakes Water	1.9	1.5
收集雨水	Collected Rainwater	3.2	3.5
桶装水	Barrels Water	0.1	0.1
其他	Others	4.0	3.7
七、按住户厕所类型分 (%)	By Household Lavatory Type (%)	100.0	100.0
水冲式卫生厕所	Sanitary Water Closet	7.8	9.3
水冲式非卫生厕所	Insanitary Water Closet	1.8	2.2
卫生旱厕	Sanitary Latrine	11.5	11.1
普通旱厕	Latrine	76.2	75.7
无厕所	No Lavatory	2.7	1.7
八、按住户主要取暖设备状况分 (%)	By Heating Facilities Condition (%)	100.0	100.0
由市政或小区集中供暖	Central Heating	0.5	0.9
自行供暖	Self Heating	54.9	56.1
无取暖设备	Without Heating Equipment	44.6	43.0
九、按主要炊用能源状况分 (%)	By Cooking Fuel Condition (%)	100.0	100.0
柴草	Firewood	53.2	53.5
煤炭	Coal	22.4	19.6
罐装液化石油气	Canned Liquified Petroleum Gas	6.3	6.1
管道液化石油气	Pipeline Liquified Petroleum Gas		0.0
管道煤气	Pipeline Gas		0.0
管道天然气	Pipeline Natural Gas	0.3	1.4
电	Electricity	15.9	17.6
沼气	Methane	1.7	1.7
其他	Others	0.2	0.1

10-24 各县(市、区)城乡居民人均收入(2014年)
Per Capita Income in Urban and Rural Households by County (City and District)(2014)

单位：元 (yuan)

地 区	Region	城镇居民人均可支配收入 Per Capita Annual Disposable Income of Urban Households	农村居民人均纯收入 Per Capita Annual Net Income of Rural Households	地 区	Region	城镇居民人均可支配收入 Per Capita Annual Disposable Income of Urban Households	农村居民人均纯收入 Per Capita Annual Net Income of Rural Households
西安市	**Xi'an**	**36100**	**14462**	麟游县	Linyou	26304	8512
新城区	Xincheng	37029		凤　县	Fengxian	33548	11765
碑林区	Beilin	37765		太白县	Taibai	25497	8463
莲湖区	Lianhu	37757		**咸阳市**	**Xianyang**	**31530**	**9612**
灞桥区	Baqiao	35147	16982	秦都区	Qindu	35738	12211
未央区	Weiyang	36462	18364	渭城区	Weicheng	35545	11979
雁塔区	Yanta	38345		三原县	Sanyuan	32561	10846
阎良区	Yanliang	37503	17007	泾阳县	Jingyang	32431	10794
临潼区	Lintong	29804	13595	乾　县	Qianxian	30421	10700
长安区	Chang'an	32377	14206	礼泉县	Liquan	30584	10796
蓝田县	Lantian	23907	9911	永寿县	Yongshou	26024	8232
周至县	Zhouzhi	24445	9961	彬　县	Binxian	31126	10271
户　县	Huxian	27026	12218	长武县	Changwu	26936	8508
高陵县	Gaoling	28581	13615	旬邑县	Xunyi	26229	8741
铜川市	**Tongchuan**	**27237**	**9169**	淳化县	Chunhua	24654	8451
王益区	Wangyi	27992	10398	武功县	Wugong	29585	10521
印台区	Yintai	26348	8934	兴平市	Xingping	33600	10936
耀州区	Yaozhou	31894	10227	**渭南市**	**Weinan**	**26725**	**8534**
宜君县	Yijun	26246	8417	临渭区	Linwei	29149	8940
宝鸡市	**Baoji**	**31560**	**9421**	华　县	Huaxian	27348	8438
渭滨区	Weibin	32519	13069	潼关县	Tongguan	26101	8381
金台区	Jintai	31329	11883	大荔县	Dali	26168	9184
陈仓区	Chencang	31797	11081	合阳县	Heyang	25563	7620
凤翔县	Fengxiang	32428	11716	澄城县	Chengcheng	27374	7691
岐山县	Qishan	32100	11791	蒲城县	Pucheng	27677	8590
扶风县	Fufeng	29608	9736	白水县	Baishui	25824	8218
眉　县	Meixian	32981	10755	富平县	Fuping	27321	8476
陇　县	Longxian	25464	8568	韩城市	Hancheng	30071	11400
千阳县	Qianyang	27703	8955	华阴市	Huayin	26719	8241

10-24 续表 continued

单位：元 (yuan)

地 区	Region	城镇居民人均可支配收入 Per Capita Annual Disposable Income of Urban Households	农村居民人均纯收入 Per Capita Annual Net Income of Rural Households	地 区	Region	城镇居民人均可支配收入 Per Capita Annual Disposable Income of Urban Households	农村居民人均纯收入 Per Capita Annual Net Income of Rural Households
延安市	**Yan'an**	**30588**	**9779**	横山县	Hengshan	29021	9364
宝塔区	Baota	31358	9529	靖边县	Jingbian	33205	13086
延长县	Yanchang	27615	8007	定边县	Dingbian	30911	11829
延川县	Yanchuan	26089	7634	绥德县	Suide	27426	8227
子长县	Zichang	32570	9335	米脂县	Mizhi	27710	8903
安塞县	Ansai	32852	10374	佳 县	Jiaxian	26405	8162
志丹县	Zhidan	33403	10001	吴堡县	Wubu	26904	8242
吴起县	Wuqi	33198	10358	清涧县	Qingjian	26705	8234
甘泉县	Ganquan	28607	9662	子洲县	Zizhou	26822	8296
富 县	Fuxian	27136	10313	**安康市**	**Ankang**	**25011**	**7468**
洛川县	Luochuan	28993	11742	汉滨区	Hanbin	27890	7572
宜川县	Yichuan	28772	9626	汉阴县	Hanyin	25420	7797
黄龙县	Huanglong	21975	8503	石泉县	Shiquan	25747	7675
黄陵县	Huangling	30213	11267	宁陕县	Ningshan	24116	7315
汉中市	**Hanzhong**	**24605**	**7933**	紫阳县	Ziyang	24749	7794
汉台区	Hantai	26030	10497	岚皋县	Langao	25786	7348
南郑县	Nanzheng	25465	9368	平利县	Pingli	25097	8147
城固县	Chenggu	25437	9473	镇坪县	Zhenping	24853	7360
洋 县	Yangxian	24700	7419	旬阳县	Xunyang	25174	7655
西乡县	Xixiang	24914	7541	白河县	Baihe	24617	7416
勉 县	Mianxian	25188	8556	**商洛市**	**Shangluo**	**24727**	**7035**
宁强县	Ningqiang	24985	7373	商州区	Shangzhou	26196	7066
略阳县	Lueyang	24675	7277	洛南县	Luonan	25302	7301
镇巴县	Zhenba	23924	7042	丹凤县	Danfeng	25447	7149
留坝县	Liuba	23649	7047	商南县	Shangnan	24783	7219
佛坪县	Foping	23674	7050	山阳县	Shanyang	24443	7380
榆林市	**Yulin**	**29665**	**9730**	镇安县	Zhen'an	25037	7276
榆阳区	Yuyang	32217	12656	柞水县	Zhashui	24822	7168
神木县	Shenmu	32610	13622	**杨凌示范区**	**Yangling**	**36008**	**14046**
府谷县	Fugu	32732	13409	杨陵区	Yangling	36008	14046

主要统计指标解释

住户 指居住在一个住宅内，共同分享生活开支或收入的一群人。居住在同一房间内、不共同分享生活开支的人群，每个人都视为一个住户。住家保姆、住家家庭帮工视为单独的住户。

常住居民 指住户成员中，经常在家居住、或者调查期内居住时间超过一半的人员，以及本住户供养的学生。常住居民是住户收支的调查对象。

整、半劳动力 整劳动力是指男子18周岁到50周岁，女子18周岁到45周岁；半劳动力是指男子16周岁到17周岁，51周岁到60周岁；女子16周岁到17周岁，46周岁到55周岁，同时具有劳动能力的人。虽然在劳动年龄之内，但已丧失劳动能力的人，不应算为劳动力；超过劳动年龄，但能经常参加劳动，计入半劳动力数内。常住人口中的职工，若这些职工为劳动力，就包括在本户的整半劳动力中。

居民人均可支配收入 指调查期内居民家庭成员人均获得的、可用于最终消费支出和储蓄的总和，即居民可以用来自由支配的收入，既包括现金收入，也包括实物收入。全体居民可支配收入可以体现各地区城乡一体的居民收入及生活水平变化情况。按照收入的来源，可支配收入包含四项，分别为：工资性收入、经营净收入、财产净收入、转移净收入。

工资性收入 指就业人员通过各种途径得到的全部劳动报酬和各种福利，包括受雇于单位或个人、从事各种自由职业、兼职和零星劳动得到的全部劳动报酬和福利。

经营净收入 指住户或住户成员从事生产经营活动所获得的净收入，是全部经营收入中扣除经营费用、生产性固定资产折旧和生产税净额（生产税减去生产补贴）之后得到的净收入。计算公式为：

经营净收入 = 经营收入 - 经营费用 - 生产性固定资产折旧 - 生产税净额（生产税-生产补贴）

财产净收入 指住户或住户成员将其所拥有的金融资产和自然资源交由其他机构单位、住户或个人支配而获得的回报并扣除相关的费用之后得到的净收入。计算公式为：财产净收入 = 财产性收入 - 财产性支出

转移净收入 指国家、单位、社会团体对住户的各种经常性转移支付和住户之间的经常性收入转移。包括政府、非行政事业单位、社会团体对居民转移的养老金或退休金、社会救济和补助、政策性生活补贴、救灾款、经常性捐赠和赔偿以及报销医疗费等；住户之间的赡养收入、经常性捐赠和赔偿以及农村地区（村委会）在外（含国外）工作的本住户非常住成员寄回带回的收入等。计算公式为：转移净收入=转移性收入-转移性支出

居民收入五等份分组 指将所有调查户按人均收入水平从低到高顺序排列，平均分为五个等份，处于最高20%的收入群体为高收入组，依此类推依次为中高收入组、中等收入组、中低收入组、低收入组。

居民人均生活消费支出 指住户用于满足家庭日常生活消费需要的全部支出，包括用于消费品的支出和用于服务性消费的支出。根据用途不同，消费支出可划分为食品烟酒、衣着、居住、生活用品及服务、交通通信、教育文化娱乐、医疗保健、其他用品及服务八大类。

城镇居民人均可支配收入（老口径） 指城镇家庭总收入扣除交纳的个人所得税和个人交纳的各项社会保障支出之后，按照城镇居民家庭人口平均的收入水平。其中家庭总收入是指该家庭中生活在一起的所有家庭人员从各种渠道得到的所有收入之和。计算公式为：

可支配收入= 家庭总收入- 交纳个人所得税-个人交纳的社会保障支出-记账补贴

农村居民人均纯收入（老口径） 指农村住户当年从各个来源得到的家庭总收入扣除有关费用性支出后，最终归农村居民所有的收入总和，按照农村住户人口平均的纯收入水平。计算公式为：

纯收入＝总收入-家庭经营费用支出-税费支出-生产性固定资产折旧-赠送农村内部亲友

Explanatory Notes on Main Statistical Indicators

Households refer to persons living and sharing economically together in one house. When people don't share living expenses, every single person are deemed to be one household. Live-in Nanny and family helpers are deemed to be one household.

Usual Resident Population refers to persons staying at home regularly or for over half of time in survey period and students provided by the household. Usual resident population is the respondent of household living expenses.

Full/Semi Labour Force Full labour force refers to persons capable of work, aged 18-50 for males and 18-45 for females. Semi labour force refers to persons capable of work, aged 16-17 and 51-60 for males and 16-17 and 46-55 for females. Persons at their working ages but not capable of work are not to be included as labour force. Persons not at working ages but participating regularly in work are included in semi labour force. For staff and workers who are usual residents, are included as full or semi labour force of the household if they are in the labour force.

Disposable Income of Residents refers to the actual income at the disposal of members of the households which can be used for final consumption and savings in survey period, residents can use that at their disposal. It includes cash income and physical income. This income demonstrates the situation about incomes of both rural and urban residents and living standard in various regions. According to the source of income, disposable income include wage income, net business income, net property income and net transferability income.

Wages Income refers to the work reward and all benefits received in various ways by the members of rural households,include the work reward and all benefits received from employed by other units or individuals,liberal professions, part-time job and sporadic labor.

Net Business Income refers to the net income received by households engaged in manufacturing & managing activities.This equals to total business income minus operating costs, depreciation for productive plant assets and net product tax(production taxes minus production subsidies).The following formula is used:

Net business income=business income-operating costs-depreciation for productive plant assets- net product tax(production taxes-production subsidies)

Net Property Income refers to the income received as returns by owners of financial assets or nature sources by providing nature sources to other institutional units,households and individuals. The following formula is used:

Net property income = property income - property expenditure

Net Transferability Income refers to various current transfers of nation, units and social organizations pay to households and recurring revenue transfer between households. This income includes pension transferred from government, the non administrative institutions and social organizations to households, social assistance, policy living allowance, disaster relief funds, regular donation and compensation, recoverable medical cost; alimony income, regular donation and compensation, income from the ones who are not resident in rural areas between the households.The following formula is used:

Net transferability income = transfer income - transfer expenditure

Five Equal Groups of Resident Income According to income per head, all investigative households are arranged from low to high. Divided five groups equally, the maximum 20% of the income groups is high-income groups, and so on, there are middle and upper-income groups, middle-income groups, medium-low-income groups and low-income groups.

Consumption Expenditure of Households refers to total expenditure of households for consumption in daily life, including expenditure on the eight categories of food; clothing; housing; household appliances and services; health care and medical services; transport and communications; recreation, education and cultural services; and miscellaneous goods and services.

The per capita disposable income(the old range) This equals to total income minus income tax, personal contribution to social security and subsidy for keeping diaries in being a sample household. The following formula is used:

Disposable income = total household income - income tax - personal contribution to social security - subsidy for keeping diaries for a sampled household

The Average Per Capita Net Income of Rural Residents(the old range) refers to the total income of rural households from all sources minus all corresponding expenses. The formula for calculation is as follows:

Net income = total income - household operation expenses - taxes and fees paid - taxes and fees depreciation of fixed assets for production - gifts to non-rural relatives

十一、环境和城市

资料整理：冉妮平　梁珠荣

简 要 说 明

一、本篇资料主要反映陕西环境保护事业发展情况和城市公用事业基本情况。

环境保护事业发展情况主要包括供水、用水情况以及工业废水和生活污水的排放及治理情况；城市空气质量，废气排放及处理情况；工业固体废物的产生、处理及利用情况；城市生活垃圾清运及处理情况；城市道路交通和区域环境噪声监测情况；造林及自然保护基本情况；地质、地震、海洋、森林灾害及突发环境事件情况；环境污染治理投资等情况。

城市公用事业基本情况主要包括城市建设、供水、供气、供热、市政设施、城市绿化、环境卫生等情况。

二、本篇资料由省国土资源厅、省环境保护厅、省住房和城乡建设厅、省水利厅、省林业厅提供。

Brief Introduction

I. This chapter reflects the development of environment protection and public utilities in Shaanxi Province.

The development of environment protection mainly include water supply and utilization, discharge and treatment of industrial and other waste water; urban air quality, emission and treatment of waste gas; production, treatment and utilization of industrial solid wastes, collection and disposal of consumption wastes in cities; national monitoring of road traffic noise and urban environmental noise in key cities; forestation, grassland construction and natural protection; incidences of geological, seismic, marine and forest disasters, environmental emergency investment in environment pollution treatment, etc.

The public utilities mainly include urban construction, water supply, gas supply, heat supply, public facilities, urban greening and environmental hygiene, etc.

Ⅱ. The data resources are provided by Shaanxi Province Department of Land and Resources, Shaanxi Province Environmental Protection Department, Shaanxi Province Housing and Urban-Rural Development, Shaanxi Province Department of Water Resources and Shaanxi Province Forestry Department.

11.环境和城市

2014年全省城市		
人均公园绿地面积	12.58	平方米
人均城市道路面积	15.47	平方米
人均日生活用水量	157.09	升
用水普及率	96.25	%
燃气普及率	95.77	%

城市人均公园绿地面积（平方米）

（2014年）

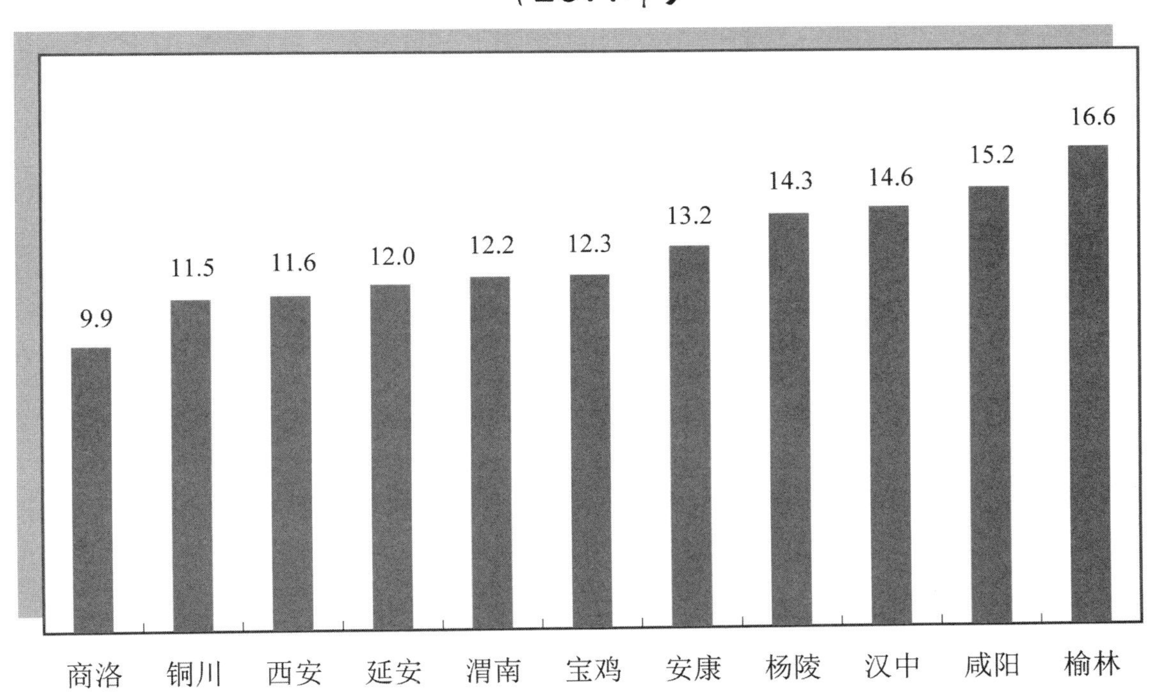

11-1 环境保护基本情况
Basic Statistics on Environmental Protection

指　　标	Item	2013	2014
水环境	**Water Environment Conditions**		
水资源总量 (亿立方米)	Total Amount of Water Resources (100 million cu. m)	353.77	351.64
地表水资源量	Surface Water	331.47	325.85
地下水资源量	Ground-Water	118.52	124.12
地表水与地下水资源重复量	Duplicated Measurement between Surface and Underground	96.22	98.33
人均水资源量 (立方米/人)	Per Capita Water Resources (cu.m/person)	941.26	932.84
用水总量 (亿立方米)	Water Consumption (100 million cu. m)	89.21	89.81
# 农业用水	Water Consumption of Agriculture	58.06	57.86
工业用水	Water Consumption of Industry	13.76	14.02
生活用水	Water Consumption of Consumption	12.46	12.75
生态环境补水	Water Consumption of Ecological Protection	2.26	2.52
废水排放总量 (万吨)	Total Volume of Waste Water Discharged (10 000 tons)	132169.34	145785.38
# 工业废水排放量	Volume of Industrial Waste Water Discharged	34870.56	36163.40
城镇生活污水排放量	Volume of Consumption Waste Water Discharged	97166.06	109536.33
集中式治理设施污水排放量	Volume of Sewage Discharged from Centralized Treatment Facilities	132.72	85.65
化学需氧量(COD)排放量 (吨)	COD Discharge (ton)	519261	504916
# 工业废水中COD排放量	COD Discharge by Industrial Waste Water	95400	95565
农业COD排放量	COD Discharge by Agriculture	192494	189456
城镇生活污水中COD排放量	COD Discharge by Consumption Waste Water	226166	216952
集中式治理设施COD排放量	Volume of COD Discharged by Centralized Treatment Facilities	5201	2943
氨氮排放量 (吨)	Ammonia Nitrogen Discharge (ton)	59560	58237
# 工业废水中氨氮排放量	Ammonia Nitrogen Discharge by Industrial Waste Water	8346	8675
农业氨氮排放量	Ammonia Nitrogen Discharge by Agriculture	15027	14827
生活污水中氨氮排放量	Ammonia Nitrogen Discharge by Consumption Waste Water	35547	34441
集中式治理设施氨氮排放量	Volume of Ammonia Nitrogen Discharged by Centralized Treatment Facilities	619	294
大气环境	**Atmospheric Environment Conditions**		
二氧化硫(SO_2)排放量 (吨)	Sulphur Dioxide (SO_2) Emission (ton)	806152	780954
# 工业SO_2排放量	Volume of Sulphur Dioxide Emission by Industry	707146	671642
城镇生活SO_2排放量	Volume of Sulphur Dioxide Emission by Consumption	98999	109286
集中式治理设施SO_2排放量	Volume of SO_2 Discharged by Centralized Treatment Facilities	7	27
氮氧化物排放量 (吨)	Volume of Nitrogen oxides (ton)	758897	705756
# 工业氮氧化物排放量	Volume of Nitrogen oxides by Industry	552078	509575
城镇生活氮氧化物排放量	Volume of Nitrogen oxides by Consumption	26595	25901
机动车氮氧化物排放量	Volume of Nitrogen oxides by Motor Vehicles	180202	170248
集中式治理设施氮氧化物排放量	Volume of Nitrogen oxides by Centralized Treatment Facilities	23	33
烟(粉)尘排放量 (吨)	Volume of Soot Emission (ton)	537739	709137
# 工业烟(粉)尘排放量	Volume of Industrial Soot Emission	468507	537753
城镇生活烟尘排放量	Volume of Consumption Soot Emission	54973	157821
机动车烟尘排放量	Volume of Soot Emission by Motor Vehicles	14215	13517
集中式治理设施烟尘排放量	Volume of Soot Emission by Centralized Treatment Facilities	43	47

11-1 续表 1 continued

指 标		Item		2013	2014
固体废物		**Solid Wastes**			
一般工业固体废物产生量	(万吨)	Volume of Industrial Solid Wastes Produced	(10 000 tons)	7491.10	8682.50
一般工业固体废物综合利用量	(万吨)	Volume of Industrial Solid Wastes Utilized	(10 000 tons)	4752.46	5464.23
# 综合利用往年贮存量		The Comprehensive Utilization Stored Quantity in Early Years		18.65	9.24
一般工业固体废物综合利用率	(%)	Ratio of Industrial Solid Wastes Utilized	(%)	63.52	62.93
一般工业固体废物处置量	(万吨)	Volume of Industrial Solid Wastes Treated	(10 000 tons)	1621.81	2136.13
# 处置往年贮存量		Stored Quantity Treated in Early Years		1.43	1.31
一般工业固体废物处置率	(%)	Ratio of Industrial Solid Wastes Treated	(%)	21.65	24.60
一般工业固体废物贮存量	(万吨)	Industrial Solid Wastes Stored Quantity	(10 000 tons)	1130.68	1092.66
危险废物产生量	(吨)	Volume of Hazardous Wastes	(ton)	303388	636994
危险废物综合利用量	(吨)	Volume of Hazardous Wastes Utilized	(ton)	95703	212088
# 综合利用往年贮存量		The Comprehensive Utilization Stored Quantity in Early Years		1159	20087
危险废物综合利用率	(%)	Ratio of Hazardous Wastes Utilized	(%)	32.00	33.30
危险废物处置量	(吨)	Volume of Hazardous Wastes Treated	(ton)	119042	347842
危险废物处置率	(%)	Ratio of Hazardous Wastes Treated	(%)	39.00	54.60
危险废物贮存量	(吨)	Hazardous Wastes Stored Quantity	(ton)	92098	100216
生态环境		**Ecological Environment Conditions**			
森林面积	(万公顷)	Area of Forest	(1 0000 hectares)	853.24	887.00
森林覆盖率	(%)	Forest Coverage Rate	(%)	41.42	43.06
累计水土流失治理面积	(千公顷)	Accumulative Area of Water and Soil Conservation	(1 000 hectares)	6784.91	7039.06
当年造林面积	(公顷)	The Area of Afforestation	(hectare)	343981	335362
# 人工造林		Man-made Forests		215732	251125
飞播造林		Afforestation by Air Seeding		54001	32000
无林地和疏林地新封山育林		Non-forest Land and Close Hillsides to Facilitate Afforestation		74248	52237
自然保护区数	(个)	Number of Nature Reserves	(unit)	61	61
# 国家级		Nation Level		23	23
自然保护区面积	(万公顷)	Area of Nature Reserves	(10 000 hectares)	115.74	115.74
自然灾害		**Natural Disasters**			
地质灾害次数	(次)	Number of Geologic Hazards	(time)	345	172
地质灾害受伤人数	(人)	Number of Geologic Hazard Injured	(person)	41	11
地质灾害死亡人数	(人)	Number of Geologic Hazard Deaths	(person)	29	44
地质灾害直接经济损失	(万元)	Direct Economic Losses of Geologic Hazard	(10 000 yuan)	9011	4717
森林火灾次数	(次)	Number of Forest Fires	(time)	187	109
森林火灾受害森林面积	(公顷)	Damaged Forest Area	(hectare)	1013	288
环境污染与治理		**Investment in the Treatment of Environmental Pollution**			
突发环境事件次数	(次)	Environmental Disasters	(time)	118	82
环境污染治理投资总额	(万元)	Total Investment in the Treatment of Environmental Pollution	(10 000 yuan)	2216819	2763183
城镇环境基础设施投资		Investment in Urban Environmental Infrastructure		1411093	2035119
燃 气		Gas		160659	180220
集中供热		Centralized Heating		248402	369105
排 水		Drainage Works		284329	384572
园林绿化		Gardening and Greening		646553	841574
市容环境卫生		Environmental Sanitation		71150	259648

11-1 续表 2 continued

指　　标		Item	2013	2014
工业污染防治投资		Investment in the Treatment of Industrial Pollution	417562	377310
治理废水		Treatment of Waste Water	60626	74340
治理废气		Treatment of Waste Gas	321029	265076
治理固体废物		Treatment of Solid Waste	9832	2196
治理噪声		Treatment of Noise Pollution	851	1557
治理其他		Treatment of Other Pollution	25224	34141
完成环保验收项目环保投资	（万元）	Investment in Completion Acceptance of Environmental Protection (10 000 yuan)	388164	350754
环境污染治理投资占GDP比重	（%）	Total Investment in the Treatment of Environmental Pollution as Percent of GDP (%)	1.38	1.56
工业废气治理设施运行费用	（万元）	Operating Costs of Industrial Waste Gas Treatment Facilities (10 000 yuan)	319057	363506
工业废水治理设施运行费用	（万元）	Operating Costs of Industrial Waste Water Treatment Facilities (10 000 yuan)	106477	100511
排污费收入总额	（万元）	Total Pollution Charges (10 000 yuan)	64497	63400
本年林业投资完成额	（万元）	Investment Completed This Year for Afforestation (10 000 yuan)	1012633	1091744
生态建设与保护		Ecological Construction and Protection	625860	693360
林业支撑与保障		Forestry Support and Protection	29883	38482
林业产业发展		Development of Forestry	68122	137308
林业民生工程		Forestry of the People's Livelihood Projects	63560	29548
其　他		Others	225208	193046
城市环境		**Urban Environmental**		
城区面积	（平方公里）	Total Urban Area (sq.km)	1555.04	1424.92
# 建成区面积		Developed Areas	915.02	910.46
城市建设用地面积	（平方公里）	City Areas and Floor Space of Buildings (sq.km)	885.04	890.68
城市供水总量	（万立方米）	Total Water Supply (10 000 cu.m)	88990.29	87921.00
城市用水普及率	（%）	Coverage Rate of Urban Population with Access to Tap Water (%)	96.52	96.25
城市污水排放量	（万立方米）	Volume of City Sewage (10 000 cu.m)	77504	83149
城市污水处理量	（万立方米）	Disposal of City Sewage (10 000 cu.m)	69007	76490
城市污水处理厂集中处理率	（%）	Treatment Rate of City Sewage (%)	89.04	91.99
城市生活垃圾清运量)	（万吨）	Urban Consumption Wastes Collected and Transported (10 000 tons)	437.30	497.00
城市生活垃圾无害化处理量	（万吨）	Volume of City Consumption Wastes (10 000 tons)	421.75	477.00
城市生活垃圾无害化处理率	（%）	Treatment Rate of City Consumption Wastes (%)	96.44	95.84
城市燃气普及率	（%）	Coverage Rate of Urban Population with Access to Gas (%)	93.75	95.77
城市集中供热面积	（万平方米）	Area of Centralized Heating in Urban (10 000 sq.m)	15963	19782
城市人均公园绿地面积	（平方米）	Per Capita Public Green Area (sq.m)	11.77	12.58
建成区绿化覆盖率	（%）	Green Covered Area as % of Completed Area (%)	40.19	40.76

注：城市环境部分，2013年数据为全省设区市和兴平、华阴、韩城三个县级市，2014年数据为全省设区市和杨凌示范区，不包括县级市。
a)Data of urban enviromental in 2013 include those of cities at prefecture level and Xingping,Huayin,Hancheng.Data of urban enviromental in 2014 include those of cities at prefecture level and Yangling.

11-2 各市(区)工业固体废物排放及处理情况(2014年)
Production and Treatment of Industrial Solid Wastes by City(District)(2014)

地　区	Region	一般工业固体废物产生量(万吨) Volume of Industrial Solid Wastes Produced (10 000 tons)	#危险废物产生量 Volume of Hazardous Wastes Produced	一般工业固体废物贮存量(万吨) Volume of Industrial Solid Wastes in Stocks (10 000 tons)	#危险废物贮存量 Volume of Hazardous Wastes in Stocks	一般工业固体废物处置量(万吨) Volume of Industrial Solid Wastes Disposed (10 000 tons)	#处置往年贮存量 Storage Capacity Disposed in Former Years	#危险废物处置量 Volume of Hazardous Wastes Disposed	一般工业固体废物综合利用量(万吨) Volume of Industrial Solid Wastes Utilized (10 000 tons)
全　省	**Shaanxi**	**8682.50**	**63.70**	**1092.66**	**10.02**	**2136.13**	**1.31**	**34.78**	**5464.23**
西安市	Xi'an	249.37	3.29	1.61		14.55	0.02	2.99	233.23
铜川市	Tongchuan	141.44				2.00			139.44
宝鸡市	Baoji	603.83	0.88	10.78	0.10	264.28		0.88	328.93
咸阳市	Xianyang	551.96	0.16	21.50	0.01	50.05	0.63	0.15	483.67
渭南市	Weinan	3191.66	7.64	2.20		1773.33		1.52	1416.13
延安市	Yan'an	108.26	12.45	0.22	0.36	13.79		11.98	94.25
汉中市	Hanzhong	636.24	13.64	285.27	8.65	14.08	0.31	0.10	338.13
榆林市	Yulin	2140.56	24.06	22.78	0.47	2.04		16.58	2115.75
安康市	Ankang	113.11	0.06	8.14	0.04	1.43	0.04	0.04	106.65
商洛市	Shangluo	944.92	1.52	740.16	0.39	0.59	0.30	0.54	206.92
杨凌示范区	Yangling	1.15							1.13

11-3 各市(区)工业废水排放及处理量(2014年)
Discharge and Treatment of Industrial Waste Water by City(District)(2014)

地　区	Region	工业用水总量(万吨) Total Water Use in Industry (10 000 tons)	工业废水排放总量(万吨) Total Volume of Industrial Waste Water Discharged (10 000 tons)	化学需氧量排放量(吨) COD Discharge (ton)	氨氮排放量(吨) Ammonia Nitrogen Discharge (ton)	工业废水处理量(万吨) Volume of Treated Industrial Waste Water (10 000 tons)	废水治理设施数(套) Number of Facilities for Treatment of Waste Water (set)	废水治理设施处理能力(万吨/日) Treatment Capacity of Facilities for Treatment of Waste Water (10 000 tons/day)	废水治理设施运行费用(万元) Operate Expenditure for Facilities for Treatment of Waste Water (10 000 yuan)
全　省	**Shaanxi**	**720041.41**	**36163.40**	**95565.24**	**8674.67**	**61842.91**	**1893**	**348.68**	**100510.93**
西安市	Xi'an	36994.88	6339.85	20137.42	1582.74	5818.27	305	25.16	10216.00
铜川市	Tongchuan	12635.38	402.46	1489.61	24.57	285.47	25	2.94	1040.30
宝鸡市	Baoji	110672.64	4687.37	14073.14	922.68	8610.70	209	45.55	12272.30
咸阳市	Xianyang	121939.74	4705.92	14564.03	1346.01	4369.66	235	32.11	12025.03
渭南市	Weinan	346098.54	5849.43	20966.50	1015.12	10901.41	175	60.31	17310.10
延安市	Yan'an	7926.78	2114.39	5188.63	259.33	3798.18	138	16.98	15730.10
汉中市	Hanzhong	48475.75	2511.50	5547.23	1211.65	9843.43	231	68.44	6404.60
榆林市	Yulin	26852.77	6254.68	3816.00	773.44	13004.93	381	57.61	18202.50
安康市	Ankang	2462.75	464.45	4293.79	267.55	558.16	92	4.40	879.20
商洛市	Shangluo	5743.53	2695.93	5049.41	1259.98	4547.67	93	34.65	6055.90
杨凌示范区	Yangling	238.64	137.42	439.47	11.60	105.03	9	0.52	374.90

11-4 各市(区)工业废气排放及处理情况(2014年)
Emission and Treatment of Industrial Waste Gas by City(District)(2014)

地区 Region	工业废气排放总量(亿立方米) Total Volume of Industrial Waste Gas Emission (100 million cu.m)	二氧化硫排放量(吨) Volume of Industrial Sulphur Dioxide Emission (ton)	氮氧化物排放量(吨) Volume of Nitrogen Oxides Emission (ton)	烟(粉)尘排放量(吨) Volume of Soot Emission (ton)	废气治理设施数(套) Number of Facilities for Treatment of Waste Gas (set)	废气治理设施处理能力(万立方米/时) Treatment Capacity of Facilities for Treatment of Waste Gas (10 000 cu.m/hour)	废气治理设施运行费用(万元) Operate Expenditure for Facilities for Treatment of Waste Gas (10 000 yuan)	空气日报优良率(%) Air Quality Fine Rate (%)
全　省 Shaanxi	**16542.54**	**671641.80**	**509574.96**	**537752.70**	**4284**	**35306.50**	**363505.80**	-
西安市 Xi'an	901.23	62604.03	31823.37	21985.41	740	4497.76	40420.60	57.8
铜川市 Tongchuan	922.18	17261.50	36892.85	51568.83	105	352.21	39822.20	62.7
宝鸡市 Baoji	1503.21	28183.83	48406.42	27280.48	567	4446.19	58987.70	66.3
咸阳市 Xianyang	1428.29	57182.78	62110.73	41483.40	495	3391.54	30475.30	59.5
渭南市 Weinan	4171.31	235067.60	141648.63	78517.14	657	10067.47	100201.70	60.3
延安市 Yan'an	185.39	16332.14	5914.74	8363.95	305	180.76	5083.50	69.3
汉中市 Hanzhong	1608.40	28349.70	18373.76	37873.52	326	3088.03	22271.10	97.3
榆林市 Yulin	5272.07	198408.64	154373.89	253988.99	662	7717.91	53291.30	92.1
安康市 Ankang	290.77	9301.29	5714.95	10776.70	193	864.31	3497.70	98.4
商洛市 Shangluo	251.13	18463.35	4240.97	5710.82	209	648.16	9249.10	99.2
杨凌示范区 Yangling	8.56	486.95	74.64	203.48	25	52.15	205.60	65.8

11-5 城市设施水平(2014年)
Level of Public Facilities in Cities(2014)

城市 City	人均公园绿地面积(平方米) Per Capita Public Green Area (sq.m)	人均城市道路面积(平方米) Per Capita Area of Paved Roads (sq.m)	人均日生活用水量(升) Per Capita Daily Consumption of Tap Water for Residential Use (liter)	用水普及率(%) Coverage Rate of Population with Access to Tap Water (%)	燃气普及率(%) Coverage Rate of Population with Access to Gas (%)
全　省 Shaanxi	**12.58**	**15.47**	**157.09**	**96.25**	**95.77**
西安市 Xi'an	11.60	18.07	187.40	100.00	100.00
铜川市 Tongchuan	11.49	11.54	60.82	92.94	91.20
宝鸡市 Baoji	12.27	15.90	139.02	100.00	98.59
咸阳市 Xianyang	15.23	12.57	125.04	91.94	96.89
渭南市 Weinan	12.22	9.51	159.54	99.33	88.11
延安市 Yan'an	11.97	6.96	168.22	81.24	99.57
汉中市 Hanzhong	14.57	7.91	163.25	79.71	99.95
榆林市 Yulin	16.60	20.82	87.11	93.89	92.20
安康市 Ankang	13.24	16.08	103.11	94.39	81.22
商洛市 Shangluo	9.88	11.23	118.42	92.12	48.48
杨凌示范区 Yangling	14.34	18.38	165.64	93.80	65.89

11-6 城市市政设施(2014年)
Municipal Infrastructure in Cities(2014)

城 市	City	道路长度 (公里) Length of Paved Roads (km)	道路面积 (万平方米) Area of Paved Roads (10 000 sq.m)	城市桥梁 (座) City Bridges (set)	#立交桥 Flyover	城市道路照明灯盏数 (盏) Number of Street Lights (unit)	城市排水管道长度 (公里) Length of City Sewage Pipes (km)
全 省	**Shaanxi**	**5793.56**	**12910.80**	**645**	**136**	**601068**	**6924.95**
西 安 市	Xi'an	3145.73	7199.75	417	100	314339	4373.41
铜 川 市	Tongchuan	296.99	465.50	32	4	27423	203.47
宝 鸡 市	Baoji	514.91	1303.47	53	1	60443	585.60
咸 阳 市	Xianyang	321.50	1181.62	33	12	52681	295.43
渭 南 市	Weinan	314.00	427.92	5	4	22898	359.48
延 安 市	Yan'an	133.88	227.09	6		23380	91.50
汉 中 市	Hanzhong	201.99	312.70	7	1	14076	153.84
榆 林 市	Yulin	420.00	851.60	30	4	52147	446.32
安 康 市	Ankang	201.91	518.70	13		23024	185.99
商 洛 市	Shangluo	135.80	185.30	25	1	6737	84.91
杨凌示范区	Yangling	106.85	237.15	24	9	3920	145.00

11-7 城市供水情况(2014年)
Basic Statistics on Tap Water Supply in Cities (2014)

城 市	City	综合生产能力 (万立方米/日) Production Capacity (10 000 cu.m/day)	#地下水 Groundwater	全年供水总量 (万立方米) Annual Volume of Tap Water Supply (10 000 cu.m)	#生产运营用水 Water Consumption of Production and Operations	#公共服务用水 Water Consumption of Public Services	#居民家庭用水 Water Consumption of Household
全 省	**Shaanxi**	**349.47**	**143.51**	**87921.14**	**27641.91**	**5014.30**	**40749.84**
西 安 市	Xi'an	183.60	47.83	50743.34	15187.91	449.25	26799.38
铜 川 市	Tongchuan	14.20	1.20	1651.10	74.00	120.00	712.50
宝 鸡 市	Baoji	28.40	10.70	6484.00	1392.00	1064.00	3050.00
咸 阳 市	Xianyang	46.80	41.30	12687.51	7328.74	588.70	3344.63
渭 南 市	Weinan	21.10	14.10	5320.00	2140.56	1021.40	1371.60
延 安 市	Yan'an	6.50		2076.94	10.00	575.25	1051.88
汉 中 市	Hanzhong	10.00	10.00	2588.00	29.00	580.00	1280.00
榆 林 市	Yulin	10.40	5.40	2673.00	897.00	236.00	985.00
安 康 市	Ankang	10.49		1571.00	289.00	109.00	1037.00
商 洛 市	Shangluo	6.10	6.10	1009.00	105.00	70.00	587.00
杨凌示范区	Yangling	11.88	6.88	1117.25	188.70	200.70	530.85

11-8 城市园林绿化情况(2014年)

Basic Statistics on Parks, Gardens and Green Areas in Cities(2014)

城 市	City	园林绿化覆盖面积(公顷) Covered area of Gardening and Greening (hectare)	# 建成区 Developed Areas	园林绿地面积(公顷) Areas of Green Land (hectare)	# 建成区 Developed Areas	公园绿地面积(公顷) Capita Public Green Area (hectare)	公园个数(个) Number of Parks (unit)	公园面积(公顷) Area of Parks (hectare)
全 省	**Shaanxi**	**41843**	**37108**	**34496**	**31221**	**10492**	**174**	**5252**
西 安 市	Xi'an	20456	18700	16777	14916	4621	75	2373
铜 川 市	Tongchuan	1958	1911	1874	1690	464	14	58
宝 鸡 市	Baoji	4619	3559	3935	3281	1006	26	850
咸 阳 市	Xianyang	3087	2900	2756	2475	1431	5	490
渭 南 市	Weinan	1856	1790	1626	1573	550	4	358
延 安 市	Yan'an	1502	1493	1384	1383	391	12	259
汉 中 市	Hanzhong	1453	1300	1063	1017	576	3	78
榆 林 市	Yulin	2779	2455	2298	2153	679	5	531
安 康 市	Ankang	1695	1695	1575	1575	427	19	137
商 洛 市	Shangluo	1419	568	517	485	163	6	109
杨凌示范区	Yangling	1019	738	692	673	185	5	9

11-9 城市环境卫生情况(2014年)

Basic Statistics on Urban Sanitation in Cities(2014)

城 市	City	道路清扫保洁面积(万平方米) Area of Paved Roads under Cleaning Program (10 000 sq.m)	#机 械 清 扫 Machinery Cleaning	生活垃圾清运量(万吨) Consumption Wastes Collected and Transported (10 000 tons)	粪 便 清运量(万吨) Volume of Disposal of Excrement and Urine (10 000 tons)	公厕数量(座) Number of Public Lavatories (set)	# 三类以上 Third Grade and Above	市容环卫专用车辆设备总数(辆) Number of Special Vehicles for Environmental Sanitation (coach)
全 省	**Shaanxi**	**14898**	**9327**	**497.33**	**15.97**	**3669**	**3593**	**2866**
西 安 市	Xi'an	9303	6441	308.08	2.90	2016	2016	1888
铜 川 市	Tongchuan	418	225	14.06	1.55	162	162	78
宝 鸡 市	Baoji	1180	422	36.34		313	308	192
咸 阳 市	Xianyang	875	413	28.89	3.05	331	331	196
渭 南 市	Weinan	528	210	18.40	0.19	43	43	63
延 安 市	Yan'an	330	168	12.69	1.07	142	116	100
汉 中 市	Hanzhong	450	105	12.50	0.05	123	112	49
榆 林 市	Yulin	1110	901	28.23	6.48	387	355	169
安 康 市	Ankang	223	74	14.13	0.68	98	96	84
商 洛 市	Shangluo	139	60	6.98		16	16	29
杨凌示范区	Yangling	342	308	17.03		38	38	18

11-10 城市燃气情况(2014年)
Basic Statistics on Supply of Gas in Cities(2014)

城市	City	天然气 Natural Gas				液化石油气 Liquefied Petroleum Gas			
		供气总量(万立方米) Volume of Gas Supply (10 000 cu.m)	销售气量(万立方米) Volume of Gas Sold (10 000 cu.m)	#居民家庭 Consumption for Residential Use	用气人口(万人) Population with Access to Gas (10 000 persons)	供气总量(吨) Volume of Gas Supply (ton)	销售气量(吨) Volume of Gas Sold (ton)	#居民家庭 Consumption for Residential Use	用气人口(万人) Population with Access to Gas (10 000 persons)
全　省	**Shaanxi**	**279088**	**272330**	**87514**	**744.92**	**27455**	**27079**	**16028**	**54.15**
西安市	Xi'an	178125	171616	54177	397.36	1885	1875	1097	1.00
铜川市	Tongchuan	11051	11051	2842	36.80				
宝鸡市	Baoji	19826	19693	5677	76.62	847	847	489	4.20
咸阳市	Xianyang	18040	18040	4997	85.05	9136	9136	5912	6.00
渭南市	Weinan	9525	9445	2582	33.70	2390	2380	2230	5.95
延安市	Yan'an	13136	13136	8363	32.48	6541	6541		
汉中市	Hanzhong	2437	2436	891	14.50	4080	3800	3800	25.00
榆林市	Yulin	22782	22753	7046	37.71				
安康市	Ankang	765	760	320	14.20	2565	2500	2500	12.00
商洛市	Shangluo	802	800	89	8.00				
杨凌示范区	Yangling	2600	2600	530	8.50				

11-11 国家级风景名胜区(2014年)
State Scenic Spots at National Level (2014)

风景区名称	Name of Scenic Spots	风景区面积(平方公里) Area of Scenic Spots (sq.km)	# 供游览面积 Area of Visiting	游人量(万人次) Number of Visitor (10 000 person-times)	# 境外游人 Number of Oversea Visitor Arrivals
总　计	**Total**	**879**	**368**	**2811.4**	**156.6**
骊山风景区	LishanHill Scenic Spot	120	91	2281.0	155.0
宝鸡天台山	BaojiTiantaishan	134	40	13.8	
合阳洽川风景区	Heyangqiachuan Scenic Spot	177	165	127.6	
华　山	Mountain Hua	148	50	220.0	1.6
黄河壶口瀑布	The Yellow River Hu-kou Falls	178	12	96.0	
黄帝陵	The Huangdi Tomb	122	10	73.0	

主要统计指标解释

水资源总量 指评价区内降水形成的地表和地下产水总量，即地表产流量与降水入渗补给地下水量之和，不包括过境水量。

地表水资源量 指评价区内河流、湖泊、冰川等地表水体中可以逐年更新的动态水量，即当地天然河川径流量。

地下水资源量 指评价区内降水和地表水对饱水岩土层的补给量，包括降水入渗补给量和河道、湖库、渠系、渠灌田间等地表水体的入渗补给量。

地表水与地下水资源重复量 指地表水和地下水相互转化的部分，即天然河川径流量中的地下水排泄量和地下水补给量中来源于地表水的入渗补给量。

用水总量 指分配给各类用户的包括输水损失在内的毛用水量之和，不包括海水直接利用量。

农业用水 指农田灌溉用水、林果地灌溉用水、草地灌溉用水和鱼塘补水。

工业用水 指工矿企业在生产过程中用于制造、加工、冷却、空调、净化、洗涤等方面的用水，按新水取用量计，不包括企业内部的重复利用水量。

生活用水 包括城镇生活用水和农村生活用水。城镇生活用水由居民用水和公共用水（含第三产业及建筑业等用水）组成；农村生活用水除居民生活用水外，还包括牲畜用水在内。

生态补水 仅包括人为措施供给的城镇环境用水和部分河湖、湿地补水，而不包括降水、径流自然满足的水量。

工业废水排放量 指经过企业厂区所有排放口排到企业外部的工业废水量。包括生产废水、外排的直接冷却水、超标排放的矿井地下水和与工业废水混排的厂区生活污水，不包括外排的间接冷却水(清污不分流的间接冷却水应计算在内)。

工业废水排放达标量 指报告期内废水中各项污染物指标都达到国家或地方排放标准的外排工业废水量，包括未经处理外排达标的，经废水处理设施处理后达标排放的，以及经污水处理厂处理后达标排放的。

生活污水排放量 指城镇居民每年排放的生活污水。用人均系数法测算。测算公式为:

$$\frac{\text{生活污水}}{\text{排放量}}=\frac{\text{城镇生活污水}}{\text{排放系数}}\times\frac{\text{市镇非}}{\text{农业人口}}\times 365$$

化学需氧量(COD) 指用化学氧化剂氧化水中有机污染物时所需的氧量。COD 值越高，表示水中有机污染物污染越重。

工业废气排放量 指报告期内企业厂区内燃料燃烧和生产工艺过程中产生的各种排入大气的含有污染物的气体的总量，以标准状态(273K，101325Pa)计算。测算公式为:

$$\frac{\text{工业废气}}{\text{排放量}}=\frac{\text{燃料燃烧过程}}{\text{中废气排放量}}+\frac{\text{生产工艺过程}}{\text{中废气排放量}}$$

生活及其他 SO_2 排放量 以生活及其他煤炭消费量和其含硫量为基础，根据以下公式计算:

$$\frac{\text{生活及其他}}{SO_2\text{排放量}}=\frac{\text{生活及其他}}{\text{煤炭消费量}}\times\text{含硫量}\times 0.8\times 2$$

工业 SO_2 排放量 指报告期内企业在燃料燃烧和生产工艺过程中排入大气的 SO_2 总量，计算公式为:

$$\frac{\text{工业}SO_2}{\text{排放量}}=\frac{\text{燃料燃烧过程}}{\text{中}SO_2\text{排放量}}+\frac{\text{生产工艺过程}}{\text{中}SO_2\text{排放量}}$$

工业烟尘排放量 指企业厂区内燃料燃烧过程中产生的烟气中夹带的颗粒物排放量。

生活及其他烟尘排放量 指除工业生产活动以外的所有社会、经济活动及公共设施的经营活动中燃烧所排放的烟尘纯重量。以生活及其他煤炭消费量为基础进行测算。

工业粉尘排放量 指企业在生产工艺过程中排放的能在空气中悬浮一定时间的固体颗粒物排放量。如钢铁企业的耐火材料粉尘、焦化企业的筛焦系统粉尘、烧结机的粉尘、石灰窑的粉尘、建材企业的水泥粉尘等。不包括电厂排入大气的烟尘。

工业固体废物产生量 指报告期内企业在生产过程中产生的固体状、半固体状和高浓度液体状废弃物的总量，包括危险废物、冶炼废渣、粉煤灰、炉渣、煤矸石、尾矿、放射性废物和其他废物等；不包括矿山开采的剥离废石和掘进废石(煤矸石和呈酸性或碱性的废石除外)。酸性或碱性废石指采掘的废石其流经水、雨淋水的 pH 值小于 4 或 pH 值大于 10.5 者。

危险废物 指列入国家危险废物名录或根据国家规定的危险废物鉴别标准和鉴别方法认定的，具有爆炸性、易燃性、易氧化性、毒性、腐蚀性、易传染疾病等危险特性之一的废物。

工业固体废物综合利用量 指报告期内企业通过回收、加工、循环、交换等方式，从固体废物中提取或者使其转化为可以利用的资源、能源和其他原材料的固体废物量(包括当年利用往年的工业固体废物贮存量)，如用作农业肥料、生产建筑材料、筑路等。综合利用量由原产生固体废物的单位统计。

工业固体废物综合利用率 指工业固体废物综合利用量占工业固体废物产生量(包括综合利用往年贮存量)的百分率。计算公式为:

$$\text{工业固体废物综合利用率}=\frac{\text{工业固体废物综合利用量}}{\text{工业固体废物产生量}+\text{综合利用往年贮存量}}\times 100\%$$

工业固体废物贮存量 指报告期内企业以综合利用或处置为目的，将固体废物暂时贮存或堆存在专设的贮存设施或专设的集中堆存场所内的数量。专设的固体废物贮存场所或贮存设施必须有防扩散、防流失、防渗漏、防止污染大气、水体的措施。

工业固体废物处置量 指报告期内企业将固体废物焚烧或者最终置于符合环境保护规定要求的场所，并不再回取的工业固体废物量(包括当年处置往年的工业固体废物贮存量)。处置方式有填埋(其中危险废物应安全填埋)、焚烧、专业贮存场(库)封场处理、深层灌注、回填矿井及海洋处置(经海洋管理部门同意投海处置)等。

工业固体废物排放量 指报告期内企业将所产生的固体废物排到固体废物污染防治设施、场所以外的数量，不包括矿山开采的剥离废石和掘进废石(煤矸石和呈酸性或碱性的废石除外)。

"三废"综合利用产品产值 指报告期内利用"三废"作为主要原料生产的产品价值(现行价)；已经销售或准备销售的应计算产品价值，留作生产自用的不应计算产品价值。

自然保护区 指为了保护自然环境和自然资源，促进国民经济的持续发展，将一定面积的陆地和水体划分出来，并经各级人民政府批准而进行特殊保护和管理的区域个数。根据保护对象，自然保护区分为自然生态系统类、野生生物类、自然遗迹类。风景名胜区、文物保护区不计在内。

湿地 指天然或人工、长久或暂时性的沼泽地、泥炭地或水域地带，包括静止或流动、淡水、半咸水、咸水体，低潮时水深不超过 6 米的水域以及海岸地带地区的珊瑚滩和海草床、滩涂、红树林、河口、河流、淡水沼泽、沼泽森林、湖泊、盐沼及盐湖。

环境突发事件 指由于违反环境保护法规的经济、社会活动与行为，以及意外因素的影响或不可抗拒的自然灾害等原因，致使环境受到污染，国家重点保护的野生动植物、自然保护区受到破坏，人体健康受到危害，社会经济和人民财产受到损失，造成不良社会影响的突发性事件。

环境污染治理投资 指在污染源治理和城市环境基础设施建设的资金投入中，用于形成固定资产的资金，其中污染源治理投资包括工业污染源治理投资和"三同时"项目环保投资两部分。环境污染治理投资为城市环境基础设施投资、工业污染源治理投资与"三同时"项目环保投资之和。

城市桥梁 指为跨越天然或人工障碍物而修建的构筑物。包括跨河桥、立交桥、人行天桥以及人行地下通道等。按使用年限分为永久性桥和半永久性桥。

城市园林绿地面积 指报告期末用作园林和绿化的各种绿地面积。包括公园绿地、生产绿地、防护绿地、附属绿地和其他绿地的面积。

Explanatory Notes on Main Statistical Indicators

Total Water Resources refers to total volume of water resources measured as run-off for surface water from rainfall and recharge for groundwater in a given area, excluding transit water.

Surface Water Resources refers to total renewable resources which exist in rivers, lakes, glaciers and other collectors from rainfall and are measured as run-off of rivers.

Groundwater Resources refers to replenishment of aquifers with rainfall and surface water.

Duplicated Measurement between Surface Water and Groundwater refers to mutual exchange between surface water and groundwater, i.e. run-off of rivers includes some depletion into groundwater while groundwater includes some replenishment from surface water.

Water Use refers to gross water use distributed to users, including loss during transportation, broken down into use by agriculture, industry, living consumption and ecological protection.

Water Use by Agriculture includes uses of water by irrigation of farming fields and by forestry, animal husbandry and fishing. Water use by forestry, animal husbandry and fishery includes irrigation of forestry and orchards, irrigation of grassland and replenishment of fishing farms.

Water Use by Industry refers to new withdrawals of water, excluding reuse of water within enterprises.

Water Use by Living Consumption includes use of water for living consumption in both urban and rural areas. Urban water use by living consumption is composed of household use and public use (including services, commerce, restaurants, cargo transportation, posts, telecommunications and construction). Rural water use by living consumption includes both households and animals.

Water Use by Ecological Protection includes replenishment of rivers and lakes and use for urban environment.

Waste Water Discharged by Industry refers to the volume of waste water discharged by industrial enterprises through all their outlets, including waste water from production process, directly cooled water, groundwater from mining wells which does not meet discharge standards and sewage from households mixed with waste water produced by industrial activities, but excluding indirectly cooled water discharged (It should be included if the discharge is not separated from waste water).

Industrial Waste Water Meeting Discharge Standards refers to volume of industrial waste water discharge which, with or without treatment, reaches national or local standards with regard to all pollutants.

Urban Non-industrial Waste Water Discharge refers to annual discharge of non-industrial waste water by urban households. It is estimated by per capita coefficient using the formula:

$$\begin{matrix}\text{Urban non - industrial}\\ \text{waste water discharge}\end{matrix} = \begin{matrix}\text{urban non - industrial waste}\\ \text{water discharge coefficient}\end{matrix} \times \begin{matrix}\text{urban non - agricultural}\\ \text{population}\end{matrix} \times 365$$

Chemical Oxygen Demand (COD) refers to the amount of oxygen required when chemical oxidants are used to oxidize organic pollutants in water. A higher value of COD corresponds to more serious pollution by organic pollutants.

Industrial Waste Air Emission refers to the discharge into atmosphere of waste air containing pollutants generated from fuel burning and production processes in enterprises within a given period of time. It is calculated at standard status (273K, 101325Pa) as:

$$\begin{matrix}\text{Industrial waste}\\ \text{air emission}\end{matrix} = \begin{matrix}\text{emission through}\\ \text{fuel burning}\end{matrix} + \begin{matrix}\text{emission through}\\ \text{production process}\end{matrix}$$

SO_2 Emission through Non-industrial and Other Activities is calculated on the basis of consumption of coal by households and other activities and the sulphur content of coal with the following formula:

$$\begin{matrix}SO_2\text{ emission}\\ \text{through non -}\\ \text{industrial and}\\ \text{other activities}\end{matrix} = \begin{matrix}\text{of coal by}\\ \text{households}\\ \text{and other}\\ \text{activities}\end{matrix} \times \begin{matrix}\text{sulphur}\\ \text{content}\end{matrix} \times 0.8 \times 2$$

SO_2 Emission through Industrial Activities refers to volume of sulphur dioxide emission from fuel burning and production process by enterprises during a given period of time. It is calculated as:

$$\begin{matrix}SO_2\text{ emission}\\ \text{through industrial}\\ \text{activities}\end{matrix} = \begin{matrix}SO_2\text{ emission from}\\ \text{fuel burning}\end{matrix} + \begin{matrix}SO_2\text{ emission from}\\ \text{production process}\end{matrix}$$

Industrial Soot Emission refers to the volume of soot in smoke emitted in the process of fuel burning in the premises of enterprises.

Soot Emission by Consumption and Others refers to the net volume of soot emitted by fuel burning from all social and economic activities and operations of public facilities other than industrial activities. It is calculated on the basis of coal consumption by households and others.

Industrial Dust Emission refers to volume of dust emitted by production process of enterprises and suspended in the air for a given period of time, including dust from refractory material of iron and steel works, dust from coke-screening systems and sintering machines of coke plants, dust from lime kilns and dust from cement production in building material enterprises, but excluding soot and dust emitted from power plants.

Industrial Solid Wastes Produced refers to total volume of solid, semi-solid and high concentration liquid residues produced by industrial enterprises from production process in a given period of time, including hazardous wastes, slag, coal ash, gangue, tailings, radioactive residues and other wastes, but excluding stones stripped or dug out in mining - gangue and acid or alkaline stones not included (a stone is acid or alkaline according to the pH value of the water being below 4 or above 10.5 when the stone is in, or soaked by water).

Hazardous Wastes refers to those included in the national hazardous wastes catalogue or specified as any one of the following properties in the national hazardous wastes identification standards: explosive, ignitable, oxidizable, toxic, corrosive or liable to cause infectious diseases or lead to other dangers.

Industrial Solid Wastes Utilized refers to volume of solid wastes from which useful materials can be extracted or which can be converted into usable resources, energy or other materials by means of reclamation, processing, recycling and exchange (including utilizing in the year the stocks of industrial solid wastes of the previous year). Examples of such utilizations include fertilizers, building materials and road materials. The information shall be collected by the producing units of the wastes.

Rate of Utilization of Industrial Solid Wastes refers to the percentage of industrial solid wastes utilized over industrial solid wastes produced (including stocks of the previous years). It is calculated as:

$$\text{Rate of utilization of industrial solid wastes} = \frac{\text{volume of industrial solid wastes utilized}}{\text{industrial solid wastes produced + stock of previous years}} \times 100\%$$

Stock of Industrial Solid Wastes refers to the volume of solid wastes placed in special facilities or special sites for purposes of utilization or disposal. The sites or facilities should take measures against dispersion, loss, seepage, and air and water contamination.

Industrial Solid Wastes Disposed refers to the quantity of industrial solid wastes which are burnt or placed ultimately in the sites meeting the requirements for environmental protection and not salvaged or recycled (including disposition in the year of those wastes of previous years). The disposition includes landfill (Safe landfills should be conducted for hazardous wastes), incineration, containment spaces, deep underground disposal, backfill in mining pits and disposal at sea.

Natural Reserves refer to certain areas of land, waters or sea demarked and approved by relevant governments at all levels to put under special protection and management in order to protect the natural environment and natural resources and to promote the sustainable development of the national economy. According to the objects be protected, the natural reserves are classified into classes of natural ecosystem, wild life and natural heritage. Scenic spots and cultural preservation zones are not included.

Wetlands refer to marshland and peat bog, whether natural or man-made, permanent or temporary; water covered areas, whether stagnant or flowing, with fresh or semi-fresh or salty water that is less than 6 meters deep at low tide; as well as coral beach, weed beach, mud beach, mangrove, river outlet, rivers, fresh-water marshland, marshland forests, lakes, salty bog and salt lakes along the coastal areas.

Sudden Accidents Effecting Environment refer to sudden accidents, due to economic or social activities that are contrary to environment protection laws or due to unforeseen factors or natural disasters, that lead to environment pollution, destruction of protected wild animals, plants or nature reserves, damage to human health, economic and property losses, and other negative impacts on the society.

Investment in Environment Pollution Harnessing Projects refers to the proportion of investment in fixed assets in the total investment in harnessing pollution and in the construction of urban environment infrastructure facilities. The investment in harnessing pollution It includes investment in harnessing sources of industrial pollution and investment in environment protection facilities designed concurrently with construction projects. Investment in environment pollution harnessing is the total of investment in harnessing pollution and investment in urban environment infrastructure facilities.

Urban Bridges refer to bridges built to cross over natural or man-made barriers, including bridges over rivers, overpasses for traffic and for pedestrians, underpasses for pedestrians, etc. Both permanent and semi-permanent bridges are included.

Area of Parks and Green Land refers to the total area occupied for green projects at the end of the reference period, including park green land, production green land, protection green land, green land attached to institutions, and other green areas.

十二、农 业

资料整理：魏静怡　孔庆惠　赵胜利
郑月霞　姜亦武　陈　伟

简 要 说 明

一、本篇资料反映陕西农业生产和农村经济的基本情况，内容主要包括耕地、农林牧渔业产值、主要农产品产量、造林、水利水保、农业机械拥有量、农业基地县等方面的统计资料。

二、农业统计范围包括除县城关镇以外所有乡镇的社会经济活动。

三、粮食播种面积及产量、主要畜禽产品产量全省为抽样调查数。

四、造林情况及2010年以后林产品产量由省林业厅提供，水利水保情况由省水利厅提供，灾情由省民政厅提供。

Brief Introduction

I. This chapter reflects the basic conditions of agricultural production and rural economy of Shaanxi Province, mainly including cultivated land, output of agriculture, forestry, animal husbandry and fishery, output of major products, forestation, water conservancy and protection, quantity of agricultural machinery and agricultural base county.

Ⅱ. Rural social and economic statistics cover social and economic activities in all townships except county towns.

Ⅲ. The sown area and output of grain and output of main animal products of Shaanxi Province are collected with sample survey.

Ⅳ. The forestation situation and output of forest product after 2010 are provided by Shaanxi Province Forestry Department. The situation of water conservancy and protection are provided by Shaanxi Province Department of Water Resources Department. The data on disasters are provided by Shaanxi Provincial Department of Civil Affairs.

12.农 业

2014年全省

年末耕地面积	2865.99	千公顷	占全省土地面积	13.9%
农林牧渔业总产值	2741.82	亿 元	比上年增长	5.1%
农作物播种面积	4262.13	千公顷		
粮食产量	1197.78	万 吨		
水果产量	1553.98	万 吨		

果园面积和水果产量

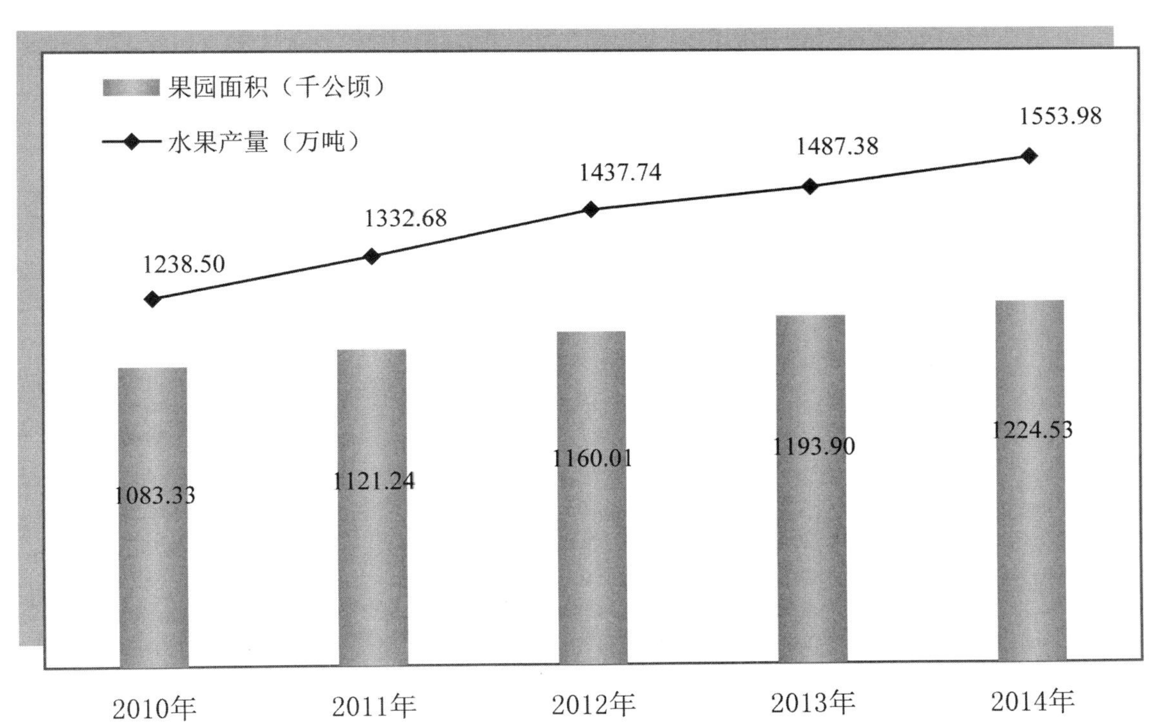

12-1 常用耕地面积
Area of Cultivated Land

年份 Year	年末常用耕地面积(千公顷) Area of Cultivated Land (1 000 hectares)	# 水田 Paddy Field	# 水浇地 Irrigated Field	每一乡村人口占有耕地(公顷) The Average Area of Cultivated Land per Rural Person (hectare)	# 水田、水浇地 Paddy Field and Irrigated Field
1978	3853.60	170.07	1047.93	0.16	0.05
1980	3815.67	169.93	1095.80	0.16	0.05
1985	3627.07	166.13	1003.33	0.15	0.05
1990	3533.00	171.47	998.20	0.13	0.04
1995	3393.44	176.04	995.59	0.12	0.04
1996	3358.98	173.54	996.37	0.12	0.04
1997	3325.01	174.00	976.83	0.12	0.04
1998	3302.47	171.09	992.42	0.12	0.04
1999	3238.28	170.88	1007.75	0.12	0.04
2000	3113.96	172.53	997.22	0.11	0.04
2001	2965.83	163.95	968.66	0.11	0.04
2002	2854.81	159.27	974.22	0.10	0.04
2003	2795.82	154.22	916.21	0.10	0.04
2004	2795.52	156.68	897.56	0.10	0.04
2005	2788.45	155.04	926.44	0.10	0.04
2006	2783.30	153.45	921.44	0.10	0.04
2007	2840.73	152.64	900.97	0.10	0.04
2008	2848.37	151.69	899.50	0.10	0.04
2009	2860.04	148.22	906.41	0.10	0.04
2010	2860.53	146.65	900.43	0.10	0.04
2011	2860.98	144.65	934.44	0.10	0.04
2012	2864.29	143.76	965.95	0.11	0.04
2013	2870.98	141.97	958.44	0.11	0.04
2014	2865.99	142.70	979.39	0.11	0.04

12-2 各市(区)常用耕地面积(2014年)
Area of Cultivated Land by City(District)(2014)

地区	Region	年末常用耕地面积(千公顷) Cultivated Land (1 000 hectares)	# 水田 Paddy Field	# 水浇地 Irrigated Field	每一乡村人口占有耕地(公顷) The Average Area of Cultivated Land per Rural Person (hectare)	# 水田、水浇地 Paddy Field and Irrigated Field
全省	**Shaanxi**	**2865.99**	**142.70**	**979.39**	**0.68**	**0.27**
西安市	Xi'an	240.49	1.61	158.17	0.41	0.27
铜川市	Tongchuan	64.64		6.62	0.74	0.08
宝鸡市	Baoji	298.36	0.45	114.14	0.84	0.32
咸阳市	Xianyang	353.96	0.17	193.99	0.71	0.39
渭南市	Weinan	511.14	0.78	327.60	0.67	0.43
# 韩城市	Hancheng	25.30	0.33	14.38	0.77	0.45
延安市	Yan'an	244.87	0.99	6.41	0.77	0.02
汉中市	Hanzhong	205.15	98.20	4.86	0.43	0.22
榆林市	Yulin	602.62	4.61	137.02	1.15	0.27
安康市	Ankang	197.30	33.98	1.17	0.56	0.10
商洛市	Shangluo	133.39	1.91	17.62	0.52	0.08
杨凌示范区	Yangling	5.46		5.46	0.48	0.48

12-3 农林牧渔业总产值

Gross Output Value of Agriculture, Forestry, Animal Husbandry and Fishery

单位：万元 (10 000 yuan)

年 份 Year	农林牧渔业总产值 Total	农 业 Farming	林 业 Forestry	牧 业 Animal Husbandry	渔 业 Fishery	农林牧渔服务业 Service in Support of Agriculture
1978	362748	309084	11717	41802	145	
1980	418773	349984	16625	51996	168	
1985	795777	611883	50751	131815	1328	
1990	1699568	1243236	90170	357676	8486	
1995	3816465	2578674	168848	1046501	22442	
1996	4484603	3229267	190692	1036321	28323	
1997	4555898	3214059	186349	1124778	30712	
1998	4793422	3408731	192286	1158870	33535	
1999	4524685	3276525	222862	989843	35455	
2000	4648889	3277761	272175	1063900	35053	
2001	4788356	3374163	235930	1140722	37541	
2002	5090762	3532131	266225	1251170	41236	
2003	5112543	3343544	268260	1455952	44787	
2004	6512051	4137371	263525	1794364	51236	265555
2005	7307239	4729047	250070	1989982	54879	283261
2006	8215406	5234189	289488	2141302	34427	516000
2007	10028501	6293403	337745	2740463	42427	614463
2008	12778611	7758512	414721	3852637	60582	692159
2009	13372200	8236000	456300	3879000	65000	735900
2010	16660575	11072354	351824	4349944	82909	803544
2011	20586024	13606649	423402	5534045	106249	915679
2012	23032043	15262805	584353	5987160	146109	1051616
2013	25625051	17147882	676185	6436731	177625	1186628
2014	27418168	18707841	735734	6482713	198949	1292931

注：1.2002年及以前农林牧渔业总产值含农民家庭兼营工业产值，按当年市场价格计算。
2.2003年及以后不含农民家庭兼营工业产值，按生产者价格计算，2004年及以后含农林牧渔服务业产值.

a) Before 2002 Gross Output Value of Agriculture, Forestry, Animal Husbandry and Fishery included commodity industry run by Rural Household, Data in this table are calculated at current prices.

b) Since 2003 it exclude commodity industry run by Rural Household,Data in this table are calculated at producer's price. Since 2004 it include services for Agriculture, Forestry,Animal Husbandry and Fishery.

12-4 各市(区)农林牧渔业总产值(2014年)

Gross Output Value of Agriculture, Forestry, Animal Husbandry and Fishery by City(District)(2014)

单位：万元 (10 000 yuan)

地 区	Region	农林牧渔业总产值 Total	农 业 Farming	林 业 Forestry	牧 业 Animal Husbandry	渔 业 Fishery	农林牧渔服务业 Service in Support of Agriculture
全 省	**Shaanxi**	**27418168**	**18707841**	**735734**	**6482713**	**198949**	**1292931**
西 安 市	Xi'an	3672101	2363649	86889	879515	24030	318018
铜 川 市	Tongchuan	418808	323040	5378	71572	2322	16496
宝 鸡 市	Baoji	2809042	1597093	93336	996384	10287	111942
咸 阳 市	Xianyang	5599917	4235744	72146	995202	13956	282869
渭 南 市	Weinan	3844624	2776511	73313	797990	32788	164022
# 韩城市	Hancheng	276872	208232	5792	37102	764	24982
延 安 市	Yan'an	2032025	1603899	73382	300691	5271	48782
汉 中 市	Hanzhong	3255057	1925455	141154	1025309	44992	118147
榆 林 市	Yulin	2500345	1347836	78748	974504	10242	89015
安 康 市	Ankang	1637491	996916	90810	453673	55915	40177
商 洛 市	Shangluo	1659191	906945	102616	581719	4606	63305
杨凌示范区	Yangling	118614	74731	9958	26698		7227

注：本表按当年价格计算。

a) Data in this table are calculated at current prices.

12-5 农林牧渔业总产值指数(1978年=100)

Indices of Gross Output Value of Agriculture, Forestry, Animal Husbandry and Fishery (year of 1978=100)

年 份 Year	农林牧渔业 总产值 Total	农 业 Farming	林 业 Forestry	牧 业 Animal Husbandry	渔 业 Fishery	农林牧渔服务业 Service in Support of Agriculture
1978	100.0	100.0	100.0	100.0	100.0	
1980	97.0	92.0	123.3	107.7	113.7	
1985	148.2	152.7	189.0	159.6	303.5	
1990	191.7	204.0	176.7	231.9	992.9	
1995	250.8	250.8	251.7	364.6	1834.7	
1996	277.1	294.5	263.1	346.4	2144.8	
1997	281.5	294.8	249.6	373.4	2348.5	
1998	306.6	321.9	274.1	402.6	2463.6	
1999	306.0	324.5	305.3	378.0	2803.6	
2000	320.0	336.8	322.1	403.7	2795.2	
2001	328.0	341.5	328.6	426.3	2937.7	
2002	348.4	361.7	363.4	452.3	3193.3	
2003	366.1	371.8	389.2	503.4	3404.1	
2004	399.8	416.8	383.6	526.1	3482.4	
2005	432.2	448.9	359.7	587.1	3844.6	
2006	463.8	484.4	367.9	627.1	4063.7	
2007	487.0	508.1	409.9	652.1	4336.0	
2008	525.4	547.7	446.8	707.6	4713.2	
2009	551.2	568.5	499.0	755.0	5080.8	
2010	583.1	605.7	512.4	789.1	5540.0	
2011	615.8	645.7	562.1	788.3	6925.0	
2012	652.7	683.8	617.2	831.7	8213.1	
2013	684.0	709.8	719.0	875.8	9592.9	
2014	718.9	748.1	764.3	905.6	10772.8	

注：本表按可比价格计算。

a) Data in this table are calculated at constant prices.

12-6 农林牧渔业总产值指数(上年=100)

Indices of Gross Output Value of Agriculture, Forestry, Animal Husbandry and Fishery (preceding year=100)

年 份 Year	农林牧渔业 总产值 Total	农 业 Farming	林 业 Forestry	牧 业 Animal Husbandry	渔 业 Fishery	农林牧渔服务业 Service in Support of Agriculture
1978	102.7	101.6	94.4	100.5	94.3	
1980	85.9	81.2	109.2	95.7	100.6	
1985	102.8	100.8	113.7	115.6	148.9	
1990	106.1	107.6	93.8	108.6	115.3	
1995	104.0	104.8	100.0	102.8	113.1	
1996	110.5	117.4	104.5	95.0	116.9	
1997	101.6	100.1	94.9	107.8	109.5	
1998	108.9	109.2	109.8	107.8	104.9	
1999	99.8	100.8	111.4	93.9	113.8	
2000	104.6	103.8	105.5	106.8	99.7	
2001	102.5	101.4	102.0	105.6	105.1	
2002	106.2	105.9	110.6	106.1	108.7	
2003	105.1	102.8	107.1	111.3	106.6	
2004	109.2	112.1	98.6	104.5	102.3	
2005	108.1	107.7	93.8	111.6	110.4	104.2
2006	107.3	107.9	102.3	106.8	105.7	105.8
2007	105.0	104.9	111.4	104.0	106.7	106.1
2008	107.9	107.8	109.0	108.5	108.7	106.2
2009	104.9	103.8	111.7	106.7	107.8	105.5
2010	105.8	106.5	102.7	104.5	109.0	105.2
2011	105.6	106.6	109.7	99.9	125.0	107.0
2012	106.0	105.9	109.8	105.5	118.6	107.6
2013	104.8	103.8	116.5	105.3	116.8	107.8
2014	105.1	105.4	106.3	103.4	112.3	108.2

注：本表按可比价格计算。

a) Data in this table are calculated at constant prices.

12-7 农林牧渔业分项产值

Gross Output Value of Agriculture, Forestry, Animal Husbandry and Fishery by Item

单位：万元 (10 000 yuan)

指 标	Item	2010	2011	2012	2013	2014
农林牧渔业总产值	**Gross Output Value of Agriculture,Forestry, Animal Husbandry and Fishery**	**16660575**	**20586024**	**23032043**	**25625051**	**27418168**
一、农业总产值	Output Value of Farming	11072354	13606649	15262805	17147882	**18707841**
# 粮食作物	Grain	3103357	3385911	3635733	3767141	3783488
(一) 谷物及其他作物	Cereals and Other Crops	3859367	4301323	4603723	4797823	4797428
1.谷 物	Cereal	2342359	2546428	2754503	2909639	2940598
2.薯 类	Tubers	548719	588160	616013	663714	679115
3.豆 类	Beans	211779	251323	265217	193788	163775
4.油 料	Oil-bearing	295515	396254	421253	430316	423636
5.棉 花	Cotton	95503	96634	93699	103992	72287
6.麻 类	Fiber Crops	333	737	663	710	704
7.糖 料	Sugar Crops	403	216	847	324	424
8.烟 草	Tobacco	95736	115371	116948	129028	109962
9.其他农作物	Others	268420	306200	334580	366312	406927
(二)蔬菜、园艺作物	Vegetables Gardening Crops	2912902	3712867	4194385	4905901	5199073
# 1.蔬 菜	Vegetables	2860449	3635456	4151458	4826254	5103123
2.花 卉	Flowers	52453	31929	29380	34634	42721
(三)水果、坚果、茶叶和香料作物	Fruits,Nuts Tea and Spices Crops	3928041	5120495	5444801	6830577	8033493
# 1.水 果	Fruits	3536584	4537842	5229613	5977161	7048394
# 园林水果	Garden Fruit	3203009	4114382	4738566	5470034	6277382
# 苹 果	Apples	2188454	2877250	3172407	3589931	4104869
果用瓜类	Melon	333575	423460	491047	507127	771012
2.坚 果	Nuts	137565	252597	323582	363359	402833
3.茶 叶	Tea	153710	183000	226603	293448	352101
4.香料作物	Spices Crops	100182	147056	156050	196609	230165
(四)中药材	Chinese Herbal Medicines	372044	471964	528849	613581	677847
二、林业产值	Output Value of Forestry	351824	423402	584353	676185	735734
(一)林木的培育和种植	Cultivation and Planting of Trees	198270	232767	336971	402415	456365
(二)竹木采运	Logging andTransport of Bamboo	31304	42459	47175	41792	40088
(三)林产品	Forestry Products	122250	148176	200207	231978	239281
三、牧业产值	Output Value of Animal Husbandry	4349944	5534045	5987160	6436731	6482713
(一)牲畜的饲养	Stock Breeding	1589937	1922945	2132462	2327127	2400109
1.牛的饲养	Cattle	326123	435484	505828	519114	553840
2.羊的饲养	Sheep	423122	551843	577830	659883	712248
3.其他牲畜饲养	Others	23689	35456	42364	54178	68363
4.奶产品	Milk Products	764107	826649	906605	990989	952047
5.毛绒产品	Feather and Cashmere Products	52896	73513	99835	102963	113611
(二)猪的饲养	Pigs Breeding	1965196	2703848	2881879	2999724	2939376
(三)家 禽	Poultry Breeding	645022	690133	715861	842138	907535
# 禽 蛋	Egg	412596	469131	475850	575052	629475
(四)狩猎和捕捉动物	Animal Hunting and Trapping	4138	6217	3929	3407	2209
(五)其它畜牧业	Other Animal Husbandry	145651	210902	253029	264335	233484
四、渔业产值	Output Value of Fishery	82909	106249	146109	177625	198949
五、农林牧渔服务业	Service in Support of Agriculture	803544	915679	1051616	1186628	1292931

注：1.本表按当年生产者价格计算。
2.由于核算制度的变化，2010年起林产品不含核桃板栗和花椒等。

a) Data in this table are calculated at producer's price.

b) Because the changes of national accounts, forestry Products exclude walnuts, chestnuts and pepper etc.

12-8 农林牧渔业增加值
Value Added of Agriculture, Forestry, Animal Husbandry and Fishery

单位：万元 (10 000 yuan)

指　标	Item	2010	2011	2012	2013	2014
农林牧渔业增加值	**Total**	**9884525**	**12209264**	**13701582**	**15260453**	**16358457**
农　业	Farming	6848658	8415524	9440605	10606594	11571486
林　业	Forestry	223675	269181	371506	429888	467747
牧　业	Animal Husbandry	2336965	2974000	3229479	3471977	3496780
渔　业	Fishery	47194	60279	83257	101215	113366
农林牧渔服务业	Service in Support of Agriculture	428033	490280	576735	650779	709078

12-9 各市(区)农林牧渔业增加值(2014年)
Value Added of Farming, Forestry, Animal Husbandry Fishery by City(District)(2014)

单位：万元 (10 000 yuan)

地　区	Region	农林牧渔业增加值 Total	农业 Farming	林业 Forestry	牧业 Animal Husbandry	渔业 Fishery	农林牧渔服务业 Service in Support of Agriculture	农林牧渔业增加值比上年增长% Growth Rate as Last Year (%)
全　省	**Shaanxi**	**16358457**	**11571486**	**467747**	**3496780**	**113366**	**709078**	**5.2**
西安市	Xi'an	2336074	1586842	47388	499021	12229	190594	5.2
铜川市	Tongchuan	234731	181394	3066	40366	1309	8596	4.9
宝鸡市	Baoji	1682587	959888	56602	590936	5901	69260	5.1
咸阳市	Xianyang	3393183	2626850	39716	542318	8350	175949	5.1
渭南市	Weinan	2172991	1534671	41168	476444	19346	101362	5.0
# 韩城市	Hancheng	152324	111293	3010	23441	433	14147	4.6
延安市	Yan'an	1163495	932186	41688	160088	3020	26513	5.6
汉中市	Hanzhong	1904888	1182629	90709	540214	26242	65094	5.3
榆林市	Yulin	1502183	849319	47898	547184	5990	51792	5.4
安康市	Ankang	949185	609268	48342	238270	34195	19110	5.5
商洛市	Shangluo	945059	542823	67994	294632	2702	36908	4.8
杨凌示范区	Yangling	72315	51787	3186	14234		3108	5.0

注：本表按当年价格计算，增长速度按可比价计算。

a) Data in this table are calculated at current prices. Growth rate are calculated at constant prices.

12-10 主要农作物播种面积
Total Sown Areas of Major Farm Crops

单位：千公顷 (1 000 hectares)

年 份 Year	总播种面积 Total Sown Area	粮食作物播种面积 Sown Area of Grain Crops	夏 粮 Summer Grain	#小 麦 Wheat	秋 粮 Autumn Grain	#稻 谷 Rice	#玉 米 Corn	#大 豆 Soja
1978	5254.67	4488.00	1949.33	1604.67	2493.33	160.00	1090.67	206.00
1980	5072.67	4310.37	1906.67	1590.67	2404.00	162.67	1076.67	211.33
1985	4663.33	3965.33	1928.00	1693.33	2037.33	156.67	950.67	202.00
1990	4860.00	4134.67	1925.33	1690.67	2209.33	159.33	1024.67	288.67
1995	4496.85	3807.73	1805.33	1600.23	2002.40	139.35	902.63	240.51
1996	4777.32	4052.85	1813.62	1597.84	2239.23	156.87	1087.38	277.12
1997	4504.04	3811.46	1810.73	1602.80	2000.74	153.86	915.92	255.85
1998	4697.17	4030.12	1820.73	1610.54	2209.39	159.97	1065.18	291.77
1999	4726.34	4026.97	1787.79	1589.45	2239.17	154.59	1123.41	273.24
2000	4555.49	3821.59	1716.62	1537.26	2104.97	144.81	1056.96	246.96
2001	4264.84	3517.63	1590.29	1424.24	1927.34	140.78	1005.06	229.06
2002	4198.37	3397.29	1512.25	1356.75	1885.04	130.52	999.93	224.25
2003	4090.26	3157.28	1402.71	1255.11	1754.57	123.35	940.53	198.19
2004	4303.04	3362.01	1324.90	1152.70	2037.11	135.25	1132.56	237.58
2005	4391.24	3453.33	1389.53	1211.53	2063.77	133.79	1148.37	232.51
2006	3983.48	3081.27	1338.76	1181.61	1742.51	106.50	1041.63	180.77
2007	4044.74	3099.81	1329.43	1167.22	1770.38	109.70	1060.32	171.21
2008	4274.45	3234.70	1317.33	1140.00	1917.37	119.01	1112.90	184.25
2009	4154.10	3133.97	1319.33	1145.97	1814.64	125.33	1164.00	187.33
2010	4185.58	3159.70	1320.67	1148.90	1839.03	121.60	1182.40	178.60
2011	4181.04	3134.87	1314.67	1136.67	1820.20	120.93	1177.80	151.79
2012	4190.27	3127.53	1286.73	1127.60	1840.80	123.33	1167.40	166.80
2013	4183.48	3105.13	1237.40	1094.80	1867.73	123.72	1166.23	153.13
2014	4262.13	3076.47	1223.07	1082.87	1853.40	123.42	1153.73	112.45

12-10 续表 continued

单位：千公顷 (1 000 hectares)

年 份 Year	棉 花 Cotton	油 料 Oil-bearing	#油菜籽 Rapeseeds	#花 生 Peanuts	麻 类 Fiber Crops	糖 料 Sugar Crops	烤 烟 Flue-cured Tobacco	蔬 菜 Vegetables	瓜 类 Melon
1978	252.67	130.00	73.33	4.7	7.13	2.60	7.60	78.67	14.67
1980	242.00	160.00	89.33	8.7	3.73	3.30	3.33	79.33	20.27
1985	94.67	240.00	114.00	47.67	2.20	4.33	34.67	121.33	30.60
1990	112.67	269.33	132.00	39.56	2.88	3.53	72.13	145.33	22.87
1995	72.75	302.18	169.77	32.87	1.50	2.28	48.33	174.23	27.63
1996	59.55	312.91	168.20	31.26	1.40	2.20	62.36	194.28	26.68
1997	39.86	296.68	160.29	28.17	1.20	3.50	87.04	182.74	25.26
1998	35.22	284.72	136.76	31.56	1.10	2.10	54.03	193.12	34.19
1999	27.74	308.15	153.47	31.78	1.01	1.77	46.73	216.95	31.91
2000	30.09	303.63	163.75	33.45	0.91	1.43	47.08	228.71	33.49
2001	50.38	291.14	167.70	30.86	0.75	1.52	40.60	219.43	37.07
2002	42.81	280.63	166.05	29.63	0.68	1.27	31.26	263.70	37.56
2003	65.06	285.58	165.82	29.51	0.51	0.33	30.95	276.80	43.52
2004	80.09	283.32	173.21	28.04	0.76	0.24	30.40	301.30	44.87
2005	70.23	276.86	178.71	29.55	1.06	0.10	32.58	331.70	51.04
2006	85.30	249.21	160.60	28.87	1.05	0.09	32.93	356.38	59.92
2007	89.13	252.12	163.39	27.57	0.68	0.09	31.18	368.91	61.84
2008	85.15	277.16	178.31	32.56	0.51	0.19	33.42	385.59	58.60
2009	61.84	295.48	194.63	31.14	0.38	0.06	36.81	428.67	64.83
2010	50.88	301.24	201.78	31.15	0.49	0.07	31.06	443.99	70.37
2011	50.28	300.84	203.32	32.05	0.49	0.05	35.74	458.28	78.42
2012	48.30	302.30	202.09	32.92	0.49	0.06	40.01	477.10	74.26
2013	36.72	298.82	204.42	32.71	0.48	0.05	36.61	489.96	76.91
2014	31.04	300.83	203.64	33.92	0.48	0.07	32.71	502.61	84.74

注：2009年及以后粮食播种面积为抽样调查数。

a) Since 2009 sown area of grain crops are sample survey data.

12-11　各市(区)主要农作物播种面积(2014年)
Total Sown Areas of Major Farm Crops by City(District)(2014)

单位：千公顷　　(1 000 hectares)

地　区	Region	总播种面积 Total Sown Area	粮食作物播种面积 Sown Area of Grain Crops	夏粮 Summer Grain	# 小麦 Wheat	秋粮 Autumn Grain	# 稻谷 Rice	# 玉米 Corn	# 大豆 Soja
全　省	**Shaanxi**	**4262.13**	**3076.47**	**1223.07**	**1082.9**	**1853.40**	**123.42**	**1153.73**	**112.45**
西安市	Xi'an	457.43	367.64	195.33	193.7	172.31	0.36	159.10	7.14
铜川市	Tongchuan	78.73	60.06	24.80	24.8	35.26		31.71	1.95
宝鸡市	Baoji	412.33	332.97	189.52	187.2	143.45	0.16	126.26	9.20
咸阳市	Xianyang	518.45	390.99	223.68	223.3	167.31		154.56	5.12
渭南市	Weinan	690.47	512.98	292.71	291.8	220.27		198.99	9.04
# 韩城市	Hancheng	26.86	22.95	13.36	13.4	9.58		8.44	0.27
延安市	Yan'an	244.58	200.40	8.92	4.0	191.48	0.47	81.37	23.74
汉中市	Hanzhong	517.53	268.25	88.11	44.0	180.14	78.74	73.87	14.93
榆林市	Yulin	590.47	476.37	15.01	2.7	461.36	1.16	148.57	51.06
安康市	Ankang	477.00	268.70	116.72	47.9	151.98	29.61	80.65	11.19
商洛市	Shangluo	282.88	209.53	98.36	59.5	111.17	0.53	75.44	21.44
杨凌示范区	Yangling	5.70	3.15	1.47	1.5	1.68		1.65	

12-11　续表　continued

单位：千公顷　　(1 000 hectares)

地　区	Region	棉花 Cotton	油料 Oil-bearing	# 油菜籽 Rapeseeds	# 花生 Peanuts	麻类 Fiber Crops	糖料 Sugar Crops	烤烟 Flue-cured Tobacco	蔬菜 Vegetables
全　省	**Shaanxi**	**31.04**	**300.83**	**203.64**	**33.92**	**0.48**	**0.07**	**32.71**	**502.61**
西安市	Xi'an	0.25	4.69	4.12	0.24				67.70
铜川市	Tongchuan		5.53	5.52				0.03	7.09
宝鸡市	Baoji	0.04	10.80	9.84	0.01	0.20		3.30	50.53
咸阳市	Xianyang	0.18	24.07	22.45	0.14			1.28	92.11
渭南市	Weinan	28.96	29.52	18.80	8.71			0.01	77.41
# 韩城市	Hancheng	0.05	0.63	0.59	0.02				3.13
延安市	Yan'an	1.08	10.70	2.21	2.37			1.77	23.43
汉中市	Hanzhong		83.66	77.24	3.86	0.01	0.01	4.09	62.81
榆林市	Yulin	0.22	47.28		7.04	0.09	0.04		26.77
安康市	Ankang	0.03	72.54	58.08	6.61	0.13	0.03	12.91	71.78
商洛市	Shangluo		11.91	5.38	4.84	0.05		9.32	20.64
杨凌示范区	Yangling		0.02	0.02					2.15

注：本表全省粮食面积为抽样调查数。

a) The sown area of grain crops of Shaanxi in this table are sample survey data.

12-12　主要农作物产品产量
Output of Major Farm Products

单位：万吨　　(10 000 tons)

年份 Year	粮食 Grain	夏粮 Summer Grain	#小麦 Wheat	秋粮 Autumn Grain	#稻谷 Rice	#玉米 Corn	#大豆 Soja
1978	800.00	293.50	251.00	542.00	81.50	292.00	19.95
1980	757.00	264.00	229.90	493.00	75.70	274.70	17.86
1985	951.90	459.20	423.30	492.70	88.30	291.60	18.35
1990	1070.70	501.70	463.70	569.00	100.40	333.80	30.75
1995	913.40	457.80	410.40	455.60	64.20	282.30	20.46
1996	1217.30	433.90	405.70	783.40	104.70	472.30	39.80
1997	1044.40	584.90	562.70	459.50	93.40	271.40	17.30
1998	1303.10	525.90	504.20	777.20	101.30	481.10	41.10
1999	1081.60	432.70	405.50	648.90	86.10	440.40	29.30
2000	1089.10	445.50	418.60	643.60	94.70	413.70	22.20
2001	976.61	432.74	406.63	543.87	92.05	352.81	19.60
2002	1005.60	440.10	405.30	565.50	80.30	374.50	21.20
2003	968.40	440.60	395.50	527.80	75.50	373.20	15.90
2004	1160.36	449.00	407.90	711.40	80.83	475.36	30.18
2005	1139.50	436.80	401.20	702.70	79.30	470.10	31.79
2006	1041.90	429.39	392.63	612.51	66.36	448.57	22.12
2007	1067.91	393.29	356.99	674.62	66.93	498.77	22.93
2008	1150.90	438.80	391.50	712.10	67.88	504.31	24.56
2009	1131.40	426.00	383.10	705.40	82.50	526.10	42.36
2010	1164.90	449.30	403.80	715.60	81.01	532.20	39.71
2011	1194.70	455.10	410.10	739.60	84.50	550.70	24.39
2012	1245.10	472.50	435.50	772.60	87.35	566.90	36.01
2013	1215.80	423.60	389.80	792.20	90.95	586.73	24.95
2014	1197.78	451.30	417.24	746.48	90.87	539.57	18.11

12-12　续表　continued

单位：万吨　　(10 000 tons)

年份 Year	棉花 Cotton	油料 Oil-bearing	#油菜籽 Rapeseeds	#花生 Peanuts	麻类 Fiber Crops	糖料 Sugar Crops	烤烟 Flue-cured Tobacco	蔬菜 Vegetables
1978	10.54	5.65	4.01	0.51	0.50	1.89	1.38	
1980	8.08	10.97	7.72	1.15	0.27	3.11	0.57	
1985	4.30	29.86	16.40	10.05	0.24	7.85	6.26	297.16
1990	7.78	33.39	19.25	7.03	0.18	5.92	12.32	367.30
1995	3.99	38.15	25.45	6.02	0.11	1.03	6.34	362.86
1996	3.12	37.42	19.05	6.63	0.12	2.75	11.09	430.93
1997	2.06	36.71	25.77	4.66	0.08	3.43	12.17	391.14
1998	2.29	35.48	17.58	6.94	0.10	4.96	8.53	459.58
1999	1.95	31.92	16.75	6.68	0.09	1.81	7.46	500.11
2000	2.74	38.76	22.40	7.33	0.09	1.79	7.36	556.53
2001	4.98	37.54	23.13	7.09	0.07	1.94	6.29	525.46
2002	4.30	41.08	24.58	7.01	0.11	3.10	5.10	660.48
2003	5.27	41.33	27.05	6.90	0.07	0.80	4.88	708.94
2004	8.23	46.06	29.45	7.18	0.11	0.67	5.32	785.34
2005	7.78	45.35	30.33	7.58	0.09	0.30	5.88	869.93
2006	8.83	41.36	27.29	7.55	0.14	0.24	5.99	848.48
2007	8.98	39.15	26.97	6.94	0.08	0.31	5.56	928.10
2008	10.07	49.46	33.35	8.20	0.06	0.30	7.14	1067.12
2009	8.58	54.38	35.63	9.71	0.05	0.17	7.31	1257.59
2010	6.92	56.08	37.27	8.98	0.06	0.20	6.73	1384.02
2011	6.74	58.97	38.36	9.28	0.06	0.16	7.67	1432.50
2012	6.72	60.33	39.94	9.76	0.07	0.17	9.15	1525.62
2013	5.79	59.52	39.67	9.64	0.07	0.16	8.54	1629.36
2014	4.22	62.30	41.56	10.13	0.06	0.15	7.20	1724.68

注：2009年及以后粮食产量为抽样调查数。
a) Since 2009 grain products are sample survey data.

12-13 各市(区)主要农产品产量(2014年)
Output of Major Farm Products by City(District)(2014)

地区	Region	粮食(万吨) Grain (10 000 tons)	夏粮 Summer Grain	#小麦 Wheat	秋粮 Autumn Grain	#稻谷 Rice	#玉米 Corn	#大豆 Soja
全省	**Shaanxi**	**1197.78**	**451.30**	**417.24**	**746.48**	**90.87**	**539.57**	**18.1[illegible]**
西安市	Xi'an	175.61	88.05	87.35	87.56	0.25	83.30	1.40
铜川市	Tongchuan	23.39	6.86	6.86	16.53		15.54	0.35
宝鸡市	Baoji	144.32	79.73	78.92	64.59	0.09	60.85	1.35
咸阳市	Xianyang	184.14	95.78	95.64	88.36		84.44	1.04
渭南市	Weinan	206.01	104.01	103.72	102.00		95.52	1.83
#韩城市	Hancheng	7.28	3.78	3.78	3.50		3.08	0.08
延安市	Yan'an	78.68	2.93	1.41	75.75	0.28	51.80	4.62
汉中市	Hanzhong	101.75	25.01	13.14	76.74	50.18	21.27	1.72
榆林市	Yulin	158.10	4.51	0.51	153.59	0.73	78.46	8.47
安康市	Ankang	86.04	30.01	12.01	56.03	20.81	24.44	2.14
商洛市	Shangluo	52.20	25.08	13.57	27.12	0.32	19.99	2.60
杨凌示范区	Yangling	1.93	0.88	0.88	1.05		1.04	

12-13 续表 continued

地区	Region	棉花(吨) Cotton (ton)	油料(吨) Oil-bearing (ton)	#油菜籽 Rapeseeds	#花生 Peanuts	麻类(吨) Fiber Crops (ton)	糖料(吨) Sugar Crops (ton)	烤烟(吨) Flue-cured Tobacco (ton)	蔬菜(万吨) Vegetables (10 000 tons)
全省	**Shaanxi**	**42171**	**622994**	**415629**	**101304**	**631**	**1478**	**71967**	**1724.68**
西安市	Xi'an	328	9785	8026	795				316.28
铜川市	Tongchuan		8049	8049				50	16.45
宝鸡市	Baoji	60	19236	18141	21	189		6283	136.36
咸阳市	Xianyang	130	47684	44518	377			3237	411.85
渭南市	Weinan	40219	73583	36624	30418			9	238.81
#韩城市	Hancheng	120	1205	1156	48				11.29
延安市	Yan'an	931	22701	4297	4820			4222	113.00
汉中市	Hanzhong	1	189144	173841	11336	5	457	11346	214.34
榆林市	Yulin	120	83182		23361	188	88		75.66
安康市	Ankang	35	147893	114430	18743	203	933	28497	140.03
商洛市	Shangluo	2	21609	7639	11433	46		18323	47.13
杨凌示范区	Yangling		128	64					14.06

注：全省粮食产量为抽样调查数。

a) The sown area of grain crops of Shaanxi in this table are sample survey data.

12-14　主要农产品单位面积产量
Output of Major Farm Products Per Hectare

单位：公斤/公顷　　(kg/hectare)

年份 Year	粮食 Grain	夏粮 Summer Grain	#小麦 Wheat	秋粮 Autumn Grain	#稻谷 Rice	#玉米 Corn	#大豆 Soja
1978	1785	1395	1470	2175	5130	2520	970
1980	1755	1380	1440	2055	4650	2550	844
1985	2400	2385	2550	2415	5640	3060	908
1990	2595	2610	2745	2580	6300	3255	1066
1995	2399	2536	2565	2275	4609	3128	851
1996	3003	2392	2539	3498	6674	4343	1436
1997	2740	3230	3511	2297	6070	2963	676
1998	3233	2888	3131	3518	6332	4517	1408
1999	2686	2420	2551	2898	5570	3920	1072
2000	2850	2595	2723	3057	6540	3914	899
2001	2776	2721	2855	2822	6539	3510	856
2002	2960	2910	2987	3000	6153	3745	945
2003	3067	3141	3151	3008	6121	3968	802
2004	3452	3389	3539	3492	5977	4197	1270
2005	3300	3144	3312	3405	5927	4094	1367
2006	3381	3207	3323	3515	6231	4307	1224
2007	3445	2958	3059	3811	6203	4704	1339
2008	3558	3331	3434	3714	5704	4531	1333
2009	3610	3229	3343	3887	6582	4520	2261
2010	3687	3402	3515	3891	6662	4501	2223
2011	3811	3462	3608	4063	6988	4676	1607
2012	3981	3672	3862	4197	7082	4856	2159
2013	3915	3423	3560	4242	7351	5031	1629
2014	3893	3690	3853	4028	7363	4677	1610

12-14　续表　continued

单位：公斤/公顷　　(kg/hectare)

年份 Year	棉花 Cotton	油料 Oil-bearing	#油菜籽 Rapeseeds	#花生 Peanuts	麻类 Fiber Crops	糖料 Sugar Crops	烤烟 Flue-cured Tobacco	蔬菜 Vegetables
1978	420	435	555	1080	1065	7260	1815	
1980	330	690	855	1320	735	9600	1830	
1985	450	1245	1440	2155	1095	18210	1815	24450
1990	690	1245	1455	1770	615	16755	1710	25245
1995	548	1263	1499	1830	726	4531	1312	20827
1996	524	1196	1133	2120	841	12399	1777	22180
1997	516	1237	1608	1654	712	9805	1398	21404
1998	650	1246	1285	2199	927	23370	1579	23798
1999	704	1036	1092	2103	899	10211	1596	23052
2000	911	1277	1368	2192	985	12578	1564	24334
2001	989	1290	1379	2297	960	12724	1550	23946
2002	1004	1464	1480	2367	1573	24389	1628	25047
2003	811	1447	1631	2340	1283	24147	1576	25612
2004	1027	1626	1700	2563	1451	27630	1749	26066
2005	1107	1638	1697	2563	883	29208	1805	26227
2006	1035	1660	1699	2615	1453	28565	1820	23808
2007	1007	1553	1650	2517	1240	33468	1783	25158
2008	1183	1785	1871	2520	1110	15898	2137	27675
2009	1395	1840	1831	3120	1275	28755	2040	29340
2010	1361	1861	1847	2884	1139	28144	2175	31172
2011	1341	1960	1887	2895	1335	31120	2147	31258
2012	1391	1996	1976	2966	1416	28350	2287	31977
2013	1577	1992	1940	2947	1438	35036	2332	33255
2014	1358	2071	2041	2987	1317	19777	2200	34314

注：2009年及以后粮食单产为抽样调查数。

a) Since 2009 grain products per hectare are sample survey data.

12-15 各市(区)主要农作物单位面积产量(2014年)
Output of Major Farm Products Per Hectare by City(District)(2014)

单位：公斤／公顷 (kg/hectare)

地区	Region	粮食 Grain	夏粮 Summer Grain	# 小麦 Wheat	秋粮 Autumn Grain	# 稻谷 Rice	# 玉米 Corn	# 大豆 Soja
全省	**Shaanxi**	**3893**	**3690**	**3853**	**4028**	**7363**	**4677**	**1610**
西安市	Xi'an	4777	4508	4510	5081	6809	5236	1964
铜川市	Tongchuan	3895	2768	2768	4688		4900	1804
宝鸡市	Baoji	4334	4207	4215	4503	5821	4819	1463
咸阳市	Xianyang	4710	4282	4283	5281		5463	2038
渭南市	Weinan	4016	3553	3555	4631		4800	2023
# 韩城市	Hancheng	3172	2828	2828	3652		3646	2882
延安市	Yan'an	3926	3285	3479	3956	5978	6366	1946
汉中市	Hanzhong	3793	2838	2986	4260	6373	2879	1153
榆林市	Yulin	3319	3003	1914	3329	6242	5281	1659
安康市	Ankang	3202	2571	2506	3687	7029	3031	1914
商洛市	Shangluo	2491	2550	2281	2439	6046	2649	1213
杨凌示范区	Yangling	6132	5980	5980	6265		6258	

12-15 续表 continued

单位：公斤／公顷 (kg/hectare)

地区	Region	棉花 Cotton	油料 Oil-bearing	# 油菜籽 Rapeseeds	# 花生 Peanuts	麻类 Fiber Crops	糖料 Sugar Crops	烤烟 Flue-cured Tobacco	蔬菜 Vegetables
全省	**Shaanxi**	**1358**	**2071**	**2041**	**2987**	**1317**	**19777**	**2200**	**34314**
西安市	Xi'an	1333	2085	1949	3280				46715
铜川市	Tongchuan		1456	1459				1630	23203
宝鸡市	Baoji	1382	1781	1844	2763	950		1906	26988
咸阳市	Xianyang	705	1981	1983	2685			2521	44715
渭南市	Weinan	1389	2493	1948	3491			1688	30850
# 韩城市	Hancheng	2192	1917	1956	2057				36046
延安市	Yan'an	863	2122	1947	2038			2381	48232
汉中市	Hanzhong	500	2261	2251	2940	493	34621	2776	34126
榆林市	Yulin	539	1759		3316	2060	2477		28258
安康市	Ankang	1385	2039	1970	2835	1598	35885	2207	19509
商洛市	Shangluo	1500	1814	1421	2362	889		1965	22835
杨凌示范区	Yangling		6000	3000					65341

注：全省粮食单产为抽样调查数。

a) The grain products per hectare of Shaanxi in this table are sample survey data.

12-16　茶、桑、果面积及产量
Areas and Output of Tea Plantation, Cocoon, Orchards

年　份 Year	茶园面积 (千公顷) Area of Tea Plantations (1 000 hectares)	茶叶产量 (吨) Output of Tea (ton)	桑园面积 (千公顷) Area of Mulberry Field (1 000 hectares)	果园面积 (千公顷) Area of Orchards (1 000 hectares)	水果产量 (万吨) Output of Fruits (10 000 tons)	# 苹果 Apples	# 柑桔 Citrus	# 猕猴桃 Kiwi
1978	31.07	1408	12.00	98.60	33.41	9.92	0.12	
1980	24.00	1428	17.40	104.27	28.00	8.93	0.30	
1985	26.16	2822	46.75	109.93	33.53	14.09	0.52	
1990	29.19	4548	37.31	304.78	62.03	34.93	0.89	
1995	30.64	5252	76.83	685.35	283.96	233.76	1.12	1.61
1996	30.96	5831	74.99	702.19	362.15	295.89	1.52	
1997	28.06	6316	66.03	691.23	326.55	263.65	2.01	
1998	28.49	6288	53.86	663.84	430.77	347.35	2.77	
1999	30.33	6215	53.81	649.32	493.49	399.27	2.96	10.80
2000	35.28	6126	58.76	664.76	493.79	388.57	3.52	16.47
2001	38.23	6273	65.59	680.11	534.19	408.57	5.85	16.04
2002	43.28	7003	71.43	703.75	577.35	440.59	6.40	19.49
2003	50.86	7952	75.23	750.51	621.14	461.79	9.86	20.47
2004	56.34	10239	78.30	788.47	735.61	555.21	11.75	23.17
2005	59.47	11382	79.83	817.45	765.74	560.12	16.76	24.03
2006	62.94	12827	97.50	860.49	881.95	649.98	16.32	27.76
2007	67.33	14400	91.75	884.91	940.23	701.57	22.43	29.81
2008	69.06	16025	104.47	950.69	1067.67	745.51	23.73	34.98
2009	78.12	20153	105.96	1011.36	1150.45	805.17	30.80	50.03
2010	85.38	25052	105.83	1083.33	1238.50	856.01	28.68	62.93
2011	90.79	28430	101.59	1121.24	1332.68	902.93	34.28	73.57
2012	97.14	35195	97.49	1160.01	1437.74	965.09	36.80	82.29
2013	109.74	40656	94.72	1193.90	1487.38	942.82	47.69	103.38
2014	121.39	49128	82.89	1224.53	1553.98	988.01	50.36	120.59

12-17　水果生产情况
Production of Fruit

品　种	Item	2010		2013		2014	
		面　积 (公顷) Area of Orchards (hectare)	产　量 (吨) Output (ton)	面　积 (公顷) Area of Orchards (hectare)	产　量 (吨) Output (ton)	面　积 (公顷) Area of Orchards (hectare)	产　量 (吨) Output (ton)
水果合计	**Total**	**1083326**	**12385021**	**1193900**	**14873834**	**1224527**	**15539830**
1.苹　果	Apples	601518	8560132	665220	9428230	681803	9880128
2.柑　桔	Citrus	33944	286765	37650	476854	38181	503630
3.梨	Pears	48954	799909	49274	972591	48632	1015019
4.葡　萄	Grapes	28839	322292	40228	606559	46615	595144
5.桃	Peach	31192	593502	32015	708089	35455	724872
6.红　枣	Jujube	162479	500320	181858	675998	185314	644592
7.杏	Apricot	60672	149347	56902	203596	55065	184126
8.柿　子	Persimmon	31786	320383	30426	396380	30034	395570
9.猕猴桃	Kiwi	47239	629341	60967	1033774	62003	1205886
10.石　榴	Pomegranate	3083	59409	4615	98205	4651	94894
11.其他水果	Others	33619	163621	34745	273558	36774	295969

注：本表为果业监测结果。

a) Data in this table are the results of fruits monitoring.

12-18 各市(区)茶、桑、果面积及产量(2014年)
Areas and Output of Tea Plantation, Cocoon, Orchards by City(District)(2014)

地 区	Region	茶园面积 (公顷) Area of Tea Plantations (Hectares)	茶叶产量 (吨) Output of Tea (ton)	桑园面积 (公顷) Area of Orchards (Hectares)	果园面积 (公顷) Area of Orchards (Hectares)	水果产量 (吨) Output of Fruits (ton)		
							苹 果 Apples	柑 桔 Citrus
全 省	**Shaanxi**	**121387**	**49128**	**82886**	**1224527**	**15539830**	**9880128**	**503630**
西 安 市	Xi'an				54152	996570	26047	
铜 川 市	Tongchuan				61751	690593	663312	
宝 鸡 市	Baoji	7		153	76866	1319702	680618	
咸 阳 市	Xianyang				280501	5617342	4615995	
渭 南 市	Weinan				183255	2920632	1937295	
# 韩城市	Hancheng				5859	114326	100752	
延 安 市	Yan'an			3820	289118	2702089	2614373	
汉 中 市	Hanzhong	63787	33025	8423	38360	430669	4593	337809
榆 林 市	Yulin			16846	203783	606125	200161	
安 康 市	Ankang	36523	13763	48715	31143	211874	5172	84397
商 洛 市	Shangluo	21071	2340	4929	4368	67201	9249	2021
杨凌示范区	Yangling				1230	38647	6897	

12-18 续表 continued

地 区	Region	梨 Pears	葡 萄 Grapes	桃 Peach	红 枣 Jujube	杏 Apricot	柿 子 Persimmon	猕猴桃 Kiwi	石 榴 Pomegranate	其它水果 Others
全 省	**Shaanxi**	**1015019**	**595144**	**724872**	**644592**	**184126**	**395570**	**1205886**	**94894**	**295969**
西 安 市	Xi'an	48757	99889	125147	44053	61145	43705	410614	32793	104420
铜 川 市	Tongchuan	305	517	5296	493	1326	11801		8	7535
宝 鸡 市	Baoji	7019	33356	34468	1	3918	23549	531507	7	5259
咸 阳 市	Xianyang	295562	172220	262609	33544	63111	91946	14965	25353	42037
渭 南 市	Weinan	423420	147105	110075	149915	25591	102960	3749	219	20303
# 韩城市	Hancheng	450	3100	3650	205	2200	3366		93	510
延 安 市	Yan'an	23886	4460	3233	47334	4256	3679			868
汉 中 市	Hanzhong	21440	2335	17174	581	2838	14461	9771		19667
榆 林 市	Yulin	20693	8129	10180	319305	13658				33999
安 康 市	Ankang	6787	1566	21134	1378	4946	22289	1644	68	62493
商 洛 市	Shangluo	1388	1670	4371	584	1316	37542	1110	35	7915
杨凌示范区	Yangling	20	1079	850		21		29745		35

注：本表全省水果产量为果业监测数据。
a) Data in this table are the results of fruits monitoring.

12-19 主要林产品产量
Output of Major Forest Products

单位：吨 (ton)

年 份 Year	生 漆 Lacquer	油桐籽 Tung-oil Seeds	五倍籽 Chinese Gall	棕 片 Palm Sheet	核 桃 Walnuts	板 栗 Chestnut	花 椒 Pepper
1978	668	14800	50		28275	3460	577
1980	930	17685	83		25700	2715	539
1985	635	17718	337	1448	12826	1777	694
1990	685	18672	1589	2265	16833	4770	2501
1995	773	15460	2922	3015	30599	8019	7135
1996	978	15409	2260	3358	30433	10635	8411
1997	1222	14265	2432	3078	26222	8116	
1998	1223	11046	1771	3217	32519	18385	9747
1999	1027	12456	1009	2735	33257	14689	9747
2000	1176	12968	863	2962	34866	20098	16298
2001	893	13003	968	3060	10474	11211	16471
2002	821	9278	934	3183	34779	21352	25112
2003	975	9634	1034	3177	44091	24022	22781
2004	995	12068	1513	3059	54243	26290	28441
2005	1060	12562	1963	3044	55206	27855	28178
2006	1613	11631	2241	3333	43492	29232	31507
2007	1851	11496	2383	3511	46717	35778	34904
2008	1697	14534	2785	4164	74069	40435	44000
2009	2552	17871	3386	3989	88773	46315	48571
2010	1915	17096	3152	3202	60453	52037	44789
2011	2434	19664	3441	3147	141362	69132	52974
2012	3494	22622	3969	2987	162981	71985	61698
2013	4516	28421	4265	2536	161500	74491	52537
2014	2864	29114	4590	3473	181771	78984	61072

注：2010年以后为林业部门统计数据。
a) Data in this table are from forestry authorities.

12-20 各市(区)主要林产品产量(2014年)
Output of Major Forest Products by City(District)(2014)

单位：吨 (ton)

地 区	Region	生 漆 Lacquer	油桐籽 Tung-oil Seeds	五倍籽 Chinese Gall	棕 片 Palm Sheet	核 桃 Walnut	板 栗 Chestnut	花 椒 Pepper
全 省	**Shaanxi**	**2864**	**29114**	**4590**	**3473**	**181771**	**78984**	**61072**
西 安 市	Xi'an					16695	5240	198
铜 川 市	Tongchuan					16054		3507
宝 鸡 市	Baoji					30600	3526	6409
咸 阳 市	Xianyang					9985		731
渭 南 市	Weinan					15414	565	44295
延 安 市	Yan'an					9511	100	2756
汉 中 市	Hanzhong	708	1629	2745	2439	19941	13756	829
榆 林 市	Yulin					121		34
安 康 市	Ankang	1940	22462	1554	1034	15727	31628	1520
商 洛 市	Shangluo	216	5023	291		47723	24169	793
杨凌示范区	Yangling							

注：本表为林业部门统计数据。
a) Data in this table are from forestry authorities.

12-21 各市(区)造林情况(2014年)
Area of Afforestation by City(District)(2014)

地 区	Region	荒山荒(沙)地造林面积(公顷) Afforestation of Barren Hills and Wasteland Area (hectare)	按造林方式分 By Approach		按林种用途分 By Function of Forest		按经济成份分 By Economic Composition	
			# 人工造林 Manual Planting	# 飞播造林 Airplane Planting	# 经济林 By-product Forests	# 防护林 Protection Forests	公有经济造林 Afforestation of State-owned	非公有经济造林 Afforestation of Non-state-owned
全 省	**Shaanxi**	**335363**	**251125**	**32001**	**70697**	**253794**	**298174**	**37189**
西安市	Xi'an	9798	7665		1829	7969	9798	
铜川市	Tongchuan	8834	6834		1338	5130	8100	734
宝鸡市	Baoji	23634	11568	4334	3528	20106	22511	1123
咸阳市	Xianyang	25338	18205	2133	6239	19099	18523	6815
渭南市	Weinan	30260	22193	667	11858	18402	21757	8503
延安市	Yan'an	82481	69994	4667	3385	79096	78247	4234
汉中市	Hanzhong	13016	7949		5459	5248	6915	6101
榆林市	Yulin	74390	62437	5333	7715	66675	70524	3866
安康市	Ankang	44212	31212	7334	23975	16676	39099	5113
商洛市	Shangluo	21700	12368	7533	5337	13727	21000	700
杨凌示范区	Yangling	134	134		34	100	134	

12-21 续表 continued

地 区	Region	四旁(零星)植树(万株) Four-side Tree Planting (10 000 trees)	幼林抚育作业面积(公顷) Area of Tending Growing Forest (hectares)	育苗面积(公顷) Area of Tending Seedlings (hectares)	当年苗木产量(万株) Output of Nursery Stock (10 000 trees)	年末核桃面积(公顷) Walnut Acreage (hectares)	年末板栗面积(公顷) Chestnut Acreage (hectares)	年末花椒面积(公顷) Pepper Acreage (hectares)
全 省	**Shaanxi**	**10226**	**161398**	**35637**	**8893**	**635294**	**304342**	**139821**
西安市	Xi'an	480	6068	11817	1800	22649	3644	837
铜川市	Tongchuan	211	2000	132	76	64967		19494
宝鸡市	Baoji	1186	14733	1225	265	94193	3909	50140
咸阳市	Xianyang	849	9400	3424	457	44032		1244
渭南市	Weinan	1256	12801	2106	1798	43576	333	52130
延安市	Yan'an	1041	44665	5305	1235	30388	1333	7938
汉中市	Hanzhong	1190	13666	2899	960	66562	51292	2081
榆林市	Yulin	1012	17066	5556	938	9431		142
安康市	Ankang	1094	14666	1336	730	71574	67262	2162
商洛市	Shangluo	1902	8000	566	188	187921	176570	3653
杨凌示范区	Yangling	5		1025	444			

注：本表为林业部门统计数据。

a) Data in this table are from forestry authorities.

12-22 畜牧业和渔业生产情况
Production of Animal Husbandry and Fishery

指 标		Item		2010	2011	2012	2013	2014
一、牲畜年末头数		**Number of Large Animals**	**(year-end)**					
(一)大牲畜	(万头)	Large Animals	(10 000 heads)	186.35	170.14	165.82	160.88	168.17
1.牛		Cattle and Buffaloes		165.00	150.10	146.80	143.13	150.60
# 奶 牛		Muich Cows		41.30	45.20	46.90	46.53	45.50
2.马		Horses		0.71	0.72	0.70	0.67	0.78
3.驴		Donkeys		15.23	14.16	13.49	13.04	12.90
4.骡		Mules		5.41	5.12	4.83	4.05	3.89
(二)猪存栏数	(万头)	Hogs	(10 000 heads)	884.40	880.00	900.24	897.90	879.40
# 母 猪		Sow		80.00	85.00	88.32	89.45	85.30
(三)羊存栏数	(万只)	Sheep and Goats	(10 000 heads)	635.20	643.00	644.93	638.84	700.20
1.山 羊		Goats		526.70	529.51	542.90	526.40	567.10
# 奶山羊		Muich Goats		101.81	99.76	105.77	100.98	105.09
2.绵 羊		Sheep		108.50	113.49	102.03	112.44	133.00
(四)家禽存栏数	(万只)	Poultry	(10 000 heads)	5726.71	6255.00	6749.21	6708.40	6623.50
(五)养蜂箱数	(万箱)	Bee	(10 000 heads)	32.16	36.91	42.19	45.79	53.39
(六)家兔存栏数	(万只)	Rabbit	(10 000 heads)	297.02	267.74	295.39	294.15	310.74
二、畜产品产量		**Output of Livestock Products**						
肉类总产量	(万吨)	Output of Meat	(10 000 tons)	102.64	99.60	107.09	112.52	116.76
# 猪 肉		Pork		79.10	77.30	83.45	88.34	91.80
牛 肉		Beef		7.30	7.39	7.50	7.52	7.70
羊 肉		Mutton		7.30	6.70	6.85	7.04	7.50
奶类产量	(万吨)	Milk	(10 000 tons)	177.62	182.37	189.08	188.51	192.34
# 牛 奶		Cow Milk		137.50	140.50	141.76	141.05	144.70
山羊毛产量	(吨)	Goat Wool	(ton)	3317	3872	4595	4827	5074
# 山羊绒		Cashmere		1497	1639	1714	1714	2205
绵羊毛产量	(吨)	Sheep Wool	(ton)	6921	6062	6682	6854	7185
禽蛋产量	(万吨)	Poultry Eggs	(10 000 tons)	47.07	50.30	51.86	55.40	54.50
蜂蜜产量	(吨)	Honey	(ton)	4272	4220	4989	5308	6266
蚕茧产量	(吨)	Silkworm Cocoon	(ton)	25477	20266	16357	13427	12376
三、渔 业		**Fisheries**						
1.水产品产量	(吨)	Output of Aquatic Products	(ton)	60373	81800	105429	125150	139320
2.水产养殖面积	(公顷)	Cultivatable area of Aquatic Products	(hectare)	39838	45531	47757	47932	48350

注：本表主要畜禽存栏和畜禽产品产量为抽样调查数。

a) The number of main livestock and the output of livestock products are sample survey data.

12-23　各市(区)牲畜存栏情况（2014年）
Livestock by City(District)(2014)

地　区	Region	大牲畜年末头数(头) Large Animals (year-end) (head)	牛 Cattle and Buffaloes	# 奶牛 Dairy cow	马 Horses	驴 Donkeys	骡 Mules	家禽(万只) Poultry (10 000 heads)
全　省	**Shaanxi**	**1681671**	**1506000**	**455000**	**7769**	**129021**	**38881**	**6623.50**
西安市	Xi'an	217257	216326	126174	513	59	359	1161.16
铜川市	Tongchuan	78879	78879	16179				179.07
宝鸡市	Baoji	513023	508384	215398	2243	1999	397	933.55
咸阳市	Xianyang	469165	466212	248046	242	169	2542	1099.33
渭南市	Weinan	292709	291773	115025	290	200	446	1189.50
# 韩城市	Hancheng	10702	10554	580	50	35	63	39.39
延安市	Yan'an	203973	148576	1940	325	41323	13749	376.39
汉中市	Hanzhong	302171	301501	3854	584	44	42	1097.63
榆林市	Yulin	257115	147033	27784	3523	85225	21334	552.62
安康市	Ankang	255252	255189	51	49	2	12	931.96
商洛市	Shangluo	130565	130565	270				798.22
杨凌示范区	Yangling	17163	17163	6629				18.60

12-23　续表　continued

地　区	Region	猪年末头数(头) Hogs (year-end) (head)	# 母猪 Sow	羊(只) Sheep and Goats (head)	# 山羊 Goats	# 奶山羊 Dairy Goat	蜂(箱) Bee (box)	兔(万只) Rabbit (10 000 heads)
全　省	**Shaanxi**	**8794000**	**853000**	**7002000**	**5671000**	**1050880**	**533890**	**310.74**
西安市	Xi'an	819498	90333	279207	271722	224901	20663	20.77
铜川市	Tongchuan	76290	10804	76009	75925	18558	67	0.50
宝鸡市	Baoji	1084722	105317	568229	563202	289488	109078	18.40
咸阳市	Xianyang	2022741	180506	1195954	1022981	723756	6981	154.54
渭南市	Weinan	2111326	229564	1055561	656159	549439	20686	40.33
# 韩城市	Hancheng	78754	11025	62732	22551	1255	2610	1.00
延安市	Yan'an	710327	73184	620714	567069	9274	64284	11.68
汉中市	Hanzhong	2589799	241847	349372	348533	3788	140671	20.72
榆林市	Yulin	983965	121907	6491824	5162415	33754	36835	26.55
安康市	Ankang	2386476	231200	971562	971232		103549	10.65
商洛市	Shangluo	1046189	111511	383666	372287	887	31076	6.60
杨凌示范区	Yangling	43615	11382	2304	1764	1695		

注：本表全省主要畜禽存栏为抽样调查数。
a) The number of main livestock of Shaanxi in this table are sample survey data.

12-24 各市(区)主要畜产品和水产品产量(2014年)
Output of Livestock and Aquatic Products by City(District)(2014)

地 区	Region	肉类总产量(吨) Output of Meat (ton)	#猪肉 Pork	#牛肉 Beef	#羊肉 Mutton	#禽肉 Poultry	奶类产量(吨) Milk (ton)	牛奶 Cow Milk	羊奶 Sheep Milk
全 省	**Shaanxi**	**1167560**	**918000**	**77000**	**75000**	**81000**	**1923428**	**1447000**	**476428**
西 安 市	Xi'an	144209	97995	12288	4198	20887	658016	514587	143429
铜 川 市	Tongchuan	17278	8362	5405	1137	2308	30292	28400	1892
宝 鸡 市	Baoji	186692	121098	33475	8407	17522	662356	597891	64465
咸 阳 市	Xianyang	218664	164907	14872	11122	16559	809917	700515	109402
渭 南 市	Weinan	222017	181356	12860	10481	16246	402279	251677	150602
#韩城市	Hancheng	9625	7628	722	705	494	1824	1726	98
延 安 市	Yan'an	76254	56425	6772	5632	5616	7379	5471	1908
汉 中 市	Hanzhong	316589	273662	14926	4379	23179	13967	12213	1754
榆 林 市	Yulin	184294	107322	5612	60609	7981	92029	89286	2743
安 康 市	Ankang	281145	231065	11613	16400	21931	82	82	
商 洛 市	Shangluo	152654	124236	9066	6580	12094	1395	1162	233
杨凌示范区	Yangling	5325	4309	424	22	561	23721	23721	

12-24 续表 continued

地 区	Region	山羊毛(吨) Goat Wool (ton)	#山羊绒 Cashmere	绵羊毛(吨) Sheep Wool (ton)	禽蛋(吨) Poultry Eggs (ton)	蜂蜜(公斤) Honey (kg)	蚕茧(吨) Silkworm Cocoon (ton)	水产品(吨) Aquatic Products (ton)	水产养殖面积(公顷) Water Area for Breeding Aquatics(hactare)
全 省	**Shaanxi**	**5074**	**2205**	**7185**	**545000**	**6266173**	**12376**	**139320**	**48350**
西 安 市	Xi'an				135191	250464		14168	1540
铜 川 市	Tongchuan				17039	610		1327	574
宝 鸡 市	Baoji	3		2	74994	747014	461	7467	3067
咸 阳 市	Xianyang	71	10	216	112063	110020		9905	2096
渭 南 市	Weinan	35	5	469	105138	332190		29823	5973
#韩城市	Hancheng	10	4	55	2950	30500		720	251
延 安 市	Yan'an	413	170	108	27782	988039	405	3030	2001
汉 中 市	Hanzhong				71434	1539785	1588	35100	7615
榆 林 市	Yulin	4545	2020	6384	52260	671341	97	8310	12114
安 康 市	Ankang				37744	1295284	8816	42356	14955
商 洛 市	Shangluo	7		6	72852	331426	1009	2880	577
杨凌示范区	Yangling				2115				

注：本表全省主要畜禽产品产量为抽样调查数。水产品产量及面积为渔业部门数据。

a) The output of livestock products of Shaanxi in this table are sample survey data.

12-25 粮食生产大县情况
Large County of Food Production

县 区	Region	2010		2013		2014	
		播种面积 (千公顷) Sown Area (1 000 hectares)	产 量 (万吨) Output (10 000 tons)	播种面积 (千公顷) Sown Area (1 000 hectares)	产 量 (万吨) Output (10 000 tons)	播种面积 (千公顷) Sown Area (1 000 hectares)	产 量 (万吨) Output (10 000 tons)
全 省	**Shaanxi**	**3159.70**	**1164.90**	**3105.13**	**1215.80**	**3076.54**	**1197.78**
生产大县合计	Total of Large Counties	1640.80	819.01	1511.34	687.91	1486.48	672.55
生产大县占全省%	As Percentage of Shaanxi	51.9	70.3	48.7	56.6	48.3	56.2
阎良区	Yanliang	14.94	9.60	14.25	8.54	14.17	8.10
临潼区	Lintong	79.15	40.10	70.81	32.68	68.99	31.79
长安区	Changan	79.98	41.49	73.74	35.77	69.96	33.84
蓝田县	Lantian	69.44	33.53	64.09	26.46	63.83	25.06
周至县	Zhouzhi	58.49	28.86	52.68	23.07	51.34	22.50
户 县	Huxian	61.87	37.15	59.87	30.34	58.79	29.60
高陵县	Gaoling	29.38	20.90	27.96	19.82	27.54	19.04
陈仓区	Chencang	59.81	29.11	58.90	23.11	58.12	22.48
凤翔县	Fengxiang	62.53	30.88	56.13	26.00	55.27	25.64
岐山县	Qishan	49.40	29.03	48.63	26.50	48.29	26.58
扶风县	Fufeng	50.81	28.99	48.47	27.30	48.43	26.55
眉 县	Meixian	27.22	14.40	23.40	12.60	22.59	12.62
千阳县	Qianyang	19.82	6.95	19.51	5.50	19.00	5.63
三原县	Sanyuan	45.18	23.60	42.06	20.00	40.83	19.51
泾阳县	Jingyang	55.29	28.79	51.53	24.24	50.82	23.98
乾 县	Qianxian	60.57	30.57	55.85	25.31	54.85	25.01
武功县	Wugong	44.62	24.29	40.49	20.00	39.65	19.72
兴平市	Xingping	46.90	25.22	44.26	22.20	43.15	21.72
临渭区	Linwei	95.57	43.00	85.89	33.77	83.58	33.31
华 县	Huaxian	31.02	14.79	27.70	11.23	27.63	11.01
大荔县	Dali	68.20	34.60	63.37	27.81	62.27	27.05
合阳县	Heyang	57.15	27.49	50.71	20.70	50.46	19.74
澄城县	Chengcheng	49.41	21.20	43.57	17.51	43.40	16.73
蒲城县	Pucheng	94.91	40.64	84.68	33.01	83.78	32.97
富平县	Fuping	93.27	44.17	81.37	36.00	80.18	35.50
韩城市	Hancheng	27.19	8.73	23.36	7.76	22.95	7.28
汉台区	Hantai	18.94	11.66	17.80	10.48	17.73	10.39
南郑县	Nanzheng	36.28	16.59	34.22	14.93	34.09	14.80
城固县	Chenggu	28.85	15.70	27.17	14.16	27.06	14.03
洋 县	Yangxian	35.28	17.66	33.26	15.76	33.13	15.62
勉 县	Mianxian	32.74	15.05	30.85	13.47	30.74	13.35
汉滨区	Hanbin	56.59	24.24	54.75	21.86	53.85	21.42

注：全省为抽样调查数。
a) The data of Shaanxi are sample survey data.

12-26 商品棉基地县情况
Base County of Marketable Cotton

县 区	Region	2010		2013		2014	
		播种面积(公顷) Sown Area (hectare)	产 量(吨) Output (ton)	播种面积(公顷) Sown Area (hectare)	产 量(吨) Output (ton)	播种面积(公顷) Sown Area (hectare)	产 量(吨) Output (ton)
全 省	**Shaanxi**	**50876**	**69240**	**36723**	**57917**	**31042**	**42171**
基地县合计	Total of Base Counties	39456	52828	22537	38937	18003	24383
基地县占全省%	As Percentage of Shaanxi	77.6	76.3	61.4	67.2	58.0	57.8
阎良区	Yanliang	3092	4344	1409	2028	40	61
临潼区	Lintong	788	1142	33	48		
临渭区	Linwei	7010	10409	5350	7865	5601	6930
华 县	Huaxian	727	926	143	193	316	450
大荔县	Dali	15353	16811	8332	18237	5380	7102
蒲城县	Pucheng	11689	18000	6996	10074	6327	9206
富平县	Fuping	798	1196	274	492	338	634

12-27 烤烟主产县情况
Base County of Flue-cured Tobacco

县 区	Region	2010		2013		2014	
		播种面积(公顷) Sown Area (hectare)	产 量(吨) Output (ton)	播种面积(公顷) Sown Area (hectare)	产 量(吨) Output (ton)	播种面积(公顷) Sown Area (hectare)	产 量(吨) Output (ton)
全 省	**Shaanxi**	**31063**	**67331**	**36614**	**85377**	**32714**	**71967**
基地县合计	Total of Base Counties	21636	46417	23699	55932	21795	47666
基地县占全省%	As Percentage of Shaanxi	69.7	68.9	64.7	65.5	66.6	66.2
宜君县	Yijun	135	312				
陇 县	Longxian	3886	7333	2790	5995	2435	4556
乾 县	Qianxian	402	814	333			
永寿县	Yongshou	333	700	121	406		
彬 县	Binxian	413	1052	249	702	255	693
长武县	Changwu	400	1050	482	1352	475	1339
旬邑县	Xunyi	1333	2980	599	1302	554	1205
合阳县	Heyang	129	405	5	30		
澄城县	Chengcheng	373	1029	205	1540	5	9
宝塔区	Baota	7	6	154	355	187	442
富 县	Fuxian	1200	2250	867	1475	793	1793
洛川县	Luochuan						
宜川县	Yichuan	711	1784	697	2075	323	735
黄龙县	Huanglong	509	1172	460	1030	469	1252
洋 县	Yangxian	275	1681	816	4304	780	4349
西乡县	Xixiang	487	1096	1440	3370	1194	3070
平利县	Pingli	478	1263	796	1806	948	1837
旬阳县	Xunyang	6655	13298	7531	15656	7156	13952
洛南县	Luonan	3908	8192	6155	14534	6220	12434

12-28 苹果基地县情况
Base County of Apple

县区	Region	2010 苹果园面积(公顷) Area of Apple Orchards (hectare)	2010 产量(吨) Output (ton)	2013 苹果园面积(公顷) Area of Apple Orchards (hectare)	2013 产量(吨) Output (ton)	2014 苹果园面积(公顷) Area of Apple Orchards (hectare)	2014 产量(吨) Output (ton)
全　省	**Shaanxi**	**601518**	**8560132**	**665220**	**9428230**	**681803**	**9880128**
基地县合计	Total of Base Counties	507135	7451893	558022	9165478	562813	9408140
基地县占全省%	As Percentage of Shaanxi	84.3	87.1	83.9	97.2	82.5	95.2
印台区	Yintai	20474	179782	20605	222360	20470	230068
耀洲区	Yaozhou	15019	152982	17198	220224	17944	226843
宜君县	Yijun	13200	141603	17132	170720	16335	171220
陈仓区	Chencang	5727	88273	7046	83271	7156	85900
凤翔县	Fengxiang	5704	98048	7227	126349	8404	131649
岐山县	Qishan	4962	102980	5593	89988	5600	92500
扶风县	Fufeng	4907	161180	8500	265861	8770	269805
陇　县	Longxian	3469	20750	4608	26577	4441	26067
千阳县	Qianyang	1726	10393	5414	15227	6101	16299
乾　县	Qianxian	24683	489400	27720	480816	28493	495840
礼泉县	Liquan	30015	1010000	30516	1160650	30312	1179254
永寿县	Yongshou	24670	363000	26923	422400	26950	426800
彬　县	Binxian	19308	321640	20606	418154	21432	422381
长武县	Changwu	16000	240000	17333	264800	18620	274050
旬邑县	Xunyi	33533	505000	33533	535040	33530	548494
淳化县	Chunhua	36667	725000	36667	823000	34046	827000
合阳县	Heyang	16772	284673	15356	292768	13503	267148
澄城县	Chengcheng	19630	292909	24097	325335	25540	363804
蒲城县	Pucheng	10219	168519	13403	177300	13984	167900
白水县	Baishui	21632	486000	22627	530177	22716	535277
富平县	Fuping	9002	189112	11404	213698	11823	221605
韩城市	Hancheng	4702	80230	4646	98045	4646	100752
宝塔区	Baota	27533	241400	31468	160500	31708	228000
延长县	Yanchang	18667	140000	19817	217838	20150	230900
延川县	Yanchuan	7556	40741	11546	50115	12380	65095
安塞县	Ansai	23342	65000	26667	29100	26667	32000
富　县	Fuxian	24166	433000	24006	479017	24006	489800
洛川县	Luochuan	33593	676500	33858	763500	33889	793000
宜川县	Yichuan	16761	333949	17672	403078	17698	417878
黄陵县	Huangling	13498	225000	14832	260670	15498	270500

注：本表基地县产量为监测推算结果。
a) The outputs of Base Counties are calculateed results by monitoring.

12-29 梨基地县情况
Base County of Pear

县 区	Region	2010		2013		2014	
		梨园面积 (公顷) Area of Pears Orchards (hectare)	产 量 (吨) Output (ton)	梨园面积 (公顷) Area of Pears Orchards (hectare)	产 量 (吨) Output (ton)	梨园面积 (公顷) Area of Pears Orchards (hectare)	产 量 (吨) Output (ton)
全 省	**Shaanxi**	**48954**	**799909**	**49274**	**972591**	**48632**	**1015019**
基地县合计	Total of Base Counties	27010	485283	26842	556665	26819	611681
基地县占全省%	As Percentage of Shaanxi	55.2	60.7	54.5	57.2	55.1	60.3
秦都区	Qindu	800	29900	791	24310	780	24340
乾 县	Qianxian	1533	30000	1600	30100	1600	32000
礼泉县	Liquan	4303	160000	3938	153500	3938	173658
彬 县	Binxian	1301	6438	1539	12101	1525	14389
临渭区	Linwei	3163	77419	2835	74590	2671	72132
蒲城县	Pucheng	8030	112645	10205	121280	10875	137760
富平县	Fuping	683	20665	846	24823	865	26032
子长县	Zichang	3800	11926	2990	8600	2623	5654
宜川县	Yichuan	1480	3908	713	7950	584	4875
洋 县	Yangxian	1918	12302	1385	12276	1359	12752

注：本表基地县产量为监测推算结果。
a) The outputs of Base Counties are calculateed results by monitoring.

12-30 猕猴桃基地县情况
Base County of Kiwi

县 区	Region	2010		2013		2014	
		猕猴桃园面积 (公顷) Area of Kiwi Orchards (hectare)	产 量 (吨) Output (ton)	猕猴桃园面积 (公顷) Area of Kiwi Orchards (hectare)	产 量 (吨) Output (ton)	猕猴桃园面积 (公顷) Area of Kiwi Orchards (hectare)	产 量 (吨) Output (ton)
全 省	**Shaanxi**	**47239**	**629341**	**60967**	**1033774**	**62003**	**1205886**
基地县合计	Total of Base Counties	38042	556112	44398	803381	44961	967621
基地县占全省%	As Percentage of Shaanxi	80.5	88.4	72.7	77.7	72.5	80.2
灞桥区	Baqiao	552	19222	496	17642	503	20685
长安区	Chang'an	261	4951	211	4473	213	4543
周至县	Zhouzhi	21400	246519	24311	338741	24682	351181
户 县	Huxian	914	22771	851	24500	718	22060
眉 县	Meixian	14467	250964	17830	411713	18079	445759
城固县	Chenggu	449	5672	698	6312	765	6380

注：本表基地县产量为监测推算结果。
a) The outputs of Base Counties are calculateed results by monitoring.

12-31 各市(区)灾情(2014年)
Conditions in Natural Disaster by City(District)(2014)

地 区	Region	受灾人口(万人次) Disaster Population Covered (10 000 persons-times)	死亡失踪人口(人) Population of Death and Abscondence (persons)	农作物受灾面积(千公顷) Disaster Areas of Farm Crops (1 000 hectares)	农作物绝收面积(千公顷) Disaster Areas of Farm Crops of No Harvest (1 000 hectares)	倒塌民房(万间) Broken Civil Buildings (10 000 units)	直接经济损失(亿元) Direct Economic Losses (100 million yuan)
全 省	**Shaanxi**	**2354.78**	**74**	**2371.08**	**335.02**	**9.48**	**187.70**
西安市	Xi'an	161.70		109.24	22.02	0.42	10.04
铜川市	Tongchuan	13.12		18.62	1.16	0.32	2.00
宝鸡市	Baoji	142.74	2	141.36	11.88	0.68	8.28
咸阳市	Xianyang	250.76		255.00	29.10	1.12	17.94
渭南市	Weinan	695.68	2	710.94	55.30	2.26	31.98
延安市	Yan'an	82.16	20	106.26	24.04	0.62	20.58
汉中市	Hanzhong	179.44	4	135.94	21.22	1.88	25.06
榆林市	Yulin	180.24	6	376.58	75.34	0.46	21.90
安康市	Ankang	272.14	10	204.88	49.38	1.08	17.42
商洛市	Shangluo	375.82	30	310.96	45.58	0.52	32.28
杨凌示范区	Yangling	0.98		1.30		0.12	0.12

12-32 农业现代化情况
Agriculture Modernization

指 标	Item	2010	2013	2014
农业机械总动力合计 (万千瓦)	**Total Agricultural Machinery Power (10 000 kw)**	**1889.27**	**2326.08**	**2552.13**
大中型拖拉机 (台)	Number of Large and Medium Tractors (unit)	78261	100524	101663
小型拖拉机 (万台)	Number of Small Tractors (10 000 units)	17.47	20.03	20.43
大中型拖拉机配套农具 (万部)	Large and Medium Tractors Towing (10 000 units)	12.99	17.21	18.56
小型拖拉机配套农具 (万部)	Small Tractors Towing Farm Machinery (10 000 units)	25.27	29.69	30.02
农用电动机 (万台)	Number of Agricultural Motor (10 000 units)	28.19	32.14	33.06
农用柴油机 (万台)	Number of Diesel Engines (10 000 units)	4.68	5.37	5.56
联合收割机 (台)	Number of Combine Harvesters (unit)	23357	31320	37408
机动脱粒机 (万台)	Number of Mobile Thresher (10 000 units)	24.65	36.09	38.72
农用运输车 (辆)	Number of Farm Vehicles (unit)	501505	479844	500424
节水灌溉类机械 (套)	Watersaving Irrigation Machinery (unit)	9972	22575	31476
农用水泵 (万台)	Number of Agricultural Pumps (10 000 units)	29.14	31.75	32.52
当年机耕地面积 (千公顷)	Area Cultivated by Mechanical (1 000 hectares)	2078.6	2395.1	2862.6
当年机械播种面积 (千公顷)	Area Sown by Mechanical (1 000 hectares)	1740.6	1907.3	2002.8
当年机械收获面积 (千公顷)	Mechanical harvest Area (1 000 hectares)	1243.5	1578.1	1811.5
农用化肥施用量(折纯量) (万吨)	Consumption of Chemical Fertilizers (10 000 tons)	196.79	241.73	230.19
氮 肥	Nitrogenous Fertilizer	87.67	98.69	96.12
磷 肥	Phosphate Fertilizer	17.98	18.45	18.44
钾 肥	Potash Fertilizer	19.99	23.33	23.81
复合肥	Compound Fertilizer	56.43	101.26	91.82
农用塑料薄膜使用量 (吨)	Plastic Film Consumption (ton)	36811	40847	41479
# 地膜使用量	Film Consumption	19547	21377	21096
地膜覆盖面积 (千公顷)	Film Coverage Area (1 000 hectares)	427.1	450.63	447.89
农用柴油使用量 (万吨)	Diesel Consumption (10 000 tons)	70.36	91.03	91.21
农药使用量 (吨)	Pesticides Consumption (10 000 tons)	12408	12998	12793

注：本表2014年为农机部门数据。
a) Data in this table come from Agricultural Machinery Bureau in 2014.

12-33 各市(区)农业现代化情况（2014）
Agriculture Modernization by City(District) (2014)

地 区	Region	农用机械总动力合计（万千瓦）Total Agricultural Machinery Power (10 000 kw)	大中型拖拉机（台）Large and Medium Tractors (unit)	小 型拖拉机（台）Small Tractors (unit)	大中型机配农具（部）Large and Medium Tractors Towing Farm Machinery (unit)	小 型机配农具（部）Small Tractors Towing Farm Machinery (unit)	农用排灌电动机（台）Agricultural Drainage and Irrigation Motor (unit)	农用排灌柴油机（台）Agricultural Drainage and Irrigation Diesel Engine (unit)
全 省	**Shaanxi**	**2552.13**	**101663**	**204290**	**185632**	**300242**	**330628**	**55583**
西安市	Xi'an	320.33	9946	7538	31451	21806	85244	2409
铜川市	Tongchuan	53.40	3515	4536	7834	7542	906	177
宝鸡市	Baoji	265.84	17578	39667	34973	62133	19728	2398
咸阳市	Xianyang	345.20	14260	12470	31248	21271	36712	5020
渭南市	Weinan	525.87	23212	59617	51092	93274	63527	12738
延安市	Yan'an	215.05	5892	44907	8350	54546	9976	5676
汉中市	Hanzhong	192.72	5669	4628	3428	4906	32700	6008
榆林市	Yulin	350.81	19048	20363	14909	24865	37393	6955
安康市	Ankang	175.64	1429	6772	693	2995	21267	12420
商洛市	Shangluo	93.69	342	3027	607	5453	22673	1782
杨凌示范区	Yangling	11.21	658	765	1047	1451	502	

12-33 续表 continued

地 区	Region	联 合收割机（台）Combine Harvesters (unit)	机 动脱粒机（台）Mobile Thresher (unit)	农 用运输车（辆）Farm Vehicles (unit)	节水灌溉类机械（套）Watersaving Irrigation Machinery (unit)	农 用水 泵（台）Pumps (unit)	化肥施用折纯量（吨）Consumption of Chemical Fertilizers (ton)	农用塑料薄膜使用量（吨）Plastic Film Consumption (ton)
全 省	**Shaanxi**	**37408**	**387155**	**500424**	**31476**	**325202**	**2301891**	**41479**
西安市	Xi'an	7815	14749	51410	2562	79849	251217	2658
铜川市	Tongchuan	244	2621	18552	1700	1064	51929	630
宝鸡市	Baoji	6131	31408	34303	278	20249	253936	1636
咸阳市	Xianyang	6952	18465	94148	1983	31051	475877	7617
渭南市	Weinan	14657	29133	98542	12829	47553	657838	13374
延安市	Yan'an	152	5838	54641	6518	13247	152578	3851
汉中市	Hanzhong	588	82556	22624	838	36217	150791	2273
榆林市	Yulin	472	34740	81410	605	53561	133088	4391
安康市	Ankang	153	96731	20046	1291	21645	111744	2883
商洛市	Shangluo	18	70841	22991	2872	20264	58220	1469
杨凌示范区	Yangling	177	73	1757		502	4673	698

注：本表为农机部门数据。
a) Data in this table come from Agricultural Machinery Bureau.

12-34 各市、县(市、区)农村经济主要指标(2014年)
Main Indicators of Rural Economy by City and County (City and District) (2014)

地 区	Region	农林牧渔业总产值(万元) Gross Output Value of Farming, Forestry, Animal Husbandry and Fishery (10 000 yuan)	农林牧渔业增加值(万元) Value Added of Farming, Forestry, Animal Husbandry and Fishery (10 000 yuan)	年末常用耕地面积(公顷) Area of Cultivated Land (hectare)	农用机械总动力(千瓦) Total Agricultural Machinery Power (kw)	农用化肥施用折纯量(吨) Consumption of Chemical Fertilizers (ton)	农用塑料薄膜使用量(吨) Plastic Film Consumption (ton)
全 省	**Shaanxi**	**27418168**	**16358457**	**2865995**	**25521306**	**2301891**	**41479**
西安市	**Xi'an**	**3672101**	**2336074**	**240489**	**3203302**	**251217**	**2658**
新城区	Xincheng						
碑林区	Beilin						
莲湖区	Lianhu						
灞桥区	Baqiao	300728	197505	9241	181659	8616	190
未央区	Weiyang	19090	11590	1047	47814	1524	18
雁塔区	Yanta	26798	19290	434	92415	115	
阎良区	Yanliang	354330	240604	15632	190369	24039	1117
临潼区	Lintong	538221	342404	46492	608868	39641	224
长安区	Chang'an	538210	362858	41980	427840	29920	180
蓝田县	Lantian	462420	280332	39733	309780	46013	184
周至县	Zhouzhi	482477	295943	33269	453137	47017	99
户 县	Huxian	481686	299470	37535	495146	33755	601
高陵县	Gaoling	468141	286078	15126	278953	20577	46
铜川市	**Tongchuan**	**418808**	**234731**	**64642**	**534036**	**51929**	**630**
王益区	Wangyi	21575	12329	3977	71104	1834	14
印台区	Yintai	90846	51531	9208	114112	7216	103
耀州区	Yaozhou	194054	106984	32154	229770	30320	195
宜君县	Yijun	112333	63887	19302	119050	12559	319
宝鸡市	**Baoji**	**2809042**	**1682587**	**298361**	**2658360**	**253936**	**1636**
渭滨区	Weibin	74374	41790	5969	77980	7231	17
金台区	Jintai	43570	27167	10176	139376	5431	4
陈仓区	Chencang	419956	245466	44968	408175	30721	180
凤翔县	Fengxiang	398017	249535	46332	427722	42299	106
岐山县	Qishan	375889	235829	35237	379286	24571	139
扶风县	Fufeng	350702	202117	32395	434260	50924	38
眉 县	Meixian	363300	208243	23161	220502	41974	124
陇 县	Longxian	305299	182345	35442	170833	13492	439
千阳县	Qianyang	160611	96316	18552	142659	12955	155
麟游县	Linyou	107561	70075	30045	77818	14824	147
凤 县	Fengxian	118555	68272	9624	109469	5130	154
太白县	Taibai	91208	55432	6460	70281	4384	133
咸阳市	**Xianyang**	**5599917**	**3393183**	**353964**	**3452000**	**475877**	**7617**
秦都区	Qindu	285600	172350	8891	234471	13447	363
渭城区	Weicheng	232705	142764	12421	233304	8393	127
三原县	Sanyuan	509048	307696	33055	293525	28160	420
泾阳县	Jingyang	737796	457574	43100	468058	36610	2540
乾 县	Qianxian	513509	303218	48443	380061	90307	147
礼泉县	Liquan	781606	513798	28865	392988	108311	803

注：全省粮食和猪牛羊禽相关数据为抽样调查数据。
a) The Shaanxi data of grain, pig, cattle, sheep are sample survey data.

12-34 续表 1 continued

地 区	Region	农林牧渔业总产值(万元) Gross Output Value of Farming, Forestry, Animal Husbandry and Fishery (10 000 yuan)	农林牧渔业增加值(万元) Value Added of Farming, Forestry, Animal Husbandry and Fishery (10 000 yuan)	年末常用耕地面积(公顷) Area of Cultivated Land (hectare)	农用机械总动力(千瓦) Total Agricultural Machinery Power (kw)	农用化肥施用折纯量(吨) Consumption of Chemical Fertilizers (ton)	农用塑料薄膜使用量(吨) Plastic Film Consumption (ton)
永寿县	Yongshou	273123	147979	20402	179823	30806	148
彬 县	Binxian	297830	172153	31283	128530	20626	930
长武县	Changwu	292219	150362	11666	136886	31389	700
旬邑县	Xunyi	486744	290208	27678	116497	33440	785
淳化县	Chunhua	456662	261693	27330	242760	30758	390
武功县	Wugong	348078	222599	26906	323911	26703	156
兴平市	Xingping	384997	250789	33924	321186	16927	108
渭南市	**Weinan**	**3844624**	**2172991**	**511137**	**5258697**	**657838**	**13374**
临渭区	Linwei	630349	350711	65963	805999	67203	1371
华 县	Huaxian	166851	95967	23922	330000	26694	378
潼关县	Tongguan	64299	36257	10661	102265	11506	45
大荔县	Dali	584115	321024	74380	1032065	82593	1986
合阳县	Heyang	332370	184044	58395	312315	24909	886
澄城县	Chengcheng	368722	206432	46925	350502	33529	736
蒲城县	Pucheng	440782	257513.0	93352.0	937671.0	67727.0	5175.0
白水县	Baishui	398236	232921	28718	396813	53742	737
富平县	Fuping	477479	275056	70814	612398	264735	1598
韩城市	Hancheng	276872	152324	25305	304622	17612	214
华阴市	Huayin	104549	60742	12703	74047	7588	248
延安市	**Yan'an**	**2032025**	**1163495**	**244873**	**2150533**	**152578**	**3851**
宝塔区	Baota	214744	125044	32431	174224	7424	212
延长县	Yanchang	153645	87741	16570	107637	5166	110
延川县	Yanchuan	109300	62284	24805	113000	4060	173
子长县	Zichang	128972	74640	31263	145350	8247	788
安塞县	Ansai	131228	75010	27200	105723	5309	323
志丹县	Zhidan	85421	52866	24417	145458	2658	310
吴起县	Wuqi	83532	50933	25066	184047	3314	863
甘泉县	Ganquan	78243	43832	6110	86033	3333	240
富 县	Fuxian	227397	127308	9864	179300	11897	338
洛川县	Luochuan	400197	223336	10471	297107	61468	70
宜川县	Yichuan	196008	113070	14851	266973	17917	65
黄龙县	Huanglong	80656	46710	12050	78107	10562	118
黄陵县	Huangling	142682	80721	9774	267574	11223	242
汉中市	**Hanzhong**	**3255057**	**1904888**	**205153**	**1927187**	**150791**	**2273**
汉台区	Hantai	294765	173593	14773	152823	8948	239
南郑县	Nanzheng	392411	223656	30446	220026	21735	433
城固县	Chenggu	726539	431398	24150	240409	37016	227
洋 县	Yangxian	380783	227521	27636	219178	23897	424
西乡县	Xixiang	313732	181401	21950	330112	13607	145
勉 县	Mianxian	359608	202443	26321	173118	21516	159
宁强县	Ningqiang	301567	179906	21263	169815	11890	184

12-34 续表 2 continued

地　区	Region	农林牧渔业总产值(万元) Gross Output Value of Farming, Forestry, Animal Husbandry and Fishery (10 000 yuan)	农林牧渔业增加值(万元) Value Added of Farming, Forestry, Animal Husbandry and Fishery (10 000 yuan)	年末常用耕地面积(公顷) Area of Cultivated Land (hectare)	农用机械总动力(千瓦) Total Agricultural Machinery Power (kw)	农用化肥施用折纯量(吨) Consumption of Chemical Fertilizers (ton)	农用塑料薄膜使用量(吨) Plastic Film Consumption (ton)
略阳县	Lueyang	155719	88701	10046	250500	3642	136
镇巴县	Zhenba	257282	154357	23631	100858	7150	263
留坝县	Liuba	50856	29817	3066	30188	829	50
佛坪县	Foping	21795	12095	1871	40160	561	15
榆林市	**Yulin**	**2500345**	**1502183**	**602617**	**3508143**	**133088**	**4391**
榆阳区	Yuyang	430033	251728	65069	476312	23922	361
神木县	Shenmu	214584	126737	48474	395570	7302	229
府谷县	Fugu	101206	61134	43263	324900	6060	58
横山县	Hengshan	246554	145934	60619	281016	11881	201
靖边县	Jingbian	350910	206999	80154	552500	8891	1460
定边县	Dingbian	323520	187424	138925	610853	30184	777
绥德县	Suide	171872	106634	41741	176227	15013	153
米脂县	Mizhi	100865	62066	27865	183000	5237	192
佳　县	Jiaxian	155538	97950	30844	138526	4091	205
吴堡县	Wubu	39133	25422	8101	72318	957	19
清涧县	Qingjian	197172	124299	27078	171563	5207	320
子洲县	Zizhou	168958	105856	30484	125358	14343	416
安康市	**Ankang**	**1637491**	**949185**	**197296**	**1756421**	**111744**	**2883**
汉滨区	Hanbin	376875	226372	42740	525216	48469	608
汉阴县	Hanyin	200726	118655	23041	215000	10967	217
石泉县	Shiquan	110801	64794	13100	123442	5538	202
宁陕县	Ningshan	74604	41484	3392	52482	348	56
紫阳县	Ziyang	193078	112150	24249	155337	5153	189
岚皋县	Langao	106117	61731	17180	91237	4654	455
平利县	Pingli	176836	99136	18332	132000	4789	452
镇坪县	Zhenping	55179	30129	4966	42007	1398	54
旬阳县	Xunyang	222456	123056	36410	287000	24555	459
白河县	Baihe	120819	71678	13885	132700	5873	191
商洛市	**Shangluo**	**1659191**	**945059**	**133395**	**936898**	**58220**	**1469**
商州区	Shangzhou	243724	143284	21230	166135	6582	203
洛南县	Luonan	364527	203591	31794	173903	18407	471
丹凤县	Danfeng	207058	114921	12163	91278	5542	117
商南县	Shangnan	227986	125471	14138	102967	5294	155
山阳县	Shanyang	282881	169978	24003	185036	8853	133
镇安县	Zhen'an	216494	121067	21586	147740	8638	240
柞水县	Zhashui	116521	66747	8481	69839	4904	149
杨凌示范区	**Yangling**	**118614**	**72315**	**5463**	**112132**	**4673**	**698**

12-34 续表 3 continued

地 区	Region	粮食播种面积(公顷) Sown Area of Grain (hectare)	粮食产量(吨) Output of Grain (ton)	油料产量(吨) Output of Oil-bearing (ton)	棉花产量(吨) Output of Cotton (ton)	蔬菜产量(吨) Output of Vegetables (ton)	水果产量(吨) Output of Fruits (ton)	# 苹果 Output of Apples
全 省	**Shaanxi**	**3076540**	**11977800**	**622994**	**42171**	**17246847**	**15539830**	**9880128**
西安市	**Xi'an**	**367640**	**1756058**	**9785**	**328**	**3162770**	**996570**	**26047**
新城区	Xincheng							
碑林区	Beilin							
莲湖区	Lianhu							
灞桥区	Baqiao	12072	52853	433	48	286513	103857	
未央区	Weiyang	953	3997			25259	1327	15
雁塔区	Yanta					18901	2329	460
阎良区	Yanliang	14167	81003	103	61	762011	67520	5788
临潼区	Lintong	68987	317870	1375		445169	55304	3836
长安区	Chang'an	69960	338400	2558	8	586105	79109	2786
蓝田县	Lantian	63832	250600	2335	210	168036	130439	7283
周至县	Zhouzhi	51341	224955	2156		198111	404056	2818
户 县	Huxian	58790	296007	825	1	276778	94895	810
高陵县	Gaoling	27538	190373			395887	57734	2251
铜川市	**Tongchuan**	**60057**	**233941**	**8049**		**164540**	**690593**	**663312**
王益区	Wangyi	3823	9967	320		15009	40215	35181
印台区	Yintai	10351	36091	1300		27700	233380	230068
耀州区	Yaozhou	29921	90347	5549		94243	245698	226843
宜君县	Yijun	15962	97536	880		27588	171300	171220
宝鸡市	**Baoji**	**332970**	**1443160**	**19236**	**60**	**1363597**	**1319702**	**680618**
渭滨区	Weibin	7385	20000	1074		18540	23611	142
金台区	Jintai	11684	33019	1097		2464	3490	847
陈仓区	Chencang	58118	224800	2769		184687	118738	85900
凤翔县	Fengxiang	55271	256353	5168		145678	140399	131649
岐山县	Qishan	48292	265783	2445	21	169767	158485	92500
扶风县	Fufeng	48427	265514	944	39	33936	296186	269805
眉 县	Meixian	22594	126173	1037		36979	468456	2414
陇 县	Longxian	32679	100101	1936		106199	33394	26067
千阳县	Qianyang	19004	56297	842		101503	18550	16299
麟游县	Linyou	21370	66326	919		18381	1035	823
凤 县	Fengxian	5982	22389	670		112286	54984	54000
太白县	Taibai	2164	6405	335		433177	2374	172
咸阳市	**Xianyang**	**390990**	**1841442**	**47684**	**130**	**4118459**	**5617342**	**4615995**
秦都区	Qindu	13101	58922	275		250816	93233	56964
渭城区	Weicheng	20663	92962	1127		131648	74941	31040
三原县	Sanyuan	40834	195125	3822		1063361	191371	105411
泾阳县	Jingyang	50815	239839	2838	122	1808544	165332	31710
乾 县	Qianxian	54853	250097	7988		42287	574880	495840
礼泉县	Liquan	26865	120567	4948		72864	1554681	1179254

12-34 续表 4 continued

地 区	Region	粮食播种面积(公顷) Sown Area of Grain (hectare)	粮食产量(吨) Output of Grain (ton)	油料产量(吨) Output of Oil-bearing (ton)	棉花产量(吨) Output of Cotton (ton)	蔬菜产量(吨) Output of Vegetables (ton)	水果产量(吨) Output of Fruits (ton)	# 苹果 Output of Apples
永寿县	Yongshou	18939	81018	2827		23443	451141	426800
彬 县	Binxian	26643	115331	10906		42959	473802	422381
长武县	Changwu	12016	55175	1378		20155	293620	274050
旬邑县	Xunyi	20216	108028	2575		72697	566967	548494
淳化县	Chunhua	23240	110000	5733		45248	921731	827000
武功县	Wugong	39655	197222	2258	8	190013	90394	74899
兴平市	Xingping	43151	217156	1009		354424	165249	142152
渭南市	**Weinan**	**512975**	**2060061**	**73583**	**40219**	**2388148**	**2920632**	**1937295**
临渭区	Linwei	83581	333084	5782	6930	558672	262448	70731
华 县	Huaxian	27629	110102	1405	450	557826	25930	1615
潼关县	Tongguan	13180	42009	3543	659	35380	11263	9455
大荔县	Dali	62274	270535	27663	7102	338856	513982	198708
合阳县	Heyang	50459	197372	3708	5586	180462	355301	267148
澄城县	Chengcheng	43397	167303	12694	8062	57670	456174	363804
蒲城县	Pucheng	83783	329654	4056	9206	136050	312829	167900
白水县	Baishui	27516	105208	7348		65210	537348	535277
富平县	Fuping	80181	355004	5014	634	300929	322681	221605
韩城市	Hancheng	22947	72790	1205	120	112930	114326	100752
华阴市	Huayin	18028	77000	1165	1470	44163	8350	300
延安市	**Yan'an**	**200403**	**786774**	**22701**	**931**	**1130010**	**2702089**	**2614373**
宝塔区	Baota	27077	89917	989		150838	232348	228000
延长县	Yanchang	10423	40077	3520	560	101608	234791	230900
延川县	Yanchuan	16966	43018	1008	358	31510	116313	65095
子长县	Zichang	25475	77657	6420		116033	24441	17100
安塞县	Ansai	28410	71490	4312		240184	33640	32000
志丹县	Zhidan	18200	53180	600		68108	16018	12100
吴起县	Wuqi	17062	62146	900		76200	9593	9000
甘泉县	Ganquan	9409	42427	76		132027	4047	3500
富 县	Fuxian	6241	36257	315		96000	490763	489800
洛川县	Luochuan	12815	99282	780		33142	795456	793000
宜川县	Yichuan	6784	37235	878	13	43100	425400	417878
黄龙县	Huanglong	11197	86149	227		4460	45840	45500
黄陵县	Huangling	10345	47939	2676		36800	273439	270500
汉中市	**Hanzhong**	**268247**	**1017512**	**189144**	**1**	**2143397**	**430669**	**4593**
汉台区	Hantai	17729	103886	16710		216102	34668	
南郑县	Nanzheng	34094	148007	34596		175818	12004	60
城固县	Chenggu	27061	140327	22987		614345	268831	153
洋 县	Yangxian	33131	156204	28182		661077	78668	1507
西乡县	Xixiang	29996	98670	25924	1	93868	5914	
勉 县	Mianxian	30736	133513	30220		127018	8125	37
宁强县	Ningqiang	30818	82549	12653		52240	4319	412

12-34 续表 5 continued

地 区	Region	粮食播种面积(公顷) Sown Area of Grain (hectare)	粮食产量(吨) Output of Grain (ton)	油料产量(吨) Output of Oil-bearing (ton)	棉花产量(吨) Output of Cotton (ton)	蔬菜产量(吨) Output of Vegetables (ton)	水果产量(吨) Output of Fruits (ton)	# 苹果 Output of Apples
略阳县	Lueyang	20243	47119	4966		52894	8331	1433
镇巴县	Zhenba	38464	86865	11521		108384	8312	683
留坝县	Liuba	3180	11791	916		24659	762	231
佛坪县	Foping	2794	8581	469		16992	735	77
榆林市	**Yulin**	**476366**	**1580959**	**83182**	**120**	**756590**	**606125**	**200161**
榆阳区	Yuyang	44691	239639	2106		80310	4410	1600
神木县	Shenmu	31598	124121	6799		21579	3689	92
府谷县	Fugu	30716	67214	2433	67	42080	28514	830
横山县	Hengshan	62543	161313	1520		44298	21298	7577
靖边县	Jingbian	51863	237461	7170		248802	13124	11028
定边县	Dingbian	111142	298472	14971		122989	1791	1560
绥德县	Suide	25854	89895	22104		52048	127958	80480
米脂县	Mizhi	26783.00	88080	3919		16130	44076	26023.00
佳 县	Jiaxian	24908	74931	3224		19733	106017	2312
吴堡县	Wubu	5576	18816	1242	7	12877	22829	773
清涧县	Qingjian	28440	75119	8856	46	55801	210884	53323
子洲县	Zizhou	32251	105898	8838		39943	21535	14563
安康市	**Ankang**	**268702**	**860382**	**147893**	**35**	**1400304**	**211874**	**5172**
汉滨区	Hanbin	53852	214162	43984	21	388683	55470	855
汉阴县	Hanyin	25913	103270	28839	14	187009	35771	97
石泉县	Shiquan	19138	66859	13746		63582	5546	598
宁陕县	Ningshan	4946	19212	854		41215	2332	261
紫阳县	Ziyang	42022	109089	12527		208511	6031	132
岚皋县	Langao	24693	65530	7022		145074	4170	120
平利县	Pingli	24771	74132	11597		103681	7858	358
镇坪县	Zhenping	9351.00	27056	1693		35311	1405	310.00
旬阳县	Xunyang	45169	123708	21038		140735	49512	2132
白河县	Baihe	18846	57364	6593		86503	43779	309
商洛市	**Shangluo**	**209531**	**521983**	**21609**	**2**	**471275**	**67201**	**9249**
商州区	Shangzhou	34635	81183	361		48060	11167	533
洛南县	Luonan	50728	142081	1046		155675	7992	434
丹凤县	Danfeng	21781	51142	1096		20361	8588	1446
商南县	Shangnan	19560	49332	10642		74799	6501	597
山阳县	Shanyang	37320	86812	2859		68125	10962	1235
镇安县	Zhen'an	32467	75641	5269	2	67827	13368	3886
柞水县	Zhashui	13039	35792	336		36428	8623	1118
杨凌示范区	**Yangling**	**3155**	**19345**	**128**		**140613**	**38647**	**6897**

12-34 续表 6 continued

地区	Region	肉类产量（吨） Output of Meat (ton)	禽蛋产量（吨） Output of Poultry Eggs (ton)	奶类产量（吨） Output of Milk (ton)	牛存栏（万头） Stocked Cattle (10 000 heads)	# 奶牛 Dairy cow	猪存栏（万头） Stocked Hogs (10 000 heads)	羊存栏（万只） Stocked (10 000 heads)	家禽存栏（万只） Stocked (10 000 heads)
全 省	**Shaanxi**	**1167560**	**545000**	**1923428**	**150.60**	**45.50**	**879.40**	**700.20**	**6623.50**
西安市	**Xi'an**	**144209**	**135191**	**658016**	**21.63**	**12.62**	**81.95**	**27.92**	**1161.16**
新城区	Xincheng								
碑林区	Beilin								
莲湖区	Lianhu								
灞桥区	Baqiao	7335	5648	66295	1.33	1.29	4.92	1.18	44.76
未央区	Weiyang	1325	103	6931	0.62	0.55	2.18	0.16	5.60
雁塔区	Yanta	750	260	950	0.02	0.02	0.40		2.70
阎良区	Yanliang	7205	7025	98354	1.92	1.79	3.83	5.55	61.52
临潼区	Lintong	26988	33652	335356	7.33	6.56	10.70	8.22	265.00
长安区	Chang'an	21704	40492	24316	1.08	0.43	11.66	1.66	286.58
蓝田县	Lantian	18801	6491	41570	3.84	0.30	8.00	7.23	127.00
周至县	Zhouzhi	30179	10275	13293	3.32	0.28	20.05	1.30	97.50
户 县	Huxian	19975	14857	26785	0.97	0.53	15.16	0.72	130.50
高陵县	Gaoling	9947	16388	44166	1.20	0.87	5.05	1.89	140.00
铜川市	**Tongchuan**	**17278**	**17039**	**30292**	**7.89**	**1.62**	**7.63**	**7.60**	**179.07**
王益区	Wangyi	1406	890	1214	0.34	0.10	1.20	0.36	23.41
印台区	Yintai	5589	9881	4146	1.00	0.19	2.58	1.46	98.11
耀州区	Yaozhou	5330	5852	24932	4.04	1.32	2.86	3.12	37.29
宜君县	Yijun	4953	416		2.51		0.98	2.66	20.26
宝鸡市	**Baoji**	**186692**	**74994**	**662356**	**50.84**	**21.54**	**108.47**	**56.82**	**933.55**
渭滨区	Weibin	2167	956	867	0.16	0.02	1.38	0.66	29.26
金台区	Jintai	3609	987	9078	0.75	0.24	2.39	1.04	15.20
陈仓区	Chencang	55829	23706	63671	6.38	1.31	28.24	4.37	193.46
凤翔县	Fengxiang	22108	11026	86472	9.09	2.65	9.29	8.40	128.30
岐山县	Qishan	21972	13562	61421	5.81	2.82	19.56	4.53	129.20
扶风县	Fufeng	24552	15193	23342	1.64	0.78	18.78	2.82	255.83
眉 县	Meixian	16894	4394	66372	3.83	2.79	13.98	3.68	73.67
陇 县	Longxian	9304	2392	204469	8.76	6.30	2.60	7.63	25.50
千阳县	Qianyang	7404	1790	146534	6.49	4.61	1.89	6.46	21.41
麟游县	Linyou	8034	213	5	5.62		1.05	12.33	19.57
凤 县	Fengxian	11251	158		1.49		7.11	2.51	31.48
太白县	Taibai	3568	617	125	0.81	0.01	2.22	2.39	10.67
咸阳市	**Xianyang**	**218664**	**112063**	**809917**	**46.62**	**24.80**	**202.27**	**119.60**	**1099.33**
秦都区	Qindu	9419	3518	21041	0.84	0.77	7.26	0.82	37.00
渭城区	Weicheng	9485	13459	64875	1.42	1.42	6.53	0.71	94.88
三原县	Sanyuan	16057	22286	50253	4.99	0.80	12.55	18.18	184.00
泾阳县	Jingyang	25186	16123	228616	7.78	7.78	19.50	18.64	210.00
乾 县	Qianxian	17569	4775	137926	5.13	4.92	16.92	5.47	49.00
礼泉县	Liquan	8952	2212	31120	1.96	1.28	7.70	10.73	23.60

12-34　续表 7　continued

地　区	Region	肉类产量（吨） Output of Meat (ton)	禽蛋产量（吨） Output of Poultry Eggs (ton)	奶类产量（吨） Output of Milk (ton)	牛存栏（万头） Stocked Cattle (10 000 heads)	#奶牛 Dairy Cow	猪存栏（万头） Stocked Hogs (10 000 heads)	羊存栏（万只） Stocked (10 000 heads)	家禽存栏（万只） Stocked (10 000 heads)
永寿县	Yongshou	10166	2420	11555	5.86	0.10	5.92	16.74	38.01
彬　县	Binxian	6169	5646	6158	1.82	0.08	3.56	4.50	30.60
长武县	Changwu	4807	3161	14600	2.66	0.59	2.32	7.65	49.60
旬邑县	Xunyi	28170	5490	7928	4.19	0.16	50.66	10.38	52.58
淳化县	Chunhua	14832	10402	41394	2.86	0.71	8.83	19.31	99.06
武功县	Wugong	23889	8514	169583	5.19	5.09	28.12	3.23	92.00
兴平市	Xingping	43963	14057	24868	1.91	1.13	32.42	3.24	139.00
渭南市	**Weinan**	**222017**	**105138**	**402279**	**29.18**	**11.50**	**211.13**	**105.56**	**1189.50**
临渭区	Linwei	33089	30722	118625	8.51	3.29	28.12	11.25	266.25
华　县	Huaxian	8189	4870	4870	1.09	0.13	7.29	2.73	86.80
潼关县	Tongguan	7098	1038		0.41		7.00	0.77	14.91
大荔县	Dali	40825	17510	16786	5.92	0.97	36.46	24.43	145.05
合阳县	Heyang	11443	4455	54552	3.87	3.43	12.02	5.32	62.60
澄城县	Chengcheng	55178	9178	821	1.05	0.02	61.19	4.56	84.11
蒲城县	Pucheng	15939	5825	38510	2.08	0.97	15.03	8.22	207.00
白水县	Baishui	16438	1455	1969	0.99	0.03	17.62	4.22	36.00
富平县	Fuping	19965	22570	150822	3.32	2.06	15.27	35.88	208.00
韩城市	Hancheng	9625	2950	1824	1.06	0.06	7.88	6.27	39.39
华阴市	Huayin	4228	4565	13500	0.89	0.53	3.25	1.91	39.39
延安市	**Yan'an**	**76254**	**27782**	**7379**	**14.86**	**0.19**	**71.03**	**62.07**	**376.39**
宝塔区	Baota	7113	3812	3509	1.83	0.11	4.35	2.39	55.42
延长县	Yanchang	3232	1512	90	2.12	0.01	2.00	6.82	24.77
延川县	Yanchuan	3163	1340	425	1.24	0.01	3.03	3.26	20.01
子长县	Zichang	9115	2405	550	2.70	0.03	7.14	7.85	25.80
安塞县	Ansai	3276	1958	165	0.33	0.01	3.35	6.57	25.03
志丹县	Zhidan	3311	1595	98	0.45	0.01	3.23	13.35	23.10
吴起县	Wuqi	5745	1598	110	0.51		3.83	13.07	21.03
甘泉县	Ganquan	4478	6378	154	0.33	0.01	2.22	5.55	94.25
富　县	Fuxian	2993	1721	52	1.91		2.25	0.26	22.03
洛川县	Luochuan	25741	1365	1823	0.50	0.01	32.48	0.86	17.15
宜川县	Yichuan	2518	1382	75	0.57		2.40	0.83	14.55
黄龙县	Huanglong	2526	961		0.82		1.74	0.72	14.27
黄陵县	Huangling	3043	1755	328	0.56		3.01	0.54	18.98
汉中市	**Hanzhong**	**316589**	**71434**	**13967**	**30.15**	**0.39**	**258.98**	**34.94**	**1097.63**
汉台区	Hantai	18836	9494	6562	0.98	0.19	11.57	0.25	131.30
南郑县	Nanzheng	39131	6568	905	3.54	0.04	32.51	2.59	101.12
城固县	Chenggu	49339	10667	416	3.25	0.03	31.95	1.48	160.05
洋　县	Yangxian	45253	7775	765	6.36	0.02	39.47	5.17	109.02
西乡县	Xixiang	31743	4930	31	3.21		28.96	6.04	73.10
勉　县	Mianxian	43464	13821	5273	2.90	0.11	38.10	1.03	158.17
宁强县	Ningqiang	34781	6554	15	3.89		31.55	2.03	109.15

12-34 续表 8 continued

地 区	Region	肉类产量(吨) Output of Meat (ton)	禽蛋产量(吨) Output of Poultry Eggs (ton)	奶类产量(吨) Output of Milk (ton)	牛存栏(万头) Stocked Cattle (10 000 heads)	#奶牛 Dairy Cow	猪存栏(万头) Stocked Hogs (10 000 heads)	羊存栏(万只) Stocked (10 000 heads)	家禽存栏(万只) Stocked (10 000 heads)
略阳县	Lueyang	15754	7413		1.65		9.85	2.32	168.87
镇巴县	Zhenba	31931	3271		3.75		30.82	13.43	67.23
留坝县	Liuba	3814	685		0.52		2.85	0.25	14.30
佛坪县	Foping	2543	256		0.10		1.35	0.36	5.32
榆林市	**Yulin**	**184294**	**52260**	**92029**	**14.70**	**2.78**	**98.40**	**649.18**	**552.62**
榆阳区	Yuyang	63370	10088	23152	3.41	0.65	40.31	134.73	123.18
神木县	Shenmu	18256	5670	16815	3.76	0.48	7.48	91.00	42.32
府谷县	Fugu	6401	3435	602	1.01	0.02	3.34	21.56	27.08
横山县	Hengshan	19621	9014	1002	0.92	0.03	6.83	95.91	53.70
靖边县	Jingbian	30173	5300	13712	1.00	0.43	16.15	128.52	73.55
定边县	Dingbian	19948	2973	14353	0.73	0.52	9.98	85.23	47.53
绥德县	Suide	4380	4186	6478	0.61	0.18	2.05	14.36	46.25
米脂县	Mizhi	4828	3056	2423	0.89	0.08	1.99	16.76	51.78
佳 县	Jiaxian	4418	3415	1105	0.91	0.03	2.24	16.57	26.87
吴堡县	Wubu	951	1333	471	0.09	0.01	0.52	3.13	8.13
清涧县	Qingjian	5449	1695	3328	0.89	0.09	3.63	11.85	21.98
子洲县	Zizhou	6499	2095	8588	0.47	0.26	3.88	29.57	30.25
安康市	**Ankang**	**281145**	**37744**	**82**	**25.52**	**0.01**	**238.65**	**97.16**	**931.96**
汉滨区	Hanbin	58445	8482	73	5.28		51.46	13.73	192.39
汉阴县	Hanyin	33963	7380		3.62		29.13	5.40	127.20
石泉县	Shiquan	21066	2552		3.25		18.32	5.82	67.37
宁陕县	Ningshan	4745	600	9	0.43		4.01	2.74	21.57
紫阳县	Ziyang	33255	4095		0.70		29.63	10.57	85.48
岚皋县	Langao	21778	4253		0.21		19.52	8.98	119.58
平利县	Pingli	30411	2491		0.79		20.47	15.14	71.46
镇坪县	Zhenping	15956	476		0.37		13.68	2.66	34.38
旬阳县	Xunyang	46260	4309		9.79		39.50	22.91	150.15
白河县	Baihe	15266	3106		1.08		12.93	9.20	62.38
商洛市	**Shangluo**	**152654**	**72852**	**1395**	**13.06**	**0.03**	**104.62**	**38.37**	**798.22**
商州区	Shangzhou	16737	7678	1164	1.50	0.02	14.36	2.45	57.13
洛南县	Luonan	34725	11409	39	4.45		29.01	5.50	100.94
丹凤县	Danfeng	24802	6635	134	1.54		13.17	3.37	295.25
商南县	Shangnan	23421	13987		1.63		14.75	4.17	95.23
山阳县	Shanyang	32080	22798		1.30		21.34	10.11	136.35
镇安县	Zhen'an	12456	5732	58	1.64		7.19	9.76	47.61
柞水县	Zhashui	8433	4613		1.00		4.80	3.01	65.71
杨凌示范区	**Yangling**	**5325**	**2115**	**23721**	**1.72**	**0.66**	**4.36**	**0.23**	**18.60**

主要统计指标解释

农林牧渔业总产值　指以货币表现的农、林、牧、渔业全部产品和对农林牧渔业生产活动进行的各种支持性服务活动的价值总量，它反映一定时期内农林牧渔业生产总规模和总成果。1957 年以前的农林牧渔业总产值中包括了厩肥和农民自给性手工业(如农民自制衣服、鞋、袜，自己从事粮食初步加工等)。1958 年及以后，林业中增加了村及村以下竹木采伐产值；牧业中取消了厩肥产值；副业中取消了农民自给性手工业产值，增加了村及村以下办的工业产值；渔业中增加了海洋捕捞水产品产值。1980 年及以后，在副业中增加了农民家庭兼营工业商品部分的产值。从 1984 年起村及村以下工业产值划归工业。从 1993 年起取消副业，将野生动物的捕猎划入牧业，野生植物采集和农民家庭兼营商品性工业划归农业。从 2003 年起，执行新的国民经济行业分类标准，农林牧渔业总产值中包括了农林牧渔服务业产值。林业中增加了森林采运业产值。农业中取消了家庭兼营商品性工业产值，将野生林产品的采集划归林业。第一次农业普查以后，由于畜牧业产品年报数据与普查数据之间存在一定的差距，根据农业普查结果对畜牧业年报数据进行了修正，对畜牧业产值进行了相应修正。

农林牧渔业总产值的计算方法通常是按农、林、牧、渔业产品及其副产品的产量分别乘以各自单位产品价格求得；少数生产周期较长，当年没有产品或产品产量不易统计的，则采用间接方法匡算其产值；然后将四业产品产值及农林牧渔服务业产值相加即为农林牧渔业总产值。

粮食产量　指全社会的产量。包括国有经济经营的、集体统一经营的和农民家庭经营的粮食产量，还包括工矿企业办的农场和其他生产单位的产量。粮食除包括稻谷、小麦、玉米、高粱、谷子及其他杂粮外，还包括薯类和豆类。其产量计算方法，豆类按去豆荚后的干豆计算；薯类(包括甘薯和马铃薯，不包括芋头和木薯)1963 年以前按每 4 公斤鲜薯折 1 公斤粮食计算，从 1964 年开始改为按 5 公斤鲜薯折 1 公斤粮食计算。城市郊区作为蔬菜的薯类(如马铃薯等)按鲜品计算，并且不作粮食统计。其他粮食一律按脱粒后的原粮计算。1989 年以前全国粮食产量数据主要靠全面报表取得，1989 年开始使用抽样调查数据。

棉花产量　指全社会的产量。包括春播棉和夏播棉。产量按皮棉计算。不包括木棉。

油料产量　指全部油料作物的生产量。包括花生、油菜籽、芝麻、向日葵籽、胡麻籽（亚麻籽）和其他油料。不包括大豆、木本油料和野生油料。花生以带壳干花生计算。

水产品产量　指人工养殖的水产品和天然生长的水产品的捕捞量。包括海水的鱼类、虾蟹类、贝类和藻类以及内陆水域的鱼类、虾蟹类和贝类，不包括淡水生植物。水产品产量是通过各级水产和统计部门逐级上报取得数据。1995 年及以前，贝类中牡蛎按鲜肉计算；蚶、蛤、蛏按 5 斤鲜品折 1 斤计算。1996 年以后则统一按鲜品计算。

猪、牛、羊肉产量　指当年出栏并已屠宰、除去头蹄下水后带骨肉(即胴体重)的重量。包括全社会范围内的产量。1996 年前为各级逐级上报数据。1996 年第一次农业普查以后，由于畜牧业产品年报数据与普查数据之间存在一定的差距，根据普查结果对畜牧业年报数据进行了修正。1999 年以后，国家统计局在部分地区开展了猪、牛、羊、禽等主要畜禽品种的抽样调查，并用抽样数据作为国家定案数据使用。未开展抽样调查的地区和品种，仍使用各级统计部门逐级上报数据。2007 年，根据第二次农业普查结果，对 2000—2006 年畜牧业年报数据进行了修正。2008 年，建立了主要畜禽监测调查制度，猪、牛、羊、禽等主要畜牧业数据均以抽样调查数为法定数据。

期初(末)畜禽存栏头(只)数　指报告期初(末)农村各种合作经济组织和国营农场、农民个人、机关、团体、学校、工矿企业、部队等单位以及城镇居民饲养的大牲畜、猪、羊、家禽等畜禽的存栏数。数据上报方式及数据调整情况同猪、牛、羊肉产量。

农作物播种面积　指实际播种或移植有农作物的面积。凡是实际种植有农作物的面积，不论种植在耕地上还是种植在非耕地上，均包括在农作物播种面积中。在播种季节基本结束后，因遭灾而重新改种和补种的农作物面积，也包括在内。它是反映我国耕地面积利用情况的一个重要指标。目前，农作物播种面积主要包括粮食、棉花、油料、糖料、麻类、烟叶、蔬菜和瓜类、药材和其他农作物九大类。

农用化肥施用量　指本年内实际用于农业生产的化肥数量，包括氮肥、磷肥、钾肥和复合肥。化肥施用量要求按折纯量计算数量。折纯量是指把氮肥、磷肥、钾肥分别按含氮、含五氧化二磷、含氧化钾的百分之百成份进行折算后的数量。复合肥按其所含主要成分折算。公式为:

折纯量=实物量 × 某种化肥有效成份含量的百分比

农业机械总动力　指主要用于农、林、牧、渔业的各种动力机械的动力总和。包括耕作机械、排灌机械、收获机械、农用运输机械、植物保护机械、牧业机械、林业机械、渔业机械和其他农业机械〔内燃机按引擎马力折成瓦(特)计算、电动机按功率折成瓦(特)计算〕。不包括专门用于乡、镇、村、组办工业、基本建设、非农业运输、科学试验和教学等非农业生产方面用的动力机械与作业机械。这个指标的统计数据主要来源于农机部门。

Explanatory Notes on Main Statistical Indicators

Gross Output Value of Agriculture, Forestry, Animal Husbandry and Fishery refers to the total value of products of agriculture, forestry, animal husbandry and fishery, and total value of services in support of agriculture, forestry, animal husbandry and fishery activities. It reflects the total scale and results of agricultural production during a given period. Prior to 1957, China's gross agricultural output value included barnyard manure and handicraft products for self-consumption (clothes, shoes, stockings, and initial grain processing undertaken by peasants). Since 1958, cutting and felling of bamboo and trees by villages and other cooperative organizations under villages have been included in forestry; value of barnyard manure has been excluded from animal husbandry; self consumed handicrafts have not been included from sideline occupations, while the output value of industries run by villages and cooperative organizations under village has been included in sideline occupations; and the output value of fish catches by motor fishing boats has been added to fishery. Since 1980, the value of handicraft products made for sale by individuals in households has been added to sideline occupations. Since 1984, industries run by villages and under villages have been included in the sector of industry. Since 1993, the subdivision of sideline occupations has been cancelled, and the hunting of wild animals has been classified into animal husbandry, and the gathering of wild plants and commodity industry run by rural household have been included in farming. A new industrial classification of economic activities was introduced in 2003. Under the new classification, value of services to agriculture, forestry, animal husbandry and fishery is included in the gross output value of agriculture, value of wood felling and transport is included in forestry, value of industrial output by rural households is not included in agriculture, and the collection of wild forest products is taken from agriculture and included in forestry. The First Agriculture Census of China revealed some discrepancy between the production of animal products from the annual reports and that from the census. According to the result of the First Agriculture census, efforts were made to adjust the output value of animal husbandry to make the figures from the annual reports consistent with the census data.

Gross output value of agriculture is obtained by multiplying the output of each product or by-product by its price, resulting in the output value of each single item. For a small number of products, annual output of which is not available or difficult to get due to the long production (growing) process involved, the output value is estimated through an indirect approach. The sum of output values of all products of agriculture, forestry, animal husbandry and fishery and services in support to those industries is then equal to the gross output value of agriculture.

Grain Output refers to the total output in the whole country including grains produced by State farms, collective units, rural households, as well as by farms affiliated to industrial and mining enterprises and other production units. Grain includes rice, wheat, corn, sorghum, millet and other miscellaneous grains as well as tubers and beans. Output of beans refers to dry beans without pods. The output of tubers (sweet potatoes and potatoes, not including taros and cassava) are converted into that of grain at the ratio 4:1, i.e. 4 kilograms of fresh tubers were equivalent to 1 kilogram of grain up to 1963. Since 1964 the ratio for conversion has been 5:1. Tubers supplied as vegetables (such as potatoes) in cities and suburbs are calculated as fresh vegetables and their output is not included in the output of grain. Output of all other grains refers to husked grain. Data on grain production before 1989 were obtained through the Comprehensive Statistical Reporting System. Since 1989, data from sample surveys are used.

Cotton Output refers to cotton production in the whole country including cotton planted in spring and in autumn. Output is measured as the weight of ginned cotton. Ceiba is not included.

Output of Oil-bearing Crops refers to the total production of oil-bearing crops of various kinds, including peanuts (dry, in shell), rapeseeds, sesame, sunflower seeds, flax seeds, and other oil-bearing crops. Soybeans, oil-bearing woody plants, and wild oil-bearing crops are not included.

Output of Aquatic Products refers to catches of both artificially cultured and naturally grown aquatic products, including fish, shrimps, crabs and shellfish in sea and inland water as well as seaweed. Freshwater plants are not included. Data on output of aquatic products are reported by aquatic product and statistical agencies level by level. Before 1995, among the shellfish, oyster was counted as fresh meat; 5 kilograms of ark shell, clams and frogs are equivalent to 1 kilogram of fresh aquatic products; they have all been counted as fresh aquatic products since 1996.

Output of Pork, Beef, and Mutton refers to the meat of slaughtered hogs, cattle, sheep and goats with head, feet, and offal taken away. Data refers to the production of the whole country. The First Agricultural Census of China in 1996 revealed some discrepancy between the production of animal products from the annual reports and that from the census. Efforts were made to adjust the output value of animal husbandry to make the figures from the annual reports consistent with the census data. Since 1999, the NBS conducted sample surveys for the major animal husbandry products, such as hogs, cattle, sheep and goats and fowls, and the data from sample surveys are used as national finalized data. Those products, which are not covered by the sample survey, are still reported by statistical agencies level by level. In 2007, the data on animal husbandry from 2000 to 2006 were revised according to the results of the Second Agriculture Census of China. In 2008, A Monitoring and Survey Program was set up on main livestock, the data on the main livestock such as hog, cattle, sheep and poultry became the official data based on the sampling survey.

Number of Livestock or Poultry in Stock at Beginning (or End) of Period refers to the total number of large animals, pigs, sheep, fowls, etc. raised by rural cooperative organizations, State farms, rural individuals, government agencies, schools, industrial and mining enterprises, army, and urban residents at the beginning (or end) of the reference period. Data reporting system and data adjustment are the same as that in the output of pork, beef and mutton.

Sown Area of Crops refers to area of land sown or transplanted with crops regardless of being in cultivated area or non-cultivated area. Area of land re-sown due to natural disasters is also included. This is an important indicator that can reflect the utilization condition of the cultivated land in China. At present, the sown area of crops mainly include the following 9 categories of crops: grain, cotton, oil-bearing crops, sugar crops, flax crops, tobacco, vegetables and melons, medicinal materials and other farm crops.

Consumption of Chemical Fertilizers in Agriculture refers to the quantity of chemical fertilizers applied in agriculture in the year, including nitrogenous fertilizer, phosphate fertilizer, potash fertilizer, and compound fertilizer. The consumption of chemical fertilizers is calculated in terms of volume of effective components by means of converting the gross weight of the respective fertilizers into weight containing effective component (e.g. nitrogen content in nitrogenous fertilizer, phosphorous pentoxide contents in phosphate fertilizer, and potassium oxide contents in potash fertilizer). Compound fertilizer is converted in regard to its major components. The formula is:

Volume of effective component= physical quantity × effective component of certain chemical fertilizer (%)

Total Power of Agricultural Machinery refers to total mechanical power of machinery used in agriculture, forestry, animal husbandry and fishery, including machinery for ploughing, irrigation and drainage, harvesting, transport, plant protection, animal husbandry, forestry and fishery and other agricultural machineries. (For the power of internal combustion engines, it is converted from its horsepower into watts while for electric motors the output power is converted into watts.) Machinery employed for non-agricultural purposes, such as the machines used in township-run and village-run industry, construction, non-agricultural transport, scientific experiments and teaching, are not included. Data are mainly from agricultural machinery agencies.

十三、工　业

资料整理：杨　琨

简 要 说 明

一、本篇资料反映陕西工业经济方面的基本情况，内容包括全部工业总产值，规模以上工业企业按企业登记注册类型、轻重工业、企业规模、工业行业大类分组的主要经济指标和经济效益指标，主要工业产品产量。

二、规模以上工业企业统计范围

1998年至2006年为全部国有及年主营业务收入在500万元以上非国有工业企业。

2007至2010年为年主营业务收入在500万元以上工业企业。

2011年起提高到年主营业务收入在2000万元以上工业企业。

三、按照 2011 年《统计上大中小微型企业划分办法》，工业企业大中小微型划分标准是：

大型：从业人员 1000 人及以上、营业收入 40000 万元及以上。

中型：从业人员 300–1000 人、营业收入 2000–40000 万元。

小型：从业人员 20–300 人、营业收入 300–2000 万元。

微型：从业人员20人以下、营业收入300万元以下。

Brief Introduction

I. This chapter reflects the basic conditions of the industrial sector, mainly including economic indicators of industrial enterprises above designated size; as well as their economic indicators, efficiency indicators, output and production capacity of key industrial products classified by type of registration, by light and heavy industries, by size of enterprise, by branch of industry.

II. The Scopes of Industrial Statistics

The scopes of industrial statistics are all State-owned industrial enterprises and non-State-owned industrial enterprises with revenue from principal business over 5 million yuan from 1998 to 2006.

The scopes of industrial statistics are all industrial enterprises with revenue from principal business over 5 million yuan form 2007 to 2010.

The scopes of industrial statistics are raised to all industrial enterprises with revenue from principal business over 20 million yuan from 2011.

III. According to "*the Division Standard of Large/Medium/Small/Mini Sized Enterprises*" in 2011, the division standard of large/medium/small/mini sized enterprises is:

Large sized enterprises:

Number of employed persons:1000 person and above.

Amount of operating revenue:400 million yuan and above.

Medium sized enterprises:

Number of employed persons: 300-1000 person.

Amount of operating revenue: 20-400 million yuan.

Small sized enterprises:

Number of employed persons: 20-300 person.

Amount of operating revenue: 3-20 million yuan.

Mini sized enterprises:

Number of employed persons: 20 person and below.

Amount of operating revenue: 3 million yuan and below.

13.工　业

2014年全省

规模以上工业企业单位数	5017	个
# 大中型工业企业	927	个
全部工业总产值	21944.58	亿元
# 规模以上工业	20015.88	亿元

规模以上工业企业利税总额（亿元）

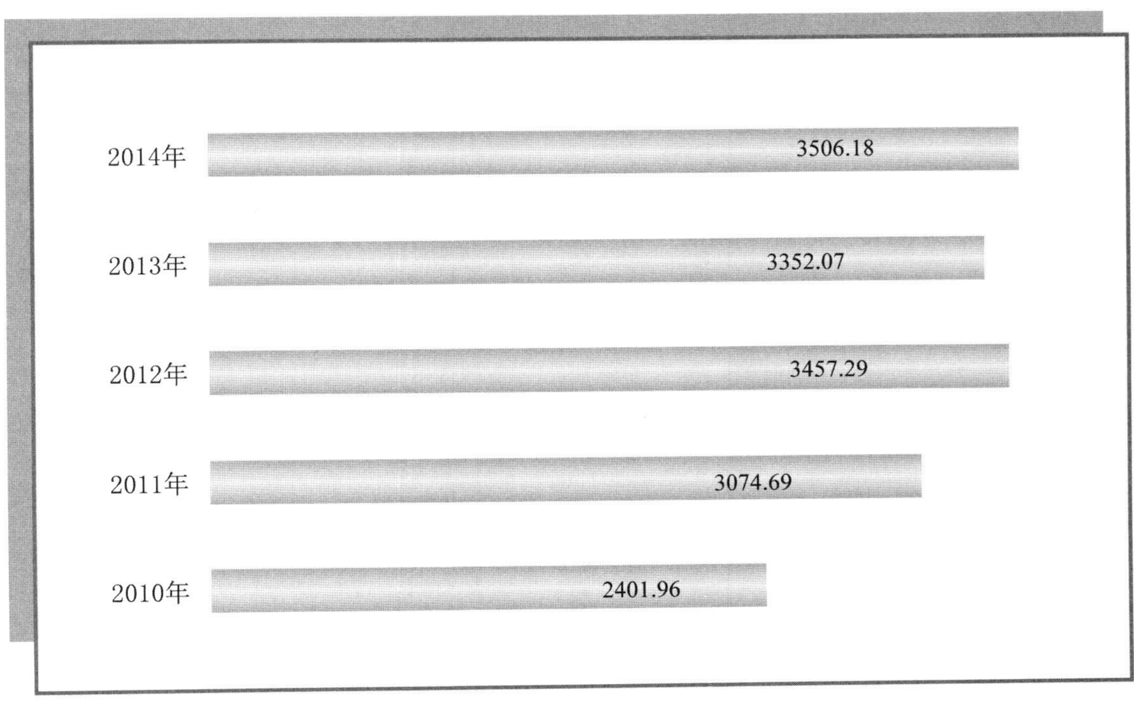

13-1 全部工业总产值
Gross Industrial Output Value

单位：亿元 (100 million yuan)

年份 Year	全部工业总产值 Gross Industrial Output Value	国有工业 State-owned Enterprises	集体工业 Collective-owned Enterprises	其他经济类型工业 Other Enterprises	城乡个体工业 Urban and Rural Individual-owned Enterprises	轻工业 Light Industry	重工业 Heavy Industry
1978	96.48	81.26	15.22			43.06	53.42
1979	105.79	90.19	15.61			47.23	58.56
1980	109.96	92.57	17.37	0.02		55.09	54.86
1981	108.64	91.22	17.32	0.10		59.24	49.39
1982	117.71	98.16	19.41	0.13		58.99	58.72
1983	131.77	110.38	21.24	0.15		61.86	69.90
1984	150.70	119.65	29.14	0.22	1.68	64.55	86.14
1985	192.08	145.69	42.39	0.29	3.72	80.11	111.98
1986	219.26	159.66	51.48	0.53	7.60	92.44	126.82
1987	258.44	185.25	60.79	0.81	11.59	108.09	150.35
1988	331.74	235.54	78.10	1.11	16.99	139.95	191.79
1989	406.71	284.91	94.48	2.36	24.95	168.70	238.01
1990	442.58	304.17	102.86	3.72	31.83	188.02	254.55
1991	508.81	348.64	114.40	8.17	37.59	214.41	294.40
1992	599.54	396.02	137.54	15.07	50.92	239.85	359.69
1993	793.78	483.97	194.74	37.70	77.37	281.03	512.75
1994	1009.76	585.08	257.39	57.81	109.48	370.67	639.08
1995	1068.71	627.99	266.78	112.73	61.21	398.13	670.58
1996	1168.54	671.48	309.90	115.30	71.87	426.52	742.02
1997	1284.14	680.18	335.03	172.10	96.82	489.77	794.37
1998	1318.81	727.42	361.64	140.92	88.82	508.72	810.09
1999	1501.05	839.29	401.43	159.79	100.54	581.16	919.90
2000	1714.18	974.75	446.00	183.38	110.04	602.35	1111.82
2001	1946.94	1106.23	483.07	233.73	123.91	674.97	1271.98
2002	2205.98	1247.29	521.63	299.00	138.05	736.57	1469.42
2003	2708.86	1526.71	603.29	424.87	153.99	816.83	1892.03
2004	3389.88	1878.00	687.52	651.98	172.38	932.13	2457.75
2005	4109.32	2332.47	785.71	822.00	169.15	988.16	3121.16
2006	5248.39	3165.22	954.71	936.98	191.49	1152.02	4096.37
2007	6587.41	4010.54	1136.90	1227.20	212.76	1371.40	5216.01
2008	8358.86	4900.65	1463.22	1748.76	246.24	1639.11	6719.76
2009	9553.70	5221.58	1642.76	2431.86	257.50	1920.50	7633.20
2010	12421.80	6900.46	1955.27	3275.61	290.46	2345.73	10076.07
2011	15811.48	8797.96	2338.01	4312.30	363.21	2958.11	12853.37
2012	18591.89	10216.05	2809.09	5170.89	395.87	3510.70	15081.19
2013	20820.07	10934.77	3075.93	6372.57	436.80	4139.23	16680.84
2014	21944.58	12286.42	3131.29	6068.42	458.45	4672.00	17272.58

13-2 规模以上工业企业主要经济指标(1998-2014年)
Main Indicators of Industrial Enterprises above Designated Size (1998-2014)

单位：亿元 (100 million yuan)

年 份 Year	企业单位数(个) Number of Enterprises (unit)	工业总产值 Gross Industrial Output Value	资产总计 Total Assets	主营业务收入 Revenue from Principal Business	利润总额 Total Profits	税金总额 Total Taxes
1998	2685	960.81	2158.36	867.48	-11.40	64.71
1999	2589	1097.45	2514.49	950.36	6.92	81.34
2000	2553	1268.43	2683.07	1133.82	63.80	91.71
2001	2440	1457.62	3071.06	1292.71	62.96	99.09
2002	2461	1667.10	3227.24	1503.30	93.18	119.94
2003	2493	2118.17	3672.72	1843.33	158.62	151.96
2004	3012	2735.22	4432.45	2632.18	253.90	212.45
2005	2997	3397.71	5085.90	3302.50	400.70	275.80
2006	3375	4442.81	6130.02	4380.18	523.95	339.49
2007	3372	5692.33	7494.03	5512.63	691.83	405.97
2008	3526	7322.92	9163.02	6944.88	872.63	469.13
2009	4480	8470.40	12119.26	8188.52	854.11	699.82
2010	4564	11199.84	14688.70	10888.80	1469.57	932.39
2011	3684	14283.48	17234.61	13790.12	1933.92	1140.77
2012	4284	16926.49	20591.16	16328.25	2057.22	1400.07
2013	4489	18982.47	22443.11	17763.00	1973.32	1378.75
2014	5017	20015.88	24371.44	18622.14	1846.98	1659.20

13-3 规模以上工业企业主要经济效益指标(1998-2014年)
Main Indicators on Economic Benefit of Industrial Enterprises above Designated Size(1998-2014)

年 份 Year	总资产贡献率(%) Ratio of Profits, Taxes and Interests to Average Assets (%)	资产负债率(%) Ratio of Debts to Assets (%)	流动资产周转次数(次/年) Turnover of Current Assets (times/year)	成本费用利润率(%) Ratio of Profits to Total Industrial Costs (%)	产品销售率(%) Sales Ratio of Products (%)
1998	4.96	71.53	0.99	-1.31	95.79
1999	6.06	68.86	1.03	0.74	96.00
2000	7.83	68.17	1.12	6.06	96.70
2001	7.58	66.01	1.15	5.19	97.17
2002	8.40	65.75	1.29	6.74	97.69
2003	10.40	63.94	1.34	9.71	97.59
2004	14.10	65.40	1.60	10.90	97.40
2005	15.38	62.15	1.72	14.46	97.74
2006	16.60	59.80	1.90	14.00	98.20
2007	17.27	57.35	1.97	14.54	97.49
2008	17.30	55.80	1.90	14.80	96.60
2009	13.60	56.00	1.60	12.30	95.90
2010	17.11	56.84	1.67	16.14	96.91
2011	18.84	56.61	1.82	16.97	96.52
2012	18.03	56.91	1.87	14.95	96.34
2013	16.00	56.06	2.02	12.86	95.20
2014	15.67	56.79	2.19	11.50	95.52

13-4 规模以上工业企业主要经济指标(2014年)

单位：万元

分 组	Item	企业单位数(个) Number of Enterprises (unit)	#亏损企业 Unprofitable Enterprises	工业总产值 Gross Industrial Output Value	工业销售产值 Sales Output Value
总 计	**Total**	**5017**	**860**	**200158820**	**191182693**
按登记注册类型分	**By Status of Registration**				
内资企业	Domestic Funded	4796	803	186334597	178567964
国有企业	State-owned Enterprises	141	41	16460716	15648976
中央企业	Central	29	4	11147228	10599751
地方企业	Local	112	37	5313488	5049225
集体企业	Collective-owned Enterprises	69	14	1229406	1196292
股份合作企业	Cooperative Enterprises	25	2	446593	436379
联营企业	Joint Ownership Enterprises	7	2	192221	188863
国有联营企业	State Joint Ownership Enterprises	2		112648	115901
集体联营企业	Collective Joint Ownership Enterprises	2	1	15747	16030
国有与集体联营企业	Joint State-collective Enterprises	1		44206	38505
其他联营企业	Other Joint Ownership Enterprises	2	1	19620	18427
有限责任公司	Limited Liability Corporations	2555	486	101748824	97068551
国有独资公司	State Sole Funded Corporations	96	30	22759506	22664588
其他有限责任公司	Other Limited Liability Corporations	2459	456	78989319	74403963
股份有限公司	Share-holding Corporations Limited	261	41	37054078	35909757
私营企业	Private Enterprises	1715	217	28814393	27752902
私营独资企业	Private-funded Enterprises	101	11	1667109	1587597
私营合作企业	Private Partnership Enterprises	49	12	1061746	1033434
私营有限责任公司	Private Limited Liability Corporations	1443	179	23017158	22221818
私营股份有限公司	Private Share-holding Corporations Ltd.	122	15	3068380	2910053
其他企业	Other Enterprises	23		388365	366244
港、澳、台商投资企业	Enterprises with Funds from Hong Kong, Macao and Taiwan	59	18	2457550	2221974
合资经营企业(港或澳、台资)	Joint-venture Enterprises	26	8	1151518	1017001
合作经营企业(港或澳、台资)	Cooperative Enterprises	2		293914	293740
港澳台商独资经营企业	Enterprises with Sole Investment	28	10	919660	818894
港澳台商投资股份有限公司	Share-holding Corporations Ltd.	3		92458	92339
外商投资企业	Foreign Funded Enterprises	162	39	11366673	10392755
中外合资经营企业	Joint-venture Enterprises	90	20	7619021	7032283
中外合作经营企业	Cooperation Enterprises	4		259967	259561
外资企业	Enterprises with Sole Funds	60	18	2978200	2685880
外商投资股份有限公司	Share-holding Corporations Ltd.	6	1	430672	359611

Main Indicators of Industrial Enterprises above Designated Size(2014)

(10 000 yuan)

资产总计 Total Assets	流动资产合计 Total Current Assets	#应收账款 Accounts Receivable	#存货 Inventories	#产成品 Finished products	固定资产合计 Total of Fixed Assets	固定资产原价 Original Value of Fixed Assets	累计折旧 Total Depreciation	负债合计 Total Liabilities	#流动负债 Total Working Liabilities
243714377	**84915479**	**17516199**	**18442887**	**7908792**	**111614224**	**174436931**	**69004715**	**138404283**	**90879252**
227979246	79181272	16169412	17085247	7384332	103611266	163020251	65252625	129836128	84338338
28076968	7736357	1771509	1486663	712673	14461575	21609293	7532204	18711285	11653849
14691167	4051129	1221017	954907	444981	8726007	14798890	6121248	8440624	5916541
13385801	3685228	550492	531757	267692	5735567	6810403	1410956	10270661	5737308
638636	311160	79102	54001	18273	266788	532914	329745	327377	241398
638741	296440	30731	117723	43057	189580	245259	58361	351463	292978
101443	53825	10949	11309	8929	34643	91258	56625	53190	35952
74833	42962	9056	9182	7565	24738	71682	46943	34372	24717
11037	6773	1415	571	481	403	7453	7060	9838	6923
4903	982	236	746	231	3921	4683	762	1300	1300
10670	3108	243	810	652	5581	7440	1860	7681	3013
121214726	49978253	9790301	11199397	4607736	42916694	62824560	24263613	71631374	49244680
45891468	17740677	2466955	3368748	1326622	11614686	17420594	6390526	25596915	15695501
75323259	32237576	7323346	7830650	3281114	31302008	45403966	17873088	46034459	33549179
58291207	12819484	2434043	2292240	879186	38052994	66072519	28408141	29212039	15957125
18705376	7911062	2038697	1904255	1100274	7509837	11331839	4467289	9367424	6763780
977560	324750	73815	67337	43915	474526	752376	239842	410198	238684
1173778	453755	138506	30745	22391	467613	492075	105705	535595	326474
14325951	6261884	1648617	1605448	905888	5750825	9074468	3855391	7440520	5426273
2228087	870673	177759	200725	128080	816873	1012919	266352	981111	772348
312148	74692	14081	19658	14204	179155	312609	136647	181978	148575
2471545	1290319	216184	224425	67092	862614	1904061	1064481	1095360	899164
909602	459475	114757	88772	31798	319299	527898	219894	382022	279770
250228	127099	24626	11812		86189	643868	557679	82857	80812
1068825	616204	63383	110721	32523	323681	569762	257821	452991	361922
242889	87542	13419	13120	2771	133446	162532	29087	177490	176661
13263586	4443888	1130602	1133215	457368	7140343	9512620	2687609	7472795	5641751
6320501	2826920	598140	591848	263467	2463434	3494852	1252261	3687741	2807100
134041	35036	24359	4140	688	86590	185540	102319	47818	17062
6242322	1347670	455734	427180	93090	4291984	5191265	967144	3381348	2540251
492843	223505	49569	103559	100123	237781	539032	321979	283966	206277

13-4 续表 1

单位：万元

分　组	Item	企业单位数（个） Number of Enterprises (unit)	#亏损企业 Unprofitable Enterprises	工业总产值 Gross Industrial Output Value	工业销售产值 Sales Output Value
按经济组织类型分	**By Economic Type of Orgnization**				
独资企业	Appropratorship	399	94	23255092	21937639
国有企业	State-owned Enterprises	141	41	16460716	15648976
集体企业	Collective-owned Enterprises	69	14	1229406	1196292
私营独资企业	Private-funded Enterprises	101	11	1667109	1587597
港澳台商独资经营企业	Enterprises with Sole Investment	28	10	919660	818894
外资企业	Enterprises with Sole Funds	60	18	2978200	2685880
合作、合伙企业	Partnership	110	16	2642806	2578221
股份合作企业	Cooperative Enterprises	25	2	446593	436379
国有联营企业	State Joint Ownership Enterprises	2		112648	115901
集体联营企业	Collective Joint Ownership Enterprises	2	1	15747	16030
国有与集体联营企业	Joint State-collective Enterprises	1		44206	38505
其他联营企业	Other Joint Ownership Enterprises	2	1	19620	18427
私营合伙企业	Private Partnership Enterprises	49	12	1061746	1033434
合作经营企业(港或澳、台资)	Cooperative Enterprises	2		293914	293740
中外合作经营企业	Cooperation Enterprises	4		259967	259561
其他企业(内资)	Other Enterprises	23		388365	366244
股份有限公司	Share-holding Corporations Limited	392	57	40645588	39271761
股份有限公司(内资)	Share-holding Corporations Ltd.	261	41	37054078	35909757
私营股份有限公司	Private Share-holding Corporations Ltd.	122	15	3068380	2910053
港澳台商投资股份有限公司	Share-holding Corporations Ltd.with Funds from Hong Kong, Macao and Taiwan	3		92458	92339
外商投资股份有限公司	Share-holding Corporations Ltd.with Foreign Investment	6	1	430672	359611
有限责任公司	Limited Liability Corporations	4114	693	133536521	127339652
国有独资公司	State Sole Funded Corporations	96	30	22759506	22664588
私营有限责任公司	Private Limited Liability Corporations	1443	179	23017158	22221818
合资经营企业(港或澳、台资)	Joint-venture Enterprises	26	8	1151518	1017001
中外合资经营企业	Joint-venture Enterprises	90	20	7619021	7032283
其他有限责任公司	Other Corporations	2459	456	78989319	74403963
按轻重工业分	**Grouped by Light & Heavy Industries**				
轻工业	Light Industry	1589	164	35928915	33923093
重工业	Heavy Industry	3428	696	164229905	157259600
按企业规模分	**Grouped by Size of Enterprises**				
大型企业	Large Enterprises	172	28	99450686	96237624
中型企业	Medium-sized Enterprises	755	138	44554666	41478023
小型企业	Small Enterprises	3879	631	54563961	51982591
微型企业	Mini Enterprises	211	63	1589506	1484455

continued

(10 000 yuan)

资产总计 Total Assets	流动资产合计 Total Current Assets	#应收账款 Accounts Receivable	#存货 Inventories	#产成品 Finished products	固定资产合计 Total of Fixed Assets	固定资产原价 Original Value of Fixed Assets	累计折旧 Total Depreciation	负债合计 Total Liabilities	#流动负债 Total Working Liabilities
37004311	10336141	2443543	2145902	900473	19818553	28655610	9326756	23283198	15036105
28076968	7736357	1771509	1486663	712673	14461575	21609293	7532204	18711285	11653849
638636	311160	79102	54001	18273	266788	532914	329745	327377	241398
977560	324750	73815	67337	43915	474526	752376	239842	410198	238684
1068825	616204	63383	110721	32523	323681	569762	257821	452991	361922
6242322	1347670	455734	427180	93090	4291984	5191265	967144	3381348	2540251
2610379	1040846	243252	195387	89269	1043770	1970609	1017336	1252901	901853
638741	296440	30731	117723	43057	189580	245259	58361	351463	292978
74833	42962	9056	9182	7565	24738	71682	46943	34372	24717
11037	6773	1415	571	481	403	7453	7060	9838	6923
4903	982	236	746	231	3921	4683	762	1300	1300
10670	3108	243	810	652	5581	7440	1860	7681	3013
1173778	453755	138506	30745	22391	467613	492075	105705	535595	326474
250228	127099	24626	11812		86189	643868	557679	82857	80812
134041	35036	24359	4140	688	86590	185540	102319	47818	17062
312148	74692	14081	19658	14204	179155	312609	136647	181978	148575
61255027	14001203	2674789	2609644	1110161	39241094	67787002	29025559	30654606	17112411
58291207	12819484	2434043	2292240	879186	38052994	66072519	28408141	29212039	15957125
2228087	870673	177759	200725	128080	816873	1012919	266352	981111	772348
242889	87542	13419	13120	2771	133446	162532	29087	177490	176661
492843	223505	49569	103559	100123	237781	539032	321979	283966	206277
142770780	59526532	12151815	13485465	5808889	51450253	75921779	29591159	83141656	57757822
45891468	17740677	2466955	3368748	1326622	11614686	17420594	6390526	25596915	15695501
14325951	6261884	1648617	1605448	905888	5750825	9074468	3855391	7440520	5426273
909602	459475	114757	88772	31798	319299	527898	219894	382022	279770
6320501	2826920	598140	591848	263467	2463434	3494852	1252261	3687741	2807100
75323259	32237576	7323346	7830650	3281114	31302008	45403966	17873088	46034459	33549179
21135481	10786815	2109225	3701024	1592903	7404800	12558362	5985901	9770589	7355920
222578896	74128665	15406973	14741863	6315889	104209424	161878569	63018814	128633694	83523332
152782675	47407233	7785091	9474599	3645627	74416219	119753246	47822634	86435975	55728660
46133983	17140320	3735628	4157464	1908301	20290831	31176336	13025670	27615385	18357495
42937012	19456152	5797395	4587610	2235074	16532238	22878241	7829857	22998940	16397222
1860707	911774	198085	223214	119790	374936	629109	326554	1353982	395876

13-4 续表 2

单位：万元

分　组	Item	所有者权益合　计 Owners' Equity	主营业务收　入 Revenue from Principal Business	主营业务成　本 Cost of Principal Business	主营业务税金及附加 Tax and Extra Charges from Principal Business
总　计	**Total**	**105199889**	**186221351**	**143675613**	**7188756**
按登记注册类型分	**By Status of Registration**				
内资企业	Domestic Funded	98046479	174341568	134180434	7072647
国有企业	State-owned Enterprises	9349190	14547527	11750040	275233
中央企业	Central	6250543	10333450	8658277	200622
地方企业	Local	3098646	4214077	3091764	74611
集体企业	Collective-owned Enterprises	304582	1204841	1012883	13387
股份合作企业	Cooperative Enterprises	284958	385797	308665	5975
联营企业	Joint Ownership Enterprises	48253	134817	98580	3481
国有联营企业	State Joint Ownership Enterprises	40461	65643	42728	1899
集体联营企业	Collective Joint Ownership Enterprises	1199	13127	12755	10
国有与集体联营企业	Joint State-collective Enterprises	3603	39411	29558	493
其他联营企业	Other Joint Ownership Enterprises	2989	16636	13538	1080
有限责任公司	Limited Liability Corporations	49459116	98289827	79478898	3352018
国有独资公司	State Sole Funded Corporations	20294086	26283744	20102134	2755046
其他有限责任公司	Other Limited Liability Corporations	29165030	72006083	59376764	596972
股份有限公司	Share-holding Corporations Limited	29063036	33024670	19775587	3120704
私营企业	Private Enterprises	9408144	26356105	21442801	292767
私营独资企业	Private-funded Enterprises	751799	1552855	1203021	31289
私营合作企业	Private Partnership Enterprises	637747	990724	650422	23901
私营有限责任公司	Private Limited Liability Corporations	6811843	20998888	17319080	199990
私营股份有限公司	Private Share-holding Corporations Ltd.	1206756	2813639	2270278	37587
其他企业	Other Enterprises	129201	397985	312980	9083
港、澳、台商投资企业	Enterprises with Funds from Hong Kong, Macao and Taiwan	1375686	2218424	1806666	13255
合资经营企业(港或澳、台资)	Joint-venture Enterprises	527081	1011812	883615	6341
合作经营企业(港或澳、台资)	Cooperative Enterprises	167372	287060	210352	2505
港澳台商独资经营企业	Enterprises with Sole Investment	615835	811318	635991	3956
港澳台商投资股份有限公司	Share-holding Corporations Ltd.	65399	108234	76708	453
外商投资企业	Foreign Funded Enterprises	5777724	9661359	7688513	102854
中外合资经营企业	Joint-venture Enterprises	2632746	6405490	5147596	84149
中外合作经营企业	Cooperation Enterprises	73173	259557	201755	1196
外资企业	Enterprises with Sole Funds	2860971	2670548	2079367	15096
外商投资股份有限公司	Share-holding Corporations Ltd.	208877	283767	224323	1948

continued

(10 000 yuan)

销售费用 Operating Expenses	管理费用 Manage-ment Expenses	财务费用 Financial Expenses	利润总额 Total Profits	亏损企业亏损额 Losses of Unprofitable Enterprises	利税总额 Total Profits and Taxes	本年应交增值税 Value Added Tax Payable	全部从业人员年平均人数(人) Annual Average Employed Persons (person)
4765311	**8993971**	**3134243**	**18469820**	**1303035**	**35061771**	**9403194**	**1547285**
4187400	8301792	3039709	17311435	1193625	33267643	8883561	1431300
328475	821912	304638	985027	260422	2045764	785504	147798
176930	421046	186205	813037	50134	1493927	480268	81099
151545	400867	118433	171990	210238	551837	305236	66699
27118	49772	4744	93383	4118	161884	55115	18141
11107	21857	6053	34576	331	59506	18955	4381
5976	21557	971	9365	107	25208	12362	1646
3452	16050	356	6302		16458	8258	961
30	264	27	11	15	125	103	185
1892	3744	591	3133		6191	2565	121
602	1500	-2	-81	93	2435	1436	379
2535008	3921924	1824496	6676281	682264	13972186	3943887	766779
501042	986469	589224	1561042	87783	5571890	1255802	148901
2033966	2935455	1235272	5115239	594481	8400296	2688085	617878
464816	2501660	591198	7001400	157135	13100216	2978112	237936
803100	951330	303819	2463588	89248	3826047	1069692	250208
46707	67614	9025	191584	4310	312707	89834	15362
63162	76071	13681	159722	11209	282784	99161	9271
619170	713940	250551	1861484	67366	2819430	757956	201840
74062	93705	30563	250798	6362	411126	122741	23735
11800	11781	3789	47817		76833	19933	4411
61670	101283	5091	239709	33126	352105	99141	21112
18616	38877	5576	83616	7898	131915	41958	7949
	6976	-2242	71556		92433	18372	2335
35077	41311	1139	74138	25229	113358	35264	8480
7977	14119	619	10399		14399	3547	2348
516241	590895	89443	918677	76284	1442023	420493	94873
367504	323009	52010	577306	50266	986099	324644	65537
1536	6073	1621	43090		59077	14791	1019
136137	248319	22048	262329	24566	340722	63297	25643
10654	10962	11563	32735	1453	49460	14776	2116

13-4 续表 3

单位：万元

分 组	Item	所有者权益合 计 Owners' Equity	主营业务收 入 Revenue from Principal Business	主营业务成 本 Cost of Principal Business	主营业务税金及附加 Tax and Extra Charges from Principal Business
按经济组织类型分	**By Economic Type of Orgnization**				
独资企业	Appropratorship	13882376	20787089	16681302	338960
国有企业	State-owned Enterprises	9349190	14547527	11750040	275233
集体企业	Collective-owned Enterprises	304582	1204841	1012883	13387
私营独资企业	Private-funded Enterprises	751799	1552855	1203021	31289
港澳台商独资经营企业	Enterprises with Sole Investment	615835	811318	635991	3956
外资企业	Enterprises with Sole Funds	2860971	2670548	2079367	15096
合作、合伙企业	Partnership	1340704	2455939	1782753	46141
股份合作企业	Cooperative Enterprises	284958	385797	308665	5975
国有联营企业	State Joint Ownership Enterprises	40461	65643	42728	1899
集体联营企业	Collective Joint Ownership Enterprises	1199	13127	12755	10
国有与集体联营企业	Joint State-collective Enterprises	3603	39411	29558	493
其他联营企业	Other Joint Ownership Enterprises	2989	16636	13538	1080
私营合伙企业	Private Partnership Enterprises	637747	990724	650422	23901
合作经营企业(港或澳、台资)	Cooperative Enterprises	167372	287060	210352	2505
中外合作经营企业	Cooperation Enterprises	73173	259557	201755	1196
其他企业(内资)	Other Enterprises	129201	397985	312980	9083
股份有限公司	Share-holding Corporations Limited	30544068	36230309	22346896	3160692
股份有限公司(内资)	Share-holding Corporations Ltd.	29063036	33024670	19775587	3120704
私营股份有限公司	Private Share-holding Corporations Ltd.	1206756	2813639	2270278	37587
港澳台商投资股份有限公司	Share-holding Corporations Ltd.with Funds from Hong Kong, Macao and Taiwan	65399	108234	76708	453
外商投资股份有限公司	Share-holding Corporations Ltd.with Foreign Investment	208877	283767	224323	1948
有限责任公司	Limited Liability Corporations	59430785	126706016	102829189	3642499
国有独资公司	State Sole Funded Corporations	20294086	26283744	20102134	2755046
私营有限责任公司	Private Limited Liability Corporations	6811843	20998888	17319080	199990
合资经营企业(港或澳、台资)	Joint-venture Enterprises	527081	1011812	883615	6341
中外合资经营企业	Joint-venture Enterprises	2632746	6405490	5147596	84149
其他有限责任公司	Other Corporations	29165030	72006083	59376764	596972
按轻重工业分	**Grouped by Light & Heavy Industries**				
轻工业	Light Industry	11287327	32436116	24770131	1321693
重工业	Heavy Industry	93912562	153785236	118905482	5867063
按企业规模分	**Grouped by Size of Enterprises**				
大型企业	Large Enterprises	66346690	96154389	70759650	5786973
中型企业	Medium-sized Enterprises	18505793	38839180	30092258	911133
小型企业	Small Enterprises	20069327	49694124	41485810	473876
微型企业	Mini Enterprises	278080	1533658	1337895	16774

continued

(10 000 yuan)

销售费用 Operating Expenses	管理费用 Manage-ment Expenses	财务费用 Financial Expenses	利润总额 Total Profits	亏损企业亏损额 Losses of Unprofitable Enterprises	利税总额 Total Profits and Taxes	本年应交增值税 Value Added Tax Payable	全部从业人员年平均人数(人) Annual Average Employed Persons (person)
573514	1228929	341593	1606460	318644	2974434	1029014	215424
328475	821912	304638	985027	260422	2045764	785504	147798
27118	49772	4744	93383	4118	161884	55115	18141
46707	67614	9025	191584	4310	312707	89834	15362
35077	41311	1139	74138	25229	113358	35264	8480
136137	248319	22048	262329	24566	340722	63297	25643
93581	144314	23874	366126	11647	595841	183574	23063
11107	21857	6053	34576	331	59506	18955	4381
3452	16050	356	6302		16458	8258	961
30	264	27	11	15	125	103	185
1892	3744	591	3133		6191	2565	121
602	1500	-2	-81	93	2435	1436	379
63162	76071	13681	159722	11209	282784	99161	9271
	6976	-2242	71556		92433	18372	2335
1536	6073	1621	43090		59077	14791	1019
11800	11781	3789	47817		76833	19933	4411
557508	2620446	633943	7295332	164951	13575201	3119176	266135
464816	2501660	591198	7001400	157135	13100216	2978112	237936
74062	93705	30563	250798	6362	411126	122741	23735
7977	14119	619	10399		14399	3547	2348
10654	10962	11563	32735	1453	49460	14776	2116
3540298	4997749	2132632	9198686	807793	17909630	5068445	1042105
501042	986469	589224	1561042	87783	5571890	1255802	148901
619170	713940	250551	1861484	67366	2819430	757956	201840
18616	38877	5576	83616	7898	131915	41958	7949
367504	323009	52010	577306	50256	986099	324644	65537
2033966	2935455	1235272	5115239	594431	8400296	2688085	617878
1680409	1287610	264692	3125548	73537	5871646	1424405	331672
3084903	7706360	2869551	15344272	1229449	29190125	7978790	1215613
2009639	5084914	1810016	10880409	433760	22261312	5593930	713026
1226664	1832179	739136	3912824	464302	6795512	1971555	407532
1488962	2004844	559402	3634994	378945	5887988	1779119	423440
40047	72034	25689	41594	26028	116958	58590	3287

13-5 规模以上工业企业分行业主要经济指标(2014年)

单位：万元

分组	Item	企业单位数（个）Number of Enterprises (unit)	#亏损企业 Unprofitable Enterprises	工业总产值 Gross Industrial Output Value
总　　计	**Total**	**5017**	**860**	**200158820**
煤炭开采和洗选业	Mining and Washing of Coal	468	127	23152244
石油和天然气开采业	Extraction of Petroleum and Natural Gas	8	1	19543748
黑色金属矿采选业	Mining and Processing of Ferrous Metal Ores	63	18	1674232
有色金属矿采选业	Mining and Processing of Non-Ferrous Metal Ores	97	14	2419957
非金属矿采选业	Mining and Processing of Non-metal Ores	73	5	952949
开采辅助活动	Support Activities for Mining	27	1	1099780
农副食品加工业	Processing of Food from Agricultural Products	493	45	10386543
食品制造业	Manufacture of Foods	198	14	4352639
酒、饮料和精制茶制造业	Manufacture of Liquor, Beverages and Refined Tea	208	12	4780989
烟草制品业	Manufacture of Tobacco	3		2179499
纺织业	Manufacture of Textile	120	18	2205452
纺织服装、服饰业	Manufacture of Textile, Wearing Apparel and Accessories	38	1	565103
皮革、毛皮、羽毛及其制品和制鞋业	Manufacture of Leather, Fur, Feather and Related Products and Footwear	9	1	126728
木材加工和木、竹、藤、棕、草制品业	Processing of Timber, Manufacture of Wood, Bamboo, Rattan, Palm and Straw Products	33	4	599907
家具制造业	Manufacture of Furniture	23	2	211811
造纸及纸制品业	Manufacture of Paper and Paper Products	68	6	1193100
印刷和记录媒介复制业	Printing and Reproduction of Recording Media	52	4	932174
文教、工美、体育和娱乐用品制造业	Manufacture of Articles for Culture, Education, Arts and Crafts, Sport and Entertainment Activities	15	3	541335
石油加工、炼焦及核燃料加工业	Processing of Petroleum, Coking and Processing of Nuclear Fuel	107	57	18198964
化学原料及化学制品制造业	Manufacture of Raw Chemical Materials and Chemical Products	306	64	8498350
医药制造业	Manufacture of Medicines	182	27	5108033
化学纤维制造业	Manufacture of Chemical Fibres	8	2	170743
橡胶和塑料制品业	Manufacture of Rubber and Plastics Products	133	10	3864436
非金属矿物制品业	Manufacture of Non-metallic Mineral Products	588	100	10903279
黑色金属冶炼和压延加工业	Smelting and Pressing of Ferrous Metals	120	33	9070138
有色金属冶炼和压延加工业	Smelting and Pressing of Non-ferrous Metals	175	43	14355528
金属制品业	Manufacture of Metal Products	144	17	2358334
通用设备制造业	Manufacture of General Purpose Machinery	224	27	4897682
专用设备制造业	Manufacture of Special Purpose Machinery	246	48	5164971
汽车制造业	Manufacture of Automobiles	109	24	11643957
铁路、船舶、航空航天和其他运输设备制造业	Manufacture of Railway, Ship, Aerospace and Other Transport Equipments	79	8	2799299
电气机械和器材制造业	Manufacture of Electrical Machinery and Apparatus	221	35	7227854
计算机、通信和其他电子设备制造业	Manufacture of Computers, Communication and Other Electronic Equipment	93	15	3004571
仪器仪表制造业	Manufacture of Measuring Instruments and Machinery	50	10	1155533
其他制造业	Other Manufacture	19	5	257039
废弃资源综合利用业	Utilization of Waste Resources	11		132310
金属制品、机械和设备修理业	Repair Service of Metal Products, Machinery and Equipment	6	1	23026
电力、热力生产和供应业	Production and Supply of Electric Power and Heat Power	131	40	12680432
燃气生产和供应业	Production and Supply of Gas	44	8	1528146
水的生产和供应业	Production and Supply of Water	25	10	198010

Main Indicators of Industrial Enterprises above Designated Size by Industrial Sector (2014)

(10 000 yuan)

工业销售产值 Sales Output Value	资产总计 Total Assets	流动资产合计 Total Current Assets	#应收账款 Accounts Receivable	#存货 Inventories	#产成品 Finished products	固定资产合计 Total of Fixed Assets	固定资产原价 Original Value of Fixed Assets	累计折旧 Total Depreciation	负债合计 Total Liabilities	#流动负债 Total Working Liabilities
191182693	**243714377**	**84915479**	**17516199**	**18442887**	**7908792**	**111614224**	**174436931**	**69004715**	**138404283**	**90879252**
22308953	36317808	13791565	2734578	1034728	382488	13974655	18029971	5937228	17270061	11594759
19405714	38871434	3639816	97593	456802	162754	31827542	56552845	24782632	20521258	9932925
1398714	1426661	550523	110014	101138	80154	554500	597734	169452	870463	698837
2234630	1607920	640132	80225	189236	83761	572037	764838	271180	957797	734460
914955	491763	205926	43426	48137	31459	201342	247581	53715	197338	140592
1090894	898922	537419	386077	32187	15177	334357	446518	117366	591227	476990
9909609	4024808	2051673	318962	884906	394326	1386295	1952627	723081	2064004	1618853
4114540	2029156	956343	209567	202303	99547	808570	1239459	496338	875536	700515
4470619	3280577	1492347	295445	588278	399294	1310159	1932234	757157	1611789	1248695
2155226	1500006	1013384	91645	639020	33554	334500	676186	341686	235983	235914
2084265	1280267	546890	81565	275003	122488	630402	912441	369095	665061	565974
516795	343061	210305	45139	97372	28631	108521	143121	47006	161585	115616
109142	75962	47110	5864	16611	11721	8159	12318	5021	36300	28362
549284	478200	195147	24039	51566	23265	167930	229000	93889	252610	118327
201834	109715	53096	11256	14653	6346	42103	49180	18435	42002	38887
1122074	561068	179164	43150	59408	29816	311301	788094	509440	234284	167947
895773	823875	378124	69338	77643	35292	343463	553277	262822	297780	243725
537359	211802	188831	172651	8055	3136	16208	22566	6668	182328	178667
18161690	27501591	10029519	933162	1405615	740546	4852936	6857444	2525811	14852558	10653343
8077668	18412727	4536969	839825	815320	412211	8701014	11398284	2987900	13258039	6602367
4738787	3856532	2246957	458369	580720	298904	1063563	2361695	1478051	1737411	1441294
168934	106021	54157	9814	13850	6431	36083	82614	46542	21795	21337
3377060	2533266	1166864	268003	359360	220339	1100003	2618776	1738891	1497851	1086799
10314205	7248772	2655322	821357	665615	307801	3997989	6553606	2960715	4013056	3115846
8522465	6177828	2693438	333542	831129	420589	3008474	4003805	1473271	4637106	4096899
13391074	13005479	6277611	776743	2308667	774432	4396702	5975834	1715263	6905923	5157454
2213103	3381405	1100968	318038	276212	133768	1641988	2054719	460646	1786870	1093631
4636574	4937931	3169944	801591	857136	341935	1046299	2674014	1692852	2549182	2266193
4750943	7260668	4514682	1635563	1427150	655913	1898862	2795174	1009137	4171997	3567878
11108829	8602877	4762676	781860	1082144	639240	2120837	3077578	1140829	5577973	4864617
2624646	2679056	1766956	691571	484112	144477	490285	791429	372088	1409084	1212268
6941872	8080977	5318509	1919878	1136109	530880	1832325	3891608	2143595	4334762	3564028
2834311	6867946	1826014	681597	480299	110294	3866438	4805079	983964	3664754	2758307
1053507	1364051	878012	377635	174556	71138	227580	431298	211679	613844	492283
232007	275321	177656	68595	25602	8519	84169	109936	30196	91184	82018
132068	102094	56375	9883	6384	3903	32286	37871	8622	54498	42670
19693	28504	24225	12823	6772	2447	2986	4669	1684	17424	16622
12178885	23959927	3910617	872087	663286	129222	17021515	27047554	10520944	18385082	8834824
1491200	1887807	736835	45838	58025	12365	852523	1090863	280325	1072788	826907
192793	1110593	333377	37891	7780	235	406725	623096	259501	683699	241624

13-5 续表

单位：万元

分组	Item	所有者权益合计 Owners' Equity	主营业务收入 Revenue from Principal Business	主营业务成本 Cost of Principal Business
总　计	**Total**	**105199889**	**186221351**	**143675613**
煤炭开采和洗选业	Mining and Washing of Coal	18954013	19792151	13045005
石油和天然气开采业	Extraction of Petroleum and Natural Gas	18349192	18077610	8535098
黑色金属矿采选业	Mining and Processing of Ferrous Metal Ores	555707	1215321	1012566
有色金属矿采选业	Mining and Processing of Non-Ferrous Metal Ores	644511	2144474	1744639
非金属矿采选业	Mining and Processing of Non-metal Ores	251253	885661	668757
开采辅助活动	Support Activities for Mining	307696	1255569	1168670
农副食品加工业	Processing of Food from Agricultural Products	1896228	9236586	8058982
食品制造业	Manufacture of Foods	1148797	3869371	3106594
酒、饮料和精制茶制造业	Manufacture of Liquor, Beverages and Refined Tea	1659550	4345752	3015837
烟草制品业	Manufacture of Tobacco	1264024	2139159	714302
纺织业	Manufacture of Textile	607149	2098779	1755470
纺织服装、服饰业	Manufacture of Textile, Wearing Apparel and Accessories	175999	507978	396383
皮革、毛皮、羽毛及其制品和制鞋业	Manufacture of Leather, Fur, Feather and Related Products and Footwear	39662	119838	100223
木材加工和木、竹、藤、棕、草制品业	Processing of Timber, Manufacture of Wood, Bamboo, Rattan, Palm and Straw Products	225590	500535	423844
家具制造业	Manufacture of Furniture	67709	203696	158683
造纸及纸制品业	Manufacture of Paper and Paper Products	326783	1047109	881178
印刷和记录媒介复制业	Printing and Reproduction of Recording Media	526086	852430	639527
文教、工美、体育和娱乐用品制造业	Manufacture of Articles for Culture, Education, Arts and Crafts, Sport and Entertainment Activities	29202	492511	477942
石油加工、炼焦及核燃料加工业	Processing of Petroleum, Coking and Processing of Nuclear Fuel	12647166	20972552	16212628
化学原料及化学制品制造业	Manufacture of Raw Chemical Materials and Chemical Products	5146695	7793618	6331376
医药制造业	Manufacture of Medicines	2104201	4521571	3010808
化学纤维制造业	Manufacture of Chemical Fibres	84226	166105	137403
橡胶和塑料制品业	Manufacture of Rubber and Plastics Products	1032730	3437386	2908293
非金属矿物制品业	Manufacture of Non-metallic Mineral Products	3209429	9624609	8151397
黑色金属冶炼和压延加工业	Smelting and Pressing of Ferrous Metals	1547123	9156965	8210364
有色金属冶炼和压延加工业	Smelting and Pressing of Non-ferrous Metals	6094803	14284614	12707272
金属制品业	Manufacture of Metal Products	1585831	2145538	1851622
通用设备制造业	Manufacture of General Purpose Machinery	2378006	4079546	3399233
专用设备制造业	Manufacture of Special Purpose Machinery	3088587	4509256	3591981
汽车制造业	Manufacture of Automobiles	3016390	9209279	8247920
铁路、船舶、航空航天和其他运输设备制造业	Manufacture of Railway, Ship, Aerospace and Other Transport Equipments	1267059	2486646	2021548
电气机械和器材制造业	Manufacture of Electrical Machinery and Apparatus	3976663	6280629	5342325
计算机、通信和其他电子设备制造业	Manufacture of Computers, Communication and Other Electronic Equipment	3200014	2793516	2313597
仪器仪表制造业	Manufacture of Measuring Instruments and Machinery	749439	907851	687194
其他制造业	Other Manufacture	184137	241752	199900
废弃资源综合利用业	Utilization of Waste Resources	43921	192545	182377
金属制品、机械和设备修理业	Repair Service of Metal Products, Machinery and Equipment	11080	30258	22002
电力、热力生产和供应业	Production and Supply of Electric Power and Heat Power	5574378	13040712	11037496
燃气生产和供应业	Production and Supply of Gas	815019	1365336	1054809
水的生产和供应业	Production and Supply of Water	413845	196538	150369

continued

(10 000 yuan)

主营业务税金及附加 Tax and Extra Charges from Principal Business	销售费用 Operating Expenses	管理费用 Management Expenses	财务费用 Financial Expenses	利润总额 Total Profits	亏损企业亏损额 Losses of Unprofitable Enterprises	利税总额 Total Profits and Taxes	本年应交增值税 Value Added Tax Payable	全部从业人员年平均人数(人) Annual Average Employed Persons (person)
7188756	**4765311**	**8993971**	**3134243**	**18469820**	**1303035**	**35061771**	**9403194**	**1547285**
514550	567070	1573903	456858	3616518	220932	6122547	1991480	200680
2430310	18777	1728502	395425	5343883	506	9862604	2088411	117119
17440	23800	51448	17297	73068	5782	167389	76881	13718
29463	20500	121689	18355	205752	4933	317315	82100	18752
13851	69657	55570	8666	69048	1501	134034	51135	9920
11374	4524	16705	3006	47929	3249	64583	5280	17392
42664	208968	198195	77702	598084	9145	881081	240332	63606
32973	209939	143850	11597	366535	4185	517703	118196	39748
130832	328032	234283	34541	605772	13284	957482	220878	37996
1004592	48754	114782	832	258703		1516851	253556	10010
16972	19658	45374	24757	246375	19045	334596	71248	48971
6217	19049	19106	9425	58231	24	80285	15837	9195
610	2597	4486	691	9267	103	15174	5297	1977
4888	15933	17552	6942	34941	920	62299	22469	4588
2155	7698	7284	1557	22658	21	30990	6177	3674
12105	21286	27332	10564	96573	1050	140879	32201	17411
10864	28127	73137	8469	102220	808	162218	49133	12904
1488	1187	1772	387	8124	141	33608	23996	1435
2308053	432351	452947	418624	931358	152788	4033045	793634	57337
43663	276500	395398	217458	242719	171281	480098	193715	72792
40321	645496	258869	45041	546533	12198	874404	287550	45273
594	1115	4307	155	23410	189	30518	6514	1214
31029	83738	178578	25803	268903	2752	387673	87741	30782
75892	267668	370379	138259	599663	88896	1010330	334775	96953
25190	102751	153115	94668	130412	127187	280370	124767	51360
63756	197729	355726	214271	656699	86388	1102654	382200	79621
16817	40502	93467	29891	110563	19732	207829	80448	22658
29146	125080	279503	26517	261936	28813	412934	121851	55113
24857	194779	345038	88495	273035	76805	433393	135501	61028
70599	241363	351238	58521	421449	41151	734037	241988	98604
11236	52521	176238	9584	220025	1966	348520	117260	24784
30299	253939	379385	42032	302709	57748	561583	228575	64819
9646	69449	269681	38008	203132	45211	256015	43237	31989
8578	32038	71768	4462	109340	4921	165788	47870	14153
2808	5591	8524	3206	16616	838	34149	14725	1735
1500	688	2693	1156	4350		7654	1804	1350
347	1536	3807	51	2198	143	4135	1590	615
99053	50849	316842	562960	1182588	86141	2036526	754885	88489
10702	59862	65932	19970	191997	8141	241557	38858	9878
1323	14212	25566	8040	6505	4120	16925	9097	7642

13-6 国有及国有控股工业企业主要经济指标(2014年)

单位：万元

分 组	Item	企业单位数 (个) Number of Enterprises (unit)	#亏损企业 Unprofitable Enterprises	工业总产值 Gross Industrial Output Value
总 计	**Total**	**678**	**178**	**106403531**
煤炭开采和洗选业	Mining and Washing of Coal	74	13	14230047
石油和天然气开采业	Extraction of Petroleum and Natural Gas	6	1	19528348
黑色金属矿采选业	Mining and Processing of Ferrous Metal Ores	12	2	670406
有色金属矿采选业	Mining and Processing of Non-Ferrous Metal Ores	14	1	796609
非金属矿采选业	Mining and Processing of Non-metal Ores	5	1	79204
开采辅助活动	Support Activities for Mining	3		919503
农副食品加工业	Processing of Food from Agricultural Products	14	4	328668
食品制造业	Manufacture of Foods	8		478674
酒、饮料和精制茶制造业	Manufacture of Liquor, Beverages and Refined Tea	8	1	964752
烟草制品业	Manufacture of Tobacco	3		2179499
纺织业	Manufacture of Textile	9	6	180896
纺织服装、服饰业	Manufacture of Textile, Wearing Apparel and Accessories	2		16232
皮革、毛皮、羽毛及其制品和制鞋业	Manufacture of Leather, Fur, Feather and Related Products and Footwear	1		37558
木材加工和木、竹、藤、棕、草制品业	Processing of Timber, Manufacture of Wood, Bamboo, Rattan, Palm and Straw Products	2		4564
造纸及纸制品业	Manufacture of Paper and Paper Products	1		4624
印刷和记录媒介复制业	Printing and Reproduction of Recording Media	3	1	220708
石油加工、炼焦及核燃料加工业	Processing of Petroleum, Coking and Processing of Nuclear Fuel	11	7	13126374
化学原料及化学制品制造业	Manufacture of Raw Chemical Materials and Chemical Products	58	14	4158742
医药制造业	Manufacture of Medicines	13	4	249638
化学纤维制造业	Manufacture of Chemical Fibres	2	1	99513
橡胶和塑料制品业	Manufacture of Rubber and Plastics Products	12	4	768054
非金属矿物制品业	Manufacture of Non-metallic Mineral Products	37	10	987225
黑色金属冶炼和压延加工业	Smelting and Pressing of Ferrous Metals	14	7	5572309
有色金属冶炼和压延加工业	Smelting and Pressing of Non-ferrous Metals	45	12	8654299
金属制品业	Manufacture of Metal Products	23	2	637641
通用设备制造业	Manufacture of General Purpose Machinery	31	9	2203513
专用设备制造业	Manufacture of Special Purpose Machinery	37	15	2247581
汽车制造业	Manufacture of Automobiles	24	7	7955006
铁路、船舶、航空航天和其他运输设备制造业	Manufacture of Railway, Ship, Aerospace and Other Transport Equipments	29	3	2026416
电气机械和器材制造业	Manufacture of Electrical Machinery and Apparatus	37	12	3169015
计算机、通信和其他电子设备制造业	Manufacture of Computers, Communication and Other Electronic Equipment	18	6	498672
仪器仪表制造业	Manufacture of Measuring Instruments and Machinery	9	2	589151
其他制造业	Other Manufacture	2	1	21358
废弃资源综合利用业	Utilization of Waste Resources	1		2569
金属制品、机械和设备修理业	Repair Service of Metal Products, Machinery and Equipment	2		7186
电力、热力生产和供应业	Production and Supply of Electric Power and Heat Power	78	22	11905810
燃气生产和供应业	Production and Supply of Gas	10		705347
水的生产和供应业	Production and Supply of Water	20	10	177821

Main Indicators of State-owned and State-holding Industrial Enterprises (2014)

(10 000 yuan)

工业销售产值 Sales Output Value	资产总计 Total Assets	流动资产合计 Total Current Assets	#应收账款 Accounts Receivable	#存货 Inventories	#产成品 Finished products	固定资产合计 Total of Fixed Assets	固定资产原价 Original Value of Fixed Assets	累计折旧 Total Depreciation	负债合计 Total Liabilities	#流动负债 Total Working Liabilities
102846357	**170773476**	**53113408**	**9839582**	**10738920**	**4292248**	**81719464**	**128526403**	**50327751**	**100480587**	**61912232**
13575486	25522464	9186628	2141095	601089	124741	10328089	13786142	5004297	12006297	8093124
19390660	38845318	3635485	97295	456777	162729	31805758	56528242	24779813	20509080	9930629
518802	614803	245022	48429	39072	32411	194570	235610	78608	417618	369879
777965	774073	251246	38889	61607	19059	264622	389038	153075	553662	434479
76454	84065	27878	6645	6142	3257	53010	74653	21643	54026	28880
921219	444397	353200	285577	16926	11571	87709	149850	64626	426923	332870
302861	167463	88166	18734	33971	12596	65406	80529	33401	121705	107271
472771	79303	52330	19839	11690	2884	23442	69050	43337	35641	35531
920064	648793	392919	37262	140733	78212	124050	180865	88006	302402	263680
2155226	1500006	1013384	91645	639020	33554	334500	676186	341686	235983	235914
170084	254921	139605	9604	69353	34768	89128	222115	143986	189214	168737
15992	6370	3791	839	1490	1028	2179	2961	782	1293	881
37873	46324	24123	886	9669	6846	3017	5770	2753	21956	17467
4564	54922	8135	317	592	358	7861	5656	3512	13517	7103
4624	394	381	134	122	122				94	
225319	306838	142792	16742	32791	15022	158014	283739	144459	39621	39607
13483939	22007209	7601482	447305	774648	423636	2651588	4543732	1923130	11290449	7648574
3953550	14320869	2699047	295409	412065	212424	6965369	8567413	1782655	10832357	4696106
218127	265839	151743	25483	60528	26341	81849	99775	25994	111082	102623
98128	74541	37806	4481	9114	4231	25674	70141	44467	10464	10006
724173	1407587	761063	140157	219358	132692	425732	427991	176083	1025370	724146
959081	1574895	387240	117506	109834	44765	1055985	1328028	475740	1089427	902003
5133185	4442456	1935764	190982	567898	304033	2236688	2585401	732953	3552025	3191864
8145318	9301595	4662387	380054	1903246	567002	3004600	3967665	1036385	5245045	3698976
601824	697443	414001	151463	161051	62020	186701	318963	140616	435075	336868
2083533	3113297	2256023	483558	527957	227435	476800	1039811	563872	1727378	1600095
2023076	4594411	3017756	1176953	1034724	492843	1021199	1409356	453653	2900353	2523007
7496079	5966135	3698974	634365	868082	566566	1278585	1865342	641602	3894851	3540382
1876505	2022709	1331935	512695	385572	118758	382049	603551	284394	1130049	976811
3168304	5207594	3638397	1327323	739553	346269	990536	1856808	877517	2656795	2172034
451339	1547249	575267	169230	107310	52968	297000	424342	149727	817522	624550
510258	708869	423583	192878	84475	32693	163459	336141	173166	286411	274314
21298	12676	9709	3277	2733	1147	2450	3904	1454	6278	6278
2942	10320	7817	294	407	356	1735	1735	4	6111	6111
4138	4498	3823	2541	407	109	669	1047	378	2958	2958
11446890	22177501	3253738	723769	601478	127581	16166718	25325250	9579311	17289756	8129467
701130	956799	377242	29097	39801	9012	379893	474787	115880	601918	459600
173576	1008534	303529	16832	7640	213	382832	584817	244787	639883	219410

13-6 续表

单位：万元

行 业	Sector	所有者权益合计 Owners' Equity	主营业务收入 Revenue from Principal Business	主营业务成本 Cost of Principal Business
总 计	**Total**	**70268404**	**102546595**	**75600591**
煤炭开采和洗选业	Mining and Washing of Coal	13460928	11252557	6920674
石油和天然气开采业	Extraction of Petroleum and Natural Gas	18336238	18062760	8520918
黑色金属矿采选业	Mining and Processing of Ferrous Metal Ores	197184	451617	354893
有色金属矿采选业	Mining and Processing of Non-Ferrous Metal Ores	220411	782731	631171
非金属矿采选业	Mining and Processing of Non-metal Ores	30039	76501	30226
开采辅助活动	Support Activities for Mining	17474	1073030	1051453
农副食品加工业	Processing of Food from Agricultural Products	45758	268338	242393
食品制造业	Manufacture of Foods	43663	445461	371685
酒、饮料和精制茶制造业	Manufacture of Liquor, Beverages and Refined Tea	346391	993829	584328
烟草制品业	Manufacture of Tobacco	1264024	2139159	714302
纺织业	Manufacture of Textile	65707	163194	160186
纺织服装、服饰业	Manufacture of Textile, Wearing Apparel and Accessories	5077	15992	13210
皮革、毛皮、羽毛及其制品和制鞋业	Manufacture of Leather, Fur, Feather and Related Products and Footwear	24368	37873	32745
木材加工和木、竹、藤、棕、草制品业	Processing of Timber, Manufacture of Wood, Bamboo, Rattan, Palm and Straw Products	41406	5526	5990
造纸及纸制品业	Manufacture of Paper and Paper Products	300	1792	1580
印刷和记录媒介复制业	Printing and Reproduction of Recording Media	267209	225196	171510
石油加工、炼焦及核燃料加工业	Processing of Petroleum, Coking and Processing of Nuclear Fuel	10716759	16621836	12778921
化学原料及化学制品制造业	Manufacture of Raw Chemical Materials and Chemical Products	3488512	3884800	3032027
医药制造业	Manufacture of Medicines	154757	205297	146997
化学纤维制造业	Manufacture of Chemical Fibres	64076	98141	80086
橡胶和塑料制品业	Manufacture of Rubber and Plastics Products	382217	771799	673754
非金属矿物制品业	Manufacture of Non-metallic Mineral Products	483278	927906	759068
黑色金属冶炼和压延加工业	Smelting and Pressing of Ferrous Metals	890528	5772848	5170727
有色金属冶炼和压延加工业	Smelting and Pressing of Non-ferrous Metals	4054346	9324959	8524898
金属制品业	Manufacture of Metal Products	262368	557993	478496
通用设备制造业	Manufacture of General Purpose Machinery	1385918	1775598	1485781
专用设备制造业	Manufacture of Special Purpose Machinery	1694058	1865159	1541812
汽车制造业	Manufacture of Automobiles	2066782	6251866	5596787
铁路、船舶、航空航天和其他运输设备制造业	Manufacture of Railway, Ship, Aerospace and Other Transport Equipments	892655	1783190	1470627
电气机械和器材制造业	Manufacture of Electrical Machinery and Apparatus	2590834	2750650	2274863
计算机、通信和其他电子设备制造业	Manufacture of Computers, Communication and Other Electronic Equipment	729727	418278	343828
仪器仪表制造业	Manufacture of Measuring Instruments and Machinery	422458	409397	329981
其他制造业	Other Manufacture	6398	20687	18861
废弃资源综合利用业	Utilization of Waste Resources	4209	2942	2569
金属制品、机械和设备修理业	Repair Service of Metal Products, Machinery and Equipment	1540	7185	5718
电力、热力生产和供应业	Production and Supply of Electric Power and Heat Power	4887278	12295134	10462182
燃气生产和供应业	Production and Supply of Gas	354880	625017	476733
水的生产和供应业	Production and Supply of Water	368651	180354	138610

continued

(10 000 yuan)

主营业务税金及附加 Taxes and Other Charges on Principal Business	销售费用 Eelling Expenses	管理费用 Manage-ment Expenses	财务费用 Financial Expenses	利润总额 Total Profits	亏损企业亏损额 Losses of Unpro-fitable Enterprises	利税总额 Total Profits and Taxes	本年应交增值税 Value Added Tax Payable	全部从业人员年平均人数(人) Annual Average Employed Persons (person)
6337842	**1788678**	**5651152**	**2163010**	**11218061**	**833628**	**23602720**	**6046818**	**743927**
293028	232501	1036899	303013	2458415	146512	4032581	1281138	129598
2430280	18508	1728298	395395	5343747	506	9862359	2088333	116911
8890	11528	23885	8783	45462	691	96001	41649	3980
4186	4765	46247	8277	78010	789	99805	17610	8025
2806	22953	11003	3315	6695	359	16081	6580	1141
474	103	4861	-109	11959		12781	348	13083
253	10049	9738	1181	8438	618	21023	12332	2356
906	39037	33125	154	17246		28809	10656	2048
75605	123203	94785	-2398	126083	535	250780	49093	7110
1004592	48754	114782	832	258703		1516851	253556	10010
786	3780	12734	5407	-12923	13676	-7836	4300	18691
25	343	840	119	1455		1600	120	600
180	896	1520	145	2760		3301	361	881
48	85	578	-0.4	56		130	26	473
4	76	81	2	49		89	36	36
1888	3368	33189	-921	17373	171	34504	15243	2990
2284826	227559	347747	309915	808739	62875	3733619	640055	26281
21883	147505	238566	168738	-1320	145141	125883	105321	37395
1758	18129	9767	1013	42646	3284	51627	7223	2895
362	330	2873	-181	14840	181	19763	4561	383
3942	25633	30260	11557	34435	2132	58051	19673	10006
6370	25159	72695	29594	24883	56405	74882	43629	13240
7407	66984	90605	66166	-48394	89681	14143	55130	22699
15903	130318	247429	166137	156142	69223	322611	150566	39358
3043	14491	32863	10301	16756	14421	49901	30102	8755
9245	51746	188309	1568	83355	9576	139709	47109	25977
9138	76960	175657	52450	40392	46852	108131	58602	26891
19856	183687	262019	37423	220256	26262	378276	138164	54217
8147	31664	135934	5920	134612	717	224791	82032	16631
17104	150140	240331	14002	95796	21608	216387	103488	33391
1794	28660	57677	21505	-659	41952	16186	15052	9777
5263	2950	30844	-548	43617	1716	78314	29434	7201
80	384	630	130	742	66	1329	507	291
0	131	227		15		17	2	67
109	173	511	1	678		1195	409	248
91992	41944	280350	537217	1070605	73561	1870878	708281	78147
4420	30986	29677	-924	111318		133112	17375	5089
1251	13198	23620	7834	5080	4120	15056	8725	7055

13-7 外商及港澳台商投资工业企业主要经济指标(2014年)

单位：万元

行业	Sector	企业单位数(个) Number of Enterprises (unit)	#亏损企业 Unprofitable Enterprises	工业总产值 Gross Industrial Output Value (at current prices)
总计	**Total**	**221**	**57**	**13824223**
煤炭开采和洗选业	Mining and Washing of Coal	2		181234
黑色金属矿采选业	Mining and Processing of Ferrous Metal Ores	1		6500
有色金属矿采选业	Mining and Processing of Non-Ferrous Metal Ores	1		31589
非金属矿采选业	Mining and Processing of Non-metal Ores	1	1	3027
农副食品加工业	Processing of Food from Agricultural Products	11	2	795098
食品制造业	Manufacture of Foods	16	3	1586004
酒、饮料和精制茶制造业	Manufacture of Liquor, Beverages and Refined Tea	26	7	1446093
纺织业	Manufacture of Textile	4	3	94957
纺织服装、服饰业	Manufacture of Textile, Wearing Apparel and Accessories	1		40178
造纸及纸制品业	Manufacture of Paper and Paper Products	4		147980
印刷和记录媒介复制业	Printing and Reproduction of Recording Media	1		43600
文教、工美、体育和娱乐用品制造业	Manufacture of Articles for Culture, Education, Arts and Crafts, Sport and Entertainment Activities	2	1	9410
石油加工、炼焦及核燃料加工业	Processing of Petroleum, Coking and Processing of Nuclear Fuel	3		304098
化学原料及化学制品制造业	Manufacture of Raw Chemical Materials and Chemical Products	16	8	256657
医药制造业	Manufacture of Medicines	12	4	930738
化学纤维制造业	Manufacture of Chemical Fibres	1		93369
橡胶和塑料制品业	Manufacture of Rubber and Plastics Products	4		701835
非金属矿物制品业	Manufacture of Non-metallic Mineral Products	16	2	781263
黑色金属冶炼和压延加工业	Smelting and Pressing of Ferrous Metals	3	2	63463
有色金属冶炼和压延加工业	Smelting and Pressing of Non-ferrous Metals	5	2	102372
金属制品业	Manufacture of Metal Products	5	2	36427
通用设备制造业	Manufacture of General Purpose Machinery	7	1	125099
专用设备制造业	Manufacture of Special Purpose Machinery	12	3	480955
汽车制造业	Manufacture of Automobiles	6	2	2402722
铁路、船舶、航空航天和其他运输设备制造业	Manufacture of Railway, Ship, Aerospace and Other Transport Equipments	10	1	274154
电气机械和器材制造业	Manufacture of Electrical Machinery and Apparatus	18	6	711885
计算机、通信和其他电子设备制造业	Manufacture of Computers, Communication and Other Electronic Equipment	15	3	1185695
仪器仪表制造业	Manufacture of Measuring Instruments and Machinery	4	1	102894
其他制造业	Other Manufacture	4	2	46487
金属制品、机械和设备修理业	Repair Service of Metal Products, Machinery and Equipment	2		11203
电力、热力生产和供应业	Production and Supply of Electric Power and Heat Power	4	1	466324
燃气生产和供应业	Production and Supply of Gas	2		353853
水的生产和供应业	Production and Supply of Water	2		7063

Main Indicators of Industrial Enterprises with Hong Kong, Macao, Taiwan and Foreign Funds (2014)

(10 000 yuan)

工业销售产值 Sales Output Value (at current prices)	资产总计 Total Assets	流动资产合计 Total Working Capitals	#应收账款 Accounts Receivable	#存货 Inventories	#产成品 Finished products	固定资产合计 Total of Fixed Assets	固定资产原价 Original Value of Fixed Assets	累计折旧 Total Depreciation	负债合计 Total Liabilities	#流动负债 Total Working Liabilities
12614729	**15735131**	**5734207**	**1346786**	**1357640**	**524460**	**8002957**	**11416680**	**3752090**	**8568154**	**6540915**
158869	259776	93342	17773	3397		161433	200511	39079	67615	43087
6435	1736	719		91		578	121	58	893	893
29993	4029	1342	345	573	533	2102	1825	192	1539	220
2700	10324	1836	600	519	151	6877	11661	4784	4773	4773
672479	224211	93509	21868	46995	5712	105639	133077	43369	112436	106126
1474763	829159	466482	95102	55056	18676	239885	421363	192034	371170	332629
1336850	1286566	512840	153364	207296	180070	598640	1093272	524711	653099	519547
82891	118279	72300	2394	52817	9716	37444	90632	53200	78589	78589
39447	7685	878	318	301	253	6707	6845	2806	406	
144758	52298	18377	5340	2992	914	20426	24586	7992	16458	14719
43484	42546	18278	8047	3035	789	9864	19692	9829	16148	15318
9410	7871	6046	3968	827		1800	2316	516	5454	5369
304098	162948	38584	7686	15483	6844	123671	115022	29251	94313	79276
247522	487989	184011	52941	27808	16840	263617	392852	138261	252356	116468
891437	978700	673968	86322	111775	77529	204567	315850	146486	457885	414467
91984	48963	33827	3977	7849	4072	14658	58564	43906	9404	9404
426461	185937	35778	13570	6565	5627	149505	235285	87777	158003	157967
728693	950243	254851	30952	65543	23523	626065	954751	366695	483029	408337
22040	75289	63239	6683	33414	18158	11438	42002	30966	43984	43984
84982	55847	40731	14536	15358	7586	5816	16271	10454	21602	14144
38454	67280	16171	6069	5459	1651	46096	61868	15773	39945	36268
111684	171030	120142	33268	33218	16534	25726	56769	36845	43335	43088
445933	559719	289214	51723	95023	25315	238385	318737	88490	305380	288291
2381690	1962050	673349	28559	115732	30160	637207	767183	234903	1359765	1063025
272460	331851	297760	126110	67402	18257	30185	48068	28965	174981	137777
635591	476196	313040	99901	53829	20327	75492	133993	59433	257187	159516
982197	4482793	744034	297851	253180	22490	3344904	3942460	615013	2506866	1866669
94071	154491	121677	42411	14997	9835	23795	37187	14822	64669	55706
46271	152125	100948	44117	1062	376	48940	68325	19986	23447	15397
11203	17308	16110	7515	5603	2338	462	1335	873	9417	9417
466324	907527	196830	50377	18652		660416	1490022	829606	565466	171849
322494	606638	211329	12773	35745	186	275735	344122	69786	338548	317724
7063	55728	22666	20327	46		4884	10114	5231	29992	10873

13-7 续表

单位：万元

行　业	Sector	所有者权益合　计 Owners' Equity	主营业务收　入 Revenue from Principal Business	主营业务成　本 Cost of Principal Business
总　计	**Total**	**7153410**	**11879783**	**9495179**
煤炭开采和洗选业	Mining and Washing of Coal	192161	98761	58722
黑色金属矿采选业	Mining and Processing of Ferrous Metal Ores	843	5945	5450
有色金属矿采选业	Mining and Processing of Non-Ferrous Metal Ores	2490	30142	27398
非金属矿采选业	Mining and Processing of Non-metal Ores	5551	2127	2574
农副食品加工业	Processing of Food from Agricultural Products	111773	673784	583069
食品制造业	Manufacture of Foods	457989	1377349	1114372
酒、饮料和精制茶制造业	Manufacture of Liquor, Beverages and Refined Tea	633455	1199241	867685
纺织业	Manufacture of Textile	39690	84329	79413
纺织服装、服饰业	Manufacture of Textile, Wearing Apparel and Accessories	7280	37872	21746
造纸及纸制品业	Manufacture of Paper and Paper Products	35840	144788	113713
印刷和记录媒介复制业	Printing and Reproduction of Recording Media	26398	30497	23517
文教、工美、体育和娱乐用品制造业	Manufacture of Articles for Culture, Education, Arts and Crafts, Sport and Entertainment Activities	2417	11637	11397
石油加工、炼焦及核燃料加工业	Processing of Petroleum, Coking and Processing of Nuclear Fuel	68635	249394	221612
化学原料及化学制品制造业	Manufacture of Raw Chemical Materials and Chemical Products	235631	235417	202850
医药制造业	Manufacture of Medicines	520814	940504	571074
化学纤维制造业	Manufacture of Chemical Fibres	39559	91997	74355
橡胶和塑料制品业	Manufacture of Rubber and Plastics Products	27934	545754	474096
非金属矿物制品业	Manufacture of Non-metallic Mineral Products	467214	651853	522870
黑色金属冶炼和压延加工业	Smelting and Pressing of Ferrous Metals	31304	63902	57677
有色金属冶炼和压延加工业	Smelting and Pressing of Non-ferrous Metals	34246	95683	85457
金属制品业	Manufacture of Metal Products	27336	40575	33281
通用设备制造业	Manufacture of General Purpose Machinery	127695	127461	108241
专用设备制造业	Manufacture of Special Purpose Machinery	254339	504367	380109
汽车制造业	Manufacture of Automobiles	602285	1747845	1622351
铁路、船舶、航空航天和其他运输设备制造业	Manufacture of Railway, Ship, Aerospace and Other Transport Equipments	156870	261901	180669
电气机械和器材制造业	Manufacture of Electrical Machinery and Apparatus	219009	702476	630373
计算机、通信和其他电子设备制造业	Manufacture of Computers, Communication and Other Electronic Equipment	1975427	971902	736670
仪器仪表制造业	Manufacture of Measuring Instruments and Machinery	89821	98075	62861
其他制造业	Other Manufacture	128679	48422	27015
金属制品、机械和设备修理业	Repair Service of Metal Products, Machinery and Equipment	7892	18753	13213
电力、热力生产和供应业	Production and Supply of Electric Power and Heat Power	342061	463263	322858
燃气生产和供应业	Production and Supply of Gas	268089	316705	252623
水的生产和供应业	Production and Supply of Water	12686	7065	5871

continued

(10 000 yuan)

主营业务税金及附加 Taxes and Other Charges on Principal Business	销售费用 Eelling Expenses	管理费用 Manage-ment Expenses	财务费用 Financial Expenses	利润总额 Total Profits	亏损企业亏损额 Losses of Unpro-fitable Enterprises	利税总额 Total Profits and Taxes	本年应交增值税 Value Added Tax Payable	全部从业人员年平均人数(人) Annual Average Employed Persons (person)
116109	**577911**	**692178**	**94534**	**1158385**	**109411**	**1794128**	**519634**	**115985**
4626	9106	8490	537	17065		36374	14683	840
109	156	101	-0.2	129		339	101	38
211	201	230	163	2210		4414	1993	208
9	65	383	9	-809	809	-680	120	110
2388	16668	12109	2969	55537	1137	71872	13947	3598
4540	114600	56658	-7251	93416	1951	132157	34201	8523
15846	87300	36964	15144	171555	12151	254020	66620	9795
679	689	2632	1367	1697	3003	4251	1876	4012
356	4627	3537	3837	3769		5200	1075	446
3910	2384	3451	734	22509		36426	10007	1196
195	1924	1109	659	3997		5811	1620	902
	100	257	13	-52	57	230	282	215
1297	6369	8858	1222	9883		52384	41204	4160
1152	8208	11516	7483	6428	6827	9477	1897	1395
7549	184731	59444	13592	102929	4090	208590	98112	7095
362	202	2224	-169	15021		19944	4561	261
7801	7699	85060	751	16611		26918	2505	1940
5634	6160	45087	9149	80881	5167	124630	38115	5673
273	3209	4047	1337	-5937	6184	-3617	2047	539
54	2051	2965	1306	4069	1600	7074	2951	405
187	1790	5172	1300	-927	3679	34	774	854
263	5938	6836	259	6905	245	9361	2193	1672
2756	17005	42094	2991	49977	23109	64565	11832	5213
41296	33835	49761	12802	84632	19944	182126	56198	32366
2242	9619	15341	-1286	50349	853	69849	17258	1728
1473	15599	26484	2980	43152	5572	77829	33204	3676
1967	12472	157949	8882	129033	2008	135519	4519	10896
845	7568	6972	1251	19324	803	23597	3429	1162
676	2091	1312	764	9880	175	17189	6634	328
99	1253	2665	32	1169		2175	907	290
4146		12611	16842	105062	10049	147275	38068	3059
3146	14293	19376	-5187	58261		67928	6522	3341
23		483	54	664		869	181	49

13-8 大中型工业企业主要经济指标(2014年)

单位：万元

行业	Sector	企业单位数(个) Number of Enterprises (unit)	#亏损企业 Unprofitable Enterprises	工业总产值 Gross Industrial Output Value (at current prices)
总计	**Total**	**927**	**166**	**144005353**
煤炭开采和洗选业	Mining and Washing of Coal	131	25	18024703
石油和天然气开采业	Extraction of Petroleum and Natural Gas	3		19473778
黑色金属矿采选业	Mining and Processing of Ferrous Metal Ores	11	4	830008
有色金属矿采选业	Mining and Processing of Non-Ferrous Metal Ores	14	3	1124315
非金属矿采选业	Mining and Processing of Non-metal Ores	8		139606
开采辅助活动	Support Activities for Mining	4		202974
农副食品加工业	Processing of Food from Agricultural Products	44	3	4019243
食品制造业	Manufacture of Foods	37	3	2525483
酒、饮料和精制茶制造业	Manufacture of Liquor, Beverages and Refined Tea	28	3	2588471
烟草制品业	Manufacture of Tobacco	2		2169636
纺织业	Manufacture of Textile	44	10	1437224
纺织服装、服饰业	Manufacture of Textile, Wearing Apparel and Accessories	10		273166
皮革、毛皮、羽毛及其制品和制鞋业	Manufacture of Leather, Fur, Feather and Related Products and Footwear	2		68786
木材加工和木、竹、藤、棕、草制品业	Processing of Timber, Manufacture of Wood, Bamboo, Rattan, Palm and Straw Products	5		303272
家具制造业	Manufacture of Furniture	4		70729
造纸及纸制品业	Manufacture of Paper and Paper Products	12		652247
印刷和记录媒介复制业	Printing and Reproduction of Recording Media	12	1	550012
石油加工、炼焦及核燃料加工业	Processing of Petroleum, Coking and Processing of Nuclear Fuel	38	18	16638444
化学原料及化学制品制造业	Manufacture of Raw Chemical Materials and Chemical Products	52	15	4899029
医药制造业	Manufacture of Medicines	36	1	3133277
橡胶和塑料制品业	Manufacture of Rubber and Plastics Products	22	1	2398444
非金属矿物制品业	Manufacture of Non-metallic Mineral Products	63	10	4350366
黑色金属冶炼和压延加工业	Smelting and Pressing of Ferrous Metals	24	10	7243053
有色金属冶炼和压延加工业	Smelting and Pressing of Non-ferrous Metals	52	12	12269646
金属制品业	Manufacture of Metal Products	17	2	436257
通用设备制造业	Manufacture of General Purpose Machinery	34	6	3074045
专用设备制造业	Manufacture of Special Purpose Machinery	43	10	3072801
汽车制造业	Manufacture of Automobiles	27	6	10542737
铁路、船舶、航空航天和其他运输设备制造业	Manufacture of Railway, Ship, Aerospace and Other Transport Equipments	18	1	1944565
电气机械和器材制造业	Manufacture of Electrical Machinery and Apparatus	34	6	4015559
计算机、通信和其他电子设备制造业	Manufacture of Computers, Communication and Other Electronic Equipment	29	4	2069208
仪器仪表制造业	Manufacture of Measuring Instruments and Machinery	9	1	794529
废弃资源综合利用业	Utilization of Waste Resources	1		66373
电力、热力生产和供应业	Production and Supply of Electric Power and Heat Power	43	7	11826377
燃气生产和供应业	Production and Supply of Gas	9	1	670649
水的生产和供应业	Production and Supply of Water	5	3	106342

Main Indicators of Large and Medium-sized Industrial Enterprises(2014)

(10 000 yuan)

工业销售产值 Sales Output Value (at current prices)	资产总计 Total Assets	流动资产合计 Total Working Capitals	#应收账款 Accounts Receivable	#存货 Inventories	#产成品 Finished products	固定资产合计 Total of Fixed Assets	固定资产原价 Original Value of Fixed Assets	累计折旧 Total Depreciation	负债合计 Total Liabilities	#流动负债 Total Working Liabilities
137715647	**198916658**	**64547554**	**11520719**	**13632063**	**5553928**	**94707050**	**150929581**	**60848304**	**114051360**	**74086155**
17312307	29773948	11100457	2207191	774419	224295	11792884	15770135	5480744	13754736	9486952
19337623	38741773	3625939	92266	455202	161231	31722817	56399593	24734105	20470680	9916391
654328	843453	346693	75130	40795	34868	301323	324050	123873	545162	448038
1066063	843185	311103	33834	73993	30692	278086	440251	171008	553083	424646
136953	90099	32471	7296	7726	3397	52676	70178	18044	58761	33936
195269	340964	142419	42359	17929	10261	184299	265319	80980	202706	102195
3800002	1453473	820712	104145	374596	153691	460823	677722	256283	880274	759045
2378740	1175554	565029	130117	97502	44977	485824	778140	316479	502886	392978
2417191	1936450	855964	180960	347510	237497	794088	1306662	594052	1013673	822771
2144938	1477744	1004145	88941	638306	33318	330736	669443	338707	221857	221788
1366077	799753	343149	38533	184286	86693	403133	669081	324142	466385	412619
244979	184534	110227	16134	50008	8004	66344	76705	17094	100757	66713
68599	51136	26288	1782	10860	7234	4716	7563	3084	24458	19969
269131	365434	137965	3972	26123	10486	116519	153842	68095	199945	81029
70979	35616	17833	1666	5194	1827	14994	26419	12965	16864	16823
598655	256789	59213	14397	23828	11926	193325	569304	392981	86192	65896
535383	515849	257101	42678	51876	22925	229569	378515	186404	134349	114508
16715462	25871609	9283870	709403	1195381	617275	4216255	6128625	2366886	13910317	9919231
4649183	15555063	3125533	365250	501141	242702	7743756	9922652	2388026	11572370	5417002
2929380	2373077	1457238	266224	331912	176156	615466	1634221	1137079	1011954	855983
2022581	1824506	848879	182105	255703	157040	792182	1681185	1075453	1187876	860885
4044588	3349345	964550	170827	245067	117623	2179627	3748506	1816211	2019550	1562010
6778527	5319119	2327348	247674	694368	342446	2630419	3455647	1287491	4075441	3692000
11462709	11635317	5494703	549756	2078450	642183	4025626	5432783	1489486	6172081	4556587
403971	706238	386044	162369	122783	55784	216681	377197	174503	403062	331909
2937443	3652052	2424987	525415	624733	261041	685012	1821574	1163811	1924786	1763515
2793732	5165876	3308353	1261347	1114779	541746	1495902	2172814	750581	3131837	2669046
10056970	7849988	4315402	666311	959600	584066	1909621	2767869	1006162	5172564	4546693
1783127	1905960	1289654	494718	355514	108194	314707	535310	285747	1028678	896862
3958376	6007973	3949017	1334572	845214	389006	1416171	3248479	1919750	2989532	2598512
1695140	6217939	1391403	527195	372977	66135	3740387	4485104	783825	3391333	2530412
709643	888163	535321	238913	89855	36352	159542	339345	180124	393720	297040
66373	26430	17445				8369	8373	2244	14891	14891
11367426	20409031	3134117	703807	616004	127876	14624084	23821313	9584044	15755754	7630983
638713	1054495	436299	27155	43556	4971	391041	504660	142511	547879	479431
105088	218723	100685	6279	4873	9	110050	261006	175330	114970	76869

13-8 续表

单位：万元

行　业	Sector	所有者权益合　计 Owners' Equity	主营业务收　入 Revenue from Principal Business	主营业务成　本 Cost of Principal Business
总　计	**Total**	**84852483**	**134993569**	**100851909**
煤炭开采和洗选业	Mining and Washing of Coal	16019211	14770379	9342750
石油和天然气开采业	Extraction of Petroleum and Natural Gas	18271093	18011644	8479867
黑色金属矿采选业	Mining and Processing of Ferrous Metal Ores	298291	565795	449177
有色金属矿采选业	Mining and Processing of Non-Ferrous Metal Ores	290102	1023629	837861
非金属矿采选业	Mining and Processing of Non-metal Ores	31339	136758	80315
开采辅助活动	Support Activities for Mining	138258	389112	339126
农副食品加工业	Processing of Food from Agricultural Products	572514	3559529	3089591
食品制造业	Manufacture of Foods	672662	2285264	1775688
酒、饮料和精制茶制造业	Manufacture of Liquor, Beverages and Refined Tea	922767	2385469	1536768
烟草制品业	Manufacture of Tobacco	1255887	2128180	709086
纺织业	Manufacture of Textile	332354	1351772	1125611
纺织服装、服饰业	Manufacture of Textile, Wearing Apparel and Accessories	83776	233556	163410
皮革、毛皮、羽毛及其制品和制鞋业	Manufacture of Leather, Fur, Feather and Related Products and Footwear	26678	68599	58244
木材加工和木、竹、藤、棕、草制品业	Processing of Timber, Manufacture of Wood, Bamboo, Rattan, Palm and Straw Products	165490	229502	202905
家具制造业	Manufacture of Furniture	18752	69916	53376
造纸及纸制品业	Manufacture of Paper and Paper Products	170597	560231	473233
印刷和记录媒介复制业	Printing and Reproduction of Recording Media	381491	506222	370481
石油加工、炼焦及核燃料加工业	Processing of Petroleum, Coking and Processing of Nuclear Fuel	11961291	19566427	14940757
化学原料及化学制品制造业	Manufacture of Raw Chemical Materials and Chemical Products	3982692	4562669	3592905
医药制造业	Manufacture of Medicines	1350968	2799788	1751268
橡胶和塑料制品业	Manufacture of Rubber and Plastics Products	636630	2146324	1828302
非金属矿物制品业	Manufacture of Non-metallic Mineral Products	1329795	3591853	3100420
黑色金属冶炼和压延加工业	Smelting and Pressing of Ferrous Metals	1243678	7540008	6745855
有色金属冶炼和压延加工业	Smelting and Pressing of Non-ferrous Metals	5463219	12466275	11101752
金属制品业	Manufacture of Metal Products	303176	466409	394097
通用设备制造业	Manufacture of General Purpose Machinery	1727266	2509350	2067012
专用设备制造业	Manufacture of Special Purpose Machinery	2034038	2630160	2019586
汽车制造业	Manufacture of Automobiles	2677425	8190991	7391167
铁路、船舶、航空航天和其他运输设备制造业	Manufacture of Railway, Ship, Aerospace and Other Transport Equipments	877282	1697957	1393163
电气机械和器材制造业	Manufacture of Electrical Machinery and Apparatus	3017528	3333795	2703740
计算机、通信和其他电子设备制造业	Manufacture of Computers, Communication and Other Electronic Equipment	2826606	1620338	1265880
仪器仪表制造业	Manufacture of Measuring Instruments and Machinery	494444	561823	419722
废弃资源综合利用业	Utilization of Waste Resources	11539	129392	128652
金属制品、机械和设备修理业	Repair Service of Metal Products, Machinery and Equipment	4653276	12235115	10417479
电力、热力生产和供应业	Production and Supply of Electric Power and Heat Power	506616	569628	419182
燃气生产和供应业	Production and Supply of Gas	103754	99711	83481
水的生产和供应业	Production and Supply of Water			

continued

(10 000 yuan)

主营业务税金及附加 Taxes and Other Charges on Principal Business	销售费用 Eelling Expenses	管理费用 Manage-ment Expenses	财务费用 Financial Expenses	利润总额 Total Profits	亏损企业亏损额 Losses of Unpro-fitable Enterprises	利税总额 Total Profits and Taxes	本年应交增值税 Value Added Tax Payable	全部从业人员年平均人数(人) Annual Average Employed Persons (person)
6698107	**3236302**	**6917093**	**2549152**	**14793233**	**898062**	**29056825**	**7565485**	**1120558**
380056	343800	1238323	362085	3111217	161510	5125930	1634657	169290
2424443	16191	1727455	394854	5343073		9853782	2086266	116572
8860	12246	34763	11504	30272	1520	87632	48500	7948
5095	6728	69964	10690	87248	2400	113991	21649	10494
2875	27603	13603	3360	8949		20440	8617	3160
8420	171	5039	863	30943		40353	990	14309
16805	79049	57494	31639	264168	2967	389286	108314	27168
21577	162239	91537	-556	240390	1796	346050	84084	21781
91381	226787	146709	15618	371417	4669	591172	128374	20024
1004473	48589	112756	847	255056		1512147	252618	9713
12145	11824	32414	17597	162812	16923	228746	53789	38368
4400	11750	10347	7246	35933		49151	8818	5407
354	1474	3136	311	5452		6976	1169	1401
2212	3779	6336	3527	17733		32957	13012	2166
1253	1941	2382	810	8983		12932	2696	1439
7421	8794	12963	5283	52079		78594	19094	10758
8937	18809	53755	6203	59912	22	103789	34940	8005
2295999	367879	414481	392999	947771	107195	4003178	759408	50239
25715	173585	277051	184825	46351	150525	178364	106298	47385
27487	486300	155273	25102	353506	26	589294	208301	28573
19053	53725	134598	14851	149896	1233	220030	51081	18396
25152	91871	135198	86926	174741	34110	324786	124893	43247
13256	88118	119817	81204	51956	104807	153740	88529	40701
53900	173382	287647	193293	566211	72666	959177	339066	66495
5422	15623	31635	9972	9729	14421	44338	29187	9801
16731	80766	203020	12584	172643	16745	267665	78291	35723
15779	140330	246660	70966	156954	44250	250773	78040	38606
62055	212102	296673	51259	334964	35599	589907	192889	88289
7905	29704	131755	3504	140389	513	229380	81086	17793
21042	190824	291349	26070	166880	40064	328650	140728	45808
5407	50540	220974	32101	151724	39712	182063	24932	23459
6220	14679	39331	938	81857	1329	124707	36630	8688
14		75	630	21		179	144	456
90751	43406	259378	483760	1112936	40115	1900850	697162	78127
4963	37494	39141	6430	88541	1290	110191	16688	6297
551	4203	14050	-141	529	1657	5628	4548	4472

13-9 八大工业支柱产业主要经济指标(2014年)

单位：万元

行　业	Sector	企业单位数（个）Number of Enterprises (unit)	#亏损企业 Unprofitable Enterprises	工业总产值 Gross Industrial Output Value (at current prices)
全省总计	**Provincial Total**	**5017**	**860**	**200158820**
八大工业合计	Total Mainstay Property of 8 Large Industries	4648	812	193589014
八大工业占全省比重(%)	Mainstay Property of 8 Large Industries Rate in Total (%)	92.6	94.4	96.7
1.通信设备、计算机及其他电子设备制造业	Manufacture of Communication Equipment, Computer and Other Electronic Equipment	93	15	3004571
2.能源化工工业	Energy and Chemical Industry	1188	302	87208697
3.装备制造工业	Equipment Manufacturing Industry	1073	169	35247629
4.医药制造业	Manufacture of Medicines Industry	182	27	5108033
5.食品工业	Foods Industry	902	71	21699669
6.纺织服装工业	Textile Wearing Apparel Industry	167	20	2897283
7.非金属矿物制品业	Manufacture of Non-metallic Mineral Products	588	100	10903279
8.有色冶金工业	Non-ferrous Metallurgy Industry	455	108	27519854

13-9 续表

单位：万元

行　业	Sector	所有者权益合计 Owners' Equity	主营业务收入 Revenue from Principal Business	主营业务成本 Cost of Principal Business
全省总计	**Provincial Total**	**105199889**	**186221351**	**143675613**
八大工业合计	Total Mainstay Property of 8 Large Industries	102305266	180212980	138816226
八大工业占全省比重(%)	Mainstay Property of 8 Large Industries Rate in Total (%)	97.3	96.8	96.6
1.通信设备、计算机及其他电子设备制造业	Manufacture of Communication Equipment, Computer and Other Electronic Equipment	3200014	2793516	2313597
2.能源化工工业	Energy and Chemical Industry	62096095	84535703	59375969
3.装备制造工业	Equipment Manufacturing Industry	16061974	29618745	25141823
4.医药制造业	Manufacture of Medicines Industry	2104201	4521571	3010808
5.食品工业	Foods Industry	5968599	19590868	14895715
6.纺织服装工业	Textile Wearing Apparel Industry	822809	2726595	2252075
7.非金属矿物制品业	Manufacture of Non-metallic Mineral Products	3209429	9624609	8151397
8.有色冶金工业	Non-ferrous Metallurgy Industry	8842145	26801373	23674841

Main Indicators of Industrial Enterprises(2014)

(10 000 yuan)

工业销售产值 Sales Output Value (at current prices)	资产总计 Total Assets	流动资产合计 Total Working Capitals	#应收账款 Accounts Receivable	#存货 Inventories	#产成品 Finished products	固定资产合计 Total of Fixed Assets	固定资产原价 Original Value of Fixed Assets	累计折旧 Total Depreci-ation	负债合计 Total Liabilities	#流动负债 Total Working Liabilities
191182693	**243714377**	**84915479**	**17516199**	**18442887**	**7908792**	**111614224**	**174436931**	**69004715**	**138404283**	**90879252**
184893653	237633634	82386723	16977308	18078862	7752010	109152689	170680799	67479419	135278348	88781267
96.7	97.5	97.0	96.9	98.0	98.0	97.8	97.9	97.8	97.7	97.7
2834311	6867946	1826014	681597	480299	110294	3866438	4805079	983964	3664754	2758307
84769798	148601697	37666928	6141138	4781148	2069166	77843105	123034005	48657313	86397870	49203344
33329473	36306964	21511747	6526137	5437419	2517350	9253175	15715818	7030826	20443712	17060898
4738787	3856532	2246957	458369	580720	298904	1063563	2361695	1478051	1737411	1441294
20649995	10834547	5513747	915618	2314507	926720	3839623	5800505	2318263	4787311	3803977
2710202	1699289	804305	132568	388985	162840	747083	1067880	421123	862946	709952
10314205	7248772	2655322	821357	665615	307801	3997989	6553606	2960715	4013056	3115846
25546883	22217888	10161703	1300524	3430170	1358936	8531713	11342211	3629165	13371289	10687651

continued

(10 000 yuan)

主营业务税金及附加 Taxes and Other Charges on Principal Business	销售费用 Eelling Expenses	管理费用 Manage-ment Expenses	财务费用 Financial Expenses	利润总额 Total Profits	亏损企业亏损额 Losses of Unpro-fitable Enterprises	利税总额 Total Profits and Taxes	本年应交增值税 Value Added Tax Payable	全部从业人员年平均人数(人) Annual Average Employed Persons (person)
7188756	**4765311**	**8993971**	**3134243**	**18469820**	**1303035**	**35061771**	**9403194**	**1547285**
7126725	4539536	8704802	3065236	17914591	1285353	34193325	9152008	1476133
99.1	95.3	96.8	97.8	97.0	98.6	97.5	97.3	95.4
9646	69449	269681	38008	203132	45211	256015	43237	31989
5438626	1434924	4667181	2080289	11657307	637837	23017594	5921661	585805
191532	940222	1696638	259503	1699057	231135	2864083	973494	341159
40321	645496	258869	45041	546533	12198	874404	287550	45273
1211061	795694	691110	124672	1829095	26613	3873117	832961	151360
23799	41303	68966	34873	313873	19172	430055	92383	60143
75892	267668	370379	138259	599663	88896	1010330	334775	96953
135849	344779	681977	344591	1065931	224290	1867728	665948	163451

13-10 规模以上工业企业主要经济效益指标(2014年)
Main Indicators on Economic Benefit of Industrial Enterprises above Designated Size (2014)

分组	Item	总资产贡献率(%) Ratio of Profits, Taxes and Interests to Average Assets (%)	资产负债率(%) Ratio of Debts to Assets (%)	流动资产周转率(次/年) Turnover of Current Assets (times/year)	成本费用利润率(%) Ratio of Profits to Total Industrial Cost (%)	工业产品销售率(%) Sales Ratio of Products (%)
总计	**Total**	**15.67**	**56.79**	**2.19**	**11.50**	**95.52**
按登记注册类型分	**By Status of Registration**					
内资企业	Domestic Funded	15.92	56.95	2.20	11.56	95.83
国有企业	State-owned Enterprises	8.43	66.64	1.88	7.46	95.07
中央企业	Central	11.47	57.45	2.55	8.61	95.09
地方企业	Local	5.08	76.73	1.14	4.57	95.03
集体企业	Collective-owned Enterprises	26.08	51.26	3.87	8.53	97.31
股份合作企业	Cooperative Enterprises	10.27	55.02	1.30	9.94	97.71
联营企业	Joint Ownership Enterprises	25.31	52.43	2.50	7.37	98.25
国有联营企业	State Joint Ownership Enterprises	22.47	45.93	1.53	10.07	102.89
集体联营企业	Collective Joint Ownership Enterprises	1.37	89.13	1.94	0.08	101.80
国有与集体联营企业	Joint State-collective Enterprises	128.07	26.51	40.13	8.76	87.10
其他联营企业	Other Joint Ownership Enterprises	22.82	71.99	5.35	-0.52	93.92
有限责任公司	Limited Liability Corporations	13.01	59.09	1.97	7.61	95.40
国有独资公司	State Sole Funded Corporations	13.54	55.78	1.48	7.04	99.58
其他有限责任公司	Other Limited Liability Corporations	12.69	61.12	2.23	7.80	94.19
股份有限公司	Share-holding Corporations Limited	23.56	50.11	2.58	30.01	96.91
私营企业	Private Enterprises	21.79	50.08	3.33	10.48	96.32
私营独资企业	Private-funded Enterprises	32.85	41.96	4.78	14.44	95.23
私营合作企业	Private Partnership Enterprises	24.92	45.63	2.18	19.88	97.33
私营有限责任公司	Private Limited Liability Corporations	21.08	51.94	3.35	9.85	96.54
私营股份有限公司	Private Share-holding Corporations Ltd.	19.86	44.03	3.23	10.16	94.84
其他企业	Other Enterprises	25.72	58.30	5.33	14.05	94.30
港、澳、台商投资企业	Enterprises with Funds from Hong Kong, Macao and Taiwan	14.69	44.32	1.72	12.14	90.41
合资经营企业(港或澳、台资)	Joint-venture Enterprises	15.25	42.00	2.20	8.83	88.32
合作经营企业(港或澳、台资)	Cooperative Enterprises	37.02	33.11	2.26	33.27	99.94
港澳台商独资经营企业	Enterprises with Sole Investment	10.91	42.38	1.32	10.39	89.04
港澳台商投资股份有限公司	Share-holding Corporations Ltd.	6.21	73.07	1.24	10.46	99.87
外商投资企业	Foreign Funded Enterprises	11.54	56.34	2.17	10.34	91.43
中外合资经营企业	Joint-venture Enterprises	16.41	58.35	2.27	9.80	92.30
中外合作经营企业	Cooperation Enterprises	45.31	35.67	7.41	20.42	99.84
外资企业	Enterprises with Sole Funds	5.82	54.17	1.98	10.55	90.18
外商投资股份有限公司	Share-holding Corporations Ltd.	12.29	57.62	1.27	12.71	83.50

13-10 续表 continued

分 组	Item	总资产贡献率(%) Ratio of Profits, Taxes and Interests to Average Assets (%)	资产负债率(%) Ratio of Debts to Assets (%)	流动资产周转率(次/年) Turnover of Current Assets (times/year)	成本费用利润率(%) Ratio of Profits to Total Industrial Cost (%)	工业产品销售率(%) Sales Ratio of Products (%)
按经济组织类型分	**By Economic Type of Orgnization**					
独资企业	Appropratorship	9.01	62.92	2.01	8.53	94.33
国有企业	State-owned Enterprises	8.43	66.64	1.88	7.46	95.07
集体企业	Collective-owned Enterprises	26.08	51.26	3.87	8.53	97.31
私营独资企业	Private-funded Enterprises	32.85	41.96	4.78	14.44	95.23
港澳台商独资经营企业	Enterprises with Sole Investment	10.91	42.38	1.32	10.39	89.04
外资企业	Enterprises with Sole Funds	5.82	54.17	1.98	10.55	90.18
合作、合伙企业	Partnership	23.65	48.00	2.36	17.91	97.56
股份合作企业	Cooperative Enterprises	10.27	55.02	1.30	9.94	97.71
国有联营企业	State Joint Ownership Enterprises	22.47	45.93	1.53	10.07	102.89
集体联营企业	Collective Joint Ownership Enterprises	1.37	89.13	1.94	0.08	101.80
国有与集体联营企业	Joint State-collective Enterprises	128.07	26.51	40.13	8.76	87.10
其他联营企业	Other Joint Ownership Enterprises	22.82	71.99	5.35	-0.52	93.92
私营合伙企业	Private Partnership Enterprises	24.92	45.63	2.18	19.88	97.33
合作经营企业(港或澳、台资)	Cooperative Enterprises	37.02	33.11	2.26	33.27	99.94
中外合作经营企业	Cooperation Enterprises	45.31	35.67	7.41	20.42	99.84
其他企业(内资)	Other Enterprises	25.72	58.30	5.33	14.05	94.30
股份有限公司	Share-holding Corporations Limited	23.27	50.04	2.59	27.89	96.62
股份有限公司(内资)	Share-holding Corporations Ltd.	23.56	50.11	2.58	30.01	96.91
私营股份有限公司	Private Share-holding Corporations Ltd.	19.86	44.03	3.23	10.16	94.84
港澳台商投资股份有限公司	Share-holding Corporations Ltd.with Funds from Hong Kong, Macao and Taiwan	6.21	73.07	1.24	10.46	99.87
外商投资股份有限公司	Share-holding Corporations Ltd.with Foreign Investment	12.29	57.62	1.27	12.71	83.50
有限责任公司	Limited Liability Corporations	13.99	58.23	2.13	8.10	95.36
国有独资公司	State Sole Funded Corporations	13.54	55.78	1.48	7.04	99.58
私营有限责任公司	Private Limited Liability Corporations	21.08	51.94	3.35	9.85	96.54
合资经营企业(港或澳、台资)	Joint-venture Enterprises	15.25	42.00	2.20	8.83	88.32
中外合资经营企业	Joint-venture Enterprises	16.41	58.35	2.27	9.80	92.30
其他有限责任公司	Other Corporations	12.69	61.12	2.23	7.80	94.19
按轻重工业分	**Grouped by Light & Heavy Industries**					
轻工业	Light Industry	28.95	46.23	3.01	11.16	94.42
重工业	Heavy Industry	14.41	57.79	2.07	11.57	95.76
按企业规模分	**Grouped by Size of Enterprises**					
大型企业	Large Enterprises	15.83	56.57	2.03	13.66	96.77
中型企业	Medium-sized Enterprises	16.27	59.86	2.27	11.55	93.09
小型企业	Small Enterprises	14.79	53.56	2.55	7.98	95.27
微型企业	Mini Enterprises	7.28	72.77	1.68	2.82	93.39

13-11 规模以上工业企业分行业主要经济效益指标(2014年)
Main Indicators on Economic Benefit of Industrial Enterprises above Designated Size by Industrial Sector (2014)

分　组	Item	总资产贡献率(%) Ratio of Profits, Taxes and Interests to Average Assets(%)	资　产负债率(%) Ratio of Debts to Assets (%)	流动资产周转率(次/年) Turnover of Current Assets (times/year)	成本费用利润率(%) Ratio of Profits to Total Industrial Cost (%)	工业产品销售率(%) Sales Ratio of Products (%)
总　计	**Total**	**15.67**	**56.79**	**2.19**	**11.50**	**95.52**
煤炭开采和洗选业	Mining and Washing of Coal	17.97	47.55	1.44	23.12	96.36
石油和天然气开采业	Extraction of Petroleum and Natural Gas	26.54	52.79	4.97	50.05	99.29
黑色金属矿采选业	Mining and Processing of Ferrous Metal Ores	12.58	61.01	2.21	6.61	83.54
有色金属矿采选业	Mining and Processing of Non-Ferrous Metal Ores	20.88	59.57	3.35	10.80	92.34
非金属矿采选业	Mining and Processing of Non-metal Ores	28.71	40.13	4.30	8.60	96.01
开采辅助活动	Support Activities for Mining	7.53	65.77	2.34	4.02	99.19
农副食品加工业	Processing of Food from Agricultural Products	23.62	51.28	4.50	7.00	95.41
食品制造业	Manufacture of Foods	26.40	43.15	4.05	10.56	94.53
酒、饮料和精制茶制造业	Manufacture of Liquor, Beverages and Refined Tea	30.22	49.13	2.91	16.77	93.51
烟草制品业	Manufacture of Tobacco	101.31	15.73	2.11	29.44	98.89
纺织业	Manufacture of Textile	28.07	51.95	3.84	13.35	94.51
纺织服装、服饰业	Manufacture of Textile, Wearing Apparel and Accessories	25.18	47.10	2.42	13.12	91.45
皮革、毛皮、羽毛及其制品和制鞋业	Manufacture of Leather, Fur, Feather and Related Products and Footwear	20.61	47.79	2.54	8.58	86.12
木材加工和木、竹、藤、棕、草制品业	Processing of Timber, Manufacture of Wood, Bamboo, Rattan, Palm and Straw Products	14.20	52.83	2.56	7.53	91.56
家具制造业	Manufacture of Furniture	29.55	38.28	3.84	12.93	95.29
造纸及纸制品业	Manufacture of Paper and Paper Products	26.96	41.76	5.84	10.27	94.05
印刷和记录媒介复制业	Printing and Reproduction of Recording Media	20.64	36.14	2.25	13.64	96.10
文教、工美、体育和娱乐用品制造业	Manufacture of Articles for Culture, Education, Arts and Crafts, Sport and Entertainment Activities	16.01	86.08	2.61	1.69	99.27
石油加工、炼焦及核燃料	Processing of Petroleum, Coking and Processing of Nuclear Fuel	16.14	54.01	2.09	5.32	99.80
化学原料及化学制品制造业	Manufacture of Raw Chemical Materials and Chemical Products	3.91	72.00	1.72	3.36	95.05
医药制造业	Manufacture of Medicines	23.50	45.05	2.01	13.80	92.77
化学纤维制造业	Manufacture of Chemical Fibres	29.11	20.56	3.07	16.37	98.94
橡胶和塑料制品业	Manufacture of Rubber and Plastics Products	16.41	59.13	2.95	8.41	87.39
非金属矿物制品业	Manufacture of Non-metallic Mineral Products	15.79	55.36	3.62	6.72	94.60
黑色金属冶炼和压延加工业	Smelting and Pressing of Ferrous Metals	5.75	75.06	3.40	1.52	93.96
有色金属冶炼和压延加工业	Smelting and Pressing of Non-ferrous Metals	10.16	53.10	2.28	4.87	93.28
金属制品业	Manufacture of Metal Products	7.00	52.84	1.95	5.49	93.84
通用设备制造业	Manufacture of General Purpose Machinery	8.99	51.62	1.29	6.84	94.67
专用设备制造业	Manufacture of Special Purpose Machinery	7.17	57.46	1.00	6.47	91.98
汽车制造业	Manufacture of Automobiles	9.32	64.84	1.93	4.74	95.40
铁路、船舶、航空航天和其他运输设备制造业	Manufacture of Railway, Ship, Aerospace and Other Transport Equipments	13.53	52.60	1.41	9.74	93.76
电气机械和器材制造业	Manufacture of Electrical Machinery and Apparatus	7.54	53.64	1.18	5.03	96.04
计算机、通信和其他电子设备制造业	Manufacture of Computers, Communication and Other Electronic Equipment	4.28	53.36	1.53	7.55	94.33
仪器仪表制造业	Manufacture of Measuring Instruments and Machinery	12.57	45.00	1.03	13.75	91.17
其他制造业	Other Manufacture	13.56	33.12	1.36	7.65	90.26
废弃资源综合利用业	Utilization of Waste Resources	8.40	53.38	3.42	2.33	99.82
金属制品、机械和设备修理业	Repair Service of Metal Products, Machinery and Equipment	14.75	61.13	1.25	8.02	85.53
电力、热力生产和供应业	Production and Supply of Electric Power and Heat Power	10.80	76.73	3.33	9.88	96.04
燃气生产和供应业	Production and Supply of Gas	13.98	56.83	1.85	15.99	97.58
水的生产和供应业	Production and Supply of Water	2.27	61.56	0.59	3.28	97.37

13-12　国有及国有控股工业企业主要经济效益指标(2014年)
Main Indicators on Economic Benefit of State-owned and State-holding Industrial Enterprises(2014)

分　组	Item	总资产贡献率(%) Ratio of Profits, Taxes and Interests to Average Assets(%)	资　产负债率(%) Ratio of Debts to Assets (%)	流动资产周转率(次/年) Turnover of Current Assets (times/year)	成本费用利润率(%) Ratio of Profits to Total Industrial Cost (%)	工业产品销售率(%) Sales Ratio of Products (%)
总　计	**Total**	**15.16**	**58.84**	**1.93**	**13.17**	**96.66**
煤炭开采和洗选业	Mining and Washing of Coal	16.95	47.04	1.22	28.95	95.40
石油和天然气开采业	Extraction of Petroleum and Natural Gas	26.56	52.80	4.97	50.11	99.29
黑色金属矿采选业	Mining and Processing of Ferrous Metal Ores	16.35	67.93	1.84	11.39	77.39
有色金属矿采选业	Mining and Processing of Non-Ferrous Metal Ores	13.90	71.53	3.12	11.30	97.66
非金属矿采选业	Mining and Processing of Non-metal Ores	22.10	64.27	2.74	9.92	96.53
开采辅助活动	Support Activities for Mining	2.88	96.07	3.04	1.13	100.19
农副食品加工业	Processing of Food from Agricultural Products	13.28	72.68	3.04	3.20	92.15
食品制造业	Manufacture of Foods	36.38	44.94	8.51	3.88	98.77
酒、饮料和精制茶制造业	Manufacture of Liquor, Beverages and Refined Tea	38.85	46.61	2.53	15.76	95.37
烟草制品业	Manufacture of Tobacco	101.31	15.73	2.11	29.44	98.89
纺织业	Manufacture of Textile	-0.95	74.22	1.17	-7.10	94.02
纺织服装、服饰业	Manufacture of Textile, Wearing Apparel and Accessories	26.96	20.30	4.22	10.03	98.52
皮革、毛皮、羽毛及其制品和制鞋业	Manufacture of Leather, Fur, Feather and Related Products and Footwear	7.59	47.40	1.57	7.82	100.84
木材加工和木、竹、藤、棕、草制品业	Processing of Timber, Manufacture of Wood, Bamboo, Rattan, Palm and Straw Products	0.24	24.61	0.68	0.85	100.00
造纸及纸制品业	Manufacture of Paper and Paper Products	23.07	23.76	4.70	2.82	100.00
印刷和记录媒介复制业	Printing and Reproduction of Recording Media	11.32	12.91	1.58	8.39	102.09
石油加工、炼焦及核燃料加工业	Processing of Petroleum, Coking and Processing of Nuclear Fuel	18.36	51.30	2.19	5.92	102.72
化学原料及化学制品制造业	Manufacture of Raw Chemical Materials and Chemical Products	2.28	75.64	1.44	-0.04	95.07
医药制造业	Manufacture of Medicines	19.91	41.79	1.35	24.24	87.38
化学纤维制造业	Manufacture of Chemical Fibres	26.53	14.04	2.60	17.86	98.61
橡胶和塑料制品业	Manufacture of Rubber and Plastics Products	5.25	72.85	1.01	4.65	94.29
非金属矿物制品业	Manufacture of Non-metallic Mineral Products	6.58	69.17	2.40	2.81	97.15
黑色金属冶炼和压延加工业	Smelting and Pressing of Ferrous Metals	1.50	79.96	2.98	-0.90	92.12
有色金属冶炼和压延加工业	Smelting and Pressing of Non-ferrous Metals	5.40	56.39	2.00	1.72	94.12
金属制品业	Manufacture of Metal Products	8.57	62.38	1.35	3.13	94.38
通用设备制造业	Manufacture of General Purpose Machinery	4.85	55.48	0.79	4.83	94.56
专用设备制造业	Manufacture of Special Purpose Machinery	3.66	63.13	0.62	2.19	90.01
汽车制造业	Manufacture of Automobiles	7.15	65.28	1.69	3.62	94.23
铁路、船舶、航空航天和其他运输设备制造业	Manufacture of Railway, Ship, Aerospace and Other Transport Equipments	11.58	55.87	1.34	8.19	92.60
电气机械和器材制造业	Manufacture of Electrical Machinery and Apparatus	4.63	51.02	0.76	3.58	99.98
计算机、通信和其他电子设备制造业	Manufacture of Computers, Communication and Other Electronic Equipment	2.46	52.84	0.73	-0.15	90.51
仪器仪表制造业	Manufacture of Measuring Instruments and Machinery	11.14	40.40	0.97	12.01	86.61
其他制造业	Other Manufacture	11.56	49.53	2.13	3.71	99.72
废弃资源综合利用业	Utilization of Waste Resources	0.16	59.22	0.38	0.50	114.52
金属制品、机械和设备修理业	Repair Service of Metal Products, Machinery and Equipment	26.57	65.76	1.88	10.59	57.59
电力、热力生产和供应业	Production and Supply of Electric Power and Heat Power	10.82	77.96	3.78	9.46	96.15
燃气生产和供应业	Production and Supply of Gas	14.43	62.91	1.66	20.75	99.40
水的生产和供应业	Production and Supply of Water	2.29	63.45	0.59	2.77	97.61

13-13 外商及港澳台商投资工业企业主要经济效益指标(2014年)

Main Indicators on Economic Benefit of Industrial Enterprises with Hong Kong, Macao, Taiwan and Foreign Funds (2014)

分 组	Item	总资产贡献率(%) Ratio of Profits, Taxes and Interests to Average Assets(%)	资 产负债率(%) Ratio of Debts to Assets (%)	流动资产周转率(次/年) Turnover of Current Assets (times/year)	成本费用利润率(%) Ratio of Profits to Total Industrial Cost (%)	工业产品销售率(%) Sales Ratio of Products (%)
总 计	**Total**	**12.04**	**54.45**	**2.07**	**10.67**	**91.25**
煤炭开采和洗选业	Mining and Washing of Coal	14.00	26.03	1.06	22.20	87.66
黑色金属矿采选业	Mining and Processing of Ferrous Metal Ores	19.52	51.45	8.27	2.27	99.00
有色金属矿采选业	Mining and Processing of Non-Ferrous Metal Ores	110.31	38.20	22.46	7.90	94.94
非金属矿采选业	Mining and Processing of Non-metal Ores	-6.48	46.23	1.16	-26.70	89.19
农副食品加工业	Processing of Food from Agricultural Products	32.76	50.15	7.21	9.03	84.58
食品制造业	Manufacture of Foods	16.13	44.76	2.95	7.31	92.99
酒、饮料和精制茶制造业	Manufacture of Liquor, Beverages and Refined Tea	21.00	50.76	2.34	17.03	92.45
纺织业	Manufacture of Textile	4.76	66.44	1.17	2.02	87.29
纺织服装、服饰业	Manufacture of Textile, Wearing Apparel and Accessories	84.85	5.28	43.13	11.17	98.18
造纸及纸制品业	Manufacture of Paper and Paper Products	71.45	31.47	7.88	18.71	97.82
印刷和记录媒介复制业	Printing and Reproduction of Recording Media	15.25	37.95	1.67	14.69	99.73
文教、工美、体育和娱乐用品制造业	Manufacture of Articles for Culture, Education, Arts and Crafts, Sport and Entertainment Activities	2.92	69.29	1.92	-0.45	100.00
石油加工、炼焦及核燃料加工业	Processing of Petroleum, Coking and Processing of Nuclear Fuel	33.40	57.88	6.46	4.15	100.00
化学原料及化学制品制造业	Manufacture of Raw Chemical Materials and Chemical Products	2.64	51.71	1.28	2.79	96.44
医药制造业	Manufacture of Medicines	21.45	46.79	1.40	12.42	95.78
化学纤维制造业	Manufacture of Chemical Fibres	40.73	19.21	2.72	19.61	98.52
橡胶和塑料制品业	Manufacture of Rubber and Plastics Products	14.87	84.98	15.25	2.93	60.76
非金属矿物制品业	Manufacture of Non-metallic Mineral Products	14.48	50.83	2.56	13.87	93.27
黑色金属冶炼和压延加工业	Smelting and Pressing of Ferrous Metals	-3.06	58.42	1.01	-8.96	34.73
有色金属冶炼和压延加工业	Smelting and Pressing of Non-ferrous Metals	13.37	38.68	2.35	4.43	83.01
金属制品业	Manufacture of Metal Products	0.14	59.37	2.51	-2.23	105.57
通用设备制造业	Manufacture of General Purpose Machinery	5.71	25.34	1.06	5.69	89.28
专用设备制造业	Manufacture of Special Purpose Machinery	12.03	54.56	1.74	11.30	92.72
汽车制造业	Manufacture of Automobiles	9.93	69.30	2.60	4.92	99.12
铁路、船舶、航空航天和其他运输设备制造业	Manufacture of Railway, Ship, Aerospace and Other Transport Equipments	21.57	52.73	0.88	24.64	99.38
电气机械和器材制造业	Manufacture of Electrical Machinery and Apparatus	17.07	54.01	2.24	6.39	89.28
计算机、通信和其他电子设备制造业	Manufacture of Computers, Communication and Other Electronic Equipment	3.25	55.92	1.31	14.09	82.84
仪器仪表制造业	Manufacture of Measuring Instruments and Machinery	16.57	41.86	0.81	24.57	91.42
其他制造业	Other Manufacture	11.80	15.41	0.48	31.68	99.54
金属制品、机械和设备修理业	Repair Service of Metal Products, Machinery and Equipment	12.87	54.41	1.16	6.81	100.00
电力、热力生产和供应业	Production and Supply of Electric Power and Heat Power	18.39	62.31	2.35	29.82	100.00
燃气生产和供应业	Production and Supply of Gas	11.22	55.81	1.50	20.73	91.14
水的生产和供应业	Production and Supply of Water	1.75	53.82	0.31	10.37	100.00

13-14 大中型工业企业主要经济效益指标(2014年)

Main Indicators on Economic Benefit of Large and Medium-sized Industrial Enterprises(2014)

分 组	Item	总资产贡献率(%) Ratio of Profits, Taxes and Interests to Average Assets(%)	资产负债率(%) Ratio of Debts to Assets (%)	流动资产周转率(次/年) Turnover of Current Assets (times/year)	成本费用利润率(%) Ratio of Profits to Total Industrial Cost (%)	工业产品销售率(%) Sales Ratio of Products (%)
总 计	**Total**	**15.93**	**57.34**	**2.09**	**13.03**	**95.63**
煤炭开采和洗选业	Mining and Washing of Coal	18.36	46.20	1.33	27.56	96.05
石油和天然气开采业	Extraction of Petroleum and Natural Gas	26.61	52.84	4.97	50.32	99.30
黑色金属矿采选业	Mining and Processing of Ferrous Metal Ores	11.22	64.63	1.63	5.96	78.83
有色金属矿采选业	Mining and Processing of Non-Ferrous Metal Ores	14.87	65.59	3.29	9.43	94.82
非金属矿采选业	Mining and Processing of Non-metal Ores	25.51	65.22	4.21	7.17	98.10
开采辅助活动	Support Activities for Mining	12.09	59.45	2.73	8.96	96.20
农副食品加工业	Processing of Food from Agricultural Products	28.76	60.56	4.34	8.11	94.55
食品制造业	Manufacture of Foods	30.09	42.78	4.04	11.85	94.19
酒、饮料和精制茶制造业	Manufacture of Liquor, Beverages and Refined Tea	31.58	52.35	2.79	19.29	93.38
烟草制品业	Manufacture of Tobacco	102.51	15.01	2.12	29.27	98.86
纺织业	Manufacture of Textile	30.82	58.32	3.94	13.71	95.05
纺织服装、服饰业	Manufacture of Textile,Wearing Apparel and Accessories	29.32	54.60	2.12	18.64	89.68
皮革、毛皮、羽毛及其制品和制鞋业	Manufacture of Leather,Fur,Feather and Related Products and Footwear	14.36	47.83	2.61	8.63	99.73
木材加工和木、竹、藤、棕、草制品业	Processing of Timber,Manufacture of Wood,Bamboo, Rattan,Palm and Straw Products	9.79	54.71	1.66	8.19	88.74
家具制造业	Manufacture of Furniture	38.55	47.35	3.92	15.35	100.35
造纸及纸制品业	Manufacture of Paper and Paper Products	32.74	33.57	9.46	10.41	91.78
印刷和记录媒介复制业	Printing and Reproduction of Recording Media	20.98	26.04	1.97	13.34	97.34
石油加工、炼焦及核燃料加工业	Processing of Petroleum, Coking and Processing of Nuclear Fuel	16.95	53.77	2.11	5.88	100.46
化学原料及化学制品制造业	Manufacture of Raw Chemical Materials and Chemical Products	2.52	74.40	1.46	1.10	94.90
医药制造业	Manufacture of Medicines	25.50	42.64	1.92	14.62	93.49
橡胶和塑料制品业	Manufacture of Rubber and Plastics Products	13.11	65.11	2.53	7.38	84.33
非金属矿物制品业	Manufacture of Non-metallic Mineral Products	12.38	60.30	3.72	5.12	92.97
黑色金属冶炼和压延加工业	Smelting and Pressing of Ferrous Metals	4.14	76.62	3.24	0.74	93.59
有色金属冶炼和压延加工业	Smelting and Pressing of Non-ferrous Metals	9.98	53.05	2.27	4.82	93.42
金属制品业	Manufacture of Metal Products	7.68	57.07	1.21	2.16	92.60
通用设备制造业	Manufacture of General Purpose Machinery	7.90	52.70	1.03	7.30	95.56
专用设备制造业	Manufacture of Special Purpose Machinery	6.24	60.63	0.80	6.34	90.92
汽车制造业	Manufacture of Automobiles	8.31	65.89	1.90	4.21	95.39
铁路、船舶、航空航天和其他运输设备制造业	Manufacture of Railway,Ship,Aerospace and Other Transport Equipments	12.40	53.97	1.32	9.01	91.70
电气机械和器材制造业	Manufacture of Electrical Machinery and Apparatus	6.04	49.76	0.84	5.20	98.58
计算机、通信和其他电子设备制造业	Manufacture of Computers, Communication and Other Electronic Equipment	3.47	54.54	1.16	9.67	81.92
仪器仪表制造业	Manufacture of Measuring Instruments and Machinery	14.36	44.33	1.05	17.25	89.32
废弃资源综合利用业	Utilization of Waste Resources	3.34	56.34	7.42	0.02	100.00
电力、热力生产和供应业	Production and Supply of Electric Power and Heat Power	11.70	77.20	3.90	9.93	96.12
燃气生产和供应业	Production and Supply of Gas	11.29	51.96	1.31	17.63	95.24
水的生产和供应业	Production and Supply of Water	2.67	52.56	0.99	0.52	98.82

13-15 主要工业产品产量

Output of Major Industrial Products

产品名称	Item	2012	2013	2014
天然原油 (万吨)	Crude Petroleum Oil (10 000 tons)	3527.56	3688.04	3767.81
天然气 (亿立方米)	Natural Gas (100 million cu.m)	309.62	371.65	410.11
铁矿石原矿 (万吨)	Crude Quantity of Iron Ore (10 000 tons)	1329.50	1498.77	1497.05
锌金属含量 (万吨)	Zinc Metal Content (10 000 tons)	29.63	44.25	54.90
钼精矿折合量 (万吨)	Reduced Quantity of Molybdenum Concentrate (10 000 tons)	4.98	4.94	4.91
发电量 (亿千瓦小时)	Electricity (100 million kwh)	1330.50	1493.66	1600.88
小麦粉 (万吨)	Wheat Meal (10 000 tons)	419.91	523.25	568.01
精制食用植物油 (万吨)	Refined Edible Vegetable Oil (10 000 tons)	121.94	133.29	146.21
饲　料 (万吨)	Feed (10 000 tons)	246.75	311.95	436.71
乳制品 (万吨)	Dairy Products (10 000 tons)	172.10	183.98	161.34
白　酒 (万千升)	Spirits (10 000 kiloliter)	9.31	10.49	11.92
啤　酒 (万千升)	Beer (10 000 kiloliter)	102.09	102.18	95.99
软饮料 (万吨)	Soft Drinks (10 000 tons)	419.84	523.89	560.93
卷　烟 (亿支)	Cigarettes (100 million pieces)	879.50	899.50	914.50
化学纤维 (吨)	Chemical Fiber (ton)	27876	25029	29367
纱 (万吨)	Yarn (10 000 tons)	28.86	35.55	40.05
布 (万米)	Cloth (10 000 m)	65006.43	57399.20	60967.85
印染布 (万米)	Dyed Fabric (10 000 m)	7438.84		2426.10
服　装 (万件)	Garments (10 000 cases)	1960.71	1974.20	2218.82
机制纸及纸板 (万吨)	Machine-made Paper and Paperboard (10 000 tons)	80.35	80.42	70.77
纸制品 (万吨)	Paper Products (10 000 tons)	50.18	48.05	73.39
原油加工量 (万吨)	Crude Runs (10 000 tons)	2124.05	2078.59	2095.79
#汽　油	Gasoline	737.65	745.21	766.18
柴　油	Diesel Oil	921.51	883.97	895.75
机械化焦炉生产的焦炭 (万吨)	Coke (10 000 tons)	2041.77	2447.37	3797.54
硫酸(折100%) (万吨)	Sulfuric Acid (10 000 tons)	134.76	128.71	132.49
氢氧化钠(烧碱) (万吨)	Caustic Soda (10 000 tons)	50.94	67.77	92.41
碳化钙(电石) (万吨)	Soda Ash (10 000 tons)	146.71	167.32	208.35
合成氨 (万吨)	Synthetic Ammonia (10 000 tons)	135.26	140.81	178.76

13-15 续表 continued

产品名称	Item	2012	2013	2014
化肥总计 (万吨)	Chemical Fertilizers (10 000 tons)	97.89	103.04	179.33
氮 肥	Nitrogen Fertilizers	74.01	80.63	163.66
磷 肥	Phosphate Fertilizers	23.88	22.40	15.44
合成洗涤剂 (吨)	Synthetic Detergents (ton)	149673		134337
化学药品原药 (吨)	Chemical Medicines (ton)	12569	16112	15241
精甲醇 (万吨)	Extract Methanol (10 000 tons)	269.40	292.35	338.96
中成药 (吨)	Traditional Chinese Medicine (ton)	32373	40194	49061
塑料制品 (万吨)	Plastic Articles (10 000 tons)	42.14	44.86	58.97
水 泥 (万吨)	Cement (10 000 tons)	7552.71	8545.52	9083.49
平板玻璃 (万重量箱)	Plain Glass (10 000 weight cases)	1360.84	1837.85	2283.01
生 铁 (万吨)	Pig Iron (10 000 tons)	803.12	882.54	884.02
粗 钢 (万吨)	Crude Steel (10 000 tons)	828.69	980.08	1038.26
钢 材 (万吨)	Rolled Steel (10 000 tons)	1283.55	1565.22	1683.92
铝 材 (万吨)	Rolled Aluminum (10 000 tons)	15.48	16.54	11.81
铁合金 (万吨)	Ferroalloy (10 000 tons)	51.44	57.26	68.79
十种有色金属 (万吨)	Ten Kinds of Nonferrous Metals (10 000 tons)	124.29	159.61	204.74
原铝(电解铝) (万吨)	Electrolyzed Aluminum (10 000 tons)	29.89	44.36	66.83
锌 (万吨)	Zinc Metal (10 000 tons)	61.92	71.78	84.21
金属切削机床 (台)	Metal-cutting Machine Tools (unit)	19781	16271	20660
# 数控机床	Computer Numerical Control Machine Tools	8670	8161	10022
金属成型机床(锻压设备) (台)	Metal Forming Machines(Forging Equipment) (unit)	4458	4671	6122
汽 车 (万辆)	Motor Vehicles (unit)	54.46	42.44	37.47
#基本型乘用车(轿车)	Basic Type Passenger Vehicle(Car)	36.62	31.70	26.71
载货汽车	Trucks	7.89	10.34	10.65
交流电动机 (万千瓦)	Alternating Current Motors (10 000 kw)	449.54	582.32	795.99
变压器 (万千伏安)	Transformers (10 000 KVA)	11278.66	12858.19	15536.35
光 缆 (万芯千米)	Fiber Optic Cable (10 000 Core.km)	156.93	334.77	513.96
电子元件 (万只)	Electronic Components (10 000 units)	41475.30	109917.55	822958.80

13-16 各市(区)规模以上工业企业工业总产值(1995-2014年)
Gross Industrial Output Value above Designated Size by City(District)(1995-2014)

单位：亿元 (100 million yuan)

年 份 Year	全 省 Shaanxi	西安市 Xi'an	铜川市 Tongchuan	宝鸡市 Baoji	咸阳市 Xianyang	渭南市 Weinan
1995	761.35	240.63	15.80	115.84	135.02	74.74
1996	814.82	281.51	21.98	123.29	151.78	79.99
1997	900.78	303.94	25.47	124.26	173.04	87.40
1998	960.81	355.15	26.97	125.62	182.22	89.60
1999	1097.45	376.72	29.21	126.21	202.89	95.79
2000	1268.43	433.43	30.84	139.98	208.70	100.27
2001	1457.62	505.02	30.11	155.13	217.24	112.93
2002	1667.10	546.24	33.38	183.76	231.22	136.04
2003	2118.17	676.93	42.13	252.95	286.13	191.74
2004	2735.22	892.60	59.91	315.47	309.65	257.79
2005	3397.71	952.18	70.49	409.95	359.16	337.71
2006	4442.81	1194.60	99.53	536.67	458.52	377.63
2007	5692.33	1623.85	124.34	672.20	565.61	474.27
2008	7480.79	2030.76	166.84	895.77	860.24	638.00
2009	8470.40	2490.50	195.02	995.99	1038.83	767.22
2010	11199.84	3130.15	249.05	1340.45	1401.92	1039.83
2011	14283.48	3552.21	335.76	1701.80	1854.54	1360.03
2012	16926.49	4066.31	461.80	1986.69	2293.52	1634.36
2013	18982.47	4497.62	549.66	2258.52	2633.00	1728.47
2014	20015.88	4420.06	565.91	2274.97	3002.05	1959.32

13-16 续表 continued

单位：亿元 (100 million yuan)

年 份 Year	延安市 Yan'an	汉中市 Hanzhong	榆林市 Yulin	安康市 Ankang	商洛市 Shangluo	杨凌示范区 Yangling
1995	33.39	53.33	16.75	12.49	5.61	1.61
1996	56.96	56.62	18.19	16.13	6.43	1.95
1997	75.33	62.91	20.15	19.04	6.92	2.32
1998	69.83	63.80	22.48	15.93	7.92	1.29
1999	83.90	62.58	24.60	16.37	9.45	1.28
2000	131.00	68.43	36.61	20.06	11.47	2.07
2001	160.78	76.31	68.20	20.63	14.19	3.58
2002	188.52	89.11	119.20	25.03	16.40	5.52
2003	255.93	110.07	142.27	30.45	22.00	13.34
2004	348.10	142.76	278.39	37.71	26.82	16.29
2005	537.00	165.41	360.04	43.57	32.76	16.53
2006	764.07	204.37	528.20	56.28	41.39	19.57
2007	905.20	241.11	773.87	81.56	60.08	28.17
2008	1053.51	260.60	1269.86	97.48	74.43	34.74
2009	969.50	310.79	1392.56	132.47	104.56	40.30
2010	1227.31	404.41	1917.70	192.15	176.99	40.09
2011	1504.86	545.42	2613.53	309.22	265.07	60.26
2012	1646.76	718.09	3130.98	482.20	365.04	79.87
2013	1612.32	856.10	3120.82	634.82	479.93	88.32
2014	1708.57	873.56	3449.20	787.97	634.11	110.86

13-17　各市(区)规模以上工业企业主要经济指标(2014年)

Main Indicators of Industrial Enterprises above Designated Size by City(District)(2014)

单位：万元　　　　(10 000 yuan)

地　区	Sector	企业单位数(个) Number of Enterprises (unit)	#亏损企业 Unprofitable Enterprises	资产总计 Total Assets	负债合计 Total Liabilities	所有者权益合计 Owners' Equity	主营业务收入 Revenue from Principal Business	主营业务成本 Cost of Principal Business
全　省	**Shaanxi**	**5017**	**860**	**243714377**	**138404283**	**105199889**	**186221351**	**143675613**
西安市	Xi'an	1113	220	47071356	28065355	18974844	37675319	31873831
铜川市	Tongchuan	153	30	4899285	2993085	1791945	4960735	4281377
宝鸡市	Baoji	536	69	19160981	10876897	8262176	18710346	15007530
咸阳市	Xianyang	774	48	21637734	10603712	11041786	27882030	21968382
渭南市	Weinan	450	99	23156879	15552801	7555020	17214164	14687928
#韩城市	Hancheng	79	36	7731225	5591148	2140076	6613718	5181729
延安市	Yan'an	129	34	33691928	17908859	15778418	19021940	12903247
汉中市	Hanzhong	392	80	7746836	5289577	2431044	9273152	8072080
榆林市	Yulin	704	218	64120662	35373926	28723402	31435568	20667942
安康市	Ankang	460	11	4455825	2015087	2416203	7399116	5805997
商洛市	Shangluo	207	36	4695958	3053702	1825822	5670793	5010451
杨凌示范区	Yangling	94	15	1066844	556327	504093	930154	778647

13-17　续表　continued

单位：万元　　　　(10 000 yuan)

地　区	Sector	主营业务税金及附加 Taxes and Other Charges on Principal Business	销售费用 Eelling Expenses	管理费用 Management Expenses	财务费用 Financial Expenses	利润总额 Total Profits	亏损企业亏损额 Losses of Unprofitable Enterprises	本年应交增值税 Value Added Tax Payable	全部从业人员年平均人数(人) Annual Average Employed Persons (person)
全　省	**Shaanxi**	**7188756**	**4765311**	**8993971**	**3134243**	**18469820**	**1303035**	**9403194**	**1547285**
西安市	Xi'an	310746	1497181	1973885	414245	2051446	269804	1346262	377472
铜川市	Tongchuan	44692	122189	249157	137779	157144	47278	198145	49353
宝鸡市	Baoji	612342	575713	1071875	248057	1353368	54891	734457	166827
咸阳市	Xianyang	857287	650650	853387	320516	3216082	133295	1350597	249046
渭南市	Weinan	89128	256804	506002	379401	492658	271354	361230	155038
#韩城市	Hancheng	18779	83484	99054	150212	161344	56494	120205	39311
延安市	Yan'an	2109617	254980	1482889	357440	2295155	39781	1340981	111472
汉中市	Hanzhong	314393	163176	271150	147685	272337	109327	238862	80980
榆林市	Yulin	1729497	862784	1881681	810584	5330298	264976	2493206	225684
安康市	Ankang	146719	230480	286009	84474	847078	17634	405446	57274
商洛市	Shangluo	49155	98302	165159	70330	235686	89868	203581	37924
杨凌示范区	Yangling	3101	50190	40364	12583	53241	4829	47413	10648

主要统计指标解释

工业 指从事自然资源的开采，对采掘品和农产品进行加工和再加工的物质生产部门。具体包括：(1)对自然资源的开采，如采矿、晒盐等(但不包括禽兽捕猎和水产捕捞)；(2)对农副产品的加工、再加工，如粮油加工、食品加工、缫丝、纺织、制革等；(3)对采掘品的加工、再加工，如炼铁、炼钢、化工生产、石油加工、机器制造、木材加工等，以及电力、自来水、煤气的生产和供应等；(4)对工业品的修理、翻新，如机器设备的修理、交通运输工具(如汽车)的修理等。

轻工业 指主要提供生活消费品和制作手工工具的工业。按其所使用的原料不同，可分为两大类：(1)以农产品为原料的轻工业，是指直接或间接以农产品为基本原料的轻工业。主要包括食品制造、饮料制造、烟草加工、纺织、缝纫、皮革和毛皮制作、造纸以及印刷等工业；(2)以非农产品为原料的轻工业，是指以工业品为原料的轻工业。主要包括文教体育用品、化学药品制造、合成纤维制造、日用化学制品、日用玻璃制品、日用金属制品、手工工具制造、医疗器械制造、文化和办公用机械制造等工业。

重工业 指为国民经济各部门提供物质技术基础的主要生产资料的工业。按其生产性质和产品用途，可以分为下列三类：(1)采掘(伐)工业，是指对自然资源的开采，包括石油开采、煤炭开采、金属矿开采、非金属矿开采等工业；(2)原材料工业，指向国民经济各部门提供基本材料、动力和燃料的工业。包括金属冶炼及加工、炼焦及焦炭、化学、化工原料、水泥、人造板以及电力、石油和煤炭加工等工业；(3)加工工业，是指对工业原材料进行再加工制造的工业。包括装备国民经济各部门的机械设备制造工业、金属结构、水泥制品等工业，以及为农业提供的生产资料如化肥、农药等工业。

根据上述划分原则，修理业中以重工业产品为修理作业对象的划为重工业，反之划为轻工业。

国有及国有控股企业 指国有企业加上国有控股企业。国有企业(即原全民所有制工业或国营工业)指企业全部资产归国家所有，并按《中华人民共和国企业法人登记管理条例》规定登记注册的非公司制的经济组织。包括国有企业、国有独资公司和国有联营企业。1957 年以前的公私合营和私营工业，后均改造为国营工业，1992 年改为国有工业，这部分工业的资料不单独分列时，均包括在国有企业内。国有控股企业是对混合所有制经济的企业进行的“国有控股”分类。它是指这些企业的全部资产中国有资产(股份)相对其他所有者中的任何一个所有者占资(股)最多的企业。该分组反映了国有经济控股情况。

工业总产值

(1)定义：

工业总产值是以货币形式表现的，工业企业在一定时期内生产的工业最终产品或提供工业性劳务活动的总价值量。它反映一定时间内工业生产的总规模和总水平。

(2)计算原则：

工业生产的原则，即凡是企业在报告期生产的经检验合格的产品，不管是否在报告期销售，均包括在内。

最终产品的原则，即凡是计入工业总产值的产品，必须是本企业生产的经检验合格的，不需要再进行任何加工的最终产品。如果企业有中间产品(半成品)对外销售，则对外销售的中间产品应视为企业的最终产品。

工厂法原则，即工业总产值是以工业企业作为基本计算(核算)单位，即按企业的最终产品计算工业总产值。按这种方法计算的工业总产值，不允许同一产品价值在企业内部重复计算，不能把企业内部各个车间(分厂)生产的成果相加，但允许企业间的重复计算。

(3)内容及计算方法：

1995 年全国工业普查对工业总产值(原规定)的内容及计算原则和方法做了某些修订，修订后的工业总产值(新规定)包括三项内容：即本期生产成品价值、对外加工费收入、在制品半成品期末期初差额价值三部分。

工业增加值 指工业企业在报告期内以货币表现的工业生产活动的最终成果。

工业增加值有两种计算方法：一是生产法，即工业总产出减去工业中间投入加上应交增值税；二是收入法，即从收入的角度出发，根据生产要素在生产过程中应得到的收入份额计算，具体构成项目有固定资产折旧、劳动者报酬、生产税净额、营业盈余，这种方法也称要素分配法。本年鉴中的工业增加值是以生产法计算的。

生产法工业增加值的计算方法为：

工业增加值=工业总产出-工业中间投入+应交增值税

资产总计 指企业拥有或控制的能以货币计量的经济资源，包括各种财产、债权和其他权利。资产按流动性分为流动资产、长期投资、固定资产、无形资产、递延资产和其他资产。该指标根据企业会计“资产负债表”中“资产总计”项目的期末数增列。

流动资产 指企业可以在一年内或者超过一年的一个生产周期内变现或者耗用的资产，包括现金及各种存款、短期投资，应收及预付款项、存货等。

流动资产平均余额 指企业在报告期内全部流动资产的平均余额。

固定资产原价 指企业在建造、购置、安装、改建、扩建、技术改造某项固定资产时所支出的全部货币总额。它一般包括买价、包装费、运杂费和安装费等。

固定资产净值年平均余额　指固定资产净值在报告期内余额的平均数。计算公式为：

$$\text{固定资产净值年平均余额}=\frac{\text{1至12月各月月初、月末固定资产净值之和}}{24}$$

固定资产净值　指固定资产原价减去历年已提折旧额后的净额。计算公式为：

固定资产净值=固定资产原价-累计折旧

负债合计　指企业所承担的能以货币计量，将以资产或劳务偿付的债务，偿还形式包括货币、资产或提供劳务。负债一般按偿还期长短分为流动负债和长期负债。根据会计“资产负债表”中“负债合计”的年末数填列。

所有者权益　指企业投资人对企业净资产的所有权。企业净资产等于企业全部资产减去全部负债后的余额，包括企业投资人对企业的最初投入的实际到位的资产及资本公积金、盈余公积金和未分配利润。所有者权益合计数小于零，表示企业资不抵债。

主营业务收入　指会计“利润表”中对应指标的本年累计数。未执行 2001 年《企业会计制度》的企业，用“产品销售收入”的本期累计数代替。

主营业务成本　指会计“利润表”中对应指标的本年累计数。未执行 2001 年《企业会计制度》的企业，用“产品销售成本”的本期累计数代替。

主营业务税金及附加　指会计“利润表”中对应指标的本年累计数。未执行 2001 年《企业会计制度》的企业，用“产品销售税金及附加”　的本期累计数代替。

利润总额　指企业生产经营活动的最终成果，是企业在一定时期内实现的盈亏相抵后的利润总额(亏损以“-”号表示)，它等于营业利润加上补贴收入加上投资收益加上营业外净收入再加上以前年度损益调整。

本年应交增值税　指企业在报告期内应交纳的增值税额。它等于本年销项税额加上出口退税加上进项税额转出数减去本年进项税额。小规模纳税企业直接按全年计税销售额乘以征收率计算取得。

从业人员平均人数　是指报告期内每天拥有的从业人员人数。其计算公式为：

$$\text{月平均人数}=\frac{\text{报告月内每天实有人数之和}}{\text{报告月日历日数}}$$

$$\text{季平均人数}=\frac{\text{季内各月平均人数之和}}{3}$$

$$\text{年平均人数}=\frac{\text{年内各月平均人数之和}}{12}$$

总资产贡献率　反映企业全部资产的获利能力，是企业经营业绩和管理水平的集中体现，是评价和考核企业盈利能力的核心指标。计算公式为：

$$\text{总资产贡献率(\%)}=\frac{\text{利润总额}+\text{税金总额}+\text{利息支出}}{\text{平均资金总额}}\times 100\%$$

公式中：税金总额为产品销售税金及附加与应交增值税之和；平均资产总额为期初期末资产之和的算术平均值。

资产负债率　该指标既反映企业经营风险的大小，也反映企业利用债权人提供的资金从事经营活动的能力。计算公式为：

$$\text{资产负债率(\%)}=\frac{\text{负债总额}}{\text{资产总额}}\times 100\%$$

资产与负债均为报告期期末数。

流动资产周转次数　指一定时期内流动资产完成的周转次数，反映投入工业企业流动资金的周转速度。计算公式为：

$$\text{流动资产周转次数}=\frac{\text{产品销售收入}}{\text{全部流动资产平均余额}}$$

公式中：全部流动资产平均余额为期初和期末的流动资产之和的算术平均值。

成本费用利润率　反映企业投入的生产成本及费用的经济效益，同时也反映企业降低成本所取得的经济效益。计算公式为：

$$\text{成本费用利润率(\%)}=\frac{\text{利润总额}}{\text{成本费用总额}}\times 100\%$$

公式中：成本费用总额为产品销售成本、销售费用、管理费用、财务费用之和。

产品销售率　该指标反映工业产品已实现销售的程度，是分析工业产销衔接情况，研究工业产品满足社会需求的指标。计算公式为：

$$\text{产品销售率(\%)}=\frac{\text{工业销售产值}}{\text{工业总产值(现价)}}\times 100\%$$

Explanatory Notes on Main Statistical Indicators

Industry refers to the material production sector which is engaged in the extraction of natural resources and processing and reprocessing of minerals and agricultural products, including (1) extraction of natural resources, such as mining, salt production (but not including hunting and fishing); (2) processing and reprocessing of farm and sideline produces, such as rice husking, flour milling, wine making, oil pressing, silk reeling, spinning and weaving, and leather making; (3) manufacture of industrial products, such as steel making, iron smelting, chemicals manufacturing, petroleum processing, machine building, timber processing; water and gas production and electricity generation and supply; (4)repairing of industrial products such as the repairing of machinery and means of transport (including cars).

Light Industry refers to the industry that produces consumer goods and hand tools. It consists of two categories, depending on the materials used:

(1) Industries using farm products as raw materials. These are the branches of light industry which directly or indirectly use farm products as basic raw materials, including the manufacture of food and beverages, tobacco processing, textile, clothing, fur and leather manufacturing, paper making, printing, etc.

(2) Industries using non-farm products as raw materials. These are the branches of light industry which use manufactured goods as raw materials, including the manufacture of cultural, educational articles and sports goods, chemicals, synthetic fibre, chemical products for daily use, glass products for daily use, metal products for daily use, hand tools, medical apparatus and instruments, and the manufacture of cultural and office machinery.

Heavy Industry refers to the industry which produces capital goods, and provides various sectors of the national economy with necessary material and technical basis for production. It consists of the following three branches according to the purpose of production or the use of products:

(1) Mining, quarrying and logging industry, which refers to the industry that extracts natural resources, including extraction of petroleum, coal, metal and non-metal ores.

(2) Raw materials industry refers to the industry that provides various sectors of the national economy with raw materials, fuels and power. It includes smelting and processing of metals, coking and coke chemistry, chemical materials and building materials such as cement, plywood, and power, petroleum refining and coal dressing.

(3) Manufacturing industry which refers to the industry that processes raw materials. It includes machine-building industries which equip sectors of the national economy; industries producing metal structure and cement products; and industries producing means of agricultural production, such as chemical fertilizers and pesticides.

In accordance with the above principles of classification, the repairing trades, which are engaged primarily in repairing products of heavy industry, are classified as heavy industry while those which are engaged in repairing products of light industry are classified as light industry.

State-owned and State-holding Enterprises refer to state-owned enterprises plus State-holding enterprises. State-owned enterprises (originally known as State-run enterprises with ownership by the whole society) are non-corporate economic entities registered in accordance with the *Regulation of the People's Republic of China on the Management of Registration of Legal Enterprises*, where all assets are owned by the State. Included in this category are State-owned enterprises, State-funded corporations and State-owned joint-operation enterprises. Joint State-private industries and private industries, which existed before 1957, were transformed into state-run industries since 1957, and into State-owned industries after 1992. Statistics on those enterprises are included in the State-owned industries instead of being grouped them separately. State-holding enterprises are a sub-classification of enterprises with mixed ownership, referring to enterprises where the percentage of State assets (or shares by the State) is larger than any other single share holder of the same enterprise. This sub-classification illustrates the control of the State over a particular industry.

Gross Industrial Output Value

(1) Definition: Gross industrial output value is the total volume of final industrial products produced and industrial services provided during a given period. It reflects the total achievements and overall scale of industrial production during a given period.

(2) Principles for calculation:

Statistics on industrial production follow the principle that all products produced by the enterprises and accepted through quality check during the reference period are to be included no matter whether they are sold or not during the reference period.

Determination of final products follows the principle that all products that are included in the calculation of gross industrial output value are the final products of the enterprise which have been accepted through quality check and require no further processing. If an enterprise has intermediate (semi-finished) products to sell, these intermediate products are considered as the final products of the enterprise.

Gross industrial output value is calculated following the principle of factory approach, i.e. industrial enterprise is used as the basic accounting unit in calculating the gross industrial output value. By this approach, value of the same product is not to be double-counted, and the output value of different workshops (branch factories) within the enterprise should not be added. However, this approach allows the possibility of double counting between enterprises.

(3) Content and method of calculation: The old definition of gross industrial output value was modified during the 1995 National Industrial Census. The revised (new) definition of gross industrial output value consists of 3 components: value of the finished products during the reference period, income from processing for external parties, and value of change in semi-finished products between the end and the beginning of the reference period.

Value-added of Industry refers to the final results of industrial production of industrial enterprises in money terms during the reference period.

Industrial value-added can be calculated by two approaches: the production approach, i.e. gross industrial output value minus intermediate input plus value-added tax, and the income approach, i.e. income for various factors used in the course of production, including depreciation of fixed assets, remuneration of labourers, net of production tax, and operating surplus. Value-added of industry in the Yearbook is calculated by the production approach as follows:

Value-added of industry = gross industrial output - industrial intermediate input + value-added tax

Total Assets refer to all economic resources, in monetary term, these are owned or controlled by enterprises, including properties, creditor's equity and other economic rights of all forms. Classified by the degree of liquidity, total assets include working capitals, long-term investment, fixed assets, intangible assets, deferred assets and other assets. Data on this indicator can be obtained by the year-end figures of total assets in the *Assets and Liability Table* of accounting records of enterprises.

Working Capital refers to capital that an enterprise can cash or use during one year or one production cycle that may exceed one year, including cash and savings deposits of various forms, short-term investment, money receivable and prepaid money, inventories, etc.

Annual Average Value of Working Capital refers to the average value of all working capital of the enterprise during the reference period.

Original Value of Fixed Assets refers to the total value, in monetary terms, that an enterprise spent on fixed assets, through construction, purchase, installation, transformation, expansion or technical upgrading. Generally, it covers cost of purchase, packing, transportation and installation, etc.

Annual Average of Net Value of Fixed Assets refers to the average of the net value of fixed assets during the reference period, calculated with the following formula:

$$\text{Annual Average of Net Value of Fixed Assets} = \frac{\text{sum of net value of fixed assets at the beginning and at the end of each month from January to December}}{24}$$

Net value of fixed assets refers to the original value of fixed assets minus depreciation over the years, i.e.:

Net value of fixed assets = original value of fixed assets - cumulative depreciation

Total Liabilities refer to payable liabilities of enterprises that have to be repaid in terms of money, assets or labour services. In terms of payment, it can be divided into liquid liabilities and long-term liabilities. Data on this item is obtained from the ending figures on total liabilities from the Assets and Liability Table from the enterprises.

Owner's Equity refers to the ownership of net assets of enterprise by its investors. Net assets equal total assets minus total liabilities of the enterprise, including the actual assets invested into the enterprise by investors, accumulation of capital and operating surplus and non-distributed profits. The enterprise's assets are less than its liabilities if the sum of owner's equity is smaller than zero.

Revenue from Principal Business refers to the annual accumulation of the corresponding item in the "profit table" of the accountant. For enterprises that do not follow the *2001 Enterprise Accounting Standards*, the year-end accumulation of revenue from the sales of products is used as a substitute.

Cost of Principal Business refers to the annual accumulation of the corresponding item in the "profit table" of the accountant. For enterprises that do not follow the *2001 Enterprise Accounting Standards*, the year-end accumulation of cost for the sales of products is used as a substitute.

Tax and Extra Charges from Principal Business refer to the annual accumulation of the corresponding item in the "profit table" of the accountant. For enterprises that do not follow the *2001 Enterprise Accounting Standards*, the year-end accumulation of tax and extra charges from the sales of products is used as a substitute.

Total Profits refer to the final achievement of production and operation activities of the enterprises, represented by total profits after deducting losses (loss is expressed by the negative figure). It is the sum of profits from operation, income from subsidies, investment earnings, net income from activities other than operation, and adjustment of profits and losses of previous years.

Value-added Tax Payable in the Current Year refers to the amount of the value-added tax which should be paid by the enterprises during the reference period. It is the sum of tax on sales, export rebate, and transferred tax on purchases of the current year, minus the tax on purchases of the current year. Value-added tax payable of small-size enterprises is determined by the taxable sales of the year multiplied by the tax rate.

Average Annual Number of Employed Persons Employed persons refer to all those who are employed in enterprises and receive remunerations there from, including currently working employees, retirees who are re-employed, teachers of local-run schools, as well as foreigners, staff from Hong Kong, Macao and Taiwan, part-time employees and persons with second job who are employed by the enterprise, and employees of other units temporarily working in the enterprises, but excluding former employees who left the

enterprise with their employment records still being kept by the enterprises.

Average number of employed persons refers to the number of employee everyday during the reference period, calculated with the following formula:

$$\text{Monthly average number} = \frac{\text{sum of actual employees everyday in reference month}}{\text{number of calendar dates in reference month}}$$

$$\text{Quarterly average number} = \frac{\text{sum of monthly average number in reference quarter}}{3}$$

$$\text{Annual average number} = \frac{\text{sum of monthly average number in reference year}}{12}$$

Ratio of Profits, Taxes and Interests to Average Assets reflects the profit-making capability of all assets of the enterprise and is a key indicator manifesting the performance and management and evaluating the profit-making potential of the enterprise. It is calculated as follows:

$$\text{Ratio of Profits, Taxes and Interests to Average Assets (\%)} = \frac{\text{total profits + total taxes + interest payment}}{\text{average assets}} \times 100\%$$

In the above formula, total taxes is the sum of tax and extra charges on the sales of products and value-added tax payable; and average assets is the arithmetic mean of the sum of beginning assets and ending assets.

Ratio of Debts to Assets reflects both the operation risk and the capability of the enterprise in making use of the capital from the creditors. It is calculated as follows:

$$\text{Ratio of Debts to Assets (\%)} = \frac{\text{total debts}}{\text{total assets}} \times 100\%$$

Both assets and debts are figures at the end of the reference period.

Turnover of Working Capital refers to the number of times of turnover of working capital in a given period of time, which reflects the speed of the turnover of working capital of industrial enterprises, and is calculated as follows:

$$\text{Turnover of Working Capital} = \frac{\text{sales revenue of products}}{\text{average balance of total working capital}}$$

In the above formula, average balance of total working capital refers to the arithmetic mean of the sum of working capital at the beginning and at the end of the reference period.

Ratio of Profits to Total Industrial Costs refers to the ratio of profits realized in a given period to the total costs in the same period, which reflects the economic efficiency of input cost and is calculated as follows:

$$\text{Ratio of Profits to Total Industrial Cost (\%)} = \frac{\text{total profits}}{\text{total costs}} \times 100\%$$

Total costs in the above formula are the sum of cost of products sold, marketing cost, management cost and financial cost.

Sales Ratio of Products is an indicator reflecting the actual sale of industrial products, analyzing the production-selling and supply-demand relations. It is calculated as:

$$\text{Sales Ratio of Products (\%)} = \frac{\text{value of industrial sales}}{\text{gross industrial output value (current prices)}} \times 100\%$$

十四、建筑业

Construction

资料整理：王　东　郭　涛　陈晓峰

简 要 说 明

一、本篇资料反映陕西建筑业概况和发展情况。内容包括建筑业企业基本情况和生产经营情况。主要指标有企业个数、从业人员数、建筑业总产值、建筑业增加值、房屋建筑面积、利润税金、劳动生产率等。此外，还包括勘察设计企业基本情况。

二、建筑业统计范围为具有建筑业资质的独立核算建筑业企业。

三、勘察设计企业资料由省住房和城乡建设厅提供。

Brief Introduction

I. This chapter reflects the general situation and the development of the construction industry of Shaanxi Province. They cover the situation of production and management of the construction enterprises, including the number of enterprises, number of employed persons, gross output value and value added of the construction industry, floor space of buildings under construction, profits and taxes and labour productivity etc. They also cover main indicators on the situation of prospecting and designing institutions and personnel.

II. The scope of Statistics is all the construction enterprises of various types of ownership with qualification certificates and independent accounting systems.

III. Data on prospecting and designing institutions are provided by Shaanxi Province Housing and Urban-Rural Development.

14.建筑业

2014年全省具有建筑业资质等级的建筑施工企业		
企业个数	1752	个
#国有及国有控股企业	246	个
总产值	4566.37	亿 元
#国有及国有控股企业	2804.31	亿 元
房屋建筑竣工面积（不含劳务分包企业）	6917.76	万平方米
房屋建筑面积竣工率（不含劳务分包企业）	30.0	%

建筑施工企业总产值（亿元）

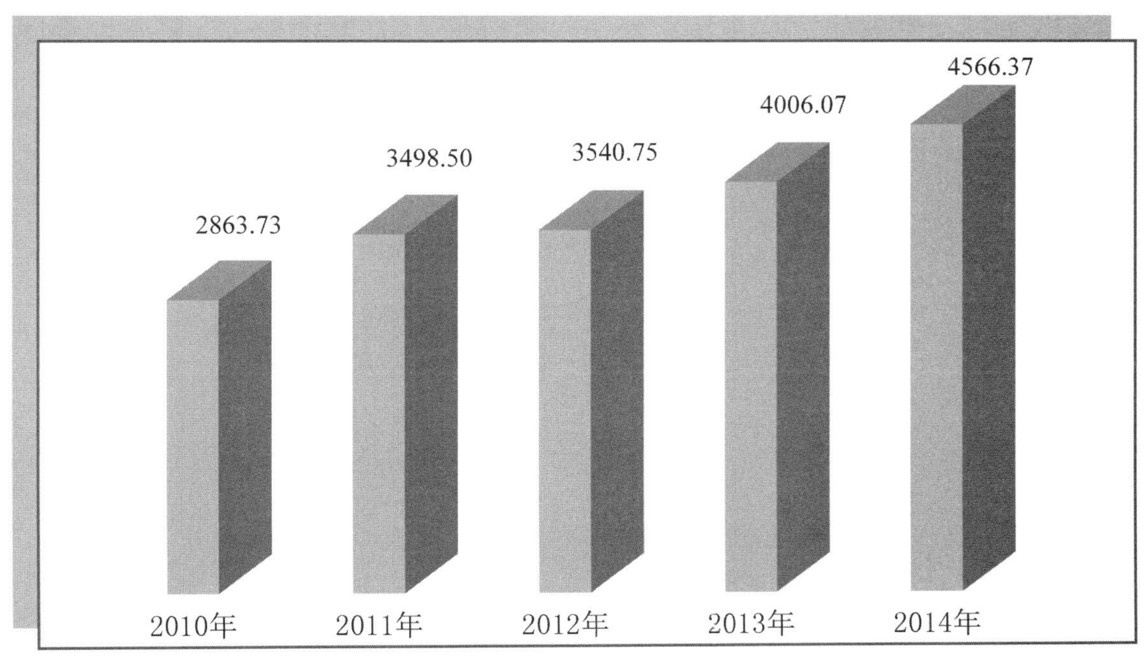

14-1 建筑业总产值
Gross Output Value of Construction

单位：万元 (10 000 yuan)

年份 Year	建筑业总产值 Gross Output Value of Construction	#地方属企业 Local-owned	国有企业 State-owned	集体企业 Collective-owned
1978	86642	60131	75082	11560
1979	91932	66057	77854	14078
1980	97607	71142	80505	17102
1981	82528	65171	65789	16739
1982	98176	70799	79749	18427
1983	110401	75874	85828	24573
1984	139234	92633	111271	27963
1985	164405	100322	132119	32286
1986	183081	112965	150795	38357
1987	208180	125264	165971	42209
1988	242409	134927	197920	44489
1989	273554	144417	230069	43485
1990	325034	155840	278358	46676
1991	360774	173400	306098	54676
1992	479806	228929	410445	69361
1993	751613	331449	650865	100649
1994	980260	414949	856685	121941
1995	1065612	501076	914782	143870
1996	1294502	735145	940012	335948
1997	1642493	928341	1158205	461272
1998	1879804	983440	1399161	394712
1999	2183009	1188225	1640515	432628
2000	2423046	1205275	1843456	439089
2001	2797388	1424557	1970842	479810
2002	3473536	1735125	2474524	490351
2003	4409564	2076800	3138878	456851
2004	5231639	2688405	3878423	439996
2005	6586411	3011102	5068215	443869
2006	8306966	3918215	6108524	686188
2007	11734648	5906626	7794313	931517
2008	16556239	8501607	11138979	1036447
2009	23092674	11391659	16741395	1201810
2010	28637317	15426858	20021853	2220240
2011	34984999	20712510	24518351	3152250
2012	35407509	24154390	22000114	3849886
2013	40060698	15161904	24898794	2184911
2014	45663737	17620612	28043125	2177236

注：1.1996年以后建筑业年报统计范围由往年的县及县以上(含县级建制镇)各种经济类型的建筑企业，改为具有建筑业资质等级四级及以上的各种经济类型的建筑施工企业；2002年改为具有建筑业资质等级的各种经济类型的建筑施工企业。

2.1998年以后国有经济为国有及国有控股企业。

3.本表资料含劳务分包企业。

a) Since 1996, the statistical range of construction annual report have changed from construction enterprises of all economic types in counties and above counties level (contain county towns) to the construction enterprises of all economic types at fourth or higher quality grades, since 2002 which have changed to the all economic types construction enterprises which possess qualification grades.

b) Since 1998, the state-owned enterprises are the state-owned and the state holding enterprises.

c) Data in the table include the subcontractor of labour services.

14-2 具有资质等级的建筑业企业主要指标(2014年)

指　　标	Item	企业数(个) Number of Enterprises (unit)	总产值(万元) Total Output Value (10 000 yuan)	直接从事生产经营活动平均人数(人) Annual Average of Persons Employed (person)	年末从业人数(人) Number of Engaged Persons (person)
总　　计	**Total**	**1752**	**45663737**	**1395067**	**896335**
# 国有及国有控股企业	State-owned and State-holding Enterprises	246	28043125	708264	361804
按登记注册类型分	**By Status of Registration**				
内资企业	Domestic Funded	1748	45207646	1384661	886381
国有企业	State-owned Enterprises	89	4438757	184976	94352
集体企业	Collective-owned Enterprises	124	2177236	93814	84296
股份合作企业	Cooperative Enterprises	3	69102	3091	2751
联营企业	Joint Ownership Enterprises	3	99242	3456	3210
有限责任公司	Limited Liability Corporations	695	28224442	715233	428711
股份有限公司	Share-holding Corporations Limited	68	2523640	59236	40152
私营企业	Private Enterprises	763	7674150	324740	232770
其他企业	Other Enterprises	3	1077	115	139
港、澳、台商投资企业	Enterprises with Funds from Hong Kong, Macao and Taiwan	1	510	14	15
合资经营企业(港或澳、台资)	Joint-venture Enterprises	1	510	14	15
外商投资企业	Foreign-invested Enterprise	3	455581	10392	9939
中外合资经营企业	Joint-venture Enterprises	2	453599	10184	9730
外资企业	Enterprises with Sole Funds	1	1982	208	209
按国民经济行业分	**By Sector**				
房屋建筑业	Building	1078	25136729	860809	612630
土木工程建筑业	Building and Civil Engineering	392	16560055	451329	232022
铁路、道路、隧道和桥梁工程建筑	Railway Road Tunnel and Bridge Engineering Construction	242	13238746	368603	178173
水利和内河港口工程建筑	Water Conservancy and Inland Port	47	1613746	37454	25342
工矿工程建筑	Industrial and Mining Engineering	39	670048	19351	10849
架线和管道工程建筑	Wiring and Piping Engineering	36	669310	14812	12973
其他土木工程建筑	Other Civil Engineering Construction	28	368205	11109	4685
建筑安装业	Construction Installation	126	2520300	50752	33871
电气安装	Electrical Installation	49	460088	14589	6026
管道和设备安装	Piping and Equipment Installation	29	139270	6945	4562
其他建筑安装业	Other Construction and Installation Industry	48	1920941	29218	23283
建筑装饰和其他建筑业	Building Decoration and Other Construction	155	1428934	31635	17510
建筑装饰业	Construction Decoration	103	487677	16655	8644
工程准备活动	Engineering Preparation	22	717399	10284	4942
提供施工设备服务	Construction Equipment Services	6	64842	502	257
其他未列明的建筑活动	Other Construction Activities Unlisted	24	159015	4194	3667

Main Production Indicators of Construction Enterprises Which Possess Qualification Grades(2014)

利润总额 (万元) Total Profits (10 000 yuan)	税金 (万元) Tax (10 000 yuan)	按总产值计算劳动生产率 (元/人) Overall Labor Productivity by Gross Output Value (yuan/person)	产值利润率 (%) Ratio of Profit to Gross Output Value (%)	产值利税率 (%) Ratio of Pre-tax Profit to Gross Output Value (%)	资产总计 (万元) Total Assets (10 000 yuan)	负债合计 (万元) Total Liabilities (10 000 yuan)	实收资本 (万元) Paid-in Capitals (10 000 yuan)	资产负债率 (%) Assets-Liability Ratio (%)
1300835	**1565607**	**327323**	**2.8**	**3.4**	**40338742**	**28707709**	**8561536**	**71.2**
526989	994445	395942	1.9	3.5	27078263	22022692	3443605	81.3
1297390	1538498	326489	2.9	3.4	39976265	28389917	8526275	71.0
119799	144229	239964	2.7	3.2	4386091	3041873	797922	69.4
126373	78200	232080	5.8	3.6	1094114	449118	489376	41.0
1303	2395	223559	1.9	3.5	74976	69739	5215	93.0
20141	2679	287159	20.3	2.7	58239	41757	10300	71.7
602084	1005133	394619	2.1	3.6	26094646	20430282	4114859	78.3
67340	67048	426031	2.7	2.7	1790544	1306451	377269	73.0
360125	238776	236317	4.7	3.1	6476662	3050554	2730652	47.1
226	36	93609	21.0	3.4	994	145	680	14.6
-54	19	364214	-10.6	3.7	174	310	661	178.3
-54	19	364214	-10.6	3.7	174	310	661	178.3
3499	15510	438396	0.8	3.4	362302	317482	34600	87.6
3072	15440	445403	0.7	3.4	359082	316651	31600	88.2
428	70	95308	21.6	3.5	3221	830	3000	25.8
795809	815766	292013	3.2	3.2	16108452	9649397	4755795	59.9
655691	392146	366918	4.0	2.4	21228632	16988687	3116261	80.0
546838	307926	359160	4.1	2.3	17641849	14375977	2420831	81.5
55062	42322	430861	3.4	2.6	1442841	1080855	241582	74.9
23070	4188	346260	3.4	0.6	1124281	811898	265207	72.2
21005	24296	451870	3.1	3.6	713426	533629	124769	74.8
9716	13414	331448	2.6	3.6	306235	186329	63872	60.8
66287	59684	496591	2.6	2.4	2077189	1475730	433068	71.0
12056	3567	315367	2.6	0.8	475556	353362	96895	74.3
5017	7647	200533	3.6	5.5	204458	131332	52390	64.2
49214	48471	657451	2.6	2.5	1397175	991037	283783	70.9
35735	32915	451694	2.5	2.3	913348	584041	255764	63.9
14621	22367	292811	3.0	4.6	488497	284797	165849	58.3
19439	8852	697588	2.7	1.2	343492	270058	41240	78.6
343	-67	1291681	0.5	-0.1	7691	5935	1686	77.2
1333	1763	379148	0.8	1.1	73667	23251	46990	31.6

14-2 续表

指　　标	Item	企业数 (个) Number of Enterprises (unit)	总产值 (万元) Total Output Value (10 000 yuan)	直接从事生产经营活动平均人数(人) Annual Average of Persons Employed (person)	年末从业人数(人) Number of Engaged Persons (person)
按隶属关系分	**By Jurisdiction of Management**				
中　央	Central	63	14119300	376207	147127
省	Provincial	86	10048545	203198	127397
市及以下	Cities at Prefecture Level and Below	539	9827093	368851	303573
其　他	Others	1064	11668800	446811	318238
按企业资质等级分	**By Qualification Grade**				
施工总承包	TheGeneralContractor	1406	41914911	1303302	842873
特　级	Special Grade	6	2656290	26520	17258
一　级	First Grade	202	26675389	738193	399660
二　级	Second Grade	803	9714757	426545	329145
三级及以下	Third Grade and Below	395	2868474	112044	96810
专业承包	The Specialized Contractor	317	3662188	83869	53462
一　级	First Grade	101	2178500	44248	22683
二　级	Second Grade	109	1040861	26742	20769
三级及以下	Third Grade and Below	107	442827	12879	10010
劳务分包	The Subcontractor of Labour Services	29	86638	7896	
一　级	First Grade	21	54443	3601	
二　级	Second Grade	5	31467	4221	
三级及以下	Third Grade and Below	3	728	74	
按营业状态分	**By Business State**				
营　业	Operating	1722	45632164	1393752	895515
停业(歇业)	Suspension	26	27632	1102	629
当年关闭	Closure in This Year	3	141	15	10
其　他	Others	1	3800	198	181
按控股情况分	**By Holding Situation**				
国有控股	State-holding	246	28043125	708264	361804
集体控股	Group Holdings	185	4383117	153055	126759
私人控股	Private Holdings	1244	12429050	506092	383859
港澳台商控股	Holdings Hong Kong, Macao,Taiwan	2	82867	535	516
外商控股	Foreign Holdings	4	7431	523	384
其　他	Others	71	718146	26598	23013

continued

利润总额 (万元) Total Profits (10 000 yuan)	税金 (万元) Tax (10 000 yuan)	按总产值计算劳动生产率 (元/人) Overall Labor Productivity by Gross Output Value (yuan/person)	产值利润率 (%) Ratio of Profit to Gross Output Value (%)	产值利税率 (%) Ratio of Pre-tax Profit to Gross Output Value (%)	资产总计 (万元) Total Assets (10 000 yuan)	负债合计 (万元) Total Liabilities (10 000 yuan)	实收资本 (万元) Paid-in Capitals (10 000 yuan)	资产负债率 (%) Assets-Liability Ratio (%)
311433	568368	375307	2.2	4.0	17427039	14788065	1830126	84.9
124194	308904	494520	1.2	3.1	6336535	5033863	1044645	79.4
415968	318188	266424	4.2	3.2	6695622	3594029	2024678	53.7
449241	370147	261157	3.8	3.2	9879545	5291753	3662087	53.6
1192055	1465070	321606	2.8	3.5	37500420	26786707	7898889	71.4
134918	180079	1001618	5.1	6.8	7833939	6628656	824270	84.6
418296	850631	361361	1.6	3.2	20343984	15522230	3491240	76.3
493499	336801	227755	5.1	3.5	7531489	3716970	2964523	49.4
145342	97559	256013	5.1	3.4	1791009	918850	618855	51.3
101153	97201	436656	2.8	2.7	2796652	1894438	658386	67.7
39574	54649	492339	1.8	2.5	1506075	1121841	300786	
54646	31475	389223	5.3	3.0	903923	527467	241985	58.4
6933	11077	343837	1.6	2.5	386655	245130	115615	63.4
7627	3336	109724	8.8	3.9	41669	26565	4262	63.8
1729	1780	151189	3.2	3.3	35497	26356	4032	74.2
5660	1504	74549	18.0	4.8	5811	56	102	1.0
238	51	98378	32.7	7.0	361	153	128	42.4
1300762	1564542	327405	2.9	3.4	40271334	28679730	8524435	71.2
-14	983	250745	-0.05	3.6	64807	26794	35814	41.3
4	0.3	94000	3.1	0.2	1846	1029	688	55.8
82	82	191919	2.2	2.2	755	155	600	20.6
526989	994445	395942	1.9	3.5	27078263	22022692	3443605	81.3
178809	141133	286375	4.1	3.2	2653458	1674539	713540	63.1
567729	404286	245589	4.6	3.3	9888863	4563117	4198734	46.1
-3997	1559	1548920	-4.8	1.9	5545	3379	2961	60.9
637	215	142092	8.6	2.9	11496	3610	8003	31.4
30669	23970	270000	4.3	3.3	701117	440374	194694	62.8

14-3 施工总承包和专业承包建筑业企业主要指标(2014年)

指标	Item	企业数(个) Number of Enter-prises (unit)	直接从事生产经营活动平均人数(人) Annual Average of Employed Persons (person)	年末从业人数(人) Number of Engaged Persons at Year-end (person)	# 工程技术人员 Engineer	# 一级建造师 First Engineer
总计	**Total**	**1723**	**1387171**	**896335**	**215776**	**12241**
# 国有及国有控股企业	State-owned and State-holding Enterprises	246	708264	361804	99269	5514
按登记注册类型分	**By Status of Registration**					
内资企业	Domestic Funded	1719	1376765	886381	214645	12180
国有企业	State-owned Enterprises	89	184976	94352	29352	925
集体企业	Collective-owned Enterprises	124	93814	84296	16228	426
股份合作企业	Cooperative Enterprises	3	3091	2751	213	14
联营企业	Joint Ownership Enterprises	3	3456	3210	183	20
有限责任公司	Limited Liability Corporations	683	714393	428711	107886	6410
股份有限公司	Share-holding Corporations Limited	68	59236	40152	8098	417
私营企业	Private Enterprises	746	317684	232770	52668	3968
其他企业	Other Enterprises	3	115	139	17	
港、澳、台商投资企业	Enterprises with Funds from Hong Kong, Macao and Taiwan	1	14	15	3	
合资经营企业(港或澳、台资)	Joint-venture Enterprises	1	14	15	3	
外商投资企业	Foreign-invested Enterprise	3	10392	9939	1128	61
中外合资经营企业	Joint-venture Enterprises	2	10184	9730	1025	61
外资企业	Enterprises with Sole Funds	1	208	209	103	
按国民经济行业分	**By Sector**					
房屋建筑业	Building	1065	857952	612630	142672	6805
土木工程建筑业	Building and Civil Engineering	388	447161	232022	59792	3934
铁路、道路、隧道和桥梁工程建筑	Railway Road Tunnel and Bridge Engineering Construction	240	365723	178173	44923	2742
水利和内河港口工程建筑	Water Conservancy and Inland Port Engineering Construction	47	37454	25342	8026	470
工矿工程建筑	Industrial and Mining Engineering	39	19351	10849	3190	413
架线和管道工程建筑	Wiring and Piping Engineering	36	14812	12973	2572	235
其他土木工程建筑	Other Civil Engineering Construction	26	9821	4685	1081	74
建筑安装业	Construction Installation	123	50300	33871	8431	885
电气安装	Electrical Installation	48	14531	6026	1833	210
管道和设备安装	Piping and Equipment Installation	28	6734	4562	1522	102
其他建筑安装业	Other Construction and Installation Industry	47	29035	23283	5076	573
建筑装饰和其他建筑业	Building Decoration and Other Construction	146	31216	17510	4828	612
建筑装饰业	Construction Decoration	98	16315	8644	2731	440
工程准备活动	Engineering Preparation	22	10284	4942	1447	137
提供施工设备服务	Construction Equipment Services	5	452	257	121	2
其他未列明的建筑活动	Other Construction Activities Unlisted	21	4165	3667	529	33

Main Indicators of General Contracting and Professional Contracting in Construction Enterprises (2014)

建筑业总产值(万元) Total Output Value (10 000 yuan)	建筑工程 Construction	安装工程 Installation	其他 Others	竣工产值(万元) Output Value of Completed Construction (10 000 yuan)	房屋建筑施工面积(万平方米) Floor Space of Buildings under Construction (10 000 sq.m)	# 本年新开工面积 New Buildings	房屋建筑竣工面积(万平方米) Floor Space of Buildings Completed (10 000 sq.m)	# 住宅 Residential Housing	房屋建筑面积竣工率(%) Rate of Floor Space of Buildings Completed (%)
45577098	**39988490**	**3962470**	**1626139**	**20488434**	**23031.28**	**8486.03**	**6917.76**	**5075.99**	**30.0**
28043125	25243536	1984358	815231	12280098	12731.31	3660.44	2811.43	2041.41	22.1
45121008	39534431	3960437	1626139	20485540	23031.28	8486.03	6917.76	5075.99	30.0
4438757	3645204	405725	387828	1818219	2005.52	572.89	442.14	316.11	22.0
2177236	1848198	261277	67761	1208352	1359.85	777.02	705.86	508.76	51.9
69102	68270		832	50802	36.99	35.56	30.43	23.24	82.3
99242	72230	14710	12302	63922	29.22	20.45	18.27	8.86	62.5
28217515	25272330	2134493	810692	13457473	14565.69	4801.79	3855.54	2825.69	26.5
2523640	2049165	337174	137302	447144	807.84	270.47	311.34	204.02	38.5
7594438	6577957	807059	209422	3438551	4224.76	2007.28	1553.40	1189.30	36.8
1077	1077			1077	1.40	0.57	0.80		57.0
510	510			412					
510	510			412					
455581	453549	2032		2483					
453599	453549	50		350					
1982		1982		2133					
25100064	22937681	1522852	639531	12205449	21625.59	8007.90	6493.91	4806.84	30.0
16528465	15090102	1070873	367491	6750902	1041.62	353.61	300.29	192.78	28.8
13218792	12883387	46502	288902	5958440	618.30	197.47	184.68	86.11	29.9
1613746	1340651	245658	27437	174541	120.45	55.18	4.13	3.27	3.4
670048	444180	178117	47751	245481	249.38	91.87	64.10	57.25	25.7
669310	72949	595475	887	231868	1.26	0.99	0.57		44.8
356569	348934	5121	2514	140571	52.22	8.09	46.82	46.15	89.6
2515833	1092458	1151557	271818	739418	122.64	55.39	51.67	36.93	42.1
459500	240096	168515	50889	169404	16.80	13.30	13.38	12.55	79.6
135942	44998	72314	18631	52879	14.78	13.94	7.26	7.18	49.1
1920391	807364	910729	202298	517135	91.06	28.16	31.04	17.20	34.1
1415017	850530	217188	347300	755998	220.05	66.14	54.73	23.44	24.9
475165	324509	131383	19274	257217	9.03	3.26	5.03	3.69	55.7
717399	375537	40674	301188	454387	155.18	23.33	26.46	17.25	17.1
64758	64758			3221					
157694	85726	45130	26838	41173	55.84	39.55	23.24	2.50	41.6

14-3 续表 1

指　标	Item	企业数(个) Number of Enter-prises (unit)	直接从事生产经营活动平均人数(人) Annual Average of Employed Persons (person)	年末从业人数(人) Number of Engaged Persons at Year-end (person)	#工程技术人员 Engineer	#一级建造师 First Engineer
按隶属关系分	**By Jurisdiction of Management**					
中　央	Central	63	376207	147127	30708	2780
省	Provincial	86	203198	127397	38023	2014
市及以下	Cities at Prefecture Level and Below	534	368317	303573	72648	2187
其　他	Others	1040	439449	318238	74397	5260
按企业资质等级分	**By Qualification Grade**					
施工总承包	TheGeneralContractor	1406	1303302	842873	202426	10914
特　级	Special Grade	6	26520	17258	5587	1007
一　级	First Grade	202	738193	399660	101912	5700
二　级	Second Grade	803	426545	329145	75293	3347
三级及以下	Third Grade and Below	395	112044	96810	19634	860
专业承包	The Specialized Contractor	317	83869	53462	13350	1327
一　级	First Grade	101	44248	22683	7044	831
二　级	Second Grade	109	26742	20769	4001	345
三级及以下	Third Grade and Below	107	12879	10010	2305	151
按营业状态分	**By Business State**					
营　业	Operating	1694	1386067	895515	215478	12237
停业(歇业)	Suspension	25	891	629	263	3
当年关闭	Closure in This Year	3	15	10	5	1
其　他	Others	1	198	181	30	
按控股情况分	**By Holding Situation**					
国有控股	State-holding	246	708264	361804	99269	5514
集体控股	Group Holdings	185	153055	126759	23989	703
私人控股	Private Holdings	1217	498443	383859	85206	5737
港澳台商控股	Holdings Hong Kong, Macao,Taiwan	2	535	516	148	22
外商控股	Foreign Holdings	4	523	384	189	8
其　他	Others	69	26351	23013	6975	257

continued

建筑业总产值(万元) Total Output Value (10 000 yuan)	建筑工程 Construction	安装工程 Installation	其 他 Others	竣工产值(万元) Output Value ofCompleted Construction (10 000 yuan)	房屋建筑施工面积(万平方米) Floor Space of Buildings under Construction (10 000 sq.m)	# 本年新开工面积 New Buildings	房屋建筑竣工面积(万平方米) Floor Space of Buildings Completed (10 000 sq.m)	# 住宅 Residential Housing	房屋建筑面积竣工率(%) Rate of Floor Space of Buildings Completed (%)
14119300	13244439	772606	102255	5802993	2799.97	840.96	347.60	215.04	12.4
10048545	8477234	939260	632051	4795733	7322.35	2075.53	1965.33	1462.83	26.8
9821937	8582709	896574	342654	5043368	7051.71	2977.62	2416.50	1860.81	34.3
11587317	9684107	1354030	549180	4846340	5857.25	2591.91	2188.32	1537.32	37.4
41914911	37780177	3005192	1129542	19133783	22528.85	8250.80	6768.47	4941.19	30.0
2656290	2400303	222008	33980	393120	998.32	285.35	196.04	90.60	19.6
26675389	24280076	1707603	687710	12212475	14122.25	4335.23	3364.19	2495.99	23.8
9714757	8569694	831397	313666	5249147	6047.75	2903.63	2582.42	1866.37	42.7
2868474	2530104	244184	94186	1279040	1360.53	726.59	625.82	488.23	46.0
3662188	2208313	957278	496597	1354651	502.43	235.23	149.29	134.81	29.7
2178500	1467418	350564	360518	1007550	183.59	68.39	40.65	39.63	22.1
1040861	537531	412028	91302	244663	270.29	137.11	95.27	86.46	35.2
442827	203364	194686	44777	102438	48.55	29.73	13.37	8.71	27.5
45548853	39963002	3960356	1625496	20467242	23016.28	8473.75	6906.16	5072.03	30.0
24304	21547	2114	644	21066	11.93	9.23	11.60	3.96	97.2
141	141			126	0.10	0.08			
3800	3800				2.97	2.97			
28043125	25243536	1984358	815231	12280098	12731.31	3660.44	2811.43	2041.41	22.1
4383117	3531567	548473	303078	1954654	2484.04	1243.20	1163.62	838.44	46.8
12345514	10551596	1316365	477553	5774166	7395.31	3382.40	2762.03	2042.28	37.3
82867	510	82357		63698					
7431	4550	2881		3332	1.33				
715043	656731	28035	30277	412486	419.29	199.99	180.67	153.87	43.1

14-3 续表 2

单位：万元

指 标	Item	资产总计 Total Assets	# 流动资产 Circulating Funds	# 固定资产 Fixed Assets	固定资产原价 Original Value of Fixed Assets
总 计	**Total**	**40297072**	**32488638**	**3738961**	**5234190**
# 国有及国有控股企业	State-owned and State-holding Enterprises	27078263	22973829	1503346	2848970
按登记注册类型分	**By Status of Registration**				
内资企业	Domestic Funded	39934596	32187059	3717399	5174263
国有企业	State-owned Enterprises	4386091	3652136	316409	509341
集体企业	Collective-owned Enterprises	1094114	801855	224657	257655
股份合作企业	Cooperative Enterprises	74976	26174	4291	4407
联营企业	Joint Ownership Enterprises	58239	16612	14975	16669
有限责任公司	Limited Liability Corporations	26080368	21655092	1968619	3088133
股份有限公司	Share-holding Corporations Limited	1790544	1507694	174384	219539
私营企业	Private Enterprises	6449271	4526967	1013598	1077900
其他企业	Other Enterprises	994	528	466	620
港、澳、台商投资企业	Enterprises with Funds from Hong Kong, Macao and Taiwan	174	159	15	143
合资经营企业(港或澳、台资)	Joint-venture Enterprises	174	159	15	143
外商投资企业	Foreign-invested enterprise	362302	301420	21547	59783
中外合资经营企业	Joint-venture Enterprises	359082	298214	21533	59738
外资企业	Enterprises with Sole Funds	3221	3207	14	45
按国民经济行业分	**By Sector**				
房屋建筑业	Building	16090240	12586515	2010633	2214393
土木工程建筑业	Building and Civil Engineering	21222979	17394855	1476535	2684274
铁路、道路、隧道和桥梁工程建筑	Railway Road Tunnel and Bridge Engineering Construction	17638208	14606035	1086845	2060226
水利和内河港口工程建筑	Water Conservancy and Inland Port Engineering Construction	1442841	1072035	179434	316156
工矿工程建筑	Industrial and Mining Engineering	1124281	857170	125017	169952
架线和管道工程建筑	Wiring and Piping Engineering	713426	636919	43710	79995
其他土木工程建筑	Other Civil Engineering Construction	304223	222696	41530	57944
建筑安装业	Construction Installation	2074755	1765290	163620	232123
电气安装	Electrical Installation	475239	407813	29978	37998
管道和设备安装	Piping and Equipment Installation	204384	164517	33173	41407
其他建筑安装业	Other Construction and Installation Industry	1395132	1192961	100469	152718
建筑装饰和其他建筑业	Building Decoration and Other Construction	897977	731804	87226	101934
建筑装饰业	Construction Decoration	475169	389051	57895	63673
工程准备活动	Engineering Preparation	343492	310241	16541	23188
提供施工设备服务	Construction Equipment Services	7691	5568	1585	3304
其他未列明的建筑活动	Other Construction Activities Unlisted	71624	26944	11206	11769

continued

(10 000 yuan)

负债合计 Total Liabilities	# 流动负债 Liquid Liabilities	所有者权益合计 Owners' Equity	# 实收资本 Paid-in Capitals	主营业务收入 Revenue from Principal Business	主营业务成本 Cost of Principal Business	主营业务税金及附加 Taxes and Other Charges on Principal Business	管理费用 Management Expenses	# 税金 Tax	营业利润 Operating Profit	利润总额 Total Profits	应付职工薪酬 Accrued Employee Payroll
28681145	**26603503**	**11615928**	**8557274**	**46074912**	**41290496**	**1491072**	**1407291**	**59619**	**1287600**	**1293208**	**5352299**
22022692	20822181	5055571	3443605	31465199	28975611	971796	845483	19763	513796	526989	3296302
28363353	26289349	11571243	8522013	45617331	40860602	1475774	1402603	59388	1284194	1289763	5298696
3041873	2768669	1344218	797922	4345141	3911854	139747	147633	4483	119297	119799	756349
449118	358250	644996	489376	2020400	1601839	72300	82243	5901	127736	126373	312678
69739	69620	5237	5215	69772	60821	2376	4304	20	1302	1303	13471
41757	27001	16481	10300	83286	59103	2616	1307	63	20141	20141	8528
20421310	19261717	5659058	4112831	30527564	27847219	973784	887371	31113	590299	600674	3117238
1306451	1247989	484093	377269	2125204	1898106	64975	50816	2073	66775	67340	186241
3032960	2555958	3416310	2728419	6444888	5480939	219940	228847	15736	358418	353907	904046
145	145	849	680	1077	721	36	82		226	226	144
310	310	-136	661	510	455	18	85	2	-54	-54	55
310	310	-136	661	510	455	18	85	2	-54	-54	55
317482	313843	44821	34600	457071	429439	15281	4603	229	3460	3499	53548
316651	313013	42430	31600	455089	428011	15215	4541	226	3033	3072	52761
830	830	2390	3000	1982	1429	67	62	4	428	428	787
9637452	8638698	6452788	4753438	21881247	19213388	753472	622249	41106	820510	814845	3125959
16988687	15976546	4234292	3116261	20792576	19029963	639485	648529	14700	375403	386521	1926057
14375977	13485680	3262231	2420831	17319355	15934293	536526	481257	9381	294986	304702	1547217
1080855	1001436	361986	241582	1876976	1709842	53154	55846	1908	40964	42322	175441
811898	794687	312383	265207	687655	619423	21603	38978	1467	4504	4188	102327
533629	522038	179798	124769	623786	514952	19899	59922	1106	24028	24296	72466
186329	172705	117894	63872	284804	251453	8304	12526	838	10922	11012	28608
1473821	1422519	600934	432643	2279948	2036668	63459	102837	2680	59280	59529	192791
353345	347697	121895	96595	390958	328883	11667	32988	370	3176	3545	35375
131287	114635	73097	52365	151539	126982	4489	9506	416	7196	7503	17737
989190	960186	405942	283683	1737451	1580803	47304	60342	1894	48908	48481	139679
571330	555886	326646	254284	1106322	996643	34158	33512	1126	32082	31990	105308
273251	264886	201918	165247	465518	407819	13579	16023	609	21579	21442	41330
270058	264928	73434	41240	566311	522903	19020	13390	419	8759	8852	56449
5935	5516	1756	1686	10954	10157	335	475	8	-71	-69	740
22086	20556	49538	46112	63538	55763	1225	3624	91	1815	1766	6789

14-3 续表 3

单位：万元

指　　标	Item	资产总计 Total Assets	# 流动资产 Circulating Funds	# 固定资产 Fixed Assets	固定资产原价 Original Value of Fixed Assets
按隶属关系分	**By Jurisdiction of Management**				
中　央	Central	17427039	14531631	961325	1990397
省	Provincial	6336535	5530438	275634	475525
市及以下	Cities at Prefecture Level and Below	6683985	5225631	1011347	1101181
其　他	Others	9849513	7200938	1490655	1667087
按企业资质等级分	**By Qualification Grade**				
施工总承包	TheGeneralContractor	37500420	30148173	3443396	4915959
特　级	Special Grade	7833939	6000984	254919	396718
一　级	First Grade	20343984	17711915	1394676	2579555
二　级	Second Grade	7531489	5235644	1401970	1511523
三级以下	Third Grade and Below	1791009	1199630	391831	428162
专业承包	The Specialized Contractor	2796652	2340465	295565	318231
一　级	First Grade	1506075	1361977	109486	180305
二　级	Second Grade	903923	658673	141401	86951
三级以下	Third Grade and Below	386655	319815	44679	50975
按营业状态分	**By Business State**				
营　业	Operating	40229738	32443870	3724192	5219371
停业(歇业)	Suspension	64733	44431	14039	13841
当年关闭	Closure in This Year	1846	4	331	579
其　他	Others	755	333	399	399
按控股情况分	**By Holding Situation**				
国有控股	State-holding	27078263	22973829	1503346	2848970
集体控股	Group Holdings	2653458	2020831	373882	458250
私人控股	Private Holdings	9854654	6939580	1746302	1814008
港澳台商控股	Holdings Hong Kong, Macao,Taiwan	5545	4799	146	409
外商控股	Foreign Holdings	11496	9068	2399	2490
其　他	Others	693656	540532	112887	110062

continued

(10 000 yuan)

负债合计 Total Liabilities	# 流动负债 Liquid Liabilities	所有者权益合计 Owners' Equity	# 实收资本 Paid-in Capitals	主营业务收入 Revenue from Principal Business	主营业务成本 Cost of Principal Business	主营业务税金及附加 Taxes and Other Charges on Principal Business	管理费用 Management Expenses	# 税金 Tax	营业利润 Operating Profit	利润总额 Total Profits	应付职工薪酬 Accrued Employee Payroll
14788065	13967232	2638975	1830126	18655222	17242303	561012	517677	6269	298535	311433	1796658
5033863	4831613	1302672	1044645	9506465	8774416	299415	213526	7363	124050	124194	1069643
3587075	3147283	3096911	2023178	8104879	6867840	293649	306827	22419	417940	414779	1139786
5272143	4657375	4577370	3659325	9808347	8405937	336996	369262	23568	447075	442803	1346212
26786707	24767711	10713713	7898889	43066612	38657760	1399559	1259135	55437	1186753	1192055	5119748
6628656	5908689	1205283	824270	6626788	6240760	178376	156155	1502	123214	134918	359278
15522230	14863198	4821754	3491240	25512650	23373902	825531	668707	22231	417492	418296	3185681
3716970	3193897	3814519	2964523	8519124	7027662	308766	337865	21698	501436	493499	1248939
918850	801927	872158	618855	2408050	2015437	86887	96408	10006	144612	145342	325850
1894438	1835791	902214	658386	3008300	2632736	91514	148156	4182	100846	101153	232551
1121841	1089822	384234	300786	1850248	1663728	51963	74438	2130	39208	39574	118346
527467	513680	376456	241985	867116	724236	29939	49487	1363	54690	54646	77606
245130	232289	141524	115615	290936	244772	9611	24231	689	6949	6933	36599
28653211	26580980	11576528	8520198	46057484	41276724	1490774	1406064	59556	1287464	1293279	5349430
26749	22347	37983	35789	14913	11440	217	1220	63	49	-158	2475
1029	20	817	688	15	10	0.2	0.2	0.1	4	4	54
155	155	600	600	2501	2323	82	7		82	82	340
22022692	20822181	5055571	3443605	31465199	28975611	971796	845483	19763	513796	526989	3296302
1674539	1478453	978920	713540	3738133	3123316	130459	147907	8736	180214	178809	495389
4542615	3882473	5312040	4194772	10202226	8617098	365195	379259	29120	567436	560960	1470791
3379	3379	2166	2961	62808	48127	1443	11002	116	-4063	-3997	3141
3610	3610	7886	8003	5439	4325	191	279	24	638	637	1554
434311	413406	259346	194394	601107	522019	21989	23363	1860	29580	29811	85121

14-4 劳务分包建筑业企业主要指标(2014年)

单位：万元

指 标	Item	企业数(个) Number of Enterprises (unit)	建筑业总产值 Total Output Value	直接从事生产经营活动平均人数(人) Number of Engaged Persons (person)	#工程技术人员 Engineer	#现场施工人员 Site Construction Personnel
总 计	**Total**	**29**	**86638**	**7896**	**738**	**6077**
按登记注册类型分	**By Status of Registration**					
内资企业	Domestic Funded	29	86638	7896	738	6077
有限责任公司	Limited Liability Corporations	12	6927	840	118	555
私营企业	Private Enterprises	17	79711	7056	620	5522
按国民经济行业分	**By Sector**					
房屋建筑业	Building	13	36665	2857	561	2327
土木工程建筑业	Building and Civil Engineering	4	31591	4168	39	3096
铁路、道路、隧道和桥梁工程建筑	Railway Road Tunnel and Bridge Engineering Construction	2	19955	2880	21	1790
其他土木工程建筑	Construction Installation	2	11636	1288	18	1306
建筑安装业	Construction Installation	3	4467	452	97	314
电气安装	Electrical Installation	1	589	58	3	48
管道和设备安装	Piping and Equipment Installation	1	3328	211	56	151
其他建筑安装业	Other Construction and Installation Industry	1	550	183	38	115
建筑装饰和其他建筑业	Building Decoration and Other Construction	9	13916	419	41	340
建筑装饰业	Construction Decoration	5	12512	340	36	320
提供施工设备服务	Construction Equipment Services	1	84	50	1	4
其他未列明的建筑活动	Other Construction Activities Unlisted	3	1320	29	4	16
按隶属关系分	**By Jurisdiction of Management**					
市及以下	Cities at Prefecture Level and Below	5	5155	534	56	361
其 他	Others	24	81483	7362	682	5716
按企业资质等级分	**By Qualification Grade**					
一 级	First Grade	21	54443	3601	674	2905
二 级	Second Grade	5	31467	4221	41	3135
三级及以下	Third Grade and Below	3	728	74	23	37
按营业状态分	**By Business State**					
营 业	Operating	28	83310	7685	682	5926
停业(歇业)	Suspension	1	3328	211	56	151
按控股情况分	**By Holding Situation**					
私人控股	Private Holdings	27	83536	7649	713	5841
其 他	Others	2	3103	247	25	236

Main Production Indicators of Labor Subcontracting in Construction Enterprises (2014)

(10 000 yuan)

固定资产原价 Original Value of Fixed Assets	本年折旧 Depreciation of Fixed Assets	资产总计 Total Assets	负债合计 Total Liabilities	实收资本 Paid-in Capitals	主营业务收入 Revenue from Principal Business	主营业务成本 Cost of Principal Business	主营业务税金及附加 Taxes and Other Charges on Principal Business	营业利润 Operating Profit	利润总额 Total Profits
4988	**385**	**41669**	**26565**	**4262**	**86590**	**72954**	**3336**	**7694**	**7627**
4988	385	41669	26565	4262	86590	72954	3336	7694	7627
2639	177	14278	8972	2028	6849	4587	236	1465	1410
2349	207	27392	17593	2234	79741	68367	3100	6229	6218
2740	146	18211	11945	2357	36695	33025	1232	966	922
1111	118	5653			31591	23747	1506	5625	5625
89	67	3641			19955	15230	931	3224	3224
1022	51	2012			11636	8517	574	2402	2402
540	10	2434	1909	425	4359	3855	148	166	156
21	4	317	17	300	555	433	20	22	22
500	5	74	45	25	3328	2995	112	144	144
19		2043	1847	100	476	427	16		-10
598	111	15371	12711	1480	13946	12326	451	937	925
402	76	13329	11546	602	12542	10982	433	935	925
165	15				84	79		2	2
31	21	2043	1165	878	1320	1265	17	0	-3
1819	166	11637	6954	1500	5218	3455	155	1234	1189
3168	219	30032	19610	2762	81372	69499	3181	6461	6438
3489	251	35497	26356	4032	54428	49019	1780	1796	1729
1229	122	5811	56	102	31467	23605	1504	5660	5660
270	12	361	153	128	695	331	51	238	238
4488	379	41595	26520	4237	83262	69959	3224	7551	7483
500	5	74	45	25	3328	2995	112	144	144
4778	320	34208	20502	3962	83521	71014	3226	6835	6769
210	65	7461	6063	300	3069	1940	110	859	858

14-5 各市(区)建筑业企业个数(2014年)
Number of Construction Enterprises by City(District) (2014)

单位：个 (unit)

地区	Region	企业个数 Number of Enterprises	中央企业 Central	地方企业 Local	施工总承包 General Contracting	专业承包 Professional Contracting	国有及国有控股企业 State-owned and State-holding	集体企业 Collective Owned
全省	**Shaanxi**	**1723**	**246**	**1477**	**1406**	**317**	**246**	**185**
西安市	Xi'an	531	123	408	333	198	123	55
铜川市	Tongchuan	31	11	20	29	2	11	8
宝鸡市	Baoji	146	17	129	105	41	17	20
咸阳市	Xianyang	106	20	86	92	14	20	18
渭南市	Weinan	116	22	94	111	5	22	17
延安市	Yan'an	131	16	115	129	2	16	14
汉中市	Hanzhong	114	15	99	99	15	15	12
榆林市	Yulin	356	4	352	334	22	4	14
安康市	Ankang	88	9	79	78	10	9	14
商洛市	Shangluo	73	6	67	73		6	13
杨凌示范区	Yangling	31	3	28	23	8	3	

注：本表资料不含劳务分包企业，下表同。

a) Data in the table do not include the subcontractor of labour services. The same applies to the table following.

14-6 各市(区)建筑业企业直接从事生产经营活动平均人数(2014年)
Number of Employed Persons at Year-end of Construction Enterprises by City(District)(2014)

单位：人 (person)

地区	Region	直接从事生产经营活动平均人数 Number of Employed Persons at Year-end	中央企业 Central	地方企业 Local	施工总承包 General Contracting	专业承包 Professional Contracting	国有及国有控股企业 State-owned and State-holding	集体企业 Collective Owned
全省	**Shaanxi**	**1387171**	**708264**	**678907**	**1303302**	**83869**	**708264**	**153055**
西安市	Xi'an	744840	540208	204632	692498	52342	540208	57054
铜川市	Tongchuan	14042	7377	6665	11874	2168	7377	3760
宝鸡市	Baoji	95733	30770	64963	83277	12456	30770	22145
咸阳市	Xianyang	114121	41362	72759	103977	10144	41362	25485
渭南市	Weinan	79865	29836	50029	78772	1093	29836	9642
延安市	Yan'an	63582	20362	43220	63291	291	20362	5127
汉中市	Hanzhong	51419	9001	42418	49904	1515	9001	3900
榆林市	Yulin	86173	8222	77951	84511	1662	8222	7903
安康市	Ankang	40383	2530	37853	38676	1707	2530	10915
商洛市	Shangluo	48545	12064	36481	48545		12064	7124
杨凌示范区	Yangling	48468	6532	41936	47977	491	6532	

14-7 各市(区)建筑业企业年末从业人数(2014年)
Annual Average Persons of Construction Enterprises by City(District)(2014)

单位：人　　(person)

地区 Region	年末从业人数 Annual Average Persons	中央企业 Central	地方企业 Local	施工总承包 General Contracting	专业承包 Professional Contracting	国有及国有控股企业 State-owned and State-holding	集体企业 Collective Owned
全　省 Shaanxi	**896335**	**361804**	**534531**	**842873**	**53462**	**361804**	**126759**
西安市 Xi'an	394070	233624	160446	361329	32741	233624	46669
铜川市 Tongchuan	6582	1599	4983	6308	274	1599	2809
宝鸡市 Baoji	66273	13848	52425	61769	4504	13848	12674
咸阳市 Xianyang	107097	36522	70575	97211	9886	36522	25367
渭南市 Weinan	71229	22617	48612	70084	1145	22617	8128
延安市 Yan'an	45702	21654	24048	45535	167	21654	4943
汉中市 Hanzhong	51407	9001	42406	49820	1587	9001	3977
榆林市 Yulin	51235	737	50498	49997	1238	737	4936
安康市 Ankang	36310	1841	34469	34767	1543	1841	10494
商洛市 Shangluo	51714	14171	37543	51714		14171	6762
杨凌示范区 Yangling	14716	6190	8526	14339	377	6190	

注：本表资料不含劳务分包企业，下表同。
a) Data in the table do not include the subcontractor of labour services. The same applies to the table following.

14-8 各市(区)建筑业企业总产值(2014年)
Gross Output Value of Construction Enterprises by City(District)(2014)

单位：万元　　(10 000 yuan)

地区 Region	总产值 Gross Output Value	中央企业 Central	地方企业 Local	施工总承包 General Contracting	专业承包 Professional Contracting	国有及国有控股企业 State-owned and State-holding	集体企业 Collective Owned
全　省 Shaanxi	**45577098**	**28043125**	**17533973**	**41914911**	**3662188**	**28043125**	**4383117**
西安市 Xi'an	25863267	19812354	6050913	23404469	2458798	19812354	1709441
铜川市 Tongchuan	319594	155808	163786	315014	4580	155808	89654
宝鸡市 Baoji	4335332	1856444	2478888	3709163	626170	1856444	842815
咸阳市 Xianyang	5475139	3032654	2442485	5065854	409285	3032654	706065
渭南市 Weinan	2392090	1502012	890078	2368041	24049	1502012	180391
延安市 Yan'an	1011569	233490	778079	1004641	6928	233490	88027
汉中市 Hanzhong	1208732	384220	824511	1169667	39065	384220	71340
榆林市 Yulin	2012710	177905	1834804	1971523	41187	177905	239263
安康市 Ankang	890049	57761	832288	853595	36454	57761	260489
商洛市 Shangluo	1146898	312049	834850	1146898		312049	195632
杨凌示范区 Yangling	921719	518428	403291	906047	15672	518428	

14-9 各市(区)建筑业企业劳动生产率(2014年)
Labor Productivity of Construction Enterprises by City(District)(2014)

单位：元/人 (yuan/person)

地 区	Region	劳动生产率 Overall Labor Productivity	中央企业 Central	地方企业 Local	施工总承包 General Contracting	专业承包 Professional Contracting	国有及国有控股企业 State-owned and State-holding	集体企业 Collective Owned
全 省	**Shaanxi**	**328561**	**395942**	**258268**	**321606**	**436656**	**395942**	**286375**
西安市	Xi'an	347233	366754	295697	337972	469756	366754	299618
铜川市	Tongchuan	227599	211208	245741	265297	21126	211208	238441
宝鸡市	Baoji	452857	603329	381585	445401	502705	603329	380589
咸阳市	Xianyang	479766	733198	335695	487209	403475	733198	277051
渭南市	Weinan	299517	503423	177912	300620	220025	503423	187089
延安市	Yan'an	159097	114670	180028	158734	238082	114670	171694
汉中市	Hanzhong	235075	426864	194378	234383	257854	426864	182923
榆林市	Yulin	233566	216377	235379	233286	247814	216377	302749
安康市	Ankang	220402	228305	219874	220704	213557	228305	238652
商洛市	Shangluo	236255	258661	228845	236255		258661	274610
杨凌示范区	Yangling	190171	793674	96168	188850	319193	793674	

注：本表资料不含劳务分包企业，下表同。
a) Data in the table do not include the subcontractor of labour services. The same applies to the table following.

14-10 各市(区)建筑业企业竣工产值(2014年)
Output Value of Buildings Completed in Construction Enterprises by City(District)(2014)

单位：万元 (10 000 yuan)

地 区	Region	竣工产值 Output Value of Buildings Completed	中央企业 Central	地方企业 Local	施工总承包 General Contracting	专业承包 Professional Contracting	国有及国有控股企业 State-owned and State-holding	集体企业 Collective Owned
全 省	**Shaanxi**	**20488434**	**12280098**	**8208336**	**19133783**	**1354651**	**12280098**	**1954654**
西安市	Xi'an	11202911	8816257	2386655	10223409	979502	8816257	498793
铜川市	Tongchuan	171609	52364	119244	167995	3614	52364	84271
宝鸡市	Baoji	1230455	412317	818138	1122379	108076	412317	242176
咸阳市	Xianyang	3034196	1693615	1340582	2844204	189993	1693615	405376
渭南市	Weinan	1077277	474827	602450	1073257	4020	474827	149832
延安市	Yan'an	450194	109446	340749	448466	1728	109446	55632
汉中市	Hanzhong	839460	301067	538392	825148	14311	301067	54399
榆林市	Yulin	1151904	119842	1032062	1115687	36217	119842	160750
安康市	Ankang	521529	49520	472009	507567	13961	49520	188264
商洛市	Shangluo	670259	249999	420261	670259		249999	115162
杨凌示范区	Yangling	138641	846	137795	135412	3229	846	

14-11 各市(区)建筑业企业房屋建筑施工面积(2014年)
Floor Space of Building under Construction in Construction Enterprises by City(District)(2014)

单位：万平方米 (10 000 sq.m)

地区	Region	房屋建筑施工面积 Floor Space of Building under Construction	中央企业 Central	地方企业 Local	施工总承包 General Contracting	专业承包 Professional Contracting	国有及国有控股企业 State-owned and State-holding	集体企业 Collective Owned
全　　省	**Shaanxi**	**23031.28**	**12731.31**	**10299.97**	**22528.85**	**502.43**	**12731.31**	**2484.04**
西安市	Xi'an	11182.18	8524.90	2657.28	11000.65	181.53	8524.90	550.25
铜川市	Tongchuan	391.22	203.01	188.21	391.22		203.01	117.53
宝鸡市	Baoji	2152.05	859.65	1292.40	2119.64	32.41	859.65	604.10
咸阳市	Xianyang	3176.40	1544.09	1632.30	2956.22	220.17	1544.09	392.57
渭南市	Weinan	1388.51	721.06	667.44	1385.89	2.61	721.06	189.12
延安市	Yan'an	659.02	123.28	535.74	659.02		123.28	36.07
汉中市	Hanzhong	1347.01	496.44	850.56	1314.72	32.29	496.44	68.32
榆林市	Yulin	1244.15	155.63	1088.52	1228.56	15.60	155.63	148.96
安康市	Ankang	830.37	30.54	799.83	814.50	15.87	30.54	252.54
商洛市	Shangluo	580.54	72.71	507.83	580.54		72.71	124.58
杨凌示范区	Yangling	79.84		79.84	77.90	1.94		

注：本表资料不含劳务分包企业，下表同。

a) Data in the table do not include the subcontractor of labour services. The same applies to the table following.

14-12 各市(区)建筑业企业房屋建筑竣工面积(2014年)
Floor Space of Building Completed in Construction Enterprises by City(District)(2014)

单位：万平方米 (10 000 sq.m)

地区	Region	房屋建筑竣工面积 Floor Space of Building Completed	中央企业 Central	地方企业 Local	施工总承包 General Contracting	专业承包 Professional Contracting	国有及国有控股企业 State-owned and State-holding	集体企业 Collective Owned
全　　省	**Shaanxi**	**6917.76**	**2811.43**	**4106.32**	**6768.47**	**149.29**	**2811.43**	**1163.62**
西安市	Xi'an	2536.71	1714.93	821.78	2507.26	29.45	1714.93	242.98
铜川市	Tongchuan	94.21	26.53	67.68	94.21		26.53	50.88
宝鸡市	Baoji	806.56	242.52	564.04	780.96	25.61	242.52	216.23
咸阳市	Xianyang	1141.69	346.46	795.22	1065.50	76.19	346.46	272.64
渭南市	Weinan	546.06	164.39	381.67	544.10	1.96	164.39	98.08
延安市	Yan'an	176.20	30.12	146.08	176.20		30.12	24.85
汉中市	Hanzhong	482.91	162.31	320.60	476.79	6.12	162.31	42.07
榆林市	Yulin	502.89	45.94	456.94	499.36	3.53	45.94	52.25
安康市	Ankang	275.24	23.01	252.23	270.65	4.59	23.01	107.87
商洛市	Shangluo	303.49	55.21	248.28	303.49		55.21	55.77
杨凌示范区	Yangling	51.80		51.80	49.94	1.86		

14-13 各市(区)建筑业企业竣工房屋价值(2014年)
Valuation of Building Completed in Construction Enterprises by City(District)(2014)

单位：万元 (10 000 yuan)

地 区	Region	竣工房屋价值 Valuation of Building Completed	中央企业 Central	地方企业 Local	施工总承包 General Contracting	专业承包 Professional Contracting	国有及国有控股企业 State-owned and State-holding	集体企业 Collective Owned
全 省	**Shaanxi**	**10771702**	**4932879**	**5838823**	**10540591**	**231112**	**4932879**	**1594887**
西 安 市	Xi'an	4498535	3169734	1328802	4453479	45057	3169734	419762
铜 川 市	Tongchuan	149426	37608	111819	149426		37608	82475
宝 鸡 市	Baoji	992181	307903	684277	946333	45847	307903	212332
咸 阳 市	Xianyang	1719886	570942	1148945	1597441	122446	570942	363739
渭 南 市	Weinan	805895	296066	509829	802371	3524	296066	122171
延 安 市	Yan'an	282173	54187	227986	282173		54187	34704
汉 中 市	Hanzhong	684094	282396	401698	677490	6604	282396	47818
榆 林 市	Yulin	730874	96472	634402	730121	753	96472	84917
安 康 市	Ankang	404936	41237	363699	398513	6423	41237	147012
商 洛 市	Shangluo	426306	76336	349970	426306		76336	79958
杨凌示范区	Yangling	77396		77396	76939	457		

注：本表资料不含劳务分包企业，下表同。
a) Data in the table do not include the subcontractor of labour services. The same applies to the table following.

14-14 各市(区)建筑业企业资产合计(2014年)
Total Assets of Construction Enterprises by City(District)(2014)

单位：万元 (10 000 yuan)

地 区	Region	资产合计 Total Assets	中央企业 Central	地方企业 Local	施工总承包 General Contracting	专业承包 Professional Contracting	国有及国有控股企业 State-owned and State-holding	集体企业 Collective Owned
全 省	**Shaanxi**	**40297072**	**27078263**	**13218810**	**37500420**	**2796652**	**27078263**	**2653458**
西 安 市	Xi'an	27262571	21431358	5831212	25106498	2156073	21431358	1512750
铜 川 市	Tongchuan	238123	130061	108062	224995	13128	130061	62926
宝 鸡 市	Baoji	2000933	1043981	956952	1693350	307584	1043981	321165
咸 阳 市	Xianyang	2710102	1823670	886432	2613099	97003	1823670	246029
渭 南 市	Weinan	1531876	1082003	449873	1517180	14696	1082003	64302
延 安 市	Yan'an	998540	123507	875032	989308	9231	123507	45232
汉 中 市	Hanzhong	669279	144231	525048	638981	30298	144231	47305
榆 林 市	Yulin	2773417	189714	2583703	2654135	119282	189714	125443
安 康 市	Ankang	602400	60395	542005	566795	35605	60395	124975
商 洛 市	Shangluo	878068	572830	305237	878068		572830	103330
杨凌示范区	Yangling	631764	476512	155253	618012	13752	476512	

14-15 各市(区)建筑业企业负债合计(2014年)

Total Liability of Construction Enterprises by City(District)(2014)

单位：万元 (10 000 yuan)

地区	Reion	负债合计 Total Liability	中央企业 Central	地方企业 Local	施工总承包 General Contracting	专业承包 Professional Contracting	国有及国有控股企业 State-owned and State-holding	集体企业 Collective Owned
全省	**Shaanxi**	**28681145**	**22022692**	**6658453**	**26786707**	**1894438**	**22022692**	**1674539**
西安市	Xi'an	21241384	17878191	3363193	19708706	1532678	17878191	1063581
铜川市	Tongchuan	167765	105990	61775	156695	11070	105990	41107
宝鸡市	Baoji	1520417	945252	575165	1265889	254528	945252	228442
咸阳市	Xianyang	1848352	1469224	379128	1830044	18308	1469224	93798
渭南市	Weinan	982273	827749	154525	981213	1060	827749	26922
延安市	Yan'an	431787	89093	342694	426780	5007	89093	23576
汉中市	Hanzhong	380325	107621	272704	360141	20184	107621	26462
榆林市	Yulin	1196163	139292	1056871	1164918	31245	139292	46865
安康市	Ankang	307573	48387	259186	291439	16134	48387	75731
商洛市	Shangluo	217404	94327	123076	217404		94327	48055
杨凌示范区	Yangling	387703	317566	70137	383478	4224	317566	

注：本表资料不含劳务分包企业，下表同。

a) Data in the table do not include the subcontractor of labour services. The same applies to the table following.

14-16 各市(区)建筑业企业固定资产(2014年)

Fixed Assets of Construction Enterprises by City(District)(2014)

单位：万元 (10 000 yuan)

地区	Region	固定资产合计 Total Fixed Assets	中央企业 Central	地方企业 Local	施工总承包 General Contracting	专业承包 Professional Contracting	国有及国有控股企业 State-owned and State-holding	集体企业 Collective Owned
全省	**Shaanxi**	**3738961**	**1503346**	**2235615**	**3443396**	**295565**	**1503346**	**373882**
西安市	Xi'an	1612105	1067435	544669	1433557	178548	1067435	99656
铜川市	Tongchuan	22637	2476	20161	22479	158	2476	11587
宝鸡市	Baoji	252758	59455	193304	225096	27662	59455	31301
咸阳市	Xianyang	448201	168427	279775	393363	54839	168427	93336
渭南市	Weinan	162076	58375	103702	153784	8292	58375	17822
延安市	Yan'an	249822	13570	236252	246864	2958	13570	11793
汉中市	Hanzhong	107888	8710	99178	104790	3098	8710	10517
榆林市	Yulin	535853	1308	534545	523611	12242	1308	35840
安康市	Ankang	122195	7070	115125	115914	6281	7070	28423
商洛市	Shangluo	161522	74176	87346	161522		74176	33607
杨凌示范区	Yangling	63905	42345	21560	62417	1488	42345	

14-17 各市(区)建筑业企业流动资产(2014年)
Circulating Assets of Construction Enterprises by City(District)(2014)

单位：万元 (10 000 yuan)

地区	Region	流动资产合计 Circulating Assets	中央企业 Central	地方企业 Local	施工总承包 General Contracting	专业承包 Professional Contracting	国有及国有控股企业 State-owned and State-holding	集体企业 Collective Owned
全省	**Shaanxi**	**32488638**	**22973829**	**9514809**	**30148173**	**2340465**	**22973829**	**2020831**
西安市	Xi'an	22600158	17934937	4665222	20697700	1902459	17934937	1324973
铜川市	Tongchuan	206212	126771	79442	193262	12951	126771	49477
宝鸡市	Baoji	1627088	970174	656915	1365160	261929	970174	222457
咸阳市	Xianyang	2079169	1608268	470901	2038822	40347	1608268	101818
渭南市	Weinan	1297138	993103	304036	1292228	4910	993103	32722
延安市	Yan'an	660492	82157	578334	654221	6271	82157	32073
汉中市	Hanzhong	532708	128401	404307	510453	22256	128401	35893
榆林市	Yulin	1878360	179338	1699022	1825843	52516	179338	85265
安康市	Ankang	397304	43988	353316	371910	25394	43988	70054
商洛市	Shangluo	679448	497674	181774	679448		497674	66100
杨凌示范区	Yangling	530560	409019	121541	519127	11433	409019	

注：本表资料不含劳务分包企业，下表同。
a) Data in the table do not include the subcontractor of labour services. The same applies to the table following.

14-18 各市(区)建筑业企业实收资本(2014年)
Contributed Capital of Construction Enterprises by City(District)(2014)

单位：万元 (10 000 yuan)

地区	Region	实收资本 Contributed Capital	中央企业 Central	地方企业 Local	施工总承包 General Contracting	专业承包 Professional Contracting	国有及国有控股企业 State-owned and State-holding	集体企业 Collective Owned
全省	**Shaanxi**	**8557274**	**3443605**	**5113670**	**7898889**	**658386**	**3443605**	**713540**
西安市	Xi'an	4582374	2573588	2008787	4137714	444660	2573588	391458
铜川市	Tongchuan	52412	13958	38454	51196	1216	13958	20678
宝鸡市	Baoji	432022	87335	344687	342196	89826	87335	68480
咸阳市	Xianyang	479853	205047	274806	457205	22648	205047	60530
渭南市	Weinan	445962	228160	217802	436010	9952	228160	30686
延安市	Yan'an	351866	18963	332903	349531	2335	18963	17945
汉中市	Hanzhong	232803	31229	201575	222568	10235	31229	18405
榆林市	Yulin	1379178	47911	1331267	1321322	57856	47911	49367
安康市	Ankang	182195	10743	171453	170856	11340	10743	25871
商洛市	Shangluo	251551	124171	127380	251551		124171	30121
杨凌示范区	Yangling	167058	102500	64558	158739	8319	102500	

14-19 各市(区)建筑业主营业务收入(2014年)

Revenue from Principal Business of Construction Enterprises by City(District)(2014)

单位：万元 (10 000 yuan)

地 区	Region	主营业务收入 Revenue from Principal Business	中央企业 Central	地方企业 Local	施工总承包 General Contracting	专业承包 Professional Contracting	国有及国有控股企业 State-owned and State-holding	集体企业 Collective Owned
全 省	**Shaanxi**	**46074912**	**31465199**	**14609713**	**43066612**	**3008300**	**31465199**	**3738133**
西安市	Xi'an	29351276	23818792	5532484	27189600	2161676	23818792	1665747
铜川市	Tongchuan	304588	148187	156400	300974	3614	148187	80208
宝鸡市	Baoji	2821412	1505139	1316273	2519117	302295	1505139	415361
咸阳市	Xianyang	5235123	2868055	2367067	4847785	387338	2868055	700708
渭南市	Weinan	2353673	1584150	769523	2329821	23852	1584150	139969
延安市	Yan'an	903086	201075	702011	895854	7233	201075	74929
汉中市	Hanzhong	1023834	345408	678426	999434	24400	345408	63369
榆林市	Yulin	1779514	163111	1616403	1732043	47471	163111	196867
安康市	Ankang	712560	57926	654633	671288	41271	57926	218190
商洛市	Shangluo	981460	311312	670148	981460		311312	182787
杨凌示范区	Yangling	608387	462043	146344	599237	9150	462043	

注：本表资料不含劳务分包企业，下表同。

a) Data in the table do not include the subcontractor of labour services. The same applies to the table following.

14-20 各市(区)建筑业企业利润总额(2014年)

Total Profits of Construction Enterprises by City(District)(2014)

单位：万元 (10 000 yuan)

地 区	Region	利润总额 Total Profits	中央企业 Central	地方企业 Local	施工总承包 General Contracting	专业承包 Professional Contracting	国有及国有控股企业 State-owned and State-holding	集体企业 Collective Owned
全 省	**Shaanxi**	**1293208**	**526989**	**766219**	**1192055**	**101153**	**526989**	**178809**
西安市	Xi'an	587357	385467	201890	507039	80318	385467	47292
铜川市	Tongchuan	3262	2477	785	3299	-37	2477	109
宝鸡市	Baoji	60615	13170	47445	54852	5764	13170	9038
咸阳市	Xianyang	233759	51897	181862	227853	5906	51897	51362
渭南市	Weinan	41488	9562	31926	40733	756	9562	5355
延安市	Yan'an	55247	-332	55579	55046	202	-332	4591
汉中市	Hanzhong	24261	3499	20763	23267	994	3499	1764
榆林市	Yulin	131958	4768	127190	129149	2809	4768	23220
安康市	Ankang	53226	1376	51851	50035	3191	1376	25263
商洛市	Shangluo	71787	31599	40188	71787		31599	10815
杨凌示范区	Yangling	30247	23507	6740	28997	1251	23507	

14-21 各市(区)建筑业企业税金总额(2014年)
Total Tax of Construction Enterprises by City(District)(2014)

单位：万元 (10 000 yuan)

地区	Region	税金总额 Total Tax	中央企业 Central	地方企业 Local	施工总承包 General Contracting	专业承包 Professional Contracting	国有及国有控股企业 State-owned and State-holding	集体企业 Collective Owned
全 省	**Shaanxi**	**1550691**	**991559**	**559132**	**1454996**	**95696**	**991559**	**139194**
西安市	Xi'an	925161	737586	187575	859498	65663	737586	58455
铜川市	Tongchuan	10744	5634	5110	10666	78	5634	2657
宝鸡市	Baoji	99079	51588	47491	88998	10081	51588	13636
咸阳市	Xianyang	196913	93996	102917	182030	14883	93996	30327
渭南市	Weinan	78437	53370	25067	77431	1006	53370	3949
延安市	Yan'an	35302	6946	28356	35012	290	6946	2910
汉中市	Hanzhong	38297	12344	25953	37405	892	12344	2271
榆林市	Yulin	82011	5196	76816	80690	1321	5196	9061
安康市	Ankang	27614	1909	25705	26302	1312	1909	8252
商洛市	Shangluo	42043	13216	28828	42043		13216	7677
杨凌示范区	Yangling	15091	9776	5315	14920	171	9776	

注：本表资料不含劳务分包企业，下表同。

a) Data in the table do not include the subcontractor of labour services. The same applies to the table following.

14-22 各市(区)建筑业企业年末应收工程款(2014年)
Account Receivable of Projects at Year-end of Construction Enterprises by City(District)(2014)

单位：万元 (10 000 yuan)

地区	Region	年末应收工程款 Account Receivable of Projects at Year-end	中央企业 Central	地方企业 Local	施工总承包 General Contracting	专业承包 Professional Contracting	国有及国有控股企业 State-owned and State-holding	集体企业 Collective Owned
全 省	**Shaanxi**	**10389953**	**7763818**	**2626135**	**9733362**	**656592**	**7763818**	**540292**
西安市	Xi'an	6789450	5694988	1094462	6246443	543007	5694988	246850
铜川市	Tongchuan	80274	53419	26854	73992	6282	53419	15973
宝鸡市	Baoji	686745	423503	263243	622501	64245	423503	113064
咸阳市	Xianyang	868933	722304	146629	856930	12004	722304	42386
渭南市	Weinan	373909	264489	109420	372363	1546	264489	7613
延安市	Yan'an	239970	46595	193375	237234	2736	46595	5438
汉中市	Hanzhong	183265	44560	138706	178397	4869	44560	11627
榆林市	Yulin	528425	81959	446467	519051	9374	81959	46577
安康市	Ankang	110038	7722	102316	102772	7266	7722	20086
商洛市	Shangluo	301747	219264	82483	301747		219264	30679
杨凌示范区	Yangling	227197	205015	22182	221934	5263	205015	

14-23 各市(区)建筑业企业主要经济效益指标(2014年)
Main Indicators on Economic Efficiency of Construction Enterprises by City(District)(2014)

地区	Region	人均利润(元/人) Per Capita Profits (yuan/person)	人均利税(元/人) Per Capita Pre-tax Profit (yuan/person)	人均竣工产值(元/人) Per Capita Output Value ofCompleted Construction (yuan/person)	人均施工面积(平方米/人) Per Capita Floor Space of Buildings under Construction (sq.m/person)	人均竣工面积(平方米/人) Per Capita Floor Space of Buildings Completed (sq.m/person)
全　省	**Shaanxi**	**14428**	**17300**	**228580**	**256.9**	**77.2**
西安市	Xi'an	14905	23477	284287	283.8	64.4
铜川市	Tongchuan	4956	16323	260724	594.4	143.1
宝鸡市	Baoji	9146	14950	185665	324.7	121.7
咸阳市	Xianyang	21827	18386	283313	296.6	106.6
渭南市	Weinan	5825	11012	151241	194.9	76.7
延安市	Yan'an	12089	7724	98506	144.2	38.6
汉中市	Hanzhong	4719	7450	163297	262.0	93.9
榆林市	Yulin	25755	16007	224827	242.8	98.2
安康市	Ankang	14659	7605	143632	228.7	75.8
商洛市	Shangluo	13881	8130	129609	112.3	58.7
杨凌示范区	Yangling	20554	10255	94211	54.3	35.2

14-23 续表 continued

地区	Region	产值利润率(%) Ratio of Profits to Output Value (%)	产值利税率(%) Ratio of Pre-tax Profit to Gross Output Value (%)	资本利润率(%) Ratio of Profits to Captitals (%)	资本利税率(%) Ratio of Pre-tax Profits to Captitals (%)	资产负债率(%) Assets-Liability Ratio (%)
全　省	**Shaanxi**	**2.8**	**3.4**	**15.1**	**18.1**	**71.2**
西安市	Xi'an	2.3	3.6	12.8	20.2	77.9
铜川市	Tongchuan	1.0	3.4	6.2	20.5	70.5
宝鸡市	Baoji	1.4	2.3	14.0	22.9	76.0
咸阳市	Xianyang	4.3	3.6	48.7	41.0	68.2
渭南市	Weinan	1.7	3.3	9.3	17.6	64.1
延安市	Yan'an	5.5	3.5	15.7	10.0	43.2
汉中市	Hanzhong	2.0	3.2	10.4	16.5	56.8
榆林市	Yulin	6.6	4.1	9.6	5.9	43.1
安康市	Ankang	6.0	3.1	29.2	15.2	51.1
商洛市	Shangluo	6.3	3.7	28.5	16.7	24.8
杨凌示范区	Yangling	3.3	1.6	18.1	9.0	61.4

注：本表资料不含劳务分包企业。

a) Data in the table do not include the subcontractor of labour services. The same applies to the table following.

主要统计指标解释

建筑业统计单位 指从事房屋、构筑物建造和设备安装活动的法人企业。建筑业法人企业应具有建筑业资质并能够独立核算，同时其应具备以下条件：①依法成立，有自己的名称、组织机构和场所，能够承担民事责任；②独立拥有和使用资产，承担负债，有权与其他单位签订合同；③独立核算盈亏，能够编制资产负债表。

建筑业总产值 是以货币形式表现的建筑业企业在一定时期内生产的建筑业产品和提供的服务的总和。建筑业总产值包括：

⑴建筑工程产值：指列入建筑工程预算内的各种工程价值。

⑵安装工程产值：指设备安装工程价值，不包括被安装设备本身的价值。

⑶其他产值：建筑业总产值中除建筑工程、安装工程以外的产值。包括房屋构筑物修理产值、非标准设备制造产值、总包企业向分包企业收取的管理费以及不能明确划分的施工活动所完成的产值。

a.房屋构筑物修理产值：指房屋和构筑物修理所完成的产值，但不包括被修理房屋、构筑物本身价值和生产设备的修理价值。

b.非标准设备制造产值：指加工制造没有定型的非标准生产设备的加工费和原材料价值(如化工厂、炼油厂用的各种罐、槽，矿井生产统一使用的各种漏斗、三角槽、阀门等)以及附属加工厂为本企业承建工程制作的非标准设备的价值。

建筑业增加值 指建筑业企业在报告期内以货币形式表现的建筑业生产经营活动的最终成果。

从 2004 年第一次全国经济普查开始，建筑业现价增加值按生产法和分配法(收入法)两种方法计算，以收入法的计算结果为准，即从收入的角度出发，根据生产要素在生产过程中应得的收入份额计算。具体计算方法：经济普查年度建筑业增加值按照《经济普查年度 GDP 核算方案》计算，非经济普查年度建筑业增加值按照《非经济普查年度 GDP 核算方案》计算。

房屋建筑施工面积 指在报告期内施过工的全部房屋建筑面积，包括本期新开工的房屋面积、上期施工跨入本期继续施工的房屋面积、上期停缓建在本期恢复施工的房屋面积、本期竣工的房屋面积及本期施工后又停缓建的房屋面积。

房屋建筑竣工面积 指在报告期内房屋建筑按照设计要求全部完工，达到了使用条件，经验收鉴定合格，正式移交使用单位的房屋建筑面积。

Explanatory Notes on Main Statistical Indicators

Statistical Unit in the Construction Industry refers to a corporate enterprise engaged in the construction of buildings and structures and in the installation of equipment. A corporate construction enterprise should have qualification certificates with independent accounting system, and should meet the following 3 requirements: a) being set up in line with relevant legal basis, having its full name, organization and location, and capable of taking civil liabilities; b) independently possessing and using its assets and assuming its liabilities, and entitled to sign contracts with other institutions; and c) making independent accounts of its profits and losses, and capable of compiling its own balance sheet.

Gross Output Value of Construction refers to total of construction products and services, expressed in money terms, produced or rendered by construction and installation enterprises during a given period of time. It includes:

(1) Output value of construction projects: the value of projects covered by the project budgets;

(2) Output value of installation projects: the value of the installation of equipment, (excluding the value of the equipment to be installed);

(3) Other output values: the output value of construction industry apart from that of construction projects and installation projects. It includes: output value of repair of buildings and structures; output value of non-standard equipment manufacturing; overhead expenses received by contracted enterprises from the sub-contracted enterprises and the completed output value of construction activities for which there is no clear definition.

a. Output value of repair of buildings and structures: the value created through the repairs of buildings or structures. It does not include the value of buildings or structures being repaired and the value of the repair of production equipment;

b. Output value of manufactured non-standard equipment: the value of non-standard production equipment, including raw materials and manufacturing cost, made for the construction project (i.e., chemical plant; kettles or tanks used by refineries; various fillers, triangle tanks, valves used by mines). It also includes the output value of equipment manufactured by subsidiary workshops.

Value-added of Construction refers to the final result of the activities of production and operation of enterprises of the construction industry in monetary terms during the reference period.

Starting from the 2004 economic census, value-added of construction is calculated by both production approach and income approach, with the figures from the income approach as the final figures. Under the income approach, calculation starts from the perspective of income and is based on the share of income derived from the production process by the relevant factors of production. Specifically, value-added of construction for the Census years is calculated in accordance with the *Programme of Compilation of GDP and National Accounts for the Year of Economic Census*, and value-added of construction for other years is calculated in accordance with the *Programme of Compilation of GDP and National Accounts for the Non Economic Census Years*.

Floor Space of Buildings Under Construction refers to floor space of buildings under construction during the reference period, including the floor space of buildings for which construction has newly started; buildings for which construction has started earlier and is continuing during the reference period; and buildings for which construction has been suspended earlier but has restarted during the reference period; buildings completed during the reference period; and buildings under construction but construction has subsequently been during the reference period.

Floor Space of Buildings Completed refers to the floor space of buildings that are completed in the reference period in accordance with the requirements of the design, up to the standard for being put into use, and having been checked and accepted by departments concerned as qualified ones.

十五、运输和邮电

Transport, Post and
Telecommunication Services

资料整理：张西莉　巨振强　王晓飞

简 要 说 明

一、本篇资料反映陕西交通运输业和邮政、通信业发展的基本状况。

交通运输业资料主要包括：各种运输方式的线路里程、运输设备拥有量、各种运输方式完成的货物运输量和旅客运输量，城市公共交通情况等资料。

邮电通信业资料主要包括：邮电业务完成情况，邮电通信发展水平等资料。

二、本篇的资料来源：

交通运输资料分别来源于西安铁路局、西延铁路公司、神华神朔铁路公司、省交通运输厅、东方航空公司西北分公司、长安航空有限责任公司、省公安厅车管所等。

邮电通信业资料来源于省通信管理局、省电信公司、省移动通信公司、省联通公司、省邮政管理局、省邮政公司等。

Brief Introduction

I. This chapter reflects the basic conditions of transportation industry, post and communication industry of Shaanxi Province.

Data on transportation industry mainly include: routes of various transport modes, quantity of transportation equipment, freight and passenger traffic volume of various transport modes, urban public transport situation, etc.

Data on post and telecommunication mainly include: completion of post and telephone service and development of posts and telecommunications, etc.

II. Sources of Data:

Data on transportation industry are obtained from Xi'an Railway Bureau, Xi Yan Railway Company, Shenhua Shenshuo Railway Company, the Ministry of Transport of Shaanxi Province, Northwest Branch of China Eastern Airlines, Chang'an Airlines and the DMV (deportment of motor vehicles) of Public Security Department of Shaanxi Province, etc.

Data on post and telecommunication are obtained from Shaanxi Communications Administration, Shaanxi Telecommunication Company, Shaanxi Mobile Communication Company, Shaanxi Unicom Company, Shanxi Provincial Postal Administration and Shaanxi Post, etc.

15.运输和邮电

2014年全省		
客运量	75208	万　　人
旅客周转量	964.66	亿人公里
货运量	157074	万　　吨
货物周转量	3522.54	亿吨公里
邮电业务总量	566.66	亿　　元
每百人拥有固定电话	19.89	部
每百人拥有移动电话	95.55	部

高速公路里程（公里）

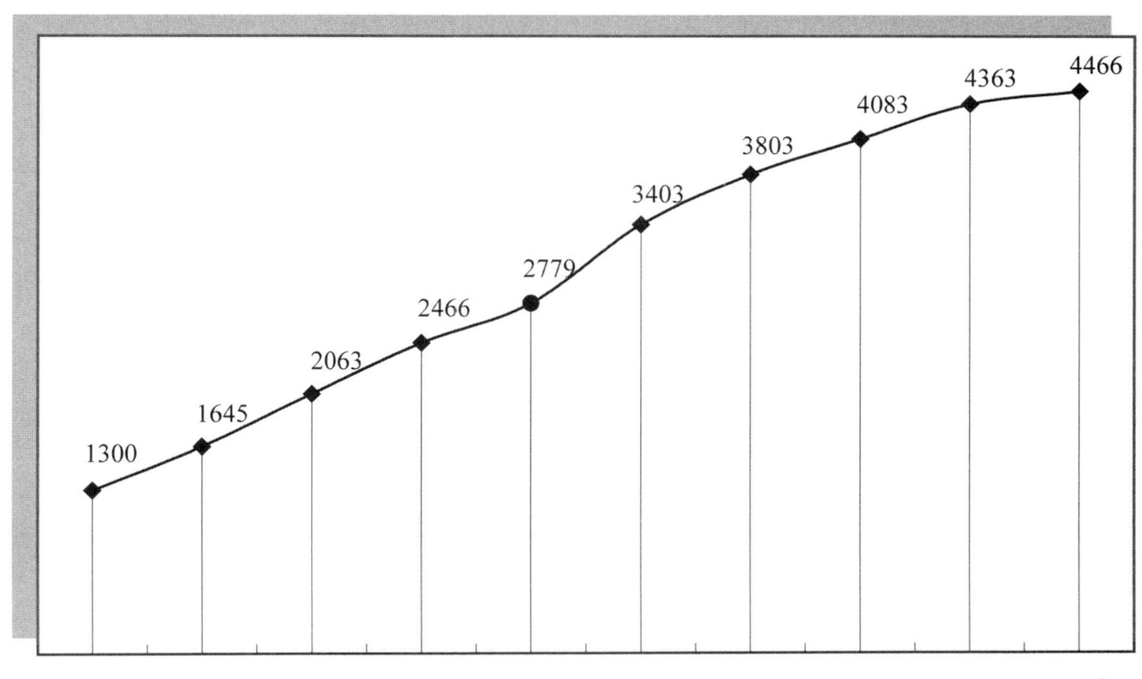

15-1 运输线路里程、质量和运输网密度
Length, Quality and Density of Transportation Routes

指　标	Item	2012	2013	2014
一、运输线路里程	**Length of Transport Routes**			
铁路正线延展里程　(公里)	Extension Length of the Trunk Lines　(km)	8804	9625	9964
# 营业里程	Railways in Operation	4464	4803	4924
公路通车里程　(公里)	Total Length of Highways　(km)	161411	165249	167145
内河航道里程　(公里)	Navigable Inland Waterways　(km)	1066	1066	1066
# 机动船航道	Motor Vessels	558	558	558
民航通航里程　(公里)	Total Civil Aviation Routes　(km)	981450	70643568	78626210
# 不重复里程	Unique Mileage	833752	66157513	73519837
二、运输线路质量	**Quality of Transport Routes**			
铁路营业里程　(公里)	Length of Railways in Operation　(km)	4464	4803	4924
# 复线里程	Double-Tracking Length	2453	2817	2999
复线里程比重　(%)	Proportion　(%)	55.0	58.7	60.9
公路线路里程　(公里)	Length of Highways　(km)	161411	165249	167145
# 等级公路	Expressway and Class I to IV Highways	146290	148991	151189
等级公路比重　(%)	Proportion　(%)	90.6	90.2	90.5
内河航道里程　(公里)	Length of Navigable Inland Waterways　(km)	1066	1066	1066
# 水深一米以上	Depth of Water Above 1 m	558	558	558
水深一米以上比重 (%)	Proportion　(%)	50.7	50.7	50.7
三、运输网密度	**Transport Density**			
1.铁　路	Railways			
省内营业里程　(公里)	Length of Province Railways in Operation(km)	4094	4421	4422
密　度　(公里/平方公里)	Density　(km/sq.km)	0.020	0.022	0.022
2.公　路	Highways			
线路长度　(公里)	Length of Routes　(km)	161411	165249	167145
密　度　(公里/平方公里)	Density　(km/sq.km)	0.785	0.804	0.813
3.水　路	Waterways			
通航里程　(公里)	Length of Waterways in Operation　(km)	1066	1066	1066
密　度　(公里/平方公里)	Density　(km/sq.km)	0.005	0.005	0.005

注：1.铁路线路为中央在陕铁路局管线路；民航通航里程为陕西民航飞机飞行航线里程。
2.铁路线路里程含神华神朔铁路有限责任公司专用铁路线路。
3.2013、2014年中国东方航空股份有限公司西北分公司通航里程由运输生产数调整为执管飞行数。

a) The transport routes are managed by the railway bureau in Shaanxi; Total civil aviation routes is the Shaanxi civil aviation's routes.
b) Length of railways includes dedicated railway line in Shenhuashenshuo Railway Co., Ltd.
c) Navigable mileage of Northwest Branch of China Eastern Airlines Corporation Limited has been adjusted from transport production numbers to administration flight numbers in 2013 and 2014.

15-2 铁路、公路线路长度及民航航线

Length of Railways, Highways and Civil Aviation

指　标	Item	2012	2013	2014
一、铁路线路长度	**Railways**			
正线延展里程　(公里)	Extension Length (km)	8804	9625	9964
# 省境内	In Shaanxi	5920	6657	6929
营业里程　(公里)	Length of Railways in operation (km)	4464	4803	4924
# 省境内	In Shaanxi	4094	4421	4524
电气化里程(省境内)(公里)	Provincal Electrified Railways (km)	3192	3513	3661
省内复线里程　(公里)	Provincal Double-Tracking Length (km)	2054	2331	2507
二、公路线路长度	**Highways**			
公路线路里程　(公里)	Length of Highways (km)	161411	165249	167145
# 高级及次高级路面	High Class and Sub-senior Class Pavement	88628	92603	97062
等级公路　(公里)	Expressway and Class Ⅰ to Ⅳ Highways (km)	146290	148991	151189
# 高速公路	Expressway	4083	4363	4466
一级公路	Class Ⅰ Highway	974	1011	1186
二级公路	Class Ⅱ Highway	8377	8441	8409
三级公路	Class Ⅲ Highway	14795	14731	15081
四级公路	Class Ⅳ Highway	118061	120445	122047
三、民用航空	**Civil Aviation**			
航线里程　(公里)	Length of Civil Aviation Routes (km)	981450	70643568	78626210
# 国际航线	International Routes	156197	6576226	6221566
港澳航线	Regional Routes	23390	2379620	2606220
航线条数　(条)	Numbers of Routes (line)	563	632	698
# 国际航线	International Routes	80	24	49
港澳航线	Regional Routes	15	14	20
通航城市　(个)	Number of Cities (unit)	150	88	177
# 国　际	International Routes	31	10	22
港　澳	Regional Routes	3	2	3

注：1.铁路线路长度含神华神朔铁路有限责任公司专用铁路线路。
2.公路线路有路面里程仅指高级路面。
3.2013、2014年中国东方航空股份有限公司西北分公司通航里程由运输生产数调整为执管飞行数。

a) Length of railways includes dedicated railway line in Shenhuashenshuo Railway Co., Ltd.
b) Length of highways with pavement only includes high class pavement.
c) Navigable mileage of Northwest Branch of China Eastern Airlines Corporation Limited has been adjusted from transport production numbers to administration flight numbers in 2013 and 2014.

15-3 运 输 工 具
Transportation

指 标		Item		2012	2013	2014
一、铁路运输工具		**Means of Railway Transportations**				
机 车	(台)	Locomotives	(unit)	1102	1353	1444
# 蒸 汽		Steam Locomotives				
内 燃		Diesel Locomotives		253	263	259
电 力		Electric Locomotives		848	1090	1185
客 车	(辆)	Passenger Coaches	(coach)	2494	2535	2508
二、公路运输工具		**Means of Highway Transportations**				
民用汽车	(辆)	Civil Vehicles	(coach)	3188389	3641318	4030291
# 新注册		New Registrations		556934	608133	648735
载客汽车	(辆)	Passenger Vehicles	(coach)	2356141	2845156	3316381
载货汽车	(辆)	Trucks	(coach)	455418	478785	498575
特种车	(辆)	Special Vehicle	(coach)			
汽车挂车	(辆)	Trailer Trucks	(coach)	34330	38601	4830
拖拉机	(辆)	Tractors	(coach)	278901	297981	306343
三、水运运输工具		**Means of Waterway Transportations**				
机动船	(艘)	Motor Vessels	(unit)	1210	1094	1175
客船载客量	(客位)	Passenger Capacity of Passenger Ships	(seat)	18180	19863	20102
货船净载重量	(吨)	Dead Weight Tonnage of Cargo Ships	(ton)	21384	21527	22841
拖轮功率	(千瓦)	Drawing Power	(kw)	282	335	519
驳 船	(艘)	Barges	(unit)	249	251	267
四、民航运输工具		**Means of Civil Aviation Transportations**				
民航飞机	(架)	Civil Aircraft	(unit)	33	49	56

注：铁路运输工具含神华神朔铁路有限责任公司机车数。
a) Means of railway transportations includes locomotives in Shenhuashenshuo Railway Co., Ltd.

15-4 各市(区)公路里程(2014年末)
Length of Highways by City(District)(2014)

单位：公里 (km)

地 区	Region	公路里程 Length of Highways	# 等级公路 Expressway and Class Ⅰ to Ⅳ Highways	# 高速公路 Expressway	# 一级公路 Class Ⅰ Highway	# 二级公路 Class Ⅱ Highway	# 三级公路 Class Ⅲ Highway
全 省	**Shaanxi**	**167145**	**151189**	**4466**	**1186**	**8409**	**15081**
西 安 市	Xi'an	13251	12733	471	325	1471	1211
铜 川 市	Tongchuan	3767	3307	152	2	328	317
宝 鸡 市	Baoji	15936	14642	241	113	854	1515
咸 阳 市	Xianyang	15511	13686	449	225	644	1915
渭 南 市	Weinan	18402	15389	324	191	699	1292
延 安 市	Yan'an	17110	16277	537	4	1546	2689
汉 中 市	Hanzhong	18828	16791	465	66	776	853
榆 林 市	Yulin	27773	26548	936	227	1269	3145
安 康 市	Ankang	22695	19065	516	2	419	983
商 洛 市	Shangluo	13482	12373	364	20	341	1068
杨凌示范区	Yangling	389	379	12	9	63	92

15-5 客运量、旅客周转量及构成
Passenger Traffic, Passenger-Kilometers and Composition

指 标	Item	2012	2013	2014
一、客运量 （万人）	**Passenger Traffic (10 000 persons)**	**112570**	**118312**	**75208**
铁 路	Railways	5757	6123	7077
公 路	Highways	105647	110963	66720
水 运	Waterways	369	377	391
民用航空	Civil Aviation	797	849	1020
二、旅客周转量(百万人公里)	**Passenger-Kilometers (million passenger-km)**	**100453**	**105114**	**96466**
铁 路	Railways	40884	42138	46474
公 路	Highways	48855	51490	33902
水 运	Waterways	58	60	66
民用航空	Civil Aviation	10655	11426	16024
三、客运量构成 (%)	**Composition of Passenger Traffic(%)**	**100.00**	**100.00**	**100.00**
铁 路	Railways	5.11	5.18	9.41
公 路	Highways	93.85	93.79	88.71
水 运	Waterways	0.33	0.32	0.52
民用航空	Civil Aviation	0.71	0.72	1.36
四、旅客周转量构成 (%)	**Composition of passenger-Kilometers (%)**	**100.00**	**100.00**	**100.00**
铁 路	Railways	40.70	40.09	48.18
公 路	Highways	48.64	48.98	35.14
水 运	Waterways	0.06	0.06	0.07
民用航空	Civil Aviation	10.61	10.87	16.61

注：本表资料为全社会口径。中央铁路部分为国家返馈陕西省境数。

a) Data in this table refer to those of the whole society system. Data of national railways refer to those responsed to Shaanxi.

15-6 货运量、货物周转量及构成

Freight Traffic, Freight Ton-Kilometers and Composition

指　　标	Item	2012	2013	2014
一、货运量　　　　（万吨）	**Freight Traffic　　(10 000 tons)**	**136734**	**152712**	**157074**
铁　路	Railways	31942	35804	37483
公　路	Highways	104593	116711	119343
水　运	Waterways	192	191	186
民用航空	Civil Aviation	7	6	7
二、货物周转量（百万吨公里）	**Freight Ton-Kilometers (million ton-km)**	**319312**	**347292**	**352254**
铁　路	Railways	144675	151469	160338
公　路	Highways	174465	195654	191745
水　运	Waterways	74	73	62
民用航空	Civil Aviation	98	96	107
三、货运量构成　　　（%）	**Composition of Freight Traffic (%)**	**100.00**	**100.00**	**100.00**
铁　路	Railways	23.36	23.45	23.86
公　路	Highways	76.49	76.43	76.01
水　运	Waterways	0.14	0.13	0.12
民用航空	Civil Aviation	0.005	0.004	0.005
四、货物周转量构成　（%）	**Composition of Freight Ton-Kilometers (%)**	**100.00**	**100.00**	**100.00**
铁　路	Railways	45.31	43.61	45.52
公　路	Highways	54.64	56.34	54.43
水　运	Waterways	0.02	0.02	0.02
民用航空	Civil Aviation	0.03	0.03	0.03

注：1.本表资料为全社会口径。中央铁路部分为国家返馈陕西省境数。
　　2.铁路货运量和货物周转量含神华神朔铁路有限责任公司专用铁路货运量和货物周转量。

a) Data in this table refer to those of the whole society system. Data of national railways refer to those responsed to Shaanxi.

b) Freight traffic and freight ton-Kilometers includes dedicated railway line in Shenhuashenshuo Railway co., ltd .

15-7 民用汽车拥有量(2014年末)
Possession of Civil Vehicles(2014)

单位：辆 (unit)

地　区	Region	民用汽车总计 Total	# 新注册 New Registrations	载客汽车 Passenger Vehicles	载货汽车 Trucks	其他汽车 Others	摩托车 Motorcycles	# 普通 Normal Motorcycles
全　省	**Shaanxi**	**4030291**	**648735**	**3316381**	**498575**	**215335**	**1604983**	**1559376**
西安市	Xi'an	1924402	342009	1657141	224314	42947	190862	184231
铜川市	Tongchuan	69349	10446	50680	11432	7237	43662	42978
宝鸡市	Baoji	204682	32870	174406	23134	7142	94147	89848
咸阳市	Xianyang	270589	44358	228964	28598	13027	109251	106912
渭南市	Weinan	394396	55801	298838	55231	40327	156314	154303
延安市	Yan'an	246119	39499	191439	35661	19019	55042	52534
汉中市	Hanzhong	174218	28533	134542	20965	18711	371639	358486
榆林市	Yulin	509566	61758	397344	73775	38447	123125	119823
安康市	Ankang	93639	17160	67831	14690	11118	328397	318430
商洛市	Shangluo	66634	9084	44656	7053	14925	120370	119719
杨凌示范区	Yangling	52442	6120	48186	3467	789	8869	8807

15-8 私人车辆拥有量(2014年末)
Possession of Private Vehicles(2014)

单位：辆 (unit)

地　区	Region	汽车总计 Total	# 载客汽车 Passenger Vehicles	# 载货汽车 Trucks	摩托车 Motorcycles	# 普通 Normal Motorcycles
全　省	**Shaanxi**	**3470904**	**2938311**	**367196**	**1595463**	**1549997**
西安市	Xi'an	1703443	1489896	181721	189980	183358
铜川市	Tongchuan	55854	41848	7239	43541	42871
宝鸡市	Baoji	165958	145425	15102	93967	89669
咸阳市	Xianyang	229999	203333	17086	108952	106625
渭南市	Weinan	316876	264474	32915	154578	152578
延安市	Yan'an	208855	170136	24385	54832	52325
汉中市	Hanzhong	150810	116446	16580	371005	357880
榆林市	Yulin	457959	368530	53446	122691	119390
安康市	Ankang	79779	57495	12388	327032	317128
商洛市	Shangluo	56253	36511	5527	120028	119378
杨凌示范区	Yangling	45116	44215	807	8856	8794

15-9 公路部门营运载客车拥有量(2014年末)
Possession of Vehicles in Operation for Highway Transportation(2014)

地 区	Region	载客汽车合 计(辆) Total (unit)	班车客运车辆 Scheduled Coach		# 高 级 Senior		# 中 级 Medium	
			辆 数 (unit)	客 位 (seat)	辆 数 (unit)	客 位 (seat)	辆 数 (unit)	客 位 (seat)
全 省	**Shaanxi**	**74732**	**18772**	**486840**	**5276**	**191785**	**8248**	**190780**
西 安 市	Xi'an	31587	2963	115011	1132	49519	985	22289
铜 川 市	Tongchuan	1930	518	11836	139	5483	80	1829
宝 鸡 市	Baoji	7055	2302	52625	272	8820	945	24538
咸 阳 市	Xianyang	5875	2082	55478	972	34790	830	17524
渭 南 市	Weinan	6251	2350	58257	509	20274	1133	24980
延 安 市	Yan'an	4528	1534	37083	136	4531	1398	32552
汉 中 市	Hanzhong	4283	1614	41823	750	21342	710	18836
榆 林 市	Yulin	6200	1694	45284	694	22020	955	22499
安 康 市	Ankang	4109	2472	35991	309	10663	454	9161
商 洛 市	Shangluo	2550	1139	30445	325	12643	692	15265
杨凌示范区	Yangling	364	104	3007	38	1700	66	1307

15-9 续表 continued

地 区	Region	# 普 通 Ordinary		旅游客车 Tourist Bus		其它客车 Others		公共汽车(辆) Bus (unit)	出租客车(辆) Taxi (unit)
		辆 数 (unit)	客 位 (seat)	辆 数 (unit)	客 位 (seat)	辆 数 (unit)	客 位 (seat)		
全 省	**Shaanxi**	**5248**	**104275**	**2107**	**75560**	**5126**	**30284**	**13200**	**35527**
西 安 市	Xi'an	846	43203	1751	63533	4937	28960	7777	14159
铜 川 市	Tongchuan	299	4524					331	1081
宝 鸡 市	Baoji	1085	19267	187	5227			1068	3498
咸 阳 市	Xianyang	280	3164	10	400			641	3142
渭 南 市	Weinan	708	13003	26	1077			678	3197
延 安 市	Yan'an			26	910			589	2379
汉 中 市	Hanzhong	154	1645	47	2155	34	549	725	1863
榆 林 市	Yulin	45	765	18	777			789	3699
安 康 市	Ankang	1709	16167	20	664			267	1350
商 洛 市	Shangluo	122	2537	22	817	155	775	275	959
杨凌示范区	Yangling							60	200

注：本表数字为在运管部门注册登记的全社会载客汽车数。
a) Data in this table refers to the whole society's for-hire vehicles registered in operation administration departments.

15-10 公路部门营运载货车拥有量(2014年末)

Possession of Vehicles in Operation for Highway Transportation(2014)

地 区 Region	载货汽车合计 Total		普通载货车辆 Ordinary Trucks		# 大 型 Heavy		# 重 型 Heavy		# 中 型 Medium	
	辆 数 (unit)	吨 位 (ton)	辆 数 (unit)	吨 位 (ton)	辆 数 (unit)	吨 位 (ton)	辆 数 (unit)	吨 位 (ton)	辆 数 (unit)	吨 位 (ton)
全 省 Shaanxi	**387968**	**2392569**	**315572**	**1479895**	**89999**	**1179249**	**71850**	**1070401**	**11620**	**38360**
西 安 市 Xi'an	206074	716472	194696	548613	31445	348642	25952	324840	3470	11719
铜 川 市 Tongchuan	11460	116148	8119	69830	5269	64803	4778	61350	203	741
宝 鸡 市 Baoji	19338	131217	16006	86180	6110	71470	4198	58567	646	1947
咸 阳 市 Xianyang	21705	204846	13775	123626	8097	115706	6472	102869	575	1812
渭 南 市 Weinan	43117	416653	29527	204285	17541	183768	12715	152377	1489	4777
延 安 市 Yan'an	9278	89319	6285	48132	3696	44471	3198	41673	198	624
汉 中 市 Hanzhong	16645	67389	14208	35004	2168	20463	1068	12565	513	1529
榆 林 市 Yulin	39411	506679	13257	232997	10232	226573	9507	221213	712	2105
安 康 市 Ankang	13042	38644	12787	36327	1812	15869	745	10027	2749	9250
商 洛 市 Shangluo	6174	96839	5724	89513	3262	84021	3027	82620	742	2597
杨凌示范区 Yangling	1724	8363	1188	5388	367	3463	190	2300	323	1259

15-10 续表 continued

地 区 Region	专用载货车辆 Dedicated Trucks		# 集装箱 Container		其他机动车 Others		轮胎式拖拉机 Wheeled Tractor	
	辆 数 (unit)	吨 位 (ton)	辆 数 (unit)	TEU (ton)	辆 数 (unit)	吨 位 (ton)	辆 数 (unit)	吨 位 (ton)
全 省 Shaanxi	**11041**	**158436**	**61**	**1701**	**36970**	**41041**	**2327**	**3584**
西 安 市 Xi'an	4758	69643	61	1701				
铜 川 市 Tongchuan	602	7787			254	177		
宝 鸡 市 Baoji	287	2267			492	294	197	507
咸 阳 市 Xianyang	626	8928						
渭 南 市 Weinan	1383	19988			15133	18477	1611	1723
延 安 市 Yan'an	1981	34185			3054	1819	15	15
汉 中 市 Hanzhong	326	2721			5191	7181	474	1301
榆 林 市 Yulin	488	6344						
安 康 市 Ankang	155	959			5580	9194	29	36
商 洛 市 Shangluo	209	3912			7266	3899	1	2
杨凌示范区 Yangling	226	1702						

注：本表数字为在运管部门注册登记的全社会营运载货车数。

a) Data in this table refers to the whole society's for-hire vehicles registered in operation administration departments.

15-11 城市公共汽车情况(2014年)
Basic Statistics on Bus in Cities (2014)

地 区 Region	运营车数 (辆) Number of Operations (unit)	# 汽油车 Gasoline	# 柴油车 Diesel Cars	# 天然气车 Natural Gas Vehicles	# 双燃料车 Dual-fuel Vehicles	标准运营车数 (标台) Number of Standard Operations (unit)	运营线路总长度 (公里) Network Length (km)	客运量 (万人次) Passengers Transported (10 000 person-times)	运营里程 (万公里) Operating Distance (10 000 km)
全 省 Shaanxi	**13200**	**116**	**1610**	**7684**	**3437**	**14880**	**14323**	**259359**	**89726**
西安市 Xi'an	7777		89	5374	2109	9007	6125	169767	48465
铜川市 Tongchuan	331		64	65	202	324	209	3912	2098
宝鸡市 Baoji	1068	38	58	487	485	1304	1101	19145	8003
咸阳市 Xianyang	641		109	527	5	819	581	14702	4417
渭南市 Weinan	678		191	201	262	624	1010	9382	5865
延安市 Yan'an	589	16	109	362	102	663	942	12305	4624
汉中市 Hanzhong	725	58	489	91	6	706	1261	8017	6245
榆林市 Yulin	789		75	445	226	855	1470	16043	5959
安康市 Ankang	267		189	78		257	852	2258	1597
商洛市 Shangluo	275	4	237	34		265	579	3751	2155
杨凌示范区 Yangling	60			20	40	56	194	77	301

15-12 城市出租汽车情况(2014年)
Basic Statistics on Taxi in Cities (2014)

地 区	Region	运营车数 (辆) Number of Operations (unit)	客运量 (万人次) Passengers Transported (10 000 person-times)	运营里程 (万公里) Operating Distance (10 000 km)	载客里程 (万公里) Passenger Milesdistance (10 000 km)
全 省	**Shaanxi**	**35527**	**122262**	**471030**	**329560**
西安市	Xi'an	14159	46549	202866	141048
铜川市	Tongchuan	1081	5106	15039	10795
宝鸡市	Baoji	3498	11059	43659	28047
咸阳市	Xianyang	3142	12155	40387	27365
渭南市	Weinan	3197	12432	43408	31391
延安市	Yan'an	2379	9545	36327	27222
汉中市	Hanzhong	1863	2794	19917	12497
榆林市	Yulin	3699	12680	44558	34575
安康市	Ankang	1350	5590	11057	8191
商洛市	Shangluo	959	3661	10077	7075
杨凌示范区	Yangling	200	691	3734	1354

15-13 铁路客货运输量
Passenger and Freight Traffic of Railways

指 标	Item	2012	2013	2014
一、路局范围	Railways Bureau			
客运量 (万人)	Passenger Traffic (10 000 persons)	5852	6225	7168
旅客周转量(百万人公里)	passenger-Kilometers(million passenger-km)	46860	48557	52903
货运量 (万吨)	Freight Traffic (10 000 tons)	11786	12259	12857
货物周转量(百万吨公里)	Freight Ton-Kilometers (million ton-km)	148036	153340	158341
二、省境内	In Shaanxi Province			
客运量 (万人)	Passenger Traffic (10 000 persons)	5757	6123	7077
旅客周转量(百万人公里)	Passenger-Kilometers(million passenger-km)	40884	42138	46474
货运量 (万吨)	Freight Traffic (10 000 tons)	31942	35804	37483
货物周转量(百万吨公里)	Freight Ton-Kilometers (million ton-km)	144675	151469	160338

注：本表路局范围为西安铁路局数字，省境内及合资铁路为国家反馈数。

a) Bureau means jointly owned railway bureau of Xi'an. The data in Shaanxi province refer to the number responsed from nation.

15-14 全省公路客货运输量(2014年)
Passenger and Freight Traffic of Highway Departments(2014)

地 区	Region	客运量 (万人) Passenger Traffic (10 000 persons)	客运周转量 (万人公里) passenger-Kilometers (10 000 passenger-km)	货运量 (万吨) Freight Traffic (10 000 tons)	货运周转量 (万吨公里) Freight Ton-Kilometers (10 000 ton-km)
全 省	**Shaanxi**	**66720**	**3390244**	**119343**	**19174527**
西安市	Xi'an	19282	1067456	41120	3863974
铜川市	Tongchuan	1823	86967	4598	599210
宝鸡市	Baoji	7939	279411	10055	1075598
咸阳市	Xianyang	7575	314799	11188	2017036
渭南市	Weinan	10138	373300	14343	3846914
延安市	Yan'an	3020	189407	5787	657361
汉中市	Hanzhong	4251	239391	6907	776755
榆林市	Yulin	3284	382066	15108	5220045
安康市	Ankang	4855	233960	6534	602972
商洛市	Shangluo	4167	208745	3439	481783
杨凌示范区	Yangling	386	14741	264	32879

15-15 铁路运输主要经济技术指标
Principal Economic and Technical Indicators of Railway Transport

指　　标		Item		2012	2013	2014
货车平均静载重	(吨)	Average Static Load of Freight Cars	(ton)	63.4	63.6	64.1
货车周转时间	(天)	Turning Around Time of Freight Cars	(day)	2.24	2.3	2.3
货运机车日产量	(万吨公里)	Average Daily Ton-kilometers of Freight Locomotives	(10 000 ton-km)	92.5	89.2	95.8
内燃机车耗油	(公斤/万吨公里)	Oil Consumption of Diesel Locomotives	(kg/10 000 ton-km)	47.19	46.9	47.1
电力机车耗电	(千瓦小时/万吨公里)	Electricity Consumption of Electric Locomotives	(kwh/10 000 ton-km)	142.81	146.1	131.7
货物列车出发正点率	(%)	Punctuality Rate of Freight Trains at Departure	(%)	98.9	99.4	98.7
货物列车运行正点率	(%)	Punctuality Rate of Freight Trains in Running	(%)	99.8	99.8	99.5
旅客列车出发正点率	(%)	Punctuality Rate of Passenger Trains at Departure	(%)	99.8	99.7	99.9
旅客列车运行正点率	(%)	Punctuality Rate of Passenger Trains in Running	(%)	99.6	99.7	99.9
客运密度	(万人公里/公里)	Density of Passenger Traffic	(10 000 person-km/km)	1118.5	1072.3	1137.9
每万名旅客拥有座卧车数	(辆)	Number of Seat Trains and Sleeping Trains Per 10 000 Passengers	(unit)	5.7	5.9	6.5
每百万旅客人公里拥有座卧车数	(辆)	Number of Seat Trains and Sleeping Trains Per million Passenger-km	(unit)	18.8	19.2	21.1
货物列车旅行速度	(公里/小时)	Running Speed of Freight Trains	(km/hr)	29.7	29.9	30.9
货运密度	(万吨公里/公里)	Density of Freight Traffic	(10 000 ton-km/km)	3533.6	3386.2	3405.7
一次货物作业时间	(小时)	Handling Time of Freigh	(hour)	15.9	15.7	15.3

15-16 铁路分品类货物发送量及装车数
Volume of Freight Dispatched and Loaded Cars of Railways by Category of Cargo

品　种	Item	货物发送量(万吨) Volume of Freight Dispatched (10000 tons)			装　车　数(车) Loaded Cars (unit)		
		2012	2013	2014	2012	2013	2014
合　　计	**Total**	**32478**	**36959**	**38419**	**4864921**	**5442378**	**5538933**
煤	Coal	28593	32961	34504	4174485	4740325	4862771
焦　炭	Coke	636	703	664	99093	109170	102084
石　油	Petroleum	1055	958	1035	205569	185415	198421
钢铁及有色金属	Steel and Iron, and Non-Ferrous Metal	381	418	405	75373	78304	67196
金属矿石	Metal Ores	170	119	144	25930	17641	21081
非金属矿石	Non-metal Ores	168	146	140	26309	22991	21879
矿建材料	Mineral Building Materials	267	367	270	40899	57162	41130
水　泥	Cement	0.1	13	7		1967	1094
木　材	Timber	10	9	6	1644	1536	1036
化肥及农药	Chemical Fertilizers and Pesticides	173	179	244	28122	28930	38750
粮　食	Grain	228	260	200	37078	41858	31981
棉　花	Cotton						
其　他	Others	797	825	801	150419	157079	151510

注：本表含神华神朔铁路有限责任公司。

a) Data in this table includes those of Shenhuashenshuo Railway co., ltd.

15-17 邮电业务总量
Total Business Volume of Post and Telecommunication Services

年 份 Year	邮电业务总量（万元） Business Volume of Postal and Telecommunication Services (10 000 yuan)	函 件（万件） Number of Letters (10 000 pcs)	报 刊 期发数（万份） Number of Newspapers and Magazines Issued (10 000 copies)	快 递（万件） Pieces of Express Mail Services (10 000 pcs)	移动电话（户） Number of Subscribers of Mobile Telephones (subscriber)	城市电话（户） Number of Urban Fixed Telephone Subscribers (subscriber)	乡村电话（户） Number of Rural Fixed Telephone Subscribers (subscriber)	互联网宽带用户（户） Number of Internet Users (subscriber)
1978	5025	9188	319			32356	14100	
1980	5595	10386	494			36521	14668	
1985	7871	13275	869			53828	15978	
1990	16936	15955	506			96573	21184	
1995	145408	24277	1017			601136	78244	
1996	206467	26456	1122			882485	153767	
1997	278942	15787	888			1174607	237720	
1998	395410	14281	1335			1507041	311724	
1999	538640	15678	521		601260	1822476	499096	
2000	850392	17444	454	227	1516687	2528584	923865	198744
2001	945861	18518	386	285	2917135	2905202	1285409	697869
2002	1331745	20323	347	298	4813341	3444609	1798321	1106756
2003	1741428	20307	312	335	6110004	4577207	2147725	1687600
2004	2447665	19915	283	366	7886903	5412164	2507240	1946200
2005	3311322	15119	286	397	9381001	5618420	2974747	2369000
2006	4242336	16072	276	489	11835813	5805703	3339014	1613600
2007	5294031	11677	279	607	16126583	5834313	3422573	1936310
2008	6287289	11219	301	767	19122464	5647062	3165318	2351717
2009	7455960	8690	365	883	23373712	5257253	2892457	2550542
2010	9028500	9734	517	2600	25182317	5195501	2623352	3688265
2011	3482544	5877	335	3942	29071848	5190462	2564357	3890780
2012	3855369	6061	337	5085	32647663	5413043	2307643	4395866
2013	4174992	4914	346	9552	35124609	5550224	2142652	5062419
2014	5666602	3310	375	13762	36072076	5566123	1941734	5524403

注：邮电业务总量按不变价格计算，2011年起按2010年不变价格计算。

a) Business volume of post and telecommunication services are calculated at constant prices.2011 are calculated at constant prices in 2010.

15-18 邮电通信水平
Level of Post and Telecommunication Services

指 标	Item	2012	2013	2014
邮政通信水平	**Postal Services Available**			
平均每一营业网点服务面积(平方公里)	Average Area Served by Every Postal Office (sq.km)	144.79	147.49	121.08
平均每一营业网点服务人口 （万人）	Average People Served by Every Postal Office (10 000 persons)	2.64	2.7	2.22
平均每人每年发函件数 （件）	Annual Number of Letters Mailed per Capita (piece)	1.61	1.31	0.88
平均每百人订有报刊数 （份）	Number of Newspaper and Magazine Subscribed per 100 Persons(copy)	9.00	9.19	9.93
电信通信水平	**Telecommunication Services Available**			
电话普及率(包括移动电话)(部/百人)	Popularization Rate of Telephone (sets/100 persons)	107.56	113.76	115.44
固定电话普及率 （部/百人）	Popularization Rate of Fixed Telephone (sets/100 persons)	20.57	20.44	19.89
城 市	City	28.84	28.74	28.05
乡 村	Rural Area	12.30	11.69	10.84
移动电话数普及率 （部/百人）	Popularization Rate of Mobile Telephone (sets/100 persons)	86.99	93.32	95.55

15-19 各市(区)邮政业务量(2014年)
Total Business Volume of Post Services by City(District)(2014)

地 区 Region		邮政业务总量(万元) Business Volume of Postal cation Services (10 000 yuan)	函件(万件) Number of Letters (10 000 pcs)	包裹(万件) Package (10 000 pcs)	快递(万件) Pieces of Express Mail Services (10 000 pcs)	报刊累计数(万份) Number of Total Newspapers and Magazines (10 000 copies)
全 省	**Shaanxi**	**459444**	**3310**	**160**	**13762**	**48550**
西安市	Xi'an	226679	2112	71	10679	15910
铜川市	Tongchuan	6593	31	2	92	1746
宝鸡市	Baoji	37592	215	16	1022	4239
咸阳市	Xianyang	39992	341	16	632	3486
渭南市	Weinan	33606	173	16	379	7221
延安市	Yan'an	15690	40	6	165	3142
汉中市	Hanzhong	44472	119	12	307	3232
榆林市	Yulin	17714	77	8	195	4392
安康市	Ankang	22080	66	9	210	2046
商洛市	Shangluo	15027	136	4	81	3137

15-20 各市(区)电信业务量(2014年)
Total Business Volume of Telecommunication Services by City(District)(2014)

地 区 Region		电信业务总量(万元) Business Volume of Telecommuni-cation Services (10 000 yuan)	移动电话用户(户) Number of Subscribers of Mobile Telephones (subscriber)	固定电话用户(户) Number of Subscribers of Fixed Telephones (subscriber)	城市电话 Number of Urban Fixed Telephone Subscribers	乡村电话 Number of Rural Fixed Telephone Subscribers	# 小灵通 Handphone	互联网宽带用户(户) Number of Subscribers of Internet Services (subscriber)
全 省	**Shaanxi**	**5207159**	**36072076**	**7507857**	**5566123**	**1941734**	**107706**	**5524403**
西安市	Xi'an	2244643	14623198	3229092	2278843	794971	94746	2461233
铜川市	Tongchuan	92928	667060	134341	101558	35428	206	94231
宝鸡市	Baoji	365080	2664618	649068	472412	164800	485	423086
咸阳市	Xianyang	453296	3678757	616723	473600	165215	1587	505696
渭南市	Weinan	465876	3629805	824603	638457	222725	26	658379
延安市	Yan'an	329487	2137526	347028	261727	91303	168	233563
汉中市	Hanzhong	304581	2346314	533081	420710	146764		354910
榆林市	Yulin	564039	3380433	537452	410050	143045	10480	345645
安康市	Ankang	239503	1742154	366879	286583	99974	4	274051
商洛市	Shangluo	147726	1202211	269590	222183	77508	4	173609

15-21 各市(区)邮电局所及邮递线路(2014年)

Postal and Telecommunication Offices and Postal Routes by City(District)(2014)

地区 Region	邮电局所总计(个) Total Number of Postal and Telecommunication Offices(unit)	邮政自办局(所) Number of Self-postal Offices	邮政代办所 Number of Sub-postal Offices	电信自办局(所) Number of Self-Telecommunication Offices	电信代办所 Number of Sub-Telecommunication Offices	邮路长度(公里) Length of Postal Routes (km)	农村投递线路总长度(公里) Total Length of Rural Delivery Routes(km)
全　省 Shaanxi	**36859**	**1031**	**667**	**1576**	**33585**	**55788**	**125548**
西安市 Xi'an	8943	234	46	405	8258	29992.1	12042
铜川市 Tongchuan	1012	22	25	65	900	795.5	3182
宝鸡市 Baoji	3108	123	46	160	2779	3207.3	9540
咸阳市 Xianyang	4091	126	52	122	3791	2121.8	14492
渭南市 Weinan	5315	126	50	197	4942	2365	16871
延安市 Yan'an	2801	70	94	116	2521	3662	10874
汉中市 Hanzhong	3681	130	93	189	3269	3229.7	15749
榆林市 Yulin	3053	39	144	120	2750	5417	19663
安康市 Ankang	2704	91	73	120	2420	2960	11437
商洛市 Shangluo	2151	70	44	82	1955	2037.6	11699

15-22 邮电通信企业主要财务指标

Principal Financial Indicators of Postal and Telecommunication Services Enterprises

单位：万元　　(10 000 yuan)

指　标	Item	2012	2013	2014
邮电业务收入总计	Total Revenue from Postal and Telecommunication Services	3476266	3966286	3996307
# 主营业务收入	Revenue from Principal Business	3262603	3694789	3879433
业务支出	Business Expenditure	1907738	2581877	1642815
营业外损益净额	Net Amount of Non Operating Profit and Loss	25265	9798	-3206
税　金	Tax	208751	148218	196970
教育附加费	Extra Charges for Education	4114	4769	4461
收支差额	Balance of Revenue and Expenditure	12527	673776	457038
年末固定资产原值	Original Value of Fixed Assets at Year-end	7601562	8439914	9109208

主要统计指标解释

铁路营业里程 又称营业长度(包括正式营业和临时营业里程)，指办理客货运输业务的铁路正线总长度。凡是全线或部分建成双线及以上的线路，以第一线的实际长度计算；复线、站线、段管线、岔线和特殊用途线以及不计算运费的联络线都不计算营业里程。该指标可以反映铁路运输业基础设施的发展水平，也是计算客货周转量、运输密度和机车车辆运用效率等指标的基础资料。

铁路电气化里程 指在全部铁路营业里程中已安装了供电线路及设备，可以供电力机车牵引列车运行的区段的总里程。

公路里程 指在一定时期内实际达到《公路工程[WTBZ]技术标准 JTJ01-88》规定的等级公路，并经公路主管部门正式验收交付使用的公路里程数。包括大中城市的郊区公路以及通过小城镇街道部分的公路里程和桥梁、渡口的长度，不包括大中城市的街道、厂矿、林区生产用道和农业生产用道的里程。两条或多条公路共同经由同一路段，只计算一次，不得重复计算里程长度。该指标可以反映公路建设的发展规模，也是计算运输网密度等指标的基础资料。

内河航道里程 也称内河通航里程，指在一定时期内，能通航运输船舶及排筏的天然河流、湖泊水库、运河及通航渠道的长度。包括全年季节性通航累计三个月以上的航道，不包括仅供零散流放竹、木排的河道。该指标可以反映内河水运网的规模、水平和发展情况。

民用航空航线里程 指统计期间内全部民用航空航线的航线总长度。航线长度指民用航空航线的计费距离。计算航线里程可按重复和不重复两种方法，前者是指各航线长度相加的总和；后者则要扣除各航线之间相同航段重复计算的部分。

货(客)运量 指在一定时期内，各种运输工具实际运送的货物(旅客)数量。该指标是反映运输业为国民经济和人民生活服务的数量指标，也是制定和检查运输生产计划、研究运输发展规模和速度的重要指标。货运按吨计算，客运按人计算。货物不论运输距离长短、货物类别，均按实际重量统计。旅客不论行程远近或票价多少，均按一人一次客运量统计；半价票、小孩票也按一人统计。

货物(旅客)周转量 指在一定时期内，由各种运输工具运送的货物(旅客)数量与其相应运输距离的乘积之总和。该指标可以反映运输业生产的总成果，也是编制和检查运输生产计划，计算运输效率、劳动生产率以及核算运输单位成本的主要基础资料。计算货物周转量通常按发出站与到达站之间的最短距离，也就是计费距离计算。计算公式为：

$$\text{货物（旅客）周转量} = \Sigma\text{（货物（旅客）运输量} \times \text{运输距离）}$$

铁路货车平均静载重 指铁路货车在始发站静止状态下平均每车装载的货物重量，用以分析货车完成装车时车辆载重力的利用情况。计算公式为：

$$\text{货车平均静载量} = \frac{\text{货物发送吨数}}{\text{装车数}}$$

静载重的多少取决于运送货物的性质、种类、车辆的类型和装载技术的高低。根据货车的平均标记载重与静载重进行对比，可以反映货车载重能力的利用程度。计算公式为：

$$\text{货车载重力利用率}(\%) = \frac{\text{货车平均静载重}}{\text{货车平均标记载重}} \times 100\%$$

铁路货运机车日产量 指在一定时期内，平均每台货运机车在一昼夜内所完成的总重吨公里数，包括载运货物的重量和车辆本身的自重。该指标从时间和牵引能力两方面反映了机车运用效率。计算公式为：

$$\text{货运机车平均日产量} = \frac{\text{货运总重吨公里数}}{\text{货运机车台日数}}$$

民用汽车拥有量 指报告期末，在公安交通管理部门按照《机动车注册登记工作规范》，已注册登记领有民用车辆牌照的全部汽车数量。汽车拥有量统计的主要分类：根据汽车结构分为载客汽车、载货汽车及其他汽车；根据汽车所有者不同分为个人(私人)汽车、单位汽车；根据汽车的使用性质分为营运汽车、非营运汽车；根据汽车大小规格不同载客汽车分为大型、中型、小型和微型，载货汽车分为重型、中型、轻型和微型。

邮电业务总量 指以货币形式表示的邮电企业为社会提供各类邮电服务的总数量，是用于观察邮电业务发展变化总趋势的综合性总量指标。分别按邮政业务总量和电信业务总量统计。邮电业务总量是以各类业务的实物量分别乘以相应的不变单价，得出各类业务的货币量再加总求得。

移动电话用户 指在电信运营企业营业网点办理开户登记手续，通过移动电话交换机进入移动电话网，占用移动电话号码的各类电话用户。包括 GSM 数字移动电话用户、CDMA 数字移动电话用户和电信运营企业发行的报告期末已激活充值的能异地漫游的各种智能卡用户。

固定电话用户 指在电信运营企业营业网点办理开户登记手续并已接入固定电话网上的全部电话用户。包括普通电话用户、公用电话用户、窄带综合业务数字网（N—ISDN）用户、智能网专用接入终端用户等。按行政区划分为城市电话用户和农村电话用户。

城市电话用户 指直辖市、省辖市、地级市、县级市的市区、市郊区及县城范围内接入局用交换机的电话用户。包括分布在农村地区县团级以上建制的独立工矿区、林区、驻军等电话用户。

农村电话用户 指县城关镇以下的集镇和农村接入局用交换机的电话用户。

Explanatory Notes on Main Statistical Indicators

Length of Railways in Operation refers to the total length of the trunk line for passenger and freight transportation (including both full operation and temporary operation). The calculation is based on the actual length of the first line if this line has a full or partial double (or more). Not included are double tracks, station sidings, tracks under the charge of stations, branch lines, special-purpose lines and non-payable connecting lines. The length of railways in operation is an important indicator to show the development of the infrastructure of railway transport. It is also essential data to calculate volume of passenger freight transport, traffic density and utilization efficiency of locomotives and carriages.

Length of Electrified Railways refers to the length of the section of railways in operation in which the power supply lines and other equipment are installed for the running of electrified locomotives. The proportion of the length of electrified railways to the total length of railways in operation is an important indicator to show the modernization of railways.

Length of Highways refers to the length of highways which are built in conformity with the grades specified by the highway engineering standard [Highways WTBZ-Technical Standard JTJ01-88] formulated by the Ministry of Transport, and have been formally checked and accepted by the departments of highways and put into use. The length of highways includes that of the suburb highways at large and medium-sized cities, highways passing through streets at small cities and towns, and also the length of bridges and ferry piers. It does not include the length of streets in big and medium-sized cities and highways built for the production purpose at factories, mines, forest areas and agricultural areas. If two or more highways go the same section of the way, the length of the section is only calculated for once and no duplication is allowed. The length of highways is an indicator to show the development of the scale of highway construction and to provide essential information to calculate the transport network density.

Length of Navigable Inland Waterways is an indicator reflecting the size and development of inland water network. It refers to the length of the natural rivers, lakes, reservoirs, canals, and ditches open to navigation during a given period, which enables transportation by ships and rafts. It includes the channels open to navigation for over an accumulated period of 3 months in a year, yet this does not include the river courses which are only used to float odd logs and bamboo rafts. This indicator can reflect the scale, level and development situation of the inland waterway network.

Length of Civil Aviation Routes refers to the length of all routes for civil aviation flights, which is used to account the freight, during the period of statistics.. There are usually two ways to calculate the route length: duplicated calculation and non-duplicated calculation, the former is the sum of length of all civil aviation routes, and the latter should deduct the duplication length of same route among all routes.

Freight (Passenger) Traffic refers to the volume of freight (passenger) transported with various means within a specific period of time. This indicator reflects the service of the transport industry towards the national economy and people's living conditions, as well as an important indicator used in formulating and monitoring transport production plans and research into the scale and pace of transport development. Freight transport is calculated in tons and passenger traffic is calculated in terms of number of persons. Freight transport is calculated in terms of the actual weight of the goods and takes no account of the type of freight and distance of travel. Passenger traffic is calculated by the principle that one person can be counted only once in one trip and takes no account of the travelling distance and ticket price. The passengers who travel with a half price ticket or a child's ticket is also calculated as one person.

Freight Ton-kilometres (Passenger-kilometres) refers to the sum of the product of the volume of transported cargo (passengers) multiplied by the transport distance. It is an important indicator to reflect the achievement of the transportation industry. This is an important indicator to show the total results of the transport industry; to prepare and examine the transport plan; and to serve as the main basic data for calculating the efficiency, labour productivity and unit cost of transport. Normally, the shortest distance between the departure station and the destination station (i.e., the payable distance) is the basis in calculating the freight ton-kilometres. The formula is as follows:

$$\begin{matrix}\text{Freight ton-kilometres} \\ \text{(passenger-kilometres)}\end{matrix} = \Sigma \begin{matrix}\text{freight} \\ \text{(passenger) traffic}\end{matrix} \times \begin{matrix}\text{distance of} \\ \text{transportation}\end{matrix}$$

Average Static Load of Freight Cars refers to the average cargo weight as loaded by each freight car under the static condition at the departure station. It is used to show the utilization extent of the loading capacity of the freight cars. The formula is:

$$\begin{matrix}\text{Static load (ton)} \\ \text{of freight car}\end{matrix} = \frac{\text{tonnage of goods dispatched}}{\text{number of freight cars loaded}}$$

The static load of freight cars is determined by the nature and type of goods loaded the type of vehicles, and the technique of loading. Comparison of the average marked load with the static load of freight cars provides indication on the degree of utilization of loading capacity of freight cars. For its calculation the following formula is applied:

$$\begin{matrix}\text{Utilization rate of} \\ \text{capacity of freight cars (\%)}\end{matrix} = \frac{\text{Average static load}}{\text{Average marked load}} \times 100\%$$

Average Daily Haul of Freight Locomotives refers to the average total ton-kilometres accomplished by each freight transport locomotive over one day and night during a given period of time. It includes both the weight of the goods carried and the dead weight of the train itself. It is a comprehensive indicator reflecting the locomotive efficiency in terms of both time and the pulling force.

$$\begin{array}{c}\text{Average daily haul of}\\ \text{freight transport locomotive}\\ \text{(ton - kilometre)}\end{array} = \frac{\begin{array}{c}\text{Total ton - kilometres}\\ \text{of freight}\end{array}}{\begin{array}{c}\text{Daily number of freight}\\ \text{transport locomotive}\end{array}}$$

Possession of Civil Motor Vehicles refer to the total numbers of vehicles that are registered and received vehicles license tags according to the *Work Standard for Motor Vehicles Registration* formulated by the Transport Management Office under the department of public security at the end of the reference period. They are divided into categories. According to the structure of motor vehicles, they are divided into passenger vehicles, trucks and others; according to ownership into private vehicles and vehicles for the unit's use; according to kind of usage into working vehicles and non-working vehicles; and according to size of vehicles into large passenger vehicles, medium-sized passenger vehicles, small passenger vehicles and mini passenger vehicles, heavy trucks, light-heavy trucks, light trucks and mini-trucks.

Business Volume of Post and Telecommunications refers to the total amount of postal and telecommunication services, expressed in value terms, provided by the post and telecommunications departments for society. This indicator reflects the overall results of development of postal and telecommunication services. It can be classificated as postal services and telecommunication services. Business volume of post and telecommunications is the sum of all services in kind multiplying with the unit price (constant price) to get the total business value.

Mobile Telephone Subscribers refer to persons who have gone through registration procedures in the operation points of enterprises engaged in telecommunications and are hence connected with the mobile telephone communication network through the mobile telephone switchboards and occupy mobile phone numbers. Included are GSM digital mobile phone subscribers, CDMA digital mobile phone subscribers and subscribers to intelligent phone cards with roaming facility issued by telecommunications enterprises and which have been subscribed to and activated at the end of the reference period.

Local Telephone Subscribers refer to all subscribers who have gone through registration procedures in the operation points of enterprises engaged in telecommunications and are hence connected to the local telecommunications service provider through fixed line network. Included are general subscribers, public telephones subscribers, N-ISDN subscribers and intelligent network terminal subscribers. They are also classified in terms of administrative districts as urban telephone subscribers and rural telephone subscribers according to location.

Urban Telephone Subscribers refer to the number of telephone subscribers, located at the different administrative districts of municipalities directly under the Central Government, cities under the jurisdiction of province, cities at prefecture level, downtown and suburb of city at county level town and county towns, that are connected to the public line telephone network, including rural mineral area, forest area, military area.

Rural Telephone Subscribers refer to telephone subscribers, located at the towns below the level of county town and villages, that are connected to the public line telephone network.

十六、国内贸易

Domestic Trade

资料整理：张　兵

简 要 说 明

一、本篇资料反映陕西国内市场发展情况，主要内容包括：限额以上批发和零售业、住宿和餐饮业基本情况、连锁经营情况，社会消费品零售总额，成品油购进、销售与库存情况等。

二、限额以上企业指年主营业务收入2000万元及以上的批发企业（单位）；500万元及以上的零售业企业（单位）；200万元及以上的住宿和餐饮业企业（单位）。

三、批发业、零售业、住宿业、餐饮业大中小微型划分标准按照 2011 年《统计上大中小微型企业划分办法》标准执行。

Brief Introduction

I. This chapter reflects the development of domestic markets in Shaanxi, mainly including: enterprises above designated size of wholesale and retail trades of commodity circulation, the basic conditions of the wholesale and retail trades above designated size, development of chain stores of retail trades, total retail sales of consumer goods, purchase, sale and stock of refined oil product, etc.

II. Enterprises above designated size cover wholesale enterprises with revenue from principal business over 20 million yuan, retail enterprises with revenue from principal business over 5 million yuan, wholesale and retail enterprises with revenue from principal business over 2 million yuan.

III. The division standard of large/medium/small/mini sized enterprises of wholesale, retail trades,hotels and catering services is based on *the Division Standard of Large/Medium/Small/Mini Sized Enterprises* in 2011.

16.国内贸易

2014年全省			
限额以上法人企业	5092	个	
批发业	864	个	
零售业	2542	个	
住宿业	718	个	
餐饮业	968	个	
社会消费品零售总额	5918.71	亿元	比上年增长 12.8%
商品零售	5336.86	亿元	比上年增长 13.4%
餐饮收入	581.85	亿元	比上年增长 8.1%

社会消费品零售总额（亿元）

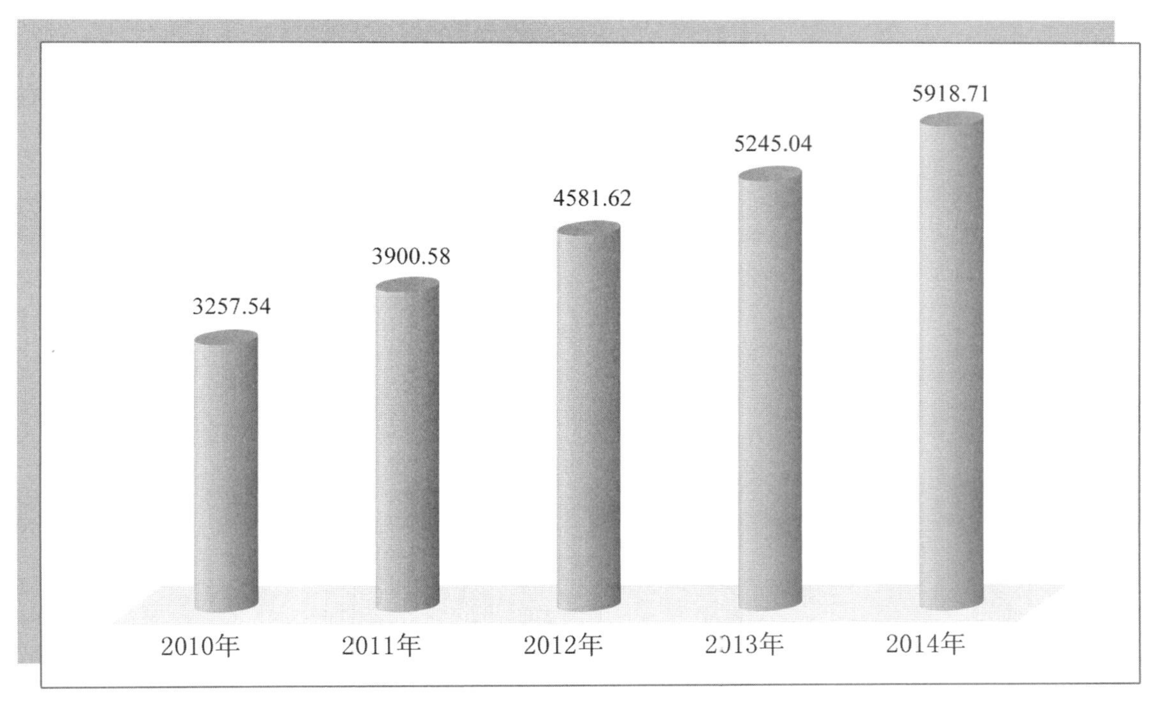

16-1 限额以上批发和零售业、住宿和餐饮业法人企业数和从业人员数(2014年) Number of Corporation Enterprises above Designated Size in Wholesale and Retail Trades, Hotels and Catering Services and Employed Persons(2014)

地 区	Region	法人企业数(个) Number of Corporation Enterprises (unit)	批发业 Wholesale Trade	零售业 Retail Trade	住宿业 Hotels	餐饮业 Catering Service
全 省	**Shaanxi**	**5092**	**864**	**2542**	**718**	**968**
西 安 市	Xi'an	1341	342	461	223	315
铜 川 市	Tongchuan	143	10	87	28	18
宝 鸡 市	Baoji	608	85	341	74	108
咸 阳 市	Xianyang	596	50	337	67	142
渭 南 市	Weinan	510	45	310	54	101
# 韩城市	Hancheng	45	4	25	5	11
延 安 市	Yan'an	329	70	155	59	45
汉 中 市	Hanzhong	372	52	215	53	52
榆 林 市	Yulin	559	118	293	75	73
安 康 市	Ankang	460	65	249	53	93
商 洛 市	Shangluo	132	22	68	27	15
杨凌示范区	Yangling	42	5	26	5	6

16-1 续表 continued

地 区	Region	从业人员数(人) Number of Employed Persons (person)	批发业 Wholesale Trade	零售业 Retail Trade	住宿业 Hotels	餐饮业 Catering Service
全 省	**Shaanxi**	**447994**	**84310**	**204312**	**72452**	**86920**
西 安 市	Xi'an	219260	46462	92449	33993	46356
铜 川 市	Tongchuan	9835	1975	5425	1485	950
宝 鸡 市	Baoji	37346	5580	19934	4716	7116
咸 阳 市	Xianyang	36489	4554	18468	5547	7920
渭 南 市	Weinan	35187	4254	19374	4301	7258
# 韩城市	Hancheng	3822	72	2778	444	528
延 安 市	Yan'an	19387	3026	8780	4671	2910
汉 中 市	Hanzhong	22779	4146	12056	4288	2289
榆 林 市	Yulin	36056	8109	14696	7588	5663
安 康 市	Ankang	20538	3780	9672	2414	4672
商 洛 市	Shangluo	9074	2208	2727	2888	1251
杨凌示范区	Yangling	2043	216	731	561	535

16-2 社会消费品零售总额

Total Retail Sales of Consumer Goods in the Whole Province

单位：亿元 (100 million yuan)

年份 Year	社会消费品零售总额 Total Retail Sales of Consumer Goods	按地区分 By Region			按行业分 By Sector	
		市的零售额 City	县的零售额 County	县以下的零售额 Under County Level	# 批发和零售业 Wholesale and Retail TradesTrades	# 住宿和餐饮业 Hotels and Catering Services
1978	33.37	11.93	9.79	11.65	28.29	1.32
1980	43.38	17.47	12.18	13.73	35.86	1.78
1985	80.01	39.83	19.45	20.73	61.23	3.84
1990	159.67	91.21	34.29	34.17	118.55	7.99
1991	176.60	102.21	36.98	37.41	126.83	9.29
1992	227.53	132.25	47.31	47.97	156.17	16.22
1993	259.87	154.35	52.41	53.12	172.50	19.63
1994	318.70	192.44	62.69	63.58	203.73	24.57
1995	398.87	242.85	80.30	75.73	253.42	31.22
1996	474.87	289.83	93.90	91.14	308.35	39.50
1997	552.37	344.26	104.09	104.03	358.21	50.15
1998	601.89	371.47	114.28	116.14	386.19	62.37
1999	657.80	407.97	124.74	125.08	427.36	69.88
2000	725.64	454.84	135.78	135.02	476.18	81.27
2001	809.31	514.23	147.77	147.31	536.74	95.08
2002	907.64	585.01	162.28	160.36	616.17	105.10
2003	1010.95	649.27	183.56	178.12	878.03	113.87
2004	1162.80	756.54	206.49	199.77	1012.57	126.59
2005	1331.35	874.47	232.07	224.81	1162.77	141.93
2006	1542.37	1006.11	275.80	260.46	1344.44	167.76
2007	1837.25	1221.28	311.78	304.20	1598.15	204.31
2008	2317.11	1542.33	401.04	373.74	2013.65	262.94

年份 Year	社会消费品零售总额 Total Retail Sales of Consumer Goods	按销售单位所在地分By Location of Establishments			按消费形态分By Consumption Patterns	
		城镇 Urban Areas	# 城区 Urban District	乡村 Rural Areas	商品零售 Retail Sales	餐饮收入 Catering income
2009	2725.67	2367.26	1588.16	358.42	2412.13	313.55
2010	3257.54	2834.08	1935.09	423.46	2886.52	371.02
2011	3900.58	3442.78	2492.10	457.80	3471.61	428.96
2012	4581.62	4037.26	3086.68	544.36	4078.21	503.41
2013	5245.04	4620.77	3552.88	624.27	4706.69	538.35
2014	5918.71	5233.56	3921.36	685.14	5336.86	581.85

注：2009-2013年数据依据第三次经济普查结果进行了修订。

a) Data from 2009 to 2013 were adjusted according to the 3rd national economic census.

16-3 各市(区)社会消费品零售总额
Total Retail Sales of Consumer Goods by City(District)

单位：亿元 (100 million yuan)

年份 Year	全省 Shaanxi	西安市 Xi'an	铜川市 Tongchuan	宝鸡市 Baoji	咸阳市 Xianyang	渭南市 Weinan
1992	227.53	100.84	5.89	25.87	24.49	21.36
1993	259.87	116.73	6.43	30.58	25.75	23.61
1994	318.70	148.03	7.44	33.48	31.53	26.18
1995	398.87	186.60	9.06	42.04	40.49	33.87
1996	474.87	222.94	10.53	49.21	48.68	41.41
1997	552.37	264.47	11.90	55.60	55.54	48.04
1998	601.89	291.45	12.31	59.76	58.21	52.79
1999	657.80	323.37	12.95	65.01	63.78	55.15
2000	725.64	360.42	13.79	71.89	70.35	58.53
2001	809.31	406.21	14.64	80.61	79.16	62.37
2002	907.64	459.76	15.96	91.19	88.83	66.68
2003	1010.95	502.65	17.73	105.06	101.56	73.21
2004	1162.80	578.60	19.94	122.91	119.07	81.58
2005	1331.35	670.56	21.76	137.48	133.03	93.02
2006	1542.37	784.95	24.12	155.23	148.88	108.65
2007	1837.25	936.21	27.58	179.81	173.11	131.96
2008	2317.11	1176.58	33.54	220.90	212.67	175.03
2009	2725.67	1398.37	40.56	260.10	250.59	202.80
2010	3257.54	1678.01	49.15	307.52	296.35	240.77
2011	3900.58	2039.24	59.15	358.23	345.10	284.08
2012	4581.62	2400.67	71.12	412.83	401.08	335.00
2013	5245.04	2742.89	84.70	473.39	462.68	387.70
2014	5918.71	3093.89	96.64	539.67	528.84	441.98

16-3 续表 continued

单位：亿元 (100 million yuan)

年份 Year	延安市 Yan'an	汉中市 Hanzhong	榆林市 Yulin	安康市 Ankang	商洛市 Shangluo	杨凌示范区 Yangling
1992	6.65	17.92	8.68	8.93	6.19	0.72
1993	7.99	20.96	9.63	10.33	7.06	0.80
1994	10.33	27.06	13.03	12.31	8.42	0.89
1995	12.13	31.19	16.17	15.50	10.66	1.15
1996	14.02	34.97	20.59	18.54	12.63	1.15
1997	15.99	36.95	26.25	22.24	13.96	1.37
1998	17.79	38.82	29.18	24.55	15.59	1.43
1999	20.36	40.50	31.85	25.76	17.50	1.42
2000	22.63	42.91	35.77	27.68	19.91	1.55
2001	26.22	45.22	40.40	29.88	22.59	1.77
2002	30.78	48.31	46.02	32.36	25.40	2.01
2003	34.99	52.69	55.55	36.06	28.65	2.35
2004	41.10	57.23	65.08	41.19	32.71	2.79
2005	47.53	65.30	76.33	46.75	35.97	3.38
2006	54.70	76.10	91.98	53.83	40.01	3.62
2007	65.85	91.80	116.02	64.12	46.22	3.92
2008	84.80	116.66	154.11	80.72	56.70	4.57
2009	96.86	133.02	176.72	93.56	66.79	5.40
2010	117.06	157.50	213.64	110.78	79.19	6.30
2011	140.48	184.44	259.18	129.72	92.18	7.54
2012	168.30	216.05	307.70	151.49	107.28	8.76
2013	192.28	248.15	348.27	171.72	121.82	10.11
2014	218.24	281.65	374.74	193.18	136.92	11.44

注：2009-2013年数据依据第三次经济普查结果进行了修订。

a) Data from 2009 to 2013 were adjusted according to the 3rd national economic census.

16-4 各市(区)按销售单位所在地和消费形态分的社会消费品零售总额(2014年)

Total Retail Sales of Consumer Goods by Location of Establishments and Consumption Patterns by City(District)(2014)

单位：万元 (10 000 yuan)

地区	Region	社会消费品零售总额 Total Retail Sales of Consumer Goods	# 限额以上企业消费品零售额 Retail Sales of Enterprises above Designated Size	按销售单位所在地分 By Location of Establishments 城镇 Urban Areas	# 城区 Urban District	乡村 Rural Areas	按消费形态分 By Consumption Patterns 商品零售 Retail Sales	餐饮收入 Catering Income
全省	**Shaanxi**	**59187052**	**37322589**	**52335648**	**39213571**	**6851404**	**53368581**	**5818471**
西安市	Xi'an	30938908	22825308	29964290	25960042	974618	28650659	2288249
铜川市	Tongchuan	966407	467718	737739	547944	228668	795393	171013
宝鸡市	Baoji	5396667	2727717	4877986	4151528	518681	4818232	578435
咸阳市	Xianyang	5288432	2502944	3976046	2123098	1312386	4351920	936512
渭南市	Weinan	4419777	2712377	3322911	1967867	1096866	3906966	512811
# 韩城市	Hancheng	369903	195204	246601	156400	123302	318466	51437
延安市	Yan'an	2182431	1022240	1749518	834760	432912	1975716	206715
汉中市	Hanzhong	2816481	1441959	2314884	998372	501597	2503756	312725
榆林市	Yulin	3747362	2310451	2619809	1579486	1127553	3416328	331035
安康市	Ankang	1931831	953230	1613410	635339	318421	1614540	317291
商洛市	Shangluo	1369246	301216	1059078	315159	310167	1227053	142192
杨凌示范区	Yangling	129511	57430	99976	99976	29534	108017	21494

16-5 各市、县(市、区)社会消费品零售总额
Total Retail Sales of Consumer Goods by City and County(City and District)

单位：万元 (10 000 yuan)

地 区	Region	2013	2014	2014年比2013年增长% Growth Rate in 2014 over 2013(%)
全 省	**Shaanxi**	**52450412**	**59187052**	**12.8**
西安市	**Xi'an**	**27428926**	**30938908**	**12.8**
新城区	Xincheng	4460631	4997780	12.0
碑林区	Beilin	4451118	5058665	13.6
莲湖区	Lianhu	3686210	4130029	12.0
灞桥区	Baqiao	1322583	1542793	16.6
未央区	Weiyang	4237165	4807887	13.5
雁塔区	Yanta	5343029	5964957	11.6
阎良区	Yanliang	313725	349333	11.3
临潼区	Lintong	640802	726349	13.3
长安区	Chang'an	1449431	1640031	13.1
蓝田县	Lantian	457356	515669	12.7
周至县	Zhouzhi	307116	346273	12.7
户 县	Huxian	509672	575164	12.8
高陵县	Gaoling	250091	283978	13.5
铜川市	**Tongchuan**	**846982**	**966407**	**14.1**
王益区	Wangyi	353287	400996	13.5
印台区	Yintai	158907	180058	13.3
耀州区	Yaozhou	281070	324645	15.5
宜君县	Yijun	53719	60708	13.0
宝鸡市	**Baoji**	**4733919**	**5396667**	**14.0**
渭滨区	Weibin	1379329	1578642	14.5
金台区	Jintai	1351437	1544017	14.3
陈仓区	Chencang	431748	491545	13.9
凤翔县	Fengxiang	334402	378042	13.1
岐山县	Qishan	359149	406844	13.3
扶风县	Fufeng	224141	256305	14.4
眉 县	Meixian	218455	249803	14.4
陇 县	Longxian	144955	162712	12.3
千阳县	Qianyang	67805	76043	12.2
麟游县	Linyou	46577	52609	13.0
凤 县	Fengxian	142611	162648	14.1
太白县	Taibai	33309	37456	12.5
咸阳市	**Xianyang**	**4626800**	**5288432**	**14.3**
秦都区	Qindu	938524	1091781	16.3
渭城区	Weicheng	759967	862483	13.5
三原县	Sanyuan	327427	362789	10.8
泾阳县	Jingyang	328745	378386	15.1
乾 县	Qianxian	465009	526390	13.2

16-5 续表 1 continued

单位：万元 (10 000 yuan)

地　区	Region	2013	2014	2014年比2013年增长% Growth Rate in 2014 over 2013(%)
礼泉县	Liquan	361727	410561	13.5
永寿县	Yongshou	124291	143928	15.8
彬　县	Binxian	217726	252562	16.0
长武县	Changwu	114505	132024	15.3
旬邑县	Xunyi	147196	169129	14.9
淳化县	Chunhua	115805	133871	15.6
武功县	Wugong	292646	327179	11.8
兴平市	Xingping	433232	497350	14.8
渭南市	**Weinan**	**3876997**	**4419777**	**14.0**
临渭区	Linwei	1037532	1196605	15.3
华　县	Huaxian	155118	175058	12.9
潼关县	Tongguan	105972	121674	14.8
大荔县	Dali	475266	537858	13.2
合阳县	Heyang	250669	286438	14.3
澄城县	Chengcheng	234267	265571	13.4
蒲城县	Pucheng	466659	529634	13.5
白水县	Baishui	177284	202726	14.4
富平县	Fuping	451395	511263	13.3
韩城市	Hancheng	326808	369903	13.2
华阴市	Huayin	196026	223045	13.8
延安市	**Yan'an**	**1922846**	**2182431**	**13.5**
宝塔区	Baota	881976	1014119	15.0
延长县	Yanchang	68369	76493	11.9
延川县	Yanchuan	84996	95486	12.3
子长县	Zichang	124394	139086	11.8
安塞县	Ansai	97133	108438	11.6
志丹县	Zhidan	99128	111056	12.0
吴起县	Wuqi	67763	76089	12.3
甘泉县	Ganquan	45795	51286	12.0
富　县	Fuxian	86492	97440	12.7
洛川县	Luochuan	163235	183797	12.6
宜川县	Yichuan	50902	57255	12.5
黄龙县	Huanglong	21331	23777	11.5
黄陵县	Huangling	131332	148109	12.8
汉中市	**Hanzhong**	**2481481**	**2816481**	**13.5**
汉台区	Hantai	990676	1124390	13.5
南郑县	Nanzheng	237114	268842	13.4
城固县	Chenggu	280159	318687	13.8
洋　县	Yangxian	135736	154241	13.6
西乡县	Xixiang	132255	151181	14.3

16-5 续表 2 continued

单位：万元 (10 000 yuan)

地 区	Region	2013	2014	2014年比2013年增长% Growth Rate in 2014 over 2013(%)
勉 县	Mianxian	243200	275434	13.3
宁强县	Ningqiang	146315	165795	13.3
略阳县	Lueyang	139827	157943	13.0
镇巴县	Zhenba	128378	145780	13.6
留坝县	Liuba	29098	33019	13.5
佛坪县	Foping	18724	21170	13.1
榆林市	**Yulin**	**3482679**	**3747362**	**7.6**
榆阳区	Yuyang	688580	720187	4.6
神木县	Shenmu	583890	616309	5.6
府谷县	Fugu	464210	496371	6.9
横山县	Hengshan	281149	310369	10.4
靖边县	Jingbian	447549	481497	7.6
定边县	Dingbian	343176	380694	10.9
绥德县	Suide	182724	197828	8.3
米脂县	Mizhi	130517	145774	11.7
佳 县	Jiaxian	64861	71347	10.0
吴堡县	Wubu	69823	77085	10.4
清涧县	Qingjian	103566	114682	10.7
子洲县	Zizhou	122632	135220	10.3
安康市	**Ankang**	**1717183**	**1931831**	**12.5**
汉滨区	Hanbin	812667	895950	10.2
汉阴县	Hanyin	116006	133329	14.9
石泉县	Shiquan	82491	95063	15.2
宁陕县	Ningshan	38955	41460	6.4
紫阳县	Ziyang	153215	176112	14.9
岚皋县	Langao	72773	83284	14.4
平利县	Pingli	93507	107381	14.8
镇坪县	Zhenping	26269	28852	9.8
旬阳县	Xunyang	231488	267014	15.3
白河县	Baihe	89812	103387	15.1
商洛市	**Shangluo**	**1218190**	**1369246**	**12.4**
商州区	Shangzhou	300428	338138	12.6
洛南县	Luonan	219222	246696	12.5
丹凤县	Danfeng	166546	186966	12.3
商南县	Shangnan	109329	122459	12.0
山阳县	Shanyang	192135	216392	12.6
镇安县	Zhen'an	151574	170091	12.2
柞水县	Zhashui	78957	88503	12.1
杨凌示范区	**Yangling**	**114409**	**129511**	**13.2**

16-6 限额以上批发和零售企业(单位)商品零售类值
Total Sales of Enterprises above Designated Size in Retail Trades by Category of Commodities

单位：万元 (10 000 yuan)

类　别	Item	2013	2014
合　计	**Total**	**29806776**	**35409263**
1.食品、饮料、烟酒类	Food, Beverages, Tobacco and Liquor	2966556	3697488
(1)粮油、食品类	Food	1785479	2294893
#粮油类	Grain and Oil	691538	806981
肉禽蛋类	Meat, Poultry and Eggs	197813	239844
水产品类	Aquatic Products	147656	207067
蔬菜类	Vegetables	189842	287529
干鲜果品类	Dried and Fresh Melons and Fruits	199833	331153
(2)饮料类	Beverages	581347	680479
(3)烟酒类	Tobacco and Liquor	599731	722116
2.服装、鞋帽、针纺织品类	Garments, Shoes and Hats, Knitwear and Textiles	4702193	5150697
(1)服装类	Garments	3745460	4090357
(2)鞋帽类	Shoes and Hats	583324	669619
(3)针、纺织品类	Knitwear and Textiles	373409	390721
3.化妆品类	Cosmetics	423054	522350
4.金银珠宝类	Gold, Silver and Jewellery	671938	732628
5.日用品类	Daily Consumer Articles	845780	950204
#洗涤用品类	Washing Articles	245893	278007
儿童玩具类	Children Toys	96451	108878
6.五金、电料类	Hardware	329569	353927
7.体育、娱乐用品类	Sports and Recreation Articles	208309	225968
8.书报杂志类	Newspapers and Magazines	305182	336842
9.电子出版物及音像制品类	E-journals and Video Products	20004	44499
10.家用电器和音像器材类	Household Appliances and Audio/Video Equipments	1806007	1915688
11.中西药品类	Traditional Chinese and Western Medicines	707938	871065
#西药类	Western Medicine	554306	619206
中草药及中成药类	Traditional Chinese Medicines	114722	156412
12.文化办公用品类	Cultural and Office Appliances	389967	527489
13.家具类	Furniture	1100180	1260936
14.通讯器材类	Communication Appliances	321387	569720
15.煤炭及制品类	Coal and Related Products	1277331	1527802
16.木材及制品类	Wood and Wooden Products		
17.石油及制品类	Petroleum and Related Products	5042307	5846207
18.化工材料及制品类	Chemical Materials and Related Products		
#化肥类	Fertilizers		
19.金属材料类	Metal Materials		
20.建筑及装潢材料类	Building and Decoration Materials	1302735	1496905
21.机电产品及设备类	Mechanical and Electrical Products	84152	80532
#农机类	Agricultural Machinery	597	
22.汽车类	Automobiles	6906832	8579910
23.种子饲料类	Seeds and Feedstuff		
24.棉麻类	Cotton and Hemp	204	334
25.其他类	Others	395152	718075

16-7 限额以上批发业商品购进、销售、库存总额(2014年)

单位：万元

指　　标	Item	商品购进总额 Total Purchases Value	# 进口 Imports
总　　计	**Total**	**52598228**	**3013160**
按批发行业分	**By Wholesale Trade Sector**		
农、林、牧产品批发	Wholesale of Farming, Forestry, Animal Husbandry Products	207197	
谷物、豆及薯类批发	Wholesale of Cereals, Beans and Tubers	158287	
种子批发	Wholesale of Seeds and Forages	16342	
饲料批发	Wholesale of Feedstuff	60	
棉、麻批发	Wholesale of Cotton and Hemp	3054	
林业产品批发	Wholesale of Forestry Products	3360	
牲畜批发	Wholesale of Livestock	1500	
其他农牧产品批发	Others	24594	
食品、饮料及烟草制品批发	Wholesale of Food, Beverages and Tobaccos	4848494	1
米、面制品及食用油批发	Wholesale of Rice, Flour and Edible Oil	165449	
糕点、糖果及糖批发	Wholesale of Cake and Sugar	52988	
果品、蔬菜批发	Wholesale of Vegetables and Fruits	524005	1
肉禽蛋奶及水产品批发	Wholesale of Poultry, Egg and Milk & Marine Products	37807	
盐及调味品批发	Wholesale of Salt and Condiments	65691	
酒、饮料及茶叶批发	Wholesale of Wines, Beverages and Tea	876027	
烟草制品批发	Wholesale of Tobaccos	3088024	
其他食品批发	Others	38504	
纺织服装及家庭用品批发	Wholesale of Textiles, Garments and Daily Consumer Articles	3007426	
纺织品、针织品及原料批发	Wholesale of Textiles, Knitwear and Textile Materials	40355	
服装批发	Wholesale of Garments	2081740	
鞋帽批发	Wholesale of Shoes and Hats	69565	
化妆品及卫生用品批发	Wholesale of Cosmetics and Health Consumer Articles	167533	
厨房、卫生间用具及日用杂货批发	Wholesale of Kitchen and Washroom Appliance and Various Household Supplies	52772	
家用电器批发	Wholesale of Domestic Appliances	595460	
文化、体育用品及器材批发	Wholesale of Culture, Sports Appliances and Equipment	351475	
文具用品批发	Wholesale of Stationary	81283	
体育用品及器材批发	Wholesale of Sports Goods and Equipments	13998	
图书批发	Wholesale of Books	149988	
首饰、工艺品及收藏品批发	Wholesale of Jewelry, Artwork and Collections	106206	
医药及医疗器材批发	Wholesale of Medicines and Medical Appliances	2384225	126646
西药批发	Wholesale of Western Medicine	1825818	118346
中药批发	Wholesale of Traditional Chinese Medicinal	513792	
医疗用品及器材批发	Wholesale of Medical Treatment and Equipment	44615	8300
矿产品、建材及化工产品批发	Wholesale of Mineral Products, Building Materials and Chemical Products	39062669	2797120
煤炭及制品批发	Wholesale of Coal and Related Products	12566586	
石油及制品批发	Wholesale of Petroleum and Related Products	15728655	20782
非金属矿及制品批发	Wholesale of Metal Materials	18961	37
金属及金属矿批发	Wholesale of Metal Mine and Its Manufacture	8656658	2772839
建材批发	Wholesale of Building Materials	1529783	3462
化肥批发	Wholesale of Garments	202912	
农药批发	Wholesale of Pesticides	16318	
农用薄膜批发	Wholesale of Agricultural Film	2366	
其他化工产品批发	Others	340432	
机械设备、五金交电及电子产品批发	Wholesale of Machinery, Hardware and Electronic Equipment	2541294	86202
农业机械批发	Wholesale of Agricultural Machinery	59907	
汽车批发	Wholesale of Vehicles	1175633	

Total Purchases, Sales and Inventory of Enterprises above Designated Size in Wholesale Trades(2014)

(10 000 yuan)

商品销售总额 Total Sales	# 公共网络商品销售额 Sales of Public Network	# 银行卡支付商品销售额 Sales of Bank Card Payment	# 批发 Wholesale Trades	# 出口 Exports	年末库存 Stock at Year-end
55630081	**3024096**	**8623902**	**48296835**	**905053**	**2397182**
281659		8834	260357	16967	48477
207866			195945	15533	41964
19577		8834	19332		4247
3707			3707		251
3054			3054		160
6161			6161		896
15051			7639		75
26243			24519	1435	885
6094885	2881709	2861454	5683288	7057	345125
173953	3021	6999	128188		17128
54562			49414		5312
548320	8426	26680	441565	6903	44335
41854		16492	40976		1646
79152			79152		7313
979242	50	4412	731238		41541
4178221	2870211	2806871	4174320		214267
39582			38437	154	13583
3081084	1551	134192	2078440	49554	221987
41374			41374		2084
2112704			1190436	982	2057
99018		30815	51192		44808
186611		82677	179121		32507
53807		1503	30062		922
587570	1551	19197	586256	48572	139610
379516	145	72670	373883	7100	27131
91994		205	87314	2600	6908
14883			14093		3
165358	145		165196		18905
107280		72465	107280	4500	1314
2585393	29784	56655	2373385		192075
1957566	21200	38993	1779466		148521
577251	8584	10662	543745		39212
50577		7000	50174		4343
40197064	14970	4835931	35053457	104059	1338186
12726579		475063	11669871	53497	444919
16321770		973455	12735147	11336	407119
22433		2930	22430	18711	1096
8960419	12000	3096881	3518285	11315	371464
1577695		233041	1548504		44212
212933		984	204602		47925
16307			16307		555
2970	2970		2970	2970	
355957		53577	335341	6230	20896
2803432	95938	629543	2287535	651822	217210
73922			51496		9348
1324913		555753	978472	419076	74368

16-7 续表

单位：万元

指　　标	Item	商品购进总额 Total Purchases Value	# 进口 Imports
汽车零配件批发	Wholesale of Vehicle Parts	54486	
摩托车及零配件批发	Wholesale of Motorcycles and Motorcycle Parts	20307	
五金产品批发	Wholesale of Hardware Products	169854	58264
电气设备批发	Wholesale of Electrical Equipments	245317	21620
计算机、软件及辅助设备批发	Wholesale of Computer, Software and Peripherals	409138	
通讯及广播电视设备批发	Wholesale of Communications and Broadcast and Television Equipments	34428	
其他机械设备及电子产品批发	Others	372224	6318
贸易经纪与代理	Trade Broker and Agency	82180	3191
贸易代理	Trade Agency	82180	3191
其他批发	Others	113269	
再生物资回收与批发	Recovery and Wholesale of Regeneration Material	55842	
其他未列明的批发	Any Other Wholesale	57427	
按登记注册类型分	**By Status of Registration**		
内资企业	Domestic Funded Enterprises	48874433	300981
国有企业	State-owned Enterprises	6503541	12003
集体企业	Collective-owned Enterprises	205493	
股份合作企业	Cooperative Enterprises	28072	
联营企业	State Joint Ownership Enterprises		
国有联营企业	State Joint Ownership Enterprises		
有限责任公司	Limited Liability Corporations	19840908	230541
国有独资公司	State Sole Funded Corporations	4933240	35416
其他有限责任公司	Other Limited Liability Corporations	14907668	195125
股份有限公司	Share-holding Corporations Ltd.	19011647	
私营企业	Private Enterprises	3206332	58437
私营独资企业	Private-funded Enterprises	16340	
私营合伙企业	Private Partnership Enterprises	10300	
私营有限责任公司	Private Limited Liability Corporations	3005976	48655
私营股份有限公司	Private Share-holding Corporations Ltd.	173716	9782
其他企业	Other Enterprises	78439	
港、澳、台商投资企业	Enterprises with Funds from Hong Kong, Macao & Taiwan	362247	
与港澳台商合资经营企业	Joint-venture Enterprises	243940	
港澳台商独资经营企业	Enterprises with Sole Investment	118307	
外商投资企业	Foreign Funded Enterprises	3361547	2712179
中外合资经营企业	Joint-venture Enterprises	3241474	2712179
外资企业	Enterprises with Sole Fund	120073	
按控股情况分	**By Status of Share Holding**		
国有控股	State-holding	31390166	221688
集体控股	Collective-holding	429688	
私人控股	Private-holding	9450213	77783
港澳台商控股	Hong Kong, Macao & Taiwan-holding	362247	
外商控股	Foreign-holding	161581	
其　　他	Others	10804333	2713689
按经营形式分	**By Form of Management**		
独立门店	Independent Stores	37863230	2867848
连锁总店	General Chain Stores	2030736	
连锁门店	Branch Chain Stores	1080355	
其　　他	Others	11623907	145313
按单位规模分	**By scale**		
大　型	Large	25048397	150966
中　型	Medium	22590779	2786064
小　型	Small	4732896	72667
微　型	Mini	226156	3463

continued

(10 000 yuan)

商品销售总额 Total Sales	# 公共网络商品销售额 Sales of Public Network	# 银行卡支付商品销售额 Sales of Bank Card Payment	# 批发 Wholesale Trades	# 出口 Exports	年末库存 Stock at Year-end
59740			51972		4442
20482			20482		2987
187806		5355	179017	77477	13421
260893			255437	118895	30509
423212	95938		307717	12177	13194
34186			34186		22115
418279		68434	408756	24197	46827
86708		20739	86708	68494	2449
86708		20739	86708	68494	2449
120342		3885	99781		4542
56449			42537		2426
63893		3885	57244		2117
51939919	2928158	5504283	44772003	905053	2248249
7899281	2870211	3391556	7392150	26850	379369
210208		775	181078		4006
30333			28465		348
20514454	41875	1152541	17306735	333480	1040712
4919012		34335	3408239	45269	306210
15595442	41875	1118206	13898496	288211	734502
19759019		817834	16596573	469067	584458
3442564	16047	136311	3201194	74222	233305
16202		826	12214		1241
10299					26
3232272	16047	129275	3039730	74222	223531
183792		6210	149250		8508
84060	25	5265	65808	1435	6051
410750		30815	284419		44808
260345			181840		
150405		30815	102579		44808
3279413	95938	3088804	3240413		104125
3154811		3087752	3154811		98716
124602	95938	1053	85602		5409
33440682	2891411	4839109	28506636	736905	1306147
451227		8194	407678		26352
10165852	35295	528928	8473715	166825	507808
410750		30815	284419		44808
166532	95938	1053	127532		10489
10995038	1452	3215802	10496855	1323	501578
39250945	1043936	5817221	34166789	443396	1592217
2550671	1206684	1572520	2206627		133868
1247038		561359	740402		42660
12581427	773477	672801	11183017	461657	628438
27120741	2853391	4341367	20793602	540575	1091044
23255925	156093	4034975	22477362	232056	992822
5017900	14213	204188	4795134	132422	305528
235516	400	43372	230737		7789

16-8 限额以上零售业商品购进、销售、库存总额(2014年)

单位：万元

指标	Item	商品购进总额 Total Purchases Value	# 进口 Imports
总计	**Total**	**25181440**	**944280**
按零售行业分	**By Retail Trades Sector**		
综合零售	Integrated Retail	5456366	5787
百货零售	Retail of General Merchandise	2719705	5779
超级市场零售	Retail of Supermarkets	2485664	8
其他综合零售	Others	250997	
食品、饮料及烟草制品专门零售	Special Retail of Food, Beverages and Tobaccos	1019191	2595
粮油零售	Retail of Grain and Oil	49157	
糕点、面包零售	Retail of Cake and Bread	4362	
果品、蔬菜零售	Retail of Melons and Fruits,Vegetables	173819	8
肉、禽、蛋及水产品零售	Retail of Meat, Poultry, Eggs and Aquatic Products	440943	
营养和保健品零售	Retail of Nourishment and Health Products	661	
酒、饮料及茶叶零售	Retail of Beverages and Tea	149528	79
烟草制品零售	Retail of Tobaccos	59478	
其他食品零售	Others	141245	2508
纺织、服装及日用品专门零售	Special Retail of Textiles, Garments and Daily Consumer Articles	1781717	0.3
纺织品及针织品零售	Retail of Textiles and Knitwear	57106	
服装零售	Retail of Garments	1493011	0.3
鞋帽零售	Retail of Shoes and Hats	11028	
化妆品及卫生用品零售	Retail of Cosmetics and Health Consumer Articles	114251	
钟表、眼镜零售	Retail of Clocks and Watches,Spectacles	54593	
自行车零售	Retail of Bicycles	577	
其他日用品零售	Others	51152	
文化、体育用品及器材专门零售	Special Retail of Culture, Sports Appliances and Equipments	599233	2421
文具用品零售	Retail of Stationery	1192	
体育用品零售	Retail of Sports Goods	120364	200
图书、报刊零售	Retail of Books	351182	836
珠宝首饰零售	Retail of Jewelry	114054	1384
工艺美术品及收藏品零售	Retail of Artwork and Collections	7738	
乐器零售	Retail of Musical Instrument	4703	
医药及医疗器材专门零售	Special Retail of Medicines and Medical Appliances	673558	83
药品零售	Retail of Medicines	664462	83
医疗用品及器材零售	Retail of Medical Supplies and Appliances	9096	
汽车、摩托车、燃料及零配件专门零售	Special Retail of Motor Vehicles, Motorcycles, Fuel and Parts	10869698	909194
汽车零售	Retail of Motor Vehicles	8511387	908073
汽车零配件零售	Retail of Motor Vehicles and Parts	60670	
摩托车及零配件零售	Retail of Motorcycles and Parts	53183	
机动车燃料零售	Retail of Fuel of Motor Vehicles	2244457	1121

Total Purchases, Sales and Inventory of Enterprises above Designated Size in Retail Trades (2014)

(10 000 yuan)

商品销售总额 Total Sales	# 公共网络商品销售额 Sales of Public Network	# 银行卡支付商品销售额 Sales of Bank Card Payment	# 批发 Wholesale Trades	# 出口 Exports	年末库存 Stock at Year-end
28258177	**413987**	**5401476**	**881977**	**14890**	**2226941**
6741168	72518	1058724	64717		450919
3521342	71621	741211	44108		151530
2959927	896	312738	13555		281377
259898		4776	7055		18012
1361009	14146	34690	132092	480	153209
55008	1758	4972	521		12185
4688			787		714
183805	75	374	19572		12815
642405	8000	3354	9058		23621
598	598				80
267572	2627	10508	29069	3	81936
58105		7700	228		11534
148828	1088	7783	72857	477	10325
1920069	268	192339	72420	0.3	86252
57188	85	14672	473		3493
1592382	59	145130	71296	0.3	41834
11822		85	110		778
137621			509		4531
52649	125	32452	32		29540
625					494
67781					5582
623350		118350	43369		124685
1242		1000			326
139941		104874	37000		23553
332721		5826	3839		79782
135909		5448	2524		19324
8787			6		274
4750		1203			1427
737951	8243	16640	95821	0.1	102931
729934	8243	16640	95821	0.1	101030
8017					1901
11579612	16988	2640014	214673	5788	1063005
9168400	8222	2393121	62867	5788	1010503
62761	7944	1049	6297		6354
54237		1265	3908		7980
2294213	822	244580	141600		38167

16-8 续表 1

单位：万元

指标	Item	商品购进总额 Total Purchases Value	# 进口 Imports
家用电器及电子产品专门零售	Special Retail of Household Appliances and Electronic Products	2317257	0.1
家用视听设备零售	Retail of Home Audio-visual Equipment	229061	
日用家电设备零售	Retail of Household Appliances	1546219	0.1
计算机、软件及辅助设备零售	Retail of Computer, Software and Peripherals	402469	
通信设备零售	Retail of Communication Equipment	107435	
其他电子产品零售	Others	32072	
五金、家具及室内装修材料专门零售	Special Retail of Hardware, Furniture and Decoration Materials	2036260	24200
五金零售	Retail of Hardware	99578	6120
灯具零售	Retail of Light Fittings	113450	
家具零售	Retail of Furniture	1146418	
涂料零售	Retail of Dope	515	
卫生洁具零售	Retail of Sanitary	526	
木质装饰材料零售	Retail of Wooden Decorating Materials	8790	
陶瓷、石材装饰材料零售	Retail of Porcelainou Sand Stone Finishing Decorating Materials	35807	
其他室内装修材料零售	Other Domestic Decorating Materials	631177	18080
货摊无店铺及其他零售业	Non-shop and Other non-mentiones-above Retails	428161	
互联网零售	E-commerce Retails	238323	
邮购及电视电话零售	Mail-order & Phone-order Retails	117536	
生活用燃料零售	Retail of Life Fuels	50192	
其他未列明的零售	Other Retail Not Classified Elsewhere	22111	
按登记注册类型分	**By Status of Registration**		
内资企业	Domestic Funded Enterprises	21129553	504558
国有企业	State-owned Enterprises	619882	4771
集体企业	Collective-owned Enterprises	450498	
股份合作企业	Cooperative Enterprises	52823	
联营企业	Joint Ownership Enterprises	6290	
集体联营企业	Collective Joint Ownership Enterprises	6290	
有限责任公司	Limited Liability Corporations	13079606	300414
国有独资公司	State Sole Funded Corporations	278224	
其他有限责任公司	Other Limited Liability Corporations	12801382	300414
股份有限公司	Share-holding Corporations Ltd.	1850357	37860
私营企业	Private Enterprises	4960839	161505
私营独资企业	Private-funded Enterprises	249846	
私营合伙企业	Private Partnership Enterprises	76199	
私营有限责任公司	Private Limited Liability Corporations	4283448	97325
私营股份有限公司	Private Share-holding Corporations Ltd.	351347	64180
其他企业	Other Enterprises	109257	8
港、澳、台商投资企业	Enterprises with Funds from Hong Kong, Macao & Taiwan	1633298	381858
与港澳台商合资经营企业	Joint-venture Enterprises	727565	247715
与港澳台商合作经营企业	Cooperative Enterprises	12	
港澳台商独资经营企业	Enterprises with Sole Investment	905721	134143

continued

(10 000 yuan)

商品销售总额 Total Sales	#公共网络商品销售额 Sales of Public Network	#银行卡支付商品销售额 Sales of Bank Card Payment	#批发 Wholesale Trades	#出口 Exports	年末库存 Stock at Year-end
2645958	51609	727462	211525	622	159398
268278	2283	106600	60507		14767
1828493	48463	426327	134221	77	94458
403662	864	192984	11562		18364
119823		1551	3906		21686
25702			1328	545	10122
2197922		502994	33689	8000	78542
102850		2118	2905		9514
112968					669
1321824		473699	1148		25304
842					111
507		41			28
10708		2061			2841
37810		14534	7000		1046
610414		10542	22636	8000	39030
451138	250215	110262	13671		8001
250215	250215				1515
117687		98458	628		1356
59386		11706	12123		2706
23850		98	920		2425
23494038	140381	4088335	803473	14890	1980929
640576	3075	54712	35049		68181
456169	5	681	24458		29567
52350			203		1784
6258					125
6258					125
14544785	73284	3006778	518508	9550	1326797
276142		33530	531		52669
14268643	73284	2973247	517976	9550	1274128
2031869		170531	155550		138412
5642778	63998	845852	64661	5341	407588
250115		6011	4059		15334
76710		2922	1		3249
4949541	63913	629058	57569	5341	358057
366411	85	207861	3032		30948
119254	20	9783	5047		8475
2129510	23390	903362	26075		166382
838283		629894	11384		78202
4591					11
1286636	23390	273468	14691		88169

16-8 续表 2

单位：万元

指标	Item	商品购进总额 Total Purchases Value	# 进口 Imports
外商投资企业	Foreign Funded Enterprises	2418590	57864
中外合资经营企业	Joint-venture Enterprises	1487285	
外资企业	Enterprises with Sole Fund	850276	57864
外商投资股份有限公司	Share-holding Corporations Ltd. with Foreign Investment	60067	
其他外商投资企业	Other Foreign Funded Enterprises	20961	
按控股情况分	**By Status of Share Holding**		
国有控股	State-holding	3324992	23636
集体控股	Collective-holding	1170940	
私人控股	Private-holding	14533388	419207
港澳台商控股	Hong Kong, Macao & Taiwan-holding	1735760	381858
外商控股	Foreign-holding	1017298	62828
其　他	Others	3399063	56752
按经营形式分	**By Form of Management**		
独立门店	Independent Stores	20245772	798210
连锁总店	General Chain Stores	1420265	
连锁门店	Branch Chain Stores	1221621	
其　他	Others	2293783	146070
按单位规模分	**By Scale**		
大　型	Large	8152703	170348
中　型	Medium	12566383	669304
小　型	Small	4050370	104629
微　型	Mini	411985	0.1
按零售业态分	**By Business Categories**		
有店铺零售	Shop Retails	24768018	944280
食杂店	Grocery Store	107429	
便利店	Convenience Store	204471	
超　市	Supermarket	1101206	837
大型超市	Hypermarket	1956479	8
仓储会员店	Warehouse Club	12668	
百货店	Department Store	2937859	10979
专业店	Specialty Store	8187912	351181
专卖店	Franchised Store	6187047	581276
家居建材商店	Building Material Store	1497561	
购物中心	Shopping Center	2012205	0.1
厂家直销中心	Factory Outlets Center	563181	
无店铺零售	Non-shop Retails	413423	
# 电视购物	TV Shopping	117536	
网上商店	Web Storefronts	242673	

continued

(10 000 yuan)

商品销售总额 Total Sales	# 公共网络商品销售额 Sales of Public Network	# 银行卡支付商品销售额 Sales of Bank Card Payment	# 批发 Wholesale Trades	# 出口 Exports	年末库存 Stock at Year-end
2634629	250215	409779	52429		79630
1612243		237058			23128
946678	250215	112664			48670
60056		60056	52429		48
15652					7785
3390578	6743	374239	200446		218140
1192218	5	64954	95357		65561
15885336	130059	2695278	381140	14890	1265350
2219957	23390	881166	14691		158464
1236318	250215	210165	63813		110860
4333770	3575	1175675	126530	0.2	408567
22435851	157196	4139799	496640	14345	1723922
1752306	3793	218055	60394		169068
1434904	990	485425	140907		114238
2635117	252008	558198	184038	545	219712
9337081	302027	2222462	376909		433816
14013047	80826	2845559	308601	4864	1351552
4471104	29970	302068	171822	9548	406098
436946	1164	31387	24645	478	35475
27829960	160237	5302518	875606	14890	2221358
108782			67820		4673
234735	20	1130	34905		10865
1171669	3076	26204	17839		127416
2265691	6	223496	7207		218449
14049	1800	1265	2015		3525
3880371	68507	932249	51912	0.1	181302
9127412	79308	1528322	369629	13886	821265
6764871	3764	1905235	127286	1004	701086
1596807		492204	19033		45322
2096511		188640	145186	0.1	40217
569063	3756	3773	32773		67238
428217	253749	98958	6372		5583
117687		98458	628		1356
254342	253749	500			2315

16-9 各市(区)限额以上批发业商品购进总额(2014年)

Total Purchases of Enterprises above Designated Size in Wholesale Trades by City(District)(2014)

单位：亿元 (100 million yuan)

地 区	Region	合 计 Total	#国有控股 State-holding	内资企业 Domestic Funded Enterprises	国有企业 State-owned Enterprises	集体企业 Collective-owned Enterprises	股份合作企业 Cooperative Enterprises
全 省	**Shaanxi**	**5259.82**	**3139.02**	**4887.44**	**650.35**	**20.55**	**2.81**
西安市	Xi'an	2586.33	1200.39	2214.09	332.51	1.22	
铜川市	Tongchuan	28.53	26.79	28.53	5.86		0.04
宝鸡市	Baoji	508.51	141.91	508.51	34.91	1.19	
咸阳市	Xianyang	515.43	481.35	515.43	34.62	2.59	
渭南市	Weinan	218.80	159.03	218.80	36.42	1.42	
#韩城市	Hancheng	32.82		32.82			
延安市	Yan'an	132.32	79.94	132.32	18.26		
汉中市	Hanzhong	119.56	65.13	119.56	24.71	12.36	
榆林市	Yulin	1013.48	887.50	1013.34	89.47	1.39	2.30
安康市	Ankang	83.47	52.79	83.47	30.81	0.38	
商洛市	Shangluo	50.80	42.24	50.80	40.83		0.47
杨凌示范区	Yangling	2.60	1.94	2.60	1.94		

16-9 续表 continued

单位：亿元 (100 million yuan)

地 区	Region	联营企业 State Joint Ownership Enterprises	有限责任公司 Limited Liability Corporations	股份有限公司 Share-holding Corporations Ltd.	私营企业 Private Enterprises	港、澳、台商投资企业 Enterprises with Funds from Hong Kong, Macao & Taiwan	外商投资企业 Enterprises with Foreign Investment
全 省	**Shaanxi**		**1984.09**	**1901.16**	**320.63**	**36.22**	**336.15**
西安市	Xi'an		1281.67	345.95	251.40	36.22	336.01
铜川市	Tongchuan		1.41	20.93	0.29		
宝鸡市	Baoji		48.32	415.69	5.97		
咸阳市	Xianyang		34.09	435.95	7.85		
渭南市	Weinan		169.00	0.23	10.62		
#韩城市	Hancheng		32.56		0.26		
延安市	Yan'an		50.69	45.96	17.06		
汉中市	Hanzhong		78.75		3.48		
榆林市	Yulin		292.23	612.67	13.25		0.14
安康市	Ankang		21.88	23.79	6.61		
商洛市	Shangluo		5.38		4.12		
杨凌示范区	Yangling		0.66				

16-10 各市(区)限额以上零售业商品购进总额(2014年)
Total Purchases of Enterprises above Designated Size in Retail Trades by City(District)(2014)

单位：亿元 (100 million yuan)

地区	Region	合计 Total	# 国有控股 State-holding	内资企业 Domestic Funded Enterprises	国有企业 State-owned Enterprises	集体企业 Collective-owned Enterprises	股份合作企业 Cooperative Enterprises
全省	**Shaanxi**	**2518.14**	**332.50**	**2112.96**	**61.99**	**45.05**	**5.28**
西安市	Xi'an	1574.32	194.99	1182.62	28.35	4.78	
铜川市	Tongchuan	28.62	5.40	28.62	0.89	0.97	
宝鸡市	Baoji	148.59	15.35	143.44	1.85	6.91	
咸阳市	Xianyang	171.70	31.65	166.87	9.42	5.10	5.12
渭南市	Weinan	160.95	18.92	160.95	10.39	13.55	
# 韩城市	Hancheng	15.41	0.73	15.41	0.35	0.35	
延安市	Yan'an	68.94	9.33	68.41	0.86	1.13	
汉中市	Hanzhong	129.70	19.85	128.51	8.47	11.10	
榆林市	Yulin	158.44	32.76	157.15	1.11	0.17	0.08
安康市	Ankang	61.33	1.95	61.33	0.39	1.22	0.09
商洛市	Shangluo	11.49	1.83	10.97	0.13	0.13	
杨凌示范区	Yangling	4.08	0.47	4.03	0.12		

16-10 续表 continued

单位：亿元 (100 million yuan)

地区	Region	联营企业 State Joint Ownership Enterprises	有限责任公司 Limited Liability Corporations	股份有限公司 Share-holding Corporations Ltd.	私营企业 Private Enterprises	港、澳、台商投资企业 Enterprises with Funds from Hong Kong, Macao & Taiwan	外商投资企业 Enterprises with Foreign Investment
全省	**Shaanxi**	**0.63**	**1307.96**	**185.04**	**496.08**	**163.33**	**241.86**
西安市	Xi'an		789.76	99.75	259.22	160.33	231.37
铜川市	Tongchuan		18.58	2.61	4.31		
宝鸡市	Baoji	0.05	107.61	10.83	14.65		5.14
咸阳市	Xianyang	0.57	74.74	8.89	61.75		4.83
渭南市	Weinan		68.67	31.50	33.00		
# 韩城市	Hancheng		10.95	1.60	1.29		
延安市	Yan'an		62.56		3.54	0.53	
汉中市	Hanzhong		57.36		50.93	1.18	
榆林市	Yulin		84.63	29.99	40.43	1.28	
安康市	Ankang		35.06	0.91	23.62		
商洛市	Shangluo		5.87	0.54	3.78		0.52
杨凌示范区	Yangling		3.10		0.86		

16-11 各市(区)限额以上批发业商品销售总额(2014年)

Total Sales of Enterprises above Designated Size in Wholesale Trades by City(District)(2014)

单位：亿元 (100 million yuan)

地区	Region	合计 Total	# 国有控股 State-holding	内资企业 Domestic Funded Enterprises	国有企业 State-owned Enterprises	集体企业 Collective-owned Enterprises	股份合作企业 Cooperative Enterprises
全　省	**Shaanxi**	**5563.01**	**3344.07**	**5193.99**	**789.93**	**21.02**	**3.03**
西安市	Xi'an	2716.25	1293.24	2347.43	375.28	1.23	
铜川市	Tongchuan	41.64	34.55	41.64	8.05		0.02
宝鸡市	Baoji	562.48	175.09	562.48	47.36	1.20	
咸阳市	Xianyang	531.70	496.97	531.70	46.27	2.58	
渭南市	Weinan	216.57	151.10	216.57	47.80	1.79	
# 韩城市	Hancheng	32.84		32.84			
延安市	Yan'an	152.27	94.72	152.27	29.80		
汉中市	Hanzhong	144.65	87.72	144.65	32.36	12.36	
榆林市	Yulin	1031.40	890.50	1031.20	108.42	1.39	2.55
安康市	Ankang	100.12	64.33	100.12	40.62	0.47	
商洛市	Shangluo	63.02	53.95	63.02	52.06		0.47
杨凌示范区	Yangling	2.92	1.91	2.92	1.91		

16-11 续表 continued

单位：亿元 (100 million yuan)

地区	Region	联营企业 State Joint Ownership Enterprises	有限责任公司 Limited Liability Corporations	股份有限公司 Share-holding Corporations Ltd.	私营企业 Private Enterprises	港、澳、台商投资企业 Enterprises with Funds from Hong Kong, Macao & Taiwan	外商投资企业 Enterprises with Foreign Investment
全　省	**Shaanxi**		**2051.45**	**1975.90**	**344.26**	**41.08**	**327.94**
西安市	Xi'an		1321.98	375.60	271.86	41.08	327.75
铜川市	Tongchuan		6.76	26.50	0.31		
宝鸡市	Baoji		56.01	449.38	5.78		
咸阳市	Xianyang		34.87	439.59	8.07		
渭南市	Weinan		155.00	0.23	10.69		
# 韩城市	Hancheng		32.59		0.25		
延安市	Yan'an		55.34	49.10	17.62		
汉中市	Hanzhong		95.82		3.81		
榆林市	Yulin		293.01	609.79	13.98		0.19
安康市	Ankang		25.68	25.72	7.63		
商洛市	Shangluo		5.98		4.52		
杨凌示范区	Yangling		1.01				

16-12 各市(区)限额以上零售业商品销售总额（2014年）
Total Sales of Enterprises above Designated Size in Retail Trades by City(District)(2014)

单位：亿元 (100 million yuan)

地区	Region	合计 Total	# 国有控股 State-holding	内资企业 Domestic Funded Enterprises	国有企业 State-owned Enterprises	集体企业 Collective-owned Enterprises	股份合作企业 Cooperative Enterprises
全 省	**Shaanxi**	**2825.82**	**339.06**	**2349.40**	**64.06**	**45.62**	**5.23**
西 安 市	Xi'an	1789.72	195.77	1326.53	29.10	5.01	
铜 川 市	Tongchuan	30.68	5.63	30.68	1.20	0.92	
宝 鸡 市	Baoji	169.47	16.12	165.28	2.14	7.11	
咸 阳 市	Xianyang	178.32	32.27	173.03	9.31	5.20	5.07
渭 南 市	Weinan	169.48	19.37	169.48	10.94	13.42	
# 韩城市	Hancheng	15.01	0.69	15.01	0.32	0.33	
延 安 市	Yan'an	72.65	11.14	72.02	0.89	1.13	
汉 中 市	Hanzhong	160.38	21.12	158.78	8.68	11.29	
榆 林 市	Yulin	170.46	32.93	169.63	1.08	0.17	0.08
安 康 市	Ankang	67.57	1.99	67.57	0.40	1.23	0.09
商 洛 市	Shangluo	12.39	2.23	11.71	0.17	0.13	
杨凌示范区	Yangling	4.69	0.49	4.69	0.15		

16-12 续表 continued

单位：亿元 (100 million yuan)

地区	Region	联营企业 State Joint Ownership Enterprises	有限责任公司 Limited Liability Corporations	股份有限公司 Share-holding Corporations Ltd.	私营企业 Private Enterprises	港、澳、台商投资企业 Enterprises with Funds from Hong Kong, Macao & Taiwan	外商投资企业 Enterprises with Foreign Investment
全 省	**Shaanxi**	**0.63**	**1454.48**	**203.19**	**564.28**	**212.95**	**263.46**
西 安 市	Xi'an		878.99	116.13	296.51	209.89	253.31
铜 川 市	Tongchuan		20.07	2.40	4.71		
宝 鸡 市	Baoji	0.05	128.57	10.82	14.67		4.19
咸 阳 市	Xianyang	0.57	77.92	10.30	63.40		5.30
渭 南 市	Weinan		74.20	31.74	35.13		
# 韩城市	Hancheng		10.62	1.58	1.31		
延 安 市	Yan'an		65.79		3.83	0.63	
汉 中 市	Hanzhong		66.26		71.83	1.60	
榆 林 市	Yulin		92.98	30.37	44.23	0.83	
安 康 市	Ankang		39.58	0.88	25.34		
商 洛 市	Shangluo		6.45	0.56	3.77		0.67
杨凌示范区	Yangling		3.67		0.86		

16-13 各市(区)限额以上批发业商品库存总额(2014年)
Total Inventory of Enterprises above Designated Size in Wholesale Trades by City(District)(2014)

单位：亿元 (100 million yuan)

地区	Region	合计 Total	# 国有控股 State-holding	内资企业 Domestic Funded Enterprises	国有企业 State-owned Enterprises	集体企业 Collective-owned Enterprises	股份合作企业 Cooperative Enterprises
全省	**Shaanxi**	**239.72**	**130.61**	**224.82**	**37.94**	**0.40**	**0.03**
西安市	Xi'an	107.41	38.02	92.53	15.38	0.13	
铜川市	Tongchuan	0.82	0.64	0.82	0.38		0.02
宝鸡市	Baoji	33.63	11.63	33.63	10.29	0.10	
咸阳市	Xianyang	5.52	4.37	5.52	1.82	0.08	
渭南市	Weinan	29.78	27.81	29.78	2.10	0.07	
# 韩城市	Hancheng	0.03		0.03			
延安市	Yan'an	5.96	2.35	5.96	1.82		
汉中市	Hanzhong	4.24	2.05	4.24	1.09	0.00	
榆林市	Yulin	46.78	40.98	46.77	2.90	0.01	0.02
安康市	Ankang	3.65	1.42	3.65	1.07	0.01	
商洛市	Shangluo	1.64	1.19	1.64	0.95		0.00
杨凌示范区	Yangling	0.27	0.16	0.27	0.16		

16-13 续表 continued

单位：亿元 (100 million yuan)

地区	Region	联营企业 State Joint Ownership Enterprises	有限责任公司 Limited Liability Corporations	股份有限公司 Share-holding Corporations Ltd.	私营企业 Private Enterprises	港、澳、台商投资企业 Enterprises with Funds from Hong Kong, Macao & Taiwan	外商投资企业 Enterprises with Foreign Investment
全省	**Shaanxi**		**104.07**	**58.45**	**23.33**	**4.48**	**10.41**
西安市	Xi'an		55.26	2.97	18.78	4.48	10.40
铜川市	Tongchuan		0.11	0.26	0.05		
宝鸡市	Baoji		2.10	19.02	1.63		
咸阳市	Xianyang		0.64	2.50	0.47		
渭南市	Weinan		27.37	0.00	0.16		
# 韩城市	Hancheng		0.02		0.02		
延安市	Yan'an		2.97	0.52	0.63		
汉中市	Hanzhong		3.06		0.08		
榆林市	Yulin		10.75	32.51	0.58		0.02
安康市	Ankang		1.33	0.65	0.61		
商洛市	Shangluo		0.36		0.33		
杨凌示范区	Yangling		0.11				

16-14 各市(区)限额以上零售业商品库存总额(2014年)
Total Inventory of Enterprises above Designated Size in Retail Trades by City(District)(2014)

单位：亿元 (100 million yuan)

地区	Region	合计 Total	#国有控股 State-holding	内资企业 Domestic Funded Enterprises	国有企业 State-owned Enterprises	集体企业 Collective-owned Enterprises	股份合作企业 Cooperative Enterprises
全省	**Shaanxi**	**222.69**	**21.81**	**198.09**	**6.82**	**2.96**	**0.18**
西安市	Xi'an	122.06	10.91	99.40	4.57	0.21	
铜川市	Tongchuan	3.96	0.43	3.96	0.17	0.06	
宝鸡市	Baoji	19.75	1.11	18.54	0.22	0.54	
咸阳市	Xianyang	12.80	2.14	12.67	0.52	0.13	0.17
渭南市	Weinan	11.77	1.26	11.77	0.54	1.41	
#韩城市	Hancheng	0.95	0.07	0.95	0.05	0.04	
延安市	Yan'an	10.48	0.23	10.44	0.16	0.01	
汉中市	Hanzhong	12.85	3.94	12.68	0.54	0.43	
榆林市	Yulin	19.27	1.21	18.92	0.06	0.00	0.00
安康市	Ankang	7.60	0.26	7.60	0.02	0.14	0.01
商洛市	Shangluo	1.77	0.23	1.71	0.02	0.02	
杨凌示范区	Yangling	0.39	0.10	0.39	0.00		

16-14 续表 continued

单位：亿元 (100 million yuan)

地区	Region	联营企业 State Joint Ownership Enterprises	有限责任公司 Limited Liability Corporations	股份有限公司 Share-holding Corporations Ltd.	私营企业 Private Enterprises	港、澳、台商投资企业 Enterprises with Funds from Hong Kong, Macao & Taiwan	外商投资企业 Enterprises with Foreign Investment
全省	**Shaanxi**	**0.01**	**132.68**	**13.34**	**40.76**	**16.64**	**7.96**
西安市	Xi'an		65.66	10.34	18.58	16.09	6.57
铜川市	Tongchuan		3.07	0.22	0.30		
宝鸡市	Baoji	0.00	14.75	0.59	2.24		1.20
咸阳市	Xianyang	0.01	6.84	0.27	4.71		0.13
渭南市	Weinan		5.84	1.68	1.95		
#韩城市	Hancheng		0.77	0.04	0.05		
延安市	Yan'an		9.90		0.37	0.04	
汉中市	Hanzhong		8.67		3.04	0.17	
榆林市	Yulin		11.71	0.60	6.47	0.35	
安康市	Ankang		4.81	0.11	2.51		
商洛市	Shangluo		1.07	0.02	0.56		0.06
杨凌示范区	Yangling		0.37		0.02		

16-15 限额以上住宿业经营情况(2014年)

指 标	Item	企业数(个) Number of Enterprises (unit)	营业额(万元) Business Value (10 000 yuan)	#银行卡支付营业额 Business Value of Bank Card Payment
总 计	**Total**	**718**	**1049208**	**150502**
按住宿行业分	**By Hotels**			
旅游饭店	Tour Restaurant	468	807030	118024
一般旅馆	General Restaurant	221	203923	22948
其他住宿服务	Other Hotel Services	29	38255	9531
按登记注册类型分	**By Status of Registration**			
内资企业	Domestic Funded Enterprises	699	929040	128965
国有企业	State-owned Enterprises	70	99226	12877
集体企业	Collective-owned Enterprises	11	8200	346
股份合作企业	Cooperative Enterprises	2	5133	3652
有限责任公司	Limited Liability Corporations	317	470629	73987
国有独资公司	State Sole Funded Corporations	10	30918	5252
其他有限责任公司	Other Limited Liability Corporations	307	439712	68736
股份有限公司	Share-holding Corporations Ltd.	23	19860	1701
私营企业	Private Enterprises	259	308793	36322
私营独资企业	Private-funded Enterprises	38	35624	461
私营合伙企业	Private Partnership Enterprises	13	10580	144
私营有限责任公司	Private Limited Liability Corporations	188	237007	33848
私营股份有限公司	Private Share-holding Corporations Ltd.	20	25582	1870
其他企业	Other Enterprises	17	17200	79
港、澳、台商投资企业	Enterprises with Funds from Hong Kong, Macao & Taiwan	8	54763	12669
与港澳台商合资经营企业	Joint-venture Enterprises	4	34695	7928
与港澳台商合作经营企业	Cooperative Enterprises	1	5766	
港澳台商独资经营企业	Enterprises with Sole Investment	3	14302	4740
外商投资企业	Foreign Funded Enterprises	11	65405	8869
中外合资经营企业	Joint-venture Enterprises	4	20002	2678
中外合作经营企业	Cooperation Enterprises	3	8586	
外资企业	Enterprises with Sole Fund	3	34601	5036
外商投资股份有限公司	Share-holding Corporations Ltd. with Foreign Investment	1	2216	1155
按控股情况分	**By Status of Share Holding**			
国有控股	State-holding	114	216899	31590
集体控股	Collective-holding	25	27925	436
私人控股	Private-holding	472	499817	66292
港澳台商控股	Hong Kong, Macao & Taiwan-holding	8	54763	12669
外商控股	Foreign-holding	11	62302	10448
其 他	Others	88	187501	29068
按经营形式分	**By Form of Management**			
独立门店	Independent Stores	691	1007035	145713
连锁总店(总部)	General Chain Stores	2	1197	
连锁门店	Branch Chain Stores	11	12870	3898
其 他	Others	14	28105	891
按单位规模分	**By Scale**			
大 型	Large	7	107731	50
中 型	Medium	103	448689	97684
小 型	Small	593	490687	52719
微 型	Mini	15	2100	50
按星级分	**By Star Rating**			
五 星	Five-star Level	14	115700	13086
四 星	Four-star Level	56	137172	30791
三 星	Three-star Level	156	226232	21657
二 星	Two-star Level	53	46123	4725
一 星	One-star Level	3	1581	644
其 他	Others	436	522400	79600

Management of Enterprises above Designated Size of Hotels(2014)

#客房收入 From Hotel Rooms	#公共网络客房收入 Public Network Income	#餐费收入 From Meals	#公共网络餐费收入 Public Network Income	#商品销售收入 From Commodities	客房间数(间) Number of Hotel Rooms (unit)	床位数(个) Number of Beds (unit)	餐位数(位) Number of Dining-seats (seat)	餐饮营业面积(平方米) Operating Area (sq.m)
487514	**21726**	**456872**	**6682**	**41647**	**90758**	**157239**	**242858**	**1399625**
382008	19074	340294	4523	33735	67582	117510	182692	972581
90174	2645	101617	1814	7126	20260	35015	52708	361636
15331	7	14961	345	786	2916	4714	7458	65408
430341	16502	414678	6463	34818	84573	147052	231349	1347477
42917	1673	45639	307	4925	8552	16119	29814	138332
3806	145	2053	15	762	716	1324	2530	16200
880		4253			157	340	194	700
236635	8286	191054	2091	16272	45758	79297	103102	635635
12337	344	14307	33	703	2339	4033	7384	29106
224298	7942	176747	2057	15570	43419	75264	95718	606529
8327	357	9427	66	491	2489	4545	9529	57384
131764	6041	153229	3984	11735	25343	42756	80089	442062
10258	146	22712	58	2323	2536	4668	8262	50420
4154	6	5390		590	897	1694	4252	23459
110841	5873	107030	3926	7907	20131	33199	59450	323293
6511	16	18097		915	1779	3195	8125	44890
6012	0	9024		632	1558	2671	6091	57164
21304	2486	17925	113	4809	2436	4011	5663	24112
8228	1548	11785	40	4691	1051	1901	3258	16320
2685		2539		118	382	603	180	3265
10392	938	3601	72		1003	1507	2225	4527
35869	2738	24269	106	2021	3749	6176	5846	28036
13076	1449	5407	70	699	1628	2996	3203	7321
3880	319	4519		169	932	1563	1025	10665
17259	651	13785	35	1153	932	1286	1168	7850
1654	319	559	1		257	331	450	2200
96972	3271	96840	796	7425	17859	31729	51880	249557
9955	403	12657	15	2621	2787	5233	8031	47229
236759	9450	225982	4386	16057	49878	86042	134654	818462
21304	2486	17925	113	4809	2436	4011	5663	24112
35383	3484	22260	106	1550	3583	5860	4619	24275
87141	2632	81207	1266	9187	14215	24364	38011	235990
466717	19213	439873	6575	39884	86475	149307	233110	1354242
634		377		180	175	380	438	1730
10798	1953	1189	70	281	2319	4559	2659	4190
9365	560	15434	36	1302	1789	2993	6651	39463
50884		43943		3375	3535	6057	10356	37587
191405	13166	210498	3890	14438	27932	46362	67057	333704
243790	8549	201893	2791	23707	58174	102926	164215	1009920
1435	11	538		128	1117	1894	1230	18414
56187	2138	51572	130	1912	5327	8110	12305	49189
71266	3687	56204	104	2062	11913	20228	29749	156583
85217	3063	113562	1243	9415	20359	36829	57215	328247
16454	241	26601	223	2545	4796	9052	19636	85014
1138	0.4	300		114	243	385	110	2200
257252	12597	208633	4982	25601	48120	82635	123843	778392

16-16 限额以上餐饮业经营情况(2014年)

指 标	Item	企业数(个) Number of Enter-prises (unit)	营业额(万元) Business Value (10 000 yuan)	#银行卡支付营业额 Business Value of Bank Card Payment
总 计	**Total**	**968**	**1288542**	**117000**
按餐饮行业分	**By Catering Services**			
正餐服务	Restaurant	932	1181910	111570
快餐服务	Fast Food	19	86167	1294
饮料及冷饮服务	Beverages and Cold Drinks	2	2036	
茶馆服务	Teahouse	1	456	
咖啡馆服务	Café	1	1580	
其他餐饮服务	Others	15	18429	4135
小吃服务	Snack	9	8219	278
餐饮配送服务	Catering Distribution	2	558	
其他未列明餐饮业	Other Catering Service not Classified	4	9652	3857
按登记注册类型分	**By Status of Registration**			
内资企业	Domestic Funded Enterprises	948	1110298	112210
国有企业	State-owned Enterprises	16	19498	402
集体企业	Collective-owned Enterprises	7	11451	4
股份合作企业	Cooperative Enterprises	1	2720	
联营企业	State Joint Ownership Enterprises	1	938	
集体联营企业	Collective State Joint Ownership Enterprises	1	938	
有限责任公司	Limited Liability Corporations	436	558643	58386
国有独资公司	State Sole Funded Corporations	8	10245	1060
其他有限责任公司	Other Limited Liability Corporations	428	548398	57325
股份有限公司	Share-holding Corporations Ltd.	27	89936	15249
私营企业	Private Enterprises	433	392291	33458
私营独资企业	Private-funded Enterprises	94	79325	3269
私营合伙企业	Private Partnership Enterprises	7	5084	4
私营有限责任公司	Private Limited Liability Corporations	307	287222	29359
私营股份有限公司	Private Share-holding Corporations Ltd.	25	20660	826
其他企业	Other Enterprises	27	34821	4711
港、澳、台商投资企业	Enterprises with Funds from Hong Kong, Macao & Taiwan	8	70301	2814
与港澳台商合资经营企业	Joint-venture Enterprises	2	11223	1508
与港澳台商合作经营企业	Cooperative Enterprises	1	16214	
港澳台商独资经营企业	Enterprises with Sole Investment	5	42864	1306
外商投资企业	Foreign Funded Enterprises	12	107942	1977
中外合资经营企业	Joint-venture Enterprises	4	1786	1058
外资企业	Enterprises with Sole Fund	5	99994	
外商投资股份有限公司	Share-holding Corporations Ltd. with Foreign Investment	1	2341	919
其他外商投资企业	Other Foreign Funded Enterprises	2	3822	
按控股情况分	**By Status of Share Holding**			
国有控股	State-holding	37	99781	21794
集体控股	Collective-holding	17	29452	574
私人控股	Private-holding	792	823172	72945
港澳台商控股	Hong Kong, Macao & Taiwan-holding	6	59078	1306
外商控股	Foreign-holding	8	102601	919
其 他	Others	108	174459	19462
按经营形式分	**By Form of Management**			
独立门店	Independent Stores	922	1062317	108147
连锁总店	General Chain Stores	11	141655	1877
连锁门店	Branch Chain Stores	10	57353	1457
其 他	Others	25	27217	5520
按单位规模分	**By Scale**			
大 型	Large	8	268022	24256
中 型	Medium	72	318523	36741
小 型	Small	849	691023	55977
微 型	Mini	39	10974	26

Management of Enterprises above Designated Size of Catering Services(2014)

# 客房收入 From Hotel Rooms	# 公共网络客房收入 Public Network Income	# 餐费收入 From Meals	# 公共网络餐费收入 Public Network Income	# 商品销售收入 From Commo-dities	客房间数(间) Number of Hotel Rooms (unit)	床位数(个) Number of Beds (unit)	餐位数(位) Number of Dining-seats (seat)	餐饮营业面积(平方米) Operating Area (sq.m)
108036	**1601**	**1055578**	**12057**	**92582**	**24675**	**44460**	**411140**	**2023801**
104465	1245	962481	11883	91753	24335	43877	392246	1938927
615		76282	116	138	120	200	13346	53204
		1410		627			203	1358
		456					80	1000
		953		627			123	358
2955	356	15405	58	65	220	383	5345	30312
28		8191			25	48	3385	9062
		515		38			510	9050
2927	356	6699	58	26	195	335	1450	12200
106847	1601	889089	6658	91209	24412	44055	385932	1899082
4072	63	12121	121	2454	879	1699	6260	30035
1802		8782		867	163	309	2075	14200
787		1837		96	70	100	500	2040
		938					220	3000
		938					220	3000
57712	1186	438181	3852	47976	12886	23062	183595	935384
2487	56	5010	100	1521	768	1256	2354	6581
55225	1130	433171	3752	46456	12118	21806	181241	928803
5864	64	71777	333	7493	1152	2216	21396	191393
31214	188	330019	2312	28717	8300	14935	163309	676510
8100	1	62029	530	8395	1259	2291	33338	110731
198		3817		1069	94	168	2390	13010
20529	187	247456	1758	17826	6348	11408	118283	517151
2388		16717	24	1428	599	1068	9298	35618
5396	100	25433	41	3606	962	1734	8577	46520
1031		67481	300	1173	179	305	10382	65361
416		9074		1117	59	105	2557	24761
		16214					340	6745
615		42192	300	56	120	200	7485	33855
157		99008	5100	200	84	100	14826	59358
157		1629			84	100	467	4400
		91410	4500	78			13199	46284
		2147	60	122			400	3000
		3822	540				760	5674
7331	120	70940	870	10178	1944	3533	24965	210956
4188	158	21422	321	2651	978	1807	10472	66400
75525	799	688062	4532	50024	17998	32409	297104	1347413
615		58406	300	56	120	200	7825	40600
		93824	4560	200			13949	50484
20377	525	122923	1474	29473	3635	6511	56825	307948
105721	1601	839406	6870	88431	23985	43224	369516	1842850
218		138607	4512	2829	62	109	25289	84588
781		56472	540	89	205	338	8172	42945
1315		21092	135	1231	423	789	8163	53418
7533	1	225677	4662	30214	220	376	34120	255796
23141	827	254019	2079	20568	3387	6225	61802	298853
77188	773	565303	4665	41585	20984	37698	308425	1428723
173		10579	653	214	84	161	6793	40429

16-17 各市(区)限额以上住宿业和餐饮业经营情况(2014年)

地区	Region	企业数(个) Number of Enterprises (unit)	营业额(万元) Business Value (10 000 yuan)	# 银行卡支付营业额 Business Value of Bank Card Payment	# 客房收入 From Hotel Rooms	# 公共网络客房收入 Public Network Income
一、住宿业	**Hotels**					
全 省	**Shaanxi**	**718**	**1049208**	**150502**	**487514**	**21726**
西安市	Xi'an	223	548075	98721	290751	16599
铜川市	Tongchuan	28	20263	5069	8124	341
宝鸡市	Baoji	74	54040	5499	21467	960
咸阳市	Xianyang	67	79773	9670	34489	518
渭南市	Weinan	54	108390	1609	22168	10
# 韩城市	Hancheng	5	4729	901	2198	9
延安市	Yan'an	59	43614	3444	24876	811
汉中市	Hanzhong	53	46665	6156	17714	880
榆林市	Yulin	75	87095	13572	36658	1406
安康市	Ankang	53	33640	3878	19835	126
商洛市	Shangluo	27	22771	2885	9418	76
杨凌示范区	Yangling	5	4882		2015	
二、餐饮业	**Catering Services**					
全 省	**Shaanxi**	**968**	**1288542**	**117000**	**108036**	**1601**
西安市	Xi'an	315	687196	88083	28507	615
铜川市	Tongchuan	18	14162	365	2129	
宝鸡市	Baoji	108	86556	5440	10843	211
咸阳市	Xianyang	142	180594	9606	15546	168
渭南市	Weinan	101	122461	3219	14057	7
# 韩城市	Hancheng	11	7998	478	680	
延安市	Yan'an	45	28344	932	6407	189
汉中市	Hanzhong	52	25796	2343	2373	186
榆林市	Yulin	73	54888	2583	11397	39
安康市	Ankang	93	73402	3784	12815	183
商洛市	Shangluo	15	10505	411	3200	4
杨凌示范区	Yangling	6	4638	233	763	1

Management of Enterprises above Designated Size in Hotels and Catering Services by City(District)(2014)

# 餐费收入 From Meals	# 公共网络餐费收入 Public Network Income	# 商品销售收入 From Commo-dities	客房间数(间) Number of Hotel Rooms (unit)	床位数(个) Number of Beds (unit)	餐位数(位) Number of Dining-seats (seat)	餐饮营业面积(平方米) Operating Area (sq.m)
456872	**6682**	**41647**	**90758**	**157239**	**242858**	**1399625**
205181	2667	14090	42427	71482	75105	370117
10639	63	124	2149	3696	5839	57496
22331	1019	9162	7761	13378	31635	184165
38377	75	3259	6005	10403	22316	136285
73870		7164	5268	9934	20419	131730
2531			590	1136	1848	10740
16214	568	359	6753	12406	14626	107127
25356	276	1421	4664	8098	25150	90889
41701	1942	2633	8276	14100	25457	185177
10750	23	2044	3398	6546	10592	70001
10022	49	1211	3365	5885	10549	51545
2432		181	692	1311	1170	15093
1055578	**12057**	**92582**	**24675**	**44460**	**411140**	**2023801**
587597	9358	47264	4664	7956	156601	868804
11677	106	352	247	441	7753	42820
70418	1696	3454	2990	5394	44758	191305
147232	105	16668	3891	6879	51002	213473
94446	30	12524	3151	6016	47274	175314
7318	30		228	408	3400	10900
21382	416	260	1553	2876	17834	72117
20755	147	2276	935	1579	18987	81002
39538	40	2915	3894	7112	32991	182343
53513	156	5813	2135	3910	26975	151075
5224		1043	974	1829	4065	26068
3796	3	13	241	468	2900	19480

16-18 限额以上批发业主要财务指标(2014年)

单位：万元

指标	Item	企业数(个) Number of Enterprises (unit)
总计	**Total**	**864**
按批发行业小类分	**By Subitem of Wholesale Trade**	
农、林、牧产品批发	Wholesale of Farm Produce and Livestock Products	38
谷物、豆及薯类批发	Wholesale of Cereals,Beans and Tubers	20
种子批发	Wholesale of Seeds and Forages	7
饲料批发	Wholesale of Feedstuff	1
棉、麻批发	Wholesale of Cotton and Hemp	1
林业产品批发	Wholesale of Forestry Products	2
牲畜批发	Wholesale of Livestock	1
其他农牧产品批发	Others	6
食品、饮料及烟草制品批发	Wholesale of Food, Beverages and Tobaccos	156
米、面制品及食用油批发	Wholesale of Rice, Flour and Edible Oil	20
糕点、糖果及糖批发	Wholesale of Cake and Sugar	5
果品、蔬菜批发	Wholesale of Vegetables and Fruits	69
肉、禽、蛋、奶及水产品批发	Wholesale of Meat, Poultry, Eggs and AquaticProducts	6
盐及调味品批发	Wholesale of Salt and Condiments	9
酒、饮料及茶叶批发	Wholesale of Beverages and Tea	31
烟草制品批发	Wholesale of Tobaccos	11
其他食品批发	Others	5
纺织、服装及日用品批发	Wholesale of Textiles, Garments and Daily Consumer Articles	34
纺织品、针织品及原料批发	Wholesale of Textiles, Knitwear and Textile Materials	4
服装批发	Wholesale of Garments	7
鞋帽批发	Wholesale of Shoes and hats	1
化妆品及卫生用品批发	Wholesale of Cosmetics and Health Consumer Articles	11
厨房、卫生间用具及日用杂货批发	Wholesale of Livestock Kitchen, Bathroom Appliances and Groceries	2
家用电器批发	Wholesale of Household Appliances	9
文化、体育用品及器材批发	Wholesale of Culture, Sports Appliances and Equipment	17
文具用品批发	Wholesale of Stationary	7
体育用品及器材批发	Wholesale of Sports Goods	1
图书批发	Wholesale of Books	5
首饰、工艺品及收藏品批发	Wholesale of Jewelry, Artwork and Collections	4
医药及医疗器材批发	Wholesale of Medicines and Medical Appliances	85
西药批发	Wholesale of Western Medicine	51
中药批发	Wholesale of Traditional Chinese Medicinal Materials and Medicines	26
医疗用品及器材批发	Wholesale of Medical Materials and Medical Instruments	8
矿产品、建材及化工产品批发	Wholesale of Mineral Products, Building Materials and Chemical Products	408
煤炭及制品批发	Wholesale of Coal and Related Products	126
石油及制品批发	Wholesale of Petroleum and Related Products	72
非金属矿及制品批发	Wholesale of Metal Materials	3
金属及金属矿批发	Wholesale of Metal Materials	95
建材批发	Wholesale of Building Materials	45
化肥批发	Wholesale of Garments	29
农药批发	Wholesale of Pesticides	2
农用薄膜批发	Wholesale of Agricultural Film	1
其他化工产品批发	Others	35
机械设备、五金交电及电子产品批发	Wholesale of Machinery, Hardware and Electronic Equipment	104
农业机械批发	Wholesale of Agricultural Machinery	11
汽车批发	Wholesale of Motor Vehicles	22
汽车零配件批发	Wholesale of Motor Parts	6

Main Financial Indicators of Enterprises above Designated Size in Wholesale Trades(2014)

(10 000 yuan)

资产合计 Total Assets	# 流动资产 Working Capital	# 固定资产 Fixed Assets	负债合计 Total Liabilities	主营业务收入 Business Revenue	主营业务成本 Cost of Principal Business	销售费用 Business Expenditure	营业利润 Profits from Principal Business	利润总额 Total Profits
18701136	**13698696**	**1116601**	**13703212**	**50966148**	**47660939**	**1144327**	**1282435**	**1060236**
207095	128160	38447	157998	279853	257190	5437	5121	8212
99792	72849	22732	73614	207866	197565	2329	1603	3963
30875	18106	7398	10826	18752	16087	1118	60	841
2437	2436	1	2337	3707	3474	179	20	20
64682	30657	5269	68107	3054	1586	506	-74	175
707	634	74	50	5180	4726	191	150	7
1800	35	140	200	15051	12300	260	1061	1061
6802	3444	2833	2865	26243	21452	855	2302	2146
1805520	1287567	290851	501199	5445831	4157639	289391	521910	527992
88032	41729	13557	49674	170471	154918	6919	291	2724
11423	10037	854	8736	46373	41453	2715	-629	-614
278037	166019	76845	133328	477582	416306	10977	32027	30889
10172	8031	2141	6706	39981	34085	3968	716	749
78257	53105	6556	27176	70755	53555	3308	9296	10120
235870	160947	21847	157161	956914	719105	165189	20174	20780
1073692	832459	161401	102818	3643726	2703339	94762	458785	462092
30038	15241	7650	15600	40030	34878	1554	1250	1253
610648	553234	31265	523789	2620350	2463530	57303	69206	53618
16348	13293	3051	11746	39193	38286	319	-21	-17
53681	26797	23077	31151	1759852	1694837	11331	41021	24157
50503	48478	2002	37658	90945	58128	16499	9408	9408
64552	56048	1608	47163	164815	145805	14727	1543	1255
14416	1265	391	3336	53261	37293	613	12313	12313
411148	407353	1136	392736	512285	489181	13814	4941	6503
221389	138121	21266	135816	337243	301626	9725	14215	14339
52332	49293	866	36699	80495	75078	2874	50	127
6153	6117	37	5374	14883	14125	529	47	47
132079	68652	5714	66294	134585	119973	5501	4057	4095
30824	14060	14649	27449	107280	92450	822	10060	10071
1117916	1044066	21261	997749	2356113	2241879	47772	16389	14045
869365	807364	17810	792620	1775319	1687131	37114	11713	9122
214391	205935	3061	180071	534520	512997	8677	4377	4502
34160	30768	390	25058	46274	41751	1982	300	422
13202009	9180539	621931	10040469	37326934	35820542	664289	603980	417654
5138033	3687392	196526	3437739	11945192	11213454	284544	403700	391866
3557042	1686724	365030	2981032	15055963	14488616	288360	157390	-12878
13389	13265	123	13299	22433	19457	2447	-3	-4
3896055	3285391	31886	3166953	8482261	8371193	63926	14992	14378
356342	314772	5858	277815	1258056	1228644	5285	8769	2578
95159	80350	9551	75946	213946	198315	7964	-782	2519
1134	673	211	318	16307	14539	158	1401	535
557	544	12	487	2970	2380		-49	-16
144300	111428	12734	86881	329805	283944	11605	18562	18676
1483138	1324548	85336	1314694	2394913	2233952	62007	47063	20306
32341	22618	4302	14096	68499	53680	2643	1783	1748
557191	505349	19905	532264	1086916	1023324	22716	28430	2226
78720	15596	50668	54567	47159	41323	755	1883	1887

16-18 续表

单位：万元

指 标	Item	企业数(个) Number of Enterprises (unit)
摩托车及零配件批发	Hardware	2
五金产品批发	Wholesale of Household Appliances	16
电气设备批发	Wholesale of Electrical Appliance	3
计算机、软件及辅助设备批发	Wholesale of Computer, Software and Peripherals	7
通讯及广播电视设备批发	Wholesale of Communications and Broadcast and Television Equipments	3
其他机械设备及电子产品批发	Others	34
贸易经纪与代理	Trade Broker and Agency	3
贸易代理	Trade Agency	3
其他批发	Others	19
再生物资回收与批发	Recovery and Wholesale of Regeneration Material	5
其他未列明的批发	Any other Wholesale	14
按登记注册类型分	**By Status of Registration**	
内资企业	Domestic Funded Enterprises	852
国有企业	State-owned Enterprises	73
集体企业	Collective-owned Enterprises	16
股份合作企业	Cooperative Enterprises	3
有限责任公司	Limited Liability Corporations	506
国有独资公司	State Sole Funded Corporations	24
其他有限责任公司	Other Limited Liability Corporations	482
股份有限公司	Share-holding Corporations Ltd.	30
私营企业	Private Enterprises	207
私营独资企业	Private-funded Enterprises	4
私营合伙企业	Private Partnership Enterprises	1
私营有限责任公司	Private Limited Liability Corporations	193
私营股份有限公司	Private Share-holding Corporations Ltd.	9
其他企业	Other Enterprises	17
港、澳、台商投资企业	Enterprises with Funds from Hong Kong, Macao & Taiwan	4
与港澳台商合资经营企业	Joint-venture Enterprises	2
港澳台商独资经营企业	Enterprises with Sole Investment	2
外商投资企业	Foreign Funded Enterprises	8
中外合资经营企业	Joint-venture Enterprises	4
外资企业	Enterprises with Sole Fund	4
按控股情况分	**By Status of Share Holding**	
国有控股	State-holding	167
集体控股	Collective-holding	35
私人控股	Private-holding	555
港澳台商控股	Hong Kong, Macao & Taiwan-holding	4
外商控股	Foreign-holding	6
其　　他	Others	97
按经营形式分	**By Form of Management**	
独立门店	Independent Stores	676
连锁总店	General Chain Stores	12
连锁门店	Branch Chain Stores	7
其　　他	Others	169
按单位规模分	**By Scale**	
大　型	Large	55
中　型	Medium	302
小　型	Small	468
微　型	Mini	39

continued

(10 000 yuan)

资产合计 Total Assets	# 流动资产 Working Capital	# 固定资产 Fixed Assets	负债合计 Total Liabilities	主营业务收入 Business Revenue	主营业务成本 Cost of Principal Business	销售费用 Business Expenditure	营业利润 Profits from Principal Business	利润总额 Total Profits
5349	5254	95	4879	19592	18723	352	24	24
88708	81710	1067	62043	173206	158392	3602	5632	3507
233112	227554	2096	208516	248313	236854	3884	4243	5207
233960	226807	183	226315	348064	333665	10919	1833	1640
11328	10777	539	9129	32050	30840	848	100	108
242428	228884	6482	202887	371112	337152	16289	3137	3961
20135	19671	429	15322	87923	83351	2494	1317	1091
20135	19671	429	15322	87923	83351	2494	1317	1091
33286	22789	5816	16176	116989	101230	5910	3234	2979
9381	5865	828	4311	57619	52662	350	2087	2035
23905	16924	4987	11866	59370	48568	5560	1147	944
17164095	12493132	1103916	12382131	47435803	44202099	1106197	1271854	1048998
2366732	1741469	238419	1044194	7080194	5944136	212389	481634	494460
122640	77745	14222	109681	151313	130618	2895	13124	12954
14851	14595	192	11670	31609	28354	31	1384	1385
8154642	5556622	468393	5842147	18523327	17096702	584264	582933	413953
1351550	941297	111468	1012379	4379932	4043940	94560	188846	32270
6803093	4615324	356925	4829768	14143395	13052763	489704	394087	381683
4712132	3639678	249629	3964842	18405078	17943785	244946	155092	105942
1760909	1443259	121876	1396275	3158026	2984195	59517	33318	16565
4762	4048	474	3305	15166	13390	612	706	587
150	111	28	30	10299	9000	612	310	
1664732	1365745	119714	1337458	2946783	2794248	53922	23753	11780
91266	73355	1661	55482	185779	167558	4371	8549	4198
32190	19766	11183	13322	86257	74309	2155	4369	3739
140401	132536	6918	120527	357385	308284	29202	10243	10257
80454	74693	4837	73274	222519	208496	10843	910	907
59947	57844	2081	47253	134866	99788	18360	9333	9351
1396639	1073028	5768	1200554	3172960	3150557	8928	338	980
1366157	1046350	3699	1182740	3076622	3061206	2945	527	1168
30483	26677	2069	17814	96338	89351	5983	-190	-188
9500441	6564262	656728	6428190	30487089	28221798	670111	1068347	876579
202634	136977	26332	165824	376786	333081	14472	14637	16243
4710494	3339443	361760	3601998	9451174	8699118	342622	142874	105477
140401	132536	6918	120527	357385	308284	29202	10243	10257
61553	57560	2211	44647	132078	122932	8693	-738	-102
4085614	3467918	62652	3342026	10161636	9975727	79227	47073	51782
12601223	9144591	802406	9475912	36427728	34503548	753140	686909	481755
722518	458221	110533	211015	2203119	1739833	55411	240671	240718
311064	246415	14650	306621	939603	897284	24268	9789	11103
5066331	3849469	189013	3709663	11395699	10520274	311508	345065	326660
7903488	5518564	573086	5457086	24042198	21825702	692876	925836	710242
7819175	6202573	328652	5999744	22073325	21259988	348299	300087	309614
2796855	1818453	211045	2095558	4638961	4368005	101510	56228	40367
181618	159105	3819	150824	211665	207243	1643	283	12

16-19 限额以上零售业主要财务指标(2014年)

单位：万元

指　　标	Item	企业数(个) Number of Enterprises (unit)
总　计	**Total**	**2542**
按零售行业小类分	**By Retail Trades**	
综合零售	Integrated Retail	631
百货零售	Retail of General Merchandise	290
超级市场零售	Retail of Supermarkets	268
其他综合零售	Others	73
食品、饮料及烟草制品专门零售	Special Retail of Food, Beverages and Tobaccos	251
粮油零售	Retail of Grain and Oil	34
糕点、面包零售	Retail of Cake and Bread	5
果品、蔬菜零售	Retail of Melons and Fruits, Vegetables	61
肉、禽、蛋及水产品零售	Retail of Meat, Poultry, Eggs and Aquatic Products	23
营养和保健品零售	Retail of Nourishment and Health Products	1
酒、饮料及茶叶零售	Retail of Beverages and Tea	77
烟草制品零售	Retail of Tobaccos	13
其他食品零售	Others	37
纺织、服装及日用品专门零售	Special Retail of Textiles, Garments and Daily Consumer Articles	115
纺织品及针织品零售	Retail of Textiles and Knitwear	8
服装零售	Retail of Garments	78
鞋帽零售	Retail of Shoes and Hats	6
化妆品及卫生用品零售	Retail of Cosmetics and Health Consumer Articles	8
钟表、眼镜零售	Retail of Clocks and Watches,Spectacles	8
自行车零售	Retail of Bicycles	1
其他日用品零售	Others	6
文化、体育用品及器材专门零售	Special Retail of Culture, Sports Appliances and Equipments	125
文具用品零售	Retail of Stationery	2
体育用品及器材零售	Retail of Sports Goods	5
图书、报刊零售	Retail of Books	77
珠宝首饰零售	Retail of Jewelry	35
工艺美术品及收藏品零售	Retail of Artwork and Collections	4
乐器零售	Retail of Musical Instrument	2
医药及医疗器材专门零售	Special Retail of Medicines and Medical Appliances	120
药品零售	Retail of Medicines	116
医疗用品及器材零售	Retail of Medical Supplies and Appliances	4
汽车、摩托车、燃料及零配件专门零售	Special Retail of Motor Vehicles, Motorcycles, Fuel and Parts	819
汽车零售	Retail of Motor Vehicles	575
汽车零配件零售	Retail of Motor Vehicles and Parts	17
摩托车及零配件零售	Retail of Motorcycles and Parts	30
机动车燃料零售	Retail of Fuel of Motor Vehicles	197
家用电器及电子产品专门零售	Special Retail of Household Appliances and Electronic Products	256
家用视听设备零售	Retail of Home Audio-visual Equipment	32
日用家电设备零售	Retail of Household Appliances	159
计算机、软件及辅助设备零售	Retail of Computer, Software and Peripherals	40
通信设备零售	Retail of Communication Equipment	14
其他电子产品零售	Others	11
五金、家具及室内装修材料专门零售	Special Retail of Hardware, Furniture and Decoration Materials	184
五金零售	Retail of Hardware	49
灯具零售	Retail of Light Fittings	2
家具零售	Retail of Furniture	80
涂料零售	Retail of Dope	1
卫生洁具零售	Retail of Sanitary	1
木质装饰材料零售	Retail of Dooden Decorating Materials	4
陶瓷、石材装饰材料零售	Retail of Porcelainous, Stone Finishing Decorating Materials	10
其他室内装修材料零售	Others	37
货摊、无店铺及其他零售	Non-shop and Other Retails	41
互联网零售	E-commerce Retails	1
邮购及电视、电话零售	Mail-order & Phone-order Retails	2
生活用燃料零售	Retail of Life Fuels	26
其他未列明的零售	Other Retail not Classified Elsewhere	12

Main Financial Indicators of Enterprises above Designated Size in Retail Trades(2014)

(10 000 yuan)

资产合计 Total Assets	# 流动资产 Working Capital	# 固定资产 Fixed Assets	负债合计 Total Liabilities	主营业务收入 Business Revenue	主营业务成本 Cost of Principal Business	销售费用 Business Expenditure	营业利润 Profits from Principal Business	利润总额 Total Profits
12972289	**8300971**	**2016054**	**9082522**	**24594599**	**21459101**	**1256602**	**955617**	**863990**
4095991	2503263	769991	2798975	5863202	4913656	525950	229725	225405
2478925	1336447	576153	1723395	2928189	2426819	212763	115807	114209
1541211	1121300	180794	1045131	2679267	2277795	300721	99347	103733
75855	45516	13044	30449	255746	209042	12466	14572	7463
955551	592467	247255	723100	793720	671001	46136	23512	20816
43876	26183	9956	30890	57077	50937	2501	64	1194
5448	2622	2143	1988	4688	3547	355	111	218
123034	68056	45729	37425	182801	145302	8356	13688	7804
36822	20231	15363	19161	80676	73097	3898	-2340	-1140
297	100	196	102	598	402	68	79	
676823	430752	156117	592973	265958	217694	23656	6111	8208
25880	17515	4367	16528	55406	46706	2339	1991	1351
43372	27009	13384	24034	146516	133317	4964	3809	3183
466617	179402	102846	180481	1635322	1318602	90887	122868	81937
14460	9681	1986	6728	56028	39901	1281	11156	10839
364257	115932	92051	134022	1330121	1078724	62245	99545	58082
12470	2913	3228	741	11822	8004	929	1204	73
14372	10153	2372	8042	123915	102940	9196	9100	11169
36862	31285	1317	17014	44198	34980	6159	2087	1994
1217	1201	16	957	625	500	29	-5	-4
22979	8236	1874	12978	68613	53552	11048	-219	-217
492389	370716	76175	265799	588539	480599	43098	31661	15182
797	763	34	481	1937	1819		6	6
150140	133362	15301	56890	134900	104299	7779	16486	3392
284069	195354	55805	179298	309261	246301	29463	14090	13380
54164	38980	4422	27269	129206	117883	5301	-32	-2010
1094	427	569	215	8783	6546	298	1045	334
2126	1831	44	1646	4452	3751	257	67	79
386510	332380	28066	331430	656382	571269	45933	10906	9739
377074	325224	27238	325561	648304	565244	45693	10320	9432
9436	7156	828	5868	8078	6025	240	586	307
5008006	3212184	510167	3927539	10374482	9535500	313355	216189	206530
4267682	2998527	366510	3471332	8190221	7565240	206504	165008	162860
25027	19161	3606	16947	60167	54774	1849	996	512
32990	25078	3025	20826	53727	46791	1747	2401	2118
682307	169418	137026	418434	2070367	1868696	103255	47784	41040
912260	735902	111350	454334	2327473	1989610	125961	137635	138212
47788	39992	3998	24233	235592	211866	13294	6159	5644
647873	533264	78120	344777	1563582	1356815	97861	46213	51285
129145	83795	28093	46328	394386	304317	4399	79126	78378
62769	58669	562	28749	107958	97861	8072	3624	3597
24685	20181	578	10248	25956	18751	2334	2513	-691
525736	301674	136743	335190	1946866	1642622	41375	144084	124897
63121	46074	8474	32554	103012	87202	3547	4245	4081
7345	1325	4410	6957	96639	69909	191	24695	24695
369924	214028	90616	251565	1154036	977741	22026	89214	82484
141		113	41	842	700	40	64	64
254	250	1	32	507	432	18	16	
4208	3700	248	2996	8259	6182	909	748	749
15150	11535	2202	10223	35378	29612	4943	-558	-742
65593	24762	30680	30822	548193	470843	9701	25661	13566
129230	72983	33460	65675	408613	336242	23908	39038	41273
17404	15788	979	-535	213981	200203	15802	-3186	-2065
11167	2440	6613	10064	117361	71597	3769	39048	39148
70139	29306	21784	39934	57592	47833	3110	2153	2106
30521	25450	4085	16212	19680	16609	1226	1022	2082

16-19 续表

单位：万元

指　　标	Item	企业数（个）Number of Enterprises (unit)
按登记注册类型分	**By Status of Registration**	
内资企业	Domestic Funded Enterprises	2487
国有企业	State-owned Enterprises	83
集体企业	Collective-owned Enterprises	107
股份合作企业	Cooperative Enterprises	6
联营企业	Joint Ownership Enterprises	2
集体联营企业	Collective Joint Ownership Enterprises	2
有限责任公司	Limited Liability Corporations	1363
国有独资公司	State Sole Funded Corporations	50
其他有限责任公司	Other Limited Liability Corporations	1313
股份有限公司	Share-holding Corporations Ltd.	64
私营企业	Private Enterprises	822
私营独资企业	Private-funded Enterprises	129
私营合伙企业	Private Partnership Enterprises	23
私营有限责任公司	Private Limited Liability Corporations	623
私营股份有限公司	Private Share-holding Corporations Ltd.	47
其他企业	Other Enterprises	40
港、澳、台商投资企业	Enterprises with Funds from Hong Kong, Macao & Taiwan	25
与港澳台商合资经营企业	Joint-venture Enterprises	6
与港澳台商合作经营企业	Cooperative Enterprises	1
港澳台商独资经营企业	Enterprises with Sole Investment	18
外商投资企业	Foreign Funded Enterprises	30
中外合资经营企业	Joint-venture Enterprises	7
外资企业	Enterprises with Sole Fund	21
外商投资股份有限公司	Share-holding Corporations Ltd. with Foreign Investment	1
其他外商投资企业	Other Foreign Funded Enterprises	1
按控股情况分	**By Status of Share Holding**	
国有控股	State-holding	201
集体控股	Collective-holding	162
私人控股	Private-holding	1831
港澳台商控股	Hong Kong, Macao & Taiwan-holding	26
外商控股	Foreign-holding	28
其　他	Others	294
按经营形式分	**By Form of Management**	
独立门店	Independent Stores	2304
连锁总店	General Chain Stores	62
连锁门店	Branch Chain Stores	52
其　他	Others	124
按单位规模分	**By Scale**	
大　型	Large	56
中　型	Medium	822
小　型	Small	1318
微　型	Mini	346
按零售业态分	**By Business Categories**	
有店铺零售	Shop Retails	2524
食杂店	Grocery Store	13
便利店	Convenience Store	38
超　市	Supermarket	356
大型超市	Hypermarket	66
仓储会员店	Warehouse Club	5
百货店	Department Store	315
专业店	Specialty Store	858
专卖店	Franchised Store	712
家居建材商店	Building Material Store	84
购物中心	Shopping Center	30
厂家直销中心	Factory Outlets Center	47
无店铺零售	Non-shop Retails	18
#电视购物	TV shopping	2
网上商店	Web Storefronts	7

continued

(10 000 yuan)

资产合计 Total Assets	# 流动资产 Working Capital	# 固定资产 Fixed Assets	负债合计 Total Liabilities	主营业务收入 Business Revenue	主营业务成本 Cost of Principal Business	销售费用 Business Expenditure	营业利润 Profits from Principal Business	利润总额 Total Profits
10535935	7064921	1803254	7428383	20361723	17780695	968284	757000	660345
288721	203869	58149	206350	597149	519637	25940	20173	17256
92180	54061	25261	57135	443982	384219	17504	13106	7305
9330	3651	5680	726	52350	35215	3499	5780	5780
317	50	266	158	6258	4984	5	302	302
317	50	266	158	6258	4984	5	302	302
6362875	4314611	1082235	4389857	12675066	11132155	637308	445364	424030
219003	140551	48215	135486	260074	215681	21545	11777	12360
6143872	4174060	1034020	4254371	12414991	10916474	615763	433587	411670
1800511	1058314	328506	1444072	1890092	1641123	88255	70924	27171
1936268	1406428	285476	1307849	4579803	3964154	189076	195066	172599
69836	37356	16909	27387	246374	208543	8253	17921	15240
21512	13119	7226	4968	75509	62625	3182	4240	4208
1694423	1262651	223594	1169750	3896486	3400209	166252	127473	108459
150497	93302	37748	105744	361434	292778	11388	45432	44692
45733	23939	17683	22236	117024	99209	6698	6285	5902
1815824	944915	115921	1326997	1977642	1663661	128532	156395	162204
418087	330168	31789	233675	729160	576127	32375	104092	103472
25537	668	24853	26788	3924	3418	1245	-2245	-2209
1372200	614079	59279	1066533	1244558	1084117	94913	54548	60941
620530	291135	96879	327143	2255233	2014745	159786	42222	41441
402484	132185	60076	159140	1369994	1227611	78800	39242	36987
207218	151379	33546	159082	821321	727848	77413	3050	4446
6533	6469	64	3939	49337	47160	3573	438	511
4295	1102	3193	4982	14582	12126		-508	-503
1255516	559839	255354	820727	3070771	2732777	170626	74662	66566
332669	212470	74992	223214	1070428	911762	44092	47114	41067
5816688	4069764	961997	4089963	13697841	11963052	555463	539339	464969
1770796	895959	119421	1300349	2046008	1726691	134732	159769	165586
422824	335535	59865	254953	1064557	933319	95463	21648	23313
3373796	2227405	544424	2393317	3644995	3191502	256226	113086	102488
9636559	5947173	1559877	6633117	19537047	17200442	872185	710680	613939
1433933	988843	174225	1083558	1398805	1150102	143704	31657	36593
735673	542439	76950	540395	1304013	1143771	113010	54812	54343
1166124	822516	205003	825453	2354734	1964786	127703	158468	159115
4135457	2501522	622738	2760321	7941358	6366002	542252	377119	387531
6831322	4475268	971524	5147132	12516560	10979132	563504	448804	378797
1800430	1188625	385215	1044507	3730873	3258516	138343	113240	85518
205080	135555	36578	130563	405807	355451	12503	16454	12145
12924858	8269420	2004670	9062532	24203415	21132944	1234386	919058	825976
16692	10161	5285	8700	108132	103649	1321	836	679
104753	34082	12340	88261	217337	185864	14370	3491	3471
431518	243614	118861	229787	1138782	945620	79917	50181	44280
1258373	952976	116528	893995	2025709	1732540	255927	65283	66584
17600	16216	1024	3684	13362	11228	405	711	813
2746380	1446137	611369	1834463	3180752	2642189	208348	137169	125273
4074734	2773177	618282	2897676	7652263	6870343	371190	133524	142517
3375054	2265808	310927	2609112	6130673	5499416	189691	222286	198066
382620	215597	94450	261482	1397697	1170890	23662	143418	124981
317689	151072	90249	92738	1845328	1521915	74892	157783	117822
199446	160580	25355	142635	493381	449291	14662	4376	1490
47431	31551	11384	19991	391184	326157	22216	36559	38014
11167	2440	6613	10064	117361	71597	3769	39048	39148
19935	16644	2437	475	217775	202438	16091	-2457	-1764

16-20 限额以上住宿业主要财务指标(2014年)

单位：万元

指标	Item	企业数(个) Number of Enterprises (unit)
总计	**Total**	**718**
按住宿行业小类分	**By Subitem of Hotels**	
旅游饭店	Tour Restaurant	468
一般旅馆	General Restaurant	221
其他住宿服务	Other Hotel Services	29
按登记注册类型分	**By Status of Registration**	
内资企业	Domestic Funded Enterprises	699
国有企业	State-owned Enterprises	70
集体企业	Collective-owned Enterprises	11
股份合作企业	Cooperative Enterprises	2
有限责任公司	Limited Liability Corporations	317
国有独资公司	State Sole Funded Corporations	10
其他有限责任公司	Other Limited Liability Corporations	307
股份有限公司	Share-holding Corporations Ltd.	23
私营企业	Private Enterprises	259
私营独资企业	Private-funded Enterprises	38
私营合伙企业	Private Partnership Enterprises	13
私营有限责任公司	Private Limited Liability Corporations	188
私营股份有限公司	Private Share-holding Corporations Ltd.	20
其他企业	Other Enterprises	17
港、澳、台商投资企业	Enterprises with Funds from Hong Kong, Macao & Taiwan	8
与港澳台商合资经营企业	Joint-venture Enterprises	4
与港澳台商合作经营企业	Cooperative Enterprises	1
港澳台商独资经营企业	Enterprises with Sole Investment	3
外商投资企业	Foreign Funded Enterprises	11
中外合资经营企业	Joint-venture Enterprises	4
中外合作经营企业	Enterprises with Sole Fund	3
外资企业	Share-holding Corporations Ltd. with Foreign Investment	3
外商投资股份有限公司	Other Foreign Funded Enterprises	1
按控股情况分	**By Status of Share Holding**	
国有控股	State-holding	114
集体控股	Collective-holding	25
私人控股	Private-holding	472
港澳台商控股	Hong Kong, Macao & Taiwan-holding	8
外商控股	Foreign-holding	11
其他	Others	88
按经营形式分	**By Form of Management**	
独立门店	Independent Stores	691
连锁总店(总部)	General Chain Stores	2
连锁门店	Branch Chain Stores	11
其他	Others	14
按单位规模分	**By Scale**	
大型	Large	7
中型	Medium	103
小型	Small	593
微型	Mini	15
按星级分	**By Star Rating**	
五星	Five-star Level	14
四星	Four-star Level	56
三星	Three-star Level	156
二星	Two-star Level	53
一星	One-star Level	3
其他	Others	436

Main Financial Indicators in Hotels above Designated Size(2014)

(10 000 yuan)

资产合计 Total Assets	# 流动资产 Working Capital	# 固定资产 Fixed Assets	负债合计 Total Liabilities	主营业务收入 Business Revenue	主营业务成本 Cost of Principal Business	销售费用 Business Expenditure	营业利润 Profits from Principal Business	利润总额 Total Profits
3038247	**955709**	**1508130**	**2326750**	**1029497**	**442512**	**289046**	**-37072**	**-115921**
2659866	805749	1363503	2091655	791360	315357	238860	-44593	-119758
267826	96562	111592	175169	199626	111353	41110	5059	2626
110555	53398	33035	59926	38510	15802	9076	2462	1212
2603643	799359	1267537	1915455	911564	401188	258772	-39661	-118398
257410	45448	144986	151494	96584	41727	26246	-5121	-3574
22037	12506	6942	26068	7736	4271	1322	-364	-392
1478	271	495	911	4465	3245	167	660	0
1670860	440094	878664	1300613	462962	180501	153087	-38616	-111851
131030	26974	57200	118743	29528	9100	10108	-1779	-2540
1539830	413120	821464	1181870	433434	171401	142979	-36837	-109311
40200	7716	28285	32434	19443	7699	6941	-399	-1327
578638	286585	190161	385183	303493	155254	68050	3166	-1553
28587	10842	16232	8498	35712	24053	2333	3969	3350
9547	3331	4552	2592	10599	6010	2076	818	589
511323	263572	159033	359043	231768	108252	61203	-3279	-6333
29180	8841	10343	15050	25415	16938	2438	1659	841
33020	6738	18005	18753	16882	8492	2959	1012	299
211179	46854	137495	144081	54332	22170	12472	-1195	-862
150673	36113	91814	92596	34689	16692	7598	-888	-630
17249	2207	15042	15007	5341	2660	1540	-1607	-1615
43256	8534	30638	36479	14302	2817	3334	1301	1383
223426	109496	103098	267213	63601	19154	17802	3784	3339
43397	8147	32803	76555	19828	6828	4436	-161	-581
15096	8327	6710	87554	8616	1693	4197	-1302	-1272
157483	92280	62185	94190	32943	10222	6931	6777	6722
7450	741	1401	8915	2213	411	2237	-1530	-1531
629259	149232	332294	381549	212594	78829	69651	-14790	-13437
57358	18691	31874	56807	27698	14489	5377	-789	-852
1045869	492242	362986	735866	490895	234192	123693	-5054	-84697
211179	46854	137495	144081	54332	22170	12472	-1195	-862
196578	108547	76666	241520	60498	16156	18017	5729	5684
898004	140145	566816	766926	183480	76676	59836	-20975	-21757
2893440	928357	1481641	2228088	988606	420053	278368	-38101	-116898
552	126	335	167	927	720	65	22	22
24775	9479	7834	6350	12106	2552	5642	2069	1959
119480	17747	18320	92144	27858	19187	4971	-1062	-1003
657698	105817	462057	405639	105626	43943	31746	3963	3393
1277902	392079	610132	1117284	441928	168936	119363	-24841	-25931
1086359	456432	422053	779895	480412	228772	137785	-15336	-92524
16288	1381	13889	23931	1530	861	152	-858	-859
493647	169286	274387	395877	113136	32375	34047	-2476	-3334
392385	122795	199035	361186	137645	34298	47294	-12662	-11359
432654	143224	211216	352293	221402	107827	61044	-7135	-81276
66220	21713	26183	39918	44273	23100	7106	5564	3463
2080	183	1757	1224	1543	498	566	23	146
1651261	498508	795553	1176252	511499	244415	138989	-20387	-23561

16-21　限额以上餐饮业主要财务指标(2014年)

单位：万元

指　　标	Item	企业数(个) Number of Enterprises (unit)
总　　计	**Total**	**968**
按餐饮行业小类分	**By Catering Services**	
正餐服务	Restaurant	932
快餐服务	Fast Food	19
饮料及冷饮服务	Beverages and Cold Drinks	2
茶馆服务	Teahouse	1
咖啡馆服务	Café	1
其他餐饮服务	Others	15
小吃服务	Snack	9
餐饮配送服务	Catering Distribution	2
其他未列明餐饮业	Other Catering Service not Classified	4
按登记注册类型分	**By Status of Registration**	
内资企业	Domestic Funded Enterprises	948
国有企业	State-owned Enterprises	16
集体企业	Collective-owned Enterprises	7
股份合作企业	Cooperative Enterprises	1
联营企业	Joint Ownership Enterprises	1
集体联营企业	Collective Joint Ownership Enterprises	1
有限责任公司	Limited Liability Corporations	436
国有独资公司	State Sole Funded Corporations	8
其他有限责任公司	Other Limited Liability Corporations	428
股份有限公司	Share-holding Corporations Ltd.	27
私营企业	Private Enterprises	433
私营独资企业	Private-funded Enterprises	94
私营合伙企业	Private Partnership Enterprises	7
私营有限责任公司	Private Limited Liability Corporations	307
私营股份有限公司	Private Share-holding Corporations Ltd.	25
其他企业	Other Enterprises	27
港、澳、台商投资企业	Enterprises with Funds from Hong Kong, Macao & Taiwan	8
与港澳台商合资经营企业	Joint-venture Enterprises	2
与港澳台商合作经营企业	Cooperative Enterprises	1
港澳台商独资经营企业	Enterprises with Sole Investment	5
外商投资企业	Foreign Funded Enterprises	12
中外合资经营企业	Joint-venture Enterprises	4
外资企业	Enterprises with Sole Fund	5
外商投资股份有限公司	Share-holding Corporations Ltd. with Foreign Investment	1
其他外商投资企业	Other Foreign Funded Enterprises	2
按控股情况分	**By Status of Share Holding**	
国有控股	State-holding	37
集体控股	Collective-holding	17
私人控股	Private-holding	792
港澳台商控股	Hong Kong, Macao & Taiwan-holding	6
外商控股	Foreign-holding	8
其　他	Others	108
按经营形式分	**By Form of Management**	
独立门店	Independent Stores	922
连锁总店	General Chain Stores	11
连锁门店	Branch Chain Stores	10
其　他	Others	25
按单位规模分	**By Scale**	
大　型	Large	8
中　型	Medium	72
小　型	Small	849
微　型	Mini	39

Main Financial Indicators of Enterprises above Designated Size in Catering Services(2014)

(10 000 yuan)

资产合计 Total Assets	# 流动资产 Working Capital	# 固定资产 Fixed Assets	负债合计 Total Liabilities	主营业务收入 Business Revenue	主营业务成本 Cost of Principal Business	销售费用 Business Expenditure	营业利润 Profits from Principal Business	利润总额 Total Profits
1562612	**630038**	**543413**	**1022919**	**1262434**	**694342**	**335859**	**13514**	**5422**
1392789	563846	475309	901581	1165426	648882	296829	15043	7973
110956	44331	33500	75607	76529	35242	35845	-2386	-2633
543	154	103	295	2036	1214	12	710	40
265	72	103	141	456	350	12	40	40
278	82		154	1580	864		669	
58324	21708	34501	45436	18443	9003	3173	147	41
3125	1467	1181	1683	8219	5101	912	613	508
6040	4176	456	2691	553	411	96	-147	-146
49159	16064	32864	41062	9671	3491	2166	-319	-322
1396200	572215	494427	899049	1096916	621566	266328	15725	8215
20575	5465	12000	9318	18948	10785	3953	1496	1303
2550	1063	1225	1707	10054	8107	367	478	425
1570	200	935	1510	2720	1908	92	353	353
53	31	10	11	938	580		342	342
53	31	10	11	938	580		342	342
801157	351785	276948	576077	549357	301171	154202	-9757	-13114
14674	4044	4605	15773	9977	6773	2646	-1419	-1944
786484	347741	272343	560304	539381	294398	151556	-8338	-11170
134110	48749	18056	46220	89925	52616	23941	3331	7101
398699	150392	166055	240149	390464	224210	79181	18274	10973
51075	19907	22676	26916	78223	47126	8765	10054	7865
1638	844	656	496	5084	3314	458	417	417
328282	121248	136192	205221	286416	161069	65316	7469	2489
17704	8392	6531	7517	20741	12702	4641	334	201
37485	14531	19198	24057	34510	22189	4592	1210	833
106154	43194	31074	81026	69774	28041	37251	-8924	-8776
16922	7744	5647	14396	11223	3885	4544	-638	-954
13016	1505	5543	10175	16259	5696	10086	-1418	-1418
76216	33944	19883	56455	42292	18460	22621	-6868	-6404
60259	14630	17912	42845	95744	44735	32280	6712	5983
1384	1198	96	2056	1786	696	985	-151	-146
55554	11897	17382	38255	87795	41665	28285	6549	6236
1838	679	257	1689	2341	989	1275	-96	-96
1483	856	178	845	3822	1384	1736	410	-12
182680	70374	40920	90063	98068	48204	35554	-938	3005
70982	20106	30840	55855	28102	17236	4969	1878	1672
866107	346458	338627	554235	816817	470288	183231	19704	8503
89232	35450	25427	66630	58551	24156	32707	-8286	-7822
57441	12625	17639	40450	90403	42768	29711	6432	6119
296170	145026	89962	215686	170493	91690	49689	-5277	-6055
1368178	544963	494860	883170	1040291	586575	253115	16431	8836
76667	33596	16141	58670	142075	73056	43249	2911	2470
86544	33816	24388	65148	53723	19222	32387	-6745	-6134
31223	17662	8024	15931	26345	15489	7109	916	250
303149	133599	44759	174387	268066	122459	105083	1186	5931
397495	165694	162108	265186	306322	176011	77926	743	-3291
855932	328966	333732	581259	680774	391498	152110	10462	1882
6037	1779	2813	2087	7271	4374	740	1123	900

16-22 批发和零售业、住宿和餐饮业连锁经营情况(2014年)
Chain Management of Enterprises of Wholesale, Retail Trades, Hotels and and Catering Services(2014)

类　别	Item	合　计 Total	直营店 Regular Chain	加盟店 Franchise Chain
批发和零售业	**Wholesale and Retail Trades**			
门店总数(个)	Number of Stores(unit)	2206	2037	169
年末零售营业面积(平方米)	Retail Operating Area at year-end(sq.m)	2521254	2351280	169974
年末从业人员数(人)	Number of Employed Persons at year-end(person)	36124	34011	2113
连锁门店商品购进总额(万元)	Total Purchases Value of General Chain Stores	8780683	8639552	141131
# 统一配送商品购进额	Centralized Purchase and Delivery	6277895	6258157	19738
# 自有配送商品购进额	Self Centralized Purchase and Delivery	3742894	17568	3725326
非自有配送商品购进额	Non-self Centralized Purchase and Delivery	298419	298419	
连锁门店商品销售额	Total Sale of General Chain Stores	10366963	10159230	207733
# 零售额	Retail Value	3542421	3334688	207733
住宿和餐饮业	**Hotels and Catering Services**			
门店总数(个)	Number of Stores(unit)	181	181	
年末从业人员数(人)	Number of Employed Persons at year-end(person)	11049	11049	
连锁门店商品购进总额(万元)	Total Purchases Value of General Chain Stores	69358	69358	
# 统一配送商品购进额	Centralized Purchase and Delivery	62848	62848	
自有配送商品购进额	Self Centralized Purchase and Delivery	59842	59842	
年末餐饮营业面积(平方米)	Retail Operating Area at year-end(sq.m)	77203	77203	
餐位数(位)	Number of Dining-seats(seat)	23110	23110	
连锁门店营业额	Business Revenue of General Chain Stores	132962	132962	
# 餐费收入	Revenue From Meals	132108	132108	
商品销售额	Total Sales of Commodities	854	854	

16-23 限额以上产业活动单位和个体户批发业商品购、销、存总额(2014年) Total Purchases, Sales and Inventory of Industrial Activity Units and Individuals above Designated Size in Wholesale Trades(2014)

单位：万元 (10 000 yuan)

指标	Item	商品购进总额 Total Purchases Value	商品销售总额 Total Sales	年末库存 Stock at Year-end
总计	**Total**	**95920**	**101943**	**3825**
按批发行业分	**By Wholesale Trade Sector**			
食品、饮料及烟草制品批发	Wholesale of Food, Beverages and Tobaccos	21503	23527	3262
米、面制品及食用油批发	Wholesale of Rice, Flour and Edible Oil	2895	3857	239
果品、蔬菜批发	Wholesale of Fruit and Vegetables	12072	14164	1513
肉、禽、蛋、奶及水产品批发	Wholesale of Meat, Poultry, Eggs, Milk and Aquatic Products	3300	2300	1300
酒、饮料及茶叶批发	Wholesale of Beverages and Tea	3236	3206	210
纺织服装及家庭用品批发	Wholesale of Textiles, Garments and Daily	14575	14573	22
厨房、卫生间用具及	Wholesale of Kitchen and Washroom	14575	14573	22
医药及医疗器材批发	Wholesale of Medicines and Medical Appliances	2339	2817	260
西药批发	Wholesale of Western Medicine	2339	2817	260
矿产品、建材及化工产品批发	Wholesale of Mineral Products, Building Materials and Chemical Products	4080	3851	281
建材批发	Wholesale of Building Materials	2574	2510	129
化肥批发	Wholesale of Garments	1506	1341	152
机械设备、五金交电及电子产品批发	Wholesale of Machinery, Hardware and Electronic Equipment	53422	57175	
农业机械批发	Wholesale of Agricultural Machinery	11116	12783	
其他机械设备及电子产品批发	Others	42306	44391	
按登记注册类型分	**By Status of Registration**			
内资企业	Domestic Funded Enterprises	76388	83023	41
集体企业	Collective-owned Enterprises	8390	11276	19
有限责任公司	Limited Liability Corporations	42306	44391	
其他有限责任公司	Other Limited Liability Corporations	42306	44391	
股份有限公司	Share-holding Corporations Ltd.	25691	27356	22
个体经营	Individual Business	19532	18920	3784
个体户	Individual	19532	18920	3784
按经营形式分	**By Form of Management**			
独立门店	Independent Stores	77663	84482	2309
其他	Others	18257	17460	1516

16-24 限额以上产业活动单位和个体户零售业商品购、销、存总额(2014年) Total Purchases, Sales and Inventory of Industrial Activity Units and Individuals above Designated Size in Retail Trades(2014)

单位：万元 (10 000 yuan)

指　　标	Item	商品购进总额 Total Purchases Value	商品销售总额 Total Sales	年末库存 Stock at year-end
总　　计	**Total**	**1319328**	**1372649**	**76165**
按零售行业分	**By Retail Trades Sector**			
综合零售	Integrated Retail	210943	216747	16763
百货零售	Retail of General Merchandise	89954	92789	6425
超级市场零售	Retail of Supermarkets	104285	106060	9207
其他综合零售	Others	16705	17899	1131
食品、饮料及烟草制品专门零售	Special Retail of Food, Beverages and Tobaccos	243216	249850	6710
粮油零售	Retail of Grain and Oil	63047	62770	663
糕点、面包零售	Retail of Cake and Bread	2489	2673	524
果品、蔬菜零售	Retail of Melons and Fruits,Vegetables	6305	6245	543
肉、禽、蛋及水产品零售	Retail of Meat, Poultry, Eggs and Aquatic Products	131260	133804	1965
营养和保健品零售	Retail of Nourishment and Health Products	2200	2110	112
酒、饮料及茶叶零售	Retail of Beverages and Tea	31148	35068	2609
烟草制品零售	Retail of Tobaccos	2802	2800	62
其他食品零售	Others	3965	4382	223
纺织、服装及日用品专门零售	Special Retail of Textiles, Garments and Daily Consumer Articles	164012	166306	13801
纺织品及针织品零售	Retail of Textiles and Knitwear	3227	3237	283
服装零售	Retail of Garments	59195	62017	8671
鞋帽零售	Retail of Shoes and Hats	32079	32075	137
化妆品及卫生用品零售	Retail of Cosmetics and Health Consumer Articles	15375	13857	2461
厨房用具及日用杂品零售	Retail of Kitchenware and Daily Groceries	2155	2000	550
自行车零售	Retail of Bicycle	1614	1615	19
其他日用品零售	Others	50367	51505	1680
文化、体育用品及器材专门零售	Special Retail of Culture, Sports Appliances and Equipments	52336	52456	2937
文具用品零售	Retail of Stationary	2632	2711	84
体育用品及器材零售	Retail of Sports Goods	1905	2203	213
图书、报刊零售	Retail of Books	1129	1132	42
珠宝首饰零售	Retail of Jewelry	45110	44846	2527
工艺美术品及收藏品零售	Retail of Artwork and Collections	1560	1565	72
医药及医疗器材专门零售	Special Retail of Medicines and Medical Appliances	37178	37537	4187
药品零售	Retail of Medicines	37178	37537	4187
汽车、摩托车、燃料及零配件专门零售	Special Retail of Motor Vehicles, Motorcycles, Fuel and Parts	117137	149868	2969
汽车零售	Retail of Motor Vehicles	20337	20066	704
摩托车及零配件零售	Retail of Motor Vehicles and Parts	7617	7199	639
机动车燃料零售	Retail of Fuel of Motor Vehicles	89184	122604	1625
家用电器及电子产品专门零售	Special Retail of Household Appliances and Electronic Products	340422	346486	17943
家用视听设备零售	Retail of Home Audio-visual Equipment	22512	23109	885
日用家电设备零售	Retail of Household Appliances	126118	127076	7973
计算机、软件及辅助设备零售	Retail of Computer, Software and Peripherals	18322	16500	3432

16-24 续表 continued

单位：万元 (10 000 yuan)

指　　标	Item	商品购进总额 Total Purchases Value	商品销售总额 Total Sales	年末库存 Stock at year-end
通信设备零售	Retail of Communication Equipment	171136	177773	5244
其他电子产品零售	Others	2335	2028	410
五金、家具及室内装修材料	Special Retail of Hardware, Furniture and Decoration Materials	150506	149710	10632
五金零售	Retail of Hardware	13184	12838	1065
灯具零售	Retail of Light Fittings	2635	2532	550
家具零售	Retail of Furniture	28074	28185	2916
卫生洁具零售	Retail of Sanitary	1155	1448	17
木质装饰材料零售	Retail of Dooden Decorating Materials	7511	7362	567
陶瓷、石材装饰材料零售	Retail of Porcelainous, Stone Finishing Decorating Materials	17312	17868	1299
其他室内装修材料零售	Others	80635	79477	4217
货摊无店铺及其他零售业	Non-shop and Other Retails	3578	3690	224
生活用燃料零售	Retail of Life Fuels	714	713	6
其他未列明的零售	Other Retail Not Classified Elsewhere	2864	2977	218
按登记注册类型分	**By Status of Registration**			
内资企业	Domestic Funded Enterprises	31595	38518	811
国有企业	State-owned Enterprises	27058	33502	543
集体企业	Collective-owned Enterprises	2851	3231	82
私营企业	Private Enterprises	1685	1785	186
私营有限责任公司	Private Limited Liability Corporations	1685	1785	186
外商投资企业	Foreign Funded Enterprises	29619	29615	5
外商投资股份有限公司	Share-holding Corporations Ltd. with Foreign Investment	29619	29615	5
个体经营	Individual Business	1258114	1304516	75350
个体户	Individual	1164034	1206896	73177
个人合伙	Individual Partnership	94080	97620	2173
按经营形式分	**By Form of Management**			
独立门店	Independent Stores	1296465	1348307	74711
连锁总店	General Chain Stores			
连锁门店	Branch Chain Stores	4723	6392	712
其　　他	Others	18141	17950	743
按零售业态分	**By Business Categories**			
有店铺零售	Shop Retails	1319328	1372649	76166
食杂店	Grocery Store	8022	8179	435
便利店	Convenience Store	16431	16731	1487
折扣店	Discount Store	424	702	122
超　市	Supermarket	241307	246710	14950
大型超市	Hypermarket	3160	2977	183
百货店	Department Store	54544	59835	4230
专业店	Specialty Store	673118	709599	33599
专卖店	Franchised Store	286788	291869	18083
家居建材商店	Building Material Store	31042	31612	2376
购物中心	Shopping Center	3458	3385	532
厂家直销中心	Factory Outlets Center	1036	1051	170

16-25 限额以上产业活动单位和个体户住宿业经营情况(2014年)
Management of Industrial Activity Units and Individuals above Designated Size of Hotels(2014)

单位：万元　　(10 000 yuan)

指　　标	Item	营业额 Business Value	# 客房收入 From Hotel Rooms	# 餐费收入 From Meals	# 商品销售收入 From Commodities
总　　计	**Total**	**181028**	**72717**	**79744**	**20128**
按住宿行业分	**By Hotels**				
旅游饭店	Tour Restaurant	137557	51934	62778	14974
一般旅馆	General Restaurant	42035	20245	16077	5146
其他住宿服务	Other Hotel Services	1436	538	889	8
按登记注册类型分	**By Status of Registration**				
内资企业	Domestic Funded Enterprises	125667	43840	60424	14948
国有企业	State-owned Enterprises	55759	8471	29692	14296
有限责任公司	Limited Liability Corporations	54436	28184	22917	360
其他有限责任公司	Other Limited Liability Corporations	54436	28184	22917	360
股份有限公司	Share-holding Corporations Ltd.	10449	5004	5155	129
私营企业	Private Enterprises	5023	2180	2661	164
私营有限责任公司	Private Limited Liability Corporations	5023	2180	2661	164
港澳台商投资企业	Enterprises with Funds from Hong Kong, Macao & Taiwan	13545	7431	5146	
港澳台商独资企业	Enterprises with Sole Investment	13545	7431	5146	
个体经营	Individual Business	41817	21446	14174	5180
个体户	Individual	41817	21446	14174	5180
按经营形式分	**By Form of Management**				
独立门店	Independent Stores	168979	66017	75193	19847
其　　他	Others	12050	6701	4551	281
按星级分	**By Star Rating**				
五　星	Five-star Level	34913	20105	13094	
四　星	Four-star Level	42916	3781	25209	13800
三　星	Three-star Level	4937	2285	2379	79
二　星	Two-star Level	2720	1007	1601	91
一　星	One-star Level	4368	1590	2075	703
其　他	Others	91174	43949	35387	5455

16-26 限额以上产业活动单位和个体户餐饮业经营情况(2014年)
Management of Industrial Activity Units and Individuals above Designated Size of Catering Services(2014)

单位：万元 (10 000 yuan)

指　　标	Item	营业额 Business Revenue	# 客房收入 From Hotel Rooms	# 餐费收入 From Meals	# 商品销售收入 From Commo-dities
总　计	**Total**	**347067**	**14019**	**307752**	**22773**
按餐饮行业分	**By Catering Services**				
正餐服务	Restaurant	334015	14012	294984	22563
快餐服务	Fast Food	329		329	
其他餐饮服务	Others	12723	7	12439	210
小吃服务	Snack	8035	7	7750	210
其他未列明餐饮业	Other Catering Service not Classified	4688		4688	
按登记注册类型分	**By Status of Registration**				
内资企业	Domestic Funded Enterprises	25228	4304	17697	2939
国有企业	State-owned Enterprises	8105	1034	5658	1413
集体企业	Collective-owned Enterprises	486	173	313	
有限责任公司	Limited Liability Corporations	13809	2651	9672	1253
其他有限责任公司	Other Limited Liability Corporations	13809	2651	9672	1253
股份有限公司	Share-holding Corporations Limited	551	171	380	
私营企业	Private Enterprises	1602	84	1190	273
私营有限责任公司	Private Limited Liability Corporations	1602	84	1190	273
其他企业	Other Enterprises	675	191	484	
个体经营	Individual Business	321838	9715	290054	19834
个体户	Individual	318457	9715	286673	19834
个人合伙	Individual Partnership	3382		3382	
按经营形式分	**By Form of Management**				
独立门店	Independent Stores	337070	12334	300782	21442
连锁门店	Branch Chain Stores	3079		2309	769
其　他	Others	6918	1685	4660	562

16-27 重点交易市场情况(2014年)
Focus on Transaction Markets(2014)

分类	Item	市场数(个) Number of Markets (unit)	摊位数(个) Number of Booths (unit)	年末出租摊位数(个) Number of Rented Stall(unit)	营业面积(平方米) Operating Area (sq.m)	成交额(万元) Turnover (10 000 yuan)
总计	**Total**	**52**	**36721**	**34117**	**2468845**	**4475601**
按市场类别分	**By Type of Markets**					
1.综合市场	Integrated Markets	6	5915	5550	225500	143734
工业消费品综合市场	Industrial Consumable Comprehensive Markets	2	2780	2575	123000	54943
农产品综合市场	Farm Produce Comprehensive Markets	2	2183	2036	53300	26915
其他综合市场	Other Comprehensive Markets	2	952	939	49200	61876
2.专业市场	Special Markets	46	30806	28567	2243345	4331867
生产资料市场	Production Markets	8	3591	3381	678500	768544
建材市场	Building Material Markets	6	2581	2512	493300	157544
金属材料市场	Metallic Material Markets	1	210	79	5200	450000
机械设备市场	Mechanical Equipment Markets	1	800	790	180000	161000
农产品市场	Farm Produce Markets	12	6469	5745	385312	1597035
粮油市场	Grain and Oil Markets	1	232	232	5496	274987
肉禽蛋市场	Meat, Poultry and Eggs Markets	1	1200	1006	31526	17032
水产品市场	Aquatic Product Markets	1	720	720	23000	21319
蔬菜市场	Vegetables Markets	8	3987	3662	286990	1245797
干鲜果品市场	Dried and Fresh Melons and Fruits Markets	1	330	125	38300	37900
食品、饮料及烟酒市场	Food, Beverages, Tobacco and Liquor Markets	1	1616	1616	51000	73090
茶叶市场	Tea Markets	1	1616	1616	51000	73090
纺织、服装、鞋帽市场	Textiles, Clothing, Shoes and Hats Markets	9	11041	10484	528942	740033
布料及纺织品市场	Cloth and Textiles Markets	1	1000	700	20000	36000
服装市场	Clothing Markets	6	7525	7268	342500	465510
鞋帽市场	Shoes and Hats Markets	1	2109	2109	150182	228500
其他纺织服装鞋帽市场	Others	1	407	407	16260	10023
电器、通讯器材、电子设备市场	Electrical Appliances, Communication Appliances and Electronical Appliances Markets	5	2940	2560	115699	278987
家电市场	Household Appliances Markets	1	160	160	5699	13600
通讯器材市场	Communication Appliances Markets	1	800	800	5000	11000
计算机及辅助设备市场	Computer and Auxillary Equipments Markets	3	1980	1600	105000	254387
医药、医疗用品及器材市场	Medicine, Medical Materials and Medical Instruments Markets	2	490	450	14000	64312
中药材市场	Chinese Medicine Markets	2	490	450	14000	64312
家具、五金及装饰材料市场	Furniture,Hardware and Decoration Materials Markets	5	2659	2467	363352	90966
家具市场	Furniture Markets	1	675	595	151180	14200
装饰材料市场	Decoration Materials Markets	2	842	842	169172	33132
灯具市场	Light Fittings Markets	1	230	230	10000	22634
五金材料市场	Hardware Materials Markets	1	912	800	33000	21000
汽车、摩托车及零配件市场	Cars, Motorcycles and Spare Parts Markets	4	2000	1864	106540	718900
汽车市场	Cars Markets	2	1050	970	85140	521900
机动车零配件市场	Motor Vehicle Spare Parts Markets	2	950	894	21400	197000
按营业状态分	**By Operating Status**					
常年营业	Perennial Operating	52	36721	34117	2468845	4475601
按经营方式分	**By Mode of Management**					
以批发为主	Wholesale Trade	30	20753	19159	1468453	2621667
以零售为主	Retail Trade	22	15968	14958	1000392	1853934
按经营环境分	**By Environment of Management**					
露天式	Open air	12	6278	5689	375124	1280593
封闭式	Closed	32	25653	23790	1816019	2909624
其他	Others	8	4790	4638	277702	285384

16-28 重点交易市场商品销售类值(2014年)
Total Sales at Main Trade Markets by Category of Commodities(2014)

类别	Item	摊位数(个) Number of Booths (unit)	成交额(万元) Turnover (10 000 yuan)
总计	**Total**	**34117**	**4475601**
粮油、食品类	Food	7897	1633118
# 粮油类	Grain and Oil	582	304680
肉禽蛋类	Meat, Poultry and Eggs	1499	135559
水产品类	Aquatic Products	951	57576
蔬菜类	Vegetables	3858	1060407
干鲜果品类	Dried and Fresh Melons and Fruits	920	70316
饮料类	Beverages	2004	87092
烟酒类	Tobacco and Liquor	95	2215
服装、鞋帽、针纺织品类	Garments, Shoes and Hats, Knitwear and Textiles	11276	748003
服装类	Garments	7965	480014
鞋帽类	Shoes and Hats	1771	182880
针纺织品类	Knitwear and Textiles	1540	85109
化妆品类	Cosmetics	147	4403
金银珠宝类	Gold, Silver and Jewelry	50	1100
日用品类	Daily Consumer Articles	1018	36714
# 儿童玩具类	Children Toys	117	1808
五金、电料类	Hardware	1083	41107
体育、娱乐用品类	Sports and Recreation Articles	109	2956
书报杂志类	Newspapers and Magazines	6	55
电子出版物及音像制品类	E-journals and Video Products	104	9446
家用电器和音像器材类	Household Appliances and Audio/Video Equipments	386	27672
中西药品类	Traditional Chinese and Western Medicines	450	64312
# 中草药及中成药类	Traditional Chinese Medicines	450	64312
文化办公用品类	Cultural and Office Appliances	1128	163522
# 计算机及其配套产品	Computer and Auxillary Equipments	972	158329
家具类	Furniture	581	23583
通讯器材类	Communication Appliances	1160	62680
化工材料及制品类	Chemical Materials and Products	24	170000
金属材料类	Metal Materials	55	280000
建筑及装潢材料类	Building and Decoration Materials	3485	196892
机电产品及设备类	Mechanical and Electrical Products and Equipments	790	161000
汽车类	Automobiles	1864	718900
种子饲料类	Seeds and Feedstuff	5	79
其他类	Others	400	40752

16-29 重点交易市场成交情况(2014年)
Turnover of Main Commodity Transaction Markets(2014)

市场 Market	摊位数（个） Number of Booths (unit)	成交额（万元） Turnover (10 000 yuan)	市场 Market	摊位数（个） Number of Booths (unit)	成交额（万元） Turnover (10 000 yuan)
海星手机市场	800	11000	西安万寿路中药材批发市场南二区实业有限公司	220	27572
陕西义乌商城物业管理有限公司	975	23795	（西安市灞桥区万北物业管理服务处）		
西安金康茶叶街市场	1616	73090	西安万寿路中药材批发市场北二区实业有限公司	230	36740
（西安金康茶文化传播有限公司）			西安大明宫灞桥建材家具股份有限公司	595	14200
陕西银邦经营管理有限公司	2378	326723	西安大明宫五金机电灯饰城	800	21000
陕西多彩商城市场	2480	40300	西安大明国际汽车配件城	474	120000
（陕西多彩企业集团有限公司）			（西安大明国际汽车配件城有限责任公司）		
昌安商贸服装批发市场	199	11990	西北管材铝塑型材批发基地	119	21931
陕西时丹达服装城管理有限公司	416	17600	（西安源兴实业有限公司）		
陕西丹尼尔商贸城有限公司	839	31650	大明宫管业暖通交易中心	550	14760
锦绣国际商贸城有限公司	2109	228500	（西安源鑫置业有限公司）		
西安胡家庙果品批发市场	125	37900	西安朱雀农产品交易中心	822	230815
西安粮油批发交易市场	232	274987	西安五龙汽车城有限公司	90	42000
西安和信实业开发有限责任公司家电市场	160	13600	宝鸡市恒丰园农产品发展有限公司	482	59849
（西安和信实业有限责任公司）			宝鸡市冠森大世界现代家居建材(城)有限公司	426	18521
西安胡家庙蔬菜批发市场	307	48000	咸阳市秦都区嘉惠商业区	956	37247
西安铁路局西铁大市场	235	12395	咸阳南郊装饰建材市场	367	31022
西安赛格电脑城	1050	215487	咸阳天元建材市场	600	53310
（西安赛格商贸有限公司）			咸阳新阳光西北农副产品交易中心	725	543000
西安东新科技贸易中心	360	28300	陕西泾云现代农业股份有限公司	300	95000
西安赛博数码广场有限公司	190	10600	大荔县同州农副产品批发市场	1801	14520
西安市文艺南路纺织品批发市场	700	36000	陕西省汉中市汽车运输总公司运达批发市场	1600	31148
西安市玉林汽配批发市场有限责任公司	420	77000	汉中皇冠过街楼蔬菜批发市场	353	165900
西安海纳汽车服务有限公司西安汽配市场	880	479900	城固县蔬菜瓜果批发市场	236	93159
西安蔚蓝机电市场有限公司	790	161000	陕西城固经贸市场	734	36428
陕西三盟庆安建材市场	450	18000	绥德县五一商城综合批发市场	205	25448
西安市方欣冷冻市场	720	21319	安康市满意建材市场有限公司	462	22532
西安国亨市场	1006	17032	安康市安运运输集团汽车运输有限公司批发市场	407	10023
陕西省生产资料第一交易市场	79	450000	安康市汉滨区兴安副食品批发市场	437	10074
同泰灯具城（陕西同泰实业有限公司）	230	22634	陕西省安康市兴华建设集团有限公司综合批发市场	380	10600

16-30 成品油批发企业能源购进、销售与库存(2014年)

Total Purchases, Sales and Inventory of Energy of Petroleum Products Enterprises in Wholesale Trades in the Whole Province(2014)

单位：吨 (ton)

能源品种	Type of Energy	年初库存量 Stock at the Beginning of the Year	本年购进量 Purchases (This Year)	# 购自省外 Purchases outside the Province	本年销售量 Sales (This Year)	# 销往省外 Sales outside the Province	# 售予省内批发和零售企业 Sale to Wholesale and Retail Enterprises in the Province	年末库存量 Stock at Year-end
汽　油	Gasoline	142361	11814027	523934	9338288	2454579	6370633	189050
# 93"	# 93"	103053	7770053	420379	7830030	2409156	5151737	54394
柴　油	Diesel Oil	349490	14964124	2137014	14964759	3047010	10350318	278340
# 0"	# 0"	334870	13355871	1092830	13333455	2007545	9792618	258796
煤　油	Kerosene	23762	1442663	427273	1412503	431332	359964	15741
燃料油	Fuel Oil	10	23793	13619	23765	22316	1449	38
润滑油	Lubricant oil	3106	8390	1973	8061	2021	5284	2537

16-31 各市(区)成品油批发企业能源购进量(2014年)

Total Purchases of Energy of Petroleum Products Enterprises in Wholesale Trades by City(District)(2014)

单位：吨 (ton)

地　区	Region	企业数(个) Number of Enterprises (unit)	汽　油 Gasoline	# 93"	柴　油 Diesel Oil	# 0"	煤　油 Kerosene	燃料油 Fuel Oil	润滑油 Lubricant Oil
全　省	**Shaanxi**	**59**	**11814027**	**7770053**	**14964124**	**13355871**	**1442663**	**23793**	**8390**
西安市	Xi'an	20	7841672	4396277	7967553	6641037	1020388	10383	713
铜川市	Tongchuan	2	45550	29111	124382	113891			457
宝鸡市	Baoji	2	259863	217193	674397	657795			1641
咸阳市	Xianyang	7	2317310	2192401	3621868	3554261	358629		218
渭南市	Weinan	2	3449		35743				
# 韩城市	Hancheng	1	3449		2842				
延安市	Yan'an	3	481679	261117	838740	795964			894
汉中市	Hanzhong	10	259756	251196	357577	346510	13007	13410	2944
榆林市	Yulin	7	458806	303345	1067585	991569			801
安康市	Ankang	3	107323	84507	187110	165675			165
商洛市	Shangluo	2	27741	25011	76229	76229	50639		557
杨凌示范区	Yangling	1	10877	9895	12940	12940			

16-32 各市(区)成品油批发企业能源销售量(2014年)
Total Sales of Energy of Petroleum Products Enterprises in Wholesale Trades by City(District)(2014)

单位：吨 (ton)

地区	Region	企业数(个) Number of Enterprises (unit)	汽油 Gasoline	#93"	柴油 Diesel Oil	#0"	煤油 Kerosene	燃料油 Fuel Oil	润滑油 Lubricant Oil
全省	**Shaanxi**	**59**	**9338288**	**7830030**	**14964759**	**13333455**	**1412503**	**23765**	**8061**
西安市	Xi'an	20	5304243	4430771	7909902	6590401	1040852	10383	687
铜川市	Tongchuan	2	88659	30027	125297	116375			492
宝鸡市	Baoji	2	259697	216867	674907	657716			1615
咸阳市	Xianyang	7	2330144	2213967	3622948	3555459	358629		157
渭南市	Weinan	2	3439		35778				
#韩城市	Hancheng	1	3439		2834				
延安市	Yan'an	3	482739	262270	842937	800223			822
汉中市	Hanzhong	10	258192	247599	349509	338442	13022	13382	2695
榆林市	Yulin	7	462086	303735	1103938	996493			726
安康市	Ankang	3	106512	84352	188877	167680			173
商洛市	Shangluo	2	31721	30995	97870	97870			694
杨凌示范区	Yangling	1	10856	9447	12796	12796			

16-33 各市(区)成品油批发企业能源年末库存量(2014年)
Inventory of Energy of Petroleum Products Enterprises in Wholesale Trades by City(District) at Year-end(2014)

单位：吨 (ton)

地区	Region	企业数(个) Number of Enterprises (unit)	汽油 Gasoline	#93"	柴油 Diesel Oil	#0"	煤油 Kerosene	燃料油 Fuel Oil	润滑油 Lubricant Oil
全省	**Shaanxi**	**59**	**189050**	**54394**	**278340**	**258796**	**15741**	**38**	**2537**
西安市	Xi'an	20	134700	22242	184697	180109	15732		281
铜川市	Tongchuan	2	2531	255	1888	916			173
宝鸡市	Baoji	2	4214	3454	9384	8490			410
咸阳市	Xianyang	7	16962	6258	29827	29350			370
渭南市	Weinan	2	10		251				
#韩城市	Hancheng	1	10		8				
延安市	Yan'an	3	3107	2168	3621	1814			348
汉中市	Hanzhong	10	6147	5971	7279	7133	9	38	551
榆林市	Yulin	7	18077	12026	34416	26659			294
安康市	Ankang	3	1909	1032	3812	2235			91
商洛市	Shangluo	2	1248	896	2797	1721			110
杨凌示范区	Yangling	1	146	91	368	368			

主要统计指标解释

批发业　指批发商向批发、零售单位及其他企事业、机关单位批量销售生活用品和生产资料的活动，以及从事进出口贸易和贸易经纪与代理的活动。批发商可以对所批发的货物拥有所有权，并以本单位、公司的名义进行交易活动；也可以不拥有货物的所有权，而以中介身份做代理销售商。还包括各类商品批发市场中固定摊位的批发活动。

零售业　指百货商店、超级市场、专门零售商店、品牌专卖店、售货摊等主要面向最终消费者（如居民等）的销售活动。包括以互联网、邮政、电话、售货机等方式的销售活动，还包括在同地点，后面加工生产，前面销售的店铺（如前店后厂的面包房）。不包括：谷物、种子、饲料、牲畜、矿产品、生产用原料、化工原料、农用化工产品、机械设备（用车、计算机及通信设备等除外）等生产资料的销售（批发业）；非零售单位附带的零售活动（如汽车修理单位销售汽车零件）；商业零售单位所在商厦的物业管理(物业管理)；商业零售单位所在的商品市场、商业大厦的市场管理活动（市场管理）。

住宿业　指有偿为顾客提供临时住宿的服务活动，不包括提供长期住宿场所的活动（如出租房屋、公寓等）。

餐饮业　指在一定场所，对食物进行现场烹饪、调制，并出售给顾客主要供现场消费的服务活动。

社会消费品零售总额　指批发和零售业、餐饮业、新闻出版业、邮政业和其他服务业等，售予城乡居民用于生活消费的商品和社会集团用于公共消费的商品之总量。社会消费品零售总额包括：

一、批发和零售业企业（单位）售予城乡居民用于生活消费和社会集团用于公共消费的商品。包括：

1.售予城乡居民的各种生活消费品；

2.售予入境旅游的外国人、华侨、港澳台同胞的各类商品；

3.售予行政事业单位、社会团体、军队和武警等机构的商品，以及以零售方式售予各类企业的商品。具体包括：用于非生产和社会交往的办公用品，如通讯设备、计算器具和设备、电讯网络设备、文印设备、音像视听器材和设备、纸张、本册、文具及装订文印材料、家具、日用电器、针纺织品、清洁卫生用品、文体用品、奖品、纪念品、礼品等；供内部人员乘坐的交通工具和燃料；用于办公设施修缮的各类配件、材料、工具等；用于取暖和防暑降温的设备、燃料、材料及食品等；专用于教学的用品和设备；非营利医疗机构的中、西药品、中药材和医疗设备器材；非专用的劳动保护用品；不对外营业的内部食堂用的餐具、炊具、设备、清洁卫生工具和食品、燃料等；军队、武警用于其人员生活的衣着品和个人用品；其他各类非生产性设备和用品。

二、餐饮业出售的主食、菜肴、烟酒饮料和其他商品。

三、新闻出版业、邮政业售予城乡居民、企事业单位、军队和武警等机构的书报杂志、音像制品、邮品等。

四、其他服务业出售的食品、烟酒饮料、服装鞋帽、日常生活用品、医药保健用品、艺术品、工艺美术品、玩具、殡葬用品以及其他消费品。

批发和零售业商品购进、销售、库存总额　指各种登记注册类型的批发和零售业企业(单位)以本企业(单位)为总体的，从国内、国外市场购进的商品总量，销售和出口的商品总量、库存的商品总量等情况。该指标可以反映商品流转过程中商品的购进、销售、库存之间的比例关系和存在的问题。

购进总额　指从本企业(单位)以外的单位和个人购进(包括从境外直接进口)作为转卖或加工后转卖的商品总额。它反映批发和零售业从国内、国外市场上购进商品的总量。商品购进包括：(1)从工农业生产者购进的商品；(2)从出版社、报社的出版发行部门购进的图书、杂志和报纸；(3)从各种登记注册类型的批发和零售业企业(单位)购进的商品；(4)从其他单位购进的商品，如从机关、团体、企业等单位购进的剩余物资，从住宿和餐饮业、其他服务业购进的商品，从海关、市场管理部门购进的缉私和没收的商品，从居民手中收购的废旧商品等；(5)从国(境)外直接进口的商品。不包括企业(单位)为自身经营用和未通过买卖行为而收入的商品以及销售退回、商品升溢等。

销售总额　指对本企业(单位)以外的单位和个人出售(包括对境外直接出口)的商品总额。它反映批发和零售业在国内市场上销售商品以及出口商品的总量。商品销售包括：(1)售给城乡居民和社会集团消费用的商品；(2)售给工业、农业、建筑业、运输邮电业、批发和零售业、住宿和餐饮业、其他服务业等作为生产、经营使用的商品；(3)售给批发和零售业作为转卖或加工后转卖的商品；(4)对国(境)外直接出口的商品。不包括出售本企业(单位)自用的废旧包装用品，未通过买卖行为付出的商品，经本单位介绍、由买卖双方直接结算、本单位只收取手续费的业务，购货退出的商品以及商品损耗和损失等。

库存总额　指报告期末各种登记注册类型的批发和零售业企业(单位)已取得所有权的商品。它反映批发和零售业企业(单位)的商品库存情况和对市场商品供应的保证程度。商品库存包括：(1)存放在批发和零售业经营单位(如门市部、批发站、经营处)仓库、货场、货柜和货架中的商品；(2)挑选、整理、包装中的商品；(3)已记入购进而尚未运到本单位的商品，即发货单或银行承兑凭证已到而货未到的商品；(4)寄放他处的商品，如因购货方拒绝承付而暂时存放在购货方的商品和已办完加工成品收回手续而未提回的商品；(5)委托其他单位代销(未作销售或调出)尚未售出的商品；(6)代其他单位购进尚未交付的商品。不包括所有权不属于本单位的商品、委托外单位加工生产尚未收回成品的商品、外贸企业代理其他单位从国外进口尚未付给订货单位的商品、代国家物资储备部门保管的商品等。

住宿和餐饮业营业额 指住宿和餐饮业法人企业（单位）在经营活动中因提供服务或销售商品等取得的收入。包括：客房收入、餐费收入、商品销售额和其他收入。客房收入指住宿和餐饮业法人企业（单位）在经营活动中因提供住宿服务取得的收入。餐费收入指住宿和餐饮业法人企业、（单位）因为顾客提供就餐服务取得的收入，包括经烹饪、调制加工后出售的各种食品，如主食、炒菜、凉拌菜等的收入。商品销售额指住宿和餐饮业法人企业（单位）伴随服务而出售商品所取得的收入（含增值税）。其他收入指营业收入中除客房收入、餐费收入、商品销售额以外的其他收入，包括娱乐、健身和商务服务等。

连锁企业（或称连锁店、连锁公司） 指在核心企业或总店的领导下，由分散的、经营同类商品或服务的企业或活动单位，采取共同方针，实行集中采购和分散销售的有机结合，通过规范化经营，实现规模效益的经济联合组织形式。一般连锁店应由若干个分店组成。其经营特征：(1)经营同类商品；(2)使用统一商号；(3)统一采购配送，采购与销售相分离（部分商品可根据物流合理和保质保鲜原则，由供应商直接送货到门店，其余均由总部统一配送）。

连锁门店的形式分为直营连锁和加盟连锁。

直营连锁也叫正规连锁。指连锁门店均由总部独资或控股开设，在总部的直接领导下统一经营。总部采取纵深似的管理方式，直接下令掌管所有的零售门店，零售门店也必须完全接受总部指挥。这是大型垄断商业资本通过吞并、兼并或独资、控股等途径，发展壮大自身实力和规模的一种形式。

加盟连锁包括特许连锁和自由连锁两种形式。

特许连锁指各连锁门店（被特许人）通过合同形式，取得使用总部（特许人）商标、商号、经营技术和销售总部开发的商品的特许权，各加盟连锁门店为独立法人，在总部指导下统一经营。

自由连锁也称自愿连锁。指连锁公司的门店均为独立法人，各自的资产所有权关系不变，在公司总部的指导下共同经营。各成员店使用共同的店名，与总部订阅有关购、销、宣传等方面的合同，并按合同开展经营活动。在合同规定的范围之外，各成员店可以自由活动。根据自愿原则，各成员店可自由加入连锁体系，也可自由退出。

Explanatory Notes on Main Statistical Indicators

Wholesale Trade refers to the activities of wholesaler selling at wholesale commodities for daily use and capital goods to enterprises of wholesale and retail trades and other enterprises, institutions and government offices, including the activities of wholesaler engaged in import and export and acting as a trade agent. The wholesaler may have the right of ownership over the commodities of wholesale and trade in the name of its own or a company, the wholesaler may not have the right of ownership, only acts an agent. The wholesale trade also include the activities of wholesaler at the fixed stalls of the wholesale market of different commodities.

Retail Trade refers to the activities of department store, supermarket, franchised store, brand store, retail stall and on-the-spot-making-selling store selling commodities to the final consumers (citizens) by any means including internet, post, telephone, sales machine. Retail trade excludes the activities of sales of capital goods such a grain, seed, feed, livestock, mineral products, raw material for production, industrial chemicals, chemical products for farm, machine and equipment (vehicle, computer and communication equipment), and the activities of supplementary sales of non-retailer such as the sales of spare parts of car repair business

Hotel Services refer to the activities of enterprises providing paid services of lodging to the customer, excluding the activities of providing long period of services of lodging (such as leased house and apartments).

Catering Services refer to the activities of enterprises providing on-the-spot services of selling food cooked and prepared to the customer in certain sites

Total Retail Sales of Consumer Goods refer to the sum of retail sales of commodities sold by wholesale and retail trades, catering services, publishing, post and telecommunications and other service industries to urban and rural households for household consumption and to social institutions for public consumption. Retail sales of consumer goods include:

1) Sales sold by wholesale and retail trades to urban and rural households for household consumption and to social institutions for public consumption.

a) Of commodities to urban and rural households;

b) Of commodities to foreigners, overseas Chinese and Chinese compatriots from Hong Kong, Macao and Taiwan visiting China;

c) Of commodities to government agencies, institutions, social organizations, military and armed police units, and commodities to enterprises in the form of retail sales. More specifically, they include: office facilities and articles for non-production purposes such as communications equipment, computing equipment and instruments, TV and network equipment, printing and copying equipment, audio-visual equipment and instruments, paper, notebooks, stationeries, furniture, electric appliances, knitwear, sanitation and cleaning articles, cultural and sport articles, articles for prizes, souvenirs, etc.; transport vehicles and fuels for employees; materials, spare parts and tools for the maintenance of office facilities; equipment, fuels, materials and food for winter heating or summer cooling purposes; articles and equipment for teaching purpose; Chinese and western medicines and medical equipment and facilities purchased by non profit-making medical institutes; non-specialized work safety articles; cooking utensils, tableware, equipment, cleaning articles, food and fuels purchased by in-house cafeterias; clothes and personal articles purchased by military or armed police units for their officials and soldiers; and other equipment and articles for non-production purposes.

2) Sales of stable food, cooked dishes, beverages, tobaccos and other articles by catering units.

3) Sales of books, newspapers, magazines, audio-visual products and post products by publishing, post and telecommunications departments to urban and rural households and to enterprises, institutions, military and armed police units.

4) Sales of food, beverages, tobaccos, clothing, hats, footwear, articles for daily use, medicines, medical and health articles, work of art, handicrafts, toys, funeral articles and other articles by other service industries.

Purchase, Sales and Stock of Commodities by Wholesale and Retail Trades refer to the total volume of commodities purchased, total volume of sales and exports, and the stock of commodities by wholesale and retail enterprises (establishments) of different status of registration from domestic and overseas markets. This indicator reflects the relationship among purchase, sales and stock of commodities in the circulation of goods and reveals the existing problems.

Total Purchases of Commodities refer to the total value of purchases of commodities by enterprises (establishments) from other establishments or individuals (including direct import from abroad) for the purpose of re-selling, either with or without further processing of the commodities purchased. The commodities include: (1) commodities purchased from agricultural and industrial producer, wholesaler, retailer, publishing house and other service business; (2) commodities purchased from institutions and government departments; (3) confiscated goods purchased from the customs authorities or market management agencies; (4) second-hand goods and wastes purchased from residents; The commodities exclude 1 commodities purchased by enterprises (establishments) for use in their own business operation, commodities obtained without buying or selling procedures such as materials, consumable goods of low value, office appliances, etc. 2 received goods without trading, such as goods handed over from others, borrowed goods, preserved goods for others, donated goods from others, processed and retrieved goods, etc. 3. Goods of direct settlement between buyer and seller with handling fees introduced by others, 4. Goods returned or refused to pay by the buyer, 5. Excessive goods.

Total Sales of Commodities refer to value of commodities sold by the establishments to other establishments and individuals (including goods sold for self consumption, including the value-added tax). The commodities include: (1) Commodities sold to urban and rural residents and social groups for their consumption; (2) Commodities sold to establishments in all industries for their production and operation, including agriculture, industry, construction, transportation, post and telecommunications, catering services, and public utility including commodities sold to wholesale and retail establishments for re-selling, with or without further processing; and (3) Commodities for direct export to abroad. Excluded are (1) Extended commodities without trading, such as goods handed over to other enterprises and institutions because of the change of organizations, lent goods, returned goods preserved for others, extended processing materials and samples donated to others, (2) Goods of direct settlement between buyer and seller with handling fees introduced by others, 3. Goods returned after purchase, (4) Damaged and spoiled goods, (5) waste and used goods of self use,

Total Stock of Commodities refers to total commodities possessed by wholesaler and retailer of various types of registration status at the end of the reference period, reflecting the commodity stock level of various wholesaler and retailer and the potential for market supply. It includes: (1) Commodities located in storage, garages, counters, and shelves of operating places (such as sale stores, wholesale centres, and operating offices); (2) Commodities in the process of being selected, sorted, and packed; (3) Commodities not arrived but recorded as purchase in the account, i.e. commodities not arrived but payment receipts for the commodities from the sellers or the banks arrived; (4)Commodities deposited in other places rather than places mentioned above, for instance: commodities in the hold of purchasers temporarily due to the refusal of payment and commodities not taken back after going through the formalities; (5) Commodities entrusted to other units to sell but not sold yet; (6) Commodities purchased for other units but not delivered yet. Commodities not included as stock are those not owned by the enterprises (units), commodities on commission for processing but not yet delivered, imported commodities of agency of foreign trade enterprise but not yet delivered to ordering units and finally those put in stock on behalf of the state material reserves units.

Business Revenue of Hotels and Catering Services refers to revenue received from providing services or selling commodities by corporate enterprises and establishments engaged in hotels and catering services, including income from hotels, from catering services, from selling of commodities and from other services. Income from hotels refers to income of corporate enterprises and establishments engaged in hotels and catering services by providing lodging services. Income from catering services refers to income of corporate enterprises and establishments engaged in hotels and catering services by providing catering services, including selling of cooked or prepared foods such as staple food, cooked dishes or cold dishes. Income from selling of commodities refers to income of corporate enterprises and establishments engaged in hotels and catering services by selling commodities (including value-added tax) that accompany the services they provide. Income from other activities refers to income received other than income from hotels, catering services or selling of commodities, such as income from providing recreation, fitness or business services.

Chain Head Stores (headquarter) refer to the core leading stores responsible for development, allocation, administration and utilization of resources (name of stores, brand of stores, operation model, service standard, management way, ect.) of chain stores. Chain stores refers to the stores engaged in providing homogeneous commodities or services, with the central leadership of head store and guided by common policies, conduct centralized purchase and distributed selling of commodities, in order to gain better efficiency through standardized operation. The chain stores include regular chain stores, franchise chain stores and voluntary chain stores.

Regular Chain store refers to chain stores that are invested or controlled by the headquarters. They operate under direct and unified management from the headquarters.

Franchise chain store refers to the chain stores (franchisees) which are franchised with operation resources such as trade marks, names, patent and operation know-how by the franchisors in form of contract and pay the operation fees to the franchisors

Voluntary chain store refers the stores operate jointly on the voluntary bases while maintaining their status of independent legal entities with full ownership of their assets. They sell goods of same brand from same channel of resource to the consumers.

十七、对外经济贸易和旅游

Foreign Trade and Tourism

资料整理：岳　洋

简 要 说 明

一、本篇资料反映陕西对外贸易和旅游业发展状况，内容包括进出口总值，进出口货物的品种、数(重)量、金额，利用外资、旅游人数和旅游收入，星级饭店基本情况等。

二、进出口商品总值按经营单位所在地统计。经营单位所在地是指境内进出口企业报关注册的登记地。

三、本篇资料由西安海关、省商务厅、省旅游局提供。

Brief Introduction

I. This chapter reflects development of international trades and tourism of Shaanxi, including kind, quantity(weight) and value of imported and exported products, utilization of foreign funds, tourist number and tourism revenue, basic conditions of star hotels, etc.

II. Total value of imported and exported commodities are calculated according to the location of operating units. The location of operating units is the place of registration where the resident imported and exported enterprises declare and register at customs.

III. The data sources are provided by Xi'an Customs District, the Department of Commerce Shaanxi Province and Tourism Administration of Shaanxi Province.

17.对外经济贸易和旅游

2014年全省				
进出口总额	1680.83	亿　元	比上年增长	34.8%
#出　口	855.57	亿　元	比上年增长	34.9%
实际利用外商直接投资额	41.76	亿美元	比上年增长	13.5%
入境旅游人数	266.30	万　人	比上年增长	5.1%
国际旅游收入	14.16	亿美元	比上年增长	5.5%

进出口总额（亿美元）

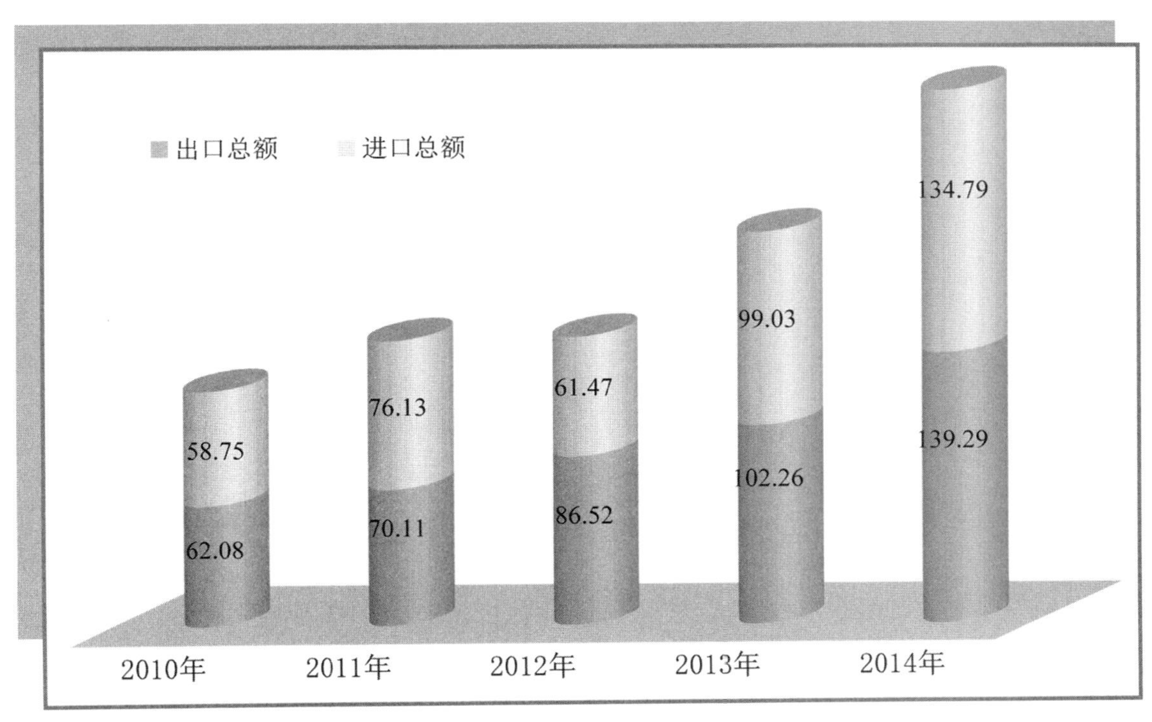

17-1 外贸进出口总值

Total Value of Imports and Exports in Foreign Trade

单位：万美元 (USD 10 000)

年 份 Year	进出口总值 Total Value of Imports and Exports	出 口 Exports	进 口 Imports
1978		1190	
1980		973	
1985	15712	10359	5353
1990	57728	46059	11669
1991	81359	60502	20857
1992	111885	76531	35354
1993	149599	99347	50252
1994	160061	121615	38446
1995	173323	128261	45062
1996	178406	126922	51484
1997	173413	123120	50293
1998	205148	117668	87480
1999	200834	115225	85609
2000	214009	131003	83006
2001	206444	111044	95400
2002	222517	137717	84800
2003	278371	173523	104848
2004	364238	239658	124580
2005	457684	307581	150103
2006	536025	362960	173065
2007	688804	467244	221560
2008	832867	538066	294801
2009	840539	398815	441724
2010	1208283	620773	587510
2011	1462344	701085	761258
2012	1479854	865178	614677
2013	2012881	1022617	990265
2014	2740847	1392926	1347921

注：2014年数据来源于《中国统计摘要－2015》。
a)Data of 2014 are from "China Statistical Abstract-2015".

17-2 按贸易方式分外贸进口总值
Total Value of Imports in Foreign Trade by Type of Trade

单位：万元 (10 000 yuan)

贸易方式类别	Type of Trade	2014	2014年比2013年增长(%) Growth Rate in 2014 over 2013(%)
进口总值	**Total Imports**	**8252555**	**34.6**
1.一般贸易	General Trade	1707564	-18.0
2.国家间、国际组织无偿援助和赠送的物资	Between Countries, International Organizations Aid and Donated Materials		
3.华侨、港澳台同胞、外籍华人捐赠物资	The overseas Chinese, Hong Kong, Macao, Taiwan,Chinese of foreign Donated Materials		
4.来料加工装配贸易	Assembly Processing Trade	30731	-13.1
5.进料加工贸易	Processing With Imported Trade	4371260	60.7
6.来料加工装配进口的设备	Assembly Processing Trade Equipment		
7.租赁贸易	Lease Trade	20	-56.1
8.外商投资企业作为投资进口的设备、物品	Foreign-invested Enterprises as the Import Investment of Equipment, Goods	8092	-9.2
9.出料加工贸易	Material Processing		
10.易货贸易	Barter		
11.保税监管场所进出境货物(保税仓库进出境货物)	Inward and Outward Goods of Free Trade Storehouse	28049	-74.8
12.海关特殊监管区域物流货物(保税区仓储转口货物)	Re-export Goods of Free Trade Zone Re-exports	1575182	46.3
13.海关特殊监管区域进口设备(出口加工区进口设备)	Export Processing Zones Imported Equipment	509730	563.7
14.其　他	Other	22293	49.6

17-3 按贸易方式分外贸出口总值
Total Value of Exports in Foreign Trade by Type of Trade

单位：万元 (10 000 yuan)

贸易方式类别	Type of Trade	2014	2014年比2013年增长(%) Growth Rate in 2014 over 2013(%)
出口总值	**Total Exports**	**8555749**	**34.9**
1.一般贸易	General Trade	3367086	6.2
2.国家间、国际组织无偿援助和赠送的物资	Between Countries, International Organizations Aid and Donated Materials	170	-98.8
3.来料加工装配贸易	Assembly Processing Trade	35836	-22.5
4.进料加工贸易	Processing With Imported Trade	4986773	150.6
5.对外承包工程出口货物	Exports Contracted Projects	90774	-25.2
6.租赁贸易	Lease Trade	1431	447.9
7.易货贸易	Barter		
8.出料加工贸易	Material Processing	65	
9.保税监管场所进出境货物(保税仓库进出境货物)	Inward and Outward Goods of Free Trade Storehouse	5876	-87.3
10.海关特殊监管区域物流货物	Re-export Goods of Free Trade Zone	64732	-93.2
11.其　他	Others	3174	-13.5

17-4 按国别(地区)分外贸进出口总值(2014年)
Total Value of Imports and Exports in Foreign Trade by Country (Region)(2014)

单位：万元 (10 000 yuan)

国别(地区)	Country(Region)	进出口 Total	出口 Exports	进口 Imports
总值	**Total**	**16808305**	**8555749**	**8252555**
阿富汗	Afghanistan	478	478	
巴林	Bahrain	3311	3311	
孟加拉国	Bangladesh	17126	16671	455
不丹	Bhutan	47	47	
文莱	Brunei	8809	8809	
缅甸	Myanmar	19231	19231	
柬埔寨	Cambodia	18415	18412	3
塞浦路斯	Cyprus	737	737	
朝鲜	Korea DPR	4420	4420	
中国香港	Hong Kong, China	1762375	1740993	21383
印度	India	151431	116141	35289
印尼	Indonesia	60380	52066	8314
伊朗	Iran	216968	214169	2799
伊拉克	Iraq	12263	12263	
以色列	Israel	61957	12395	49562
日本	Japan	962956	344188	618768
约旦	Jordan	5222	4959	263
科威特	Kuwait	12714	12714	
老挝	Laos	4066	4066	
黎巴嫩	Lebanon	1593	1593	
中国澳门	Macao, China	600	600	
马来西亚	Malaysia	281834	143613	138221
马尔代夫	Maldives	18	18	
蒙古	Mongolia	9419	9419	
尼泊尔联邦民主共和国	Nepal	1088	1084	4
阿曼	Oman	6033	6033	
巴基斯坦	Pakistan	25293	25080	213
巴勒斯坦	Palestine	79	79	
菲律宾	Philippines	70289	39798	30491
卡塔尔	Qatar	3827	3827	
沙特阿拉伯	Saudi Arabia	56543	56543	
新加坡	Singapore	643972	319222	324750
韩国	Korea Rep.	1753092	829443	923648
斯里兰卡	Sri Lanka	9563	9290	273
叙利亚	Syria	1087	1087	
泰国	Thailand	108295	90076	18219
土耳其	Turkey	44770	40137	4633
阿拉伯联合酋长国	United Arab Emirates	61205	61204	2
也门	Republic of Yemen	1408	1407	1
越南	Vietnam	118098	114561	3537
中国	P. R. China	62480		62480
中国台湾	Taiwan, China	2648700	497224	2151475
哈萨克斯坦	Kazakhstan	64816	64816	
吉尔吉斯	Kirghizia	3259	3259	
塔吉克斯坦	Tadzhikistan	16692	16692	
土库曼斯坦	Turkmenistan	21551	21551	

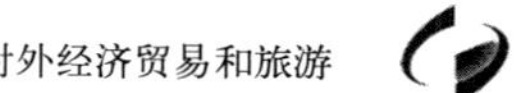

17-4 续表 1 continued

单位：万元 (10 000 yuan)

国别(地区)	Country(Region)	进出口 Total	出口 Exports	进口 Imports
乌兹别克斯坦	Uzbekistan	17736	17736	
阿尔及利亚	Algeria	131513	131512	2
安哥拉	Angola	41049	41049	
贝 宁	Benin	5655	4819	836
博茨瓦纳	Botswana	225	225	
布隆迪	Burundi	83	83	
喀麦隆	Cameroon	8131	7009	1122
佛得角	Cape Verde	3	3	
中 非	Central Africa	1071	1071	
乍 得	Chad	153	153	
科摩罗	Comoros	55	55	
刚 果	Congo	2205	2205	
吉布提	Djibouti	1946	1946	
埃 及	Egypt	38652	38571	81
赤道几内亚	Eq. Guinea	2802	2802	
埃塞俄比亚	Ethiopia	24252	24252	
加 蓬	Gabon	221	221	
冈比亚	Gambia	93	93	
加 纳	Gambia	8715	6256	2459
几内亚	Guinea	965	965	
可特迪瓦	Cote d'lvoire	344	258	85
肯尼亚	Kenya	6341	6334	7
利比里亚	Liberia	9335	79	9255
利比亚	Libya	3443	3443	
马达加斯加	Madagascar	730	712	19
马拉维	Malawi	31	31	
马 里	Mali	776	393	382
毛里塔尼亚	Mauritania	34746	502	34244
毛里求斯	Mauritius	444	444	
摩洛哥	Morocco	6772	3122	3650
莫桑比克	Mozambique	11678	11642	36
纳米比亚	Namibia	663	591	72
尼日尔	Niger	132	132	
尼日利亚	Nigeria	26298	26228	70
留尼汪	Reunion	45	45	
卢旺达	Rwanda	1648	1648	
塞内加尔	Senegal	1	1	
塞舌尔	Seychelles	1130	1130	
塞拉利昂	Sierra Leone	60	60	
索马里	Somalia	4056	867	3190
南 非	South Africa	30	30	
西撒哈拉	Western Sahara	317596	46489	271107
苏 丹	Sudan	5858	5803	56
坦桑尼亚	Tanzania	4577	4577	
多 哥	Togo	3853	3853	
突尼斯	Tunisia	2183	2025	157
乌干达	Uganda	1091	1091	
布基纳法索	Burkina Faso	604	1	603
扎伊尔	Zaire	6507	1259	5249
赞比亚	Zambia	7628	5631	1997
津巴布韦	Zimbabwe	554	554	
莱索托	Lesotho	5	5	
斯威士兰	Swaziland	65	57	8
厄立特里亚	Eritrea	6	6	

17-4 续表 2 continued

单位：万元 (10 000 yuan)

国别(地区)	Country(Region)	进出口 Total	出 口 Exports	进 口 Imports
比利时	Belgium	157484	46931	110553
丹 麦	Denmark	25696	4273	21424
英 国	United Kingdom	381043	331353	49691
德 国	Germany	404513	120061	284451
法 国	France	279901	214235	65666
爱尔兰	Ireland	46782	4278	42504
意大利	Italy	127754	59274	68481
卢森堡	Luxembourg	921	60	860
荷 兰	Netherlands	339359	116485	222874
希 腊	Greece	15237	15235	3
葡萄牙	Portugal	2525	2223	302
西班牙	Spain	34734	23880	10854
阿尔巴尼亚	Albania	625	625	
奥地利	Austria	14550	1664	12886
保加利亚	Bulgaria	5613	1827	3785
芬 兰	Finland	20782	7949	12834
匈牙利	Hungary	8305	6203	2102
冰 岛	Iceland	65	65	
列支敦士登	Liechtenstein	210		210
马耳他	Malta	596	596	
摩纳哥	Monaco	28	28	
挪 威	Norway	18631	5442	13190
波 兰	Poland	18238	15156	3082
罗马尼亚	Romania	14724	12126	2597
瑞 典	Sweden	27499	11140	16360
瑞 士	Switzerland	50395	3564	46831
爱沙尼亚	Estonia	2601	2512	89
拉脱维亚	Latvia	2338	2119	219
立陶宛	Lithuania	4325	1428	2897
格鲁吉亚	Georgia	1591	1516	76
亚美尼亚	Armenia	401	401	
阿塞拜疆	Azerbaijan	3472	3472	
白俄罗斯	Byelorussia	4780	4740	41
摩尔多瓦	Moldavia	277	229	48
俄罗斯	Russia	106184	93465	12719
乌克兰	Ukraine	12352	6375	5977
斯洛文尼亚共和国	Slovenia	3295	3219	77
克罗地亚共和国	Croatia	1650	1569	82
捷 克	Czech	14292	4626	9666
斯洛伐克	Slovak	16203	7713	8490
前南斯拉夫马其顿	Macedonia	5	5	
波斯尼亚-黑塞哥维那	Bosnia & Herzegovina	44	43	1
塞尔维亚	Serbia	2236	698	1539
黑 山	Montenegro	1170	37	1133
阿根廷	Argentina	9607	8435	1172
阿鲁巴岛	Aruba	36	36	
巴哈马	Bahamas	203	203	
巴巴多斯	Barbados	118	118	
伯利兹	Belize	22	22	
玻利维亚	Bolivia	290	290	

17-4 续表 3 continued

单位：万元 (10 000 yuan)

国别(地区)	Country(Region)	进出口 Total	出口 Exports	进口 Imports
巴　西	Brazil	61515	28770	32745
智　利	Chile	60733	11110	49627
哥伦比亚	Colombia	10342	10332	10
多米尼克	Dominica	22	22	
哥斯达黎加	Costa Rica	1968	1547	421
古　巴	Cuba	114	114	
库腊索岛	Curacao	2	2	
多米尼加	Dominica Rep.	1399	1387	13
厄瓜多尔	Ecuador	9273	9273	
格林纳达	Grenada	58	58	
瓜德罗普	Guadeloupe	36	36	
危地马拉	Guatemala	17082	17082	
圭亚那	Guyana	175	175	
海　地	Haiti	97	97	1
洪都拉斯	Honduras	261	214	48
牙买加	Jamaica	613	612	1
马提尼克	Martinique	2	2	
墨西哥	Mexico	77257	73286	3970
尼加拉瓜	Nicaragua	1146	1146	
巴拿马	Panama	6907	6907	
巴拉圭	Paraguay	2645	2645	
秘　鲁	Peru	31423	14441	16983
波多黎各	Puerto Rico	280000	267020	12980
圣卢西亚	Saint Lucia	171	171	
圣文森特和格林纳丁斯	Saint Vincent & the Grenadines	29	29	
萨尔瓦多	El Salvador	651	650	
苏里南	Surinam	417	417	
特立尼达和多巴哥	Trinidad and Tobago	240	240	
乌拉圭	Uruguay	20696	20696	
委内瑞拉	Venezuela	18179	18179	
加拿大	Canada	116899	58808	58092
美　国	United States	3532887	1446120	2086767
澳大利亚	Australia	276619	52568	224051
斐　济	Fiji	2149	2149	
新喀里多尼亚	New Caledonia (Fr)	305	305	
瓦努阿图	Vanuatu	3	3	
新西兰	New Zealand	7130	4979	2150
巴布亚新几内亚	Papua New Guinea	2048	2048	
所罗门群岛	Solomon Is.	6	6	
汤　加	Tonga	23	23	
萨摩亚	Samoa	16	16	
贝劳共和国	The Republic of Palau	9	9	
法属波利尼西亚	Polynesia (F)	137	137	
国(地)别不详	Others	115		107

17-5 进出口商品分类金额(2014年)
Value of Imports and Exports by HS Section and Division(2014)

单位：万元 (10 000 yuan)

商品分类	HS Section and Division	出口 Exports	进口 Imports
总　　值	**Total**	**8555749**	**8252555**
第一类 活动物；动物产品	**Live Animals; Animal Products**		
第1章 活动物	Live Animals	211	12511
第2章 肉及食用杂碎	Meat and Edible Meat Offal	1	400
第3章 鱼、甲壳动物、软体动物及其他水生无脊椎动物	Fish and Crustaceans Molluscs and Other Aquatic Invertebrates		212
第4章 乳品；蛋品；天然蜂蜜；其他食用动物产品	Dairy Produce; Birds' Eggs; Natural Honey; Edible Products of Animal Origin, not ElsewhereSpecified or Included	7402	1119
第5章 其他动物产品	Products of Animal Origin, not Elsewhere Specified or Included	1928	
第二类 植物产品	**Vegetable Products**		
第6章 活树及其他活植物；鳞茎、根及类似品；插花及装饰用簇叶	Live Tree and Other Plants; Bulbs, Roots and the Like; Cut Flowers and Ornamental Foliage	143	2769
第7章 食用蔬菜、根及块茎	Edible Vegetables and Certain Roots and Tubers	13091	2177
第8章 食用水果及坚果；甜瓜或柑桔属水果的果皮	Edible Fruit and Nuts; Peel of Citrus Fruit or Melons	33940	2130
第9章 咖啡、茶、马黛茶及调味香料	Coffee, Tea, Mate and Spices	2792	66
第10章 谷物	Cereals	814	
第11章 制粉工业产品；麦芽；淀粉；菊粉；面筋	Products of The Milling Industry; Malt; Starches;Inulin; Wheat Gluten	622	189
第12章 含油子仁及果实；杂项子仁及果实；工业用或药用植物；稻草、秸秆及饲料	Oil Seeds and Oleaginous Fruits; Miscellaneous Grains, Seeds and Fruit; Industrial or Medicinal Plants; Straw and Fodder	18107	43785
第13章 虫胶；树胶、树脂及其他	Lac; Gums, Resins And Other Vegetable Saps and Extracts	43146	1035
第14章 编结用植物材料；其他植物产品	Vegetable Plaiting Materials; Vegetable Products Not Elsewhere Specified or Included	19	12
第三类 动、植物油、脂及其分解产品；精制的食用油脂	**Animal or Vegetable Fats and Oils and their Cleavage Products; Prepared**		
第15章 动、植物油、脂及其分解产品；精制的食用油脂；动、植物蜡	Animal or Vegetable Fats and Oils and Their Products; Prepared Edible Fats; Animal or Vegetable Waxes	166	142
第四类 食品；饮料、酒及醋；烟草、烟草及烟草代用品的制品	**Prepared Foodstuffs; Beverages, Spirits And Vinegar; Tobacco and Manufactured Tobacco Substitutes**		
第16章 肉、鱼、甲壳动物、软体动物及其他水生无脊椎动物的制品	Preparations of Meat, of Fish or of Crustaceans, Molluscs or other Aquatic Invertebrates	1	
第17章 糖及糖食	Sugars and Sugar Confectionery	1506	
第18章 可可及可可制品	Cocoa and Cocoa Preparations		
第19章 谷物、粮食粉、淀粉或乳的制品；糕饼点心	Preparations of Cereals, Flour, Starch or Milk; Pastry-Cooks' Products	83	253
第20章 蔬菜、水果、坚果或植物其他部分的制品	Preparations of Vegetables, Fruit, Nuts or Other Parts of Plants	200038	302
第21章 杂项食品	Miscellaneous Edible Preparations	2892	320
第22章 饮料、酒及醋	Beverages, Spirits and Vinegar	218	2467
第23章 食品工业的残渣及废料；配制的动物饲料	Residues and Waste from The Food Industries; Prepared Animal Fodder	1490	1490
第24章 烟草、烟草及烟草代用品的制品	Tobacco and Manufactured Tobacco Substitutes	11305	

17-5 续表 1 continued

单位：万元 (10 000 yuan)

商品分类	HS Section and Division	出口 Exports	进口 Imports
第五类 矿产品	**Mineral Products**		
第25章 盐；硫磺；泥土及石料；石膏料、石灰及水泥	Salt; Sulphur; Earths and Stone; Plastering Materials, Lime and Cement	13350	1244
第26章 矿砂、矿渣及矿灰	Ores, Slag and Ash	15064	340879
第27章 矿物燃料、矿物油及其蒸馏产品；沥青物质；矿物蜡	Mineral Fuels, Mineral Oils and Products cf Their Distillation; Bituminous Substances Mineral Waxes	1143	12928
第六类 化学工业及其相关工业的产品	**Products of The Chemical or Industries Allied**		
第28章 无机化学品；贵金属、稀土金属、放射性元素及其同位素的有机及无机化合物	Inorganic Chemicals; Organic or Inorganic Compounds of Precious Metals, of Rare-Earth Metals, of Radioactive Elements or of Isotopes	82230	166757
第29章 有机化学品	Organic Chemicals	159047	102352
第30章 药品	Pharmaceutical Products	6753	110899
第31章 肥料	Fertilizers	9352	1
第32章 鞣料浸膏及染料浸膏；鞣酸及其衍生物；染料、颜料及其他着色料；油漆及清漆；油灰及其他类似胶粘剂；墨水、油墨	Tanning or Dyeing Extracts; Tannins and Their Derivatives; Dyes, Pigments and Other Colouring Matter;Paints and Varnishes; Futty and Other Mastics; Inks	7144	3871
第33章 精油及香膏；芳香料制品及化妆盥洗品	Essential Oils and Retinoid; Perfumery, Cosmetic or Toilet Preparations	2401	174
第34章 肥皂、有机表面活性剂、洗涤剂、润滑剂、人造蜡、调制蜡、光洁剂、蜡烛及类似品、塑型用膏、“牙科 用蜡”及牙科用熟石膏制剂	Soap,Organic Surface-Active Agents,Washing Preparations,Lubricating Preparations, Waxes, Polishing or Scouring Preparations, Candles and Similar Articles, Modelling Pastes, "Dental Waxes" And Dental Preparations With a Basis of Plast	1204	9020
第35章 蛋白类物质；改性淀粉；胶；酶	Albuminoidal Substances; Modified Starches; Glues; Enzymes	1964	2712
第36章 炸药；烟火制品；火柴；引火合金；易燃材料制品	Explosives; Pyrotechnic Products; Matches; Pyrophoric Alloys; Certain Combustible Preparations	48	7756
第37章 照相及电影用品	Photographic or Cinematographic Goods	829	17035
第38章 杂项化学产品	Miscellaneous Chemical Products	246886	48147
第七类 塑料及其制品；橡胶及其制品	**Plastics and Articles Thereof Rubber and Articles Thereof**		
第39章 塑料及其制品	Plastics and Articles Thereof	77450	38990
第40章 橡胶及其制品	Rubber and Articles Thereof	43715	21571
第八类 生皮、皮革、毛皮及其制品；鞍具及挽具；旅行用品、手提包及类似品；动物肠线(蚕胶丝除外)制品	**Raw Hides and Skins, Leather, Fur Skins and Thereof; Saddlery and Harness; Travel Goods,Articles Handbags and Similar Containers; Articles of Animal Gut (Other Than Silk- Worm Gut)**		
第41章 生皮(毛皮除外)及皮革	Raw Hides and Skins(Other Than Fur Skins) and Leather	15	
第42章 皮革制品；鞍具及挽具；旅行用品、手提包及类似容器；动物肠线(蚕胶丝除外)制品	Articles of Leather; Saddlery and Harness; Travel Goods, Handbags and Similar Containers; Articles of Animal Gut(Other Than Silk-Worm Gut)	43326	241
第43章 毛皮、人造毛皮及其制品	Fur Skins and Artificial Fur; Manufactures Thereof	833	3

17-5 续表 2 continued

单位：万元 (10 000 yuan)

商品分类	HS Section and Division	出口 Exports	进口 Imports
第九类 木及木制品；木炭；软木及软木制品；稻草，秸秆、针茅或其他编结材料制品；篮筐及柳条编结品	**Wood and Articles of Wood; Wood Charcoal; Cork and Articles of Cork; Manufactures of Straw, of Esparto or of Other Plaiting Materials; Basket Ware and Wickerwork**		
第44章 木及木制品；木炭	Wood and Articles of Wood; Wood Charcoal	5498	1029
第45章 软木及软木制品	Cork and Articles of Cork	1878	342
第46章 稻草、秸秆、针茅或其他编结材料制品；篮筐及柳条编结品	Manufactures of Straw, of Esparto or of Other Plaiting Materials; Basket Ware and Wickerwork	285	
第十类 木浆及其他纤维状纤维素浆；纸及纸板的废碎品；纸、纸板及其制品	**Pulp of Wood or of Other Fibrous Cellulosic Material; Waste and Scrap of Paper or Paperboard; Paper and Paperboard and Articles Thereof**		
第47章 木浆及其他纤维状纤维素浆；回收(废碎)纸或纸板	Pulp of Wood or of Other Fibrous Cellulosic Material; Waste and Scrap of Paper or Paperboard	4249	108
第48章 纸及纸板；纸浆、纸或纸板制品	Paper and Paperboard; Articles of Paper Pulp, of Paper or Paperboard	25784	5431
第49章 书籍、报纸、印刷图画及其他印刷品；手稿、打字稿及设计图纸	Printed Books, Newspapers, Pictures and Other Products of The Printing Industry; Manuscripts, Typescripts and Plans	3268	8601
第十一类 纺织原料及纺织制品	**Textiles and Textile Articles**		
第50章 蚕丝	Silk	2604	31
第51章 羊毛、动物细毛或粗毛；马毛纱线及其机织物	Wool, Fine or Coarse Animal Hair; Horsehair Yarn and Woven Fabric	24769	
第52章 棉花	Cotton	35666	12101
第53章 其他植物纺织纤维；纸纱线及其机织物	Other Vegetable Textile Fibres; Paper Yarn and Woven Fabrics of Paper Yarn		
第54章 化学纤维长丝	Man-Made Filaments	1985	202
第55章 化学纤维短纤	Man-Made Short Fibres	66570	70
第56章 絮胎、毡呢及无纺织物；特种纱线；线、绳、索、缆及其制品	Wadding, Felt and Nonwoven; Special Yarns; Twine, Cordage, Ropes and Cables and Articles Thereof	5441	651
第57章 地毯及纺织材料的其他铺地制品	Carpets and Other Textile Floor Coverings	1692	
第58章 特种机织物；簇绒织物；花边；装饰毯；装饰带；刺绣品	Special Woven Fabrics; Tufted Textile Fabrics; Lace; Tapestries; Trimmings; Embroidery	2372	131
第59章 浸渍、涂布、包覆或层压的纺织物；工业用纺织制品	Impregnated, Coated, Covered or Laminated Textile Fabrics; Textile Articles of a Kind Suitable for Industrial Use	2725	581
第60章 针织物及钩编织物	Knitted or Crocheted Fabrics	13259	6
第61章 针织或钩编的服装及衣着附件	Articles of Apparel and Clothing Accessories, Knitted or Crocheted	61986	974
第62章 非针织或非钩编的服装及衣着附件	Articles of Apparel and Clothing Accessories, not Knitted or Crocheted	61665	255
第63章 其他纺织制成品；成套物品；旧衣着及旧纺织品；碎织物	Other Made Up Textile Articles; Sets; Worn Clothing And Worn Textile Articles; Rags Articles; Rags	24229	637

17-5 续表 3 continued

单位：万元 (10 000 yuan)

商品分类	HS Section and Division	出口 Exports	进口 Imports
第十二类 鞋、帽、伞、杖、鞭及其零件；已加工的羽毛及其制品；人造花；人发制品	**Footwear, Headgear, Umbrellas, Sun Umbrellas, Walking-Sticks, Seat-Sticks, Whips, Riding-Crops and Parts Thereof; Prepared Feathers and Articles Made Therewith; Artificial Flowers; Articles of Human Hair**		
第64章 鞋靴、护腿和类似品及其零件	Footwear, Gaiters and The Like; Parts of Such Articles	43770	438
第65章 帽类及其零件	Headgear and Parts Thereof	2438	86
第66章 雨伞、阳伞、手杖、鞭子、马鞭及其零件	Umbrellas, Sun Umbrellas, Walking-Sticks, Seat-Sticks, Whips, Riding-Crops And Parts Thereof	1169	238
第67章 已加工羽毛、羽绒及其制品；人造花；人发制品	Prepared Feathers and Down and Articles Made of Feathers or of Down; Artificial Flowers; Articles of Human Hair	7877	334
第十三类 石料、石膏、水泥、石棉、云母及类似材料的制品；陶瓷产品；玻璃及其制品	**Articles of Stone, Plaster, Cement, Asbestos, Mica or Similar Materials; Ceramic Products; Glass and Glassware**		
第68章 石料、石膏、水泥、石棉、云母及类似材料的制品	Articles of Stone, Plaster, Cement, Asbestos, Mica or Similar Materials; Ceramic Products; Glass and Glassware	16551	4193
第69章 陶瓷产品	Ceramic Products	43323	6496
第70章 玻璃及其制品	Glass and Glassware	64050	18431
第十四类 天然或养殖珍珠、宝石或半宝石、贵金属、包贵金属及其制品；仿首饰；硬币	**Natural or Cultured Pearls, Precious or Semi-Precious Stones, Precious Metals, Metals Clad With Precious Metal and Stones, Precious Metals, Metals Clad With Precious Metal and Articles Thereof; Imitation Jewellery; Coin**		
第71章 天然或养殖珍珠、宝石或半宝石、 贵金属、包贵金属及其制品；仿首饰；硬币	Natural or Cultured Pearls, Precious or Semi-Precious Stones, Precious Metals, Metals Clad With Precious Metal and Articles Thereof; Imitation Jewellery; Coin	285859	25396
第十五类 贱金属及其制品	**Base Metals and Articles of Base Metal**		
第72章 钢铁	Iron and Steel	36807	12644
第73章 钢铁制品	Articles of Iron or Steel	180735	40676
第74章 铜及其制品	Copper and Articles Thereof	34482	174651
第75章 镍及其制品	Nickel and Articles Thereof	993	13159
第76章 铝及其制品	Aluminium and Articles Thereof	42005	46590
第78章 铅及其制品	Lead and Articles Thereof	5	8
第79章 锌及其制品	Zinc and Articles Thereof	176	37
第80章 锡及其制品	Tin and Articles Thereof	65	46
第81章 其他贱金属、金属陶瓷及其制品	Other Base Metals; Cermets; Articles Thereof	167821	20194
第82章 贱金属工具、器具、利口器、餐匙、餐叉及其零件	Tools, Implements, Cutlery, Spoons and Forks, of Base Metal; Parts Thereof of Base Metal	38690	17189
第83章 贱金属杂项制品	Miscellaneous Articles of Base Metal	40519	2815
第十六类 机器、机械器具、电气设备及其零件； 录音机及放声机、电视图像	**Machinery and Mechanical Appliances; Electrical Equipment; Parts Thereof; Sound Recorders and Reproducers, Television Image and Sound Recorders and Reproducers; and and Accessories of Recorders and Reproducers; and Parts and Accessories of Such Artic**		
第84章 核反应堆、锅炉、机器、机械器具及其零件	Nuclear Reactors, Boilers, Machinery and Mechanical Appliances; Parts Thereof	2023532	2023532

17-5 续表 4 continued

单位：万元 (10 000 yuan)

商品分类	HS Section and Division	出口 Exports	进口 Imports
第85章 电机、电气设备及其零件；录音机及放声机、电视图像、声音的录制和重放设备及其零件、附件	Electrical Machinery and Equipment and Parts Thereof; Sound Recorders and Reproducers, Television Image and Sound Recorders and Reproducers, and Parts and Accessories of Such Articles	3401193	4000490
第十七类 车辆、航空器、船舶及有关运输设备	**Vehicles, Aircraft, Vessels and Associated Transport Equipment**		
第86章 铁道及电车道机车、车辆及其零件；铁道及电车轨道固定装置及其零件、附件；各种机械(包括电动机械)交通信号设备	Railway or Tramway Locomotives, Rolling-Stock and Parts Thereof; Railway or Tramway Track Fixtures And Fittings and Parts Thereof; Mechanical(Including Electro-Mechanical) Traffic Signalling Equipment of All Kinds	11195	15891
第87章 车辆及其零件、附件，但铁道及电车道车辆除外	Vehicles Other Than Railway or Tramway Rolling-Associated Stock, and Parts and Accessories Thereof	394497	17521
第88章 航空器、航天器及其零件	Aircraft, Spacecraft, and Parts Thereof	40245	43199
第89章 船舶及浮动结构体	Ships, Boats and Floating Structures	67	105
第十八类 光学、照相、电影、计量、检验、医疗或外科用仪器及设备、精密仪器及设备；钟表；乐器；上述物品的零件、附件	**Optical, Photographic, Cinematographic, Measuring, Checking, Precision, Medical or Surgical Instruments and Apparatus; Clocks And Watches; Musical Instruments; Parts and Accessories Thereof**		
第90章 光学、照相、电影、计量、检验、医疗或外科用仪器及设备、精密仪器及设备；上述物品的零件、附件	Optical, Photographic, Cinematographic, Measuring, Checking, Precision Medical or Surgical Instruments and Apparatus; Parts and Accessories Thereof	123398	470769
第91章 钟表及其零件	Clocks and Watches and Parts Thereof	7969	300
第92章 乐器及其零件、附件	Musical Instruments; Parts and Accessories of Such Articles	1275	324
第十九类 武器、弹药及其零件、附件	**Arms and Ammunition; Parts and Accessories Thereof**		
第93章 武器、弹药及其零件、附件	Arms and Ammunition; Parts and Accessories Thereof	412	
第二十类 杂项制品	**Miscellaneous Manufactured Articles**		
第94章 家具；寝具、褥垫、弹簧床垫、软坐垫及类似的填充制品；未列名灯具及照明装置；发光标志、发光名牌及类似品；活动房屋	Furniture; Bedding, Mattresses, Mattress Supports, Cushions and Similar Stuffed Furnishings; Lamps and Lighting Fittings, not Elsewhere Specified or Included; Illuminated Signs, Illuminated	104419	4246
第95章 玩具、游戏品、运动用品及其零件、附件	Toys, Games and Sports Requisites; Parts and Accessories Thereof	25209	195
第96章 杂项制品	Miscellaneous Manufactured Articles	15734	718
第二十一类 艺术品、收藏品及古物	**Works of Art, Collectors' Pieces and Antiques**		
第97章 艺术品、收藏品及古物	Works of Art, Collectors' Pieces and Antiques	705	3
第二十二类 特殊交易品及未分类商品	**Commodities and Transactions not Classified According to Kind**		
第98章 特殊交易品及未分类商品	Commodities and Transactions not Classified According to Kind		269280

17-6 主要出口商品数量、金额(2014年)
Main Export Commodities in Volume and Value(2014)

商品名称	Item	数 量 Volume	金 额 (万元) Value (10 000 yuan)
水海产品	(千克) Aquatic and Seawater Products (kg)	20000	141
谷物及谷物粉	(千克) Cereals and Cereals Flour (kg)	2162529	868
#稻谷和大米	Rice	20000	15
蔬 菜	(千克) Vegetable (kg)	10220017	3525
#鲜或冷冻蔬菜	Fresh Vegetables	8572012	1721
干的食用菌类	Dry Edible Fungus	47580	481
干 豆	(千克) Dried Beans (kg)	8381849	9898
鲜的、干水果及坚果	(千克) Fresh, Dried Fruits and Nuts (kg)	45679370	33833
#橘、橙	Mandarins and Oranges	3577879	2792
鲜苹果	Apples	35265193	23719
食用油籽	(千克) Edible Oil Seeds (kg)	21723505	10682
#大 豆	Soybean	21704705	10658
花生、花生仁	Peanuts	18800	24
食用植物油(包括棕榈油)	(千克) Edible Vegetable Oil (kg)	23760	26
#菜子油	Rapeseed Oil	23760	26
烘焙花生	(千克) Roasted Peanut (kg)	1000	1
食 糖	(千克) Sugar (kg)	150	3
天然蜂蜜	(千克) Natural Honey (kg)	4906420	7046
茶 叶	(千克) Tea (kg)	6040	9
啤 酒	(升) Beer (liter)	316796	156
猪 鬃	(千克) Bristles (kg)	3400	37
药 材	(千克) Medical Materials (kg)	752146	3448
烤 烟	(千克) Flue-cured Tobacco (kg)	3084121	6167
锯 材	(立方米) Wood Sawn (cu.m)	278977	267
生 丝	(千克) Raw Silk (kg)	79915	2553
山羊绒	(千克) Cashmere (kg)	147549	12050
黏土及其他耐火矿物	(千克) Clay and Other Refractory Minerals (kg)	2668672	368
#天然石墨	Natural Graphite	113750	45
天然碳酸镁; 氧化镁	Natural Magnesium Carbonate	135950	23
天然硫酸钡(重晶石)	(千克) Barite (kg)	3095150	340
滑 石	(千克) Talcum (kg)	5500	1
氧化铝	(千克) Aluminum Oxide (kg)	58310	57
焦炭、半焦炭	(千克) Coke and Semi-coke (kg)	7432071	944
成品油	(千克) Petroleum Products Refined (kg)	79905	122
放射性元素、同位素及化合物	(克) Radioactive Elements, Isotope and Compounds (g)	4095	1079
糠 醛	(千克) Furfural (kg)	3930400	3538
合成有机染料	(千克) Synthetic Organic Dyestuffs (kg)	49711	202
锌钡白(立德粉)	(千克) lithopone (kg)	64750	42
医药品	(千克) Medical and Pharmaceutical Products (kg)	1482965	41967
#抗菌素(制剂除外)	Antibiotics(Except Preparations)	355936	7030
中式成药	Medicaments of Chinese Type	34141	1062
医用敷料	Pharmaceutical Goods	101222	591
美容化妆品及护肤品	Cosmetics and skin care products		2
洗衣粉	(千克) Washing Powder (kg)	11625	5

17-6 续表 1 continued

商品名称		Item		数量 Volume	金额（万元） Value (10 000 yuan)
松香及树脂酸	(千克)	Rosin and Resin Acids	(kg)	626640	848
初级形状的聚氯乙烯	(千克)	The Primary PVC	(kg)	75500	45
新的充气橡胶轮胎	(条)	Rubber Tyres	(unit)	23023010	36026
家用或装饰用木制品	(千克)	Wood Articles for Household or Decoration Use	(kg)	488810	1454
纸及纸板(未切成型的)	(千克)	Paper and Paperboard in Rolls	(kg)	5109664	10378
纺织纱线、织物及制品		Textiles			171061
#棉纱线	(千克)	Cotton Yarn	(kg)	88507	315
含合成短纤85%及以上的纱线	(千克)	Containing 85% or More by Synthetic Staple Fibers of Yarn	(kg)	3069211	7305
合成短纤与棉混纺纱线	(千克)	Synthetic Staple Fibers and Cotton Blended Yarn	(kg)	30034	52
丝织物	(米)	Silk fabrics	(m)	3569	20
毛纺机织物	(米)	Wool Fabric	(m)	68159	378
棉机织物	(米)	Cotton Cloth	(m)	55644156	35351
合成短纤与棉混纺机织物	(米)	Synthetic Short Fibre and Cotton-fibre Mixture Woven Fabric	(m)	55877996	28457
人造纤维短纤机织物	(米)	Man-made Short Fibre Fabric	(m)	5703636	2557
地　毯	(米)	Carpets	(m)	765449	1692
棉浴巾	(米)	Cotton Towel	(m)	460689	621
针织或钩编台布、盘垫	(件)	Tablecloth and Plate Pad,Knitted or Crocheted	(unit)	105246	60
塑料编织带(周转带除外)	(条)	Bags of PP or PE Strip (Except Turnover Bags)	(unit)	10457489	1752
水　泥	(千克)	Cement	(kg)	96300	25
花岗岩石材及制品	(千克)	Granite Material and Products	(kg)	192265	119
平板玻璃	(平方米)	Plate Glass	(sq.m)	405604	101
玻璃制品		Glass Products			48836
家用陶瓷器皿	(千克)	Porcelain and Pottery Wares for Household Use	(kg)	2029616	8316
装饰用陶瓷制品	(千克)	Porcelain and Pottery Wares for Decoration Use	(kg)	782284	4786
珍珠、宝石及半宝石	(千克)	Pearls、Gems and Semi-gems	(kg)	15337	18448
硅　铁	(千克)	Ferrosilicon	(kg)	7026876	6402
钢坯及粗锻件	(千克)	Billet and Crude Forgings	(kg)	4119	27
钢　材	(千克)	Rolled Steel	(kg)	152441389	113770
#钢铁棒材		Steel Bar		1530348	923
角钢及型钢		Angle Iron and Steel		960615	910
钢铁板材		Steel Plate		7896744	7946
钢铁线材		Steel Wire		12497994	7505
钢铁管配件		Steel Tube Accessories		25964137	35341
未锻造的铜及铜材	(千克)	Unwrought Copper and its Alloys	(kg)	9122092	33453
未锻造的铜(包括铜合金)		Unwrought Copper		78	1
铜　材		Rolled Copper		9122014	33452
未锻造的铝及铝材	(千克)	Unwrought Aluminum and its Alloys	(kg)	5057855	10452
铝　材		Rolled Aluminum		5057855	10452
钢铁或铜制标准紧固件	(千克)	Iron or Copper Nails, Bolts, etc.	(kg)	3930141	6343

17-6 续表 2 continued

商品名称	Item	数 量 Volume	金 额（万元） Value (10 000 yuan)
不锈钢厨具、餐具等家用器具 （千克）	Stainless Steel Kitchenware, Tableware and Other Household Appliances (kg)	799586	3864
餐桌、厨房及其他家用搪瓷器 （千克）	Table, Enamel Kitchen and other Household Devices (kg)	68168	144
手用或机用工具 （千克）	Hand Tools and Tools for Machines (kg)	10403259	28131
锁 （千克）	Lock (kg)	787473	2905
电 扇 （台）	Fans (unit)	611058	4255
纺织机械及零件	Textile Machinery		3229
普通缝纫机 （台）	Sewing Machines (unit)	3273	94
工业用缝纫机 （台）	Industrial Use Sewing Machines (unit)	256082	72138
金属加工机床 （台）	Machine Tools (unit)	42730	20355
#车 床	Lathes	1694	10534
铣 床	Milling Machines	50	262
电子计算器(包括具有计算功能) （台）	Electric Calculator (unit)	879186	423
自动数据处理设备及其部件 （台）	Automatic Data Processing Machines and Components (unit)	4023630	363700
#数字式自动数据处理设备	Digital Automatic Processing Equipments	42534	3361
数字式中央处理部件	Digital Central Processing Unit	362	771
输入或输出部件	Input or Output Components	249723	597
键盘、鼠标器	Keyboard, Mouse	247871	478
自动数据处理设备零件	Parts for Auto Data Processing Equipment		1089036
轴 承 （套）	Bearings (unit)	43257143	21900
电动机及发电机 （台）	Electric Motors and Generators (unit)	1698065	13243
变压器 （个）	Transformers (unit)	1539621	16328
静止式变流气 （个）	Static Converters (unit)	4727811	15281
原电池 （个）	Primary Cells and Batteries (unit)	5608677	354
蓄电池 （个）	Electric Accumulators (unit)	142191	2840
手电筒 （个）	Flashlights (unit)	1134150	1013
有线电话机(包括无绳电话机) （台）	Wireless Telephone Sets (unit)	680704	18768
扬声器 （个）	Loudspeakers (unit)	5058195	12132
录、放像机 （台）	VCR and videoplayers (unit)	721547	10822
录音机及收录(放)音组合机 （台）	Sound Recording Apparatus (unit)	45347	614
收音机 （台）	Radio Sets (unit)	43777	185
录放音、像机及唱机的零附件 （千克）	Parts of Sound Recorders, Video Tape Recorders and Phonographs (kg)	60271	258
电视、收音机及无线电讯设备的零件附件 （千克）	Parts of Television, Radio and Wireless Telecommunication Equipment (kg)	1377407	11611
电容器 （千克）	Electrical Capacitors (kg)	1816304	60273
印刷电路 （块）	Printed Circuit (unit)	26600236	14524
通断保护电路装置及零件	Electrical Apparatus for Swithing or Protecting Electrical Circuit		74625
二极管及类似半导体器件 （个）	Diode and Semi Conductors (unit)	393330410	245744
电线和电缆 （千克）	Insulated Wire or Cable (kg)	2586857	49226
集装箱 （个）	Container (unit)	37	2426
汽 车 （辆）	Motor Vehicles (unit)	20497	244641
汽车零件	Parts of Motor Vehicles		84473

17-6 续表 3 continued

商品名称		Item		数 量 Volume	金 额（万元） Value (10 000 yuan)
摩托车	（辆）	Motorcycle	(unit)	2319	1524
自行车	（辆）	Bicycles	(unit)	9021	183
摩托车及自行车的零件		Parts of Motorcycles and Bicycles			4609
船 舶	（艘）	Ships	(unit)	151	58
医疗仪器和器械		Medical Instruments and Appliances			12702
手 表	（只）	Wrist Watches	(set)	1224050	1357
电动手表		Electric Watches		1224050	1357
日用钟	（只）	Clocks	(set)	278063	1258
家具及其零件		Furniture			39564
床垫、寝具及类似品		Mattresses and Bedding Articles			4385
灯具、照明装置及类似品		Lights and Lighting Apparatus			57718
旅行用品及箱包		Boxes,Bags and Travel Goods			41218
服装及衣着附件		Garments and Clothing Accessories			129120
#织物制服装		Textile Garments			113940
非针织钩编织物服装		Garments(Excluding Knitwear and Crochet)			55365
针织或钩编的服装		Garments, Knitted or Crocheted			58575
皮革服装	（件）	Leather Garment	(unit)	2477	24
裘皮服装	（千克）	Fur clothing	(kg)	881	157
皮革手套	（双）	Leather Gloves	(pair)	305153	1295
织物制手套	（双）	Textiles Gloves	(pair)	6884674	2589
织物制袜子	（双）	Textiles Socks	(pair)	1578257	689
手 帕	（条）	Handkerchieves	(unit)	3761	9
帽 类	（个）	Hats	(unit)	3289283	2402
鞋 类		Footwear			43770
鞋	（双）	Shoes	(pair)	4749781	41685
鞋靴零件；护腿及类似品	（千克）	Shose Accessories, Leg Guards and Analogs	(kg)	398555	2085
塑料制品	（千克）	Plastic Articles	(kg)	17623579	56223
玩 具		Toys			996
游戏机	（台）	Play Station	(unit)	16474	725
圣诞用品	（千克）	Articles for Christmas	(kg)	865924	8206
足球、篮球、排球	（个）	Football,Basketball,Volleyball	(unit)	379685	535
铅 笔	（吨）	Penciles	(ton)	1260.971	3829
艺术品、收藏品及古董		Artwork, Collections and Antiques			705
贵金属或包贵金属的首饰		Precious Metal or Jewelry Clad with Precious Metal			12252
伞	（把）	Umbrellas	(unit)	133341	518
鬃 刷	（把）	Bristles Brushes	(unit)	1919420	349
人造花	（千克）	Artificial Flowers	(kg)	437177	7406
热水瓶	（个）	Thermos	(unit)	61481	161
机电产品		Machanical and Electrical Products			6339219
金属制品		Metal Products			252282
机械设备		Machinery and Equipments			2023532
电器及电子产品		Electric and Electronic Products			3401193
运输工具		Transport Equipments			446004
仪器仪表		Instruments and Meters			123398
其 他		Others			92809

17-6 续表 4 continued

商品名称		Item		数量 Volume	金额（万元） Value (10 000 yuan)
高新技术产品		High and New-tech Products			4928537
生物技术		Biotechnology			17557
生命科学技术		Life Sciences Technology			73596
光电技术		Photoelectric Technology			9926
计算机与通信技术		Computer and Communication Technology			1552519
电子技术		Electronic Technology			2825438
计算机集成制造技术		Computer Integrated Manufacturing			34244
材料技术		Material Technology			236657
航空航天技术		Aerospace Technology			175815
其他技术		Others			2481
钼矿砂及其精矿	（千克）	Molybdenum Ore	(kg)	1490000	14961
粮 食	（千克）	Grain	(kg)	36927135	22042
#淀粉块茎及薯类		Tubers		4678052	617
豆 类		Beans		30086554	20556
苹 果	（千克）	Apples	(kg)	35265193	23719
乳 品	（千克）	Milk and Dairy Products	(kg)	43000	315
果蔬汁	（千克）	Vegetable and Fruit Juice	(kg)	225382533	193645
#苹果汁		Apple Juice		207717531	178676
菜子油和芥子油	（千克）	Rapeseed Oil and Mustard Oil	(kg)	23760	26
稀土及其制品	（千克）	Rare earth and its products	(kg)	10000	59
钨 品	（千克）	Tungsten Products	(kg)	114208	5260
钨及其制品		Tungsten and its Products		114208	5260
碳酸钠（纯碱）	（千克）	Sodium carbonate	(kg)	26000	12
维生素C	（千克）	Vitamin C	(kg)	11085	68
农 药	（千克）	Pesticide	(kg)	280471	1088
初级形状的聚氯乙烯	（千克）	The Primary PVC	(kg)	75500	45
新闻纸	（千克）	Newsprint	(kg)	6500	10
牛皮纸	（千克）	Kraft Paper	(kg)	266327	637
铁合金	（千克）	Ferroalloy	(kg)	10645792	19546
冰 箱	（台）	Refrigerator	(unit)	170	269
洗衣机	（台）	Washing Machine	(unit)	1451	63
微波炉	（个）	Microwave Oven	(unit)	7211	153
打印机(包括多功能一体机)	（台）	Printer(Including Multi-function Printer)	(unit)	61	131
液晶显示板	（个）	Liquid Crystal Display	(unit)	53874	688
节能灯	（只）	Energy-saving Lamps	(unit)	1310267	888
处理器及控制器	（个）	Processor and controller	(unit)	24658599	5843
存储器	（个）	Memorizer	(unit)	1287439815	2518943
放大器	（个）	Amplifier	(unit)	720862	59
装有引擎的汽车底盘	（台）	Chassis with Engines	(unit)	93	2564
照相机	（架）	Cameras	(unit)	1	5
数字式照相机		Digital Cameras		1	5
箱包及类似容器		Suitcases,Bags and Similar Containers			41218
小轿车(包括整套散件)	（辆）	Cars(including a Complete Set of Spare Parts)	(unit)	12891	49887
小客车(9座及以下)	（辆）	Small Passenger Cars (9 and under)	(unit)	22	68
货车(包括整套散件)	（辆）	Trucks(including a Complete Set of Spare Parts)	(unit)	6681	161322
打火机	（个）	Lighters	(unit)	3563552	230

17-7 主要进口商品数量、金额(2014年)
Main Import Commodities in Volume and Value(2014)

商品名称	Item		数量 Volume	金额（万元） Value (10 000 yuan)
冻　鱼	（千克）Frozen Chicken	(kg)	41568	28
大　豆	（千克）Soybean	(kg)	73445015	22344
食用植物油	（千克）Edible Vegetable Oil	(kg)	65191	122
#菜子油及芥子油	Rapeseed Oil and Mustard Oil		43660	24
饲料用鱼粉	（千克）The Fishmeal for Feed	(kg)	608980	554
配制的动物饲料	（千克）Animal Feed	(kg)	850617	2467
天然橡胶(包括胶乳)	（千克）Natural Rubber (including Latex)	(kg)	11511360	13274
合成橡胶（包括胶乳）	（千克）Synthetic Rubber (including Latex)	(kg)	46800	74
原　木	（立方米）Logs	(cu.m)	497916	103
锯　材	（立方米）Wood Sawn	(cu.m)	1642517	794
纸　浆	（千克）Pulp	(kg)	103822	108
棉　花	（千克）Cotton	(kg)	9118889	11280
铁矿砂及其精矿	（千克）Iron Ore	(kg)	4428184979	257052
锰矿砂及其精矿	（千克）Manganese ores and concentrates	(kg)	16244880	1368
铜矿砂及其精矿	（千克）Copper Ores	(kg)	2278623	640
氧化铝	（千克）Aluminum Oxide	(kg)	535491	2308
成品油	（千克）Petroleum Products Refined	(kg)	20280	167
碳酸钠（纯碱）	（千克）Sodium carbonate	(kg)	2	1
乙二醇	（千克）Glycol	(kg)	357	6
医药品	（千克）Pharmaceutical Products	(kg)	187195	111034
#抗菌素（制剂除外）	Antibiotic preparation		1	5
肥　料	（千克）Fertilizer	(kg)	129	1
聚合物油漆及清漆	（千克）Polymer Paint	(kg)	104813	778
感光材料	Photosensitive Materials			713
初级形状的塑料	（千克）Plastic in primary Forms	(kg)	2771932	7327
#初级形状的聚乙烯	The Primary PVC		901	1
初级形状的聚丙烯	Polyethylene in primary Forms		9842	29
初级形状的聚苯乙烯	The primary shape of polystyrene		100	5
非泡沫塑料的板、片、膜、箔	（千克）Non-Form-Plastic Plates,Sheets,Films and Foils	(kg)	873348	6496
农　药	（千克）Pesticides	(kg)	245913	177
胶合板及类似多层板	（立方米）Plywood and Similiar Boards	(cu.m)	52056	18
纸及纸板(未切成型的)	（千克）Paper and Paperboard (Unchopped in Shape)	(kg)	3924132	3886
#牛皮纸	Kraft Papers		1389426	776
无机物涂布纸	Inorganic Coated Papers		1968303	1511
棉纱线	（千克）Cotton yarn	(kg)	197325	374
合成纤维纱线	（千克）Fiber Yarns	(kg)	920	16
丝织物	（米）Silk	(m)	56727	31
棉机织物	（米）Cotton Cloth	(m)	181435	448
合成纤维长丝机织物	（米）Synthetic Fibers Long Silk Woven Fabric	(m)	40038	170
合成短纤与棉混纺机织物	（米）Synthetic Short Fibre and Cotton-fibre Mixture Woven Fabric	(m)	7285	17
涂覆浸渍塑料的织物	（千克）Coated plastic impregnated fabric	(kg)	14943	93

17-7 续表 1 continued

商品名称	Item	数　量 Volume	金额（万元） Value (10 000 yuan)
针织或钩编织物　（千克）	Knitted or crocheted fabrics　(kg)	1386	6
鞋靴零件；护腿及类似品　（千克）	Shose Accessories, Leg Guards and Analogs　(kg)	644	19
玻璃纤维及其制品　（千克）	Glass Fibers and Relative Products　(kg)	1393098	6027
钻　石　（克）	Diamonds　(g)	34971	20460
其他宝石及半宝石　（千克）	Other Precious and Semi-precious Stones　(kg)	2777875	4
钢坯及粗锻件　（千克）	Billet and Crude Forgings　(kg)	319427	574
钢　材　（千克）	Rolled Steel　(kg)	3969450	23936
#钢铁棒材	Steel Bar	1876889	8394
角钢及型钢	Angle Iron and Steel	1332	31
钢铁板材	Steel Plate	1320608	3396
钢铁管材及空心异型材	Steel Tube Accessories	570815	3870
钢铁制标准坚固件　（千克）	Standard Fastener Made of Steel　(kg)	288043	10237
未锻造的铜及铜材　（千克）	Unforged Copper and Rolled Copper　(kg)	38728054	172442
未锻造的铜（包括铜合金）	Unforged Copper (Including Copper Alloys)	37247679	157751
铜　材	Rolled Copper	1480375	14691
未锻造的铝及铝材　（千克）	Unforged Aluminum　(kg)	7626078	35752
未锻造的铝（包括铝合金）	Unwrought aluminum (aluminum alloy)	4700	180
铝　材	Rolled Aluminum	7621378	35573
钢铁或铝制结构体及其部件　（千克）	Structure and Relative Parts Made of Steel or Aluminum　(kg)	909313	4561
钢铁或铝制绞股线及类似品　（千克）	Wires and Relative Products Made of Steel or Aluminum　(kg)	124842	469
活塞式内燃机的零件　（千克）	Parts of Piston Combustion Engines　(kg)	2425591	22314
涡轮喷气发动机　（台）	Turbojet EngineS　(unit)	7	67
液泵及液体提升机　（台）	Liquid Pumps and Elevators　(unit)	10949	20779
制冷设备用压缩机　（台）	Compressors for Refrigerating Equipment　(unit)	172	6326
空气调节器　（台）	Air Conditioning　(unit)	149	2252
冷冻机和制冷设备	Refrigerators and Refrigerating Equipment		169
非家用型水的过滤、净化机器　（台）	Non-family Machinery for Filtering and Purifing　(unit)	2742	2001
饮料及液体食品灌装设备　（台）	Canned Equipment for Beverage and Liquid Food　(unit)	2	95
机械提升搬运装卸设备及零件	Mechanical Elevators for Transport and Relative Parts		13346
建筑及采矿用机械及零件	Machinery and parts for Construction and Mining		16031
食品加工机械及零件	Machinery and parts for Food Processing		3308
制造纸及纸制品用机械及零件	Machinery for Paper and Paper Products Manufacturing and Relative Parts		2738
印刷、装订机械及零件	Machinery and parts for Printing and Binding		1470
纺织机械及零件	Textile Machinery and Relative Parts		14325
#纺织纱线生产及预处理机　（台）	Textile Yarn and Pre-production Machines　(unit)	20	1243
织　机　（台）	Knitting machine　(unit)	386	10833
纱线织物等后整理机器　（台）	Yarn, Fabric and other Finishing Machines　(unit)	68	150
工业用缝纫机　（台）	Industrial Use Sewing Machines　(unit)	314	651
金属加工机床　（台）	Machine Tools　(unit)	182	38313

17-7 续表 2 continued

商品名称		Item		数量 Volume	金额(万元) Value (10 000 yuan)
金属冶炼铸造设备及零件		Metal Smelting and Forging Equipment and Relative Parts			675
金属轧机及零件		Metal Mills and Relative Parts			1107
玻璃热加工机械及零件		Machinery and parts for Glass Hot Processing			1806
橡胶或塑料加工机械及零件		Machinery and for Rubber or Plastic Processing			3866
型模及金属铸造用型箱		Casting Molds for Metal Forging			2987
阀门	(套)	Valves	(unit)	303195	32970
自动数据处理设备及其部件	(台)	Automatic Data Processing Machines and Components	(unit)	97384	24291
#数字式自动数据处理设备		Automatic Data Processing Equipments		149	2368
数字式中央处理部件		Digital Central Processing Unit		613	6693
输入或输出部件		Input and Output Operations		6316	492
自动数据处理设备的零件	(千克)	Parts of Data Processing Machines	(kg)	113240	28255
电动机及发电机	(台)	Electric Motors and Generators	(unit)	11323	8311
发电机组及旋转式变流机	(台)	Dynamo Units and Rotated Converters	(unit)	171	23187
旋转式电力设备的零件	(千克)	Parts of Rotated Electric Equipment	(kg)	98139	1915
变压、整流、电感器及零件		Transformers, Rectifiers, Inductancers and Relative Parts			49790
电池	(个)	Batteries	(unit)	359563	892
焊接机器及零件		Welders and Relative Parts			4668
未录的磁带及类似品		Unrecorded Tapes and The Analogs			27490
无线电导航雷达及遥控设备	(台)	Radar for Radio Navigationequipment and Control Equipment	(unit)	230	583
录、放像机机	(台)	Record, like machine	(unit)	49	273
录放音、像机及唱机的零附件	(千克)	Parts of Sound Recorders, Video Tape Recorders and Phonographs	(kg)	24	34
电视、收音机及无线电讯设备的零附件	(千克)	Parts of Television, Radio and Wireless Telecommunication Equipment	(kg)	2174	1163
电容器	(千克)	Electrical Capacitors	(kg)	132505	11516
电阻器	(千克)	Resistor	(kg)	149500	14067
印刷电路	(块)	Printed Circuit	(unit)	49561257	32757
断路保护电路装置及零件		Breaking-off and Safety CircuitSets and Parts			67699
二极管及类似半导体器件	(个)	Diodes Transistors and Semiconductor Devices	(unit)	479016950	82924
电线和电缆	(千克)	Insulated Wire or Cable	(kg)	910076	15784
汽车和汽车底盘	(辆)	Motor Vehicles and Chassis	(unit)	14	2390
货车(包括整套散件)		Trucks (including a Complete Set of Spare Parts)		1	515
专用汽车		Special Purpose Vehicles		1	1328
装有引擎的汽车底盘	(台)	Automobile chassis with the engine	(unit)	12	547
汽车零件		Auto parts			14429
飞机	(架)	Airplanes	(unit)	68	9861
航空器零件	(千克)	Parts of Air Craft	(kg)	181738	31391

17-7 续表 3 continued

商品名称		Item		数量 Volume	金额(万元) Value (10 000 yuan)
船舶	(艘)	Camera Accessories	(unit)	1	87
医疗仪器及器械		Medical Instruments and Appliances			20743
计量检测分析自控仪器及器具		Measuring, Checking and Analyzing Auto-controlling Apparatus			393545
计钟表机芯及钟表零件		Design Watch Movement and Watch Parts			65
印刷品	(千克)	Presswork	(kg)	121272	8601
塑料制品	(千克)	Plastic Articles	(kg)	2267608	15630
玩具		Toys			132
纽扣及其零件	(千克)	Buckles and Relative Parts	(kg)	107	6
拉链及其零件	(千克)	Zippers and Relative Parts	(kg)	117617	34
机电产品		Machanical and Electrical Products			6689453
金属制品		Metal Products			78270
机械设备		Machinery and Equipments			2057904
电器及电子产品		Electric and Electronic Products			4000490
运输工具		Transport Equipments			76718
仪器仪表		Instruments and Meters			470769
其他		0thers			4966
高新技术产品		High and New-tech Products			5934906
生物技术		Biotechnology			246
生命科学技术		Life Sciences Technology			242865
光电技术		Photoelectric Technology			176692
计算机与通信技术		Computer and Communication Technology			84549
电子技术		Electronic Technology			3703319
计算机集成制造技术		Computer Integrated Manufacturing Technology			1588108
材料技术		Material Technology			24537
航空航天技术		Aerospace Technology			109954
其他技术		Others			4731
其他燃料油	(千克)	Other Fuel Oil	(kg)	382	2
橄榄油	(千克)	Olive Oil	(kg)	21287	98
酒类		Liquor			2447
#啤酒		Beer			18
葡萄酒		Wine			2428
二甲苯		Dimethylbenzene			3
美容化妆品及护肤品		Cosmetics and skin care products			1
涂布纸		Coated Papers			1631
加工中心		Machining Center			19498
数控铣床		NC Milling Machine			11952
制造单晶柱或晶圆用的机器及装置		Boules or Wafers of a Single Plant and Equipment			49479
制造半导体器件或集成电路用的机器及装置		Semiconductor Devices or Integrated Circuits Used in Machinery and Equipment			1266296
制造平板显示器用的机器及装置		Flat Panel Display Manufacturing Machines and Equipment			9
蓄电池		Electric Accumulators			693

17-8 利用外资情况
Utilization of Foreign Capital

单位：万美元 (USD 10 000)

年份 Year	签订合同项目(个) Number of Signed Projects (unit)	签订外商直接投资合同 Contracts of Direct Foreign Investments		实际利用外商直接投资 Amount of FDI Actually Utilized	
		金额 Value	比上年增长% Growth Rate as Preceding Year(%)	金额 Value	比上年增长% Growth Rate as Preceding Year(%)
1983	2	823		25	
1984	7	154	-81.3	129	416.0
1985	50	42848	27723.4	818	534.1
1986	34	34786	-18.8	942	15.2
1987	18	17381	-50.0	2890	206.8
1988	14	2096	-87.9	18007	523.1
1989	22	2650	26.4	9679	-46.2
1990	24	1134	-57.2	4191	-56.7
1991	54	2068	82.4	3159	-24.6
1992	424	52290	2428.5	4583	45.1
1993	790	92204	76.3	23432	411.3
1994	444	41142	-55.4	23809	1.6
1995	272	41518	0.9	32407	36.1
1996	280	60054	44.6	33008	1.9
1997	182	64954	8.2	61016	84.9
1998	196	37582	-42.1	30010	-50.8
1999	157	42693	13.6	24197	-19.4
2000	215	49931	17.0	28842	19.2
2001	223	73009	46.2	36455	26.4
2002	203	84060	15.1	41064	12.6
2003	229	83428	-0.8	46602	13.5
2004	271	104877	25.7	52664	13.0
2005	256	158237	50.9	62839	19.3
2006	255	203530	28.6	92489	47.2
2007	184	197311	-3.1	119516	29.2
2008	156	181781	-7.9	136954	14.6
2009	101	140117	-22.9	151053	10.3
2010	139	221030	57.8	182006	20.5
2011	138	254910	15.3	235483	29.4
2012	144	515036	102.1	293609	24.7
2013	204	372078	-27.8	367800	25.3
2014	141	585453	57.4	417557	13.5

17-9 外商投资情况
Foreign Investment

单位：万美元 (USD 10 000)

分组	Groups	项目数(个) Number of Projects (unit)		合同外资 Contracted Foreign Investments		实际外资 Actually Utilized Foreign Investments	
		2013	2014	2013	2014	2013	2014
总计	**Total**	**204**	**141**	**372078**	**585453**	**367800**	**417557**
按投资方式分	**By Investment Form**						
中外合资企业	Equity Joint Venture	73	43	155217	168213	120326	133175
中外合作企业	Contractural Joint Venture	5	1	-3302	-860	549	1199
外资企业	Wholly Foreign-owned Enterprise	125	97	164803	418066	191274	283183
外商投资股份制	FDI Shareholding Inc.	1		55360	34	55651	
按国民经济行业分	**By Sector**						
农、林、牧、渔业	Agriculture, Forestry, Animal Husbandry and Fishery	6	5	9667	4043	2802	2635
采矿业	Mining	2		724	-164	1593	1288
制造业	Mining	54	43	198871	216414	248381	244421
电力、燃气及水的生产和	Production and Supply of Electricity,	2	5	3179	14159	7586	1410
建筑业	Construction	6	7	4130	2130	3941	5
交通运输、仓储和邮政业	Transport, Storage and Post	8	3	12799	10825	4044	7762
信息传输、计算机服务和软件业	Information Transmission, Computer Services and Software	10	9	975	6532	243	6765
批发和零售业	Wholesale and Retail Trades	52	25	34793	33766	29362	23479
住宿和餐饮业	Hotels and Catering Services	13	7	4070	615	2793	2225
金融业	Financial Intermediation	2	4	3799	10319	1650	4190
房地产业	Real Estate	10	5	83502	229840	57916	73610
租赁和商务服务业	Leasing and Business Services	25	22	6147	44176	1845	39903
科学研究、技术服务和	Scientific Research, Technical Service	2	1	2107	7943		8181
水利、环境和公共设施	Management of Water Conservancy,Environment	4		3217	2599	1092	1597
居民服务和其他服务业	Services to Households and Other Services	2	2	234	783	129	11
教育	Education			30	42		72
卫生、社会保障和社会福利业	Health, Social Security and Social Welfare				1071	4423	
文化、体育和娱乐业	Culture, Sports and Entertainment	6	3	3834	360		1

17-9 续表 continued

单位：万美元 (USD 10 000)

分组	Groups	项目数(个) Number of Projects (unit) 2013	2014	合同外资 Contracted Foreign Investments 2013	2014	实际外资 Actually Utilized Foreign Investments 2013	2014
按国别(地区)分	**By Country(Region)**						
文　莱	Brunei			344		344	
朝　鲜	Korea DPR	3		59		11	
香　港	Hong Kong, China	73	63	238959	414531	176637	234261
印　尼	Indonesia			79		79	
伊　朗	Iran	1		8			8
日　本	Japan	5	1	3878	469	8777	2055
澳　门	Macao, China	3		891		234	
马来西亚	Malaysia	1	2	55	531	400	158
新加坡	Singapore	9	6	82485	21175	62876	12550
韩　国	Korea Rep.	63	37	3969	75181	73397	132957
毛里求斯	Mauritius			6000	7418	6000	7418
泰　国	Thailand		1		10		
台湾省	Taiwan, China	7	6	119	145	165	58
塞舌尔	Seychelles	2	1	620	100	600	14
英　国	United Kingdom	2	1	763	12	300	361
德　国	Germany	2	2	460	1164	388	317
法　国	France	1	1	113	1251	54	1593
意大利	Italy		1	-122	6	53	
荷　兰	Netherlands				5717		5329
冰　岛	Iceland			489	722	1528	
挪　威	Norway		1				
瑞　士	Switzerland	1		283			211
阿根廷	Argentina	1		648			
开曼群岛	Cayman Islands	1		200	-4104	110	200
巴拿马	Panama						2
维尔京群岛	Virgin Is. (E)	6	1	7370	8561	11959	4265
加拿大	Canada	4	3	156	270	7	58
美　国	United States	8	4	-1314	1095	2273	2056
百慕大	Bermuda	1		644	4338	1534	3518
澳大利亚	Australia	3		982	-774	11	313
库克群岛	Cook Is.				-190		
新西兰	New Zealand			1528	2737	1346	1037
萨摩亚	Samoa	2	2	57	4222	299	52
投资性公司投资	Investment Companies	5	8	22355	40866	18418	8766

17-10 旅游总收入和总人数
Total Income and Number of Visitors

年 份 Year	总收入 (亿元) Total Income (100 million yuan)	国内旅游收入 (亿元) Domestic Tourism (100 million yuan)	国际旅游收入 (万美元) International Tourism (USD 10 000)	总人数 (万人) Total Number (10 000 persons)	国内游客 Domestic Vistiors	国际游客 International Vistiors
1991	27	23	5482	1532	1500	32
1992	31	25	7505	1594	1550	44
1993	35	28	8900	1746	1700	46
1994	39	30	11279	1794	1750	44
1995	54	42	14090	2144	2100	44
1996	77	61	19820	2350	2300	50
1997	86	67	22464	2554	2500	54
1998	95	74	24717	2604	2550	54
1999	111	88	27189	2663	2600	63
2000	150	127	28000	3131	3060	71
2001	168	142	30871	3436	3360	76
2002	187	158	35097	3818	3733	85
2003	160	144	19800	3347	3300	47
2004	301	271	36136	5312	5232	80
2005	353	316	44625	6081	5988	93
2006	418	378	51000	7056	6950	106
2007	504	458	61200	8138	8015	123
2008	607	561	66011	9182	9056	126
2009	767	715	77107	11555	11410	145
2010	984	916	101596	14566	14354	212
2011	1324	1240	129505	18406	18135	270
2012	1713	1610	159747	23276	22941	335
2013	2135	2031	167620	28514	28161	352
2014	2521	2435	141630	33219	32953	266

17-11 旅游业发展情况
Development of Tourism

指 标	Item	2010	2011	2012	2013	2014
入境旅游人数 (万人次)	Number of Overseas Visitor Arrivals (10 000 person-times)	212.17	270.41	335.24	352.06	266.30
1.港澳同胞	Chinese Compatriots From Hong Kong and Macao	32.90	46.96	60.34	59.97	46.46
2.台湾同胞	Chinese Compatriots From Taiwan Province	24.04	33.54	41.23	40.97	34.00
3.外 国 人	Foreigners	155.24	189.91	233.66	251.13	185.83
国际旅游外汇收入(万美元)	Foreign Exchange Earnings from International Tourism (USD 10 000)	101596	129505	159747	167620	141630
1.长途交通	Long Distance Transportation	36879	52838	57349	60176	52828
飞 机	Civil Aviation	29260	40017	44569	49280	42206
火 车	Railway	5588	5439	7189	9219	9772
汽 车	Highway	2032	7382	5591	1676	850
2.景区游览	Sightseeing	6502	7770	9904	10728	9489
3.住 宿	Accommodation	12496	13857	19968	20953	19120
4.餐 饮	Food and Beverage	9448	4921	7348	8213	8781
5.购 物	Shopping	19405	23829	30512	30172	23935
6.娱 乐	Entertainment	3962	7123	11182	12069	10197
7.邮电通讯	Postal and Communication Services	2438	2979	3385	3352	3257
8.市内交通	Local Transportation	4165	5180	5911	7375	6090
9.其他服务	Other Service	6299	11008	14217	14583	7931
入境游客在陕人均天花费 (美元/人天)	Per Capita Days Spent of Visitors in Shaanxi (USD/per-day)	186	188	188	186	188
国内旅游人数 (万人次)	Number of Domestic Visitors (10 000 person-times)	14354	18135	22941	28161	32953
国内旅游收入 (亿元)	Earnings from Domestic Tourism (100 million yuan)	916	1240	1610	2031	2435
旅行社数 (个)	Number of Travel Agencies (unit)	615	660	716	730	735

注：2014年入境旅游人数和外汇收入为入境过夜人数和收入。

a) The data of overseas visitor arrivals and foreign exchange earnings of 2014 are oversea visitor arrivals and earnings.

17-12 分国别入境旅游人数
Number of Oversea Visitor Arrivals by Country/Region

单位：人 (person)

国别和地区	Country and Region	2010	2011	2012	2013	2014
总　　计	**Total**	**2121721**	**2704071**	**3352365**	**3520663**	**2663015**
港澳同胞	Chinese Compatriots From Hong Kong and Macao	328951	469588	603423	599709	464644
台湾同胞	Chinese Compatriots From Taiwan Province	240414	335390	412320	409679	340025
日　　本	Japan	183516	186715	183751	123623	104793
韩　　国	Korea Rep.	161262	169337	226323	250518	229839
蒙　　古	Mongolia		30472	35649	36297	20334
菲 律 宾	Philippines		18543	22923	23081	17094
印　　度	India		25488	28763	29671	22468
越　　南	Vietnam		2892	8071	8751	
缅　　甸	Myanmar		1030		4772	
朝　　鲜	Korea DPR		384		7020	
巴基斯坦	Pakistan		3112		7580	6438
英　　国	United Kingdom	88275	91032	101833	99891	78693
法　　国	France	83549	82170	101525	92517	63344
德　　国	Germany	80517	83101	98644	93660	68041
意 大 利	Italy	32781	39122	44622	38324	27566
瑞　　士	Switzerland	14447	14511	18574	21719	15197
瑞　　典	Sweden	13187	16310	17590	17458	10352
俄 罗 斯	Russia	26015	33933	47328	40822	30136
西 班 牙	Spain	30619	38955	40709	32563	27449
美　　国	United States	211869	231349	261415	273831	192320
加 拿 大	Canada	72192	88490	90882	88572	53441
澳大利亚	Australia	55577	63355	78231	76771	59882
新 西 兰	New Zealand		14477	18036	19299	10701
泰　　国	Thailand	19647	20585	29224	39369	21458
新 加 坡	Singapore	39486	48552	52001	50022	42738
印度尼西亚	Indonesia	26020	31064	37139	32186	25270
马来西亚	Malaysia	31183	39264	45979	44980	81747
其　　他	Others	382214	524850	747410	957978	649045

17-13 各市(区)对外经济和国际旅游情况(2014年)
Foreign Economy Trade and International Tourism by City(District)(2014)

地　　区	Region	进出口总值 (万元) Total Value of Imports and Exports (10 000 yuan)	# 出　口 Exports	外商投资 Foreign Capital 项目数 (个) Number of Projects (unit)	合同外资 (万美元) Contracts of Foreign Investments (USD 10 000)	实际外资 (万美元) Actually Utilized Foreign Investments (USD 10 000)	星级饭店数 (个) Number of Star-rated Hotel (unit)
全　　省	**Shaanxi**	**16808305**	**8555749**	**141**	**585453**	**417557**	**375**
西 安 市	Xi'an	15321514	7346822	92	480457	370318	109
铜 川 市	Tongchuan	13651	13642	1	2100	2100	13
宝 鸡 市	Baoji	524327	412095	10	14101	8008	34
咸 阳 市	Xianyang	353851	282767	2	11824	10356	23
渭 南 市	Weinan	141684	119111		813	1216	29
延 安 市	Yan'an	71390	71390	1	1252	1063	48
汉 中 市	Hanzhong	63730	45362	6	3316	4005	29
榆 林 市	Yulin	29308	25498	3	9982	7266	29
安 康 市	Ankang	21731	21731	1	489	3000	30
商 洛 市	Shangluo	224659	183170	1	1046	473	19
杨凌示范区	Yangling	42458	34160		1002	611	6
西咸新区	Xixian New Area					8020	
其　　他	Others			24	59071	9141	6

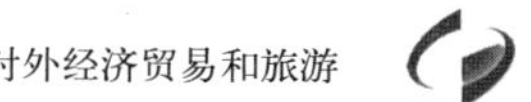

17-14 主要星级饭店基本情况(2014年)
Basic Conditions of Main Star-Degree-Hotels(2014)

饭店名称	Name of Hotel	地址	Address
五星级	**Five Star**		
维景(阿房宫)饭店	Hyatt Regency Hotel	西安市东大街158号	No.158 East Street,Xi'an
西安喜来登大酒店	Sharaton Hotel	西安市沣镐东路262号	No.262 East Fenghao Avenue,Xi'an
西安金花大酒店	Golden Flower Hotel,Xi'an	西安市长乐西路8号	No.8 West Changle Avenue,Xi'an
西安君樂城堡酒店	Grand Park Hotel,Xi'an	西安市环城南路西段12号	No.12 West Section ,South City Ring Road,Xi'an
索菲特人民大厦	Sofitel,Renmin Square, Xi'an	西安市东新街319号	No.319 East New Street,Xi'an
西安香格里拉大酒店	Shangri-la Hotel,Xi'an	西安市科技路38号乙	No.38 Keji Road,Xi'an
陕西世纪金源大饭店	Empark Grand Hotel	西安市建工路19号	No.19 Jiangong Road,Xi'an
天域凯莱大酒店	Tian-yu Gloria Plaza Hotel	西安市雁塔北路15号	No.15 North Yanta Road,Xi'an
建国饭店	Jianguo Hotel	西安市互助路2号	No.2 Huzhu Road,Xi'an
西安瑞斯丽大酒店	Swisstouches Hotel	西安市高新区沣惠南路22号	No.22 West Fenghui Avenue,Xi'an
西安阳光国际大酒店		西安市解放路177号	No.177 Jiefang Road,Xi'an
西安赛瑞喜来登大酒店	Sheraton Xian North City Hotel	西安市未央路32号	No.32 Jiefang Road,Xi'an
西安新兴戴斯大酒店	Days Inn	西安市金花北路189号	No.189 North Jinhua Road,Xi'an
榆林永昌国际大酒店	Yongchang International Hotel,Yulin	榆林市高新技术产业园朝阳路	Zhaoyang Road,High Technology Industry Park,Yulin
四星级	**Four Star**		
唐华宾馆	Xi'an Garden Hotel	西安市雁引路40号	No.40 Yanyin Road,Xi'an
古都新世界大酒店	Grand New World Hotel	西安市莲湖路172号	No.172 Lianhu Road,Xi'an
西安宾馆	Xi'an Hotel	西安市长安北路58号	No.58 North Chang'an Road,Xi'an
西安骊苑大酒店	Le Garden Hotel,xian	西安市劳动南路8号	No.8 South Laodong Road,Xi'an
唐城宾馆	Tangcheng Hotel	西安市含光路南段229号	No.229 South Hanguang Road,Xi'an
钟楼饭店	Bell Tower Hotel,Xian	西安市南大街110号	No.110 South Street,Xi'an
陕西皇城豪门酒店	Imperial City Haomen Hotel	西安市东大街334号	No.334 East Street,Xi'an
东方大酒店	East Hotel	西安市朱雀大街393号	No.393 Zhuque Street,Xi'an
润天宾馆	Runtian Hotel	西安市阎良区润天大道15号	No.15 Runtian Road,Yanlian District,Xi'an
高速神州酒店	Sino Pearl Hotel	西安市环城东路9号	No.9 East City Ring Road,Xi'an
陕西奥罗国际大酒店	Aurum International Hotel	西安市南新街30号	No.30 South New Street,Xi'an
西京国际饭店	West Capital International Hotel	西安市西大街241号	No.241 West Street,Xi'an
天翼新商务酒店	Tianyi Commercial Hotel,Xi'an	西安市西二环南段281号	No.281 South Section ,West Second
西安美居人民大厦	Mercure on Renmin Square,Xi'an	西安市东新街319号	No.319 East New Street,Xi'an
西安富凯酒店	Fukai Hotel,Xi'an	西安市南新街27号	No.27 South New Street,Xi'an
西安志诚丽柏酒店	Ziction Liberal Hotel,Xi'an	西安市高新路46号	No.46 Gaoxin Road,Xi'an

17-14 续表 continued

饭店名称	Name of Hotel	地址	Address
万年饭店	Eternity Hotel,Xi'an	西安市长乐中路副11号	No.11 Changle Road,Xi'an
陕西中江之旅时代大酒店	ZhongJiang Journey Time Hotel,Shaanxi	西安市文景路18号	No.18 Wenjing Road,Xi'an
西安皇后大酒店	Xi'an Empress Hotel	西安市兴庆路45号	No.45 Xingqing Road,Xi'an
西安美华金唐国际酒店	Meihua Jintang International Hotel,Xi'an	西安市西大街79号	No.79 West Street,Xi'an
西安军安王朝大酒店	King Dynasty Hotel,Xi'an	西安市大庆路1号	No.1 Daqing Road,Xi'an
西安唐朝酒店	The Tang Dynasty Hotel	西安市凤城三路198号	No.198 Fengcheng 3 Road,Xi'an
西安绿地假日酒店	Green Holiday Hotel,Xi'an	西安市锦业路5号	No.5 Jinye Road, Xi'an
西安雁塔国际大酒店	Yanta International Hotel, Xi'an	西安市西影路西段609号	No.609 West of Xiying Road, Xi'an
陕西华山国际酒店	Huashan International Hotel,Shaanxi	西安市北大街199号	No.199 South Street,Xi'an
长庆宾馆	Changqing Hotel	西安市未央路151号	No.151 Jiefang Road,Xi'an
西安长征国际酒店	Long March international Hotel	西安市高新区西部大道1号	
怡和酒店	Jardine Matheson Hotel	宝鸡市火炬路中段	Middle Section ,Huoju Road,Baoji
高新君悦国际酒店	Gaoxin Junyue International Hotel	宝鸡市高新区高新大道69号	No.69,New&Hi Avenue,New&Hi-tech Industrial Development Zone,Baoji
红螺湾假日酒店	Red screw holiday Hotel	咸阳市渭阳西路中段	Middle Section ,West Weiyang Road, Xianyang
国贸大酒店	International Trade Hotel	咸阳市渭阳中路	Weiyang Zhong Road,Xianyang
邮政大酒店	Post Hotel	汉中市天汉大道中段	Middle Section,Tianhan Avenue,Hanzhong
红叶大酒店	Red Leaf Hotel	汉中市劳动东路中段33号	Middle Section,East Laodong Road, Hanzhong
金江大酒店	Jinjian Hotel	汉中市人民路北段123号	No.123 North Renmin Road,Hanzhong
明江国际酒店	MingJiang International Hotel	安康市滨江大道3号	No.3 Binjiang Avenue,AnKang
光明大酒店	GuangMing Hotel	渭南市朝阳大街82号	No.82 Zhaoyang Street,Weinan
延安旅游大厦	Yan'an Tourism Hotel	延安市中心街	Central Street,Yanan
延安丽森酒店	Lisen Hotel,Yan'an	延安市双拥大道	Double Support Avenue,Yanan
黄陵桥山滨湖酒店	Huangling Bridge Lake Hotel	黄陵县黄帝陵西侧	West Tomb of Huangdi,Huangling
延安高第华苑大酒店		延安市大桥街6号	No.6 Daqiao Street,Yanan
延安维也纳国际大酒店	Vienna international hotel,Yan'an	延安市火车站南侧	
亚华商务酒店	Yahua Business Hotel	神木县东新街南端	South Section, East New Street,Shenmu
五洲国际大饭店	Wuzhou International Hotel	神木县东兴街北段	Nouth Section,Dongxing Street,Shenmu
天峰国际酒店	Tianfeng International Hotel	神木县中兴街东段	East Section,Zhongxing Street,Shenmu
正阳国际大酒店	Zhengyang International Hotel	铜川新区正阳路16号	No.16 Zhengyang Road, New Zone of Tongchuan
杨凌国际会展中心酒店	International Exhibition Centers	杨凌示范区新桥北路1号	No.1 North New Bridge Road,Yangling

主要统计指标解释

进出口总额 指实际进出我国国境的货物总金额。包括对外贸易实际进出口货物，来料加工装配进出口货物，国家间、联合国及国际组织无偿援助物资和赠送品，华侨、港澳台同胞和外籍华人捐赠品，租赁期满归承租人所有的租赁货物，进料加工进出口货物，边境地方贸易及边境地区小额贸易进出口货物(边民互市贸易除外)，中外合资企业、中外合作经营企业、外商独资经营企业进出口货物和公用物品，到、离岸价格在规定限额以上的进出口货样和广告品(无商业价值、无使用价值和免费提供出口的除外)，从保税仓库提取在中国境内销售的进口货物，以及其他进出口货物。该指标可以观察一个国家在对外贸易方面的总规模。我国规定出口货物按离岸价格统计，进口货物按到岸价格统计。

商品经营单位所在地进、出口额 指在所在地海关注册登记的有进出口经营权的企业实际进、出口额。

商品目的地进口额和商品货源地出口额 目的地进口额指进口货物的消费、使用或最终抵运地的实际进口额；货源地出口额指出口货物的产地或原始发货地的实际出口额。

利用外资 指我国各级政府、部门、企业和其他经济组织通过对外借款、吸收外商直接投资以及用其他方式筹措的境外现汇、设备、技术等。

外商直接投资 指外国企业和经济组织或个人(包括华侨、港澳台胞以及我国在境外注册的企业)按我国有关政策、法规，用现汇、实物、技术等在我国境内开办外商独资企业、与我国境内的企业或经济组织共同举办中外合资经营企业、合作经营企业或合作开发资源的投资(包括外商投资收益的再投资)，以及经政府有关部门批准的项目投资总额内企业从境外借入的资金。

旅游人数

(1)入境旅游人数：指报告期内来我国观光、度假、探亲访友、就医疗养、购物、参加会议或从事经济、文化、体育、宗教活动的外国人、港澳台同胞等入境游客。统计时，外国人、港澳台同胞每入境一次统计 1 人次。

(2)出境人数：指中国（大陆）居民因公或因私出境前往其他国家、中国香港特别行政区、澳门特别行政区和台湾省观光、度假、探亲访友、就医疗养、购物、参加会议或从事经济、文化、体育、宗教活动的人数，即出境游客。统计时，按每出境一次统计 1 人次。

(3)国内旅游人数：指在报告期内在中国（大陆）观光游览、度假、探亲访友、就医疗养、购物、参加会议或从事经济、文化、体育、宗教活动的中国（大陆）居民人数，其出游的目的不是通过所从事的活动谋取报酬。统计时，国内游客按每出游一次统计 1 人次。

国际旅游(外汇)收入 指入境游客在中国（大陆）境内旅行、游览过程中用于交通、参观游览、住宿、餐饮、购物、娱乐等全部花费。

国内旅游收入 又称旅游总花费指国内游客在国内旅行、游览过程中用于交通、参观游览、住宿、餐饮、购物、娱乐等全部花费。

国际旅行社 指经营业务范围包括入境旅游业务、出境旅游业务和国内旅游业务的旅行社。

国内旅行社 指经营范围仅限于国内旅游业务的旅行社。

星级饭店 指设备、设施、服务符合《旅游饭店星级的划分与评定》(GB/T14308-2003)，通过相关旅游管理部门评定，并取得星级饭店称号的饭店（含预备星级饭店）。

Explanatory Notes on Main Statistical Indicators

Total Imports and Exports at Customs refer to the real value of commodities imported and exported across the border of China. They include the actual imports and exports through foreign trade, imported and exported goods under the processing and assembling trades and materials, supplies and gifts as aid given gratis between governments and by the United Nations and other international organizations, and contributions donated by overseas Chinese, compatriots in Hong Kong and Macao and Chinese with foreign citizenship, leasing commodities owned by tenant at the expiration of leasing period, the imported and exported commodities processed with imported materials, commodities trading in border areas (excluding mutual exchange goods), the imported and exported commodities and articles for public use of the Sino-foreign joint ventures, cooperative enterprises and ventures with sole foreign investment. Also included is import or export of samples and advertising goods for which CIF or FOB value are beyond the permitted ceiling (excluding goods of no trading or use value and free commodities for export), imported goods sold in China from bonded warehouses and other imported or exported goods. The indicator of the total imports and exports at customs can be used to observe the total size of external trade in a country. In accordance with the stipulation of the Chinese government, imports are calculated at CIF, while exports are calculated at FOB.

Import Export Value by Location of China's Foreign Trade Managing Units refers to actual value of imports and exports carried out by corporations which have been registered by the local Customs house and are vested with right to run import export business.

Import Value of Commodities by Place of Destination and Export Value of Commodities by Place of Origin in China The former indicator refers to the value of import commodities of the places of their consumption, utilization or the places of their final destination. The latter indicator refers to the value of export commodities of the places of their origin or the places of the commodities dispatched.

Utilization of Foreign Capitals refers to remittance, equipment and technology financed from abroad, by loans, foreign direct investment and other forms undertaken by the Chinese governments at all levels, by various departments, enterprises and other economic units.

Foreign Borrowings refer to funds borrowed from abroad through formal signing of borrowing agreements with foreign institutions, including loans of foreign governments, loans of international financial institutions, commercial loans of foreign banks, export credit, and funds raised by Chinese bonds (and shares before 1996) issued abroad. It is an important part of China's utilization of foreign capitals.

Foreign Direct Investment refers to the investments inside China by foreign enterprises and economic organizations or individuals (including overseas Chinese, compatriots from Hong Kong, Macao and Taiwan, and Chinese enterprises registered abroad), following the relevant policies and laws of China, for the establishment of ventures exclusively with foreign own investment, Sino-foreign joint ventures and cooperative enterprises or for co-operative exploration of resources with enterprises or economic organizations in China.

Number of Tourists

(1) Visitor arrivals refer to the number of foreigners, Chinese compatriots from Hong Kong, Macao and Taiwan Chinese (mainland) who come to China (mainland) for sight-seeing, vacation, visiting relatives, medical treatment, shopping, attending conference, or to engage in economic, cultural, sports and religious activities. In compiling statistics, each time of entering China is counted as one person-time.

(2) Number of Chinese residents going abroad refer to the number of Chinese (mainland) residents going to other countries, Hong Kong Special Administrative region, Macao Special Administrative region and Taiwan for on official or private purposes, for sight-seeing, vacation, visiting relatives, medical treatment, shopping, attending conference, or to engage in economic, cultural, sports and religious activities. In compiling statistics, each time of leaving is counted as one person-time.

(3) Number of domestic tourists refers to the number of Chinese (mainland) residents who travel within China (mainland) for sight-seeing, vacation, visiting relatives, medical treatment, shopping, attending conference, or to engage in economic, cultural, sports and religious activities. In compiling statistics, each time of travelling is counted as one person-time.

Foreign Exchange Earnings from International Tourism refer to the total expenditure of foreigners, overseas Chinese, Chinese compatriots from Hong Kong, Macao and Taiwan during their stay in the mainland of China on transportation, sighting, accommodation, food, shopping and entertainment.

Income from Domestic Tourism refer to expenditure of domestic tourists on transportation, sighting, accommodation, food, shopping and entertainment while they travel.

International Travel Agencies refer to travel agencies engaged in tourism entering China, Chinese residents going abroad and domestic tourism.

Domestic Travel Agencies refer to travel agencies only engaged in domestic tourism.

Star-rated Hotels refer to hotels rated with stars as assessed by the relevant tourism authorities according to GB/T14308-2003 standard with reference to their infrastructure, facilities and service levels.

十八、金融和保险

资料整理：张应剑

简 要 说 明

一、本篇资料反映陕西金融、证券、保险业务发展情况。

二、资料来源:

金融、证券、保险资料分别由中国人民银行西安分行、中国证券监督管理委员会陕西监管局、中国保险监督管理委员会陕西监管局提供。

Brief Introduction

I. This chapter reflects the development of banking, bond and insurance of Shaanxi Province.

II. The data sources:

The data on banking, bond and insurance are provided by Xi'an Branch of the People's Bank of China, Shaanxi Bureau of China Securities Regulatory Commission and Shaanxi Bureau of China Insurance Regulatory Commission.

18.金融和保险

2014年底全省		
金融机构(含外资)人民币存款余额	28111.34	亿元
# 个人储蓄存款	13428.86	亿元
金融机构(含外资)人民币贷款余额	18837.20	亿元
保险业保费收入		
财 产 险	160.00	亿元
人 身 险	316.75	亿元

金融机构（含外资）人民币年底存贷款余额（亿元）

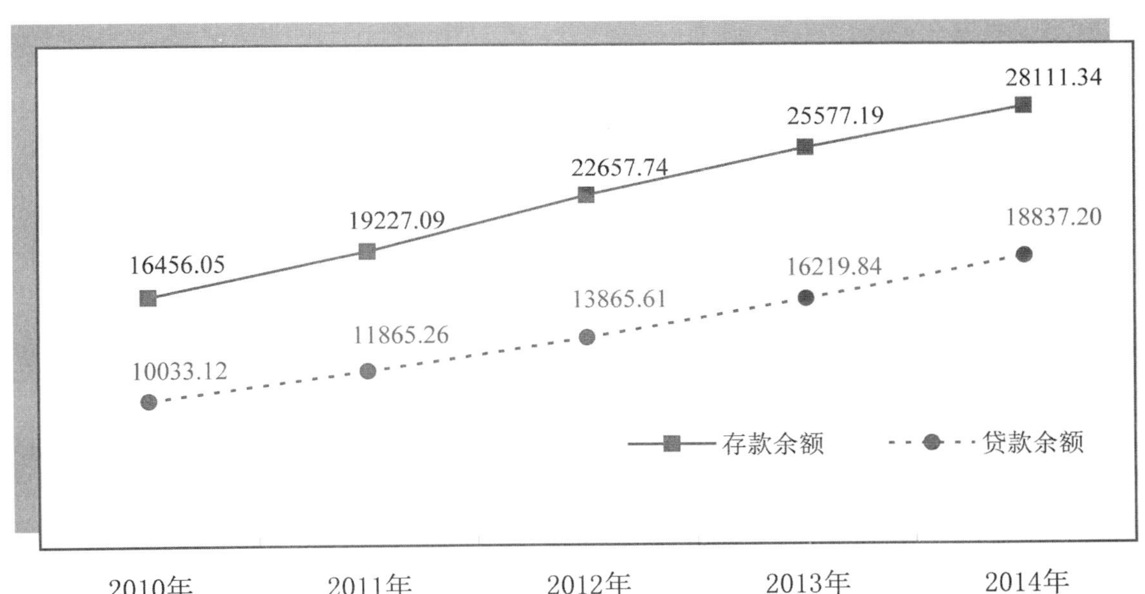

18-1 金融机构(含外资)人民币信贷收支(年底余额)
Summary of Sources & Uses of Funds of Financial Institutions in RMB (Uncluding Foreign Currency at Year-end)

单位：亿元 (100 million yuan)

项　　目	Item	2012	2013	2014
资金来源总计	**Total Funds Sources**	**21627.24**	**24329.16**	**27094.65**
一、各项存款合计	Total Deposits	22657.74	25577.19	28111.34
1.单位存款	Corporate Deposits	11103.19	12270.61	13338.57
2.个人存款	Personal Deposits	10934.76	12654.39	13972.54
# 储蓄存款	Savings Deposits	10770.05	12249.36	13428.86
3.财政性存款	Fiscal Deposits	344.42	322.72	385.04
4.临时性存款	Temporary Deposits	38.30	39.25	17.35
5.委托存款	Entrusted Deposits	25.72	94.67	110.44
6.其他存款	Other Deposits	211.36	195.55	287.41
二、金融债券	Financial Bond			10.17
三、中长期借款	Medium & Long-term Loans	0.89	0.87	0.85
四、应付及暂收款	Accounts Payable and Temporary	424.40	538.08	658.29
五、同业往来	Business with Counterpart	90.85	164.81	444.92
六、系统内资金往来	Funds Transactions in the System			
七、外汇买卖	Foreign Exchange Trading	55.00	119.01	125.35
八、各项准备	All Provisions	368.60	422.59	522.64
九、所有者权益	Owner's Equity	636.91	833.90	983.97
十、其他	Others	-2607.16	-3327.29	-3762.89
资金运用总计	**Total Use of Funds**	**21627.24**	**24329.16**	**27094.65**
一、各项贷款合计	Total Loans	13865.61	16219.84	18837.20
1.境内贷款	Domestic Loans	13863.99	16218.13	18836.43
短期贷款	Short-term Loans	3964.40	4697.04	5052.02
中长期贷款	Medium & Long-term Loans	9385.20	11026.40	12965.17
融资租赁	Financial Lease	1.08	0.28	3.10
票据融资	Bill Financing	512.80	493.60	810.17
各项垫款	Miscellaneous Advances	0.51	0.81	5.98
2.境外贷款	Overseas Loans	1.63	1.71	0.77
二、有价证券	Portfolio Investments	299.38	583.00	781.45
三、股权及其他投资	Shares and Other Investments	184.85	253.58	402.81
四、应收及预付款	Receivables and Prepayments	117.08	230.81	261.93
五、同业往来	Business with Counterpart	117.98	154.50	69.50
六、系统内资金往来	Funds Transactions in the System	6630.12	6373.70	6187.78
七、金银占款	Position for Bullion and Silver Purchase			
八、外汇买卖	Foreign Exchange Trading	55.43	119.52	126.26
九、固定资产	Fixed Assets	208.80	238.56	263.56
十、库存现金	Cash in Vault	147.59	155.27	163.75
十一、投资性房地产	Investment Real Estates	0.40	0.38	0.40

18-2 证券业主要情况
General Statistics on Securities Markets

指　　标	Item	2013	2014
上市公司情况	**Listed Companies**		
上市公司 (户)	Number of Listed Companies (accounts)	39	42
# A 股 (只)	A Shares (number)	39	42
上市公司总股本 (亿股)	Total Issued Capital of Listed Companies (100 million shares)	276.36	406.38
# 流通股本	Negotiable Shares	237.4	256.96
上市公司股票市价总值(亿元)	Total Market Capitalization of Listed Companies(100 million yuan)	2207.05	4845.87
# 股票流通市值	Negotiable Market Capitalization	1847.57	3187.22
证券公司及交易情况	**Securities Companies and Trading**		
证券公司 (个)	Number of Securities Companies (number)	3	3
证券营业部 (个)	Security Exchange (number)	139	179
(含外地公司在陕营业部)	(include Nonlocal Exchange in Shaanxi)		
证券交易开户数 (万户)	Total Stock Investors (10 000 accounts)	234	248
证券交易额 (亿元)	Trading Volume (100 million yuan)	15508.02	23096.3
# 股票、基金	Stocks and Funds	11077.55	17339.79
期货交易情况	**Futures Trading**		
期货代理交易额 (亿元)	Agent's Turnover of Futures (100 million yuan)	50145.68	45318.02

18-3 保险业保费收入(2014年)
Premium of Insurance Transactions (2014)

单位：万元 (10 000 yuan)

地　区	Region	保费收入 Premium		赔款与给付 Payment	
		人身险 Life Insurance	财产险 Property Insurance	人身险 Life Insurance	财产险 Property Insurance
全　省	**Shaanxi**	**3167477**	**1600038**	**945983**	**851461**
省本级	The Same Level	788	54500	284	35926
西安市	Xi'an	1453162	741762	434746	372906
铜川市	Tongchuan	44263	28009	12556	14713
宝鸡市	Baoji	339312	103671	107036	52800
咸阳市	Xianyang	369438	142551	119296	66947
渭南市	Weinan	339214	123907	94887	71148
延安市	Yan'an	95787	89555	24390	55363
汉中市	Hanzhong	213399	69601	74588	33705
榆林市	Yulin	118844	170790	19596	104473
安康市	Ankang	107464	46470	25959	24583
商洛市	Shangluo	85807	29222	32645	18896

主要统计指标解释

信贷资金 指金融机构以信用方式积聚和分配的货币资金。金融机构信贷资金的来源有各项存款、金融债券、对国际金融机构负债、流通中现金、其他项目等；信贷资金的运用有各项贷款、有价证券及投资、金银占款、外汇占款、财政借款及在国际金融机构中的资产等。

存款 指企业、机关、团体或居民根据资金必须收回的原则，把货币资金存入银行或其他信贷机构保管并取得一定利息的一种信用活动形式。根据存款对象或性质的不同可划分为单位存款、个人存款、财政性存款、临时性存款、委托存款、其他存款等科目。它是银行信贷资金的主要来源。

贷款 指银行或其他信贷机构根据资金必须归还的原则，按一定利率，为企业、个人等提供资金的一种信用活动形式。银行贷款分为境内贷款和境外贷款，境内贷款有短期贷款、中长期贷款、融资租赁、票据融资等。

保险公司 在中国境内的、经过保险监督管理部门批准设立，并依法登记注册的各类商业保险公司。

保险金额 指保险人承担赔偿或者给付保险金责任的最高限额。

保费 指投保人为取得保险人在约定范围内所承担赔偿责任而支付给保险人的费用。

赔款 指保险人根据保险合同的规定，向被保险人支付的赔偿保险责任损失的金额。

给付 包括死伤医疗给付和满期给付。死伤医疗给付是指保险人根据人寿保险及长期健康保险合同的规定，因被保险人在保险期内发生保险责任范围内的保险事故支付给被保险人(或受益人)的金额。满期给付是指被保险人生存期满，保险人按人寿保险合同规定支付给被保险人的满期保险金额。

Explanatory Notes on Main Statistical Indicators

Credit Funds refer to the monetary funds accumulated and distributed in the means of credit by the financial institutions. The sources of credit funds include various deposits, financial bonds, liabilities to international financial institutions, currency in circulation, other items. The uses of credit funds include loans, securities and investment, position for bullion and silver purchase, position for foreign exchange purchase, advances to treasury, and assets with international financial institutions.

Deposit is a form of credit by which enterprises, institutions, organizations or households can put money into banks and other credit institutions for safekeeping and interest earning under the principle of free withdrawal. According to different depositors, deposits are divided into corporate deposits, personal deposits, fiscal deposits, temporary deposits, entrusted deposits, other deposits and etc. Deposits are major sources of the credit funds of banks.

Loan is a form of credit by which banks and other credit institutions provide funds at certain interest rate to enterprises and individuals in the light of the principle of unconditional repayment. Loans from Chinese banks include short-term loan, medium- term and long-term loans, entrusted loans, and other loans.The bank loans are divided into domestic loans and overseas loans. The domestic loans include short-term loans, medium & long-term loans, financial lease, bill financing and etc.

Insurance Companies refer to commercial insurance companies of various forms registered by law and established in China with the approval of insurance regulatory agencies.

Amount Insured refers to the maximum that the insurant will get for the claim of the case insured.

Premium is the fee paid by the insurant to the insurer to obtain the obligation of compensation from the insurance within the agreed terms.

Settled Claim is the compensation paid by the insurer to the insurant in accordance with the insurance contract.

Payment includes payment for death, injury or medical treatment and payment at maturity. Payment for death, injury or medical treatment refers to the money paid to the insurant (or the beneficiary) in accordance with the life or health insurance contract when the insurant encounters accidents within the insured period covered in the contract. Payment at maturity refers to the payment to the insurant in accordance with the life insurance contract at the end of the insured period.

十九、教育、科技和文化

Education, Science, Technology and Culture

资料整理：杨小侠　宋　鑫　董清刚

简要说明

一、本篇资料反映陕西教育、科学技术活动和文化事业的基本情况。

二、本篇资料主要包括:

1. 各级各类教育基本情况，指标主要包括各级各类的学校数、在校生数、招生数、毕业生数、教职工数和专任教师数等。

2. 科技活动情况，科技成果及科技人员情况，专利申请和授权，规模以上工业企业研究与试验发展（R&D）活动发展情况等。

3. 文化艺术、文物、图书馆、新闻出版、广播、电影、电视等文化事业的机构、人员及业务活动开展情况等。

三、本篇资料来源:

教育统计资料由省教育厅提供。

科技统计资料由省科技厅、省人力资源和社会保障厅提供（其中规模以上工业企业科技活动由统计局根据统计年报整理）。

文化统计资料由省文化厅、省新闻出版局、省广播电影电视局、省文物局等有关部门提供。

Brief Introduction

Ⅰ. This chapter reflects the basic conditions on the development Shaanxi's education, science and technology.

Ⅱ. The data in this chapter mainly include:

1. The data on tertiary, secondary, primary, and kindergarten education and various types of adult education at all levels, including the number of schools, the number of students enrolled, the number of new enrollments, the number of graduates, the number of staff and workers, and the number of full-time teachers of various levels and categories.

2. The data on scientific and technological, including personnel, achievements and prizes of scientific and technical, numbers of patent applications accepted and granted, R&D activities development of industrial enterprises above designated size, etc.

3. The data on institutions, personnel and business activities of culture and arts, cultural relics, libraries, news and publication, radio, film and television, etc.

III. Data sources:

Data on education are provided by Shaanxi Provincial Department of Education.

Data on science and technology are provided by Shaanxi Provincial Department of Science and Technology, Shaanxi Provincial Department of Human Resources and Social Security. (Science and technology activities of industrial enterprises above designated size are processed and prepared in accordance with the annual statistical reports provided by Shaanxi Provincial Bureau of Statistics.

Data on culture are provided by Shaanxi Provincial Department of Culture, Shaanxi Provincial Administration of Press and Publication, Shaanxi Provincial Administration of Radio, Film and Television, Shaanxi Provincial Cultural Heritage Bureau and the related departments.

19.教育、科技和文化

2014年全省

普通高等学校在校学生	109.96	万人
普通高等学校毕业生	27.74	万人
从事科技活动人员	24.91	万人
图书出版量	18925	万册
杂志出版量	5305	万份
报纸出版量	68245	万份

高等学校在校学生数（万人）

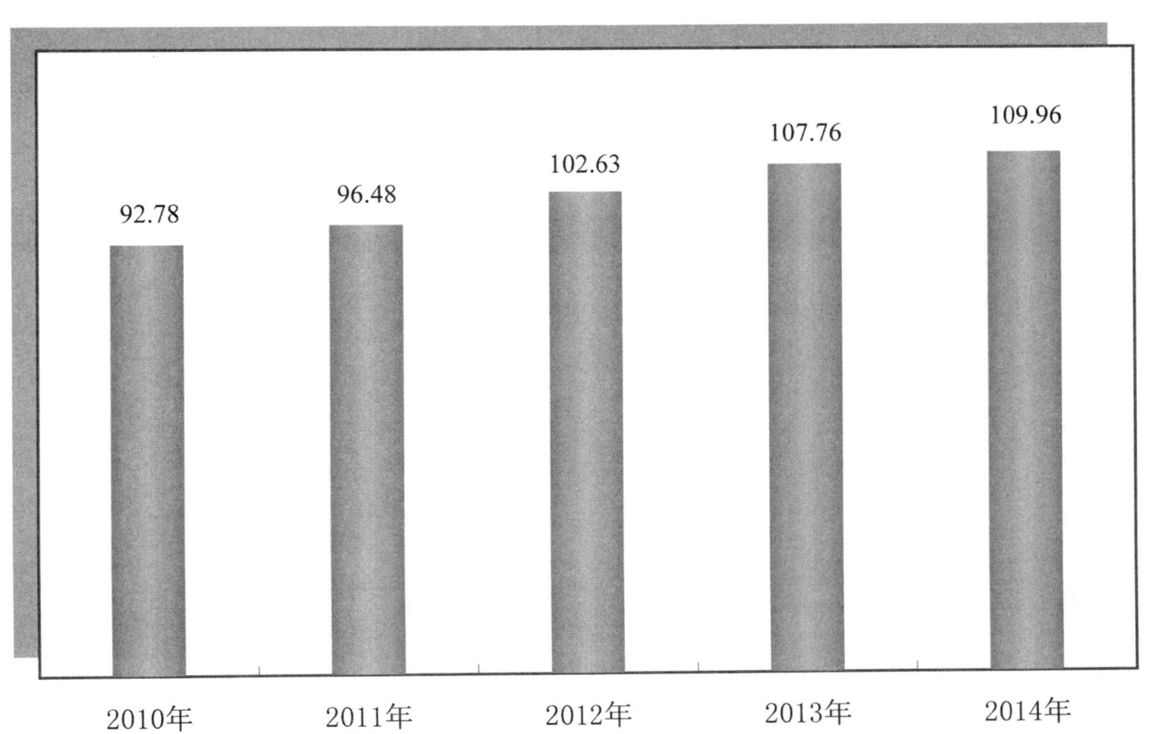

19-1 各级各类教育基本情况(2014年)
Basic Statistics on Schools by Level and Type of School(2014)

指 标	Item	学校数(所) Number of Schools (unit)	毕业生数(人) Graduates (person)	招生数(人) New Enrollment (person)	在校学生数(人) Total Enrollment (person)	教职工数(人) Teachers and Staff (person)	# 专任教师 Full-time Teachers
一、高等教育	Higher Education	118	413827	472639	1514562	106131	67261
1.研究生(含科研机构)	Institutions Providing Postgraduate Programs (Include Research Institutions)	49	27083	32217	98756		15062
# 普通高校	Regular Institutions of Higher Education	27	26865	32012	98044		14487
2.普通高等教育	Regular Higher Education	80	277356	306410	1099613	103332	64970
# 地方院校	Local Universities	74	249791	277335	983559	80379	52443
(1)本 科	Enrolled in Full Undergraduate Courses	37	150931	172958	705800		
# 地方院校	Local Universities	31	123366	143883	589746		
(2)专 科	Enrolled in Specialized Courses	37	126425	133452	393813		
# 地方院校	Local Universities	37	126425	133452	393813		
3.成人高等教育	Higher Education for Adult		62484	62495	176361		
# 成人高等学校	Institutions of Higher Education for Adult	16	6222	6014	18846	2799	1716
4.网络本专科	Students Enrolled in Internet-based Courses		46904	71517	139617		
# 本 科	Enrolled in Full Undergraduate Courses		20431	30078	60159		
5.自考助学班	Students Taking Unified Exams after Completing Self-learning Programs				215		
二、中等职业教育学校	Vocational Secondary Education	491	224331	177052	502557	37306	27483
普通中等专业学校	Regular Specialized Secondary Schools	45	42500	26656	88747	5231	3279
成人中等专业学校	Adult Specialized Secondary Schools	10	3737	1287	5412	1630	1034
职业高中学校	Vocational Senior Secondary Schools	252	114392	107356	282976	18115	13287
技工学校	Technical Schools	184	63702	41753	125422	12330	9883
三、普通中学	Regular Secondary Schools	2220	711722	639352	1968328	203128	164374
高 中	Senior Secondary Schools	506	304394	279795	851044		56924
初 中	Junior Secondary Schools	1714	407328	359557	1117284		107450
四、小 学	Primary Schools	6574	374597	405034	2264095	160287	147511
五、幼儿园(含学前班)	Kindergartens(include Pre-schools)	6970	447848	682780	1327552	115173	68118
六、特殊教育学校	Special Education	52	883	1376	7852	1287	1035
七、工读学校	Schools for Juvenile Delinquents	1	12	15	31	40	20
八、成人中、小学	Adult High and Primary Schools	1677	104065		90306	3086	1822
九、职业技术培训机构	Vocational and Technical Training Institution	8781	1329375		1382338	28033	16273

注：1.研究生培养机构中所含24所普通高等学校的教职工数已计入高等学校教职工总数中。
2.12所独立学院未计入普通高等学校数中，其学生及教职工数等已分别计入高等教育相应指标总数中。

a) Teachers and staff of regular institutions of higher education include the 24 regular institutions of higher education in institutions providing postgraduate programs.

b) 12 non-university tertiary don't count the number of regular institutions of higher education schools. But its students and teachers count corresponding item of regular institutions of higher education respectively.

19-2 普通高等学校基本情况
Basic Statistics on Regular Institutions of Higher Education

年 份 Year	学校数 (所) Number of Schools (unit)	招生数 (万人) New Enrollment (10 000 persons)	在校学生数 (万人) Total Enrollment (10 000 persons)	毕业生数 (万人) Graduates (10 000 persons)	教职工数 (人) Teachers and Staff (person)	# 专任教师 Full-time Teachers
1978	30	1.37	3.44	0.82	27210	10699
1980	34	1.44	5.39	0.38	31694	12066
1985	45	2.86	8.21	1.47	43210	16516
1990	47	2.62	9.54	2.81	51130	19558
1995	46	4.07	12.83	3.75	52440	20200
1996	43	4.28	13.56	3.71	50981	19730
1997	43	4.30	14.10	3.52	50400	19302
1998	42	4.53	15.09	3.44	49279	19250
1999	43	6.90	18.19	3.68	50819	19750
2000	39	9.52	24.17	3.51	52220	20723
2001	47	11.55	31.74	4.35	58846	23613
2002	52	14.70	41.16	5.16	63412	27637
2003	57	16.84	49.97	7.98	67405	35716
2004	62	19.98	58.39	11.10	74607	37145
2005	72	20.89	66.69	14.06	82317	42864
2006	76	21.91	72.62	16.23	87981	47549
2007	76	24.36	77.65	19.55	90306	50741
2008	76	27.64	83.97	21.73	94196	53740
2009	77	27.30	89.37	21.20	96485	56171
2010	78	27.44	92.78	23.55	98536	58288
2011	78	29.69	96.48	25.89	99010	59171
2012	79	32.45	102.63	26.53	100881	61500
2013	80	31.13	107.76	25.38	102017	64171
2014	80	30.64	109.96	27.74	103332	64970

19-3 中等职业学校基本情况
Basic Statistics on Vocational Secondary Schools

年 份 Year	学校数 (所) Number of Schools (unit)	招生数 (万人) New Enrollment (10 000 persons)	在校学生数 (万人) Total Enrollment (10 000 persons)	毕业生数 (万人) Graduates (10 000 persons)	教职工数 (人) Teachers and Staff (person)	# 专任教师 Full-time Teachers
1978	89	1.77	2.93	0.45	10401	3297
1980	162	2.54	6.55	0.92	15246	5699
1985	382	5.54	11.92	3.14	29279	11893
1990	499	7.48	17.99	5.89	39880	17960
1995	569	11.64	27.01	8.39	41736	20926
1996	591	13.08	29.56	8.76	43031	21689
1997	588	13.96	32.54	9.02	40318	21095
1998	652	14.23	34.70	10.24	42719	22628
1999	658	14.90	37.37	10.72	41037	21606
2000	648	13.66	36.37	11.38	40692	21693
2001	535	13.07	34.43	11.49	38050	20746
2002	533	17.26	38.54	10.80	37540	22760
2003	607	20.12	45.57	12.14	41265	25043
2004	588	22.61	50.88	13.33	41817	23868
2005	563	25.43	55.84	15.92	40698	28525
2006	573	28.78	63.55	18.12	40347	25902
2007	691	37.18	76.44	23.09	31986	20916
2008	676	37.19	84.99	25.41	49713	35742
2009	680	35.23	89.91	25.98	52727	36834
2010	663	35.20	89.93	27.35	51534	34619
2011	616	31.45	84.67	30.59	48923	33274
2012	564	24.98	73.31	29.09	44041	30063
2013	520	21.43	60.56	25.76	43440	33025
2014	491	17.71	50.26	22.43	37306	27483

19-4 普通中学基本情况
Basic Statistics on Regular Secondary Schools

年份 Year	学校数 (所) Number of Schools (unit)	招生数 (万人) New Enrollment (10 000 persons)	在校学生数 (万人) Total Enrollment (10 000 persons)	毕业生数 (万人) Graduates (10 000 persons)	教职工数 (人) Teachers and Staff (person)	# 专任教师 Full-time Teachers
1978	7558	90.52	193.47	73.47	116097	91701
1980	5838	52.56	180.85	31.21	127056	97643
1985	3103	56.24	170.33	41.32	122187	93102
1990	3041	47.18	132.64	45.95	127861	98272
1995	2788	55.71	145.07	37.48	129046	100084
1996	2697	56.16	157.21	39.74	131298	102723
1997	2645	65.12	169.01	44.03	134072	105457
1998	2614	70.11	183.60	47.78	137332	109569
1999	2586	78.84	204.41	51.28	142131	115007
2000	2599	88.94	230.52	56.25	149267	122279
2001	2680	97.02	254.75	63.42	160109	131183
2002	2699	103.01	278.26	72.35	169628	140192
2003	2714	104.15	295.41	80.51	178330	148437
2004	2719	103.73	302.56	90.27	185508	154242
2005	2727	102.44	304.56	97.20	191041	159138
2006	2688	102.32	307.93	97.72	193560	162876
2007	2637	96.95	300.09	101.67	195705	166340
2008	2583	93.73	288.87	101.84	198259	169126
2009	2509	88.08	274.68	98.86	198656	170177
2010	2436	83.18	259.91	93.76	198543	170482
2011	2363	79.47	246.80	89.61	210135	170878
2012	2295	73.02	225.70	83.86	207578	168822
2013	2252	68.31	210.13	77.35	206168	167457
2014	2220	63.94	196.83	71.17	203128	164374

19-5 普通小学基本情况
Basic Statistics on Regular Primary Schools

年份 Year	学校数 (所) Number of Schools (unit)	招生数 (万人) New Enrollment (10 000 persons)	在校学生数 (万人) Total Enrollment (10 000 persons)	毕业生数 (万人) Graduates (10 000 persons)	教职工数 (人) Teachers and Staff (person)	# 专任教师 Full-time Teachers
1978	39747	117.01	450.51	67.91	180682	173003
1980	40800	87.10	452.14	58.76	198082	187394
1985	38815	59.93	367.87	61.41	186208	169225
1990	37155	58.42	353.75	42.74	193292	176756
1995	36471	86.30	451.58	50.12	200359	183152
1996	36201	85.97	474.27	53.79	198460	181326
1997	36025	83.05	489.93	59.33	199093	180704
1998	34634	77.31	496.58	66.00	193177	175173
1999	34336	71.57	492.18	71.73	196011	178655
2000	33336	68.22	480.93	77.00	199395	182297
2001	29359	66.87	461.57	81.32	200185	183464
2002	26989	59.51	433.22	83.04	203733	188394
2003	24922	53.01	401.48	80.62	206447	190964
2004	22988	48.16	370.97	76.57	204007	188062
2005	20711	43.59	340.09	72.46	203262	186644
2006	18590	48.52	325.11	67.98	200256	184573
2007	16316	45.43	305.53	65.26	198058	182940
2008	14185	43.18	286.48	61.79	196323	180898
2009	11583	40.99	271.44	55.56	193530	178320
2010	9710	40.86	261.04	50.59	190545	175184
2011	8867	40.77	253.60	46.46	173769	171011
2012	7994	37.89	234.62	44.86	169723	166822
2013	7356	38.81	227.33	40.05	163908	162841
2014	6574	40.50	226.41	37.46	160287	147511

19-6 技工学校基本情况(2014年)
Basic Statistics on Technical Schools(2014)

指　标	Item	学校数(所) Number of Schools (unit)	招生数(人) New Enrollment (person)	在校学生数(人) Total Enrollment (person)	毕业生数(人) Graduates (person)	教职工数(人) Teachers and Staff (person)	# 专任教师 Full-time Teachers
总　计	**Total**	**184**	**41753**	**125422**	**63702**	**12330**	**9883**
一、劳动部门办校	Run by Labour Department	11	2772	8239	2922	1244	933
二、国有经济单位办校	Run by State-owned Unit	58	17871	52511	24363	5450	4512
行业办校	Run by Sector	28	9731	27589	14076	2826	2394
企业办校	Run by Enterprise	30	8140	24922	10287	2624	2118
三、民　办	Run by Private	115	21110	64672	36417	5636	4438

19-7 全省科技活动情况
Scientific and Technological Activities in the Whole Province

指　标		Item		2012	2013	2014
一、从事科技活动人员	(人)	Personnel Engaged in S&T Activities	(person)	220279	229359	249058
中　央		Central		113611	118472	123878
地　方		Local		106668	110887	125180
二、机构数	(个)	Number of Institutions	(unit)			
1.科研院所		Research Institutions		111	111	113
2.高等院校		Regular Institutions of Higher Education		316	358	387
3.规模以上工业企业		Large and Medium-sized Industrial Enterprises		453	558	574
4.其　他		Others		102	100	100
三、R&D经费内部支出	(万元)	Internal Expenditure on R&D	(10 000 yuan)	2872035	3427454	3667730
1.按来源构成分		By Composition of Source				
政府资金		Government Funds		1618303	1920210	1999843
企业资金		Self-raised Funds by Enterprises		1145198	1328656	1552916
境外资金		Foreign capital		964	2142	1191
其他资金		Others		107571	176446	113781
2.按隶属关系分		By Jurisdiction of Management				
中　央		Central		2234057	2544284	2652539
地　方		Local		637979	883170	1015191
四、科技成果与著作情况		Achievements and Books in S&T				
1.科技论文	(篇)	Technical and Scientific Papers	(piece)	64336	64353	64798
2.出版科技著作	(种)	Kinds of Published Scientific Books	(unit)	1516	1384	1454

19-8 全省地方登记的科技成果

Achievements in Science and Technology in the Whole Province

单位：项 (unit)

行 业	Sector	2012	2013	2014
总 计	**Total**	**3281**	**2826**	**2462**
农、林、牧、渔业	Agriculture, Forestry, Animal Husbandry and Fishery	635	304	217
采矿业	Mining	95	118	84
制造业	Manufacturing	454	670	447
电力、燃气及水的生产和供应业	Production and Distribution of Electricity,Gas and Water	158	153	142
建筑业	Construction	52	61	40
批发和零售业	Wholesale and Retail Trades	30	35	1
交通运输、仓储和邮政业	Traffic, Transport, Storage and Post	127	97	46
住宿和餐饮业	Hotels and Catering Services	7		1
信息传输、软件和信息技术服务业	Information Transmission, Software and Information Services	347	267	185
金融业	Financial Intermediation	3	1	2
房地产业	Real Estate	11	1	1
租赁和商务服务业	Leasing and Business Services	1	3	
科学研究和技术服务业	Scientific Research, Technology Services	159	488	888
水利、环境和公共设施管理业	Management of Water Conservancy, Environment and Public Facilities	84	47	56
居民服务、修理和其他服务业	Residents Service, Repair and other Services	16	48	25
教 育	Education	65	12	24
卫生和社会工作	Health, Social Work	781	497	271
文化、体育和娱乐业	Culture, Sports and Entertainment	23	6	18
公共管理、社会保障和社会组织	Public Management, Social Security and Social Organization	229	16	14
国际组织	International Organizations	4	2	

19-9 地方公有经济企业专业技术人才分行业情况(2014年)

Situation of Professional and Technical Personnel in Local Public Economy Enterprises(2014)

单位：人 (person)

行 业	Sector	总 计 Total	#工程技术人员 Engineering	#农业技术人员 Agriculture	#科学研究人员 Scientific Research	#卫生技术人员 Health Care	#教学人员 Teaching
总 计	**Total**	**159701**	**88397**	**1303**	**1269**	**8206**	**2277**
农、林、牧、渔业	Agriculture, Forestry, Animal Husbandry and Fishery	3463	965	1001	53	257	45
采矿业	Mining	37752	21019	107	50	3118	1029
制造业	Manufacturing	44074	24761	38	703	1593	591
电力、燃气及水的生产和供应业	Production and Distribution of Electricity, Gas and Water	9680	6370	5	1	16	58
建筑业	Construction	27560	21839	17	9	225	33
批发和零售业	Wholesale and Retail Trades	4566	218	27		1894	4
交通运输、仓储和邮政业	Traffic, Transport, Storage and Post	9146	4717	15	12	51	37
住宿和餐饮业	Hotels and Catering Services	1721	252		3	14	10
信息传输、软件和信息技术服务业	Information Transmission, Software and Information Services	556	162			5	10
金融业	Financial Intermediation	3743	99		11	2	7
房地产业	Real Estate	1278	622	1			1
租赁和商务服务业	Leasing and Business Services	286	63	1			
科学研究和技术服务业	Scientific Research, Technology Services	8218	6449	3	400	95	93
水利.环境和公共设施管理业	Management of Water Conservancy, Environment and Public Facilities	800	448	25	5	25	4
居民服务、修理和其他服务业	Residents Service, Repair and other Services	1581	216			99	4
教 育	Education	739					337
卫生和社会工作	Health, Social Work	867	1			809	
文化、体育和娱乐业	Culture, Sports and Entertainment	3130	196	3	22	3	14
公共管理、社会保障和社会组织	Public Management, Social Security and Social Organization	541		60			

19-10 规模以上工业企业研究与试验发展(R&D)人员和经费支出情况(2014年)
R&D Personnel and Expenditure of Industrial Enterprises above Designated (2014)

分 组	Item	R&D人员(人) R&D Personnel (person)	#研究人员 Research Personnel	R&D经费内部支出(万元) R&D Internal Expenditure (10 000 yuan)	#政府资金 Government Funds	#企业资金 Enterprises Funds	#境外资金 Foreign Funds
总 计	**Total**	**75835**	**33670**	**1606946**	**337761**	**1252833**	**175**
按企业规模分	**Grouped by Size of Enterprises**						
大 型	Large Enterprises	51331	24565	1135358	309596	822106	77
中 型	Medium-sized Enterprises	13402	5345	220101	16775	197363	
小 型	Small Enterprises	11062	3733	251067	11330	233004	99
微 型	Micro Enterprises	40	27	419	60	359	
按登记注册类型分	**By Status of Registration**						
内资企业	Domestic Funded	74071	32921	1569201	335397	1217721	175
国有企业	State-owned Enterprises	17722	8713	293111	66351	223778	
集体企业	Collective-owned Enterprises	47	12	346	10	336	
股份合作企业	Cooperative Enterprises	24	7	502	50	452	
有限责任公司	Limited Liability Corporations	45420	19801	1053665	257642	784911	99
国有独资公司	State Sole Funded Corporations	15389	6941	334390	90810	242577	
其他有限责任公司	Other Limited Liability Corporations	30031	12860	719276	166832	542334	99
股份有限公司	Share-holding Corporations Limited	7325	3212	143419	6865	135411	77
私营企业	Private Enterprises	3465	1150	77385	4479	72384	
私营独资企业	Private-funded Enterprises	56	28	2699	20	2679	
私营有限责任公司	Private Limited Liability Corporations	2948	934	65723	3728	61473	
私营股份有限公司	Private Share-holding Corporations Ltd.	461	188	8963	731	8233	
其他企业	Other Enterprises	68	26	774		450	
港、澳、台商投资企业	Enterprises with Funds from Hong Kong, Macao and Taiwan	476	122	11479	825	10385	
合资经营企业(港或澳、台资)	Joint-venture Enterprises	323	80	4726	825	3633	
港澳台商独资经营企业	Enterprises with Sole Investment	125	36	6077		6077	
港澳台商投资股份有限公司	Share-holding Corporations Ltd.	28	6	675		675	
外商投资企业	Foreign Funded Enterprises	1288	627	26266	1539	24727	
中外合资经营企业	Joint-venture Enterprises	664	349	13289	1401	11888	
外资企业	Enterprises with Sole Funds	575	261	10919		10919	
外商投资股份有限公司	Share-holding Corporations Ltd.	49	17	2058	138	1921	
按国民经济行业分	**By Sector**						
采矿业	Mining	3994	1920	69530	1578	67647	
煤炭开采和洗选业	Mining and Washing of Coal	1561	515	23986	114	23567	
石油和天然气开采业	Extraction of Petroleum and Natural Gas	1576	1209	31593	1439	30154	
黑色金属矿采选业	Mining and Processing of Ferrous Metal Ores	43	14	264		264	
有色金属矿采选业	Mining and Processing of Non-Ferrous Metal Ores	794	173	13186	26	13160	
非金属矿采选业	Mining and Processing of Nonmetal Ores	20	9	503		503	
制造业	Manufacturing	69905	31103	1524840	331631	1172662	175
农副食品加工业	Processing of Food from Agricultural Products	869	300	24865	859	23088	
食品制造业	Manufacture of Foods	575	180	23467	228	22495	

19-10 续表 continued

分组	Item	R&D人员(人) R&D Personnel (person)	#研究人员 Research Personnel	R&D经费内部支出(万元) R&D Internal Expenditure (10 000 yuan)	#政府资金 Government Funds	#企业资金 Enterprises Funds	#境外资金 Foreign Funds
酒、饮料和精制茶制造业	Manufacture of Wine,Beverages and Refined Tea	519	195	16240	317	15909	
烟草制品业	Manufacture of Tobacco	124	45	4773		4773	
纺织业	Manufacture of Textile	453	162	7124	109	6953	
纺织服装、服饰业	Manufacture of Textile and Clothing	14	4	30	5	25	
皮革、毛皮、羽毛及其制品和制鞋业	Manufacture of Leather, Fur, Feather and Related Products and Footwear	39	4	409		409	
木材加工和木、竹、藤、棕、草制品业	Processing of Timber, Manufacture of Wood, Bamboo, Rattan,Palm and Straw Products	66	29	3485		3485	
造纸和纸制品业	Manufacture of Paper and Paper Products	79	20	6156	55	6097	
印刷和记录媒介复制业	Printing, Reproduction of Recording Media	122	76	3672	75	3589	
文教、工美、体育和娱乐用品制造业	Manufacture of Articles for Culture, Education, Arts and Crafts, Sport and Entertainment Activities	18	12	555		555	
石油加工、炼焦和核燃料加工业	Processing of Petroleum, Coking, Processing Nuclear Fuel	1661	661	74896	2057	72838	
化学原料和化学制品制造业	Manufacture of Chemical Raw Material and Chemical Products	3814	1630	71517	6115	64098	
医药制造业	Manufacture of Medicines	2423	992	41452	1063	40225	
化学纤维制造业	Manufacture of Chemical Fibers	16	8	1174		1174	
橡胶和塑料制品业	Manufacture of Rubber and Plastics	621	99	17492	4153	13340	
非金属矿物制品业	Manufacture of Non-metallic Mineral Products	606	239	17335	1121	15834	
黑色金属冶炼和压延加工业	Smelting and Pressing of Ferrous Metals	694	179	40978	697	40250	
有色金属冶炼和压延加工业	Smelting and Pressing of Non-ferrous Metals	3165	1675	81354	8469	72197	
金属制品业	Manufacture of Metal Products	3439	1938	56639	11847	44761	
通用设备制造业	Manufacture of General Purpose Machinery	3892	1609	52033	6386	45484	99
专用设备制造业	Manufacture of Special Purpose Machinery	6171	3196	92924	12394	78862	77
汽车制造业	Automotive Industry	5000	1083	74912	8346	66426	
铁路、船舶、航空航天和其他运输设备制造业	Manufacture of Railway,Shipping,Aerospace and Other Transport Equipments	17796	8985	486045	243836	237407	
电气机械和器材制造业	Manufacture of Electrical Machinery and Equipment	5581	2114	135772	6157	128580	
计算机、通信和其他电子设备制造业	Manufacture of Computers,Communication and Other Electronic Equipment	5900	2793	95927	12151	80648	
仪器仪表制造业	Manufacture of Measuring Instrument and Machinery	5925	2838	90430	9615	80050	
其他制造业	Other Manufacturing	97	18	2635	39	2596	
金属制品、机械和设备修理业	Industry of Metalwork,Machinery, and Equipment Repair	226	19	552	37	515	
电力、热力、燃气及水生产和供应业	Production and Distribution of Electricity, Gas and Water	1936	647	12575	51	12524	
电力、热力生产和供应业	Production and Supply of Electric Power and Heat Power	1921	644	12014	17	11997	
燃气生产和供应业	Production and Supply of Gas	15	3	561	34	527	

19-11 规模以上工业企业研究与试验发展(R&D)项目情况(2014年)
The Situation of Industrial Enterprises above Designated Projects (2014)

分 组	Item	项目数 (项) Number of R&D Projects (item)	参加项目人员 (人) R&D Personnel (person)	项目人员全时当量 (人年) Full-time Equivalent of R&D Personnel (man-year)	项目经费内部支出 (万元) Expenditure on R&D Projects (10 000 yuan)
总 计	**Total**	**6668**	**66848**	**44756**	**1321262**
按企业规模分	**Grouped by Size of Enterprises**				
大 型	Large Enterprises	3936	44888	32301	907577
中 型	Medium-sized Enterprises	1465	11923	7275	193078
小 型	Small Enterprises	1251	10001	5168	220210
微 型	Micro Enterprises	16	36	12	396
按登记注册类型分	**By Status of Registration**				
内资企业	Domestic Funded	6519	65196	43802	1287845
国有企业	State-owned Enterprises	1847	15390	11327	247291
集体企业	Collective-owned Enterprises	2	39	30	332
股份合作企业	Cooperative Enterprises	4	23	13	379
有限责任公司	Limited Liability Corporations	3555	40147	26798	867336
国有独资公司	State Sole Funded Corporations	1234	13395	9568	277635
其他有限责任公司	Other Limited Liability Corporations	2321	26752	17230	589702
股份有限公司	Share-holding Corporations Limited	762	6443	4050	105998
私营企业	Private Enterprises	343	3094	1580	65874
私营独资企业	Private-funded Enterprises	5	48	25	2392
私营有限责任公司	Private Limited Liability Corporations	324	2642	1366	56777
私营股份有限公司	Private Share-holding Corporations Ltd.	14	404	190	6704
其他企业	Other Enterprises	6	60	5	635
港、澳、台商投资企业	Enterprises with Funds from Hong Kong, Macao and Taiwan	42	451	212	11322
合资经营企业(港或澳、台资)	Joint-venture Enterprises	34	314	113	4726
港、澳、台商独资经营企业	Enterprises with Sole Investment	6	109	97	5947
港、澳、台商投资股份有限公司	Share-holding Corporations Ltd.	2	28	2	649
外商投资企业	Foreign Funded Enterprises	107	1201	743	22095
中外合资经营企业	Joint-venture Enterprises	63	617	337	11659
外资企业	Enterprises with Sole Funds	38	542	393	8984
外商投资股份有限公司	Share-holding Corporations Ltd.	6	42	12	1452
按国民经济行业分	**By Sector**				
采矿业	Mining	294	3572	2223	43658
煤炭开采和洗选业	Mining and Washing of Coal	149	1458	944	20781
石油和天然气开采业	Extraction of Petroleum and Natural Gas	104	1354	809	10602
黑色金属矿采选业	Mining and Processing of Ferrous Metal Ores	1	30	8	264
有色金属矿采选业	Mining and Processing of Non-Ferrous Metal Ores	38	714	453	11831
非金属矿采选业	Mining and Processing of Non-metal Ores	2	16	10	180
制造业	Manufacturing	6278	61390	42265	1266129
农副食品加工业	Processing of Food from Agricultural Products	72	745	225	19794
食品制造业	Manufacture of Foods	56	527	264	17425

19-11 续表 continued

分组	Item	项目数 (项) Number of R&D Projects (item)	参加项目人员 (人) R&D Personnel (person)	项目人员全时当量 (人年) Full-time Equivalent of R&D Personnel (man-year)	项目经费内部支出 (万元) Expenditure on R&D Projects (10 000 yuan)
酒、饮料和精制茶制造业	Manufacture of Wine,Beverages and Refined Tea	55	442	240	13158
烟草制品业	Manufacture of Tobacco	23	118	29	2589
纺织业	Manufacture of Textile	29	353	157	6439
纺织服装、服饰业	Manufacture of Textile and Clothing	1	12	1	23
皮革、毛皮、羽毛及其制品和制鞋业	Manufacture of Leather, Fur, Feather and Related Products and Footwear	7	37	12	287
木材加工和木、竹、藤、棕、草制品业	Processing of Timber, Manufacture of Wood, Bamboo, Rattan,Palm and Straw Products	3	60	25.5	2608
造纸和纸制品业	Manufacture of Paper and Paper Products	6	74	35	5845
印刷和记录媒介复制业	Printing, Reproduction of Recording Media	27	108	67	3199
文教、工美、体育和娱乐用品制造业	Manufacture of Articles for Culture, Education, Arts and Crafts, Sport and Entertainment Activities	1	15	1	400
石油加工、炼焦和核燃料加工业	Processing of Petroleum, Coking, Processing Nuclear Fuel	115	1475	1101	53622
化学原料和化学制品制造业	Manufacture of Chemical Raw Material and Chemical Products	592	3246	2642	64122
医药制造业	Manufacture of Medicines	298	2197	1425	36828
化学纤维制造业	Manufacture of Chemical Fibers	1	12	7	900
橡胶和塑料制品业	Manufacture of Rubber and Plastics	120	568	229	13657
非金属矿物制品业	Manufacture of Non-metallic Mineral Products	43	544	234	15834
黑色金属冶炼和压延加工业	Smelting and Pressing of Ferrous Metals	34	665	553	37739
有色金属冶炼和压延加工业	Smelting and Pressing of Non-ferrous Metals	285	2583	1513	64815
金属制品业	Manufacture of Metal Products	279	2952	2227	41322
通用设备制造业	Manufacture of General Purpose Machinery	425	3460	2347	42794
专用设备制造业	Manufacture of Special Purpose Machinery	556	5519	3611	79732
汽车制造业	Automotive Industry	348	4623	2438	66978
铁路、船舶、航空航天和其他运输设备制造业	Manufacture of Railway,Shipping,Aerospace and Other Transport Equipments	785	15240	11589	402281
电气机械和器材制造业	Manufacture of Electrical Machinery and Equipment	1018	4768	2346	121615
计算机、通信和其他电子设备制造业	Manufacture of Computers,Communication and Other Electronic Equipment	617	5467	4492	71768
仪器仪表制造业	Manufacture of Measuring Instrument and Machinery	467	5261	4406	77648
其他制造业	Other Manufacturing	6	95	42	2191
金属制品、机械和设备修理业	Industry of Metalwork,Machinery, and Equipment Repair	9	224	8	515
电力、热力、燃气及水生产和供应业	Production and Distribution of Electricity, Gas and Water	96	1886	269	11475
电力、热力生产和供应业	Production and Supply of Electric Power and Heat Power	92	1873	267	10915
燃气生产和供应业	Production and Supply of Gas	4	13	1	561

19-12 规模以上工业企业新产品开发、生产及销售情况(2014年)
Developing, Producing and Sales of Industrial Enterprises above Designated (2014)

分 组	Item	新产品开发项目数(项) Number of New products Development Project (item)	新产品开发经费支出(万元) New products Development Expenditure (10 000 yuan)	新产品产 值(万元) New products Output Value (10 000 yuan)	新产品销售收入(万元) New products Sales Income (10 000 yuan)
总 计	**Total**	**6684**	**1710125**	**12787332**	**11267648**
按企业规模分	**Grouped by Size of Enterprises**				
大 型	Large Enterprises	3495	1152131	9560219	8269399
中 型	Medium-sized Enterprises	1761	252308	1984372	1736561
小 型	Small Enterprises	1413	304120	1239648	1258440
微 型	Micro Enterprises	15	1566	3093	3248
按登记注册类型分	**By Status of Registration**				
内资企业	Domestic Funded	6430	1617348	11180505	9909472
国有企业	State-owned Enterprises	1628	320097	1301075	1121689
集体企业	Collective-owned Enterprises	4	1065	120	120
股份合作企业	Cooperative Enterprises	3	199	1800	1800
有限责任公司	Limited Liability Corporations	3520	1091554	8882202	7699585
国有独资公司	State Sole Funded Corporations	1203	322153	2105974	1872834
其他有限责任公司	Other Limited Liability Corporations	2317	769401	6776228	5826751
股份有限公司	Share-holding Corporations Limited	847	127200	710693	772179
私营企业	Private Enterprises	422	76460	284615	314099
私营独资企业	Private-funded Enterprises	5	2711	3183	3595
私营有限责任公司	Private Limited Liability Corporations	390	66776	267410	294899
私营股份有限公司	Private Share-holding Corporations Ltd.	27	6972	14023	15605
其他企业	Other Enterprises	6	774		
港、澳、台商投资企业	Enterprises with Funds from Hong Kong, Macao and Taiwan	56	15115	27332	26965
合资经营企业(港或澳、台资)	Joint-venture Enterprises	51	9674	27332	26965
港、澳、台商独资经营企业	Enterprises with Sole Investment	5	5441		
外商投资企业	Foreign Funded Enterprises	198	77662	1579495	1331212
中外合资经营企业	Joint-venture Enterprises	128	27126	760382	719197
外资企业	Enterprises with Sole Funds	65	50058	810835	604536
外商投资股份有限公司	Share-holding Corporations Ltd.	5	478	8278	7479
按国民经济行业分	**By Sector**				
采矿业	Mining	151	36487	13817	13611
煤炭开采和洗选业	Mining and Washing of Coal	87	23353	800	1005
石油和天然气开采业	Extraction of Petroleum and Natural Gas	53	7217		
黑色金属矿采选业	Mining and Processing of Ferrous Metal Ores				
有色金属矿采选业	Mining and Processing of Non-Ferrous Metal Ores	9	5294		
非金属矿采选业	Mining and Processing of Nonmetal Ores	2	623	13016	12606
制造业	Manufacturing	6476	1666073	12773515	11254038
农副食品加工业	Processing of Food from Agricultural Products	93	37274	165466	144871
食品制造业	Manufacture of Foods	55	23026	74675	66421

19-12 续表 continued

分　组	Item	新产品开发项目数（项）Number of New products Development Project (item)	新产品开发经费支出（万元）New products Development Expenditure (10 000 yuan)	新产品产值（万元）New products Output Value (10 000 yuan)	新产品销售收入（万元）New products Sales Income (10 000 yuan)
酒、饮料和精制茶制造业	Manufacture of Wine,Beverages and Refined Tea	41	8807	181909	210322
烟草制品业	Manufacture of Tobacco	24	5090	44672	47977
纺织业	Manufacture of Textile	33	5704	26842	26651
纺织服装、服饰业	Manufacture of Textile and Clothing	3	1006	11021	10932
皮革、毛皮、羽毛及其制品和制鞋业	Manufacture of Leather, Fur, Feather and Related Products and Footwear	8	477	9712	9712
木材加工和木、竹、藤、棕、草制品业	Processing of Timber, Manufacture of Wood, Bamboo, Rattan, Palm and Straw Products	6	10328	1477	5063
造纸和纸制品业	Manufacture of Paper and Paper Products	6	6455	3183	3595
印刷和记录媒介复制业	Printing, Reproduction of Recording Media	23	1687	5404	3976
文教、工美、体育和娱乐用品制造业	Manufacture of Articles for Culture, Education, Arts and Crafts, Sport and Entertainment Activities	1	555	31	31
石油加工、炼焦和核燃料加工业	Processing of Petroleum, Coking, Processing Nuclear Fuel	33	15168	32941	32941
化学原料和化学制品制造业	Manufacture of Chemical Raw Material and Chemical Products	605	81691	393113	388230
医药制造业	Manufacture of Medicines	309	61065	479334	453165
化学纤维制造业	Manufacture of Chemical Fibers	1	1174		
橡胶和塑料制品业	Manufacture of Rubber and Plastics	119	19284	58653	61485
非金属矿物制品业	Manufacture of Non-metallic Mineral Products	55	18136	87959	109952
黑色金属冶炼和压延加工业	Smelting and Pressing of Ferrous Metals	43	44300	1015218	990310
有色金属冶炼和压延加工业	Smelting and Pressing of Non-ferrous Metals	311	58102	871971	849722
金属制品业	Manufacture of Metal Products	277	58472	312911	300770
通用设备制造业	Manufacture of General Purpose Machinery	409	72185	552998	541299
专用设备制造业	Manufacture of Special Purpose Machinery	521	102032	674194	647250
汽车制造业	Automotive Industry	434	129861	2934467	2124401
铁路、船舶、航空航天和其他运输设备制造业	Manufacture of Railway,Shipping,Aerospace and Other Transport Equipments	771	517955	2173568	1964132
电气机械和器材制造业	Manufacture of Electrical Machinery and Equipment	930	134003	1049554	974917
计算机、通信和其他电子设备制造业	Manufacture of Computers,Communication and Other Electronic Equipment	854	152996	1297742	1068029
仪器仪表制造业	Manufacture of Measuring Instrument and Machinery	490	95037	270113	173523
其他制造业	Other Manufacturing	11	3646	3078	3048
金属制品、机械和设备修理业	Industry of Metalwork,Machinery, and Equipment Repair	10	556	41312	41312
电力、热力、燃气及水生产和供应业	Production and Distribution of Electricity, Gas and Water	57	7566		
电力、热力生产和供应业	Production and Supply of Electric Power and Heat Power	53	7005		
燃气生产和供应业	Production and Supply of Gas	4	561		

19-13 规模以上工业企业自主知识产权保护情况(2014年)

分组	Item	专利申请数 (件) Number of Patent Application (piece)	#发明专利 Patent of Invention
总计	**Total**	**7354**	**3171**
按企业规模分	Grouped by Size of Enterprises		
大型	Large Enterprises	3638	1669
中型	Medium-sized Enterprises	1378	568
小型	Small Enterprises	2333	931
微型	**Micro Enterprises**	**5**	**3**
按登记注册类型分	By Status of Registration		
内资企业	Domestic Funded	7110	3075
国有企业	State-owned Enterprises	1212	673
集体企业	Collective-owned Enterprises	16	2
股份合作企业	Cooperative Enterprises		
有限责任公司	Limited Liability Corporations	4036	1611
国有独资公司	State Sole Funded Corporations	1089	462
其他有限责任公司	Other Limited Liability Corporations	2947	1149
股份有限公司	Share-holding Corporations Limited	1046	388
私营企业	Private Enterprises	800	401
私营独资企业	Private-funded Enterprises		
私营有限责任公司	Private Limited Liability Corporations	761	369
私营股份有限公司	Private Share-holding Corporations Ltd.	39	32
港、澳、台商投资企业	Enterprises with Funds from Hong Kong, Macao and Taiwan	62	29
合资经营企业(港或澳、台资)	Joint-venture Enterprises	56	27
港、澳、台商独资经营企业	Enterprises with Sole Investment	3	2
港、澳、台商投资股份有限公司	Share-holding Corporations Ltd.	3	
外商投资企业	Foreign Funded Enterprises	182	67
中外合资经营企业	Joint-venture Enterprises	155	59
外资企业	**Enterprises with Sole Funds**	**22**	**7**
外商投资股份有限公司	Share-holding Corporations Ltd.	**5**	**1**
按国民经济行业分	By Sector		
采矿业	Mining	311	97
煤炭开采和洗选业	Mining and Washing of Coal	166	25
石油和天然气开采业	Extraction of Petroleum and Natural Gas	133	60
有色金属矿采选业	Mining and Processing of Non-Ferrous Metal Ores	3	3
非金属矿采选业	Mining and Processing of Nonmetal Ores	3	3
开采辅助活动		6	6

Proprietary Intellectual Property Rights of Industrial Enterprises above Designated (2014)

有效发明专利数（件）Number of Effective Patent Invention (piece)	#境外授权 Abroad Authorization	专利所有权转让及许可数（项）Number of Patent Ownership Transfer and Permission (item)	专利所有权转让与许可收入（万元）Income of Patent Ownership Transfer and Permission (10 000 yuan)	发表科技论文（篇）Pulish Technical Thesis (piece)	拥有注册商标数（件）Number of Registered Trademark (piece)	#境外注册 Abroad Register	形成国家或行业标准数（项）Number of National and Trade Standards (item)
6675	**45**	**217**	**27654**	**5571**	**5429**	**404**	**906**
3097	19	31	24303	4139	1947	329	514
1419	14	60	1740	801	1061	34	202
2148	12	125	1611	610	2414	41	190
11		**1**		**21**	**7**		
6458	45	216	27354	5529	5088	392	904
1203	1	17	2040	1413	177	23	161
16					2		1
13		1			3		
3419	29	61	25023	2636	3182	133	565
1024	16	3		797	647	97	331
2395	13	58	25023.4	1839	2535	36	234
1101	12	82	5	1257	928	228	70
706	3	55	286	223	796	8	107
					1		
629	3	54	286	168	760	8	98
77		1		55	35		9
64		1	300	17	6		2
59		1	300	11	5		2
5				6	1		
153				25	335	12	
131				19	83		
19					**251**	**12**	
3				**6**	**1**		
145		2		1278	5		
42				538	3		
96		2		732			
				7			
1				1	2		
6							

19-13 续表

分组	Item	专利申请数 (件) Number of Patent Application (piece)	#发明专利 Patent of Invention
制造业	Manufacturing	6846	3004
农副食品加工业	Processing of Food from Agricultural Products	89	47
食品制造业	Manufacture of Foods	16	12
酒、饮料和精制茶制造业	Manufacture of Wine,Beverages and Refined Tea	38	14
烟草制品业	Manufacture of Tobacco	12	5
纺织业	Manufacture of Textile	12	3
纺织服装、服饰业	Manufacture of Textile and Clothing	8	6
皮革、毛皮、羽毛及其制品和制鞋业	Manufacture of Leather, Fur, Feather and Related Products and Footwear	12	4
木材加工和木、竹、藤、棕、草制品业	Processing of Timber, Manufacture of Wood, Bamboo, Rattan,Palm and Straw Products	7	1
造纸和纸制品业	Manufacture of Paper and Paper Products	1	
印刷和记录媒介复制业	Printing, Reproduction of Recording Media	13	6
石油加工、炼焦和核燃料加工业	Processing of Petroleum, Coking, Processing Nuclear Fuel	130	63
化学原料和化学制品制造业	Manufacture of Chemical Raw Material and Chemical Products	683	468
医药制造业	Manufacture of Medicines	181	118
化学纤维制造业	Manufacture of Chemical Fibers		
橡胶和塑料制品业	Manufacture of Rubber and Plastics	53	16
非金属矿物制品业	Manufacture of Non-metallic Mineral Products	37	20
黑色金属冶炼和压延加工业	Smelting and Pressing of Ferrous Metals	50	12
有色金属冶炼和压延加工业	Smelting and Pressing of Non-ferrous Metals	275	142
金属制品业	Manufacture of Metal Products	205	109
通用设备制造业	Manufacture of General Purpose Machinery	474	111
专用设备制造业	Manufacture of Special Purpose Machinery	888	303
汽车制造业	Automotive Industry	823	199
铁路、船舶、航空航天和其他运输设备制造业	Manufacture of Railway,Shipping,Aerospace and Other Transport Equipments	856	518
电气机械和器材制造业	Manufacture of Electrical Machinery and Equipment	763	165
计算机、通信和其他电子设备制造业	Manufacture of Computers,Communication and Other Electronic Equipment	814	439
仪器仪表制造业	Manufacture of Measuring Instrument and Machinery	299	153
其他制造业	Other Manufacturing	81	49
金属制品、机械和设备修理业	Industry of Metalwork,Machinery, and Equipment Repair	26	21
电力、热力、燃气及水生产和供应业	Production and Distribution of Electricity, Gas and Water	197	70
电力、热力生产和供应业	Production and Supply of Electric Power and Heat Power	197	70

continued

有效发明专利数(件) Number of Effective Patent Invention (piece)	#境外授权 Abroad Authorization	专利所有权转让及许可数(项) Number of Patent Ownership Transfer and Permission (item)	专利所有权转让与许可收入(万元) Income of Patent Ownership Transfer and Permission (10 000 yuan)	发表科技论文(篇) Pulish Technical Thesis (piece)	拥有注册商标数(件) Number of Registered Trademark (piece)	#境外注册 Abroad Register	形成国家或行业标准数(项) Number of National and Trade Standards (item)
6451	45	215	27654	3950	5399	404	894
47		5	170	12	56		51
17				11	39		99
15				23	211	6	14
11				71	179		
1				26	5	1	
6			5		6		1
2					5		
7							
1					2		
20				3			5
73		2	24000	130	18		26
528		28	1944	346	1277	164	55
327	7	95	3.0	79	1072	34	62
90				40	17		8
84		2	231	42	52		17
60				234	5		23
483				348	231	3	59
275		17	303	156	101		18
337		12		148	254	40	37
778	11	18	695	291	325	64	48
483	15	11		241	342	54	4
837	6			682	187	1	81
582	1	11	0.2	416	171	24	65
883	5	14	303.5	478	622	13	22
473				162	207		199
16				3	13		
15				8	2		
79				343	25		12
79				343	25		12

19-14 专 利 项 目
Patent Items

单位:件 (piece)

指 标	Item	2012	2013	2014
一、申请量总计	**Patents Application Accepted**	**43608**	**57287**	**57512**
发明专利	Inventions	17043	26487	24399
实用新型专利	Utility Models	16392	26157	16067
外观设计专利	Designs	10173	4643	17046
二、授权量总计	**Patents Application Granted**	**14908**	**20836**	**22820**
发明专利	Inventions	4018	4133	4885
实用新型专利	Utility Models	9158	13936	15405
外观设计专利	Designs	1732	2767	2530

19-15 各类技术合同签定情况
Statistics on Technical Contracts Signed by Type

指 标	Item	合同数(项) Number of Contracts (unit)		成交金额(亿元) Turnover Fulfilled (100 million yuan)	
		2013	2014	2013	2014
合 计	**Total**	**19288**	**25963**	**533.31**	**639.98**
技术开发合同	Technical Development Contracts	8112	9894	251.82	320.02
技术转让合同	Technology Transfer Contracts	378	330	22.34	25.02
技术咨询合同	Technical Consultation Contracts	827	797	8.77	41.05
技术服务合同	Technical Service Contracts	9971	14942	250.38	253.88

19-16 文 化 事 业
Development of Culture Industry

指　　标	Item	2012	2013	2014
艺术表演团体演出场次(万场次)	Number of Performance of Art Troupes (10 000 shows)	2.3	2.5	2.4
观众人次 (万人次)	Number of Spectators (10 000 person-times)	2418	2681	2110
图书馆藏书量 (万册)	Total Collections in Public Libraries (10 000 volumes)	1400	1377	1514
书刊文献外借人次 (万人次)	Number of Books Borrowed by the Readers (10 000 person-times)	299	335	354
书刊文献外借册数 (万册次)	Number of Books and Magazines Lent to Readers (10 000 volume-times)	497	609	635

注：2013年公共图书馆藏书量不含电子图书。
a)The public library hldings don't include electronic book.

19-17 文化事业机构和人员
Number of Institution and Personnel in Cultural Industry

指　　标	Item	2012		2013		2014	
		机构数(个) Number of Institutions (unit)	人　数(人) Number of Persons (person)	机构数(个) Number of Institutions (unit)	人　数(人) Number of Persons (person)	机构数(个) Number of Institutions (unit)	人　数(人) Number of Persons (person)
总　　计	**Total**	**2340**	**21478**	**2318**	**21963**	**2136**	**22019**
# 一、艺术事业	Arts	136	3030	179	7757	177	7841
# 表演团体	Arts Performance Troupes	64	4151	92	6142	91	6137
表演场所	Arts Performance Places	72	755	84	1588	83	1687
二、图书馆事业	Public Libraries	112	2163	114	2231	114	2167
三、群众文化事业	Mass Culture	1772	7375	1772	7567	1772	7590
四、艺术教育事业	Culture and Education	5	224	5	228	5	217

19-18 群众艺术馆、文化馆(站)活动情况
Activities Statistics on Mass Art Centers and Cultural Centers(Stations)

指 标	Item	2012	2013	2014
机构数 (个)	Number of Institutions (unit)	1772	1772	1772
举办展览次数 (次)	Number of Exhibitions (unit)	4571	5441	5299
组织文艺活动次数 (次)	Art Performances and Story-telling Sessions (time)	16961	18113	20186
举办训练班班次 (次)	Number of Training Courses (time)	8985	11147	12222
举办训练班结业人数(万人次)	Number of Training Course Completers (10 000 person-times)	70	94	103
藏 书 (万册)	Books Collected (10 000 volumes)	378	475	515
总收入 (万元)	Total Income (10 000 yuan)	49504	51503	56658
总支出 (万元)	Total Expenditure (10 000 yuan)	47509	52184	57618

注：本表含乡镇文化站的活动情况。

a) Data in this table include those of township cultural stations.

19-19 文 物 事 业
Development of Cultural Relics

指 标	Item	2012	2013	2014
文物机构	**Cultural Relics Institutions**			
机构数 (个)	Number of Institutions (unit)	458	476	493
人员数 (人)	Number of Persons (person)	10141	11555	13054
藏品件数 (件)	Number of Collections (piece)	1212481	1355289	1636437
# 一级品	Grade One	8009	8070	8180
二级品	Grade Two	15839	15878	14592
三级品	Grade Three	82427	83058	86507
参观人次 (万人次)	Number of Spectators (10 000 person-times)	3476	3968	4927
# **博物馆**	**Museums**			
机构数 (个)	Number of Institutions (unit)	210	221	238
人员数 (人)	Number of Persons (person)	5519	6225	7101
藏品件数 (件)	Number of Collections (piece)	1028725	1174563	1436898
# 一级品	Grade One	7462	7517	7630
二级品	Grade Two	14395	14415	13141
三级品	Grade Three	71328	72303	74626
参观人次 (万人次)	Number of Spectators (10 000 person-times)	2565	2874	3831
基本陈列 (个)	Permanent Exhibition (unit)	492	425	531
举办展览 (个)	Exhibition Hold (unit)	406	422	259

注：1.博物馆含民营博物馆、行业博物馆。
2.2014年规范了临时展览的统计口径，由承办展览单位填报，出展单位不再重复填报。

a) Museums include those run by private institutions and Industry museums.

b) The statistic scope of temporary exhibition was revised in 2014,which refers to number reported by the organizer.

19-20 广播电视基本情况
Basic Statistics on Radio and Television

指标	Item	2012	2013	2014
一、无线广播宣传基本情况	**Radio**			
广播电台 (座)	Number of Broadcasting Stations (set)	10	10	10
调频广播发射台 (座)	Relaying Stations of Frequency Modulation Broadcasting (unit)	172	171	171
调频广播发射机部数和功率 (部／千瓦)	Stations and Power of Frequency Modulation Broadcasting (unit/kw)	383/446.65	378/465.85	381/476.95
节目套数 (套)	Number of Radio Programs (set)	107	107	107
全年播出时间(时: 分)	Length of Public Radio Programs Broadcasted(hour:minute)	417565:53	458272:55	484669：18
广播人口覆盖率 (%)	Radio Coverage of Population (%)	97.15	97.37	97.77
全年制作广播节目(时)	Length of Radio Programs Produced (hour)	229064	254575	241756
新闻节目	News Programs	43355	51025	45578
专题节目	Special Subject Programs	57197	70035	63228
文艺节目	General Entertainment Programs	52632	61688	58997
其他类	Others	75880	71827	73953
二、电视宣传基本情况	**Television**			
电视台 (座)	Number of TV Stations (set)	10	10	10
发射台及转播台 (座)	TV Transmission and Relaying Stations (unit)	123	124	124
发射机功率(部／千瓦)	Power of Transmision (unit/kw)	273/644.20	238/537.44	238/537.44
节目套数 (套)	Number of TV Programs (set)	123	123	123
全年播出时间(时: 分)	Length of Public TV Programs Broadcasted (hour:minute)	597998:33	611538:34	611069
电视人口覆盖率 (%)	TV Coverage of Population (%)	98.12	98.26	98.49
制作电视节目 (时)	Length of TV Programs Produced (hour)	102136	118154	110336
新闻节目	News Programs	30512	36690	35747
专题节目	Special Subject Programs	25247	26453	27729
文艺节目	General Entertainment Programs	16446	16868	14638
影视剧节目	TV Play Programs	2124	1837	486
其他节目	Others	27807	36306	31735
三、县广播电视台 (个)	Number of Broadcasting Stations (unit)	88	88	88

注：1.2012年省广播电台电视台合并，广播电台和电视台中均未包括。
2.国家新闻出版广电总局调整统计口径，2013年起制作影视剧节目时间只计算以第一出品人拍摄、制作的电视剧时间数。
(2012年以前影视剧类节目制作时间包括以第一出品人拍摄的以及参与制作的影视剧)。

a) In 2012, radio station and TV station of province are merged, which are not included in the data of radio station and TV station.

b)The statistical range were adjusted by the State Administration of Press,Publication,Radio,Flim and Television,from 2013 time of making movie or tv only compute the time of movie or tv shooted and made by the first producer.

(Time of making movie or tv include movie or tv shooted and made by the first producer before 2012)

19-21 图 书 出 版
Number of Books Published

类 别	Category	图书种数(种) Number of Publications (kind)		总印数(万册) Printed Copies (10 000 copies)	
		2013	2014	2013	2014
图书总计	**Total**	**9395**	**9334**	**19328**	**18925**
一、使用“中国标准书号”部分合计	Publications with "China International Standard Book Number"	9385	9332	19325	18925
A.马列主义、毛泽东思想	Marxism-Leninism, Mao Zedong Thought	15	18	16	15
B.哲　学	Philosophy	123	112	56	55
C.社会科学总论	General Social Sciences	51	60	17	19
D.政治、法律	Politics and Law	181	159	252	386
E.军　事	Military Affairs	35	39	26	18
F.经　济	Economics	235	273	67	67
G.文化、科学、教育、体育	Culture, Science, Education and Sports	5264	5077	17040	16770
H.语言、文字	Languages	407	351	288	225
I.文　学	Literature	934	668	586	397
J.艺　术	Arts	274	287	169	91
K.历史、地理	History and Geography	350	366	155	156
N.自然科学总论	General Natural Sciences	5	8	3	5
O.数理科学、化学	Mathematics and Chemistry	166	200	100	91
P.天文学、地球科学	Astronomy and Geology	21	25	39	23
Q.生物科学	Biology	56	60	33	33
R.医药、卫生	Medicine and Health Care	414	637	156	226
S.农业科学	Agricultural Science	70	91	22	25
T.工业技术	Industrial Technology	679	763	219	249
U.交通运输	Transportation	25	41	45	22
Y.航空、航天	Aeronautics and Aerospace	19	26	4	14
X.环境科学	Environmental Science	20	22	16	15
Z.综合性图书	General Books	41	49	16	20
二、不使用“中国标准书号”部分合计	Publications without "China International Standard Book Number"	10	2	3	0.1

19-22 杂志、报纸出版
Number of Magazines and Newspapers Published

类 别	Category	种 数(种) Number of Publications (kind)		总印数(万份) Printed Copies (10 000 copies)		总印张(千印张) Printed Sheets (1 000 sheets)	
		2013	2014	2013	2014	2013	2014
一、杂 志	**Magazines**	**267**	**267**	**5498**	**5305**	**389092**	**378577**
1.综 合	Synthesis	4	4	7	7	412	405
2.哲学、社会科学	Philosophy and Social Science	49	49	1701	1698	102404	108428
3.自然科学技术	Natural Science and Technology	158	158	646	527	55900	41732
4.文化教育	Culture and Education	38	38	1990	1903	183817	175328
5.文学、艺术	Literature and Arts	12	12	276	223	18117	15415
6.少年儿童	Children's Books	4	4	864	928	27276	35372
7.画 刊	Pictorials	2	2	14	20	1166	1897
二、报 纸	**Newspapers**	**44**	**43**	**68281**	**68245**	**4344767**	**4355040**
1.省 级	Provincial-level Newspapers	29	27	41652	43445	3398831	3526870
2.市 级	City-level Newspapers	15	15	26629	24530	945936	825468

19-23 各市(区)文化事业情况(2014年)
Basic Statistics on Cultural Industry by City(District)(2014)

地 区	Region	公共图书馆 (个) Public Libraries (unit)	公共图书馆藏书量 (千册) Total Collections (1000 volumes)	群众艺术馆文化馆 (个) Art Centers Cultural Centers (unit)	文化站 (个) Cultural Stations (unit)	广播人口覆盖率 (%) Radio Coverage of Population (%)	电视人口覆盖率 (%) TV Coverage of Population (%)
全 省	**Shaanxi**	**114**	**15141**	**122**	**1650**	**97.77**	**98.49**
西 安 市	Xi'an	14	1839	15	183	99.49	98.96
铜 川 市	Tongchuan	5	711	5	41	99.63	99.95
宝 鸡 市	Baoji	13	1470	14	122	99.92	99.95
咸 阳 市	Xianyang	12	1196	14	171	99.45	99.60
渭 南 市	Weinan	11	929	12	193	95.02	96.70
#韩城市	Hancheng	1	140	1	16	99.60	99.95
延 安 市	Yan'an	14	1145	15	176	99.29	99.74
汉 中 市	Hanzhong	12	796	13	207	97.92	98.88
榆 林 市	Yulin	12	1241	13	226	96.55	96.49
安 康 市	Ankang	11	777	11	200	94.17	97.09
商 洛 市	Shangluo	8	578	8	126	95.45	98.87
杨凌示范区	Yangling	1	12	1	5	100.00	100.00
省直单位	Others	1	4447	1	-		

注：公共图书馆藏书量不含电子图书。
a)The public library hldings don't include electronic book.

主要统计指标解释

普通高等学校 指按国家规定的设置标准和审批程序批准举办的，通过全国普通高等学校统一招生考试，招收高中毕业生为主要培养对象，实施高等学历教育的全日制大学、独立设置的学院和高等专科学校、高等职业学校及其他机构（独立学院和分校、大专班）。

大学、独立设置的学院主要实施本科层次以上教育。高等专科学校、高等职业学校实施专科层次教育。其他机构是承担国家普通招生计划任务不计校数的机构，包括独立学院、普通高等学校分校、大专班和批准筹建的普通高等学校等。独立学院指由普通本科高校按新机制、新模式举办的本科层次的二级学院，一些普通本科高校按公办机制和模式建立的二级学院，“分校”或其他类似的二级办学机构不属此范畴。

成人高等学校 指按照国家规定的设置标准和审批程序批准举办的，通过全国成人高等教育统一招生考试，招收具有高中毕业或同等学历的人员为主要培养对象，利用函授、业余、脱产等多种形式对其实施高等学历教育的学校。包括职工高等学校、农民高等学校、管理干部学院、教育学院、独立函授学院、广播电视大学、其他机构等。其他机构是承担国家成人招生计划任务不计校数的机构。

小学学龄儿童净入学率 指调查范围内已入小学学习的学龄儿童占校内外学龄儿童总数(包括弱智儿童，不包括盲聋哑儿童)的比重。计算公式为:

$$\begin{matrix}\text{小学学龄儿童}\\\text{净入学率}\end{matrix}=\frac{\text{已入学的小学学龄儿童数}}{\text{校内外小学学龄儿童总数}}\times100\%$$

研究与试验发展(R&D) 指在科学技术领域，为增加知识总量，以及运用这些知识去创造新的应用进行的系统的创造性的活动，包括基础研究、应用研究、试验发展三类活动。国际上通常采用 R&D 活动的规模和强度指标反映一国的科技实力和核心竞争力。

R&D 人员 指参与研究与试验发展项目研究、管理和辅助工作的人员，包括项目(课题)组人员，企业科技行政管理人员和直接为项目(课题)活动提供服务的辅助人员。反映投入从事拥有自主知识产权的研究开发活动的人力规模。

R&D 人员全时当量 指全时人员数加非全时人员按工作量折算为全时人员数的总和。例如：有两个全时人员和三个非全时人员(工作时间分别为 20%、30%和 70%)，则全时当量为 2+0.2+0.3+0.7=3.2 人年。为国际上比较科技人力投入而制定的可比指标。

R&D 经费支出合计 指调查单位用于内部开展 R&D 活动（基础研究、应用研究和试验发展）的实际支出。包括用于 R&D 项目（课题）活动的直接支出，以及间接用于 R&D 活动的管理费、服务费、与 R&D 有关的基本建设支出以及外协加工费等。不包括生产性活动支出、归还贷款支出以及与外单位合作或委托外单位进行 R&D 活动而转拨给对方的经费支出。

专业技术人员 指从事专业技术工作和专业技术管理工作的人员，即企事业单位中已经聘任专业技术职务从事专业技术工作和专业技术管理工作的人员，以及未聘任专业技术职务，现在专业技术岗位上工作的人员。包括工程技术人员，农业技术人员，科学研究人员，卫生技术人员，教学人员，经济人员，会计人员，统计人员，翻译人员，图书资料、档案、文博人员，新闻出版人员，律师、公证人员，广播电视播音人员，工艺美术人员，体育人员，艺术人员及企业政治思想工作人员，共十七个专业技术职务类别。用来反映科技人力资源情况。

专利 是专利权的简称，是对发明人的发明创造经审查合格后，由专利局依据专利法授予发明人和设计人对该项发明创造享有的专有权。包括发明、实用新型和外观设计。反映拥有自主知识产权的科技和设计成果情况。

发明（专利） 指对产品、方法或者其改进所提出的新的技术方案。是国际通行的反映拥有自主知识产权技术的核心指标。

实用新型（专利） 指对产品的形状、构造或者其结合所提出的适于实用的新的技术方案。反映具有一定技术含量的技术成果情况。

外观设计（专利） 指对产品的形状、图案、色彩或者其结合所作出的富有美感并适于工业上应用的新设计。反映拥有自主知识产权的外观设计成果情况。

艺术表演团体 指由文化部门主办或实行行业管理(经文化市场行政部门审批或已申报登记并领取相关许可证)，专门从事表演艺术等活动的各类专业艺术表演团体，含民间职业剧团。如话剧团、方言话剧团、滑稽剧团、儿童剧团、歌剧团、木偶团、皮影团等以及由若干剧种组成的综合性专业艺术表演团体。不包括群众业余文艺表演团体。

艺术表演场馆 指由文化部门主办或实行行业管理(经文化市场行政部门审批或已申报登记并领取相关许可证)，有观众席、舞台、灯光设备，公开售票、专供文艺团体演出的文化活动场所。附属于文化部门机构内非独立核算的剧场、排演场，公开营业的也应单独统计。

广播/电视节目综合人口覆盖率 指根据原国家广电总局制定的《广播电视人口覆盖率统计技术标准和方法》进行统计调查的，在对象区内能接收到由中央、省、地市或县通过无线、有线或卫星等各种技术方式转播的各级广播/电视节目的人口数占全国总人口数的百分比。

Explanatory Notes on Main Statistical Indicators

Regular Institutions of Higher Education refer to educational establishments set up according to the government evaluation and approval procedures, recruiting graduates from senior secondary schools as the main target by National Matriculation TEST. They include full-time universities, colleges, institutions of higher professional education, institutions of higher vocational education, institutions of higher vocational education and others (non-university tertiary, branch schools and undergraduate classes).

Universities and colleges primarily provide undergraduate courses; institutions of higher professional education and institutions of higher vocational education primarily provide professional trainings; and others refer to educational establishments, which are responsible for enrolling higher education students under the State Plan but not enumerated in the total number of schools, including: branch schools of universities and colleges, and universities and colleges that have been approved and under plan for construction. Non-university tertiary refers to the regular undergraduate branch college which is running in new mechanism and mode, excluding the branch schools and other similar branches of educational institutions.

Institutions of Higher Education for Adults refer to educational establishments, set up in line with relevant rules approved by the government, enrolling staff and workers with senior secondary school or equivalent education, and providing higher education courses in many forms of correspondence, spare time, or full time for adults. Professionals thus trained receive a qualification equivalent to graduates studying regular courses at regular universities, colleges and professional colleges. Institutions of higher learning for adults include schools of higher education for staff and workers, schools of higher education for peasants, colleges for management cadres, pedagogical colleges, independent correspondence colleges, Radio and TV universities and other educational establishments. Other educational establishments have undertakings to enrol adult students but not enumerated in the schools under the State Plan.

Net Enrolment Ratio of Primary Schools refers to the proportion of school age children enrolled at schools to the total number of school age children both in and outside schools (including retarded children, but excluding blind, deaf and mute children). The formula is:

$$\text{Net Enrolment Ratio of Primary Schools} = \frac{\text{Total Primary School - age Children at Schools}}{\text{Total Primary School - age Children Whether or Not Attending School}} \times 100\%$$

Research and Development (R&D) refers to systematic and creative activities in the field of science and technology aiming at increasing the knowledge and using the knowledge for new application. R&D includes 3 categories of activities: basic research, applied research and experimentation for development. The scale and intensity of R&D are widely used internationally to reflect the strength of S&T and the core competitiveness of a country in the world.

R & D Personnel refer to persons engaged in research, management and supporting activities of R & D, including persons in the project teams, persons engaged in the management of S&T activities of enterprises and supporting staff providing direct service to the research projects. This indicator reflects the size of personnel engaged in R&D activities with independent intellectual property.

Full-time Equivalent of R&D Personnel refers to the sum of the full-time persons and the full-time equivalent of part-time persons converted by workload. For instance, if there are 2 full-time persons and 3 part-time workers (20%, 30% and 70% of working hours respectively on R&D activities), the full-time equivalent are 2+0.2+0.3+0.7=3.2 person-years. This is an internationally comparable indicator of S&T manpower input.

Total Expenditure of Funds on R&D refers to the real expenditure of surveyed units on their own R&D activities (basic research, application study, test and development) including direct expenditure on R&D activities, indirect expenditure of management and services on R&D activities, expenditure on capital construction and material processing by others. Excluding the expenditure on production activities, return of loan, and fees transferred to cooperated and entrusted agencies on R&D activities.

Professional and Technical Personnel refer to persons engaged in professional and technical work or in the management of professional and technical activities, i.e., people with professional or technical positions who are engaged in professional and technical work or in the management of professional and technical activities, and people without professional or technical positions but are working on professional or technical posts. They include professionals and technicians working in 17 categories of technical occupations including engineering, agriculture, scientific researches, medical service, teaching, economic research and application, accounting, statistics, translation, libraries, archives, cultural and museum service, journalism and publication, lawyers, notarization service, radio and television broadcasting, handicraft and fine arts, sports, performing art, and political workers in enterprises. This indicator reflects the condition of human resources in S&T.

Patent is an abbreviation for the patent right and refers to the exclusive right of ownership by the inventors or designers for the creation or inventions, given from the patent offices after due process of assessment and approval in accordance with the Patent Law. Patents are granted for inventions, utility models and designs. This indicator reflects the achievements of S&T and design with independent intellectual property.

Patented Inventions refer to new technical proposals to the products or methods or their modifications. This is universal core indicator reflecting the technologies with independent intellectual property.

Patented Utility Models refer to the practical and new technical proposals on the shape and structure of the product or the combination of both. This indicator reflects the condition of technological results with certain technical content.

Designs refer to the aesthetics and industrially applicable new designs for the shape, pattern and colour of the product, or their combinations. This indicator reflects the appearance design achievements with independent intellectual property.

Arts Performance Troupes refer to the various professional performing arts groups, which sponsored by the cultural sectors or guided by the cultural society (approved by the cultural market administration, or registered and permitted with the relative certificate), including non-governmental troupes, such as drama troupes, dialect troupes, comedy troupes, children troupes, Opera troupes, puppetry troupes, Shadowgraph troupes, etc., comprehensive professional arts performance troupes. The mass sparetime arts performance troupes are not included.

Arts Performance Places refer to the various sites for cultural activities, which sponsored by the cultural sectors or guided by the cultural society (approved by the cultural market administration, or registered and permitted with the relative certificate), with the facility of auditorium, stage, and lighting, and selling tickets in public, including the opera halls and rehearse sites, etc. which are affiliated to the culture sectors without independent financial accounts and open to the public.

The Population Coverage Rate of Radio/Television refers to the percentage of the whole country's population who can receive radio/television programmes transmitted by national, provincial, municipal or county stations through wireless, cable or satellite techniques, according to *Statistical Standard and Method on Television and Radio Coverage of Population* established by the former State Administration of Broadcasting, Film and Television.

二十、体育、卫生和其他

Sports, Public Health and Others

资料整理：杨小侠

简 要 说 明

一、本篇资料反映陕西体育、卫生、社会福利、安全生产等情况。

二、本篇资料主要内容及资料来源:

体育部分主要包括体育系统职工人数、群众体育活动开展情况及运动竞技成绩等，资料由省体育局提供。

卫生部分主要包括卫生机构、床位及人员数，农村合作医疗情况等，资料由省卫生厅提供。

社会福利部分主要包括各种社会福利事业的机构数、收养救济人数、婚姻登记状况等，资料由省民政厅提供。

交通、火灾、伤亡事故情况由省公安厅、省安全生产监督管理局提供。

律师、公证及人民调解工作等资料由省司法厅提供。

Brief Introduction

Ⅰ. This chapter reflects the development of Shaanxi's sports, public health, social welfare, safe production and other undertakings.

Ⅱ. Primary coverage and data sources:

The data on sports mainly include the number of staff and workers in sports departments, mass sports and athletics sports, etc. The data are provided by Shaanxi Provincial Bureau of Sports.

The data on public health mainly include the number of health institutions, hospital beds and personnel, situation of rural cooperative medical service and etc. The data are provided by Shaanxi Provincial Department of Public Health.

The data on social welfare mainly include the number of institutions, the number of persons receiving social welfare relief funds and marriage registration status, etc. The data are provided by Shaanxi Provincial Department of Civil Affairs.

The data on traffic, fire and casualties accident are provided by Shaanxi Provincial Department of Public Security and Shaanxi Provincial Bureau of Work Safety.

The data on lawyer, notarization and the people's mediation work are provided by Shaanxi Province Federation of Trade Unions, Shaanxi Women's Federation and Shaanxi Provincial Department of Justice.

20.体育、卫生和其他

2014年全省		
等级运动员发展人数	832	人
等级裁判员发展人数	2403	人
卫生机构数（含个体诊所）	37250	个
#医 院	2587	个
卫生技术人员	25.26	万人
#执业(助理)医师	7.65	万人

卫生技术人员和医生数（万人）

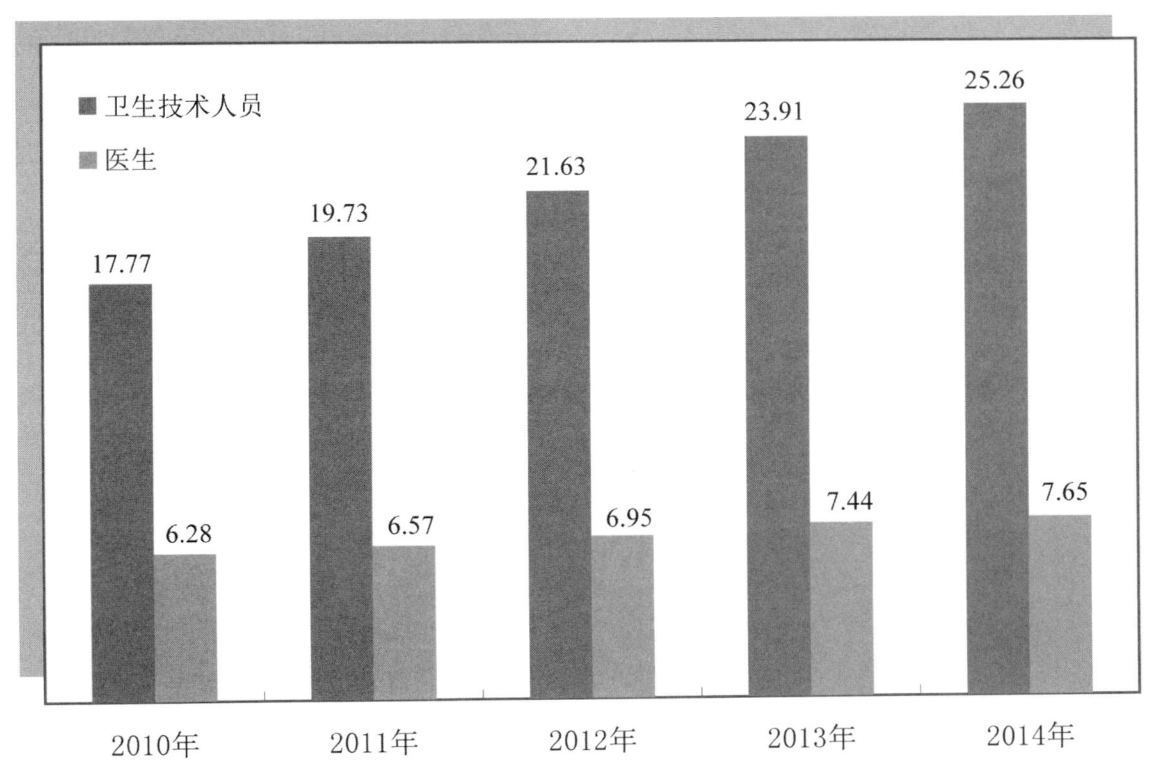

20-1 体 育 事 业
Statistics on Sports Industry

指 标	Item		2011	2012	2013	2014
一、体育系统职工人数 (人)	Employees Sports System	(person)	5393	5770	5172	5514
二、等级运动员发展人数 (人)	Number of Class Athlete Development	(person)	466	496	685	832
#女运动员	Female Athletes		180	152	245	348
#国际健将	International Masters Sports		4	5	1	5
运动健将	Masters of Sports		35	21	35	30
三、等级裁判员发展人数 (人)	Number of Graded Referees	(person)	519	965	1191	2403
#女裁判员	Female Referees		135	255	271	672
#国家级	National Referees		16			17
四、少年儿童业余体校 (所)	Spare-time Sports School	(unit)	66	82	65	81
#重点体校	Key Sports School		26	8	8	10
在校学生 (人)	Number of Students in School	(person)	8967	9822	10233	10835
五、取得冠军次数 (次)	Number of Champions	(time)	41	26	35	26
世界冠军	International Champion		16	10	16	7
亚洲冠军	Asian Champions			2	2	10
全国冠军	National Champion		25	14	17	9

20-2 等级运动员发展人数(2014年)
Number of Athletes in Grades by Type of Sports (2014)

单位：人 (person)

地 区	Region	等级运动员 Number of Athletes in Grades	#女 Women	#国际级健将 International Masters Sports	#运动健将 Masters of Sports	#一 级 First Grade	#二 级 Second Grade
全 省	**Shaanxi**	**685**	**245**	**5**	**30**	**408**	**389**
省级直属	Directly under the Provincial	91	47	5	30	408	10
西 安 市	Xi'an	434	134				123
铜 川 市	Tongchuan	25	15				12
宝 鸡 市	Baoji	15	5				77
咸 阳 市	Xianyang	8	3				37
渭 南 市	Weinan	24	7				7
延 安 市	Yan'an						36
汉 中 市	Hanzhong	36	21				32
榆 林 市	Yulin						30
安 康 市	Ankang	31	5				15
商 洛 市	Shangluo	21	8				10

20-3 卫生机构、床位及人员数
Number of Health Units, Beds and Staff

年份 Year	卫生机构(个) Health Institutions (unit)	#医院 Hospitals	卫生机构床位(万张) Number of Hospital Beds (10 000 beds)	#医院 Hospitals	卫生技术人员(万人) Medical Technical Personnel (10 000 persons)	#医生 Doctors	#护士(师) Nurses
1978	5598	3064	5.39	4.99	7.12	3.43	1.11
1979	5780	3078	5.78	5.32	7.58	3.60	1.17
1980	5845	3095	6.08	5.52	8.05	3.72	1.19
1981	6158	3109	6.37	5.72	8.84	4.07	1.40
1982	6369	3113	6.51	5.92	9.23	4.20	1.57
1983	6280	3106	6.66	6.06	9.57	4.38	1.73
1984	6251	3119	6.87	6.23	10.01	4.63	1.81
1985	6346	2218	7.20	6.46	10.61	4.97	1.88
1986	6309	2439	7.45	6.70	10.89	5.12	1.93
1987	6293	2559	7.68	6.95	11.22	5.29	2.04
1988	6248	2502	8.03	7.22	11.48	5.70	2.41
1989	6312	2515	8.29	7.47	11.63	5.84	2.64
1990	6416	2521	8.55	7.80	11.82	5.91	2.72
1991	6433	2577	9.02	8.22	11.99	5.87	2.81
1992	6404	2604	9.29	8.51	12.33	5.97	2.87
1993	6215	2389	9.56	8.81	12.28	5.89	2.91
1994	6227	3040	9.84	9.07	12.60	6.20	3.03
1995	6215	3313	9.88	9.05	12.80	6.28	3.10
1996	6033	3315	9.59	9.05	12.82	6.30	3.10
1997	5947	3217	9.48	9.04	12.99	6.23	3.25
1998	5639	2779	9.48	9.09	13.03	6.17	3.37
1999	5493	2753	9.68	9.22	13.28	6.37	3.48
2000	5572	2779	9.69	9.25	13.34	6.43	3.56
2001	5563	2780	9.91	9.43	13.53	6.60	3.62
2002	5240	2748	10.00	9.53	13.53	5.95	3.65
2003	5039	2740	10.27	9.89	13.47	6.03	3.72
2004	5138	2710	10.31	9.97	13.46	5.97	3.75
2005	5366	2674	10.67	10.34	13.66	6.03	3.85
2006	5385	2672	11.12	10.90	13.91	6.06	4.07
2007	4753	2645	11.78	11.42	14.17	5.93	4.25
2008	4429	2629	12.52	12.31	14.82	5.81	4.69
2009	4421	2660	13.45	13.05	16.29	6.13	5.44
2010	4638	2639	14.24	13.72	17.77	6.28	6.13
2011	4669	2611	15.38	14.69	19.73	6.57	7.02
2012	4684	2603	16.92	16.31	21.63	6.95	7.94
2013	6290	2634	18.51	17.93	23.91	7.44	8.96
2014	6314	2587	19.94	18.57	25.26	7.65	9.72

注：1.本表卫生机构不含个体诊所，医院、医院床位数含卫生院、妇幼保健院和专科疾病防治院。2013年起新增计划生育技术服务机构。
2.2002年起医生为执业医师和执业助理医师，护士(师)为注册护师。

a) The health institutions in the table does not include private clinics.Hospitals and hospital beds include health center, women and children care agencies and specialized disease prevention &treatment institutes. Since 2013, Family Flanning Technical Service Institutions.

b) Since 2002, doctors refer to practicing physicians, practicing physician assistants, nurses (division) refer to registered nurses.

20-4 各类卫生机构、床位及人员数(2014年)
Number of Various Health Units, Beds and Staff (2014)

指标	Item	机构数(个) Health Institutions (unit)	床位数(张) Beds (bed)	人员合计(人) Persons Engaged (person)	卫生技术人员 Medical Technical Personnel	其他技术人员 Other Technical Personnel	管理人员 Management	工勤人员 Support Staff
总计	**Total**	**37247**	**199372**	**336288**	**252611**	**4258**	**23786**	**22261**
一、医院	Hospitals	977	154871	193005	162033	1666	14182	15124
综合医院	Comprehensive Hospitals	694	118116	150521	127061	1170	10837	11453
中医医院	Hospitals of Traditional Chinese Medicine	144	23702	28604	24123	320	1904	2257
中西医结合医院	Hospitals Combined by Medium Doctors	8	1316	1425	1163	53	132	77
专科医院	Specialized Hospitals	129	11685	11411	8804	140	1279	1188
二、基层医疗卫生机构	Basic Medical and Health Institutions	34202	34900	105056	64852	420	3173	3239
社区卫生服务中心(站)	Community Health Service Center (station)	589	3878	11269	9478	46	948	797
社区卫生服务中心	Community Health Service Center	245	3193	8171	6777	41	637	716
社区卫生服务站	Community Health Service station	344	685	3098	2701	5	311	81
卫生院	Commune Hospitals	1610	30917	38554	34034	374	2225	1921
街道卫生院	Hospitals in the Streets	9	86	180	155		12	13
乡镇卫生院	Township Hospitals	1601	30831	38374	33879	374	2213	1908
中心卫生院	Center Hospital	642	18346	21583	19257	206	1016	1104
乡卫生院	Rural Hospitals	959	12485	16791	14622	168	1197	804
村卫生室	Village Clinic	25969		36717	3345			
门诊部	Outpatient Departments	245	105	3329	3015			314
综合门诊部	Comprehensive Outpatient Departments	160	70	2363	2134			229
中医门诊部	Chinese Medical Outpatient Department	26	10	294	270			24
中西医结合门诊部	Combination of Traditional Chinese and Western Medicine Outpatient Department	5		50	47			3
专科门诊部	Specialist OutPatient Department	54	25	622	564			58
诊所、卫生所、医务室	Clinics, Health Institute, Medical Office	5789		15187	14980			207
诊所	Clinics	4964		12398	12286			112
卫生所、医务室	Health Institute, Medical Office	825		2789	2694			95
三、专业公共卫生机构	Specialty Public Health Agency	1949	8035	35347	24056	1806	5878	3607
疾病预防控制中心	Disease Prevention and Controlling Center	119		6227	4656	247	694	630
专科疾病防治院(所、站)	Specialized Disease Prevention and Treatment Centers (stations)	6	890	674	493	1	92	88
健康教育所(站、中心)	Health Education Offices (stations or centers)	4		102	56	23	19	4
妇幼保健院(所、站)	Maternity and Child Care Centers (stations)	118	7145	12886	10616	136	1109	1025
急救中心(站)	First-aid Center (station)	4		183	68	4	52	59
采供血机构	Blood Collecting and Supply Organizations	10		801	518	39	126	118
卫生监督所(中心)	Health Supervision Centers	115		2851	2262	36	303	250
计划生育技术服务机构	Family Planning Technical Service Institutions	1573		11623	5387	1320	3483	1433
四、其他卫生机构	Other Health Institutions	119	1566	2880	1670	366	553	291
疗养院	Sanatoriums	5	1566	414	285	18	63	48
医学科学研究机构	Research Institutes of Medical Science	11		283	178	19	53	33
医学在职培训机构	Medical On-the-job Training Organizations	42		1287	650	256	250	131
统计信息中心	Statistical Information Center	1		6			6	
其他	Others	60		890	557	73	181	79

注：本表人员合计中含乡村医生和卫生员。

a) Summation-personnel in this table includes country doctors and medical orderlies.

20-5 传染病发病率和死亡率(2014年)
The Incidence and Death of Infectious Diseases(2014)

病 名	Diseases	发病率 (1/10万) Incidence (1/100 000)	死亡率 (1/10万) Death Rate (1/100 000)	病死率 (%) Mortality Rate (%)
合 计	**Total**	**201.45**	**0.40**	**0.20**
鼠 疫	The Plague	-	-	-
霍 乱	Cholera	-	-	-
肝 炎	Hepatitis	89.55	0.03	0.04
痢 疾	Dysentery	16.78	-	-
伤寒+副伤寒	Typhoid and Paratyphoid Fever	0.09	-	-
艾滋病	AIDS	1.41	0.20	14.13
淋 病	Gonorrhea	3.37	-	-
梅 毒	Syphilis	22.71	-	0.01
脊 灰	Poliomyelitis	-	-	-
麻 疹	Measles	0.21	-	-
百日咳	Pertussis	0.50	-	-
白 喉	Diphtheria			
流 脑	Epidemic Encephalitis			
猩红热	Scarlet Fever	2.36	-	-
出血热	Hemorrhagic Fever	2.76	0.01	0.38
狂犬病	Hydrophobia	0.08	0.08	95.72
血吸虫病	Schistosomiasis	-	-	-
布 病	Brucellosis	3.91	-	-
炭 疽	Anthrax	-	-	-
斑疹伤寒	Typhus	0.10	-	-
乙 脑	JE	0.14	0.01	5.57
黑热病	Black Fever	0.03	-	-
疟 疾	Malaria	0.15	-	-
新生儿破伤风	Newborn Tetanus	0.010	-	-
登革热	Dengue Fever	0.01	-	-
肺结核	Pulmonary Tuberculosis	57.39	0.06	0.11
非 典	SARS			

20-6　出院病人前十位疾病构成（2014年）
Discharged Patients Diseases of the Top Ten (2014)

序号 NO.	城市 Urban		
	疾病	Disease	构成(%) Constitute
1	循环系统疾病小计	Pregnancy, Childbirth and the Puerperium	17.83
2	呼吸系统疾病小计	Respiratory System Diseases	13.31
3	消化系统疾病小计	Digestive Disease	9.05
4	损伤、中毒和外因的某些其他后果小计	Injury, Poisoning and Certain Consequences Caused by the External	8.24
5	妊娠、分娩和产褥期小计	Circulatory System Diseases	7.93
6	影响健康状态和与保健机构接触的因素小计	Musculoskeletal System and Connective Ttssue Diseases	6.20
7	肿瘤小计	Genitourinary System Diseases	5.39
8	肌肉骨骼系统和结缔组织疾病小计	Influencing Health Status and Factors Access to Health Care Institutions	4.68
9	泌尿生殖系统疾病小计	Cancer	4.57
10	眼和附器疾病	Diseases of the Eye and Adnexa	3.71
	构成合计	Total of the Constitute	80.92

20-6　续表 continued

序号 NO.	农村 Rural		
	疾病	Disease	构成(%) Constitute
1	循环系统疾病小计	Respiratory System Diseases	21.09
2	呼吸系统疾病小计	Circulatory System Diseases	20.63
3	妊娠、分娩和产褥期小计	Pregnancy, Childbirth and the Puerperium	9.77
4	损伤、中毒和外因的某些其他后果小计	Injury, Poisoning and Certain Consequences Caused by the External	9.36
5	消化系统疾病小计	Digestive Disease	9.34
6	泌尿生殖系统疾病小计	Some Cases Originating In the Perinatal Period	4.00
7	影响健康状态和与保健机构接触的因素小计	Genitourinary System Diseases	3.93
8	某些传染病和寄生虫病小计	Musculoskeletal System and Connective Ttssue Diseases	3.72
9	肌肉骨骼系统和结缔组织疾病小计	Cancer	3.20
10	肿瘤小计	Influencing Health Status and Factors Access to Health Care Institutions	2.24
	构成合计	Total of the Constitute	87.28

20-7 各市(区)卫生机构、床位及人员数(2014年)
Number of Health Institutions, Beds and Persons Engaged by City(District) (2014)

地区	Region	机构数 (个) Health Institu-tions (unit)	床位数 (张) Beds Total (bed)	人员数 (人) Total Staff (person)	卫生技术人员 (人) Medical Technical Personnel (person)	#执业(助理)医师 Lecensed (Assistant) Doctors	#注册护士 Registered Nurses
全省	**Shaanxi**	**37247**	**199372**	**336288**	**252611**	**76460**	**97221**
西安市	Xi'an	5742	51065	96816	76375	24931	32210
铜川市	Tongchuan	947	5179	8901	7048	2156	2895
宝鸡市	Baoji	2916	21478	30133	22784	7554	8388
咸阳市	Xianyang	4683	27148	46584	37596	9690	14141
渭南市	Weinan	4203	20832	36625	25780	7266	8891
延安市	Yan'an	3571	11971	20958	13835	4269	5351
汉中市	Hanzhong	3858	19805	27126	20065	6191	7237
榆林市	Yulin	4939	17248	29875	21245	5852	8098
安康市	Ankang	3190	12595	19717	14351	4288	5381
商洛市	Shangluo	3007	10991	17435	11771	3757	3865
杨凌示范区	Yangling	191	1060	2118	1761	506	764

20-8 农村村级卫生组织情况(2014年)
Situations of Health Institutions in Rural Village (2014)

地区	Region	村卫生室 (个) Village Health Room (unit)	乡村医生和卫生员 (人) Rural Doctors and Health Workers (person)	乡村医生 Rural Doctors	卫生员 Health Workers
全省	**Shaanxi**	**25969**	**33372**	**31857**	**1515**
西安市	Xi'an	2944	3708	3327	381
铜川市	Tongchuan	543	511	511	
宝鸡市	Baoji	1816	3075	2878	197
咸阳市	Xianyang	3259	3567	3512	55
渭南市	Weinan	3222	5984	5863	121
延安市	Yan'an	2812	2806	2789	17
汉中市	Hanzhong	2683	3395	3319	76
榆林市	Yulin	3855	4109	3751	358
安康市	Ankang	2432	2723	2654	69
商洛市	Shangluo	2287	3363	3128	235
杨凌示范区	Yangling	116	131	125	6

20-9 社区卫生服务中心(站)情况(2014年)
Statistics on Community Health Service Centers (Stations) (2014)

地 区	Region	社区卫生服务中心(站)(个) Community Health Service Center(station) (unit)	床位数(张) Beds (bed)	人员数(人) Persons Engaged (person)	卫生技术人员(人) Medical Technical Personnel (person)	# 执业(助理)医师 Lecensed (Assistant) Doctors	# 注册护士 Registered Nurses
全 省	**Shaanxi**	**589**	**3878**	**11269**	**9478**	**3362**	**3222**
西安市	Xi'an	202	1798	5706	4689	1560	1523
铜川市	Tongchuan	40	172	301	248	88	101
宝鸡市	Baoji	75	785	1201	1020	427	349
咸阳市	Xianyang	101	534	1576	1433	484	566
渭南市	Weinan	66	283	890	753	323	235
延安市	Yan'an	29	113	375	307	130	113
汉中市	Hanzhong	18	30	326	259	102	84
榆林市	Yulin	38	123	541	461	115	145
安康市	Ankang	16		249	219	92	76
商洛市	Shangluo	4	40	104	89	41	30
杨凌示范区	Yangling						

20-10 新型农村合作医疗情况
Statistics on New Cooperative Medical System

年 份 Years	实行新型农村合作医疗县(区)(个) Number of Counties Implementing NCMS (unit)	参加新农合人数(万人) Number of Enrollees (10 000 persons)	参合率(%) Rate of Enrollees (%)
2007	104	2434.95	90.05
2008	104	2495.47	91.58
2009	104	2566.11	92.97
2010	104	2581.38	95.00
2011	104	2631.66	97.10
2012	104	2649.65	98.70
2013	91	2550.35	99.40
2014	91	2569.95	99.80

20-11　社会福利事业、企业单位机构和人员
Social Welfare, Business Unit Organizations and Personnel

指　　标	Item	机　构 (个) Institutions (unit)		工作人员(人) Staff (person)	
		2013	2014	2013	2014
总　　计	**Total**	**1393**	**1148**	**24615**	**23372**
一、收养性社会福利事业单位	Adopting Social Welfare Institutions	918	706	6809	7577
二、社会福利企业单位	Social Welfare Enterprises	240	200	14068	12104
(工商部门登记)	(the business sector registered)				
福利工厂	Welfare Factories	193	166	11653	9906
假肢厂	Artificial Limb Factory	1	1	97	88
安置农场	Placement Farms	1		34	
其他福利企业	Other Welfare Enterprises	45	33	2284	2110
三、烈士纪念建筑物管理单位	Martyrs Memorial Building Management Unit	39	41	358	352
四、救助站	Relief Stations	90	90	902	901
五、殡葬事业单位	Funeral Institutions	106	111	2478	2438

20-12　社会福利事业单位基本情况(2014年)
Basic Statistics on Social Welfare Institutions (2014)

指　　标	Item	院　数 (个) Number of Homes (unit)	工作人员 (人) Number of Staff and Workers (person)	床　位 (张) Number of Beds (bed)	年在院总人数 (万人) Number of Persons Housed (10 000 persons)
一、民政部门办收养性社会福利事业单位	Adopting Social Welfare Institutions Established by the Home Department	368	3441	41741	611.4
#优抚休、疗养院	Convalescent Homes Founded by the Home Department	27	720	2278	50.9
城市福利院	Urban Welfare	48	1295	10682	232.5
二、老年收养性机构	Adoption of the Old Institutions	630	5532	71474	1378.3

注：1.优抚休、疗养院包括荣誉军人康复医院、复退军人慢性疗养院、复退军人精神病院和国家办光荣院。
2.城市福利院包括社会福利院、社会儿童福利院、社会精神病人福利院。
3.老年收养性机构包括城镇、农村的敬老院、养老院、老年性公寓。

a) Convalescent Homes include the honor military rehabilitation hospital, Futuijunren chronic nursing homes, psychiatric hospitals and the state office of honor Futuijunren hospital.
b) Urban welfare include social welfare, social welfare homes, social welfare of mental patients.
c) Old adoption of institutions include urban and rural areas of the nursing home, nursing homes, senile apartment.

20-13 社会福利企业基本情况(2014年)
Basic Statistics on Social Welfare Enterprises (2014)

地 区	Region	单位数 (个) Number of Homes (unit)	年末职工人数 (人) Number of Workers (person)	# 残疾职工 Disabled Employees	# 女 性 Female
全 省	**Shaanxi**	**200**	**12104**	**4488**	**1558**
西安市	Xi'an	74	4334	1716	544
铜川市	Tongchuan	3	71	47	13
宝鸡市	Baoji	38	2468	675	213
咸阳市	Xianyang	21	1271	588	197
渭南市	Weinan	16	1739	783	313
延安市	Yan'an	6	608	140	68
汉中市	Hanzhong	19	597	254	89
榆林市	Yulin	13	774	213	81
安康市	Ankang	1	22	17	13
商洛市	Shangluo	7	115	41	21
杨凌示范区	Yangling				
厅级小计	Others	2	105	14	6

20-14 城镇社区服务设施(2014年)
Urban Welfare Facilities (2014)

地 区	Region	城镇社区服务设施数 (个) Urban Welfare Facilities (unit)	便民利民服务网点 (个) Convenience Services (unit)
全 省	**Shaanxi**	**3811**	**2493**
西安市	Xi'an	958	868
铜川市	Tongchuan	198	273
宝鸡市	Baoji	377	590
咸阳市	Xianyang	616	263
渭南市	Weinan	309	52
延安市	Yan'an	273	14
汉中市	Hanzhong	197	114
榆林市	Yulin	166	4
安康市	Ankang	550	293
商洛市	Shangluo	167	22
杨凌示范区	Yangling		

20-15 律师、公证及人民调解工作(2014年)
Lawyers, Notarization and Mediation of Civil Disputes (2014)

项　　目	Item	实有数 Number
一、律师工作	**Lawyers**	
律师人员(人)	Number of Lawyers(person)	6567
# 专　职	Full-time Lawyers	5914
兼　职	Part-time Lawyers	489
刑事诉讼辩护及代理(件)	Agent of Criminal Defense(case)	17695
民事诉讼代理(件)	Agent of Civil Case(case)	44679
行政诉讼代理(件)	Agent of Administrative Action (case)	4311
担任法律顾问(家)	As Legal Advisers(unit)	6693
代写法律文书(件)	Legal Document Written on Behalf of Clients(case)	26533
律师事务所(个)	Number of Law Offices(unit)	454
二、公证工作	**Notarial Personnel**	
公证处(个)	Number of Notary Offices(unit)	117
# 涉外公证处	Foreign-related Notary Offices	24
公证人员(人)	Notarial Personnel(person)	477
办理公证文书(件)	Notarized Documents (case)	252400
三、人民调解工作	**Number of People's Mediation**	
人民调解委员会(个)	Number of People's Mediation Committees(unit)	31060
调解委员(人)	Member of a Mediation Committee(person)	118281
调解民间纠纷(件)	Number of Civil Disputes Mediated(case)	145974

20-16 国内公证文书分类(2014年)
Domestic Notarized Documents by Type (2014)

分　类	Type	办证件数(件) Number of Notarial Documents Issued (case)	分　类	Type	办证件数(件) Number of Notarial Documents Issued (case)
合　计	**Total**	**187380**	赠　与	Presentation Documents	2510
合同(协议)	Contracts	87729	遗　嘱	Testaments	885
买卖合同	Sale and Purchase Contracts	3599	保证(担保)	Guarantees	128
赠与合同	Gift Contracts	4185	承诺(要约)	Offer(Acceptance)	380
借款合同	Loan Contracts	43434	其　他	Others	739
租赁合同	Lease Contracts	1160	现场监督	Field Supervision	1285
承揽合同	Work Contracts	130	招标投标	Bidding	811
建设工程合同	Engineering and Construction Contracts	91	拍　卖	Auctions	115
			开奖、评选	Lottery	87
委托合同	Application Contracts	5602	公司会议	Corporate Meeting	14
担保合同	Guaranty Contracts	13444	抽签(摇号)	Draw Lots	201
土地使用权合同	Land Use Rights Contracts	351	其　他	Others	57
知识产权合同	Intellectual Property Contracts	9	保全证据	Evidence Preservation	5211
承包合同	Contracts	154	公司章程	Corporation Constitutions	137
企业经营合同	Operation Enterprises Contracts	41	组织资格	Organization Qualification	112
劳动(劳务)合同	Labor contracts	934	财产权	Property Right	80
其他合同	Other contracts	6091	身　份	Status	87
合伙协议	Partnership Agreements	120	收养关系	Adoption Relationship	90
财产分割协议	Property Partitioning Contracts	406	婚姻状况	Marital Status	319
财产约定协议	Property Agreements	902	亲属关系	Kindred Relationship	1750
扶养协议	Legacy-support Agreements	106	有无违法犯罪记录	have or no Illegal and Criminal Record	1252
出国留学协议	Foreign Study Agreements	763	其他有法律意义事实	Other Facts of Legal Significance	870
拆迁安置协议	Compensation and Resettlement Agreements	412	证书(执照)	Certificate(License)	515
			签名(印鉴)	Signatures and Seals	11116
赔偿协议	Indemity Agreements	464	文本相符	Text Conformity	1654
还款协议	Payment Contracts	3877	赋予执行效力	Given Executory Effect	18656
其　他	Others	1454	执行证书	Execution Certificate	1365
继　承	Inheritances	10479	抵押登记	Mortgage Registration	338
单方法律行为	Unilateral Legal Act	37387	提　存	Drawing	28
委　托	Proxy	22532	保　管	Reserve	9
声　明	Announcement	10213	其　他	Others	6911

20-17 婚姻登记情况
Registered Marriages

指　　标	Item	2012	2013	2014
一、登记结婚数　　(对)	**Number of Registered Marriages　(couples)**	**374046**	**396187**	**381682**
1.内地居民登记结婚数(对)	Registered Marriages in the Mainland (couples)	373626	395718	381221
初婚数　　(人)	Number of First Marriages　(person)	656169	688904	655587
再婚数　　(人)	Number of Re-marriages　(person)	91083	102532	106855
#恢复结婚数	Restoration of Marriages	800	1501	1910
2.涉外婚姻数　　(对)	Number of Marriages with Foreigner (couples)	420	469	461
二、登记离婚数(对)	**Number of Registered Divorces　(couples)**	**55006**	**63292**	**68328**
1.内地居民登记离婚数(对)	Registered Divorces in the Mainland (couples)	54928	63243	68281
2.涉外婚姻数　　(对)	Number of Divorces with Foreigner (couples)	78	49	47

20-18 各市(区)婚姻登记情况(2014年)
Registered Marriages by City(District) (2014)

地　区	Region	准予登记结婚数(对) Number of Marriages Registered (couples)	初婚数(人) Number of First Marriages (person)	再婚数(人) Number of Re-marriages (person)	#恢复结婚数 Restoration of Marriages	登记离婚数(对) Number of Divorces Registered (couples)	#涉外婚姻离婚数 Number of Divorces with Foreigner
全　省	**Shaanxi**	**381221**	**655587**	**106855**	**1910**	**68328**	**47**
西安市	Xi'an	86192	146609	25775	530	17442	
铜川市	Tongchuan	6308	10353	2263	16	1561	
宝鸡市	Baoji	33301	57146	9456	83	5090	
咸阳市	Xianyang	60208	104826	15590	254	8965	
渭南市	Weinan	56539	96291	16787	330	10223	
延安市	Yan'an	22817	40055	5579	78	4118	
汉中市	Hanzhong	27353	44430	10276	43	6010	
榆林市	Yulin	38787	68982	8592	491	7336	
安康市	Ankang	26357	45468	7246	57	4652	
商洛市	Shangluo	22898	40778	5018	28	2884	
杨凌示范区	Yangling						
厅级小计	Others	461	649	273		47	47

20-19　交通事故情况
Basic Statistics on Traffic Accidents

地　区	Region	事故次数(起) Number of Accidents (case)		死亡人数(人) Number of Deaths (person)		受伤人数(人) Number of Injuries (person)		损失折款(万元) Converted into Cash Losses (10 000 yuan)	
		2013	2014	2013	2014	2013	2014	2013	2014
全　省	**Shaanxi**	**5952**	**5055**	**1800**	**1655**	**5452**	**4609**	**3696**	**3652**
西安市	Xi'an	2306	1970	516	483	2249	1832	1173	1264
铜川市	Tongchuan	210	204	40	32	292	273	189	149
宝鸡市	Baoji	971	902	165	154	722	771	534	516
咸阳市	Xianyang	177	157	125	117	182	103	113	271
渭南市	Weinan	441	457	173	154	389	448	214	262
延安市	Yan'an	318	262	218	203	242	169	245	241
汉中市	Hanzhong	439	296	159	149	440	285	107	148
榆林市	Yulin	605	393	203	190	499	319	730	547
安康市	Ankang	251	150	95	79	209	131	318	184
商洛市	Shangluo	212	188	101	90	204	186	67	56
杨凌示范区	Yangling	22	75	5	4	24	92	6	9

20-20　火灾事故情况
Basic Statistics on Fires

地　区	Region	事故次数(起) Number of Accidents (case)		死亡人数(人) Number of Deaths (person)		受伤人数(人) Number of Injuries (person)		损失折款(万元) Losses Converted into Cash (10 000 yuan)	
		2013	2014	2013	2014	2013	2014	2013	2014
全　省	**Shaanxi**	**12127**	**13137**	**51**	**39**	**23**	**16**	**16220**	**13875**
西安市	Xi'an	4163	2274	26	17	6	5	3245	4400
铜川市	Tongchuan	300	300	2	3	4		185	167
宝鸡市	Baoji	1561	2102	6	2	4		905	1707
咸阳市	Xianyang	1885	2392	4	4	6	2	1778	1314
渭南市	Weinan	1199	1278	5	5		1	1695	1379
延安市	Yan'an	563	477				4	980	495
汉中市	Hanzhong	561	682		4	2		1772	1334
榆林市	Yulin	1364	1688	4	1			4579	1789
安康市	Ankang	199	338	1	1	1	3	446	355
商洛市	Shangluo	250	490	3	1		1	413	665
杨凌示范区	Yangling	82	116					222	266

20-21 各类伤亡事故情况(2014年)
Statistics on Various Fatal Accident (2014)

类别	Type	总计 Total		一次死亡3-9人 Number of Deaths each Time(3-9 people)		一次死亡10-29人 Number of Deaths each Time(10-29 people)	
		起数(起) Times (time)	死亡(人) Deaths (person)	起数(起) Times (time)	死亡(人) Deaths (person)	起数(起) Times (time)	死亡(人) Deaths (person)
全　省	**Shaanxi**	**8965**	**1879**	**20**	**65**	**1**	**13**
#工矿商贸	Industry, Mining, Commerce	118	171	13	42	1	13
1.煤　矿	Coal Mine	32	54	3	10	1	13
2.金属与非金属矿	Metallic and Nonmetallic Mine	27	33	1	3		
3.建筑施工业	Construction Industry	28	42	4	12		
4.危险化学品	Hazardous Chemicals	5	3				
5.烟花爆竹	Fireworks	26	39				
6.工商贸其它	Others	3434	7	5	17		
铁路交通	Rail Transport	5055	1655				
农业机械	Agricultural Machinery	44	36	7	23		
水上交通	Waterborne Traffic	314	10				

20-22 社会捐赠和收养登记情况(2014年)
Statistics on Social Donation and Adopting Registration (2014)

地区	Region	捐赠款数额(万元) Donated Fund (10 000 yuan)	捐赠其他物资价值(万元) Value of Other Donated Materials (10 000 yuan)	收养登记合计(人) Number of Registered Adoption (person)	中国公民 Adoption by Chinese	外国人 Adoption by Foreigners
全　省	**Shaanxi**	**364.1**	**28.3**	**328**	**157**	**171**
西安市	Xi'an			69	69	
铜川市	Tongchuan					
宝鸡市	Baoji	6.6		5	5	
咸阳市	Xianyang	195.8		6	6	
渭南市	Weinan	11.3		9	9	
延安市	Yan'an					
汉中市	Hanzhong		28.3	20	20	
榆林市	Yulin	20.0		7	7	
安康市	Ankang			31	31	
商洛市	Shangluo	130.4		10	10	
杨凌示范区	Yangling					
厅级小计	Others			171		171

主要统计指标解释

卫生机构 指从卫生行政部门取得《医疗机构执业许可证》，或从民政、工商行政、机构编制管理部门取得法人单位登记证书，为社会提供医疗保健、疾病控制、卫生监督服务或从事医学科研和教育等工作的单位。卫生机构包括医院、疗养院、社区卫生服务中心(站)、卫生院、门诊部、诊所(卫生所、医务室)、急救中心(站)、采供血机构、妇幼保健院(所、站)、专科疾病防治院(所、站)、疾病预防控制中心(防疫站)、卫生监督所、卫生监督检验(监测、检测)机构、医学科研机构、医学在职培训机构、健康教育所(站)等其他卫生机构。

卫生技术人员 包括执业(助理)医师、注册护士、药剂人员、检验和影像人员等卫生专业人员。不包括从事管理工作的卫生技术人员(一律计入管理人员)。

执业医师 指具有《医师执业证》及其“级别”为“执业医师”且实际从事医疗、预防保健工作的人员，不包括实际从事管理工作的执业医师。执业医师类别分为临床、中医、口腔和公共卫生。

执业助理医师 指具有《医师执业证》及其“级别”为“执业助理医师”且实际从事医疗、预防保健工作的人员，不包括实际从事管理工作的执业助理医师。执业助理医师类别同样分为临床、中医、口腔和公共卫生四类。

社区卫生服务中心(站) 指为本社区居民提供预防、医疗、保健、康复、健康教育、计划生育技术服务等的基层卫生机构。包括社区卫生服务中心和社区卫生服务站。

社会福利企业 指以集中安置有一定劳动能力的残疾人员就业为目（残疾职工占生产人员10%以上）、带有社会福利性质的企业总称。主要包括福利工厂、假肢厂和其他福利企业。

城镇社区服务设施数 指报告期末城镇（街道办事处、居委会）设立的以非盈利为目的，为本社区居民服务，特别是为老年人、残疾人、儿童服务的社区服务中心、活动站、服务站、养老院、老年公寓（托老所），残疾人工疗站、残疾儿童日托所、家务服务站、婚姻介绍所等福利性设施以及职工社会保险管理服务的机构数。几种不同类型的社区服务单位，共用一个场所的，只能统计为一个社区服务设施。成为社区服务设施的条件:（1）是独立核算单位;（2）有固定的从业人员;（3）有一定的服务项目;（4）有一定的场所。

公证人员 指在公证处工作的人员总称，包括公证处主任、副主任、公证员、公证员助理(助理公证员)和其他从事辅助性工作的人员。

公证文书 指公证处根据当事人申请，依照事实和法律，按照法定程序制作的，具有法律效力的司法证明文书。

受理劳动争议案件数 指劳动争议仲裁委员会根据国家有关规定，对劳动争议当事人的申请予以审查，符合受理条件而正式立案、准备处理的劳动争议案件数。

Explanatory Notes on Main Statistical Indicators

Health Care Institutions refer to the units which have been qualified the Certification of Health Care Institution by the administration of public health, or qualified the Certification of Corporate Unit by the civil affairs, administration for industry and commerce, commission office for public sector reform, and engaging in medical care, disease prevention and control, health supervision and inspection, medicine research and health education, etc., including: hospitals, sanatoriums, community health service centers (stations), health centers, clinics (health stations and infirmaries), first-aid canters (stations), blood gathering and supplying institutions, women and children care agencies (centers and stations), special disease prevention and curing agencies (canters and stations), disease prevention and control centers (epidemic prevention stations), health supervision and inspection agencies, sanitary inspection institutions, medicinal scientific research and on-job training institutions, health education canters and so on.

Medical Technical Personnel refer to the professional staff engaged in health care, including licensed (assistant) doctors, registered nurse, pharmacists, laboratory technician, and imaging staff, excluding the medical technical personnel engaged in management job (included as the management staff).

Licensed Doctors refer to the medical workers who have obtained the licenses of qualified doctors and are employed in medical treatment, disease prevention or healthcare institutions, excluding the licensed doctors engaged in management job. The classification of licensed doctors is clinician, Chinese medicine, dentist and public health.

Licensed Assistant Doctors refer to the medical workers who have obtained the licenses of qualified assistant doctors and are employed in medical treatment, disease prevention or healthcare institutions, excluding the licensed assistant doctors engaged in management job. The classification of licensed assistant doctors is clinician, Chinese medicine, dentist and public health.

Community Health Service Centers (stations) refer to the primary units that provide the health care for community residents, such as disease prevention and control, medical treatment, health care, rehabilitation, health education, family planning technical services, including community health service centers and community health service stations.

Social Welfare Enterprises refers to those welfare-oriented enterprises employing a significant number of handicapped people with certain labour ability (handicapped employees shall exceed 10% of the production staff), including welfare factories, artificial limb plants as well as other welfare enterprises.

Number of Service Facilities in Urban Communities refers to the number non-profit welfare facilities set up by urban communities (community offices and residents' committees) to serve the community residents, including, among others, community-based centers that serve senior citizens, the handicapped or children, recreational centers, service centers, nursing homes, apartments for the elderly (nursery for the aged), work and treatment stations for the handicapped, day-care centers for handicapped children, domestic help agencies and dating services, as well as social insurance management agencies for the employees. Different types of community service providers that share the same premise are regarded as one community service facility. The requirements for a social service facility of communities include: (1) independent accounting; (2) fixed employees; (3) provision of services; and (4) premises.

Notary Personnel refers to people working for notary offices including: directors, deputy directors, notaries, assistant notaries and other people providing assistance.

Notary Documents refer to the judicial notary documents drawn up at the request of the interested party and are in accordance with facts and the law and following certain legal proceedings.

Number of Labour Disputes Cases Accepted refers to the number of cases of labour disputes submitted that, after being reviewed by the labour dispute arbitration committees in line with the relevant national regulations, are accepted and registered for treatment.

二十一、水　利

Irrigation

资料整理：陈　艳　郭力涛　文　燕

简 要 说 明

一、本篇资料反映陕西水利建设基本情况。主要内容包括水利建设投资，水利工程供水，水库，灌区，灌溉面积，水土保持，农村饮水等情况。

二、本篇资料由省水利厅提供。

Brief Introduction

Ⅰ. This chapter reflects the basic conditions of Shaanxi's water conservancy, mainly including investment in water conservancy projects, water supply of water conservancy projects, reservoir, irrigated area, water and soil conservation, drinking water in rural areas and etc.

Ⅱ. The data are provided by Shaanxi Province Department of Water Resources.

21.水利

2014年全省

设施灌溉面积	1525.08	千公顷
解决农村饮水安全人口	264.53	万人
水利工程供水总量	89.81	亿立方米

水利建设投资（亿元）

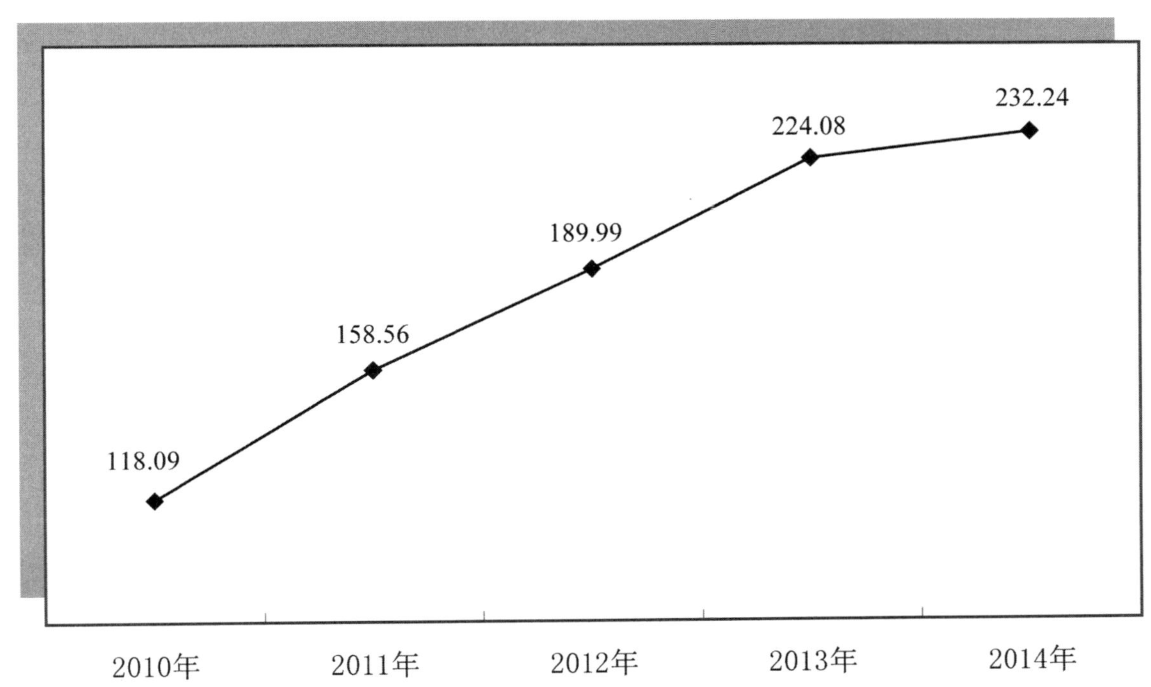

21-1 水利建设投资情况(2014年)
Construction Investment Situation of Hydroproject(2014)

单位：万元 (10 000 yuan)

地　区	Region	水利建设投资总计 Total	中　央 Central Level	省　级 Provincial Level	市　级 City Level	县及县以下 at and below County Level	民间投资 Nongovernment Investment
全　省	**Shaanxi**	**2322367**	**666296**	**680812**	**508350**	**186749**	**280160**
省　属	Provincial	381636	34493	347143			
西安市	Xi'an	388120	41447	28574	234206	23020	60874
铜川市	Tongchuan	25121	13538	6239	3605	1430	309
宝鸡市	Baoji	177650	74282	33424	8654	27478	33812
咸阳市	Xianyang	198978	64727	44560	14131	46058	29502
渭南市	Weinan	247490	120584	58244	62268	6395	
#韩城市	Hancheng	17126	7746	3821		5559	
延安市	Yan'an	190024	59970	25633	85581	18841	
汉中市	Hanzhong	219173	81286	47997	10798	5815	73276
榆林市	Yulin	222170	61118	30661	84936	45455	
安康市	Ankang	160286	76281	42422		8308	33275
商洛市	Shangluo	105419	37014	15343	257	3692	49112
杨凌示范区	Yangling	6298	1555	572	3915	256	

注：水利建设投资主要包括：防洪、险库、重点水源及枢纽、灌排、饮水、水土保持、农村小水电、渔业等。

a)Construction investment of hydroproject mainly includes flood protection ,dangerous reservoir,key water source and key position,irrigation and drainage ,potable water,water and soil conservation ,rual small hydropower ,fishery industry etc.

21-2　灌溉面积(2014年)
Irrigated Areas(2014)

单位：千公顷　(1 000 hectares)

地　区	Region	设施灌溉面积 Irrigated Areas by Facilities	本年灌溉面积 Irrigated Areas This Year	有效灌溉 Effective Irrigated Areas	林地灌溉 Irrigated Wooded-land Areas	园地灌溉 Garden Plot Irrigated Areas	牧草地灌溉 Irrigated Pasture	其他灌溉 Others
全　省	**Shaanxi**	**1525.08**	**1347.87**	**1226.49**	**10.17**	**95.14**	**1.46**	**14.61**
西安市	Xi'an	187.16	180.66	165.56	2.35	11.54		1.21
铜川市	Tongchuan	28.42	22.04	18.25		3.53		0.26
宝鸡市	Baoji	193.23	173.93	149.53	0.68	23.53	0.01	0.18
咸阳市	Xianyang	287.32	243.88	229.86	1.69	11.78	0.35	0.2
渭南市	Weinan	421.27	369.44	329.65	1.79	34.66		3.34
#韩城市	Hancheng	16.90	12.86	12.74		0.12		
延安市	Yan'an	32.53	29.09	26.96	0.10	2.02		0.01
汉中市	Hanzhong	125.28	115.18	109.29	0.6	4.45		0.84
榆林市	Yulin	168.82	139.24	129.7	1.64	2.27	0.97	4.66
安康市	Ankang	54.07	47.19	40.76	1.29	1.10	0.13	3.91
商洛市	Shangluo	21.06	21.46	21.46				
杨凌示范区	Yangling	5.92	5.76	5.47	0.03	0.26		

21-2　续表　Continued

单位：千公顷　(1 000 hectares)

地　区	Region	节水灌溉面积 Water Saving Irrigation Areas	喷灌 Spray Irrigation	微灌 Micro Irrigation	低压管灌 Low Pressure Pipe Irrigation	渠道防渗 Canal Seepage Control	有效实灌面积 Effectively Irrigated Areas	旱涝保收面积 Stable-harvest Farming Areas
全　省	**Shaanxi**	**850.62**	**27.50**	**34.16**	**270.79**	**518.17**	**1009.53**	**735.31**
西安市	Xi'an	137.96	5.21	2.58	63.3	66.87	140.5	126.46
铜川市	Tongchuan	18.03	0.73	4.78	10.37	2.15	8.28	4.01
宝鸡市	Baoji	137.98	5.76	5.3	38.75	88.17	117.5	113.32
咸阳市	Xianyang	159.13	2.653	6.24	56.26	93.97	181.63	136.03
渭南市	Weinan	221.56	2.21	6.57	37.58	175.2	276.53	168.43
#韩城市	Hancheng	10.48	0.02	0.01	1.95	8.5	9.28	8.5
延安市	Yan'an	22.66	3.84	4.42	14.4		19.72	11.42
汉中市	Hanzhong	65.83	1.99	0.95	1.96	60.93	97.81	78.78
榆林市	Yulin	42.163	2.76	0.42	38.98		114.67	61.71
安康市	Ankang	33.84	1.09	1.76	4.64	26.353	34.19	23.22
商洛市	Shangluo	7.52	1.22	0.14	2.8	3.36	13.35	7.41
杨凌示范区	Yangling	3.95	0.03	1	1.75	1.17	5.35	4.52

21-3 易涝耕地面积治理情况(2014年)
Management Situation of Areas of Floating Plowland (2014)

单位：千公顷 (1 000 hectares)

地　区	Region	易涝耕地面积 Areas of Floating Plowland	除涝面积 Area of Waterlogging Control	# 本年新增 New-added in This Year	# 本年减少 Decrease in This Year
全　省	**Shaanxi**	**165.28**	**132.5**	**1.62**	**1.71**
西安市	Xi'an	50.81	44.07	1.13	1.60
铜川市	Tongchuan				
宝鸡市	Baoji	3.91	2.95	0.06	
咸阳市	Xianyang	28.09	24.24		
渭南市	Weinan	35.38	30.36	0.42	0.11
# 韩城市	Hancheng	0.40	0.36	0.02	0.02
延安市	Yan'an				
汉中市	Hanzhong	13.35	9.6	0.01	
榆林市	Yulin	22.80	19.40		
安康市	Ankang				
商洛市	Shangluo	10.71	1.65		
杨凌示范区	Yangling	0.23	0.23		

21-4 用水总量(2014年)
Water Use (2014)

单位：万立方米 (10 000 cu.m)

地　区	Region	用水总量 Water Use	农田灌溉用水量 Farmland Irrigation Water	林牧渔畜用水量 Water Consumption of Forestry, Animal Husbandry, Fishery and Livestock	工业用水量 Consumption of Industry Water	城镇公共用水 Consumption of Town Public Water	乡村生活用水量 Residents Living Water	生态环境用水量 Ecological Environment Water
全　省	**Shaanxi**	**898103**	**492374**	**86201**	**140228**	**26611**	**51327**	**25226**
西安市	Xi'an	174604	54098	9791	40731	12444	8983	16365
铜川市	Tongchuan	9076	1681	1196	3538	321	572	172
宝鸡市	Baoji	76827	42454	8614	9326	1527	5629	1103
咸阳市	Xianyang	110100	61692	12231	18759	2939	6523	1489
渭南市	Weinan	158175	103293	18721	17421	2312	5874	1614
# 韩城市	Hancheng	8798	2237	738	4100	165	382	251
延安市	Yan'an	26171	6136	4948	7889	1284	2671	503
汉中市	Hanzhong	162663	127738	10620	11209	1648	6316	975
榆林市	Yulin	75918	42810	5268	16631	1607	4202	1504
安康市	Ankang	72180	40459	10821	8277	1504	7415	454
商洛市	Shangluo	28659	10089	3583	6266	843	2978	864
杨凌示范区	Yangling	3730	1924	408	181	182	164	183

21-5　水利工程供水总量(2014年)
Water Supply by Water Projects(2014)

单位：万立方米　　(10 000 cu.m)

地　区	Region	供水总量 Water Supply	地表水源供水量 Surface Water Supply	蓄　水 Reserve Water	引　水 Channel Water	提　水 Draw Water	人工载运 Artificial Ferried
全　省	**Shaanxi**	**898103**	**551604**	**201991**	**237010.3**	**112398**	**205**
西安市	Xi'an	174604	78865	50301	25180	3384	
铜川市	Tongchuan	9076	5761	3066	1633	1040	22
宝鸡市	Baoji	76827	36291	25862	6838	3574	17
咸阳市	Xianyang	110100	46963	6872	30968	9120	3
渭南市	Weinan	158175	95135	18946	14289	61880	20
# 韩城市	Hancheng	8798	2966	2696	119	151	
延安市	Yan'an	26171	16101	5429	5369	5254	49
汉中市	Hanzhong	162663	140173	54156	74004	12011	2
榆林市	Yulin	75918	43205	9570	24169	9448	18
安康市	Ankang	72180	67304	20761	40439	6030	74
商洛市	Shangluo	28659	20809	7028	13189	592	
杨凌示范区	Yangling	3730	997		932	65	

21-5　续表　continued

单位：万立方米　　(10 000 cu.m)

地　区	Region	地下水源供水量 Groundwater Supply	深层水 Deep Water	浅层水 Shallow Water	微咸水 A Little Salty Water	其他水源供水量 Other Walter Supply	污水处理回用 Waste Water reuse	雨水利用 Rain Use
全　省	**Shaanxi**	**333009**	**45435**	**285068**	**2506**	**13490**	**12354**	**1136**
西安市	Xi'an	87144	13719	72732	693	8594.7	8534.1	60.6
铜川市	Tongchuan	3107	120	2987		208	19	189
宝鸡市	Baoji	39406	691	38715		1130	896	234
咸阳市	Xianyang	60845	5399	55446		2292	2174	118
渭南市	Weinan	62799	11122	50662	1015	241	231	10
# 韩城市	Hancheng	5832	290	5542				
延安市	Yan'an	9579	2892	6687		491	436	55
汉中市	Hanzhong	22259		22259		231	24	207
榆林市	Yulin	32578	11492	20288	798	135	40	95
安康市	Ankang	4799		4799		77		77
商洛市	Shangluo	7760		7760		90		90
杨凌示范区	Yangling	2733		2733				

21-6 堤防情况(2014年)
Dikes Situation(2014)

地 区	Region	堤防总长度(公里) Dikes Total Length (km)	1级堤防 Level 1 Dikes	2级堤防 Level 2 Dikes	3级堤防 Level 3 Dikes	4级堤防 Level 4 Dikes	5级堤防 Level 5 Dikes	5级以下堤防 Other Grades Dikes	达标堤防长度(公里) Length of Standard Dikes (km)	1级堤防 Level 1 Dikes	2级堤防 Level 2 Dikes
全 省	**Shaanxi**	**9112.46**	**405.82**	**420.38**	**761.91**	**1423.02**	**1747.37**	**4353.95**	**3883.02**	**399.43**	**350.34**
西 安 市	Xi'an	995.92	192.34	117.02	101.31	210.10	305.34	69.81	636.16	192.34	90.09
铜 川 市	Tongchuan	177.13		1.24	39.71	73.60	59.39	3.18	61.12		
宝 鸡 市	Baoji	432.71	100.03	72.27	54.59	125.55	37.21	43.06	364.47	96.43	72.27
咸 阳 市	Xianyang	229.71	37.27	32.31	26.47	49.77	82.06	1.83	224.11	34.48	32.31
渭 南 市	Weinan	427.85	50.11	86.77	9.00	75.96	163.09	42.92	343.14	50.11	75.89
# 韩城市	Hancheng	3.00			3.00				3.00		
延 安 市	Yan'an	394.33		41.51	261.04	48.51	29.66	13.61	338.26		14.52
汉 中 市	Hanzhong	1123.39	10.04	50.29	71.56	361.52	161.56	468.42	402.45	10.04	46.34
榆 林 市	Yulin	483.38		16.31	108.94	54.26	96.91	206.96	269.47		16.26
安 康 市	Ankang	953.12	4.24	1.57	32.31	202.03	218.18	494.79	409.18	4.24	1.57
商 洛 市	Shangluo	3872.54			54.88	214.32	593.97	3009.37	819.68		
杨凌示范区	Yangling	22.38	11.79	1.09	2.10	7.40			14.98	11.79	1.09

21-6 续表 continued

地 区	Region	3级堤防 Level 3 Dikes	4级堤防 Level 4 Dikes	5级堤防 Level 5 Dikes	本年新增堤防达标长度(公里) Newly Increased Standard Dikes Length This Year(km)	本年减少达标堤防长度(公里) Newly Reduced This Year Standard Dikes Length(km)	全部堤防保护人口(万人) All the Dikes Protected the Population (10 000 persons)	# 本年新增 Newly Increased This Year	全部堤防保护耕地(千公顷) All the Dikes Protected the Farmland (1 000 hectares)	# 本年新增 Newly Increased This Year
全 省	**Shaanxi**	**690.69**	**1094.90**	**1347.66**	**413.92**	**40.21**	**1040.03**	**76.18**	**590.39**	**37.78**
西 安 市	Xi'an	101.31	204.44	47.98	37.99		240.50	1.63	97.70	
铜 川 市	Tongchuan	0.54	5.83	54.75	0.24		37.25	0.30	5.70	0.04
宝 鸡 市	Baoji	47.89	117.92	29.96	63.53		134.09	13.25	62.11	15.61
咸 阳 市	Xianyang	25.49	46.27	85.56	3.99		95.34	11.84	17.76	11.26
渭 南 市	Weinan	9.00	67.65	140.49	16.33		77.85	2.41	86.20	1.98
# 韩城市	Hancheng	3.00					2.20		1.50	
延 安 市	Yan'an	254.82	47.85	21.07	37.93		113.19	8.89	147.28	0.62
汉 中 市	Hanzhong	56.55	176.12	113.40	33.71	31.71	113.13	4.35	94.80	1.04
榆 林 市	Yulin	106.15	54.26	92.80	24.26		71.91	8.61	9.25	1.09
安 康 市	Ankang	31.96	177.64	193.77	68.15	3.00	61.19	12.10	22.75	1.43
商 洛 市	Shangluo	54.88	196.92	567.88	125.69	5.50	89.48	12.50	44.05	4.72
杨凌示范区	Yangling	2.10			2.10		6.10	0.30	2.80	

21-7　水库情况(2014年)
Situation of Reservoir (2014)

地　区	Region	水库数量(座) Reservoir Volume (block)	水库库容(万立方米) Reservoir Storage Capacity (10 000cu.m)	# 兴利库容 Hennessy Capacity	# 防洪库容 flood control Storage	已淤积库容(万立方米) Storage Capacity Sedimented (10 000cu.m)	灌溉面积(万亩) Irrigated Area (10 000acres) 设计 Design Irrigation	本年实灌 Actual Irrigation This Year
全　省	**Shaanxi**	**1092**	**899985**	**490763**	**191052**	**173968**	**6849**	**693**
西安市	Xi'an	93	38087	27715	24602	5233	83	18
铜川市	Tongchuan	32	11740	6037	2016	3659	33	19
宝鸡市	Baoji	104	86735	57120	22925	16739	568	341
咸阳市	Xianyang	73	50604	20529	16854	8878	375	108
渭南市	Weinan	112	28296	17174	10321	3812	86	25
# 韩城市	hancheng	11	6615	4370	3056	911	15	6
延安市	Yan'an	41	64209	16238	12988	30619	5561	107
汉中市	Hanzhong	342	60646	37702	7564	10246	91	52
榆林市	Yulin	94	139459	83035	35342	59005	21	11
安康市	Ankang	149	405894	217480	54080	33324	19	9
商洛市	Shangluo	52	14315	7734	4360	2453	12	1

21-8　万亩以上灌区基本情况(2014年)
Basic Irrigated Area above 10 000 Acres (2014)

地　区	Region	灌区数(处) Irrigated Areas (unit)	设施灌溉面积(千公顷) Facilities Irrigation (1 000 hectares)	农田灌溉面积(千公顷) Farmland Irrigation Facilities (1 000hectares)	渠道长度(公里) Channel Length (km) 干渠 Trunk	支渠 Branch Canal	斗渠 Douqu	实际灌溉面积(千公顷) Actual Irrigated Area (1 000 hectares)	节水灌溉面积(千公顷) Water-saving Irrigation Area (1 000 hectares)
全　省	**Shaanxi**	**186**	**1760**	**1220**	**4785**	**7939**	**24353**	**889**	**408**
省　属	Directly under the provincial	5	641	475	761	1601	5593	405	238
西安市	Xi'an	25	102	54	303	431	1170	30	5
铜川市	Tongchuan	3	6	3	33	48	65	2	2
宝鸡市	Baoji	20	191	152	469	1000	2513	48	14
咸阳市	Xianyang	27	110	70	306	922	1843	42	12
渭南市	Weinan	46	486	288	1122	2066	8719	229	102
# 韩城市	Hancheng	3	23	18	36	186	305	9	
延安市	Yan'an	9	19	14	197	144	173	6	4
汉中市	Hanzhong	20	144	116	676	695	2641	92	25
榆林市	Yulin	16	31	26	489	251	908	21	4
安康市	Ankang	7	18	13	218	308	540	7	1
商洛市	Shangluo	8	12	10	211	474	189	6	3

21-9 农村饮水安全达标情况(2014年)
Basic Statistics on Rural Drinking Water Safety Standards(2014)

单位：万人 (10 000 persons)

地区	Region	饮水安全达标人口 Population by Drinking Water Safety Standards	集中式供水 Centralized Water Supply	联户供水 Joint Household Water Supply	单户供水 Single-family Water Supply	饮水安全达标当年新增人口 Newly Increased Population by Drinking Water Safety Standards in this year	饮水安全达标当年减少人口 Reduce Population by Drinking Water Safety Standards in this year	"十二五"初期饮水安全未达标人口 Population by Drinking Water Safety Below Standards at the early stage of the 12th Five-year Plan Period	"十二五"累计饮水安全达标人口 Population by Drinking Water Safety Standards in the 12th Five-year Plan
全　省	**Shaanxi**	**2574.82**	**2500.81**	**12.88**	**61.13**	**264.53**	**145.42**	**1069.16**	**892.44**
西安市	Xi'an	384.01	381.71	2.30		27.04	7.07	134.54	114.01
铜川市	Tongchuan	42.25	39.31		2.94	1.21	0.58	9.50	8.09
宝鸡市	Baoji	254.76	251.84	1.36	1.56	14.01	15.45	81.27	63.77
咸阳市	Xianyang	362.24	362.06		0.18	36.53	30.92	191.61	172.66
渭南市	Weinan	415.07	415.07			48.03	45.47	177.69	145.36
#韩城市	Hancheng	24.96	24.96			2.05		11.67	11.49
延安市	Yan'an	144.22	115.14	5.47	23.61	14.04	8.60	43.55	30.55
汉中市	Hanzhong	270.93	270.93			43.81	8.61	130.03	104.58
榆林市	Yulin	282.79	251.88		30.91	30.06	6.33	93.80	79.42
安康市	Ankang	227.46	227.46			36.61	12.65	112.18	98.71
商洛市	Shangluo	179.35	173.67	3.75	1.93	13.12	9.73	93.84	74.34
杨凌示范区	Yangling	11.74	11.74			0.07		1.15	0.95

21-10 水土保持情况(2014年)
Basic Statistics on Soil and Water Conservation(2014)

单位：千公顷 (1 000 hectares)

地区	Region	累计水土流失治理面积 Total Area of Soil Erosion under Control	#小流域治理面积 Area of Small Watershed under Control	本年新增治理面积 Area of Newly Increased Soil Erosion under Control This Year	#小流域治理面积 Area of Small Watershed under Control	本年减少水土流失面积 Area of Decreased Soil Erosion This Year	#因植被死亡或破坏 For Death or Destruction of Vegetation	#因开发建设或开荒、过牧 For Development and Construction or Land Clearing and Overgrazing
全　省	**Shaanxi**	**7039.1**	**2581.5**	**665.2**	**237.8**	**411.0**	**223.3**	**108.2**
西安市	Xi'an	178.3	23.6	31.2	4.8	26.7	11.4	9.3
铜川市	Tongchuan	190.1	65.2	20.8	7.5	12.4	6.9	3.2
宝鸡市	Baoji	557.5	146.9	40.6	10.9	22.5	11.0	4.9
咸阳市	Xianyang	429.8	173.4	50.9	16.9	11.1	6.6	3.4
渭南市	Weinan	443.6	162.8	60.1	19.0	39.7	9.5	11.1
#韩城市	Hancheng	64.2	19.4	4.0	0.5	1.0		0.5
延安市	Yan'an	1445.8	359.1	104.5	34.4	66.4	35.4	4.0
汉中市	Hanzhong	775.6	296.5	85.0	27.9	40.5	26.0	12.2
榆林市	Yulin	1751.2	732.1	116.3	37.9	99.4	60.3	30.8
安康市	Ankang	584.8	272.7	85.2	50.2	56.2	37.2	15.7
商洛市	Shangluo	676.7	343.9	70.2	28.4	36.0	19.1	13.4
杨凌示范区	Yangling	5.6	5.3	0.5	0.2	0.2	0.0	0.2

21-11 农村水电装机情况(2014年)
Basic Statistics on Rural Hydropower Installed Capacity(2014)

地 区	Region	处 数 (处) Number (unit)	容 量 (千瓦) Capacity (kw)	1(含)~5万千瓦(含) 10 000 kw (inclusive) - 50 000 kw (inclusive)		0.1(含)~1万千瓦 1 000 kw (inclusive) - 10 000 kw	
				处 数 (处) Number (unit)	容 量 (千瓦) Capacity (kw)	处 数 (处) Number (unit)	容 量 (千瓦) Capacity (kw)
全 省	**Shaanxi**	**659**	**1308112**	**24**	**467500**	**214**	**708900**
省 属	Directly under the Provincial Government	10	67350	2	37400	7	29450
西安市	Xi'an	48	80633	1	20000	16	50500
铜川市	Tongchuan	1	4200			1	4200
宝鸡市	Baoji	122	157145	1	26000	36	95430
咸阳市	Xianyang	9	87100	1	48000	7	38300
渭南市	Weinan	9	36080			8	35830
延安市	Yan'an	10	5790			1	1500
汉中市	Hanzhong	194	403882	10	186100	55	183030
榆林市	Yulin	4	13000			3	12100
安康市	Ankang	168	400265	9	150000	65	222190
商洛市	Shangluo	83	51947			15	36370
杨凌示范区	Yangling	1	720				

21-11 续表 continued

地 区	Region	0.1万千瓦以下 Under 1 000 kw		本年新增装机 Newly Increased Hydropower Installed Capacity This Year		全年发电量 (万千瓦时) Annual Electricity Generation (10 000 kwh)	年利用小时 (小时) Annual Use Hours (hour)
		处 数 (处) Number (unit)	容 量 (千瓦) Capacity (kw)	处 数 (处) Number (unit)	容 量 (千瓦) Capacity (kw)		
全 省	**Shaanxi**	**421**	**131712**	**14**	**49265**	**363784**	**2784**
省 属	Directly under the Provincial Government	1	500			23926	3552
西安市	Xi'an	31	10133			25526	3166
铜川市	Tongchuan					1018	2424
宝鸡市	Baoji	85	35715	7	17305	33532	2134
咸阳市	Xianyang	1	800			26764	3073
渭南市	Weinan	1	250			11225	3111
延安市	Yan'an	9	4290			1349	2330
汉中市	Hanzhong	129	34752	4	17200	106305	2643
榆林市	Yulin	1	900			5784	3449
安康市	Ankang	94	28075	3	11960	119001	2973
商洛市	Shangluo	68	15577		2800	270	3750
杨凌示范区	Yangling	1	720			9084	1749

主要统计指标解释

灌溉面积 指一个地区当年农、林、牧等灌溉面积的总和。总灌溉面积=有效灌溉面积（耕地）+林地灌溉面积+园地灌溉面积+牧草灌溉面积+其他灌溉面积。

有效灌溉面积（农田或耕地灌溉面积） 指灌溉工程或设备已基本配套，有一定水源，土地比较平整，在一般年景可以进行正常灌溉的农田或耕地灌溉面积。

有效实灌面积 指利用灌溉工程和设施，在有效灌溉面积中当年实际已进行正常（灌水一次以上）灌溉的耕地面积。在同一亩耕地上，报告期内无论灌水几次，都应按一亩计算，而不应按灌溉亩次计算。凡是肩挑、人抬、马拉抗旱点种的面积，一律不算实灌面积。

旱涝保收面积 指有效灌溉面积中，遇旱能灌，遇涝能排的面积。灌溉设施的抗旱能力，按各地不同情况，应达到三十天到五十天，适宜发展双季稻的地方，应达到五十到七十天，除涝达到五年一遇以上标准，防洪一般达到二十年一遇标准的有效灌溉面积。

机电排灌面积 是指由固定站、流动站、机电井、喷灌机械等所有机械、电动力设备进行排水、灌溉的耕地面积。其中，只要有固定的机械排灌的设施，能够进行正常排灌，不论当年是否进行排灌，都应统计为机电排灌面积（含灌排结合面积）。

纯排面积 指在机电排灌面积中，机电设备只单纯用于排水（不需灌溉）的耕地面积。一般地，这部分面积的灌溉往往通过自流方式灌溉，不需要机电灌溉设备来完成。

节水灌溉面积 是指在给农作物进行灌溉时采用先进的设备和手段，在满足农作物需要用水的同时减少了用水。一般要有水源保证，利用渠道防渗、管灌、喷滴灌等工程节水措施，当年已进行正常灌溉的农田、果园、林地、牧草等面积，不包括农作物种植方式、种植品种改变等非工程节水措施的灌溉面积。节水灌溉面积包括渠道防渗面积、低压管道输水灌溉面积、喷灌面积、微灌面积和其他工程节水灌溉面积。在同一灌溉面积上，采用多种节水灌溉工程措施时，只能依主要工程或措施统计一种，不得重复计算。

易涝面积 一些地区由于地势低洼，降雨径流不能及时排走，田间积水超过农作物的耐淹能力，造成农业损失，即为涝。形成的受淹农田面积称为易涝面积，易涝耕地面积是指抗涝能力标准低的低洼涝耕地面积。

除涝面积 通过水利工程如围埝、抽水等对易涝面积进行治理，使易涝耕地免除淹涝称除涝面积。按除涝的标准分为3－5年、5－10年和10年以上。易涝面积虽经过治理，但标准尚未达到三年一遇标准的，不作为除涝面积统计。

水土流失 是由于水力、重力、风力等外力引起的水土资源和土地生产力遭到破坏和损失的现象。造成水土流失的原因可分为自然原因和人类活动原因两类。遭到水土流失侵害和损失的土地面积称水土流失面积。

水土流失治理面积（又称水土保持面积） 是指在水土流失面积上，按照综合治理的原则，采取各种治理措施如：坡改梯、淤地坝、谷坊、造林、种草、封山育林育草（指有种林、种草补植任务的）等，以及按小流域综合治理措施所治理的水土流失面积总和。

农村饮水安全标准 农村饮用水安全卫生评价指标体系分安全和基本安全两个档次，由水质、水量、方便程度和保证率四项指标组成。四项指标中只要有一项低于安全或基本安全最低值，就不能定为饮用水安全或基本安全。水质：符合国家《生活饮用水卫生标准》要求的为安全；符合《农村实施〈生活饮用水卫生标准〉准则》要求的为基本安全。水量：每人每天可获得的水量不低于40～60升为安全；不低于20～40升为基本安全。方便程度：人力取水往返时间不超过10分钟为安全；取水往返时间不超过20分钟为基本安全。保证率：供水保证率不低于95%为安全；不低于90%为基本安全。

农村饮水安全达标人口 是指满足农村饮水基本安全标准的农村地区（即城市及县城关镇以外地区）年末常住人口。农村饮水包括农村居民餐饮、洗涤以及散养畜禽等日常生活用水。

灌区 是指在蓄水灌溉工程、引水灌溉工程、提水灌溉工程等灌溉工程中，灌溉设备齐全、渠系配套完整，自成灌溉体系，有统一管理，设计灌溉面积为万亩及以上和有效灌溉面积达到万亩及以上的灌溉区域。灌区由各省水利厅审定、备案。

堤防 是指修筑在江、河、湖、海岸适用于防止洪水的工程。堤防工程按防洪标准分为五个级别：防洪标准[重现期(年)]>=100为1级，100-50为2级，50-30为3级，30-20为4级，20-10为5级。

供水量 指各种水利供水工程为农业灌溉、工业生产、城镇生活、乡村生活、生态环境等方面的实际供水量，它包括输水损失的毛水量，按供水对象所在区域进行统计。供水量来源包括地表水供水量（蓄水、引水、提水、调水）、地下水供水量和其他水源供水量。

农业灌溉供水量 是指水利工程为农田、林地、果园、牧草灌溉实际毛供水量的总和。

工业生产供水量 是指水利工程为城市及县以下乡镇工业的供水。1991年以前乡镇工业供水统计在农业供水中，从1992年开始统计在工业供水中。乡镇企业供水指水利工程为乡镇工业及农副产品加工实际毛供水量。

城镇生活供水量 是指水利工程对城镇居民生活供水，

还包括用于餐饮、服务以及市政环卫等公共服务方面的供水。生活供水主要统计各类水利工程向自来水厂或城镇居民供应的原水量，即未经任何处理的水量。

乡村生活供水量　除居民生活用水外，还包括牲畜用水。

生态环境供水　主要指通过水利工程设施向城镇、乡村生态脆弱地区或恶化地区以及其他地区补水，以维持、控制、恢复、改善原有的生态环境状态，如为了避免湿地萎缩、维持地下水位、防止海水入侵、维持河川基流、恢复原有湖泊、保护植被等目的，以及为了维持人类居住地的生态环境需要所进行的补水。

水利发电供水量　指水利工程为水电站的供水，全国水电供水量 2400 亿立方米/年，但它基本不消耗水量，如果和工业、农业供水等并列计入供水总量，将影响水资源的平衡核算研究。现行水利统计报表制度规定、水电供水量单独进行统计，不计入供水量总计。

水库　在江河上筑坝（闸）所形成的拦洪蓄水和调节水流的水利工程建筑物，可以用来灌溉、发电、防洪和养鱼。总库容在 1 亿立方米及以上为大型水库，1000（含 1000）万立方米至 1 亿立方米为中型水库，10 万立方米至 1000 万立方米为小型水库。

水库库容　校核洪水位以下的水库容积，包括死库容、兴利库容、调洪库容（减掉和兴利库容重复部分）之总和，称为总库容。它是一项表示水库工程规模的代表性指标，是划分水库等级、确定工程安全标准的重要依据。

兴利库容　水库在正常运用情况下，为满足兴利要求在开始供水时应蓄到的水位，称正常蓄水位，又称正常高水位、兴利水位，或设计蓄水位。正常蓄水位至死水位之间的水库容就是兴利库容，即调节库容。它主要用以调节径流，提供水库的供水量。

死库容　水库死水位以下的水库容积。除特殊情况外，死库容不参与径流调节，即不动用这部分库容内的水量。

Explanatory Notes on Main Statistical Indicators

Irrigated Area The sum of irrigated areas for agricultural, forest, pasture and grazing areas in a particular region. The total irrigation area is equal to the sum of effective irrigated areas (arable land), forest irrigated areas, orchard irrigated areas, grazing irrigated areas and other irrigated areas.

Effective Irrigated Areas (irrigated areas of farmland or cultivated land) The effective irrigated area refers to farmland or cultivated land with irrigation in normal years, equipped with installed irrigation facilities, water source and relatively leveled land.

Actual Effective Irrigated Area The area of effective irrigated land has been applied irrigation (once or more than once) in the current year, taking the advantage of irrigation works or facilities. No matter how many times irrigation is made in the same area of land within report period, it is all counted as one mu, but not be counted according to the irrigation times. All non-mechanized irrigated areas such as irrigated area with drought-relief measures of people or animal carrying water for irrigation are not included.

Farmlands with Stable Yields Despite of Drought or Waterlogging Farmlands, within effective irrigation areas, can irrigate in drought season and drain in flood season. According to drought-resistant capacity of irrigation facilities under varied conditions of different regions, irrigation may last for 30 days to 50 days, and may last for 50 days to 70 days in the regions suitable for double cropping rice. Waterlogging control in the effective irrigated areas should reach the standard of once in five years return period and flood control should reach the standard of once in twenty years return period.

Electromechanical Irrigation and Drainage Areas The areas are drainage or irrigated by electromechanical facilities, such as fixed and movable irrigation and drainage facilities, electromechanical wells and sprinklers. No matter whether farmlands were irrigated in the current year, whenever fixed irrigation facilities are placed, the area is included in electromechanical irrigation and drainage areas.

Pure Drainage Areas It refers to the area of cultivated land that the electromechanical equipment is used only for drainage in Electromechanical irrigation and drainage areas. Generally speaking, the irrigation of this part is self irrigation, with no need of electromechanical equipment.

Water-saving Irrigated Areas It refers to reducing water consumption by advanced equipment and measures when irrigating, which also meeting the need of plants. Generally, there are actual water resources, and taking measures of leakage free channel, pipe irrigation, jetting and dropping irrigation to save water. The normal irrigation area of arable land, forest areas, orchard areas, grazing areas etc., which do not take water saving measures, such as non engineering measures of planting manner and planting variety in the current year are not included in this indicator. It includes leakage free channel, jetting and dropping irrigation, tiny irrigation, and others. In the same area, with more than two water saving measures taken, only one main project can be counted.

Prone-waterlogging Farmland In some area, for low lying, rain can not be drained in time, plants submerged into water are over endurance, leading to agricultural losses. Farmland of waterlogging are called prone- waterlogging farmland, which refers to low lying farmland with low standard of preventing waterlogging.

Waterlogging Control Areas The controlled area of prone-waterlogging farmland by waterworks such as cofferdams and water pump. The standard of waterlogging control can be divided into 3-5 years, 5-10 years and above 10 years. The area of waterlogging farmland with control measures but has not reached to the standard of once in three years return period, are excluded from waterlogging control areas.

Soil Erosion Damage or losses of water resources and land productivity caused by external forces, such as water power, gravity and wind etc. Soil erosion is usually caused by two reasons of nature or human activities. The damaged or lost farmland areas caused by soil erosion are termed as soil erosion areas.

Improved Eroded Area (also named soil and water conservation area) The sum of improved eroded areas in Mountinous or hilly areas, has implemented comprehensive control measures, including terraced fields, silt retention dam, check dam, reforestation, grass plantation, enclosed reforestation and grass planting (refers to the area with tasks of planting forest and grass) and small watershed comprehensive management, in line with the principle of integrated management.

Standard of Safe Drinking Water in Rural Areas The evaluation index system of drinking water safety in rural areas divides the water into two levels of safe and generally safe, which is formed by four elements of water quality, water quantity, convenience of access to water and guarantee rate. If the value of one of the four indices is lower than the minimum level of safety or generally safety, the drinking water can not be deemed as safe or generally safe. Water quality: water quality that meets the "National Sanitary Standards for Drinking Water" is deemed as safe; water quality that meets the "Implementing Rules of National Sanitary Standards for Drinking Water in Rural Areas" is deemed as generally safe. Water quantity: each person can get 40-60 L water per day or above is deemed as safe; each person get no less than 20-40 L water per day is deemed as generally safe. Convenience of access to water: manpower getting water with no more than 10 minutes is deemed as safe and no more than 20 minutes as generally safe. Guarantee rate: 95% of water supply or more than 95% of water supply is guaranteed is deemed as safe; the guarantee rate is not lower than 90% is deemed as generally safe.

Rural Population with Safe Drinking Water Permanent residential population in the rural areas (outside of urban areas and counties) where drinking water safety standard has been met at the end of the year. Rural drinking water includes daily water use of rural residents for cooking, washing and raising livestock etc.

Irrigation District Irrigation area has above 10,000 mu of designed and effective irrigated area, with complete irrigation facilities, sub-canal system, self-established irrigation system and unified management system, under water storage irrigation project, water diversion irrigation project or pumping irrigation projects. Irrigation districts are approved and recorded by provincial departments of water resources.

Embankment Embankment project is constructed along the banks of river, lake or coast to prevent flood disasters. Embankment project can divided into five classes according to the standard of preventing flood disasters. Class 1: with reappear year over 100 years, class 2: 100-50, class 3: 50-30; class 4: 30-20, class 5: 20-10.

Quantity of Water Supply Actual quantity of water supply provided by all kinds of water supply projects for irrigation, industrial, domestic water use in urban and rural areas and ecological environment etc, including gross water loss in water transportation and data are sorted according to water consumption region for statistics. The quantity of water supply consists of quantity of surface water (water storage, water diversion, pumping and water transfer), groundwater and quantity of water supply of other water sources.

Quantity of Water Supply for Irrigation The sum of actual gross water provided by water projects for farmlands, forests, orchards and grazing irrigation.

Quantity of Water Supply for Industries Water supply provided by water projects for industrial water use in urban and rural areas. Before 1991, the quantity of water supply for township industries is included in agricultural water supply, but from 1992 it began to be counted in industrial water supply. Water supply for township enterprise means actual gross quantity of water supply provided by water projects for township industries and processing of agricultural products and by-products.

Quantity of Urban Water Supply Water supply for urban residents, including restaurants, service industry, municipal environment, sanitation and other public utilities. The quantity of urban water supply is the original quantity of water provided by all kinds of water projects to water plants or urban residents, i.e. quantity of untreated water.

Quantity of Rural Water Supply Quantity of water supply for both rural residents and livestock or big animals.

Water Supply for Ecological Environment. Refers to water recharged to ecological frailty area or ecological deterioration area through water projects, in order to sustain, control, restore and improve the original ecosystem and environment, such as prevent wetlands shrinking, sustain groundwater level, prevent seawater intrusion, keep base-flow of rivers, restore original lake and vegetations, and consider the needs of sustaining ecological environment of living places of human being.

Water Supply for Hydropower Generation Water supply provided by water projects for hydropower generation. In China, the annual water supply for hydropower generation is 2.4×10^{11} m^3, but power generation does not consume water resources. If it is included in the total quantity of water supply as industrial and agricultural water supply, it shall exert impact on water balance calculation. According to the current statistic regulation of water resources, water supply for hydropower generation is calculated independently and excluded from the total quantity of water supply.

Reservoir Storage area that is formed by constructing dams (gates) to detain and store water resources and regulate water flow. Large reservoir: the total storage capacity is over 100 million m^3.Medium reservoir: the total storage capacity is between 10 million m^3 (including 10 million m^3) to 100 million m^3.Small reservoir: the total storage capacity is between 0.1 million m^3 to 10 million m^3.

Storage Capacity of Reservoir It is also called total storage capacity. It refers to storage capacity above the check water level, including dead storage capacity, usable storage capacity, and flood control storage capacity (deducting the repeating part of usable storage). It is a key index for the total scale of a reservoir, and is a key index for dividing the class of reservoir and deciding standard of project safety.

Usable Storage Capacity of Reservoir refers to the water level which called normal water level, that should be reached for providing water in normal conditions. Storage capacity of reservoir between normal water level and dead storage capacity level are called usable storage capacity, which also called adjusting capacity. It is used for adjusting runoff, providing quantity of reservoir.

Dead Storage Capacity of Reservoir It refers to storage below the dead storage water level. It does not take part in adjusting of runoff, it can't be moved.

二十二、全国各省、市、自治区主要指标

Main Indicators of National Economy by Countrywide, Province, Municipality and Autonomous Region

资料整理：孙士梅

简 要 说 明

一、本篇资料反映全国各省、市、自治区经济发展情况，包括生产总值、人口、固定资产投资、居民消费价格指数、城乡居民收入及消费支出、主要产品产量、社会消费品零售总额、进出口总额等指标。

二、本篇资料主要来源于《中国统计摘要-2015》。

Brief Introduction

Ⅰ. This chapter reflects economic development of China's provinces, cities and autonomous region, including gross domestic product, population, investment in fixed assets, consumer price indices, incomes and consumptions of both rural and urban residents, output of major products, total retail sales of consumer goods, total export import volume, etc.

Ⅱ. The data sources are obtained from "Chinese statistical abstract-2015".

22-1 生 产 总 值(2014年)
Gross Domestic Product(2014)

地　区	Region	生产总值(亿元) Gross Domestic Product (100 million yuan)	第一产业 Primary Industry	第二产业 Secondary Industry	第三产业 Tertiary Industry	生产总值比上年增长% GDP Growth over the Previous Year (%)	人均生产总值(元) Per Capita GDP (yuan)
全　国	**National Total**	**636462.7**	**58331.6**	**271392.4**	**306738.7**	**7.4**	**46652**
北　京	Beijing	21330.8	159.0	4545.5	16626.3	7.3	99995
天　津	Tianjin	15722.5	199.8	7731.4	7791.3	10.0	105202
河　北	Hebei	29421.2	3447.5	15020.2	10953.5	6.5	39984
山　西	Shanxi	12759.4	788.1	6343.3	5628.0	4.9	35064
内蒙古	Inner Mongolia	17769.5	1627.2	9119.8	7022.6	7.8	71044
辽　宁	Liaoning	28626.6	2285.8	14384.6	11956.2	5.8	65201
吉　林	Jilin	13803.8	1524.6	7287.3	4992.0	6.5	50162
黑龙江	Heilongjiang	15039.4	2611.5	5504.0	6923.9	5.6	39226
上　海	Shanghai	23560.9	124.3	8164.8	15271.9	7.0	97343
江　苏	Jiangsu	65088.3	3634.3	31057.5	30396.5	8.7	81874
浙　江	Zhejiang	40153.5	1779.3	19152.7	19221.5	7.6	72967
安　徽	Anhui	20848.8	2392.4	11204.0	7252.3	9.2	34427
福　建	Fujian	24055.8	2014.9	12515.4	9525.5	9.9	63472
江　西	Jiangxi	15708.6	1683.7	8388.3	5636.6	9.7	34661
山　东	Shandong	59426.6	4798.4	28788.1	25840.1	8.7	60879
河　南	Henan	34939.4	4160.8	17902.7	12875.9	8.9	37073
湖　北	Hubei	27367.0	3176.9	12840.2	11349.9	9.7	47124
湖　南	Hunan	27048.5	3148.8	12481.9	11417.8	9.5	40287
广　东	Guangdong	67792.2	3166.7	31345.8	33279.8	7.8	63452
广　西	Guangxi	15673.0	2412.2	7335.6	5925.2	8.5	33090
海　南	Hainan	3500.7	809.6	874.4	1816.7	8.5	38924
重　庆	Chongqing	14265.4	1061.0	6531.9	6672.5	10.9	47859
四　川	Sichuan	28536.7	3531.1	14519.4	10486.2	8.5	35128
贵　州	Guizhou	9251.0	1275.5	3847.1	4128.5	10.8	26393
云　南	Yunnan	12814.6	1991.2	5281.8	5541.6	8.1	27264
西　藏	Tibet	920.8	91.6	336.8	492.4	10.8	29252
陕　西	**Shaanxi**	**17689.9**	**1564.9**	**9577.2**	**6547.8**	**9.7**	**46929**
甘　肃	Gansu	6835.3	900.8	2924.9	3009.6	8.9	26427
青　海	Qinghai	2301.1	215.9	1232.1	853.1	9.2	39633
宁　夏	Ningxia	2752.1	216.8	1343.2	1192.1	8.0	41834
新　疆	Xinjiang	9264.1	1538.6	3927.8	3797.7	10.0	40607

注：本表绝对数按当年价格计算，增长速度按不变价格计算。

a) Level data in this table are calculated at current prices, while the growth rate are at constant prices.

22-2 年末常住人口
Resident Population and Per Capita GDP

地 区	Region	年末常住人口(万人) Resident Population at year-end (10 000 persons)		城镇人口比重(%) Proportion of Urban Population(%)	
		2013	2014	2013	2014
全 国	**National Total**	**136072**	**136782**	**53.73**	**54.77**
北 京	Beijing	2115	2152	86.30	86.35
天 津	Tianjin	1472	1517	82.01	82.27
河 北	Hebei	7333	7384	48.12	49.33
山 西	Shanxi	3630	3648	52.56	53.79
内蒙古	Inner Mongolia	2498	2505	58.71	59.51
辽 宁	Liaoning	4390	4391	66.45	67.05
吉 林	Jilin	2751	2752	54.20	54.81
黑龙江	Heilongjiang	3835	3833	57.40	58.01
上 海	Shanghai	2415	2426	89.60	89.60
江 苏	Jiangsu	7939	7960	64.11	65.21
浙 江	Zhejiang	5498	5508	64.00	64.87
安 徽	Anhui	6030	6083	47.86	49.15
福 建	Fujian	3774	3806	60.77	61.80
江 西	Jiangxi	4522	4542	48.87	50.22
山 东	Shandong	9733	9789	53.75	55.01
河 南	Henan	9413	9436	43.80	45.20
湖 北	Hubei	5799	5816	54.51	55.67
湖 南	Hunan	6691	6737	47.96	49.28
广 东	Guangdong	10644	10724	67.76	68.00
广 西	Guangxi	4719	4754	44.81	46.01
海 南	Hainan	895	903	52.74	53.76
重 庆	Chongqing	2970	2991	58.34	59.60
四 川	Sichuan	8107	8140	44.90	46.30
贵 州	Guizhou	3502	3508	37.83	40.01
云 南	Yunnan	4687	4714	40.48	41.73
西 藏	Tibet	312	318	23.71	25.75
陕 西	**Shaanxi**	**3764**	**3775**	**51.31**	**52.57**
甘 肃	Gansu	2582	2591	40.13	41.68
青 海	Qinghai	578	583	48.51	49.78
宁 夏	Ningxia	654	662	52.01	53.61
新 疆	Xinjiang	2264	2298	44.47	46.07

22-3 固定资产投资
Investment in Fixed Assets

单位：亿元 (100 million yuan)

地区	Region	全社会固定资产投资 Total Investment in Fixed Assets in the Whole Province		固定资产投资(不含农户) Investment in Fixed Assets (Excluding Rural Households)	
		2013	2014	2013	2014
全　国	**National Total**	**446294.1**	**512760.7**	**435747.4**	**502004.9**
北　京	Beijing	6847.1	6924.2	6797.5	6873.4
天　津	Tianjin	9130.2	10518.2	9103.0	10490.4
河　北	Hebei	23194.2	26671.9	22629.8	26147.2
山　西	Shanxi	11031.9	12296.1	10745.3	11977.0
内蒙古	Inner Mongolia	14217.4	17585.0	14072.4	17431.0
辽　宁	Liaoning	25107.7	24730.8	24791.4	24426.8
吉　林	Jilin	9979.3	11486.5	9725.8	11254.8
黑龙江	Heilongjiang	11453.1	9878.2	11121.3	9587.1
上　海	Shanghai	5647.8	6016.5	5644.1	6013.0
江　苏	Jiangsu	36373.3	41938.7	35982.5	41552.8
浙　江	Zhejiang	20782.1	24262.8	20194.1	23554.8
安　徽	Anhui	18621.9	21688.5	18091.2	21069.2
福　建	Fujian	15327.4	18219.8	15045.8	17911.7
江　西	Jiangxi	12850.3	15109.9	12434.9	14677.0
山　东	Shandong	36789.1	42495.5	35875.9	41599.1
河　南	Henan	26087.5	30782.2	25188.1	30012.3
湖　北	Hubei	19307.3	22965.3	18796.9	22491.7
湖　南	Hunan	17841.4	21269.7	17225.2	20575.3
广　东	Guangdong	22308.4	26294.0	21795.5	25843.1
广　西	Guangxi	11907.7	13843.2	11383.9	13287.6
海　南	Hainan	2697.9	3112.3	2625.6	3039.5
重　庆	Chongqing	10435.2	12281.1	10291.0	12136.5
四　川	Sichuan	20326.1	23318.7	19755.3	22662.3
贵　州	Guizhou	7373.6	9025.7	7102.8	8778.4
云　南	Yunnan	9968.3	11498.5	9621.8	11073.9
西　藏	Tibet	876.0	1069.2	876.0	1069.2
		(15934.2)	**(18709.5)**	**(15583.6)**	**(18357.8)**
陕　西	**Shaanxi**	**14884.1**	**17192.1**	**14533.5**	**16840.4**
甘　肃	Gansu	6527.9	7884.1	6407.2	7759.6
青　海	Qinghai	2361.1	2861.2	2285.3	2788.9
宁　夏	Ningxia	2651.1	3173.8	2577.8	3093.9
新　疆	Xinjiang	7732.3	9438.3	7371.2	9058.3

注：本表各地区固定资产投资不含跨省项目，括号内数据为陕西含跨省项目投资额。

a) This table, investment in fixed assets by region do not include inter-provincial projects, data in the brackets are investment of Shaanxi that include inter-provincial projects.

22-4 房地产开发企业投资和商品房销售额

Total Investment in Real Estate Development and Total Sale of Commercialized Buildings

单位: 亿元 (100 million yuan)

地区	Region	房地产开发投资额 Total Investment in Real Estate Development		商品房销售额 Total Sale of Commercialized Buildings		# 住宅 Residential Buildings	
		2013	2014	2013	2014	2013	2014
全　国	**National Total**	**86013.4**	**95035.6**	**81428.3**	**76292.4**	**67694.9**	**62395.6**
北　京	Beijing	3483.4	3715.3	3530.8	2738.7	2434.7	2102.5
天　津	Tianjin	1480.8	1699.6	1615.5	1486.9	1443.3	1294.3
河　北	Hebei	3445.4	4059.7	2779.7	2928.0	2329.1	2501.6
山　西	Shanxi	1308.6	1403.6	728.3	746.1	625.1	639.8
内蒙古	Inner Mongolia	1479.0	1370.9	1177.4	1064.8	874.4	765.0
辽　宁	Liaoning	6450.8	5301.3	4759.2	3092.1	3941.9	2518.9
吉　林	Jilin	1252.4	1030.1	993.0	808.6	839.7	667.6
黑龙江	Heilongjiang	1604.8	1324.1	1582.3	1208.5	1305.9	962.7
上　海	Shanghai	2819.6	3206.5	3911.6	3499.5	3264.0	2923.4
江　苏	Jiangsu	7241.5	8240.2	7913.7	6898.4	6777.7	5969.6
浙　江	Zhejiang	6216.2	7262.4	5396.0	4923.0	4513.9	4172.6
安　徽	Anhui	3946.2	4339.0	3182.9	3345.2	2662.0	2691.8
福　建	Fujian	3703.0	4567.4	4232.1	3763.5	3410.6	2939.6
江　西	Jiangxi	1174.6	1322.5	1647.9	1621.8	1396.1	1379.5
山　东	Shandong	5444.5	5818.0	5215.1	4879.7	4461.1	4009.5
河　南	Henan	3843.8	4375.7	3074.1	3440.6	2516.3	2739.7
湖　北	Hubei	3286.0	3983.8	2790.3	3088.3	2310.0	2543.8
湖　南	Hunan	2628.3	2883.6	2525.6	2299.1	2115.0	1858.6
广　东	Guangdong	6489.6	7638.5	8941.1	8461.8	7476.1	6960.3
广　西	Guangxi	1614.6	1838.5	1375.8	1532.1	1166.7	1274.6
海　南	Hainan	1196.8	1431.7	1032.7	935.2	997.0	873.2
重　庆	Chongqing	3012.8	3630.2	2682.8	2815.0	2283.6	2253.3
四　川	Sichuan	3853.0	4380.1	4020.3	3997.4	3308.6	3145.0
贵　州	Guizhou	1942.5	2187.7	1276.7	1370.3	988.8	1000.0
云　南	Yunnan	2488.3	2846.7	1487.2	1596.4	1192.6	1165.4
西　藏	Tibet	9.7	52.9	10.6	34.3	8.8	28.6
陕　西	**Shaanxi**	**2240.2**	**2426.5**	**1608.1**	**1598.0**	**1413.2**	**1368.1**
甘　肃	Gansu	724.6	721.5	474.1	602.3	418.1	513.5
青　海	Qinghai	247.6	308.3	158.8	211.3	146.3	155.8
宁　夏	Ningxia	559.0	654.8	443.7	465.0	363.6	352.0
新　疆	Xinjiang	825.7	1014.8	861.0	840.5	710.7	625.3

22-5 居民消费价格分类指数(2014年)
Consumer Price Index by Category(2014)

(上年=100) (preceding year=100)

地区	Region	居民消费价格指数 Consumer Price Index	食品 Food	烟酒及用品 Tobacco and Liquor	衣着 Clothes	家庭设备用品及服务 Household Facilities and Services	医疗保健和个人用品 Health Care and Personal Products	交通和通信 Transportation and Communication	娱乐教育文化 Recreational, Education, Culture	居住 Living
全国	**National Total**	**102.0**	**103.1**	**99.4**	**102.4**	**101.2**	**101.3**	**99.9**	**101.9**	**102.0**
北京	Beijing	101.6	103.2	99.7	100.4	100.3	99.9	99.2	103.2	101.4
天津	Tianjin	101.9	103.0	98.7	101.8	103.3	100.4	99.7	101.7	102.0
河北	Hebei	101.7	102.3	98.8	104.1	101.2	101.5	100.0	101.9	101.1
山西	Shanxi	101.7	102.8	100.1	102.4	101.4	100.9	99.8	101.8	100.8
内蒙古	Inner Mongolia	101.6	102.9	100.4	102.1	100.6	100.8	99.4	101.2	101.0
辽宁	Liaoning	101.7	102.7	100.3	102.2	100.3	101.6	100.4	101.1	101.3
吉林	Jilin	102.0	103.0	100.1	103.1	100.8	100.6	100.2	101.8	102.0
黑龙江	Heilongjiang	101.5	102.0	100.9	102.9	100.8	102.2	99.6	100.9	100.6
上海	Shanghai	102.7	103.2	101.0	103.7	101.8	100.4	100.1	101.8	104.6
江苏	Jiangsu	102.2	102.6	98.6	103.9	103.3	101.8	99.8	102.6	102.4
浙江	Zhejiang	102.1	103.1	99.6	101.8	101.5	101.9	99.7	102.2	102.4
安徽	Anhui	101.6	102.5	97.5	101.0	101.3	101.6	99.2	102.4	102.0
福建	Fujian	102.0	103.3	99.2	102.6	100.4	100.7	100.2	101.7	102.3
江西	Jiangxi	102.3	103.7	100.1	102.4	99.9	101.0	99.7	102.8	102.5
山东	Shandong	101.9	102.6	100.3	102.9	101.1	101.2	99.8	102.0	102.1
河南	Henan	101.9	102.6	98.3	102.5	100.9	101.0	99.9	103.2	102.2
湖北	Hubei	102.0	102.3	99.7	102.0	101.5	100.7	100.2	101.7	103.3
湖南	Hunan	101.9	102.6	99.5	101.7	101.3	102.1	100.2	103.0	101.4
广东	Guangdong	102.3	104.4	99.6	103.0	100.8	100.9	99.6	101.1	101.9
广西	Guangxi	102.1	104.3	99.2	100.4	100.3	101.0	99.9	101.5	101.5
海南	Hainan	102.4	103.7	97.9	102.3	101.4	102.0	100.0	101.7	102.6
重庆	Chongqing	101.8	103.3	97.8	102.0	100.5	101.7	100.3	100.1	101.6
四川	Sichuan	101.6	102.1	97.9	102.5	101.2	101.1	100.3	101.6	101.9
贵州	Guizhou	102.4	104.2	99.8	102.1	100.7	101.6	100.2	102.4	101.8
云南	Yunnan	102.4	104.3	100.5	100.9	101.3	101.1	100.3	100.6	102.7
西藏	Tibet	102.9	105.3	100.1	102.3	101.3	101.0	100.6	101.7	102.4
陕西	**Shaanxi**	**101.6**	**102.8**	**98.8**	**101.1**	**101.0**	**102.7**	**99.9**	**100.7**	**101.2**
甘肃	Gansu	102.1	103.6	99.9	102.4	102.2	101.2	100.0	101.4	101.5
青海	Qinghai	102.8	104.0	98.7	104.9	99.8	101.4	100.3	102.6	103.0
宁夏	Ningxia	101.9	102.7	99.1	102.7	101.1	101.6	99.6	102.8	101.2
新疆	Xinjiang	102.1	103.6	100.6	101.9	101.1	101.3	100.4	100.4	101.9

22-6 城乡居民人均收入
Per Capita Income of Urban and Rural Residents

单位：元 (yuan)

地 区	Region	城镇居民人均可支配收入 Per Capita Disposable Income of Urban Residents		农村居民人均可支配收入 Per Capita Disposable Income of Rural Residents	
		2013	2014	2013	2014
全 国	**National Total**	**26467**	**28844**	**9430**	**10489**
北 京	Beijing	44564	48532	17101	18867
天 津	Tianjin	28980	31506	15353	17014
河 北	Hebei	22227	24141	9188	10186
山 西	Shanxi	22258	24069	7949	8809
内蒙古	Inner Mongolia	26004	28350	8985	9976
辽 宁	Liaoning	26697	29082	10161	11191
吉 林	Jilin	21331	23218	9781	10780
黑龙江	Heilongjiang	20848	22609	9369	10453
上 海	Shanghai	44878	48841	19208	21192
江 苏	Jiangsu	31585	34346	13521	14958
浙 江	Zhejiang	37080	40393	17494	19373
安 徽	Anhui	22789	24839	8850	9916
福 建	Fujian	28174	30722	11405	12650
江 西	Jiangxi	22120	24309	9089	10117
山 东	Shandong	26882	29222	10687	11882
河 南	Henan	21741	23672	8969	9966
湖 北	Hubei	22668	24852	9692	10849
湖 南	Hunan	24352	26570	9029	10060
广 东	Guangdong	29537	32148	11068	12246
广 西	Guangxi	22689	24669	7793	8683
海 南	Hainan	22411	24487	8802	9913
重 庆	Chongqing	23058	25147	8493	9490
四 川	Sichuan	22228	24234	8381	9348
贵 州	Guizhou	20565	22548	5898	6671
云 南	Yunnan	22460	24299	6724	7456
西 藏	Tibet	20394	22016	6553	7359
陕 西	**Shaanxi**	**22346**	**24366**	**7092**	**7932**
甘 肃	Gansu	19873	21804	5589	6277
青 海	Qinghai	20352	22307	6462	7283
宁 夏	Ningxia	21476	23285	7599	8410
新 疆	Xinjiang	21091	23214	7847	8724

22-7 农林牧渔业总产值(2014年)
Gross Output Value of Farming, Forestry, Animal Husbandry and Fishery (2014)

地 区	Region	农林牧渔业总产值(亿元) Total Gross Output Value (100 million yuan)	#农 业 Farming	#林 业 Forestry	#牧 业 Animal Husbandry	#渔 业 Fishery	农林牧渔业总产值比上年增长(%) Total Gross Output Value Over the Previous Year (%)
全 国	**National Total**	**102226.1**	**54771.5**	**4256.0**	**28956.3**	**10334.3**	**4.2**
北 京	Beijing	420.1	155.1	90.7	152.7	13.2	0.0
天 津	Tianjin	441.7	230.7	3.2	117.6	79.5	3.0
河 北	Hebei	5994.8	3453.4	108.1	1952.0	191.0	4.0
山 西	Shanxi	1530.5	984.0	98.5	354.6	9.8	4.0
内蒙古	Inner Mongolia	2779.8	1408.4	96.4	1205.7	29.1	3.1
辽 宁	Liaoning	4498.4	1734.1	152.4	1717.5	699.8	2.4
吉 林	Jilin	2763.0	1342.5	104.4	1195.0	40.1	4.1
黑龙江	Heilongjiang	4894.8	3015.6	195.7	1486.1	102.7	5.5
上 海	Shanghai	322.2	169.5	8.3	69.9	62.5	1.0
江 苏	Jiangsu	6443.4	3362.8	118.2	1182.7	1426.7	3.1
浙 江	Zhejiang	2844.6	1386.0	147.0	472.2	779.4	1.0
安 徽	Anhui	4223.7	2119.2	283.1	1182.1	459.7	4.6
福 建	Fujian	3522.3	1529.6	323.3	522.9	1025.2	4.5
江 西	Jiangxi	2726.5	1144.1	274.2	814.9	400.7	4.8
山 东	Shandong	9198.3	4765.8	131.5	2418.3	1481.7	4.0
河 南	Henan	7549.1	4492.0	152.4	2505.2	105.1	4.2
湖 北	Hubei	5452.8	2761.7	157.0	1427.7	844.2	5.6
湖 南	Hunan	5304.8	2884.7	304.8	1503.2	338.9	4.7
广 东	Guangdong	5234.2	2613.2	279.8	1077.4	1080.3	3.0
广 西	Guangxi	3947.7	1994.0	303.2	1087.2	413.1	3.7
海 南	Hainan	1252.2	568.2	103.2	228.0	310.2	4.9
重 庆	Chongqing	1595.0	967.9	53.6	486.4	64.9	4.3
四 川	Sichuan	5888.1	3078.6	196.0	2318.8	192.4	4.0
贵 州	Guizhou	2118.5	1321.9	99.6	569.3	47.0	6.6
云 南	Yunnan	3263.3	1806.3	303.1	975.8	78.1	6.2
西 藏	Tibet	138.7	63.3	2.6	69.3	0.2	4.2
陕 西	**Shaanxi**	**2741.8**	**1870.8**	**73.6**	**648.3**	**19.9**	**5.1**
甘 肃	Gansu	1618.8	1174.9	25.5	268.4	2.1	5.4
青 海	Qinghai	327.5	144.2	6.6	169.1	2.2	5.4
宁 夏	Ningxia	445.5	274.0	10.0	126.8	14.9	6.1
新 疆	Xinjiang	2744.0	1955.1	49.4	651.2	19.6	6.8

注：本表绝对数按当年价格计算，增长速度按可比价格计算。
a) Level data in this table are calculated at current prices, while the growth rate are at constant prices.

22-8 主要农产品产量(2014年)
Output of Major Farm Crops (2014)

单位：万吨 (10 000 tons)

地 区	Region	粮 食 Grain	油 料 Oil-bearing Crops	棉 花 Cotton	蔬 菜 Vegetables	水 果 Fruit	肉 类 Meat	奶 类 Milk
全 国	**National Total**	**60702.6**	**3507.4**	**617.8**	**76005.5**	**26142.2**	**8706.7**	**3841.2**
北 京	Beijing	63.9	0.7	0.01	236.2	96.5	39.3	59.5
天 津	Tianjin	176.0	0.5	3.8	460.2	62.7	46.4	68.9
河 北	Hebei	3360.2	150.2	43.1	8125.7	2019.0	468.1	496.1
山 西	Shanxi	1330.8	17.3	2.4	1271.4	770.8	87.5	97.2
内蒙古	Inner Mongolia	2753.0	170.3	0.2	1472.7	322.3	252.3	797.1
辽 宁	Liaoning	1753.9	63.7	0.01	3090.1	870.6	429.2	134.5
吉 林	Jilin	3532.8	85.7	0.1	876.0	229.7	262.0	49.8
黑龙江	Heilongjiang	6242.2	17.1		985.6	258.7	230.2	560.1
上 海	Shanghai	112.5	1.3	0.1	393.2	86.2	23.4	27.1
江 苏	Jiangsu	3490.6	146.6	16.0	5417.0	861.6	379.5	60.7
浙 江	Zhejiang	757.4	30.7	2.5	1762.8	714.8	157.1	15.9
安 徽	Anhui	3415.8	228.8	26.3	2551.0	965.3	414.0	27.9
福 建	Fujian	667.0	29.8	0.01	1801.4	790.8	213.7	15.4
江 西	Jiangxi	2143.5	121.7	13.4	1312.4	627.1	339.8	12.9
山 东	Shandong	4596.6	335.9	66.5	9973.7	3134.0	770.2	289.6
河 南	Henan	5772.3	584.3	14.7	7272.5	2560.2	719.0	342.4
湖 北	Hubei	2584.2	341.7	36.0	3671.5	972.3	440.4	16.4
湖 南	Hunan	3001.3	233.8	12.9	3763.5	920.0	546.5	9.3
广 东	Guangdong	1357.3	105.5		3274.7	1560.7	429.4	13.8
广 西	Guangxi	1534.4	61.3	0.3	2610.1	1560.6	420.0	9.7
海 南	Hainan	186.6	11.6		551.5	413.0	79.5	0.2
重 庆	Chongqing	1144.5	56.9		1689.1	347.6	214.2	5.7
四 川	Sichuan	3374.9	300.8	1.2	4069.3	884.5	714.7	71.3
贵 州	Guizhou	1138.5	98.0	0.1	1625.6	196.4	201.8	5.7
云 南	Yunnan	1860.7	64.7	0.03	1735.5	669.0	378.5	64.6
西 藏	Tibet	98.0	6.4		68.2	1.4	26.4	34.3
陕 西	**Shaanxi**	**1197.8**	**62.3**	**4.2**	**1724.7**	**1849.9**	**116.8**	**192.3**
甘 肃	Gansu	1158.7	72.4	6.4	1705.2	636.6	95.5	40.3
青 海	Qinghai	104.8	31.5		158.6	2.6	33.4	31.3
宁 夏	Ningxia	377.9	16.5		540.8	290.2	28.5	135.7
新 疆	Xinjiang	1414.5	59.3	367.7	1815.4	1466.9	149.3	155.6

注：水果产量含果用瓜。

a) The fruit production includes melons for fruits use.

22-9 主要工业产品产量(2014年)
Output of Major Industrial Products(2014)

地 区	Region	原 油 (万吨) Crude oil (10 000 tons)	天然气 (亿立方米) Natural Gas (100 million sq.m)	水 泥 (万吨) Cement (10 000 tons)	生 铁 (万吨) Pig Iron (10 000 tons)	粗 钢 (万吨) Crude Steel (10 000 tons)	钢 材 (万吨) Steel Products (10 000 tons)	汽 车 (万辆) Automotive (10 000 units)	发电量 (亿千瓦小时) Electricity (100 million kwh)
全 国	**National Total**	**21142.9**	**1301.6**	**247613.5**	**71159.9**	**82269.8**	**112557.2**	**2372.5**	**56495.8**
北 京	Beijing		12.8	703.6		2.1	195.0	206.3	364.0
天 津	Tianjin	3074.8	21.2	957.9	2182.5	2287.1	7303.9	51.2	625.5
河 北	Hebei	592.3	17.5	10677.4	16932.6	18530.3	23995.2	97.8	2499.9
山 西	Shanxi		31.6	4700.0	4052.0	4325.4	4701.0		2647.0
内蒙古	Inner Mongolia	21.5	15.5	6294.0	1330.7	1661.5	1763.2	2.4	3857.8
辽 宁	Liaoning	1021.9	8.1	5807.6	6167.7	6511.4	6946.0	112.1	1647.8
吉 林	Jilin	663.9	22.3	3702.7	1132.8	1264.8	1412.2	237.4	771.7
黑龙江	Heilongjiang	4000.0	35.4	3702.6	456.7	476.3	483.5	10.8	881.3
上 海	Shanghai	5.7	2.1	686.0	1643.3	1774.5	2309.1	247.4	792.3
江 苏	Jiangsu	206.0	0.5	19395.8	7080.1	10195.5	13255.2	121.6	4347.6
浙 江	Zhejiang			12390.0	1140.3	1748.3	4171.0	30.9	2885.3
安 徽	Anhui			12921.0	1998.6	2451.4	3265.7	93.4	2033.9
福 建	Fujian			7760.9	907.7	1820.8	3019.6	18.1	1873.4
江 西	Jiangxi		0.4	9831.2	2075.3	2235.3	2611.1	46.2	873.3
山 东	Shandong	2713.2	4.9	16496.3	6719.1	6411.0	8939.4	103.0	3691.1
河 南	Henan	470.5	4.9	17080.7	2779.6	2882.2	4704.1	40.9	2729.9
湖 北	Hubei	79.0	1.5	11418.1	2437.6	3056.4	3429.0	174.5	2382.3
湖 南	Hunan			12060.1	1780.7	1917.6	1989.3	29.5	1313.7
广 东	Guangdong	1245.4	83.7	14783.4	1082.4	1710.4	3447.1	216.8	3948.4
广 西	Guangxi	58.7	0.2	10706.5	1231.7	2084.3	3262.6	209.2	1310.0
海 南	Hainan	28.5	1.6	2151.6		22.4	29.7	9.0	244.6
重 庆	Chongqing		7.8	6688.8	444.6	785.6	1322.0	231.4	675.8
四 川	Sichuan	19.2	253.5	14612.7	1931.4	2243.0	2935.2	32.4	3079.4
贵 州	Guizhou		0.4	9456.4	498.6	551.6	552.4		1747.7
云 南	Yunnan		0.02	9596.9	1704.9	1689.1	1935.1	11.0	2550.0
西 藏	Tibet			342.2			1.1		32.3
陕 西	**Shaanxi**	**3767.8**	**410.1**	**9083.5**	**884.0**	**1038.3**	**1683.9**	**37.5**	**1600.9**
甘 肃	Gansu	71.2	0.2	4931.5	898.8	1074.0	1108.1	0.7	1241.1
青 海	Qinghai	220.0	68.9	1859.6	127.0	144.3	131.4		580.3
宁 夏	Ningxia	7.9		1793.9	201.7	161.5	165.6		1156.6
新 疆	Xinjiang	2875.3	296.7	4974.6	1337.5	1213.4	1489.5	1.1	2090.9

22-10 社会消费品零售总额和进出口总额
Total Retail Sales of Consumer Goods and Total Import and Export

地区	Region	社会消费品零售总额(亿元) Total Retail Sales of Consumer Goods(100 million yuan)		进出口总额(亿美元) Total Import and Export (100 million USD)		出口总额(亿美元) Total Exports (100 million USD)	
		2013	2014	2013	2014	2013	2014
全国	**National Total**	**242842.8**	**271896.1**	**41589.9**	**43030.4**	**22090.0**	**23427.5**
北京	Beijing	8872.1	9638.0	4290.0	4156.5	631.0	623.5
天津	Tianjin	4470.4	4738.7	1285.0	1339.1	490.0	526.0
河北	Hebei	10516.7	11820.5	549.1	598.8	309.6	357.1
山西	Shanxi	5139.3	5717.9	157.9	162.5	80.0	89.4
内蒙古	Inner Mongolia	5114.2	5657.6	119.9	145.5	40.9	63.9
辽宁	Liaoning	10581.4	11857.0	1144.8	1139.6	645.2	587.6
吉林	Jilin	5426.4	6080.9	258.3	263.8	67.4	57.8
黑龙江	Heilongjiang	6251.2	7015.3	388.8	389.0	162.3	173.4
上海	Shanghai	8557.0	9303.5	4412.7	4664.1	2041.8	2101.6
江苏	Jiangsu	20878.2	23458.1	5508.0	5637.6	3288.0	3418.7
浙江	Zhejiang	15970.8	17835.3	3357.9	3551.5	2487.5	2733.5
安徽	Anhui	7044.7	7957.0	455.2	492.7	282.5	314.9
福建	Fujian	8275.3	9346.7	1693.2	1775.0	1064.7	1134.6
江西	Jiangxi	4696.1	5292.6	367.5	427.8	281.7	320.4
山东	Shandong	22294.8	25111.5	2665.3	2771.2	1341.9	1447.5
河南	Henan	12426.6	14005.0	599.6	650.3	359.9	393.8
湖北	Hubei	11035.9	12449.3	363.8	430.6	228.4	266.5
湖南	Hunan	9509.5	10723.5	251.8	310.3	148.2	200.2
广东	Guangdong	25453.9	28471.1	10915.8	10767.3	6363.6	6462.2
广西	Guangxi	5133.1	5772.8	328.3	405.5	186.9	243.3
海南	Hainan	1090.9	1224.5	149.9	158.7	37.1	44.2
重庆	Chongqing	5055.8	5710.7	686.9	954.5	468.0	634.1
四川	Sichuan	11001.0	12393.0	645.7	702.5	419.5	448.5
贵州	Guizhou	2601.2	2936.9	82.9	108.1	68.9	94.0
云南	Yunnan	4112.6	4632.9	253.0	296.2	156.7	188.0
西藏	Tibet	322.2	364.5	33.2	22.5	32.7	21.0
陕西	**Shaanxi**	**5245.0**	**5918.7**	**201.3**	**274.1**	**102.3**	**139.3**
甘肃	Gansu	2368.8	2668.3	102.4	86.5	46.8	53.3
青海	Qinghai	549.6	620.8	14.0	17.2	8.5	11.3
宁夏	Ningxia	668.5	737.2	32.2	54.4	25.5	43.0
新疆	Xinjiang	2179.5	2436.5	275.6	276.7	222.7	234.8

2014 年陕西省统计局大事记

1 月 1 日，陕西省委常委、常务副省长、省政府第三次经济普查领导小组组长江泽林检查指导经济普查入户登记工作，标志着我省第三次全国经济普查入户登记全面展开。

1 月 13 日，省统计局统计数据移动查询客户端“数据陕西”正式上线运行，这是省统计局在全国统计系统首创的数据发布平台。

1 月 21 日，全省统计工作会议召开，江泽林常务副省长对会议及 2013 年全省统计工作作出重要批示，省统计局局长丁云祥作大会报告并布置 2014 年全省统计工作 7 项重点任务。

2 月 7 日至 8 日,省统计局党组召开会议集中听取局机关各单位汇报 2013 年工作亮点、2014 年工作思路，部署全年各项工作任务。

2 月 8 日，省统计局印发《关于表彰 2013 年度目标责任考核优秀单位和个人的通知》(陕统办字〔2014〕4 号)，对 12 个目标责任考核先进单位、51 名目标责任考核先进个人、8 名连续三个年度考核优秀记三等功人员进行表彰。

2 月 27 日，省委、省政府发出《关于表彰 2013 年度目标责任考核优秀单位的决定》，省统计局被评为 2013 年度全省目标责任考核优秀单位。

3 月 5 日，省统计局党组召开专题会议，分析研究全省统计系统党风廉政建设工作情况，部署 2014 年度党风廉政建设工作。

3 月 13 日，全省第三次经济普查办公室主任会议在西安召开，传达全国三经普办公室主任暨普查中心主任会议精神，部署个体户抽样调查工作，安排下阶段重点工作。

3 月 14 日，省统计局召开目标责任考核工作总结和部署会，丁云祥局长对 2013 年省统计局目标责任考核工作进行回顾，对 2014 年度目标责任考核工作提出 5 点要求。

3 月 17 日，省统计局召开党的群众路线教育实践活动总结暨深化整改工作部署会，省委第六督导组到会指导，会议全面总结了省统计局党的群众路线教育实践活动。

3 月 18 日，省统计局与西咸新区联合召开西咸新区统计监测工作会议，交流业务开展情况。

3 月 31 日至 4 月 3 日，国家统计局党组成员、纪检组长高建华来陕西调研。

4 月 17 日，省统计局召开全省统计信息化工作会议，总结 2013 工作，对 2014 年全省统计信息化工作进行部署。

4 月 20 日到 25 日，省统计局举办“2014 年度全省统计系统新进人员培训班”，52 名新进人员参加培训。

4 月 28 日，陕西省人民政府任命晁文庆为陕西省统计局副巡视员（陕政任字〔2014〕60 号)。

4 月 29 日，陕西省统计局印发《关于成立全面深化统计改革领导小组及办公室的通知》(陕统办字〔2014〕

14 号)，成立统计改革领导机构，安排开展深化统计改革工作。

5 月 8 日，省统计局成立党的群众路线教育实践活动党员代表监督小组，围绕局教育实践活动整改方案开展“五查”。

5 月 9 日，中共陕西省委办公厅、陕西省人民政府办公厅印发《关于 2013 年度全省党政领导干部优秀调研成果的通报》，省统计局丁云祥局长的调研报告《对陕西转型换档期发展的思考》获一等奖。

5 月 19 日至 23 日，省统计局在省委党校举办机关处级以上干部学习贯彻习近平总书记系列重要讲话精神培训班。

5 月份，省统计局结合党的群众路线教育实践活动，在全系统开展“走基层、察民情、转作风”为主题的业务调研活动。

6 月 13 日，省统计局印发《关于开展“制度建设年”工作实施方案》，以此切实推进局机关各项制度建设，巩固党的群众路线教育实践活动成果。

6 月 15 日，陕西省人民政府办公厅印发经省机构编制委员会审核的《陕西省统计局主要职责内设机构和人员编制规定》(陕政办发〔2014〕63 号)，对省统计局的职能转变、主要职责、内设机构、人员编制做出进一步的明确。

6 月 17 至 18 日，国家统计局副局长张为民在陕西省督导第三次全国经济普查事后质量抽查工作。

6 月 30 日，省政府办公厅印发《陕西省人民政府办公厅关于开展全省农业农村普查的通知》(陕政办发〔2014〕100 号)，决定开展全省农业农村普查。

7 月 1 日，省统计局召开庆祝中国共产党成立 93 周年大会，对 4 个先进党支部、8 名优秀党务工作者、20 名优秀共产党员进行了表彰。

7 月 5 日，省委书记赵正永、省长娄勤俭在西安会见国家统计局局长马建堂一行。

7 月 7 日，德国联邦统计局局长罗德里希•埃格勒先生率代表团一行到省统计局进行座谈，双方就统计工作进行了广泛交流。

7 月 14 日，省政府办公厅发出《关于进一步加强部门统计工作的通知》(陕政办发〔2014〕104 号)，要求全省各设区市人民政府，省人民政府各工作部门、各直属机构进一步加强统计工作。

8 月 12 日至 14 日，国家统计局副局长李强来陕西调研服务业统计工作。

8 月 12 日，省政府决定免去刘松年、晁文庆的陕西省统计局副巡视员职务，退休(陕政任字〔2014〕113 号)。

8 月 15 日，省统计局与省委宣传部联合印发《关于进一步加强文化产业统计和规模以上文化企业培育工作的通知》，就进一步加强文化产业统计和规模以上文化企业培育工作作出安排部署。

9 月 2 日，省委书记赵正永对省统计局统计专报《目前全省商品房住宅待售面积与消化库存情况》做出批示，要求各市书记、市长高度关注商品房待售面积与消化库存问题。

9 月 6 日，陕西省政府办公厅印发《关于认真做好 2015 年全国 1%人口抽样调查工作的通知》（陕政办函〔2014〕194 号），部署 2015 年开展全省 1%人口抽样调查工作。

9 月，省统计局编印完成《陕西省统计局工作制度》，这标志着省统计局“制度建设年”取得重大成果。2014 年，省统计局新制订制度 40 项，修订制度 24 项，审定 65 项机关工作制度和 32 项统计业务制度，举办制度培训会 2 次，机关制度建设得到进一步增强。

10 月 27 日至 31 日，省统计局在西北大学举办全省统计系统干部能力提升培训班，旨在适应统计改革发展的新形势和统计工作的新要求，进一步提升统计干部的素质能力。

10 月 23 日，省统计局印发《陕西省统计局关于贾志让等 9 名同志任职的通知》（陕统任免〔2014〕12 号），省统计局统计执法监督处、统计设计管理处、省地方社会经济调查中心社情民意调查处正式挂牌。

11 月 6 日，省统计局成立公务用车制度改革领导小组，并制定《陕西省统计局公务用车制度改革实施方案》，报省公务用车制度改革领导小组，省统计局公务用车制度改革工作进入实施阶段。

11 月 19 日，省统计局召开全省县域经济监测部门工作会议，总结 2014 年度工作，部署安排 2015 年县域经济社会发展监测考评工作任务。

11 月 30 日，省委书记赵正永、省长娄勤俭在西安会见来陕出席陕西调查总队主要领导调整宣布大会的国家统计局局长马建堂一行。

12 月 4 日，省统计局联合咸阳市统计局开展国家宪法日和法治统计宣传活动。

12 月 9 日至 10 日，省统计局举办全省第一届统计从业人员师资大赛暨统计从业人员师资培训班。

12 月 16 日，省委第二巡回督导组对省统计局群众路线教育实践活动整改情况进行巡回督导，督导组对省统计局群众路线教育实践活动整改工作给予充分肯定。

12 月 20 日，2014 年度目标责任考核市(区)和省直部门工作满意度调查在省统计局社情民意调查中心启动。

12 月 28 日，省委书记赵正永、省长娄勤俭在西安会见了来陕出席中国（西安）丝绸之路研究院揭牌仪式的国家统计局局长马建堂一行。

（苏　明）

2014 年陕西调查总队大事记

1 月 7 日，调查总队发布《2013 年陕西统计调查工作十大亮点》。

1 月 20 至 21 日，调查总队召开陕西国家统计调查工作会议。丁远忠总队长作题为《勇于面对挑战深化业务改革 奋力推进陕西国家统计调查工作再上新台阶》的工作报告。

2 月 19 日，调查总队印发《深入开展第二批党的群众路线教育实践活动安排意见》，启动陕西国家统计调查系统党的群众路线教育实践活动。

2 月 20 日,调查总队召开党的群众路线教育实践活动第一批总结暨第二批动员部署会议，总结机关第一批党的群众路线教育实践活动，启动第二批市县调查队实践教育活动。国家统计局教育实践活动第二督导组参加。

2 月 22 日，调查总队完成 2014 年公务员招录面试工作。

2 月 28 日，调查总队、省统计局联合发布《2013 年陕西省国民经济和社会发展统计公报》。

2 月 28 日，调查总队首次发布陕西城乡一体化调查“全省居民人均可支配收入”数据。

3 月初，调查总队印发《国家统计局陕西调查总队 2014 年审计工作安排》，规范系统财务审计工作。

3 月 4 日，调查总队印发《陕西省“三经普”个体经营户抽样调查预防风险工作预案》、《陕西省“三经普”个体经营户抽样调查数据质量控制办法》，规范“三经普”个体经营户抽样调查工作。

3 月 19 日，王恩斗副总队长陪同国家统计局第二巡视组一行参加西安调查队党的群众路线教育实践活动动员会。

3 月 19－20 日，丁远忠总队长陪同国家统计局第二巡视组一行对汉中调查队党的群众路线教育实践活动进行巡视督导。

3 月 20 日，调查总队与省扶贫办、省发改委、省统计局联合印发《陕西省片区规划实施监测和评估工作方案》。

3 月 24 日，副省长祝列克召开专题会议，听取调查总队关于陕西农民收入和农业生产情况汇报。

3 月 27 日，调查总队下发《陕西国家统计调查系统工作考核办法》，进一步规范系统工作业务，提升水平。

3 月 27 日，调查总队开展“宝鸡西周、汉中两汉三国”旅游文化景区建设调查。

3 月 31 日，国家统计局纪检组长高建华视察调查总队工作，与总队领导和部分机关干部座谈，听取工作汇报并对陕西调查工作提出新要求。

3 月底，陕西省委省政府分别授予调查总队“全省党委系统信息工作先进单位”和“全省政务信息工作先进单位”称号。

4 月 1 日至 3 日，国家统计局高建华纪检组长来陕督查三经普个体户抽样调查，与总队及部分市县调查队代表座谈。

4 月 2 日，陕西国家统计调查系统党风廉政和行风作风建设工作会议召开，国家统计局高建华纪检组长出席并作重要讲话。

4 月 11 日，马建堂局长对调查总队《'市带县'管理模式的探索》作出批示，对调查总队在改进系统管理方面的积极尝试给予肯定。

4 月 11 日，调查总队首次对外发布全省一体化住户调查季度数据。

4 月 28 日，调查总队印发第二批党的群众路线教育实践活动专项整治方案。

5 月 7 日至 16 日，国家统计局巡视组到调查总队开展巡视工作。

5 月 9 日，调查总队向省政府专题汇报陕西畜牧业生产形势以及畜禽监测调查工作。

5 月 14 日，调查总队建立陕西以县为总体的粮食产量抽样调查制度，开展县级粮食产量抽样调查。

5 月 16 日，调查总队成立固定资产投资统计制度方法改革试点工作领导小组。

5 月 20 日，调查总队调研报告《陕北农村耕地撂荒问题亟待关注》荣获 2013 年度全省党政领导干部优秀调研成果一等奖。

5 月中旬，调查总队完成全省投资环境调查。

5 月 22 日，总队印发《关于进一步加强工作纪律的通知》，参与、配合省直机关"庸懒散浮"专项整治活动。

5 月 29 日，调查总队印发《第二批党的群众路线教育实践活动查摆问题、开展批评环节工作方案》，对第二批市县调查队教育实践深入开展提出明确要求。

5 月 29 日，调查总队在系统组织开展青年干部优秀统计分析报告评选，鼓励青年干部深入一线学习业务、积极参与统计分析和课题研究工作。

6 月 8 日，罗卫国副总队长陪同国家统计局第二巡回督导组检查、指导延安调查队党的群众路线教育实践活动。

6 月 18 日，国家统计局党组副书记、副局长张为民到宝鸡调查队检查指导党的群众路线教育实践活动。省统计局局长丁云祥、陕西调查总队副队长罗卫国陪同。

6 月 15 日至 22 日，调查总队领导带队，兵分五路开展了为期一周的专项督导工作，以听、看、点、谈等方式检查教育实践活动第二环节落实情况。

6 月中旬，调查总队党组成员按照国家统计局"四必谈"的要求，分赴各市县调查队检查指导第二批党的群众路线教育实践活动。

6 月，调查总队开展"应届大学毕业生就业状况"专题调查。

6 月，调查总队开展全省专利产品产值调查。

6月，调查总队开展系统保密宣传月活动，通过基层检查、调研、宣教等方式提高系统保密工作水平，强化系统人员保密意识。

6月24日,娄勤俭省长、江泽林常务副省长对陕西居民收入调查工作作出重要指示。

7月4日-6日，马建堂局长在西安接待来华访问的德国联邦统计局局长罗德里希.暖格勒先生，丁远忠总队长与丁云祥局长陪同。

7月8日至9日，调查总队组织开展调查系统基层统计人员岗位知识培训试点，重点对培训内容、授课方式和培训效果进行测试并征求意见。

7月15日，陕西省委省政府联合发文，明确调查总队为2014年陕西省农民收入倍增、农民收入普查、扶贫机制建设等工作任务落实开展的责任单位之一。

7月25日，调查总队与省旅游局等部门共同举办新闻发布会，发布有关调查数据。

7月31日，调查总队成为省社会救助联席会议成员单位。配合有关部门指导各地完善社会救助标准，科学制定动态调整机制和社会保障标准与物价上涨挂钩的联动机制。

8月1日，调查总队印发《在第二批党的群众路线教育实践活动中开好专题民主（组织）生活会并开展民主评议党员工作的通知》，号召系统各级调查队按照延安整风精神开好专题民主（组织）生活会。

8月4日，调查总队完成2013年度全省企业专利产品产值调查工作。

8月13日，国家统计局副局长李强参加咸阳调查队党的群众路线教育实践活动党组专题民主生活会，丁远忠总队长陪同。

8月27日，调查总队成立陕西国家统计调查系统全面深化统计调查改革领导小组。

8月28日至29日，调查总队召开陕西国家统计调查系统年中工作座谈会。

8月，调查总队开展陕西国家统计调查系统“最美调查员”、“最美辅调员”、“最美记账户”评选宣传活动。

9月初，调查总队建立农业生产“快速反应报告机制”要求各级调查队对影响粮食生产的因素变化迅速反应，及时汇报，为准确推算全国和分省数据打好基础，也为地方政府保障粮食生产提供统计调查分析服务。

9月上旬，调查总队撰写的专题调研报告《“更难就业季”存喜，结构性就业有忧》，被国务院发展研究中心主办的《经济要参》2014年第34期全文刊载。

9月中旬，调查总队举办主题为“最美调查人•情系统计梦”的统计开放日活动。

9月28日至29日，调查总队召开“陕西国家统计调查系统纪检监察工作会”，对全面落实党风廉政建设主体责任和监督责任暂行规定及问题线索处置流程进行专题培训。

9月，陕西国家统计调查系统青联开展了“统计人•统计情•统计梦”征文，号召系统青年干部投身统计工作、服务基层统计、奉献统计事业。

10 月 15 日，调查总队开展国有企业反腐倡廉民意调查工作。

10 月 21 日，国家统计局第二巡回督导组一行参加西安调查队党的群众路线教育实践活动总结大会，罗卫国巡视员陪同。

10 月 22 日，调查总队成立新设立小微企业和个体经营户跟踪调查工作办公室。

10 月 28 日，调查总队与省统计局联合印发《关于做好小微企业和个体经营户抽样调查工作的通知》。

11 月中旬，调查总队科研课题《土地流转对“三农”的影响统计研究》获得 2014 年度全国统计科学研究项目“重点项目”立项。

11 月 24 日，马建堂局长对宝鸡调查队呈报的《关于调查队系统承担小微企业调查工作情况、问题和建议》作出批示。

11 月 26 日，国家统计局任命孙法臣为调查总队党组书记、总队长。

11 月 30 日，国家统计局马建堂局长参加陕西调查总队全体干部大会，宣布孙法臣为调查总队党组书记、总队长。

11 月，调查总队撰写的《对陕西居民收入翻番的思考》被《2014 中国发展报告》全文收录。

11 月，调查总队完成国有企业反腐倡廉民意调查。

12 月上旬，调查总队开展注册资本登记制度改革实施情况调研。

12 月中旬，调查总队开展国家宪法日和法治统计宣传教育活动。

12 月下旬，调查总队开展网购用户专项调查。

（袁　琦）

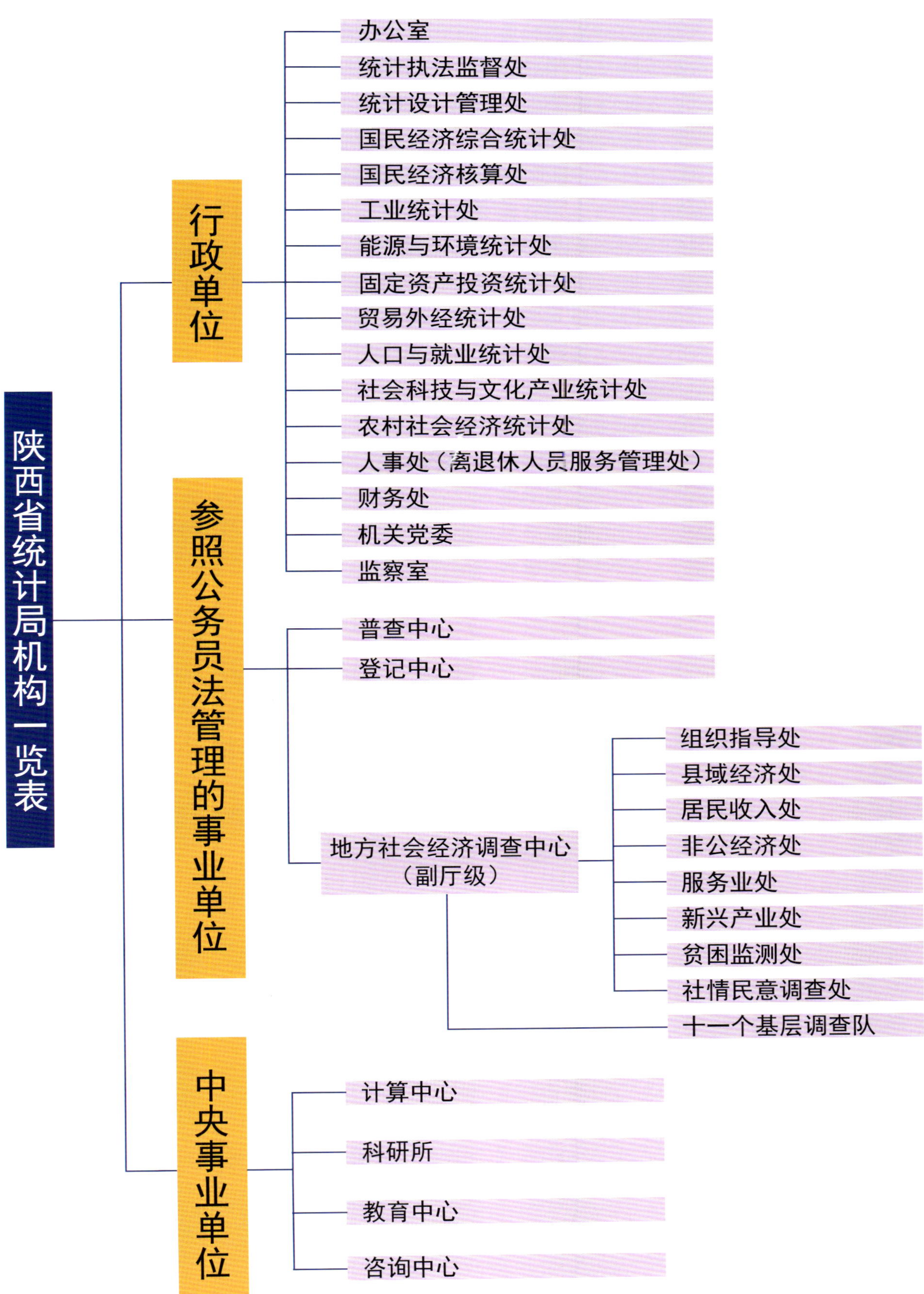
陕西省统计局机构一览表
行政单位
办公室
统计执法监督处
统计设计管理处
国民经济综合统计处
国民经济核算处
工业统计处
能源与环境统计处
固定资产投资统计处
贸易外经统计处
人口与就业统计处
社会科技与文化产业统计处
农村社会经济统计处
人事处（离退休人员服务管理处）
财务处
机关党委
监察室
参照公务员法管理的事业单位
普查中心
登记中心
地方社会经济调查中心（副厅级）
组织指导处
县域经济处
居民收入处
非公经济处
服务业处
新兴产业处
贫困监测处
社情民意调查处
十一个基层调查队
中央事业单位
计算中心
科研所
教育中心
咨询中心

陕西调查总队机构一览表

总队机关

- 办公室
- 综合处
- 农业调查处
- 住户专项调查处
- 商业和投资建筑业调查处
- 统计监测处
- 消费价格调查处
- 人事教育处
- 纪检监察室
- 信息技术应用处
- 信息网络办公室
- 法规制度处
- 居民收支调查处
- 工业调查处
- 服务业调查处
- 专项调查处
- 生产投资价格调查处
- 财务管理处
- 机关党委

市级调查队

- 西安调查队
- 咸阳调查队
- 渭南调查队
- 榆林调查队
- 安康调查队
- 杨凌调查队
- 宝鸡调查队
- 铜川调查队
- 延安调查队
- 汉中调查队
- 商洛调查队

县级调查队

长安　临潼　周至　户县　蓝田　未央

陈仓　凤翔　扶风　眉县

三原　泾阳　礼泉　彬县　旬邑

耀州　宜君

大荔　蒲城　澄城　合阳　富平

子长　志丹

神木　定边　绥德　清涧　子洲

城固　略阳

汉阴　紫阳　旬阳

洛南

社会经济调查队

铜川　户县　陇县　临渭　华阴　蒲城

略阳　西乡　洛南　宝塔　绥德

统计职业道德规范

忠诚统计
乐于奉献
实事求是
不出假数
依法统计
严守秘密
公正透明
服务社会

陕西统计人精神

严谨　求实　卓越　奉献

严谨：是统计人的科学态度。严谨即严肃谨慎、严密周到。体现在统计人在工作中不浮夸、不马虎、不好高骛远、不粗枝大叶，认真求证每一个统计数据和统计指标、仔细核对每一张统计报表、深入分析每一次统计调查，努力提高统计数据质量、维护政府统计公信力。

求实：是统计人的职业素养。“求”是探究、求证；“实”，真也，是反映在统计数据中的真理、规律。求实，是贯穿于统计生产全过程的一种工作理念。

卓越：是统计人的工作标准。卓越，意味着杰出与超越。是社会发展对统计工作提出的要求，也是检验统计工作好坏的标准。

奉献：是统计人的职业要求。奉献就是付出、给予、呈现。展现统计人在平凡的岗位上，将甘于奉献化作对工作的无限热爱，受得清苦、耐得寂寞、吃苦耐劳、无怨无悔。